CZECHOSLOVAKIA'S INTERRUPTED REVOLUTION

Czechoslovakia's Interrupted Revolution

H. GORDON SKILLING

Princeton University Press · Princeton, New Jersey

Library of Congress Cataloging in Publication Data will
be found on the last printed page of this book

This book has been composed in Linotype Times Roman

Printed in the United States of America
by Princeton University Press, Princeton, New Jersey

Written under the auspices of the
Centre for Russian and East European Studies,
University of Toronto

A list of other Centre publications appears
at the back of this book

To

Alexander · Antonín · Ivan · Jan
Jaroslav · Jiří · Jiřina · Josef · Karol
Lisa · Michal · Olga · Pavel
Václav · Vladimír · Vilém · Zdeněk

For the human character is such that men wish to be
governed in a human fashion, rather led than dragged,
rather persuaded than compelled, for man was created in
the image of God, a reasoning, free and independent being.
The art of government is thus based upon wisdom and not upon
force, upon caution and foresight and not upon trickery.

J. A. Komenský (1668)

CONTENTS

CONTENTS

CONTENTS

x

WHEN I first visited Czechoslovakia in the summer of 1937, at a high point in the history of the First Republic, I could not foresee that that country would soon experience the catastrophe of Munich and the German occupation. Thirty years later, in 1967, when I again spent a summer there, equally unforeseeable events were ahead—the outburst of reform and the Soviet invasion in the following year. In each case there were, of course, warning signals of impending calamity, but the blow, when it came, was unanticipated and produced the same collapse of high hopes and the same anger and hatred of the outside intervener.

At the time of the invasion in 1968 I was taking part in a conference on Change in Communist Systems in the idyllic surroundings of the Institute for Behavioral Studies in Stanford, California. Few of the participants expected such a drastic interruption of the course of change then under way in Czechoslovakia. On the day of the intervention Robert Tucker, of Princeton University, and I exchanged views on the implications of the event for the two countries (the USSR and Czechoslovakia) to which we had devoted many years of study. Having already embarked on a program of research on group conflict in Czechoslovakia, I was easily persuaded to expand this into a more complete study of the 1968 events. We were both convinced that the short-lived experiment in the reform of communism in Czechoslovakia was of decisive historical importance, not only for the Czech and Slovak peoples, but also for Soviet Russia and world communism.

My intention was to avoid elaborate theoretical schemes and to prepare an empirical case study, based on a systematic examination of all available sources. I was under no illusions that I could attain complete objectivity in the analysis of a subject so controversial, but could only hope, following the standards of scholarly research, to portray events as fully and fairly as possible. Although my attitude to the reform movement was sympathetic, I have taken account of all standpoints, favorable and unfavorable, and have tried to analyze its failings as well as its virtues. I have refrained from extensive personal interpretations and have sought to achieve a judgment more detached than was perhaps possible for protagonists and critics personally involved in these events.

I am fully aware that a study of a historical episode at such close range cannot be in any sense definitive. In spite of the extraordinary freedom of expression that prevailed during 1968, much remained concealed or obscure and may never be fully revealed. After the manuscript had been completed, the appearance, in 1975, of Smrkovský's final testimony and a memorandum by Zdeněk Mlynář (both of which are summarized in appendices) underlined the perils of writing contemporary history, without access to confidential documents and personal memoirs. No doubt the future historian will have the benefit of much fuller documentation and of later revelations. The contemporary observer has at least the advantage of having been able to follow events closely as they occurred and to discuss them on the spot with participants and observers, and may hopefully capture the spirit of the times better than a retrospective analyst. During visits to Czechoslovakia during May and June 1968, and also in the summer of 1967, the fall of 1968, and the spring of 1969, I conducted many interviews with Czechs and Slovaks which gave life to the written sources. Earlier trips before World War II, and in 1948, 1950, 1958, 1961, and 1962, provided a valuable perspective for interpreting more recent developments.

Even before I began to write this book, I had thought of a possible title—The Interrupted Revolution. I am conscious of the ambiguities of these words, and the controversiality of the concept embodied in them, but for reasons set forth in my conclusions, have retained the title as expressing most fully the meaning of 1968. While writing and rewriting the conclusions I had the benefit of discussing them, and the title, on a number of occasions, in particular in seminars at the Russian Research Center, at Harvard University; at the York-Toronto Colloquium on the Politics of Socialism, and at Carleton University, Ottawa; in Great Britain, at the centers for Russian and East European studies at Birmingham, Glasgow, Swansea, and St. Antony's College, Oxford; at Cambridge and the London School of Economics and Political Science; and further afield, at the Hebrew University in Jerusalem. Those who offered criticisms and observations may recognize some of their points in the final version of my concluding chapter.

Appreciation must be expressed to many persons for assistance in preparing the book. First and foremost comes my wife, Sally, who accompanied me on many visits to Czechoslovakia over the years and who encouraged and helped me in the long and arduous task of research and writing. As always, her splendid editing of the manuscript has given it whatever lucidity and style that it may possess, and her construction of the index has made its contents readily accessible. Also invaluable was the contribution of my colleague at the University of Toronto, Dušan Pokorný, who, in making his gentle but cogent comments on the entire manuscript, drew upon his wide knowledge of the economics, politics, philosophy, journalism, and diplomacy of his native country, and his long experience in both Slovakia and the Czech lands. Karel Kovanda, then a Ph.D. student at MIT, also read the manuscript, checking the spelling of Czech and Slovak names and words, and offering critical observations. Others who made valuable comments on the book as a whole were Stanley Pech, of the University of British Columbia, and Zvi Gitelman, of the University of Michigan. Jan Štepan, of Harvard University, and Oldřich Kýn, of Boston University, read chapters XIII and XIV, respectively.

Thanks go to many others, especially Czechs and Slovaks who offered their own ideas and useful information and gave other invaluable aid. They must remain anonymous but are represented by the first names of some of them in the dedication. Those who assisted me in research included: Douglas Evans and my wife (English-language materials); Lida Havrlant and Hilarion Kukšin (Czech and Slovak); Stefania Stanislawska-Fiszman and David Paul (Polish, Russian, and other languages, for chapter XXI). Special appreciation must be voiced to the expert typists of countless drafts and of the final version of the manuscript, Lila Fernandez, of Waban, Mass., and Ahnna Lowry, of Toronto, and to the latter also for her patience and skill in performing the many administrative tasks involved. My gratitude is expressed to Sanford Thatcher, of Princeton University Press, for his encouragement and support from the beginning; to Polly Hanford, for her skilled editing; and to other members of the staff of the Press for contributing to the fine technical quality of the book.

Appreciation is recorded for permission to use, in revised forms, parts of the following articles of mine: "The Fall of Novotný in Czechoslovakia," *Canadian Slavonic Papers* (Ottawa, Canada), 12, no. 3 (Fall 1970), 225-42; "Communism and Czechoslovak Tradition," *Journal of International Affairs*, XX, no. 1 (1966), 118-36; "Czechoslovakia," in Adam Bromke and Teresa Rakowska-Harmstone, eds., *The Communist States in Disarray, 1965-1971* (University of Minnesota Press, Minneapolis, 1972), pp. 62-71. Appreciation is also expressed to Praeger Publishers, Inc., for permission to use tables, in original and revised form, from Jaroslav A. Piekalkiewicz, *Public Opinion Polling in Czechoslovakia, 1968-69* (New York, 1972), and to the Palach Press Ltd., London, for permission to use the materials by Josef Smrkovský and Zdeněk Mlynář in the appendices.

Finally I wish to record my gratefulness to various institutions (and to their responsible officers) for financial and other support: to the Canada Council, for the initial generous Killam award and subsequent research grants; to the University of Toronto, for supplementary aid and for two full years of sabbatical leave, the latter taken in two separate parts; to the institutions which provided me with congenial workplaces during these later leaves: the Center for International Studies of the Massachusetts Institute of Technology, and the Russian Research Center of Harvard University, in 1972, and St. Antony's College, Oxford, in 1975; and to the Centre for Russian and East European Studies at the University of Toronto (in particular to Franklyn Griffiths and Donald Schwartz who served as acting directors during my absences).

Toronto, Canada   H. GORDON SKILLING

LIST OF ABBREVIATIONS

PERIODICALS AND NEWSPAPERS

AER—*American Economic Review*
AJS—*American Journal of Sociology*
APSR—*American Political Science Review*
ASEER—*American Slavic and East European Review*
BBC—British Broadcasting Corporation, Monitoring Service, Summary of World Broadcasts
ČČH—*Československý časopis historický*
CDSP—*The Current Digest of the Soviet Press*
CEP—*Czechoslovak Economic Papers*
CH—*Current History*
CJEPS—*The Canadian Journal of Economics and Political Science*
CJPS—*Canadian Journal of Political Science*
CSM—*The Christian Science Monitor*
CSP—*Canadian Slavonic Papers*
DAS—*Dějiny a současnost*
EČ—*Ekonomický časopis*
EE—*East Europe*
EEE—*Eastern European Economics*
EEQ—*East European Quarterly*
FČ—*Filosofický časopis*
HČ—*Historický časopis*
HN—*Hospodářské noviny*
IJ—*International Journal*
IR—*International Relations*
JCEA—*Journal of Central European Affairs*
JIA—*Journal of International Affairs*
JP—*Journal of Politics*
Kat. nov.—*Katolické noviny*
KN—*Kulturní noviny*
KT—*Kulturní tvorba*
KZ—*Krasnaya zvezda*
KŽ—*Kultúrny život*
LD—*Lidová democracie*
LG—*Literaturnaya gazeta*
LL—*Literární listy*
LN—*Literární noviny*
MF—*Mladá fronta*

MN—*Magyar Nemzet*
MT—*Moravskoslezský týden*
MV—*Mezinárodní vztahy*
NA—*Narodna armiya*
NBIC—*News From Behind the Iron Curtain*
ND—*Neues Deutschland*
NLR—*New Left Review*
NM—*Nová mysl*
NS—*Nové slovo*
NTCE—*New Trends in Czechoslovak Economics*
NYT—*The New York Times*
OL—*Obrana lidu*
PC—*Problems of Communism*
PE—*Politická ekonomie*
PH—*Plánované hospodářství*
PKD KSČ—*Příspěvky k dějinám KSČ*
PO—*Právny obzor*
PSQ—*Political Science Quarterly*
PU—*Pravda Ukrainy*
RD—*Rabotnichesko delo*
Rep.—*Reportér*
Reprints—*Reprints from the Soviet Press*
RN—*Roľnícke noviny*
RP—*Rudé právo*
SCC—*Studies in Comparative Communism*
SČ—*Sociologický časopis*
SEER—*Slavonic and East European Review*
SR—*Sovetskaya Rossia*
SS—*Svobodné slovo*
SZ—*Socialistická zákonnost*
TL—*Trybuna Ludu*
U.S. JPRS,—*U.S. Joint Publication Research Service, East Europe Eastern Europe*
VN—*Východoslovenské noviny*
VP—*Večerní Praha*
WT—*The World Today*
ZIP—*Zëri i Popullit*
ZN—*Zemědělské noviny*
ŽS—*Život strany*

ABBREVIATIONS

ARS—Akademická rada studentů (Academic Council of Students)
CC—Central Committee
CMEA or COMECON—Council for Mutual Economic Assistance
ČNR—Česká národní rada (Czech National Council)
CPCz—Communist Party of Czechoslovakia
CPS—Communist Party of Slovakia
CPSU—Communist Party of the Soviet Union
ČSL—Československá strana lidová (Czechoslovak People's Party)
ČSM—Československý svaz mládeže (Czechoslovak Union of Youth)
ČSS—Československá strana socialistická (Czechoslovak Socialist Party)
ČSSR—Československá socialistická republika (Czechoslovak Socialist Republic)
ČSTV—Československý svaz tělesné výchovy (Czechoslovak Union of Physical Training)
ČTK—Československá tisková kancelář (Czechoslovak Press Agency)
GDR—German Democratic Republic
GFR—German Federal Republic
JZD—Jednotné zemědělské družstvo (collective farm)
K231—Club 231
KRK—Kontrolní a revizní komise (Commission of Supervision and Auditing)
KSK—Komise stranické kontroly (Commission of Party Control)
KSUT—Kulturna spilka ukrayinskykh trudyashchykh (Cultural Union of the Ukrainian Working People)
KAN—Klub angažovaných nestraníků (Club of the Non-party Engagés)
KSČ—Komunistická strana Československa (Communist Party of Czechoslovakia) —in English, CPCz
LCY—League of Communists of Yugoslavia
MFA—Ministry of Foreign Affairs
MPA—Main Political Administration
NF—Národní fronta (National Front)
RFE—Radio Free Europe
ROH—Revoluční odborové hnutí (Revolutionary Trade Union Movement)
RSFSR—Russian Soviet Federative Socialist Republic
RŠO—Rok šedesátý osmý v usneseních a dokumentech ÚV KSČ (The Year Sixty-eight in Decisions and Documents)
StB—Státní bezpečnost (State Security)
SČSS—Svaz československých spisovatelů (Union of Czechoslovak Writers)
SED—Socialist Unity Party of Germany (GDR)
SKŘO—Státní komise pro řízení a organisac (State Commission for Management and Organization)
SNB—Sbor národní bezpečnosti (Corps of National Security)
SNR—Slovenská narodná rada (Slovak National Council)
ÚKRK—Ústřední kontrolní a revizní komise (Central Commission of Supervision and Auditing)
ÚMPE—Ústav pro mezinárodní politiku a ekonomii (Institute of International Politics and Economics)
ÚPS—Ústřední publikační správa (Central Publication Administration)
ÚRO—Ústřední rada odborů (Central Council of Trade Unions)
ÚV—Ústřední výbor (Central Committee)
ÚVVM—Ústav pro výzkum veřejného mínění (Institute for Public Opinion Research)
VB—Veřejná bezpečnost (Public Security)
WTO—Warsaw Treaty Organization

PART ONE

THE HISTORICAL SETTING

CHAPTER I

Communism and Czechoslovak Traditions

COMMUNIST regimes have almost without exception repudiated the dominant traditions of their countries' history and claimed to have established brand-new patterns of politics and society. At the same time they have sought to depict communism as a projection of the "revolutionary" and "progressive" elements of their national heritage and to incorporate these in the mythology of the new order. In most cases, as, for instance, Soviet Russia, the past thus rejected was autocratic and reactionary, and only selected radical traditions were regarded as the forerunners of communism. In Czechoslovakia, however, the dominant tradition was democratic, deeply rooted in the feelings of the people, and regarded positively by most Czechs and by many Slovaks. The communists, therefore, had to renounce the advanced and progressive features of the past, such as the legacy of Masaryk, since these were integral elements of the dominant tradition.[1] In another respect, also, Czechoslovakia seemed to stand in stark contrast to other communist countries. The regimes have usually, willy-nilly, been affected and influenced, often unconsciously, by their own historical backgrounds, including those elements which were condemned. For a decade or more, Czechoslovak communism seemed to have been successful in erasing the dominant national traditions and to have escaped even their indirect influence. In the sixties, however, the forces of the past began once more to make themselves felt.

NATIONAL TRADITIONS AND THE COMMUNISTS

The strongest traditions with which the Czechoslovak communists had to grapple were those that had evolved during the twenty years of the First Republic between the two World Wars.[2] Created largely as a result

---

[1] Few scholars have attempted to discuss Czechoslovak communism in relation to Czech and Slovak traditions. The standard works by Edward Taborsky, *Communism in Czechoslovakia, 1948-1960* (Princeton, 1961) and V. Busek and N. Spulber, eds., *Czechoslovakia* (New York, 1957) are completely lacking in historical background. Of two major studies of the communist victory in 1948, Paul E. Zinner, *Communist Strategy and Tactics in Czechoslovakia, 1918-48* (New York, 1963) and Josef Korbel, *The Communist Subversion of Czechoslovakia, 1938-1948: The Failure of Co-existence* (Princeton, 1959), only Zinner, in a brief introduction, indicates some of the historical factors that affected the rise of communism to power. Korbel explains it almost exclusively in terms of the communist strategy of deceit. See also William E. Griffith, "Myth and Reality in Czechoslovak History," *East Europe* 11 (March 1962), 3-11, 34-36, 40-41.

[2] For this period, see R. W. Seton-Watson, *A History of the Czechs and Slovaks*

of the victory of the Entente and the decisions of the Paris Peace Conference, Czechoslovakia emerged as an independent state after three centuries of subservience and brought Czechs and Slovaks together in a single political entity for the first time in history. Modeled politically in the image of the Western democracies by its two great leaders, the first President, Tomáš G. Masaryk, and his successor, Edvard Beneš, Czechoslovakia, the new state, alone in Eastern Europe, maintained a democratic system during the two decades between the wars. True, many of the "traditions" of Czechoslovakia were new and broke with the historical experience of the Czechs and Slovaks within the Austro-Hungarian Monarchy. There were, however, important elements of continuity, so that the Republic could be regarded as a logical culmination of the national awakening and of decades of striving for a democratic life, social advance, and self-government.[3]

There were great disparities in the pasts of the Czechs and Slovaks, and their union in a single state, although not without historical justification, represented a new departure. Before 1919 the Czechs had risen to a high level of economic, social, and cultural development and had played an important political part in Austria; the Slovaks had remained at a lower level of development in all respects and possessed almost no political rights in Hungary. Their nationalism was less pronounced than that of the Czechs and was strongly influenced by the pressures of the Magyar environment and by the authority of the Catholic Church. The national movement, insofar as it existed, was mainly inspired and led by those Protestants and Catholics conscious of Slovak linguistic and cultural links with the Czech nation. After 1919, leadership by the larger nation, the Czech, led to the dominance of their traditional values, as represented by Masaryk and Beneš, and the subordination of the distinctive ideals of Slovak nationalism. The concept of a "Czechoslovak" nation asserted by Czech leaders even denied that a separate Slovak nation existed. Many Slovaks, including General Milan Štefánik, cofounder of the Republic, accepted the notion of Czechoslovak national unity.[4] Others increasingly stressed separate Slovak identity and urged

---

(London, 1943), chap. 16; S. Harrison Thomson, *Czechoslovakia in European History* (Princeton, 1943), chap. 13; Robert J. Kerner, ed., *Czechoslovakia: Twenty Years of Independence* (Berkeley and Los Angeles, 1940); and esp., Victor S. Mamatey and Radomír Luža, eds., *A History of the Czechoslovak Republic, 1918-1948* (Princeton, 1973). On Slovakia, see Jozef Lettrich, *History of Modern Slovakia* (New York, 1955); J. Mikus, *Slovakia: A Political History, 1918-50* (Milwaukee, 1963); Joseph M. Kirschbaum, ed., *Slovakia in the 19th and 20th centuries* (Toronto, 1973); and esp. C. A. Macartney, *Hungary and Her Successors: The Treaty of Trianon and Its Consequences, 1919-1937* (London, 1937).

[3] Thomson, *Czechoslovakia*, p. 157.
[4] General Štefánik perished in a plane crash in 1919.

autonomy for Slovakia. Other minorities, such as the Germans, Magyars, Poles, and Ruthenians had to reconcile themselves to the supremacy of the "Czechoslovaks" as the state-nation and to life within a community reflecting the spirit and ideas of the Czechs.

The concept of an independent Czechoslovak state had not attracted the left-wing socialists who eventually formed the Communist Party of Czechoslovakia (CPCz), as they had hoped for either a socialist revolution in the Austro-Hungarian Monarchy as a whole, or the incorporation of the Eastern European peoples in a continent-wide Soviet federation.[5] When independence was achieved, they accepted the new state as a political reality but viewed it as an "imperialist" state subordinated to the general interests of the ruling classes of the Western powers. Bohumír Šmeral, a leading pre-war socialist, and eventual founder of the Communist Party, endorsed the doctrine of proletarian dictatorship and pressed for membership in the Communist International, but openly recognized that conditions in Czechoslovakia were not ripe for revolution. By preserving a large party he hoped ultimately to win mass support for revolution. Although opposed to the new political and social order, Šmeral defended the territorial integrity of the new state and rejected the idea of self-determination for the national minorities.

The democracy established by Masaryk and the major Czechoslovak parties was treated by the communists as a façade which veiled the dominance of the bourgeoisie and condemned the workers to wage slavery and exploitation.[6] The "Castle" (*Hrad*), i.e. the President's office, was considered the pinnacle of power of the ruling classes, and Masaryk, and later Beneš, as the personification of capitalist rule. Although the communists benefited from the democratic rights established by the constitution, and functioned, subject to some restrictions, as a legal party during the life of the Republic, they considered themselves as outside the existing system and as its avowed enemy, and used its parliamentary and elec-

[5] There is no full history of Czechoslovak communism. See Zinner, *Communist Strategy*, chaps. 2-4 and H. Gordon Skilling, "The Formation of a Communist Party in Czechoslovakia," *American Slavic and East European Review* 14 (Oct. 1955), 346-58; "The Comintern and Czechoslovak Communism: 1921-1929," ibid. 19 (April 1960), 234-47; "Gottwald and the Bolshevization of the Communist Party of Czechoslovakia, 1929-1939," ibid. 20 (Dec. 1961), 641-55.

[6] For a communist interpretation of the First Republic, see M. Gosiorovský, ed., *Přehled československých dějin, III, 1918-1945, These* (Prague, 1956), esp. pp. 16, 29, 40. Czech communists, for some years, denied that the achievement of independence was due to the "foreign action" of Masaryk and Beneš and the support of the Western powers, but claimed that it was the product of the impact of the October revolution in Russia and the revolutionary actions of the masses at home. The birthday of the Republic was taken to be not October 28, 1918, when the National Committee in Prague proclaimed independence, but October 14, when the Socialist Council carried through a mass demonstration in the name of independence. See O. Říha, ed., *Přehled československých dějin, II (do roku 1918), These* (Prague, 1955), pp. 157-58.

toral opportunities as a means for its ultimate abolition. Always in radical opposition, they were treated by their opponents as outsiders, and not as legitimate participants in the democratic process. Although the communists functioned within a working democracy for two decades, this experience did not exert a strong influence on their thinking and behavior when they eventually achieved power.

When the CPCz was formed in 1921, it was a massive party, representing a substantial part, perhaps a majority, of the members of the post-war Czechoslovak Social Democratic Party and could therefore be regarded as a legitimate heir of Austrian social democracy. This movement had been originally Marxist in outlook and international in its appeal and included representatives of all the nationalities of the Monarchy. But Czech socialism had become increasingly nationalist in orientation and like the rest of the movement, revisionist or evolutionary in strategy and tactics. Although after 1918, many Czech socialists, under Šmeral's leadership, at first inclined toward the Comintern and its revolutionary program, at heart they were really left-wing socialists, rather than Bolsheviks. The left-wing element soon lost their dominant position to the more moderate wing of social democracy, which endorsed the Masaryk program of national liberation and became a governing party. There was also a substantial pre-war non-Marxist socialist tradition among Czechs, so that under these influences and Masaryk's leadership, the new state was "socialistic," but in a sense that was unacceptable to the communists with their dogmatic, revolutionary approach.[7]

The efforts of the Comintern were bent toward transforming the Czechoslovak movement, with its strong social democratic traditions, into a "Bolshevik" party, on the Leninist model. This required a constant struggle against so-called social democratic vestiges within its ranks and culminated in 1929 in the appointment of Moscow's choice, Klement Gottwald, as leader. Hostile to the existing Republic and its "bourgeois" democracy, the party, under his direction, devoted itself to the attainment of a proletarian revolution and the establishment of a Soviet Czechoslovakia. Successive purges produced a strong corps of pro-Moscow leading cadres and reduced the party to a small, sectarian, Moscow-oriented movement, shorn of its original social democratic and national heritage and lacking in popular appeal. Marx was replaced by Lenin in their pantheon, just as he was replaced by Masaryk in more moderate socialist circles. When the Comintern in 1924 adopted the doctrine of national self-determination, including even the right of secession,

---

[7] See T. G. Masaryk's critique of Marxism before 1914, in *Otázka sociální* (Prague, 1898); in English, E. V. Kohák, trans., *Masaryk on Marx* (Lewisburg, Pa., 1972). Cf. R. R. Betts, "Masaryk's Philosophy of History," *Slavonic and East European Review* 26 (Nov. 1947), 30-43.

and the CPCz incorporated this in their program, their ultimate objective became the disintegration of Czechoslovakia as a multinational state. As a result, communism's appeal was not so much to members of the ruling Czech nation as to the minority peoples, especially the Magyars in Slovakia and the Ruthenians. Nonetheless, in the years of deepening economic crisis, the party, with its radical program, began to gain support among the working class, and even among the intellectuals, and became a significant political factor, well represented in parliament.[8]

In the closing years of the Republic, the rise of Hitler to power, the danger of German aggression, and the formulation of the policy of the Popular Front by the Comintern led the Czechoslovak communists to adopt a more positive attitude toward the state and its democratic system. Still under Gottwald's leadership, in 1935, they embarked on a campaign for the defense of the Republic and its independence against the external threat from Germany, and of its democratic order against internal foes. This involved communist support for Edvard Beneš, who was elected as President in that year. The conclusion of the Czechoslovak-Soviet pact of mutual assistance in the same year removed any contradiction between the party's line and the foreign policy of the state. After Munich, the CPCz bitterly condemned what they called Beneš' capitulation to the ultimatum of the Great Powers and opposed the partition of the country, the subsequent Nazi occupation of Bohemia and Moravia, and the formation of a separate Slovak state. This enhanced the patriotic image of the party and widened its popular appeal. From 1939 to 1941, however, this policy was abandoned, the war was denounced as "imperialist" and Beneš' liberation movement was condemned. When the Soviet Union became involved in hostilities in 1941, however, the communists revived the democratic and nationalist approach and launched a crusade for the reconstitution of Czechoslovakia in its pre-war form.

Their willingness to cooperate with Beneš and to take part in the restored democratic system in 1945 suggested that they had abandoned their earlier hostility to Czech traditions and had themselves absorbed and been influenced by them. Until 1948 Gottwald seemed to have been successful in fusing Czech national interests with communist beliefs and objectives and by following what he called "a national path to socialism," won substantial support and sympathy for the Communist Party. The

---

[8] In the general elections of 1929 and 1935, the Communist Party was in each case the fourth strongest party, with thirty seats (almost one-quarter of the total) in the House of Deputies, and with a popular vote of approximately 750,-000 and 850,000 (in each case about 10 percent of the total). In 1925 they had been the second strongest party, with over 933,000 votes (13 percent of the total), and forty-one seats. For details, see Mamatey and Luža, eds., *Czechoslovak Republic*, pp. 128, 140, 154; Charles Hoch, *The Political Parties in Czechoslovakia*, 2nd ed. (Prague, 1936), table.

seizure of power in 1948 indicated, however, that the conversion of the communists, if there had been one, was superficial and that their repudiation of the nation's democratic past was total and permanent. Thereafter for twenty years, communism became the dominant, indeed the exclusive, political force and established new traditions of crucial significance for the future and in particular for the events after January 1968.

CZECHS AND SLOVAKS

In one important respect there was striking continuity between the communist and pre-communist periods, namely, the restoration of Czechoslovakia after World War II mainly in the form and within the boundaries established by the Paris peace settlement of 1919.[9] Masaryk's strategy of a union of Czechs and Slovaks was thus confirmed by the communists and has been continued ever since. Moreover, the long-standing Czech belief in the territorial integrity of Bohemia and Moravia, and the argument of Masaryk and Beneš for incorporating the whole of these regions, in spite of a large German minority, into the liberated Republic, were again endorsed in 1945, although with the important change, to be discussed later, of the expulsion of the Germans. The less ancient tradition of including in the state Polish and Magyar minorities and the lands where they lived, largely within the 1919 frontiers, was also reaffirmed. The only exception to the restoration of the pre-war territorial structure was the cession of Subcarpathian Ruthenia to the USSR. This area had been assigned to Czechoslovakia in 1919 primarily for strategic considerations and had always been a heavy burden on the resources of Prague governments. Its loss, unlike the cession of Poland's eastern territories, did not represent the reversal of a deep historic tradition and was little lamented. Indeed, it was accepted by President Beneš and other non-communists as a sacrifice well worth making in return for the assurance of the integrity of the rest of the Republic.

The reunification of Czechs and Slovaks in a single state brought to an end the "independence" which Slovaks had enjoyed after 1939. During the First Republic the Slovaks had experienced great cultural and political development as contrasted with their lot under the Magyars, and many of them had identified strongly with the new Czechoslovakia. Their failure to secure the autonomy which they had expected and the assumption by the Czechs of a dominating role in the Republic had caused other Slovaks, led by Andrej Hlinka and his successor, Jozef Tiso, to expound a more pronounced Slovak nationalism and to demand home rule, or even independence. In successive elections the Slovak People's Party

[9] See H. G. Skilling, "The Czechoslovak Struggle for National Liberation in World War II," *SEER* 39 (Dec. 1960), 174-97.

8

proved to be the strongest in Slovakia but was always outvoted by the combined votes of parties with a Czech or Czechoslovak orientation.[10] Only after Munich was Slovakia granted the long-desired autonomy, but important elements in the People's Party began to turn toward complete independence as a preferable goal. The establishment, in 1939, for the first time in history, of a separate Slovak state, even under the suzerainty of Nazi Germany and under conservative, clerical-fascist leadership, created a distinctive tradition that was bound to have a continuing impact on Slovak thought.

During the war the communists had formed a separate illegal Slovak party and some of its leaders had at first flirted with the notion of a future Slovak Soviet state. The CPCz leadership in Moscow, and eventually the leading Slovak communists at home, such as Gustáv Husák and the poet, Laco Novomeský, however, committed themselves fully to the restoration of the pre-war Republic. During the Slovak Uprising of 1944, both communists and non-communists endorsed this policy and accepted the authority of the Beneš government in London. They insisted, however, that the Slovaks must be recognized as a distinct nation and must be guaranteed home rule in a liberated Czechoslovakia. They rejected, therefore, not only the brief experience of Slovak independence, and the nationalist philosophy of Fathers Hlinka and Tiso, but also the pre-war concept of a single "Czechoslovak" nation and the very limited autonomy granted to the Slovaks in the First Republic. The Košice government program of 1945 proclaimed anew the principle of Czech-Slovak unity but at the same time asserted the doctrine of Slovak equality and autonomy, thus forecasting a substantial change in Czech-Slovak relations.

In the early post-war months the communists, both Czech and Slovak, were vigorous advocates of a distinct Slovak identity and of Slovak autonomy, but conscious of their own political weakness in the Slovak regions, they soon turned toward centralist rule in the Republic as a whole. Even after 1948 the communists continued to recognize the separate identity of the Slovak nation and to protect its cultural and linguistic rights, and in the 1948 constitution provided for organs of Slovak self-government. Nonetheless the powers of the government in Prague waxed steadily and the reality of home rule waned. Moreover, the Com-

---

[10] In the elections of 1925, 1929, and 1935, the People's Party won the following votes: 489,000, 404,000, and 490,000, representing approximately 34, 28, and 30 percent of the total vote in Slovakia. The parties of Czech or Czechoslovak orientation received 400,000 (28 percent), 579,000 (40 percent), and 628,000 (39 percent). Slovak communists in these three elections accounted for 189,000, 152,000, and 211,000 votes, resp. (Kirschbaum, ed., *Slovakia*, p. 123; Mamatey and Luža, eds., *Czechoslovak Republic*, pp. 128, 141, 154; Macartney, *Hungary and Her Successors*, pp. 118, 144.)

munist Party, having reunited its Czech and Slovak branches in 1948, was predominantly Czech in membership and in leadership. The campaign against Slovak nationalism in the fifties resulted in the execution of Vladimír Clementis, the imprisonment of Husák and others, and the subordination of the Slovak party to Prague. Czechoslovakia again became a state ruled by Czechs, but this time with even greater indifference to Slovak rights than before 1939. The 1960 constitution openly articulated extreme centralism and reduced even the forms of Slovak self-government to nil. After 1963 there was a resurgence of Slovak cultural nationalism and a certain advance in the political position of the Slovaks, but they continued to be minor partners in a predominantly Czech state and party.

GERMANS AND HUNGARIANS

Conflict with the Germans has always been a central issue in Czech political life and a salient factor in the nation's historical tradition.[11] The clash of the two nations within the Austro-Hungarian Monarchy was followed by the reversal of roles after 1919 when the Czechs became the rulers, and the Germans the ruled. The latter enjoyed the full freedom of a democratic society and substantial cultural rights but were relegated to the status of a minority within a predominantly Slavic state and fell easy prey, later, to Nazi propaganda. By 1937 the majority supported the autonomist and implicitly secessionist demands of Konrad Henlein, Sudeten German supporter of Hitler. The Munich partition in September 1938, Germany's ruthless occupation of the rump of Bohemia and Moravia, and the wartime struggle against Nazi rule contributed to the decision of the Czechoslovak government-in-exile that the Germans must be expelled from their historic homelands. This marked a sharp break with the past since, in spite of continuing hostility, the Czechs had always sought a basis of cohabitation with the Germans within a single political entity and, during some periods of the Republic, had even won the cooperation of certain German parties in coalition governments. It was also decided, after the war, to remove all or most of the Hungarians from Slovakia by exchanging them for Slovaks repatriated from Hungary.

The Communist Party between the wars had included both Germans and Hungarians in its ranks; it had a number of German-speaking leaders, and tended to support the complaints of the German and other minorities. After 1945, the communists might have been expected either

[11] For the view of the Czech historian, František Palacký, that the conflict with the Germans was the central question in Czech history, see the translation of essential passages from his works in M. Weatherall, "The Mainspring of Czech History," *Central European Observer*, June 26, 1942, p. 203.

to favor a multinational state, recognizing the autonomous rights of the Germans and other minorities, as in the USSR, or to advocate the break-up of Czechoslovakia and the cession of the German areas to Germany. Instead, the CPCz endorsed Beneš' policy of expulsion and transfer, aiming at the establishment of a largely Slavic state of Czechs and Slovaks, and even outdid their colleagues in pressing this nationalistic policy. After the war they took an active part in resettling the vacated territories with Czechs and Slovaks from other parts of the Republic, and even from abroad, and were as adamant as the non-communists in insisting on the maintenance of the boundaries of the pre-Munich Republic.

This gave the Czechs, like the Poles, a powerful national interest in an alliance with the Soviet Union as a guarantor of their territorial integrity against the threat of German revisionism. Although their hatred of the Germans was not as intense as that of the Poles, there was a similar apprehension of pressures by refugees and revanchist elements in West Germany, so that communist policy received strong backing from the population. Cooperation with East Germany was only in partial contradiction to this, as the existence of such a state, which recognized Czechoslovakia's western frontiers and weakened the position of the German nation by keeping it divided, served both the ends of communist policy and Czech national interests.

THE BREAK WITH THE PAST

In the matters so far discussed, the communists, even when they retained certain traditional attitudes, significantly modified them in actual practice. As far as the political aspect was concerned, the break with the past was even more complete. The constitution of 1920 had provided Czechoslovakia with a government modeled on British, French, and American patterns, and included elements of both parliamentary and presidential systems. Although not without serious defects, this structure had functioned between the wars with considerable success as an effective democracy.[12] This democratic tradition was prolonged for a few years after 1945 in the altered conditions of the National Front. In 1948, however, the communists took advantage of a crisis within the coalition government to seize power, under a constitutional guise, and to eliminate their partners from all political participation. The constitution of 1948, adopted after the February coup, preserved on paper some elements of

[12] There has been little Western analysis of the Czechoslovak political system between the wars. See the chapters by Malbone W. Graham, in Kerner, ed., *Czechoslovakia*, chaps. 7 and 8, and also Graham, *New Governments of Central Europe* (New York, 1926), chaps. 12-14. The fullest analysis is by E. Taborsky, *Naše nová ústava* (Prague, 1948) and *Czechoslovak Democracy at Work* (London, 1945).

the pre-war system but could not conceal the reality of the dominance of a single party. Not even lip service was paid to the ideas of Masaryk and Beneš, which had no effect, even indirectly or unconsciously, on communist political behavior. In the fifties a series of political trials represented the complete destruction of pre-communist legal traditions and even of the "socialist legality" professed by the communists. The constitution of 1960 moved Czechoslovakia still further away from its national past and closer to the Soviet pattern. The Russian autocratic tradition, as developed under communism, had thus more effect on Czechoslovak political life than indigenous national traditions.

An equally sharp rupture with the past occurred in the economic and social field. Between the wars Czechoslovakia remained primarily a system based on free enterprise and private property but advanced far in the direction of a welfare state. The mixed economy of the early post-war years included a substantial private sector in agriculture, trade, and even part of industry, but after 1948, was transformed into a full-blown "socialist" system on the Soviet model. Czechoslovakia was unique among communist states in inheriting a well-developed industry, a skilled proletariat, and an experienced managerial class, but these were subjected to draconic and far-reaching changes. The economy was fundamentally reshaped, with the emphasis no longer on textiles, glass and other industries, and on trade with the West, but on heavy industrial products and dependence on the East. The position of the workers was basically modified as a result of the destruction of the free trade union movement and the harnessing of the labor force to the goals of the state through the transmission belts of party-controlled unions. Managerial talents were often squandered through the dismissal or emigration of managers, the appointment of party men without business experience as directors or state officials, and a downgrading of pay for white-collar workers.

The economy was at first able, despite this radical transformation, to maintain a higher standard of living than other bloc countries and to stimulate productive growth in the favored sectors. The ultimate outcome, however, was an economic crisis from 1961 on and the recognition of the need for fundamental revision by economists and political leaders. This represented not a return to pre-war capitalism, but the restoration of some traditional elements of a market economy within the framework of a planned and state-owned system.

In the intellectual realm, too, the transition to full communism after 1948 led to a basic reorientation of Czech and Slovak life. Prior to 1914 their culture, like that of most small nations, had been composed of many foreign ingredients, as well as native traditions. While they could not escape the impact of the German-Austrian and Hungarian worlds within which they were embedded, Czechs and Slovaks were also subject to the influences of more remote European cultures. As Slavs, they often felt the pull of Russian civilization and of pan-Slav attractions, especially in literature. In the latter half of the 19th century, however, Western cultures, including French, English, and American, had a more profound impact than Eastern or Slavic. Czechoslovak civilization, reflecting these influences and its own unique history as expounded by František Palacký and Masaryk, was identified with the ideas of freedom and humanity.[13] Especially after 1919 Czech life was dominated by the views of Masaryk, an intellectual as well as a political leader, and was strongly Western as well as profoundly national, democratic, and humanist in its orientation.[14] Karel Čapek, the writer, who was a close friend of Masaryk, personified this trend most fully.[15] There were also strong Marxist and socialist elements in Czech culture, and a powerful attraction to the Soviet Union and communism among the intellectuals.[16] In Slovakia, other traditions competed with the liberal, Czech-oriented tendency, for instance, the more conservative, anti-Czech "populist" school of thought and the radical and nationalistic wing of Slovak communism.

For a short time after the second World War, there was a return to the intermingling of diverse cultural elements, marked by a substantial advance in Soviet or Russian influence, and a decline in Western and traditional Czech currents of thought.[17] After the coup of 1948, however, the wheel was made to turn exclusively in one direction, with the Soviet pattern proclaimed as the model in all spheres and with Western elements almost excluded.[18] This was part of a full-scale effort to mold education, scholarship, and the creative arts according to Soviet concepts of socialist realism and historical materialism. All indigenous traditions, as typified by Masaryk, Beneš, and Štefánik, among both Czechs and Slovaks, and by Hlinka and Tiso, and even Clementis, Husák, and Novomeský, among Slovaks, had to be eliminated in the drive against liberalism, social democracy, nationalism, and religion. Some threads of the past, such as the Hussite tradition or literary nationalism as repre-

[13] See Hans Kohn, *Not By Arms Alone* (Cambridge, Mass., 1941) and Václav Beneš, "Background of Czechoslovak Democracy," in M. Rechcigl, Jr., ed., *The Czechoslovak Contribution to World Culture* (The Hague, 1964), pp. 267-76.

[14] This is not to say that there were not Czechs who rejected the dominant Masaryk influence, and, among historians, some who challenged his interpretations of Czech history. See O. Odložilík, "Modern Czechoslovak Historiography," *SEER* 30 (June 1952), 376-92; S. Harrison Thomson, "T. G. Masaryk and Czech Historiography," *Journal of Central European Affairs* 10 (April 1950), 37-52.

[15] See W. E. Harkins, *Anthology of Czech Literature* (New York, 1953), p. 177; Milada Součková, *A Literature in Crisis: Czech Literature 1938-1950* (New York, 1954), pp. 102, 137-38.

[16] Harkins, *Anthology*, pp. 172-73.

[17] Součková, *Literature in Crisis*, pp. 5 ff., 31-39, 138-39.

[18] Ibid., pp. 40-53, 139-43.

13

sented by Alois Jirásek, were preserved, but were interwoven with radical democratic or left-wing socialist historical trends and embroidered with Russian and Soviet features.

In spite of unremitting indoctrination, many of the old patterns of thought remained buried in the consciousness of the people, and came to the surface with the restoration of a certain degree of intellectual freedom after 1963.[19] Rehabilitation of such literary figures as Čapek, Novomeský, and Franz Kafka represented a revival of some components of the national tradition. There were substantial obstacles in the way of a full, or even a partial, rehabilitation of Masaryk and Beneš, since they embodied the main cultural orientation before the war and represented the antithesis of communist ideals and ideology. Yet vestiges of "Masarykism," of which the communists constantly complained, persisted, and were manifested in the sixties in the rebirth of critical realism and the search for truth among communist intellectuals.

East and West in Foreign Relations

The position taken by Czechoslovakia in world affairs has also reflected a counterpoint of East and West. It has been argued that from the outset Czech historical experience has always represented a mingling of elements of West and East, with the former predominant, but the latter never absent.[20] Certainly in the modern period, the Czechs looked in both directions for succor and support—before 1914 as a counterpoise to the Austro-German context of their lives, and after 1919 as bulwarks against the threat of Germany. This balance was also present in the two World Wars in the effort that was made to win independence with the aid of both Eastern and Western powers. Yet there was a sharp contrast between the quarter of a century after 1914, and the one after 1939. In the earlier period, the pendulum swung heavily in a Western direction, as indicated by the alliance with France, the shaping of the state in a Western mold, and widespread sympathy with the USA, Great Britain, and France. The Eastern orientation was expressed in the alliance with the USSR after 1935 and the sympathy of many Czechs for Soviet communism and was continued during the war in Beneš' policy of close co-

[19] See Skilling, *Communism National and International: Eastern Europe after Stalin* (Toronto, 1964), chap. 7.

[20] O. Odložilík, "Components of Czechoslovak Tradition," *SEER* 23 (Jan. 1945), 97-106. See also Karel Čapek and Ferdinand Peroutka, in Čapek et al., *At the Cross-Roads of Europe: A Historical Outline of the Democratic Idea in Czechoslovakia* (Prague, 1938), pp. 8-10, 261, resp. For the views of Masaryk and Beneš, see T. G. Masaryk, *The Making of a State: Memories and Observations, 1914-1918* (London, 1927), pp. 377-85, and Edvard Beneš, *My War Memoirs* (London, 1928), pp. 490-99.

operation with the USSR. In the post-1945 years, there were renewed efforts to achieve an equilibrium between East and West, but the balance tipped toward the East. After 1948, the weight was shifted entirely in that direction, with intimate association with the USSR and complete elimination of ties with the West.

The swing to the East has sometimes been interpreted as a logical continuation of strong pro-Russian and pro-Soviet historical sympathies among Czechs, a proposition which greatly exaggerates the realities of the past. In fact what distinguished Czechs and Slovaks from Poles or Hungarians was the *absence* of a long-standing anti-Russian tradition, rather than the *presence* of a dominant pro-Russian one, and a somewhat less intense anti-Soviet attitude, rather than a strongly pro-Soviet one. What united the Czechs was a powerful anti-German historical tradition, reinforced by the experience of two World Wars and the occupation by Nazi Germany, which caused them to look favorably, albeit rather sentimentally, to the Russians as a counterweight against the main enemy. The communists, pro-Soviet rather than pro-Russian, took advantage of the lack of deep anti-Russian feelings and of vague pro-Soviet sentiments to justify a close alliance with the USSR. They also exploited to the full the discrediting of the Western powers caused by the Munich betrayal— a factor which profoundly affected Beneš in his assessment of the balance between East and West and which contributed to a more positive Czech attitude toward communism and the Soviet alliance. After 1948, however, the communists transformed the relationship into a slavish subservience to the USSR and to all things Russian, which was entirely alien to the Czech past.

The sequence of events after 1938 took the heart out of Czech and Slovak national spirit. Having achieved independence in 1919 largely with the aid of the West, they saw it undermined by the Western governments in 1938 and liquidated by Germany the following year. Munich was a crushing blow which negated the essence of at least two decades of Czechoslovak history and sapped faith in the West and its ideas. Similarly, having regained their independence in 1945 largely with the aid of the East, they lost it again in 1948 by the actions of the Czechoslovak communists. The February coup thus weakened another strand of Czechoslovak tradition by discrediting Russia and communism. Yet an appeal to the West in 1948 was excluded by the experience of Munich. Moreover, Germany and the Germans were still the main sources of danger in the consciousness of most Czechs and could not therefore be brought into the balance against Russia. In a new crisis, in 1956, communists and non-communists found their will to act paralyzed by successive disappointments and disillusionments. Neither communists nor non-communists could find much sustenance in their own national traditions, so badly shaken by past experience. Continued subservience to Moscow, and conformity with the Soviet pattern, was therefore the path of least resistance, and the one preferred by the regime's leaders. In the sixties there was a rebirth of Czechoslovak intellectual and economic interest in the West and some evidence of a desire on the part of the communist government to restore a more balanced orientation toward East and West, thus suggesting the continuing strength of the pro-Western tradition.

A NATION OF ŠVEJKS?

Another facet of the Czech tradition has often been cited but so far not seriously analyzed by Western or Czech scholars—namely, the supposed willingness of the Czech nation and its leaders to adapt passively to a given political system, and their unwillingness to resist even unpopular or hated rulers by violent or revolutionary means. The celebrated character of Jaroslav Hašek's novel, *The Good Soldier Švejk*, has often been considered the typical model of Czech behavior toward authority, foreign or native, and is offered as an explanation of the conformity of Czechoslovak communism, and of the passive acceptance of the regime by the population even during its Stalinist phases. This is not the place for a full examination of this facile, but unconvincing, interpretation of Czech history, which has been prevalent both in some Western circles, and among Eastern European communists, including the Czechs. Enough must be said, however, to indicate that it involves not only a misinterpretation of the meaning of Švejkism but a distortion of Czechoslovak history. The Švejk myth, it should be noted, relates only to the Czechs and not to the Slovaks, who possess, in their history, the figure of Jánošík, a kind of Robin Hood of the 18th century, who became, in literature and folklore, a legendary symbol of Slovak nationalism and rebelliousness against social injustice.

It must be admitted that Czechs lack an ancient revolutionary past, such as the Poles or Hungarians possess, and that their history has been more peaceful in content and reformist in methods. For at least a century theirs has been a tradition, not of violent nationalism or of extreme revolutionism, but of tolerance and democracy, moderate rather than radical.[21] In the modern period, after a brief revolt in Prague in 1848, the Czechs eventually adopted a nonviolent course, seeking to secure and improve their position through piecemeal reform attained through cooperation with Austrian authorities. National radicalism gave way to cautious

[21] Peroutka (Čapek et al., *Cross-Roads of Europe*, p. 253) wrote: "The spirit of revolution was never at home in modern Bohemia as it was in Ireland or in Russia."

realism or opportunism, and revolutionary socialism to reformism. This involved practical work to improve their position within the Austrian system, rather than an effort to overthrow it by revolution. Strong nationalist feelings were, however, intensified by the persistent resistance of the Austrian Germans to their demands.[22] During the years of war (in both World Wars) there was a readiness, on the part of some Czechs (and Slovaks), to adapt themselves to the prevailing system and to collaborate with their German rulers. When independence came in 1918 (and again in 1945), it was largely the result of decisions by the Great Powers, supported by the diplomatic actions of Czech exiles, and seemed therefore to be a gift from outside rather than a product of native struggle at home. Similarly, between the wars, Masaryk and Beneš eschewed force and violence, based their political system on democratic procedures and moderate social reform, and founded their foreign policy on diplomatic compromise.

It is also true that the communists themselves have been a party of reform, not of revolution. Although repudiating the pre-war Republic in words, they did not attempt its revolutionary overthrow. During the second World War, there was courageous resistance by communists, as well as by non-communists, but eventual liberation was effected by the tanks and planes of the Soviet army. The communist leaders, like their World War I predecessors, and like Beneš in World War II, returned to the homeland as a result of an Allied victory and did not take control by their own efforts. After the war the communists at first chose to pursue a gradual approach, rather than to seize the reins at once by force. Even the 1948 coup was not so much a revolution as a consolidation of strength by a party already in power, and without bloodshed.[23] The presence in the neighborhood of the Soviet army and the unwillingness of the West to intervene were important contributing factors, so that communist victory, like liberation in 1919 and 1945, was in considerable degree conditioned by outside forces. The acquiescence of Beneš was a kind of second Munich, and like its forerunner, did not produce open revolt or popular resistance. The brilliantly successful communist strategy sapped the will of non-communists to resist, either then or later. In a similar way Czech communists, remote from the mainstream of Czech nationalism but influenced by the realist tradition, were unwilling to risk taking a stand against Stalinism, as their counterparts did in some other communist countries. The extreme terror of the fifties resulted in a failure of will which, although understandable under the circumstances, continued for

[22] See Skilling, "The Politics of the Czech Eighties," in Peter Brock and H. Gordon Skilling, eds., *The Czech Renascence of the Nineteenth Century* (Toronto, 1970).

[23] See Skilling, "The Prague Overturn in 1948," *Canadian Slavonic Papers* 4 (1960), 88-114.

some years after the death of Stalin and contributed to the absence of overt action in 1956.

Nonetheless, there is another side to the picture. The Czechs have not been as passive and adaptive to authority as suggested by their description as "a nation of Švejks." For one thing, Švejk was in essence a radical and revolutionary figure, ridiculing not only state power and militarism, but also religion, nationalism, and all established conventions. Evincing outward conformity to the Austrian system, Švejk rejected it inwardly in every aspect and sought to destroy it by bringing it into derision and contempt. Moreover, in their long history, Czechs have often shown a readiness to challenge authority, not only by passive resistance but, when appropriate, by force or by active opposition. They possess as rich and deep a national past as any people of Eastern Europe, including such glorious episodes as the Hussite movement, and a galaxy of celebrated figures such as Jan Hus, Jan Žižka, Jan Amos Komenský, and King George of Poděbrady, and, in the modern period, Karel Havlíček, Palacký, and Masaryk.

It is true that the tragedy of Bílá Hora in 1620 initiated three centuries of subjugation, during which the opportunity for heroic action was excluded. When the occasion presented itself, however, the Czechs did resist—by force in 1848, and after 1860 by abstention from participation in Austrian politics. In 1879, the Czechs entered the phase of "organic cooperation" (as the Poles have called their own comparable tactics) but this was accompanied by mounting nationalism and by a growing opposition to Austria, implicit until 1914 but explicit in 1918. When independence came, it was the result not merely of action by the Great Powers but also of brave acts of defiance by some Czechs and Slovaks at home and abroad, eventually endorsed by the people at large. The precedent of a liberation movement abroad was repeated in the second World War. Although in neither period was there widespread resistance, mass defection from the Austrian army; military action by the Czechoslovak Legions on the Allied side in World War I; the Slovak and Prague revolts; and the formation of military units abroad in World War II can hardly be reconciled with the myth of consistently passive adaptation to foreign rule.

Although, for reasons discussed above, the latter theme did loom large in 1938, and again in 1948, events in the sixties indicated that the Czechs had not permanently reconciled themselves to their fate or rejected the possibility of changing it by their own actions. Although de-Stalinization was belated and strongly opposed by the communist leaders, it came as a result of independent thinking and courageous speaking by individuals, especially writers, scholars, and other professional persons. Resistance that was slight and abortive in 1953 and 1956 was more active and successful after 1963. A new generation which had not lived through the days of Munich and the German occupation, and had not even personally experienced the worst phases of Stalinism, sought not to overthrow communism, but to reform it. Their ranks were strengthened by some members of the older generation, often the victims of the terror of the fifties who, having escaped with their lives and been rehabilitated, added their voices to the demand for change. Although resembling Švejk in their outward display of loyalty to the communist system, and acting in its name, they went beyond him in their blunt criticism of past and present defects and in their open insistence on the need for fundamental reform.[24]

SOVEREIGNTY AND ITS BENEFITS

There is one other example of the formal retention by the communists of a national tradition which, although vastly altered in substance, was of great actual and potential significance. Since 1945 Czechoslovakia has been a sovereign state, thus repeating the experience between the two World Wars. Its formal independence in 1918 was, however, primarily the product of a change in the balance of power and a function of Western support and German and Soviet weakness, and came to an abrupt end in 1938-39. For twenty years, however, Czechoslovakia, within the limits imposed on every small state, had been able to formulate its own domestic policy and to follow a somewhat independent course in foreign affairs. After 1948, in spite of formal independence, Czechoslovakia was in fact a political satellite, in the sense of being governed indirectly by the Soviet Union through the intermediary of a thoroughly submissive and loyal CPCz and its leaders.[25] In a sense, its status was hardly different from what it would have been as a Union Republic within the USSR. Nonetheless, as later events demonstrated, the maintenance of Czechoslovakia and other communist satellites as sovereign states, at least in form, was to have profound repercussions. The preservation of the nation-state, and indeed its exaltation as the main vehicle of political action, made possible the rise of national communism in Yugoslavia, Poland, Rumania, and Albania.[26]

For twenty years the communists rulers of Czechoslovakia did not take advantage of the possibilities of independent action. Submission to

[24] See Skilling, "Czechoslovakia" in Adam Bromke, ed., *The Communist States at the Crossroads: Between Moscow and Peking* (New York, 1965), pp. 102-5.

[25] For this definition, see Ferenc A. Váli, *Rift and Revolt in Hungary* (Cambridge, Mass., 1961), pp. 13-17.

[26] See Paul Shoup, "Communism, Nationalism and the Growth of the Communist Community of Nations after World War II," *American Political Science Review* 56 (Dec. 1962), 886-98.

Moscow was their own choice, although alternative courses were possible. Just as they had accepted Soviet direction and policy, Czech and Slovak communists could, if they had wished, have rejected the former and criticized the latter—in other words, have ceased to act like a satellite. If they were to have shown greater initiative, and reflected the changing temper of their people, national traditions, suitably refashioned to reflect modern conditions, would inevitably have exerted a growing influence. In fact this was precisely what happened in the sixties, culminating in 1968, when many apparently extinct traditions were revived and began to have an impact on all spheres of Czech and Slovak life.[27]

[27] This chapter was originally published in a slightly different version in *Journal of International Affairs* 20, no. 1 (1966), 118-36. It was severely criticized by Jaromír Obzina, *Život strany*, no. 21 (1970), pp. 45-48; ibid., no. 17 (1972), pp. 12-14. Obzina's first article was a sharp critique of Masaryk's *Sociální otázka* and his concepts of "bourgeois reformism" and "humanist democracy," which formed the basis of bourgeois rule under the First Republic and were revived again in 1945-1948 and 1968-1969. Skilling's article, he wrote, provided the "opportunists" and "revisionists" with helpful argumentation for their efforts in 1968-1969 to achieve "a renaissance of Marxism-Leninism with the aid of Masarykism" and thus to justify the conception of "national communism." In his second article Obzina criticized the efforts of the revisionists of 1968-1969 to effect the "erosion" of a socialism based on the general patterns of social development as set forth by Marxism-Leninism and to formulate "a specific Czechoslovak model" based on the conceptions of Masaryk (in effect the "Skilling model of socialism").

CHAPTER II

The Dualism of Czechoslovak Communism
From Gottwald to Novotný

THIS BRIEF excursion into the background of Czechoslovak communism brings out its ambivalent and erratic past, illustrated by the extraordinary shifts of policy between 1921 and 1929, between 1935 and 1940, and between 1945 and 1948. At times communism was in tune with the democratic and national views of Czechs and Slovaks and gained widespread sympathy and support. At other times it was at odds with the dominant national attitudes and became a dogmatic sect, isolated from the mainstream of national life. On some occasions it supported Czechoslovak democracy and the independence and territorial integrity of the Republic; on other occasions it opposed both. As a result, the degree of its "legitimacy," i.e. of its acceptance in Czechoslovak political life, varied greatly. Sometimes it was supported by a substantial part of the population, as in the early years under Šmeral, and in the Popular Front period under Klement Gottwald. At other times, it was rejected by the bulk of the Czech and Slovak nations who regarded it as a force primarily imposed and controlled from outside, by the Comintern or the Soviet party. Yet paradoxically even when it had widespread support, it simultaneously met with strong opposition; when its policy was generally condemned, it managed to retain the loyalty of a hard core of "genuine believers."

A critical element in this contradictory and shifting pattern of communist behavior was the relationship with the USSR and with the CPSU. In all periods, without exception, the Czechoslovak party remained a loyal and devoted follower of the CPSU and of its policies. Moscow was able to exercise direct control of the CPCz through the intermediary of leaders who were ready to accept without reservation and usually without reluctance all Soviet directives, and to purge from their ranks any who held divergent views. Yet the Soviet impact did not always tend in the same direction. At certain times Soviet influence reinforced the nationalist and democratic tendencies, at other times, the dogmatic and sectarian trends, of Czech and Slovak communists. The analysis is complicated further by the fact that the non-communist attitudes toward Russia were ambivalent, ranging from open antipathy to substantial sympathy. During and after World War I Masaryk adopted policies that could hardly be regarded as friendly to the Soviet Union; Beneš, from 1935 on, and again during World War II and its aftermath, based his strategy on close co-operation with the Soviet Union.

The theme of duplexity, if not duplicity, of Czechoslovak communism may be further illustrated by a closer examination of the almost quarter of a century of communist rule under Klement Gottwald and his principal successor, Antonín Novotný. This is not a matter of contrasting the two leaders with each other, but rather of recognizing the duality that runs like a red thread through the tenure of each of them. In the case of Gottwald, two phases may be noted: from 1945 to 1948, when, with Soviet approval, he won a certain legitimacy by following policies favorable to democratic processes and national needs and circumstances; and from 1948 to 1953, when, under Soviet pressure, Gottwald gradually destroyed important elements of this legitimacy by his subservience to Soviet views and interests and by thorough Stalinization of Czech and Slovak life. In the case of Novotný, two phases, not so clearly marked, may also be discerned. In the first, from 1953 to 1961, Novotný continued the main lines of Gottwald's second phase, even though this was no longer appropriate in the light of the evolution of post-Stalin Russia. Although he experimented with a modest "New Course" for a brief time after 1953, he increasingly resorted to coercive measures to secure obedience and thereby weakened the legitimacy of his regime. In the second period, from 1961 to 1967, political terror gave way to less violent forms of repression but was not replaced by more persuasive means or by spontaneous loyalty. Under the impact of continued de-Stalinization in the Soviet Union, however, Novotný made successive retreats and concessions to the developing forces of opposition at home. The balance of this chapter will seek to develop this theme of duality as a background to a more detailed examination of the decline and fall of Novotný in the following chapters.

THE NATIONAL PATH TO SOCIALISM

During the period from 1945 to 1948 the Communist Party, under Gottwald, emerged as the dominant, but not the exclusive, political force in liberated Czechoslovakia. Refraining from an attempt at violent and total revolution on the Soviet pattern, the party, with the sanction of the Soviet Union, opted for a more moderate course, more in line with the predominant national traditions of the country. Accepting the leadership of Beneš as President and cooperating responsibly with other parties within the National Front, the Communist Party of Czechoslovakia espoused a program which represented a blend of continuity and revolution.[1] Nationalization of a sector of industry, radical land reform, and a

[1] See Skilling, "Revolution and Continuity in Czechoslovakia, 1945-1946,"

limited system of short-term planning produced a mixed economy which included substantial elements of both capitalism and socialism. The pre-war constitutional system was, in broad outline, preserved, although with some significant changes, including a broadened Slovak autonomy and a reformed system of local government in the form of the national committees. Non-communist parties were permitted, in the Czech areas as continuants of pre-war predecessors—the Czechoslovak National Socialist, People's, and Social Democratic Parties—and in Slovakia, the Labor Party and the newly established Democratic Party. Other leading pre-war parties, such as the Czechoslovak Agrarian and the Slovak People's Parties, were, however, banned. The National Front, grouping the main political parties as a basis for the coalition government, was an unusual political formation, permitting no opposition to the Front as such, but allowing sharp conflicts and some electoral competition between its constituent elements. In spite of these limitations, political life took place within a general context of democratic freedom, in which the press, scholarship, and cultural life were largely free of party or government control. The "people's democracy" thus established was certainly not a complete nor a perfect democracy, but it embodied important democratic elements, far more genuine than in the neighboring "people's democracies" or in Soviet Russia and it retained important features of pre-communist Czechoslovak politics.

This "national and democratic revolution," as Gottwald called it, continued the pre-war strategy of the Popular Front and identified the communists with important aspects of Czechoslovak tradition. Moreover, President Beneš and the non-communist parties were prepared to accept, in the main, certain revolutionary changes advocated by the Communist Party. As a result the latter had a broad popular appeal and became a dominant factor in post-war politics. Numbering over a million members, it emerged from the elections in 1946, in relatively free competition with the other parties, as the leading party.[2] The polls, however, also revealed some of the weaknesses of the CPCz and the continuing appeal of the non-communist parties. Moreover, although the communists were in almost full control of the trade union movement, headed by Antonín Zápotocký, other significant organizations, such as the United Farmers' Association, the Association of University Students, and the Sokol gymnastic movement, were not in their hands. It was soon clear that the goals of the party reached far beyond the limited post-war reforms and clashed with those of other segments of opinion. Within the

---

Journal of Central European Affairs 20 (Jan. 1961), 357-77, and "Revolutions in Prague," *International Journal* 4 (Spring 1949), 119-36.

[2] The communists secured 38 percent of the total vote (43 percent in the Czech lands), and 114 of the 300 parliamentary seats.

National Front divergence of views on fundamental issues became more and more evident and gradually led to a more or less open struggle for power.[3]

In Slovakia the communists were much less successful in making an effective appeal. In the 1946 elections the Democratic Party, which was to some extent an heir of the Slovak People's Party, emerged as the predominant political force, thus documenting the continuing strength of conservative nationalism and the relative weakness of communism among Slovaks.[4] An indirect consequence was that the Czech parties, including the Communist Party, failed to implement their wartime promises of far-reaching Slovak autonomy for fear of the domination of Slovakia by conservatives and even the ultimate victory of separatism. The destruction of the Democratic Party by extra-parliamentary maneuvers and pressures became the first order on the agenda of the Communist Party and their success in achieving this goal in 1947 prepared the way for the seizure of power in Prague a few months later.

The post-war revolution in Czechoslovakia occurred within the context of the changed balance of power in Europe and of the dominant influence of the Soviet Union in Eastern Europe. This was expressed, as far as Czechoslovakia was concerned, in the alliance with the Soviet Union, which had been concluded by Beneš during the war years, and was the keystone of her foreign policy. The communists regarded the bond with the Soviet Union as crucial and sought to make it the exclusive one, whereas the non-communist parties preferred to balance it by ties with the West. Although this primacy of Soviet influence was distasteful to many Czechs and Slovaks, they were consoled by the fact that the Soviet Union at the time favored the "national path" to socialism proclaimed by Gottwald and approved, if it did not initiate, the moderate course followed by their Czechoslovak comrades. For some of the latter, the general line of moderacy was much more to their taste than what followed and was presumably considered by them to be a permanent strategy. For other communists, doubtless including Gottwald, these were temporary tactics, designed to conciliate the non-communist forces (and some communists) and to prepare the ground for more radical steps

---

[3] For the political conflict leading up to the 1948 seizure of power, see the following: Hubert Ripka, *Czechoslovakia Enslaved: The Story of the Communist Coup d'État* (London, 1950); Josef Korbel, *The Communist Subversion of Czechoslovakia, 1938-1948* (Princeton, 1959); Paul E. Zinner, *Communist Strategy and Tactics in Czechoslovakia, 1918-48* (New York, 1963); William Diamond, *Czechoslovakia Between East and West* (London, 1947); Skilling, "The Break-up of the Czechoslovak Coalition, 1947-8," *The Canadian Journal of Economics and Political Science* 26 (Aug. 1960), 396-412.

[4] The Democratic Party polled 62 percent of the votes, as compared with 30 percent for the communists, and secured 43 seats to 21 for the Slovak Communist Party.

when appropriate. By 1948, with the drastic change in the international situation exemplified by the beginning of the "cold war" and the assertion of independence by Yugoslavia, the time had come for a shift in course in foreign and domestic affairs. Although the new policy, no doubt imposed by Moscow, represented a volte-face in Czech communist politics, it was willingly adopted by Gottwald and accepted by the bulk of the party.[5]

FOLLOWING THE SOVIET MODEL

February 1948 was the initial step in the break of Czechoslovak communism with national traditions and the ultimate undermining of the legitimacy which the movement had acquired in the early post-war years. The seizure of power, accomplished by forcing President Beneš, through the use of extra-parliamentary pressures, to accept the hegemony of the Communist Party, has often been described and needs no further elaboration.[6] The full impact and the ultimate implications of the February events were not immediately apparent to all, including even the communists. For most members and for other sympathetic sections of the population, February at first constituted a triumph over the "forces of reaction" represented by the other parties and their leaders. Although manipulation and deceit played an important part in Gottwald's victory, it must be conceded that he was able, by propaganda and masterly organization, to mobilize substantial support for the seizure of power, not only among the huge party membership, but also within the trade union movement and even among the intelligentsia and peasantry. Perhaps more moderate and nationalist communists, who had favored the post-1945 tactics of the party, had inner misgivings about the ruthless tactics pursued, but they offered no serious opposition to the new line. Although Gottwald destroyed much of his previous appeal to the non-communist majority, as well as among communists and other sympathizers, his personal reputation as the foe of Munich and of Hitler, and as the post-war leader of the coalition, was enhanced by his newly won fame as the victor in February.

The breach of continuity with the past was at once made evident by Gottwald's coercion and ultimate elimination of Edvard Beneš as President and the transformation of the National Front and the coalition into

---

[5] Taborsky writes of Gottwald as "a national communist at heart," but offers no evidence for a characterization that runs counter to all the evidence of Gottwald's continued loyalty to Moscow from 1928 onward. See Edward Taborsky, *Communism in Czechoslovakia, 1948-1960* (Princeton, 1961), pp. 101-2.

[6] For the February conquest of power see the sources listed in n. 3 above. Cf. Skilling, "The Prague Overturn in 1948," *Canadian Slavonic Papers* 4 (1960), 88-114.

a façade for communist domination. Through the action committees, the non-communist parties were purged and remolded into satellites which had little or no support among their former adherents. The Social Democratic Party, some of whose leaders were purged, was merged with the Communist Party and ceased to be an independent force, although some of its former leaders, such as Zdeněk Fierlinger, Evžen Erban, and Ludmila Jankovcová, were given high positions in the party and state hierarchies. The presence of Jan Masaryk in the immediate post-February cabinet represented an important personal bond with the past and with non-communist opinion, but his death within weeks, whether by suicide or assassination, brought this to an abrupt end.

In the aftermath of February, down to his death in 1953, Gottwald seemed obsessed with an almost suicidal drive to extirpate not only national traditions but also those of the party itself, thereby causing even some communists to question the legitimacy of his regime. The concept of a "people's democracy," as a distinctive form of government and society, was emptied of meaning by its identification with the Leninist doctrine of "the dictatorship of the proletariat."[7] The "national path" to socialism which Gottwald had himself espoused with vigor was treated as heresy and linked with the Titoist deviation. Under the slogan, "The Soviet Union, Our Model," Gottwald embarked on a slavish adoption of Soviet practice in every sphere and the elimination of distinctive national patterns. This was followed by a vindictive denigration of Masaryk, Beneš, and Štefánik, and a campaign against "bourgeois nationalism" in Slovakia. The significance of the Slovak Uprising was minimized in historical writings and official propaganda, and Czechoslovakia's liberation was explained mainly in terms of Soviet military action. The reputation of the Czechoslovak army in World War II and of the Prague revolt at the end of the war, was also besmirched, with the removal of General Ludvík Svoboda, wartime commander-in-chief, from the Ministry of National Defense in 1950 and his relegation to a job as an accountant on a collective farm, and with the expulsion from the party and the imprisonment of Josef Smrkovský, the communist leader of the 1945 revolt. Still another important segment of the party's leadership, those of Jewish origin, was singled out for attack, notably in the trial of Rudolf Slánský (the party's general secretary), Vladimír Clementis, and thirteen others, most of whom were executed. Twelve of the victims were Jewish.

In the political trials beginning in 1950 and culminating in the case against Slánský and his associates, Gottwald showed most strikingly his

[7] See Skilling, "People's Democracy: The Proletarian Dictatorship and the Czechoslovak Path to Socialism," *American Slavic and East European Review* 10 (April 1951), 100-116.

subservience to Soviet will and his apparent impulse to destroy his own handiwork, the Communist Party and its prestige. Later evidence revealed that these trials were conducted at the command of Stalin and his associates and were managed and directed by agents of the Soviet security police.[8] Gottwald at first opposed the trial of Slánský, but eventually he became an accomplice in a grim spectacle in which some of his closest comrades were liquidated. If he felt any reluctance, it was overcome by Soviet pressure, blind trust in Moscow's leadership, and his own fears of a similar fate. Perhaps he was brought to believe that Slánský, who had been at his side from his assumption of leadership in 1929 and who had shared power with him since 1945, *had* conspired against him and the regime. Many other party members were so imbued with faith in their own leaders and in the CPSU that they accepted without question the necessity of the trials and the justice of the verdicts. An intensive propaganda effort successfully persuaded broad segments of the population of the rightness of the condemnations. If doubts were entertained within the party ranks, they were hidden, or if revealed, ruthlessly punished. Nonetheless, the trials delivered another damaging blow at the legitimacy of Gottwald's rule within his own party as well as in the nation as a whole, a blow the impact of which was felt most seriously in the subsequent period of de-Stalinization. The system of terror, embodied in a succession of trials of communists and non-communists alike, provided a cruel and crude means of securing obedience, based on fear and coercion.

A full analysis of the second Gottwald period is not appropriate in this brief historical review.[9] During those years the political framework with-

---

[8] For an early Western analysis of the trial see Paul Barton, *Prague à l'heure de Moscou* (Paris, 1954). See also the post-January communist analysis by K. Kaplan, "Thoughts on the Political Trials," *Nová mysl*, nos. 6, 7, and 8 (1968), pp. 765-94, 906-40, 1054-78, resp. The trials were fully analyzed in the Piller report prepared in 1968 and published abroad in 1970 and discussed in detail below, chap. XIII. The members of the Political Secretariat during 1951 and 1952 were K. Bacílek, A. Čepička, J. Dolanský, K. Gottwald, R. Slánský (until Dec. 1951), V. Široký, A. Zápotocký, and from December, V. Kopecký and A. Novotný. Members of the Organizational Secretariat were G. Bareš, S. Bašťovanský, J. Frank (all three to early 1952), V. David, K. Gottwald, J. Hendrych (to 1952), A. Novotný; J. Tesla and J. Uher (after Jan. 1952); B. Voda-Pexa (after Feb. 1952).

[9] See V. Busek and N. Spulber, eds., *Czechoslovakia* (New York, 1957); I. Gadourek, *The Political Control of Czechoslovakia* (Leiden, 1953); V. Chalupa, *Rise and Development of a Totalitarian State* (Leiden, 1959). See also Skilling, "The Czechoslovak Constitutional System: The Soviet Impact," *Political Science Quarterly* 57 (June 1952), 198-224; Skilling, "Czechoslovakia: Government in Communist Hands," *The Journal of Politics* 17 (Aug. 1955), 424-47; L. Feierabend, "The Gottwald Era in Czechoslovakia," *JCEA* 13 (Oct. 1953), 246-56; P. B., "Sovietization of the Czechoslovak Economy: The Effects in Industry," *The World Today* 9 (Feb. 1953), 72-81; J. A., "Sovietization of the Czechoslovak Economy: The Effects in Agriculture," ibid. 9 (April 1953), 174-84. For a severe post-January criticism of this period, see the first two articles in the series by

in which his successors continued to work for fifteen more years was established. The constitution enacted in 1948 made some concessions to the continuity of Czechoslovak traditions, some not without importance, as for example the retention of the presidency. In the main, however, it was a meaningless document, hardly affecting the actual practice of politics. As we have noted, the National Front and the other parties became nonentities, and in Slovakia, mere ciphers. The National Assembly was nothing more than a rubber stamp; the executive departments, mere administrative agencies; and the local government bodies, including Slovak organs, tools of the central power. Even the presidency degenerated into a post held more or less ex officio by the party leader and lacked independent authority. The mass associations, including the large trade union movement, became transmission belts of the party. "Socialist legality" and the judicial system became a façade for terror and injustice, accompanied by extensive Soviet interference in the security police. The party itself was transformed, the Secretariat and Presidium dominating the making of policy, and the Central Committee apparatus directly controlling all other government and party bodies, as well as the mass organizations. The apparatus also subjected culture, education, and scholarship to its control and conducted a barrage of propaganda in the press, radio, and television. Religion was countered by an intensive atheistic campaign; the churches were placed under official controls; and their dignitaries often subjected to persecution and imprisonment. In the economy, the almost total collectivization of agriculture, and the nationalization of the whole of industry and commerce, including even small trades and crafts, proceeded apace. Under the five year plan the economy was drastically reorganized and mobilized at breakneck speed to achieve ever higher goals, especially in heavy industry.

These harsh measures generated dissatisfaction among many sectors of the population and awakened doubts, even in communist ranks, of the correctness of the course followed. As a result of the system of terror, little or no open opposition was expressed and many retreated into apathy and political indifference. There were some groups who enjoyed special economic and social privileges, and certain individuals who attained a favored status through opportunism and hypocrisy. Moreover, in spite of the ills of society and the evils of the system, many communists supported Gottwald's policies, some even with enthusiasm. On the surface the regime seemed stable, but it had many weaknesses which were gradu-

V. Mencl and F. Ouředník, "Jak to bylo v lednu," *Život strany*, no. 14 (July 1968), pp. 22-26 and no. 15 (July 1968), pp. 10-13. See also Z. Eliáš and J. Netík, "Czechoslovakia," in William E. Griffith, ed., *Communism in Europe* (Cambridge, Mass., 1967), vol. II, chap. 8.

ally to mature into a deepening crisis in the economy, in politics, and in society generally.

The Transition to Novotný

The sequel to Gottwald's death in 1953 was a four-year period of dual rule by Antonín Zápotocký, veteran party leader, and Prime Minister under Gottwald, who succeeded to the presidency, and Antonín Novotný, party functionary and a relative newcomer to the highest party circles, who became First Secretary. Closely associated in the top rank of what was described as a collective leadership were Viliam Široký, elevated to the premiership, and Karol Bacílek, Slovak First Secretary.

It is difficult to determine the degree to which Novotný, as First Secretary, was the dominant figure and the degree to which his power was shared or influenced by others, in particular, Zápotocký. There were striking personal differences between Gottwald's two principal successors. Zápotocký enjoyed considerable prestige by virtue of his long association with pre-war social democracy and the trade union movement, and as a founder of the Communist Party, one of its inter-war leaders, a wartime concentration camp victim, and a writer of historical novels about the working-class movement. He was widely respected, even by non-communists, as a man of sincere convictions and humane attitudes, and often regarded, even in the absence of evidence, as being unsympathetic with the harsh policies of his associates. Novotný, on the other hand, a minor party functionary between the wars, was almost unknown to the general public until he became regional secretary in Prague after 1945, and a member of the party's leading bodies in 1951 after Slánský's fall. His previous life had been bounded by the narrow horizons of the lower levels of the party apparatus.[10] He shared with Zápotocký a working-class origin, the absence of middle school education, and concentration camp imprisonment, but lacked the personal appeal of his older colleague. He had no reputation based on past achievements or prominence in the Gottwald era, and soon acquired the image of a person lacking in intellectual ability or qualities of leadership and primarily preoccupied with the maintenance of his own power. His very weaknesses may have been a reason for his selection by Gottwald after the removal of Slánský, and for his endorsement as First Secretary by the

[10] Novotný, as regional secretary, had been a member of the Central Committee from 1946. Appointed to the Organizational Secretariat and the Political Secretariat in September and December 1951, respectively, he was entrusted with the direction of the work of the Secretariat in March 1953 and appointed First Secretary in September 1953.

Soviet leaders. His lack of decisive will and of popular support would hardly qualify him to follow an independent course of his own.

The contrasts in personal character and background between Novotný and Zápotocký were not serious enough to produce an open conflict between advocates of a "hard" and a "soft" line such as occurred in the USSR and in other bloc countries. The customary dualism of Czechoslovak communism exhibited itself, therefore, not in a clash of personalities, but in the distinctive policies of the two major phases of the post-Gottwald era. Whatever conflicts there may have been behind the scenes, Novotný appeared to be as closely identified with the relaxations of the first year or two as was Zápotocký with the more repressive period that followed.

A NEW COURSE?

The Zápotocký-Novotný duumvirate coincided at the outset with the Malenkov-Khrushchev partnership in Moscow and the "New Course" in the USSR and some other bloc countries. In Czechoslovakia, however, changes of policy came somewhat later and were more modest than those in Hungary and Poland, or even in the USSR.[11] The initial step was Siroký's policy statement in September 1953, which provided mainly for economic relaxations and proposed no serious changes in the political system. The measures introduced were a product in part of the customary practice of following the Soviet example, and in part of the necessity of rectifying some of the difficulties resulting from Gottwald's post-1948 policies of industrialization and collectivization. The economic chaos and exhaustion which had resulted, and the currency reform in June, produced a serious riot in Pilsen, amounting almost to a rebellion, which shook the new leaders' confidence.

In what may be termed the Czechoslovak "New Course," an effort was made to relax the frantic drive for industrialization and collectivization of the previous five years; to place somewhat greater emphasis on agriculture, light industry, and consumer goods; to pay more attention to improving the standard of living; and in general to employ conciliation and propaganda to win the allegiance of the population. In agriculture, for instance, forceful collectivization was suspended and farmers were even permitted to leave collective farms.[12] Some took advantage of this,

[11] On this period, see G. L., "New Policy in Czechoslovakia," WT 9 (Oct. 1953), 439-49; J. A., "Politics and Economics in Czechoslovakia: The Tenth Congress of the Czechoslovak Communist Party," ibid. 10 (Aug. 1954), 356-66; Ivo Duchacek, "Czechoslovakia: New Course or No Course?" Problems of Communism 4 (Jan.-Feb. 1955), 12-19.

[12] Zápotocký was later criticized for allegedly encouraging departures from the collective farms. See Dějiny Komunistické strany Československa (Prague,

until the opportunity was withdrawn in 1954, but not on the same scale as in Hungary and Poland, so that the decline in the number of collective farms was relatively slight. But a year later, in September 1954, the desirability of establishing collective farms without the use of force was again proclaimed, and in the following June a renewed campaign for collectivization began. The economic measures introduced in 1953 and early 1954 were on the whole shifts in emphasis rather than basic changes of direction, and were not broadened or deepened in the subsequent two years. As a result, it is difficult to identify the date of the ending of the "New Course" which in a sense simply petered out during 1955 and early 1956.

In the political field there were even fewer relaxations. Collective leadership was proclaimed, and the cult of personality was condemned, although without censure of its Czech embodiment, Klement Gottwald. The Soviet Union continued to be taken as the model, although more emphasis was laid on adapting it to Czechoslovak national conditions. Nor was there any admission that the party's line had been in any respect mistaken, although shortcomings in its implementation were acknowledged. The policies launched in September were described as continuations of previous ones, adapted to the circumstances of 1953. Changes in leadership were minimal, and the Gottwald team continued in power. The structure of government, inherited from Gottwald, remained unaltered. The elections of the national committees in May and of the National Assembly in November took place, without competition, on the basis of single National Front lists and did not produce any modification in the function and character of these bodies.

The 10th CPCz Congress held in June 1954 was anticlimactic. The proceedings were mainly devoted to agricultural and industrial shortcomings, and there was no major revision in policies. The most significant changes in leadership were the appointments of Rudolf Barák as full member, and Otakar Šimůnek, as candidate, to the Politburo, and of Jiří Hendrych to the Secretariat.[13] Although serious defects in the work of the party were castigated, its leading role in society and its controlling

---

1961), p. 590. See also criticism of Zápotocký, *ŽS*, no. 24 (Dec. 1964), p. 1496. Conflicts between Zápotocký and Novotný in 1953-54 on the issues of collectivization and the New Course, and in 1956 on the question of de-Stalinization, were referred to by Mencl and Ouředník, *ŽS*, no. 15 (July 1968), pp. 12-13 and no. 16 (Aug. 1968), p. 18.

Cf. a later sympathetic analysis of Zápotocký which cited, however, little evidence of a distinctive policy (*Reportér*, April 24-May 1, 1968, p. 14).

[13] Fierlinger and Jankovcová who had been members of the broader Presidium from 1949, but not of the Political Secretariat created in 1951, were also named to the 1954 Politburo. The latter body consisted, on June 15, 1954, of K. Bacílek, R. Barák, A. Čepička, J. Dolanský, Z. Fierlinger, V. Kopecký, A. Novotný, V. Široký, and A. Zápotocký, and as candidates, L. Jankovcová, and O. Šimůnek.

function in relation to scholarship and the creative arts were reasserted. The congress was replete with attacks on "liberalistic" tendencies in art, films, music, architecture, and education, thus implying the existence of opposition to party control and socialist realism among intellectuals and scholars.

Even more noteworthy was the continuing onslaught on so-called bourgeois nationalism, especially in Slovakia, which suggested the persistence of dissatisfaction with Prague centralism among Slovak communists. This campaign, dating from 1950, when Husák and Novomeský were expelled from the party, culminated, in April 1954, with their trial and long-term imprisonment. This trial, and that of Slánský's deputy, Marie Švermová, in January 1954, indicated that the policy of terror in Czechoslovakia still prevailed one year after Stalin's death. However, in an effort to follow to some extent the Soviet example of rectifying the injustices of the Stalin period, a committee, headed by the Minister of the Interior, Barák, was established in 1955 to investigate the political trials of the years 1949 to 1952.[14] A number of the victims were quietly released, but without public rehabilitation.

CRISIS AVERTED

By the time of the 20th Party Congress of the CPSU the Czechoslovak Party had overcome the difficulties created by the deaths of Stalin and Gottwald, the Pilsen riots, and the New Course, and was committed to a relatively hard line even in the economic field. Symbolic of this was the unveiling of a gigantic statue of Stalin on the bank of the Vltava on May 1, 1955. The fall of Malenkov in the USSR had no counterpart in Czechoslovakia where the leadership remained intact. It was comparatively easy to damp down a mild ferment among writers occasioned by Khrushchev's rapprochement with Tito and his policy of conciliation with the United States. More serious were the repercussions of the assault on Stalin at the 20th Party Congress in February 1956, which raised questions concerning the whole system of Stalinist communism and stirred up a wave of controversy throughout the Soviet bloc. The immediate reaction of the Czechoslovak party hierarchy was to join cautiously in the chorus of denunciation of the cult of personality but to exempt Gottwald from personal responsibility. Blame was placed primarily on Slánský, and the trials conducted while he was in power were

---

[14] Later evidence based on party archives indicated that the committee's mandate expressly excluded the Slánský case (*Rudé právo*, July 25, 1968). This was confirmed by K. Kaplan, *NM*, no. 8 (1968), pp. 1069-70. A second Barák commission to investigate the Slánský trial was formed in 1956 and reported in 1957 (ibid., pp. 1072-73).

condemned as unjust. Slánský was not rehabilitated, but the anti-Titoist and the anti-Zionist charges against him were withdrawn. The only leader singled out for punishment was Alexej Čepička, member of the Politburo and Minister of National Defense, who was accused of introducing the cult of personality in the army and was removed from all posts. The party's line concerning Slovak nationalism was defended as correct by Široký, and Clementis was not rehabilitated. Some criticism of the campaign against bourgeois nationalism was expressed, however, and Slovakia was promised a wider autonomy.

Such modest and ambiguous concessions were insufficient to allay the unrest of the youth generally and of students and writers. During April and May the dissatisfaction of young people was expressed in specific complaints and demands for reform at a series of meetings and demonstrations in Prague and Bratislava. The party-controlled newspapers and official critics sharply condemned these attitudes and actions. The most telling outburst of dissent occurred at the 2nd congress of Czechoslovak writers in late April 1956, when grave criticism of party policy in cultural affairs was voiced and the distinguished poet, Jaroslav Seifert, called on the writers to be "the conscience of the people." Spokesmen for the regime, including Zápotocký, vigorously defended the party's role. Even more widespread and acute was the dissatisfaction within party organizations, which expressed itself in "completely wrong demands" for an extraordinary congress, a change in the party line, and the abolition of press control.[15] At a party conference in June, Novotný and Zápotocký justified the general line, endorsed party control of national life, and denied the charges made by students, writers, and party organizations. Novotný reiterated that there was no need to rehabilitate Slánský. After paying lip service to the principles of the 20th Party Congress of the CPSU, Novotný proclaimed the continuance of the class struggle and rejected abstract bourgeois concepts of freedom. The conference approved the directives of a second five year plan (1956-60) which emphasized heavy industry and proposed the completion of collectivization by 1960. It was clear that Czechoslovakia was not to be permitted even a shadow of the liberalization that was taking place in Poland and Hungary.[16]

[15] See the later speech by B. Köhler, *ŽS*, no. 6 (March 1957), pp. 334-36. Cf. *Dějiny KSČ*, pp. 615-16.

[16] For reports on these events, see *News from Behind the Iron Curtain* 5, no. 7 (1956), pp. 3-9, and no. 8 (1956), 15-21; *WT* 12 (Aug. 1956), 339-48. See also Taborsky, "Czechoslovakia in the Khrushchev-Bulganin Era," *ASEER* 16 (Feb. 1957), 50-65 and "Political Developments in Czechoslovakia Since 1953," *JP* 20 (Feb. 1958), 89-113.

For a severely critical analysis of CPCz policy from 1953 to 1960, see Erik Polák, in a collection of party lectures given in 1968, published by the CC

When the dissent in Poland and Hungary culminated in the crisis of October 1956, the firm stand taken by the Czechoslovak leaders prevented the involvement of their country in the revolt against Moscow and was a crucial factor in the maintenance of Soviet hegemony in Eastern Europe. So, too, was Czechoslovak approval of Moscow's military action against Hungary and their immediate support of Kádár and the new Hungarian regime. The discontent of the spring had not been dissipated but did not express itself in any movement of solidarity with the Hungarians or the Poles. The Czechoslovak leaders could, with some justification, claim that their strict line in 1953 and early 1956 had been vindicated and had averted more drastic developments[17] which might have proved fatal to the regime.

There were other reasons for the relative passivity of Czechs and Slovaks during those tumultuous times. As a result of comparatively satisfactory economic conditions, no serious unrest occurred among peasants and workers, as in Hungary and Poland, so that no simultaneous movements of protest by dissenting intellectuals and the broader masses took place. Among intellectuals the task of reassessing the system was hindered not only by severe restrictions on freedom of expression, but by a continuing belief in socialism and its merits, persisting faith in the Soviet Union, as well as fear of Western "imperialism."[18] The absence of a revolutionary tradition, or of a deep historical hostility toward the Russians, and the memories of British and French betrayal in 1938 and Western inaction in 1948, contributed to the failure of the Czechs and Slovaks to join the Hungarians and the Poles in resistance. In fact, the democratic tradition proved to be as impotent in 1956 as it had been in 1948 and may even have been a hindrance to militant action against dictatorial repression. Of crucial importance was the solidarity of the old core of leaders, among whom there was no person, such as Gomułka or Nagy, capable of heading a movement for reform and national independence. Zápotocký, in spite of earlier signs of a tendency toward concilia-

Ideological Department, *50 let Československa 1918/1968: K některým politickým a ekonomickým problémům let 1948-1968* (Prague, 1968), pp. 41-65. Polák described the inadequacies of the New Course and the "half-hearted and inconsistent measures" taken after February 1956, blaming this on the failure of the leadership to take advantage of the opportunities presented by the 20th CPSU Congress.

[17] See for instance V. Kopecký, *RP*, April 20, 1957, and J. Hendrych, ibid., June 19, 1957. See also *Dějiny KSČ*, pp. 623-25.

[18] For discussions of the reasons for Czechoslovak inaction, see, in addition to Taborsky's articles cited above, anonymous articles in *WT* 13 (April 1957), 145-52, and 14 (March 1958), 101-9; Duchacek, "A 'Loyal' Satellite: The Case of Czechoslovakia," *Annals of the American Academy of Political and Social Science*, no. 317 (May 1958), pp. 115-22; Otto Pick, "Czechoslovakia—'Stable Satellite,'" *PC* 7 (Sept.-Oct. 1958), 32-39.

tion, proved eventually as firm and unyielding to internal dissent as Novotný and his colleagues. Perhaps, too, the insecurity felt by the party leaders due to the events of 1953 and 1956 made them realize their dependence on the Soviet Union for maintaining their own power and discouraged them from any independent action.

At the Central Committee in December 1956, Novotný set the tone of Czechoslovak policy by lashing out at "revisionism" and "national communism" in both its Polish and Yugoslav forms, and strongly supporting both Soviet policy and the Kádár regime. This refrain was repeated at the Slovak Party Congress in April 1957, when it was supplemented by denunciation of Slovak nationalism by Bacílek, and again at the CPCz Central Committee session in June. Repeated references to "incorrect opinions" and "mistakes" by writers, journalists, Slovaks, the youth, and others suggested that there was in fact good reason for the campaign against revisionism and nationalism. Criticism of the cult of personality was also continued but with warnings against the misuse of "de-Stalinization" as a cloak for opposition to socialism and the Soviet alliance. The anti-religious campaign, somewhat relaxed in 1956, was resumed. Some steps toward decentralization were announced both in local government and in industry, but the basic structure of the political and economic system remained unchanged. Collectivization proceeded apace, and the revised draft five year plan again placed the emphasis on heavy industry. In October 1957, the Barák commission reaffirmed the guilt of Slánský and most of the other victims of the trials of the early fifties and exonerated only a few. Some were released; others remained in prison.[19]

NOVOTNÝ SUPREME

The death of Zápotocký in November 1957 and the immediate succession of Novotný to the presidency initiated the period of the latter's unrestricted personal power that was to last for a decade. The struggle of Khrushchev with the "anti-Party group" in the summer of 1957 had had no repercussions in Prague, so that Novotný acquired the supreme state and party posts without a power conflict, and several months before his mentor in Moscow. The hard line already endorsed by the Czechoslovak party fitted in well with the general direction of Soviet policy as set forth at the world communist conference held a few days before Zápotocký's death. The Moscow meeting's condemnation of revisionism and national communism was endorsed by the CPCz Central Committee in December, and was amplified by an intensive propaganda campaign

[19] *Dějiny KSČ*, p. 636; Kaplan, *NM*, no. 8 (1968), pp. 1073-74. See fuller discussion below, chap. XIII.

in ensuing months against Yugoslav deviations, Czech and Slovak revisionism, and Slovak nationalism. Spokesmen for the regime, from Novotný down, in repeated speeches revealed their concern over the continued influence of "bourgeois democratic" ideas and of Slovak "populist" views and proclaimed war on these dangerous tendencies.[20]

An economic reform introduced in April 1958 was but a faint echo of Soviet decentralization measures and constituted a minimal attempt to modify the centralized system of planning without any fundamental recasting of economic management or diminishing of party control. A new climax in the ideological crusade was reached in May and June at the 10th Slovak and the 11th Czechoslovak Party Congresses. The latter set forth the goal of the "completion of socialist construction" and accelerated the tempo of economic development. The addition to the CPCz Politburo of Hendrych, leading ideologue, Šimůnek, economic planner, and Pavol David, Slovak Presidium (Buro) member from 1953, and to the Secretariat of Vladimír Koucký, prominent theoretician, suggested the continuance of the hard line. Moscow *Pravda*, during a visit of Novotný to the USSR, referred to "the total identity of views" between the two parties, thus indicating full Soviet endorsement of the Czechoslovak leader and his policies.[21]

During the next two years Novotný pursued a course that involved a minimum of de-Stalinization and avoided any serious relaxation of the system, or basic changes in leadership. Any possible challenge by Široký, who remained Prime Minister, was excluded by a decisive purge of state organs in 1958 and 1959. The dominant role of the party was constantly reiterated as the cardinal principle of statecraft and was taken to justify continued strict control of the mass associations. As a result congresses or conferences of the trade unions, the youth league, the journalists, and the writers, passed uneventfully. In agriculture the drive for collectivization won gradual success, without provoking open unrest among peasants. On the model of the Soviet Union, heavy agricultural machinery was to be transferred to the collective farms from the machine tractor stations. A revision of wage norms in industry was carried through without overt resistance by the workers. In October 1959 a draft five year plan for 1961-65 was approved, continuing to accent heavy industry and integrating the economy more than ever with the Soviet bloc. These relatively harsh measures were coupled with other actions designed to improve somewhat the living standards of both workers and peasants.

In the cultural and intellectual spheres the years 1958 to 1960 were marked by a sustained effort to stamp out dissident and heretical ideas and to coerce the intellectuals into acceptance of the orthodox party line.

[20] For example, K. Bacílek, *Práca*, Jan. 12, 1958.
[21] July 2, 1958.

The shock of de-Stalinization had galvanized some intellectuals to recall democratic traditions and to reexamine hitherto sacrosanct concepts and principles. Scarcely any professional group escaped criticism—writers, artists, composers, film makers, dramatists, philosophers, journalists, publishing houses, the cultural newspapers, the social science departments at the universities, and the youth.[22] A seminar on revisionism in October 1958 set the tone for a campaign against unorthodox ideas which reached its peak in June 1959 at the Congress of Socialist Culture, when Ladislav Štoll and Hendrych were the chief spokesmen. In June 1960 a Committee on Socialist Culture, headed by the former, was established to enforce the party's line in the arts and scholarship. "Administrative measures," i.e. the removal of certain editors or professors, or the closing down of newspapers, were also used to curb heretical opinions.

By 1960 the Czechoslovak regime, after twelve years of communist rule, had reached what it chose to describe as a new and higher stage of development.[23] Following the example of Khrushchev's proclamation that the Soviet Union was entering on the period of transition from socialism to communism, Novotný declared that Czechoslovakia, too, had completed the building of socialism and was about to begin to lay the foundations of communist society, and that a new constitution was required to document this achievement. Novotný sought thus to establish himself as the architect of the successful building of socialism and as the leader authorized to guide the country in the next phase. He also presumably hoped to make Czechoslovakia appear *not* as a backward, conformist regime, lagging behind others, but as a state in the van of communist evolution, prepared to move, with the USSR, into the higher stage of communism.

The special party conference in July 1960 was to be the turning point, with the approval of the draft of the third five year plan (1961-66) and of the text of the new constitution.[24] The fundamental law went further than its Soviet counterpart in describing the party as "the leading force in society and in the state," in requiring that cultural policy and education be directed "in the spirit of the scientific world outlook, Marxism-Leninism," and in endorsing the "fraternal cooperation" of the countries

[22] Cf. the speeches of V. Koucký, *RP*, Nov. 1, 1958, and L. Štoll, ibid., Nov. 21, 1958. Koucký regretted the "vestiges of the years-old traditions of social democratism, Masarykism and nationalism"; Štoll lamented the existence of "a very numerous intelligentsia class which all too easily succumbs to the political and ideological influence of the bourgeoisie." See Pick, "Socialist Realism Obdurate," *WT* 15 (Sept. 1959), 364-74; *Osteuropa* 9, nos. 5-6 (1959), 382-88.

[23] See Taborsky, "Czechoslovakia's March to Communism," *PC* 10 (March-April 1961), 34-41.

[24] For an analysis of the constitution see Skilling, "The Czechoslovak Constitution of 1960 and the Transition to Communism," *JP* 24 (Feb. 1962), 142-66, and Josef Kalivoda, "Czechoslovakia's Socialist Constitution," *ASEER* 20 (April 1961), 220-36.

belonging to "the world socialist system." The constitution was trumpeted as the embodiment of "socialist democracy," although the elections to the representative bodies, which had already been held in June, were conducted in the old style, without competition. The constitution completely subordinated Slovakia to the Prague organs of government, thus reversing the slight advance toward Slovak autonomy in 1956. It also confirmed the revamping of the system of local government, carried out earlier in the year, which had established fewer and larger regions and districts, endowed with somewhat greater autonomy, but still subject to strict control from above.[25]

When the party celebrated its fortieth anniversary in May 1961, it seemed to have weathered the storms of the transition from Stalinism to Khrushchevism in the Soviet Union and of the succession from Gottwald to Novotný in Czechoslovakia. The latter had survived the impact of critical events in the USSR and of turmoil in neighboring Hungary and Poland and, with the evident endorsement of Khrushchev, was steering a relatively conservative course. While proclaiming faithfulness to the Soviet example, the Czechoslovak leader was able to follow a path that was in fact much less oriented to reform than Moscow's. When it suited the Prague hierarchy the Soviet model was followed, for example, in the revision of the educational system in the spirit of Khrushchev's reform, and in the decisions to merge the collective farms and to establish "people's courts" patterned after the "comradely courts." But on more sensitive issues such as rehabilitation, economic reform, or cultural freedom, as well as leadership, the regime took advantage of the somewhat freer relationship with the USSR and avoided significant reforms. Most important from the point of view of the Soviet leaders, Czechoslovakia had made quite clear its unwavering loyalty to the USSR, its acceptance of the obligations of the Warsaw Pact and of Comecon, and had given strong support to Moscow in the emerging conflict with Peking.

SHAM DE-STALINIZATION

An initial shock came from the proceedings of the 22nd Congress of the Communist Party of the Soviet Union, when Khrushchev assaulted Albania and renewed his onslaught on Stalin's heritage. The attack on Albania brought the Sino-Soviet conflict, simmering below the surface, into the open and confronted all communist parties with the necessity of choosing their allegiance. For the Czechs and Slovaks, this decision was relatively easy and had in fact already been made in the earlier hidden stage of the dispute. There was no evidence of a desire on the part of any

[25] For a full description of the political system of 1960, see Taborsky, *Communism in Czechoslovakia*.

of the leaders, or of the rank and file, to follow the model of Albania and to opt for China. Czechoslovak communism throughout its existence had been so bound up with Soviet communism, was so dependent on the Soviet Union for support, and was so easily subject to Soviet counterpressures, that the choice of Moscow in preference to Peking was a foregone conclusion. In the years that followed, as the Sino-Soviet dispute became more and more intractable, Prague remained a pillar of loyalty to Moscow and evinced no sympathy for Peking, nor did it show any sign of mediating between the two rivals.[26]

More embarrassing was Khrushchev's call for a new offensive against Stalinism. An acceleration of de-Stalinization in Prague might easily have produced crises comparable to those in Budapest and Warsaw and might have threatened the position of Novotný and his colleagues, who were deeply involved personally in the wrongs and failures of the old order. The Prague leaders were apparently confident that while paying homage in words to the crusade against the "cult of personality," they could avoid serious measures in this direction. As far as is known, none of them chose, as did Molotov or Rákosi, to reject outright the very notion of an anti-Stalin course. If there were some among them, such as Barák, who would have preferred a more drastic assault on the legacy of Stalinism and on its chief exponents, they were effectively silenced.[27]

In his report to the Central Committee in November 1961, Novotný adopted a clever line of symbolic de-Stalinization which was designed to associate himself verbally with current Soviet policy and to ward off criticism of his own responsibility during his eight years in power.[28] He declared his fervent support of the CPSU program and of the Khrushchevian strategy, and bitterly attacked both Albania and dogmatism, *and* Yugoslavia and revisionism, declaring that the latter was "the main danger." Admitting that "the cult of personality" had permeated the Czechoslovak party and in particular had led to its subordination to the security organs, he cunningly placed the blame for this on Slánský and his associates, who had been caught up between the "millstones" which they themselves had set in motion, and on Gottwald, who after 1948 had permitted the use of the methods of "the cult" and had been affected by it himself. He reminded his listeners that he (Novotný) had not been in the topmost leadership at the time, thus adroitly dissociating himself

[26] See Skilling, "Czechoslovakia," in Adam Bromke, ed., *The Communist States at the Crossroads* (New York, 1965), chap. 5.

[27] See below in this chapter.

[28] For a fuller discussion, see Skilling, *Communism National and International* (Toronto, 1964), chap. 6. For Novotný's speech, see the official publication of decisions and documents, *Usnesení a dokumenty ÚV KSČ, Od celostátní konference KSČ 1960 do XII. sjezdu KSČ* (Prague, 1962), II, 5-57. See also Duchacek, "Czechoslovakia: The Past Reburied," *PC* 11 (May-June 1962), 22-26.

from the actions of that period, and argued that everyone was in some measure responsible for the failures of the past, again diverting the finger of accusation from himself and his colleagues.

According to his argument the liquidation of the Slánský group had been the first step in the elimination of Stalinist methods. The party had become fully aware of the danger of these methods in 1953, in the aftermath of the currency reform, Novotný said, and had taken substantial corrective steps, especially after 1956. In other words, the Czechoslovak party, far from lagging behind in de-Stalinization, had begun to eliminate the errors of the past from the time of Novotný's assumption of power. The process of restoring "socialist legality," Leninist methods of party work, and democratic political procedures must now, he declared, be carried further. As a symbol of this intent, the Prague monument of Stalin was to be removed, and Gottwald's embalmed body, which had been displayed à la Lenin in a special mausoleum, was to be buried. Contradictorily, however, while announcing that some victims of the trials (unnamed) had been released and rehabilitated, Novotný declared that there was no need to revise the verdicts and rejected demands for any further widespread rehabilitation. These involved and contradictory arguments left much unexplained. Moreover, by admitting that these past events had been "a black mark" on the party's record and that the party had, as a result, become "isolated" from the people, Novotný sullied the reputation of the party in the post-1948 years of triumph; by criticizing Gottwald's role, he weakened further the legitimacy of Czechoslovak communism and the prestige of its greatest personal embodiment.[29]

The sudden dismissal of Rudolf Barák from his party and government posts in February 1962, and his condemnation to fifteen years' imprisonment at a secret military trial in April, hinted at a crisis at the topmost level and seemed to be related to the matters just discussed.[30] The case against him was limited to the charge of economic sabotage resulting from misappropriation of state funds and did not include accusations that he was seeking to advance his political power. Nonetheless, such

[29] Novotný, referring to unnamed individuals in high office, spoke of "the strengthening of their personal power, the defense of their personal ambitions, and the creation of their personal untouchability," and admitted that their actions had "deadened the work of the party, inner party democracy, criticism and initiative." As a result, "the party is managed in an administrative and bureaucratic fashion, and is separated from the working people; the leadership of the party ceases to feel the pulse of the daily life of the country, and a barrier is formed between leadership and people" (*Usnesení KSČ, 1960 do XII. sjezdu*, II, 25). Cf. *XII. sjezd Komunistické strany Československa* (Prague, 1963), p. 92.

[30] For further discussion of the Barák case, see Duchacek, "Czechoslovakia"; Eliáš and Netík in Griffith, ed., *Communism in Europe*, pp. 242 ff.; Pavel Tigrid, "The Ghost of Rudolf Slánský," *New Leader*, Dec. 24, 1962, pp. 11-14.

allegations were made or hinted at on a number of occasions.[31] Barák, as Minister of the Interior from 1953 to 1961, a member of the Politburo from 1953, and chairman of the commission to investigate the trials, had been deeply involved both in the conduct of major political trials and in their subsequent reexamination. It does not seem farfetched to assume that his removal may have been linked with the question of de-Stalinization and perhaps with a struggle for power with Novotný. The latter, who at the 12th Congress accused Barák of concealing facts uncovered by the commission,[32] may in fact have wished to avoid further revelations that would have proven his own complicity in these events. Whether Barák had tried to reopen the Slánský and other cases, as he himself later argued, and had hoped to oust Novotný and to initiate, with Khrushchev's support, a more thorough-going program of de-Stalinization, cannot at present be determined owing to lack of evidence.[33] Novotný admitted later that there was some criticism within the party of Barák's dismissal and referred on another occasion to opposition to the party's policy.[34] The elimination of Barák removed any threat to Novotný's position and cleared the way for the appointment of a new commission of investigation into the trials and past revisions, under the direction of Drahomír Kolder. Novotný presumably felt he would be able to influence its work sufficiently to avoid unpleasant personal complications.[35]

The 12th Party Congress, held in December 1962, after a postponement of several months, offered testimony of the apparent success of Novotný's strategy. The old team of leaders continued without significant change, other than the addition of Kolder and Jozef Lenárt to the Politburo and of Alexander Dubček and Antonín Kapek as candidate members. The session was devoted largely to the deepening economic crisis and adopted a policy of intensified centralism as the recipe for economic ills. There was a slight relaxation in the hostility expressed toward Yugoslavia, and open attacks were made on China and dogmatism. This was

[31] Novotný in a radio speech on Feb. 22, 1962 charged Barák with aiming at "seizing political power." This was not included in the newspaper report of his speech. L. Štrougal, at the 12th Congress, referred to Barák's ambition to attain "the highest office in the state" (*XII. sjezd KSČ*, pp. 536-37).

[32] *XII. sjezd KSČ*, pp. 91-92.

[33] Barák's case was reexamined by the Supreme Court in July 1968. The proceedings resulted in his release and the cancellation of the charges of "economic sabotage" (*RP*, July 17-19, 1968). Barák and his defense lawyer, on this occasion, described the trial in political terms, as a product of Novotný's fear of a revelation of his own complicity in the earlier trials and of other conflicts with Barák. For full discussion, see below, chap. XIII.

[34] *Usnesení KSČ, 1960 do XII. sjezdu*, II, 244-45, 344-45.

[35] The Kolder commission began its work in the fall of 1962 and had not completed it at the time of the 12th Congress. For its report, see below, chap. III, and more fully, chap. XIII.

41

accompanied by a reassertion of the leading role of the party in the new party statute and repeated warnings of the dangers of revisionism and bourgeois ideas. Belated progress with symbolic de-Stalinization had already been achieved with the demolition of the Stalin monument and the interment of the body of Gottwald in October. At the congress, Novotný referred to the "incorrectness of the trials" and the release of some thirty victims, and promised the completion of a full review of all trials held between 1949 and 1954 within four months. Hendrych, however, contradictorily asserted that there was no need to change the evaluation of Slánský which had already been made.[36]

[36] *XII. sjezd KSČ*, pp. 92, 175. See also below, chap. v. For a fuller account see Galia Golan, *The Czechoslovak Reform Movement: Communism in Crisis, 1962-1968* (Cambridge, 1971), chap. 1.

The Presidium members were K. Bacílek, J. Dolanský, Z. Fierlinger, J. Hendrych, D. Kolder, J. Lenárt, A. Novotný, O. Šimůnek and V. Široký. Candidate members were A. Dubček, L. Jankovcová, and A. Kapek. The Secretaries were A. Novotný (First Secretary), J. Hendrych, D. Kolder, V. Koucký, B. Köhler, and V. Slavík. The majority of these had held high positions most of the time since 1954, and in some cases during the Gottwald period.

PART TWO

STALINISM IN DECLINE

CHAPTER III

The Mounting Crisis

AT THE end of 1964 Novotný, having just attained his sixtieth year and having completed eleven years as First Secretary and seven as President, was reelected to the latter office by unanimous vote of the National Assembly. His reelection was not attended by a glorification of Novotný as an individual and was interpreted officially as an expression of confidence in the party and its successes during the previous decade. Errors and shortcomings were conveniently ignored. It was claimed that the union of the two positions, the presidency and the first secretaryship, had been proven correct, since the party had exercised "a direct and immediate influence on state policy at the highest level."[1] In spite of repeated rumors of his impending fall, Novotný had thus survived all difficulties and met with no insuperable challenge to his position, either from his colleagues at the topmost level, or from dissenting forces within society. As a functioning system of power, the Novotný regime had shown itself to be no less stable than other communist states, and indeed stabler than some.

Yet during the years 1963 and 1964 the signs of a deepening crisis were already revealed, and in retrospect these years marked the beginning of a process of decline which culminated in the fall of Novotný in 1968.[2] The seeds of crisis, it was gradually recognized, had been sown in the years after 1948 when the moderate national path to socialism was abandoned and the Soviet model, in its Stalinist form, had been imposed on a country whose national tradition and special circumstances made it entirely inappropriate. It was a crisis of many dimensions, affecting all

[1] Leading article, *Život strany*, no. 23 (Dec. 1964), pp. 1413-16. See also Z. Mlynář's review of the three-volume edition of Novotný's speeches and articles, *Literární noviny*, Dec. 12, 1964, and the review by K. Innemann, *ŽS*, no. 24 (Dec. 1964), pp. 1580-81.

[2] The fullest account of the crisis is given by Galia Golan, *The Czechoslovak Reform Movement* (Cambridge, 1971). For contemporary comment, see Viktor A. Velen, "Czech Stalinists Die Hard," *Foreign Affairs* 42 (Jan. 1964), 320-28; Frank Osvald, "Cross-Currents in Prague," *Survey*, no. 49 (Oct. 1963), pp. 35-63; H. Hanak, "Recent Trends in Czechoslovakia," *The World Today* 22 (Feb. 1966), 78-88, and 22 (March 1966), 130-34; E. Taborsky, "Changes in Czechoslovakia," *Current History* 48 (March 1965), 168-74; P. Tigrid, "Ferment in Czechoslovakia," *New Leader*, Sept. 27, 1965, pp. 14-17; E. Taborsky, "Where is Czechoslovakia Going?" *East Europe* 16 (Feb. 1967), 2-12. See also Barbara Jancar, "The Case for a Loyal Opposition: Czechoslovakia and Yugoslavia," *Orbis* 12 (Summer 1968), 415-40; R. V. Burks, "The Decline of Communism in Czechoslovakia," *Studies in Comparative Communism* 2 (Jan. 1969), 21-49.

spheres of life. No one factor, unless it be the economic, can be singled out as the decisive cause of the final collapse. The snail's pace of rehabilitation, Slovak discontent, the economic crisis, open dissent of the writers, political apathy of the youth, restiveness among students, muffled criticism of foreign policy, and even strains in Czechoslovak-Soviet relations after the fall of Khrushchev (to be discussed in this chapter)—all contributed to the sapping of the foundations of the system. The intellectual awakening in all fields of scholarship (chapter IV) was steadily undermining the legitimacy of the regime and its ideology and was expanding the limits imposed on freedom of thought and expression. All of these forces of dissent ultimately converged on the political system, as the focal point of all other faults (chapter V). Several years were to pass before the accumulation of discontents and unsolved problems reached a climax in the latter part of 1967, when the crisis penetrated the highest party organs and affected the person of Novotný himself (chapter VI).

Dropping the Stalinists

Most remarkable had been Novotný's ability to ward off any challenge to his personal position of supremacy or even to his team of close associates. He had himself entered the topmost leadership at the very time of the removal of the Slánský group and of the early trials and had been directly responsible as First Secretary for the trials that followed in 1953 and 1954.[3] Although he had eventually admitted the failures and indeed the crimes of his predecessors, Gottwald and Slánský, those who had worked most closely with these discredited leaders had remained in the highest places.

During 1963, however, Novotný demonstrated his capacity for political maneuver and intrigue by ridding himself of his most tarnished colleagues while still maintaining his own position. In early April, in a move announced only six weeks later, Karol Bacílek was displaced as Slovak First Secretary and removed from the CPCz Presidium. He had been a Presidium member from 1951, First Secretary of the Slovak Communist Party (CPS) from 1953, and, as Minister of Public Security after January 1952, had played a prominent part in the Slánský trials. At the same time, Bruno Köhler, one of the party's "founding fathers," Comintern delegate and official between the wars, and a CC Secretary from 1953, was dropped from the Secretariat. A pre-war associate of Gottwald, he had been a key figure in the preparation of the trials. Both Bacílek and

---

[3] During the year prior to the Slánský trial, Novotný, as regional secretary in Prague, had, according to the public testimony of Bacílek, assisted substantially in the preparation of the case against Slánský (*Nová mysl*, no. 12, 1952, pp. 107-8).

Köhler remained in the Central Committee, however. Four months later, in August, Viliam Široký, another veteran comrade of Gottwald's, who had been the chief architect of the trials against the Slovak leaders and had been associated with Novotný, as Prime Minister, from 1953, lost this position and his seat on the Presidium. Ludmila Jankovcová, former Social Democrat, who had been in the top party ranks since 1948, was removed from the Presidium and from her government post.

By 1964 Novotný had almost completely dissociated himself from the Gottwald old guard. Only four persons in leading party posts had occu- pied high office between 1949 and 1954, namely Jaromír Dolanský (Po- litburo member from 1946); Fierlinger (Politburo member, 1948 to 1949, and from 1954); Šimůnek (Politburo candidate from 1954, full member from 1958); and Hendrych (Secretariat from 1954, Politburo member and Secretary from 1958).[4] Prominent among the newcomers in the Presidium were two Slovaks, Alexander Dubček, who succeeded Bacílek as CPS First Secretary, and Jozef Lenárt, who replaced Široký as Prime Minister, and a Czech, Drahomír Kolder, regional secretary of North Moravia. The new head of the Slovak National Council (*Slovenská národná rada*, SNR), succeeding Lenárt, was Michal Chudík, who a year later also joined the Presidium. These men had as yet no clear-cut political profile but represented at least a potential for future change.[5]

When Bacílek was dismissed, no explanation was given nor was there any public criticism of his record. When Široký was removed, there were only vague references to "inadequacies" in his work and to "some errors in his political activity in the past," as well as to his health. It seemed clear, however, that these changes in leadership were closely related to the question of the reexamination of the trials. At the time of Bacílek's ouster, the Central Committee received and approved the final report of the Kolder commission on the Slánský trials, and a brief editorial article in *Rudé právo* indicated that the victims of the trials from 1949 to 1954 would be civically and judicially rehabilitated.[6]

[4] Dolanský ceased to be deputy Prime Minister in September 1963 but re- tained his Presidium seat and was made head of the party's Commission on Liv- ing Standards.

[5] It has been reported without confirmation that Novotný opposed the replace- ment of Bacílek by Dubček in 1964 and later tried to get him removed and replaced by Chudík (L. Kohout, *Pravda*, April 14, 1968). The Presidium mem- bers as of May 1964, were M. Chudík, J. Dolanský, A. Dubček, Z. Fier- linger, J. Hendrych, D. Kolder, B. Laštovička, J. Lenárt, A. Novotný, O. Šimůnek, and as candidates, A. Kapek, M. Sabolčík, and M. Vaculík. The Secre- taries were A. Novotný, J. Hendrych, D. Kolder, V. Koucký, and F. Penc. Later changes included the replacement of Penc by L. Štrougal in 1965; of Fierlinger by O. Černík, and the addition of two candidates, M. Pastyřík and Š. Sádovský, in 1966.

[6] *Rudé právo*, May 14, 1963.

Certain parts of the Kolder report were divulged to members through brief versions distributed through party channels.[7] Rank-and-file communists thus learned for the first time officially that no anti-state conspiracy had ever existed and that the trials, including the later ones, had been artificially constructed by the use of illegal methods of interrogation. They were informed that the leadership was recommending that the Supreme Court cancel the sentences but had decided that Slánský and some others were not to be restored to party membership. They were blamed for having introduced the unlawful methods of which they had later become the victims and for having committed other political errors. Apart from Slánský and some of his fellow victims, the responsibility for the trials and the breach of "socialist legality" was placed on Gottwald and the entire political leadership, in particular on Ladislav Kopřiva, Čepička, Bacílek, and Köhler, and for the later trials and the failure of rehabilitation, on Barák. The report blamed Stalin for his methods and doctrines, Beria's security officers, and Rákosi for direct pressure on the Czechoslovak leaders.

Meanwhile none of this was revealed to the general public. There were persistent demands for a complete and systematic implementation of de-Stalinization and for a public exoneration of the victims, many of whom had already been released.[8] The congresses of writers and journalists in April and May 1963 were dominated by this theme and provided a forum for bitter denunciation of the Stalinist past and the slowness of changes in policy.[9] In June the Slovak party organ, *Pravda*, published the startling speech by Miroslav Hysko, lecturer in journalism and former chief editor of *Pravda*, directly attacking Široký, then Prime Minister, and criticizing the failure to carry through de-Stalinization since 1956.[10]

[7] The shortest version, some twenty pages, destined for local party organizations, was later published abroad, with commentary, in *Svědectví*, no. 28 (1966), pp. 350-90. The full text was published in German, J. Pelikán, ed., *Pervertierte Justiz* (Vienna, 1972). The decision of the Supreme Court on May 14 rescinding the sentences was also published abroad, *Svědectví*, no. 31 (Spring 1967), as a supplement, 1-45 pp. For the text of the Supreme Court decision in the Evžen Löbl retrial, see Löbl, *Sentenced and Tried: The Stalinist Purges in Czechoslovakia* (London, 1969), pp. 63-81.

[8] M. Hysko, *Pravda*, March 28, May 8, 1963, and L. Novomeský, *Kultúrny život*, April 5, 1963, and the defensive statement on behalf of the regime by J. Fojtík, *RP*, March 29, 1963.

[9] For the congresses, see *LN*, May 25, June 1, 8, 1963, and *Kulturní tvorba*, April 27, May 4, June 1, 1963.

[10] *Pravda*, June 3, 1963. Hysko wrote a letter, then unpublished, to the Central Committees of the Czechoslovak and Slovak parties, bitterly condemning the failure to proceed with rehabilitation and placing the blame on persons still in office (naming Bacílek and P. David), who were directly involved in the crimes of the fifties. He also criticized the continued exclusion of Husák from public life (text, *Nové slovo*, July 11, 18, 1968). Hysko was attacked by Novotný who ordered him expelled from the party. He was not expelled, however, and also

Only in late August was a laconic announcement published in the press revealing that the sentences of the victims of the major trials from 1949 to 1954 had been canceled, and giving the names of some of those exonerated.[11] None of the report's conclusions concerning illegal methods or the analysis of responsibility was, however, revealed. Nor was the judicial exoneration coupled with political rehabilitation in all cases. Slánský and others were still treated as guilty of serious political failings and were not readmitted to the party, even posthumously, nor, in the case of the survivors, were they restored to posts commensurate with their previous status. Moreover, only a few hundred of the leading party victims had been exonerated by name, and thousands of others had not been publicly absolved of charges of serious crimes or compensated in any way. No action was taken against those who were responsible for the trials and dismissals of the fifties, either those at the topmost political level, or at the lower administrative level, among judges, security police investigators, etc. Novotný, who was deeply implicated in these past events, still held the highest offices in party and state, and had been able to shift the blame to his former associates, Bacílek, Köhler, and Široký. Little could be said openly about these matters, but resentment ran deep.

THE SLOVAK QUESTION UNSOLVED

This was especially true of the Slovaks among whom there was an outburst of angry discussion in the spring and summer of 1963 and demands that the charges of "bourgeois nationalism" be dropped.[12] Hysko and the

---

found support among his colleagues in the university and at *Kultúrny život* (*Pravda*, March 23, 1968).

[11] *RP*, Aug. 22, 1963. For further details of the decision, see the later Piller report in Jiří Pelikán, *The Czechoslovak Political Trials, 1950-1954* (London, 1971), pp. 160-61. For a fuller discussion, see below, chap. XIII. Expulsion from the party was confirmed in the following cases: Slánský, O. Šling, B. Reicin, O. Fischl, K. Šváb, and J. Taussigová. Expulsion from the Central Committee was confirmed in the case of the preceding persons, together with M. Švermová, Smrkovský, V. Nový, Clementis, Husák, Novomeský, and others. According to the unpublished Kolder report, Kopřiva and Čepička were expelled from the party.

[12] E.g., P. Števček, *KŽ*, Aug. 31, 1963. The role of the Slovaks has often been underestimated in Western accounts. J. M. Kirschbaum, on the other hand, placed undue stress on the Slovak contribution in "Slovakia in the de-Stalinization and Federalization Process of Czechoslovakia," *Canadian Slavonic Papers* 10 (Winter 1968), 533-56. A more balanced treatment is given by the Slovak journalist in exile, Eugen Steiner, *The Slovak Dilemma* (Cambridge, 1973), from chap. 12 on. See also a useful study, Robert W. Dean, *Nationalism and Political Change in Eastern Europe: The Slovak Question and the Czechoslovak Reform Movement* (Denver, 1973). For a useful brief analysis of pre-1968 developments, see Stanley Riveles, "Slovakia: Catalyst of Crisis," *Problems of Communism* 17 (May-June, 1968), 1-9.

writer, Roman Kaliský, were the targets of bitter attack by Novotný in a speech in Košice in June, when he upheld the political "guilt" of the Slovak leaders and defended the status quo in Czech-Slovak relations.[13] Dubček, the Slovak First Secretary, also asserted the legitimacy of the charges of bourgeois nationalism but revealed that the victims were to regain their membership in the party, although not in the Central Committee.[14] Meanwhile a special party commission, assisted by a team of Czech and Slovak experts (named the Barnabite commission after the former monastery in which it held its sessions) began work and in December 1963 presented a report which declared that the entire campaign against "bourgeois nationalism" had been unjustified. This report was approved by the CPCz Central Committee but its contents were not published for some months and then only in briefest summary form.[15]

The volte-face of the regime on the charges of "bourgeois nationalism" left many matters still unsettled. For one thing, the surviving leaders of the Slovak National Uprising, especially Gustáv Husák and Laco Novomeský, were not restored to their membership in the Central Committee (from which they had been removed in 1951) and were kept on the political sidelines. Novomeský had been named a member of the party's Ideological Commission but Husák received no political appointment of any kind. Both were eventually given research posts in the Slovak Academy of Sciences. At the 13th Party Congress in 1966, and at the Slovak Congress immediately preceding, neither was elected to the Central Committee of either party. Meanwhile both threw themselves into the effort to rehabilitate some of the basic traditions of the Slovak past, particularly the Uprising. A special effort was made to restore the reputation of Clementis, as a personification of Slovak communism and a symbol of the injustices perpetrated in the 1950s. With the support of historians, both Czech and Slovak, the Uprising was gradually cleared of some of the derogatory features attached to it during the campaign against "bourgeois nationalism."[16] The Czechoslovak and Slovak parties, in a joint set of theses on the Uprising published in April 1964, admitted previous distortions in its treatment and sought to rehabilitate this historic event but strongly warned of the danger of nationalism, especially

---

[13] *RP*, June 13, 1963. [14] Ibid., June 27, 1963.

[15] *RP* and *Pravda*, Feb. 29, 1964. See chap. XIII below for fuller discussion.

[16] See, for instance, S. Falt'an, *K problémom národnej a demokratickej revolucie na Slovensku* (Bratislava, 1965); also Husák's book on the Slovak Uprising, *Svedectvo o Slovenskom národnom povstaní* (Bratislava, 1964). Husák's book was critically reviewed by the Czech historian, V. Král (*KT*, Feb. 24, 1966); the latter in turn was sharply censured by Falt'an for his negative attitude to the new spirit of Slovak historiography (*Historický časopis* 14, no. 4, 1966). See also a report on the conference of Czech and Slovak historians in June 1963, F. Beer et al., *Dějinná křižovatka* (Prague, 1964). Cf. M. Gosiorovský, *KŽ*, June 10, 1963, and L. Novomeský, ibid., April 4, June 20, 1964.

"narrow demands for regional nationalism."[17] A year later the CPCz, in theses issued on the anniversary of the 1945 liberation, managed to avoid even a mention of the Uprising in its account of the party's past triumphs.[18] Although Novotný, with Khrushchev at his side, attended the celebration of the 20th anniversary of the Uprising in Bratislava, it was evident that he was not willing to draw the full implications of the change of attitude toward Slovak nationalism or to meet the rising tide of Slovak complaints.

This discontent was particularly acute with regard to the place of Slovakia in the system of political authority. The constitution of 1960 had shorn the Slovak organs of government of what little power they had previously enjoyed and had intensified the strictly centralist system of government. At first there were official criticisms of the Slovak organs for failing to use fully the powers which they possessed. Then on May 7, 1964, a joint resolution of both Central Committees, Slovak and Czechoslovak, sought to broaden somewhat the role of the Slovak National Council and its commissions, which resulted in a modest expansion of their activity. There was, however, still no readiness to countenance any serious change in the constitution, nor to restore the Board of Commissioners, abolished in 1960, as an executive body or cabinet. Stress continued to be laid on maintaining the unified character of the political structure of the country as a whole and on improving the asymmetrical system in which Slovak organs, weak as they were, had no counterpart in Czech organs of autonomy. The notion of federalism was rejected by Slovak leaders as a retrogressive step in comparison with the existing system which, it was argued, reflected the special conditions of Czech-Slovak relations.[19] Although open discussion of this subject was taboo, federalism was a live issue in the minds of the Slovaks and in private discussions, and was alluded to indirectly in public debates.[20]

[17] *RP*, April 26, 1964. Cf. speech by Dubček, ibid., June 11, 1964.

[18] Ibid., April 3, 1965.

[19] M. Chudík, in an interview, characterized the Slovak National Council as not merely "a Slovak national organ into whose competence fall matters of a national and regional character," but "a national link in the all-state political and economic order for the territory of Slovakia, whose task is directly and jointly to create and also implement all-state policy" (*Pravda*, Jan. 18, 1966). He criticized individuals who underestimated the significance of the Council and also those who "mechanically see the only solution in the federative form of organizing the state." M. Pecho and Bil'ak also expressly condemned federation (*NM*, Feb. 22, 1966 and *RP*, March 2, 1966, resp., both cited in Steiner, *Slovak Dilemma*, pp. 139-40). Dubček, in his report to the Slovak Party Congress in May 1966, referred to the improved position of the Slovak National Council as "an organic component of the system of all-state direction" (*Sjazd Komunistickej strany Slovenska*, Bratislava, 1966, pp. 29-30, 42-43). See also Chudík's speech, ibid., pp. 166-67; Dubček, *RP*, June 11, 1964.

[20] The idea of federalism was broached in a confidential memorandum by Prof. M. Gosiorovský sent to *Nová mysl* and Central Committee members in

Official pronouncements treated the Slovak question as solved, citing in particular the extraordinary economic development that had occurred in this relatively backward region and predicting a steady equalization of economic standards in the Czech and Slovak areas and a gradual "approximation" of the two nations. Slovakia was not regarded as a region requiring differentiated treatment so that all policies were to be applied more or less in the same way as in the Czech regions.[21]

The sharp attacks on nationalism that the party leaders, Czech and Slovak, constantly felt obliged to make were eloquent testimony that the Slovak question was by no means settled and that deep dissatisfaction still prevailed.[22] Although the economic development of Slovakia under communist rule was not denied, there was keen awareness of the continued inferiority of the Slovak standard of living and some concern as to the effect on Slovakia of the introduction of the new economic model. There was a growing feeling that only if Slovakia were treated as a special national political region and its organs of government given greater authority, could the Slovaks hope to attain a position of genuine equal-

---

1963. In a historical review of the Slovak question in communist policy from 1921 on, Gosiorovský severely criticized the 1960 constitution and advocated its revision, indicating his own preference for a federal solution. The document indirectly criticized Novotný, under whose auspices the constitution had been introduced, and explicitly criticized Lenárt. Although it could not be published, the memorandum was widely known among intellectuals at the time. Its text was published later in *HČ* 16, no. 3 (1968), 354-404.

According to Gosiorovský, Novotný attacked his memorandum as nationalistic and ordered strict party penalties for him. The CPS imposed a lesser penalty, and Gosiorovský was not removed as chief secretary of the Slovak Academy of Sciences, or as member of the presidium of the Czechoslovak Academy. He was later elected chairman of the Slovak Historical Association and vice-president of the Czechoslovak Historical Society (*Práce*, March 28, 1968).

In a series of interviews in 1969, J. Zrak, then a member of the Slovak Presidium, noted that "the idea of a federal constitutional arrangement was already (in the sixties) circulating intensively in the political atmosphere." The Slovak leadership at the time, he said, followed a policy of "consistently fulfilling the asymmetrical model" and had an "uncrystallized attitude" toward the idea of a federal solution (*Pravda*, Jan. 29, 1969).

[21] See the theses for the 13th congress (*RP*, Dec. 23, 1965).

[22] The following is based in part on conversations in Bratislava during the summer of 1967 and the fall of 1968. See articles by R. Kaliský, *KŽ*, June 1, 1963; J. Krajčí and J. Boček, *KT*, June 20, 1963; A. J. Liehm, *LN*, Sept. 7, 1963; D. Havlíček, *KT*, March 10, 1966. An article by the Slovak party's ideological head, M. Pecho, referred to what he called a "suffocating atmosphere" of criticism, especially among the younger and better educated generation (*NM*, Dec. 1964, pp. 1441-48). See also Pecho, ibid., no. 4 (Feb. 22, 1966), pp. 3-7. See A. Hykisch, "The Everyday Life of a Younger Brother" (*Plamen*, no. 1, Jan. 1968, pp. 22-30) in which he deplored the inadequacies of mutual informedness of Czechs and Slovaks, including the lack of knowledge of the Slovak language and literature among Czechs, and "trifles" of daily behavior. He blamed this not on Czech nationalism, but on the lack of national feeling among Czechs.

ity.[23] There was resentment of alleged Czech superiority and smugness, and of discrimination against Slovaks. In almost all institutions, for instance, the trade unions, the Academy of Sciences, the youth league, and the cultural associations, Slovaks were in a subordinate position, subject to bureaucratic rule from Prague. There were demands for the federalization of institutions such as the Writers' Union, the Academy of Sciences, and the Union of Youth. Although it could not be publicly expressed, there was a mounting dislike, even hatred, of Novotný, who was blamed for his part in the original campaign against nationalism as well as for his continuing opposition to the resumption of political activity by such persons as Husák, and who was condemned for his arrogant attitude toward the Slovaks and his rigid rejection of greater power for Slovak organs.[24] This discontent could not be openly expressed, except occasionally in the columns of newspapers such as the organ of the Slovak Writers' Union, *Kultúrny život*. This newspaper became a kind of tribune for the discussion of national issues as well as of questions of de-Stalinization and liberalization in general and provided a forum for Gustáv Husák to publish his views on Slovak history, the Uprising, and Clementis, at a time when he had no other means of influencing public opinion.[25]

By 1967 the question of constitutional relations of Czechs and Slovaks could be addressed more openly, as at a special symposium of leading Czech and Slovak scholars, organized by the Slovak Institute of Party History. There were references to continuing political centralism and vestiges of "Czechoslovakism," and frank mention of earlier programs for autonomy, such as that of the People's Party. Gosiorovský argued that the solution of the unsolved problems in the relations of the two nations was a key aspect of democratization. In a state made up of several nations, he said, "each nation should have, within its ethnic territory, its own national-state (*národnoštátna*) organization." The form that this would take (an independent state, some form of federation, or some

[23] See articles by the Slovak economists, V. Pavlenda, *Pravda*, Oct. 19, 26, Nov. 2, 9, 16, 1966; H. Kočtúch, *Slovenské pohľady*, no. 1 (1967); Pavlenda, *KT*, July 30, 1967; P. Turčan, *KŽ*, Nov. 17, 1967; Z. Šulc, *RP*, July 13, 1967.

[24] In particular a visit by Novotný in August 1967 to the Matica Slovenská in Martin aroused great bitterness because of his behavior on that occasion. According to reports of this episode (in 1968), he was said to have been angered by criticisms of the representation of Slovak culture abroad by the Czechoslovak Foreign Institute and of the keeping of Slovak historical documents in Prague and described these charges as threats to Czechoslovak unity. He later refused to receive a gift sent to him by the Matica and did not respond to the proposal of a visit by a Matica delegation. See T. Goldbergerová, *Reportér*, March 3-10, 1968, p. 16; P. Vongrej, *RP*, April 14, 1968. Other trips by Novotný to Slovakia during which he rejected criticisms of party policy were reported by M. Ruttkay, *Pravda*, March 17, 1968; and by V. Šalgovič, ibid., April 5, 1968.

[25] See his series on Clementis, *KŽ*, Aug. 4-25 incl., Sept. 8 and 22, 1967.

form of autonomy) would depend on the advantages to the nations concerned, although it was beyond all doubt that the best solution for the Slovak nation was a common state with their Czech brother-nation. Another participant, Gustáv Husák, stated that national equality could be guaranteed, not by a mere declaration, but by "concrete constitutional solutions in practice." He defined the right of self-determination as "the right of a nation to a state of its own or a common state shared with another nation"—"the democratic right of a nation to full state and political life, to the assertion of national and state sovereignty, to democratic self-government in various spheres."[26]

The Communist Party of Slovakia occupied a peculiar position in this struggle between Prague centralism and Slovak nationalism. As an integral part of the unified Czechoslovak party, the Slovak section enjoyed no autonomy whatever and had to follow all party decisions to the letter. It was unable, even if it had wished, to advocate a federal reform or urge more attention to Slovak needs and desires. Its most discredited leaders, Bacílek and Široký, who scarcely deserved to be regarded as Slovaks, had been removed.[27] In their place a new generation of leaders had come to the top, most of them becoming members of the Slovak Presidium either in 1958 or 1962. The four top figures, Dubček, Chudík, Lenárt, and Bil'ak, consolidated their position in 1963 and 1964 when old-time leaders, such as Bacílek, L'udovít Benada, Pavol David, František Župka, and Jozef Kríž, were dropped. The supremacy of the "big four" in the Slovak party and their high rank in the all-national party was confirmed at the congresses of 1966 when they were reelected.[28]

The new Slovak leaders did not show any signs of actively articulating Slovak national interests or a more liberal viewpoint. Various observers have argued that from 1963-1964 there began to be a change of political conceptions by the Slovak party; that there were distinct cleavages

[26] *HČ*, no. 4 (1967), pp. 559-72. The historian, J. Mlynárik, published an article on Šmeral's advocacy of a federal solution of Czech-Slovak relations (*Československý časopis historický* 15, Oct. 1967, pp. 653-66).

[27] Bacílek was a Czech who had become Slovakized. Široký's nationality was doubtful, but was probably mixed Magyar and Slovak.

[28] The members of the Slovak Presidium after 1966 were as follows (date in parentheses indicates the year of membership if earlier than 1966): F. Barbírek (1963), V. Bil'ak (1962), V. Daubner (1955), Dubček (cand. 1958, full member, 1962), H. Ďurkovič, Chudík (1957), J. Janík (cand. 1964), J. Lörincz (1964) and M. Sabolčík (1962), and as candidates, K. Boda, F. Dvorský (cand. 1958) and M. Hruškovič (1963). The Secretariat consisted of Dubček (1962), Bil'ak (1962), Janík (1964), Sabolčík (1963), and J. Zrak. The chairman of the Slovak Central Commission of Supervision and Auditing (ÚKRK) was V. Šalgovič, member of the Slovak CC from 1950 and of the ÚKRK from 1962. Slovak members of the CPCz Presidium, as of 1966, were Dubček (cand. 1963, full member, 1964), Chudík (1964) and Lenárt (1962); candidates, Sabolčík (cand. 1963) and Sádovský.

among the Slovak leaders, and sharp conflicts between Dubček and Novotný behind the scenes, but there is little evidence for these assertions. In the later words of Jozef Zrak, "Slovak politics . . . had really ceased to exist as a factor."[29] Neither Lenárt, Czechoslovak Prime Minister, nor Chudík, SNR chairman, nor Dubček, as party chief, revealed, in their public utterances, a distinctively Slovak viewpoint or expressed dissent or reservations concerning the Czechoslovak party line.[30] Dubček, it is true, in a number of addresses on important anniversaries, including that of the Slovak National Uprising and the founding of the Matica Slovenská, in 1963, and the birth of L'udovít Štúr, in 1964, emphasized the Slovak "national heritage" but was careful always to link this with the need for cooperation with the Czechs and the unity of the two nations, and even praised the policy of the CPCz, making no mention of the campaign against bourgeois nationalism.[31] Only later, in

[29] Zrak, *Pravda*, Jan. 29, 1969. For the assumed change of conception, see J. Hrabina, *NM*, no. 5 (1968), pp. 646-49. Cf. M. Pecho, ibid., no. 4 (1968), pp. 423-27. According to Hrabina, materials were prepared on the national question by the time of the 13th congress but were not discussed by the Central Committee. This presumably refers to a brief document of the CPCz Presidium which treated the Czech-Slovak relationship as merely a part of the nationality question in general and included no significant proposals (ibid., no. 12, June 13, 1967, pp. 7-8). See below, chap. XVIII.

Concerning party divisions, Zrak stated that the leadership was divided, some oriented toward Novotný and even toward Bacílek; others hesitating; and others, headed by Dubček, forming a group with a more progressive policy. Zrak admitted the serious failings of the Slovak leadership and the difficulties of the conditions of their work. The more progressive wing sought to develop a program of advancing Slovak interests, but accepted the party line in order to avoid a premature conflict with Novotný (*Pravda*, Jan. 29, 1969).

For the conflict of Dubček and Novotný, see Kohout, *Pravda*, April 14, 1968. This conflict, and Dubček's progressive role before 1968, are discounted by Steiner (*Slovak Dilemma*, pp. 124, 126, 155). Ján Uher reports that Dubček, in spite of many disagreements, sought to avoid open clashes with Novotný and to follow "a form of political struggle oriented to the long run" (*Výber*, no. 1, 1969, p. 35).

For a more positive assessment of the position of the CPS and its conflict with the all-Czechoslovak party, see Dean, *The Slovak Question*, pp. 14 ff.

[30] See as typical examples Dubček's speech at the CPCz 13th congress, *XIII. sjezd Komunistické strany Československa* (Prague, 1966), pp. 165-72; and his main report to the Slovak Party Congress, *Sjazd KSS*, 1966, pp. 14-67.

William Shawcross, in his *Dubček* (London, 1970), cites a number of Dubček's speeches indicating his general support of Novotný's line but assumes, without offering evidence, that Dubček was, by 1964, pursuing a course of moderate reform which brought him into conflict with Novotný and prepared him for his post-January role (pp. 57-58, 70, 89-93, 152-53). Doubt is cast on this theory by a Czech writing under the pseudonym Moravus, in *Listy* (Nov. 1971), pp. 25 ff., also given in J. Pelikán, ed., *Ici Prague* (Paris, 1973), pp. 358 ff.

[31] These addresses were published under the title *Komunisti a národné dedičstvo* (Bratislava, Nov. 1968). In the Matica speech Dubček expounded at length on the great economic and cultural advance of Slovakia since 1948. Admitting undefined errors of party policy in 1938-1939 and 1944, and wrong interpretations of the Uprising and of the role of Husák and Novomeský (pp. 42-45), Dubček

1967, did Dubček exhibit, in several of his statements, a significant difference in approach.[32]

Nonetheless, there was some evidence that the line followed by the CPS in Slovakia, especially in dealing with cultural and intellectual dissent, was somewhat different than that adopted in Prague. Although there was no readiness to relax the leading role of the party, there seems to have been a genuine effort to implement it in a more moderate and less repressive manner. Dubček, for instance, at the Slovak Congress in 1966, in an otherwise orthodox report, expressed a positive attitude toward the intelligentsia and the use of objective scientific knowledge. He laid stress on the use of persuasion, rather than administrative methods, and urged the support of "progressive" tendencies and persons in the struggle against "the old." Dubček was also critical of sectarian as well as rightist views and referred to some who criticized the policy of "patient winning over" as "compromisingness" (*kompromisníctvo*). Bil'ak, on the same occasion, asserted the leading role of the party in the field of art and culture, but also urged the need to win over the artists by the more difficult process of persuasion rather than the easier method of administrative action.[33]

It was later revealed that a serious crisis had developed in 1964 within the Slovak party, especially its important Bratislava organization. At the municipal conference of that year there was open censure of party decisions, dissatisfaction with the slow progress of ending the cult of personality and its consequences, reservations on cadre questions, and "even tendencies to negate everything in the past." Husák delivered an important speech which was not, however, published, then or later. The next year at the Bratislava conference disagreement with the Slovak Central Committee was again expressed. By 1966 the crisis had been largely overcome, it was said, through the use of persuasion rather than administrative methods, and with unspecified assistance from the CPCz Central Committee.[34]

---

paid tribute to the policy of the Czechoslovak party, especially its wartime directives concerning the Uprising (pp. 38-41) and its later decisions from 1962 on (pp. 90, 93-94). He made no reference to the idea of federation, or even to the desirability of expanding the powers of the Slovak national organs.

[32] See Dubček's article, *NM*, no. 4, Feb. 21, 1967, pp. 6-10, discussed in chap. v below. See also his speeches of November and December 1967, cited by Riveles, "Slovakia," p. 6.

[33] *Sjazd KSS* (1966), pp. 52-53, 233-38, resp. But compare the severe criticism by the former editor-in-chief of *Kultúrny život*, J. Spitzer, of Bil'ak's treatment of the press, including the censorship of many articles on Czech-Slovak relations (written before the occupation, *KŽ*, Aug. 30, 1968). Bil'ak's role in the sixties is sharply censured by Steiner, *Slovak Dilemma*, pp. 127, 139-43.

[34] This is based on the speech at the Slovak congress in 1966 by Zrak in *Sjazd KSS* (1966), pp. 178-83. F. Dvorský later reported that Prague exerted intense

ECONOMIC CRISIS AND REFORM

Even more acute and pressing was the problem of the economy. The highly centralized system of directive planning had achieved rapid growth in industry, especially in preferred branches of heavy industry, and enhanced living standards for certain workers, but had also produced severe distortions in the economy, a standing crisis in agriculture, and serious deprivations for consumers. In 1961-1963 the swift advance in economic growth had ground to a complete halt, an event without parallel in the communist world. The national income actually fell between 1962 and 1963. Throughout 1961 serious consumer goods shortages offered dramatic testimony of the deepening crisis. Official admission of the serious state of affairs was delayed until the summer of 1962, when the regime announced that the five year plan, hardly begun, was to be abandoned, and a one year plan was to be introduced to solve the most pressing problems.[35] The initial response of the regime was to blame the economic difficulties on the modest trend toward decentralization launched in 1958, and at the party congress at the end of 1962, to seek a cure in a renewal of centralization. It soon became obvious that more radical steps would be required if economic growth were to be restored and a balanced economy established.[36]

---

pressure on Bratislava to expel Husák from the party after his speech in 1964, but the CPS did not comply (*Pravda*, April 12, 1968). A summary of Husák's speech is given in A. Ostrý, *Československý problém* (Cologne, 1972), pp. 11-13.

[35] Novotný's address of April 12, 1962 revealed the dimensions of the crisis to the Central Committee but was not published at the time (*Usnesení a dokumenty ÚV KSČ, Od celostátní konference KSČ 1960 do XII. sjezdu KSČ*, Prague, 1962, II, 224 ff.). See also John M. Montias, "A Plan for all Seasons," *Survey*, no. 51 (April 1964), pp. 63-76.

[36] For a discussion of the economic reforms at various stages, see V. Holesovsky, "Czechoslovakia's Economic Quandary," *EE* 13 (Nov. 1964), 7-13; V. Holesovsky, "Czechoslovakia's Economic Debate," ibid. (Dec. 1964), 13-19; Edward Taborsky, "Change in Czechoslovakia," *CH* 48 (March 1965), 168-74; Vaclav E. Mares, "Czechoslovakia's Half Century," ibid. 52 (April 1967), 200-207; Harry G. Shaffer, "Czechoslovakia's New Economic Model, Out of Stalinism," *PC* 14 (Sept.-Oct. 1965), 31-40; V. Holesovsky, "Problems and Prospects," ibid., 41-45; Montias, "Economic Reform in Perspective," *Survey*, no. 59 (April 1966), pp. 48-60; Jan Michal, "The New Economic Model," ibid., pp. 61-71; Holesovsky, "Prague's Economic Model," *EE* 16 (Feb. 1967), 13-16; George J. Staller, "Czechoslovakia: The New Model of Planning and Management," *American Economic Review* 58 (May 1968), 559-67; V. Holesovsky, "Planning Reforms in Czechoslovakia," *Soviet Studies* 19, no. 4 (1968), 544-56; L. Urbanek, "Some Difficulties in Implementing Economic Reforms in Czechoslovakia," ibid., pp. 557-66. For a later explanation of the economic recession as a result of the centralized planning system, see M. Bernasek, "The Czechoslovak Economic Recession, 1962-65," ibid. 20, no. 4 (1969), 444-61; and for a reply denying this hypothesis, see Josef C. Brada, ibid. 22, no. 3 (1971), 402-5. Fuller studies, all completed prior to 1968, are available in book form: Kurt Wessely, "Wirtschaftsreformen in der Tschechoslowakei," in Karl C. Thalheim, ed., *Wirtschaftsreformen*

The initiative in urging drastic change in the system of planning and in the institutions and procedures of economic life was taken by the professional economists, especially those in the Institute of Economics, headed by Ota Šik.[37] The party leadership, however, was not easily won over to the idea of economic reform. When a lecturer at the Technical College in Prague, Radoslav Selucký, criticized the previous methods of planning and attacked the so-called cult of the plan, he was condemned by Novotný who defended the high "authority" of the plan.[38] A turning point was reached, however, at the end of 1963, when the party's Economic Commission appointed a team of experts, under Šik, to examine the question of management and planning. Thus Šik, who had been a candidate member of the Central Committee from 1958 and a full member from 1962, had not only a technical base in his institute, but also a degree of political authority to proceed with a consideration of economic reform. In the CC session in December, he had severely censured the centralized planning system and advocated the expanded use of "profits" and other economic criteria at the enterprise level. He had warned against any compromise solution such as that of 1958.[39] Less than a year later, in September 1964, the Central Committee accepted a draft of the

---

in Osteuropa (Cologne, 1968); K. Paul Hensel et al., Die sozialistische Marktwirtschaft in der Tschechoslowakei (Stuttgart, 1968); George R. Feiwel, New Economic Patterns in Czechoslovakia (New York, 1968). See also contributions by Holesovsky, Shaffer, Michal, and Montias, in Feiwel, ed., New Currents in Soviet-type Economies (Scranton, Pa., 1968).

For retrospective analysis, see Ivo Moravcik, "The Czechoslovak Economic Reform," CSP 10 (Winter 1968), 430-50; B. Korda and I. Moravcik, "Reflections on the 1965-1968 Czechoslovak Economic Reform," CSP 13 (Spring 1971), 45-65; O. Kýn, "The Rise and Fall of Economic Reform in Czechoslovakia," AER 60 (May 1970), 300-306; O. Kýn, "The Fate of Economic Reform in Czechoslovakia" (mimeo.), an earlier version of which appeared in German, in Hans-Hermann Höhmann, M. Kaser, and K. C. Thalheim, eds., Die Wirtschaftsordnungen Osteuropas im Wandel, 2 vols. (Freiburg, 1972), i, 139-80; J. Kosta and J. Slama, "Die tschechoslowakische Wirtschaft in den sechziger Jahren, Das Schicksal einer Wirtschaftsreform," Jahrbücher für Nationalökonomie und Statistik 185 (July 1971), 481-510; Šik, "The Economic Impact of Stalinism," PC 20 (May-June 1971), 1-10; Kosta and Bernasek, papers given at the Reading (England) conference, 1971, in V. V. Kusin, ed., The Czechoslovak Reform Movement 1968 (London, 1973), pp. 179-204, 205-20. See also R. Selucký, Czechoslovakia: The Plan that failed (London, 1970); V. Holesovsky, Planning and Market in the Czechoslovak Reform (New Haven, 1972); George W. Wheeler, The Human Face of Socialism: The Political Economy of Change in Czechoslovakia (New York, 1973); Benjamin B. Page, The Czechoslovak Reform Movement 1963-1968: A Study in the Theory of Socialism (Amsterdam, 1973).

[37] See below, chap. iv.

[38] Selucký's article was published in the party's cultural journal, KT, Feb. 7, 1963. Cf. similar radical criticisms by E. Löbl, KŽ, Sept. 28, Oct. 5 and 12, 1963. For Novotný's reply, RP, March 24, 1963.

[39] RP, Dec. 22-23, 1963.

principles of an improved system of planned management,[40] and in January 1965, a project for the "improvement" of the planning system.[41] The 13th Party Congress in June 1966 confirmed a CC decision in April to accelerate the introduction of the improved system in the whole economy, including agriculture.[42] Detailed procedures for implementing the reform were approved by the party and set forth in successive government decrees.[43]

By 1967 then the party had committed itself on paper to a project of economic reform which went far beyond that contemplated by the Soviet Union and most other communist countries, although not as far as Šik and others would have liked. The party leadership had implicitly accepted the arguments of the reformers that the Soviet command model was no longer appropriate for Czechoslovakia and that a return to the modest decentralization of 1958-1959 was an inadequate solution. A decisive step was to be taken from a command to a regulated market system, which would facilitate a shift also from an extensive to an intensive pattern of growth. The basic plan would formulate the objectives of long-run developments; actual production would be under the control of enterprises seeking to maximize their profits and to compete both at home and abroad on the basis of quality and efficiency. Wages and prices would more and more be adjusted by natural market processes, although the state would still regulate the general conditions of the market. Wage rewards would be differentiated according to skills and productivity. There would be greater emphasis on technical innovation and on skilled management. Economic criteria would thus partially supplant political considerations in the making of crucial decisions. These measures did not, of course, mean the abandonment of central planning, still less of socialism, but sought to combine planning and other indirect central controls of the economy with a greater development of market relations, including the use of profit as an incentive.

[40] For the text, ibid., Oct. 17, 1964; in English, in *Eastern European Economics* 3 (Summer 1965), 3-18. Cf. Šik's exposition of the reforms in *NM*, no. 10 (1964), pp. 1165-80; in English, in *Czechoslovak Economic Papers*, no. 5 (Prague, 1965), pp. 7-33. For a full summary of the principles and subsequent controversy among economists, see Golan, *Czechoslovak Reform*, pp. 53 ff.

[41] Text in *RP*, Jan. 30, 1965; in English, in *Economic Discussion in Czechoslovakia, Documents*, no. 5 (Prague, 1965). See Šik's exposition in the world communist organ, *Problemy mira i sotsializma*, no. 3 (March 1965), pp. 23-32; in English, in *EEE* 4 (Fall 1965), 3-12.

[42] *XIII. sjezd Komunistické strany Československa* (Prague, 1967), pp. 586-94.

[43] *Sbírka zákonů*, no. 90/1965; 242/1966; 100/1966. The latter two documents are given in full in German in Hensel, *Soz. Marktwirtschaft*. The Central Committee in March 1966 approved a version of the agricultural reforms, and in October the general conditions of enterprise management and a revised five year plan.

The prospects for the establishment of the new economic model were still uncertain, however. The scheme of economic reform adopted by the party had been of a compromise character and its initial realization was slow and incomplete. The absence of a thoroughgoing price revision, an integral part of the program, was a serious handicap. A limited price reform, affecting mainly wholesale prices and providing for a restricted category of "free" prices, was introduced in 1966, but most prices remained frozen and were fixed centrally. The determination of wages was left to the individual enterprise but excessive increases were discouraged by "stabilization taxes" on the enterprise's wage fund. Although the annual plan did not contain binding obligations in 1966 or 1967, central controls, indirect and direct, were maintained and enterprises continued to feel bound by them. The enterprises were subject to uniform taxes rather than arbitrary transfers of funds to the state, and could use their own resources and bank credits for some of their investment. The old system of subsidies for weak enterprises had not, however, been fully replaced. The continuance in office of incompetent directors, persisting intervention by the party in enterprise affairs, the monopolistic position of the general directorates, and old habits of acting and thinking hampered the successful implementation of the new system.[44]

It was becoming increasingly evident that it was hard to introduce the reform gradually within the old system in circumstances not propitious for the radical institutional and structural changes required. Continuing economic difficulties necessitated frequent reservations and exceptions in the application of the principles of the reform. The fear of inflation, for instance, discouraged the introduction of complete price flexibility and led to continuing price controls. Meanwhile recovery in the rate of growth in 1966 and 1967 made the revisions seem less urgent and strengthened the hands of the opponents of reform. The reformers, on the other hand, emphasized the essential weaknesses of the economy, criticized the inadequacy of steps taken, and warned against delays or half-measures. Since few responsible spokesmen openly opposed reforms, controversy centered on the question of timing, with the more conservative stressing the difficulties to be overcome and arguing for a gradual and relatively long transition period, and the reform-oriented emphasizing the need for swift and simultaneous action on many fronts.[45]

[44] For the above, see the sources in n. 36, especially Holesovsky and Urbanek (*Soviet Studies*), both of whom were skeptical of the ultimate success of the reform. See also Moravcik, *CSP*; Kýn, *AER*; Feiwel, *New Econ. Patterns*, pp. 383-99. For a full analysis of persisting economic problems, see Šik, *NM*, no. 8, April 18, 1967; in English, *New Trends in Czechoslovak Economics*, no. 5 (1967), pp. 15-41.

[45] Kýn, "Fate of Econ. Reform." M. Kohoutek, deputy chairman of the State Planning Commission, is cited by Kýn (*AER*, p. 302) as an example of the re-

It was also clear that, in addition to economic obstacles, there were political impediments to the early implementation of reform, particularly the unrelenting opposition of more conservative elements who were disturbed by the criticism of the old system and unable to accept the new ideas. Even at the topmost level there was evidently a difference of view, with Lenárt, the Prime Minister, usually regarded as more sympathetic, and Oldřich Černík, planning head, and Kolder, chief of the Economic Commission, as favoring a slower, more moderate approach. The need for maintaining and even strengthening central direction of the economy was regularly stressed by Novotný in his speeches.[46] Official statements hinted that the introduction of the reforms would be "a long, slow process."

At somewhat lower levels, the economists, who bore the main burden of the defense of reforms, had support from some of the managers, who hoped to benefit from greater freedom of action, and from some party *apparatchiki* who recognized the urgency of a solution. Others were apprehensive, including many ministers, planning officials, and trust directors, who foresaw a reduction in their authority and a challenge to their traditional procedures; incompetent managers who feared the loss of their positions in a system favoring economic expertness and initiative rather than political reliability and administrative practices; party *apparatchiki* who envisaged a decline in the role of the party at all levels, and hence a loss of their own power; and entrenched trade union bureaucrats whose functions as instruments of mobilizing the workers would no longer be necessary. Paradoxically, some sections of the working class were apprehensive, perceiving dangers of dismissals or transfers, greater wage inequalities, and the necessity of harder work. Many had been corrupted by a system offering an assured income for a minimum amount of work and were unwilling to sacrifice what they had for what was promised. Some workers, as well as party *apparatchiki* and trade unionists of proletarian origin, were accustomed to think of themselves as the ruling class and saw a threat to this traditional concept in a reform stressing the value of expertise and knowledge. The general public, worn down by years of

---

orientation of economic thinking among top economic administrators. Although Kohoutek did endorse reform, he emphasized the need for a "gradual carrying out of economic reform" and opposed "an instantaneous liberalization of market relations." He rejected criticism that they were not moving forward fast enough or putting fully into effect the theoretically formulated target model of management and argued that it was impossible to disregard "real problems" and the concrete economic situation (*Plánované hospodáství*, no. 9, 1967, pp. 17-25; in English, *CEP*, no. 10, 1968, pp. 125-37, quotation at p. 135). Cf. Turek's argument for an immediate introduction of reform at one stroke (below, chap. IV). See also Šimon's estimate of a five-year transition (below, chap. IV).

[46] For instance, *RP*, March 18, 1964; Oct. 29, 1965; Nov. 4, 1965.

hardship and unable to express their views openly, were apathetic and entertained little hope of serious improvement in their economic situation.[47]

The more radical critics were frank in deploring the "inertia" of old ideas and practices and warning of the danger of a return to the "old system." In particular, Šik drew attention to the resistance of "conservatives" and urged the need to accelerate the implementation of the principles of the reform.[48] Some of the reformers began to realize that economic reforms could only be achieved if accompanied by political changes.[49]

THE WRITERS AND FREEDOM OF THE PRESS

Another intractable problem which confronted Novotný throughout the sixties was the persistent struggle for greater freedom of expression waged by the more liberal writers, conducted in the main through their association, the Union of Czechoslovak Writers (SČSS) and its principal organs, the Czech *Literární noviny* and the Slovak *Kultúrny život*. During the decade the writers managed to some extent to escape the restrictions imposed by the canons of socialist realism and by censorship. After long years of suppression and isolation from world currents, Czech and Slovak cultural life experienced a veritable renaissance, extending beyond prose and poetry to the theatre, the film industry, radio, and television.[50] For reasons of space, we must skirt the broad question of the

[47] These comments are based on discussions in Prague during 1967. See also V. Meier, "Czechoslovakia: The Struggle for Reform," *EE* 14 (Aug. 1965), 26-28; A. Korbonski, "Bureaucracy and Interest Groups in Communist Societies: The Case of Czechoslovakia," *SCC* 4 (Jan. 1971), 57-79. For Italian communist discussion of opposition, see *Rinascita*, Dec. 1, 1967, quoted by Feiwel, *New Econ. Patterns*, pp. 399-400.

[48] Šik, *RP*, Feb. 18, 22, 23, 1966; Šik, *KT*, Oct. 27, 1966; J. Kantůrek, ibid., Jan. 5, 1967; Löbl, *KŽ*, Jan. 20, 1967. In his speech at the 13th congress (*XIII. sjezd KSČ*, 1967, pp. 535-43) Šik referred to "some comrades" who "can imagine only one, the hitherto so to speak unchangeable form of the plan" and "consider the transition to the new system of management as an attempt to liquidate planning." "He who would wish to confine the new system merely to a certain system of motives or market relations and at the same time to preserve the old administrative character and method of drawing up the plan, indicates that he has not advanced in his thinking further than we already were in 1958" (pp. 540-41).

[49] Šik, *XIII. sjezd KSČ* (1967), p. 543. See also the panel discussion on "Market, Planning and Democracy," in Josef Sládek, ed., *O lidech, ekonomice a demokracie* (Prague, 1968). Cf. M. Gamarnikow, "Political Patterns and Economic Reforms," *PC* 18 (March-April 1969), 16-17.

[50] The fullest treatment of this renaissance is given by Golan, *Czechoslovak Reform*. For a personal account of the "new wave" in film making, see Josef Škvorecký, *All the Bright Young Men and Women: A Personal History of the Czech Cinema* (Toronto, 1971). See also A. J. Liehm, ed., *Closely Watched Films: The*

relationship of literature and politics and concentrate on the more overt political activity of the union and its organs, and the closely connected problem of freedom of expression in the media of communications.[51] The efforts of the government to harness the press, radio, and television to its purposes and to curb the cultural periodicals generated bitter resistance and resulted in a deadlock which contributed to the weakening of the regime and its ultimate collapse.

The doctrine of the "leading role of the party" was usually interpreted as endowing the party, as Novotný once put it, with "the right to direct cultural life" just as it did other aspects of the country's life.[52] This task was assigned to the CC Ideological Department and after 1962, also to the CC Ideological Committee, headed first by Jiří Hendrych, later by Vladimír Koucký, and then again by Hendrych, and in Slovakia, to the corresponding apparatus department, under the supervision of Vasil Bil'ak. As a result of the lip service that had to be paid to greater freedom of expression after the CPSU's 22nd Congress, the party adopted a somewhat less doctrinaire cultural line. Although this gave some endorsement to the ideas espoused by more liberal writers and artists and undermined the traditional rigidity of the ideologues, the latter continued to wage war against ideological deviations and mobilized all the instruments of control at their disposal for this purpose. Where "persuasion" failed, more direct "administrative measures" were used, such as the censorship of articles, the changing of editors, or the closing of journals.

The Union of Writers, like its counterparts in music, the fine arts, the theatre, and journalism had originally been established on the Soviet model as a mechanism of control over its members and its particular sphere of creative endeavor. During the Stalinist period the union and its journals were used by the party as instruments in imposing socialist realism and in transforming literature into propaganda. Under the supervision of the Ideological Department, the officers, who were almost ex-

---

Czechoslovak Experience (White Plains, N.Y., 1973), and a special issue containing extracts from this book, *International Journal of Politics* 3 (Spring-Summer, 1973). See also Hana Benesova, on Czech literature in the sixties, in E. J. Czerwinski and Jaroslaw Piekalkiewicz, eds., *The Soviet Invasion of Czechoslovakia: Its Effects on Eastern Europe* (New York, 1972); Pavel Tigrid, "Frost and Thaw: Literature in Czechoslovakia," *EE* 15 (Sept. 1966), 2-10; Vera Blackwell, "Literature and the Drama," *Survey*, no. 59 (April 1966), pp. 41-47.

[51] For the political role of the writers, see Dušan Hamšík, *Writers Against Rulers* (London, 1971), translated from the Czech, *Spisovatelé a moc* (Prague, 1969); citations from the English version. The part played by the cultural intelligentsia, especially the writers, as an "intellectual opposition," is described by A. J. Liehm, *The Politics of Culture* (New York, 1967, 1968); also in French, *Trois Générations* (Paris, 1970). See also F. L. Kaplan, "The Writer as Political Actor in Czechoslovak Society: A Historical Perspective," *East European Quarterly* 7 (Summer 1973).

[52] *RP*, March 24, 1963.

clusively party members and selected by the department, directed a financially well-off bureaucratic apparatus which served as a transmission belt for party decrees and a means of collective discipline. The members, 630 in number by 1967, were kept in step not only by ideological and administrative coercion but also by the corrupting influence of the perquisites of membership: the use of clubs and rest homes, stipends for travel and writing, and preference in the publication of their works. The union's journals, under carefully chosen editors, and its publishing house were the purveyors of the party line in cultural matters and helped to direct literature in the desired channels and to discourage nonconformist ideas or styles.[53]

In the early sixties, however, the union, its congresses, and its journals began to resist complete party control and to achieve greater leeway for free discussion, thus becoming, in the words of a Czech historian, "an oasis" of democracy.[54] Both *Kultúrny život* and *Literární noviny*, whose editorial boards consisted almost entirely of communists, appointed by the union with the approval of the party apparatus, became forums for the expression of frank views not only by writers and literary critics, but by other intellectuals, including philosophers, historians, economists, and sociologists. In their columns every aspect of economic, social, political, as well as cultural, life was subjected to critical analysis, and the urgency of drastic reforms was voiced. *Literární noviny*, in its own words, became "a political platform, an important factor in the process of social change."[55] The two papers acquired a wide readership among professionals in all fields and thus became organs for the intelligentsia as a whole.[56] Although *Kultúrny život* had a much smaller circulation, there were times when it enjoyed a large audience among Czechs because of its outspoken content and its somewhat greater freedom from restrictive controls. In addition, as we have noticed earlier, it served as a channel for the expression of Slovak national interests.

A high point in the political ferment among the writers came in the spring of 1963 with the congresses of Slovak writers, in April in Brati-

[53] For the early phase of the Writers' Union, see Z. Eis, "Writers and the Time," *Rep.*, April 3, 1969, pp. I-IV. For the transformation of the Writers' Union from a transmission belt to a genuine representative of the writers' interests and values, see Liehm, in the collection of essays, *Sborník, Systémové změny* (Cologne, 1972), pp. 159-82. According to Liehm, the Film and Television Workers' Union, unlike the other creative unions, was founded not as a transmission belt, but as an organization to defend the interests of its members.

[54] Karel Bartošek, "Revolution against Bureaucratism?" part 2 of a series, *RP*, July 24, 1968.

[55] *LN*, Dec. 23, 1963.

[56] In conversations in Prague and Bratislava in 1967 the author was told that the circulation of *Literární noviny* was approximately 100,000, and of *Kultúrny život*, 30,000. A total circulation of all cultural periodicals, including *Kulturní tvorba*, was given officially as 278,500 in 1964 (*RP*, April 3, 1964).

slava, and of Czechoslovak writers, in May in Prague, the stormy proceedings of which were fully published in the union's journals.[57] Another congress, that of the Slovak journalists, was less lively but included a sensational speech by M. Hysko, referred to above, which was carried in full in *Pravda*.[58] The Prague congress witnessed a much broader revolt than in 1956 and directly challenged the party's cultural policy as presented by Hendrych. The union was severely reproved by some for its failure to protect the interests of the writers, and the journals were criticized for their past support of party policy. The central theme of the sessions, however, was the damage done to literature, and the gross injustices to individual writers, during the period of the "cult." Speeches were not limited to purely literary matters, but included slashing critiques of Stalinism and of the delay in correcting abuses since 1956. The congresses, with their direct condemnation of the former cultural dictators, Václav Kopecký and Ladislav Štoll; eloquent denunciation of "the lies" and "the fear" pervading the fifties; and courageous demands for literary freedom, presented a damning indictment of the political system and of current cultural policies. "Art is hampered," said one Slovak writer, Vladimír Mináč, "by any terror, whether administrative, psychological or moral; our cultural policy must be fundamentally changed."[59]

Faced with this explosion the party leadership reacted vigorously. Novotný led off with a savage speech in Košice warning *Kultúrny život* editors and writers that they had entered on a "dangerous path" and cautioning *Pravda* that attacks on the party "would not be permitted." "Only with the party, and under its leadership, and in its ranks, was it possible to conduct the struggle against the remains of the cult of the personality so as to serve the interests of socialist society." Hendrych followed with a speech rejecting the claim of the writers to speak for the nation and declaring that only the party could be "the conscience of our nation and the leading ideological centre of our society."[60] Three months later, Novotný proclaimed: "In the principles and the policy of the party we shall change nothing because their correctness is confirmed by life and the results of the development of socialist Czechoslovakia. In all our work, the supreme obligation is to defend and implement the party line

[57] *LN* and *KŽ*, from the end of April to early June. For a full account, see Skilling, *Communism National and International* (Toronto, 1964), chap. 7.

[58] *Pravda*, June 3, 1963. See above, this chapter. It is, of course possible that Hysko was encouraged to make his speech by the Slovak party authorities, although evidence is lacking. The independence of *Pravda* in printing this speech was a rare case. The editor, O. Klokoč, who remained in his post to 1968, was reprimanded for his error and took no similar actions thereafter.

[59] *LN*, May 25, 1963.

[60] *Pravda* and *RP*, June 13, 1963; *RP*, June 29, 1963, resp. See also Č. Císař, *NM*, no. 4 (1963), pp. 385-97; editorial, *RP*, June 15, 1963; J. Fojtík, *RP*, July 11, 1963.

and party principles, according to which every communist must conduct himself. . . . We do not wish to combat, nor shall we ever fight against responsible criticism, which we welcome and need like salt. Our party will support every down-to-earth, constructive, critical voice, but will sharply repudiate every attempt at criticism which wished to weaken the leading role of our party in the state and which impaired the unity of socialist society."[61]

An active campaign against the dissident writers was launched by the Central Committee in December 1963, culminating in a 10,000 word statement on the cultural periodicals in April 1964.[62] Not only *Literární noviny* and *Kultúrny život*, but also the party's own cultural weekly, *Kulturní tvorba*, and many other journals were criticized for assuming the role of "autonomous interpreters of the political line of the party" and in the case of *Kultúrny život*, of "negating the party's leading role." Even the Ideological Department was reprimanded for its failings. The campaign was widened to include the media of communications as a whole in another statement damning the deficiencies of the press, radio, and television and declaring that there could be "no room for opinions which do not agree with party politics."[63] Aping Khrushchev, Novotný invited writers, journalists, and other groups to the Castle for long discussions, presumably hoping to persuade them to cooperate in implementing the party's cultural policy in their particular fields.[64]

The results of this systematic campaign were minimal. Only the Union of Journalists supported the party's statement. The Union of Writers and *Literární noviny* asserted their intention to continue to attack dogmatism and to seek to make an impact on public opinion with "our positive and progressive ideas." "Literature must be an independent, energetic and active partner of the other social forces."[65] *Kultúrny život*, describing itself as "a political periodical," defended the correctness of its orientation. "We remain the allies of everything that is really new, progressive and human in our society, whereby a critical approach will continue to be the method of our work."[66] In a later interview, published in both *Literární noviny* and *Kultúrny život*, Laco Novomeský urged, as a common objective for both Czechs and Slovaks, "absolute freedom of expression for writers to the greatest possible degree."[67]

That the problem was not solved was evident from the constant at-

---

[61] *RP*, Sept. 23, 1963.   [62] *RP*, April 3, 1964.

[63] *ŽS*, no. 5 (March 1965). Cf. the criticism of the press by A. Hradecký, head of the Union of Journalists, *NM*, no. 9 (1964), pp. 1104-10.

[64] See J. Šotola on the first meeting of this kind, *LN*, Feb. 1, 1964.

[65] Speech by J. Šotola, endorsed by the Writers' Union central committee (ibid., March 7, 1964).

[66] *KŽ*, May 1, 1964.

[67] Ibid., April 22, 1966; *LN*, April 23, 1966.

tacks on the cultural periodicals and on the press, radio, and television in the next two or three years.[68] Frequent changes had to be made in the editorial boards of the journals, and in the leadership of the Writers' Union, including its Slovak branch, and even in the direction of the CC Ideological Department. The party apparatus repeatedly interfered in the work of newspapers and periodicals, forcing the editors to modify or drop individual articles. At the end of 1965, the union's organ for young writers, *Tvář*, which had been under attack, ceased publication after the editor refused to agree to changes in the editorial board demanded by the party and transmitted by the union.

The authorities used other methods of directly controlling the mass media, and all forms of expression, including cultural organs, specialized periodicals, books, and even the theatre and cabarets. Censorship, established by an unpublished decree in 1953, required preliminary approval of all materials printed or otherwise expressed.[69] This secret, and indeed unconstitutional, practice subjected everything published to the direct control of the Chief Administration for Press Supervision, operating within the Ministry of the Interior, whose stamp was required on every page of material submitted to it. Controversial matters were also referred to the CC Ideological Department, with which editors and authors conducted long and bitter arguments, giving rise to constant frustration, persistent self-censorship, and frequent defeats. Censorship was completely arbitrary and varied in intensity at different times. It was applied more severely in the daily press, radio, and television. As a result, although much was prohibited, and the overall impact on literature and journalism was negative, the censorship did not succeed in preventing the expression of controversial and heretical opinions, especially in the cultural journals and in specialized periodicals with small circulation. Even party journals reflected the greater freedom of expression to a limited degree. Radio and television also began to display greater objectivity and to promote controversial discussions.

[68] See for instance the editorial, *ŽS*, no. 1 (1966), and the statement on the press, *NM*, no. 19, Sept. 20, 1966.

[69] For a description of the procedures and the consequences of censorship, with specific examples from the experience of *Literární noviny*, see Hamšík, *Writers*, pp. 97-117. He reported that the censor had intervened 381 times between 1963 and 1967 (pp. 140-41). Nonetheless the paper had become, by 1967, in Hamšík's words, "the sole remaining forum of critical thought" (p. 19). See also paper given by D. Havlíček at the conference in Reading, England, in Kusin, ed., *Czechoslovak Reform*, pp. 237-58.

An interesting example of censorship related to a memorandum on cultural policy prepared at the request of the Central Committee in October 1965 by the Slovak writer and CC member, Peter Karvaš, and approved by the Writers' Union central committee. Its publication in the Slovak party journal, *Predvoj*, was forbidden. The text of this interesting document was published in part in *KŽ*, Feb. 16, 23, 1968, and in full in *Rep.*, July 17-24, 1968, pp. I-XI.

Two events in 1966 offered striking examples of the party's desire to portray its intentions toward culture and the mass media in favorable colors and at the same time to keep firm control in these spheres. At the 13th Party Congress (as well as that of the Slovak party) major speeches by Novotný, Hendrych, and Bil'ak were characterized by the familiar line of defending freedom of expression but warning of its abuse. In the main resolution, the mass media were enjoined to act "in a communist spirit," to criticize negative features in society, and to seek to implement the party line. Workers in the media "must direct their sectors independently, within the framework of the party line and with full partisan and civic responsibility toward the party's organs." A resolution on socialist culture endorsed "the democratic exchange of opinions" and the recognition of diversity and called for "co-participation" of those working in culture and art in the management of this sphere. It condemned both liberalism and dogmatism, but also proclaimed the need for democratization. Nonetheless the resolution defended the principle of party direction of the cultural sector and proclaimed the responsibility of writers and editors to accept and fulfill the party line.[70]

In the fall of the year, a new law on the press and mass media illustrated again the contradictions of official policy.[71] Although, in its first article, the statute invoked freedom of the press, it placed on the publisher and the chief editor and his associates "the obligation to observe and vindicate the interests of the socialist state and society" (art. 12) and stated that the publication of information threatening these interests was an abuse of press freedom. The law provided for the registration of all newspapers and for preliminary censorship by a Central Publication Administration (ÚPS), as the former office, still under the Ministry of the Interior, was renamed. State organs were obliged to provide the press with information necessary for informing the public, although not if this constituted a state secret, harmed the interests of state or society, or was "in conflict with the rights of citizens." A citizen or an organization could also demand the publication of a correction of untrue or distorted statements, affecting their honor or good name. The ÚPS was empowered to stop the publication of state secrets and also to warn editors if information was in conflict with "other interests of society." Penalties were stipulated for editors who through negligence transgressed the criminal law. These provisions in effect legalized the existing practice of censorship and did not substantially alter the procedures. Constant interventions by censors, and supervision by the party apparatus, which was authorized by a special Presidium resolution of September 1966, continued to hinder journalists and writers in the expression of their views and in the

[70] *XIII. sjezd KSČ* (1966), esp. pp. 410, 471-72; Novotný's speech, ibid., p. 94.
[71] *Sb. z.*, no. 81/1966. For further discussion, see Hamšík, *Writers*, pp. 97-117.

publication of information. Yet once again, in March 1967, Hendrych had to utter the same warnings and issue the same injunctions as in the past.[72]

The 4th congress of the Union of Writers in June 1967 gave striking evidence of the persisting deadlock. The meeting witnessed an open confrontation between Hendrych and the more liberal writers. The preceding Slovak writers' congress had been a scene of quietude, and the relatively few Slovaks present in Prague did not take an active part comparable to their Czech colleagues. The debate on political issues was so bitter, touching not only domestic matters but even foreign policy in the Middle East, that the proceedings were not published and only selected speeches from pro-regime spokesmen appeared in the press. Nonetheless, intellectual circles in Prague and elsewhere soon became aware of the explosive character of the session. Ludvík Vaculík, in an eloquent speech, denounced the very essence of the political system in a scathing analysis of the corrupting effect of power and the failure of the regime to solve its major problems. Czechoslovak support of Arab states in the war in the Middle East was condemned by Pavel Kohout; Milan Kundera praised the Czech democratic tradition and its cultural ties with Europe; Václav Havel criticized the bureaucratic character of the Union of Writers; Antonín Liehm censured the party's dictatorship over cultural policy; Jan Procházka expounded on the necessity of "freedom of creativity." Censorship in its new form, under the press law, was harshly criticized in numerous speeches, including those of Eduard Goldstücker, Kohout, Ivan Klíma, and Alexander Kliment, and in a letter from the absent Novomeský. The letter of Aleksandr Solzhenitsyn on this subject to the Soviet Union of Writers, which had not been discussed at the Soviet writers' congress in the spring, was read. Some writers, including, for instance, Jiří Hájek, editor of *Plamen*, adopted a more moderate or even conservative approach. Others, such as Professor Eduard Goldstücker, sought to mediate between the sharply opposed camps.[73] Still others, mainly Slovaks, but including some Czechs, in a special letter to the congress, unpublished at the time, criticized the emotional tone of the

[72] *RP*, March 29, 1967.

[73] An almost complete record of the congress proceedings, omitting, however, the text of the Solzhenitsyn letter, was published in 1968, *IV. sjezd Svazu československých spisovatelů (Protokol), Praha, 27.-29. června 1967* (Prague, 1968). For Hendrych's opening address, see *LN*, July 1, 1967; for reports and excerpts from a few speeches, *LN*, July 8, 29; *NM*, July 25; *RP*, July 12, 16, 21, Aug. 12-13, 1968. Hamšík gives a detailed account of the congress and the texts of speeches by Kundera, Novomeský, and Vaculík. He describes in some detail the struggle with the party apparatus over the publication of the proceedings (*Writers*, pp. 74-93). For a re-creation of the congress in the form of a play see Pavel Kohout, *From the Diary of a Counter-revolutionary* (New York, 1972), pp. 212-35; also available in French, *Journal d'un contre-révolutionnaire* (n.p., 1971), pp. 236-62.

discussions and noted that certain matters could have "a serious foreign political effect." The letter warned against "a struggle for power" which could threaten the existence of the union as a unified body.[74]

The final resolution, citing the 13th Party Congress decision, spoke in favor of "freedom of artistic questing" and cultural tolerance, and defended "the continuity of Czechoslovak culture."[75] Specifically, in a section added to the original draft, the resolution urged a reexamination of the press law, a limitation of censorship to matters of state defense, and the guarantee of the individual author's right to defend himself against charges of violating the law. The union's central committee, elected after much debate with Hendrych, did not include a number of persons blackballed by the party.[76] The office of chairman remained vacant as a result of lack of agreement between party and union on an acceptable candidate.

The aftermath of the congress demonstrated how deep was the gulf between the party and the literary community. Novotný denounced the dissident writers for seeking to form "a third force" and declared that there could be "no compromise" with bourgeois ideology.[77] The mount-

[74] The letter was signed by, *inter alios*, V. Mihálik, J. Špitzer, M. Válek, V. Mináč, Jan Procházka, A. Lustig, and J. Drda, and was endorsed by the congress presidium. For the text, see *IV. sjezd SČSS Protokol*, pp. 157-59; also *KŽ*, March 29, 1968. Still another letter to the congress, also unpublished at the time, was even more critical of what it termed the abuse of the congress for political purposes directed against the party's policy. This second letter was signed by, among others, L. Mňačko. Its content was revealed by M. Válek, *KŽ*, May 17, 1968. For later controversy, see below, chap. IX.

[75] The text was published in *LN*, July 8, 1967; also in *IV. sjezd SČSS Protokol*, pp. 5-13, 192-98. The congress was later condemned by the writer, Jiří Hájek, as the basis of the formation of "the great coalition of intellectuals" consisting of revisionist communists and non-party people in which the "liberals" around *Literární noviny* played the leading role and gained the reputation as the forerunners of the January reform. The genuine Marxists, on "the left," particularly the Slovaks, but also some Czechs, had welcomed the 13th congress resolution on culture and had recognized the need for basic reform but had opposed the radical views of the liberals. Official policy, ignoring the wide differences between "liberals" and Marxists, had attacked all the intellectuals, thus forcing them into a defensive unity, and allowing the leadership to pass to the liberals. He also ascribed great importance to foreign Marxists, including Roger Garaudy and Ernst Fischer, whose idea of the "hegemony" of the intellectuals exercised a profound influence on Czechoslovaks (Jiří Hájek, *Mýtus a realita ledna 1968*, Prague, 1970, pp. 28-41 and 48-53).

[76] Excluded, at the insistence of Hendrych, were Vaculík, Klíma, Havel, and Kohout. Other names originally struck from the candidate list by the party (including Karel Kosík, Šotola, and Milan Jungmann) were, however, ultimately approved. None of the more conservative spokesmen, for instance Hájek, was elected. For the full list of the central committee, see *IV. sjezd SČSS Protokol*, pp. 200-202. See also Hamšík, *Writers*, pp. 43, 67, 70. A presidium was not elected until late October and did not include Kosík, Kundera, Kohout, or Procházka.

[77] *RP*, July 1, 1967.

ing tension was aggravated by three other events affecting the literary world. In July severe prison sentences were imposed on Pavel Tigrid, emigré journalist in Paris, *in absentia*, for subversive activities, and on Jan Beneš, a young Prague writer, who was charged with providing Tigrid with information. This was widely regarded as a warning to the more liberal writers. In early August, the Slovak writer, Ladislav Mňačko, author of the strongly anti-Stalinist books, *Delayed Reports* and *The Taste of Power*, left Czechoslovakia for Israel in protest against Czechoslovak support of the Arab states and against censorship, and was promptly expelled from the party and deprived of his citizenship. On September 3 the *Sunday Times* (London) published what was said to be a protest to world opinion and an appeal for support against censorship and oppression by over three hundred Czech and Slovak intellectuals, whose names were, however, not given. Although this was generally regarded in Prague as a fake and was indeed later revealed to be one, it stirred up new controversy between the party and the literary community.[78]

The climax was reached at the meeting of the CPCz Central Committee in late September.[79] The speeches published were aggressive in tone, accusing the writers of neglecting the international class struggle and the anti-communist efforts of world imperialism; condemning them for failing to discuss literature at the congress and for presenting oppositional, and even anti-communist views. Hendrych's speech, in particular, was an indictment, not only of the dissident writers, but of the Union of Writers, for becoming a platform for "oppositional political conceptions." He rejected "abstract freedom" and argued that freedom was based on class relations and must be limited by them. The plenum proceeded to take severe actions against the leading culprits, expelling Vaculík, Liehm, and Klíma from the party, and dropping Procházka as a CC candidate. As a final blow the Central Committee accused *Literární noviny* of becoming "a platform of opposition political standpoints" and, expropriating this property of the union, arbitrarily placed it under the Ministry of Culture and Information. Its name was unchanged but its editorial board was completely new owing to the unwillingness of all previous editors to serve. The Union of Journalists, at its 5th congress in the fall, condemned *Literární noviny* in the same vein as the party had

---

[78] This document was the work of a young historian, Ivan Pfaff, who was arrested but not tried before the change of regime in January 1968. He later admitted publicly that the declaration had been his own and had not been signed by others. Although he regretted the form of his action, he defended the content of the document as an expression of his belief in "absolute freedom of expression" (*Lidová democracie*, March 21, 27, 1968).

[79] See partial reports of certain speeches, *RP*, Sept. 30, Oct. 3-4, 1967; *LN*, Oct. 7, 1967.

done, and its general secretary, Adolf Hradecký, expressed approval of the press law.[80] On the other hand, the Slovak writers' journal *Kultúrny život*, which was permitted to continue to appear, protested the action of the regime against its sister organ.[81] The impasse between the party and the literary community was complete and apparently unbridgeable.

YOUTH AND THE YOUTH MOVEMENT

The attitude of the younger generation presented another difficult problem with which the party struggled without any real success throughout the sixties. The gap between the young people and the regime became more and more apparent. Distinctive attitudes toward society and its problems, and toward the political system, ripened among certain sections of the youth, especially the university students. There was a spreading discontent with their own lot under the existing system and a consciousness of the lack of perspective for the future.

Overt manifestations of the spreading malaise were the public meetings which occurred on May Day in 1962, and almost every year thereafter, at the statue of the Czech poet, Karel Hynek Mácha, on Petřín hill in Prague, often leading to parades in the downtown area, with provocative banners and slogans. In October 1964 demonstrations took place in the heart of the city on Václavské náměstí and were broken up by the police, who made numerous arrests, mainly of young workers. In 1965 the traditional student festival, Majáles, permitted for the first time after a nine-year break, was the occasion of a massive parade many features of which were disturbing to the regime. The party press sharply castigated the election as King of Majáles of the American poet, Allen Ginsberg, who was shortly thereafter expelled from the country. The following year the Majáles once more took an unorthodox course and was again censured.[82]

The deeper roots of the problem were analyzed by various writers and journalists and by scholars, including those working in the newly developed field of the "sociology of youth."[83] As Miroslav Jodl, a leading

---

[80] *RP*, Oct. 20-21, 1967.

[81] *KŽ*, Nov. 3, 1967. See the strong condemnation of the CC actions by Z. Jesenská on Oct. 16, 1967 (*KŽ*, April 26, 1968).

[82] *RP*, May 17, 20, 1965; May 16, 24, 1966; *Mladá fronta*, May 2, 16, 1965.

[83] Among the writers and journalists, L. Novomeský, *KŽ*, July 4, 11, 18, 1964; April 23, 1965; D. Bendová, ibid., April 23, 1965; M. Chorvath, ibid., April 29, 1966; J. Loukotka, *RP*, April 5, 8, 1966; among the scholars, M. Jodl, *LN*, Oct. 10, 1964; M. Kusý and J. Suchý, *Pravda*, Aug. 2, 1967. See also Prof. F. Kahuda, "Mládež v dnešní dynamice společenského vývoje," *Socialistická škola*, no. 1 (Sept. 1967), pp. 11-21; J. Šiklová, "Sociology of Youth in Czechoslovakia" (in English), *Acta Universitatis Carolinae, Philosophica et historica* 2 (1969), 79-107. For an excellent analysis of social groups based on age (including youth

sociologist, expressed it, the "problem of youth" was a reflection of the problems of society as a whole. Although for the most part, he argued, the younger generation accepted socialism as a matter of fact, they were much more prone than their elders to criticize the defects of the system, in particular the discrepancy between the ideal and the reality. Others admitted the justice of the complaints of youth concerning economic and social deficiencies and problems relating to school and education. Especially demoralizing to the youth had been the revelations of the evil features of the "cult." Whereas in the late forties and early fifties, the youth "with blue shirts and red hearts" had participated actively and enthusiastically in public affairs, in the sixties this was replaced by disillusionment and the absence of political activity. The so-called *svazácká generace* (Youth Union generation) had been succeeded by one highly critical of the shortcomings of society and of the failure of the party and the Czechoslovak Union of Youth (ČSM) to deal adequately with these problems.[84] As a new generation, living under different conditions, the young people had their own values, wrote Jodl, and should not be expected to conform to the existing system of values.

If the youth were expected to accept the adult "program" and "present conditions," and were prevented from formulating their own program for change, warned two Slovak philosophers, they would be driven to "criticism for criticism's sake" and to "protesting against everything."[85] The only solution, as an orthodox but perceptive analysis put it, was to give the younger generation "greater opportunity" to be political and to offer them "plenty of room for independence, for experiment, errors and extremes." Only "wise political leadership" could win them over and avoid driving them into "isolation and political opposition."[86] In fact, as was officially admitted in *Rudé právo*, the youth were not well represented in the national committees or in the societal organizations, such as the trade unions or even in what was supposed to be their own orga-

---

and the elderly) and their distinctive economic and social, and also political and ideological interests, expressed in "group consciousness," see D. Cahová, in P. Machonin, ed., *Sociální struktura socialistické společnosti* (Prague, 1967). Cahová also noted the failure of the youth organization to give expression to the varied interests of youth.

A poll conducted among university students throughout the nation revealed that 61 percent favored capitalism. A poll of young working people indicated that 73 percent wished the world to develop toward socialism, but 58 percent felt that the potentialities of socialism were not being realized, and 36.4 percent that they were being realized only partially. The latter opinion was shared by 75 percent of university students (*Šiklová*, "Soc. of Youth," pp. 94-95).

[84] *LN*, Jan. 16, 1965, by a former ČSM official.

[85] Kusý and Suchý, *Pravda*, Aug. 2, 1967.

[86] L. Tomášek, "Youth and the Political System," in *Vedúca úloha strany a politický systém* (Bratislava, 1968; written in early 1967), esp. pp. 133, 136, 137, 141.

nization. As a result they participated in little or no political activity and tended toward opposition and disapproval of the social system and its shortcomings.[87] The representation of youth in the party was indicative: only 9 percent of party members, in 1966, were 26 years or younger.[88]

Beginning with a special resolution on the youth adopted by the CPCz Central Committee in November 1961, there was constant upbraiding of the youth for their "wrong opinions," "bourgeois influences," "anti-socialist deeds," and "indifference, apoliticalness, and irresponsibility."[89] Decisions and statements, repeated year after year, did not, however, eliminate, or even modify the unsatisfactory attitudes of young people. The official viewpoint denied the existence of a generational problem and placed the blame for the situation on outside bourgeois influences, on the weaknesses of the ČSM and of the party in dealing with the youth, on the faults of teachers, the mass media and certain cultural periodicals, and of course, on youth itself.

The regime's objective was to win over the youth and to teach them to be examples of "communist man" through the work of the Union of Youth. The latter was defined by the party statute as "the unified social organization of youth, the active aid and reserve of the party." Its task was to train the youth in the spirit of Marxism-Leninism and to mobilize them for the implementation of party policy. The party was made responsible for the ČSM's activity, and its organs and organizations were to "direct and supervise" it.[90] The emphasis was at first placed on "education through work," with the young encouraged to engage in socialist competition, voluntary brigades, and special construction projects.[91] Later, in the sixties, there was an attempt to relate work among youth to their actual needs and interests, but the fundamental objective was still to "influence" them and guide them in the right direction.[92]

In spite of exhortations and admonitions, the ČSM did not show significant signs of improvement. Its membership, which had stood at approximately a million and a half in 1963, dropped to a little more than

[87] Loukotka, *RP*, April 8, 1966.

[88] *XIII. sjezd KSČ* (1967), p. 910. According to Koucký only 16 percent were aged 18 to 30 (*XIII. sjezd KSČ*, 1966, p. 254).

[89] *Usnesení KSČ, 1960 do XII. sjezdu*, II, 64-70; Novotný and Hendrych, at the CC plenum, *RP*, Nov. 21-22, 1961; Novotný, CC plenum, July 1962, *Usnesení KSČ, 1960 do XII. sjezdu*, II, 351-52; the pre-12th congress document, ibid., II, 390-94; Novotný's report to the 12th congress, *XII. sjezd Komunistické strany Československa* (Prague, 1963), pp. 71-72, 81; CC decision, *Usnesení a dokumenty ÚV KSČ*, 1962-63 (Prague, 1964), pp. 536-41 (final quotation above from p. 536); CC decision, January 1965, *ŽS*, no. 4 (Feb. 1965), p. 211; Novotný's report to the 13th congress, *XIII. sjezd KSČ* (1967), p. 90.

[90] CPCz statute, 1962, *XII. sjezd KSČ*, p. 683.

[91] V. Vedra, then ČSM chairman, at the 12th congress (*XII. sjezd KSČ*, pp. 498-501). See also Vedra, *ŽS*, no. 16 (Aug. 1962), pp. 986-90.

[92] CC resolution, January 1965, *ŽS*, no. 4 (Feb. 1965), p. 211.

a million in 1966, representing only something more than one-half of the total youth population.[93] Of the ČSM membership, only 7.2 percent were party members in 1966.[94] Of the working youth, 363,000 were ČSM members, about one-fourth of the total. Middle-school members numbered 293,000. A higher proportion of the students of institutes of higher learning, 66,800 from a total of approximately 90,000, were ČSM members.[95] There were periodic admissions of the lack of appeal of the ČSM to the youth and of the inadequacy of its methods of work. Even Novotný, at the 4th ČSM Congress in 1963, called for a different approach, and a new chairman, Miroslav Zavadil, was appointed. A revised ČSM statute, however, described the purpose of the Union in familiar terms and declared that it was to act according to CPCz "directives and counsel."[96] An effort was made to adapt the organizational forms of the Union to the actual needs and interests of the varied segments of youth, but there was no basic alteration in its policies or methods. Official criticism of the inadequacy of the work of the ČSM mounted with each passing year, reaching a climax in late 1965 and during 1966.[97]

STUDENT UNREST

The party and the ČSM faced a particularly thorny problem in the attitudes of students, who shared the general dissatisfaction of youth with many features of society but had their own special frustrations produced by poor dormitory conditions, restrictions on foreign travel, and by what they considered the low quality of education. Special sources of grievances were the courses in Marxism-Leninism, and some urged the re-

[93] *MF*, April 19, 1963; P. Vranovský, *Práce*, April 24, 1966. The total number of youth was variously estimated, as 1,936,000, between ages 14 and 24 years in 1961 (Loukotka) and as 2,200,000, between 15 and 24 in 1966 (Vranovský). Professor Kahuda favored 15 to 30 as the "sociological age of youth" but others, he said, preferred 15 to 24 years. In 1966, the ČSM statute set the age of membership at 15 to 30 (in place of 14 to 26).

[94] *XIII. sjezd KSČ* (1966), p. 254. In 1967, the proportion was only 6.5 percent (*ŽS*, no. 12, June 1967, p. 18).

[95] M. Zavadil, *ŽS*, no. 18, Sept. 21, 1966, pp. 23-26.

[96] *MF*, April 19, 24, 1963. V. Vedra declared that the union was "a political organization" and could not be permitted to be "a free association of cultural-educational youth groups."

[97] For a negative attitude toward ČSM see O. Baláž, *ŽS*, no. 11 (June 1965), pp. 684-89. Note also the sharp censure by Hendrych, at the ČSM central committee, when he stated that the union seemed to act as a kind of "chief administration for youth" rather than "an organization of youth" (*ŽS*, no. 21, Nov. 1965, pp. 1286-91); and the even sharper condemnation by M. Vaculík, who wrote that the ČSM had given a "completely inadequate response to the needs, interests, and thinking of the younger generation" (*NM*, no. 1, Jan. 11, 1966, pp. 19-20). Cf. a poll of students at the Liberec Higher School of Machinery and Technology, 64 percent of whom regarded the work of the *ČSM* as unsatisfactory (*NM*, no. 9, 1965, pp. 1126-32).

duction or elimination of this compulsory political training. The unsatisfactory character of this instruction was recognized in official circles and the responsible departments and teachers were often taken to task.[98] These and other complaints produced among students widespread political indifference and apathy and a general feeling of uncertainty about life.[99]

The problem was well stated by Dr. Pavel Machonin, head of the Institute for Marxism-Leninism for Higher Schools. The students, he said, formed "a real social group with its own specific position, its own interests, its social psyche, and even a developing ideology." Students were extremely critical of the concrete forms of socialist life and their demands concerning education and broader social questions were often justified. They formed, he said, a political force which must be taken into account. He noted the decline of the authority of the ČSM among students and blamed this on the negative features of its work. The only way to counter "liberal moods, exaggerated criticism, and opposition tendencies," he concluded, was to take steps (such as those recommended by the Prague university party committee) to improve relations with the students and heed their views.[100]

Public opinion polls conducted by sociologists in various faculties and universities documented the general lack of political interest among students and the unwillingness of the overwhelming majority to take an active part in public affairs or to work within a political party.[101] Few

[98] Note the severe criticism of Marxist-Leninist training at the universities in the Secretariat measure of January 1963 (*Usnesení KSČ*, 1962-63, pp. 74-96) and the Presidium decision, July 28, 1964 (*Usnesení a dokumenty ÚV KSČ*, 1964, Prague, 1965, pp. 233-61). Cf. J. Kladiva, *NM*, no. 9 (Sept. 1964), pp. 1033-41.

[99] Kahuda cited the poll of Ostrava and Nitra pedagogical students, in which indifference and apathy were expressed by 29 and 30 percent, resp., and feelings of uncertainty about life in general, by 43.9 and 35.6 percent resp. On the other hand, 74.0 and 69.6 percent, resp., expressed general feelings of personal happiness ("Mládež" cited above).

[100] *Vysoká škola*, no. 2 (Sept. 1964), pp. 5-11.

[101] In a sociological investigation of university students of various faculties only 9 percent of the respondents said that they had ever "acted in defense of general social interests" and only 12 percent were willing to advance their own views about such matters. When asked whether they devoted time to activity in social matters, 64 percent responded, "almost none"; 30 percent, "passively"; 6 percent, "actively." In "political affairs" there was somewhat greater activity: 65 percent, "passive"; 8 percent, "active"; 27 percent, "almost none." See Eliška Freiová, "Sociologický výzkum vysokoškolských studentů" (Ústav marxismu-leninismu pro vysoké školy, Prague, Research material, no. 3, report 2, mimeographed, Oct. 1967). See another report in this series by Dr. J. Šiklová, on attitudes toward Marxism-Leninism instruction and on the political opinions of men and women students (Research material, no. 3, report 2, Feb. 1968). See also *Smena*, Nov. 23, 1967, for further information on student polls.

Even in 1961-1963, when politics were said to have again become interesting to youth, their involvement, according to another study, took the form of "taking

students were party members, and most were profoundly disillusioned by the party's policy. In 1966, only 6,372, i.e. 0.4 percent of the CPCz total membership, were students.[102] In 1963, the party sought to increase its influence in the universities by establishing special university party committees (as distinct from the regular territorial district committees) including students as well as professors and instructors, in Prague, Bratislava, and Brno, but did not succeed in expanding student membership.[103]

The majority of students were members of the ČSM, no doubt largely owing to the fact that admission to the university and post-graduation job placement was dependent on recommendations from the Union.[104] The students were, however, often entirely passive members of the youth organization and were severely critical of its work, in particular its failure to treat differently the varied categories of youth, especially the students, who had little in common with the working youth or the younger boys and girls who were also members. The idea of a separate student organization was broached, but rejected by the party and the ČSM. An effort was made, however, to recognize and institutionalize the special interests of students by the establishment of university district committees of the ČSM (comparable to those in the party) as well as a national university council within the ČSM. As an unexpected consequence, the Prague ČSM district committee, especially the representatives on it from certain faculties—Philosophical, Technical and Nuclear Physics, and Mechanical Engineering—began to voice unorthodox views often unacceptable to the ČSM and the party.

A conference of university students, held in December 1965 at the call of the party and the ČSM, revealed continuing student dissatisfaction. The most radical critique of the Union and a program of reform were advanced by a student of the School of Mechanical Engineering in Prague, Jiří Müller, who urged that the Union represent the views and interests of its members vis-à-vis the decision-making authorities, if nec-

---

a critical interest in everyday events" and of "having an opinion of their own," but not in accepting a public function or working in a political party. This was based on a poll of students of the Ostrava pedagogical faculty. Similarly, 74.6 percent of the students polled at the Ostrava and Nitra pedagogical faculties did not believe they could actively intervene in public affairs with any effect (Šiklová, "Soc. of Youth," pp. 90, 94).

[102] *XIII. sjezd KSČ* (1967), p. 911. In Prague universities the percentage of party members among students dropped from 11 percent in 1958 to 5.2 percent in 1967 (V. V. Kusin, *Political Grouping in the Czechoslovak Reform Movement*, London, 1972, p. 139). In Slovakia the number of students in the CPCz dropped from 7.9 percent (of all students) in 1963 to 3 percent in 1966 (*Echo*, May 14, 1968).

[103] *ŽS*, no. 16 (Aug. 1963), p. 963.

[104] Šiklová, "Soc. of Youth," p. 91.

essary acting as "an opponent" (in the academic sense) of the policy of the party. This would require representation in the National Front and in all state bodies, including the National Assembly. This necessitated "a qualitative change" in the Union's structure, which would recognize two distinct groups, one for those under eighteen years, which would have an "interest group" character, and one for those over eighteen, "a socially engaged group," which would be "a political organization." The latter would be organized in three parts, for industrial, agricultural, and university youth respectively, each equally represented in a central federal body. This bold proposal of federalization received some support but was not endorsed by the conference. The final resolution proposed that the structure and work of the ČSM be examined by a special commission whose report would be considered at a conference to be held prior to the 5th ČSM congress. The resolution also proposed educational reforms, such as admission to the university exclusively on the basis of "knowledge," including two foreign languages, and greater opportunities for study abroad.[105]

In the year following the conference, support for the idea of federalism grew. Müller was elected to the ČSM university council in Prague and supporters of federalism gained a majority on this body. At the end of 1966, however, Müller was expelled from the ČSM and from his faculty, and a few days later, drafted into the army. His case at once became a cause célèbre among Prague students, and he was strongly supported by the ČSM university committee. His successor, Lubomír Holeček, and other so-called Prague radicals, played an important part at the city-wide ČSM conference in May 1967 and some were elected delegates to the forthcoming national congress.[106]

The response of the party and ČSM leadership was at first somewhat noncommittal and defensive. Koucký, in his speech at the 1965 student conference, did not reject outright the proposal of federalization but argued that the decision must be left to the next ČSM congress. His attitude toward the youth in general was more realistic, recognizing the legitimate interests of the varied sectors and the necessity of adopting a differentiated approach.[107] Novotný soon made clear his unalterable

---

[105] For Müller's speech, see *Student*, Jan. 26, 1966; for the resolution, *MF*, Jan. 27, 1966. For an explanation and discussion of the term "opponent" (in Czech, *oponentura*), see below, chap. IV. Müller was made a member of the commission, and his close associate, L. Holeček, its chairman.

[106] Jan Kavan, "Testament of a Prague Radical," *Ramparts*, Sept. 28, 1968, pp. 53-60; *Literární listy*, March 7, 1968, pp. 6-7.

[107] *Student*, Jan. 26, 1966. He was reported as endorsing the idea of an "*oponentura*," although expressing the view that the party was in a better position than the youth organization to develop such a solid academic *oponentura*. A fuller report of his speech in *RP*, Dec. 22, 1965, did not include his remarks on Müller's proposals.

opposition to any division of the ČSM and was supported by Zavadil, the ČSM chairman, who, however, recognized the need for a differentiated approach to various groups.[108] Although, at the 13th congress, the youth and the ČSM came in for the usual censure, no significant changes were made in the position or the methods of the Union.[109]

As the 5th ČSM congress approached, the party indicated that it realized the need for some modification of the Union's structure so as to give more attention to the differing interests of various sectors of the youth and to enlarge the share of youth in decisions on problems directly affecting them.[110] At the congress, however, which was held in June 1967, the party, and the Union, made clear that they were determined not to relax the Union's basic principles. The opposition radicals were given no opportunity to speak, and the idea of federalism was not even discussed. Zavadil, who was 35 years old, was reelected chairman, although with some unprecedented opposition. The vice chairmen and secretaries were all 28 years or older (most of them above 30); the youngest member of the presidium was 24. The new ČSM statute described it as the "unified political and interest societal organization of youth" and reasserted direct party control. There was to be a differentiated approach to social and age groups by the establishment of councils for various sectors, such as the university council, and by the authorization of separate clubs within the ČSM, for individual categories.[111] Yet the Union was to remain unified and party-dominated and was to support the party's policy rather than to defend youth interests. Its radical critics had failed in their efforts to federalize the Union and to make it a genuine spokesman of youth.[112]

In the fall of 1967, a crisis in the relations between students and the regime flared up, almost accidentally, as a result of events at the Strahov student dormitories in Prague.[113] On the evening of October 31, at about 9:30 p.m., a power failure plunged into darkness 5,000 students, mainly of the Czech Technical College, who inhabited this large dormitory com-

[108] *RP*, April 18, May 20, 1966, resp.

[109] *XIII. sjezd KSČ* (1967), pp. 90, 251-54, 409, 439-40, 734-35. The party statute was unchanged with respect to the ČSM (pp. 674-75).

[110] Standpoint of the ČSM central committee, *Smena*, Jan. 22, 1967; Hendrych, at CPCz Central Committee, *RP*, Feb. 10, 1967.

[111] *MF*, June 7, 11, 15, 1967, for the congress decision, the statutes, and the main speech of Zavadil. He was elected by 650 votes to 150 (Kavan, "Testament").

[112] In August Holeček was drafted into the army and the "radical" group more or less broke up. For a post-occupation critique of the efforts of the "radicals," charging them with seeking to create an opposition to the party, see J. Ondrouch, *Tvorba*, no. 42 (1970), supplement.

[113] For a description of the Strahov events, see the report of the governmental commission (*RP*, Dec. 15, 1967); and later reports, published after January 1968, by the Ministry of the Interior (ibid., March 12, 1968) and by the Military Procuracy (*Universita Karlová*, Dec. 4, 1968).

plex. This was but another in a series of similar breakdowns in lighting and heating at these residences dating from the end of 1965, which had led to recurrent appeals and protests by the Strahov dormitory council, and repeated failures by the firms concerned to make the promised repairs. In October alone there had been ten lighting failures and several heating breakdowns.[114] On this occasion a spontaneous demonstration of some 1,500 students, bearing lighted candles and chanting "We want light!" proceeded from Petřín toward the center of the city by way of the Nerudova ulice. At the foot of this steep narrow street, Public Security (VB) units blocked further advance, using tear gas, and arrested three students. Although two of them were released almost at once, one was detained. The students, forced to return to the dormitories, held a mass meeting for the release of their colleague. This was broken up by VB detachments, who penetrated into the residences and used what later were officially called "disproportionately severe measures," resulting in injuries to thirteen students and three VB members. Quiet was restored only at 1:00 a.m.

These events created an atmosphere of tension among students at all Prague higher schools and created "an extraordinarily delicate situation politically," in the words of the university party committee. An assemblage of students of the Philosophical Faculty of Charles University on November 8, which lasted five hours, adopted a resolution which threatened action on November 20 if their demands were not met: inter alia, that individual policemen responsible be identified and punished; that the episode be discussed in Parliament; and that the press should report accurately on the events.[115] The university party committee sharply condemned the "dilatory action" of the authorities of the Technical College and the Ministry of Education. Although describing the street demonstration as improper and justifying the steps taken by the police in "restoring public order," the committee insisted on investigations by the Ministry of the Interior of actions of individual policemen and the necessary measures against them. Every effort must be made, it was urged, to avoid similar situations in the future and to seek "a solution based on maximum patience" if one *should* arise.[116] Official statements by the rector of the Technical College and a pro-rector also censured the demonstration and justified police intervention, but recognized the legitimacy of student complaints and reproached those responsible for failing to make the necessary repairs. The press, including even the youth papers, *Mladá fronta* and *Student*, took a similar line.[117] Some commen-

---

[114] *Student*, Nov. 29, Dec. 6, 1967.

[115] F. Röll and G. Rosenberger, *ČSSR, 1962-1968, Dokumentation und Kritik* (Munich, 1968), p. 151.

[116] *Student*, Nov. 15, 1967.

[117] Ibid. Cf. *RP* and *MF*, Nov. 14, 1967.

tators went still further, denouncing the "political aims" of the students, and, in one case, laying the blame on Radio Free Europe propaganda and the writings of *Literární noviny* during the past decade.[118]

Meanwhile separate investigations were begun by the Technical College, by a special governmental commission headed by the Minister of Education, Professor Jiří Hájek,[119] and by the Ministry of Interior and the Prosecutor General. Emergency measures were taken to assure electric power at Strahov.

A second mass meeting of students at the Philosophical Faculty on November 20 was attended by the university rector, Oldřich Starý, the dean of the faculty, Jaroslav Kladiva, both of whom were members of the Central Committee, and by Professor Goldstücker, pro-rector, and by representatives of other faculties. It lasted nine hours and was more political in character than the previous assembly. The crisis was blamed on the general political and economic situation prevailing in the country and the right of public demonstration against such conditions was defended. Although the students were dissuaded by the academic authorities from organizing a public demonstration, the final resolution established a student commission and demanded that matters be settled by December 15.

The ultimate report of the Hájek commission, approved by the government, recognized that the complaints of the Strahov students were legitimate and announced punishment for those in positions of authority who were directly responsible for the "emergency situation." The resort to a demonstration was, however, condemned. The intervention of the police was described as "necessary and also legal," but the "unduly harsh" measures were censured. No criminal proceedings were to be taken against students or police, but disciplinary actions against students, after further investigation, were not excluded. A number of improvements in the training and equipment of the VB for handling such situations were announced. The report regretted "attempts to exploit the events against the interests of socialist society" and urged that students support the efforts being made by the authorities to maintain "academic order" and to improve students' conditions of life and study.[120]

[118] F. J. Kolár, *KT*, Nov. 16, 1967. This article was condemned by the Writers' Union in December in a statement published later (*LL*, March 1, 1968). The rector of the Technical College and the university rector, O. Starý, also warned students against being misused by other forces, both at home and abroad (*RP*, Nov. 14; *Student*, Dec. 6, 1967).

[119] In order to distinguish him from the writer of the same name, the minister, who later became Minister of Foreign Affairs, will be designated henceforth as Professor Hájek.

[120] *RP*, Dec. 15, 1967. The director of the construction firm and three college officials directly responsible for the failure to deal with the problem were dismissed. Other employees of the firm responsible for the electric cables were given

This report only partially satisfied the demands of the students, who had already established academic councils (ARS) at various faculties and were even less sympathetic to the ČSM and the party than before Strahov. These unplanned events, and their aftermath, had caused a breakdown in the regime's relations with the students and brought into sharp relief many aspects of the general crisis of the system, including the inefficiencies of the economy, the power of the police, the lack of protection of the right of assembly, and the absence of accurate press reporting. Above all, they revealed the inadequacy of the Union of Youth and the complete loss of student confidence in this organization, so unresponsive to their needs.[121]

CONFORMITY IN FOREIGN POLICY

As a member of the socialist bloc and of the world communist movement, Czechoslovakia, somewhat like Canada within the Commonwealth, has had two types of external relationships: one, more intimate, with the Soviet Union and her fellow bloc members, and with the fraternal parties of the communist movement; the other, more properly "foreign," with non-bloc states, including both "capitalist" and "developing" countries. For some years after 1948, the closely knit character of the bloc, under Soviet domination, excluded any autonomy of action by individual communist states. Within the bloc, the imperative of unity overrode any consideration of specific national interest. Diplomacy with non-communist states had to be conducted, in all matters of substance, within the framework of Soviet policy, and in most cases amounted to

---

reprimands and financial penalties. The original statement by the college rector did not explicitly concede that harsh measures had been used. Student complaints concentrated, however, on this point. As early as November 8 the Ministries of both Education and the Interior admitted that the actions taken had not been proportionate to student behavior and would be investigated (*Smena*, Nov. 19, 1967).

[121] For analyses of the student problem prior to January, see Kusin, *Political Grouping*, pp. 123 ff.; Golan, *Czechoslovak Reform*, pp. 100-106, 259-65. After January, much attention was paid to the Strahov events. There was criticism of the construction companies (J. Ruml, *Rep.*, Jan. 17-24, 1968); of the interpretation of the constitution and the laws by the police authorities (J. Marek, *KN*, March 8); of the actions of the police and of the December report (J. Ruml, *Rep.*, June 6-13); of Kolár's commentary (for his defense, *KŽ*, Feb. 9; for criticism by V. Maňák, ibid., Feb. 16). Professor Hájek, in an interview, justified the conclusions of his report and again characterized the demonstration as an unwise action and a breach of order (*LL*, Jan. 20, 1968).

There was also censure of the Ministry of the Interior for its arrests and trials in May 1966, and of the university authorities and the ČSM for the expulsion of Müller and Holeček (J. Ruml, *LL*, March 21). See also below, chap. XVIII for a later report by the Ministry of the Interior, and the reaction of the party's university committee (*RP*, March 12-13, 1968).

little more than declarative approval of Moscow's position. Although there were no Soviet troops on Czechoslovak soil, the alliance with the Soviet Union excluded even the slightest breach of solidarity in international or bloc relations. As Jaroslav Šedivý, foreign affairs specialist, later put it, "Czechoslovakia after 1950 did not make its own policy: on the contrary, its subordination to Soviet policy was total."[122]

In the mid-fifties, when the Soviet campaign for peaceful coexistence was launched, the possibility emerged for individual communist states and parties to defend their own standpoints and even to take some degree of initiative but this was often discouraged, or counteracted, by opposing tendencies toward unity of action. In February 1956 the CPCz Central Committee, in a rare discussion of foreign policy, is said to have criticized severely the Ministry of Foreign Affairs and to have proclaimed the desirability of a foreign policy of "initiative," which was not, it was claimed, in contradiction with the demands of unity of the socialist camp.[123] Apart from certain modest and limited actions, however, no active foreign policy was developed in subsequent years, owing partly to the unfavorable conditions after the Hungarian revolt in 1956, and partly, in Šedivý's later words, to the "lack of will, capacity, and courage" of those responsible for Czechoslovakia's foreign affairs.[124]

During the next decade complete solidarity with the Soviet Union remained the guiding principle of Czechoslovak external relations, as demonstrated by the renewal of the 1943 alliance in 1963, and by repeated proclamations of loyalty by leading spokesmen.[125] The sudden removal of Khrushchev in 1964, only a few months after a visit to Czechoslovakia

[122] *Rep.*, May 1-7, 1968, pp. 17-20. Šedivý described Czechoslovakia as "at best a co-creator but in the main a mere supporter of a foreign policy effort determined first and foremost by the Soviet Union" (*Věda a život*, no. 9, 1965, pp. 513-19).

[123] This decision was not published at the time, but was cited by Šedivý in several of his articles, and in a symposium prepared for party schooling, *Otázky mezinárodní politiky* (Prague, 1967), p. 325. According to his citation, the decision read:

Absolute and consistent unity of the lands of the socialist camp is not in the slightest contradiction with the greatest possible activity by the individual countries, and with the taking of their own initiative. On the contrary, the interests of the common struggle of the socialist camp . . . require that all countries, starting from a single common line and mutually coordinating their action, should develop their own initiative to the greatest possible extent and utilize all their own possibilities for an active struggle for the interests of socialism and world peace.

Cf. also M. Janků, *NM*, no. 5 (1968), p. 631.

[124] *LL*, April 18, 1968. In 1965, Šedivý placed the responsibility on economic difficulties, the conflict with China, and imperialism's actions against the socialist states (*Otázky*, p. 325).

[125] Cf. Novotný and Koucký, at the 13th congress, *XIII. sjezd KSČ* (1966), pp. 103, 257.

in August, undoubtedly alarmed and embarrassed Novotný. There were unconfirmed reports of an altercation by telephone with Brezhnev over the precipitate ousting of his predecessor, without prior notification or consultation, but nothing of this dispute was revealed publicly.[126] Perhaps significantly, Novotný did not attend the Moscow anniversary celebrations in November but his visit to the USSR in December seemed to confirm the close alliance of the two countries.[127] The conclusion of a five-year trade treaty, covering the years 1966 to 1970, in October 1965, was reportedly accompanied by some strains,[128] but did not alter the almost total dependence of the Czechoslovak economy on the Soviet Union. A nine-day visit by Novotný to the USSR in late 1965 demonstrated anew the intimate relations with the Soviet Union and its new leadership and Novotný's willingness to accept their strategy and directives in return for their support.[129]

Within Comecon, Czechoslovakia strongly supported Khrushchev's idea of greater integration and offered no support for Rumania's independent course. She remained an active participant in this organization's activities, but was dissatisfied with the slow progress toward economic integration. Some economists expressed disappointment at the absence of economic reform in most Comecon states and urged the need for "market relations" in their mutual trade. Proposals were reportedly made in 1966 for the development of such relations and of direct contacts between enterprises.[130] It was generally recognized, however, that, since Comecon was not a supranational organization, advance could be achieved, not by general multilateral coordination of national plans, as originally intended, but more slowly and over a longer run, by bilateral agreements, reflecting the interests of the specific countries.[131]

Within the Warsaw Treaty Organization, Czechoslovakia approved Brezhnev's advocacy of a strengthening of the pact's defensive arrange-

---

[126] See J. F. Brown, *The New Eastern Europe* (New York, 1966), p. 172, on the alleged Brezhnev-Novotný clash. At the October CC plenum, Novotný's speech dealing with relations with the CPSU was not published, nor was his report on Khrushchev's removal (*Usnesení KSČ*, 1964, pp. 316-17). For other details of the alleged clash with Brezhnev, see Moravus, *Listy* (Nov. 1971), pp. 27-28.

[127] *ŽS*, no. 24 (Dec. 1964), pp. 1474-75.

[128] Viktor Meier, "Politics in Prague," *Survey*, no. 59 (April 1966), pp. 4-5.

[129] *ŽS*, no. 19 (Oct. 1965), pp. 1160-62; *NM*, no. 10 (1965), pp. 1153-58.

[130] See the lectures given in 1967 by J. Kantůrek and J. Štěpánek, in *50 let socialismu–představy a skutečnost* (Prague, 1968); Golan, *Czechoslovak Reform*, pp. 88-89.

[131] O. Šimůnek, *RP*, Aug. 7, 1966; J. Holeček, *Slovanský přehled*, no. 1 (1966), pp. 26-32; J. Smilek, *Hospodářské noviny*, July 22, 1966; in English, *EE* 15 (Nov. 1966), 27-29; *XIII. sjezd KSČ* (1966), pp. 389, 395. See also Zdeněk Suda, *La division internationale socialiste du travail* (Leiden, 1967), esp. pp. 74-80, 126-29; Suda, *The Czechoslovak Socialist Republic* (Baltimore, 1969), pp. 93-98.

ments and evinced no sympathy with Rumania's proposals for organizational reform.[132] Full participation in Warsaw pact maneuvers, including the Vltava exercises held partly on Czechoslovak soil in August 1966, was an earnest of Prague's loyalty and of her military capacity. It is not known whether there was Soviet dissatisfaction with the Czechoslovak armed forces, as some have speculated, or whether proposals for the permanent or temporary stationing of Soviet troops on Czechoslovakia's western frontier were in fact made by Moscow and refused by Prague.[133]

Within the world communist movement Czechoslovakia had resolved with relative ease the dilemma created by Sino-Soviet tension by casting its full support to Moscow and rejecting Peking's ideological and political line.[134] The Czechoslovak party showed no inclination to follow Albania's heresy of alliance with China and gave no support to Rumania's balancing act vis-à-vis China and the USSR. After 1963, and the Soviet shift in attitude toward Yugoslavia, Prague found it possible to begin a rapprochement of her own, including an exchange of visits by Novotný and Tito in 1964 and 1965, and a second trip by the former in 1967. Novotný repeatedly endorsed the necessity of international communist unity, as set forth in the conferences of 1957 and 1960, and seconded

[132] Note Brezhnev's speech at the CPSU Central Committee plenum in September 1965, in which he spoke of "the coordination of the foreign policy of the socialist countries," particularly in the United Nations, and of "improving the activity of the Warsaw Treaty Organization, the need to set up within the framework of the Treaty a permanent and prompt mechanism for considering pressing problems" (Fritz Ermarth, *Internationalism, Security, and Legitimacy: The Challenge to Soviet Interests in East Europe, 1964-1968*, Rand Corp., Santa Monica, Cal., March 1969, pp. 33-34). The nature of the proposed Soviet measures has never been disclosed, nor have the Rumanian proposals (ibid., p. 36). See Thomas W. Wolfe, *Soviet Power and Europe: 1945-1970* (Baltimore, 1970), pp. 304-8. See below, chap. xix.

[133] John Erickson, "The 'Military Factor' and the Czechoslovak Reform Movement: 1967-1968," paper at the Reading, England, conference, published in Kusin, ed., *Czechoslovak Reform*, pp. 34-35, 42; also in Czech, *Svědectví*, no. 42 (1971), pp. 213-30. See also his article, *Sunday Times*, Sept. 1, 1971. According to Erickson, the Soviet military did lack confidence in Czechoslovak armed capacities and were convinced that in view of the Soviet shift to a strategic doctrine of flexible response, Soviet troops on the western frontier were required. See chap. xix for further discussion. See also John P. Fox, "Czechoslovakia 1968 and 1938," *Contemporary Review* 214 (March 1969), 122-27. A. Šnejdárek, one-time director of ÚMPE, in a personal interview in 1971, denied that there was a Soviet proposal for the permanent stationing of troops but stated that the idea of the free movement of troops in the bloc countries had been raised and discussed in 1967. See also Šnejdárek, in Kusin, ed., *Czechoslovak Reform*, p. 52. According to the *Neue Zürcher Zeitung*, Sept. 8, 1968, Novotný had several years earlier, in a secret agreement with the Soviet Union, reserved the right to call in Warsaw treaty troops in the event of an internal or external threat but had opposed "uninvited intervention" (Kenneth Ames, "Reform and Reaction," *PC* 17, Nov.-Dec. 1968, 46n.).

[134] See Skilling, "Czechoslovakia," in Adam Bromke, ed., *The Communist States at the Crossroads* (New York, 1965).

Soviet proposals for a new world communist conference. Koucký also supported the Soviet thesis that "respect for specific national tasks must always be interpreted in such a way as not to harm common international interests (of the fraternal parties) nor disturb their mutual unity."[135] Only with the German Democratic Republic (GDR) did occasional conflicts occur, mainly as a result of East German criticism of Prague's cultural "liberalization" and of attempts at rapprochement with West Germany.[136]

As for relations with non-communist states, Czechoslovakia associated herself with some enthusiasm with the Soviet policy of "peaceful coexistence," since it opened the way to breaking down barriers to cooperation in Europe.[137] There was little doubt that Prague, while retaining close ties with the communist bloc, strongly desired to extend its economic and cultural relations with neighboring countries.[138] Two major initiatives of Czechoslovak diplomacy were designed to support these objectives—its proposals, at the United Nations in 1962, to codify the principles of peaceful coexistence, and in the Economic Commission for Europe in 1964 and after, for all-European joint economic projects.[139] Prague also joined the Soviet campaign for a European security system and for a European conference, and advanced its own plan for a Central European security pact.[140] In all these respects, of course, Czechoslovak diplomacy was acting within the framework of basic Soviet policy. In the Middle East, Prague's breach of relations with Israel in the summer of 1967 followed immediately after similar Soviet action. Peaceful coexistence was assumed to exclude coexistence in the realm of ideas, or any relaxation of struggle against what were considered the main sources of threats to the peace, notably the United States and West Germany. Both these were blamed by Prague for the failure to solve outstanding prob-

[135] Novotný, *XIII. sjezd KSČ* (1966), pp. 103-5; Koucký, ibid., p. 256; congress decision, ibid., p. 415. Cf. also K. Douděra, *RP*, Nov. 22, 1967.

[136] A. Müller and B. Utitz, *Deutschland und die Tschechoslowakei: Zwei Nachbarvölker auf dem Weg zur Verständigung* (Freudenstadt, 1972), pp. 84 ff. See also Golan, *Czechoslovak Reform*, pp. 129-30.

[137] Skilling, in Bromke, ed., *The Communist States*, p. 93. Note the stress on peaceful coexistence and its advantages by Šedivý, *Věda a život*, and in his more orthodox article, *NM*, no. 16, Aug. 9, 1966, pp. 3-5.

[138] Richard Burks, "The Decline of Communism in Czechoslovakia," *SCC* 2 (Jan. 1969), 26. On cultural relations, see A. Ort, *Mezinárodní vztahy*, no. 3 (1966), pp. 54-60; in German in *Europa-Archiv* 13 (1968), 478-84; A. J. Liehm, *MV*, no. 1 (1968), pp. 55-62.

[139] Šedivý, *Otázky*, pp. 334-35, 340. See V. Pěchota, *MV*, no. 4 (1967), pp. 8-15.

[140] James H. Wolfe, "West Germany and Czechoslovakia: The Struggle for Reconciliation," *Orbis* 14 (Spring 1970), 154-79. This was to be a pact including Germany, Czechoslovakia, Poland, and Hungary, and providing for a reduction of forces, disbanding of pacts, an atom-free zone, and nonagression treaties (p. 175).

lems. Even in the case of Austria, responsibility for improving relations was placed on Vienna.[141]

Prague's negative and conformist policy was most evident in respect to Western Germany, toward which, at least until the end of 1966, it remained hostile and suspicious, in keeping with the attitudes of Moscow and East Berlin.[142] Bonn's refusal to meet Czechoslovakia's terms, including the recognition of "realities" such as the existence of the GDR, and the invalidity of the Munich treaty *ab initio*, as well as Bonn's tolerant attitude toward "revanchist" elements in West Germany, were said to block any "normalization" of Prague-Bonn relations, particularly the resumption of diplomatic relations. Nonetheless, substantial increases in both economic and cultural relations did in fact occur. In January 1967, within weeks of the formation of the Great Coalition under Chancellor Kiesinger, discussions were opened in Prague with a West German representative that would probably soon have led to an economic agreement and perhaps eventually to diplomatic relations. The crisis within the Soviet bloc resulting from Rumania's recognition of West Germany, and East German and Polish condemnation of this action, interrupted this promising development. Prague had to yield to pressure from her allies to the north, expressed at the Warsaw conference in February, and to abandon for the time being her approach to Bonn. The conclusion of military alliances with the GDR and Poland in March, and the stiff declaration of the Karlovy Vary conference in April, suggested that Prague had sacrificed her own interest in improving relations with West Germany to those of her allies and to bloc unity.

Yet only a few months later, renewed negotiations with Bonn led in August to the conclusion of a trade agreement covering the years 1967 to 1969, and concurrence on the establishment of trade missions in Prague and Frankfurt. Economic, not political, considerations had undoubtedly been predominant in this arrangement. A more far-reaching political and diplomatic consensus was impeded by Prague's respect for bloc unity. Yet some observers believed that the renewal of contact was bound to have eventual political repercussions.[143] Officially, however, Czechoslovakia maintained her stiff and unrelenting attitude on the conditions that must be fulfilled by West Germany for the resumption of diplomatic relations.[144]

[141] *XIII. sjezd KSČ* (1966), pp. 100-101 (Novotný); pp. 255-56 (Koucký). See also the preparatory materials, *XIII. sjezd KSČ* (1967), pp. 917, 922.

[142] See the hard-line article by V. Král, *NM*, Oct. 18, 1966, pp. 20-23. On Czechoslovak-West German relations, see Müller and Utitz, esp. pp. 114-51; James H. Wolfe, *Orbis* (Spring 1970).

[143] For a positive commentary, see A. Müller, *LN*, Aug. 11, 1967. Cf. the more reserved attitude of K. Douděra, *RP*, Aug. 5, 1967.

[144] V. David, at the UN General Assembly (quoted in J. H. Wolfe, *Orbis*, pp.

During these years the conduct of foreign policy was largely in the hands of the party Presidium, with the Central Committee seldom even discussing the subject.[145] The National Assembly and its foreign affairs committee played little or no role; even the Ministry of Foreign Affairs was often bypassed by the CC International Relations department.[146] Public opinion on international affairs could hardly express itself and had little or no influence. From time to time, however, official refutation was required to meet rumblings of criticism about the cost of defense or the Warsaw pact maneuvers, the harmful effects of trade with the Soviet Union and the Comecon link, or excessive aid for the developing countries. Occasionally, lack of understanding, especially among the youth, of the need for the close relationship with the Soviet Union, pacificism, and "neutral attitudes" in the conflict of East and West, were deplored.[147] Official support of the Arab states and the break with Israel produced widespread disapproval, sometimes overtly expressed, for instance in speeches at the Writers' Union congress in 1967, and in the departure for Israel of the Slovak author, Mňačko, as a protest.[148] A gradual change of the public attitude toward West Germany is said to have produced a major rift between the rigid official policy and specialists in foreign affairs.[149] The latter, at least in veiled fashion, expressed

---

154-55). He reiterated the oft-stated conditions—abandonment of the Hallstein doctrine, acceptance of the nonproliferation treaty, the ending of ties with West Berlin, and recognition of the sovereignty of the GDR and of the invalidity of Munich *ab initio*. Cf. Šnejdárek's firm but balanced speech in Bonn, March 1967, published in *MV*, no. 2 (1967), pp. 3-11; in English, *International Relations* (1968), pp. 13-24; Šedivý's insistence on German fulfillment of the standard conditions (*Věda a život* 9, 1965); and Ort's arguments re the invalidity of the Munich treaty, *MV*, no. 3 (1967), pp. 43-51.

[145] CC discussions were limited to the international communist movement and were usually not published. See the meetings in October 1964 (*Usnesení KSČ*, 1964, pp. 316-17) and April 1965, *ŽS*, no. 9 (1965), p. 565.

[146] These points were made by V. David, then still Minister of Foreign Affairs, in the CC plenum, *RP*, April 13, 1968. See also Josef Šedivý, *ŽS*, no. 11 (May 1968), p. 61.

[147] For instance, Novotný, *XIII. sjezd KSČ* (1966), p. 103; *XIII. sjezd KSČ* (1967), pp. 746, 770-71, 795; Hendrych, CC plenum, *RP*, Feb. 10, 1967.

[148] *IV. sjezd SČSS Protokol*, p. 40. Mňačko, in interviews in 1968, explained his action as a protest against the one-sided official attitude toward Israel and his own inability to express his opinion in Czechoslovakia. Like Kohout, he compared the position of Israel, threatened with "genocide" by the Arabs, with that of Czechoslovakia in 1938, and repudiated the charge that Israel was the aggressor. It was moreover illogical, he said, to sever diplomatic relations with Israel without breaking off with the United States or with Greece. See above in this chapter, and below, chap. XIX, pp. 633-34. According to Kusin, "public opinion almost unanimously sided with Israel" (*The Intellectual Origins of the Prague Spring*, Cambridge, 1971, p. 126).

[149] Müller and Utitz, pp. 137 passim. Müller and Utitz refer to the "unbridgeable gulf" between official quarters and the majority of communist scholars and journalists on relations with West Germany. The German question thus

dissatisfaction with the general conduct of foreign policy, as well as with specific actions in this field. These symptoms of unease about Czechoslovakia's international course contributed to the growing general crisis.[150]

became, in their view, an important "domestic political polarization factor" and a stimulus for general democratization (p. 150).

[150] See below, chap. IV. For brief accounts of foreign policy issues, see Kusin, *Intellectual Origins*, chap. 12; Golan, *Czechoslovak Reform*, pp. 86-88, 236-39, 312-15. Kusin writes of widespread dissatisfaction, largely beneath the surface and rarely expressed, but minimizes unduly the role of foreign policy dissent, especially among specialists (p. 124). Golan goes even further, stating that foreign policy was "not a significant issue in the reform movement campaign prior to 1968" (p. 312).

CHAPTER IV

Science, Scholarship, and the Party

EVER since the death of Stalin, and in particular since 1956, party leaders and ideologues had been conducting a bitter campaign against what they termed "revisionism" in almost all spheres of scholarship, especially in philosophy, history, and the social sciences. In the name of Marxism-Leninism and the traditional party domination of all fields of intellectual activity, the party sought to curb the growing tendencies among scholars toward freer inquiry and greater objectivity generated by Khrushchev's assault on Stalin at the 20th congress of the CPSU. The constitution of 1960 had given explicit endorsement of Marxism-Leninism as "the scientific world outlook" which was to direct culture and education, but the interpretation of this doctrine by scholars often clashed with official expositions by party theorists. In a decision of July 4, 1961 the CC severely criticized the situation in social science teaching and research, both at the universities and the Academy of Sciences, and at the Higher Party School and the Institute of Social Science in the Central Committee, charging lack of sufficient "party-mindedness," "unhealthy individualism," and separation from practical needs. The Institute of Economics was singled out for special censure. The decision stressed the need for strengthening the leading role of the party in this sphere and "the systematic management of the social sciences by the Central Committee in basic ideological questions."[1]

The impact of the 22nd CPSU Congress, with its renewed attack on Stalin, on official Czechoslovak attitudes toward intellectual life appeared to be negligible. True, at the 12th congress of the CPCz in 1962 there was criticism of the cult of personality and opposition to Albanian and Chinese dogmatism, and a new emphasis on the need for scientific-technical progress in the economy and for more scientific planning. This was coupled, however, with a call for a struggle against both revisionism on the "right" and dogmatism, and "peaceful coexistence" in the ideological sphere was expressly rejected.[2]

Nonetheless, the declaration of war on the cult of personality unleashed a general onslaught on dogmatism in all areas of life and pro-

[1] *Usnesení a dokumenty ÚV KSČ, Od celostátní konference KSČ 1960 do XII. sjezdu KSČ* (Prague, 1962), I, 576-89.
[2] *XII. sjezd Komunistické strany Československa* (Prague, 1963), pp. 91, 638-39, 644, 649, 654-56.

duced, in 1963, an intellectual ferment unparalleled in the history of Czechoslovak communism. The revolt in the field of scholarship was somewhat less visible, especially to the outside world, than that of the writers. Many outstanding scholars from the universities and the institutes, however, as contributors to cultural weeklies and in scholarly journals and conferences, in the daily round of lectures and discussions, and in books, were carrying through what amounted to an intellectaul revolution.[3] The party's endorsement of science legitimized, in every discipline, questioning of old dogmas, a fresh and critical attitude toward the subject of inquiry, and a greater reliance on objective findings and independent thinking. This brought a renewed interest in pre-communist Czech and Slovak intellectual traditions, hitherto condemned as bourgeois falsifications, and a less negative approach to scholarly work during the First Republic. It involved also a more open attitude toward Western non-communist scholarship, encouraged by greater ease of travel and freer access to Western literature, and a widened knowledge and appreciation of unorthodox Marxist thought in other countries. This in turn tipped the balance away from the previous dependence on Soviet scholarship and the rigidly enforced acceptance of established Soviet interpretations. This was not an easy process for Czechoslovak scholars, most of whom had been faithful, and even enthusiastic, exponents of Stalinist modes of thought. Although they remained Marxists and usually party members, they began the painful process of self-examination and reassessment of their past thinking. Burdened often by feelings of shame and guilt for their earlier endorsement of falsehoods and distortions, they boldly claimed greater freedom of thought and of interpretation in their fields of study.

Their work, whether published or not, struck hard at the legitimacy of entrenched doctrines and challenged the decisive influence of the party apparatus in the intellectual field. It threatened the position of leaders and ideologues, and more conservative scholars, who had a vested interest in the maintenance of the old system of thought. As a consequence, the party organs felt themselves obliged to intervene directly in scientific work, bypassing authorized institutions such as the Academy of Sciences and thus circumscribing the autonomy of scholarly work, especially in the social sciences. As the head of the Academy, František Šorm, later lamented, scholarly institutions became "work-places of the party." According to Zdeněk Mlynář, social sciences were identified by the party

[3] See V. V. Kusin, *The Intellectual Origins of the Prague Spring* (Cambridge, 1971), chap. 2. He denotes the year 1956 as "the beginning of reform" (p. 27). See also Edward Taborsky, *East Europe* 16 (Feb. 1967), 2-12; Robert F. Lamberg, *Osteuropa* 16 (May-June 1966), 289-99; Luciano Antonetti, "Lenin e il leninismo a Praga negli ultimi anni," *Critica marxista* 8 (May-June 1970), 194-204.

with agitation and propaganda, and ideas and proposals generated by scholars had little or no influence on public policy.[4]

PARTISANRY AND THE SCIENTIFIC SPIRIT

A feature of official policy after 1961, with profound implications for scholarship, was, however, the insistence that the party should take more account of the findings of "science" (or "scholarship," as it would be termed in English) and that public policy should be "scientific" in the sense of being based on these findings.[5] This implicitly challenged the traditional view that policy *was* "scientific" since it was based on Marxism-Leninism and the "correct" interpretation of that doctrine as enunciated by leaders and ideologists at a given time. As a prominent Czech publicist, Čestmír Císař, phrased it, this had placed "theory and science" in the background and had meant the loss of *raison d'être* for theoreticians and scientific workers. All the social sciences had suffered, including philosophy, sociology, economics, and history, and even some natural sciences. Dogmatism had "deformed" the thinking of Marxists and had led to "stagnation and backwardness of thoughts and actions." The time had come, wrote Císař, to render scientific the activity of the party and of all society."[6]

Nonetheless, Vladimír Koucký, the major spokesman in the campaign against revisionism, in his report to the special CC plenum devoted to ideological questions at the end of 1963, continued to castigate the social sciences for their shortcomings.[7] A few months later, addressing the Academy of Sciences, he was more specific in his criticism, especially of economics, history, philosophy.[8] At the end of 1964 the Presidium issued a special decision on the guidance of the social sciences, which lamented "ideological wavering . . . and even attacks on the basic principles of socialist society and on the leading role of the party" by certain scholars. Warning against the concept of "peaceful coexistence of ideologies," it proclaimed that the basis of the "scientific approach" must be a "class approach" and urged a struggle on two fronts, against the continuing remnants of dogmatism from the cult period and against liberalistic and revisionist opinions. The decision then outlined a series of con-

---

[4] F. Šorm, at a press conference, *Rudé právo*, April 12, 1968. See also the remarks of Z. Mlynář and R. Richta on that occasion.

[5] V. Mlíkovský, *Nová mysl*, no. 6 (1963), p. 643.

[6] *NM*, no. 4 (1963), esp. pp. 388-90.

[7] *RP*, Dec. 21, 1963. See also the CC decision, *Usnesení a dokumenty ÚV KSČ*, 1962-63 (Prague, 1964), p. 546. The decision asserted the need to "overcome the lagging of the social sciences behind the real needs of society" and "more closely to link them to the party's policy."

[8] *RP*, April 11, 1964. See his earlier criticism of social sciences (*NM*, no. 8, 1962, pp. 897-921).

crete measures for tighter control of social research by the party, through its Ideological Commission and the apparatus, and by the Academy of Sciences and the Ministry of Education and Culture.[9]

Responding to the challenge of scholars, the regime reasserted the traditional doctrine of "partisanry" (*stranickost*) which was to be observed in every discipline of the social sciences. At a special seminar devoted to this question at the Higher Party School in March 1965, it was argued that partisanry represented a dialectical unity of "scientificness" (*vědeckost*) and the "ideology-mindedness" (*ideologičnost*) of the working class. It was denied that scientific study must recognize "facts which in and of themselves are never of a class character"; on the contrary, "science was forced to evaluate facts . . . from the standpoint of this or that class." Moreover the ideological and scientific sides of *stranickost* were linked with "its organizational side," including disciplined acceptance of decisions by party members, "in spite of partial differences of opinions."[10]

The party's organizational journal in an article on "Scientific Work and the Party"[11] explained what this meant in practice. "The development of social theory was always, in the communist movement, an inseparable component of practical revolutionary transformation. It is not possible therefore to cultivate it as science in the old sense of the word and to develop it outside the Communist Party, from some kind of theoretical detachment separated from the actual movement." This did *not* represent "a limitation of theoretical freedom." There was "no contradiction between creative theoretical work in the field of social research and the party responsibility and discipline of a communist theorist." The theoretical worker in the social sciences was "an element and an instrument of the cognitive activity of the party" and developed science "with the mandate of the party." "The party alone, drawing on the results of all social science work centers and all other sources of knowledge, was able to develop social science as a whole and to achieve the most complex understanding of reality." Indeed the conclusions of the social scientists were to be published only after consultations with the appropriate party organs, since "the party alone is capable of judging and evaluating them."

The seriousness of the problem of scholarly independence was indicated by the "unsatisfactory situation" at the Central Committee's Higher Party School and Institute of Social Sciences which might have been

[9] *Usnesení a dokumenty ÚV KSČ*, 1964 (Prague, 1965), pp. 394-405. See V. Knapp, *NM*, no. 2 (1965), pp. 224-31.

[10] The main report by I. Hrůza and L. Hrzal, and comments by representatives of a number of scholarly disciplines, were published in a special supplement, "On Communist Partisanry," *NM*, no. 4 (1965), pp. 1-56. Quotations at pp. 2-3, 4, 9.

[11] V. Ráb, *Život strany*, no. 12 (June 1964), pp. 739-41.

expected to be citadels of right-minded and loyal attitudes. Instead the School was depicted, in a special Presidium decision in August 1964, as rife with "incorrect opinions, doubts, and reservations" about the CC's decision on ideological questions. There was even "denial of the leading role of the party in theoretical work" and in face of party criticism, "silence, passivity, and in some cases active support of incorrect standpoints." The removal of Milan Hübl, the pro-rector, in early 1964, and the transfer of many other teachers, had apparently not corrected the situation. The Presidium lamented the "passive attitude" of some of the staff "to various attacks against the leadership of the party and against the politics of the Central Committee, from the position of right-wing opportunism, liberalism, and revisionism." Some teachers, affected by "petty bourgeois intellectualism," placed "the principle of party approach in opposition to scientificness," and held "opinions as to the independence of the scientific work of the school from the politics, and in general the practice, of the party." "Scientific skepticism" was often interpreted as meaning "to doubt everything" in contemporary political activity and in the party's ideological struggle. The only solution was the removal of a number of teachers to other places of work, the statement concluded.[12]

A PHILOSOPHY OF MAN

The situation in the field of philosophy was of special concern to the party. The philosophers were few in number, but they occupied a strategic and sensitive position in the ideological system, based on Marxism-Leninism as a kind of "state religion" and on the right of political organs to formulate its correct interpretation.[13] The assault on dogmatism in 1956 inspired many philosophers to reassess sacrosanct dogmas inherited from Stalinist days and to interpret Marxism more flexibly. A reexamination of the early writings of Marx, the study of the works of prominent revisionist Marxists abroad, such as György Lukács in Hungary, and an objective appreciation of the ideas of non-Marxist philosophers, produced heretical currents of thought and "a plurality of tendencies and schools" among Marxists.[14] The Politburo regarded the situation as serious enough to require a special statement, issued in 1959, which referred to the "great shock" of the 20th congress for many philosophers and the "profound doubt" and "incorrect views" that had resulted. Ivan Sviták and Karel Kosík were singled out for special condemnation, in particular for their contributions to a series on philosoph-

[12] Usnesení KSČ, 1964, pp. 282-86. [13] J. Cvekl, RP, June 6, 1968.
[14] Cvekl, ibid.; see Kusin, Intellectual Origins, chap. 4, for detailed analysis of controversies in philosophy.

ical questions published by *Literární noviny* in 1956-1957. Revisionism, according to the Politburo, had its roots in a misinterpretation of Hegel and of the younger Marx and in the influence of foreign Marxists such as Lukács, Henri Lefebvre, etc. Although most philosophers were party members and Marxists, philosophy had become separated from politics; yet philosophy must "actively serve party policy" and must be directed by the party.[15]

The ferment in philosophy was given a fillip by Khrushchev's renewed assault on Stalinism in 1961. Czechoslovak philosophers published new works and articles condemning Stalinism and neo-Stalinism in their field and expounding an "authentic Marxism," derived from the works of the younger Marx and based on critical thinking and the search for truth. Milan Průcha, for instance, quoted Marx's *Economic and Philosophical Manuscripts* to the effect that "communism is humanism, a complete humanism." He argued that it was not a question of opposing these ideas to Marx's later studies but of "avoiding the distortion of the humanist core of Marx's concept of communism" as a result of preoccupation with his later writings.[16]

This theme, in various forms, was developed by other philosophers whose works were characterized by a search for a new philosophy and ethic, a critique of the bureaucratization of all aspects of life, and a vision of a democratic and humanist socialism.[17] Even the philosophy of Masaryk was restudied, still critically, but in an objective manner in striking contrast to the earlier unconditional condemnation.[18] Slovak philosophers, such as Miroslav Kusý and Július Strinka, drew radical conclusions concerning the need for freedom of thought and, in the case of Strinka, for an institutionalized means of expressing dissenting views.[19]

[15] The substance of this resolution was indicated in a major article in *NM*, no. 6 (June 1959), pp. 571-79. For text of a CC report on the same subject, *Usnesení a dokumenty ÚV KSČ, Od XI. sjezdu do celostátní konference, 1960* (Prague, 1960), pp. 305-19.

[16] Erich Fromm, ed., *Socialist Humanism* (Garden City, N.Y., 1965), p. 145.

[17] P. Ludz, "Philosophy in Search of Reality," *Problems of Communism* 18 (July-Oct. 1969), 35 ff. See various essays on "authentic Marxism" written before 1968 by J. Cvekl, F. Šamalík, I. Dubský, and others in *Marx a dnešek* (Prague, 1968) and by R. Kalivoda, *Moderní duchovní skutečnost a marxismus* (Prague, 1968). Cf. J. Fibich, "Institutional Alienation and the Freedom of Man," *Filosofia*, no. 6 (Nov.-Dec. 1967), pp. 607-17. See Fromm, ed., *Soc. Humanism* for essays by Sviták and Kosík.

[18] Lubomír Nový, *Filosofie T. G. Masaryka* (Prague, 1962). Cf. also Karel Kosík's discussion of "the return to Masaryk," in A. J. Liehm, ed., *The Politics of Culture* (New York, 1967, 1968), p. 407.

[19] J. Strinka, *Kultúrny život*, Nov. 26, 1965, reprinted in G. Hillmann, *Selbstkritik des Kommunismus* (Reinbek bei Hamburg, 1967), pp. 221-32; M. Kusý, *Pravda*, Oct. 19, 1966. See also Kusý, *Filosofia politiky* (Bratislava, 1966). Kusý and M. Suchý argued for the establishment of an association of philosophers

The most eminent exponent of a new approach to Marxism was Karel Kosík, whose influential book, The Dialectic of the Concrete, published in 1963,[20] was a dialectical analysis of man within the "concrete totality" of society. This work centered on the idea of man as a free individual, having the right to live his life "creatively" and "critically."[21] The cardinal question, he stated elsewhere, was "What is Man?" Through critical thought a new conception of socialism must be evolved, based on a new concept of man.[22] "Every individual," wrote Kosík, in The Dialectic of the Concrete, "*must himself and without intermediary* absorb culture and live his life" (p. 19). "In history man realizes himself. It is not only that, before history and independently of it, he does *not know* who he is; but it is first in history that he *is* man at all" (p. 234). "Neither absolute regularity nor absolute freedom rules in history; in history nothing is absolutely necessary and nothing absolutely accidental. History is the dialectic of freedom and necessity" (pp. 228-29). "Men make history" (p. 230).

Ivan Sviták went further than others in his radical rethinking of Marxism and was in fact charged with rejecting Marxism.[23] From 1956 on he had boldly assailed the role of philosophy and philosophers during the cult period and had warned of a new dogmatism based on continued official intervention. The task of philosophy, he wrote, was above all "to think." "*Science ends exactly at the point where its freedom ends.*" Philosophy was to be equated with "critical thinking; the philosopher must never give up the critical spirit, the essence of philosophy." In 1963 he argued for a socialist humanism based on the works of the later as well as the younger Marx, and on scientific anthropology as it had developed since Marx. In 1966 he urged the necessity of recognizing the diversity of interpretations of Marxism and himself opted for a "humanist-democratic interpretation," rather than the prevailing "pragmatic-economic conception."[24] Sviták, who was frequently criticized by party spokesmen, was dismissed from the Institute of Philosophy in 1964, in spite of resistance by his colleagues, and was also expelled from the party.[25]

---

since its joint statements would carry more weight than those of individuals and involve less risk (*KŽ*, April 22, 1966).

[20] *Dialektika konkretního* (Prague, 1963); in German translation, *Die Dialektik des Konkreten* (Frankfurt, 1967). Quotations are from the German edition.

[21] Ludz, "Philosophy." See also Kosík, "L'individu et l'histoire," *L'homme et la société*, no. 9 (July-Aug.-Sept. 1968), pp. 79-90.

[22] Kosík, in Liehm, ed., *Politics of Culture*, pp. 398-99, 403-5. See also Kosík, in Fromm, ed., *Soc. Humanism*, pp. 148-56.

[23] V. Mlíkovský, *NM*, no. 7 (1964), pp. 842-49.

[24] Some of Sviták's essays from the sixties may be read in English in Sviták, *Man and His World: A Marxian View* (New York, 1970). Quotations at pp. 17, 19, 24, 47, 158-59, 144, 148, resp.

[25] See his letter (not published at the time) defending socialist humanism and

In the context of these new currents of thought the works of Franz Kafka, condemned during the cult period as bourgeois and decadent, assumed an importance that went beyond the narrowly literary into the philosophical and other realms. An important discussion of Kafka took place at the Liblice conference in May 1963, with Czech as well as foreign philosophers, including Roger Garaudy and Ernst Fischer, participating.[26] Eduard Goldstücker, professor of German at Charles University and the chief proponent of a rehabilitation of Kafka, affirmed that Kafka's views of man's alienation in a hostile and absurd bureaucratic environment were relevant under socialism, because alienation existed under socialism, too.[27] Kosík compared Kafka with Jaroslav Hašek, author of *The Good Soldier Švejk*, both of whom described "the impotence of man in an objectivized alienated world." Yet "man is not reducible to a thing; he is more than a system . . . man has within himself the enormous and indestructible force of humanity."[28] According to Goldstücker, the effort to revive Kafka was a decisive event affecting the whole of Czech intellectual life and represented the central point in a struggle to break out of the cultural isolation into which the Czechs had been forced during the period of Stalinism.[29]

The independent reexamination of Marxism and of established versions of that doctrine represented a challenge to the party, striking at its so-called cognitive (*poznávací*) function. The ideologues and officially minded philosophers defended the right of "party direction" of philosophy and asserted the need for a struggle against revisionism as well as dogmatism.[30] In a more sophisticated analysis, an article in the main philosophical journal rejected "coexistence" in the ideological sphere and condemned efforts to develop a "philosophy of man" outside Marxism, such as existentialist or Catholic interpretations. Invoking the writings

---

freedom of thought and bitterly attacking Šorm, the head of the Academy of Sciences, for the decision to expel him from the institute (Sviták *Verbotene Horizonte*, Freiburg im Breisgau, 1969, pp. 9-13).

[26] Proceedings of the Liblice conference were published as *Franz Kafka* (Prague, 1963). See Kusin, *Intellectual Origins*, chap. 6, for the conference. The proceedings were severely criticized by East German political leaders. See Galia Golan, *The Czechoslovak Reform Movement* (Cambridge, 1971), pp. 129-30.

[27] Quoted in F. Röll and G. Rosenberger, *ČSSR, 1962-1968, Dokumentation und Kritik* (Munich, 1968), pp. 41-42.

[28] *Literární noviny*, Jan. 19, 1963.

[29] Liehm, ed., *Politics of Culture*, pp. 280-86. See also Goldstücker, *LN*, Feb. 16, 1963; Ivo Fleischmann, ibid., March 30, 1963; Ivan Sviták, "Kafka as Philosopher," *Survey*, no. 59 (April 1966), pp. 36-40.

[30] V. Ruml, *NM*, no. 1 (1964), pp. 9-18. Cf. V. Koucký's attack on philosophical trends, especially the emphasis on alienation, the younger Marx, and the search for a philosophical anthropology (*RP*, April 11, 1964). See also the criticism of Lukács and certain Czech philosophers in the CC statement on the cultural periodicals (ibid., April 3, 1964).

of the early Marx, the author defended what he called the humanism of Marxism but insisted on a class approach to man and to freedom.[31]

The situation in philosophy reached a point of such deterioration, from the party viewpoint, that the Presidium, like its predecessor, found it necessary to adopt a special resolution in early 1965 lamenting the fact that the 1959 decision had not been fully implemented and delivering a searing critique of the Institute of Philosophy, other centers, including the Slovak Institute of Philosophy, the chief journals of philosophy, and the cultural weeklies.[32] Even the CC department responsible for philosophy was castigated for failing to provide "consistent guidance." Once again, Kosík and Sviták were sharply criticized. Sviták's expulsion was justified and his colleagues were accused of "collegial comradeliness" for defending him. The tendencies to reduce Marxist philosophy to "a mere theory of man, to philosophical anthropology," were rejected. The decision condemned the attitude of some philosophers who denied "the cognitive function" of the party, and stressed the need for increased party guidance on the philosophical front. Almost hidden among these negative comments was a reference to the "important task" of philosophy, namely, "the study of the changes in human relations in connection with the revolutionary processes in technology, production, and science"—a reference to the studies under way in the Institute of Philosophy, under the direction of Radovan Richta, on the scientific and technological revolution, which were soon to receive official endorsement.[33]

REBIRTH OF SOCIOLOGY

Another development within philosophy was the revival of sociology as a scholarly discipline. Having existed as a field of study under the First Republic and in the early post-war years, sociology had been treated as a "bourgeois pseudo-science" during the period of the cult and eliminated from the universities and research institutes. It was replaced by dialectical and historical materialism as the all-embracing science of society. Even after 1956 and the acceptance of sociology in Poland and the USSR, Czechoslovakia lagged behind. It was only in the sixties that empirical social research began to be carried out and that rehabilitation of Marxist sociology was openly discussed. As in Poland and the USSR, the rebirth of sociology was pressed in the main by philosophers, but, in Czechoslovakia, also by instructors within the departments of Marxism-Leninism, as an outgrowth of what had been termed "scientific com-

[31] L. Hrzal, "On Some New Tasks of Philosophy," *Filosofický časopis* 12, no. 1 (1964), 1-12.
[32] *NM*, no. 4 (1965), pp. 501-7.   [33] See below in this chapter.

munism." Persistent hostility toward sociology by party ideologues and conservative scholars, who feared its implications, delayed the recognition and institutionalization of the discipline.[34]

Nonetheless, by 1964, a number of significant measures had been taken to reestablish sociology as a scholarly discipline. This development was guided by a special commission of the Academy of Sciences' Philosophical Collegium (shortly to be renamed the Philosophical and Sociological Collegium), headed by Pavel Machonin of the Institute of Marxism-Leninism for Higher Schools in Prague, in close collaboration with the party's Ideological Commission. The first significant step was the founding of a Slovak Sociological Society, and a few months later, in April 1964, of a Sociological Society for the country as a whole, headed by Jaroslav Klofáč, of the Higher Party School. Later in the same year an Institute of Sociology, under the philosopher Miloš Kaláb, was established within the Academy of Sciences. Departments of sociology were formed at many universities, including the Higher Party School, usually within the departments of philosophy or Marxism-Leninism. Research departments also came into existence at a number of specialized institutes. At the beginning of 1965, the first issue of *Sociologický časopis*, published under the Academy's auspices, appeared, with Irena Dubská, of the Institute of Philosophy, as general editor. Full endorsement of the development of sociology and an agenda of its future development were embodied in a special CC Secretariat decision in March 1965.[35] In 1966 Czech and Slovak sociologists participated in the world sociological congress in Evian, France, and later in the year held their own first conference. An associated development was the establishment, within the Academy, of an Institute for Public Opinion Research, terminating the interruption of such research since 1948.[36]

[34] For articles urging the recognition and promotion of sociology, and complaining of delays, see *inter alia* J. Klofáč, *RP*, Nov. 2, 1963; M. Jodl and others, *LN*, Jan. 11, 1964; M. Kaláb, P. Machonin, and J. Večeřa, *RP*, June 15-16, 1965. On public opinion research, see D. Slejška, *Zemědělské noviny*, Feb. 19, 1964; Slejška, *NM*, no. 6 (1964), pp. 756-62. Slejška stressed the need for studying conflicts of opinion, group opinions, and differences between official and informal opinion.

[35] The decision described sociology as "an indispensable instrument in the cognitive activity of the directive organisms of socialist society." For the text, see *NM*, no. 6 (June 1965), pp. 779-85, and for the fuller report on which it was based, *Sociologický časopis* 1, no. 4 (1965), 357-65. For a summary of the development, see P. Machonin, *SČ* 1, no. 1 (1965), 77-79; also no. 6, pp. 649-55. For a list of sociological work centers at the end of 1964, see ibid., no. 3 (1965), pp. 336-47. See also Machonin and Z. Strmiska, ibid. 3, no. 2 (1967), 201-13; ibid., pp. 213-16; no. 3 (1967), pp. 347-57.

[36] *RP*, Jan. 12, 1966; *Pravda*, Feb. 11, 1967. The director of the institute, Dr. J. Zapletalová, attributed to Šorm's efforts the fact that the institute became a part of the Academy of Sciences rather than of the Ministry of Culture and In-

From the early sixties proponents of sociology devoted much attention to the sensitive theoretical question of defining the content of Marxist sociology and its relationship with Marxism-Leninism as a whole.[37] During the cult period, it was said, historical materialism had consisted of a rigid system of dogmatic theories not based on concrete social research. Bourgeois sociology, on the other hand, was largely empirical and lacked a theoretical framework. Marxist sociology, it was argued, guided by the general theory of historical materialism, must test and expand its theoretical doctrines by concrete social research, in line with the character of the study of social phenomena by Marx and Engels, and Lenin. This involved the use of "scientific methods for acquiring accurate and comprehensive information" on new social phenomena, the analysis of this material, and its use in practical life and political management.[38] This required the development of close cooperation with other social sciences, including psychology and social psychology, and the use of modern statistical and mathematical methods. Sociology would enrich Marxism-Leninism by integrating within it the knowledge gained by the individual scholarly disciplines.[39] This broadening of the horizons of Marxist-Leninist social science encouraged a more objective appreciation of pre-communist Czechoslovak sociologists, such as I. A. Bláha and J. L. Fischer, and even T. G. Masaryk, and a wider knowledge and utilization of sociological work in foreign countries, including the non-socialist.[40]

The relationship of sociology with the party raised delicate questions comparable to those raised by the renaissance of other scholarly disciplines. The advocates of sociology and of public opinion research often argued that the principal purpose was to contribute to the "scientific" character of decision-making. As Jodl argued, "the party needs the full and undistorted truth" for making its decisions.[41] Sociology occupied, Klofáč stated, "a significant place as an element of the cognitive activity of the party."[42] Yet the 1965 Secretariat decision made clear that all sociological work must be directed by the party, "according to the needs of the party," through the Ideological Commission and the party ap-

---

formation (*Svět v obrazech*, April 30, 1968). For a detailed analysis of public opinion research from 1946 to 1948, see Č. Adamec, *SČ* 2, nos. 1, 3 (1966).

[37] E.g. J. Klofáč, *NM*, no. 3 (1965), pp. 351-60; A. Sirácky, *SČ* 1, no. 1 (1965), 41-51.

[38] Klofáč, *NM*, no. 3 (1965), p. 352.

[39] Machonin, *Kulturní tvorba*, Dec. 9, 1965.

[40] See the detailed analysis of foreign sociology by J. Klofáč and V. Tlustý, *Soudobá sociologie* (Prague, 1965). On Masaryk and the tradition of Czechoslovak sociology, see *SČ* 1, no. 5 (1965), 630-31; on I. A. Bláha, ibid., no. 4 (1965), pp. 437-50; on J. L. Fischer, ibid. 3, no. 1 (1967), pp. 12-22. For a number of articles on Czech and Slovak sociology in the past, *SČ* 4, no. 3 (1968).

[41] M. Jodl, *LN*, Jan. 11, 1964.

[42] J. Klofáč, *ŽS*, no. 14 (July 1964), pp. 876-79.

paratus.[43] Kaláb and others admitted openly that this was bound to create a problem in the relationship between central direction and the "free development of scientific research."[44]

By 1966 sociology was fully recognized as a scholarly discipline and the foundations had been laid for its growth after years of neglect. Much remained to be done, however, especially in training qualified personnel and deepening sociological knowledge. There was also a danger of "dilettantism" as a result of the sudden popularity of the discipline and of illusions as to its potentialities.[45] Research was just beginning and had not gone far by the close of the Novotný period. The first public opinion poll was conducted only at the end of 1967.

The most noteworthy example of objective sociological research was the study of the changing Czechoslovak social structure conducted by an interdisciplinary team headed by Pavel Machonin, including scholars from the Institute of Marxism-Leninism, the Institutes of Sociology and Philosophy, and other centers. This project was an outgrowth of a conference held in 1964, devoted mainly to the clarification of concepts and methods of analyzing social structure, the proceedings of which were published in 1966 under the title, The Social Structure of Socialist Society.[46] At the request of the party, the group also prepared certain materials for the 13th congress in the same year.[47] Work was well under way on this ambitious empirical analysis of Czechoslovakia's social structure but was not completed until 1968.[48]

[43] NM, no. 6 (1965), p. 784.
[44] Kaláb, Machonin, and Večeřa, RP, June 16, 1965.
[45] See the conclusions of the Czechoslovak sociological conference in 1966, SČ 3, no. 2 (1967), 213-16; P. Machonin, ibid., no. 4 (1967), pp. 389-97.
[46] P. Machonin, ed., Sociální struktura socialistické společnosti (Prague, 1967; in Czech only). See a brief resumé, in English, Summary of the Publication: The Social Structure of Socialist Society (Prague, n.d.). See also P. Machonin and others on this research project, Co-existence 5, no. 7 (1968), 7-16. A review (NM no. 26, Dec. 28, 1966, pp. 44-46) referred to the book as marking a turn of the social sciences in Czechoslovakia toward the use of "modern methods of investigation." The book's main contribution was said to be the stress on the heterogeneity of interests of various social strata, thus rendering untenable earlier notions of the homogeneity and unity of interests in a socialist society. Cf. the proceedings of a symposium in Slovakia in May 1967 on social structure, with chapters by Machonin, Kaláb, and others, Dynamika sociálnej štruktúry v ČSSR (Bratislava, 1968).
[47] A brief version was published as Změny v sociální struktuře Československa a dynamika sociálně politického vývoje (Prague, 1967).
[48] This was eventually published after the occupation, first in Slovak, then in Czech—Pavel Machonin, ed., Československá společnost (Bratislava, 1969). For a detailed summary, see Machonin, "Social Stratification in Contemporary Czechoslovakia," American Journal of Sociology 75 (March 1970), 725-41. For an excellent review article, see Ernest Gellner, "The Pluralist Anti-Levellers of Prague," Government and Opposition 6 (Winter 1972), 20-37.

REVIVAL OF HISTORY

The effervescence of ideas among historians after 1963 was so intense and explosive as to lead an outside observer to refer to the reform movement as a "retrospective revolution," "an historian's revolution."[49] The shock of the 20th congress in 1956 stirred up some discussion among historians, mainly conducted in private, but the dogmatic approach continued to dominate published work.[50] At the 3rd congress of historians in September 1959, attended by Jiří Hendrych and other party officials, Josef Macek, director of the Historical Institute, in the main address, proclaimed Marxism-Leninism as "the only theoretical basis" of historical science and condemned the influence of certain bourgeois tendencies, such as positivism and objectivism, on communist historiography. The one-sided criticism of dogmatism in 1956 was deplored and the need for a struggle against "petty-bourgeois liberalism" and other hostile ideological influences was proclaimed.[51]

Beneath the surface, however, in the years following 1956, historians began to reassess important aspects of the Czech and Slovak past, hitherto deformed or falsified by official dogmas or self-imposed intellectual fetters.[52] The real awakening began in 1963, as part of the general intellectual ferment engendered by the 22nd congress, and more directly, of the personal involvement of leading historians in the reexamination of the trials of the fifties. The evidence of the party's falsification of the charges confirmed the historians' conviction that other major historical events needed fresh analysis. A leading Slovak historian, Samo Falťan, called for an objective evaluation of historical questions, especially the Slovak Uprising of 1944. A young Czech, Jan Křen, decried the distortion of the resistance movement during World War II and urged an impartial treatment of President Beneš and his wartime role.[53] Josef Macek, in a critique of historical science as a whole, admitted that there had

---

[49] Z.A.B. Zeman, *Prague Spring: A Report on Czechoslovakia, 1968* (Harmondsworth, 1968), p. 129. Excellent discussions of the revival of history are given by Karel Bartošek, "Czechoslovakia: the State of Historiography," *Journal of Contemporary History* 2 (Jan. 1967), 143-55 and by Stanley Z. Pech, "Ferment in Czechoslovak Marxist Historiography," *Canadian Slavonic Papers* 10 (Winter 1968), 502-22. See also Antonetti, *Critica marxista* 8, no. 3 (May-June 1970), 194-204.

[50] Pech, "Ferment," pp. 503-7.

[51] For the proceedings of the congress, including the speech by Macek, see *Československý časopis historický* 8 (1960), 1-18, 54-61.

[52] Pech, "Ferment," pp. 507-8. According to him, the initial reassessment concerned Czech nationalism in the 19th century. The Czechs and Slovaks, wrote Zeman, had "to come to terms with their past, to stop rejecting large parts of it, and treating them as if they had never happened" (*Prague Spring*, p. 131). On past distortions of Czech history, see Kusin, *Intellectual Origins*, chap. 8.

[53] *KŽ*, March 23, 1963; *KT*, May 30, 1963, resp.

been "scientific simplification" under Stalin, and black and white treatment of historical events, and of figures such as Masaryk. During the years of "the cult" historical scholarship had been deformed by dogmatism, he said, so that its task was merely "to confirm the theses of the classics of Marxism-Leninism."[54] Pavel Reimann, who was appointed in 1962 as director of the party's Institute of CPCz History, called for a new evaluation of party history. To eliminate the many traces of the cult in their thinking, he said, was a difficult and long-term task, which would require an open exchange of opinions and self-criticism.[55]

This was the prelude to an avalanche of criticism of past historical scholarship, expressed not only in the cultural newspapers and the journal of popular history, *Dějiny a současnost*, but also in the organs of the party history institute and the other historical institutes.[56] Soviet historical science, it was said, had exercised a decisive influence over Czechoslovak scholars. Dogmatism had penetrated Czech and Slovak scholarship without much opposition, and indeed with the active cooperation of almost all historians. The young post-1948 scholars, lacking a real knowledge of Marxism or of the methods of historical scholarship, became "political publicists and propagandists," and their writings "mere apologia" of party decisions. Access to archives and sources had been severely limited and scholars had indulged in uncritical use of official documents. Bourgeois history was repudiated *in toto* and "a sectarian nihilism" toward the past prevailed. A "frightened self-censorship" had discouraged scholars from publishing objective studies, thus reenforcing official censorship.

The role of the Institute of CPCz History, which was established in 1950, came in for special condemnation.[57] During the cult years it had been "a guardian of dogma" and an exclusively propaganda institution. Work on the history of the party had often shown "a disrespect for facts" and in some cases had amounted to outright falsification. Documentary publications, for instance, Gottwald's *Spisy*, had been doctored by omitting significant passages to conform to contemporary political needs and to protect Gottwald's infallibility. Only in the spring of 1962 was the institute's work subjected to examination and criticism by the Secretariat, and a new director appointed to implement a fresh policy.

Among the critics of the cult, there was considerable difference of

[54] *NM*, no. 8 (1963), pp. 1043-51.
[55] *Příspěvky k dějinám KSČ* 3, no. 2 (1963), 163-176.
[56] The magazine *Dějiny a současnost* was the organ of the Socialist Academy. Apart from articles already cited, see Z. Richtová, *DAS*, no. 7 (1963); G. Bareš, *LN*, Nov. 16, 1963; M. Hájek, *PKD KSČ* 3, no. 5 (1963), 730-39.
[57] For an early criticism, see Karel Kaplan, *NM*, no. 1 (1963), pp. 62-70. See also J. Mlynárik, *ČČH* 12 (1964), 206-16; J. Měchýř and L. Niklíček, *PKD KSČ* 4, no. 1 (1964), 60-71; Jan Pachta, ibid., no. 4 (1964), pp. 563-81.

opinion, and occasionally sharp polemics, over the question of the individual historian's responsibility. Vilém Prečan, of the Historical Institute, for instance, tended to place the blame not on the "personal morality" of historians, but rather on the "social conditions" of the time. Historians had not, he said, been consciously lying or breaking the moral principle of scientific work, but had themselves been affected by the deformation of history.[58] Milan Hübl, on the other hand, insisted on the individual ethical obligations of historians, even before 1953. Responsibility for the cult lay with Stalin, Gottwald, and others, but historians as individuals (himself included), shared the blame. Especially after 1956, Hübl argued, historians, who knew the truth, for instance, about the trials in Poland and Hungary, ought to have drawn appropriate lessons concerning Czechoslovakia and had a duty, in the spirit of the 20th congress, to support progressive rather than conservative forces.[59] Yet both Prečan and Hübl shared what was becoming a generally accepted view among historians, that there must be a "turn to *facts*" and a "cult of historical truth."[60]

The swing of party policy against revisionism at the December 1963 plenum did not at first touch on historical scholarship. There were, however, serious misgivings in party circles about the tendency of historians to reevaluate important events such as the 5th Party Congress in 1929, the party's policies in the thirties, and the wartime resistance movements. Koucký, in his address to the Academy of Sciences in April 1964, gave specific examples of such dangerous trends, which were said to be grave, even if not "typical," and demanded "partisan responsibility" of historians. He denounced Hübl, a specialist on the Slovak Uprising and on Comintern history, for a brief article in *Literární noviny* in which he had condemned communists of the thirties, including the noted poet, S. K. Neumann, for their faith in Stalin and for their defense of the Moscow trials.[61] Top ideologists, such as Štoll, Koucký, and F. J. Kolár, joined in the fray against Hübl, defending Neumann and pre-war communists for their faith in Soviet policy and condemning contemporary criticisms of the Moscow trials as Trotskyist. Vilém Nový, in the same connection, censured a historical science which "distorted historical reality" and

[58] *ČČH* 12, no. 1 (1964), 44-49. This was a criticism of a review by Hübl of a book published in 1962 in which the author had been taken to task by Hübl for consciously publishing what were, it was implied, untruths.

[59] Hübl, ibid., no. 2 (1964), pp. 199-205.

[60] Křen, *KT*, May 30, 1963. Cf. J. Šedivý on the need for "objective interpretation of historical happenings" and on the "moral responsibility" of historians to "historical truth" (*LN*, Aug. 15, 1964).

[61] Koucký, *RP*, April 11, 1964. Hübl's article (*LN*, March 21, 1964) was a reply to a polemical attack by F. J. Kolár on a young poet who had severely criticized Neumann and another distinguished pre-war poet, Vítězslav Nezval, for their poems in praise of Stalin.

warned that the critics were "sowing doubts and disbelief in the party, in its past and present policies."[62]

The party was in no mood to tolerate heretical viewpoints. Although Hübl's article was the immediate pretext for his dismissal from the Higher Party School, his opposition to the plenum's ideological and cultural policy was no doubt the chief reason.[63] Novotný, in a speech at the end of May 1964, savagely attacked not only Hübl, but also Ján Mlynárik, charging him [the latter] with depicting the 5th congress as the source of the dogmatism of the fifties. Justifying Hübl's dismissal, Novotný regretted the use of administrative intervention, but called it the ultimate means for countering threats to ideological unity.[64] In the party decision on the Higher Party School, issued in early summer, the historians at the school were singled out for special criticism and several of them were transferred to other work.[65] In 1965 the entire editorial board of *Dějiny a současnost* was removed for an article of which the party disapproved.[66] In early 1965 a secretariat plan for work in the field of party history attacked the impact of the cult on history and its partial continuance after 1956, but also asserted the necessity of defending "the purity of Marxism-Leninism" in historical research. Certain questions, which had not yet been thoroughly investigated, should not, it was said, be discussed in journals with mass circulation.[67]

The party met with only partial success in its efforts to direct historical scholarship. In subsequent years, sensitive topics of modern history, including even post-war events, were treated with a new objectivity and often on the basis of access to party archives.[68] There was a frank re-

[62] *RP*, Aug. 1, 1964. See Štoll, *RP*, April 26, 1964, also in *EE* 13 (Aug. 1964), 7-9; Kolár, *RP*, April 29, Sept. 19, 1964; J. Taufer, *RP*, May 31, 1964; J. Fojtík, *RP*, June 26, 1964.

[63] See Hübl's interview, *RP*, April 17, 1968.

[64] Ibid., May 29, 1964. Mlynárik's article (n. 57 above) was a criticism of the treatment of the history of the party between the wars.

[65] *Usnesení KSČ*, 1964, pp. 282-86.

[66] Pech, "Ferment," p. 515. The article was a review (*DAS*, no. 3, 1964) criticizing a documentary collection by V. Král for omission of passages of documents. See Z. Šikl, *DAS*, no. 5 (1968), 1-3, 46-48.

[67] Text in *PKD KSČ* 5, no. 2 (1965), 199-216.

[68] Among those whose works may be mentioned are M. Reiman and Z. Sládek, on Soviet history; M. Soukup and M. Hájek, on the Comintern; Ján Mlynárik, on pre-war party history; J. Křen, on Beneš and the war; Věra Olivová, on Czechoslovak-Soviet relations; J. Opat, K. Kaplan, and J. Kladiva, on the post-1945 years; J. Šedivý and K. Kaplan, on February 1948 and post-1948. Note in particular the books by Jaroslav Opat, *O novou demokracii 1945 až 1948* (Prague, 1966) and Karel Kaplan, *Utváření generální linie výstavby socialismu v Československu* (Prague, 1966). Cf. also the proceedings of the Liblice conference on Czechoslovak history, *Československá revoluce v letech 1944-1948* (Prague, 1966). Note the controversies between the party and historians over such matters as the election of V. Král to the Academy of Sciences and the inter-

evaluation of important aspects of party history, such as the role of Šmeral, the 5th congress, and the policies of the Communist International. Certain subjects, such as the trials of the fifties, or the most recent years of Novotný's regime, were still taboo. Moreover, Masaryk, who had been the subject of ruthless denigration in the fifties, had not yet been reassessed as a major figure in Czech history, although selected aspects of his thinking and of his career were examined more objectively than in the past.[69] A similar trend toward the restoration of genuine historiography was observable among Slovak historians in their analysis of the Slovak national movement, including the Uprising, with open censure of Czech attitudes and policies. The congress of Slovak historians in June 1965 had as its theme the rise of their nation and its national consciousness.[70]

The 4th congress of historians in Brno in September 1966 was not attended by any high-ranking party leaders and represented a significant milestone in the reawakening of Czech and Slovak historians.[71] Although the main lines of the 3rd congress were endorsed and Marxism-Leninism and "partisanry" were again emphasized, a new spirit pervaded the gathering. For instance, Macek, in the principal address, also described Marxism-Leninism as the starting point and basis of history, but declared that "partisanry" involved the "maximum of objective reality and truth." Although revolution remained the central theme of the historian's work, more attention must be paid, he said, to the "continuity of the historical process"; boundaries should not be set in 1918, and still less in 1945. This point was underlined by the congress' resolution urging that on the forthcoming fiftieth anniversary of the founding of Czechoslovakia, October 28 and 30 be proclaimed as the days of the birth of the Republic.[72]

---

pretation of the 50th anniversary of the Republic in 1967 (interview with P. Oliva, *DAS*, no. 7, 1968, pp. 26-28).

[69] Lubomír Nový (see above, n. 18) paid special attention to Masaryk's philosophy of Czech history which, he said, had positive aspects and was still relevant. See also L. Nový, "T. G. Masaryk v českém myšlení," *FČ*, no. 1 (1966), pp. 22-44; Nový, *Plamen*, no. 9 (1967), pp. 76-79; K. Pichlík, *DAS*, no. 10 (1963), pp. 1-5; Pichlík, *LN*, July 25, 1964; anon., *Host do domu*, no. 12 (1967), pp. 8-23; Jan Procházka, *My 66*, no. 11 (1966).

[70] The papers were published as *Slováci a ich národný vývin* (Bratislava, 1969). See also Pech, "Ferment," pp. 518-20 and above, chap. III.

[71] For Macek's speech and the congress report and resolution, see *ČČH* 15, no. 1 (1967), 1-34, 165-70. A briefer version of Macek's address is given in *NM*, no. 20 (1966), pp. 3-8, 11. Cf. Hübl, *LN*, Oct. 8, 1966. At the Czechoslovak Historical Society, a general society of those interested in history, held in Brno at the same time, it was urged that the society become "a democratic organ of historians" and a place for "discussion in a democratic spirit." See F. Kavka, *DAS*, no. 1 (1967), pp. 1-2.

[72] October 28 had been celebrated as independence day until 1951 but thereafter merely as the anniversary of the nationalization of industry. From 1966 on, although it was not officially restored to its original purpose, October 28

LAW AND JUSTICE

The discipline of "state and law" was tardier than other branches of knowledge in recovering from its Stalinist past. Beginning in 1956, however, legal scholars began to reevaluate traditional doctrines and to criticize legal practices. This met with substantial resistance on the part of officials, judges and lawyers, and even some scholars, who could not break with old ways of thought and practice. An all-state conference of the CPCz in June 1956 proposed various reforms in criminal justice to safeguard socialist legality, especially in regard to the procedures of investigation. Many of the principles outlined were embodied in the new criminal procedure code and the amendments to the criminal code in 1956. Legal and judicial practices were again revised in 1961, with the enactment of a new criminal code and a revision of the code of criminal procedure. These changes were designed to regulate pre-trial investigation, to strengthen the right of defense, to introduce the "presumption of innocence," and to protect the independence of judges.[73] Reform-oriented jurists regarded them as serious improvements but, with increasing boldness, pointed to continuing inadequacies in judicial procedures.

In early 1962 the discipline of "state and law" was subjected to severe censure by the Politburo in a special report which criticized the influence both of dogmatist views from the Stalinist period and of bourgeois vestiges, such as "positivism" and "normativism." The field had been spared more serious revisionist tendencies, it was said, but had lagged behind in studying the problems of developing socialist democracy and legality and of protecting the fundamental rights of citizens. The report set forth measures for overcoming the failures of the discipline, including a close link with Soviet scholarship and more creative discussion.[74] Yet neither the 12th congress nor subsequent CC plena in early 1963 devoted much attention to the problem of legality other than the limited rehabilitation of the victims of the main trials.[75]

Nonetheless, these steps, and especially the Kolder report on the trials, were taken as a starting point for discussion in the law journals concern-

---

was treated in press comment as the anniversary of Czechoslovak independence (e.g. *RP*, Oct. 28, 1966, Oct. 30, 1967). October 30 was the day of the Slovak declaration of independence in 1918. See materials prepared for a conference on the 50th anniversary of the Republic by the Institute of CPCz History, *Materiály z vědecké konference věnované 50. výročí Československé Republiky* (Prague, 1968), vol. 1.

[73] See *Sbírka zákonů*, nos. 63, 64/1956; 140, 141/1961. For an excellent review of the lawyers' discussions and of legal reforms throughout the sixties, see Golan, *Czechoslovak Reform*, pp. 210-22.

[74] For the text and editorial comment, see *Právník* 101, no. 5 (1962), 344-56, 333-43, resp.

[75] For example, see Novotný's report, *XII. sjezd KSČ*, pp. 90-92, and the congress decision, ibid., p. 650.

ing the procedures of policy-making and management, and guarantees of legality and fundamental rights, and for a critical reexamination of the field of state and law.[76] In non-academic media there was a bolder treatment of the needed reform of legal practice, with emphasis on past breaches of justice and the desirability for a rule of law. Zdeněk Mlynář, a scholar at the Institute of State and Law, emerged as a vigorous but moderate protagonist of legal and political reform and the rights of the individual.[77] More orthodox statements dwelt on the necessity for "socialist legality" in a new sense, but laid great stress on what had already been accomplished since 1953.[78]

The opening shots in a campaign for reform of legal scholarship and legal procedures were fired at a special Academy of Sciences conference in February 1963.[79] Academician Viktor Knapp elaborated upon the influence of the cult period on "science" in general, which had become, he said, "mere commentary on, and justification of, decisions already prepared" and which treated an "error" as "anti-party activity." Most serious was its effect on "socialist legality," which was considered "a legality binding on citizens but not on state organs." There had been "a fetishization of the general interest" and neglect of the rights of citizens. Urging an end to dogmatism in the discipline, Knapp also underlined the importance of stability and certainty in law and the independence of the courts. Materials prepared in the Institute of State and Law and later published in *Právník* stressed the fact that in spite of improvements since 1956, only the first steps had been taken to free the discipline from copying Soviet legal thought and to move toward empirical research.[80] These articles were followed by a frank examination of the situation in criminal law which clearly revealed continued shortcomings. There were, on the other hand, repeated calls for strict measures of enforcement against "anti-socialist elements" threatening the security of citizens and the socialist order.[81]

[76] Editorial, *Právník* 102, no. 1 (1963), 1-5.

[77] E.g. Mlynář, *KT*, April 25, June 6, Aug. 15, 1963; *LN*, March 21, 1964. See also his book, *Stát a člověk* (Prague, 1964). Cf. his earlier orthodox article in *NM*, no. 9 (1962), pp. 1047-53.

[78] E.g. V. Škoda, *ŽS*, no. 15 (Aug. 1963), pp. 885-88; O. Průša, *NM*, no. 6 (1963), pp. 660-70.

[79] *Právník* 102, no. 5 (1963), 416-24. A conference on law and the guarantees of socialist legality was also held in Slovakia in November 1963. See *Právny obzor*, no. 2 (1964), for some of the papers presented.

[80] *Právník* 102, no. 8 (1968), 621-33.

[81] E.g. the editorial article in *Právník* 102, no. 7 (1963), 521-26, and the following articles in the same journal: no. 7 (1963), 583-99; J. Vieska, no. 9 (1963), 689-99; discussion, 103, no. 10 (1964), 919-37; J. Boguszak and Z. Jičínský, 104, no. 3 (1965), 197-204; J. Vieska, no. 6 (1965), 509-18. See also L. Schubert, *PO*, no. 6 (1963), pp. 321-30; S. Zdobinský, *Socialistická zákonnost* 12, no. 1 (1964), 1-3; Z. Číhal, ibid., pp. 4-7; Z. Hrazdíra, ibid., pp. 9-15; J.

The continuance of the "class approach" in the judicial sphere was criticized, and the adherence to legal concepts derived from the Soviet jurist, Andrei Vyshinsky, was condemned.[82] Too much emphasis was placed on the repressive side of law, it was charged, in particular on law as an instrument for the solution of social conflicts and for the implementation of policy through coercion. The rights of citizens continued to be disregarded and individual interests arbitrarily subordinated to the social interest. There were still breaches of legality in practice, even though the formal procedures provided by statute were satisfactory. Investigators were charged with using improper methods and ignoring the rights of the accused. The right of the defense was not respected in the pre-trial investigation or in the judicial proceedings. The idea of investigatory judges, first advanced in 1956, was again raised. The supervision of investigation by the procurators was said to be often inadequate and control by the courts was suggested. In court proceedings the principle of "presumption of innocence" was frequently ignored, and the independence of judges was often infringed by outside intervention. Apart from certain procedural exceptions specified in law, wrote Juraj Vieska, "no one else may influence the decision in a concrete case, neither the organ which elected the court, nor any state or party organs."[83] As for legal scholarship, there were frequent references to continuing dogmatism and appeals for more controversial theoretical argumentation and for the use of modern methods of research, including cybernetics.[84]

It is difficult to assess the impact of these theoretical discussions on the procedures actually employed in the judicial system. The party's Central Committee established in March 1964 a Legal Commission, headed by Koucký, to provide the central party and state organs with expert advice and to promote the observance of legality.[85] In mid-June 1965, a number of statutes were adopted, designed to enlarge the rights of defense coun-

---

Štěpán, ibid., no. 5 (1964), pp. 29-39. For an informed analysis of the discussion, see Otto Ulc, "Czechoslovakia's Restive Jurists," *EE* 14 (Dec. 1965), 18-25.

[82] The harmful effects of past Soviet influence, especially the cult of Stalin, Vyshinsky's doctrines, and Beria's practice were indicted by the editor of *Právník*, Ivan Bystřina, who proposed, however, closer cooperation with Soviet legal scholars on the basis of a free exchange of opinions. See *Právník* 102, no. 10 (1963), 757-61.

[83] Vieska, *Právník* 102, no. 9 (1963), 697.

[84] See, for instance, Knapp, *Právník* 102, no. 1 (1963), 5-23; Mlynář, 103, no. 3 (1964), 230-44, 280-84.

[85] Editorial, Mlynář, *Právník* 103, no. 5 (1964), 438-40. According to a later comment by its secretary, Mlynář, the work of this commission was ineffective, limited as it was to the making of "comments" on proposals prepared "behind closed doors," and excluding initiative by legal scholars and open discussion of conflicting views (editorial, Mlynář, ibid. 108, no. 5, 1968, 377-79).

sels and to define the role of investigators and of the procuracy, and to supervise the administration of detention and imprisonment.[86] The goal of these measures was to protect the rights of the accused during investigations, in particular to provide for the presence of his defense lawyer during this stage; to define more clearly the right of the procuracy to watch for violation of rights; to assure the presumption of innocence and the rights of prisoners through supervision by courts and procurators.

On the other hand, there was a general effort to strengthen the law in dealing with criminality, particularly by stiffer penalties against repeated violators of public order and "parasites."[87] Official statements during the 13th Party Congress also accented the need to enforce the duties and responsibilities of citizens and to protect the social order against anti-socialist activity, especially by foreign intelligence agencies.[88]

Discussions in legal circles suggested that, although substantial progress had been made, not all reforms advocated in theory, or the corrections embodied in the law, were being implemented in actual practice.[89] Experts continued to state that guaranteeing the independence of the courts and limiting the power of security organs were crucial elements in a system of genuine justice. Great attention was also given to the protection of the basic civil rights of citizens, including those of association and assembly. Although the need to limit these freedoms was admitted, commentators were severely critical of existing constitutional and legal provisions and urged that any limitations should be explicitly defined in law.[90] Concern was also expressed over the safeguarding of the individual against illegal actions by state organs and the improvement in appeal procedures, including recourse to the courts. In mid-1967 a law on ad-

[86] Sb. z. (1965), no. 56 (criminal law); no. 57 (criminal law procedure); no. 59 (deprivation of liberty); no. 60 (procuracy).

[87] Sb. z., 58/1965.

[88] XIII. sjezd Komunistické strany Československa (1966), pp. 88, 406. See also editorial, Právník 105, no. 4 (1966), 301-9. Cf. the series, "Legality, Citizens' Rights and Party Policy," RP, Aug. 11, 13, 18, 1965.

[89] E.g. M. Lakatoš, Občan, právo a demokracie (Prague, 1966), pp. 149-59. Cf. his later book, Úvahy o hodnotách demokracie (Prague, 1968), pp. 146 ff. This work, completed in 1967, laid great emphasis on judicial independence as the main guarantee for a restoration of respect for law (esp. pp. 149, 157, 178-84). Lakatoš had also stressed the independence of the courts in his earlier work. See citations below, chap. XIII, p. 410. Although Právník, under the editorship of Ivan Bystřina, had great difficulties with censorship with almost every issue, and many articles could not be published, the journal devoted much attention to problems of legal reform. See also B. Slezák and J. Štěpán, SZ 15, no. 6 (1967), 363-71 for statistics on the degree to which defense lawyers participated in preliminary investigations, revealing great variations between districts and cases.

[90] E.g. in Právník, vol. 106 for 1967: E. Kučera, no. 2, pp. 105-17; Z. Jičínský, no. 4, pp. 313-22; discussion, no. 7, pp. 674-77; P. Peška, no. 7, pp. 585-91; V. Pavlíček, no. 7, pp. 592-607.

ministrative procedures provided for increased protection against administrative illegalities, but did not incorporate the idea of judicial supervision of state organs.[91]

The continuance of the political system, largely unchanged, and the hard-line policy pursued by Novotný in the political sphere set strict limits to the implementation of these progressive ideas in judicial practice. Legal experts were gradually coming to realize, as a prominent jurist, Zdeněk Jičínský, expressed it, that political reforms, and in particular the development of "democratic forms and methods," were a necessary condition of a genuine system of justice. In a major article in *Právník*, Jičínský delivered a scathing critique of the political system as it had developed during the cult of personality, including the underestimation of democratic forms and methods, the overemphasis on organizational forms, "decree-mania," and the decline in respect for the rights and freedom of citizens, and clearly indicated his belief that the reforms after 1956 had been inadequate.[92] Other legal specialists, notably Mlynář and Lakatoš, as will be seen in the next chapter, were also active in the discussion and advocacy of political reform.

A SCIENCE OF POLITICS

The notion of reviving "political science," which had been taboo during the fifties, was discussed by a number of scholars in party organs. It was argued that, under the guidance of the party, the discipline would be a valuable "auxiliary" in solving political problems.[93] In collaboration with other disciplines, political science would deal concretely with such matters as expanding democracy in existing institutions and would make proposals for improvements in the political model. Some scholars strongly urged the recognition of a separate "political science," which would include the study of interest groups, mass associations, and public opinion, as well as political institutions. The usefulness of a critical study of

[91] *SB. z.*, 71/1967. Cf. discussion, *Právník* 105, no. 6 (1966), 387-90; 106, no. 7 (1967), 632-51. Boguszak and Jičínský argued for a constitutional court, on the model of Yugoslavia, to check on the constitutionality of laws passed by the legislature (105, no. 5, 1966, pp. 403-4).

[92] *Právník* 102, no. 5 (1963), 337-52.

[93] A. Ort, M. Had, and K. Krátký, *NM*, no. 5 (1965), pp. 684-93. This article cited the Soviet scholar, F. Burlatskii (*Pravda* [Moscow], Jan. 10, 1965) on the desirability of developing political science and referred to Czechoslovak participation in the congresses of the International Political Science Association in 1961 and 1964 as a positive factor. For the following, see also Kusin, *Intellectual Origins*, pp. 103-5; F. Kratochvíl, *NM*, no. 8, April 19, 1966, pp. 12-14; M. Formánek, ibid., no. 15, July 26, 1966, pp. 13-16; M. Soukup, ibid., no. 18, Sept. 6, 1966, pp. 13-15; a symposium, ibid., no. 26, Dec. 28, 1966, pp. 11-14; J. Fibich and T. Syllaba, *FČ* 15, no. 4 (1967), 513-30. Note the well-informed description of political science in the USA by V. Soják, *NM*, no. 24, Nov. 29, 1966, pp. 28-30.

non-socialist political systems and of bourgeois political science was recognized. Other scholars were more reserved in their acceptance of political science as a distinct branch of study and warned of the danger of neglecting Marxism as the general basis of research and of weakening the ideological character of the social sciences by the proliferation of separate disciplines.[94] But, as the editors of *Nová mysl* summed up the discussion, there was a general recognition of the value of a systematic study of politics, including the role of the party, through a special discipline, which would carry out studies for improving political forms and methods and for elaborating long-range political development.[95]

Yet there was no consensus on the exact content of the subject or the means of its institutionalization. A Czechoslovak Political Science Association had been formed, having as members scholars from many fields, and was affiliated with the International Political Science Association, but was not an influential force. The persistent suspicion of political science as an independent discipline blocked full support by the party for its development on the lines of sociology. A proposal to set up an institute of political science within the Academy of Sciences led to the party's decision to create one within its own framework. The Institute of Political Science, within the Central Committee, and headed by Václav Slavík, a CC member, was to conduct research in conjunction with the party's activities and to prepare concrete proposals for party decisions. Its work, as officially described, would concentrate on such topics as the leading role of the party, problems of socialist democracy and political structure, material and moral work incentives, classes and social groups, and nationality relations. One of its most urgent tasks was to study the problem of electoral reform. It was also to work closely with the regional and district committees, the Slovak organs, other departments of the CC *aparát* and individual CC members and to participate in the long-term preparation of a special CC plenum to be devoted to the party's work.[96]

In the autumn of 1966 an interdisciplinary team was formed within the Institute of State and Law to do research on the development of the

[94] E.g. K. Ondris, *NM*, no. 20, Oct. 4, 1966, pp. 16-18; J. Loutka and S. Kučera, ibid., no. 25, Dec. 13, 1966, pp. 24-27, 27-28, resp.; and the symposium, ibid., no. 26, Dec. 28, 1966. See also L. Révész, "Political Science in Eastern Europe," *Studies in Soviet Thought* 7 (Sept. 1967), 199-201.

[95] *NM*, no. 26, Dec. 28, 1966, pp. 14-15. For a discussion of politics as "the dialectics of group interest" and of political science and sociology as disciplines for the analysis of the interest structure of society, see M. Kaláb, *NM*, no. 9, May 3, 1966, pp. 6-8.

[96] The original decision was taken at the CC plenum in December 1966 and by the Presidium in early 1967. See the brief announcements in *ŽS*, no. 7 (March 1967), p. 61 and *RP*, June 6, 1967; and an interview with Slavík, *KT*, May 4, 1967. See also J. Hendrych, CC speech, *RP*, Feb. 10, 1967. Some information was also derived from a personal interview with Slavík in May 1968.

political system and on democracy in a socialist society. It was headed by Zdeněk Mlynář, who had taken the original initiative and secured the approval of the Academy, and of Hendrych, chief of the Ideological Commission. In view of Mlynář's membership in the party's Legal Commission, this team had an official cast but it included persons of diverse outlook, drawn from many fields—state and law, sociology, economics, history, and philosophy, as well as cybernetics and organizational theory.[97] The team's plan of work envisaged some twenty-five theoretical studies, to be prepared over a period of five to seven years, and also the preparation of a short-term report, by the end of 1968, on "the most suitable conceptual model for the development of the political system." The planned research embraced such topics as elites, industrial democracy, national committees, the role of law, and as a fundamental question, according to Mlynář, the position of the party. Inner party questions were, however, to be studied by special party institutions. Western models were to be examined as well. The entire study was closely related to the introduction of the new economic system, the success of which was thought by some to depend on political reform.

Although there were some scholars who advocated a completely new system, Mlynář, at least in public, spoke rather of "a gradual reform of the deformed system, essentially from above." The purpose, he stated, was not to devise an ideal abstract model, but rather, beginning with the existing system, to examine various alternatives for developing it. The starting point would be a study of social and interest groups and societal organizations. Although the electoral system was not satisfactory, it was not their task to submit concrete changes. Whether the party and state organs, to whom their proposals would be submitted, would act favorably on them was, of course, impossible to predict, but the long-term studies were expected at least to exert an impact on public thinking.[98] In turn, the studies were bound to be influenced by the wide-ranging discussion of the political system (to be discussed more fully in the following chapter) in which Mlynář and other team members took an active part.[99]

[97] Lakatoš, an active advocate of reform, was not a member of the Mlynář team, probably due to long-standing personal differences between the two colleagues. For the team's plans, see an interview with Mlynář and other members of the team, RP, July 6, 1967. See also the memorandum prepared by Mlynář in 1975 (Appendix E).

[98] Personal interview with Mlynář, June 17, 1967. See a discussion in which Mlynář took part, Pravda, Oct. 25, 1967, and an interview with Mlynář, Student, Sept. 27, 1967.

[99] Two chapters of the Machonin project's initial theoretical symposium (Sociální struktura) were devoted to political questions. One, by Z. Mlynář and V. Pavlíček, dealt in familiar terms with politics as a process of resolving conflicting interests and with the importance of the representative organs and the mass associations. The other, by René Rohan, discussed the party in an orthodox

Even the exposition of the ideology of the political system by party theoreticians could not escape the impact of new ideas. Their analysis displayed a curious blend of progressive ideas, paralleling the more daring thoughts of the scholars and writers, and of traditional conceptions of politics, as expounded by the party leaders. In some respects their formulations pointed to a more democratic ordering of the political system; in other respects, they seemed designed to justify the continuance of party dominance and to exclude genuine democratization of public life. The discussion was highly abstract, often obscure in meaning, and seemed to have little contact with concrete reality.[100]

This scientific study of the party was sometimes described as an independent discipline on "party doctrine (*učení o straně*)."[101] It was to be closely linked with political science,[102] but would also employ the findings of fields such as sociology, psychology, systems analysis, games theory, information theory, management theory, cybernetics, numbers theory, etc., and thus enrich Marxism with fresh content and knowledge.[103] This study was designed to develop and present a new "model"

---

manner. In the ensuing research there was to be a study by Lubomír Brokl on "Power and Social Stratification." This was described by Brokl (*SČ* 3, no. 6, 1967, pp. 708-14) as an attempt empirically to determine the share in power of individuals by examining their employment in certain institutions (party, state, economic management, etc.) and their membership in the party or in elected organs, and correlating the extent of their power with other characteristics such as income, education, generation, etc. The results, as published later (Machonin, ed., *Československá společnost*, chap. 7; English summary, pp. 593, 599, 606-8), identified a certain political elite which possessed substantial political power; the mass of the population whose power was limited; and certain "graduated sub-elites" (p. 238). The holding of power was correlated with party membership, although this was not necessarily the causal determinant. Party members constituted the "cadre elite" from whom were recruited the "core elite" (pp. 253, 257-59). For the Richta team's studies on political questions, see below, this chapter.

[100] See the following books: by René Rohan, written in 1966, *Politické strany* (Prague, 1968), esp. pp. 254-86; by Ladislav Tomášek, written in 1967, *Vedúca úloha strany a politický systém* (Bratislava, 1968); by M. Havlíček, *Dialektika vnitrostranických vztahů* (Prague, 1968); and a collection of articles from 1965 to 1967, *Strana a společnost* (Prague, 1968). An earlier study, completed in December 1965, was similar in tone—L. Tomášek, J. Litera, and J. Večeřa, *Strana a dnešek* (Prague, 1967). See also Tomášek's contribution to *Vedeckotechnická revolúcia a socializmus* (Bratislava, 1967), pp. 261-96. Cf. articles in *NM*, by J. Kučera, no. 26, Dec. 28, 1966, pp. 7-10; no. 11, May 30, 1967, pp. 30-32; no. 18, Sept. 5, 1967, pp. 7-10; F. Havlíček, no. 20, Oct. 3, 1967, pp. 3-7; Ján Paško, no. 25, Dec. 12, 1967, pp. 3-8; Jan Kolář, no. 1 (Jan. 1968) pp. 17-25. Cf. a panel discussion with Kolář, F. J. Kolár, and others, *KT*, Nov. 16, 1968.

[101] Tomášek et al., *Strana*, pp. 26-27. Cf. Rohan, *Pol. strany*, pp. 273-74.

[102] Tomášek, *Vedúca úloha*, pp. 9-19, 38. Cf. Rohan, *Pol. strany*, p. 277.

[103] Tomášek et al., *Strana*, pp. 16-17, 29-30, 132. "Social cybernetics can become a truly outstanding instrument in the hands of party management. . . . The party directs and organizes, comes to know, and programs, social reality; a series

of the party and its role of leadership, replacing the traditional "directive" and "administrative" method of party control by a new and democratic relationship between the party and the masses, and the party and other organizations. In the economy, in harmony with the spirit of the new economic mechanism, the party's task would be sharply distinguished from direct management, a function reserved for the factory directors.[104] In society as a whole, there would be recognition of the differentiation of interests, with the party elaborating and articulating the all-society interest.[105] The theoreticians also accented the need to introduce scientific methods into the political system, including the party, which in turn would require greater respect for the intelligentsia and an improvement in the educational level and technical competence of party functionaries.

All of these doctrines implied a far-reaching democratization of politics and party work and made imperative "a basic change" in the political system, not just "an evolutionary improvement," in Tomášek's words.[106] Yet none of the ideologists proposed any concrete program for such reform. There was much talk of the necessity of a "dialogue" and "an exchange of views" but this was counterbalanced by emphatic assertions of the need for unity and by references to Marxism-Leninism as the binding theoretical framework.[107] There was stress on pluralism, but this was to be "pluralism of a socialist type, based on the dialectical unity of differentiating and integrating processes," and not "a pluralism of political parties." This would involve "a constructive *oponentura* . . . which would assure not only the appropriate direct or indirect self-realization of group political interests but also socialist effectiveness, without which it is never possible to speak of dynamic and democratic socialism."[108]

Above all, the ideologues were eloquent in restating the necessity to retain the vanguard role of the party. "The question is not whether or not

---

of acts in this sphere can be accomplished with the aid of machines; cybernetics can make its contribution to the organization of party work" (pp. 225-26).

[104] V. Pešička, *Stranické organizace v oblasti výroby a ekonomiky* (Prague, 1967).

[105] Tomášek, *Vedúca úloha*, pp. 173-214. Ota Šik was credited with having theoretically rehabilitated the category of interests under socialism, thus making a great contribution to sociology and politology as well as economics (ibid., p. 176). Cf. Tomášek et al., *Strana*, pp. 74-75, 130.

[106] Tomášek, *Vedúca úloha*, p. 250.

[107] *Strana a společnost*, pp. 123 ff., 135.

[108] Tomášek, *Vedúca úloha*, pp. 28-32, 227, 252-53. The term *oponentura* was taken from academic or professional life, where it was used to refer to a system of required criticism by "opponents" of a research thesis or a new project. It was in some ways similar to the idea of a "devil's advocate" as the opponent did not normally reject nor condemn the candidate or the proposal. Cf. explanation in *ŽS*, no. 10 (May 1968), p. 4.

to direct all spheres of our life, but rather how to guide it well, rationally and effectively, and how, in an optimal fashion, to bring both expertness and politicalness into harmony." The party is "the coordinating and integrating factor of social movement."[109] "The party will be the basic integrating cement and leading force of socialist society." ". . . the party organization will be first and foremost the teacher, leader, propagator, and agitator in the ranks of the workers and peasants for the line of our party, sometimes even against the interests of the more backward part of the working class."[110] This was not in any way in contradiction to the development of socialist democracy. The party was, however, not to become a mere "discussion club" or "association concerned only with theoretical-educational matters." Although debates and exchanges of views were necessary, this did not obviate the need for discipline and for democratic centralism.[111]

FOREIGN POLICY AND INTERNATIONAL RELATIONS

The intellectual ebullition in the social sciences affected the study of foreign policy and international relations, but had little impact on the actual conduct of foreign affairs. Historical studies of Czechoslovak diplomacy under the First Republic and after 1945, and of the Communist International and the Cominform, were characterized by a more objective and less doctrinaire approach than in the past.[112] International relations as a field of research began to be developed, especially with the establishment of the Institute of International Politics and Economics (ÚMPE) in 1957, and the publication of its journal, Mezinárodní vztahy, from 1966 on. This, however, was a semi-official institution, financed by the Ministry of Foreign Affairs, and thus labored under various handicaps, such as restricted freedom of research and the lack of respect for scholarship in official circles. Nevertheless, scholars, in spite of censorship, were able with circumspection to press for a more active and independent course in foreign policy and bloc relations.[113]

---

[109] Tomášek et al., Strana, p. 337; Rohan, Pol. strany, p. 270, resp.

[110] See Vedeckotechnická revolúcia, pp. 261-96, esp. pp. 289, 296.

[111] Strana a společnost, pp. 81-82, 125. Cf. Tomášek et al., Strana, pp. 351-52.

[112] E.g. Jaroslav Šedivý, on Czechoslovak foreign policy from 1945 to 1948, Věda a život, no. 6 (1965), pp. 321-27; M. Soukup, on the Comintern and Cominform, PKD KSČ 4 (Feb. and May 1964), 3-25, 171-98, resp.

[113] Most issues of the Institute's journal, the chief editor of which was the young diplomatic historian, Jaroslav Šedivý, appeared late as a result of censorship. Selected articles were published in an English language journal, International Relations, which was issued annually in 1967 and 1968. For a review of the first decade of the Institute, see A. Ort, MV, no. 2 (1967), pp. 54-59; for an analysis of research in international relations, A. Šnejdárek, MV, no. 1 (1966), pp. 4 ff. (also IR, 1967, pp. 5-18); for an essay on the study of Czechoslovak

Šedivý, for example, in *Věda a život*, a journal published in the more liberal atmosphere of Brno, took up the theme of the 1956 CC plenum and affirmed that the first principle of Czechoslovak foreign policy should be "to develop to a maximum degree its own foreign policy initiative within the framework of the global tasks of the socialist camp." During a period of peaceful coexistence, he said, diplomacy ceased to be "a mere calculation of economic or military strength" and more and more resembled "diplomacy in the classic sense of the word, giving increasing prominence to the subjective elements—the degree of experience and skill of those forming and implementing it." "Foreign policy, relying as it must on economics, law, philosophy, history, and sociology, was becoming a science," he stated.[114] A year later, in the party's theoretical journal, Šedivý gave a more restrained exposition. While advocating "absolute unity" in basic questions and noting the limitations on peaceful coexistence, he described equality, non-interference, and sovereignty as the principles underlying coexistence, as well as within the socialist camp, and stressed the need for the recognition of specific interests and the possibility of individual initiative.[115]

Václav Kotyk, head of ÚMPE's department on the relations of the socialist countries, wrote extensively on the changing theory and practice of bloc relations after 1956, and warmly supported the principles of equality and non-interference, as proclaimed, for instance, in the Soviet declaration of October 1956 and in declarations of the 1957 and 1960 world communist conferences. He repeatedly emphasized that the differences of standpoint among socialist countries were based on objective

---

foreign policy, Šedivý, *MV*, no. 4 (1967), pp. 54-58. For a discussion of the content of the "multidiscipline" of international relations, see articles by Ort and by V. Soják, both published in *Czechoslovak Political Science On I.P.S.A. Congress in Brussels* (Prague, 1968), pp. 277-89, 291-314. See also Ort, "Are International Relations a Science?" *MV*, no. 1 (1968), pp. 62-68. Other articles on this theme, originally published in *Mezinárodní vztahy* in 1966 and 1967, included two by Ort and Š. Plaček on the relations of political science and international relations; one by V. Kotyk, on the role of history in international relations; and a round-table conference on the sociology of international relations. Note the post-occupation criticism of ÚMPE's work, charging it with exaggerating peaceful coexistence, neglecting the class approach, and underestimating peaceful forms of counterrevolution (J. Sedlák, *NM*, no. 4, 1971, pp. 629-36). On problems of research, see Šnejdárek's lecture, April 29, 1968, in Šnejdárek, *Výbor z přednášek a statí, 1968* (Prague, 1968), pp. 64-66; Kotyk, *ČČH* 13 (1965), 376-85; see also Kotyk's book, cited below, n. 117.

[114] "How to Make Foreign Policy," *Věda a život*, no. 9 (1965), pp. 513-19. He expressed a similar viewpoint in a detailed historical review of Czechoslovak foreign policy published in the symposium, *Otázky mezinárodní politiky* (Prague, 1967), pp. 297-342, and in his essay on the study of Czechoslovak foreign policy (*MV*, no. 4, 1967, p. 57).

[115] *NM*, no. 16, Aug. 9, 1966, pp. 3-5.

117

differences of conditions, and that these could best be resolved by discussion and debate and by the recognition of equality and non-interference. In *Slovanský přehled*, in 1965, he ruled out any form of pressure, such as the exclusion of a party or country from the socialist camp, its condemnation as non-socialist, or the interruption of state relations because of inter-party conflict. Unity of the socialist camp was the goal, he proclaimed, but this could be achieved only by the difficult process of harmonizing the national interests of the individual countries with the international interest of the bloc as a whole.[116]

In a later book completed in mid-1966, and "published," but not distributed, in 1967, Kotyk buttressed his thesis with a detailed historical review of bloc relations from 1945, noting the enunciation of a new relationship of socialist countries based on equality and non-interference after 1956 but regretting the failure fully to implement these principles thereafter. The book was noteworthy for its sharp criticism of Soviet policy toward the bloc under Stalin and even later (pp. 64, 96); its favorable treatment of Yugoslav views in 1948 and afterwards (pp. 65-83); its positive treatment of Khrushchev; a balanced analysis of Hungarian events in 1956 (pp. 183-88); praise of the Chinese role in 1956 (pp. 201-5); and criticism of certain features of the Moscow declaration of 1960 (pp. 273-75).[117]

The idea of "neutrality" was ruled out by Kotyk's colleague, Alexander Ort, who held that the Warsaw pact was a reliable guarantee of security and independence for the socialist states, just as NATO was for the West European. The time was not ripe to replace the pacts with a

[116] *Slovanský přehled*, no. 5 (1965), pp. 257-64. See a more restrained version of this article (*NM*, no. 15, July 26, 1966, pp. 3-7) in which he laid stress on the need for absolute unity and did not include the list of "don'ts" cited above. He emphasized, however, the desirability of "the creative contribution" and "initiative" of each state and attention to "specific" and "national" interests, and even asserted the need to recognize "the absolute independence of the communist and workers' parties, not only in the organizational sense of the word, but also in the formulation of their domestic and foreign policy." This argument was similar to that of his earlier book, *O zahraniční politice socialistických států* (Prague, 1964), chaps. 3, 7. Cf. his more orthodox exposition in *NM*, no. 2 (1963), pp. 140-49, in which he argued strongly for economic integration through Comecon.

[117] This book, *Světová socialistická soustava* (Prague, 1967) appeared in the bookstores only in early 1968. The essence of his analysis, however, was published in 1967 in the scholarly journal *ČČH* 15 (1967), pp. 576-91, and in *Slovanský přehled*, no. 5 (1967), 292-97. Kotyk's work was remarkable for its use of dissident communist statements, such as the Italian, Yugoslav, and Rumanian, and of Western non-communist sources, including, for instance, the work of Donald Zagoria, who was praised for his methodology in analyzing the Sino-Soviet conflict. In the *Slovanský přehled* article, Kotyk noted that "the creation of relations of a new type" was only "a perspective *possibility*, not an existing situation."

new form of European security. A first step in such a direction would be the development of broad cooperation among all European states, especially in the economic and cultural spheres.[118]

REFORM IN ECONOMICS

The seeds of "revolution" in the thinking of economists were sown as early as 1956 and had been fertilized by the failure of the modest reforms of 1958, but were brought to full fruition by the gravity of the economic situation after 1961. The awakening of economic science was not easy owing to the liquidation of prominent economists in the fifties, the prolonged aping of Soviet doctrines, the long isolation from Western economics, and the resulting low level of economic theory.[119] Nonetheless, economists began, during 1962 and 1963, to reassess and challenge accepted dogmas and to criticize the centralized planning system. Influential in this shift in economic thinking was the impact of Polish writings, in particular the work of W. Brus, of Yugoslav experimentation, and of reform discussions in the Soviet Union, as well as greater knowledge and more objective treatment of capitalism and Western economics.[120]

The center of reappraisal was the Institute of Economics, headed from 1962 by Dr. Ota Šik and including in its ranks a number of protagonists of reform such as K. Kouba, B. Komenda, Č. Kožušník, and O. Turek. Economists elsewhere—at the universities, including the higher party schools; at other institutes; and even within the party apparatus—took part in a broadening discussion of the failings of the old "directive" economy and of proposals for economic reform. Their views were published in scholarly journals, such as *Politická ekonomie*, but were expressed in even more uninhibited form, because uncensored, in many economic symposia and in papers and draft articles circulated among economists.[121] The journal of the Socialist Academy, *Ekonomická revue*, and

[118] See Ort's objective review of the discussion of neutralism, neutrality, and non-engagement at the IPSA conference in Brussels, in September 1967 (*MV*, no. 4, 1967, pp. 59-64). See his paper on this subject, *Czechoslovak Political Science*, pp. 213-37.

[119] B. Korda and I. Moravcik, "Reflections on the 1965-1968 Czechoslovak Economic Reform," *CSP* 13 (Spring 1971), 53-57. See also J. Sláma, *Reportér*, April 3-10, 1968, pp. I-II.

[120] Brus' book was translated into Czech—*Modely socialistického hospodářství* (Prague, 1964). For a reevaluation of capitalism, see D. Fišer, *Plánování ve vyspělých kapitalistických zemích* (Prague, 1968), and L. Smetana et al., *Kapitalismus našeho věku* (Prague, 1966).

[121] Cf. the round-table discussions published in *Hospodářské noviny*, nos. 8 and 15, 1963. See other symposia, translated into English, in special issues of *Eastern European Economics* 3 (Summer 1965), and 4 (Fall 1965); J. Kosta, *Czechoslovak Economic Papers*, no. 4 (1964), pp. 139-48; ibid., no. 10 (1968), pp. 125-37, 139-43.

the party's weekly, *Hospodářské noviny*, helped to create an atmosphere favorable to economic reform. Textbooks in political economy also played an important role in promoting the new ideas.[122] Needless to say, there were great differences of opinion, even among the reform-minded, and strong resistance by those who could not free themselves from traditional ways of thought. These views were seldom expressed in published form, unless in veiled fashion, and usually with disclaimers that the spokesmen were not opposed to reform as such.[123] Gradually a consensus emerged among most economists, Slovak as well as Czech, in favor of a revision of the planning and management system that would eliminate its centralized and administrative character and make greater use of market forces such as prices and wages.

Ota Šik has usually been identified abroad as the chief architect of economic reform. Formerly an orthodox economist, heading the economics department at the Higher Party School, and a member of the Central Committee from 1962 (a candidate from 1958), Šik eventually became a vigorous advocate of the reform ideas which had emerged among his fellow economists.[124] An earlier work, on economics, interests, and politics, which was translated into Russian, was one of the first explicit statements of the existence of conflicting interests under socialism and hence struck, as he later put it, at "certain basic Stalinist theoretical postulates" concerning the alleged unity of interests in a system based on socialist ownership.[125] In another earlier work on the problem of "socialist commodity relations," which was eventually revised as *Plan and Market Under Socialism,* Šik presented, and hence legitimized, views already developing among economists as to the need for change in the system of management. As he later observed, although the idea of "socialist market relations" originated in 1957-1958, the terms "market" and "competi-

[122] E.g. B. Urban, ed., *Politická ekonomie socialismu* (Prague, 1966), esp. the chapters by Oldřich Kýn.

[123] E.g. J. Vejvoda, *NM*, no. 2, Jan. 24, 1967, pp. 24-28. See also the polemic between Šik, Felix Oliva, and J. Vejvoda, in the Slovak journal *Ekonomický časopis* 14, no. 10 (1966), 904-18, 919-30; 15, no. 5 (1967), 434-48; no. 10 (1967), 916-27. Both Oliva and Vejvoda denied that they were opposed to the new economic system. Šik, however, argued that their abstract approach reflected obsolete ways of economic thinking and that their views were welcomed by conservative or wavering political forces. See also criticism of Oliva and Vejvoda by J. Cibulka, *EČ* 15, no. 7 (1967), 639-45.

[124] Šik, *NM*, no. 9 (1963), pp. 1025-42.

[125] O. Šik, *Ekonomika, zájmy, politika* (Prague, 1962), in Czech, translated into Russian as *Ekonomika, interesy, politika* (Moscow, 1964); later Czech edition, *Ekonomika a zájmy* (Prague, 1968). As Šik wrote in the preface to the second edition, this was a theoretical analysis of "economic interests of social strata, smaller social groups, organs of power and institutions," and helped to explain "the necessity and specifics of market relations as the form of solution of the . . . economic conflicts of socialism."

tion" could not be used, and the vaguer concept of "commodity relations" had to be substituted.[126]

When *Plan and Market Under Socialism* was eventually published, it represented a substantial revision of the earlier editions and reflected, in his words, his experience in elaborating designs for economic reform.[127] The volume, which drew heavily on the works of the Polish economists, Oskar Lange and Włodzimierz Brus, was abstract and theoretical, utilizing Marxist and technical economic concepts, and highly polemical in tone, attacking Stalin's dogma of the incompatibility of "commodity relations" with socialism and the system of "directive" planning based on that conception. The polemic extended to contemporary exponents of these entrenched theories and practices, with occasional specific references to the "incorrect" views of certain Soviet scholars and sharp criticism of unnamed Czechoslovak opponents of reform.

In a section devoted to Czechoslovakia's economic development, Šik contended that the administrative system had given rise to a pattern of "extensive growth" (i.e. growth based on increased use of the factors of production) and had prevented the necessary changeover to an intensive pattern (growth based on increased factor productivity), and had thus contributed to the cessation of growth entirely in 1962-1963 (pp. 71 ff., 96-98). Centralization had other negative results—instability in long-range plans; one-sided quantitative and uneconomic orientation of production; unnecessary investments and expensive production; wasteful consumption of material; avoidance of technical and qualitative development; growing "disproportions" or a continual state of emergency and shortages; a lag in services, science, research, and education; a retarded increase in consumption and a leveling of wage and salary scales (pp. 98, 337-38).

The bulk of the book was devoted to an exposition of the changes necessary in the planning system and of the role of market relations if growth were to be resumed (pp. 45-46). Defining socialist planning as "a unified, social, purposeful determination of the development of eco-

[126] The work appeared in two earlier editions, under the title *K problematice socialistických zbožních vztahů* (Prague, 1964, 1965), also available in German translation. For Šik's comments, see esp. the preface to the Czech edition of *Plan and Market Under Socialism* (see below), p. 6. Elsewhere Šik mentioned a study prepared in 1958, which advocated the greater use of commodity relations but which was not acted upon by the party leadership (O. Šik, *Czechoslovakia: The Bureaucratic Economy*, White Plains, N.Y., 1972, p. 45).

[127] The Czech edition, *Plán a trh za socialismu* (Prague, 1968) appeared later than the English translation, *Plan and Market Under Socialism* (White Plains, N.Y. and Prague, 1967), also available in German, *Plan und Markt im Socialismus* (Vienna, 1967). References, unless otherwise noted, are to the English edition. For a summary and analysis of the book, see Harry G. Shaffer, "An Economic Model in Eclipse," *PC* 17 (Nov.-Dec. 1968), 50-56.

nomic activity," Šik left no doubt of his belief in the absolute requirement of "a central governing body coordinating its conscious directive activity with the basic interests of all workers and assuring a uniform fundamental management of all subordinate bodies, and finally, of all economic activity" (pp. 109, 118). No one central body, however, could decide on all the details of the economy and respect the varied economic interests at work. Only through a market mechanism could individuals, groups, and enterprises be guided by their own genuine interests and these in turn be reconciled and harmonized with the general social interest (pp. 123-26, 158-59, 170-71). This would constitute "a planned regulated market" (Czech ed., p. 217) which would be subject to the guidance and direction of central organs, not only through the long-term plans but through monetary and fiscal controls.

Other major works, like that of Šik's, were published only after much delay and hence reflected an earlier stage of thinking. Only a few of the most notable books can be mentioned.[128] Otakar Turek, an active participant in economic discussions and official planning, embodied ideas that had matured from 1963 to 1967 in his book on Plan, Market, and Economic Policy.[129] The major part of this work was devoted to a detailed comparative analysis of the two main models of socialist economics, and a third which he termed "transitory." The first was the directive or administrative model, one which had actually existed in the Soviet Union, and in Czechoslovakia up to 1967, and which concentrated economic decisions at the center and used the "command" as the basic form of transmitting decisions below. The other was the "economic model of management," which did not exist in fact but was a conception of a more effective system of management toward which Czechoslovakia had taken a decisive step by 1967. In this model the center would make decisions only in fundamental questions, leaving a wide sector of free decision-making to the enterprises, and the market mechanism would play a significant role. The center would establish the general principles for the functioning of the model and influence the enterprises by the selective use of "economic instruments." The third "transitory" model, in Turek's view, varied little from the directive model and owing to its compromise character and its toleration of old methods, had a tendency to degenerate into the directive system. It was not therefore a real and stable alternative (pp. 20-22, 178-81).

[128] An outstanding Slovak work was by Ignác Rendek, *Optimálny plán* (Bratislava, 1967). See also E. Löbl, *Úvahy o duševnej práci a bohatstve národa* (Bratislava, 1967), in German, *Geistige Arbeit: Die Wahre Quelle des Reichtums* (Vienna, 1967), and V. Pavlenda, *Ekonomické základy socialistického riešenia národnostnej otázky v Československu* (Bratislava, 1968).

[129] In Czech only, *O plánu, trhu a hospodářské politice* (Prague, 1967). See review, B. Šimon, *RP*, Jan. 9, 1968.

The essential difference between the two principal models was that although both employed planning, under the directive system the plan was the main instrument, "the motor" of the economy, and the market mechanism was not used, whereas under the economic model, both plan and market were employed, with the market serving as the "motor," and the plan seeking "to perfect and enrich the market and to deprive it of its negative features" (pp. 184-85). This was therefore a socialist, not a laissez faire, market.

The economic model, in Turek's view, was not only better than the directive system, but in fact "the only solution." They were, admittedly, just at the beginning of research on the economic model, and the transition to it would not be accomplished from one day to the next. It should not, however, be prolonged over many years. The proper strategy should in fact be to create "the core of the economic system" at one stroke, "by one basic economic and political act," "by basic changes in all spheres . . . on one date." This did not exclude, indeed it required, various compromises, but these must be rare and temporary.[130]

Karel Kouba, who was an early and strong defender of the market idea, in a volume of essays on the socialist economy, which he edited, stated the case for "linking plan and market." The plan was an instrument, he said, for "perfecting" the market; the market mechanism must function "under the decisive influence of central decisions." Reverting to the debate in the thirties between Oskar Lange and the critics of socialism (F. A. von Hajek, L. von Mises et al.), Kouba rejected the contention of the critics that socialism could not function rationally in the absence of private ownership, and also Lange's counterclaim that rationality could be achieved under socialism without a genuine competitive market. Kouba pressed the case for such a market, including "a rational price structure." Without this, "optimal planning was impossible."[131]

Other important contributions to the economic debate, too numerous to discuss at length, included the study by Josef Goldmann and Karel Kouba of economic growth in Czechoslovakia, completed in 1966 and published in 1967. This applied the model of the Polish economist, M. Kalecki, to analyze quantitatively the effectiveness of the centralized system of management and the causes of fluctuations in growth. Their conclusion was that the traditional system of planning had encouraged rapid economic growth in the fifties but had had the opposite effect in the sixties. The continued growth of the Czechoslovak economy required a more effective system of planning in the form of a "regulated market sys-

[130] Turek, O plánu, pp. 217, 220-21, 223, 227, 300-301.
[131] K. Kouba et al., Úvahy o socialistické ekonomice (Prague, 1968), quotations at pp. 224, 236, 210. The contributors were, in addition to Kouba, Č. Kožušník, J. Hronovský, B. Komenda, and R. Richta.

tem," "an organic linking of central planning and a regulated market mechanism."[132]

Radoslav and Milada Selucký presented a similar argument in their book, Man and the Economy, published in 1967.[133] Condemning the "non-commodity" model of the Soviet Union which had been imposed on Czechoslovakia in the fifties, they put the case for a "commodity-model" of socialism, which would represent a synthesis of planning and market. This was a purely theoretical construction, not even Yugoslavia having so far established such a model. The authors stressed the intimate relationship of such economic decentralization with political democracy —one without the other could not be conceived. "In the long run it is unthinkable that a democratic economic system of management, with explicit elements of self-management, in which the producer is a co-participant in decision-making, should be combined with a political model which limits the democratic rights of the citizen and makes them formal matters" (p. 148).

Similar ideas were penetrating the party apparatus and the administrative bureaucracy. In a series of articles in Nová mysl at the end of 1967, B. Šimon, head of the Economics Department of the CC apparatus, presented the report of a study team which also accepted the notion of "a symbiosis of plan and market." The new system could not be introduced through spontaneous or self-regulating forces but would have to be implemented by the center through a well-defined economic policy and a complex of instruments, especially the plan itself. Various compromises and state interventions would be necessary, and the transition to the final phase of the new system would last at least five years.[134]

Similar conclusions were reached at a party conference held in the State Planning Commission in mid-1967, devoted to the theme "Plan and Market." Pavel Pelikán, economist at the Research Institute of the Economics of Industry, explained the need for both plan and market as "mutually supplementing sources, from which producers and consumers ought to derive information and motives for their rational and socially desirable, or at least socially unobjectionable, decision-making." After a number of other economists had elaborated on various aspects of the plan-market relationship, the deputy chairman of the State Planning

[132] Hospodářský růst v ČSSR (Prague, 1967; 2nd ed., 1969); in English, Economic Growth in Czechoslovakia (New York, 1969). Quotations at p. 133 (Czech).

[133] Radoslav and Milada Selucký, Člověk a hospodářství (Prague, 1967), esp. pp. 101 ff., 145-48. See also the panel discussion on "Market, Planning and Democracy," in Josef Sládek, ed., O lidech, ekonomice a demokracii (Prague, 1968).

[134] NM, nos. 21, 23-26, from Nov. 17, 1967, esp. the final article, no. 26, Dec. 28 (1967), pp. 8-11 (in English, in New Trends in Czechoslovak Economics, no. 2, 1968, pp. 23-112, esp. pp. 33-36, 96 ff., 110).

Commission, Miloslav Kohoutek warmly endorsed the new system and warned against a prolongation of the transition to a more rational system of management.[135]

THE SCIENTIFIC REVOLUTION AND SCHOLARSHIP

The 13th Party Congress, held in late May 1966, demonstrated anew the ambivalent attitude of the party toward science and scholarship. The main documents and speeches placed the customary emphasis on the importance of science and the scientific character of policy-making, but, as usual, asserted the leading role of the party, and in particular its "cognitive" function; they also paid tribute to the work accomplished by the social sciences, mentioning specifically state and law, philosophy and history, and urged the development of new disciplines such as sociology and social psychology and the utilization of Western scholarship. The principal decision also intoned the "class and party approach" in scholarship and complained vaguely of certain articles which "had nothing in common with a scientific evaluation of past and present development." Novotný, in his major address, praised, at least briefly, the work of the social sciences, although he, too, proclaimed the need for developing science on "class and party principles." In his view, the Central Committee was "the organizer and the direct active factor in the theoretical elaboration of a series of economic and ideological questions."[136]

More significant than these abstract proclamations was the positive attitude taken toward the work of Radovan Richta and a group of scholars from various institutes and higher educational institutions on the scientific and technological revolution. This interdisciplinary team had been set up in 1965, under the auspices of the Academy of Sciences, and with the endorsement of the CC's Ideological Commission. The research already completed, some twenty-three studies in all, had been examined and approved by the party apparatus. Hendrych, in his address, rejected the idea of the scientific and technological revolution as "a worldwide, autonomous supra-class current" leading to "a reconciliation of social systems," and condemned "superficial opinions of an all-human humanism concerning so-called modern man and the modern state," but endorsed the idea that this revolution would be the means by which a classless or socialist society could achieve future communism.[137] As a result

[135] But see above (chap. III, n. 45) for Kohoutek's remarks on the "timing" of reform. For the conference, see *Plánované hospodářství* 20 (1967), no. 8, pp. 91-93; no. 1, pp. 67-78 (Pelikán); no. 9, pp. 17-25 (Kohoutek).

[136] Decision in *XIII. sjezd KSČ* (1966), pp. 387, 408; Novotný, pp. 93, 95. Other documents in *XIII. sjezd KSČ* (1967), pp. 711-12, 884. See also J. Hendrych, *RP*, Jan. 9, 1966.

[137] Hendrych, *XIII. sjezd KSČ* (1966), pp. 213-15.

of the green light thus given, the Richta team was able to embark on a five- to seven-year program of further research and to publish its initial conclusions in book form, in *Civilization at the Crossroads*.[138]

This important scholarly work was a social and economic analysis of the role of science in the modern world and its impact on the economy and on society in general, embedded in a Marxist philosophical framework. The term "scientific and technological revolution," coined originally by the British scientist and Marxist, J. D. Bernal, had gradually penetrated Soviet and other communist scholarly discussions, especially among philosophers, and went beyond the customary lip service paid by the ideologists to science and scientific decision-making.[139] Drawing, on the one hand, from the analysis of the impact of science on society in the studies of a host of Western scholars, and, on the other hand, citing the writings of Marx, as well as Soviet references to the role of science in the modern world, Richta's work was a sophisticated and imaginative forecast of the future, but was sufficiently orthodox to be acceptable in other socialist countries, where it was indeed eventually published.

Richta's central thesis was that the scientific and technological revolution was different in kind from the earlier industrial revolution and represented a watershed in economic, and therefore social and human, devel-

[138] Originally published without footnotes as R. Richta et al., *Civilizace na rozcestí, Společenské a lidské souvislosti vědeckotechnické revoluce* (Prague, 1966), the later editions under the same title were somewhat expanded, but not basically changed. The third edition (Prague, 1969), completed for the press in the spring of 1968 but published only after the occupation, was used as the basis of the English translation, *Civilization at the Crossroads: Social and Human Implications of the Scientific and Technological Revolution* (Prague and New York, 1969). Citations below are to the English edition. Some translations are adjusted to the Czech original. See favorable review by J. Coufalík, *NM*, no. 24, Nov. 29, 1966, pp. 30-31. For briefer restatements of the main themes, see O. Klein and J. Zelený, "The Dynamics of Change: Leadership, the Economy, Organizational Structure, and Society," in R. B. Farrell, ed., *Political Leadership in Eastern Europe and the Soviet Union* (Chicago, 1970), pp. 199-223; R. Richta, "Révolution scientifique et technique et transformations sociales," *L'homme et la société*, no. 3 (Jan.-Feb.-March 1967), pp. 83-104; R. Richta, "La révolution scientifique et technique et les choix offerts à la civilisation moderne," ibid., no. 9 (July-Aug.-Sept. 1968), pp. 29-53; Ota Klein, "Quelques données théoriques du renouveau tchécoslovaque," ibid., no. 10 (Oct.-Nov.-Dec. 1968), pp. 65-72; R. Richta, "La dialectique de l'homme et de son oeuvre dans la civilisation moderne," ibid., no. 13 (July-Aug.-Sept. 1969), pp. 39-57. Cf. R. Richta, "Ekonomika jako civilizační dimenze," in Kouba et al., *Úvahy*, pp. 11-64. See also proceedings of a seminar organized by the Slovak party in May 1967, *Vedecko-technická revolúcia* (cited in n. 100); and a special issue devoted to this theme, *SČ*, no. 2 (1966). See earlier works by Richta, *Člověk a technika v revoluci našich dnů* (Prague, 1963); *Komunismus a proměny života* (Prague, 1963).

[139] For Soviet discussions, see V. G. Marakhov, *Voprosy filosofii* 17, no. 10 (1963), 3-12, and the report of a conference on this theme, ibid. 18, no. 9 (1964), 154-57. Cf. A. A. Zvorykin, *Nauka proizvodstvo trud* (Moscow, 1965).

opment. Accepting the Soviet dictum that science was part of the "base," "a direct productive force," Richta wrote: "Science is now penetrating all phases of production and gradually assuming the role of the central productive force of human society and, indeed, the 'decisive factor' in the growth of the productive forces" (p. 28).[140] As a consequence, the degree to which a country used science and applied its findings to industry was the primary criterion of a country's capacity to progress in competition with others (p. 229). "Socialism stands or falls with science, just as it stands or falls with the rule of the workers" (p. 246). "Everyone should realize that without a scientific and technological revolution the new society must unconditionally perish—regardless of nice wishes, firm will and the best of intentions" (p. 278).[141]

In admitting the backwardness of Czechoslovak industry in utilizing the fruits of the scientific revolution (pp. 89 ff.), Richta was presenting a damaging criticism of previous economic policy and a challenge to the party to develop a "strategy of science." Socialism would have to overcome many difficulties if it were to move into the era of the scientific revolution. Without the operation of what he called "a *developed system of interests*" it would be "impossible to throw open the doors to the scientific and technological revolution" and "enable it ultimately to prevail" (p. 81). The directive system of management was inadequate and "the thorough implementation of the new economic system of planning and management is a condition for Czechoslovakia's entry into the stream of the scientific and technological revolution" (pp. 98, 100-103). This would entail a new role for "the human factor" as an important element of economic growth (pp. 32-37, 155-61). Investment of resources in education, public health, and environmental improvement would become crucial aspects of development.

The enhanced role of science in the economy would necessitate radical changes in education, the increased technical competence of workers, better utilization of the technical and scientific intelligentsia and adequate rewards for their work (reversing previous tendencies toward "equalization"), and improved methods of consultation with scholars and scientists. An atmosphere of free discussion and of conflicting views was a prerequisite for the maximum development of science. There was no longer a place, it was said, for the "obedient specialist." This would apply not only to natural sciences, but also to the social sciences, which would constitute "*a system of sciences* of man" and would require research by interdisciplinary teams of specialists in philosophy, economics,

[140] Cf. Marakhov, p. 5; Zvorykin, p. 14. On Marx, see Richta, *Civilization*, pp. 39, 46, n. 3, 212-13.
[141] Cf. first Czech edition, pp. 274, 308-9.

sociology, social psychology, law and history, political science, ergonomics, cybernetics and the natural sciences (pp. 208-9, 254-56).[142]

Although these propositions were, in the existing context of ideas, fresh and critical, the Richta study was in other respects more moderate, even conservative, in its approach. Richta strongly endorsed the "improved" planning and management system and spoke of the employment of "economic forces," such as market relations, in conjunction with planning, but was not specific in expounding the needed changes[143] and advocated a kind of "systems-engineering" (p. 235) which was not incompatible with continued central control. Frequent homage was paid to "socialist enterprise," but no concrete reference was made to broader competence for individual enterprise directors. Cybernetics was described as "the sole possible basis for modern management and planning," constituting an "indirect" system of management. Other formulations were highly abstruse. Everything depended on "working out a system of *civilization regulators*, of means and rules for adjusting the economic, and also the social, political, psychological and cultural conditions for promoting man's creative activity and directing his interest to socialism" (p. 238). "*Regulation of the regulators*" was "a higher form of management . . . the sole means by which to make the process of modern civilization amenable to planning and control," and "a basis for widespread application of computer technology" (p. 239).

Richta also laid great stress on the changed status of the active and independent individual, freed from the alienation created by industrial civilization and rendered the authentic "subject" of the economic process (pp. 202-8). Although he envisaged the individual as an active participant in decision-making, he did not make any practical proposals for enlisting such participation, for instance, in the form of workers' councils. Indeed, the attainment of the enlarged role of the creative individual, it was admitted, would be a long and slow process, depending on the full implementation of the scientific and technical revolution.[144]

The work of the team did not touch directly on the political system

---

[142] Cf. Miroslav Král, "The Scientific-Technological Revolution and Questions of Management," *NM*, no. 21, Oct. 18, 1966, pp. 9-13. See also the symposium on science and the management of society edited by Král, *Věda a řízení společnosti* (Prague, 1967) which included chapters on cybernetics, mathematics, and functionalism.

[143] See the detailed review article of Richta's book by Dušan Pokorný, who urged far-reaching economic reforms, combining planning and market forces (*LN*, May 6, 1967).

[144] *Civilization*, pp. 252, 261-73, 306-7. Cf. Pokorný, *LN*, on the desirability of workers' representation. See Richta's "Ekonomika jako civilizační dimenze," in Kouba et al., *Úvahy*, for an abstract theoretical analysis of the causes of alienation under capitalism and socialism and the means of assuring "the creative activity of man" under socialism. On the same theme, cf. Richta, "Les choix offerts," pp. 14 ff., 47-53.

but had very substantial implications for this sphere. Long-term perspective planning, which was said to be indispensable, would necessitate "free discussion" and would require the development of democratic forms of participation. All this would affect the role of the party as "the leading center and the organizer of the scientific-technological revolution." It would have to "overcome the narrow horizon of traditional power-political government, linked with administrative means, and develop more mature, more effective forms of *society-wide* ('social-political') management" (p. 253). This would demand a rationalization of the flow of information, including public opinion probes, higher qualifications for members of the *aparát*, and "a renovation of the traditional methods of party work." The party would have to rely more on the use of science and encourage new scientific conceptions and progressive solutions (p. 286). Although the original report did not offer concrete suggestions for political reforms, its continuing program of research, launched in 1967, was to address itself to the elaboration of "an optimal model of political organization."[145]

The Richta approach was welcome to the party as a reputable scholarly analysis, based on Marx and in line with Soviet views, and offering a moderate solution, within the existing system, for the mounting ills of society. It seemed to portray the attainment of communism as a natural projection of the existing order and of the party's policy, without the drastic changes envisaged by other intellectuals. In view of the backward state of Czechoslovak technology and the great economic difficulties that had to be surmounted, Richta's vision of the consequences of the scientific and technological revolution seemed in some ways to be a dream of the distant future, only indirectly related to present reality.[146] Although open criticism of the Richta approach was hampered by its official approval, it appeared to more radical dissenters, such as Kosík, as he later wrote, as a somewhat technocratic approach and even as an apology for the existing system.[147] The party's endorsement of the Richta team's

[145] A mimeographed outline of its program included studies on the nature of politics; the decision-making process; classes and the power elite; the position of the individual; democracy; public opinion; constitutionalism; the legal order and individual rights; representative bodies; public administration; planning and democracy; industrial democracy; the societal organizations; security and the courts; the party as the leading force. Inner party relations were, however, to be dealt with by party institutions. The program also comprised historical studies, including the First Republic, and comparative studies, including bourgeois states and East European states, especially the USSR, Poland, and Yugoslavia.

[146] Šik, at the 13th congress, spoke positively of the Richta study, but called for concrete planning prognoses and warned against discussion of long-term perspectives which distracted attention from urgent immediate problems and the economic difficulties in the way of their solution (*XIII. sjezd KSČ*, 1966, pp. 302-3.

[147] *Literární listy*, May 16, 1968. Kosík spoke of the term "scientific and

129

work, as well as the use of other interdisciplinary study groups (under Šik, Machonin, and Mlynář), suggested that the regime was trying to reach a *modus vivendi* with some scholars and to enlist them in the elaboration of policy, and thus to defuse the more critical attitudes of others.[148] This prepared the ground for the post-January changes by influencing the thinking of some members of the party apparatus and the leadership and winning them to the idea of at least moderate reform. The reforms adopted or planned in 1968, however, went far beyond the thinking of the regime-sponsored team studies and embodied the views of more radical reformers, some of whom were members of the official teams, others not.[149]

The attempt to employ the talents of the scholars was a double-edged weapon, however. Scholarly participation in policy-making and theoretical discussion might render policy and ideology more scientific and objective and thereby win greater support for the regime from the intelligentsia and the population, but it might also allow dissenting and critical views to permeate the apparatus, and thus weaken or threaten the position of the ruling oligarchs. Novotný, however, was not really sincere about accepting the counsel of the scholars and was determined to keep the influence of their thinking within strict bounds. In an address to the graduating class of the Higher Party School, on June 30, while stressing the role of social science research, he lashed out at the writers and certain scholars in the economic field who ignored "the socialist principles of the national economy" and took over various capitalist methods and elements, and reiterated his usual theme that "socialist science" must be

---

technological revolution" as "a mystification," concealing the real problems of the revolution and the social conflicts accompanying it. Criticizing both the belief in the all-powerfulness of technology and the fear of it, he wrote that, although science was necessary for socialism, it could be used against socialism.

[148] R. Rohan, in reviewing a conference on the intelligentsia under socialism, condemned "permanent criticism of the social order and nonconformism to the existing system of knowledge" and spoke of "the influence of the intelligentsia on social structure through scientific and technical progress" (*NM*, no. 23, Nov. 1966, pp. 31-32).

The moderate, if not conservative, character of Richta's approach was later corroborated by the post-occupation approval of the team's work and by the translation of the book into Russian. Richta was among the first scholars of eminence to endorse the Husák regime's policy. See Richta and J. Filipec, *Tvorba*, Nov. 26, 1969. Two articles signed by a number of members of the Richta team criticized earlier errors of the group but argued that the majority had been Marxist-Leninist in their outlook (ibid., April 29, May 6, 1970).

[149] Professor Zeman goes too far in referring to the 1968 reforms as "a programmed revolution" based on the Richta and other studies (*Prague Spring*, pp. 87-90). On the conflict of opinion within the teams and the radical views of some members and non-members, communist and non-communist, see Bystřina, *Svědectví* 12, no. 47 (1974), 457-60.

based exclusively on a Marxist-Leninist view of the world.[150] The party must base its policy and propaganda, he said, "only on confirmed scientific knowledge," but could not "accept every opinion and concept of an individual scientific worker." "The non-acceptance of this or that proposal is no reason to assert that science is not recognized here." Two months later, at a ceremony for graduates of higher military schools, Novotný repeated his attack on those who were smuggling in bourgeois views and practices and condemned those scholars who were acting "against the interest of the country, of the party, of socialism, and against the international interests of the communist movement."[151]

POWER AND THE INTELLECTUALS

The renascence of the intellectuals, including the scholars dealt with above and the writers and journalists discussed in the preceding chapter, was of extraordinary importance in deepening the crisis of the regime, sapping its legitimacy, and sharpening the awareness of the urgency of reform.[152] Most of the intellectuals were Marxists and party members, often working at official expense in institutes and universities, but they were reaching independent conclusions through a flexible interpretation of Marxism. Unlike Soviet intellectuals, they had a vivid memory of the freer years between 1945 and 1948, and if they were older, of the liberty of the pre-war Republic. They were the heirs, too, of the prominent political role of intellectuals in the history of the two nations. Even those who had come to maturity in the fifties and were then imbued with fervent loyalty to the party and to socialism were shocked by the revelations of the sixties and as a result of the lessening of terror, were liberated from the fear of expressing novel or heretic ideas. Censorship and other forms of repression silenced the more radical and forced others to exercise self-censorship and to use Aesopian language to express their ideas. Nonetheless, successive waves of creative ferment in different disciplines and cultural spheres were mutually supporting and produced a cumulative broadening of freedom of expression.

In the relatively small and intimate Czech and Slovak intellectual communities no one could help being influenced by the explosion of ideas in scholarly and cultural milieux. The cultural weeklies, the scholarly journals, and even party publications, provided forums of discussion for scholars and artists from all fields, and soon had an attentive public drawn from the intelligentsia as a whole. The interdisciplinary teams brought together experts from various spheres of creative work and from

---

[150] *RP*, July 1, 1967. [151] *RP*, Sept. 2, 1967.
[152] Cf. Kusin, *Intellectual Origins*, pp. 135-37.

all parts of the Republic and helped to create a common front of intellectuals in favor of change. Even party officials, linked by career and educational associations with intellectuals outside the apparatus, and often trained in party schools and institutes by teachers who were liberal in outlook, did not entirely escape the influence of reform ideas. There were, of course, wide differences of views among the intellectuals, and some of them remained conservative and dogmatic. Yet the orientation toward reform became more and more prominent within the intellectual community as a whole, which exerted a liberating influence on the thinking of educated Czechs and Slovaks and thus became a political force of some magnitude.

The party leadership was caught within a serious dilemma, largely of its own making, by this development. In the Stalinist period the cult of the working class had led to an attitude of suspicion and hostility toward the intellectuals, which was expressed most strongly by Novotný but infected the party as a whole and all levels of society. During the sixties the reluctant acceptance of de-Stalinization and the endorsement of the scientific and technological revolution forced the leaders to reconsider their attitude toward the intellectuals and to make a conscious effort to utilize their knowledge and to raise their status and prestige. The formation of the interdisciplinary teams and the employment of specialists within the party apparatus and as outside consultants legitimized the tendency toward freer inquiry and informed analysis. Yet the leadership, and Novotný in particular, was fearful of the critical spirit spreading among the intellectuals and permeating the ranks of the party functionaries and reacted with repeated assertions of the party's leadership role, constant demands for conformity and loyalty, and repressive action against heretical ideas and their bearers. This official condemnation intensified resentment and opposition among intellectuals; stimulated a growing self-consciousness and daring; and heightened their sense of responsibility to society.

The mounting influence of the intelligentsia raised an embarrassing ideological issue in a society committed to the leading role of the working class and its vanguard, the Communist Party. Constant discussion of the theme did not resolve the problem, either in theory or in practice.[153]

153 For an excellent sociological study of the intelligentsia, see Libuše Dziedzinská, *Inteligence a dnešek* (Prague, 1968). This study touched on the social and political influence of the intellectuals, the conflict of freedom and control, and their role as leaders of society (pp. 174-90, 215-37). See Z. Valenta's more limited analysis in the Machonin collective work, *Sociální struktura*, pp. 436-70. Among many discussions in the press, see the symposia in *Plamen*, nos. 10 and 11 (Oct. and Nov. 1966), pp. 1-5, 66-73, resp.; *Rep.*, Dec. 31, 1966, pp. 4-7. An extensive opinion poll carried out in 1966 for the Institute for the Planning of Science (a sample of 1,400) revealed a generally positive attitude toward university

Ernst Fischer, the Austrian Marxist theoretician, in a major article in *Literární noviny*, entitled "The Intellectuals and Power," described the intellectuals as "a potential power" in modern society. Condemning anti-intellectualism, Fischer warned against both a failure of the intellectuals to accept responsibility and the danger of their corruption through serving those in power. He exalted the intellectuals as independent critics, as "heretics," and as "the conscience of the nation," and saw their greatest opportunity in working teams which would act as "brain trusts" for those in power but which would, by retaining their independence, serve as "a counterweight to the old power apparatuses."[154] This concept was, of course, anathema to party ideologists and conservative intellectuals such as Jan Fojtík, who sought to refute it in a long series of articles in *Rudé právo*. The intellectuals had an important role to play, but not as critics, oppositionists, and "heretics." Their "social power and influence," he declared, was dependent on their association (*sounaležitost*) with the working class and on "the degree to which they aided the party in its complex programmatic, ideological, and organizational tasks."[155]

---

teachers, scientific workers, and other branches of the scientific intelligentsia. For full results see V. Brenner and M. Hrouda, *SČ* 3, no. 5 (1967), 541-50; 4, no. 1 (1968), 43-54; in shorter form, *RP*, Aug. 8-10, 1968.

[154] *LN*, June 18, 1966.

[155] *RP*, July 29, Aug. 2, 5, 9 (quotation from the end of the final article). This may be compared with similar views expressed earlier by Jiří Hájek (*Plamen*, no. 8, Aug. 1964, pp. 19-27) who denied that the intelligentsia was "an independent political force called upon to save humanity," as suggested in the writings of Fischer. They "cannot arrogate to themselves alone the right to seek, without the party and outside the party, definite universally valid answers, especially as regards social practice and its direction. Their basic and unalterable duty continues to be to place their knowledge at the disposal of the party and to strive, within the party, for the solution of all problems which have to be solved" (p. 26).

CHAPTER V

The Political System under Fire

THE POLITICAL system inherited from Gottwald and modeled essentially on the Soviet prototype remained substantially unchanged throughout the fifteen years of Novotný's rule. The major state institutions embodied in the constitution of 1960 and the party organs incorporated in successive statutes provided a bureaucratic foundation for an extreme concentration of power in the hands of Novotný. The domination of "the party" over all aspects of political life made it in effect the only "subject" of the political system. The very term "party" was, however, a meaningless one, inasmuch as the mass of members had few rights and little influence, and even the higher organs, such as the Central Committee and the Congress, became bodies with decorative and declarative functions, without a significant share in policy-making. The party in essence was embodied in the army of functionaries at every level of its hierarchy, and the *aparát* of the Central Committee in Prague, and its subordinate Slovak arm in Bratislava, were its dominant elements.

Since these were in turn subservient to the First Secretary, Novotný occupied the position of a fulcrum, capable of directing and manipulating, from the center, every branch of the mechanism and thus every element of the political system as a whole. Novotný, however, could hardly be regarded as an autocrat who alone determined the major lines of policy, since his was a derived power, based on the backing of Moscow and on his willing acceptance of Soviet strategies and directives. Moreover, lacking, as he did, original ideas of his own, or even a grasp of the social realities around him, Novotný's power was in large part exercised, not by him personally, but by those around him, in the small oligarchic leadership corps and in the *aparát*—persons who were in turn dependent on Novotný's continued approval for the retention of their own power. Having been trained in a certain pattern of bureaucratic politics at lower levels of the apparatus, Novotný exercised his authority through familiar instruments of administrative manipulation and coercion, extending even to the slightest details of political life. As a post-1968 analysis put it, Novotný, with the "mentality" of an official, fitted well into the dominant bureaucratism of the time and relied on other officials to give effect to his policies.[1]

[1] Jan Smíšek, "Antonín Novotný, Politics and Power," *Tribuna*, Jan. 15, 22, 1969. L. Mňačko also described Novotný as "a conscientious bureaucrat," whose chief support was "the anonymous power of the bureaucracy, the *aparát*," which

The abuse of power which a centralized system like this made possible was already evident during Gottwald's tenure of office and was the subject of open criticism in the years after Stalin's death. In the carefully controlled process of de-Stalinization after 1956, however, Novotný absolved the system as such of blame and placed it on particular persons and on the faults of leadership occasioned by the "cult of personality." There was nothing essentially wrong that could not be corrected by a restoration of "Leninist norms" in the party and by "a deepening of socialist democracy." Although the party had in fact been responsible for everything that happened since 1948, and claimed credit for the "achievements" of those years, any discredit for abuses and failures of those years must be deflected from it. The defects of the entire system became increasingly obvious with the failure of the Novotný regime to deal effectively with the serious political problems discussed in the preceding chapters. Dissatisfaction with the prevailing methods of political life became more and more widespread but could not be expressed publicly, at least not until after 1961. Quite naturally, any criticism of these methods, and still more of the fundamentals of the system, was regarded by Novotný as a threat to the continuance of his personal power and the political system which he personified.

THE TWELFTH PARTY CONGRESS

The 22nd congress of the CPSU, with its renewed attack on the "cult of personality," and its clarion call for an expansion of "socialist democracy," confronted the Czechoslovak party with a dilemma: how to explain their own past employment of Stalinist methods and how to envisage the reform of their political system. There was an ideological aspect of this problem in Khrushchev's thesis, embodied in the CPSU party program, that the USSR was making a transition from a proletarian dictatorship to "a state of the entire people" and that with the transition to communism, the organs of state power would gradually be transformed into "organs of public self-government."[2] In 1960 when the constitution was enacted, Czechoslovakia had claimed to have completed the building

was "the only bearer of power in the state" (*Kultúrny život*, July 26, 1968). For an analysis of the *apparatchiki* as the principal source of Novotný's strength and as a significant force of opposition to reform, see Galia Golan, "Antonin Novotny: The Sources and Nature of His Power," *Canadian Slavonic Papers* 14 (Autumn 1972), 425-26, 435-36.

[2] See *Pravda* (Moscow) for the reports on the congress proceedings, in particular for the party program (Nov. 2, 1961). English version published as *Programme of the Communist Party of the Soviet Union* (Moscow, 1961). For a detailed theoretical analysis, see F. M. Burlatskii, *Gosudarstvo i kommunizm* (Moscow, 1963). See review of Burlatskii by O. Průša, *Nová mysl*, no. 9 (1965), pp. 1145-47.

of socialism and to have entered the stage of laying the foundations of communism. It seemed appropriate, therefore, to follow the Soviet lead by advancing almost immediately in the direction of an "all-people's state" and "a socialist democracy of the people as a whole," a step in theory which would presumably have placed political reform on the agenda.

In fact, however, there was delay and confusion in the Czechoslovak response to the Soviet challenge. When the 12th congress of the CPCz was announced at the CC plenum in November 1961, Novotný was extremely vague in explaining the "significance," as he put it, of the idea of an "all-people's state" for Czechoslovakia.[3] As the congress approached, he did not offer any clarification of this crucial question. His assertions of the traditional principles of democratic centralism, the leading role of the party, continued class conflict, and "firm central direction" suggested that his references to "the deepening of socialist democracy" did not anticipate important changes in the methods of rule. He admitted the need for criticism, but "not hostile attacks on the party and its principles under the guise of criticism" or "the creation of mistrust in the party's policies and the party's organs." Nor did the key draft document for the forthcoming congress, published in August, break new ground in theoretical analysis or in practical proposals for political change.[4]

The much heralded 12th congress was anticlimactic as far as doctrinal advance or political reform were concerned.[5] Although the idea that socialism had been completed was retained, the task of the future was said to be merely "the further development of socialist society" and earlier assumptions of a rapid transition to communism were not repeated. Novotný's report, and the final congress resolution on the main trends of socialist society, referred to the process of "the transformation of the state of the dictatorship of the proletariat into an all-people's state" but did not elaborate on the implications of this transition. Although the pre-congress draft document had stated that the direct struggle of hostile

---

[3] *Usnesení a dokumenty ÚV KSČ, Od celostátní konference KSČ 1960 do XII. sjezdu KSČ* (Prague, 1962), II, 53.

[4] CC plenum, April 1962, ibid., II, 247; CC plenum, July 1962, ibid., II, 344-45. On the latter occasion Novotný did not even mention the "all-people's state." See also "On the Prospects of the Further Development of our Socialist Society," ibid., II, 354-404.

[5] Novotný's report, and the congress resolution, *XII. sjezd Komunistické strany Československa* (Prague, 1963), pp. 21 ff., 635 ff., resp. The draft document had spoken somewhat more explicitly of the task of "developing our *socialist statehood* and further bringing together the working class, the cooperative peasants and the intelligentsia, as well as the nations of our republic, and thus of gradually creating a unified society of working people, organized in an all-people's state" (*Usnesení KSČ, 1960 do XII. sjezdu,* II, 357). It had also noted that the transition to an all-people's state was not yet finished (p. 384).

136

classes was not "decisive for the character of our society,"[6] this proposition was dropped in the congress resolution. Although once again asserting the need for "deepening socialist democracy," Novotný reiterated the continuance of the "leading role of the working class" in the transition to the all-people's state. The final resolution proclaimed the need to assure the party's "determining directive influence on all sectors of our life."[7]

There was a hint of possible reform in references to an increased activity of the national committees, but these organs were also criticized for accenting local interests and were required to protect "all-society interests." Frequent allusions were made to greater participation of the societal organizations and of all citizens in public administration, but there was no reference to the Soviet concept of developing "self-administration" through the transfer of governmental functions to the mass associations. Novotný mentioned the idea of improving electoral procedures but merely suggested that, in the nominating stage, there should be several candidates from whom the most suitable would be selected.[8] There was also repeated criticism of earlier interpretations of democratic centralism which had minimized centralism and wrongfully encouraged "decentralization."

In the pre-congress discussions there was much talk of developing party democracy through the adoption of a new statute. When the draft statute was published in July, Novotný spoke of it, however, as "an instrument for deepening the leading role of the party in all spheres of our life."[9] The final document approved by the congress confirmed that the fundamental character of the party was to be modified, if at all, in the direction of accentuating its discipline and unity and buttressing its powerful position as the "leading and directing force of society and state," as already proclaimed in the 1960 constitution. The statute, unlike the CPSU statute adopted in 1961, did not describe the party as "a party of the whole people," but defined it as "a voluntary, militant, and active union of like-minded persons, communists, which groups together the most conscious members of the working class, peasantry, and intelligentsia" (preamble). Importance was attached to the principle of democratic centralism, which required of all organizations and communists that "they actively and creatively implement party policy and the decisions of leading party organs" (art. 18). These were "unconditonally binding" on all lower organs. The minority and individuals were expected "in a disciplined manner to subordinate themselves to majority decisions."

[6] Ibid., II, 384-85.   [7] *XII. sjezd KSČ*, pp. 66, 655, resp.
[8] Ibid., pp. 69-70.
[9] CC plenum, July 1962, *Usnesení KSČ, 1960 do XII. sjezdu*, II, 347-48.

The Central Committee was empowered "to regulate and supervise the activity of the National Assembly, the government and other central state organs, the National Front and the central organs of the societal organizations through the medium of communists and party groups, and to direct their activity toward the consistent implementation and carrying out of party policy" (art. 30c). Comparable organs at lower levels had similar authority. The basic organizations were given far-reaching rights to examine and check on the actions of leaders of economic enterprises and institutions and were authorized to make decisions binding on them (art. 69). The Slovak party was to form a "regional organization" in Slovakia and to be guided by the decisions of the CPCz congress and Central Committee (art. 36). The Czechoslovak Union of Youth was described as "an active auxiliary and reserve of the party," seeking to organize the youth in carrying out party policy (art. 73). The statute was so formulated that the party, to a greater degree than in previous versions, would be a pliable and obedient instrument of the top leaders.[10]

LIMITED REFORMS

Throughout 1963 and 1964 the leadership devoted much of its attention to the campaign against the cultural periodicals, repeatedly appealing for party discipline and denouncing intellectuals "spreading ideological confusion," "the saboteurs of the intellectual front," to use Císař's words.[11] The criticisms of the "cult" were indeed implicitly or explicitly political, probing into all aspects of life and constituting a severe indictment of the party's policies and the political system as a whole, and a challenge to the regime and to Novotný himself.[12] His bitter response did not create an atmosphere propitious for political reform.

Moreover, the doctrinal interpretation of the transition from the proletarian dictatorship to a state of the whole people was not favorable to democratic changes. Some features of the all-people's state did exist,

[10] Text in *XII. sjezd KSČ*, pp. 659-84. The party statute did not contain the provisions for rotation of leading officials included in the CPSU rules and required longer periods of service for leading functionaries. Jan Kašpar, in a highly abstract theoretical analysis of the "cognitive and directing task of the party," stressed the necessity of a single directing center and a strictly centralized party organization (*Příspěvky k dějinám KSČ* 3, Oct. 1963, pp. 643-70).

[11] *Kulturní tvorba*, June 11, 1964.

[12] A penetrating analysis of the causes and the main features of the cult of personality as "a system" affecting all spheres of society was given in a memorandum prepared by three Slovak intellectuals for the Slovak party (unpublished at the time). The authors, Dr. Elena Filová-Fať'arová, Academician L. Szántó, and Dr. A. Kopčok, were extremely critical of the official attitude toward the intelligentsia, who were treated as a "hostile" force, and condemned the very slow tempo of the liquidation of the effects of the cult in Czechoslovakia. For text, see *Pravda*, June 28, 1968.

a party theoretician argued, in the form of a broadened political participation of the working people, but the false notion that the all-people's state already existed would lead to a weakening of the party's leading role. "Neither the state nor socialist democracy has yet lost its class basis here, even if eveything is passing through great changes in its development." Although the struggle of hostile classes was no longer the determining factor in domestic affairs, it remained a reality in the international arena and exerted an impact on people's thinking so that some features of the dictatorship of the proletariat continued to operate. As the state of the whole people gradually developed, there would be an ever greater participation of the masses in public affairs, and a transfer of some state functions to the societal organizations. Such transfers would not necessarily hasten the attainment of communism and might have some harmful effects by depriving society of the advantages of centralism in planning and management.[13]

In this setting it is not surprising that changes in political procedures were designed to strengthen the authority of the party. In 1963, in accordance with the decision of the 12th congress, commissions of people's control were set up at every level of the party and state hierarchy, and also in factories, to supervise the fulfillment of party and state decisions.[14] Although their elective character was stressed these organs were admittedly to be guided and directed by the party. They were to operate according to the principle of democratic centralism, so that the whole system would function as "an instrument" of the Central Commission of Supervision and Auditing (ÚKRK). The commissions were described as employing "methods of persuasion and assistance" and as designed to create "a public opinion against incorrectness and the breach of all-social interests." By 1965 there were about 5,000 commissions of people's control, with more than 50,000 members, checking up on the work of all state and economic organs and the national committees, and defending the interests of society as a whole against conflicting tendencies.[15] This system could hardly be regarded as a measure of democratization.

Later, in September 1963, in view of the allegedly unsatisfactory implementation of the 12th congress decisions, it was decided to set up four Central Committee commissions which were not, it was said, to replace the government and its ministries, but to provide them with "a binding conceptual program."[16] Novotný was later quoted as defining this as "an

[13] L. Křížkovský, *Život strany*, no. 6 (March 1964), pp. 354-58.
[14] Ibid., no. 3 (Feb. 1963), pp. 131-35; no. 5 (March 1963), pp. 277-80.
[15] V. Hromádka, *NM*, no. 1 (1965), pp. 65-73.
[16] For the text of the decision, see *Usnesení a dokumenty ÚV KSČ, 1962-63* (Prague, 1964), pp. 466-71. For further comment, see *ŽS*, no. 20 (Oct. 1963), pp. 1187-89; and no. 21 (Nov. 1963), pp. 1255-58 (D. Kolder); O. Průša, *NM*, no. 11 (1963), pp. 1281-88. The commissions and their heads were Economic

effort to improve the methods and style of managing activity and to strengthen the leading role of the party." It was intended, according to the text of the decision, to deepen the role of the Central Committee and of collective leadership and to assure participation of all CC members in the consideration of key questions and in the formulation of the binding directives of the topmost party organs. Although not much is known of the background of this significant decision, it was reported that the work of the government and ministries had been severely criticized at this plenum, thus suggesting that the commissions were also meant to tighten the party's control of the state institutions. It was later revealed that Július Ďuriš, then Minister, who was removed from the Central Committee at this time, had strongly opposed the new measure and had been charged, as a result, with attacking Novotný and the entire leadership.[17] It seems doubtful, however, that the commissions would exercise a decisive influence on basic policy conceptions or do more than exert a marginal influence within the general framework established by the policymakers.

The need for a comprehensive implementation of the provisions of the 1960 constitution had already been urged by a leading constitutional lawyer in the pages of the party's theoretical journal.[18] The first steps in this direction, concerning the representative bodies, were limited in scope. For the elections to the National Assembly and the national committees in June 1964, a new provision was made, namely that more than one person might be nominated for candidacy for a given seat. A single National Front candidate was, however, eventually to be agreed upon at a unification meeting in the electoral district[19] so that there would be no competition in the actual election. The result was a considerable number of additional nominations for national committee seats, but only in 68 cases were there several nominations for candidacy to the National Assembly.[20] Although Novotný, in a speech to the National Front on

---

(D. Kolder), Agricultural (J. Hendrych), Living Standards (J. Dolanský), and Ideological (V. Koucký). Commissions were also established at the district and regional level. In March 1964 a Legal Commission (V. Koucký) was created and Hendrych became head of the Ideological Commission. Each of the central commissions included, in addition to CC members, a number of other persons holding responsible posts within its sphere of action. For the full list of members, ŽS, no. 20 (Oct. 1963).

[17] ŽS, no. 8-9 (April 1968), pp. 40-42.

[18] Pavel Peška, "The Realization of Our Constitution," NM, no. 10 (1962), pp. 1193-1202. He argued for the exercise of the party's leading role "within the framework of the constitution" and stressed the importance of public opinion and the need for "a scientifically based" leadership.

[19] Rudé právo, Feb. 27, 1964.

[20] NM, no. 6 (1964), p. 663. For the regional committees, there were 2,349 nominations for 1,455 electoral constituencies; for the district committees, 17,407

March 4, had underlined the importance of encouraging the participation of non-party persons in public office, these electoral provisions indicated that the exclusive position of party members or party-endorsed candidates was not to be weakened.

Another move in the direction of "democratization" was taken with measures "to deepen the activity" of the National Assembly and the Slovak National Council, approved by the CC plena in May and June, and embodied in law in September 1964.[21] Official commentary linked this with the transition to "a state of the whole people," although it was admitted that this process had not proceeded as far as in the Soviet Union owing to the continuing impact of class vestiges on people's minds. The role of the assembly, its presidium and its committees, was to be elevated, especially in the initiation and discussion of legislation and in the supervision of administration. Plenary sessions would be longer and more regular, and more active and substantive. The right of interpellation by deputies was proclaimed. The committees were also to be more active, drawing in officials and experts from outside the assembly and making recommendations to state organs. Three new committees were to divide the responsibility of the previous industrial committee.

The actual effect of this measure is difficult to assess. There was some evidence of increased business and greater independence of the assembly, especially in its committees. An unprecedented amendment of a government bill was passed by a majority vote in July 1965 but in the end had no effect, as the bill became law without change.[22] This action by the legislature brought to an abrupt close the effort to vitalize the assembly. The dominant position of a single party and the absence of an effective opposition rendered a genuine revival of the legislative and the representative functions of the assembly most improbable.

A similar law to "deepen the activity" of the Slovak National Council (SNR) was adopted. Forecast in the decision of the 12th congress, this was approved by the Central Committees of the two parties and adopted by the CPCz plenum in May 1964.[23] It centered attention on the ex-

---

nominations for 10,784 constituencies; for local committees, 271,277 nominations for 227,132 constituencies.

[21] CC reports and the Presidium's decision of May 7, 1964, *Usnesení a dokumenty ÚV KSČ, 1964* (Prague, 1965), pp. 153-56, 178-87, 210-12; text of law, *Sbírka zákonů*, no. 182/1964. A new law revised the assembly's rules of procedure, *Sb. z.* 183/1964. For comments, see J. Grospič, *NM*, no. 5 (1964), pp. 538-44; V. Škoda, *ŽS*, no. 10 (May 1964), pp. 587-90; V. Veverka, *NM*, no. 11 (1964), p. 660.

[22] *RP*, July 18, 1965.

[23] For the May plenum and the CC decision, *Usnesení KSČ, 1964*, pp. 153-56, 157-75. For comment, M. Chudík, *ŽS*, no. 11 (June 1964), pp. 647-50. See above, chap. III, n. 19.

panded participation of the Slovak Council in drafting and carrying out the state plan and the budget, and provided for close cooperation of the government and the SNR presidium; of central ministers, and Slovak commissioners; and of committees of the National Assembly and of the SNR. The essential purpose, however, was not to advance autonomy or self-rule for Slovakia but to give the Slovak organs greater participation in working out and implementing all-Czechoslovak policy in spheres relating to Slovakia. The commissioners, as the executive organs of the SNR, were to have a more clearly defined competence, and a number of new commissionerships were to be established in areas not hitherto within Slovak competence. The Board of Commissioners, abolished in 1960, was not, however, restored. As in the case of the assembly, the plenary sessions of the Council and its committees were authorized to take a more vigorous part in policy-making. The National Assembly, according to its new rules of procedure, was to empower the Slovak Council to legislate on those matters which required special action in Slovakia, but the assembly could rescind SNR laws if contrary to the constitution or another law.

The New Economic System and Political Change

More indicative of a genuine change of attitude was the discussion of the principles of the new system of planning and management in the closing months of 1964. The adoption of this reform was likely to have implications in relation to law and democracy, argued Zdeněk Mlynář, who described it as another step in the direction of a state of the whole people.[24] At first the political conclusions drawn were modest, however. The CC plenum in November adopted a resolution providing for more frequent participation of leading officials in lower level party meetings and public gatherings and for speedier transmission of information to the lower party organizations. A Presidium decision in December dealt with cadre work in a manner which, while emphasizing the importance of the class approach and political maturity, stressed technical knowledge and managerial ability. The appointment of non-party persons to responsible positions was also endorsed.[25]

The Central Committee's resolution in January 1965 on the improvement of the planned direction of the national economy and on the work of the party was designed to combine continued central direction of the economy with a greater competence for enterprises and branch directorates and greater play for "commodity money relations" and "material

[24] *KT*, Nov. 26, 1964; *Literární noviny*, Jan. 16, 1965; *Věda a život*, no. 1 (1965).
[25] *Usnesení KSČ, 1964*, pp. 350-51, 378-93, resp.

interestedness." Although it was to be introduced gradually throughout 1965 and 1966 and although it did not replace, but modified, centralized planning, political procedures would inevitably be affected. A long section on the changed character of the leading role of the party and of the activity of the mass or societal organizations was included.[26]

According to the decision, the party would focus on "the solution of perspective questions and the pursuit of all-society interests," thus bringing about conditions for "a more independent solution of problems by the state and economic organs and the societal organizations." The chief responsibility would fall on the Central Committee as "the main bearer of creative political thought," and on its commissions, which would work out "conceptions and basic proposals" in consultation with scholars, experts, and the working people. The party was not to take over practical economic tasks or replace the economic organs, as had happened often in the past, but was to concentrate on political and coordinating activity. This did not, however, mean that the party's work could be separated from economic problems, but its approach to them should be "political." As a commentator explained, the party could not confine itself to "political and ideological activity divorced from production" but must exert its influence on the economic organs, "determining their main directions, conceptions and perspectives," and coordinating all-social activity. Moreover, he said, the party possessed "the right of supervision" in the sense of mobilizing and organizing communists and non-communists for the fulfillment of plans and measures.[27]

As for the societal and interest organizations, these were, according to the CC decision, to have an expanded role and to employ fresh methods in stimulating popular participation in economic and public affairs. The trade unions and the youth union would continue to function in the factories, but other associations would transfer their base to the localities. A special resolution on the trade union movement was adopted by the January plenum, criticizing its previous work and that of the communists in the unions.[28] The trade unions, "an auxiliary of the party," were to concentrate on educational duties, explaining the features of the new system and fighting against conservatism, bureaucracy, and wage-leveling. They would encourage the participation of workers in decision-making through industrial committees and would protect their material

[26] For the text, *ŽS*, no. 4 (Feb. 1965), pp. 195-212. The measure had been discussed at earlier CC and government meetings in Dec. 1964, but without public reports (*Usnesení KSČ, 1964*, p. 377). For commentary, K. Klečák, "Party Direction on a Higher Level," *ŽS*, no. 5 (March 1965), pp. 259-63; V. Kvěš, ibid., no. 24 (Dec. 1964), pp. 1515-18; R. Rohan, *NM*, no. 6 (1965), pp. 705-13.

[27] Klečák, "Party Direction," pp. 261-62.

[28] *ŽS*, no. 4 (Feb. 1965), pp. 212-20; commentary by N. Vacík, *RP*, April 3, 1965.

interests and needs. Later, in the labor code which went into effect in 1966, the trade unions were endowed with the right to express opinions on draft legislation and to initiate legislative proposals.[29] Other party and trade union documents asserted the need for the trade unions to defend the interests of their members and to participate in management and in policy-making, but also required them to promote party policy and to defend the general interests of society.[30]

The national committees were also affected by the new methods of planning and management. The need for reform in their methods of work had been under discussion for some time, and had led to certain measures by the goverment in March 1965.[31] These did not extend the jurisdiction of the national committees in general but did increase the authority of the local and municipal committees in the economic field. In 1966 the CC took further steps to enhance their role, giving them greater financial autonomy and more control of investments, and widening the authority of local, municipal, and district committees. On the other hand the committees were not to be permitted to interfere in the competence of enterprises. A new law on national committees was to be prepared.[32] Whether these measures of decentralization did in fact substantially diminish the bureaucratic character of the national committees and strengthen them as organs of democratic local government is, however, difficult to say.

Late in 1965 central organs of government were affected by several changes which, according to the CC statement, were designed "not to weaken the central direction but on the contrary, to strengthen it and improve its quality."[33] The central organs were henceforth to focus on "the solution of problems of a perspective and programmatic character" and would concern themselves with the perfection of long-term planning, the creation of conditions for the use of economic instruments, such as wages and prices, and the coordination of these two areas. The enterprises and the newly formed branch directorates would concentrate on

[29] *Sb. z.* 65/1965.

[30] For instance, 13th congress resolution, *XIII. sjezd Komunistické strany Československa* (Prague, 1966), p. 405; Novotný, ibid., p. 89. See also trade union statements, *Odbory a společnost*, no. 1 (1967), pp. 40-50, 51-55. Cf. Galia Golan, *The Czechoslovak Reform Movement* (Cambridge, 1971), pp. 96-100.

[31] For discussion, June 1964 CC plenum (*Usnesení KSČ*, 1964, p. 210) and Lenárt's article, *ŽS*, no. 22 (Nov. 1964), pp. 1347-51. For the measures, *ŽS*, no. 7 (April 1965), pp. 443-44.

[32] *RP*, March 24, 1966, for the CC decision; ibid., March 26, for Lenárt's speech; ibid., March 28, 1966, for the materials on national committees. See also 13th congress resolution on national committees, *XIII. sjezd KSČ* (1966), pp. 452-57.

[33] Text, *ŽS*, no. 22 (Nov. 1965), pp. 1346-52. This was approved by the CC plenum in early November and endorsed a week later by the National Assembly. See speeches by Lenárt, *RP*, Nov. 10 and 11, 1965.

"concrete tasks of production and management." To fulfill its tasks, the government would rely on specialized organs, some just established, such as the State Planning Commission; the State Commissions for Finance, Prices, and Wages; for Technology; for Economic and Scientific Co-operation; for Management and Organization; the Central Commission of People's Control; and in scientific matters, the Academy of Sciences. It would seek to bring the Slovak National Council more closely into the work of planning. The individual ministries would also require qualitative change so as to meet their long-term responsibilities, and certain new departments were to be established. As far as cadres were concerned, the decision placed emphasis on raising both the technical and political levels of qualification.

Nonetheless, Novotný made quite clear that these measures were not to weaken central authority.[34] The enterprises, he said, were to have "a certain room for operatively dealing with production tasks," but a firm hand would be kept on the process of planning, and "neither anarchy or spontaneity" would be tolerated. The central plan would remain "the axis" of all economic activity, and the government would exert "a decisive influence on all stages of the work on the plan." The exercise of authority by the government would be "a guarantee to the party that the decisions and directives of the Central Committee . . . will be implemented" and "that the interests of society as a whole will . . . be defended against incorrect departmental, parochial and subjective interests." Moreover, although non-communists might hold responsible positions, specialist knowledge must not be overrated at the expense of political maturity and experience.

THEORETICAL DISCUSSIONS OF REFORM

The assault on the cult of personality at the CPSU congresses in 1956 and 1961 had created, as Michal Lakatoš later put it, "a new atmosphere of thought" in which "analyses of certain conceptual questions of the political management of society began to appear" and in spite of initial resistance "won some room for themselves."[35] As Mlynář phrased it, "with the criticism of the cult of personality, people began critically to investigate the real existence and the real social functioning of the forms of the democratic system." The prospect was for a long-term struggle of two tendencies, one creating the possibility of a greater freedom of man, and the other, of limiting man and his creative powers.[36]

The official endorsement of the doctrine of the all-people's state and

[34] *RP*, Nov. 4, 1965.
[35] M. Lakatoš, *Občan, právo a demokracie* (Prague, 1966), p. 10.
[36] Z. Mlynář, *Stát a člověk* (Prague, 1964), pp. 172, 187.

of the notion of expanding socialist democracy had in fact encouraged and legitimized a far-reaching discussion of the political system. The reforms introduced, although circumscribed and piecemeal, and not changing the essential character of the political system, stimulated re-examination of specific institutions and their continuing defects and of ways to improve their operation. In particular the introduction of the new economic system prompted the idea that a more adequate political system was equally necessary and required the same kind of rational study that had been devoted to economic reform.[37] The discussion that occurred from 1964 on, even though restricted by censorship, left almost no important question untouched and dealt, for instance, with guarantees of the rights of citizens, limits on state power, the restoration of legality, independence of the courts, and the revival of public opinion. There was a much more objective treatment of bourgeois political systems, and a genuinely comparative analysis of features common to all systems, such as the problem of expertness in a democracy, or the role of interest groups. The Soviet system was no longer treated as the only viable model and its defects during the Stalinist period were sharply criticized. Even more startling, the Yugoslav pattern was openly and sympathetically studied.

A summary of these deliberations, in which Mlynář and Lakatoš played leading roles, can only bring out certain salient features relevant to our principal interest.[38] The participants took the values proclaimed by the regime, such as the deepening of democracy or the broadening of participation, as a starting point for the advocacy of reforms which often went beyond the intentions of the leadership. There was, of course, considerable difference of view, even among scholars in the field of state and law, and still more between scholars and official ideologists.[39]

[37] P. Peška, "The Future of Constitutional Law and of Constitutionalism," *Právník* 105, no. 5 (1966), 407-19.

[38] The following analysis will be based primarily on two books by Lakatoš (*Občan, právo a demokracie*) and Mlynář (*Stát a člověk*) and many articles by them from 1964 to 1966. Mlynář's book was completed in early 1964 and published later in the same year; Lakatoš's work was written in 1964 but published only in 1966. Mlynář, as secretary of the CC's Legal Commission, tended to justify official policies, but was often unorthodox and critical. His articles frequently appeared in party organs, *Rudé právo, Nová mysl*, and *Kulturní tvorba*, as well as in journals such as *Literární noviny* and, in one significant case, in the world communist journal, *Problémy míra i sotsializma*. Cf. his relatively orthodox exposition in chap. 12, *Základy vědeckého komunizmu*, 2nd ed. (Bratislava, 1968), originally published in 1965. Lakatoš, his colleague in the Institute of State and Law, held no official position and was more prone to criticize the existing system. His articles did not appear in party organs, except in Bratislava *Pravda*, but mainly in legal journals, especially *Právny obzor*.

[39] A prominent participant was the legal specialist, František Šamalík, whose book *Člověk a instituce* (Prague, 1968), was a theoretical study of the "paradox of modern democracy," drawing widely on Western sources and on the ideas of

Common to most contributions was a severe critique of the political model developed under Stalin and transplanted to Czechoslovakia and other East European communist states. The chief faults of this system were explained in terms not only of personal factors but also of objective forces, such as Russian backwardness, the negative effects of rapid industrialization and collectivization, and Stalin's distortion of Leninist doctrines.[40] The concept of the dictatorship of the proletariat, appropriate as it may have been in the struggle for power of the earlier period, had, it was argued, laid exclusive emphasis on class conflict and on the coercive aspects of government. All other forms of conflict, between the individual and the state, or between rival groups, were regarded as "counterrevolutionary" and dealt with by administrative means. As a result, the rule of law and the rights of the individual had been ignored and later completely abolished. A highly centralized bureaucratic system of administration had developed, subordinating the representative bodies and the mass associations, and even the government and the state administration, to the paramount will of the party leadership. The security organs had come to occupy a supreme position from which they could subjugate the individual and the whole of society, including even the party. This in turn had produced fear, general apathy, and passivity among the citizenry.

In the intervening years a transformation of society had taken place which required appropriate changes in political life. Class conflict had ceased to be the decisive factor, but other conflicts, including those between interest groups, constituted an essential feature of politics. A new political system was needed which would shift the balance from coercion to persuasion and would establish democratic procedures for reconciling conflicting interests. In Lakatoš's words, the state would become, not "a

---

the Italian Marxist, Antonio Gramsci. See also his study of law and society, *Právo a společnost* (Prague, 1965), and his chapter on the "political management of society" in Miloslav Král, ed., *Věda a řízení společnosti* (Prague, 1967). Among many articles by other specialists, see two by members of the Mlynář team, P. Pithart and I. Bystřina, *LN*, Nov. 12 and Dec. 17, 1966, resp. For a discussion of the implications of economic reform for political procedures, see the symposium in which leading economists and jurists participated, in *Právník* 103, nos. 6 and 7 (1964), 548-61, 635-63. The conclusions concerning political change were relatively modest, and some saw no need for any serious changes. Another important symposium, drawing more radical conclusions as to the need for expanded democracy, was devoted to the theme of "democracy and expertness in management," ibid. 104, nos. 5, 6, 7 (1965), 446-57, 552-61, 625-44, resp. Other major articles on political reform published in *Právník* included Mlynář, 104, no. 5 (1965), 397-412 (a critique of past "deformation"); J. Boguszak and Z. Jičínský, 105, no. 1 (1966), 1-9 (on the democratic control of bureaucracy, including workers' participation in management); Boguszak and Jičínský, 105, no. 5 (1966), 393-406 (on the separation of powers); Mlynář, 106, no. 10 (1967), 928-42 (in French, in *L'homme et la société*, no. 9, July-Aug.-Sept. 1968, pp. 91-112).

[40] Mlynář, *Stát*, pp. 49-52. Cf. his article in *RP*, April 6, 1965.

mere executor of orders directed to the defense of all-social interests" but "an active organ capable of coordinating these interest conflicts and shaping, under the pressure of these group interests, the interests of society as a whole" (*Občan*, p. 117). This would require broader popular participation in government, especially through the representative organs, so as to assure the citizens a part in "the formation of the will of society." Previous legislative practice had been to a large degree "formal," "a holiday affair" (p. 84). "The formation of will, expressed in law," he wrote, "represents a complicated process which must overcome conflicts between the will of the individual, of the group and of the whole society, conflicts between local and general interests, between central and local management, etc." (p. 62). He urged that the representative bodies must be created "by means of a free choice of people as candidates" (p. 62) and sharply criticized the existing electoral system (pp. 138-39). The citizen must be assured the possibility of "choosing, in accordance with his social-political interests, the person who is capable, in his opinion, of defending these interests" (p. 33).

Mlynář also argued that the representative organs must "guarantee the confrontation of varied interests and needs of social groups, strata and individuals, so that in a democratic way, the binding general social interest, 'the state will,' would be formulated" (*Stát*, p. 143). Both he and Lakatoš expressed considerable sympathy with the Yugoslav multichamber legislative system as an appropriate way of guaranteeing adequate group representation.[41] Both also advocated that the mass associations become genuine interest groups, "the institutionalized expression of group interests," in Lakatoš's words (*Občan*, p. 108). Neither, however, saw much to be gained by the transfer of political functions to these organizations (*Občan*, p. 79; *Stát*, pp. 60-61).

Much attention was devoted to the question of "expertness" in modern government and the relationship between the technical and the democratic aspects of decision-making. How could the specialized elite be assured an adequate influence on policy-making and yet be subjected to effective control? The solution was to be found in part in a representative system on the Yugoslav model, in which the experience and knowledge of those involved in each sphere would be applied to decision-making; in part it was to be found in the use of specialists in the commissions of the representative organs, and of party and government, and in consultation with scholars and specialists of all kinds. It was also found in the participation of the working people in management, i.e. self-management (*samospráva*), exercised through factory councils or industrial commit-

[41] Mlynář, *Stát*, pp. 147-59; Lakatoš, *Občan*, pp. 102-5, 116-19, 140-41. Cf. Mlynář, *LN*, Feb. 8, 1964 and Jan. 16, 1965.

tees.[42] Moreover, discussion should be free and controversial among scholars and public alike, allowing full examination of alternative solutions for a given problem.

Scholarly dialogues could not, of course, question the dominant position of the Communist Party in the political system, but could, and did, discuss it with unusual frankness. Mlynář regarded the party, in the epoch of the all-people's state, as "a vanguard" of the whole of society, "a special social organism whose mission is . . . to defend all-society needs, and which *therefore* has also a leading political position" (*Stát*, pp. 64-67). As he expressed it elsewhere, the leading role of the party was not achieved "once and for all by a single act or organizational form," but must be "constantly re-formed by the practical policies of the party."[43] Unfortunately this had been affected by the methods introduced during the cult of personality, when the party had become "a disciplined 'political elite,' directed in breach of Leninist democratic norms" (*Stát*, pp. 180 ff.). This conception continued to influence the political system harmfully and hindered the fulfillment of the party's role as the guarantor of an "active public."

Lakatoš interpreted the leading role of the party as organizing the all-society will on the basis of an understanding of the conflicting individual and group wills, through the medium of "science" and the free exchange of opinions (*Občan*, pp. 57-59). As he put it elsewhere, "the party as the leading and directing political force fulfills its function by resolving intra-class and inter-class interests."[44] In the USSR during the cult pe-

[42] Neither Mlynář nor Lakatoš devoted attention to this idea in their books, but it was widely discussed by leading scholars, e.g. in the two symposia in *Právník*, cited above, n. 39. In the first symposium, with a few exceptions, there were only general references to the desirability of workers' participation in management, without specific proposals. See, however, F. Šamalík (103, p. 557) and Karel Witz (103, p. 660). In the second, however, there were more frequent and specific references to self-management (*samospráva*), participation of the "collective" in management, "factory councils," and "industrial committees." See in particular P. Machonin (104, p. 555); K. Bertelmann (104, p. 557); D. Slejška (104, pp. 636-38); and A. Pfeifer (104, pp. 641, 643).

In 1967, *Právník* published a symposium devoted exclusively to this theme, with an introductory report by Mlynář (106, no. 1, 1967, 61-81). Mlynář proposed participation in management through organs with "decision-making," not merely consultative, competence. These would be linked with the political representative system along Yugoslav lines. Lakatoš was sharply critical of the "theses" of the conference and advocated independent organs acting separately from the trade unions (pp. 69-72). See also the defense of "self-management" exercised through an elected council of the whole "working collective," to which the enterprise manager would be responsible in matters relating to material conditions, R. Kocanda, *Plánované hospodářství* 20, no. 10 (1967), 12-24.

[43] Mlynář, *Věda a život*, no. 1 (1965).

[44] Lakatoš, *Právny obzor*, no. 1 (1965), pp. 34-35.

149

riod, and to a significant degree in Czechoslovakia as well, the leading role of the party had been implemented through "an enormous professional 'aparát' for the directive management of the economy and a political aparát which . . . became authoritative in the highest degree." This aparát, especially the security forces, escaped the control even of the highest party organs and often became a conservative force blocking the introduction of new methods of management. Similar massive aparáts, under party control, dominated the societal organizations. The only escape from this situation was "the construction of a political system which would be able to subordinate the aparát to those social forces which rule in this society and to assure effective social control" (Občan, pp. 128-30).

The possibility of a genuine multi-party system or an institutionalized form of opposition was seldom raised publicly. Out of a sense of realism, if not of conviction, it was assumed that reform of the political system must occur within the framework of a single dominant party. When, in the metaphysical language of the Marxian dialectic, Július Strinka, a Slovak philosopher, suggested the need for an institutionalized opposition, his proposal was at once condemned. Strinka had referred to the danger of the atrophy of power if "integrated power and integrated directing activity is only faced by disintegrated, scattered criticism of this power." "Thus the paradoxical situation may arise that in a society which is almost bubbling over with criticism, in which criticism is even officially encouraged, no criticism actually exists." The only solution for the situation was to confront "integrated power" by "integrated criticism," i.e. to establish "definite institutional guarantees" which would assure "timely and effective, socially constructive criticism."[45] This novel analysis was a plea presumably not for the creation of an opposition party or movement but for a greater opportunity for criticism within the party and within the political system as a whole. His argument was countered, without specific reference to Strinka, by his fellow philosopher, M. Kusý, who rejected the notion of an "institutionalized opposition" other than that which was exercised by the Communist Party itself.[46] An official ideologue went further and, citing Strinka's article, described integrated criticism as an oppositional ideological movement contrary to the leading role of the party.[47]

Lakatoš, writing in newspapers and weeklies, and in the Slovak legal

---

[45] His article, entitled "Reticent Dogmatism and Revolutionary Dialectics," was published in shortened form in KŽ, Nov. 6, 1965, and in full in Filozofia, no. 1 (1966), pp. 82-88. The full text also appeared in the Croatian monthly, Nase Teme, no. 12 (Dec. 1965).

[46] Predvoj, Feb. 24, 1966.

[47] M. Marko, NM, no. 24, Nov. 29, 1966, p. 2.

journals, expounded his ideas before a wider audience,[48] and in a book, destined not to be published until after the occupation, developed the notion of "opposition" in a novel way. He rejected the idea of a restoration of a multi-party system and suggested that the quest for an improved system must be based on the existing state of affairs, i.e. the absence of political parties of the parliamentary type, and the existence of the Communist Party as the leading force which exclusively formulated state policy.[49] Nonetheless, the party required a legal platform for "opposition," he stated in his book, because opposition would otherwise exist de facto and "outside and against the political system," and democracy would be endangered. Distinguishing two types of opposition, he argued that although the political order did not allow the legality of "basic opposition," seeking a change in the system, it should permit, and indeed required, "an opposition operating on the basis of the social political system." Such an "oponentura" should exist within the party, in the form of "a clash of opinions," and in the system as a whole, especially through the proposal of alternative courses by the non-state social organizations and within the representative organs. "For a civil society the possibility of an opposition is the possibility to express conflicting interests and to reconcile these conflicts democratically."[50]

There was no public repudiation of either the more circumspect but critical ideas of Mlynář, or the more radical ones of Lakatoš, but orthodox ideologists, such as Pavel Auersperg, then head of the CC Ideological Department, entered serious reservations. He criticized those who cast doubt on the leading role of the working class in the transition to the all-people's state.[51] The decisive force was the working class; their interests had become the interests and requirements of society as a whole. Conflicts between individual, group, and society's interests must be reconciled only on the basis of socialist principles. The role of the individual was important but was best expressed through the societal organizations and not in antagonism to them. Differences of opinion should be expressed but only in conjunction with unity, discipline, and democratic centralism. Incorrect opinions, such as the demands of some workers for equalization of wages, or of some intellectuals expressing "wrong liberalistic views with a certain touch of opposition," as well as sectarian views,

[48] Lakatoš, *LN*, July 15, 1967; *PO*, no. 2 (1967), pp. 110-18; *Pravda*, April 1, 1967.

[49] *PO*, p. 115.

[50] *Úvahy o hodnotách demokracie* (Prague, 1968), chap. 4, final quotation at p. 87. The idea of an "*oponentura*," in the sense of contests and differences of opinion, was endorsed by Josef Smrkovský, but he rejected "opposition" in the sense of "fundamental disagreement" with the party (*LN*, Sept. 15, 1967). For the term *oponentura* see above, chap. IV, n. 108.

[51] *NM*, no. 3, Feb. 8, 1966, pp. 3-7.

were condemned. The further development of democracy, he said, was sometimes "abused by individuals, groups, and by some organizations or their organs in an attempt to place partial and minority interests above the requirements of society as a whole." The all-people's state toward which society was tending must not be regarded as a return to bourgeois democracy nor a restoration of non-socialist relations.

Similarly, Jan Fojtík, in a series of articles in the party daily on "the meaning of the activity of the Communist Party," repudiated the cult of personality and dogmatism, but even more sharply condemned "liberalism" and "abstract humanism." Recognizing the pluralism of different interests, Fojtík rejected the idea of several parties or a parliamentary system, or of opposition as an end in itself, and emphasized the role of the party as "an integrating force which keeps watch over the harmony of social interests and the interests of individuals and groups." "However, if the party is to carry out this task, it must possess certain powers which would give it the right to control societal institutions and organizations from this standpoint and . . . permit authoritative intervention in case the social interest is in danger."[52]

The Thirteenth Party Congress

The Central Committee at its August 1965 plenum announced the convocation of the 13th congress of the party on May 31, 1966. During the subsequent months attention was concentrated on preparations for this meeting, especially on the discussion of the Theses published in December.[53] The congress proceedings and its major documents, however, contained no surprises and proposed no significant reforms or changes in policy.[54]

In fact the purpose of the congress was said to be to elaborate the line of the 12th congress which had been correct and needed no essential revision. The main target continued to be "the building and the development of socialist society," which was described as long-term and exception-

[52] *RP*, June 29, July 7, 13, and 20, 1967. The quotation is taken from the final article. Cf. the more sophisticated article in the government-controlled *Literární noviny* by J. Kučera (Nov. 11, 1967), who criticized the discussion of specialized matters of politics in an emotional manner by nonspecialists, as by certain writers. See his elaboration of the idea of "rationalizing" democracy through more effective organizational and informational mechanisms (ibid., Dec. 2) and V. Solecký's support of his position (ibid., Nov. 25, Dec. 9). Mlynář responded sharply, asserting the responsibility of politicians and experts to those whose interests were affected by their decisions (ibid., Dec. 9).

[53] Text, *RP*, Dec. 23, 1965.

[54] For documents, including the Theses, see *XIII. sjezd Komunistické strany Československa* (Prague, 1966). A fuller collection was published under the same title (Prague, 1967).

ally complicated and "a necessary first stage in the future development of communism." "The state of the dictatorship of the working class had fulfilled its main historic mission but its gradual change into a state of the whole people . . . could not avoid the necessary intermediate stages of development." "We are only at the beginning of this evolution," read the Theses.[55] There was the usual reference in the Theses to the fact that the class struggle had "permanently lost its domestic economic base." In Novotný's words, it was "not the main motive force."[56] Nonetheless, classes still existed, even though they were not antagonistic, and the international class conflict was a decisive reality. The leading force in society remained the working class, especially its "progressive core," although the process of differentiation had produced a variety of conflicting interests and even within the working class, as Novotný admitted, there was a backward section. The congress decision stressed that although the interests of different classes and groups must be considered, individual and group interests must not be placed above the interests of the whole society.[57]

These assumptions concerning the development of society led to no significant conclusions about the political system. The development of "socialist democracy" was analyzed in familiar terms as though this had already been achieved or was well on the way to completion. Novotný spoke of "the beginning of significant changes," not only in the methods of management, but in economic thinking and economic policy. These changes went beyond the sphere of economics and were part of the effort to "render the management of the whole of our society scientific" and would lead to a deepening of socialist democracy.[58] Yet apart from the expansion of the role of the national committees, which he described as the key question, there was not a single proposal adopted for political reform. On the contrary, Novotný warned: "We shall in no case broaden

[55] *XIII. sjezd KSČ* (1966), pp. 5-7, 31. There was criticism of views of "the unlimited possibilities of socialism without regard to its state of development and real conditions" and of "tendencies to exaggerate the level of development achieved, to skip stages and to set goals for the attainment of which the conditions had not yet ripened." It was argued that "the first stage of the building of the new society, the phase of socialism, will be essentially longer in time than was generally believed." See the document "On the Development of our Society and the Work of the Party Between the 12th and 13th Congresses of the CPCz," *XIII. sjezd KSČ* (1967), p. 807.

[56] *XIII. sjezd KSČ* (1966), pp. 29, 82, resp. The idea that the dictatorship of the proletariat was "obsolete" and that the class struggle was "slackening" was criticized, after the occupation, as incorrect (Jiří Hájek, *Mýtus a realita ledna 1968*, Prague, 1970, pp. 18-20, 22-24). Husák also later criticized the underestimation of the class conflict and the "premature orientation on the all-people's state" (*Pravda* [Moscow], April 15, 1970).

[57] *XIII. sjezd KSČ* (1966), pp. 8, 83, 403.

[58] Ibid., p. 75.

democracy for its own sake (*samoúčelně*), merely for the sake of democracy. For us it is a matter of developing socialist democracy of such a kind that presumes a unified organized approach and a system of purposeful direction. Therefore, socialist democracy is inconsistent with social irresponsibility, liberalistic arbitrariness, spontaneity, or the most varied anarchistic ideas and dogmatic rigidity." Nor could democracy be permitted to be abused for introducing bourgeois ideology and morality.[59] In harmony with this approach, the congress documents proclaimed a war against both liberalism and dogmatism, and certain wrong views were singled out for condemnation.[60] An integral element of this conception was the familiar accent on the leadership of the party. Novotný urged "the deepening of the leading role of the party in all spheres of social life, in politics, economics and ideology," and the perfection of its "cognitive, directing, and organizing function."[61] Its role in the economic sphere was reasserted as involving a "political approach," which would avoid both the tendency to replace the economic organs and the tendency to neglect economic questions.

There were no significant proposals for reform in the party's structure or activity.[62] During the congress the work of the Central Committee and its commissions was praised and there was no suggestion of any need for improvement. The party statutes adopted in 1962 were regarded as satisfactory and were amended in relatively minor ways.[63] In the preamble, there was a renewed emphasis on the leading role of the party which was said to be responsible for "elaborating, on the basis of a scientific analysis, the program and the fundamental conception of development of socialist society and for winning the working people to support its policy

[59] Ibid., p. 85.

[60] Demands for a "so-called scientific *oponentura*" or for an opposition party, and ideas of a return to democracy of a bourgeois type, were said to have been voiced during the pre-congress discussion of the Theses, especially among students, and were, of course, condemned (*XIII. sjezd KSČ*, 1967, p. 745). For other references to "wrong ideas," see ibid., pp. 738-47 passim, 781. Hendrych, in an earlier article, had referred to doubts concerning the role of the party in the economy and to demands for the autonomy of certain fields, such as culture (*RP*, Jan. 9, 1966). Elsewhere he had referred to attempts to distort or "castrate" the principle of democratic centralism (*NM*, no. 1, Jan. 11, 1966, p. 18). Although dogmatic or sectarian views were also criticized at the congress, only one speaker, O. Voleník from North Moravia, made them the main target of attack (*XIII. sjezd KSČ*, 1966, pp. 200-201).

[61] *XIII. sjezd KSČ* (1966), p. 66.

[62] V. Slavík later revealed that some party organizations had raised demands for the separation of the functions of the presidency and the first secretaryship, but no hint of this appeared in the published proceedings (*ŽS*, no. 12, 1968, p. 6). O. Voleník spoke of "reform" proposals submitted by the North Moravian party organization (*RP*, April 18, 1968).

[63] For the text of the amended statute, *XIII. sjezd KSČ* (1966), pp. 417-41. See also Novotný's speech, ibid., p. 99. For commentaries, see Jan Svoboda, *RP*, March 17, 1966; V. Bernard, *NM*, no. 10, May 17, 1966, pp. 17-18.

by the daily persuasive and organizing work of communists." In later articles even greater stress was placed on the responsibilities of party members, party groups, and all party organizations for implementing party policy and on discipline in accord with the traditional principle of democratic centralism. In cadre policy, there was explicit reference to "technical knowledge, organizing ability, and practical experience," as well as "political maturity."

The only substantive change was designed to facilitate entry into the party, namely, the abolition of the one-year period of candidacy. This might in theory have led to a substantial increase in party ranks, but was hardly likely to change the composition of membership decisively. Novotný's report proclaimed the necessity to strengthen the working class core of the party, but also to admit more cooperative farmers, intellectuals, and especially young workers—all injunctions often heard in previous years.[64] At the time of the congress the total membership had risen slightly (by 40,000), from 1962, to a total of 1,698,000, representing 17.2 percent of the total population 18 years or over. The data published on this occasion indicated that the ranks had changed but little and were still primarily working class in origin (62.5 percent).[65] According to present occupation, workers (including agricultural workers) constituted 33 percent of the membership, engineering-technical personnel and economic officials had risen from 14.6 percent in 1962 to 17 percent. The number of scientific, artistic, and cultural workers, together with teachers, professors, and students, was only 4.9 percent. As in the past, cooperative farmers were few—only 5.4 percent. The party was also relatively old and poorly educated. Forty-six percent were over 45 years of age; only 27 percent were 35 years or under. Those with an elementary education represented 70 percent; those with some university education only 5.9 percent.

The professional functionaries and leading personalities of the party presented a somewhat similar picture of a group of long-time members, mostly proletarian in origin, elderly, and often poorly educated. Members of the Central Committee were mainly proletarian in original employment (54.8 percent); those who had been white-collar workers were 12.7 percent; those who came from the intelligentsia had risen from 16.3 to 22.9 percent since 1962. In terms of current occupation, over 60 percent of the CC were functionaries of party, state, mass associations, or of the army and police. The majority were over 45 years old, and 83 percent had been party members since before 1948. About 50 percent had

[64] *XIII. sjezd KSČ* (1966), p. 99.

[65] *XIII. sjezd KSČ* (1967), pp. 909 ff., with tables at pp. 938 ff. See also Hendrych's report to the Central Committee, ibid., pp. 560-65, and *ŽS*, no. 18, Sept. 21, 1966, pp. 9, 11, 14, 21; *RP*, June 21 and July 12, 1966.

had some university education, including training at the higher party schools in Moscow or in Prague. The broader category of functionaries in CC offices, the Slovak CC and the regional and district committees, some 4,751 in number, were overwhelmingly proletarian in origin (77.6 percent), and proletarian in their original employment (72.8 percent). The social composition (present occupation) of regional and district committee members corresponded to that of CC members. Over 60 percent in each case were administrators in party, state, and other associations, or in industry and agriculture; only about 20 percent were workers; 12 to 13 percent were technical, professional, and cultural workers. These data, if reliable, suggest that neither the party members nor the officials were likely to favor political reform that would increase the role of the educated, or lower the prestige of the working class, or even less, to contemplate any diminution in the power of the apparatus, or of the party, on which their careers depended.

RESPONSE AT HIGHER LEVELS

Ota Šik alone, at the 13th congress, raised the question of the need for far-reaching political reform comparable to that being introduced in the economic field. By the next party congress, he urged, there should be "a deep analysis of the whole problem of democracy in the relations within the entire political and directing sphere" and the submission of appropriate proposals for change. Inner party democracy should also be further developed. There would be, he realized, as in the economic sphere, "conservative resistance and struggle against all new and unusual ideas." Yet the party could "maintain its leading position and strengthen its authority" only if it undertook a progressive solution of the problems that had developed.[66] His suggestion followed logically from the economic reforms adopted by the party, both in the sense that the diminution of the centralized and authoritarian procedures of planning and management required corresponding political adjustments, including greater popular participation in decision-making, but also in the sense that the economic reforms could only be fully and successfully implemented if the continuing opposition of vested interests and conservative forces was weakened by measures of political reform.

The party leadership, as we have seen, tolerated the critical examination of the political system and encouraged the study of an improved political model. Yet the atmosphere which the 13th congress created was not favorable to experiments in the political realm, and the readiness for such actions of Novotný and his ideological spokesmen was minimal.

[66] *XIII. sjezd KSČ* (1967), p. 543.

The tenor of official pronouncements continued to be hard and orthodox. For example, Hendrych, in an interview in March 1967, reasserted the leading role of the party as expressed not merely in its "generally political task," but also in its control, organizational, and cadre functions.[67]

In spite of repeated asseverations of the desirability of "deepening socialist democracy," almost no significant measure to implement this principle was introduced. The modification of the people's control commissions in early 1967 did not diminish the party's control of these bodies and in fact, by assigning the election of the commissions at the lower levels to the trade union membership and to the national committees respectively, rather than to the workers and the general public, reduced the direct participation of the masses.[68] A further reform of the national committees was designed to increase their independence from higher bodies, extend their competence at the municipal and district level, and to expand public participation in their work, but did not in reality decrease party and government control.[69] Only in regard to the electoral system was a modest step taken in the direction of democratization. By a law ultimately approved in November 1967, the procedures for the elections to the national committees and the National Assembly (which were postponed to May and November 1968 respectively), were altered to provide a somewhat wider choice by the voters. Multi-member constituencies were introduced so as to guarantee representation of the main social groups. There were to be some 30 percent more candidates than seats to be filled, although the selection of candidates was to be in the hands of the National Front organizations. The voters would also select alternates, who would automatically take up seats that became vacant. The elections to the National Assembly would be separated in time from those to the national committees and the courts. Štefan Sádovský, in introducing this proposal to the Central Committee in September, described it as an important widening of socialist democracy but made clear that it would in no way diminish the leading role of the party in all stages of the elections, expressed in "political directives both from the standpoint of cadres and substantive aspects of the elections."[70]

Yet certain leading party spokesmen were expressing, necessarily in an indirect way, viewpoints that appear, especially in retrospect, to reflect a different approach. In an important article in the party's central

[67] *ŽS*, no. 6 (March 1967), p. 4.
[68] *Sb. z.*, 21/1967.
[69] *Sb. z.*, 69/1967. See also *RP*, July 20, 1967; J. Kudrna, *Národní výbory* (Aug. 1967), pp. 2-6.
[70] *RP*, Sept. 29, 1967; also Sádovský, *NM*, no. 24, Nov. 28, 1967, pp. 3-6. For laws, *Sb. z.*, 113, 114/1967. See also Slavík (*RP*, Oct. 4, 1967) on the contribution of the Institute of Political Science to this measure and proposed research on further improvement of electoral procedures.

theoretical organ, the Slovak leader, Dubček, referred to the "key importance" of "basic and organically linked changes in the politics of the party" in all spheres, and urged the responsibility of all communists, not just those in the party's organs and *aparát*, to promote this forward movement. The decisive factor, he argued, was "the struggle of old and new." It was a question of "strengthening the new progressive tendencies and their development and expansion in the whole of society." He later referred to the difference between people who "understood the new and will be its determined protagonists," and those who "do not understand the time and stand still" and "some who, in their own way, adopt a reactionary stance against the basic tendencies of development." Dubček also termed scientific and technical knowledge as the basis of success and praised the role of the intelligentsia "whose creative activity is an indispensable component of all further advance." Political management must be founded on competence ("he who wishes to direct a given sector must be competent") and on "the possibility of the choice of the most suitable alternative." Work in the realm of ideas must be founded on "the scientific objective findings of history, economics, philosophy, sociology, and other social sciences." The new conditions required "a new political approach," he concluded. Unity and discipline were necessary, but the main method of party guidance must be "persuasion," not "administrative methods."[71]

Somewhat more guardedly, but by implication quite clearly, Josef Špaček, leading secretary in South Moravia, in the same journal, wrote of the weaknesses of past party methods, which had given rise to passivity and feelings of impotence among members.[72] Dissatisfaction could not be treated as a mere reflection of a low ideological level or of hostile propaganda; it could be dissipated only if the leading organs listened to proposals and developed a program to correct the main defects. There was no contradiction between the development of democracy and the leading role of the party, since the latter was precisely the instrument for the development of socialist democracy. The working class remained the leading class, but this did not mean that it should replace "the specific mission of the intelligentsia to be the bearer of science and technology, and of expert management of the economy and of other specific processes

[71] *NM*, no. 4, Feb. 21, 1967, pp. 6-10. Cf. his speech at the CPS Central Committee, *Pravda*, May 30, 1967.

[72] *NM*, no. 13, June 27, 1967, pp. 3-6. Other party ideologists expressed their views indirectly by laying emphasis on the weaknesses of past party work and on the urgency of new methods for the exercise of the party's leading role. See M. Kusý's contribution to a party seminar in Bratislava in May 1967, the proceedings of which were published as *Dynamika sociálnej štruktúry v ČSSR* (Bratislava, 1968), pp. 214-36. Cf. articles by M. Láb, *NM*, no. 14, July 11, 1967, pp. 3-7; *ŽS*, no. 15, July 1967, pp. 16-21; F. Srdinko, *NM*, no. 23, Nov. 14, 1967, pp. 3-7.

in society." Nor must "the party as the leading force" in society be confused with "the working class as the ruling force." "The party leads society, but does not itself represent the power of the working class, nor does it, through its organs, replace it. The system of political organization of socialist society consists of the party, the state and the non-state societal organizations, and the tasks of each of these components are given by the objectively existing relations in society."

The Writers' Congress in the early summer of 1967 produced, as we have noted in an earlier chapter, an outburst of critical discussion of the general situation in the country and of the failure of the party to deal adequately with the crucial problems of society. A high point was the speech by Ludvík Vaculík who bitterly condemned the abuse of power by those in authority, and the vassalage to which citizens had been reduced. In his scathing remarks, he sharply criticized the constitution and the neglect of the rights of citizens embodied in that document. He observed no real autonomy in the cultural field and no guarantees for the citizen's freedom. "An uncultured policy," he said, "does not understand that freedom exists only where one does not have to speak about it. It is annoyed because people talk about what they see; yet instead of changing what people see, it always wants to change their eyes. And in the meantime we are losing what alone is worth all the pathos, namely the dream of a government identical with the citizen, the dream of a citizen who governs himself almost alone. Is this dream realizable?" His answer, he concluded, was: "I do not know."[73]

The reaction of Novotný to this open defiance and to other more guarded challenges was predictable and followed stereotyped lines. At the end of June he declared that the objective was "the development of socialist democracy with a class tendency and with a struggle against all ideologies which oppose communist views. In this matter we shall agree to no compromises. And all who do not recognize this stand on the other side." "The leading role of the party," he declared, "is and will remain the standard principle of the life of socialist society. If we were to permit any weakening whatever of this principle it would cause only harm to our people. . . . We decidedly do not imagine its leading role only as an educational influence on the working people, or only as supervision. The party acts and will act as the leading, directing force in all spheres of social life without exception, beginning with the national economy and including the fields of ideology, culture, and art."[74]

Several months later he reiterated his warning—"Democracy and free-

[73] Text, *IV. sjezd Svazu československých spisovatelů* (*Protokol*) (Prague, 1968), pp. 141-51.
[74] *RP*, July 1, 1967.

dom . . . have their limits, given by the fact that in a socialist state the propagation of opinions and ideologies harmful to socialism and hostile to the Communist Party may not be permitted. Our democracy is a class democracy; our freedom is a class freedom." As for those who think of themselves as directing "some kind of process of revival in our society and in our Communist Party," he admonished: "Only the communist party—and not this or that group, which fancies itself—is called upon to follow and to direct the social process and in case of need to correct inadequacies and errors which may appear in the development of our society."[75]

[75] *RP*, Sept. 2, 1967.

CHAPTER VI

The Fall of Novotný

THE FALL of Novotný came as a surprise both to the general public and to the party membership. During fifteen years of rule he had shown an extraordinary capacity to survive. Although unable to resort to extreme measures of terror in the later years, he surmounted repeated crises and continued to govern by employing administrative coercion and manipulation, coupled with piecemeal and reluctant concessions. The regime enjoyed substantial support, primarily in the apparatus, but also in the army and police, the people's militia, the state bureaucracy, and even among the broad masses. Neither the workers nor the peasants evinced active dissent, nor did the Slovaks as a whole, nor the Slovak party, openly resist Prague rule. Above all, Soviet endorsement, avowed or implicit, buttressed the position of Novotný and made his removal, without Soviet consent, difficult. This support did not rest on the stationing of Soviet troops, but on the presence of Soviet advisers, or trustworthy Czech and Slovak party functionaries, at focal points throughout the administrative system. In the last analysis, however, wrote one of the regime's sharpest critics, Novotný lasted so long because he was in fact accepted by most of the people, despite widespread discontent and dissent in certain circles. Everyone was responsible, he said, for accepting "the authority of the office . . . , untouchable and all-powerful," even though it was occupied by "a fool."[1]

Having sought to maintain a form of Stalinism intact, long after its modification in the Soviet Union, Novotný began in the sixties to yield to pressures, both Soviet and domestic, for de-Stalinization, while at the same time resisting demands at home for a more accelerated advance and often back-tracking from steps already taken. As one of his supporters later put it, Novotný's policy was characterized by "absolute half-measures, and by the ambiguity and relativization of all political principles and measures," thus producing great dissatisfaction and general disillusionment.[2] Economic difficulties had been partly faced, but the proposed

---

[1] L. Mňačko, "Who Elected Novotný for Us?" *Kultúrny život*, July 26, 1968. See also Galia Golan, "Antonin Novotný: The Sources and Nature of His Power," *Canadian Slavonic Papers* 14 (Autumn 1972), 421-41.

[2] Jiří Hájek (the writer), in his post-occupation book, *Mýtus a realita ledna 1968* (Prague, 1970), pp. 25-26. According to a pseudonymous post-occupation critic, Novotný was filled with fear of criticism, of new ideas and of change; his regime was "a peculiar hodge-podge of hardness and 'liberalism'" (A. Ostrý, *Československý problém*, Cologne, 1972, pp. 13, 18-21).

reform was a compromise and its implementation still hung in the balance. Intellectual dissent had been smothered by coercive actions and by lip service to greater freedom for culture and scholarship, but had not been eliminated. The Slovak question had been dampened down by the removal of the most disliked leaders and by partial rehabilitations, but this was linked with a ban on all discussion of federation or fundamental reform. The apathy and resentment of youth had been met by administrative controls and limited concessions. The need for political reforms was recognized in words, but no real improvements in procedures or institutions were made. Basically the entire system remained unaltered, but it was weakened, rather than strengthened, by this combination of coercion and concessions. To use the telling phrases of a critic, Stalinism, as a system, "existed but no longer functioned" and was "not only feeble but helpless, writhing amid the contradictions between the ambitions of its chief exponent and its genuine prospects of success."[3]

There ensued the long, slow decline of the power and prestige of the regime, which, however, obstinately resisted the forces of change. At last, in 1967, with the writers' congress and the Strahov events acting as catalysts, the accumulation of discontents penetrated the topmost organs of the party and hence created the conditions for the removal of Novotný and the termination of his system of personal power. The opportunity came unexpectedly, and without concerted planning, at meetings of the Central Committee and the Presidium beginning in the fall of 1967. Largely unknown to the general public, and known only in limited and distorted form to party members, a furious controversy, unique in the history of these bodies, raged at the CC sessions at the end of October, in late December and in early January 1968, and in the intervening meetings of the Presidium.[4]

[3] Radoslav Selucký, *Czechoslovakia: The Plan that failed* (London, 1970), pp. 85-86.

[4] Nothing is known with certainty about the Presidium sessions. The minutes of the CC plena, some 1,500 pages long, have not been published. On March 4, 1968, two months after the change of leadership, the Presidium issued for party use a rather bland nineteen-page summary of the main issues of the discussion, but did not identify the position taken by individual CC members. This was published only in 1969 in a collection of decisions and documents relating to 1968, *Rok šedesátý osmý v usneseních a dokumentech ÚV KSČ* (Prague, 1969), pp. 7-25; henceforth cited as *RŠO*.

A fuller report of the CC plena, based on the minutes and citing some speakers briefly, was published in a series of articles, "What Happened in January?" by V. Mencl and F. Ouředník, in *Život strany*, nos. 14-19 (July, Aug., and Sept. 1968). Excerpts are given in R. A. Remington, ed., *Winter in Prague, Documents on Czechoslovak Communism in Crisis* (Cambridge, Mass., 1969), pp. 18-39. A fuller analysis by Mencl alone was issued in printed form, but not for public circulation, by the party's Ideological Department, under the title "The Historic

CONFLICT AT THE TOP

The threat to Novotný's position was heralded at earlier CC meetings in 1967. At the February plenum, Mária Sedláková, one of the editors of *Pravda*, blamed the passivity of the masses squarely on "those who are responsible for the management of the fate of society." Others, including Černík, were reportedly critical of the party's work.[5] After the open challenge of the writers' congress in June, Novotný resolved to take the offensive. His tough speech on September 1 was a signal for the intended renewal of a hard-line policy, which was said to have included stringent measures by the army and police against dissidents.[6] A few days later, in the Presidium, Novotný is reported to have bitterly condemned Šik and the writers for their "stormy talk" of democracy and attacked certain communists in the Central Committee who did not "recognize party principles." He is also claimed to have praised the actions of the Polish party in purging critics of its policy in the army, security, economic institutions, radio, and television.[7]

The counterattack culminated at the CC plenum at the end of September when punitive actions were taken against some writers and against *Literární noviny*, the journal of the Writers' Union. The plenum was devoted primarily to the economy, and the problems of introducing the new system, with a major report by Lubomír Štrougal, and to the electoral reforms, introduced by Štefan Sádovský, but acquired its main political significance as a result of Hendrych's condemnation of the writers' congress and his justification of the penalties taken. His hard-line policy toward the writers who had "misused" the congress for attacks against

January Plenum" in a booklet, *50 let Československa, 1918-1968* (Prague, Oct. 1968), pp. 66-125; henceforth cited as Mencl.

Another version of the proceedings, also based on the minutes but dealing primarily with December and January, appeared abroad in the Paris journal, *Svědectví* 9, no. 34-36 (Winter 1969), 147-82. A briefer version of this by Pavel Tigrid, the editor of *Svědectví*, is given in his article, "Czechoslovakia: A Post-Mortem," *Survey*, no. 73 (Autumn 1969), pp. 133-64, and in his books, *Why Dubček Fell* (London, 1971), chap. 1 and *Le printemps de Prague* (Paris, 1968), pp. 178-92.

The Mencl and *Svědectví* reports are selective and differ in many respects, but on the whole corroborate each other. The following is based mainly on these two sources, which are cited only where necessary. Although the Mencl chapter and the joint Mencl-Ouředník articles are often identical, citations are in most cases from Mencl.

See an earlier version of this chapter, Skilling, "The Fall of Novotný in Czechoslovakia," *CSP* 12 (Fall 1970), 225-42.

[5] Mencl, pp. 82-83.

[6] *Rudé právo*, Sept. 2, 1968. Mencl (pp. 85-86) refers to secret directives issued by the 8th department of the CC apparatus, supervising state administration, especially the army, security, and the courts, for an offensive against anti-socialist elements in literary and scientific circles.

[7] See *Dějiny a současnost*, no. 6 (1968), pp. 44-45; also *KŽ*, June 28, 1968.

the party and against socialism was strongly endorsed by a number of other spokesmen, including O. Švestka, J. Kladiva, K. Hoffmann, J. Fojtík, and V. Ruml. On the surface, it seemed that Novotný, who spoke only at the end, had carried the day, since the overwhelming majority of the Central Committee approved the severe measures of punishment. In a manner unprecedented in past sessions, however, some voices were raised in opposition, and several votes were cast against the proposed actions.[8] The veteran communist, František Vodsloň, for instance, according to later reports, opposed the penalties against the writers and called for "a political solution" of the conflict. The writers were, he said, "a mirror of society"; it was unwise to break the mirror for being at fault.[9] Although this small, almost token, opposition was largely concealed from the general public, it was an omen, and an example, for the future.

In retrospect, importance must be attached to Dubček's speech, scarcely noted at the time, which dealt with economic questions, especially the failure to implement 13th congress decisions on the proper exploitation of Slovak economic resources. He strongly defended the new system of management and articulated the doubts and worries expressed in the factories as to whether it would be implemented. The development of "economic instruments" could not be assured, he said, by "compromise" or by "supplements and exceptions." Most of his remarks were devoted to the problem of regional development and the special need to take cognizance of the distinctive historical development and conditions of Slovakia. As a result of relying primarily on enterprise resources for investments, he said, only 21.9 percent (instead of the planned 28 percent) had gone to Slovakia in the first half of 1967. Dubček argued that the continuance of this practice would simply perpetuate the differences between regions and proposed the establishment of a central fund to assure the development of "progressive sectors." If Slovak resources were not effectively exploited, he concluded, this would be detrimental to the Czechoslovak economy as a whole.[10]

Meanwhile, discussions were taking place within the party, at all levels, in preparation for the CC session to be held in late October which was to consider, inter alia, the official draft, "Theses on the Position and

---

[8] *RP*, Sept. 28-30, Oct. 3-4, 1967, for the published speeches and the final resolution. Neither the speeches by the critics, nor the concluding remarks by Novotný, were published, nor were any negative votes recorded. Z. Fierlinger's speech, as reported in the press, dealt generally with literature as discussed at the congress but did not condemn the writers or openly approve the penalties.

[9] Mencl, p. 83. Vodsloň's speech was later published, in *Práce*, April 7, 1968.

[10] *RP*, Sept. 29, 1967, partial translation in Remington, ed., *Winter in Prague*, pp. 13-16. None of the main speakers on the economy (Štrougal, B. Sucharda, F. Vlasák, O. Pohl, and F. Hamouz), who had spoken the day before, mentioned the problem raised by Dubček.

the Leading Role of the Party in the Present Stage of Development of Our Socialist Society." This twenty-odd page document was not published, either then or later, but was circulated within the party. Extensive materials also poured in to Prague headquarters from the party organizations, embodying many criticisms of the work of the party and proposals for reform.[11] Novotný made quite clear, however, in a speech in mid-October to district and regional secretaries, that he was not ready to make any serious concessions to the growing desire for reform. He declared that "the party would exercise its leading role everywhere, and would use those measures which it recognized as suitable in each concrete case." He rejected what he termed non-Leninist conceptions, according to which the party was to carry out "predominantly, or even exclusively, so-called programmatic (*koncepční*) work, the elaboration of objectives and program, and politico-ideological activity," whereas other organs, such as the government, had "the task of carrying out their own directing and so-called operational activity."[12]

THE OCTOBER PLENUM

The crisis came to a head in the CC sessions in October and December. At the October plenum, when Hendrych presented an outline of the discussion materials and, presumably, the draft Theses, he did so in a form that apparently differed from that originally approved by the Presidium. Although his statement was also not published at the time, or later, its content and that of the draft Theses, may be deduced from his article in a subsequent issue of *Život strany*.[13] Emphasis was placed on "the need to deepen the leading role of the party" in order to meet the conditions arising out of the technical and scientific revolution and the new economic system and to overcome the "passivity of some communists." Recognizing that in domestic affairs the "class struggle" had ceased to be the main motive force, Hendrych stated that "a regulating power which would combine varied interests in a single current of action by the whole of society" was required. In international affairs where a bitter class struggle of two opposing systems persisted, the mission of the party was to develop "socialist class consciousness and international feeling." Although he spoke of the necessity of replacing outdated methods, he gave almost no concrete indication, at least in this published version, as to what was to be changed, mentioning only greater use of "science," including the social sciences, in the management of society; better implementation of party decisions; and an improvement in the party's inner life. In general, the report suggested that no significant alteration in pre-

[11] R. Bajalski, *Borba* (Belgrade), Jan. 9, 1968.
[12] Mencl, pp. 86-87.   [13] *ŽS*, no. 24 (Nov. 1967), pp. 1-4.

vailing political procedures was contemplated, but rather that party control would be strengthened. It was bound therefore to confirm the dissatisfaction of those who were bent on achieving thorough reforms.

Bitter discussion, unknown in previous CC meetings, was touched off by Alexander Dubček, who criticized Novotný for using materials different from those approved by the Presidium and proceeded to deliver a comprehensive critique of the party's methods of operation. Although he referred approvingly to the Theses as raising "the historically significant questions," Dubček censured the document for failing to deal adequately with many questions, and drew on data submitted by certain regional party organizations, in particular those of South Moravia and East Slovakia. He proclaimed the need for the party to exercise a leading role, but also for "essential changes in the party's work," in line with what he termed the qualitatively new stage of society's development. The party must "lead, not direct, society." "The government must govern. . . ." Treading on more controversial ground, he warned that conservatism was no less a danger than "the liberal tendency" and advocated "a struggle of old and new," "progressive and conservative," a struggle which, he said, would involve "concrete people." It was necessary, he concluded, "to clarify the relations of work in the central organs, to make some further demands on the work of the Central Committee, to work out a long-term party program, and to adopt a standpoint on the cumulation of functions in the highest organs of the party, government, National Assembly and the national economy generally." Dubček also spoke at some length on the Slovak question, emphasizing both the indispensability of national equality for Czechs and Slovaks and of unity of Czechoslovak "statehood" and recommending a new program in nationality relations. With this speech, which expounded the urgency for basic changes and openly raised the sensitive question of the duplication of jobs at the highest level, Dubček had thrown down the gauntlet to Novotný.[14]

The subsequent debate revealed that Dubček was not alone in his discontent. Other speakers, notably Sedláková, Kriegel, and Špaček described the serious situation in which the party found itself and the need for drastic change.[15] When Martin Vaculík, a candidate member of the Presidium, criticized Dubček, imputing "personal" motives for his atti-

[14] Mencl, pp. 88-89. A full text was published in late 1968 in a collection of Dubček's speeches, *K otázkam obrodzovacieho procesu v KSČ* (Bratislava, Oct. 1968), pp. 3-16. It was later reported that the Theses had referred to the "harmful" effect of the cumulation of functions, without, however, relating this general idea specifically to the posts at the highest level (*RŠO*, p. 22). The separation of the functions of the presidency and the first secretaryship had apparently been raised earlier in 1966, but had not been discussed publicly at that time (V. Slavík, *ŽS*, no. 12, June 1968, p. 6).

[15] Mencl, pp. 90-95. Other critics of the party's work were reported to be V. Slavík, M. Sabolčík, V. Kadlec, and O. Voleník.

tude, it was clear for the first time that there was division within the highest ranks. After the plenum had gone into closed session, with only full members and candidates present, Novotný delivered an impassioned discourse in which he censured Dubček's work as head of the Slovak party and accused him of expressing "narrow national interests." This drew a sharp response from several Czechs (O. Voleník, I. Málek and J. Borůvka) and especially from Dubček's colleague, V. Bil'ak. The latter reminded Novotný of the damages caused in the fifties by the charge of nationalism against Slovaks and urged a CC meeting in a few weeks, with all members of the Slovak Presidium present.[16] Josef Borůvka's proposal that the session not be terminated but be reconvened after a two or three weeks' recess was, however, not adopted. Nor was František Kriegel's suggestion that voting be by secret ballot. In the end the Theses were approved, not unanimously as requested by Novotný, but with thirteen negative votes.[17] Novotný promised that there would be further discussion of the work of the central organs, especially of the government.

The official report on the October plenum, as published in *Rudé právo*, did not include even censored texts of the speeches and thus concealed the division of opinion at the apex of the party.[18] It asserted the doctrine of the leading role in traditional terms. "The party is the leading political force, the ideological center, the cognitive and directive organism of socialist society. It unifies and directs all the essential aspects of social life and organizes the working people for the realization of socialist and communist aims." It continued, in words that echoed, although somewhat ambiguously, Novotný's formulation in mid-October: "In its activity it concentrates on the conscious programming and the strategic direction of the general social process. From state and economic organs, it demands full responsibility for the operative and perspective management of their respective spheres on the basis of the political line set

[16] According to Bil'ak, the Slovak CC also opposed Novotný's reaction to Dubček's speech. See his collection of speeches and articles, *Pravda zůstala pravdou: Projevy a články, říjen 1967-prosinec 1970* (Prague, 1971), p. 43. According to F. Dvorský, leading party secretary of the West Slovak region, strong support for Dubček against the charges of nationalism was expressed by Slovak party functionaries attending a conference at that time (*Pravda*, April 12, 1968).

[17] *Svědectví*, no. 34-36, p. 149.

[18] *RP*, Nov. 1, 1967. The first post-January commentary in *ŽS* (no. 2, Jan. 1968, pp. 4-6) quoted the plenum decision explicitly as follows: ". . . excessive cumulation of functions does not contribute to the quality of their implementation and must therefore be energetically eliminated." The same wording was given in Bil'ak's speech of December 1967, as given in his later collection of speeches and articles (*Pravda zůstala pravdou*, p. 44). The decision as published in *Rudé právo* did *not* contain these words. Jan Kolář, in a major exposition of the leading role of the party in the light of the October plenum (published prior to the January session), made no mention of the problem of cumulation of functions (*Nová mysl*, Jan. 1968, pp. 17-25).

forth." It was not possible, however, "to separate the programmatic and the organizational sides of the party's activity. . . . The party's action may not be limited merely to cognitive activity, to the formation of concepts and to ideological work. The party must in its activity penetrate all spheres of social life and, through the medium of communists, influence the development of the whole of society."

It appeared that Novotný had once again scored a victory. It was evident, however, at least to those "in the know," that the top leadership was split and that the issues of the controversy had not yet been finally settled. In the weeks that followed, Novotný's position significantly worsened. The Strahov student demonstration, and its brutal suppression by the police, which occurred on the very evening of the final plenum meeting, led to widespread public criticism of the police action and further discredited the "hard-line" policy. Immediately following the plenum Novotný was in Moscow for eight days for the celebration of the 50th anniversary of the Soviet revolution. His absence permitted those opposed to his continuance in office to organize their forces. Although the evidence is scanty, it seems that by this time the Presidium was split in half over the issue of party reform, including Novotný's holding of the two top positions of party and state. Dubček, Dolanský, Černík, Kolder, and, eventually Hendrych, were said to be urging a separation of the two offices and were criticizing Novotný's work as First Secretary.[19] This created an impasse in the preparations for the December plenum, and resulted in a vague compromise resolution which referred only to the intention to "solve concretely the problems linked with the implementing of the Theses . . . in relation to the work of the central organs, including the cumulation of functions."[20]

THE CRISIS DEVELOPS

The one-day visit to Prague by Leonid Brezhnev on December 8 remains shrouded in mystery. During Novotný's trip to Moscow, he had, by his own admission, been unable to speak at length with the Soviet leader but had invited Brezhnev to visit Prague, presumably hoping that this would strengthen his own position. Later, again according to Novotný, a telephone call by Brezhnev led to an acceptance of this invitation. None of this was known to the Central Committee members or

[19] There were various reports circulating in Prague of a Presidium divided 8 to 2, or 6 to 4, and eventually, with a shift of position by Hendrych, of a deadlock of 5 to 5. The five listed above as opposing Novotný are named by Mencl (p. 97). *Svědectví*, no. 34-36, gives the same names and lists M. Chudík, B. Laštovička, J. Lenárt, and O. Šimůnek as supporting Novotný (p. 151). Špaček reported the same division (*RP*, March 19, 1968).

[20] *RŠO*, pp. 9-10.

even, seemingly, to the Presidium.[21] During his brief stay in the capital the Soviet chief did not meet with the full Presidium, as was apparently planned, but talked separately with individual members. He was generally believed to have declined to interfere in the affair and to have left the Czechoslovak leaders to settle it themselves.[22] Since Novotný was not removed at this time, Brezhnev presumably took no steps to support his ouster and may even have urged his continuance in office and have left Prague confident that Novotný would weather the storm. On the other hand, his apparent "neutrality" did not strengthen the position of Novotný, who was not able to rely on Soviet support a few weeks later.

When the Central Committee gathered on December 19, one week later than previously scheduled, it became evident that great dissatisfaction existed both with the proposed resolution submitted by the Presidium (which was in the end referred back) and with the lack of information concerning the divergencies within the topmost organ and the visit by the Soviet leader. Novotný did little to remove this dissatisfaction. Speaking somewhat defensively, he apologized for his statements disparaging the Slovak leaders, sought rather weakly to explain the visit by Brezhnev, and dealt at length with the dangers of the international situation. On the question of the separation of the top offices, he offered alternative solutions and, it seems, suggested postponement of a decision for several months.[23] Critical speeches were made by Vodsloň, Fierlinger, and Šorm, head of the Academy of Sciences, but the real challenge came from Ota Šik.

Referring to the growing "political discontent of the people" and the "declining activity and interest of party members," Šik made a devastating critique of the entire party system, including the suppression of criticism and the "immense cumulation of power in the hands of some comrades, especially comrade Novotný." Separation of the functions of President and First Secretary must be carried through without delay. Concretely, he proposed the resignation of Novotný as First Secretary and the selection of a successor by a secret vote. Two candidates for the post, as well as several new Presidium members, should be nominated by a

---

[21] For this and for Novotný's explanations, see *Svědectví*, no. 34-36, pp. 150, 152. *Rudé právo* reported "a brief friendly visit" at the invitation of the CC Presidium and the government, and described the discussions as characterized by "comradely frankness and cordial friendship" (Dec. 10, 1967).

[22] Mencl, p. 99. Cf. Kolder's statement to this effect in *Svědectví*, no. 34-36, p. 167. Hence the oft-quoted phrase, later attributed to Brezhnev, "*Eto vashe dyelo!*" ("This is your affair!") (Smrkovský, *Zemědělské noviny*, March 15, 1968). The report in *Svědectví*, however, quoting Hendrych, assumes that Brezhnev threw his support to Novotný (p. 150). For the Brezhnev visit, and Smrkovský's meetings with Novotný prior to the December plenum, see Smrkovský's testament (Appendix D).

[23] *Svědectví*, no. 34-36, pp. 151-53; Mencl, pp. 98-99.

special commission which would not include any members of the Presidium. He also advanced a series of proposals for the democratization of the party, so that the Central Committee would in fact become the supreme organ between congresses and not merely "an assembly which always unanimously approves proposals submitted in one version by the Presidium." Individual CC Secretaries would be responsible to commissions, which in turn would be responsible to the Presidium and the CC plenum. They would be limited to two terms of office and would be excluded from other state functions. All elections would be secret. Cadre policy would no longer be an instrument in the hands of one person but would be permeated with "the spirit of collective party leadership." The Presidium would be authorized to work out a political and economic action program which would assure the solution, as soon as possible, of the burning questions that had piled up.[24]

The initial reaction to Šik's speech was mixed. A number of persons, including Lenárt, Chudík, and Šimůnek, opposed his proposals, arguing that many of them fell outside the competence of the Central Committee, and defending in varying degrees Novotný's tenure of office. Both Lenárt and Chudík warned of the international repercussions of a change in leadership, especially in neighboring socialist states, particularly in the German Democratic Republic. A fervent speech in defense of Novotný was made by Věra Dočkalová, who admitted that all was not in order, but denied there was a crisis in the party and declared that the leader had the confidence of the entire nation.[25] Others took a somewhat ambiguous position. Jan Piller, for instance, was critical of Novotný but was doubtful of the wisdom of an immediate division of functions. Progressive spokesmen, such as Václav Slavík and others, spoke in favor of a separation of functions. Alois Indra, a cabinet minister, condemned the limitations placed on the actions of the government and of individual ministers by the party authorities. Dubček is not reported to have spoken. His colleague, Bil'ak, however, in a long review of the past, censured Novotný's attitude toward Slovakia and the Slovak party and urged a solution of the problem of the division of functions at once. Novotný, he said, had always considered Slovakia "a weak link" in the Republic and viewed the Slovak party with suspicion and hostility, and had severely limited the authority of the Slovak top party organs.[26]

---

[24] Partial text, Svědectví, no. 34-36, pp. 154-57; Mencl, pp. 100-102.

[25] Svědectví, no. 34-36, p. 158.

[26] His speech was published later in Bil'ak, Pravda zůstala pravdou, pp. 15-35. Bil'ak strongly defended the positive attitude of the CPS toward Czechoslovakia and its consistent campaign against "populism" and "separatism," and noted that the CPS had rejected the proposal of federation in 1963. The competence of the Slovak CC had been so severely limited that it could not call its own meetings or make changes in its Presidium without prior approval from the Central Committee

Šik's statement and the subsequent three days of sharp debate crystallized the conflicting tendencies of thought among CC members. According to a post-January reconstruction of the issues under debate, two major groupings emerged.[27] On the one hand, a "conservative" group was largely satisfied with the status quo, blamed existing problems on "Western ideological diversion," and urged an even more emphatic implementation of the methods of directive administration. A "progressive group" regarded the situation as one of grave crisis and urged the need for a thoroughgoing democratization of the party and the development of socialist democracy. The focal issue had, however, become the separation of the functions of First Secretary and President, and as it became clear that such a division was unavoidable, when, and in what form, this division should be effected. The progressives urged immediate action, whereas the conservatives sought a postponement, hoping to secure time to defend Novotný's position. The divergence of opinion thus became somewhat confused, since a number of issues—Novotný's leadership, the division of functions, and the timing of action—were intertwined. Moreover, a number of persons previously closely associated with Novotný tended to shift their ground and to move from one to another grouping on specific issues. Nonetheless, the main line of distinction—for or against Novotný—became increasingly clear as the debate proceeded.

Novotný, confronted with these realities, resorted to a defensive maneuver, informing the Presidium, and later the plenum, that he was "placing the function of First Secretary at the disposal of the plenary session of the Central Committee" and that he would carry out any decision that was made.[28] This shrewd move, which did not amount to a complete resignation, would have left the question of separation open and postponed its final resolution. Thereupon Dubček, on behalf of the Presidium, proposed that the final decision, including the choice of a successor, be deferred until January 3 when the plenum would resume its deliberations.

---

of the CPCz. He also censured Novotný for his failure to carry out party decisions, for instance with regard to the extension of the powers of the Slovak organs, and for his condemnation of bourgeois nationalism after the report of the Barnabite commission.

[27] This was given in the Presidium's "information" of March 1968, *RŠO*, pp. 13 ff. See also later interview with O. Šik, *Kulturní noviny*, March 29, 1968. Laštovička, in defending himself later against the charge of having supported Novotný, argued strongly that there were not two distinct blocs which had opposed each other for several years, but rather different groupings on different issues. Although he had supported a postponement of the decision on separation, he had realized that it must eventually come. Laštovička had criticized the Presidium's March "information" and managed to get it modified in some respects (*RP*, June 7, 1968).

[28] *Svědectví*, no. 34-36, pp. 159-60.

Once again a turbulent debate began, mainly centering on the question of postponement, with some advocating immediate action, and others accepting the delay; with some defending, and others criticizing, Novotný. During this third day of discussion the Presidium members and Secretaries were requested to speak and thus compelled openly to commit themselves. Most of them favored a division of functions, but a few, including Šimůnek and Chudík, were opposed and warmly defended Novotný.[29] In the end an overwhelming majority supported the proposal, made by Vilém Nový and accepted by the Presidium, to postpone the discussion until January 1968, and to leave the decision on separation to a consultative group, which would include, in addition to all Presidium members, a representative from each regional party organization.[30] In the brief communiqué issued after the meeting, priority was given to the question of economic development and the standard of living, and no reference at all was made to the political content of the plenum debate. The CC decision on economic questions was published the following day.[31]

During the two-week period between the plenary sessions, both sides made strenuous efforts to prepare the ground for the final struggle. It was at this time that certain steps were taken in military circles to try to influence the decisions of the Central Committee, or perhaps even to use armed force to prevent the ouster of Novotný. These activities were conducted, it would appear, primarily by Miroslav Mamula, head of the 8th department of the party Secretariat, responsible for state administration, and General Jan Šejna, the secretary of the party committee in the Ministry of National Defense. Mamula had direct supervision of all the relevant ministries, in this case National Defense, and its chief party organization, and was thus able to bypass, to a considerable extent, the joint party-army Main Political Administration in that ministry, headed by General Václav Prchlík. In September and October 1967, Mamula was already reported to have sought to implement in the armed services the

[29] Those who opposed separation were said to include Šimůnek, P. Hron, and M. Pastyřík; those in favor, Kolder, M. Vaculík, Štrougal, Koucký, A. Kapek, M. Sabolčík, Černík, Dolanský, Dubček, and perhaps Hendrych and Sádovský.

Smrkovský also supported immediate separation. Whether he spoke on this occasion or at the January sitting is not clear, as the main sources differ. *Svědectví* (pp. 160-66) places this speech in December; Mencl, in January (pp. 111-12). The content of his address, which varies little in the two sources, suggests that it was delivered in January. This was confirmed by Smrkovský (Appendix D).

[30] Mencl and Ouředník, *ŽS*, no. 19, Sept. 18, 1968; *Svědectví*, no. 34-36, p. 168. The latter reports that the consultative group was also to propose Novotný's successor, suggesting that the issue of separation had already been settled. Those appointed to the group were: J. Piller, F. Červenka, F. Samec, J. Černý, O. Paul, J. Borůvka, J. Špaček, O. Voleník (later replaced by M. Čapka), A. Perkovič, E. Rigo, and M. Hladký. F. Barbírek was added later.

[31] *RP*, Dec. 22 and 23, 1967. The plenum also welcomed the invitation of eighteen parties to a world communist conference in February 1968.

hard line set forth in Novotný's speech of September 1 and by the plenum at the end of that month. During and after the October plenum, he and General Šejna continued their intrigues but were rebuffed by the Minister, General Bohumír Lomský, and by General Prchlík. Both Mamula and Šejna were reported as being convinced of the danger of a "counterrevolution" engineered by the West and carried through by the oppositional elements within the party. The party's leading role and socialism were endangered, they believed, and a situation comparable to Hungary in 1956 existed. Both voiced strong opposition to the division of Novotný's functions and to his removal from power.[32]

In early December there was a call-up of troops for military exercises, concluding on December 18, the day before the CC plenum began. These training exercises had been decided on earlier, but holding them at this time may have been designed to exert influence on the plenum deliberations. During and after the plenum at the end of December, General Šejna continued his efforts to convince high-ranking military personnel, for instance, General Lomský, and General Martin Dzúr, the deputy Chief of Staff, that there was a threat to socialism and to the party, thus awakening fears in their minds that the armed forces might be used for political purposes.[33] Lomský, Dzúr, and Prchlík rejected Šejna's arguments and overtures, and Prchlík informed the political chiefs at lower levels to be prepared to ward off the danger of a "misuse" of the army. General Lomský later quoted himself as having said to Novotný on the telephone: "I defend the principle that the army may not be misused in the present situation. By neither side . . . ! We are not after all some-

[32] For this, see the series of articles by J. Kokoška, "What Happened in the Army," published in the journal of the Main Political Administration (MPA), *A-revue*, nos. 12 to 16, from June to August 1968. These articles were based on archival materials and interviews with many of the participants (except, of course, Gen. V. Janko, who had in the meantime committed suicide, and Gen. J. Šejna, who had defected to the USA). These later events tended to lend corroboration to the charge that these two were involved in some kind of dubious activities. Šejna, in a later interview with *The New York Times* (Aug. 26, 28, 1968), firmly denied that he had attempted a military coup. M. Mamula made a similar denial (*Reportér*, June 5-12, 1968, pp. 7-9). See also an article by Gen. E. Pepich, deputy chief of the MPA in 1967, *Obrana lidu*, Feb. 24, 1968, and an interview with Gen. M. Dzúr, ibid., April 6, 1968, the latter cited at length by Tigrid, *Le printemps*, pp. 190-91. For a brief discussion, based on Šejna's later account, see J. Erickson, paper at Reading conference, 1971, in V. V. Kusin, ed., *The Czechoslovak Reform Movement 1968* (London, 1973), pp. 36-38.

[33] Šejna is reported as declaring that "certain opinions, in their essence, tend to call forth distrust in the leadership of our party and comrade Novotný as the First Secretary of the party. There is no doubt that the dissemination of various opinions and moods, and calumnies, as well as the expression of distrust in the highest organs of the party, strike deeply at the very essence of the existence of the party as the leading force in our society, and tend to destroy its ideological and action unity, whether the bearers of such opinions or moods are aware of this or not" (*A-revue*, no. 16, p. 37).

where in Africa!"[34] General Vladimír Janko, another deputy Minister of National Defense, was apparently more receptive to Šejna's arguments.[35] Throughout the holiday season, Janko was said to have had meetings with Šejna and to have taken steps to put military units in a state of readiness. According to these reports he ordered some military leaders to Prague and arranged for a tank brigade to go to the capital at a certain time. Meanwhile, Mamula had reportedly drawn up a list of over one thousand persons to be arrested, and had warrants ready and signed.[36] Even if these moves were in fact taken, it is not entirely clear whether they were preparations for military action in defense of Novotný's position, or whether they were designed to exert a psychological influence on the military leaders and on the CC members, and thus to discourage any action which would weaken Novotný's power.[37]

CLIMAX IN JANUARY

When the plenum resumed in January, there was still strong resistance to Novotný's removal. At the outset, the Prime Minister, Jozef Lenárt, spoke at length on proposed changes in the work of the government but urged care in consideration of the question of dividing the top functions. Novotný, in his opening remarks, admitted errors in his work but in essence rejected the case of his critics. In principle, he expressed agreement with the idea of separating the two posts, but cleverly shifted the discussion to the question as to when and how this might take place, clearly seeking to delay action. The Presidium, too, had submitted an ambiguous resolution, which in effect postponed the settlement until the next plenum, when it would be considered in accordance with recommendations to be made by the Presidium and the consultative group.[38] A number of speakers, including Sedláková, V. Mináč, and Smrkovský, reacted vigorously by insisting that the decision be made at once, at that very sitting. Others, including Generals Lomský and Otakar Rytíř, Lenárt, and the Foreign Minister, Václav David, warned that the international situation argued against the removal of Novotný. General Lomský's position was, however, somewhat ambiguous, since he strongly defended Novotný, spoke of the threat from imperialism, and did not oppose or

---

[34] Ibid., no. 14, p. 38.
[35] Ibid., no. 14, pp. 36-40; no. 15, pp. 27-28, 33; no. 16, p. 40.
[36] Svědectví, no. 34-36, p. 169.
[37] The official investigation commission after January reported that, although General Šejna had been active in seeking to prevent Novotný's overthrow in December 1967, there was no evidence that the army had been misused by General Lomský. There were no orders placing the army in a state of preparedness nor were any large-scale actions undertaken. Military exercises affected small units and had been planned beforehand (RP, June 12, 1968).
[38] Partial text, Mencl and Ouředník, ŽS, no. 19, Sept. 18, 1968.

support the separation of posts.[39] Lenárt once again emphasized the danger that the removal of Novotný would pose for the GDR and for Ulbricht's position. These arguments concerning the international implications were sharply countered by other speakers, including the Slovak, Jozef Valo, General Prchlík, and Smrkovský.

The latter delivered a major speech, which was similar in many ways to Šik's earlier address, and which now helped to turn the tide against Novotný.[40] Proclaiming his own support for the closest relations with the USSR, he denied that any individual or group could arrogate the right to be the guarantor of this relationship, or that it was necessary, as Chudík apparently had suggested, to consult the Soviet leaders. They would no doubt respond, he said, that it was up to each individual party and its organs, which "know the situation best," to solve its internal problems. The party had no tradition of "separatism" toward the international communist movement and there was no reason to "doubt the international position of this Central Committee or any part of it." Smrkovský also protested the idea that any group could claim a monopoly of the interests of the working class and opposed any tendency to put the workers in opposition to the intellectuals.

He rejected the charge of nationalism against the Slovaks and stressed that Czech-Slovak relations were not entirely "in order." He rejected as absurd the charge of nationalism against "a man who felt so internationally as did Dubček" and warned, on the basis of past experience, against using, in response to Slovak demands, the "bogey of nationalism," supported, he noted, on more than one occasion by "force and cadre measures." Smrkovský dealt at length with the Slovak question, referring to "the not too happy Czech protectorship (*protektorství*), the old and irritating sermonizing (*mentorování*) of Bratislava by Prague," and proposed "a creative rethinking of the principles of 'Košice.' "

Admitting his earlier uncertainty as to whether "a sudden change in the topmost posts" might lead to "a too risky rocking of authority" and "the danger of anarchy," he said that he had come to the conclusion that a division of the two posts was necessary and must be accomplished without delay. Contributing to his decision no doubt was the fear he shared with many others that there might be a return to the practice of the fifties, including "severe acts against opposition elements within the party" and "a new use of the organs of violence, especially the security agencies, for the solution of inner-party problems."

In this "historic moment" of the party's history, there was urgent need

[39] Mencl, pp. 110-11; *A-revue*, no. 15, pp. 28-30. Lomský later said that he had favored the division of functions.
[40] Text given in *Svědectví*, no. 34-36, pp. 160-66. J. Lederer praised it as a "turning-point" and gave extensive excerpts in an article published in early 1969 (*Rep.*, Jan. 8, 1969, pp. 10-11).

for "a democratization" of society and for basic changes in the party's manner of work. This should begin with the addition of new blood to the Presidium, and a division of the functions of First Secretary and President. In favor of the latter, he said, were the greater part of the Central Committee, including half of the Presidium, the majority of the Slovak Presidium, and all the CC Secretaries. He urged that this question be settled at once, at this session, by secret ballot, with a choice between alternative candidates. It was not enough for Novotný to put his position at the disposal of the Central Committee; he ought to resign, as he should have done much earlier. "Novotný, as the highest functionary, with the greatest concentration of power, also bears the greatest share of responsibility for the existing situation." The new Secretary should act as chairman of the Presidium, as "first among equals," thus guarding against concentrating too much power in the hands of an individual. More than this would be required, however, if the party were to regain the confidence of the people—a positive program that would unite all "who wished socialism without deformations" and "a rehabilitation of the ideas for which the majority of us have dedicated our lives."

Meanwhile the arena of debate and decision was transferred to the joint meetings of the Presidium and the consultative group. On the 4th of January Černík reported that their proposal was that the issue of separation of functions be settled at this very plenum and that the Presidium should make its suggestions known on the following day. Plenum discussions on the 4th indicated that there was still opposition, for instance, by General Rytíř, the army's Chief of Staff, who described Novotný as a "firm representative" in the defense against imperialism and pressed for a delay in settling the question of division.[41]

It was more difficult to select a successor to Novotný, however. Although nothing is known with assurance of the discussions in the consultative body on this crucial matter, it has been reported that Novotný rejected Smrkovský or Šik, and that his own suggestions, including Laštovička, Lenárt, and Vaculík, were not acceptable to others.[42] Agreement was finally reached on Alexander Dubček, as a compromise candidate who was approved by all, including Novotný, and who was prevailed upon to accept the nomination. There was also concurrence on the addition of four new members to the Presidium.

This proposal was submitted to the plenum on January 5 by Novotný who declared that he was relinquishing his post in the interest of party unity and saw in Dubček a "guarantee" of "the strengthening of that unity." In the discussion that followed, some opposition voices were heard, including Oldřich Pavlovský and Viliam Šalgovič, but in the end

[41] Mencl, pp. 112-13; A-revue, no. 15, pp. 32-33.
[42] Svědectví, no. 34-36, p. 171.

the recommendations were approved unanimously. In his acceptance speech Dubček revealed his reluctance to accept the post and his intention to work as "first among equals." He pledged himself to carry out the "intentions" of the Novotný leadership, especially in strengthening both Czechoslovak statehood and the relationship with the Soviet and other communist parties. He thanked Novotný for his past work, urged that it be objectively evaluated, and expressed the hope of Novotný's continued assistance.[43]

There was an ironic epilogue associated with the efforts of General Šejna to prevent the ouster of Novotný. At meetings of the presidium of the main party committee in the Ministry of Defense on January 3 and 4, Šejna sought to persuade his colleagues of the dangers of the situation and eventually convinced them that it was necessary to send a letter to the Central Committee setting forth the views of the party members in the ministry. Early in the morning of the 5th, at about 8 a.m., more than an hour before the CC plenum was to open, an enlarged meeting of the party committee, including approximately 120 persons, began its discussion of the draft of such a letter. Šejna spoke of the threat to the party as the leading force and was supported by General Janko but was opposed by General Dzúr, General Josef Čepický, deputy Chief of Staff, and others. The content of the letter was modified, but in its final version strongly opposed the division of the functions of First Secretary and President as a threat to party unity and to the implementation of the 13th congress line and the October plenum decisions. It rejected also the slander of comrade Novotný "whom we know as a consistent defender of the party's line, and of the alliance with the Soviet Union and as a defender of the fulfillment of the international duty of our party." In the final vote, taken between 1 and 2 in the afternoon, the letter was overwhelmingly approved, only Dzúr opposing it. It was, however, too late— the plenum had already taken *its* decision and Novotný had been removed.[44]

THE PROCESS OF SUCCESSION

The overthrow of Novotný was markedly different from comparable events in other communist countries. As elsewhere, there was no established mechanism or procedure for effecting a succession during the lifetime of the incumbent. In the Soviet Union the ouster of Khrushchev was the result of action by Brezhnev and other colleagues, who predetermined the ultimate outcome by carefully arranged organizational mea-

[43] Text, ibid., pp. 173-74.
[44] The episode is described in *A-revue*, no. 16, pp. 34-43. The text of the letter is given in part. See also Dzúr's interview, *OL*, April 6, 1968.

sures. In Prague, however, the changeover was effected apparently without concerted planning, and only after a sharp clash of competing forces in which Novotný and his partisans took active part. The death-agony of the regime, in consequence, lasted three months and the result was not certain until the last moment. The overthrow of the top leader was, however, accomplished peacefully, and in a seemingly democratic fashion, through an orderly process of debate and voting in the topmost party organs.

The assaults on Novotný by Dubček, Šik, and Smrkovský seem to have been uncoordinated, a fact which itself testified to the widespread dissatisfaction with Novotný's rule. These spokesmen were very different in their background and position, and each possessed weaknesses as well as strengths. Dubček, a long-time associate of Novotný, had not previously, as head of the Slovak party, openly opposed his chief and did not have the backing of all his Slovak colleagues. Although his original intervention touched off the entire controversy, Dubček did not spearhead the subsequent movement against Novotný. Šik's dramatic speech was more decisive in carrying the struggle forward and in broadening the issues. As a once conservative economist who had enjoyed the friendship of Novotný, and as the head of the Institute of Economics, who had sponsored the economic reform, he could hardly be ignored. Nonetheless, as an intellectual, his political influence within the Central Committee was somewhat limited, although substantial among more moderate members. Finally, Smrkovský also had a somewhat ambiguous reputation, as a resistance leader in 1945 and a victim of the fifties, and on the other hand, as a colleague of Novotný from the mid-sixties. Since he was regarded as close to the working class and deeply loyal to the Soviet Union, his critical speech had great impact. A less prominent but important role in the CC debate was played by the South Moravian leader, Špaček, from whom, however, had come some of the most critical materials on the reform of the political system. Martin Vaculík, recently appointed first secretary in Prague, who had acquired a reputation for reform in South Moravia, actually opposed the initiative of Dubček and the others.

Although the ultimate decision appeared, on the surface, to be the result of a democratic process of debate and voting, ever present in the background was the potential exercise of force and coercion by one or other of the participants, a possibility which everyone took into account and sought to utilize in his own interest. General Lomský, in a manner reminiscent of General Svoboda's behavior in 1948, did not commit the army in favor of Novotný and hence in effect supported his removal. The "neutralization" of the armed forces, and also of the security forces, deprived Novotný of their use as weapons in his own defense and contributed to a peaceful changeover.

The role of the Soviet Union is still clouded in obscurity. Brezhnev's "failure to intervene" was doubtless based on his conclusion that Novotný's position was untenable and on his desire not to be in the situation of backing a sure loser. One may assume that behind the scenes, during and after his brief visit to Prague, Brezhnev bent every effort to secure a solution favorable to Soviet interests. Exercising his influence through key figures in governing circles, he presumably sought to make sure that, if Novotný were removed, his successor would be a "reliable" person, likely to pursue a policy acceptable to the Soviet leadership. Above all, he would have to be someone who would maintain intact the existing relations between Moscow and Prague. Whether Brezhnev was consulted during the process of selecting Novotný's successor, and decisively influenced the outcome, cannot be determined. Presumably, however, the choice of Dubček was approved by Moscow and was regarded at the outset as not likely to disturb the intimate alliance of the two parties and the two regimes.

PART THREE

THE POLITICS OF CHANGE

CHAPTER VII

Prelude to Change

(January and February)

On January 6 the Central Committee announced the replacement of Antonín Novotný as First Secretary by Alexander Dubček, in a brief communiqué that was at once startling and ambiguous.[1] Such a shift, removing a leader from his key post after fifteen years of rule, as in other communist countries, could have profound and incalculable repercussions. Yet at first there was little evidence of a basic change of direction and hence some reason to believe that nothing more than "a change of guard" had occurred, replacing a discredited leader with one of his faithful colleagues and supporters. As a commentator, in retrospect, later expressed it, "Novotný was defeated but not 'the spirit of the system.' "[2] For some time the general public, and even the rank and file of the party, had a minimum of information concerning the hectic struggle that had taken place during the preceding three months and were still in the dark as to the real meaning of the change in leadership.[3]

CHANGE OF THE GUARD

Many elements in the situation seemed to imply a shift of emphasis rather than of direction. For one thing, Novotný, although removed, "at his own request," as First Secretary, remained as President of the Republic and was still a member of the party's Presidium. The January communiqué contained not a single word of direct criticism of him personally and indeed expressed appreciation for his "devoted work" and praise of his "significant successes." Dubček was described as "in his own person maintaining the continuity of party leadership." The disunity within the ranks of the Central Committee during the sessions from October to January was veiled by references to the "broad discussion" that had occurred and the "complete unity of opinion" that had resulted. Although there was reference to the "existing inadequacies in the methods and style of work," including defects in "inner party democracy," the only

---

[1] Published in *Rudé právo*, Jan. 6, 1968, and later in *Rok šedesátý osmý* (Prague, 1969); henceforth *RŠO*. This communiqué was a brief version of a resolution which was not published at the time. For text of the latter, see *Tribuna*, Oct. 15, 1969, pp. 8-9. The resolution did not differ substantially from the communiqué but discussed in greater detail the changes deemed desirable in the party's work.

[2] F. Šamalík, *Politika*, Sept. 19, 1968, p. 10.

[3] See Smrkovský's testimony (Appendix D).

specific changes mentioned were the separation of the functions of the presidency and the first secretaryship and a future "improvement of the activity" of the government and the Slovak National Council. Moreover, the measures taken were said to be designed to implement the conclusions of the 13th congress in 1966, and of the Theses on the Position and Role of the Party approved at the October plenum, suggesting that an alteration of methods, rather than objectives, was envisaged.

Other changes in leadership pointed in the same direction. Apart from the promotion of two candidates to full membership, the Central Committee, selected during Novotný's tenure, remained the same. Indeed, under the rules, it could be fully renovated only at the next party congress, for which no date was set. Four new members were added to the Presidium. Two of these were veteran cadres: Jan Piller, a long-time *apparatchik*, at the time deputy Minister of Heavy Industry, who had become a candidate member of the Central Committee in 1958, and a full member in 1962, and Josef Borůvka, a pre-war party comrade, and a member of the Central Committee continuously from 1954, who had been long associated with agricultural matters, both in party posts and in the National Assembly, and was at the time a collective farm chairman. Two others, both party functionaries, were relative newcomers: Emil Rigo, who was of gypsy origin and head of the party organization in a large ironworks in eastern Slovakia, and Josef Špaček, a graduate of the Higher Party School in Prague, and leading party secretary in southern Moravia. Both had been in the Central Committee from 1966 only. Suggestive of a new orientation, however, was the fact that Rigo and Borůvka were in direct contact with the working people in factory and farm, and that Špaček had acquired a progressive reputation as party secretary in Brno.

The successor to Dubček as Slovak party chief, Vasil Bil'ak, elected at the Slovak Central Committee meeting two weeks later, also did not represent a break with the past, but as *Pravda* commented, "embodied the continuity of the work of the party in Slovakia."[4] A long-time party functionary, he had been a Slovak Secretary and Presidium member from 1962, and under Dubček, had been responsible for ideological work. Like the latter, he had taken part in the Slovak Uprising. A Ruthenian in origin, he had graduated from the Higher Party School and had later attained a doctor's degree at that institution by correspondence. He had held high posts both in the Prague government and in the Slovak organs and as Slovak First Secretary he now became a member of the CPCz Presidium. In his address to the Slovak CC plenum, not published at the time, he praised the CC sessions as "significant," but not "unusual" or

[4] Jan. 24, 1968.

184

"sensational" and described the December plenum as a logical continuation of the October meeting and the Theses then adopted.[5] Two other veterans were added to the Slovak Presidium—Miloslav Hruškovič, as full member, and Michal Pecho, as candidate, as well as party secretary, and one relative newcomer, Robert Harenčár, youth leader, as a candidate.

Dubček's past career hardly suggested that he was likely to carry through radical reforms.[6] The son of a communist worker who had emigrated to the Soviet Union in the twenties, Dubček had spent the formative years from age 4 to 17 there, as a student in elementary and high school. Returning to Slovakia in 1938 as an adult, he became a factory worker and a party member and took part in the Slovak Uprising, during which he was twice wounded and his brother was killed. Continuing after the war as an industrial worker and party activist until 1949, he then began his career as full-time functionary as a district secretary and gradually climbed up the bureaucratic ladder—leading secretary in Bratislava in 1958, a party secretary in Prague in 1960, and First Secretary of the Slovak party, succeeding Karol Bacílek, in 1963. That Dubček was early regarded as potential top leadership material was indicated by his selection for study at the Higher Political School in Moscow, where, in his mid-thirties, he spent the years 1955 to 1958. This coincided with the period of Khrushchev's de-Stalinization drive and may have left an imprint on his own thinking and prepared him for a similar role in 1968. Apart from this experience and his participation in the Slovak Uprising, he seemed, however, to be a typical *apparatchik* who, as a member of the CPCz and CPS Central Committees from 1958, and the Slovak Presidium from 1962, had loyally given his support to Novotný on all key issues.

There was nothing in Dubček's background, at least as known publicly, that distinguished him as a person of unusual standpoint, even on the Slovak question. He was largely unknown, especially among Czechs. As party secretary in Bratislava, a post which did not permit him to pursue a policy independent from the course set in Prague, he had enjoyed a reputation for a rule somewhat less obscurantist than that of Novotný's

[5] Vasil Bil'ak, *Pravda zůstala pravdou* (Prague, 1971), pp. 36-50. He singled out for special mention the declared intention to improve the party's relations with the state organs, including the Slovak, and the decision to correct the relations of Czechs and Slovaks but made no reference to federation and implied that this decision would carry forward what had already been begun in 1967.

[6] Biographical sketch in *RP*, Jan. 6, 1968. See also Deryck Viney, "Alexander Dubček," *Studies in Comparative Communism* 1 (July-Oct. 1968), 17-39. Two journalistic biographies of Dubček contain well-known facts, together with a substantial amount of speculation and undocumented information: William Shawcross, *Dubček* (London, 1970) and Ludvík Veselý, *Dubček* (Munich, 1970).

185

and was believed to have come into conflict with the latter behind the scenes, especially on matters relating to Slovak interests.[7] As we have seen, in the decisive October plenum in 1967 (although this was unknown to the public) he had taken an early stand critical of Novotný but had not played a decisive part in the subsequent struggle. His selection as First Secretary was a compromise after other candidates had been opposed by Novotný or by his critics.[8] In his acceptance speech, as briefly cited in the January announcement, he proclaimed his faith in the Leninist principles of the party, in Marxism-Leninism, and in socialist internationalism.[9] Contributing to the uncertainty about his intentions was his own failure to make any public statement of future policy for a whole month, until the beginning of February, at the Congress of Agricultural Cooperatives. This speech, although fresh in tone, was not remarkable in its content and was made after the completion of a trip to Moscow and conversations with Brezhnev which were said to have produced "complete unity of views" on all questions. Shortly thereafter Dubček held meetings, on Czechoslovak territory, with other communist leaders— János Kádár, in Komárno, and Władysław Gomułka, in Ostrava.

Everything about Dubček's behavior in the first weeks of office indicated a man who was cautious and evolutionary, pragmatic and realist, in his approach to his new task. There was little to suggest that he had a clear conception of future development and nothing to indicate how far he might go in reform. His purpose appeared to be to consolidate the communist system, shaken to its foundations by the years of Novotný rule, and, in line with much of past Czech tradition (and somewhat out of accord with the reputedly more romantic traditions of the Slovaks) to work out, step by step, a program of moderate reform. Furthermore, since he was associated in the leadership with some who had long resisted the removal of Novotný (including Novotný himself), his leeway for more substantial reform seemed strictly limited.

SIGNS OF INNOVATION

Nevertheless there were signs of more far-reaching potentialities in the situation. The January changeover was the outcome of deep conflict in

---

[7] See above, chap. III.

[8] In a major article at the time of Dubček's expulsion from the party, in 1970, his selection was severely criticized as "a compromise" and "an emergency solution." His weaknesses were said to include "political lack of preparedness" and "insufficiency of will" (*RP*, July 16, 1970). Bil'ak, at the September 1969 plenum, argued that it had been a mistake to select him since the situation required a "hard" and "more principled" man (*Svědectví* 10, no. 38, 1970, p. 281).

[9] Cf. a version of his remarks published abroad in *Svědectví* 9, no. 34-36 (1969), 173-74, which did not contain these statements. See above, chap. VI.

the Central Committee and Presidium and reflected profound discontent with the policies of Novotný and his methods of governing. The Central Committee, although unchanged in its composition, had assumed a new role as a forum of debate and as an instrument for the transition to a new leadership. The removal of Novotný undermined the system of personal rule which he had developed, and the separation of top state and party posts opened up the possibility of restoring some degree of independence also to the government and the National Assembly and to the mass organizations. Basic reforms in the party itself, such as the subordination of Presidium and Secretariat to the Central Committee and the emergence of the First Secretary as "first among equals," both of which were advocated by some during the plenum, were also possible consequences of the January decision.[10]

Dubček, as a person, although in some ways ambiguous, also symbolized the winds of change blowing in the party. At 46, he represented a generational shift in the topmost post, and as events were soon to show, introduced a marked turn in the style of leadership. Not less significant was the elevation of a Slovak to the most powerful post in a country in which Czechs had usually held the supreme positions, under communist or non-communist rule. He had already given some evidence, both in his speech at the October plenum and in other statements during 1967, of a desire for a basic change in the party's work and for the formulation of a long-term political program. In an article published at the end of the year in *Pravda*, just prior to his selection, he had rejected the use of "forceful or authoritarian methods," described the party as "an organic part of society," and spoke of "a historical turn, a transition to a new quality of socialist society."[11]

In his first major speech (unpublished at the time) at the Slovak Central Committee in late January, Dubček gave some hints of his attitude: "We are not changing the general line, either in domestic or foreign policy. . . . We are not changing the mission of the party; we must, however, adapt its activity and methods to the new quality of the development of society." Even more significantly, he went on: "Real democracy assumes discipline, too, and conscious discipline is proportional to the democratic quality of decisions and decision-making. In this sense there will never be enough democracy. Democracy is not only the right and the possibility to express one's opinion; democracy is also the condition, the method of dealing with the opinions of the people—whether functionaries, and the working people generally, have a real feeling of co-responsibility, of co-decision-making; whether they feel that they share in mak-

[10] The phrase quoted was used by Dubček and Smrkovský (chap. VI above). See also A. Hradecký in *Reportér*, Jan. 17-24, 1968.

[11] *Pravda*, Dec. 31, 1967. See above, chaps. V, VI.

ing decisions, and in the solution of tasks in their place of work and of serious social problems; whether their consciousness of this is strengthening or declining."[12]

He repeated this passage at the agricultural congress in early February in a speech that added little that was really novel but displayed an uncustomary human warmth. Admitting that errors had been committed in the past, he insisted that the general line had been correct and would not be changed. There must, however, be new methods and approaches and in particular "the development of socialist democracy, activating and unifying the social forces in all spheres of life of our society," and "opening up room for the activity of all social groups of our society without distinction as to generation or national affiliation." They were, however, "only at the beginning of this process," and treading a "new, unknown path," and must incorporate the wealth of fresh ideas in an "action program" which would express the "progressive forces of our society."[13]

Nor did Dubček's speech at the end of February, on the anniversary of the 1948 seizure of power, represent a radical break with the past or provide a clear view of the future.[14] Reviewing the two decades of communist rule in Czechoslovakia, he paid handsome tribute to Klement Gottwald and made only restrained criticism of the later periods of his rule. In the presence of Brezhnev and the leaders of other bloc states, Dubček cited Gottwald's words on following "our own specific path" and creating "a new type of democracy," but reiterated the importance of strengthening unity and fraternal cooperation with the Soviet Union and the other socialist countries. He admitted that many unsolved questions had accumulated and referred specifically to economic difficulties, the conflict with the intelligentsia, and problems of the youth. He spoke at some length about Czech-Slovak relations and as in previous speeches, stressed both national equality and Czechoslovak "statehood."[15] Although for the first time he noted the need to correct the 1960 changes in the status of the Slovak national organs, he did not broach the idea of federalism. In general, the key to reform, Dubček declared, was in the political sphere, where there must be an end to the "directive" methods

[12] See a collection of Dubček's speeches, *K otázkam obrodzovacieho procesu v KSČ* (Bratislava, Oct. 1968), pp. 61-62; henceforth cited as *K otázkam*.

[13] See *RP*, Feb. 2 and *K otázkam*, pp. 17-30. Strangely, the idea of an action program was mentioned in the unpublished January resolution but *not* in the Jan. 6 communiqué.

[14] See *RP*, Feb. 23 and *K otázkam*, pp. 31-58. Bil'ak later described this speech in its original form as "revisionist" and "liquidationist." He reported that Brezhnev had been "shocked" when its content was read to him on the telephone. Even though it was fully reworked, it had to be revised again before delivery (Bil'ak's speech of Sept. 1969, *Svědectví* 10, no. 38, 1970, pp. 282-83).

[15] Cf. his article in *Pravda*, Dec. 31, 1967, and his speeches in January and early February, *K otázkam*, pp. 64-65, 28-29, resp.

of the past and a new activity to replace previous passivity. Although the leading role of the party could not be questioned, he declared, again quoting Gottwald, that the party must "lead the masses," and not command them. The proposed action program would represent a long-term plan for the period extending after 1970, based on the 13th congress decisions but further developing them in preparation for the 14th congress, embodying "everything new in our society" but "without losing continuity with past development." The party's leading role must be implemented in such a way that "every communist would participate in the elaboration of the political line and procedure of the party."

DIVISIONS AT THE TOP

Although, apart from Dubček, most top leaders refrained from public utterances, certain prominent figures, usually below the highest level, expressed their opinions of the meaning of the changeover. In spite of what appeared to be unanimity in favor of January, there was a clear differentiation in the interpretation of its meaning.

Some, including even several who had long been in seats of power, warmly welcomed the post-January course and advocated basic alterations in the whole of public life. Kolder, for instance, in a major article in *Rudé právo*, delivered a sharp criticism of past practices in party work and expounded the changes required for a speedier implementation of the 13th congress line, especially within the party (for instance, democratic discussion), and in the party's relations with the state organs and mass associations—all of which would, he said, be set forth in the action program under preparation.[16] Fierlinger, who had been a member of every Presidium under Gottwald and Novotný from 1948 to 1966 and was still a Central Committee member, put the stress on the division of the functions of party and government as a logical result of economic reform.[17] Slavík, also a veteran party functionary under Novotný and a CC secretary, advocated more information and open discussion and the participation of the people at large in political life.[18] Gustáv Husák, who still held no political post, welcomed the selection of Dubček and the "democratic reform of our society," and in a strongly progressive article in *Kultúrny život*, demanded the abandonment of the former "kindergarten" methods of leading people by the hand.[19] Špaček, in a wide-ranging interview, urged the need "to tell the truth" in politics and for leaders to listen to others and seek the "collective wisdom" of all.[20]

[16] *RP*, Feb. 18.   [17] *Rep.*, Jan. 31-Feb. 7.
[18] *RP*, Jan. 30; *Práce*, Feb. 7.
[19] *Kultúrny život*, Jan. 12. See also other articles by Husák, ibid., Feb. 2 and *Pravda*, Feb. 25.
[20] *Obrana lidu*, Feb. 10.

Josef Smrkovský, who held only a secondary ministerial office at the time, broke new ground, in an influential article in *Práce*, when he declared that the January plenum had not been a mere "matter of persons" but "a first step" toward "the removal of bureaucratic styles and residues of the past," both in party and state, "from the supreme organs to the least village or workplace," and gave assurance that "decisions would be made on the basis of democratic principles. . . ." "The administration," he said, "must be the executor and the auxiliary of the political will of the people, the nation and the party—not the reverse." In another article he advocated profound reforms in the party, a thorough activization of the organs of government and of the assembly, and of the mass associations, and a revision of Czech-Slovak relations. The objective, he declared, was "a democratization of the party and society as a whole, a thorough and honest democratization not weakened by reservations but based on real and comprehensible guarantees."[21] These articles, and his subsequent speeches to party organizations and at public meetings, were later described as decisive steps in establishing "direct contact with the public" and in forming "the opinion of citizens" and made Smrkovský one of the most vigorous proponents of genuine reform—the person who changed the January plenum into "something which entered history as January."[22]

Other party leaders were, however, less enthusiastic. Novotný, in a speech to a large Prague factory in mid-February, ignored in the mass media, apparently made an attempt to appeal to the workers for support by insinuating that the economic reform would strike at their standard of living and would endow the director, the functionaries, and the intelligentsia with privileges at their expense.[23] A few days later, in what was to be his final major public address, on the anniversary of February 1948, Novotný praised the achievements of the past and the continuity of communist policy and spoke fleetingly of the January action as involving more effective measures for implementing the line of the 13th congress.[24] Other leading spokesmen, while endorsing January, made reservations and issued cautions that suggested a more moderate or conservative approach. Bil'ak, for example, in his speech on the February anniversary in Bratislava, warned against "unreal plans," or "anarchy and arbitrariness," and pointed to the danger of "right opportunism" as well as "conservatism."[25] Hendrych tried to minimize the achievements of the pre-January critics and to stress the continuity of the process of

---

[21] *Práce*, Jan. 21; also *Práca*, Jan. 23; *RP*, Feb. 9; *Rep.*, Feb. 14-21.
[22] J. Lederer, *Rep.*, Jan. 8, 1969.
[23] *L'Humanité*, March 27, 1968, cited by Pierre Broué, *Le printemps des peuples commence à Prague* (Paris, n.d.), pp. 35-36.
[24] *RP*, Feb. 24.   [25] *Pravda*, Feb. 24.

reform.[26] Oldřich Švestka, editor-in-chief of *Rudé právo*, roundly denied that there would be any change whatever in the "previous political course" and warned against "yielding to pressures" or the demagogy of "cheap popular actions" designed to win support.[27] Although all these spokesmen approved democratization and even attacked "conservatives," it was evident that they themselves occupied a place at the moderate end of the political spectrum and rejected a radical interpretation of January. It was also becoming clear that the process of democratization would be long and slow and would involve a strenuous struggle between the more progressive and conservative tendencies.[28]

PARTY AND PUBLIC UNCERTAINTY

Active participation in developments was initially confined mainly to the highest party organs and to individual CC members and other leading persons, who took it upon themselves, as we have seen, to comment on the meaning of January. Their statements reflected the lack of consensus and the uncertainty as to the way forward.[29] No meeting of the Central Committee was called, but the Presidium, after an initial delay of several weeks, began to meet frequently and to publish brief reports of its proceedings.[30] A group of almost one hundred people, including high party functionaries and scholars, were at work behind the scenes on an action program. The first draft was approved by the Presidium on February 19 and began to be publicly discussed, its general outline having been indicated in the party press and in official statements. Below the topmost level of the party, at district conferences and at meetings of basic organizations, the implications of the January change were evaluated with unusual frankness, but largely within the framework of the authoritative statements so far made.

[26] *RP*, Feb. 11.

[27] Ibid., Jan. 14, 21. One of his deputy editors, Fojtík, denied the need for "a radical earthquake which would proclaim everything which . . . previously existed as 'obsolete' " and expressed the desirability of "creating conditions for quiet and deliberate activity" and for avoiding "uncertainty and nervousness" in the work of leadership (*Nová mysl*, no. 3, 1968, p. 277).

[28] Cf. Husák, *Pravda*, Feb. 25.

[29] Post-occupation statements by Kolder and Indra often referred to the divisions within the leadership at this time (*RP*, Sept. 10 and 24, 1969). The 1970 article "Why Alexander Dubček Was Expelled" criticized him for failing to call leading persons to account for their unauthorized statements, for delaying a meeting of the Presidium for three weeks, and for refusing to convoke the Central Committee (ibid., July 16, 1970). Biľak added the criticism that Dubček did not go to Moscow at once, and that, when he did go, he went alone and without preparation (*Svědectví*, no. 38, 1970, p. 282).

[30] See Presidium statements of Feb. 6 and 19, *RŠO*, pp. 26-28, 28-32, respectively, which sketched out some of the reforms under study in the preparation of the action program.

191

The party's organs published commentaries, which varied in emphasis and in degree of orthodoxy, on the significance of the new course.[31] At first more stress was placed on the need to fulfill the decisions of the 13th congress and the October plenum than on the implications of January, but this was coupled with statements that the methods for implementing these policies urgently required modification. One of the strongest statements, by J. Fojtík, in *Rudé právo*, as early as January 10, was couched in orthodox and stereotyped terms, but called firmly for democratism and collective leadership within the party, a division of labor among party and state organs, and freedom and rights for the individual. A month later, an editorial in the party daily declared that what was required was not "a mere improvement," but the "gradual reconstruction" of the political system.[32]

The party's organizational journal, *Život strany*, was slow in expressing the new spirit. K. Vlč, for instance, referred to the inevitability of different opinions and the need to consider such views, but went on to say that there could be no absolute freedom and that discussion must be limited by Marxism-Leninism, by the party program, and by congress and CC decisions. J. Hendrych, in a leading article on the anniversary of February 1948, expressed himself in entirely traditional terms. Only in the following issue did a new tone begin to permeate the journal, especially in an article by Špaček, entitled "Openly, Correctly, and Critically," which urged more active participation of party members in policy-making and more independence for district and basic organizations.[33]

Gradually, with the relaxation of censorship, discussion of the future became more and more vigorous in the press, and on radio and television, and even before the end of February, public opinion began to emerge as a factor of some importance.[34] Yet an atmosphere of uncertainty continued to prevail among the general public and in party ranks, with high hopes blended with skepticism.[35] This ambivalent state of mind was no doubt due to the absence of a consensus among leading spokesmen and to lack of adequate information, even among party rank and file, let alone the general public, a deficiency which was often severely

[31] For instance, *RP*, Jan. 10, 14, 21 and Feb. 8; editorials, *Pravda*, Jan. 9 and 11. See the moderate commentaries by V. Solecký, *Literární noviny*, Jan. 13; J. Jelínek, *Mladá fronta*, Jan. 7; A. Hradecký, *Rep.*, Jan. 17-24. See the extremely conservative comment by F. J. Kolár, *Kulturní tvorba*, Jan. 25.

[32] *RP*, Jan. 10, Feb. 8.

[33] See the editorial article, *Život strany*, no. 2 (Jan. 1968), pp. 4-6 and several articles in no. 3 and 4 (Feb. 1968); Vlč, no. 4, pp. 45-47; Hendrych, no. 4, pp. 1-4; Špaček, no. 5 (March 1968), pp. 1-4.

[34] V. Jisl, *Rep.*, Feb. 7-14.   [35] See chap. XVII below.

criticized and the improvement of which was officially promised. Doubts and uncertainties were strengthened by the continuance in office in party and state, in the mass organizations, and in all spheres of administration, of the same persons who had occupied these posts under Novotný.

The only omens of impending innovation, in mid-February, were the dismissal of F. Havlíček as head of the party's Ideological Commission (succeeded by J. Kozel) and the removal of Mamula from his key position as head of the CC's 8th department for state administration. He was replaced by Gen. Václav Prchlík, formerly chief of the Main Political Administration of the Ministry of National Defense, and he in turn by Gen. Egyd Pepich, both of whom had acquired a certain progressive reputation in opposing Šejna's efforts to block the ouster of Novotný. Another hopeful sign was the selection of Professor Goldstücker to fill the post of chairman of the Writers' Union, vacant since the congress in the summer of 1967.

In the many commentaries and declarations which emanated from the general public, January was never openly opposed and was in fact warmly welcomed, for instance, by representatives of the people's militia and by informal gatherings of pre-war communists.[36] The basic issues of reform were reiterated in statement after statement: an end to the system of "directive centralism" and of the "cumulation of functions"; an improvement in Czech-Slovak relations; the revival of the independence of the government and the legislature, and of mass associations; the recognition of group and national interests; the need for a clash of opinions and the use of science in the formulation of policy; rehabilitation of the victims of terror; stricter control of the security police; removal of censorship; genuine elections; and above all, a democratization of the party and political life generally. Opposition to January was expressed only rarely, and secretly, as for instance in the so-called Libeň letter, sent in mid-February to the party leaders and circulated amongst the public. This letter, signed by five "old communists" from the Libeň district, including Josef Jodas, a party member from 1921, praised Novotný as the only pre-January leader who had defended the leading role of the party and its revolutionary tradition, and described January as "a putsch of bourgeois and neo-bourgeois elements."[37]

[36] *RP*, Feb. 25; *Rovnost* (Brno), Feb. 2. The Brno communists called for a party congress in due course and immediate preparations for it. Slavík referred to an open letter of 165 pre-war communists in support of Dubček (*RP*, Jan. 30).

[37] Other signatories were Václav Svoboda (from 1921), Ladislav Morávek (1935), Karel Šmidrkal (1921), and Karel Pospíšil (1926). Excerpts from the letter were published a month later, with a reply, in *KŽ*, March 22, 1968, and a fuller text, after the occupation, in *Rep.*, Oct. 23-30, 1968, pp. 12-13. *Rudé právo* refused to publish the views of this group at the time (*RP*, March 18, 1968).

END OF THE BEGINNING

The first phase in the emerging reform movement may be said to have been completed by the end of February. The changeover, to this point, has been described as "a revolution from above."[38] Although January had been the product of widespread dissent and the immediate post-January weeks witnessed a certain dissipation of previous apathy and indifference, the mass of the population, and even the rank and file of the party, were not yet directly involved, except as somewhat confused and skeptical observers. Leadership had, in a sense, been thrust upon Dubček, who had, at first, no clearly articulated program of reform, except as set forth in very general terms in the unpublished resolution of the January plenum. The "unity" of which the communiqué boasted was a tenuous one, based mainly on opposition to Novotný's continuance in office, and cracks were already beginning to appear. Great power still rested in the hands of those who might be called "neo-conservatives" who were ready to accept a program of cautious and moderate reform, but were fearful of more drastic steps that would threaten vested interests and privileges, old habits of thought, and established doctrine. A successful and consistent pursuit of reform would be possible only if Dubček took decisive steps to destroy the position of Novotný and his associates and shift the balance of forces toward those pressing for a more definite reform course.

During the two months after the change of guard the other parties of the Soviet bloc had not evinced any open hostility to it or to the subsequent march of events. Nor had they, for that matter, exhibited enthusiasm or warm approval. The appointment of Dubček had been reported, without comment, in Moscow *Pravda* and in the journals of the other parties.[39] In succeeding weeks there was little reporting of developments in Czechoslovakia, and no comment on her domestic affairs.[40] Nor was there any evidence, in published accounts, that formal meetings of Czechoslovak and Soviet leaders, for instance in Moscow, in January, and in Prague, in February, had been the occasion of serious disagreement. Only later was it claimed that the Soviet leaders had expressed their concern at these meetings and had received from Dubček promises of action to stabilize the situation.[41] On the surface the Czechoslovak change of course did not seem to have stirred up controversy within the bloc nor had it met with open resistance. Moreover, Czechoslovakia's

[38] Rémi Gueyt, *La mutation tchécoslovaque* (Paris, 1969), pp. 27-28.

[39] E.g. *Pravda* (Moscow), Jan. 6, 1968. The communiqué was published in full, together with a picture and biographical sketch of Dubček.

[40] See William F. Robinson, "Czechoslovakia and Its Allies," *SCC* 1 (July/Oct. 1968), 141 ff.

[41] *Pravda* (Moscow), Aug. 22, 1968.

own attitude vis-à-vis its bloc associates appeared not to have changed essentially. However, in Budapest, at the preparatory communist conference at the end of February and in early March her chief delegate, Koucký, adopted a more independent stance at a meeting which was characterized in general by sharp differences of view.[42]

[42] See below, chap. XIX.

CHAPTER VIII

Spontaneity and Consolidation

(March and Early April)

FROM THE early days of March political developments assumed a dynamic and spontaneous character that awakened the fears of some that the party was no longer fully in command of the movement for reform. There was an extraordinary outburst of public discussion, "an eruption of freedom,"[1] which included mounting criticism of the power centers of the old political system and strong pressures for change. As a result, institutions of government and the mass associations, and even some organs of the party, began to take initiatives without waiting for authorization from above. As a result, the leadership was to some extent overtaken by events and pushed into actions more radical than intended. By the time of the CC plenum in early April, however, it seemed to have been able to consolidate the situation and to prepare the way for further controlled advance.

THE EMERGENCE OF PUBLIC OPINION

The unprecedented and unexpected outburst of activity was stimulated by official appeals for participation by the public in politics and by the apparent uncertainty and hesitations of the regime as to its future course. Dubček himself, in his relatively rare published statements, was moderate in his espousal of reform and took what seemed to be a middle-of-the-road position.[2] A somewhat similar stance was assumed by Černík, who warmly advocated reform but warned against extremes on both sides.[3] Lenárt, in a major television appearance, sought to defend himself against criticism by denying that he had been opposed to the division of functions or to the appointment of Dubček (whom he claimed to have nominated) and declared that he was in favor of the new course.[4] Stronger stands in support of reform, although certainly not extreme, were taken by Šik and Špaček.[5] More conservative views were expressed

[1] K. Bartošek, "Revolution Against Bureaucracy," *Rudé právo*, July 31, 1968. See Fritz Beer, "Ten Weeks that Shook Czechoslovakia," and Vera Blackwell, "Czechoslovakia at the Crossroads," in *Survey*, no. 68 (July 1968), pp. 56-66, 66-79, resp.

[2] *RP*, March 5. [3] Ibid., March 14.

[4] Text in *Mladá fronta*, March 19. Husák condemned Lenárt (as well as Chudík) for their actions in December and January (*Práca*, March 19).

[5] *RP*, March 15, 16, resp.

by Kolder, who made a special point of rejecting the view that the party would resign its leading role and become a "debating club."[6] These differences of opinion, the continued paucity of information about the pre-January plena, and the lack of an early meeting of the Central Committee to formulate the basic lines of reform, promoted a ferment of debate, with ever sharper criticism of past policies and leading figures and more radical demands for change. The mass media, released from the hampering controls of strict censorship, moved into what was a political vacuum and facilitated an unparalleled discussion of all public issues.

A critical element touching off this verbal explosion was the defection to the USA of General Šejna, which occurred at the end of February and was publicly revealed a few days afterwards. At the time of his flight Šejna was about to be arrested in connection with criminal proceedings for his presumed involvement in the embezzlement of state property. The evident leaking of this information to Šejna, the delay required by the necessity of having his parliamentary immunity lifted, the failure of the police to keep watch on his movements, and his possession of a diplomatic passport, made it possible for him, just prior to his arrest, to cross the frontier with his son and a young woman and to make his way via Hungary, Yugoslavia, and Italy to the USA. Nothing is known with certainty as to the reasons for his defection. An official investigating commission concluded in June that he had fled primarily to evade criminal proceedings and that his action was also motivated by the failure of his plans to defend Novotný and the system of personal power to which he (Šejna) owed his career.[7]

This event, and the suicide of General Janko two weeks later, confirmed, in the minds of many, suspicions concerning the part played by the military in December and January. General Šejna was a parliamentary deputy; secretary of the party's military committee; and secretary of the party organization in the Ministry of National Defense. He had

[6] Ibid., March 10, 11.

[7] For the report, see *RP*, June 12, 1968. His successful escape was made possible, according to the commission, by serious failings in the Ministry of National Defense and the Chief Military Procuracy. He did not, however, receive help from outside the country, or from General Lomský, it was concluded. Nor was there any evidence, it was said, of an "abuse of the army" by Lomský. Šejna, in a post-occupation interview, denied that he had sought to use military means to prevent the ouster of Novotný. Although he revealed little of importance, Šejna claimed that he had fled after vainly warning Dubček of plans by Kolder, backed by Prchlík, to remove him, with Soviet support (*The New York Times*, August 26, 28). See the account, unfortunately undocumented, by J. Erickson, paper at Reading conference, 1971, in V. V. Kusin, ed., *The Czechoslovak Reform Movement 1968* (London, 1973), pp. 38-41. This episode is linked by Erickson with the replacement of Šejna and Mamula by Prchlík and Pepich and with the subsequent removal of General Lomský and J. Kudrna from office, thus eliminating Soviet influence in the armed forces and security and removing the possibility of the use of military power against Dubček.

been promoted to general's rank, it was learned, by presidential decree in November 1967. The press at once raised questions concerning the ease with which he rose to high office; his support of Novotný in the fall and winter; his friendship with Antonín Novotný, Jr.; and the conditions which made his defection possible.[8] The revelation that Šejna had advanced rapidly without any educational or even military qualifications, and the charges that he had used his power for personal enrichment, as well as for the preservation of Novotný's position, placed the pre-January regime and Novotný personally in an even more unfavorable light. His easy escape from the country aroused apprehensions that there were people in high places who might be able to frustrate the reform movement and stirred up demands for the replacement of holdovers from the past. All of these factors combined to give a powerful fillip to the pressures for reform and led to a flood of demands for the removal of Novotný from the presidency.

The open debate had already begun, to a limited degree, in late February, as journalists and speakers boldly discussed sensitive issues. In early March the party's Presidium prepared the way for the deluge by abolishing its 1966 decision concerning censorship; removing the Central Publications Board, responsible for censorship, from the jurisdiction of the Minister of the Interior; and promising a revision of the much criticized press law.[9] Shortly thereafter, the party organization in the board itself recommended the abolition of censorship.[10] By the beginning of March the censors had virtually ceased to exercise effective control. Faced with an opportunity for almost unlimited freedom of expression, journalists aired sensational news, for instance about the Šejna "scandal," and ventilated many repressed grievances. The newspapers were filled with articles and round-table discussions on the ills of the past two decades; the trials of the fifties; discriminations against Slovaks; freedom of the press; free-

---

[8] Earlier statements by the Military Procuracy indicated that investigations of embezzlement by an official in the Ministry of National Defense in late 1967 had led to the detention of a Colonel Moravec on January 26, 1968, and this, in turn, produced evidence, in early February, implicating Šejna. His arrest was delayed, it was said, by the need to secure the authorization of the National Assembly. Statements by the presidium of the National Assembly, and by the chairman of the assembly, Laštovička, laid the blame on the procuracy which had informed the chairman about Šejna on February 21 but had stressed the need for secrecy rather than swift action. When the presidium of the assembly learned about the matter at its scheduled meeting on February 27, Šejna had already escaped two days earlier. For these statements, see RP, March 8, 9, 15, 16.

A later investigation of Novotný's son by the General Procuracy led to a report which confirmed his friendship with General Šejna and the exploitation of his position for personal benefit (e.g. the building of a villa and a country cottage [chata] with the help of military personnel) but found no basis for criminal prosecution (RP, June 28).

[9] See Rok šedesátý osmý (Prague, 1969), pp. 32-33; henceforth RŠO.

[10] RP, March 16, 1968.

dom of religion; Czech traditions, including the role of T. G. Masaryk; the meaning of democracy and of genuine elections, and many issues formerly taboo. This "frenzy of negation,"[11] as it has been called, was in fact a positive process of cleansing the atmosphere of the falsities and distortions that had accumulated over the years. It marked also the emergence of public opinion as a powerful force, a fact recognized by the beginning of systematic and objective polling and research on this new phenomenon in politics.[12]

A prominent feature of politics in its altered form was the conversion of the press from organs of propaganda into forums of controversy and channels of objective reporting, not free from occasional sensationalism. A number of editors resigned or were removed from their posts.[13] Journalists sometimes expressed opinions not authorized by their publishers or their chief editors. Trade union papers, such as *Práce*, and the Slovak *Práca*, the youth dailies, *Mladá fronta* and *Smena*, agricultural newspapers, *Zemědělské noviny* and *Rol'nícke noviny*, the organs of the noncommunist parties, *Svobodné slovo* and *Lidová demokracie*, the journalists' weekly, *Reportér*, and even the military organ, *Obrana lidu*, underwent a surprising metamorphosis and their circulation greatly increased as a result. The party organs did not escape the general trend.[14] The "editorial collective" of *Rudé právo* indulged in self-criticism and proclaimed its intention, as an organ of the Central Committee and the party as a whole, to contribute freely to the development of the party's policy.[15] The theoretical journal, *Nová mysl*, censured itself for "lagging behind the progressive tendencies of theoretical thinking" and declared that it must no longer be "an apologist and a passive interpreter of the decisions of party organs but a theoretical pathfinder." In a major editorial it called for a struggle against conservative opinions without "fear of discussion or possible deviations."[16] The party's cultural weekly, *Kulturní tvorba*, was also sharply criticized.[17] The beginning of publication of the organ of the Writers' Union, under its new name *Literární listy*, brought into the fray a journal of high intellectual quality which at once started

[11] Rémi Gueyt, *La mutation tchécoslovaque* (Paris, 1969), pp. 66-67.

[12] See below, chap. XVII. O. Kýn wrote on the need for more information, transmitted both from the central organs to the citizens and from the citizens to the central organs, through public opinion research and through free expression in the mass media (*Literární listy*, March 14, 1968, p. 3).

[13] For instance, the editors of *Reportér* replaced their chief editor, A. Hradecký, by S. Budín, well-known journalist who had been expelled from the party in the thirties and had never rejoined (*Rep.*, April 3-10).

[14] This may be noted in *Nová mysl*, beginning with no. 4, sent to the press on March 28, and *Život strany*, beginning with no. 10, sent on April 30.

[15] *RP*, March 20.

[16] *Nová mysl*, no. 4 (1968), pp. 415-17, 405 resp. Cf. self-criticism by the editors of *Život strany*, no. 8-9 (April 1968), pp. 8-11.

[17] *RP*, April 2, 11; *Kulturní tvorba*, April 4.

to print, for a steadily growing circle of readers, controversial and provocative articles.[18] An even more outspoken paper was *Student*, an independent organ of a group of young intellectuals. A Slovak counterpart was the Bratislava student *Echo*.

People devoured the exciting fare offered to them in the newspapers and listened avidly to the controversial ideas expressed in other media of communication. Radio and television, although official in character and manned largely by communists, long-time purveyors of lifeless propaganda, underwent a complete transformation. There was greater objectivity of news reporting, frequent probing interviews with public figures, and panel discussions (broadcast live) which revealed the great variety of opinion among prominent figures. Even associates of the old regime were called to account, in telephone calls which were broadcast directly. Personal attacks, often justified but sometimes irresponsible and cruel, constituted, it has been said, a kind of "moral pressure" which led more conservative persons to maintain silence, although they had an opportunity to present their views.[19]

Hundreds of public meetings permitted confrontations between lively and critical audiences and progressive spokesmen. In mid-March in the *Slovanský dům* in Prague, leading reformers, such as Smrkovský, Vodsloň, Procházka, and Kohout, and victims of past injustices, such as Zdeněk Hejzlar, former youth leader who was arrested in 1952, and Marie Švermová, high party official until her imprisonment in the fifties, addressed a stormy assembly of some 2,000 young people and responded to hundreds of blunt questions. The extraordinary atmosphere of the meeting may be illustrated by a few examples. Hejzlar appealed for "freedom of speech" as the surest guarantee that there would be no return to the old order. Švermová condemned the Slánský trials (especially for their anti-Semitic aspects), but warned against similar treatment of those guilty ("We do not want an eye for an eye, a tooth for a tooth.") Smrkovský delivered an impassioned attack on anti-Semitism as "a scandal"; he unhappily admitted that he had voted for the expulsion of the writers in September 1967 and attempted to explain this action. He also warned the young people present to respect different opinions and to "learn democracy."[20]

In view of the attendance at this gathering another was called by the

[18] The first issue was that of March 1. For a collection of articles from *Literární listy*, in translation, see J. Škvorecký, ed., *Nachrichten aus der ČSSR* (Frankfurt, 1968).

[19] Gueyt, *Mutation*, pp. 57-60.

[20] *Zemědělské noviny*, March 15; *Smena*, March 26. There was a similar meeting of several thousand university students in Bratislava, at which Husák, H. Kočtúch, and others appeared and replied to questions (*Pravda*, March 21).

200

Prague Union of Youth. Held on March 20 at the Congress Palace in Fučík Park, it was attended by over 15,000 people and lasted for six or seven hours. Once again bold questions were answered frankly by such personalities as Smrkovský, Šik, Goldstücker, Husák Švermová, and Kohout. The entire proceedings were broadcast live to an astonished audience throughout the country. At the conclusion the meeting called for the resignation of Novotný and adopted a manifesto which contained demands going beyond anything so far approved by the Dubček leadership.[21] Replying to the question, "What kind of socialism shall we have in our country?" the manifesto declared that it would be "really enlightened, humane, and democratic. . . . The guarantee of such a socialism can only be democracy." Freedom of expression would make possible the formation of "a real public opinion." Equally important were freedom of assembly and association, and freedom of movement. This democratization of public life would require the abolition of all forms of censorship, the amendment of the law on association, changes in the procedures for issuing passports and visas, and the postponement of the national committee elections. There must also be legal guarantees of democracy: a constitutional court, the abolition of all laws and ordinances contrary to the spirit of the constitution, and the separation of the legislative, executive, and judicial powers. The solution of the Slovak question must be found in "the equality of Czechs and Slovaks within the framework of a federative Czechoslovak state." "The dignity and sovereignty of our state" must be defended with might and main, and "the sovereignty of all nations and all currents of thought" must be recognized. Foreign policy would continue to respect the geographical location of the Republic in central Europe and would be imbued with the "will . . . for good and equal relations with all neighbors, especially the USSR." While the alliance with the Soviet Union and other socialist countries was justified by historical experience, it must be "freed from all taboos and ballast" and "guided by the principles of state independence and by socialist, humane, and moral principles. . . ."

Two other episodes testified to the unusual circumstances of the time. In early March the birthday of T. G. Masaryk, and the tragic death of his son, Jan, were commemorated by the pilgrimage of thousands to the Masaryk grave in the village of Lány not far from Prague. At the end of the month, in a happening unique in a communist country, Dubček, on the repeated urging of a crowd of young people outside Central Committee headquarters, appeared before them just before midnight and responded to questions and complaints.[22]

[21] Text, *Rep.*, April 3-10, 1968, p. 7. On Smrkovský's urging, the declaration did not include a demand for Novotný's resignation.
[22] *NYT*, March 30.

REBELLIOUSNESS AT THE GRASS ROOTS

Another dramatic feature of the March days was the awakening of the mass associations, the non-communist political parties, and the Communist Party itself. Meetings of basic organizations, or committees at higher levels, resounded with criticism of the leadership and of the previous policies of these organizations, and with demands for resignations and for more independence in defending the interests of the social groups involved. The activization of interest groups gathered speed and was endorsed in principle by the party Presidium at its meeting on March 21.[23] Leaders of the trade union movement, the youth union, the journalists' union, the cooperatives, and the women's congress, were openly called upon, by the members and lower organizations, to resign, or were removed. The Union of Youth virtually disintegrated, as separate groups of young people, for instance the university students, demanded, or began to form, independent organizations of their own. The Slovak *Matica* pressed for rehabilitation after years of official restrictions. The demand was raised for the early establishment of a collective farmers' association.

New organizations also came into existence de facto, without legal approval, for example, the Academic Council of Students in Prague, as a parliament of students, the Club of Critical Thought within the Writers' Union, which planned to organize public debates, and most controversial, K 231. Membership in the latter was open to all who had been in prison under the 1948 law for the defense of the Republic (no. 231). Several thousand former prisoners attended a highly emotional inaugural meeting in Prague.[24] Although its primary purpose was to secure the rehabilitation of victims of past injustice, it hoped to share in safeguarding human rights. In early April, a Slovak Organization for the Defense of Human Rights was set up in Bratislava. Although primarily concerned with rehabilitation, it also proposed to defend human rights, as set forth in the Universal Declaration of Human Rights, by all constitutional means.[25] Almost at the same time, the Club of the Non-party Engagés (*Klub angažovaných nestraníků*), which came to be known as KAN, was formed to give citizens who were not members of any party an opportunity to participate in public life and to share in the building of "a new political system—hitherto never realized in history—democratic socialism."[26]

[23] *RŠO*, p. 39.

[24] A letter of greeting was read from Professor Goldstücker (*RP*, April 2 and *NYT*, April 1). See statements by Karel Nigrín, K 231 chairman, in *MF*, April 20 and *Pravda*, May 2. Cf. J. Brodsky, "Czechoslovakia's 231 Club," *East Europe* 18 (June 1969), 23-25.

[25] *Kultúrny život*, April 12.

[26] *LL*, no. 7, April 11, 1968. The hope was later expressed that KAN would be legalized as "a regular partner" in the rebirth of democracy and that there would

In the Socialist and People's Parties, local branches and the party newspapers expressed dissatisfaction with the policies and leaders of their respective parties and demanded the resignation of discredited officers, such as A. Neuman and J. Plojhar, and independence of action by their parties.[27] Many meetings of the parties and of associations raised problems that required solution at the national level, such as the rehabilitation of the victims of the fifties, and passed resolutions in favor of the resignation of leading figures, such as General Lomský, Dr. Václav Škoda, and Novotný himself. It was argued that such resignations should be considered a normal democratic procedure and should be conducted without recrimination, and in a dignified manner.[28] Catholics, headed by Bishop František Tomášek, set forth extensive demands for the correction of wrongs done to priests and believers, including permission for Cardinal Josef Beran to return from his exile in Rome, the ending of limitations on the Church's activities, and the restoration of full religious freedom.[29]

At the lower levels of the Communist Party there was a similar spirit of rebellion and controversy, especially during the district party conferences from March 9 to 19. The organizational journal spoke of the "new spirit" of the conferences and "a real renaissance of party activity."[30] Great dissatisfaction with the lack of information available to party members was expressed, and demands were made that the minutes of the pre-January plena be published. There was a barrage of criticism of district and regional officers which often culminated in their replacement, in elections conducted by secret ballot. There were attacks on higher leaders, such as Hendrych, Chudík, and Lomský, and calls for the resignation of Novotný from the presidency and of other persons from the Central Committee. In Prague, there was sharp censure of the municipal leading secretary, Martin Vaculík, for his role before and after January, and criticism of a statement by the municipal committee which had asserted that the political situation had developed since January without "the necessary influence of the party leadership."[31] In Bratislava there was similar condemnation of Chudík.[32] The discussions revealed a wide range of opinions, extending from radical reformist views, which ap-

be no obstacles, under the new electoral law, to the nomination and election of non-communists (L. Rybáček, ibid., April 25).

[27] See, for instance, *Lidová demokracie*, March 29, in which almost all the party's central committee members expressed lack of confidence in the leadership. Cf. ibid., March 9 and 16. Plojhar sought to associate himself with the reform movement and admitted the need for changes in party policy (ibid., March 17).

[28] *ZN*, March 14; *LD*, March 16.   [29] *NYT*, March 25 and 27.

[30] These were briefly reported in *RP*, March 10-13, 17-18; *Pravda*, March 16-18. See also *ŽS*, no. 7 (March 1968), pp. 1-3, 21-29.

[31] *Večerní Praha*, March 9, 18, 21.   [32] J. Zrak, *Pravda*, March 16.

proved the new course and urged accelerated action, to more cautious and conservative warnings of threatening dangers and criticisms of the mass media.[33] In a few recorded cases there was open opposition to basic features of the post-January course, for instance, in a Prague borough party meeting, where two speakers, L. Morávek and J. Jodas, charged Goldstücker, Smrkovský, and others with seeking to liquidate the party, the alliance with the USSR, and the principles of socialism, and were warmly applauded. The conference nonetheless gave its full support to the party's new line.[34] A joint meeting of the party committees in two of the largest industrial enterprises, the Kladno mines and ČKD Sokolovo plant in Prague (where Novotný had spoken), declared their support for the "process of revival" and demanded clear statements of position by leading persons.[35] Although the storminess of these meetings was muffled in the newspaper reports, there could be no mistaking the importance of this grass roots revolt within the party.

RESPONSE AT HIGHER LEVELS

The leading bodies of party and state lagged behind the unofficial movement of protest. Key positions continued to be held by the same persons who had held them under Novotný—Lenárt, Prime Minister; David, foreign minister; and Lomský, defense minister. State and party organs, encouraged by official statements, were, however, coming to life after years of moribundity. The National Assembly voiced criticism of its past record and began to plan a more independent and active role, even though for the time being there were to be no changes in its composition through elections. In mid-March the assembly's presidium expressed lack of confidence in the Minister of Interior, Jan Kudrna, and the Procurator General, Jan Bartuška, which led to their dismissal. The Slovak National Council removed its chairman, Michal Chudík, close colleague and supporter of Novotný (a step which was later approved by the party Presidium); began to discuss changes in its own position; and adopted a resolution in favor of federalization. The Prague government also indulged in self-criticism and initiated discussions of its own reform, a move which was endorsed by the party Presidium. Individual

---

[33] A controversy developed in connection with a panel discussion in a Prague factory (Tesla) in which fears of excessive criticism were voiced. *Rudé právo* asserted that many shared these views and all should have the right to express them (*RP*, March 10, 12; *Práce*, March 13, 19).

[34] *RP*, March 18. Jodas was also quoted as complaining of "anti-party, anti-communist and anti-Soviet influences" in various party institutions, including *Rudé právo* (*VP*, March 18). Karel Mestek, Minister of Agriculture and Food, was also critical of the mass media (*NYT*, March 19). Jodas was the author of the so-called Libeň letter referred to above, chap. VII.

[35] *RP*, March 16.

ministries began to display a new independence and to prepare proposals for reform, such as the draft law on rehabilitation submitted by the Ministry of Justice. The communist organizations within various departments, including even the Ministry of the Interior, severely censured the record of their department and its highest officials, and urged radical changes. On March 12 this ministry issued a report on the Strahov student demonstration in 1967 which criticized the behavior of the police and promised improvements in police procedures.[36] President Novotný was obliged to pardon Jan Beneš, the young writer condemned in the summer of 1967 for alleged subversive activity. The National Front announced that national committee elections would be held on May 19, thus taking the first step toward the renovation of elected organs. At the end of March the Czechoslovak People's Party elected new officers by secret ballot, but replaced Plojhar by A. Pospíšil, a veteran party leader, and retained Plojhar as honorary chairman and party representative in the government. The People's Party issued a proclamation declaring its determination to democratize itself and its desire to act independently within the National Front as a group of citizens of "Christian world outlook."[37] The Czechoslovak Socialist Party also elected a new leadership, retaining Neuman as honorary chairman, however, and replacing him as chairman with a party veteran, B. Kučera. The party issued a statement regretting its previous lack of participation in the democratization process and resolving to play a significant and independent part in future.[38]

The increasing public demand for the removal of Novotný, whose continuance as President seemed to personify the slowness of the reform movement and the danger of a relapse, could no longer be resisted. On March 21 he announced his intention to resign to the party Presidium, which accepted his "request" and endorsed his "retirement for reasons of health." His resignation was then accepted by the National Assembly. Thereupon, in an informal "nomination campaign" hitherto unheard of in a communist country, various organizations and meetings advanced alternative candidates, such as Smrkovský, Císař, Goldstücker, and Novomeský, for the vacant post.[39] In the end Novotný's successor was selected by an entirely conventional procedure in which the CC plenum chose General Svoboda as the party's candidate, the National Front and the other parties gave their formal approval, and he was finally elected

---

[36] See above, chap. III.   [37] *LD*, April 1.

[38] *Svobodné slovo*, March 24, 27. See a fuller statement of its principles, ibid., April 14.

[39] The central committee of the Union of Youth formally proposed Císař, who was a favorite of many students. Other students, however, distrusted him, a long-time party functionary, and preferred Goldstücker. The names of Husák, Dubček, Šorm, Černík, and Fierlinger were also advanced (*RŠO*, p. 48).

by the National Assembly, in an almost unanimous vote.[40] Although some were disappointed by the choice, there was, after the event, general satisfaction with the outcome.[41]

The new President, at 72 years of age, was a distinguished and venerable-looking person, who no doubt was expected to be little more than a symbolic and ceremonial figure. As President, however, he would possess certain significant powers under the constitution, in particular as supreme commander of the armed forces.[42] In Dubček's words to the assembly, the office of the presidency had "a democratic and progressive tradition" in Czechoslovakia, and "the person of the President" had always been regarded as "a representative of our independence and of Czechoslovak statehood." Svoboda was presumably considered a compromise figure designed to satisfy both ardent and moderate reformers and to assuage any fears that the Russians might entertain. He had fought on the Russian side in both world wars, during the second as head of the Czechoslovak army in the Soviet forces, and held high military decorations from the USSR. After the war, until 1950, he had been Minister of Defense, and in that office had facilitated the communist seizure of power in 1948. General Svoboda had joined the Communist Party in 1948 and was a CC member in 1948 and 1949. He had later become a victim of Gottwald's purge, having been removed from office in the early fifties and relegated to a collective farm.[43] In 1955 he was appointed head of the Gottwald Military Academy, a post he held until his retirement in 1959. As a man of distinguished public service, identified with the struggle for national liberation in both world wars, and persecuted during the fifties, he enjoyed considerable popularity among both Czechs and Slovaks. His career, however, and especially his close relations with the Soviet Union and his part in the seizure of power in 1948, awakened uneasiness in the minds of some, both within and outside the party.

Within the party's higher organs the spontaneous movement also made itself felt. At first, as Dubček later explained, the party sought to avoid hasty changes in cadres and to concentrate on the formulation of policy.

[40] There were 282 votes for, none against, and six abstentions. In the CC plenum, 105, of 107 present, supported Svoboda. See *RP*, March 31, for the proceedings, Dubček's speech, and Svoboda's biography. Nothing is known as to the Presidium's discussion of alternative choices or the reasons for their selection of Svoboda. For a laudatory biography of Svoboda, of no scholarly value, see Teodor Fiš, *Mein Kommandeur, General Svoboda: Vom Ural zum Hradschin* (Vienna, 1969).

[41] See laudatory article, *Rep.*, April 10-17, 1968. Public opinion polls indicated that 88 percent were satisfied with the selection of Svoboda. In polls before the election, there had been a preference for Smrkovský at an early stage, and later for Svoboda (*RP*, April 30). See also Jaroslaw A. Piekalkiewicz, *Public Opinion Polling in Czechoslovakia, 1968-69* (New York, 1972), pp. 254-55.

[42] F. Sýkora, *Pravda*, March 31.

[43] See below, chap. XIII, for later revelations of alleged Soviet disfavor.

As a result many conservatives, who were not fully in sympathy with reform, still remained in high office. It was only on March 4 that Hendrych, the executor, if not the architect, of Novotný's cultural policies, was removed as the party's ideological chief and replaced by Špaček. Ten days later Císař was appointed to head the secretariat department dealing with education, science, and culture. Within the powerful Central Commission of Supervision and Auditing (ÚKRK), there was self-criticism, followed by the resignation of its chief, Pavel Hron, and his replacement by Miloš Jakeš.[44] These were mere shifts within the apparatus and did not yet affect the highest echelons. Hendrych, for example, remained a member of the Presidium throughout March. In response to public pressures, however, especially during the campaign surrounding the presidency, two of the unofficial "candidates" were given high posts in the regime at the plenary session which endorsed Svoboda as president: Smrkovský, as member of the Presidium, and Císař as CC Secretary and member of the Secretariat. The principal leadership changes, to be discussed below, were announced only at the conclusion of the plenary session a week later.

The Presidium of the party, in this atmosphere of public excitement, had to meet more frequently to keep pace with events.[45] On March 14 and 21, it endorsed the entire "movement of revival" as "healthy" and "creative," designed to establish a democracy of "socialist character," and not to be judged by some "extreme tendencies" or "non-socialist moods." Apprehensions as to whether things were moving in "the right direction" were said to reflect "old habits" of thought and practice. Nor were fears that everything might go back to the old channels justified, it was stated. In other statements the Presidium endorsed the revival of political activity, including that of the mass associations and the work of the media of communications, and encouraged them to proceed further. It approved the need for rehabilitation, for constitutional amendments, for changes in the government's procedures, and for revisions of cultural policy. The demand frequently raised for the postponement of local elections until the end of June was also sanctioned, on the grounds that the electoral law required revision before elections were held.[46] The action program, which was to be submitted to the next CC plenum, would be a general guideline for the future, the concrete implementation and further development of which would have to be worked out by the individual organs of government and the members of the National Front. The Central Committee was, however, not scheduled until the end of March

[44] *RŠO*, pp. 41-43.
[45] Meetings were held on March 4, 12, 14, 21, 25, 26 (*RŠO*, pp. 32 ff.).
[46] The postponement was approved by 79 percent in a public opinion poll (*RP*, March 27).

on the assumption that the party leadership could then present a coherent policy to an impatient party and nation and couple this with urgently needed cadre changes. The removal of Novotný, carried through at a special meeting prior to the main part of the plenum, was an unforeseen result of public pressure. The appointment of Svoboda indicated, however, that the Presidium was still the decisive political factor.

THE INTERNATIONAL CONTEXT

On every suitable public occasion Dubček emphasized the importance of the alliance with the Soviet Union and the necessity of the unity of the socialist bloc, and proclaimed Czechoslovakia's intention to preserve these two essential features of its policy. Czechoslovak participation in the Warsaw pact conference in Sofia in early March, with a delegation consisting of Lenárt, David, and Lomský, suggested no basic change in orientation. This was further confirmed by the visits to Moscow by Černík and General Pepich later in the month, although nothing concrete is known as to what transpired on those occasions.

Press comment in the Soviet Union and bloc states, as we have seen, had been rather limited at first and without controversial implications. On March 14, in fact, *Pravda* gave a generally favorable account of Czechoslovak developments, based mainly on *Rudé právo* reports. Suddenly, however, clouds began to appear on the horizon, although their significance was not at first clear. Immediately after Černík returned from Moscow and the resignation of Novotný was announced by the Presidium, on March 23, a conference of Communist Party leaders was hurriedly called in Dresden. On this occasion the Soviet and bloc leaders apparently revealed deep misgivings about the course of events in Czechoslovakia. Dubček admitted that the Soviet leaders had expressed "worries" but stated that they had in the end evinced "understanding" and promised "support" for the Czechoslovak party's policy.[47] In his main report at the April plenum, Dubček, in referring to the Dresden talks, said that the Czechoslovak attitude was "accepted with understanding," and declared that "the principle of non-interference in internal affairs would continue to be valid."[48] Earlier, at the CC plenary session dealing with the selection of Svoboda, he made a special point that the issue of changes of leadership had not been discussed, "officially or unofficially," at Dresden and had emphasized the "responsibility" and the "sovereignty" of the CPCz in regard to "our internal development."[49]

Apart from this, nothing was revealed concerning the Dresden talks. Soviet comments in *Pravda* were sparse and factual, limited to the com-

---

[47] *RP*, March 27. [48] *RŠO*, pp. 85-86.
[49] Ibid., p. 50.

muniqué, which gave no indication of deep Soviet concern over the Czechoslovak situation, a front-page editorial in similar tone, and reports of Dubček's account and his later interview.[50] Only after the occupation were accounts given suggesting that the Dresden meeting had been an occasion for stringent criticism of Czechoslovak policies by Brezhnev and other leaders, with warnings of the dangers of counterrevolution arising out of the activity of "anti-socialist forces," and censure of the Prague regime for failing to limit such threats by decisive action.[51]

That the situation was more serious was indicated a few days after the Dresden meeting when Kurt Hager, East German leader, made a blistering attack on the trend of events in Czechoslovakia and on Smrkovský in particular, evoking a diplomatic protest by Prague. This speech was a rude shock to the general public who were made suddenly aware of the international dimension of post-January events. *Rudé právo* sharply rebuked Hager for his speech and described it as an intervention in Czechoslovakia's internal affairs.[52] An open letter to the Central Committee, signed by 134 writers and cultural figures, including Jaroslav Seifert and Eduard Goldstücker, expressed concern about the Dresden discussions and assured support to the leadership, "if you show that, while preserving the international solidarity of socialist states, you also feel a responsibility for this country primarily to its own people."[53] Špaček, however, while regretting Hager's speech, did not think the situation should be dramatized, since exchanges of opinion, without pressure from outside, were valuable. He disavowed "a narrow national concept" and saw a solution based on "the realistic conceptions of individual parties" and on "the general regularities of the development of socialism."[54]

DUBČEK SPEAKS

Dubček, in several speeches, endorsed the wave of political activity and sought to dispel fears about the future and to justify the party's strategy. In an effort to counteract moves by Novotný to appeal to the industrial workers, Dubček, in a speech in Kladno, emphasized the leading role of the working class and at the same time the need for the cooperation of the workers with the intelligentsia and the collective farm peasantry.[55] In Brno at a municipal party conference in mid-March, he declared: "Activity is returning to the party, and confidence to the people. The annual membership meetings and the district conferences of the

---

[50] *Pravda* (Moscow), March 26, 27, 28.
[51] See below, chap. xx.
[52] *RP*, March 28. For Hager's speech, see below, chap. xx.
[53] *LL*, March 28; *RP*, March 27.   [54] *RP*, April 11.
[55] *RP*, March 5.

party demand and urge the further consistent fulfilment of the conclusions of the January plenum. A lively, passionate, and sometimes even anxious discussion is taking place, full of interest in the party and in its work. The party as a whole is beginning to be conscious of the necessity to place itself at the head and to guide the bursting current of creative social activity. . . . The party is seeking out ways adequately to express the needs of the nations, of society, of social groups, and of the individual. The search is a complicated process. But without such a search it is not possible to lead society."[56]

Acknowledging that a certain vacuum had been created, and that there was some impatience with, and also some fears of, the results of spontaneity, he praised the work of the mass media, but criticized some "imprudence" and urged editors "not to accelerate too much the tempo of bringing forward problems." Recognizing that there were some dangers in the situation, he denied that there was any real possibility that "the relatively broadly tolerated democratic quality of politics" involved "the danger of weakening the bases of power, of defense, or the principles of socialism."

When the CC plenum met in the first days of April, Dubček, in his main report, again expounded his attitude in terms similar to those of the Brno address.[57] The post-January movement was "dynamic," but "expressly socialist and democratic, called forth by our Communist Party." He admitted that there had been too little information concerning the January changeover, that events had moved faster than expected, and that the leadership had not been prepared with a "concrete plan of advance." The Central Committee could not, however, have met earlier before a program had been developed and the views of the party members had been heard. The Presidium's duty was first to work out the basic program of advance, concentrating on "content," and later, on this basis, to make cadre changes, and not to proceed in the reverse order. The spontaneous activity of the masses must be understood as a consequence of the acute political crisis which had produced January and reflected the conflict of views as to the situation and the future. The party should not be afraid of this, but should learn from it. Dubček repeatedly stressed the socialist character of democratization and condemned anti-socialist forces which accompanied it but which were not a determining feature. He rejected fears that the party was "retreating before pressure" or "giving up its positions." The party was "fulfilling" and not "weakening" the line of the 13th congress; it was actively "deepening" this line and "preparing its new formulation."

[56] *RP*, March 17; also in Dubček *K otázkam obrodzovacieho procesu v KSČ* (Bratislava, 1968), pp. 68-82.
[57] *RP*, April 2 (also *RŠO*, pp. 65-88).

The main task was "to deepen, make concrete and consolidate this whole process of revival of ours," and to "create a mechanism" which could proceed "not catastrophically or through campaigns, but in a quiet, businesslike, and democratic way." It was important "to consolidate political relations and to reform the whole previous system of political direction so as to link fully socialism and democracy." The Communist Party must be the decisive political force, without the presence of opposition parties, but its authority was not "given once and for all" and must be constantly rewon by its work.

They were only at the beginning, taking the first steps, said Dubček. The Action Program was "an open document" which would have to be developed further and concretely implemented. With the party at the head, and with the program as the point of departure, democratization would have to go further; action must be oriented to "progressive demands, even if they seem perhaps at the moment too radical." The ultimate goal was "to create a more perfect type of socialist democracy corresponding to Czechoslovak conditions."

Dubček's speech, characteristically, was rambling, much more so than these brief quotations suggest. On one point, however, he expressed himself unambiguously, especially in his concluding speech.[58] The time was not yet ripe, he said, for an extraordinary congress of the party, as proposed by some. Many problems would face the next congress, including the development and concrete implementation of the Action Program, the approval of a new party statute, constitutional changes, further economic reform, and cadre problems. Time and study were needed to prepare solutions for these questions. A congress which did not deal effectively with them would be a great disappointment. It was better, he said, quoting a Czech proverb, "to measure twice and cut once." Certainly changes in cadres, including the CC membership, were needed, but that was not enough to justify an early congress. The Central Committee in its present composition had shown itself capable of taking the necessary steps. Rather than schedule an extraordinary congress, it was better to speed up the preparations for the convening, as soon as possible, of the regular 14th congress.

THE PLENUM DEBATE

The debate in the Central Committee lasted five days, and for the first time in party history, the widespread divergence of opinion was bared in the published reports.[59] The intense discussions reflected the general

---

[58] *RP*, April 6 (also *RŠO*, pp. 88-94).
[59] *RP*, April 2 *et seq.* For a full analysis of speeches and decisions, see Gueyt, *Mutation*, pp. 75-94.

atmosphere of crisis and uncertainty in the country at large and in Dubček's own words, "differences in the evaluation of the previous development and in opinions on further advance," and differences as to "the tempo and the balance of the whole process." Although no one openly repudiated the post-January trend, many speakers severely criticized certain aspects. The opinions ranged from conservative—Novotný, V. Nový, M. Jakeš, O. Rákosník, Fojtík, J. Krosnář, and B. Chňoupek— to more progressive—Císař, Smrkovský, Vodsloň, Slavík, Mlynář, Šik, Švestka, and Špaček. Several high-ranking functionaries—Koucký, Hendrych, Auersperg, Lomský, Švestka, Kolder, Hron, and Dolanský— indulged in a certain self-criticism, often coupled with attempts at self-defense, and Koucký, Šimůnek, Dolanský, and Lomský announced their intentions to resign from office. A few of the topmost leaders, notably Chudík and Černík, were not reported to have spoken at all.

"Progressive" speakers raised demands for more information; more frequent CC meetings; an early congress, even in 1968; cadre changes, including voluntary resignations; a reconstruction of the government and improvement in the working of the assembly; the postponement of local government elections; acceleration of rehabilitation; concrete measures of political reform, such as federalization, and so on. Slavík warned against stopping half-way in the process of revival.[60] Špaček complained of those who exaggerated the danger on the "right," including the efforts of progressive communists, and identified the main danger as the fear that "we may go too far." He emphasized the need for an early congress which would elaborate "a new general line" going beyond that of the 13th congress.[61]

More conservative spokesmen criticized "spontaneous" and anti-socialist or rightist tendencies, and demanded their control or elimination; urged that the party keep matters in its hands and control the course of events; pleaded for unity and stabilization; censured the "labeling" of persons and loose definitions of "conservatives"; rejected criticism of the party's entire past and emphasized "socialism" as the objective; urged caution and "justice" in cadre changes; pleaded for limits on the mass media; defended an international approach and the alliance with the Soviet Union.

Chňoupek, in one of the most conservative statements at the plenum, was disturbed by the fact that "the democratization current had gone beyond party grounds and become a public matter, for which we shall find in the past no historical parallel; that public attacks, either spontaneous or those organized by groups, have been made against comrades who in January showed personal courage in clearly defending a progres-

---

[60] *RP*, April 5.   [61] Ibid., April 11.

sive standpoint; that the first anti-Soviet assaults have appeared; that a rapid activizing movement has taken place in other political parties. . . ." He urged that the party "not act under pressure but set the tone and rhythm for the healthy progressive process, guiding it constantly in the right direction, and not permitting even for a moment attacks from the right, and especially not to yield to them."[62] Chňoupek expressed his general approval of the January decisions but also his great concern about "right-wing excesses," and criticized Špaček's proposal of a "new general line" and the idea of an extraordinary congress.

Although the tenor of most speeches was in one direction or the other, it was not easy to differentiate speakers into two entirely opposed camps. Even the more conservative speakers, although pointing to the attendant dangers, approved the January changeover. More progressive spokesmen were relatively moderate in their advocacy of reform and accented the "socialist" character of the process and the leading role of the party, albeit in a new form. They recognized, too, the accompanying "dangerous tendencies." Several, including Šik, pleaded for toleration of different views and warned against a witch hunt.[63] Whatever the differences, and they were undeniably great, there was still general agreement, at least in principle, and as expressed publicly, on the post-January policy. The general approach, even of the more progressive spokesmen, was less radical than more extreme tendencies appearing among the general public.

Novotný was given ample time to express his views, but received no explicit support.[64] In spite of admitted errors, he defended the post-1948 path as essentially correct. The line of the 13th congress was good and needed only to be concretely developed. He confirmed the necessity of the events from the October plenum on, including the January decision, and complained that his public speeches in support of this had not been published. He accepted the division of top functions and wondered whether it had been wise to combine the posts in 1957. This had, however, been the result of the difficult situation in which the party then found itself and had been designed to strengthen its leading role. Novotný denied his complicity in the trials of the fifties and justified his rehabilitation policy as a "just" one that had protected the confidence of the people in the party and in Gottwald. He argued that, if there had

[62] Ibid., April 7. His speech was published in full, in *Tvorba*, no. 23 (1970), supplement.

[63] *RP*, April 7.

[64] Ibid., April 6. See the sharp critique of his speech by five historians, ibid., April 13. They censured his failure to make any serious changes in policy in 1953, and again in 1956 and 1961, and his use of administrative measures against advocates of reform. The historians also linked Novotný with the trials of the fifties and blamed him for not carrying through a complete reexamination of the verdicts.

been a system of "personal power" under his leadership, it had been the product of "a certain process." He denied that the state had been "undemocratic," and asserted that it had been a "socialist" democracy. He was ready to admit his own errors inasmuch as he had shared responsibility for making party policy, but rejected responsibility for all actions implementing it. Could I, with a few others, Novotný asked, have directed the party and the state against the will of the elected and other organs? He rejected charges that he had tried to use the army and security forces to defend his position and denied any personal relations with General Šejna.

The post-January trend toward implementing the line of the last congress was essentially "healthy," but had been accompanied by "dangerous phenomena." Novotný described the present situation as "serious," since the party did not have things sufficiently in hand, and publicists were determining the tone of public discussions. "The healthy, socialist, progressive process initiated by the January session . . . could bring results which we do not want." Dubček's report, however, he found "good" and "quietening," "a strengthening of socialist tendencies in the very democratization process." He approved the Action Program, which should be "elaborated so as to be consistently placed on the bases of Marxist-Leninist consciousness and the interests and needs of the working people." If the Slovaks wished federalism, he was ready to accept it. The party's role must be maintained. "Without this, one cannot speak of democracy as socialist." Concerning friendship and the alliance with the Soviet Union "there could be no compromises."

ATTEMPT AT CONSOLIDATION

The concluding actions of the plenum reflected the general aims of consolidation and moderate advance. The resolution on "the present political situation," introduced by Švestka, was a relatively restrained document which reiterated the main lines of Dubček's report. "The broad current of the democratic movement" was a "socialist" one, seeking to free socialism of its previous deformations and to build "a socialism that would correspond to our conditions and traditions." "As far as non-socialist, or in some cases even anti-communist voices, are heard, they do not find a significant response or any support and cannot determine the tone of our democratization process. We must actively and decisively take steps against such tendencies. . . ."The Action Program was "an open political document," a point of departure for the state organs and the National Front. It would be the basis of an effort "to achieve the necessary stabilization of our democracy and its fully socialist character." Criticism would continue, but in a "well-thought-out system of effecting

214

and implementing social criticism and initiative, control, and responsibility."[65]

The concrete decisions taken were designed to eliminate the most glaring errors of the past and to set forth the major principles of reform. The plenum approved the full rehabilitation of all persons victimized in the years from 1949 to 1954; it was to be effected on the basis of a law which would provide for revision of the original sentences by the courts and for the payment of damages. A special commission, headed by Jan Piller, was appointed to complete the "rehabilitation" of leading party members. The CC decisions of September 1967 concerning the dissident writers were revoked; the party group in the Union of Writers and the party's Ideological Commission were to examine and evaluate the writers' congress and the actions of its communist members. The elections to the national committees were postponed until an even later time than originally considered, at the earliest in the fall. The plenum approved the basic changes proposed in the working of the government and the Slovak Council and endorsed the principle of a "symmetrical" or federative constitutional system. These decisions in most cases simply ratified those already taken by the Presidium or ÚKRK, or by the appropriate organs of government, and broke no new ground, but together constituted significant steps toward correcting the most serious deficiencies of the past.

Even more important was the ratification of the Action Program, introduced by Kolder, and the request to the National Front and the government to prepare the measures necessary to carry it out. The program, which will be discussed below, represented a rather hastily drafted compromise which embodied some radical proposals, such as freedom of the press, and other provisions more conservative in character, such as the maintenance of the Communist Party's hegemony. In many respects, as Dubček admitted, the program had been overtaken by events so that much depended on how it would actually be implemented and further elaborated by the responsible bodies.

The changes in party leadership adopted by the plenum produced a substantial shift in the balance of forces, but did not represent an unambiguous transition toward a completely new and reform-oriented team. Novotný lost his positions in the Presidium, in the Secretariat, and the National Front. Four of his closest associates and supporters, Chudík, Šimůnek, Hendrych, and Laštovička, were retired from the Presidium, and Miroslav Pastyřík and Michal Sabolčík were dropped as candidates. Dolanský, a comrade of Gottwald and Novotný for several decades, but an opponent of Novotný in the final phase before January, resigned "for reasons of age." Lenárt, however, who had backed Novotný to the end, remained as a candidate Presidium member and as a Secretary. Dubček, Kolder, and Černík, who had been long-time colleagues of Novotný, but had opposed him in the fall and winter, were the only persons from the pre-January Presidium who remained as full members. Of those added in January, Rigo, Piller, Špaček, and Bil'ak continued in the Presidium, but Borůvka, regarded as an ardent reformer, was dropped. New additions included two vigorous reformers, Smrkovský and Kriegel; the more conservative Švestka; and one other, František Barbírek, a Slovak who had been an associate of Dubček in the Slovak leadership since 1963. Two supporters of Novotný in the pre-January weeks, Kapek and M. Vaculík, were still candidate members, along with the demoted Lenárt.

Although exact identification is difficult, only three members of the new Presidium could be considered strong advocates of reform—Smrkovský, Kriegel, and Špaček. Šik, whose name had been proposed by a number of speakers in the plenum, was not appointed. Almost all of the persistent defenders of Novotný before January had been removed. Most of the members had, however, been collaborators of Novotný, or even Gottwald, and had held high party or government posts in Bratislava or Prague during the fifties or sixties. Some of them, like Dubček, could be regarded as "centrist," but others, as events were to reveal, were neo-conservatives, who had accepted January, at least in words, but were lukewarm to the basic changes advocated by the strong reformers.

Except for Kolder, Sádovský, and Dubček the Secretariat was largely new. Novotný, Hendrych, Štrougal, and Koucký were dropped. The new body consisted of some "centrist" figures such as Dubček and perhaps Sádovský and Voleník; others of more progressive orientation—Císař, Mlynář and Slavík; and some more conservative, such as Kolder, Lenárt, who had supported Novotný, and Indra, who had opposed him. Among the Secretaries (as distinct from the Secretariat), there were, apart from Dubček, several carryovers (Kolder, Sádovský, and Císař) and two new members, Indra and Lenárt. The removal of Hron from the ÚKRK chairmanship, and his replacement by Jakeš, did not appear to be a shift in a progressive direction. On the other hand, the replacement of Laštovička, as chairman of the National Assembly, by Smrkovský, and of Novotný, as chairman of the National Front, by Kriegel, elevated two vigorous reformers to positions of importance. Černík, who, in spite of his long connection with Novotný, was committed to the program of moderate reform that was emerging, was appointed to head the government.[66]

[66] For biographies of appointees, *RP*, April 5.

THE ACTION PROGRAM

The general pattern of reform envisaged by the leadership was set forth in the Action Program, approved by the plenum on April 5 and published on the 10th.[67] This lengthy document was the product of a commission of CC members chaired by Kolder, but unlike programmatic documents in the past, reflected the views of many persons, including intellectuals from outside the *aparát*, who had participated in the preliminary work in a number of subcommittees.[68]

This was an eclectic document, quite general in most of its provisions, and thus left a great deal to be concretely determined in future laws and measures.[69] This was regarded as one of its strengths, distinguishing it from previous party pronouncements which were more finally binding. As stated in the text, the program "comprised the tasks, designs, and aims of the immediate future, up to the 14th congress" and would be followed by a long-term program. Dubček, in a speech to the Prague *aktiv* on the day before its publication, called it an "open document" which "opens the door to structural changes and a new dynamism of society," corresponding to the specific national conditions of Czechoslovakia. In an interview with *Rudé právo* on the day after its publication, he again spoke of it as an "open" document which was not intended to mean that policy-making must stop.[70] In the party's theoretical organ, Dubček, noting that the program had gone far beyond the line of the 13th Party Congress, called it "a first step toward a new democratic model of socialist

[67] *RP*, April 10. An important correction of the section on science, more democratic in tone than the original version, was published a few days later, ibid., April 12. A full English version, based on a not too happy official Czech translation, is available in Paul Ello, ed., *Czechoslovakia's Blueprint for "Freedom"* (Washington, D.C., 1968), pp. 89-178. A better translation is given in R. A. Remington, ed., *Winter in Prague* (Cambridge, Mass., 1969), pp. 88-137. This does *not* include the revised section on science.

[68] R. Richta, *RP*, April 1. The final draft was prepared by an editorial committee, including Richta, Mlynář, and others and had to be approved by party authorities. An earlier draft, by Auersperg, it is said, was severely criticized.

[69] For a post-occupation criticism of the Action Program, see *RP*, Oct. 3, 1970 (originally published in Moscow *Pravda*). The program was cited as an example of the regime's yielding to "spontaneous development." See also J. Pecen and K. Roubal, *ŽS*, nos. 8, 9, and 10 (1970). Jiří Hájek also condemned the Action Program for its errors and weaknesses, and many compromise formulations, but it embodied certain valid elements, which could have been the basis for unifying political forces against the right and for winning the support of the other socialist countries (*Mýtus a realita ledna*, Prague, 1970, pp. 47-48, 61-62, and the whole of chap. 5, esp. pp. 86-87).

[70] *RP*, April 9, 11, resp. Mlynář described the program as "not a completed, all-embracing text, something like a supreme law," but "a directive for the further activity of communists and others alike." "It was to be a starting point, not at all a conclusion in the development of our new policy" (*RP*, March 31).

society" which "would be further shaped (*se dotvárat'*) and would culminate in a party line which the future congress could confirm and approve."[71]

Only a brief sketch of the program is necessary at this point, since the full text is readily available and the detailed provisions will be frequently referred to in later chapters. In general, it was not unlike programmatic statements of the past, setting forth broad goals for all spheres of life and defining the basis of the actions of party members in public institutions, associations, and other contexts. Although in some sections its language was unusual and fresh, it was on the whole worded in the traditional jargon of apparatus documents. Dubček described it as a wide platform for unifying the views of communists and non-communists, but in fact it was a declaration of CPCz policy and had not been discussed with, or approved by, other parties and organizations. As in the past, it was not assumed that the program would be eventually approved or rejected after general public debate, but rather that its goals would be endorsed as a result of the party's organizational and propagandistic work and implemented by the appropriate authorities. In spite of these limitations, the program mirrored public expectations of decisive future change and stimulated hopes that such reforms would in fact be introduced.

Although there were frequent references to the 13th congress decisions, as though the program was a continuance of previous policy, there could be no mistaking the substantially new direction in which the party was planning to move. The reforms outlined would have altered the communist system in many respects and were likely to awaken worries and fears in the minds of more conservative communists at home and abroad. Yet there were often reservations or conditions attached to individual proposals which made the Action Program less radical than customarily assumed and certainly less drastic than was desired by some reformers. For them it represented a cautious and inadequate blueprint which would not fundamentally alter Czechoslovak society. One commentator observed that the program would have been ahead of public opinion two months earlier but no longer seemed novel. It represented, he believed, the maximum to be expected from the existing Central Committee, but a minimum from the body to be elected at the next congress.[72] Another observer described it as "the program of a transitional period," which was limited by various factors, including the relationship of political forces within the party and society. It was "a first effort at reconstructing the system of direction" that would become of little significance if it were not "developed, consummated, and carried out, in its concrete Czecho-

---

[71] *NM*, no. 5 (1968), p. 537.
[72] R. Selucký, *Práce*, April 11. For the full text, Pavel Tigrid, *Le printemps de Prague* (Paris, 1968), pp. 217-20.

slovak form, in a complex program of democratic socialism," to be formulated at the 14th congress.[73]

"We are not changing our basic orientation," stated the program. The general objective was, however, "to embark on the building of a new model of socialist society, one which was profoundly democratic and conformed to Czechoslovak conditions." These aims could not be achieved "by following old paths or by using means which have long become outdated, or by crude methods which have always thrown us back . . . we cannot rely on traditional schemata. We cannot press life into stereotyped patterns even if they are well conceived. It is now our assignment to blaze a trail under unknown conditions, to experiment, and to give a new shape to socialist development, drawing on creative Marxist thinking and the knowledge of the international working-class movement, but relying on a correct understanding of the conditions of the socialist evolution in Czechoslovakia, as a country which, before the eyes of the international communist movement, bears the responsibility for evaluating and exploiting, in the interest of socialism and communism, a relatively mature material base, unusual standards of education and culture among the people, and incontestable democratic traditions."

This need not involve an abandonment of the party's leading role, but did require a basic modification of the way this was to be exercised. "The party relies on the voluntary support of the people. It does not effectuate its leading role by ruling over society, but by devotedly serving its free, progressive, socialist development. The party cannot impose its authority by force but must constantly earn it by its deeds. The party cannot carry out its line by command but only through the work of its members and through the truthfulness of its ideals." The leading role was not to be interpreted, as in the past, as "a monopolistic concentration of power in the hands of party organs," in accord with the thesis that the party was "the instrument of the proletarian dictatorship," nor as making it "the universal 'manager' of society, binding all organizations and every step in life by its directives." In performing its tasks, the party must embody democratic principles in its own inner life and establish regular working relations with the scientific community.

A somewhat more exact indication of how this was to be accomplished was given in the analysis of the National Front, which was defined as linking together the political parties and the social organizations for "the creation of state policy." The National Front would provide "a political platform which did not divide political parties into governing and opposition parties in the sense of forming an opposition against the line of state policy or of the whole National Front and of conducting a political struggle for power in the state." Nor would the political parties have a monop-

[73] Karel Kaplan, *NM*, no. 5 (1968), p. 579.

olistic position. The National Front would make possible "direct influence on state policy, its formation and execution" by all political organizations, including the "voluntary social organizations," such as the trade unions. It was clear that the Action Program did not envisage a system of free political competition among independent parties and other organizations but a kind of political partnership in which the primacy of the Communist Party would have to be recognized by all other participants and the supporting role of the latter would in turn be recognized by the party. The crucial question as to how elections would be conducted in this peculiar system of non-competitive partnership was not discussed. Elections were to be postponed until a new election law, based on "democratic principles," had been formulated.

More far-reaching and unorthodox were the provisions for the guarantee of freedom of assembly and association, and of freedom of expression, which would in each case be embodied in constitutional law. In the former, the law would guarantee the emergence of voluntary organizations, interest group associations, clubs, and so on, but would also stipulate what was to be restricted as "anti-social, forbidden, or criminal." Similarly, freedom of expression would be assured by a statute which would also define what was "anti-social." A new press law was promised for the immediate future, which would exclude preliminary censorship but specify the extent of restrictions to be set by state organs on certain information. The public would be assured complete and speedy information on political and economic matters through regular press conferences and would have access to foreign newspapers. The freedom of expression of minority interests and opinions would be more precisely guaranteed by legal norms, "within the framework of socialist laws and according to the principle that decisions would be determined by majority will." There was a provision for the guarantee of freedom of movement, especially travel, extending even to the right of permanent residence abroad, subject to some restrictions to prevent the loss of certain categories of specialists. The personal and property rights of citizens would be guaranteed, with provisions for damages caused by illegal decisions of state organs. There was to be political and civil rehabilitation, on the basis of law, of persons, both communist and non-communist, who had been victims of illegality in the fifties.

The program devoted much space to the relations of Czechs and Slovaks, which had suffered, it was said, from serious faults and fundamental distortions. There must be a crucial change in constitutional relations, specifically a new constitutional law establishing a federal system, to be enacted in the immediate future. This would assure Slovakia its own legislative and executive organs in Bratislava and guarantee Slovak equality of rights in the central organs in Prague. A constitutional law embodying the national rights of the other nationalities was promised. As in the case of the other basic legal reforms envisaged, these two laws would ultimately be incorporated in a new constitution.

Apart from general references to the new form of the leading role of the party and to the need for its democratization, the Action Program did not refer in detail to the party. Much was, however, said of the state organs. The National Assembly was to become a genuine socialist parliament, with elections held on a democratic basis. A "division and control of powers" would assure the independent power of the government, free of direct party intervention, but would make it responsible to the assembly. The reduction of the powers of the Ministry of the Interior, and especially the security apparatus, was emphasized, and guarantees of genuine "legality" in the judicial system were pledged.

In the sections devoted to the economy, the program referred to the need to implement fully the economic reforms and to establish economic democratization, including greater independence of enterprises and the right of all groups, such as workers and consumers, to defend their interests. The functions of the state would continue to be important and would encompass the drafting of the plan and the formation of economic policy, but these would be performed democratically and coordinated with a market, which would be "a socialist, not a capitalist market."

The provisions relating to science, culture, and education represented reforms of varying significance. In the section on science, emphasis was placed on freedom from "outside interference" or censorship. Although the references to education were not radical, some changes were suggested, including a new law guaranteeing democracy in the universities. As far as culture was concerned, it was said that the policy of the 13th congress, which had not been implemented, was a suitable starting point. Strong statements against censorship of artistic creation, and in favor of the autonomy of cultural organizations and workers, were included.

In a brief reference to foreign policy, the alliance with the Soviet Union and the other socialist states was proclaimed as "fundamental." Czechoslovakia's foreign policy must express the national and international interests of socialist Czechoslovakia. A more active role, both in foreign policy and in bloc relations, was envisaged but no specific actions were proposed.

CONCLUSION

By early April the second stage in the evolution of reform had been completed. The plenum represented a certain consolidation of the situa-

tion, at least temporarily, on the basis of the "centrist" position personified by Dubček.[74] The outcome represented a compromise which sought
on the one hand to calm an impatient public opinion by the adoption of
the Action Program and by the other decisions taken. On the other hand,
it sought not to alienate completely the more conservative elements in
the Central Committee and in the party by avoiding drastic cadre
changes and by deferring a party congress, and elections, until 1969.[75]
Thus the plenum reflected the contradictory tendencies of the leadership
—its desire to continue along the chosen path of reform as well as its
reluctance to take decisive action to break the back of potential resistance within the party.

Nonetheless, the fact that the CPCz had been able to elaborate a detailed program for implementation by party and state and to designate
leading personalities for the presidency, and for key positions in government, the National Assembly, and the National Front, suggested that it
was still firmly in control of events. The Action Program represented a
middle-of-the-road plan of action which disappointed some,[76] yet it
received very strong support from the population as a whole.[77] The fact
that such a program, embodying substantial changes in the previous
party line, had been elaborated, even without a party congress, encouraged many to believe that, in spite of many past disappointments, serious
reforms were in the making (conversely others, more conservative, felt
alarm at some of its provisions).[78] The phraseology of the program was
perhaps less significant than the fact that a document existed to which
party leaders at lower levels and reform spokesmen could refer in advocating innovative measures. Significant, too, was the fact that the Central
Committee, in spite of its lack of genuine consensus, had shown itself
ready to accept this program. Yet it *was* a compromise document, reflecting the contradictions of the political situation, and could even be
interpreted as a means of dampening and controlling the more radical
trends toward reform.[79]

Although the changes in the top leadership represented a certain shift
in the balance of forces toward "reform," the post-April team continued
to be an amalgam of disparate elements which reflected the contradictory
tendencies within the Central Committee and within the party as a whole.

---

[74] Kaplan used the phrase "the consolidation of a provisorium" (*RP*, April 13).
See Gueyt, *Mutation*, pp. 76, 93. See also Dalimil (pseud.), *LL*, April 18.
[75] Kaplan, *RP*, April 13.   [76] V. Blažek, *LL*, April 11.
[77] See below, chap. XVII.
[78] Conservatives later claimed that the events from March on were "a shock"
which aroused serious fears as to the party's position. See Kolder and Indra, *RP*,
Sept. 10, 24, 1969, resp.
[79] This was the interpretation of the French Trotskyist, Pierre Broué, *Le
printemps des peuples commence à Prague* (Paris, n.d.), pp. 58-59, 63.

The "synthesis" of conflicting viewpoints among the leaders was by no means stable and indeed veiled the crystallization of clearly defined wings. "Reactionaries" (such as Novotný, Bacílek, and Široký), who would have liked to turn the clock back and restore the old order, remained members of the Central Committee but had lost any serious influence. Neo-conservatives (such as Kolder, Švestka, Indra, and Bil'ak), who were ready to accept a cautious and moderate program of change, but who were alarmed by more radical demands, still held key positions. Moderate reformers (such as Dubček) and more vigorous ones (such as Smrkovský, Císař, and Kriegel) constituted a kind of divided "center," differing as to the pace and the content of further advance. Finally, the most radical reformers, communists and non-communists alike, who wished drastic, if not revolutionary, changes and were dissatisfied with many features of the plenum, held no important official posts but were influential in the press and in public life.

During this second stage a broadening of participation in the political process had occurred, since more of the middle and top elite groups, and even to some extent, the rank and file, communist and non-communist, had become involved, in a largely spontaneous manner, and were exerting considerable pressure on the leadership. A large part of the population, however, especially the non-communists, had no real role in the process of revival since elections had not been held and the major associations and organizations had little genuine autonomy. It remained an open question as to whether public confidence in the party, badly damaged by twenty years of communist rule, and only beginning to be restored by the party-led movement for reform, would be regained by the implementation of the Action Program, or would be lost through the indecisiveness of the leadership. It seemed to be Dubček's belief that by admitting the errors of the past and blaming them on specific persons and incorrect policies, he would be able to absolve the CPCz as a whole, and the system as such, of blame, and that by initiating and carrying out needed reforms he would gain popular support for the party.

Dubček also hoped to persuade the Soviet Union that the position of the party and the stability of the system would be strengthened, not weakened, by reform, and that the so-called anti-socialist forces would be kept under control. Soviet press reaction to the April plenum was limited. Having reported Novotný's removal and Svoboda's election, *Pravda* confined itself to brief summaries of Dubček's CC report and of the Action Program, without comment, and reported criticisms by Chňoupek and other speakers of anti-socialist forces.[80] More pregnant

[80] *Pravda* (Moscow), March 27, 31, April 3, 12, 17. Cf. the later description of the Action Program as "a convenient legal platform" for attacks on the Communist Party, socialism, and the USSR (ibid., Aug. 22, 1968).

with future significance was the CPSU's own April plenum, following immediately after that of the CPCz, which bitterly attacked the efforts of imperialism to "undermine socialist society from within" and emphasized the importance of the Dresden meeting.[81] It was thus uncertain whether the fears and concerns of the Soviet Union and its bloc partners would be allayed by Dubček's relatively moderate course or would be aggravated by the continued activity of more radical spontaneous forces.

Dubček was at the center of these many conflicting pressures, "incarnating," as a radical reformer later expressed it, "in contradictory fashion both continuity and discontinuity."[82] In some respects his position in the middle was a source of strength since he derived support from both reformist and conservative camps and could use the pressure from each side to avoid advancing, or retreating, too far in the other direction. Yet it had the disadvantage of leaving him subject to constant pressures and thus weakened his capacity decisively to determine the course of events. Nor was it yet clear how far, and in which direction, Dubček *wished* to move, or would *have* to move, in response to these competing pressures. The plenum had removed some of the obstacles to reform, and yet by its caution and by leaving many issues unresolved, was bound to arouse demands for further action by those who feared a slowing down, or arresting, of the tempo of change. As events were soon to indicate, this represented only a transitional stage, preparing the way for a continuing struggle of more conservative and more progressive tendencies of party and public opinion, the outcome of which would ultimately determine the fate of the reform movement.

[81] Ibid., April 11. See below, chap. xx.
[82] F. Šamalík, *Politika*, Sept. 19, 1968.

CHAPTER IX

The Step-by-Step Strategy Challenged

(April and Early June)

THE EIGHT weeks from early April to early June, between the two plenary sessions of the Central Committee, constituted a period of sharp political conflict and modest preliminary steps toward reform. Dubček hewed to a line of carefully preparing future reforms and deferring more fundamental policy changes to the regular party congress to be held in early 1969. Yet within the party clear divisions of opinion were crystallizing, especially on the issue of calling an extraordinary congress to accelerate the pace of reform. Moreover, public opinion was voicing demands often going far beyond the Action Program.

PREPARING FOR REFORM

In the two months that followed the publication of the Action Program, none of the proposed reforms was actually consummated. However, the state organs were busy preparing the ground for the eventual implementation of the major objectives. A new government under Old-řich Černík was announced on April 8 and submitted its program to the National Assembly at the opening session on April 24. Both government and assembly began to take on the character of genuine working bodies and ceased to be the mere transmission belts of the past. Although these bodies still consisted overwhelmingly of communists, the new independence of individual communists, and the autonomous position promised for the governmental institutions, combined to encourage widespread debate and initiative.

The Prime Minister, Černík, had held high positions in state and party under Novotný, but had emerged as an energetic advocate of moderate reform. His cabinet was not a brand new team, and still less a group of radical reformers, but contained new faces and some outspoken reformers.[1] The five deputy prime ministers included three newcomers to high office, Professor Šik; Gustáv Husák, strong advocate of constitutional reform; and another Slovak, Professor P. Colotka, a legal scholar, as well as two veteran officials, L. Štrougal and F. Hamouz. Two ministries of crucial importance, Foreign Affairs and National Defense, were assigned

---

[1] Biographical sketches and pictures of the government members were given in *Rudé právo*, April 10, 1968.

respectively to Professor Jiří Hájek (formerly Minister of Education), scholar and diplomat, and General M. Dzúr (former deputy defense minister), who had fought under General Svoboda in the wartime Czechoslovak army and had been imprisoned in the fifties. Other key posts were allotted to men with reputations as strong or moderate reformers: Education to Professor V. Kadlec, a well-known economist; Culture and Information to M. Galuška, prominent diplomat and journalist; Agriculture and Food to J. Borůvka, a collective farm chairman; and Interior to J. Pavel, who had fought in Spain and in the Czechoslovak forces on the western front, had been head of the People's Militia in 1948, and had been imprisoned in the fifties. All of these, and the overwhelming majority of the cabinet, were Communist Party members. The minor parties, paradoxically, had less representation than under Novotný (one from the People's Party, V. Vlček, Minister of Health, and one from the Socialist Party, B. Kučera, Minister of Justice), a fact which evoked some criticism.

The government at once began to prepare for the legislative activity which faced it. The division of responsibility of the deputy prime ministers was announced at the outset, with Černík in charge of government action in general, as well as defense, security, and foreign policy; Colotka, legislative policy and the assembly; Hamouz, Comecon questions; Husák, the constitutional system, mass organizations, and religious affairs; Šik, economic reform; and Štrougal, the Economic Council.[2] This latter body, which consisted of ministers concerned with economic affairs, was to prepare and coordinate the government's economic policies. Černík, at a press conference in mid-May, discussed the government's plans, and individual ministers, for example, Pavel and Dzúr, in statements to the press, outlined the policy they proposed to follow. By late May several draft bills were submitted to assembly committees. All of this gave the impression that the government was serious about implementing its reform program and was anxious to keep the general public informed.

In his first statement to the National Assembly Černík stressed the change in the position of the government, which would exercise an "independent competence" and would recognize its responsibility to the assembly.[3] He expounded the principles underlying future government action in all spheres and the concrete measures planned to implement the Action Program. Although no detailed information was included, the order suggested that first place was being assigned to the development of "socialist democracy." This would include a constitutional reordering

---

[2] Ibid., April 20.
[3] Text, ibid., April 25. Sections on economic and foreign policies are given in R. A. Remington, ed., *Winter in Prague* (Cambridge, Mass., 1969), pp. 147-56.

of Czech-Slovak relations, and the assurance of civil and nationality rights and religious freedom. More specifically, there would be a law on freedom of assembly and association; a new press law; regulations concerning passports to facilitate foreign travel; guarantees of legality in the judicial and the investigatory system; a reduction of the authority of the Ministry of the Interior and its subordination to the government and the assembly; provisions for compensation to citizens for damages caused by illegal actions of the government; and a law on rehabilitation. A large section of Černík's report was devoted to economic policy, with a detailed analysis of the defects in the economy that required correction. Certain immediate improvements in pensions and in maternity and child allowances were promised, but it was bluntly indicated that no general wage increase was possible. Little was said concerning economic reform, although an expansion of the role of the enterprises was mentioned. In regard to international affairs, there was reference to a "foreign policy of initiative" but no indication of a substantial change of course.

The National Assembly, despite the fact that its composition was unchanged since the Novotný days, began to show surprising signs of genuine parliamentary activity. This began with the resignation of the longtime Novotný supporter, B. Laštovička, as chairman, and the election of Smrkovský in his place. The latter remained a member of the party's Presidium. His nomination, submitted by Kriegel on behalf of the National Front and the CPCz Central Committee, was endorsed by the noncommunist parties. In secret balloting, which led to his election by a substantial majority, there was a significant opposition vote—68 of the 256 valid ballots. There were also divided votes in the election of the deputy prime ministers and certain committee chairmen, in most cases with less opposition than to Smrkovský, but in several cases with even more.[4] Although this was unprecedented in communist parliamentary procedure and suggested the revival of the assembly, it also testified to the resistance of more conservative deputies. A number of resignations from committees and other offices occurred, in most cases, however, merely to avoid duplication with other positions. In the elections to fill the vacancies, a number of veteran Novotný cadres, including Václav David, the former foreign minister, Laštovička, Šimůnek, Chudík, Lomský, and others, were elected.[5]

Smrkovský, in his inaugural speech, eloquently expressed his conception of the assembly as "a forum in which the basic problems of the life of this land will be decided in open discussion" and as "a passionate and aggressive tribune for the exchange of opinions." This would mean a cer-

---

[4] *RP*, April 19.
[5] Ibid., April 26. Others elected were Neumann, Škoda, Plojhar, and Lenárt, all of whom had been criticized in the press for their pre-January actions.

tain "rehabilitation" of the assembly as a whole and a "rebirth of the function of deputy." The assembly, Smrkovský said, would carry out "a qualified *oponentura* toward proposals of the government, ministries, etc.," an opposition which could "lead to the rejection, or to the approval, or to the improvement of draft proposals."[6]

The debate, which began on April 24 and 25, and was resumed on May 2 and 3, illustrated the metamorphosis of the assembly and its members. True, there was no opposition to the government program, which in the end was adopted unanimously. The discussion, however, was not cut-and-dried and meaningless, as in the past, but substantive and prolonged, and included various specific suggestions and questions addressed to the government. Several interpellations were raised, including one directed to the Minister of the Interior as to whether telephone wiretapping did or did not exist. In his closing address, Černík admitted that many of the demands raised could not be satisfied and pleaded that the government be given "time" to accomplish its aims.

The National Front also entered what was described as a new phase under the chairmanship of the party's nominee, Kriegel, medical doctor and Spanish Civil War veteran, who, like Smrkovský, retained his seat in the party's Presidium. At an enlarged meeting of the front's central committee in early April, Kriegel spoke of a "revival" of the front as an important policy-creating body. Speakers representing other parties and the mass associations endorsed the CPCz's Action Program and proclaimed a "partnership" of communist and non-communist parties in the creation of state policy. The National Front, however, showed few signs of real independence. It approved the government's composition as proposed by Černík and agreed to the CPCz proposal to postpone the national committee elections until the fall at the earliest.[7] The election of a new central committee of the National Front and the adoption of a program would be effected at a later date, it was announced.

In comparison with the activity of the government and assembly, the top party organs presented a picture of relative quiescence. At the five meetings of the Presidium in April and May, no new ground was broken and little was revealed of the content of the discussions.[8] The decisions that were announced were on the whole conservative, for example, the expression of confidence in the much-criticized editor-in-chief of *Rudé právo*, Švestka; the emphatic assertion of the party's leading role in the

[6] Ibid., April 19. See chap. IV (n. 108) above, for the term "*oponentura*."

[7] *RP*, April 9. The presidium of the National Assembly ratified this postponement without specifying a date for the eventual elections. There was no reference to National Assembly elections, which presumably would take place even later.

[8] Meetings were held on April 16, 30, May 7-8 (with the Secretariat), May 14, and May 21-22. See *Rok šedesátý osmý* (Prague, 1969), pp. 146-47, 152-53, 154-55, 160-62; henceforth, *RŠO*; and *RP*, May 9.

National Front; and the condemnation of the restoration of a separate Social Democratic Party. Otherwise meetings were devoted to such procedural matters as the regional conferences and preparations for the CC plenum at the end of May. The Central Commission of Supervision and Auditing (ÚKRK) devoted its attention to the rehabilitation of prominent communists, restoring to membership a number of persons expelled from the party in the fifties and early sixties.[9] The division of responsibilities among the Secretaries indicated that no transformation had occurred in the traditional role of the Secretariat as an agency supervising all spheres of life. Those assigned to these tasks, with the exception of the first two, were not strong reformers: Dubček, party organization, defense, and security; Císař, science, education, culture, and the mass media; Indra, the National Front, societal and state organizations; Kolder, economic policy and heavy industry; Lenárt, international relations and party education; and Sádovský, food and agriculture, light industry, and party management.

THE PARTY'S TACTICS CHALLENGED

In a series of speeches during April, Dubček reiterated the tactics which he had set forth at the April plenum.[10] He warned repeatedly against "sudden" decisions and called for "wise," "responsible," and "carefully prepared" actions. "Consolidation" was the watchword, and this was to be achieved primarily by the implementation of the Action Program. The urgent matters under consideration by the government and assembly could presumably be dealt with in the course of the next month or two. The longer-run problems, in particular those connected with the formulation of a new party line to succeed that of the 13th congress, required more time and careful preparation. A regular party congress could not therefore be convoked before the first half of 1969, at the earliest in the spring. He looked forward to a congress that would be a substantive and working meeting, and not merely the occasion of cadre changes. Admitting the need for the latter, he urged that they be made in a humane way, "without scandalizing," and that most of them be deferred until the congress. Presumably Dubček hoped that this carefully scheduled program would win the support of more conservative and cautious party members and would at the same time sufficiently satisfy the more radical and impatient. The party would thus be able to achieve internal unity and gain wide popular support.

Recognizing that this cautious approach aroused apprehensions that

[9] *RŠO*, pp. 148-49, 155-59.
[10] See in particular *RP*, April 9, 11, 21, 25, 27. The last three are also in Dubček, *K otázkam obrodzovacieho procesu v KSČ* (Bratislava, 1968), pp. 122-30, 131-40, 141-52.

the process of renewal was slowing down and that there were dangers of compromises or even of a return to the old ways, Dubček countered by declaring that they were only "at the beginning of the road" and could not "stop half-way." He did not underestimate the fears, he said, in view of past historical experience and the presence of vested interests. "Every one who sees the problems and recognizes their extent must admit that in one hundred days we have taken serious steps, but we could not do and solve everything." The danger was, however, that under the pressure of time, they would not make "adequate analyses" and "justified conclusions." "Real needs and possibilities" and "concrete proposals" were required, "not demagogy, various anarchistic tendencies, and irresponsible demands."[11]

Dubček admitted that there were also serious worries on the other side, fears of "anarchy and even counterrevolution."[12] Some things, he admitted, had escaped from the hands of the party, because so many problems had piled up. He expressed confidence in the party's ability to overcome these difficulties. The main current of development had been a healthy one, and extremes had been rejected. There had been "errors" and "instances of haste," but this was inevitable in the course of creative work. Otherwise there would be "stagnation and degeneration."[13] There were, he said, "functionaries and publicly active persons" who were afraid that the party had abandoned its "power positions" and who were hopeful that it would "take things firmly into its hands again." Nonetheless, he affirmed, "we must persistently continue on the path we have newly embarked upon."[14]

More than once Dubček revealed his yearning for institutional stability and measured advance. It was not enough to have "different views and criticism"; also necessary was "a functioning system of institutions," under democratic control.[15] Democracy must include "rules" and "discipline"; otherwise it would be merely a matter of "non-binding proclamations," and not "a method of deciding matters." "To understand democracy as a situation where everyone speaks about everything and does as he wishes—that is anarchy which has nothing in common with real democracy."[16] What was required was "an open confrontation of interests and standpoints and an institutionalized anchoring of this articulation of interests, their criticism and their resolution."[17]

In the latter part of April the regional party conferences made it evident that the party membership was seriously divided over questions of tactics but that a substantial part was anxious to press on more rapidly and did not agree with the relatively moderate advance recommended

[11] *RP*, April 21.   [12] Ibid., April 9.   [13] Ibid., April 17.
[14] Ibid., April 21.   [15] Ibid., April 9.   [16] Ibid., April 11.
[17] Ibid., April 21.

by Dubček. Even the sparse reports of the proceedings[18] could not conceal the discontent of many members with the actions of regional leaders, and with other aspects of party activity since January. On the other hand, conservative voices were raised expressing doubts and apprehension about the situation, including, for instance, the editorial policy followed by certain regional party newspapers.[19] Elections by secret ballot brought about substantial or complete changes in leadership, including the replacement of almost all the First Secretaries. There were frequent criticisms of the fact that the Central Committee remained unchanged. This led logically to demands for an early calling of a regular party congress, or for an extraordinary congress in 1968, which would make possible the election of a new Central Committee.[20] In the meantime, it was urged, compromised members should voluntarily resign. Certain important regional organizations—the South Moravian, West and South Bohemian, and the Prague municipal—in the end adopted resolutions calling for an extraordinary congress. The Prague resolution, which urged an extraordinary congress at the latest by the end of 1968, made open reference to the "loss of confidence in the party" and the real "danger that confidence would not be regained and that people would seek a solution of political problems outside or against the party."[21] This resolution was overwhelmingly adopted immediately after an address by Dubček in which he argued the case for a regular congress in the spring of 1969 and had promised to do everything possible to convene it in the shortest possible time. Although it was later denied that this vote was an expression of lack of confidence in Dubček, it certainly constituted strong pressure on him to change his view on this crucial question. Even at those conferences where Dubček's tactic was approved, the resolutions usually urged a regular congress as early as possible, and a minority often demanded an extraordinary congress. A substantial proportion of the party membership was clearly anxious to accelerate the holding of the meeting.[22]

---

[18] Ibid., April 20-22, 26-30. May 4; *Život strany*, no. 10 (May 1968), pp. 6-13.

[19] For instance, the editorial policy of *Nová svoboda* (North Moravia), *Průboj* (North Bohemia), and *Pochodeň* (East Bohemia) was sharply criticized. The editor-in-chief of *Nová svoboda* was reelected to the regional committee but obtained the lowest number of votes; the editor-in-chief of *Průboj* was not even elected (*ŽS*, no. 10, May 1968, pp. 6, 12, 13).

[20] See the strong statement in favor of an extraordinary congress in 1968, including open criticism of Dubček's viewpoint as "incorrect," by a member of the presidium of the Prague-West district committee (*ŽS*, no. 10, May 1968, pp. 48-49). According to Hájek (*Mýtus a realita ledna 1968*, Prague, 1970, p. 117), the first demand for an extraordinary party congress was made by L. Hrdinová, as early as April 4. In fact she then called for an ordinary congress within six months (*RP*, April 4).

[21] *RP*, April 27.

[22] This question was the focus of conflict within the editorial board of *Rudé právo*. Certain editors charged Švestka, the editor-in-chief, with concealing data on

SPONTANEOUS PUBLIC ACTIVITY

Meanwhile the flow of activity outside the central party and state organs was gathering tempo. Institutions and associations of all kinds, national and local, were following the example set by the highest public bodies but often outdistancing the measured pace of the latter. In accordance with the party's recommendations, many individual institutions, such as the Academy of Sciences, were drafting their own action programs. Important changes in personnel were made, for example, the reappointment of Milan Hübl to the Higher Party School and his designation as rector. Government ministries, and associations such as the journalists' and the writers' unions, were rehabilitating members who had suffered persecution in the past. The courts reopened a number of significant cases, including those of prominent non-communists, and usually canceled the original verdicts. In the wake of public criticism of the judicial and security systems, certain persons who had held high offices in these bodies committed suicide—Dr. J. Břešt'anský, deputy chairman of the Supreme Court, Col. J. Počepický, head of investigation in the Prague security service, and Dr. J. Sommer, chief doctor at the Ruzyně prison.

The mass associations were awakening from their previous state of dormancy as could be seen by changes in leadership, the rescinding of past decisions, and the raising of significant demands. The organizations were thus responding both to the appeal of the party leaders and to the insistence of their own members that they should become active and independent interest groups. The trade unions began to negotiate actively with the government concerning wages and living standards and permitted the forming of autonomous unions in various branches of industry, thus effecting a breach of their highly unified organizational structure. The youth movement, confronted with the formation of many separate youth organizations, sought, with some difficulty, to maintain its position as a kind of "umbrella organization."

The non-communist political parties went through a slower process of revival, but were drafting new programs, making some changes in leadership, and expanding their membership. Both the Socialist and People's Parties in the Czech lands, and the two tiny Slovak parties (Party of Freedom and Party of Slovak Revival) were voicing their desire to be treated as equal partners in the National Front and claiming their right

---

the mood of the party by preventing publication of a memorandum of late March which indicated that almost half a million party members favored either an extraordinary congress or an accelerated regular congress. For this, and Švestka's reply, see *RP*, May 8, 13; J. Hochmann, *Reportér*, May 22-29, 1968. See also R. Gueyt, *La mutation tchécoslovaque* (Paris, 1969), pp. 165-66.

to organize in factory and farm, without restrictions on the number of their members. The Czechoslovak People's Party, in a draft program, defined itself as "an independent democratic political party of . . . citizens who profess a Christian world view." The present state of society was described as "pluralist socialism," expressing "a unity of aims in a multiplicity of interests," and respecting "basic human rights and equality of all citizens without distinctions of world view, nationality, racial affiliation and social group." The National Front, in their view, was "a voluntary grouping of primarily independent and mutually equal political parties" and "a basis for dialogue and confrontation of viewpoints. . . ."[23] The Czechoslovak Socialist Party, in an outline of principles, professed "democratic socialism" as its aim and defined the Czechoslovak path to socialism as based on "humanism, democracy, and the freedom of man." The system of several political parties was described as "one of the basic guarantees of a democratic development of socialism" and the National Front as the basis for the encounter of "the political interests of the varied social strata of society." The parties, following a common basic goal, differed only "in the means of attaining this goal and in the stress on certain specific views of socialist development."[24] In later statements, the party proclaimed its readiness to participate in political life as "a political subject with full rights . . . on the basis of its own standpoints and in accordance with the interests of its members" and rejected "the right of one political party to a universal, solely justified and correct interpretation of socialism." "People of varied social strata and of varied opinions, from Marxists to Christians, from workers to intellectuals, profess the ideas of socialism," and their representatives had "the right to a voice in social progress."[25]

Even more illustrative of the unusual atmosphere was the revival of associations banned in the fifties, such as the Sokols and the Boy Scouts, and the creation of many new associations, including a union of scientific workers, a collective farm organization, and various youth groups, notably a union of university students. Within the Union of Writers, a noncommunist Club of Independent Writers was formed. More expressly political in character were K 231, an association of former political prisoners, and KAN, the Club of the Non-party Engagés (both discussed earlier), and the Society for Human Rights. The latter took the Universal Declaration of Human Rights as its starting point and declared as its main purpose the defense of the rights embodied in this document. These could be guaranteed, it was stated, through laws and institutions and by public opinion. In more general terms the organization would seek to

---

[23] *Lidová demokracie*, May 23, 1968; Pospíšil, *RP*, June 1.
[24] *Svobodné slovo*, April 14.   [25] Ibid., June 8, 9; Kučera, *RP*, June 8.

train its members to "learn to be free and to think and act democratically" and to provide "a political platform for non-party people, restoring to them a feeling of citizenship and political self-consciousness."[26] At this stage all these groups were in a preliminary phase of holding organizational meetings, drafting programs, and forming preparatory committees. Their future existence hinged on approval and registration by the Ministry of the Interior and, in most cases, on their acceptance as members by the National Front. Although all, without exception, pledged their support to socialism, many of them were expressly non-communist in membership and envisaged independent political activity.

Still more controversial was the attempt to re-form a Social Democratic Party. In a proclamation of May 18 (which as a result of a warning by the Czechoslovak Press Agency [ČTK] was not published in the press), a preparatory committee of social democrats denounced the fusion of their former party with the Communist Party in 1948 and announced their intention of reestablishing it as an independent party. Negotiations were immediately begun both at the headquarters of the CPCz (with Smrkovský) and the National Front (with Kriegel) with the purpose of having the party recognized and admitted to the front. Its organizers advanced the argument that the unification had not been legitimate, since it was carried through without the approval of the party's members, and that the Social Democratic Party still existed legally. The Communist Party spokesmen, in these private discussions, firmly rejected the idea of an independent social democratic party but offered promises of greater opportunities for social democrats to act within the party and in public affairs. The efforts to revive a separate social democratic movement were publicly denounced by a number of prominent former social democrats, some of whom, such as Fierlinger and Erban, had long held high positions in the Communist Party, and by both the party Presidium and the National Front. It was argued that such a move would be a retrogression from the unification achieved in 1948. In spite of these rebuffs, the organizers continued their endeavors to legitimize a social democratic party and preparatory committees were formed in many parts of the country.[27]

[26] *Kulturní noviny*, April 26, 1968, for the declaration of the society and an interview with its secretary, E. Ludvík. Signatories included legal specialists such as I. Bystřina, P. Pithart, and M. Průcha; leaders of the two main non-communist parties, B. Kučera and V. Vlček; and well-known intellectuals such as V. Černý, I. Sviták, J. Procházka, J. Šlitr, and J. Škvorecký.

[27] A brief note of the founding of the central preparatory committee appeared later in *SS*, June 7, and a fuller report in *Student*, June 12. Earlier meetings had been held on March 22 and April 4, and preparatory committees had already been formed in several places. Meetings were held with Kriegel on May 20, June 14 and 21, and with Smrkovský, on May 18 and 23. For the statements of former social democrats, see *RP*, May 9, and interviews with E. Erban, *Večerní Praha*,

Faced with this wave of activity the Presidium reasserted the party's leading role in the National Front and urged the maintenance of unified federative bodies in cases, such as the youth movement, where independent associations were being formed. It explicitly disapproved the setting up of youth organizations by individual political parties[28] and the creation of new political parties.[29] As to the latter, the Ministry of the Interior flatly declared that the forming of parties was contrary to the legal order, which contained no provisions for such actions, and that there was no prospect of approval of such proposals.[30]

Other events gave evidence that public opinion was becoming a major force in political life. The May Day parade, hitherto a strictly organized and conformist demonstration, became an enthusiastic march in which party members participated voluntarily and avowed their ardent support for Dubček and for reform. Unorthodox slogans appeared on the banners of the marchers: "With the Soviet Union for all time, but not a day longer"; "Long live the USSR—but at its own expense (*za své*)"; "No democracy without opposition"; "Free elections."[31] Two days later, at a mass meeting of youth in the Old Town Square, the criticism of the Communist Party was so sharp that it brought a long editorial response in *Rudé právo* and a deluge of correspondence pro and con.[32]

The press, radio, and television carried full reports of this extraordinary wave of public activity and of the rising tide of demands for reform. The Journalists' Union, for instance, insisted on an early end of censorship. The Writers' Union urged the restoration of Mňačko's citizenship. The Philosophical Faculty at Charles University pressed for a new university law protecting academic freedom. Moravian organizations ad-

---

May 17, June 13. *Student* (May 22, 29, June 19) carried on a polemic against Fierlinger, denying that he had the right to speak for former social democrats and criticizing the 1948 unification as invalid. See Fierlinger's reply, *RP*, May 23. For official condemnations, see *RP*, June 8; *RŠO*, pp. 160-62, 204, 225. For detailed informative accounts, see V. Příhoda and V. Netrefa, "Social Democracy—Instrument of Counterrevolution in Czechoslovakia," *ŽS*, nos. 43 to 49, Oct. 22 to Dec. 3, 1969; and an anonymous article, *Svědectví* 10, no. 38 (1970), 171-88.

[28] *RŠO*, pp. 160-62.   [29] Ibid., p. 208.   [30] *RP*, May 25.

[31] Some of these were even reported in *RP*, May 19. See also M. Salomon, *Prague Notebook: The Strangled Revolution* (Boston, 1971), p. 87. A sociological survey by Dr. J. Kapr (*Rep.*, May 15-21) noted that domestic issues predominated in the May Day slogans and that words such as freedom, democracy, truth, and peace were used more frequently than "socialism" or "imperialism." Many slogans stressed social and ethical values, such as "Jesus, not Caesar," "Love, not war," "Believe in one's self." Demands included the dissolution of the political police, the cessation of jamming and censorship, free elections and opposition, and an extraordinary party congress.

[32] Among other events of the evening was the reading of Karel Čapek's 1924 essay, "Why I Am Not a Communist." See J. Sekera (*RP*, May 5 and 31), who deplored the "scandalizing" of the party and the distortion of its policies at this meeting.

vanced the proposal of a special position for Moravia in a tripartite federation. The Hungarian national organization, Csemadok, and a newly formed German association, presented claims for fuller nationality rights. Religious groups, especially Roman and Greek Catholic, demanded expanded religious freedom.

The public, unaccustomed to public debate, was electrified by the uninhibited presentation of issues until recently taboo or encrusted with propaganda.[33] Almost no topic was sacrosanct. Every aspect of reform was discussed, especially rehabilitation and freedom of the press, and dissatisfaction with the progress so far achieved was often expressed. There was analysis of the political system, including bitter criticism of past practices, and diverse views were articulated on the question of opposition parties and on the role of elections. There was objective examination of historical events, hitherto distorted by ideological interpretations, such as the role of Masaryk, Beneš, and Štefánik; the Czech legions and Czechoslovak policies in World War I; the Czech National Council of 1945; the Slovak question under the Republic and after 1948, and so on. Great attention was focused on the interrogations, trials, and imprisonments of the fifties, with memoirs of prominent victims and revealing interviews with former Ministers of National Security. The delicate question of the death of Jan Masaryk in 1948 was raised by Ivan Sviták, which led to an official investigation.[34]

Radio, television, and the entire daily press, both Czech and Slovak, participated in this wave of public discussion, raising issues sometimes embarrassing to the reform leaders and disturbing to those of more conservative persuasion. Even the party publications, including regional organs, although following a course closer to the official line, were more objective in their reporting and often independent and frank in their treatment of public issues.[35] Indeed, controversy within the editorial staff of *Rudé právo* and criticism of the chief editor, Švestka, by members of his staff, obliged the party Presidium to devote part of its meeting on May 14 to this question. The Presidium expressed confidence in Švestka but called upon the newspaper to defend party decisions more vigorously and to oppose anti-socialist forces.[36]

[33] For many excerpts from the press, see Pavel Tigrid, *Le printemps de Prague* (Paris, 1968), chaps. 5, 6. See J. Hájek, *Mýtus*, pp. 54 ff., 94 ff., for a critical analysis of these discussions.

[34] See below, chap. XIII.

[35] This may be noted in *Nová mysl*, beginning with no. 4, and *Život strany*, beginning with no. 10. See also the North Bohemia party organ, *Průboj* (e.g. May 29 and June 12) in which conservative forces in the party were criticized.

[36] *RŠO*, p. 155. A series of post-occupation articles (*RP*, Sept. 16-18, 1970) defended Švestka's role and condemned the "rightist" editors who had striven to oust him and control the paper.

OPINIONS DIVIDED

The party's rank and file, and the leadership at all levels, as well as public opinion in general, was sharply divided at this point. The top party ideologist, Kozel, spoke of "the boiling cauldron of political ideas," in which anti-socialist and anti-communist views, and the glorification of bourgeois democracy, had come to the surface and called for action by the party to counteract these tendencies.[37] Z. Šulc wrote of the "specter of distrust," with some people fearing a cessation of democratization, and others, a return to the pre-1948 or even pre-Munich conditions.[38] Many party members, it was reported in *Rudé právo*, were disoriented and worried by events since January, uncertain as to the future, and often alarmed about their own personal fates.[39] Many functionaries, wrote Karel Vlč, found themselves in a difficult situation in face of the new demands and opinions, the bitter criticism of past events, and the collapse of earlier values and certainties, and, not unnaturally, reacted by "a defense of the past."[40] In another article Vlč referred to "conservative tendencies," which exaggerated the threat to socialism and to the party's leading role, as well as "extremist tendencies," sometimes taking anti-communist and anti-socialist form. Admittedly, the former was the greatest immediate danger, but "honest communists" who held these views, he said, could be won over by persuasion. The party must struggle on both fronts and eliminate the apprehensions of some that there might be a return to the pre-January situation.[41] M. Jodl, a sociologist, expressed concern that the Prague Spring was coming to an end and noted the many changes yet to be implemented, especially in the economic field. There were, he said, really "two parties within one party."[42]

During May, at conferences of party secretaries and of chairmen of basic organizations, fears concerning the anti-socialist and anti-communist forces were aired, and the mass media were taken to task for encouraging these forces.[43] A conference of the People's Militia, while pro-

---

[37] *RP*, May 16.   [38] Ibid., May 28.

[39] Reports from the Mladá Boleslav Automobile plant, and from Pardubice, ibid., May 28, 29.

[40] *ŽS*, no. 11 (May 1968), pp. 34-35. Cf. also I. Mráček (ibid., no. 12, June 1968, pp. 43-45), who wrote of "a kind of vacuum" resulting from the lack of information and the criticism of party functionaries.

[41] *ŽS*, no. 12 (June 1968), pp. 1-2. Cf. the major article by J. Sláma, an economist, in which he dealt with the danger of both anti-socialist and conservative tendencies (*RP*, May 15).

[42] *Literární listy*, May 30. He was critical of Smrkovský's speech (see below) but saw positive elements in it.

[43] *RP*, May 14, 22, resp. Dubček and Smrkovský were later reported to have revealed grave concern over anti-socialist forces at the conference. Dubček was said to have cautioned that these tendencies could lead to the forming of "an

claiming its support of Dubček and of the Action Program, warned of forces seeking to discredit 1948 and weaken the leading role of the party, and called for support of the army and security forces and for the legalization of the militia.[44] Illegal leaflets, attacking the new course, began to appear more frequently, as well as anti-communist leaflets.[45] Josef Jodas, signatory of the Libeň letter, publicly reiterated his charge that January had been an anti-socialist putsch, aimed at the destruction of the party and the liquidation of socialism, and complained that communists were "outside the law," unable to express their opinions publicly. His views were condemned by the district committee of Prague 8, as well as by the municipal party organization.[46] On the other side, there were sharp denials of the importance of anti-socialist forces and repudiations of the attacks on the mass media, and demands for the swift enactment of a new press law guaranteeing freedom of expression. In a number of factories, beginning with one in Ostrava, Committees for the Defense of Freedom of the Press were set up.[47] In Slovakia there was a similar clash of opinions, reflected, for instance, in *Pravda* by an editorial expressing fears for socialism and defending the party against unjust criticism, and by a symposium of distinguished intellectuals exhibiting a wide range of opinion as to the dangers of conservativism and of threats to socialism.[48]

Most of the topmost leaders who spoke or wrote publicly during this period also exhibited anxiety over "anti-socialist forces" but differed in

---

anti-communist, counterrevolutionary platform," abetted by the imperialist states. See *RP*, Aug. 12, 1969, for supposedly verbatim excerpts from his and other speeches. A later version of Bil'ak's address on that occasion shows him calling for "vigilance" against anti-socialist, and even counterrevolutionary forces, who were attacking the party and state *aparát*, the security, courts, procuracy, and the army, and waging "a struggle for power." (V. Bil'ak, *Pravda zůstala pravdou*, Prague, 1971, pp. 70-75.)

In a post-occupation article, K. Vlč cited a number of resolutions from April and May 1968, expressing concern over anti-socialist forces, and complained that these had not been published (*ŽS*, no. 43, Oct. 22, 1969). The leadership, it was charged in another retrospective article, had failed to heed these warnings or to take action to avert the danger (*RP*, July 16, 1970).

[44] *RP*, May 15, 21, 23. See also *Rep.*, April 24-May 1, 1968, pp. 14-15, where it was suggested that the militia might be attached to the army, and its ranks opened to non-communists.

[45] *RP*, May 17; *Mladá fronta*, June 14.

[46] *Obrana lidu*, June 8; *ŽS*, no. 10 (May 1968), pp. 46-47. The Prague municipal organization was said to have laid plans to exert pressure, through a special delegation, on the CC during its forthcoming May plenum, and particularly on its Prague members, in support of its more progressive standpoint (*RP*, Feb. 2, 1971). On the alleged plans of the municipal committee, see also Bil'ak, *Pravda zůstala pravdou*, p. 168.

[47] *RP*, May 24.

[48] *Pravda*, May 26, 31, resp. In the symposium more progressive views were expressed by Július Strinka and Pavol Števček; more conservative views, although not opposed to reform, by Andrej Kopčok, Karol Minárik, Andrej Sirácky and Ladislav Szántó.

degree of emphasis. The only published speeches by Dubček in May were two addresses on commemorative occasions, one on the 100th anniversary of the first patriotic rally held at Mount Říp, the other on the centennial of the founding of the National Theatre; in both he evoked the national traditions of the Czech nation in support of the democratization movement.[49] Smrkovský, in a major article in *Rudé právo*, drew attention to the dangers and extremes on both the anti-socialist and the conservative sides, and if anything, dwelt most on the former. He saw the solution in more rapid and decisive measures by the party to fulfill the Action Program.[50] In an interview on rehabilitation policy he roundly condemned "anti-communism" and declared: "Let no one think that we shall give up what we have fought to attain and that we are abandoning everything for which we made the revolution. Certainly not; on the contrary, we wish to perfect our order, to humanize it."[51] Another progressive, Špaček, censured anti-socialist trends and the dangers of "spontaneity" and urged the party to give "leadership" by a "decisive" policy of reform.[52] Šik cautioned against the "hidden ultra-leftist or sectarian forces" which "exaggerate the anti-socialist danger." There were also "hidden forces" seeking a restoration of capitalism, but they should not be overestimated. He advocated speedy action on economic questions.[53] Husák considered the differentiation in opinion and the existence of hostility to socialism and democracy as inevitable in a revolutionary period and was confident that the party would achieve stabilization and consolidation by its creative work. Freedom and democracy must have their limits, however, unless there were to be chaos and anarchy. He condemned "opposition for the sake of opposition"—"like small boys seeing who can spit the farthest."[54]

The views of Švestka, Kolder, and Bil'ak were more conservative. In an editorial in *Rudé právo*, Švestka deplored the negative attitudes toward the past, making the party as a whole responsible, and destroying the traditions of the revolution. He lamented the attacks on the party, the silence of many communists, and the "terrorizing" by some publicists.[55] Kolder, in a leading article, denounced the anti-socialist forces who were trying to discredit and liquidate the party. "Without the party there would not be socialism or democracy." We must struggle against the danger, he said, by policies designed to unite the party, especially by

---

[49] *RP*, May 11, 17, resp.
[50] *RP*, May 19. Cf. his even more cautious address in Pilsen, ibid., May 12.
[51] *ŽS*, no. 10 (May 1968), p. 18.   [52] *RP*, May 23.
[53] Ibid., May 22.
[54] *Pravda*, May 9. See also his interview, *NM*, no. 6 (1968), p. 663.
[55] *RP*, May 16. Švestka expressed doubts concerning the labels "conservative" and "progressive" but described as dangerous both "conservatives" within the party and "anti-socialist forces" outside it (ibid., June 23).

gradually realizing the aims of the Action Program.[56] Bil'ak, in his major addresses to the Slovak and Czechoslovak CC plena in May, identified the "rightist forces" as "the main danger" and referred to the threat of "counterrevolution," singling out K 231 for particular condemnation.[57]

Public opinion polls indicated that ordinary people were divided in their views, but were less worried about anti-socialist forces and less critical of the mass media than party leaders and functionaries. When asked in April about the existing amount of freedom of expression, 61 percent felt that there was sufficient freedom; 23 percent, too much; and 14 percent, not enough. There was some difference, although not great, between party members (whose responses were 54, 33, and 12, respectively) and non-party members (63, 23, and 15, respectively). In May, in a poll in northern Bohemia, the same question drew affirmative responses from 86 percent of non-party members; 62 percent of party members; and only 16 percent from leading secretaries of regional and district committees.[58] In Slovakia there was substantial sympathy for the press, radio, and television (65 percent, compared to 76 in the Czech lands and 73 in the whole country), but a slightly higher proportion felt that the media concerned themselves with matters not within their competence (22 percent in Slovakia; 19 percent in the Czech lands; 17 percent in Czechoslovakia as a whole).[59] When asked in May about the pos-

[56] Ibid., May 29.

[57] *Pravda*, May 23; *RP*, June 5. Bil'ak was also quoted as stating that Czechoslovakia "did not live in a vacuum" and their policies were not "our purely Czechoslovak affair." He also argued that attention to "the national specific" should not mean the ignoring of "common international interests," but denied that the CPSU had insisted that they copy Soviet experiences and adopt the Soviet model. For post-occupation versions of his speeches, see Bil'ak, *Pravda zůstala pravdou*, pp. 76-119, 120-33.

[58] For poll results, see Jaroslaw A. Piekalkiewicz, *Public Opinion Polling in Czechoslovakia, 1968-69* (New York, 1972), pp. 83, 85, resp. When asked, in March, in a poll throughout Czechoslovakia, whether the mass media were dealing with matters outside their competence, an overwhelming majority of respondents (73 percent) did not think so, as opposed to 19 percent who did (ibid., p. 40). Different results, somewhat less favorable to the media, were given in *RP*, March 27 and May 30. See J. Hudeček, *Rep.*, April 10, 1969, pp. XIII-XVI, for full information on polls dealing with mass media.

A poll conducted by the CC's Institute of Political Science reported varied degrees of criticism of the press among party and non-party members correlated with education: among communists, 45 percent of those with lower education were critical, 28 percent, with higher education; among non-communists, 19 percent and 8 percent, resp. Many communists, however, disagreed with the criticism of the press: 52 percent among those with lower education, 70 percent, with higher education; non-communists disagreed even more strongly, 77 percent and 81 percent, resp. (*RP*, June 26).

[59] April 20-21, Piekalkiewicz, *Polling*, p. 86. Other polls, in June, in Slovakia alone, indicated a high degree of satisfaction with the manner in which the press, radio, and television had contributed to publicizing and implementing the Action Program—over 80 percent fully or partially in each case (ibid., pp. 88-89).

sibility of an "overthrow" by anti-socialist forces, 70 percent of the sample saw no such possibility; 30 percent did not believe that such anti-socialist forces existed.[60]

CZECH-SLOVAK DIFFERENCES

A striking feature of political life during April and May was the growing differentiation between Slovakia and the Czech lands both at the official levels and among the populations. In Slovakia this manifested itself in a greater concern with the solution of Czech-Slovak relations and other nationality questions, less emphasis on other more general aspects of democratization, and a more conservative attitude toward the latter.

In a one-day session of the Slovak Central Committee on April 9, the plenum stressed the need for a new federal arrangement of Czech-Slovak relations and charged the Slovak National Council and a newly created CC committee with the preparation of proposals for such a system.[61] Important changes were made in the Slovak leadership, with the removal of Chudík from the Presidium and the demotion of Sabolčík to candidacy, and the appointment of four new members of relatively progressive outlook, O. Klokoč, V. Pavlenda, A. Ťažký, and J. Zrak. S. Falťan and M. Sedláková, similarly oriented, were named to the Secretariat. Bil'ak, however, remained as First Secretary. In his comparatively conservative major address he denied that Slovakia was lagging behind the Czech lands in democratization and argued that in view of the substantial political advance of Slovakia in the sixties, the Slovaks had started at a different level than the Czechs after January. Fewer changes of personnel were therefore necessary. He rejected pressures for additional cadre changes and condemned the "scandalizing" of party functionaries. He was sharply critical of the media of communications and defended the control of the press. Radio and television must serve the interests of the socialist state. On the other hand, Bil'ak praised the rehabilitation of Husák and other Slovaks and made a special plea for democratizing the judiciary, the prosecutors' agencies, and the security services. He rejected, however, any notion of rehabilitating "hostile elements."[62]

When the Slovak plenum next met in early May, little advance had been made toward a federal system beyond the enunciation of the principles of federalism in the Action Program. Nonetheless, Husák, who had

[60] Institute of Public Opinion, mimeographed, May 29, 1968; *RP*, May 30; Piekalkiewicz, *Polling*, p. 12.

[61] *Pravda*, April 10-11.

[62] Ibid., and *RP*, April 11. Bil'ak was also reported to have declared, at the regional conference at Sliač, that if an extraordinary congress were held without adequate preparations, the Slovak communists would not attend (Ota Plavková, *Kultúrny život*, June 7, 1968). See also *Student*, May 15.

meanwhile become deputy Prime Minister in charge of Czech-Slovak constitutional reform, in a speech in Bratislava in late April, revealed no dissatisfaction with Czech attitudes nor any impatience with the pace of reform. Federalization, he said, had been generally accepted among Czechs who had shown no desire to slow down or block progress.[63] The Slovak plenum, however, began to exert pressure on Prague, demanding that a constitutional law be drafted by June and be enacted into law by October 28, the anniversary of Czechoslovak independence.[64] When the Slovak plenum again convened in late May there were no special complaints of delay. The Slovak Action Program adopted on that occasion asserted the necessity for federalization and for a corresponding change in the organization of the party.[65] In early June the CPCz plenum approved the idea of federalizing the party as well as the state. Dubček, in his report, accepted the deadline of October 28 for the enactment of the new constitutional arrangement.

Although Slovak leaders rejected the notion that Slovakia was behind in the process of democratization, there was no doubt that the achievement of a new and equal position for Slovakia came first and foremost in their plans. Husák denied that Slovakia was lagging and argued that the two main objectives were not in conflict. Federalization, he believed, was an application of democratic principles in nationality policy and in turn could not function properly without a general democratization.[66] Yet there was increasing evidence that the Slovak party was not as anxious as the Czechs to press forward with democratization. The Czechoslovak Action Program was indeed approved by the CPS and taken formally as the basis of its own Action Program. This latter document, however, was a moderate version of the CPCz program and lacked its most radical proposals. Although it was approved by the Slovak Presidium in early May, it was not published until its adoption by the Slovak Central Committee in late May, on the very day of the opening of the CPCz plenum, so that it was somewhat lost sight of in the plethora of other reports.[67]

Moreover, the proceedings of the Slovak plenum in late May, as briefly reported in the press, were very conservative in tone.[68] No strongly

---

[63] *Pravda*, April 23. [64] Ibid., May 7.
[65] Ibid., May 29.
[66] *Pravda*, April 23. See also his article, ibid., May 9.
[67] Text, *Pravda* and *RP*, May 29.
[68] *Pravda*, May 23-25, 1968. A most extreme speech, not published at the time, was given by B. Chňoupek who lamented the press attacks on leading functionaries and described the situation as serious. He warned that the counterrevolution in Hungary had begun before 1956 along a "quiet path," as a "dry revolution," and compared some of its features to those accompanying the democratization process in Czechoslovakia: the split in the Central Committee; the exaggeration of the conservative danger and the underestimation of the danger on the right; the de-

progressive speech was reported. Bil'ak, in his speech cited above
(n. 57), even went so far, it was reported later, as to warn that the May
plenum would witness "an open struggle with the extreme forces" and
"even an attempt at overthrow in our party." He made only brief mention of federation as the basis of the political system.[69] The CPS "Standpoint," adopted on this occasion,[70] expressed concern with many phases
of democratization, including "one-sided criticism"; the "mass psychosis" concerning Štefánik and Masaryk; the revival of "populist" ideology;
bourgeois influence among the youth; the widespread mistrust of the
army, security, the courts, and the People's Militia; the weakening of the
authority of state organs; and "anti-socialist and anti-communist forces
in Bohemia." The plenum took certain positive steps, however, in repeal-
ing 1958 party decisions against Š. Šebesta and A. Pavlík, and in dismissing several much-criticized persons from office. F. Dvorský was removed
as candidate Presidium member, and R. Cvik as CC member. Sabolčík
was released as Secretary and as Presidium candidate, to be free for work
with the Slovak National Council.[71]

The differentiation of Slovaks from Czechs was not confined to the
party leadership but characterized to some extent the broader Slovak
community. As one commentator put it, Slovak political life, owing partly to the absence of state organs, and partly to the conservative policy of
the party leaders, was "paralyzed" and was reduced merely to the activity of the CPS and its Central Committee. Concentration on the "national revolution," especially by leaders who hoped thus to avoid other
aspects of democratization, had had the consequence of a "retardation"
in Slovakia.[72] The Slovak public, too, according to public opinion polls,
placed national equality first on the agenda of reforms, and democratization second, whereas among the Czechs, the latter stood first, and national equality in seventh place.[73] This concentration on the nationality
question, and later on federalization, combined with more conservative
national traditions, clerical and populist in character, dampened the rise
of extreme or radical views.

---

moralization of the security apparatus; the undermining of the party; and the
escape of the press and mass media from party control. He charged that "a second
center" existed which was seeking to replace the Dubček leadership. (*Tvorba*, no.
23, 1970.)

[69] Bil'ak, *Pravda zůstala pravdou*, p. 116. Bil'ak repudiated the designation of
"conservative" for those who wished to build socialism on genuinely Marxist-Leninist principles, or the term "progressive" for those who wished to return to pre-
February conditions or even to pre-war bourgeois democracy.

[70] *Pravda*, May 30; *RP*, May 31.

[71] The Presidium, at an earlier meeting, had exonerated E. Friš and others from
charges made in the fifties and had appointed M. Sedláková as editor-in-chief of
Pravda (*Pravda*, May 4).

[72] A. Hykisch, *KŽ*, June 14.   [73] *RP*, May 5.

This is not to say that reform activity did not occur in Slovakia but it was somewhat muted and restrained in comparison with Czech developments. There was a reactivization of various mass associations, but not usually in such a radical manner as among Czechs. No organizations such as KAN or K 231 appeared. The Slovak non-communist parties were too tiny to have any real significance. The Catholic Church and lay organizations, although not opposed to reform, concentrated on religious freedom and other objectives. Within the Communist Party, at the regional conferences, discussions were less sharp, although there was criticism of local and all-Slovak leaders and replacement of many of the former. No regional conference, however, supported the demand for an extraordinary congress. Certain newspapers, such as *Smena*, the organ of the youth movement, and *Práca*, the trade union daily, showed a new independence. *Kultúrny život*, the writers' weekly, served as a tribune for the discussion of democratization and the national question. Even the party daily, *Pravda*, became a lively medium of news and commentary, in some respects going even beyond *Rudé právo* in its frank and objective reporting. An indication of more radical Slovak opinion was the formation of the Club of the Young Generation of Slovakia, whose initial proclamation criticized the "slowness and one-sidedness" of democratization in Slovakia and the failure to replace leading officials, and, while supporting federalization, urged the need for other aspects of democratization.[74]

THE SPLIT OF THE SLOVAK WRITERS

Much more serious was the division in the ranks of the Slovak writers, culminating in the resignation from the editorial board of *Kultúrny život* of certain prominent figures in mid-April, the open clash at the ensuing writers' conference, and the resulting emergence of a substantial "nationalist" or "conservative" wing in the Slovak literary community, a phenomenon without any parallel among Czech writers. The roots of this crisis went back to pre-January days but did not manifest themselves at once to the general public. The Slovak Union of Writers identified itself fully with reform in its initial post-January statements. The proclamation adopted at meetings of its committee during March pressed for freedom of expression and urged that censorship, both by state and by party, must be abolished, and press, radio, and television must become genuine organs of public opinion. Other reforms, such as separation of powers, freedom of movement of citizens, and rehabilitation, were advocated. On the issue of federation, which was termed the only solution for Czech-

[74] *RP*, April 9; *LL*, April 25. This club, headed by Pavlenda, Števček, Hykisch, et al., was to use the youth newspaper, *Smena*, as its forum.

Slovak relations, the declaration contended that this was inextricably linked with democratization. Indeed the attainment of a federal system would be "a doubtful victory," it stated, "if centralistic bureaucracy and autocracy were replaced by the supremacy of Slovak bureaucracy and autocracy." The Slovak mass media were criticized for creating the impression that "errors" in Slovakia were the result of centralism only and that other problems, common to the whole Republic, did not exist.[75]

Simultaneously, signs of disunity began to appear, mainly in relation to two questions from the pre-January period, namely, the notorious "letter" initiated by leading Slovaks at the writers' congress in 1967, and Mňačko's departure for Israel later in the summer. In March, Miroslav Válek, the chief sponsor of the letter and chairman of the Slovak union's committee, responded angrily to criticism by the Slovak writer, Anton Hykisch, one-time editor-in-chief of *Kultúrny život* and a strong advocate of reform. Not only did Válek warmly defend his action at the 4th congress, but he further explained his critical attitude to the congress, especially in connection with the Solzhenitsyn letter and the discussion of the Arab-Israeli conflict. He reiterated his viewpoint that Mňačko's departure from Czechoslovakia was "a tragic error" and linked this with a denunciation of "national chauvinism" on both the Arab and Israeli sides. Other signatories, such as V. Mihálik, J. Procházka, and J. Špitzer, defended their action in signing the letter, and Hykisch again censured it as "a tactical manifesto of loyalty to the intimidator."[76]

This controversy was but the prelude to the much greater one produced by the resignations from the editorial board of *Kultúrny život* of the celebrated poet and board chairman, Novomeský, and of two other writers, Mihálik and Válek. Their explanatory statement issued to ČTK on the eve of the union's conference produced strong expressions of regret and censure by almost all the other members of the editorial board, including Dominik Tatarka, Pavol Števček, Peter Karvaš, and Zora Jesenská. A bitter debate between the rival groups ensued at the writers' conference at the end of April.[77] The chief editor of *Kultúrny život*, Jozef Bob, expressed the belief that the resulting crisis could have

[75] For the union's March statement, *KŽ*, March 22. See, in the same issue, the progressive January 23 declaration of the union's party organization, calling for the resignation of Novotný, the rehabilitation of Husák, the abolition of censorship, etc.

[76] For the controversy, see *Smena*, March 5 (Hykisch); *KŽ*, March 22 (Válek), March 29 (other signatories of the letter), and April 5 (Hykisch). For a defense of Mňačko, see J. Rozner, *KŽ*, March 15. For the text of the 1967 letter, see ibid., March 29. See also chap. III (n. 74) above.

[77] For letters of resignation, *KŽ*, May 3; for later statement issued to ČTK, ibid., May 3, also *Pravda*, April 27; for criticisms by J. Bob and others, *KŽ*, May 3. For a verbatim report of the conference see *KŽ*, May 3 (Válek's report), 10, 17, 24, 31. For a full summary, *LL*, May 9, p. 7. See also briefer reports, *RP*, May 1, 12; *Pravda*, May 5, 7. For commentaries, Š. Šugar, *RP*, May 5; Z. Eis, *Rep.*, May 15-20.

"catastrophic results," including the "disintegration" of the union. The Slovak literary community was thus rent asunder at the very time when it had an opportunity to play a significant role in the democratization process.

The split within the ranks of the Slovak writers involved a number of intermingled issues, the relative importance of which was estimated differently by the participants.[78] The main problem, in the minds of those who had resigned, was the difference of opinion on the Arab-Israeli conflict, which in turn was linked with Mňačko's leaving the Republic and with the 4th writers' congress, both of which were viewed critically. Although denying that they were opposed to Israel or that they fully approved Czechoslovak policy in the Middle East, the "conservatives" or "federalists," as Válek, Novomeský, and their supporters were sometimes called, strongly disapproved the pro-Israel position taken by their critics. Novomeský denied any disregard of the fate of the Jews during World War II or their just complaints against the Arabs, but argued that this could not legitimate "atrocities against the Arabs." He and his associates expressed keen dissatisfaction with the general policy followed by the union's weekly on this and other questions, which they termed "one-sided" and "extreme." Válek again justified his action in drafting the original letter to the 4th congress, and in his report to the conference on the work of the union's committee, reminded his listeners of the protest it made concerning the treatment of *Literární noviny* in 1967 and defended the committee's record since January.

On the other side, the "democrats," such as Števček, Tatarka, Jesenská, and others, were critical of the 1967 letter and the union's attitude toward Mňačko both before and after January, and openly condemned the failings of the union's committee since January. It had "missed its historical opportunity" (Tatarka), and had done almost "nothing" in the four months since January (Jesenská). In fact it had continued to act as a "transmission belt" and thus brought into question the very legitimacy of the union, declared Jaroslava Blažková. On the other hand, the weekly organ, *Kultúrny život*, had played a significant role in seeking to " 'radicalize' the dynamics of political life" in Slovakia, affirmed Števček.

These quarrels over the past were combined with crucial divergences over current problems of federalization and democratization, and their relative importance, and reflected, in Válek's words, "a difference of

---

[78] See esp. Novomeský, *Pravda*, April 27; *RP* and *Pravda*, April 19; *Pravda*, May 7 (also *RP*, May 12). See also V. Mináč, *RP* and *Pravda*, May 19. For Števček's views, see *Pravda*, May 7 (also *RP*, May 19). Cf. J. Strinka, *KŽ*, April 5. Strinka called for the replacement of M. Pecho, M. Sabolčík, M. Lúčan, and F. Dvorský.

world outlook." For Novomeský and others, the primary goal for Slovaks must be the attainment of national equality through federalism. They were impatient with the relative indifference of Czechs to this question and with the slow progress toward its solution. The more "nationalist" group denied that they were lukewarm to democratization and argued that democratization and federalization were so closely linked that in fact they could not be separated nor one given preference over the other. Nonetheless, somewhat contradictorily, they pressed, in the ČTK release, for a greater emphasis on federalism. Moreover, Novomeský and others were highly critical of the Czechs for both their past and present attitude toward Slovakia. Mináč went so far as to describe the First Republic as representing "almost genocide for Slovaks," a statement which stirred up heated responses by both Czechs and Slovaks.[79] Yet the "federalists" were also basically conservative in their approach to reform, evincing distinct unhappiness with the more "extreme" versions of democratization espoused in the Czech lands, and by some Slovaks, especially in the columns of *Kultúrny život*. Novomeský in fact was critical of the idea of unrestricted freedom of the press, or of democracy without limits, and declared that he did "not wish to be present at the liquidation of socialism."[80]

On the other hand, the more radical advocates of democratization, such as Števček, were dissatisfied with the slowness of democratization in Slovakia and in particular with the inadequate espousal of this cause by the Writers' Union. This was indeed, in their view, the main root of the controversy which resulted from the efforts of *Kultúrny život* to "deepen the democratization current especially in Slovakia" and to strive for "the purge of compromised people" from the Slovak political representation, and thus to carry on its best traditions from 1956 and 1963. The "liberal" wing, especially Števček and Jesenská, gave strong support to federalization but warned that it would mean little in Slovakia if it were not accompanied by democratization. In fact, said Števček, federalization "in the wrong hands" would distract attention from the need for a genuine "self-purge" and could be used against so-called Czech "extreme forces" and against Czechoslovak statehood, with its traditions of democracy and humanism. The democratization process, he argued, was "one and one only—Czechoslovak," and federation was "only one of its fruits." Hence the slogan, "federalize first, and then later democratize, i.e. federalization with any one and under anyone . . . was the sign of an impure game with the nation."[81]

Thus, although neither side rejected either federalization or democra-

---

[79] For Mináč, *Pravda*, May 5; for criticism, J. Mlynárik, *LL*, May 16; I. Dérer, *LL*, June 6; letters from readers, *LL*, June 6, 20; *Pravda*, May 16 and 23.
[80] *Pravda*, May 7.   [81] Ibid., May 7.

tization, they differed substantially as to the priority of these two principal aims and as to the substantive content of democratization. Thus two distinct wings of the literary community could be identified, one, represented by Novomeský and his associates, more conservative and nationalist in approach, and the other, represented by Števček and his colleagues, more liberal and less nationalistic. In early May the former gained an organ for the articulation of their views, the party cultural weekly, *Predvoj*, which was renamed *Nové slovo* after the wartime newspaper of that name published under Husák's direction during the Uprising. It was placed under an editorial board including Husák, Novomeský, Mináč, and others. [82] The more liberal wing continued to use *Kultúrny život* as a medium of expression. This split within the Slovak intelligentsia weakened them as a force supporting democratization and deepened the differences between the Czech lands and Slovakia on this issue. It also afforded the support of distinguished cultural personalities for the more conservative line of the Slovak party and strengthened the tendency among Slovaks to place the greatest emphasis on the achievement of federation. Husák's identification with the conservative nationalist wing gave him a platform for voicing his opinions and for seeking a return to Slovak politics, and, as later events proved, was to have momentous consequences extending far beyond the Slovak literary and cultural scene.

Bloc Relations

The new foreign minister, Professor Hájek, in his first statement to the press, emphasized "continuity" of foreign policy and expressed his confidence that Czechoslovakia by its policy would "assure our friends that the process of revival is in no case anti-Soviet and still less anti-communist."[83] His visits to Moscow and to Budapest in May were no doubt designed to underline this. During the same month the Italian communist leader, Luigi Longo, and the Yugoslav foreign affairs secretary, Marko Nikezić, paid visits to Prague and issued statements of support for Czechoslovakia in her new course. Czechoslovakia's unchanged basic orientation in international relations was demonstrated by her participation in the Budapest conference of communist parties, where the chief delegate, Lenárt, spoke with greater independence than usual, but declared Czechoslovakia's support for the proposed world communist conference, and by the visit of the Bulgarian chief, Zhivkov, in late May, for the conclusion of a twenty-year treaty of mutual assistance.[84] In early May Marshal Konev arrived for an extended stay to celebrate Soviet-Czechoslovak friendship and, a month later, a Ukrainian delegation

[82] The first issue appeared on May 23.
[83] *RP*, April 12.   [84] For the latter, *RP*, April 26-28.

toured the country in connection with the customary Days of Soviet Culture.

On the surface nothing essential seemed to have changed in Czechoslovakia's relations with its allies, including the Soviet Union. An ominous sign, however, was the one-day visit to Moscow by Dubček and several of his closest colleagues on May 4. The talks were described as "open and comradely" but their content was not revealed.[85] Dubček, in an interview, admitted that economic aid had been requested from the USSR and that the internal situation in both countries had been discussed. He noted Soviet "concern" about the possible "abuse of the democratization process against socialism" and stressed that the Czechs themselves were determined to resist "anti-socialist extremes."[86] Several weeks later Smrkovský stated that economic questions, including a loan, and international matters had been discussed, as well as the contemporary political development in Czechoslovakia. The Soviet Union had naturally wished to be informed of what was going on, he said, and the Czechs had provided "facts and arguments" explaining the party's decisions in January and April. "The Soviet friends," he reported, "recognized our arguments and consider this as an internal matter of our Republic and will not in any respect interfere in our affairs." He admitted that they had been asked in particular about "forces in action" which had aims other than those of the party. He expressed his own position that Czechoslovakia would not allow its course to be abused by such elements.[87]

Even more disturbing was a meeting in Moscow in early May of the First Secretaries from the countries of the European bloc, in the absence, however, of Czechoslovak and Rumanian delegates. The communiqué referred to "an exchange of opinions on urgent problems of the international situation and the world communist and workers' move-

---

[85] Communiqué, ibid., May 6. Note S. Budín's criticism of the secrecy of the talks, *Rep.*, May 15-21. Bil'ak later claimed that this sudden visit was the result of a Czechoslovak initiative and was related to Prague's request for economic assistance, including a hard currency loan. In the negotiations, which lasted far into the night, according to Bil'ak, economic questions were linked closely with political questions, with Soviet warnings against threatening counterrevolutionary tendencies and pleas that action be taken against them. Although full Soviet economic aid was offered, it was made clear that it would be given only on condition that the Czechs "established order" at home (*RP*, Sept. 3, 1969). For Smrkovský's later account, see Appendix D.

[86] *RP*, May 7, quoted also in *Pravda* (Moscow), May 8. Cf. Dubček's remarks regarding Soviet warnings on this occasion as quoted in *RP*, Aug. 12, 1969. Moscow *Pravda* (Aug. 22, 1968) reported that Czechoslovak leaders had themselves given a critical evaluation of the situation and said they were ready to take the necessary measures to master it.

[87] *RP*, May 16. According to Bil'ak, Dubček promised the necessary measures to control anti-socialist forces, but did not inform the Presidium of these talks.

ment" but otherwise revealed nothing concerning the discussions. These talks, coming as they did within a few days of Dubček's visit to Moscow, but excluding him from participation, were presumably devoted to an exchange of views on the Czechoslovak situation.[88] This was followed by extended visits to Czechoslovakia by the Soviet Minister of National Defense, Marshal Grechko, and the Soviet Prime Minister, Alexei Kosygin. Again no information was publicly given as to their purpose or the subjects discussed. As Czech spokesmen indicated, however, Soviet worries about the course of development were aired on these occasions.[89]

In any case, the differences in view began to be openly revealed in the press. On April 30 Moscow *Pravda*, in its first full article on Czechoslovak developments, gave a positive appraisal of the Action Program but quoted Indra and Husák on anti-socialist and anti-party forces. On May 7 Tass, in reaction to the investigation into the death of Jan Masaryk, issued an official denial of Soviet complicity. The statement referred to "enemies of socialist Czechoslovakia" who were hoping to "stir up anti-Soviet moods among politically unstable people." In mid-May Soviet newspapers began to mount a more systematic offensive, with criticism of specific articles or statements made in the Czechoslovak press. Theoretical articles strongly defending the leading role of the party, without specific reference, but with obvious relevance, to Czechoslovakia also started to appear. The Polish and East German newspapers began to publish critical reports about Czechoslovakia in early May. The Polish and GDR governments even made official protests against the tone of the Czechoslovak press in dealing with their affairs, and Prague made a similar protest to the GDR. Czech conservatives were also concerned, as was evidenced by the interpellation by V. Nový in the National Assembly concerning the comments on radio and television relating to the socialist countries and his call for action to prevent this.[90] Noteworthy, however, was the more positive treatment of Czechoslovak events in the Hungarian press.[91]

All this created a steadily increasing nervousness and tension in

[88] *Pravda*, May 9; *RP*, May 11. Cf. W. F. Robinson, "Czechoslovakia and Its Allies," *Studies in Comparative Communism* 1 (July-Oct. 1968), 159-60.

[89] In addition to Smrkovský's statement cited above, see his comments on Kosygin's visit (*RP*, May 20) and the statements by Professor Hájek (ibid., May 17) and by the deputy foreign minister, J. Pudlák (ibid., May 25). Tigrid, without offering any source, reports that an agreement was reached with Kosygin, which referred to the maintenance of the CPCz's monopoly of power; the continuance of democratization; the holding of an extraordinary party congress; the suspension of Novotný from the party; the conduct of Warsaw pact staff exercises; and the maintenance of Czechoslovakia's relations with the Warsaw pact and Comecon (*Le printemps*, p. 247).

[90] *RP*, May 16.

[91] Robinson, "Czechoslovakia," pp. 153-54. See below, chap. xx, for the above.

Czechoslovakia. Articles began to appear in the press complaining of the attitudes of their bloc allies and pleading for understanding and tolerance.[92] Official and unofficial statements tended to minimize the significance of Soviet "concern," to treat it as natural, and to give the impression that Czechoslovak leaders had been successful in explaining the situation to the satisfaction of their allies.[93] Public anxiety intensified as reports circulated of troop movements in Poland and the GDR during early May. Alarm was further heightened when it was revealed that in June staff exercises (as the Minister of Defense, General Dzúr, called them) would be held on Czechoslovak territory by the Warsaw treaty forces, involving, he said, "relatively small units."[94] This was all the more disquieting because of Western reports, denied by Czechoslovak authorities, that the permanent stationing of Soviet troops in Czechoslovakia was under discussion.[95] General Yepishev, head of the Chief Political Administration in the Soviet Ministry of National Defense, had earlier been quoted by *Le Monde* as saying that Soviet forces were ready to "perform their international duty if socialism in Czechoslovakia were threatened." Although this was later denied, the report added to the tenseness of the atmosphere.[96] On the eve of the May plenum, increasing Soviet concern over Czechoslovak developments was indubitable, and mounting external pressures on Prague were evident, but uncertainty prevailed as to what Moscow proposed to do about it.

THE MAY PLENUM

When the plenum convened at the end of May, its proceedings presented a study in contrasts and contradictions which reflected the confused political situation as described above.[97] The most striking result,

[92] For instance, M. Jodl, E. Goldstücker, and A. J. Liehm, *LL*, May 16, 23.

[93] See the statements cited in n. 89. Compare also the pacifying statements by M. Wiener, *Rep.*, May 8-15, and by S. Budín, ibid., May 15-21.

[94] See statements in *RP*, May 31, June 1 and 7. Marshal Yakubovsky, Warsaw pact chief, visited Prague in the last week of April. In early May Soviet troop movements in Poland near the border with Czechoslovakia were reported in the Western press.

[95] See below, chap. XIX.

[96] *Le Monde*, May 5; *RP*, May 20, 1968. Marshal Konev, in a speech in Kladno, was quoted as saying: "Our friendship is strong and inviolable. We shall permit no one to break the fraternal ties binding our peoples" (British Broadcasting Corporation, Monitoring Service, *Summary of World Broadcasts*, part I [USSR], May 14, 1968). Marshal Grechko, on the other hand, was quoted as saying that "the solution of the internal problems of the Czechoslovak People's Army is the internal affair of Czechoslovakia" (*RP*, May 19).

[97] Reports in *RP*, from May 30 to June 7; Dubček's report, ibid., June 4 (also in *K otázkam*, pp. 153-90). See also *RŠO*, pp. 163-224. For translations of some of the plenum materials, including Dubček's report, see Paul Ello, ed., *Czecho-*

announced in Dubček's opening report and later approved by the plenum, and described by him as "a political offensive," was the decision to convoke the 14th congress in extraordinary session on September 9. This represented a retreat by Dubček from his original position on this question.[98] Designed to prepare a new general line, a revised party statute, and a draft constitutional revision on Czech-Slovak relations, as well as to elect a new Central Committee, the congress would unquestionably have represented a long step toward the acceleration of reform and a decisive shift of the political spectrum in a progressive direction.

In explaining the decision, Dubček argued that the omission of economic matters from the agenda made it possible to prepare for the congress in this short period. More significantly, he referred to the proceedings of the regional conferences and their demands for CC changes, and "the acceleration of political movement in the past few weeks." He spoke of "the decline of the authority of the Central Committee and hence its ability to solve these questions authoritatively and to lead the party in this complicated situation." It was necessary, therefore, to elect a new Central Committee. The main question was "to strengthen the authority and influence of the party in society" and thus to counteract extreme tendencies, which could lead to attacks on socialist power. "Without an extraordinary congress, the party today would not be able quickly enough to unite and to fulfill its tasks."[99]

The seriousness of the political situation was further elaborated by

---

slovakia's Blueprint for "Freedom" (Washington, D.C., 1968), pp. 185-274. For Smrkovský's later report on the plenum, see Appendix D.

[98] According to Bil'ak, who said he had favored an early congress in February, when the situation was well in hand, Dubček was then opposed and rejected the idea again in April and May. After the Moscow conference, according to Bil'ak, Dubček decided that the congress must be called in August and he (Bil'ak) unwillingly agreed to this. See Bil'ak's speech of September 1969, as reported in *Svědectví*, no. 38 (1970), pp. 284-85. According to Indra, the decision to call the congress at an earlier date had been made on May 25, at a meeting in Dubček's office of Černík, Bil'ak, Indra, and Sádovský, and was approved by the Presidium on the 27th (*RP*, Sept. 24, 1969).

[99] *RŠO*, pp. 185-86. Mlynář, newly elected Secretary, in a post-plenum commentary, claimed that the change of view on the calling of an early congress indicated that the leadership had "reacted in time to the reality" and admitted the loss of confidence in the party and the "insufficiency of the authority of the CC itself in its previous composition." "Without a consistent break with past deformations, without the departure of people linked with these from the party's leading organs, it would not be possible to assure the advance (*nástup*) of the party and the growth of confidence in its policy" (*ŽS*, no. 13, June 1968, p. 2). Dubček later explained that the party could not risk having its forces divided and exhausted by discussion of this problem for many months (*RP*, June 4). Šimon, the Prague leader, argued that in view of the unwillingness of discredited CC members to resign voluntarily, there was no alternative but to call the congress quickly (*VP*, June 12). Otherwise, said Šimon, mistrust in the CC would continue and would result in a serious crisis in the party (*Rep.*, June 26-July 3, 1968, pp. 7-8).

Dubček, and in an even franker speech, by Černík. Dubček spoke of the "diversity of views on the evaluation of the present situation," a "polarization," as he later termed it, and the grave danger of anti-communist tendencies and of the "anti-communist and anti-Soviet atmosphere" created by them. Although there had been "certain elements of political consolidation" since the April plenum, he admitted that there had been weaknesses in their work, and that they had been slow in some respects and in others had not adequately publicized what they had done. A spontaneous process would open the way for extremist tendencies and could threaten socialism: hence the need was to "consolidate the process of democratization" and to "strengthen the position of socialism." Černík also spoke of the conflicting tendencies of opinion in the party, some "positive," and others "conservative," and blamed this on the years of deformation before January and not on the present leadership. An "enormous wave" had struck them, so that it was impossible to solve everything at once. He referred to a widespread disorientation of party members, the discrediting of the party, and the loss of authority of some CC members. The only solution, he said, echoing Dubček, was "a policy of the offensive."[100]

Despite his call for a political offensive, Dubček still adhered to his policy of step-by-step advance and warned against too radical or extreme demands, or "spontaneous and disintegrating forces." "In other words, we cannot permit that the political power structure which we have should be smashed, until we replace it, gradually and deliberately, by a new one. We must gradually transform it. Not destruction but a qualitative transformation and development of the socialist system—that is the main thing at the present time. We must distinguish the aims for which we are striving from the transition to those aims, which we are now passing through and which must take place gradually, by stages (*po etapách*)." "This does not mean giving up the final goal. This would, however, be endangered if we wished to anticipate the development, and prematurely solve problems which in the given conditions we are not capable of solving, or if we formulated demands which the people would not understand."[101]

The discussions in the plenum, although published in abbreviated form, testified to the great disunity that prevailed.[102] The announcement of the suspension of Novotný and others from the party, and of the convocation of the congress in September, removed certain important topics from the agenda but did not silence the debate. On the opening day,

---

[100] *RP*, June 7.   [101] *RŠO*, p. 183.
[102] Gueyt (*Mutation*, pp. 189-200) gives a full account of the debate and attempts a classification of the speakers, on the basis of their attitude toward the "principal danger," as center, right and left of center, and extreme right and left.

Novotný, in a speech that went unreported, attempted to defend himself but was subjected to a blistering attack by Husák, who, although not a CC member, was attending as a guest.[103] The plenum debate revealed a wide variation of viewpoint. At the outset, a series of conservative speeches—by Bil'ak, Nový, Hamouz, Kapek, Dočkalová, Rigo, and others—were made, severely criticizing anti-socialist forces. No one openly questioned the calling of the extraordinary congress, but the last two expressed great disappointment with the developments since April. Several speakers censured the party for not acting decisively enough against anti-socialist tendencies or attacked those who had criticized the Soviet Union. On the other side a number of vigorous progressive speeches were made by Smrkovský, Šik, Kladiva, Macek, Kadlec, Šimon, and others. Other speeches fell somewhere between the more clearly defined extremes. Although most of the progressive spokesmen expressed concern about anti-socialist forces, Šik and Mlynář also drew attention to "leftist forces." Quite frequently the demand was raised for voluntary resignations from the Central Committee, although no individuals were named. Smrkovský called for a "quickening of the tempo" of the party's action and outlined the reforms which were needed.

The actions taken, apart from those concerning Novotný and the congress, were few and did not represent notable steps forward. Moreover, a good deal was concealed from the public. A report by Černík on the Šejna affair was adopted but not published. Piller's interim report on the trials of the fifties was also not made public. At Piller's recommendation, however, Novotný was removed from the CC, and he; along with Bacílek, Pavol David, B. Köhler, Š. Rais, V. Široký, and J. Urválek, were suspended from party membership until their share of responsibility in the political trials had been fully examined by the commission. The Jakeš report on rehabilitation within the party was not published, although in his speech to the plenum Jakeš gave substantial information on the progress made. The decisions concerning Czech-Slovak constitutional relations represented modest advances, mainly by endorsing the proposals made by the Slovak party and by setting up state and party commissions to prepare the formation of Czech national organs and an appropriate restructuring of the CPCz. The measures adopted to prepare for the congress followed a traditional pattern; the preparatory work and the principal reports were assigned to Dubček (the party and its main tasks), Černík (matters relating to the constitution and the political system), Indra (the party statute), and Jakeš (rules of procedure and electoral principles of the CC and ÚKRK).

Shifts in the topmost organs were not striking. In the Presidium, Mar-

---

[103] His speech was published later (*RP*, June 15).

tin Vaculík, the former Prague party chief, who had been subjected to sharp public criticism, was replaced by his successor in that post, B. Šimon. Mlynář, legal scholar and advocate of political reform, was appointed Secretary, although he was not a CC member, and Erban, the former social democrat and long-time colleague of Gottwald, was named to the Secretariat. As for the Central Committee, the removal of Novotný was the most significant alteration. In spite of many appeals for voluntary resignations, only three withdrew—Cvik and Lomský, from full membership, and Škoda, from candidate membership.[104] Šik was not named to the Presidium, in spite of several suggestions to this effect in the plenum debate. Nor was Husák included in the Central Committee from which he had been removed in the fifties prior to his arrest and imprisonment. Certain changes were made in the CC commissions, including the appointment of Mlynář and Lenárt as heads of the Legal and Ideological Commissions, respectively.[105]

Other documents adopted by the plenum, the main "resolution on the present situation and the party's further advance," and the proclamation to the party and the people, were indicative of the somewhat ambiguous and relatively moderate stance taken at this point in the democratization process.[106] The implementation of the Action Program was, of course, described as the main goal, and the extraordinary congress as the principal guarantee that this would be attained. The fundamental task of the moment was to make sure that "the socialist character of power and of the social order should not be threatened from any direction, either by rightist, anti-communist tendencies, or by conservative forces. . . ." Reiterating Dubček's conception of tactics, but with more pointed criticism of those who did not share it, the resolution declared: "This final aim of the development embarked upon must be distinguished from the conditions and possibilities of the individual stages of the transition from the past to the goal. The concrete policy of the party in each period must start from the conditions of each stage of this transition as possible in reality. Therefore, efforts by comrades who do not see such a necessity and mix up the demands concerning goals with the concrete practical tasks of the present stage, are harmful to the policy of the party."[107]

Following Dubček's report in many of its phrases, the resolution stressed the need "to assure political leadership of society by the Com-

[104] Although Lomský had been much criticized publicly, he pledged support for the post-January policy in his speech of resignation and was praised by Smrkovský for his work. Note the sharp criticism of the failure of CC members "representing the past" to resign, in the main editorial in *NM*, no. 7 (1968), pp. 803-6.

[105] A number of persons (including J. Bartuška, J. Kudrna, M. Mamula, V. Škoda, K. Mestek, F. Havlíček, J. Havlín, etc.) were removed from certain commissions (*RŠO*, p. 177).

[106] *RŠO*, pp. 201-14, 214-18, resp.   [107] Ibid., pp. 202, 203.

munist Party and to rebuff all efforts to discredit the party as a whole and to deny it the moral and political right to lead our society. . . ." The CPCz was described as "the one political force in this land with a scientific socialist program," as "the main guarantee of good relations between the ČSSR and the other socialist states, and hence a guarantee of the stable international position of our republic." "It is the unifying force of both our nations, Czechs and Slovaks. It concentrates hundreds of thousands of workers, peasants, and mental workers, who enjoy personal respect and honor in their milieu; in its ranks are concentrated the overwhelming majority of the best creative forces of our society, scientists, technicians, and artists. . . . Its cadres form the dominant part of the administrative and directing structure of our society. All this creates, as a historic reality, a situation in which, in order to achieve a really democratic, socialist evolution, without conflicts, without undesirable shocks and without unleashing a struggle for power (and hence a struggle concerning its very socialist character), there is no other path forward than the one on which the CPCz as the most powerful organized political force in this land is leading the whole process of development, to be sure by new means and methods which are clearly outlined by the Action Program and which the party congress will define. . . . If anti-communist elements were to attempt an attack on this historic reality and would wish to direct the progress of our nations on another path, the party will mobilize all the forces of our people and of the socialist state and will reject and suppress such an adventurist attempt."[108]

More specifically, the National Front was declared to be the exclusive platform for political activity, and any oppositional organization or any party outside the National Front was flatly rejected. Any attempt to establish social democracy or to create a second Marxist party was condemned as "anti-communist." Dubček's own treatment of the media of communications had been almost entirely critical and had spurned the idea that journalists could be "autonomous creators" of policy. The resolution, in this spirit, demanded of the journalists "positive political activity" in implementing the party's policy. Nor could there be permitted any anti-communist pressures by the mass media on inner-party questions. There must also be no weakening of the organs of the state, and existing laws must be respected.

Relations with the Soviet Union, stated the resolution, were based on "the principles of internationalism and full respect for the special conditions in which, in every particular country and in every specific time period, the struggle for the general common aims of the communist movement takes place. Our development today is one which corresponds to

[108] Ibid., pp. 204-5.

our present-day Czechoslovak conditions. The party entered on this path also out of a feeling of responsibility to our nations." Any effort to describe this as a "binding 'model' " for all socialist lands was harmful. Impermissible also were "any exaggeration of definite differences in opinions," or "lying reports of a 'danger of military intervention.' " Confidence was expressed that negotiations would lead to "positive conclusions," including Soviet economic aid. Turning to divisions within the international communist movement, and linking this adroitly with the Czechoslovak case, the resolution proclaimed the party's desire to contribute to overcoming them. "The existence of conflicts among communist parties should not in any case negatively influence their mutual relations. In accordance with the Action Program, we shall explain and defend the standpoint that our domestic development is a sovereign affair of the ČSSR; we do not interfere in the internal questions of other lands and we demand the same, too, in relation to our country."[109]

In its conclusion, the main resolution underlined the seriousness of the situation. "There is no cause for nervousness and panic; there are, however, reasons for fears about the further successful advance of our development. We are not striving for power, for we are already the decisive force. We are, however, struggling for confidence, for the growth of confidence, and for the constant and fuller support of the masses of noncommunists. . . . Only through this confidence will a firmer socialist power and the political leading task of our party be strengthened."[110]

Dubček, in a concluding speech not reported at the time,[111] dwelt on the serious danger from the right and devoted little attention to the danger on the left. The report and the resolutions represented, he said, "the united standpoint of the Presidium." "We all agreed on them without exception." Similarly, the Central Committee, in spite of "different emphases and different approaches," had reached consensus on the plenum documents. "No one asserts," he stated, "that this danger (the formation of anti-party and anti-socialist forces) is such that we would today stand face to face with the danger of counterrevolution." Certainly, however, the danger on the right existed and lay in the fact that "a wave of spontaneous and disintegrating tendencies could assume an anti-communist direction and culmination." It was precisely in this light that the Central Committee's decisions were to be understood. If this danger were not taken into account, it could disrupt (narušiti) the united approach to the implementation of the party's Action Program. Hence the need for a struggle to win the confidence of the people and preserve party unity.

[109] Ibid., p. 211. [110] Ibid., p. 214.
[111] This was issued in printed form, for inner party circulation only, in June 1968.

Conclusion

The plenum in May seemed to constitute a victory for the moderates and, like its predecessor in April, a compromise. On the surface the plenum appeared to have overcome the crises of March and April and to have initiated a period of stabilization or consolidation. Its decisions, however, scarcely concealed the intensifying political crisis, the deepening differentiation within the party and outside of it, and the uncertainty and lack of decisiveness resulting from the divisions within the Dubček team.[112] In one sense, the plenum constituted, in Dubček's words, a "political offensive," especially in the decision to remove Novotný and to convoke an early congress, thus preparing the way for a renewed advance. But there was also an element of the "defensive,"[113] or even retreat, in the avoidance of large-scale changes in personnel, the emphasis on the danger from the right, and the criticism of the mass media.

The decision to call an extraordinary congress in early September represented a complete reversal of Dubček's position on this issue, and to that extent a challenge to Dubček's step-by-step approach to the goals of the Action Program.[114] He was, however, still resolved to pursue such a policy, but to move at a quicker tempo, reflecting his reassessment of the situation. He wished to satisfy the public, and the reformers, that the reform movement would in fact continue, but also to assure the more conservative critics that this would be achieved under the party's direction. The convocation of an early congress would meet the wishes of the former, but the session would be carefully prepared, and there would be no prior wholesale expulsions from the Central Committee. Meanwhile concrete implementation of the Action Program would proceed, item by item, in the period before the congress. The media, it was hoped, would maintain a responsible attitude, supporting the party's tactics and the reform measures. Then in due course, and by orderly procedures, the congress would select a fresh leadership and draft a new policy, which would extend the reforms further. These steps, he hoped, would solidify the party as a whole, win it broad public support, and undercut the more radical elements inside and outside the party.[115]

---

[112] In post-occupation statements, much stress was laid on the Presidium's disunity. See Kolder and Indra, *RP*, Sept. 10, 24, 1969.

[113] Gueyt, *Mutation*, p. 187.

[114] Jiří Hájek (*Mýtus*, pp. 111-19) condemned the decision to call the extraordinary congress and the arguments advanced to explain this switch in policy. Although the decision was justified in view of the decline in the CC's authority, it reduced the value of the more favorable plenum actions.

[115] Dubček, at the CC plenum in Sept. 1969, strongly defended the general conclusions of the May plenum and argued that their implementation had brought about a significant relaxation of tension. He had not believed at the time that there was a danger of counterrevolution and had wanted to settle matters, not by "power

The plenum, and especially the decision to call the 14th congress, was described by one commentator as a stage of "transitional political consolidation," in which the decisive element remained the "center," between extremist elements on both sides. Conservative forces within the party constituted, however, a dangerous brake on future advance which would have to be reduced in the preparations for the congress. Indeed authoritative commentators, including Mlynář, placed much more stress on the "conservative danger" than did Dubček or the main congress documents, and urged the primary necessity of a struggle against these forces.[116] The compromises agreed upon constituted not a permanent or stable, but a highly precarious, base for the unification of the party. The progressive reformers would hardly find the plenum fully satisfactory, in view of its emphasis on the right-wing danger and the continuance of conservatives in high places.[117] Concrete progress, in terms of leaders or policies, had been slight, and the danger of a relapse was still present. Yet the reformers could look forward hopefully to the congress and its favorable potentialities. On the conservative side, comfort could be derived from the general tenor of the plenum resolutions, including Dubček's report, and from the likelihood of greater control of "antisocialist tendencies" and of the mass media.[118] The possibilities of the forthcoming congress, however, were disturbing. Intense political struggle after the plenum was certain to occur, mainly with reference to the specific proposals of reform and to the preparations for the congress, especially the election of delegates. The domestic conflict was interwoven with the external pressures from the Soviet bloc, which gave moral support to the conservatives, worried the moderate reformers and encouraged them to be cautious, and alarmed the more radical reformers and the public generally.

The entire political situation was unstable in a wider sense. After years of political slumber, the nation had been plunged into intense activity, but leaders accustomed to take a genuinely political role were scarce, and

---

means," but by a positive and concrete program (*Svědectví*, no. 38, 1970, pp. 269-71, 274).

[116] Mlynář blamed the conservative forces ("the main danger") for playing into the hands of the anti-socialist forces in their efforts to discredit the party (*ŽS*, June 1968, p. 3). Cf. the editorial in *Nová mysl* (no. 7, 1968), the main thrust of which was directed against the conservatives, who were described as the party's "greatest ballast" in the revival process (pp. 804-5).

[117] Cf. Hykisch, *KŽ*, June 14, 1968. A declaration by communist activists in the cultural field welcomed the calling of the extraordinary congress, but urged resistance to conservative tendencies and support for progressive tendencies (*RP*, June 7).

[118] The May resolution was later praised by conservative spokesmen, who, however, severely criticized the failure to implement its provisions (Kolder and Indra, *RP*, Sept. 10, 24, 1969).

the public lacked democratic experience. Politics was still primarily concentrated within the Communist Party, especially at its higher levels. The non-communists might play a major part in the future, if genuine elections occurred and free political associations were permitted, but so far could act only as passive observers, or, to a limited extent, as "pressure groups" for reform. They found, however, much common ground with the progressive or radical communists and formed with them an unofficial and unspoken alliance for reform.[119] Would Dubček's policy and its eventual implementation satisfy the non-communist majority of the population and the reform communists, so that in future elections the leading position of the Communist Party would be confirmed? Or would the various reform groupings, communist and non-communist, be disillusioned by Dubček's moderate approach and insist on a more rapid and radical advance? Still more uncertain was the answer to the burning question— would the plenum decisions eliminate the fears and concerns of the Soviet regime as to the future of Czechoslovak communism, or be taken as renewed evidence of tendencies threatening socialism and the party's position?

[119] Hykisch, *KŽ*, June 14.

CHAPTER X

Reforms Amid Tension

(June to Mid-July)

THE DECISION to call the 14th congress was described by one analyst as the end of "phase one" of the democratization experiment which had been characterized by "a combination of 'enlightened' political *reform* from above with elements of popular initiative of the 'quiet *revolution*' type from below." A new phase was beginning, which would involve the codification of the victories already won and the first steps toward a democratic and pluralist model.[1] In the six weeks following the May plenum several concrete reforms were adopted and many others were being studied and prepared. This was accomplished amidst gathering tension in domestic politics, manifested in several domestic crises which diverted attention momentarily from reform and testified to deep discord among contending political forces. A new element of crisis, this time international in character, also distracted attention from reform but produced an impressive unity of Czechs and Slovaks behind their leadership in its refusal to yield to outside pressure.

THE FIRST REFORM MEASURES

The meeting of the National Assembly in the last week of June witnessed the enactment of a number of laws which had been under discussion within the government and in parliamentary committees for several weeks. These related to the rehabilitation of the victims of legal injustice and the abolition of censorship, as well as the preparation of federalism and several social insurance measures.[2] The passage of these reforms, and the vigorous parliamentary debate accompanying it, offered vivid testimony to the changing character of politics.

The rehabilitation law, introduced by the Minister of Justice, Dr. B. Kučera, provided for the orderly redress of injustices committed by the courts against persons wrongfully convicted between 1948 and 1965. This was to be accomplished individually, through judicial proceedings, in special tribunals established for this purpose. If the person were exonerated, he, or his heirs, was to receive material compensation. The law also provided for special proceedings to investigate those officials respon-

---

[1] A. Hykisch, *Kultúrny život*, June 14, 1968.
[2] For fuller discussion, see below, chaps. XII-XV.

sible for breaches of the law and for the dismissal of such persons from their posts.

The adoption of this law, unanimous but for one abstention, was dramatic evidence of the intense feeling on this matter which had been one of the subjects most vigorously discussed since January. The government had not, however, accepted the view that there should be a sweeping and general cancellation of all verdicts in political trials but had decided in favor of the reexamination of each case separately. It was clear that the final settlement of the many tens of thousands of cases was still far in the future. There was considerable satisfaction nonetheless that justice would at last be done to the victims of the fifties, even though many years after the event. This step was widely hailed as the first time, in a communist country, that rehabilitation had been formally guaranteed in law.

The measure ending censorship took the form of several amendments to the existing law on the press and other mass media, introduced by the Minister of Culture and Information, M. Galuška, who described it as "the legal anchoring of freedom of expression, speech, and the press." One of the provisions explicitly declared that "censorship," defined as "any intervention of the state organs against freedom of speech or depiction," was not permissible. Chief editors would, however, be responsible for seeing to it that no "state, economic, or official secrets" were published. Another amendment protected the right of an individual to secure public correction of any false information published by the media. The assembly debate indicated a division of opinion, with some opposition to the proposals. Some deputies, for example, V. Nový, expressed fears about continued press attacks on individuals; others urged penalties for journalists abusing freedom of expression. An amendment to this effect, introduced by A. Švec, was not approved but led to an understanding that this question would be left to the new press law, to be introduced in September. Although the amendments were passed by a large majority, thirty deputies voted against, and seventeen abstained.[3] This action by the assembly was widely welcomed—a public opinion poll showed 86 percent of those questioned to be in favor. Only 5 percent were opposed.[4] It was, it is true, a provisional measure, leaving final settlement to a future general press law, and did not eliminate all sources of concern

[3] For parliamentary debate see *Rudé právo*, June 13, 19, 26, 27, 1968; *Večerní Praha*, June 26.

[4] *RP*, July 18. For commentary, see Z. Kryštůfek, *Reportér*, June 26-July 3, 1968; for post-occupation criticism, *Tribuna*, Sept. 17, 1969. Deputies who voted against the amendment were criticized (*Lidová demokracie*, June 27; *RP*, June 28) and were also defended (*Pravda*, July 25). For praise of the law, see Smrkovský, *Kulturní tvorba*, June 27. In a post-occupation critique of the mass media, J. Smrčina condemned the abolition of censorship as leading to "the loss of control" of the mass media by the party and its use by "rightist forces" against the party and socialism (*Tribuna*, July 30, 1969).

on the part of those urging freedom of the press. Yet by explicitly forbidding censorship and thus ratifying the freedom of expression that already existed de facto, it was an event unique in the communist world.

Another important action of the National Assembly was the approval of a constitutional law on the preparation of the federal system, which provided inter alia for the creation of a Czech National Council as the counterpart, and partner, of the Slovak National Council in the elaboration of the final federalization law, and which endorsed in principle a federation of the two nations, Czech and Slovak.

This historic session of the assembly was brought to a close after adopting several social insurance measures, endorsing the holding of general elections by the end of 1969, and creating a sixty-member committee, under Professor Viktor Knapp, to work on a new constitution. Much remained to be done but the legislative body had taken several steps to implement the reform program, thus giving earnest of the intention of the Dubček regime to translate into deeds the words of the Action Program. Many other measures, notably the revision of the law on association and assembly, laws on freedom of travel and on non-judicial rehabilitation, the reform of the national committee system and the courts, and the definitive provisions for the setting up of works councils, were also under consideration. Although the National Assembly had shown itself capable of vigorous action, its deliberations had also indicated the presence of a core of conservative deputies openly critical of certain aspects of reform.

Emerging Political Forces

Although the shape of the new political system had not yet been fully delineated, some of its general features were beginning to appear. The National Front (NF), as already forecast by the Action Program, was, in its new form, to be a crucial element. Its exact nature and functions were to be set forth in a special statute on which work was proceeding. The major aspects of this key organization were, however, revealed at a ceremonial meeting of the main political entities of the front in mid-June, in Dubček's major speech and the common proclamation adopted.[5] As Dubček put it, the NF would provide "a basis for the democratic expression of the different interests and needs of the people, of different groups and strata (*vrstvy*) of our society, where, on the base of a common socialist program and socialist interests, there could be a democratic discussion and an exchange of views," and as a result "unity of political action." He made quite clear, however, that the party would maintain its leading role and would indeed effectuate it through the front. We respect the non-communist parties, Dubček said, as partners on the NF platform

[5] *RP*, June 16.

and within its framework. The NF statute will determine, he said, under what conditions a group could become a partner of the National Front.

As Kriegel, the front's chairman, expressed it a few days later,[6] the National Front would no longer be a transmission belt, as it was after February 1948, nor would it be a scene of "party struggles," as had been the case before February. It would be "a place of conversations, of a confrontation of opinions," which would lead, through compromises, to conclusions satisfactory to all. No organization would be admitted to membership unless it respected certain principles, such as social ownership, Czech and Slovak equality, and the alliance with the Soviet Union; and rejected fascism, racism, and anti-communism. As the proclamation stated, the statute would determine the position and functions of the member organizations and would set forth the "conditions" for admission. "Political activity directed against the principles and the common NF platform," read the proclamation, "cannot have any further legal possibility of occurring. . . ." How this would work out in practice, as far as political parties were concerned, was made crystal clear in a statement made shortly thereafter by Professor B. Rattinger, a deputy and adviser to Slavík, which was approved by the assembly's constitutional and legal committee. The National Front, he said, was "the only constitutionally permissible system of political parties," so that, in his opinion, parties outside this system "cannot develop any activity."[7]

Meanwhile the only political parties, apart from the Communist Party, which were full-fledged members of the National Front were the four which had collaborated with, or rather had been subservient to, the Communist Party ever since 1948. Two of these in Slovakia, the Party of Slovak Revival, and the Party of Freedom, were trifling in membership (less than 1,000) and in influence. Both claimed to be non-Marxist, the former with a Christian orientation, but both recognized the leading role of the Communist Party.[8] The two Czech (by name "Czechoslovak") parties, the Socialist and the People's Parties, had substantially increased their membership since January 1968 and had a not insignificant follow-

[6] Ibid., June 19.

[7] Ibid., June 19, 20. Rattinger explicitly rejected Josef Pavel's view that no political parties could be formed because there were no legal provisions for them, saying, on the contrary, that the absence of such laws would permit the formation of parties.

[8] The Party of Freedom was formed from dissidents within the Democratic Party in 1946 and had been headed since 1956 by M. Žákovič. The Party of Slovak Revival resulted from the change in name of the Democratic Party after 1948, and was headed by J. Mjartan, a leading member since 1952. Its membership had dwindled from 1,000 after 1948 to 87 in the early sixties. See interviews with Mjartan and Žákovič, Echo, June 30, 1968. The party newspapers were Sloboda and Ľud, respectively.

ing among certain groups.[9] Both had reformulated their programs, although in a way that differentiated them only in emphasis from the Communist Party, and took the latter's Action Program as the basis of their own. Nor had they shown much evidence of independence or of influence on the course of events, either in the assembly or in the government. Their newspapers, *Svobodné slovo* and *Lidová demokracie*, were, however, influential in affecting public opinion.

There were only two other organizations, which, although small and rudimentary, might represent political forces of potential significance. One was the preparatory committee for a Social Democratic Party; the other, the Club of the Non-party Engagés (KAN). The Communist Party leaders left no doubt whatever that they had no intention of recognizing or permitting social democracy to re-form, still less of admitting it to the National Front.[10] The celebration of the ninetieth anniversary of the foundation of the Social Democratic Party was the occasion for prominent communist leaders, including Dubček, and Erban, a former Social Democrat, to express their opposition to the rebirth of a separate social democratic party.[11] Nonetheless such an embryonic movement did exist in the form of a central preparatory committee in Prague and similar committees in other places. It had its defenders in the press, although it was unable to get its own views published. In view of the "illegality" of their activities, the organizers had to avoid public meetings, although one large assembly took place on June 19 in the Faculty of Philosophy of Charles University and a closed meeting of representatives of preparatory committees was held on June 21. Negotiations continued, both with Kriegel and Smrkovský, and at the Prague CPCz headquarters, leading, in the latter case, to a "gentleman's agreement" by which the social democratic spokesmen agreed to postpone any public proclamation for the time being. The social democrats also decided to postpone a founding conference scheduled for August 17.[12]

KAN was a somewhat different matter. This organization had been formed in order to defend the interests of non-party people and to provide an opportunity for their political participation. Although in its manifesto it disavowed any intention of assuming the role of a political party

---

[9] Both parties were successors to parties of the same name which had been purged in 1948 and under new leaders, had thenceforth been subservient to the CPCz. See below, chap. XVII for further discussion.

[10] See the standpoint of the CPCz Presidium, June 11, *Rok šedesátý osmý* (Prague, 1969), p. 225; henceforth *RŠO*.

[11] *RP*, June 28. See also S. Pošusta, ibid., June 26, and J. Novotný, ibid., July 9.

[12] For these developments, see *Svědectví* 10, no. 38 (1970), 179-86; *Tribuna*, April 23, 1969, p. 7; *Život strany*, nos. 47-48, Nov. 19-26, 1969; ibid., no. 49, Dec. 3, 1969. See also *Student*, June 19, 1968; *Literární listy*, July 4, p. 2.

for the time being, it expressed the wish to contribute to "maintaining the fundamental rules of democratic political life" and looked forward to elections by secret ballot, in which candidates of several parties, as well as independent candidates, would contest for seats. They also hoped for "the formation or reconstruction of political parties on the basis of principled world outlooks and standpoints elaborated from a long-term point of view." They wished to be "an independent political force of a completely new type" and, "not against, but beside, the Communist Party, to aim toward a common goal—socialism, on the basis of humanism and democracy."[13]

It was to be an association of "citizens without party affiliation" and would not admit persons who were members of any party. One of its main objectives was "the equality of non-party people in civil and public life, and in science and culture." It sought accordingly the abolition of the "cadre ceiling" restricting the holding of offices by non-party persons. Although, as a preparatory committee, KAN was somewhat limited in the activities it could carry on and was impeded by lack of funds and the absence of a journal of its own, as well as by impediments to the publication of its viewpoints, it carried on widespread activity, seeking, mainly through public meetings, to influence public opinion. It had its own views on desirable constitutional amendments and changes in the political system and the electoral law, and strongly advocated the constitutional freedoms of the individual, including a new law of assembly and association and the abolition of censorship. It worked hard to secure its own registration and acceptance into the National Front, and sought also to influence elections in the trade unions and even the selection of delegates to the CPCz congress. Party spokesmen repeatedly denied that KAN was a political party, or even a "pressure group," inasmuch as it did not seek to attain power, and described it as a political club, which did seek political participation and was not merely a discussion club. Yet the possibility of KAN becoming a party was not excluded, especially as a result of the pressures from other parties and forces.[14]

[13] For the manifesto of KAN, see *Svobodné slovo*, July 11. See also addresses on KAN's purposes by Ivan Sviták on April 18 and May 14 published in *Student*, May 1, June 19, resp. Both are given in Sviták, *The Czechoslovak Experiment, 1968-1969* (New York, 1971). Among those who signed the manifesto (including members and non-members of KAN) were Prof. V. Černý, Karel Gott (folk singer), Alexander Kliment (writer), Jaroslav Seifert (poet), Jiří Šlitr (composer and actor), Jiří Suchý (poet), Ivan Sviták (philosopher), Josef Škvorecký (novelist), Otto Wichterle (scientist), Jan Zrzavý (painter), and other prominent writers, film directors, composers, painters, and actors.

[14] Smrkovský, in an interview, suggested that further consideration of KAN was necessary "so as to get to know more exactly their ideas" (*SS*, July 3, 1968). Useful information concerning its activities is given in *RP*, May 15, 19, July 11; *Rep.*, July 3-10, 1968, p. 8; *Tribuna*, March 19, 1969; A. I. Simon, "Czechoslovakia's KAN: A Brief Venture in Democracy," *East Europe* 18 (June 1969), 20-22. See

Apart from such explicitly political organizations, the National Front system was to embrace some of the most significant interest organizations, including, of course, major associations already existing, such as the trade unions or the creative unions, other large organizations in process of formation, such as the collective farmers' association, and still others which were gradually coming into existence, often with separate Czech and Slovak sections. As previously noted, the blossoming of interest organizations, old and new, had begun soon after January and continued through the spring and early summer. The new associations were still in a preparatory stage and had not received permission to function in a permanent form. In fact, the Minister of the Interior, in a statement on June 18 to a parliamentary committee, revealed that of seventy organizations which had requested registration (31 with draft statutes) only one, the Society for Human Rights, had been approved.[15] Moreover, the degree to which any of them would be granted political status by admission into the National Front was as yet uncertain.

K 231, the organization of former political prisoners, was a special case. Its potential membership was at first estimated as 40,000, but later as high as 130,000. Although confined in the main to Bohemia and Moravia it had a sister organization in Slovakia, the Organization for the Defense of Human Rights. It had organized committees in all districts of Bohemia and Moravia, and even in some parts of Slovakia, and claimed 50,000 members by the end of May. The organization became the subject of much controversy; some of its leaders and members were accused of having been genuinely guilty of crimes, and the organization was charged with having broader political purposes.[16] Its leaders disavowed any aim of creating a political party and described its purpose as exclusively to promote and aid in the rehabilitation of former prisoners.[17] In official circles K 231 was considered as performing a tem-

---

also for many details, and excerpts from programmatic statements and draft statutes, an anonymous article, *Svědectví* 12, no. 45 (1973), 152-69.

There was strong resistance by many KAN members to the establishment of a highly organized party-like structure. The draft statute proposed a rather elaborate organization, replete with congress and central committee, but sought to avoid hierarchical authority and to preserve the independence of the individual organizations and members (draft in *Svědectví*, no. 45, pp. 157-60). See also June memorandum on organizational matters, ibid., pp. 163-64; unpublished draft perspective program (mimeo.), pp. 14 ff.

[15] *RP*, June 19.

[16] See *RP*, May 28, June 1, 3, 5, 8, 11, 26; *Pravda*, June 11; J. Prášek, *Rep.*, June 12-19, 1968. See also *Tribuna*, Jan. 22, March 12, 1969. Husák was reported as criticizing K 231, asserting that its future would depend on whether it will "create order in its own ranks and purge itself of undesirable elements" (Bratislava *Večerník*, June 11, 1968).

[17] K. Nigrín, *Pravda*, May 2; V. Hejl, *Student*, June 19; Hejl, *LL*, June 27; J. Brodský, *Rep.*, June 26-July 3, 1968. Cf. *SS*, July 4; *RP*, June 4. See also Brodsky, "Czechoslovakia's 231 Club," *EE* 18 (June 1969), 23-25.

porary function only, and as having lost justification for continued existence after the passing of the rehabilitation law.[18]

FRESH WINDS IN THE PARTY

Whatever shape the political system as a whole finally assumed, the evolution within the ruling Communist Party would be a factor of decisive importance. The necessity of fundamental reforms of party procedures was an integral part of the post-January program and had been urged insistently by prominent reform spokesmen. The membership meetings in June were disappointing owing to poor attendance and a relative political backwardness. During late June and early July, however, the district and regional conferences revealed that new currents were flowing at lower levels of the party structure.[19] As the Presidium reported, the sessions represented "a marked shift in support of progressive forces and ideas."[20] The conference delegates were to a large degree newcomers and, although divided in opinions, tended to reflect reform trends.[21]

The conference debates, as rather sketchily reported in the press, were vigorous and spirited, and were dominated by progressive spokesmen to a much greater degree than in March. For some delegates, wrote an official commentator, the "main danger" was on the right, but for most, the danger of a "freezing of the democratization process" was much greater.[22] There was criticism of many aspects of the party's work, and of specific leaders, both at lower and higher levels. There was open admission of the lack of confidence in the party and of the measures necessary to overcome it. Some of the highest leaders, for instance, Indra, Kolder, Švestka, and Bil'ak, were censured and in several cases were obliged to make speeches defending their record. There were demands for changes in the party's methods, some quite radical, as, for example, a proposal by a Košice delegate to draft a completely new party statute rather than amend the existing one, or a suggestion at Pilsen to dissolve the entire membership and begin anew with fresh applications, or the Hradec

[18] Pavel, *RP*, June 19; Kriegel, *SS*, June 25; Smrkovský, *SS*, July 3. In a statement in early June the Ministry of Interior denied that it was cooperating with K 231 or intended to do so. K 231, however, claimed to have supplied documentary materials to the ministry (*RP*, June 6).

[19] For reports of these meetings, see *RP*, June 29-30, July 1, 5-8; *Pravda*, July 14-15; for official commentaries, E. Šíp, *RP*, July 3, and F. Zdobina, ibid., July 9.

[20] June 25 meeting, *RŠO*, p. 260.

[21] For detailed analysis of delegates' opinions see *Zpráva o současné politické situaci Československé socialistické republiky a podmínkách činnosti Komunistické strany Československa* (Prague, 1968), pp. 71-81 and below, chap. XVI.

[22] Zdobina, *RP*, July 9.

Králové resolution to hold the 14th congress in public, with its proceedings broadcast. The Prague city organization decided to remain in "permanent session" until the 14th congress in view of the critical situation. Expressing lack of confidence in a significant part of the CC membership, the resolution provided for the convocation of a plenary meeting of the Prague conference in case the political situation required "drastic political action."[23] In the discussion of the party statutes there were many proposals for change which emphasized democratic principles of party organization. Above all, there were frequent calls for the withdrawal of discredited persons from the Central Committee as the chief condition of regaining the confidence of members and of the public at large.

The election of delegates to the 14th congress was crucial, since this body would elect the Central Committee. The election was conducted by secret ballot, and often after criticism, or changes, of the official list of nominees and produced a body of delegates that would almost certainly have stood firmly for accelerated reform and many changes in the composition of the Central Committee. Certain important conservative figures, notably Kolder and Indra, were not elected as delegates, although Bil'ak and Švestka were. There was also substantial opposition to the election of many others, of both progressive and conservative coloring. A striking novelty was the fact that the conferences were accorded the right to nominate CC and ÚKRK candidates from whom the congress would make the final selection. Nine hundred and thirty-five persons were nominated, on the basis, according to the Presidium's report, of "their positive and active relationship to the process of revival."[24]

Meanwhile the preparations for the 14th congress were proceeding apace and changes in the party's methods of work were being introduced. The rehabilitation of individual party members was also going forward, under the general direction of the Central Commission on Supervision and Auditing (ÚKRK), and a special committee was to investigate the activity of Miroslav Mamula.[25] The Piller Commission was examining the main political trials of the fifties and assessing the responsibilities of individual party leaders. In an interview in June, Piller, without giving any specific names, assigned the chief responsibilities to particular offices

[23] *RP*, July 8. See also J. Smrčina, ibid., Sept. 16, 1969; A. Svarovská and J. Rous, ibid., Oct. 8, 1969. Smrčina criticized this action as an attempt to create "a second center" in the party and to displace the Central Committee. J. Pal'o (*Pravda*, July 10) did not entirely disapprove of this action, but expressed the hope that it would not be repeated elsewhere.

[24] Presidium meeting of June 25, *RŠO*, p. 260.

[25] See interview with Jakeš, *RP*, June 19 and the reports of ÚKRK, ibid., July 4 and 5.

of the party and state and rejected Novotný's attempt to escape blame in his speech at the May plenum.[26] The Presidium made several key personnel changes at party institutions, such as the Higher School, the Institute of the History of the CPCz (renamed the Institute for the History of Socialism), and the party's publishing house, and announced plans for the publication of two new journals, *Politika* and *Tribuna*.[27]

A significant element in the preparations for the congress was the initiation of work on the revision of the party statute and the opening of discussion in the party press on this subject. A working group, headed by Miroslav Havlíček, of the Gottwald Military and Political Academy, elaborated a draft proposal which was considered and adopted by higher party bodies, including the Presidium, in early July and then submitted in revised form to the districts and regions for further comment.[28] The final draft statute was published in August and will be treated more fully in the following chapter. Although the initial draft was not published at the time, the general tenor of the changes envisaged became known from June 18 on as a result of discussion in the press in which members of the working group took an active part.[29]

The statute's aim, wrote Havlíček, was to stress the democratic aspects of democratic centralism and in particular to encourage the "struggle of opinions" within the party. Another member of the working group, Jindřich Fibich, condemned the conception of the party as "a monolithic disciplined base of the highest peaks of the party bureaucracy." The new statute, he wrote, must not be "a plastering over of the traditional Stalinist model" but "a completely new model of inner-party relations," based on the classic associational conception of Marx and on the findings of the theory of organization and the sociology of politics.[30]

The need for "a profound transformation" of the party was expressed in a joint statement by members of the Richta team, which declared that the old type of party, developed under the conditions of the dictatorship of the proletariat, was "a thing of the past." The party could not accomplish its tasks "without a democratization of decision-making, without freedom to judge various alternatives before every decision, without a constant renewal of cadres, without continuing ascertainment of the opinion of party members, or without secret voting. . . ." In particular,

---

[26] Ibid., June 19. The importance of the forthcoming report was emphasized by Šik in a speech at the regional conference in České Budějovice (ibid., July 7).

[27] For Presidium meetings in June and July, see *RŠO*, pp. 224-42.

[28] *RP*, July 19. A poll of party opinion on the statute was conducted between July 13 and 22. Some of its results were published during August. For the detailed questionnaire, including a variety of alternatives for reform of all phases of party life, see *ŽS*, no. 16 (Aug. 1968), insert, p. 28.

[29] For the discussion, see *RP*, beginning June 18, and *ŽS*, beginning with no. 14 (July 1968). See also *Pravda*, June 20, July 25, Aug. 6; J. Moravec, *KT*, July 4.

[30] *RP*, July 23, June 18, resp.

"groups with different opinions" must not be labeled fractions but must be allowed to express their views.[31]

The discussion included specific suggestions as to how to develop a model of the party, as one comment expressed it, which would not be based on the Soviet pattern but would conform to Czechoslovak conditions and traditions. Membership would be voluntary, based less on social origin and more on "social consciousness," and would include voluntary withdrawal. The party would thus become "an elite of politically committed progressives" from all classes and social groups.[32] Voting would be secret for officers at all levels, even the Central Committee, and election of the higher party organs would be direct. Time limits on the term of office would assure the rotation of officials; a ban on the holding of multiple posts would prevent a monopolization of power in the hands of a few. The all-pervasive role of professional functionaries in all spheres of life was frequently condemned, and the need for developing real "political personalities" was asserted.[33] There would be a maximum participation of members and organs in the formulation of policy, and substantial autonomy for lower organs within their own spheres. There would even be, in Fibich's words, "a certain plurality, variability, and relative independence of the main organs," thus averting domination by a single body. Above all, in his view, there must be a free flow of information and discussion of alternative views on policy, with protection for minority opinions. Although this would not permit the creation of organized "fractions" and would not alter the traditional binding character of decisions, it would make it possible for a minority to form a temporary group, publish its views and proposals, and revive discussion at a later point.[34]

To the discomfiture of the leaders, these matters, especially the choice of congress delegates, which were regarded as internal party matters, became the topics of public discussion. Owing to the central role of the party in political life, the critics felt that the populace had a right to know as much as possible about intra-party developments and to express an

---

[31] Ibid., July 12.

[32] *RP*, July 2. See also ibid., July 31; V. Kuš, *Pravda*, June 25.

[33] M. Hysko, *Nové slovo*, July 25; V. Smrkovský, *ŽS*, no. 12 (June 1968), pp. 40-43; L. Hrabovský, *Nová mysl*, no. 6 (1968), pp. 728-39.

[34] *LL*, Aug. 1. Havlíček advocated the right to form "temporary groups" with "their own group opinion" and to submit "alternative proposals." The real threat to unity, he argued, would arise from suppressing such opinions and driving people into "permanent opposition" and thus creating the danger of an "eruptive overthrow" and a "split" within the party (*Pravda*, June 19). Detailed proposals for amendments to the statute by party members at the Philosophical Faculty of Charles University included extensive provisions for protecting minority views, such as the right to form "informal groups" to express opinions before the taking of a decision and the right to maintain "one's own minority view" after the decision (*LL*, July 18).

interest in their outcome. After all, the election of delegates and of the Central Committee would in large measure determine the fate of the reform program. Moreover, as one commentator put it, the results would show citizens whether there were reasons to support the party in the eventual elections for the National Assembly. Public discussion of the merits and demerits of leading figures would alone provide a sound basis for eventual selection of members for the topmost party organs.[35] Writers in non-party journals expressed some doubts about the congress preparations, especially the election of delegates, since these tasks were in the hands of the apparatus, in particular of Indra. Moreover, the election was to be conducted indirectly through a four-stage procedure likely to discourage the choice of non-conformist candidates, it was thought. Despite these reservations, there was considerable praise for the actual candidates selected and for the general direction which party reforms were taking.[36]

POLARIZATION OF FORCES: THE TWO THOUSAND WORDS

The controversy stirred up by the Two Thousand Words can only be understood against the background of the polarization of forces that had been occurring throughout June. Ever since the May plenum there had been increasing worry among those elements favorable to reform that conservative forces would be able to slow down or bring to a halt the momentum of change initiated after January. This concern was aroused by the plenum resolution, with its stress on the anti-socialist danger, and aggravated by utterances of more conservative personalities, beginning with a hard-line speech by Alois Indra, in early June, which was not published but the content of which became widely known.[37] Even more alarming was an article by the extreme conservative, Josef Jodas, expressing fears for the fate of socialism and of a return to capitalism.[38] Šik's response to the Jodas article alerted a wider audience to the danger threatening from the "conservative" side.[39] On the other hand the new spirit and tone of the mass media aroused misgivings among many party

[35] J. Hanzelka, *Mladá fronta*, June 9. Hanzelka's article was followed by many letters to *Mladá fronta*, mostly in support of his position. See also Dalimil (pseud.), *LL*, June 6 and 27; I. Bystřina, ibid., June 20; I. Klíma, ibid., July 4; J. Hochman, *Rep.*, July 3-10. Cf. Hájek, for criticism of non-communist influence on congress preparations, *Mýtus a realita ledna* 1968 (Prague, 1970), pp. 123, 128.

[36] Fibich, *LL*, June 13; J. Ruml, *Rep.*, June 12-19; Hochman, ibid., July 3-10.

[37] On Indra's speech, see A. Kliment, *LL*, June 27.

[38] *Obrana lidu*, June 8.

[39] *RP*, June 18. See also his other warnings of the conservative danger, ibid., June 30, and *Práce*, July 7.

members and functionaries, unaccustomed to such free discussion.[40] In Slovakia, a letter to *Pravda*, by an old communist, in which he condemned praise for Masaryk and criticism of the communist past, produced a polemical reply by M. Gašparík, who defended the role of the progressive intelligentsia in criticizing the old order.[41]

Another influential conservative, Švestka, editor-in-chief of *Rudé právo*, published two long articles in defense of his "progressive" record under Novotný, and, in a speech at a Prague regional party conference, repudiated attacks on his post-January stand and on the party daily.[42] In a leading article on "The Meaning of January," he interpreted it as "a rebirth of the socialist revolution achieved from the positions of Marxism-Leninism," and after identifying the two dangers in the party, proceeded to make a very sharp attack on "anti-socialist efforts."[43] In the same issue, under the heading "Citizens Beware!" Professor Goldstücker published the text of a vicious anti-Semitic letter addressed to him and warned that it was high time to cleanse the party of such elements who, "while speaking as the defenders of the interests of the working class, the nation and the party," have in fact nothing but "contempt" for them.[44] The frequent use of anonymous letters and leaflets to attack some of the topmost leaders, such as Šik, Kriegel, Císař, and Goldstücker, was deplored and repudiated by the party organ itself two weeks later.[45]

Meanwhile, at the other end of the political spectrum, reform-oriented forces stepped up their pressure for political change. This progressive mood was particularly evident at the conferences of the Revolutionary

[40] E.g. a symposium conducted by Karel Vlč (*ŽS*, no. 15, July 1968, pp. 27-31). For other articles indicating the difficulties of adjustment by functionaries, see ibid., no. 11 (May 1968), pp. 34-36; no. 14 (July 1968), pp. 16-19.

[41] *Pravda*, June 19, 28.

[42] *RP*, June 18, 19, July 8. Švestka not only defended the record of *Rudé právo* under his editorship but also cited his efforts from 1964 on to secure changes in the way the leading role of the party was implemented. For a sharp refutation and condemnation of Švestka, see the statement by staff members in the paper's art and literature department, including its head, M. Vacík (*LL*, July 11).

[43] *RP*, June 23.

[44] Ibid.; text in English in R. A. Remington, ed., *Winter in Prague* (Cambridge, Mass., 1969), pp. 189-94. The letter, addressed to "the Zionist hyena bastard," was written by someone who claimed to speak for the working class and the Communist Party and was a diatribe against Jews and Zionists. For many days thereafter statements were published in *Rudé právo* condemning the letter, for instance, from a cultural *aktiv* (June 27), a people's militia unit (July 4), "old communists" in North Bohemia (July 9); and in letters to the editor, several of which, however, supported the anonymous letter (July 10).

[45] *RP*, July 5. Similar condemnatory views were expressed by party members in the Ministry of the Interior, ibid., July 13, 16. A television editor referred to the flood of anti-communist, anti-Semitic, and anti-democratic letters received, reflecting, he said, the "moral crisis" of society (*ŽS*, no. 15, July 1968, p. 31). For anonymous letters attacking P. Kohout and L. Vaculík, see *LL*, June 27 and July 4.

Trade Unions and of the Union of Journalists which met in rapid succession in June. Appeals for reform and warnings against conservative forces were issued by *aktiv* meetings of communist cultural workers and of the university communists at the end of the month.[46] In the same spirit, journals such as *Literární listy* and *Reportér* repeatedly drew attention to the conflict of progressive and conservative forces within the party, and expressed fears that the latter might triumph in the months leading up to the extraordinary congress.[47]

The progressive elements were also disturbed by the cautious attitudes of the reform leaders, typified by the address by the Prime Minister to the trade union congress. Černík referred to the tremendous wave of demands on scarce resources, called for "realism," and defended a gradual policy, aiming "not at months but years ahead."[48] Smrkovský, on his return from a lengthy trip to the USSR, was met by persistent questioning as to his remarks in Russia about anti-socialist tendencies. There was, as *Literární listy* warned, a perceptible decline in the popularity of this reform spokesman.[49] Even Dubček, who remained high in public esteem, stirred up doubts by his appearance at the conference of the People's Militia, where he praised this armed workers' unit, regarded by many as a conservative force, and expressed the view that they represented no danger to the reform movement.[50]

The legislative reforms adopted by the National Assembly at the end of June were welcomed, but the opposition to the abolition of censorship by some deputies was disquieting. The election of the Czech National Council by the assembly in early July was also disturbing inasmuch as two well-known writers, Jiří Hanzelka and Pavel Kohout, both signatories of the Two Thousand Words, were defeated, and Šik was elected by a narrow majority, thus confirming the continuing strength of conservative deputies.[51] All these worries as to the fate of reform were intensified by

[46] *RP*, June 27-28.

[47] Ruml, *Rep.*, June 12-19; Hochman, ibid., July 3-10; Dalimil, *LL*, June 27; F. Šamalík, ibid., July 11.

[48] *RP*, June 21.

[49] Dalimil, *LL*, June 20. Public opinion polls placed Smrkovský lower on the scale of popular trust than earlier. For Smrkovský's reports on his trip, ibid., June 18, 20. In an interview Smrovský expressed regrets for his critical remarks in Moscow concerning the journalists (*SS*, July 3).

[50] *RP*, June 20. See below in this chapter on this episode. R. Horčic, chief of staff of the People's Militia, denied that the militia was a "conservative force" or that it would interfere, by "armed force," in domestic political affairs. He expressed the belief that the functions of the militia should be reevaluated and that it should be given a legal basis, and did not exclude membership by non-communists (*LD*, July 14).

[51] This defeat of two candidates on the list submitted by the National Front was sharply criticized by Smrkovský, Kriegel, and Pelikán. See *Tribuna*, Sept. 17, 1969, p. 9.

the "war of nerves" occasioned by the renewal of Soviet press polemics in the middle of June and the holding of Warsaw pact maneuvers on Czechoslovak soil at the end of the month.

It was in this setting, just prior to the district party conferences and to the termination of military maneuvers, that the Two Thousand Words, drafted by the noted writer, Ludvík Vaculík, was published in *Literární listy*, which, by this time, was appearing in 300,000 copies.[52] Written at the request of a number of scholars and scientists, it was signed originally by over sixty persons, some of whom were ordinary workers and farmers, others, distinguished figures from various fields of science, scholarship, and the arts. The magnitude of the controversy, national and international, which it produced was no doubt a surprise to its signatories. The document contained sharp criticisms of the party's past record, but paid tribute to the fact that the CPCz had launched the democratization movement and that some of its leaders were seeking to redress wrongs and mistakes. Since the party alone had the necessary organization and the experienced officials, and a concrete program of reform, there could be no thought, it was stated, that the democratic revival could be carried on "without the communists or, if necessary, against them." Nonetheless many functionaries were opposed to the changes and still had great power, especially in the local communities, producing a struggle "concerning the content and text of laws and the extent of practical measures." This was "a moment of hope," but a hope that was "constantly threatened."

Although such comments were commonplace in the heady atmosphere of the early summer, the conclusions drawn from this analysis were unusual and aroused qualms within and outside the country. The people were called upon to act "at our own initiative and by our own decisions." At the center nothing more could be demanded or expected at that time, but in the districts and local communities much remained to be done. In particular, persons who had abused their power must be forced to withdraw from their positions by "public criticism, resolutions, demonstrations, demonstrative work brigades, collections for those going into re-

[52] It was published simultaneously on June 27 in *Práce, Zemědělské noviny*, and *Mladá fronta*; English text in Remington, ed., *Winter in Prague*, pp. 196-202. In the same issue of *Literární listy* (June 27), Vaculík published an article on the "revival process" in the small town of Semily which he visited in mid-May. The lagging of democratization which he reported no doubt influenced him in writing the Two Thousand Words. For an account of the writing of the statement, see Vaculík, *LL*, July 11. According to another *LL* editor (in an interview with the author in Oct. 1968) the document was a personal statement of Vaculík's, and most of the editors disagreed with its publication. For comments, see also Rémi Gueyt, *La mutation tchécoslovaque* (Paris, 1969), pp. 217, 221-27; Hájek, *Mýtus*, pp. 128-35. For Vaculík's article on Semily and other documents relating to the Two Thousand Words, see A. Oxley, A. Pravda, and A. Ritchie, *Czechoslovakia: The Party and the People* (London, 1973) pp. 6-17, 219-82.

tirement, a strike, or a boycott of their doors." All "illegal or coarse methods" should be avoided, but much could be accomplished by choosing good managers and works' council members, by activizing the National Front and the national committees, by setting up "special citizens' committees and commissions," including committees for the defense of the free press, and by holding meetings with "our own units of public order." It was this appeal for initiative and action at the community level that was later interpreted as threatening the orderly process of reform. The statement recognized federalization as the solution for the Czech-Slovak question but warned that this would not solve the problem if "government by the party-state bureaucracy" continued. The declaration also referred to "foreign forces" which were threatening to "intervene in our development" and proclaimed a readiness to stand behind the government, "if necessary with arms," combined with an assurance that the treaties of alliance, friendship, and trade would be maintained.

The original purpose of the Two Thousand Words had been to alert the public to the threats to the democratization movement and to stir people into action, especially at the lower levels of government and party, during the summer holiday season.[53] Its immediate consequence was to bring down upon the signatories the bitter denunciation of party and government leaders and to intensify the polarization of public opinion by stirring up both conservative and progressive indignation. The cascade of mutual recrimination began with an interpellation in the National Assembly by the Slovak, Gen. Samuel Kodaj, commander of Czechoslovak forces in eastern Slovakia, who called the manifesto "an open appeal for counterrevolution" and demanded legal action against the signatories.[54] A major crisis ensued. Strong statements were issued by the Presidium, the National Front, and the government, and Dubček addressed the nation on television.[55] Although the Presidium did not go as far as Kodaj in its estimate of the peril, it described the declaration as "an attack" on the party's policy, which "opened the path for anti-communist tendencies" and for "an assault on the present leadership." The Presidium especially opposed the appeals to create "various committees or commissions with political functions or aims outside the system of the National Front" and urged the population not to permit the disturbing of "the peaceful constitutional character of the reform of our political system which was now taking place."

[53] L. Vaculík, at the Prague party conference, *RP*, June 30.
[54] Text in *SS*, June 28. Kodaj stood firm on his views (*Práce*, July 4), but eventually resigned from his parliamentary seat and other public positions.
[55] Texts in *RP*, June 29. According to Moscow *Pravda* (Aug. 22, 1968), the Soviet leaders had immediately called Dubček's attention to the danger of the Two Thousand Words and had received assurance that the most resolute measures would be taken.

Although Dubček, in his television address, did not explicitly refer to the Two Thousand Words, he stressed the need for unity and argued that any weakening of the position of the party would weaken the process of democratization. Černík, the Prime Minister, in a measured statement to the assembly, warned of the dangers on both sides, conservative and "rightist," and condemned the declaration for agitating both extremes. In his address to the Prague party conference the following day, Dubček mentioned the many unsolved problems and unsatisfied demands and declared that it was "not possible to deal with them by strikes and demonstrations, without regard for the needs and possibilities of society, and outside the democratically elected and responsible organs."[56] Smrkovský, in an article entitled, "One Thousand Words," censured the "political romanticism" of the statement, which did not give enough consideration to "all components—internal and external—by which the development of our society is determined." Those with the responsibility "must take *all* connections into account and think through all the possible results. They must simply be realists." Although the main threat was from the forces seeking to restore the pre-January regime, he said, there was also the danger of "right extremists," which in turn strengthened the hands of the conservatives.[57] Indra went much further, sending out a message from the Secretariat to all party organizations warning that the Two Thousand Words could create a "counterrevolutionary situation" and was "an attempt to break up the party" and to "introduce anarchy and build institutions which could lead to the destruction of the state."[58] It was obvious that the party leaders differed in their interpretation of the statement but were determined not to let their leadership be challenged by more radical spokesmen or permit the interruption of their planned program of reform.[59]

Public reaction was intense and divided. In the district party conferences the Two Thousand Words became a major topic of debate. Císař, Šik, and Husák, condemned it and endorsed the official standpoint; others backed the declaration and censured the leadership for overreacting to it. There was criticism of the Presidium's statement and of the Indra message and considerable sympathy for the Two Thousand Words. The Prague municipal party organization issued a penetrating but bal-

[56] *RP*, June 30 (also Dubček, *K otázkam obrodzovacieho procesu v KSČ*, Bratislava, 1968, pp. 206-7). See Dubček's speech at Líšeň (Brno), *RP*, July 1.

[57] *RP*, July 5 (also in *Mladá fronta and Práce*). See also Appendix D.

[58] This message was not published at the time but its text was later given in *Student*, July 10.

[59] In 1969, Kolder reported that all members of the Presidium, including Smrkovský, had considered the declaration "counterrevolutionary" but this viewpoint had been toned down in the official statement, from which Dubček, Smrkovský, and others later moved still further away (*RP*, Sept. 10, 1969).

anced criticism of the manifesto, making no reference to the danger of counterrevolution.[60] A flood of letters poured into the newspapers, radio, and television, most of them, as admitted by *Rudé právo*, supporting the Two Thousand Words.[61] Letters often sharply censured General Kodaj and denied the threat of counterrevolution. Many thousands added their signatures to the declaration. Organs of progressive opinion, such as *Literární listy, Reportér*, and *Práce*, were especially critical of the official viewpoint. It was argued that the crisis had been artificially created by conservative forces and in fact amounted to "an open attempt at a reactionary putsch in the party."[62] The real threat was a "counterrevolution" from the conservative forces.[63] There were reports of a meeting of the communist parliamentary group, whose proceedings were not published, at which demands were allegedly made for the cancellation of the 14th congress, the immediate convocation of the Central Committee, a change in the Presidium's composition, and the mobilization of the People's Militia. In Slovakia the official reaction was negative, but unofficial comments were balanced and in some cases supported the Two Thousand Words.[64]

Although the timing of the manifesto was perhaps poorly chosen and its wording in some cases unfortunate, the Two Thousand Words was in essence an attempt to combat growing conservative resistance and to carry the democratization process to the smaller communities and to the public at large. In the eyes of the French communist, Pierre Daix, it represented "an opening of the party to the people," thus making democratization no longer just the party's business.[65] Although in that sense it might have strengthened the hands of the reform leaders in carrying through their planned reforms, they were embarrassed by the vigorous character of the offensive and sensed in it a threat to their own measured approach. Yet their public condemnation of the declaration concealed a certain sympathy on the part of at least some of the leaders for its main

[60] *VP*, June 28. See also *ŽS*, no. 15 (July 1968), for conflicting views.

[61] *RP*, July 6. See also *Práce*, June 29, 30, July 3-6.

[62] Dalimil, *LL*, July 4.

[63] Ruml, *Rep.*, July 17-24; also S. Budín, ibid., July 10-17. Cf. the statement of the artistic and cultural unions that the Two Thousand Words was "a pretext" for "a counteroffensive of the conservative forces" (*RP*, June 29).

[64] For the Slovak Presidium's statement, *Pravda*, July 2. Cf. S. Faltan, ibid., July 3; I. Hudec, ibid., July 4; *NS*, July 4; *KŽ*, July 5. Novomeský was much more critical and was particularly incensed that the authors had not considered it necessary to seek Slovak advice or Slovak signatories (*NS*, July 25). J. Inovecký was critical, but denied the danger of "counterrevolution" (*Roľnícke noviny*, July 20). Army commanders (communists) in the eastern Slovak region repudiated the attacks on General Kodaj and endorsed his fears about the fate of socialism. *Pravda*, in an editorial, responded by criticizing other actions by Kodaj after January (July 23, 24).

[65] Pierre Daix, *Journal de Prague* (Paris, 1968), pp. 241-42.

thrust. The Two Thousand Words was the conception of one, or at most several persons, and not of an organization dedicated to concerted political action, and was certainly not a political reform for counterrevolution or for illegal actions at the local level, as alleged.[66] As a matter of fact nothing very significant resulted from its appeal for local action. It did, however, stir up public opinion, mainly in favor of reform, but at the same time served as a convenient pretext for a conservative riposte, which, however, also failed to influence the course of events significantly. More serious was the belated Soviet reaction (see below), which revived a crisis that had died down by the time of the regional conferences in early July.

SLOVAKS AND THE FEDERAL QUESTION

The Two Thousand Words crisis had hardly subsided before a new one developed, this time over federalism and the Slovak question. Although the idea of federalism had been generally accepted, Slovaks were beginning to be worried about the actual form and content of the future federation and the slow progress toward this objective.[67] Their apprehensions were not fully assuaged by the passage of the procedural law on federation, since this did not represent the full draft statute which they had demanded by the end of June and a Czech National Council was not yet in existence. Nor had the expert commission on the federal order reached agreement on the division of competence between federal and national organs, or on measures to protect the Slovaks against being outvoted in federal bodies. Moreover, there were strong pressures from the South Moravian region for consideration of an alternative tripartite form of federalism which was quite unacceptable to the Slovaks. A mood of discouragement was therefore spreading among Slovaks, who felt that the constitutional talks were being needlessly delayed and that the October 28 deadline might not be met. The brief reference in the Two Thousand Words to the federal question confirmed the opinion of many Slovaks that Czechs did not share their belief in the urgency, indeed the primacy, of settling the question of Czech-Slovak relations. On more than one occasion Slovak dissatisfaction was voiced, although, until early July, this took a relatively moderate tone.[68]

Slovak anxiety over this matter became intertwined with a developing

---

[66] Pierre Broué, French Trotskyist, called the Two Thousand Words "truly revolutionary," since it called for a mass struggle against the apparatus (*Le printemps des peuples commence à Prague*, Paris, n.d., p. 89).

[67] See chap. xv below for full discussion of federation.

[68] See, for instance, Husák, *RP*, June 21; Slovak National Council, *Pravda*, June 28; the CPS Economic Commission, ibid., June 29; Bratislava district conference, ibid., June 30.

conflict among Slovak leaders. The CPS Central Committee on June 20 decided to convene an extraordinary congress of the Slovak party in October and to entrust Bil'ak, the First Secretary, with the responsibility of directing the preparations. In his address, Bil'ak rejected arguments advanced by some for a Slovak congress prior to the 14th CPCz Congress.[69] At the subsequent district conferences the federal question did not receive much attention, but Bil'ak and others censured the Two Thousand Words for neglecting it.[70] At a Presidium meeting on July 1, however, there was severe criticism both of the Two Thousand Words and also of the "slowness" of the work on federalism, and an insistence on the October 28 deadline and on safeguards against any outvoting of Slovaks.[71] Bil'ak, in an interview, spoke at length on the need for adapting the party's structure to the federal system and proposed equal representation of Czech and Slovak parties in a future CPCz Central Committee.[72]

The real storm broke at the meeting of the Bratislava municipal conference in the first week of July. Husák, who, it should be remembered, at this time held no high party position, even in Slovakia, revealed his political ambitions by mounting a major offensive on the question of federalism, coupled with open criticism of the Slovak leaders.[73] As deputy Prime Minister and chairman of the federation commission in Prague, he could speak with authority on the state of the constitutional discussions and the differences that still existed within the commission. He reported that a situation of "crisis" had arisen, mainly as a result of the Slovak demand for parity of representation in federal organs and the Czech unwillingness to accept it. Explicitly rejecting Bil'ak's arguments, Husák urged that the Slovak party congress should be held *before* the 14th CPCz Congress, so as "to adopt a firm standpoint" with regard to federalism.

Proceeding to more sensitive questions of inner-party Slovak politics, Husák warned against the danger of a new "Široký," who, speaking in the name of the Slovak Communist Party, had defended "other interests"

---

[69] *Pravda*, June 21.   [70] Ibid., June 30.   [71] Ibid., July 3.

[72] *NS*, July 4. Cf. similar views by J. Zrak, *Pravda*, July 4. Husák favored a "federalized" party but with a strong central organ (*Rep.*, June 26-July 3). V. Pavlenda recommended an earlier Slovak congress as well as parity representation in the new Central Committee (*Pravda*, July 6).

[73] *Pravda* and *RP*, July 5, 6. Husák's speech was reported differently in the two papers; a fuller text was given in *Smena*, July 7. That Husák's position was not without support was indicated by criticisms of Slovak leaders (J. Šulič, *Pravda*, June 26) and calls for speeding up the democratization process in Slovakia by the Union of Slovak Journalists (ibid., July 16). The same themes were voiced by a Slovak journalist, Ota Plávková, at the journalists' conference at the end of June. See also her article, *KŽ*, June 7. Her views were cited in an article condemnatory of Bil'ak's views by I. Černický, *Rep.*, July 3-10. For other criticisms of the Slovak leaders, see Jonáš (pseud.) *KŽ*, July 5, 19.

and prevented the Slovak leaders from "vindicating their justified standpoints." Criticizing the present Slovak leaders for not being sufficiently self-critical, Husák exploded the "legend" that the leadership had been "totally progressive" after 1963 and reminded his listeners that the process of revival had often been suppressed, not just by Novotný, but by "Slovak hands." Slovaks such as Dubček and Bil'ak had admittedly played a progressive role in the fall of 1967 and in January 1968, but individuals who had opposed Novotný were, he said, not necessarily forever progressive. A "consistent purge" in the leadership, including a recasting of the Slovak Central Committee and Presidium, was urgently needed. It was impossible to go forward in the new conditions "under the old team," Husák declared, pointedly declaring that he did not have Bil'ak in mind, although many of his remarks admittedly did concern him. In a reference to the Slovak party chief that seemed strangely condescending, Husák expressed the belief that Bil'ak "was to play a further significant political role both in Slovakia and in the state as a whole." He buttressed his line of reasoning by describing the great difference between the Czech lands, where the progressive camp dominated public life, and Slovakia, where there was little movement and few changes of leadership, and by warning that, after federalization, there might be a very different situation in Slovakia and in the Czech lands.[74]

Bil'ak found himself very much on the defensive, not only against Husák's indirect attack, but against other speakers who found fault with the pre-January and post-January policy of the Slovak leadership. He reiterated his view that the CPS congress should be held *after* the CPCz congress and expressed the opinion that a forthcoming joint session of the Slovak and Czechoslovak presidia would solve the problem of safeguards against outvoting. If this were not settled, he agreed, an earlier Slovak congress would be desirable. Also, if the regional conferences were to go on record in favor of an early congress, the Central Committee would have to decide. He sharply criticized the Czech media for neglecting the Slovak question and stressed the absolute necessity of meeting the October deadline. He restated the argument for federalizing the party and proposed equality of representation in top organs and provisions against the outvoting of Slovaks. Although accepting some of the censure of cadre policy, Bil'ak saw no point in altering the composition of the Slovak Presidium until the future of the Slovak National Council

[74] For texts of the speeches by Hruškovič and Bil'ak, see *Pravda*, July 10 and 11. Hübl, at the Prague city conference in early July, censured Bil'ak's speech in Bratislava for its unjustified criticism of Czech attitudes and for its blanket demands for parity and measures against outvoting, including parity representation at the 14th congress. A compromise solution could be reached, he said, but only on the basis of "sober reason" and not by ultimatums such as Bil'ak's. Excerpts in A. Ostrý, *Československý problém* (Cologne, 1972), pp. 87-89.

had been determined and personnel matters relating to Slovak government organs were settled. Then a new Slovak CC would select a new Presidium. Bil'ak's speech also included a severe condemnation of Novotný's treatment of Slovakia and a strong defense of the actions of the Slovak leadership after 1963. His colleague, M. Hruškovič, supported him and praised Dubček and Bil'ak as "the driving force" of reform both in Slovakia and in Czechoslovakia as a whole.

The final resolution of the Bratislava conference, which lamented the slowing down of preparations for federation and warned of the danger of outvoting of Slovaks in the federal organs, was a signal victory for Husák. The proposal for a Slovak party congress prior to the CPCz session was also approved and the anniversary of the Slovak Uprising was suggested as the date. This congress, it was said, would deepen the process of democratization by removing from the leadership those responsible for deforming public life. It would adopt a statement on federalization which would be binding on Slovak state and party representatives in their negotiations with the Czechs. Bil'ak could find some consolation in the fact that he, as well as Husák and Novomeský, were among those chosen by the Bratislava organization as delegates for both congresses.

Bil'ak's position was weakened further at other regional conferences. The West and East Slovak meetings differed on the issue of an early congress, the former favoring it, and the latter opposing.[75] Ironically, Dubček, at the Košice conference, expressed a viewpoint more "unitary" in spirit, stressing the principle of national equality and federalism, but also emphasizing the importance of safeguarding the interests of Czechoslovakia as a whole and of assuring the party's unity. The party must play the role of "an integrating factor" and must have a "really authoritative, firm center."[76] He did not express an opinion on the timing of the Slovak congress and refrained from criticism of Bil'ak or other Slovak leaders. At the Central Slovak conference a week later, however, Husák again spoke strongly in favor of an earlier congress and set forth his views on federalism in forthright terms, rejecting any "cowardly compromise" with the Czechs and insisting on an "honorable agreement."[77] The final blow at Bil'ak's position was struck when this conference also supported the idea of a prior Slovak congress, thus placing three of the four Slovak regions on this side of the issue and as Bil'ak himself admitted, two-

---

[75] *RP*, July 7 and 8; *Pravda*, July 9. Both conferences urged the federalization of the party and measures to prevent Slovak outvoting.

[76] *Pravda*, July 11; also *K otázkam*, pp. 209-19 (p. 217 for the quotation). See also Dubček's speech, *RP*, June 30 (*K otázkam*, pp. 205-6).

[77] *Pravda*, July 14, 15 (Husák), 16. Husák reiterated the desirability of changes in the Slovak party leadership so that they could defend Slovak demands effectively at the 14th congress.

thirds of the party's membership. In these circumstances Bil'ak had to beat a dignified retreat. The Slovak Central Committee, at a meeting on July 18, in the middle of the crisis over the Warsaw letter, reversed its decision to hold the congress in October and scheduled the session for August 26 in Bratislava.[78]

By mid-July progress toward federalization had apparently reached an impasse. The formation of the Czech National Council, in a vote in the National Assembly on July 10, opened the way for further advance, but left the major issues unresolved.[79] It was likely that the Slovak party, under new leaders after the August congress, would resist any settlement that did not meet their main demands. Faced with this prospect, the Czechs were beginning to favor some kind of meeting prior to the 14th Party Congress, either a congress of a newly formed Czech party, or a conference of Czech congress delegates to formulate their views on federalism.[80] There was evidence, too, of a readiness on the part of some leading personalities to accept the idea of a separate Czech party, which, while preserving the unity of the party as a whole, would function, like the Slovak party, as a territorial organization, with the division of competence defined in the party statute.[81] In the meantime, much depended on a mutually satisfactory consensus at the forthcoming meeting of the two presidia, which, however, had to be postponed owing to the crisis resulting from the Warsaw letter.[82]

[78] *Pravda*, July 19.   [79] *RP*, July 11.

[80] See, for instance, the proposals made at the district conferences at Pilsen and Ústí nad Labem (*RP*, July 7 and 8), and at the Prague city conference (*ŽS*, no. 15, July 1968, p. 3).

[81] B. Šimon, *Rep.*, June 26-July 3, p. 8. Other alternatives, less preferable in his opinion, were the formation of a party bureau for the Czech lands, or of bureaus for both Czech and Slovak lands. Šimon favored a meeting of delegates from the Czech lands after the party congress to create a Czech CC. According to a post-occupation article, Šimon, as early as the middle of May, had suggested the forming of a Czech Communist Party, to hold its founding congress before the 14th congress (*Tribuna*, Nov. 26, 1968). M. Hübl (*VP*, June 25) favored a federalized party but expressed doubts concerning parity. He proposed a constituent congress of Czech delegates after the 14th congress. M. Lab (*Pravda*, July 12) urged that the CPCz be made up of "national-territorial parties" as "exponents of national aims" but that there should be a unified Central Committee and a common program. Švestka stated that the leadership inclined toward creating a Czech Communist Party but wished the party as a whole to be "a single political force" (*Pravda*, July 8). See also Z. Hejzlar, in V. V. Kusin, ed., *The Czechoslovak Reform Movement 1968* (London, 1973), pp. 119-20.

[82] The CPCz Presidium, in its meeting on July 9, referred to an imminent meeting with the Slovak Presidium and called for an objective discussion of solutions (*RŠO*, p. 234). The CPS Presidium held a preparatory meeting on July 12 (*RP*, July 13). The Warsaw letter did not endorse or condemn federalization but welcomed the "settlement" of Czech-Slovak relations within the framework of the Republic (*RŠO*, p. 237).

MOUNTING BLOC PRESSURES

The position of the Czechoslovak leaders was not an easy one, "either domestically or internationally," as Smrkovský put it; "we stand at the point of interaction of the most varied pressures and opinions."[83] Throughout June and July, the pressures from Moscow and the other bloc capitals steadily intensified, as the withdrawal of Warsaw bloc troops was delayed, press polemics were resumed, and direct party intervention increased, culminating in the Warsaw letter of mid-July. Constant Czechoslovak efforts to demonstrate their loyalty to Moscow and the bloc and to explain and defend their position seemed to have been in vain.

The Warsaw pact maneuvers took place on Czechoslovak territory between June 20 and 30. Prior to this, there was great uncertainty as to whether they would be limited to staff exercises, as originally announced, or would be more extensive. It soon became evident that substantial forces, and not merely officers, would be involved. Some units even arrived in early June, during the CC plenum meeting. After the completion of the maneuvers, which Marshal Yakubovsky, supreme commander of the Warsaw pact forces, described as "successful," there were many contradictory official reports as to the date of troop withdrawal. The evacuation actually began on July 13 but owing to further delays, some units had not departed by the time of the conference in Warsaw. The general public was alarmed by these events and confused, and hardly pacified, by conflicting official statements.[84] Although Czechoslovak spokesmen sought to calm this uneasiness by frequent explanations, the leadership no doubt shared the general concern, but made no open protest to the Soviet Union.[85] In spite of Russian denials that the continued presence of troops constituted pressure on Prague, they weighed heavily on public attitudes and government decisions, and produced a stiffening resistance, rather than concessions, to the Soviet standpoint.

The "war of nerves," as it was described, was aggravated by the resumption of polemics in the Soviet press, and to a lesser extent in the mass media of other bloc states, often taking the form of responses to articles or speeches appearing in Czech and Slovak journals.[86] This was

[83] *RP*, July 7.

[84] See J. Hanák, *Rep.*, July 3-10, 1968. In contrast to the general reaction, a speaker at the Central Bohemia district conference was warmly applauded when he asked the rhetorical question as to why there were so many comments on the military exercises when in 1945 the presence of Soviet troops did not bother anyone (*RP*, July 8, 1968).

[85] Dubček, in his address to the Central Committee on the Warsaw letter, referred to the public confusion and doubts which resulted from the repeated changes of the time of the troop departure (Remington, ed., *Winter in Prague*, p. 236).

[86] The journalist, Jiří Hájek, later placed the blame on the Czechoslovak media

initiated by a severe condemnation in Moscow *Pravda* of the speech delivered by Císař on the celebration of the 150th anniversary of the birth of Karl Marx. He was castigated for describing Leninism as a Russian phenomenon and was branded an anti-Marxist and compared to Karl Kautsky and the Mensheviks.[87] This campaign reached a climax some two weeks after the publication of the Two Thousand Words when this document was blasted in *Pravda* by I. Aleksandrov as "an organizational preparation of the counterrevolution."[88] The Soviet Union made a formal diplomatic protest concerning an article in *Lidová demokracie* which blamed the escape of General Šejna in March on the assistance given to him by Soviet military authorities in Czechoslovakia in his passport arrangements.[89] More ominous was the Soviet exploitation of a message sent to the Soviet embassy in Prague from a conference of the People's Militia in late June. The final resolution avowed their support for Dubček and the reform program and also declared their intention to guard the achievements of 1948 and the alliance with the Soviet Union. The message delivered to the embassy struck a different note, deploring the irresponsible actions of some journalists and proclaiming full solidarity with the Soviet Union. Although not published at the time in the Czech or Slovak press, it was at once published in Moscow *Pravda* (June 21) and was made the subject of "discussion" at factory meetings throughout the Soviet Union.[90] Thousands of Soviet responses, proclaiming solidarity with the Czechoslovak workers, poured into the People's Militia headquarters in Prague.[91]

The Soviet authorities were evidently alarmed by the advancing reform movement in Czechoslovakia and neglected no opportunity to express their concern through official and unofficial channels. Czechs and Slovaks, on the other hand, complained of the Soviet lack of information about, and understanding of, Czechoslovak developments and used every occasion to elucidate and justify their actions. Smrkovský, for instance,

---

for fomenting nationalism and "anti-Sovietism," especially after June (*Mýtus*, pp. 135-49).

[87] Císař's speech was published in *RP*, May 7. The *Pravda* commentary (June 14) was written by Academician F. Konstantinov. See Císař's reply, *RP*, June 22, and the critique of Konstantinov by V. Blažek, *LL*, June 20. See below, chap. XIX, XX.

[88] July 11.

[89] *LD*, June 5. See also Moscow *Pravda*, June 11.

[90] The conference resolution was published in *RP*, June 20. The message was published later (*Pravda*, July 9; RP, July 13).

[91] See the commentary in Moscow *Pravda*, July 7, in which "alarm" was expressed over the "incessant attacks by anti-socialist and anti-Soviet elements." R. Horčic, chief of staff of the People's Militia, defended the message as a "spontaneous" expression of "love for the USSR" and not as a call for Soviet intervention. He also denied that the Soviet replies were politically significant or represented intervention in Czechoslovakia's domestic affairs (*LD*, July 14).

during his trip to the USSR, bent every effort to explain the process of democratization but admitted that it was difficult to defend certain things that had appeared in *Student*, or the report about Šejna in *Lidová demokracie*. In a statement on his return, Smrkovský recognized that the Soviet Union was perturbed by certain negative features of Czechoslovak evolution and believed that the Czechs underestimated them. He acknowledged that he was also bothered by certain phenomena, but felt it was wrong to exaggerate them. Time would be needed to achieve a better understanding, but something had been accomplished during his visit. The Soviet comrades, including those in the highest posts, shared the view, he said, that "every socialist country has its own special conditions, responsibility, and the right to solve its problems according to its own needs." But "fears and doubts" remained.[92] Professor Hájek, the foreign minister, utilized his diplomatic visits to expound upon the situation in Czechoslovakia and to try to convince the other socialist states that it did not threaten their interests. In East Berlin, he said, it was agreed that useless polemics should be avoided, and that more objective information was needed. He had contended, however, that freedom of the press in Czechoslovakia prevented any administrative limitations on journalists. In Sofia, Hájek tried to explain the Two Thousand Words and denied any anti-socialist intentions on the part of its authors. In Rumania and in Hungary, he reported, there was much more understanding of the Czechoslovak viewpoint.[93]

During these weeks the Czech regime sought to pursue a course in foreign affairs that would awaken no fears on the part of their allies and that would indeed contribute to their belief in Prague's reliability. Time and again Dubček and his colleagues reiterated their determination to keep the alliance with the Soviet Union and the other Warsaw bloc members as the keystone of Prague's foreign policy.[94] The visit of a top-ranking delegation to Budapest in mid-June led to the conclusion of a new treaty of alliance with Hungary.[95] Hájek went to Rumania in early July to discuss the renewal of the treaty of friendship between the two countries. Meanwhile Czechoslovak delegations participated in the preparatory conference of communist parties in Budapest in June, and in the regular Comecon session in Moscow in July, without giving any evidence of a dissonant attitude. Štrougal paid an important visit to Moscow in June to discuss economic relations between the two countries. The Prague leaders also attempted to allay worries among their allies about Czechoslovak

---

[92] *RP*, June 18, 20, 25, July 3. Smrkovský later reported an effort by Brezhnev to win him over against Dubček (Appendix D).

[93] *RP*, June 20, 29, July 11.

[94] E.g. Černík, at a Soviet-Czechoslovak youth rally in Děvín, and Dubček, at a peace meeting in Líšeň (*RP*, July 1).

[95] Ibid., June 15.

relations with other countries. Černík, for instance, in a press conference, denied that there was any weakness in Czechoslovak defenses on the western frontiers of the bloc, or that there was any intention of changing Prague's policy toward Israel.[96] Both Hájek and his deputy foreign minister, J. Pudlák, sought to dispel any concern about West Germany, restating the traditional Czechoslovak position on the conditions for diplomatic relations and denying that they had any thought of repatriating Sudeten Germans.[97]

Only in one case were there hints of an impending change in Czechoslovakia's role and that concerned the sensitive question of the Warsaw pact. At the very moment of the meeting of the five parties in Warsaw, General Prchlík, head of the CPCz department for state administration, held a press conference, to discuss his views on necessary changes in the Warsaw pact organization.[98] He also deplored the Warsaw meeting, then in progress, as an example of "fractional activity" by a group of member states which would lead to a breach of the fundamental principles of state sovereignty and non-interference in internal affairs. The solution to the conflict, according to Prchlík, lay, not in concessions or compromises, but in the consistent implementation of the principles of the Warsaw treaty and its pertinent provisions. The Czechoslovak leaders could take advantage of differences among the Warsaw pact members (especially the sympathetic attitude of Hungary) and exploit also the favorable views of other fraternal parties, such as the French, Italian, Rumanian, and Yugoslav. In answers to questions about the maneuvers, he apparently criticized the delays in the withdrawals of bloc troops and asserted that Czechoslovak authorities did not know the exact number of troops involved and had not participated in the command of these exercises.[99] As the whole matter became the subject of controversy at a later stage, it can best be discussed in the following chapter.[100]

THE WARSAW LETTER

Until the first week of July, the Soviet Union confined its exertions largely to indirect forms of pressure such as troop movements and press polemics. During the Czechoslovak parliamentary visit, Brezhnev had made clear the Soviet concern with Czech developments, but, "with tears in his eyes," had denied any intention of intervening.[101] In early June,

---

[96] Ibid., July 13.   [97] Ibid., June 20, 29, July 3, 9, 14.

[98] *Pravda*, July 16. A fuller version, broadcast by Prague radio, is given in Remington, ed., *Winter in Prague*, pp. 214-20.

[99] These remarks were not reported in newspaper accounts but were referred to in official refutations.

[100] See also below, chap. XIX.

[101] This was reported by a People's Party deputy, who was a member of the delegation (*LD*, June 17). See also Smrkovský's reports cited above.

287

however, in a speech delivered on the occasion of a visit by Kádár to Moscow, Brezhnev (without referring to Czechoslovakia), had declared that the Soviet Union could not be indifferent to the fate of socialism in other lands and emphasized the common features of socialism in all countries. Kádár also gave a hard-line speech emphasizing the dangers threatening from imperialism and nationalism and justifying the use of force, if necessary, to protect the socialist order.[102] Shortly thereafter, on June 12, Brezhnev is said to have suggested a meeting with Czechoslovak leaders at any place they desired.[103]

In early July it became known in Prague that letters had been received by the CPCz from Moscow and other bloc capitals which expressed grave concern with the course of events and proposed a joint meeting in Warsaw. This report became the subject of discussion at several of the municipal party conferences, especially in Prague and Brno. In the former case, in the presence of Smrkovský, a statement was adopted which supported the Presidium in its defense of "state and party sovereignty," and while not opposing discussions or suggestions from the other parties, rejected "any effort to replace concrete argumentation with political or economic pressure."[104] Although the content of these letters was not published at the time (or later), it was obvious that the Soviet Union was determined to exert maximum political pressure on the Prague leaders in the hope of forcing them to retreat. The CPCz Presidium, in two successive meetings, approved the principle of discussions but proposed bilateral talks which would prepare the way for an eventual broader meeting.[105] Kolder, according to a later revelation, had presented a written

[102] Reported in *RP*, July 4. See below, chap. xx.

[103] Bil'ak, *RP*, Sept. 3, 1969; Husák, ibid., Sept. 29, 1969.

[104] The text of this resolution and the discussion were given in a post-occupation article, in what purports to be a summary of the conference minutes (*Tribuna*, Oct. 1, 1969). The proposal that this resolution be published and be sent to other regional conferences was said to have been opposed by Smrkovský and defeated. The Prague conference also reportedly adopted a position on foreign policy which defended the right of Czechoslovakia to have "its own standpoint on all problems of world politics." Approving the previous orientation toward CMEA and WTO, the decision declared that these organizations should become "an instrument of equal partnership and not at all institutions of pressure by some members against others" (K. Beránek, *Tvorba*, Dec. 17, 1969).

[105] *RŠO*, pp. 233, 234-35, for Presidium meetings of July 8 and 12. The decision not to accept the invitation was reported to have been unanimous. Later accounts stated that some members of the Presidium, including Kolder and Bil'ak, had favored attending the Warsaw meeting. Allegedly the Presidium members were not aware of the date of the proposed meeting, although Dubček had already been informed of it. See the interviews with Bil'ak (*RP*, Sept. 3, 1969); Kolder (ibid., Sept. 10, 1969); and Černík, *Tribuna*, Aug. 27, 1969. Dubček, in his speech at the CC plenum in Sept. 1969 (as reported in *Svědectví* 10, no. 38, 1970, pp. 274-75) reviewed the entire course of events prior to the Warsaw meeting and denied that any specific date had been proposed. In any case the main issue was one of "principle." Although he admitted that certain comrades expressed different views, "we

memorandum to the Presidium, arguing for a special CC meeting to consider the invitation to Warsaw. Although he claimed that this was eventually supported by a majority in the Presidium, no plenary session was actually convoked.[106]

A few days later the Warsaw meeting of the five parties took place without the Czechs, who, they claimed, had not been informed of either time or place so that they could not possibly have attended.[107] The fact that the conference met in their absence, and the harsh content of the letter addressed by the participants to the Czechoslovak party, indicated

---

agreed on a common, unanimous standpoint" in regard to the preparations for a conference. It had been assumed that bilateral talks were not unacceptable to the Soviet leaders. Smrkovský confirmed Dubček's account in his later testimony (Appendix D). Bil'ak (ibid., no. 38, p. 286), also stated that the date was not the main reason for non-participation, but blamed it on Dubček's fear that they would be forced to agree to Soviet troops remaining in Czechoslovakia. According to Jiří Hájek, the refusal to attend the Warsaw conference was the second fateful error; the first was the decision to call the 14th extraordinary congress (*Mýtus*, pp. 151-57).

[106] Kolder's memorandum, submitted on July 11, was published in *Tribuna*, Sept. 10, 1969. It read in part as follows: "I agree in essentials with the fears expressed in the letter of the Politburo of the CPSU Central Committee, even if the causes of a number of negative phenomena of the process of revival we are going through can be evaluated differently on the basis of our experiences." While he did not agree that there was "a raging counterrevolution," as the Soviet comrades believed, he saw the cause of the situation in "the absolute incapacity or unwillingness of the party leadership to assure, in the new democratic conditions, the implementation of the goals of its decisions through ideological, political, and especially organizational means," and he accepted Soviet fears that this could lead to "political catastrophe." Kolder cited the neglect of democratic centralism, the "scandalizing" of those ready to carry out decisions, "demogogic statements" in the mass media, "the atmosphere of fear" (an example of which was the campaign against General Kodaj), the wavering of leading party functionaries, "the organized and well-managed counteractions from the right," "sectarian attacks from the left," and the facilitating of interference from outside by the mass media's detailed citing of Western bourgeois newspapers, and drew certain conclusions. "The dissatisfaction of the CPSU leadership" and their fears were "justified." The letters should not be regarded as "intervention in our internal affairs," but as "drawing attention to a serious danger which, in the leadership of the party, we still do not feel equal to recognizing, let alone effectively countering." Rejecting "back-room politics" in such a serious question, he called for an immediate meeting of the CC plenum and "a unification of forces in the Presidium" on the basis not of "unity in general" but of "unity of the healthy forces of party and society." Our attitude to the letters should be "deliberate and wise" and not based on the "psychosis of anti-Sovietism," and should lead to "principled and honorable negotiations with our friends on the basis of sovereignty and equality, and with respect for the inviolability of the common interests of socialist countries."

[107] According to post-occupation statements, Prague had learned only on July 13 that the meeting would be convened on July 14, so that the July 12 Presidium meeting had been "superfluous." A secret meeting of Dubček with Kádár, somewhere in Slovakia, apparently took place on July 13, but nothing was known of this meeting at the time, nor was anything revealed later as to its purpose (Husák, *RP*, Sept. 29, 1969; Švestka, ibid., Aug. 21, 1969). The meeting with Kádár was referred to by General Prchlík in his press conference (ibid., July 16, 1968).

289

how wide was the chasm between Czechoslovakia and its bloc allies. The message set forth for the first time publicly the reasons for Soviet concern with Czechoslovak developments, and even more ominously listed the specific actions required to dispel the danger of counterrevolution. The Warsaw letter thus constituted a new climax in the controversy and the beginning of a period of crisis which was not to end until early August, after the meetings in Čierna and Bratislava, and then only temporarily.

As the text is readily available, the Warsaw letter need only be briefly summarized.[108] Discounting any intention of interfering in purely internal affairs, or of seeking to hinder necessary reforms, the message declared that "we cannot assent to hostile forces pushing your country off the path of socialism and creating the threat that Czechoslovakia may break away from the socialist commonwealth. This is no longer your affair only. It is the common affair of all communist and workers' parties. . . . It is the common affair of our countries . . . united in the Warsaw Pact. . . ." The letter went on to remind the Czechoslovak party of the warnings issued at previous meetings and of the assurances given in reply, and referred to the "forces of reaction" in the new political organizations and clubs, and in the press, radio, and television. The Two Thousand Words, in particular, contained "an organizational-political platform of counter-revolution" which had not been rejected and had even found champions within the leadership. Could the Czechoslovak comrades fail to see "that the party was losing control over the course of events and was retreating more and more under the pressure of anti-communist forces?" "We are convinced that a situation has arisen in which the threat to the foundations of socialism in Czechoslovakia jeopardizes the vital common interests of the rest of the socialist countries. . . . Each of our parties bears a responsibility not only to its own working class and its own people but also to the international working class and the world communist movement and cannot evade the obligations derived from this." It was "not only your task but ours, too, to deal a resolute rebuff to the anti-communist forces. . . ." This required an offensive against the rightist and anti-socialist forces; a cessation of the activities of all political organizations that oppose socialism; party control over the news media; and solidarity in the ranks of the party itself. "We know there are forces in Czechoslovakia that are capable of upholding the socialist system and dealing a defeat to the anti-socialist elements. . . . The task today is to give these healthy forces a clear perspective and rally them . . . for a struggle against counterrevolution. . . ." The Czechoslovak party, in taking the necessary measures, could "count on the solidarity and general assistance of the parties of the fraternal socialist countries."

[108] For the text, see Moscow *Pravda*, July 18; *RP*, July 19; English version in Remington, ed., *Winter in Prague*, pp. 225-31.

290

The response of the Czechoslovak party leaders was swift and decisive, in the form of a letter from the Presidium which firmly rejected the major charges and insisted on bilateral talks.[109] Openly acknowledging that the process of democratization had been accompanied by certain "negative aspects," "extremist tendencies," both anti-socialist and dogmatic-sectarian, the Prague letter argued that the May plenum had recognized the possible danger to socialism from these tendencies and had set forth a political tactic for overcoming them. "We do not, however, see any real reasons which would justify calling our present situation counterrevolutionary. . . ." Denying that there had been any change in Czechoslovak foreign policy, or that there was any inclination to break away from the socialist camp, the Presidium pointed to the staff maneuvers as "a concrete proof of our faithful fulfillment of our alliance commitments."

Reiterating that the May plenum had recognized certain elements tending to discredit the party, the Prague reply saw no reason to believe that "such phenomena could rightly be judged a threat to the socialist system, or as spelling the doom of the political role of the CPCz under the pressure of reactionary, counterrevolutionary forces." The actions taken to implement the May plenum decisions had consolidated the political situation and had led to "a rise in the authority of the new democratic policy of the party." On the other hand, pressures from domestic extremist forces, both on the right and from the conservative side, which sought to have basic questions settled "elsewhere and at another time than at the fourteenth congress," *was* a threat to the consolidation of the party's role. "The evaluation of the situation contained in the letter of the five parties and the no doubt sincerely intended advice for our further advance did not take into account the whole intricacy of the dynamic social movement as analyzed by the CPCz Central Committee plenary meeting in May or the complexity of the conclusions that were adopted by this plenum." While they did not reject in principle the idea of joint conferences, they felt that bilateral meetings were a prerequisite, so that a joint meeting would not be based on "one-sided and sparse information." "We think that the common cause of socialism is not advanced by the holding of conferences at which the policy and activity of one of the fraternal parties is judged without the presence of their representatives." They urged therefore that bilateral talks be held as soon as possible, at which the possibility of a common meeting would be assessed, and the program and composition, and time and place, of such a meeting would be agreed upon.

[109] For the reply, see *RP*, July 19; also in Remington, pp. 234-43. There were some who felt that this response made damaging admissions and should properly have rejected all the criticisms in the Warsaw letter.

On the evening prior to the publication of the Presidium's response, Dubček addressed the nation on television in a speech which was stronger than the official statement in many respects. He proclaimed the intention of continuing with the post-January course and of not giving up in any way the principles of the Action Program. Affirming their loyalty to proletarian internationalism, and denying that they wished to set a pattern for others, he stated that socialism in Czechoslovakia, with due regard for "generally valid principles," must correspond to "national conditions and Czechoslovak traditions." "Who could better comprehend and understand the interests of our working people than the Czechoslovak party?" This speech and the Presidium's reply were published the following day, along with declarations similar in tone from the National Front, the government, the National Assembly presidium, and the unions and youth organizations.[110] Support was also given by the Slovak Party Presidium, although in a statement that referred more than once to antisocialist elements which must be "rebuffed and suppressed if they try to subvert socialist development."[111]

Having thus responded to the Warsaw letter, Dubček decided to call a special meeting of the Central Committee to secure that body's approval of the Presidium's action. There were some who opposed this, fearing a show of disunity, or even worse, the CC's acceptance of the Warsaw letter, and who proposed as an alternative the immediate convocation of the 14th congress.[112] In view of the composition of the Central Committee, Dubček's action was something of a gamble, but it paid off, since the plenum gave unanimous approval of the Presidium's standpoint.[113] Dubček's speech on that occasion (the only one published) boldly declared that there would be no retreat from the Action Program,

[110] *RP*, July 19.

[111] *Pravda*, July 19. Bil'ak, in his speech to the Slovak CC, was even less decisive, urging that no doubt should be left as to their attitude to the Soviet Union and that everything should be done to explain the matters in dispute at bilateral meetings. In a completely different version of his speech published later, Bil'ak was cited as recognizing Soviet criticisms as justified and regretting the Presidium's rejection of the invitation to Warsaw. He condemned the campaign concerning the presence of Soviet troops and the threat to Czechoslovak sovereignty from the Soviet Union, and declared that there was no such threat and that he would never agree to a break with the Soviet Union and the CPSU. He also cited warnings given him personally by Kádár prior to the Warsaw meeting (Bil'ak, *Pravda zůstala pravdou*, Prague, 1971, pp. 134-47).

[112] Kolder speaks of a memorandum to this effect which an unknown author submitted to the Presidium on July 17 but which Dubček withdrew (*RP*, Sept. 10, 1969). Dalimil also advocated the immediate convocation of the party congress (*LL*, July 11).

[113] Only 88 of the full membership of approximately 120 attended, together with some 40 congress delegates. During the session many delegations from factories and organizations came to the Castle to present resolutions in support of a strong stand by the Central Committee (*The New York Times*, July 20, 1968).

but firmly approved "comradely discussions" as the best method of solving problems, at home or abroad. While defending the sovereignty of Czechoslovakia and insisting on policies adapted to national conditions, he strongly asserted their desire to cooperate with the Soviet Union and to maintain the alliances with the socialist countries. Somewhat unusual, however, was his reference to the danger of conservative forces who might exploit the Warsaw letter for their own purposes. Both these, and right-wing forces, he said, must be dealt with decisively. The brief resolution adopted by the Central Committee endorsed the Presidium's action and urged that direct discussions should begin as soon as possible, in the form of bilateral talks which would prepare for "an eventual meeting of all interested communist parties."[114]

Even before the Warsaw letter and the Presidium's reply had been published, support for the leadership and for a policy of firm resistance began to pour in to official places and to the newspapers. When the position taken by the Presidium became known, the wave of support swelled from organizations such as the creative unions, the Slovak writers and journalists, and the university students; from the non-communist parties; and from the newspapers and weeklies.[115] *Literární listy* issued a special edition with a leading article declaring that the warning of the Two Thousand Words had been justified and that "the path embarked upon is still in danger" and proclaiming its full support for the party's actions.[116] In Slovakia an open letter from the Union of Slovak Writers (signed by persons from both wings of the literary community, for example Mihálik, Mináč, Novomeský, Válek, and Števček) to the writers' unions of the other European communist states defended the post-January course and warned that "any outside psychological or power (*mocenský*) pressures, directed against the process of revival" could do great harm not only to Czechoslovakia but to the whole socialist camp.[117]

The tone of this public comment was stronger than that of official

[114] For the CC proceedings, and Dubček's speech, see *RP*, July 20 (also *RŠO*, pp. 251-59). Bil'ak later claimed that many voted for the statement against their real feelings owing to the atmosphere which prevailed and the pressures to which they were subjected (*RP*, Sept. 3, 1969).

[115] For instance, *Pravda*, July 16, 17; *Práce*, July 18; V. Kotyk, *Práce*, July 11, 20; *LD*, July 18, 19; *SS*, July 19; J. Ruml, *Rep.*, July 17-24; Hochman, ibid., July 24-31; Liehm, *LL*, July 11; M. Jungmann and J. Lederer, ibid., July 18. See also the strong statement adopted by the foreign affairs and constitutional and legal committees of the National Assembly, *RP*, July 16. Note in particular the proclamation of the creative unions supporting the Presidium's reply and pledging "full support to the progressive forces in the CPCz leadership and the NF government in their effort to develop further the democratization process as well as their effort to preserve the sovereignty of the country and its full freedom of decision in our affairs" (*LL*, July 19).

[116] July 19.

[117] *Pravda*, July 17 (also *KŽ*, July 19). See also Števček, *KŽ*, July 26.

293

statements. There were frequent references to other historical occasions, such as Munich in 1938, when decisions were taken *o nás bez nás* (about us and without us), or to the Soviet denunciation of Yugoslavia in 1948. There was unconditional rejection of the Warsaw "ultimatum." Questions were sometimes raised as to whether the leadership had been firm enough and would continue to rely on the populace, but the actions of the leaders were praised and full support was offered. The effect of the crisis produced by the Warsaw conference was therefore to unite the overwhelming majority of the population, Czech and Slovak, behind Dubček and to strengthen his hand for the forthcoming bilateral talks. Certainly differences remained, but outside pressure had had a boomerang effect, creating a unity that had been absent during the crises of the preceding weeks.

This was clearly demonstrated in public opinion polls taken just prior to the Warsaw conference when foreign pressures were reaching a peak. These indicated that the overwhelming majority of the population had trust in the party leadership headed by Dubček. Significantly also, in spite of constant foreign and domestic efforts, very few of the population had been persuaded that anti-socialist tendencies represented a danger. A greater danger lay in pressures from abroad. The vast majority of the population was opposed to such pressures or to armed intervention.[118]

[118] For these polls, see below, chap. XVII.

CHAPTER XI

The Storm Gathers

(Before and After Čierna)

THE WARSAW letter and the Czechoslovak reply had exposed before the entire world the profound conflict of viewpoint between Prague and its partners in the Warsaw alliance. Prague and Moscow seemed to be embarked on a collision course comparable to the clash of wills that had produced the bloc crises of 1948 and 1956, and likely to precipitate a new breach in the international communist movement. The Rumanian and Yugoslav regimes, and the Italian party, had made clear their sympathy for Prague, but others firmly supported Moscow. The French Communist Party, alarmed by the "extreme gravity of the situation," saw a ray of hope in a general conference of European communist parties, and one of its leaders, Waldeck Rochet, journeyed to Moscow and then to Prague, to discuss their proposal to this effect.[1]

In conversations with Dubček on July 19 (the content of which was revealed in *L'Humanité* in 1970) the French leader explained their initiative in terms of the danger of a rupture of the Czechoslovak and Soviet parties which would cause great harm to the international communist movement.[2] He used the occasion to present to Dubček the major worries of the Soviet party concerning the situation in Czechoslovakia and made clear that he shared many of these anxieties. Although the French party had supported the initial post-January reform plans, they could not conceal their "great anxiety" concerning the anti-socialist forces that had developed since April and the failure of the Czechoslovak party to take adequate measures against them. In particular he agreed that the Two

[1] Rochet was accompanied by two Italian communist representatives. Fourteen European parties expressed their approval of the proposal, according to a later statement by the French party. The CPSU objected from the beginning to such a conference (Rochet, *L'Humanité*, Oct. 23, 1968). See Kevin Devlin, "The New Crisis in European Communism," *Problems of Communism*, 17 (Nov., Dec. 1968) 59-63.

[2] The text of a French transcript of the conversations in Prague was published in *L'Humanité*, May 18, 1970. This occurred as a result of a charge by the dissident French communist, Roger Garaudy, that the document had been turned over to Prague authorities by a French delegation in November 1969 as evidence in a possible trial of Dubček. The charge was denied by the French party, which, however, published the transcript. In January 1970, Indra, in a broadcast speech, referred to a French record of the talks, which was given to the Czechoslovak party. A commentary, with extensive but selected quotations from the French text, was published in *Rudé právo*, May 22, 1970. See also *Le Monde*, May 6, 13, 19, 1970.

Thousand Words was a platform for counterrevolution. Rochet also indicated his sympathy with Soviet doubts concerning foreign policy discussions in Czechoslovakia and expressed his own fear of a rupture of the alliance with the Soviet Union and a resulting shift in the balance of forces in Europe. It was urgent, he concluded, that the Czechoslovak party hold talks with the Soviet and other bloc parties to settle the issues in dispute.

Although Dubček did not reject the idea of a European conference, he reportedly argued that a meeting devoted solely to Czechoslovakia was not desirable "for the time being" and should be preceded by bilateral discussions. In the meantime, too, the other parties should acquire more information about Czechoslovak developments and their representatives should visit Czechoslovakia. The Prague government had *not* refused to go to Warsaw but in three letters to the CPSU had proposed bilateral talks and, when the meeting did occur, had advised against the publication of the Warsaw letter. Dubček denied that there were any reasons for a "rupture" and defended his party's position as an "international" party which was in favor of unity with the USSR and the other socialist countries. While admitting the presence of anti-socialist forces, he declared that such forces would not make them "depart from socialism." He minimized the importance of such matters as the Masaryk investigation, the Two Thousand Words, and K 231 and social democracy. The party was ready to take action, with the help of the People's Militia (70,000 strong) in case of necessity, but the use of force, for instance, in the Two Thousand Words case, would have produced a "catastrophe." He expressed confidence that anti-socialist forces could be handled effectively by political measures and that "administrative means" were neither necessary nor desirable.

When an alternative solution—bilateral talks between the parties directly concerned—was found, the French proposal was, by common consent, dropped. The Czechoslovak regime, in their response to the Warsaw ultimatum, had indicated its willingness to engage in bilateral talks which might lead eventually to a conference of "all interested communist parties." When the Soviet Union proposed talks between the two parties, to be held in the USSR, the Czechoslovak party countered with a suggestion that the talks be held in Czechoslovakia. Within days of the Warsaw conference, agreement was reached that a meeting would be held, on Czechoslovak soil, and at the Presidium level.[3] On July 22 the CPCz Presidium endorsed this procedure and announced their intention to invite

[3] For an ex post facto exposition of the steps leading up to the agreement, see Dubček's speech to the CC in September 1969, as reported in *Svědectví* 10, no. 38 (1970), 274-75. Dubček claims to have made the proposal that the two presidia meet.

other individual communist parties later to bilateral talks. Neither time nor place for the forthcoming Czechoslovak-Soviet negotiations was yet announced, and tension prevailed until the conference finally opened in the Slovak village of Čierna nad Tisou on August 1.

OUTSIDE PRESSURES INTENSIFY

The outlook for the forthcoming talks was not encouraging. A plenary session of the CPSU Central Committee, held on July 17, set the tone for a press polemic that was to intensify during the two weeks prior to the Čierna negotiations. From July 19 for a week, *Pravda* featured on the front page resolutions of *aktivs* held throughout the country in support of the CPSU policy at Warsaw. Although the text of the Czechoslovak reply to the Warsaw letter was not published in the bloc press, it was found seriously wanting in the commentaries of the main party organs.[4] Not a day passed without the most virulent condemnation of the Czechoslovak course, with the main themes of the Warsaw letter repeated, in various forms, over and over again. A glaring example of this was the article in Moscow *Pravda* on July 26 by Yuri Zhukov, who denounced the slogan of democratic socialism as "a social democratic slogan leading to an anti-socialist and anti-Marxist political system." The peak of aggressive comment was reached by *Neues Deutschland* on July 30 with its assertion that "a quiet counterrevolution" was taking place. In this climate, it appeared likely that, at the "comradely negotiations," in Čierna, the Soviet position would offer little opportunity for compromise.

Even more menacing were various types of military pressure employed against the Prague regime. There were hopeful signs at first, when the bloc's military maneuvers ended on July 20 and troop withdrawals from Czechoslovakia began, but these were soon counteracted by repeated delays in the departure of Soviet troops. As a result, when the talks started at the end of the month, there were still some armed forces on Czechoslovak soil. The revelation in Moscow *Pravda* on July 19 of the discovery of an arms cache in western Bohemia near the German frontier and of a secret U.S. army document on preparations for "aggressive adventures" in Eastern Europe did not contribute to a peaceful atmosphere. The Czechoslovak Minister of the Interior, Josef Pavel, denounced the former as "a provocation" and contradicted Bulgarian reports of other arms caches.[5] The United States denied plans for intervention in Eastern Europe and delivered a strong protest to the Soviet government.[6]

---

[4] See in particular *Pravda* (Moscow), July 22. For the CC plenum, ibid., July 18, 1968. See also below, chap. xx.
[5] *RP*, July 22.   [6] *The New York Times*, July 20, 23, 1968.

Equally disturbing were Western reports of troop movements in Poland, followed by the announcements, on July 23, of Soviet rear-guard military exercises along the entire western frontier of the USSR, to last until August 10; on July 25, of a second set of maneuvers, of air defense forces; and on July 29, of large-scale maneuvers in Poland and East Germany. Almost at the same time West German maneuvers, scheduled to take place in September on Germany's eastern frontiers, were shifted away from the Czechoslovak borders, to avoid any suggestion of Western pressure or possible intervention. Soviet actions were all the more alarming when coupled with Western reports that the Soviet Union had officially presented Prague with a demand for stationing Warsaw forces on Czechsolovakia's western frontiers as a guarantee of their security.[7] Although these reports were not confirmed, Prague authorities felt obliged to make emphatic statements concerning the safety of their frontiers and the capacity of the Czechoslovak armed forces to defend them in case of attack. It was also stated that fears about internal security were not justified. Nor was there any evidence, declared a deputy Minister of the Interior, that "domestic extremists were acting in conjunction with the outside."[8]

Another controversy, closely connected with the question of the Warsaw pact, arose from the "Prchlík incident." General Prchlík, in a press conference on July 15, referred directly to the question of stationing bloc troops in Czechoslovakia. He denied that this could occur without approval by the government concerned but hinted that there was a danger of such an intervention by a group of Warsaw pact states.[9] Without mentioning this issue specifically, the organ of the Soviet armed forces, *Krasnaya zvezda*, on July 23 declared that Prchlík's remarks about the Warsaw pact organization had been nothing less than "outright slander" and expressed surprise that he had not been rebuffed by Czechoslovakia's party and military leadership.[10] Western newspapers reported that a Soviet note charging that Prchlík had revealed Warsaw pact military secrets had been delivered in Prague a few days earlier.[11] Two days after the

[7] Ibid., July 23, 1968. See below, chap. xix.

[8] The statements were made by deputy Ministers of the Interior and of Defense, and by the commander of the Frontier Guard, Gen. K. Peprný, at a special meeting of the National Assembly's defense and security committee "called in view of certain doubts expressed concerning the assurance of the security of our country and its internal order" (*RP*, July 26). See the earlier statement by General Peprný that the Warsaw letter's fears of a weakening of the defense of the western frontiers were "false" (ibid., July 24). In none of these statements was any reference made to Soviet demands for the stationing of bloc troops in Czechoslovakia.

[9] See above, chap. x, and below, chap. xix.

[10] Partial text given in R. A. Remington, ed., *Winter in Prague* (Cambridge, Mass. 1969), pp. 220-23.

[11] *NYT*, July 26.

Krasnaya zvezda article, the Czechoslovak Presidium announced the abolition of the CC state administration department, of which General Prchlík had been head, and his return to army duties.[12] Although this department was destined to be abolished, or at least reorganized, as a result of the decision to bring to an end direct party control of military and security affairs, this precipitate act, at that moment, seemed to be an effort to pacify Soviet official opinion. Some days later the official press agency announced that Prchlík's remarks had not been authorized and did not represent an "official viewpoint." This anonymous ČTK release, two weeks after the event, stirred up a good deal of criticism, especially by military journalists who issued a stinging public rebuke.[13] In view of Prchlík's progressive reputation as a result of his actions during the crisis in December 1967 and his stand on political issues after January, his dismissal was considered by many as an act of political discrimination against a spokesman of progressive views and regarded as an unjustified concession to Soviet demands and a poor augury for the forthcoming Čierna talks. A strong protest signed by some ninety outstanding intellectuals was sent to Dubček, and several party organizations, including the Prague municipal committee, nominated Prchlík as a candidate for the Central Committee.[14]

General Dzúr denied that the dismissal had been due to Soviet criticism, and while noting that Prchlík had made some mistakes, evaluated his press conference statements positively.[15] On August 16, a fuller and more critical announcement was issued by the Military Council of the Ministry of Defense, charging Prchlík with providing "distorted information" and revealing some "secret data."[16] It was asserted that information on troops *was* known to the Czechoslovak authorities and that Czechoslovak officers *did* participate in the direction of the maneuvers. Defending the "firm and deliberate stand" of the army authorities in their efforts to secure a "speedier tempo of withdrawal" of bloc troops, the announcement deplored "expressions of unjustified doubts about the correctness of statements by leading army persons." Although this was no doubt designed to assuage the feelings of Soviet military and political authorities, it awakened serious misgivings among the Czechoslovak population as to the future of democratization in the critical security and military spheres and raised questions concerning the exact nature of Warsaw pact

---

[12] A week earlier General Pepich had been replaced as head of the Ministry of National Defense's Main Political Administration (*RP*, July 18).

[13] Ibid., July 29, Aug. 6. See also *Reportér*, Aug. 7-14, 1968, pp. 13-14. *ČTK* excused itself for issuing this anonymous statement and blamed it on the government's press spokesman (*RP*, Aug. 10).

[14] Remington, ed., *Winter in Prague*, p. 213.

[15] *RP*, Aug. 7.   [16] Ibid., Aug. 16.

obligations and procedures and the party's attitude toward its evident defects.

REACTION TO PRESSURE

The unremitting pressures from abroad diverted attention from domestic reforms and consumed the time and energy of leaders and people alike. As a result not much progress was made in implementing the Action Program. Behind the scenes those responsible for preparing the documents for the extraordinary party congresses continued their work. A full session of the Presidium (July 25) was devoted to these matters, but otherwise attention was concentrated on the impending talks with Soviet leaders. One important measure was under examination by the government, namely, the law for extra-judicial rehabilitation, which was to deal with past administrative injustices, such as confiscation of personal property or expulsion from family dwellings.[17]

On the international front, apart from the decisive sector of bloc relations, the scene was largely quiescent. Visits by the deputy Minister of Foreign Affairs, Pudlák, to Rome, and by the Minister of Foreign Trade, V. Valeš, to Moscow, took place without public impact. The draft treaty with Rumania was under consideration. As we have noted, Western governments sought to dissociate themselves from events in Czechoslovakia. Prague authorities adopted a defensive attitude by issuing denials of various reports, for instance, that talks were being conducted with the West German politician, Walter Scheel, or that the Ministry of National Defense was preparing plans for defense against the Soviet Union.[18] Assurances of Rumanian and Yugoslav support were quietly reported in the press and were mentioned in commentaries as favorable features of the situation.[19]

In the forefront of everyone's mind were the forthcoming negotiations, although the date and place were still not known to the public. The party's attitude was set forth in statements by Smrkovský, Šik, and Císař and by Dubček in a radio and television address to the nation.[20] These statements indicated no intention to retreat on the major issues, but also

---

[17] Ibid., July 26, 27. See chap. xiii below.

[18] Ibid., July 23, 26.

[19] A visit to Prague by President Tito, which, it was reported abroad, had been urgently requested by Prague and deliberately leaked to the press, was delayed at the request of Dubček after the announcement of bilateral talks (NYT, July 19, 20). A secret meeting of Tito and Ceauşescu shortly thereafter was also reported but not confirmed. The two leaders were said to have assured Dubček of their support and of their readiness to fly to Prague at a moment's notice (ibid., Aug. 1, 1968).

[20] RP, July 22, 27; Pravda (Bratislava), July 28, also in Dubček, K otázkam obrodzovacieho procesu v KSČ (Bratislava, 1968), pp. 233-37.

included emphatic assurances of continued solidarity with the Soviet Union and the other communist states and of the determination to preserve socialism and the leading role of the party. At the same time stress was laid on the sovereignty and equality of states and on the specific features of Czechoslovakia and its reform program. Dubček resolutely defended their intention to construct "socialism with a human face" and their resolution not to retreat one step from the path on which they had embarked.

Another common theme in official pronouncements was the hope and belief that the talks would lead to an understanding by the Soviet Union of the Czechoslovak position. In Dubček's words, "I am convinced that our friends will understand, even though this need not be by a single act, that the socialist process of revival does not threaten the common interests of the socialist countries, but on the contrary that it is the only possible path that will make our republic a really firm component of the socialist system and our frontiers the most reliable frontier of socialism." Smrkovský, describing the Warsaw letter as the expression of a desire to help the Czechoslovak party, complained that it had been based on one-sided information and hoped that, with the opening of bilateral discussions, it would "belong to the past." Císař described the Warsaw letter and the subsequent campaign as unjust but expressed confidence in the "good sense of our friends and their willingness to find a way out." He declared that the Presidium was absolutely united in its attitude, assuring his audience that "none of our representatives has an interest in harming the cause of socialism, democracy, and humanism, which we have initiated. And if someone *was* found after all, the people would turn away from him."

The firm stand of the leadership in response to the Warsaw letter generated a massive wave of popular support from all quarters, in Slovakia no less than in the Czech lands. Many organizations sent messages to their counterparts in the five bloc countries, appealing for an understanding of the Czechoslovak viewpoint and inviting them to send delegates to Czechoslovakia to observe the situation with their own eyes. The organ of the Writers' Union, *Literární listy*, took the initiative with a special issue on July 26, containing a Message from the Citizens to the Presidium. Even *Rudé právo* published this, at the head of its front page on July 27. The Slovak Writers' paper, *Kultúrny život*, reprinted it with a long list of Slovak signatories.[21] The message, drafted by the writer, Pavel Kohout, offered support to the Presidium in performing its "historic task" of averting the danger of "an unjust punishment" which hung

[21] *Kultúrny život*, Aug. 2; English text in *Studies in Comparative Communism* 1 (July-Oct. 1968), 276-78. Kohout reported that Vaculík, the author of the Two Thousand Words, had first been asked to draft the statement (*Literární listy*, Aug. 1).

over them all. "It is your mission to convince the leaders of the CPSU that the process of revival in our country must be carried through to the end in a manner in accord with the interest of our common country and in the interests of the progressive forces on all continents." The aims were expressed in four words: "Socialism! Alliance! Sovereignty! Freedom!" Calling on the members of the Presidium individually, by name, and acknowledging that they were not all of the same opinion in all matters, the manifesto declared: "It would be tragic if the personal feelings of any one of you were to prevail over the responsibility which you bear at this moment for 14,361,000 people, among whom you, by your very being, also belong. . . . Negotiate, explain, but in unity, and defend, without concessions, the road on which we have embarked and from which we will never depart alive. . . . We are thinking of you. Think of us! You are writing, for us, a fateful page in the history of Czechoslovakia. Write it with deliberation, but above all with courage!"

This proclamation was made available for public signature and was soon endorsed by over a million persons. Its four key words, alliterative in Czech and Slovak (*Socialismus! Spojenectví! Suverenita! Svoboda!*), and the phrase "We are thinking of you. Think of us!" became popular slogans which summed up the feelings of many as they awaited the beginning of the fateful negotiations.[22] Another manifestation of support was the creation of the Fund of the Republic to which voluntary donations of money and objects of value poured in during ensuing weeks. Some advocated a five-minute general strike as a token of popular resistance to Soviet demands and of backing for the leadership. This proposal was strongly denounced, however, in a joint statement by Dubček, Svoboda, Smrkovský, Černík, and Karel Poláček, trade union chief, and was given up by its proponents.[23]

An apparent break in popular unity occurred when, on the second day of the Čierna talks, Moscow *Pravda* published a letter from workers (and their families) of the Praga automobile plant in Prague.[24] This letter, addressed to "our Soviet friends," expressed agreement with their anxiety about the fate of socialism and the signatories' own fear for the country's future. It categorically opposed demands for the acceleration of the withdrawal of troops and declared that their presence made the workers feel more secure. Citing Gottwald, the letter went on: ". . . we

[22] The writer, J. Hájek, later contended that this manifesto had made the leaders "bondsmen of so-called public opinion." He noted that it had had great effect in Slovakia and had eliminated the previous differences between Slovaks and Czechs (*Mýtus a realita ledna 1968*, Prague, 1970, pp. 159-61).

[23] *RP*, July 29. The suggestion was first made in the two youth journals, *Smena* and *Mladá fronta*.

[24] July 30; English text in *SCC* 1 (July-Oct. 1968), 280-81. The text was not published in Czechoslovakia until Aug. 14. See below in this chapter.

cherish our friendship with the USSR as the apple of our eye and declare that we will allow no one to denigrate or slander this friendship no matter what post such a person may occupy. This is a friendship sealed in blood." It was soon revealed that the message had been drawn up without discussion and signed by only 99 persons (including family members) in a factory employing 4,500.[25] Although it showed the existence of pro-Soviet sympathies and dissatisfaction with the post-January course, the episode pointed up all the more sharply the massive popular support enjoyed by the leadership.

Although facts were few, the talks to be held at Čierna were the main subject of discussion in the organs of opinion. The failure of the Soviet and bloc media to publish Czechoslovak opinions and the distortion of information in the Soviet press were generally deplored. Some commentators echoed the belief of the leaders that the exchange of views would remove misunderstandings and lead to "a comradely settlement of disputes."[26] *Rudé právo*, in an unsigned editorial, expressed a similar opinion, but described the Warsaw letter, both in its content and its tone, as "quieting" and advocated "the necessity to accept the fears of our friends with understanding." Have we "done everything to explain and clarify" questions? it was asked. Have we "done everything to paralyze extremist forces" to the left and right?[27] In Bratislava, *Pravda* was firmer in tone, although at the very beginning of the conference it published two letters from readers strongly critical of anti-socialist forces.[28] Its main commentators were, however, more skeptical of the chances of a successful outcome. The problem was not a lack of information, or even misunderstanding, on the part of the Soviet Union, they said. The real problem, wrote Edo Friš, was the entirely different Soviet interpretation of the Czechoslovak process of reform and the existence of socialisms of diverse types. It was naive to think that they could convince the signatories of the Warsaw letter. The Czechoslovak representatives must defend the principle of "the coexistence of socialisms" and the right of each country to decide on its own form.[29] Vladimír Mináč also upheld the view that it was not a question of misunderstanding (*nedorozumenie*) but a lack of understanding (*neporozumenie*). We should

---

[25] *RP*, July 31.

[26] J. Šedivý, *Život strany*, no. 16 (Aug. 1968), pp. 1-3.

[27] *RP*, July 21. Apart from publishing the official statements by Dubček and others, *Rudé právo* included no other major editorial comment on the forthcoming talks. See, however, articles on the international communist movement, July 26 and 30.

[28] *Pravda*, July 30. This was followed by a flood of letters, some openly condemning, others supporting, the original letters, in a proportion of somewhat less than two to one respectively (*Pravda*, Aug. 6, 8, 9, 11, 13, 16, 20).

[29] For three major commentaries by Friš, see *Pravda*, July 24, 27, 31. Cf. M. Hysko, ibid., July 29, Aug. 1.

make no retreat, he said, from the concepts of equality and independence and must get used to the notion of being "friends in constant strife."[30]

Opinions expressed in the more radical weeklies were even sharper. Petr Pithart, in *Literární listy*, reiterated the argument that the Soviet attitude was the result not of a misunderstanding but on the contrary of a clear understanding of the process of revival and was "a reflection of the logic of an improved Stalinism."[31] Jiří Hochman, in *Reportér*, declared that the Czechoslovak "sin" was not that they were threatening socialism but rather the bureaucratic system which had buried socialism.[32] Pavol Števček, writing in *Kultúrny život* on "Democracy in its Seventh Month," warned that "the democratic child is in mortal danger" and urged "tactical wisdom and political foresightedness."[33] Dalimil (pseud.) stated that entirely different conceptions of socialism were the main issue and declared that Čierna would be neither a Constance (the Council which condemned Jan Hus) nor a Canossa.[34]

CONFRONTATION AT ČIERNA NAD TISOU

The delegations of the two parties began their meetings on July 29 in Čierna nad Tisou, a small railway junction in eastern Slovakia on the Soviet frontier. The entire Soviet Presidium, except for two members, D. S. Polyansky and A. P. Kirilenko, along with two candidate members and two Secretaries, met with the entire Czechoslovak Presidium, including all three candidates, together with President Svoboda and the head of the Commission on Supervision and Auditing, M. Jakeš. The Soviet delegation lived in a special railway carriage which each night crossed the frontier to the Soviet railway junction in Chop. Negotiations were conducted in the hastily improvised facilities of a railwaymen's club and lasted four full days instead of the one day originally scheduled. The meeting ended by publishing the briefest of communiqués, which referred to the "broad comradely exchange of opinions" and "the exchange of detailed information about the situation in their countries," and which described the aim as being "to seek ways of further developing and strengthening the traditionally friendly relations between the communist parties and peoples of our lands, based on the principles of Marxism-Leninism and proletarian internationalism." The only concrete provision was the agreement to hold a multilateral meeting with the Bulgarian, Hungarian, East German, and Polish party leaders in Bratislava one day later.[35]

[30] *Nové slovo*, July 25. [31] *LL*, July 25.
[32] *Rep.*, July 31-Aug. 7, 1968. [33] *KŽ*, July 26.
[34] *LL*, Aug. 1.
[35] *RP*, Aug. 2; in English, Remington, ed., *Winter in Prague*, p. 255.

Apart from these bare facts almost nothing is known of the course of the negotiations.[36] The press, both Czechoslovak and foreign, was kept at a distance from the conference room on the main street of the little town. There were no serious leaks of information at the time or later. The minutes, of course, have not been published. Even the government in Prague was not kept informed of the proceedings. Later reports referred to dramatic events such as a walkout by Dubček and his fellow delegates on the first day; a four-hour opening speech by Brezhnev reiterating, on the basis of detailed documentation, the familiar claims and charges; a quiet, firm reply by Dubček and an impressive response by General Svoboda; a private talk, in the railway carriage, between Dubček and an indisposed Brezhnev; a stroll by Dubček after midnight and a chat with railway workers, etc. It has also been claimed, but strongly denied, that serious divisions manifested themselves within the Czechoslovak delegation. Although none of these reports can be confirmed, it would require little imagination to reconstruct the major issues of the dialogue from the content of the Warsaw letter and the Czechoslovak reply, and from the press polemics in the organs of "the five" before the conference. The four days of discussions were undoubtedly not only "completely frank," as the communiqué noted, but stormy, difficult, and at times near the verge of breakdown.

The populace was disturbed not only by the absence of information and by the short communiqué but by the announcement of a new meeting in Bratislava with the party leaders of "the five." Would this be another Warsaw conference, but with Czechoslovakia present? President Svoboda's broadcast to an expectant nation was hardly reassuring.[37] Describing Čierna as a symbol of Czechoslovak-Soviet friendship, he dwelt almost exclusively on the need to strengthen the unity of the socialist countries and had harsh words for anyone seeking to destroy friendship with the Soviet Union. This more than outweighed his assertion that the Soviet leaders had shown full understanding and promised full support for the reform movement, based on the Action Program. That evening several thousand young people demonstrated outside the Central Committee building on the Vltava and later in the Old Town Square, demanding to know "the truth." Smrkovský, in a brief impromptu appearance, assured them that no limits on press freedom had been agreed upon and

---

[36] Pavel Tigrid's accounts of the conference, said to be based on the minutes, do not give detailed information concerning the speeches and discussion. See his *Why Dubček Fell* (London, 1971), part I, chap. 5; also *Survey*, no. 73 (Autumn 1969), pp. 133-64. A fuller report of the proceedings, with purported summaries of major speeches, is given in Gérard de Sède, ed., *Pourquoi Prague?* (Paris, 1968), pp. 292-321. For Smrkovský's account, see Appendix D.

[37] *RP*, Aug. 2.

that the Bratislava conference would not deal with Czechoslovakia. Many in the audience were not fully convinced.[38] Dubček's report on radio and television the next evening was somewhat more encouraging but did not eliminate the doubts of the skeptics.[39] "You can be satisfied with the results," he asserted; "the discussions were successful." "We have kept our promises," he declared, in a masterpiece of ambiguity, "to stand firmly on the post-January policy . . . and to remain faithful to our friends and to proletarian internationalism." We can resume our cooperation on the basis of "real internationalism," including unity and cooperation, but also respect for state sovereignty. We agreed to take "further practical steps to deepen mutual cooperation within the framework of the Comecon agreements and the Warsaw treaty" and to begin this at the Bratislava conference, which would concentrate attention on "common interests." "Our sovereignty" is not "threatened," Dubček said.

Adding to the confusion, Bil'ak, speaking in Bratislava, made no reference to the continuance of the reform program and spoke only of "the confirmation of our alliance and our common interests." All participants were convinced, he said, that "our freedom, and our state and national sovereignty, about which so much has been spoken and written in the past days, can and will be assured only in firm alliance with the Soviet Union and the other socialist countries." In a radio and television interview two weeks later, he described the purpose of the negotiations as being to avoid a deepening of the conflict of the two parties and indeed to overcome it and to create favorable external conditions for developing the January line. He had taken as his own starting point the preceding discussions in the Presidium and Central Committee—with the aim that "there should not be a worsening of the relations" of the two parties and countries. Bil'ak denied reports that he had tried to torpedo Dubček's standpoint at Čierna and stated that he, like the other delegates, had spoken not personally but on behalf of the party's highest organ.[40]

[38] *Pravda*, Aug. 2; also *NYT*, Aug. 2. In an interview broadcast on Belgrade radio (Aug. 7), Smrkovský was quoted as saying that his greatest fear at Čierna had been "whether we would find a common language and whether the Czechoslovak leadership would act in a united way." "As you know," he said, "everything went well." It had been agreed not to speak about the Warsaw letter since the two sides "could not find a common view" on this basis. Hence at Bratislava there was to be no discussion of the letter or of Czechoslovak problems but rather about "closer cooperation" between the six countries (British Broadcasting Corporation, Monitoring Service, *Summary of World Broadcasts* II, Eastern Europe, Aug. 9, 1968); hereafter, BBC.

[39] *RP*, Aug. 3; also *K otázkam*, pp. 238-41.

[40] *Pravda*, Aug. 3; *RP*, Aug. 17. The version of Bil'ak's later remarks published in 1971 omitted many parts of the original interview, including the portion paraphrased in the final sentence above, and his assertion of the "sincere relation" he

Apart from the announcement of the Bratislava meeting, the only other specific result of Čierna was an agreement to end the polemics of the past weeks. The cessation of press attacks, which did in fact take place, was more than welcome to Czechs and Slovaks, but there was anxiety as to whether this would mean limitations on freedom of expression and even a restoration of censorship. Although Smrkovský and Černík had both explicitly referred to an accord on ending polemics, the former had denied that censorship had even been discussed. Later, Soviet spokesmen and some Czechs affirmed that "concrete agreements" had been reached at Čierna but charged that the Czechs had not carried them out.[41] A year afterwards, Dubček reaffirmed that no "secret agreements" had been concluded at Čierna. Although apparently nothing was put in writing, it seems likely that the Czechoslovak spokesmen, as Dubček later admitted, had given certain indications of their future plans, for example, concerning organizations such as K 231, KAN, and the social democratic movement, and that these statements of intent were interpreted by the Soviet representatives as assurances or promises.[42] The

---

had had to Dubček then and in the past (Bil'ak, *Pravda zůstala pravdou*, Prague, 1971, pp. 148 ff.).

[41] *Pravda* (Moscow), Aug. 22, 1968. See also Švestka, *RP*, Aug. 21, 1969; Černík, *Tribuna*, Aug. 27, 1969; Rigo, *RP*, Feb. 12, 1970. A speech by Jaromír Hrbek, republished as a pamphlet, *Manifest pravdy* (Prague, 1969) listed six specific steps that were to be taken at once: control of the mass media; the cessation of anti-socialist and anti-Soviet attacks in the press and on radio and television; a ban on certain anti-socialist clubs and organizations; forbidding of the restoration of the Social Democratic Party; and measures to strengthen the leading role of the party and the position of socialism (p. 11). These are the six points which were said to have been agreed on at Čierna in the letter of August 17, 1968 from the Soviet Politburo to the CPCz Presidium, cited below, n. 79.

Bil'ak stated in Nov. 1968 that after the close of the final Čierna meeting, Brezhnev had remarked to those still in the hall: "Comrades, we are not signing any agreement; we rely on your communist word; we expect that you will act and behave as communists. If you deceive us once more, we shall consider it a crime and a betrayal and act accordingly. Never again would we sit with you at the same table" (*Pravda zůstala pravdou*, p. 169).

Tad Szulc of *The New York Times* reported that a six-point agreement had been worked out, including press control; a ban on certain political groups; measures to strengthen the People's Militia and security forces; and the removal of Kriegel and Císař from the leadership (Szulc, *Czechoslokavia Since World War II*, New York, 1971, p. 364).

[42] Dubček's speech to the Sept. 1969 plenum as reported in *Svědectví*, no. 38 (1970), pp. 275-76. Dubček admitted having talks with Brezhnev about "cadre" matters but sought to justify himself by saying that such changes could have been made only at a forthcoming CC plenum. In his address to the CC plenum on Aug. 31, 1968, Dubček referred to measures that were prepared after Čierna and Bratislava and were to be taken before the 14th congress. These included a National Front law banning the rise of new political parties; an attempt to stop anti-Soviet attacks in the information media; government action to end the activity of

Prague leaders, unlike those in Moscow, were not able to impose restrictions on the press, even if they had wished to do so, and were dependent on the voluntary cooperation of the journalists. It appears that steps were taken by the authorities to persuade the press and other mass media to avoid actions that would be contrary to the spirit of a cessation of polemics.[43] In its first meeting after Čierna, on August 6, the Presidium expressed its expectation that those working in the press and the media would "in the spirit of the policy of the CPCz and the government of the Republic henceforth respect the national and the international interests of the Czechoslovak people and state in their reporting and commenting on events, especially in the foreign policy field."[44]

The Czechoslovak leaders were, by the nature of things, unable to reveal what had transpired at Čierna or to describe the results. They professed the belief, in their public statements, that they had won a signal victory and that the Czechoslovak reform course and the independence of the country were assured. According to their version, the Soviet leaders had demonstrated "good will and an effort to understand our problem" and "to respect each party's indisputable right independently to decide its affairs."[45] It was said that they had not insisted on the ending

K 231; and a NF decision not to recognize KAN as a political organization. He did not, however, suggest that these were the results of an agreement at Čierna (*O zasedání Ústředního Výboru KSČ dne 31. srpna 1968*, Prague, 1968). In a speech in Ostrava in Sept. 1968, Černík declared that "we did not conclude agreements of any kind at Čierna. We only informed the Soviet representatives there how we would proceed in future at home so as to limit leftist and also right-wing extremes" (*Pravda*, Sept. 22). Smrkovský also denied that there were any agreements but referred to measures to curb the mass media (Appendix D).

[43] Švestka, in an interview in Aug. 1969, stated that the agreement to end polemics had been the result of Dubček's initiative. Consequently, on the evening of the very first day of the conference, instructions were issued to all chief editors, who were made responsible for carrying them out. Švestka gives what purports to be the text of these instructions, which included eight points, relating, however, mainly to the reporting of the conference itself. Only official accounts were to be published. Resolutions or foreign press information were not to be published. The newspapers were to refrain from commentaries on the course of the conference and from publishing attacks of all kinds, including cartoons, against the other countries. More general was the admonition to stress the positive sides of relations with the Soviet Union and other socialist states in all spheres, particularly in foreign affairs (*RP*, Aug. 21, 1969). Bil'ak also reported that instructions had been sent to the journalists from Čierna to stop polemics, and they had agreed to do so, but for 48 hours only (*Pravda zůstala pravdou*, p. 194).

A meeting, or meetings, were said to have been held between some party leaders and journalists on the eve of, and during, the conference at Čierna (*NYT*, Aug. 2, 4). Efforts were made by some government leaders to have the contents of forthcoming issues of certain journals, notably *Literární listy* and *Reportér*, modified, but it was said to be too late to do anything.

[44] *Rok šedesátý osmý* (Prague, 1969), p. 270.

[45] *K otázkam*, p. 239. Dubček even implied that the Czechs had won "support" for their policies (pp. 242-43).

of censorship, or the removal of certain reform leaders, or the stationing of Soviet troops at the western border. It looked as if the Warsaw letter was a thing of the past, superseded by the Čierna agreement, and that there was no further danger of Soviet intervention.[46] This optimistic view was apparently corroborated by the announcement of the completion of the withdrawal of Soviet troops from Czechoslovakia on the final day of the talks. It remained to be seen, however, whether the Bratislava conference, with its emphasis on bloc solidarity, would in fact negate and frustrate the hopeful outlook engendered by Čierna.

THE BRATISLAVA CONCLAVE

The idea of a broader conference, including the other members of "the five," was reportedly brought up by Brezhnev at the end of the Čierna meeting when the final communiqué was being drafted. The Czechoslovak representatives were taken aback by what seemed to be a reversion to the discredited Warsaw conference pattern, but apparently agreed when assured that the meeting would take place on Czechoslovak soil and would not discuss Czechoslovak affairs. Within twenty-four hours of the conclusion of the Čierna talks, the expanded meeting took place in Bratislava, in the famous Hall of Mirrors where, in 1805, Napoleon had signed the treaty of Pressburg at the end of the war against Russia and Austria-Hungary. Attending were delegations from the top organs of the six parties, including, for Czechoslovakia, Dubček, Černík, Smrkovský, Bil'ak, and Lenárt, with President Svoboda also present. A full day of negotiations, of which even less is known than of the Čierna talks, ended with the signing of a statement of common views that came to be known as the Bratislava declaration.[47] According to Dubček, in his radio and television report to the nation, "no other conclusions were accepted."[48] The deliberations, reported the Czechoslovak Presidium, represented "a common success of all the participating delegations and a new impulse for the development of mutually advantageous relations among the brotherly parties and socialist lands on the basis of Marxism-Leninism and proletarian internationalism."[49]

The conference discussions were apparently devoted almost exclusively to the elaboration of the declaration which was based on an original Soviet draft, amended according to changes suggested by various partici-

[46] A briefing for editors by Smrkovský, Černík, and Císař reported in *NYT*, Aug. 3, 1968.

[47] Text in *Pravda* (Moscow), and *RP*, Aug. 4; in English, Remington, ed., *Winter in Prague*, pp. 256-61.

[48] *RP*, Aug. 5; also *K otázkam*, pp. 242-46.

[49] *RŠO*, p. 270.

pants.[50] The final version was couched in the orthodox phraseology of past documents of this kind, thereby awakening considerable criticism in subsequent Czechoslovak comment. It represented, as Dubček explained in his address, "certain generally formulated principles and aims which were acceptable to all, and concrete themes of future collaboration." The document set forth ways in which the "fraternal cooperation" of the socialist states could be strengthened and developed and proclaimed that this would be based on "the principles of equality, respect[51] of sovereignty and national independence, territorial integrity, and fraternal mutual aid and solidarity." Reference was made to the need to follow "the general patterns" for the construction of a socialist society, primarily by strengthening the guiding role of the working class and its party, but, at the same time, to the need for each party to take into account "national particularities and conditions."[52] The declaration proclaimed "the common international duty of all socialist countries to support, strengthen, and defend" the gains achieved in the construction of socialism and communism and also mentioned specific forms which common action should take—developing economic cooperation on a bilateral and multilateral basis; improving the work of Comecon; holding an economic conference at the highest level; a "coordinated" policy in European affairs, including a congress of the peoples of Europe; steps to augment the solidarity of the international communist movement, including the proposed world conference of communist parties. The Bratislava declaration went still further, asserting the need, in view of the threat of imperialism, to "harmonize and coordinate their activity in the international sphere," and demanding "unslackening efforts to augment the defense capability of every socialist state and the whole socialist commonwealth and to strengthen political and military cooperation in the Warsaw Treaty Organization."

In sum, the principles and concrete proposals contained in the document represented little more than a restatement of the concepts often propounded by the Soviet bloc states. The emphasis on the common interests of the socialist states, however, suggested a tightening of the bonds of unity and a lessening of the independence of the members. The ambiguity of many of the provisions permitted future interpretations that might threaten the ability of the individual countries to follow their

[50] NYT (Aug. 6, 1968) for a full report on what is said to have occurred, including a summary of the main Czechoslovak amendments. See also de Sède, ed., Pourquoi Prague?, pp. 322-33, for the purported proceedings.

[51] In Russian, uvazheniye. In the Czech text, the word zachování (preservation) is used.

[52] J. Hájek (the journalist) later referred to these as binding principles which were ignored by Czechoslovak party leaders and ridiculed by the press (Mýtus, pp. 162-63).

chosen path. Although the customary references to "national conditions" and to sovereignty and independence were made, the principle of "non-interference in domestic affairs," usually present in similar documents, was replaced by that of "fraternal mutual aid and solidarity." Moreover, the assertion of the common duty of all to defend the gains of socialism contained the implication that common action might be justified to meet any threat to these gains.[53] By implication the declaration set forth the criteria the neglect of which would justify such intervention.

In their reports on the Bratislava meeting the Czechoslovak party leaders stressed the references to "national conditions" and "independence" and concluded that this made it possible to continue on the post-January path. The talks in Čierna and Bratislava, Dubček said, "opened the door to the further room required for our socialist revival process." The building of socialism by each party would be guided by "generally valid principles . . . in harmony with the concrete conditions and traditions of its own homeland." "Not a word was said about our affairs," declared Černík; no conclusions were reached that "would force us to revise anything in our basic standpoints with regard to domestic or international political questions." Emphasis was also placed on the provisions for closer cooperation with the socialist states. "What we have resolved upon in January," said Dubček, "can be carried through successfully to its goal only in partnership with the socialist lands, with whom our future is permanently linked. Otherwise it is not possible to assure our economic development, still less to guarantee the security and independence of our country, which in the present divided and disturbed world is our first duty."[54]

Bil'ak, in a radio and television interview ten days later, denied reports that the Soviet Union, at any of the conferences from Dresden to Bratislava, had expressed a desire for a return to pre-January conditions and praised the Bratislava declaration "which had significance not only for our domestic development but which also anchors the basic principles for building socialism generally and for mutual relations of fraternal communist parties." A few days later he rejected the view that anyone had been "defeated" at the conferences and asserted that "the spirit of socialist internationalism and the common effort to defend socialism and its further development" had been victorious. He repudiated the notion that the Soviet Union had any interest in threatening their sovereignty and argued that the conferences had created the "necessary room for the development of the socialist process of revival."[55]

[53] After the invasion, Jaromír Hrbek in fact interpreted the provisions concerning the common task of defense as a de facto expansion of the Warsaw treaty to cover "aid against internal threat" (*Manifest pravdy*, pp. 11-12).
[54] Dubček, *K otázkam*, p. 243; Černík, *RP*, Aug. 6.
[55] *RP*, Aug. 17; *Pravda*, Aug. 20.

311

Party journals hailed the results of the negotiations. *Rudé právo*, in an editorial by Švestka, praised the agreements as "a victory of reason and friendship" and spoke of "support of the January political line" by the Soviet party, in spite of their justified fears concerning negative phenomena. The conferences created the conditions for "an undeformed implementation of the leading role of the party and the defense of the foundations of socialism whose face must be really democratic and humane."[56] Articles in Bratislava *Pravda* called it a triumph for the entire communist movement, recognizing the right of each country to determine its own form of socialism and giving a "green light" for the process of reform.[57] *Nové slovo* expressed satisfaction that there was no mention of Czechoslovakia or of counterrevolution in the Bratislava declaration but observed that the test would come in practice, especially in connection with the proposed party statute.[58]

Statements by the journalists and the creative unions welcomed the results of Čierna and Bratislava but accented the necessity of maintaining freedom of the press.[59] Unofficial journals were critical in their analyses, thus indicating that "the end of polemics" was not stifling frank commentary. *Reportér* rejoiced that "the hope of tolerance" had replaced the dangers of excommunication and military intervention and concluded that Bratislava had been "a milestone . . . if it is not just a first round."[60] *Kultúrny život* considered it "a victory" but warned that there could be a return to the Warsaw letter. The Czechoslovak course would be safeguarded only if its ideas also conquered in the neighboring states.[61] *Práce* described it as "a victory of reason," made possible by "the unity of almost all Czechs and Slovaks in defense of our sovereignty" and by the solidarity of our foreign friends—Yugoslavia, Rumania, and almost all the communist parties of Western Europe.[62] Articles in *Literární listy* were more skeptical and restrained. The language of the Bratislava communiqué and the lack of information as to what actually happened were disturbing. The greatest achievement, believed J. Válka, had been "the recognition de facto and de jure of the new Czechoslovak regime," but

56 *RP*, Aug. 8. See sharp criticism of this editorial by M. Moravec, *MF*, Aug. 10.
57 Hysko, *Pravda*, Aug. 5. See also Friš, ibid., Aug. 10.
58 S. Štúr and B. Graca, *NS*, Aug. 8 and 15, resp.
59 *RP*, Aug. 5, 8.
60 A. Hradecký, *Rep.*, Aug. 14-21, 1968.
61 R. Olšinský, *KŽ*, Aug. 9. See also Mňačko's favorable comment (*KŽ*, Aug. 16). In the same issue E. Löbl was more critical and insisted on the need for real guarantees of Czechoslovak sovereignty and for assurances that the events of the past few months would not be repeated. Jonáš (pseud.) stated that "everything depends on how the declaration will be interpreted." R. Kaliský was concerned with the lack of information and the de facto restoration of indirect censorship during and after the conference.
62 M. Hübl, *Práce*, Aug. 4.

312

only the fall would show whether the "spring" had been "a mere episode." The result could be described as "confidence on credit," wrote L. Veselý. This was not "the end of the ideological struggle," said V. Blažek, who expressed the hope that the conferences had created the possibility for Czechoslovakia to act as "an inspiration or at least an impulse for our partners." Dalimil warned that although Czechoslovakia did not wish to change its foreign policy or weaken Soviet security, they could not sacrifice their new socialism for the sake of the balance of power and "could not agree with any pressure whatever on our domestic affairs."[63]

The public reaction to Bratislava was one of relief from tension and of general satisfaction, mingled with uncertainties and worries about the future. An opinion poll conducted by the party in northern Bohemia showed that the overwhelming majority (74 percent) was favorable to Čierna and somewhat less so (65 percent) to Bratislava, but only 40 percent were optimistic as to future relations with "the five."[64]

FOUR BILATERAL MEETINGS

In the two weeks following the Bratislava conference Czechoslovak leaders received visits from Tito, Ulbricht, Ceaușescu, and Kádár. The Tito visit had been scheduled earlier but had been postponed from day to day owing to the prolongation of the Čierna talks. Ceaușescu's trip had also been discussed during the days of crisis at the beginning of August. Dubček believed that bilateral talks with other members of "the five" had been rendered unnecessary by the Čierna and Bratislava meetings and, in any case, could not be held in the short period before the 14th Party Congress. Nonetheless, for reasons that are obscure, but probably owing to the renewal of an atmosphere of crisis, Ulbricht and Kádár came for brief and informal talks, the former held without great éclat in Karlovy Vary, and the latter in secret at Komárno in Slovakia. In contrast, the Tito and Ceaușescu negotiations took place in Prague and evoked a warm public response.[65]

Tito arrived on August 9 for a two-day visit and met with "a publicly jubilant but officially reticent welcome."[66] Massive gatherings of the pop-

---

[63] *LL*, Aug. 8: Válka, Veselý, Blažek, and Dalimil, resp. Ivan Sviták, in an article written after Bratislava but not published until after the invasion (*Student*, Aug. 29), condemned Bratislava as a compromise resembling Munich and criticized the leaders for "a capitulation" which only postponed the threat of intervention. See Sviták, *The Czechoslovak Experiment, 1968-1969* (New York, 1971), pp. 141-44.

[64] *RP*, Aug. 7. See other polls below, chap. XVII.

[65] Senator Mansfield paid a brief visit to Prague on Aug. 10 and met Smrkovský. U Thant was scheduled to come on the 23rd.

[66] *NYT*, Aug. 10.

ulace in the streets and at the Castle testified to the enthusiasm with which the Czechs greeted this pathbreaker of a national and independent communism who had unequivocally expressed support for the Czechoslovak reform movement. After the harrowing days just past, his visit was welcome evidence of his continued backing of Dubček and the Czechoslovak course. The spontaneous chanting of the slogan "Tito! Dubček!" assumed overtones of an overt demonstration of resistance to outside pressure. Both leaders, however, took pains to avoid anything that would appear as an ostentatious challenge to the Soviet Union and the bloc. Since Tito came as party chief and not as President, public ceremony and official speeches could be avoided. Nothing is known of the content of the private talks of this "working visit." The brief communiqué referred only to an exchange of information and the discussion of mutual cooperation and emphasized the value of "bilateral cooperation" in the international communist movement and of "the broadest collaboration of all progressive and peace-loving forces." In his press conference Tito ruled out a treaty between the two countries as "not necessary" in view of their friendship. He had come, he said, to demonstrate support of the Bratislava solution, which he evaluated positively. In response to many questions he indicated his favorable attitude to Czechoslovak reforms, and his opposition to any interference in the domestic affairs of a socialist country.[67] Press comment after the event was warm and friendly and paid tribute to Tito's achievements in defending Yugoslavia's independent course and building its own model of socialism.[68]

Twenty-four hours after Tito's departure, Walter Ulbricht arrived for a visit described officially as the result of a Czechoslovak invitation, "within the framework of the bilateral meetings to be effected with cer-

[67] RP, Aug. 11. Bil'ak later alleged that Tito had expressed some dissatisfaction with Czechoslovak policy and had issued some warnings (ibid., Sept. 3, 1969). The only hint of this was given in his press conference when Tito defended freedom of the press but called for "constructive" criticism. He did not think that journalists should be permitted to write articles without considering whether or not they were helpful to socialist development. In Yugoslavia there was no censorship, he said, but informal meetings were held to dissuade journalists from writing certain things.

[68] See, for instance, Olšinský, KŽ, Aug. 16; Liehm and anon. (p. 6), LL, Aug. 15; Friš, Pravda, Aug. 10. Friš wrote that the visit was not a counterweight to existing allied relationships or an effort to create a separate socialist grouping. Olšinský, however, expressed the wish that Czechoslovakia, Yugoslavia, and Rumania might form "a firm bloc of democracy, reason, and humanistic socialism." Liehm referred to Tito's triumph in Prague as an "expression of the yearning of the nation for its own Tito," P. Berta wrote of Yugoslavia's moral support for Czechoslovakia and of the lessons of the Yugoslav path (NS, Aug. 15). Práce (Aug. 11) advocated the conclusion of an alliance with Yugoslavia, to replace the one abrogated in 1948 (H. Haefs, ed., Die Ereignisse in der Tschechoslowakei, Bonn, 1969, p. 140, n. 42).

tain fraternal parties." The meeting occurred at Karlovy Vary near the East German border "in an atmosphere of chill,"[69] without any ceremonial events or public demonstrations of welcome. Eight hours were devoted, according to the final press release, to the discussion of the political situation in the two countries and the problems of the international situation and the international communist movement. The European situation was discussed in detail, "in the spirit" of the earlier Bucharest and Karlovy Vary declarations. Both sides stressed the significance of the Bratislava proclamation.[70] Ulbricht, at a concluding press conference, described it as "the most significant Marxist-Leninist document of our time." He was quoted as referring to "difficulties in view of such a great change" as "normal" and "not to be taken too tragically" and expressed the belief that they could be overcome "if we look forward to the perspective of the struggle for the victory of socialism."[71] Although the talks were said to have placed the emphasis on common interests and attitudes, there can be little doubt that they revealed serious differences of opinion on many matters.[72] At the time, however, there was no way of knowing whether they had contributed to "better mutual understanding," as the press release put it, or to a widening of the gap between the two parties. Nor has any evidence come to light to confirm speculation that Ulbricht sent an alarming report to Brezhnev which had some influence on the decision to invade.[73]

Two days after Ulbricht's departure the Rumanian leader, Ceauşescu, arrived for a visit that was designed inter alia for the renewal of the alliance between the two states. Characterized by all the pomp and circumstance of a visit by a head of state it was the occasion for an outburst of public warmth second only to that given to Tito. Both at a mass meeting in the Avia factory and at a press conference Ceauşescu made no effort to conceal his sympathy with Czechoslovak reforms, his belief that

[69] NYT, Aug. 13. [70] RP, Aug. 13.
[71] Ibid., Aug. 14; fuller report, Pravda, Aug. 14.
[72] This was implied in the commentary by I. Šetlík (RP, Aug. 14), who referred to the distinctive policies of the Socialist Unity Party (SED) as representing "a national path to socialism." In regard to European security he spoke of differences in Czechoslovakia's "possibilities" and different evaluations of such matters as "opposition" forces or "neo-Nazi" elements in West Germany.

According to post-invasion reports, Ulbricht tried to persuade the Czechoslovak leaders to fulfill the Bratislava resolutions, without success (Neues Deutschland, Aug. 25, 1968). J. Götz, head of the CPCz international relations department, later wrote that the SED delegates had been shocked by the Czechoslovak attitude toward certain parts of the Bratislava statement, such as the references to West German "revanchism" and "bourgeois ideology," and that one member of the CPCz delegation had threatened to leave the room if the Germans insisted on their formulation concerning the latter point. The final press release had been a meaningless compromise, he said (RP, Aug. 19, 1969).

[73] Tigrid, Why Dubček Fell, p. 95. See below, chap. xx, for further discussion of the visit.

315

there was no danger from anti-socialist trends, and his confidence in the ability of the leaders to direct developments. Although he did not hide his displeasure that the conference at Bratislava, like those at Dresden and Warsaw, had dealt with Comecon and Warsaw pact affairs in the absence of Rumania, like Tito, he evaluated the Bratislava conference "positively" and cited it, and the Čierna talks, as examples of settling disputes by "comradely discussion."[74] In responding to a question about the possibility of a three-sided conference of Rumania, Yugoslavia, and Czechoslovakia, he replied that there were "nine socialist states which have the same view on the development of relations among themselves" and that he was not in favor of either three-sided or four-sided conferences. The final communiqué asserted the principle of "non-interference in domestic affairs," but also stressed the strengthening of the defense unity of the Warsaw Treaty Organization.[75]

The major result of the visit was the formal signing of a twenty-year pact of friendship, cooperation, and mutual assistance. Dubček, in his speech to the Avia workers, depicted this as another link in the chain of treaties already signed with the USSR, Poland, the GDR, Bulgaria, and Hungary, all of which manifested Czechoslovakia's "adherence to the society of socialist countries."[76] The text of the treaty emphasized the importance of the cooperation of socialist states in Comecon and the Warsaw Treaty Organization. Nonetheless the conclusion of the pact at this time represented a reinforcement by a friendly Rumania of Czechoslovakia's position vis-à-vis the other bloc states.

The fourth visit in this series, that of Kádár, was held in secret in Komárno on August 17 and is said to have lasted until midnight. Nothing is known with any surety as to the purpose or the content of this meeting, reportedly arranged at Kádár's initiative.[77] It has been claimed that Kádár warned of "extreme measures" by Moscow if the Bratislava agreements were not carried out at once but that he did not actually reveal the impending invasion.[78] On the same day a letter was addressed to the Czechoslovak Central Committee by the Soviet Central Committee, which complained of the failure of the Prague leaders to carry out the "agreements" of Čierna and Bratislava and gave evidence of the deteriorating situation in Czechoslovakia.[79] Although these moves were

[74] *RP*, Aug. 17. Cf. the editorial in *Scînteia*, Aug. 8, given in Remington, ed., *Winter in Prague*, pp. 261-63.
[75] *RP*, Aug. 18. [76] Ibid., Aug. 19.
[77] Husák, ibid., Aug. 20 and Sept. 29, 1969.
[78] Tigrid, *Why Dubcek Fell*, p. 96.
[79] The content of the letter was mentioned by M. Vaculík at the opening of his speech to the illegal 14th congress after the occupation (J. Pelikán, ed., *The Secret Vysočany Congress*, London, 1971, pp. 20-21). Husák, in the speeches cited in n. 77, also referred to letters from the Soviet Politburo and from Brezhnev, on the 13th, and another from the Politburo on the 17th. Hrbek lists a series of messages

secret, it was already evident that the lull after Bratislava had come to an end. The Kádár visit to Dubček may have been a last effort to avert the necessity of an invasion but, if so, it was in vain. The general public in Czechoslovakia, although conscious of the renewed crisis, was not yet aware of the actual danger which threatened—nor indeed were the leaders, according to their own professions.[80]

Preparations for the 14th Congress

Throughout these intoxicating days the more prosaic work of preparing for the extraordinary party congress was proceeding in the working groups formed at the May plenum which were responsible for submitting the congress documents to the political commission under Dubček. The schedule provided for these papers to be completed by the end of July and then to be discussed in the party organizations, with the participation of all congress delegates, in the second half of August. The final drafts of all materials were to be ready by early September.[81]

The congress delegates had been nominated at the meetings of the basic organizations and at the district and regional conferences in June and July, as had over 900 CC and ÚKRK candidates. Although these elections had been termed "inner-party matters," they had, as noted above, awakened a great deal of public interest. The full list of CC candidates was not published, but the identity of the nominees, at least in each region, was known to the party members who had participated in their selection. The names of those included (or excluded) often leaked out to the public. There was discussion in the media of the better known

from Aug. 9 to 17, including the one from the Politburo on the 17th (*Manifest pravdy*, p. 13). Husák claimed that Dubček had not told the Presidium of the Kádár visit or of the messages from Brezhnev (*RP*, Sept. 29, 1969). Cf. also Švestka, ibid., Aug. 21, 1969; and Biľak, in his speech to the CC plenum in Sept. 1969 (*Svědectví*, no. 38, 1970, p. 288). Dubček did not deny these charges but stated that he had informed the Presidium about the Kádár meeting orally on the 20th. As to the letter of the 17th, Dubček said that he had received this on the 19th and had read it to the Presidium on the 20th (after the beginning of the invasion). There was no information in the letter that suggested he must call an immediate meeting of the Presidium to discuss it (Sept. 1969 plenum, *Svědectví*, no. 38, p. 276). The full text of this letter was later given in a Prague radio broadcast on Aug. 20, 1969 (*SCC* 3, Jan. 1970, pp. 141-44). For fuller discussion, see below, chap. xx.

[80] Z. Hoření, in a commentary on Bratislava and the four meetings published in *Rudé právo* on Aug. 20 found a common denominator in the overcoming of the immediate danger of a split and contributing to "the integration of the socialist world." Full normalization of relations would take time and placed "a heavy responsibility on us, on our communications media, and on our partners." These relations were, however, "the alpha and omega of our national future."

[81] *ŽS*, no. 14 (July 1968), pp. 1-3.

candidates, with occasional suggestions that certain more conservative figures not be elected.[82]

These preparations were, of course, rudely interrupted by the invasion. By that time the major documents had been prepared, but only one, the draft party statute, had been published, on the day of the arrival of Tito. Two other drafts were ready and had presumably been submitted to the party organizations. The first—a long document analyzing the party's activity since the 13th congress and setting forth the main tasks for the immediate future—was intended as a rough draft for the major report to be presented at the congress by Dubček.[83] The second was a short draft of a long-term party program, which, if approved by the congress, would have been the basis for subsequent elaboration and eventual consideration at the 15th congress.[84] These two documents can best be treated in the appropriate places in later chapters.

The draft statute had twice been considered by the Presidium and was the topic of further deliberation in party organizations and in the press in ensuing weeks.[85] Suggestions for amendment were to be forwarded to the district organizations by August 25 and then sent to a special CC group for analysis and amalgamation. Final approval would, of course, rest with the congress.

The August 10 draft differed in important respects from the original version as a result of changes made by Indra's group to which the May plenum had assigned the main responsibility for the statute. These changes, according to Jindřich Fibich, one of the members of the lower level working group, reflected the contradictions between "the progressive forces, mainly from below" and "certain conservative opposition, from the highest places."[86] The draft was therefore a curious mixture of

[82] E.g. the discussion with two delegates, both of whom were opposed to the inclusion of Kolder, Švestka, Indra, and Kapek (*LL*, Aug. 1). Such public evaluation of delegates was severely criticized by J. Benda, *RP*, Aug. 20, and defended in *Rep.*, Aug. 21-28, pp. 9-10.

[83] This draft was based on a series of reports prepared, under the supervision of various party leaders, by teams of specialists. These included the post-13th congress analysis (Sádovský); the party and the political system (Mlynář); the party's relations with the main interest groups (Lenárt); economic policy (Kolder); science, culture, and ideology (Císař); long-term program (Richta); international policy (Professor Hájek). The combined document was prepared by Mlynář, Hájek, Kouba, Machonin, Provazník, Richta, and Uher. The text has been published abroad in several languages: Jiří Pelikán, ed., *Vysočany Congress*, pp. 187-253; in Czech, Pelikán, ed., *Tanky proti sjezdu* (*Protokol a dokumenty XIV. sjezdu KSČ*) (Vienna, 1970). For alternative title see bibliography.

[84] This was prepared by a team of intellectuals headed by R. Richta. See Pelikán, ed., *Vysočany Congress*, pp. 100-124.

[85] *Rudé právo* and *Život strany*, from August 11 on, featured regular discussions of the draft statute.

[86] *Práce*, Aug. 21. For other criticisms, see *RP*, Aug. 20 and J. Ruml, *Rep.*, Aug. 21-28, p. 3. The original text was published in *RP*, Aug. 10; in English, Remington,

new and old. Many concepts, as Indra stated, were taken from previous statutes, including, for example, the basic structure of the party, the principles of inner-party democracy and democratic centralism, respect for Marxism-Leninism, and the recognition of the historic role of the working class.[87] Yet the statute was suffused with a fresh democratic spirit and included provisions for voluntary membership, secret voting, conflict of opinions, the rights of a minority, etc. With all its limitations it was a new model of a communist party, breaking sharply with the traditional conception adumbrated in previous statutes. It was not just "a partial renovation," wrote Jiří Sekera in *Rudé právo*, but "an essential reelaboration and modernization."[88]

The general organization of the party was altered least. The pyramidal structure, the leading organs, and the organizations at lower levels were retained, except for the regional level which was to be abolished. The most significant structural alteration related to the position of Czechs and Slovaks in the common party. Unlike the state, the party was not to become "federal" but it was to be reorganized to assure "full equality and development" of the two nationalities. There were to be two "national territorial organizations" (not "independent parties," be it noted) which together would form "the united (*jednotný*) international Communist Party of Czechoslovakia" (para. 45). A Communist Party of the Czech lands was to be created alongside the existing Communist Party of Slovakia, and each was to have its own system of organs and was to possess substantial autonomy of action.

These two national territorial organizations were, however, to be "guided by its (the CPCz) program and statutes" (para. 38); the CPCz Central Committee was to "direct" them "while respecting their rights and supporting their initiative" (para. 48c). Both were to participate in the formation of general party policy, but were not to be represented in the central organs on the basis of parity, as originally demanded by the Slovaks.[89] The exclusive jurisdiction of the party's Central Committee

---

ed., *Winter in Prague*, pp. 265-87. Both the original and draft versions are given by Pelikán, ed., *Vysočany Congress*, pp. 128-85. See below, chap. xii, for further discussion.

[87] *RP*, Aug. 15.   [88] *RP*, Aug. 11.

[89] M. Láb, a member of the working group, explicitly rejected the idea of parity and urged a CC composition based on the relative number of members in party organizations. The CC should be "an authoritative organ" representing all-society interests. Parity would deepen the division of the party and weaken the unified efforts to attain common goals, he wrote. He suggested a 4/5 majority for decisions, or joint meetings of the CC's, as safeguards against outvoting (*Rep.*, July 31-Aug. 7). The statutes did not indicate the methods of selecting congress delegates or CC members. Three members of the working group wrote that the Central Committee would be formed "on the basis of the election of delegates to the congress according to a uniform proportion valid for the whole party." See M. Havlíček, M. Láb, and M. Tícha, *Kulturní tvorba*, Aug. 15, 1968.

was ensured in certain spheres, such as the international communist movement and international relations, and the work of communists in statewide organs and in the armed forces. There were, however, provisions to safeguard the Slovaks against being outvoted. On matters affecting survival, sovereignty or sovereign national or territorial interests, a decision would require a majority vote of the representatives of the two national organizations voting separately, if an absolute majority of each had requested such a method of voting. In addition, joint meetings of the two Central Committees could be called, although the decisions of such a session would not be binding (para. 49).[90] There were, however, no similar provisions concerning actions taken by the Presidium or Secretariat of the joint party. In sum, the party was to remain "unitary," with "a united organ (the Central Committee) above the national organs, to examine national demands, or points of departure, from the viewpoint of the whole society."[91]

Gathering Crisis in Slovakia

With the extraordinary congress of the Slovak party scheduled to open on August 26, public attention was riveted on the preparations for this decisive meeting and on its probable outcome. The delegates, 638 strong, had already been chosen at the district and regional conferences. Although the date had originally been advanced to permit the Slovak party to formulate its stand on federalization before the 14th congress, this problem receded somewhat into the background and was superseded by the question of replacing leading cadres by the election of a new Central Committee.[92] The political committee responsible for congress preparations decided against publishing the names of the almost three hundred persons nominated for CC membership.[93] This was sharply criticized by some who urged that the list be made public before the congress opened.[94] Many spokesmen, including prominent delegates to the congress, advocated that certain former high functionaries be removed in the elections.

It became obvious that a struggle for power, focused particularly on

[90] The working group's version had provided, in serious matters or those affecting the interests of a national organization, for consultations with the appropriate national CC, and for a majority of 4/5 of the CC members present; in exceptionally serious matters a joint meeting of the CPCz CC and the national CC involved, or of the two national CC's, had been stipulated (para. 46).

[91] Havlíček, Láb, and Tícha, *KT*, Aug. 15, 1968. For criticism of the draft statute by Šebesta, see below, in this chapter.

[92] M. Hysko, *NS*, July 25.   [93] *Pravda*, Aug. 13.

[94] E.g. Zora Jesenská and L. Olex, both delegates (ibid., Aug. 20, 21). Sedláková defended the decision although she criticized the small number of women on the list and the absence of workers among the Bratislava nominees (ibid., Aug. 19).

the two rivals, Bil'ak and Husák, and their close associates, was under way. More and more frequently voices were raised against the continuance in high office of those who were responsible for pre-January policies and not fully sympathetic with the process of democratization. These "conservatives," as they were openly called, were charged with supporting federation as a means of maintaining their own position and of neglecting other aspects of democratization. These views were often buttressed by two other arguments, namely, that the pre-January Slovak leaders had not been as progressive as some of them made out and that Slovakia was far behind the Czech lands in reforms.[95]

Bil'ak, who had been thrown on the defensive by the decision to advance the date of the Slovak congress, made a major effort to recoup his position, in a radio and television interview on August 16 in which he defended the post-1963 Slovak leadership and denied, as he had done before, that Slovakia was lagging behind the Czech lands. Admittedly, the Slovak party, like the CPCz, had not made many changes in CC membership, but there had been extensive shifts in leadership at the level of the basic organizations, districts, and regions. Other cadre changes, in the Slovak Council and the national committees, could not be made until after the elections, he argued. In justifying the decision not to publish the list of CC nominees, Bil'ak observed that this had been taken by the political committee, which included such figures as Husák and Novomeský, and that a similar decision had been made by the Czechoslovak Presidium.[96] Bil'ak justified the concentration on federation after January arguing that they had had to make great efforts to get this idea into the Action Program and to attain its implementation during 1968 and had also pressed the demand for inclusion of this question on the 14th congress agenda.

Husák made his opposition to Bil'ak quite clear during a visit to Žiar nad Hronom in remarks which were published on the very day of the Soviet invasion. There had, he agreed, been some relaxation after 1963, but "methods of the cult" and "personal power" had continued and a basic change had occurred only after January 1968. Yet Slovakia had "stopped at mid-course" in the revival process; there had been almost no changes in leadership. Bil'ak, he complained, had surrounded himself with people who sought to slow down democratization and preserve the

[95] For instance, M. Svetlík (*Pravda*, Aug. 16); O. Pavlík (ibid., Aug. 17); I. Kuhn (ibid., Aug. 18); Jesenská (ibid., Aug. 20). Svetlík cited Bil'ak and Pecho by name as examples. Löbl went so far as to speak of the conservatives, "in the given constellation of the world," as "a potential fifth column" (*KŽ*, Aug. 16). The most critical analysis was by Števček, ibid., July 12, republished in *LL*, July 25.

[96] *Pravda*, Aug. 17. In a later speech, Bil'ak, avoiding contentious domestic political references, described the congress as involving "the authority of the whole party and not only of its leadership" (*Pravda*, Aug. 20).

321

existing situation. Michal Pecho was accused of "hiding behind Dubček's back." As for Dubček, he was "great not for what he did in the years 1963-1967 but for what he has done after January." Husák expressed the conviction that at both party congresses people would be elected who would be "capable of entering on the correct course of developing our society." As for federalism, he expected that the deadline of October 28 —"the extreme time limit of Slovak patience"—would be met and that a new constitutional order would guarantee equality of both nations.[97]

Strangely, prominent spokesmen, including Husák and Bil'ak, made no mention of the party's future structure. Due to the crisis surrounding the Čierna and Bratislava conferences, the projected joint meeting of the two presidia had not been held. Shortly thereafter the publication of the draft statute revealed that there was no plan for federalizing the party, as advocated by the Slovaks, nor any provision for parity representation in the highest organs. The draft was criticized by Štefan Šebesta, a political leader ousted in the sixties and a congress delegate (in an interview published in *Rudé právo* but not in the Bratislava party paper), who insisted on the "federalization" of the party and suggested more consistent safeguards against outvoting in all fundamental questions.[98] Apart from this single comment, this issue, which had been central in Slovak thinking a few weeks earlier, disappeared from public discussion. Meanwhile preparations for the founding of a Czech party were proceeding, with a meeting of Czech 14th congress delegates likely to take place prior to the 14th congress, and a constituent congress afterwards.[99]

Slovak opinion was more outspoken on the question of federalizing the state system. Indicative of this was the "Appeal to Czechs and Slovaks," signed by many outstanding Slovaks and published in *Nové slovo* on the 1st of August, during the Čierna conference.[100] This statement regretted the continuance in many Czech minds of the "old Czechoslovakist centralist spirit . . . which sometimes affected the consideration of federation" and warned against "any attempt at cutting down the principle of equality of rights or any efforts to postpone the constitutional

[97] Husák, ibid., Aug. 21. [98] *RP*, Aug. 19.
[99] J. Kolář, head of the CC political-organizational department, in an interview on these preparations, revealed that many aspects of the party's future organization remained unclear and would have to be settled by the forthcoming joint meeting of the two presidia. Kolář and other members of the committee favored a meeting of Czech delegates *before* the congress (*ŽS*, no. 17, Aug. 1968, pp. 62-63). A post-occupation article described at length, with substantial quotations, a programmatic proclamation drafted in late July for the Czech party's constituent congress, but reported that this was not approved by the CC apparatus (*Tribuna*, Nov. 26, 1969).
[100] The appeal was also published on the same day in *Pravda* and *Rudé právo*, but not in *Kultúrny život*. *Pravda* criticized its issuance at a time when progress was being made on federalization and when the sovereignty of the state as a whole was at stake (Aug. 1). See below, chap. xv, for fuller discussion of the appeal and of federation.

law." It also expressed resentment at Czech condemnation of the slowness of democratization in Slovakia and asserted that the Slovaks were capable of making the necessary institutional and personnel changes for achieving an optimum of freedom and socialist democracy. Demanding parity representation in the central organs, especially in the federal parliament and government, the appeal insisted on wide safeguards against outvoting in both domestic and foreign policy. The manifesto concluded by declaring that it was "high time that the principle of equality of rights of our two nations, which up to then had only been declared, should be definitively codified and introduced into state practice. . . ."

This extreme statement no doubt reflected the views of a wide segment of Slovak opinion. Some were disquieted by the lack of interest in this problem among Czechs and by the failure of the government expert commission to reach agreement, and were afraid that the whole process of federalization was slowing down and that the October 28 deadline would not be met.[101] Throughout these weeks of international crisis the columns of *Nové slovo* were filled with articles expounding Slovak complaints and demands, almost to the exclusion of other issues. Commentators reasserted the familiar theme that there could be no genuine and consistent democratization without national equality and federalization. "One without the other cannot exist," wrote one contributor.[102] Šebesta admitted that Slovaks felt more strongly about federalization than any other question and described this goal as a vital element of democratization, although not the only aspect of the latter.[103]

Another school of thought, not represented among official party spokesmen, was best expressed by the scholar, Pavol Števček, who doubted the sincerity of certain leaders in advocating federation and placed most emphasis on the democratic substance of a future federal system. "We need," he wrote, "to enrich the national program of federation . . . with our own Slovak concept of democracy under the conditions of socialism." Federation in Košice or elsewhere in Slovakia must "bear the brand name of Czechoslovak democratism."[104]

It was ironic that this spate of Slovak nationalist discontent should coincide with noticeable progress toward federalization. For one thing, the Czech National Council had held its first meeting at the end of July and had heard its chairman, Císař, outline the main features of the proposed federal system. Moreover, the government's commission of experts had reached agreement on the outline of the future constitutional system

---

[101] E.g. J. Paško, of the Slovak party *aparát*, *ŽS*, no. 17 (Aug. 1968), pp. 5-8. The presidium of the Slovak National Council, in late July, had stressed the October 28 deadline (*Pravda*, July 28).
[102] J. Šolc, *Nové slovo*, Aug. 1.
[103] *Pravda*, Aug. 7. See also M. Chorvath, ibid., Aug. 9.
[104] *KŽ*, July 12. Cf. M. Kusý, *NS*, June 20, 27.

and had submitted its report to the government and the National Assembly. This did not mean, of course, that the full bill of particulars advanced by the Slovaks had been accepted by the Czechs, or that consensus had been achieved on all contentious points. Agreement was often limited to general principles which had yet to be translated into a detailed draft statute. Although there was still a long road ahead before all controversial issues were settled, there was some hope and, indeed, optimism among those most directly concerned, that the constitutional law would in fact be adopted by the National Assembly by the deadline of October 28.

CRACKS IN POLITICAL UNITY

The international crisis extending from the receipt of the Warsaw letter to the Čierna and Bratislava conferences had produced an unparalleled national unity in support of the Dubček government. This had, it was believed, been a significant factor underlying the firmness of the leadership's resistance to Soviet pressures and may have warded off military intervention by demonstrating the absence of local support for such action.[105] This newfound unity was in part nationalist in character, a product of outrage and resentment at foreign interference, but it was also an expression of consolidation of support for reform, a major target of the outside pressures. Any illusions that this extraordinary spirit of unity could be fully preserved were, however, soon dispelled.[106]

There had been hints of future trouble in the Prchlík controversy and in the Praga letter, both of which, as noted above, had serious domestic repercussions. Although disavowed by the Ministry of Defense and indeed by the government as a whole, General Prchlík found many defenders who were greatly concerned by the implications of his dismissal for the reform movement and for bloc relations. The Praga letter had even more harmful effects. Meetings were held in the factory, where prominent editors and political leaders spoke and warned against persecution of those involved. Nonetheless, a wave of abuse and criticism of the signatories swept the press, radio, and television, and there were demands for their dismissal or punishment.[107] The sociologist, Miroslav Jodl, in a letter to *Svobodné slovo*, called the signers "traitors" and their letter "a stab in the back" of the Czechoslovak negotiators at Čierna and suggested that they should "emigrate to where they seek support and find

[105] J. Hochman, *Rep.*, July 31-Aug. 7; Aug. 7-14.
[106] See a discussion of the problem of unity by several congress delegates, *LL*, Aug. 8.
[107] *RP*, Aug. 11, 13, 14. J. Kolář (ibid., Aug. 11), spoke of "some—although not many—letters with views similar" to those in the Praga letter, which were received by the CC *aparát* and *Rudé právo*. See also *ŽS*, Dec. 3, 1969.

response." This brought bitter condemnations, including one published in *Rudé právo* calling on the Procurator and the Minister of the Interior to take the necessary action against Jodl. On August 14, *Rudé právo* published the full text of the Praga letter and an article which condemned not only Jodl's action and the demands for administrative actions against the signatories, but also the circulation of anonymous letters. In the end, it seems, few of the signatories lost their jobs, but some were removed from positions in the party, factory, or People's Militia organizations.[108]

Other signs of unrest were certain happenings in downtown Prague— demonstrations of young people, heated discussions in little Myslbek Park, and a new campaign for signatures, this time for a petition urging the abolition of the People's Militia, which was conducted outside the Dětský Dům (the House of Children Department Store) on Na příkopě. The demonstrations, which had begun during the Čierna and Bratislava conferences, had culminated in a gathering outside the Central Committee building on August 8, when, according to a later report in *Rudé právo*, the crowd called for Smrkovský's appearance; shouted insulting slogans; beat on the doors; and threw stones at the windows.[109] The discussion meetings, which became almost a nightly occurrence, gave rise to concern in some circles that they represented a threat to public order and free discussion. A well-known economist, Jiří Sláma, in *Rudé právo* (Aug. 17), praised the democratic aspects of this little "Hyde Park," but deplored its excesses, especially the tendency to silence opinions by denunciation. Observing that the atmosphere of these meetings was predominantly anti-communist, Sláma urged non-communists to support the progressive wing of the party which, he noted, had initiated the reform movement. In the same issue the organizer of the original signature campaign for the support of Dubček repudiated the new drive as undemocratic and advised people to avoid such provocative actions.

The Presidium of the party on August 13 castigated what it called "hooliganism" in downtown Prague and warned that breaches of law and public order could not be tolerated and might lead to "political provocation." The statement also rejected the attacks on the People's Militia and the campaign against the ninety-nine Praga employees.[110] *Rudé právo*, in a series of reports and commentaries, criticized these events and strongly defended the People's Militia, arguing that illegal leaflets and

---

[108] Jodl, *Svobodné slovo*, Aug. 9; his later reply, ibid., Aug. 15. See also *RP*, Aug. 11, 14. Several of the signatories explained that the letter had been drawn up and signed prior to the publication of the Warsaw letter and had been "misused" later at the time of Čierna. The party committee in the plant treated the letter as the opinion of private persons, defended their right to express it, and opposed any administrative actions against them. Only two workers, it was said, left the plant, at their own request.

[109] For this and the following, *RP*, Aug. 17.

[110] *RŠO*, pp. 292-93.

the signature campaign demonstrated the need for the militia to protect public order and the security of citizens.[111] An article by I. Aleksandrov in Moscow *Pravda* on August 18 focused on these happenings, and on press attacks on the Čierna and Bratislava conferences.[112]

Even more disturbing to national unity was the controversy which developed from a major article in *Rudé právo* on July 14 by the editor-in-chief, Švestka, on "Questions of Working Class Policy." Švestka contended that the main target of the anti-socialist forces was the working class and its position in society and that the workers themselves had so far adopted a somewhat passive and waiting attitude toward democratization. In the subsequent polemics, several prominent scholars, including Pavel Machonin, charged him with minimizing the activity of the working class after January and with distorting the meaning of democratization. Švestka, in another article on August 20, declared that "government by the working class" was the central aim of the revival process and deplored the use of the term "conservative" against critics, depicting it as an attempt to discredit the whole party *aktiv*.[113]

In the meantime Švestka had become the target of personal criticism for his comments on Čierna and Bratislava, or, as a commentator in *Rudé právo*, put it, was made the object of a campaign aimed at his "moral and social-political liquidation."[114] His editorial policy became a matter of disputation within the newspaper editorial staff, leading, it was reported in *The New York Times*, to the firing of several progressive editors and to an attempt by some of his associates to have him removed from his post. *Rudé právo* flatly denied these reports, and the *Times* correspondent was not granted an extension of his stay in Prague.[115] Whatever the truth was, Švestka had become a controversial figure who was unlikely to be elected to the Central Committee at the forthcoming congress.

Meanwhile the actions of the mass media were a continuing problem for the party leadership. On August 17 members of the Presidium, including Černík, Smrkovský, Kriegel, and Císař, met with an *aktiv* of

[111] *RP*, Aug. 17, 20. A resolution from militia members in Domažlice appealed to the party to use "other means" to preserve public order, if necessary, and argued that these events should be called, not "hooliganism," but "provocations against party and state" (ibid., Aug. 21). For post-occupation critique of the campaign against the People's Militia, see *Tribuna*, April 2, 1969, p. 5.

[112] See below, chap. xx. Aleksandrov quoted extensively from the *Rudé právo* analysis of the Prague situation, and *Rudé právo* in turn reported the Moscow article fully (Aug. 19).

[113] For fuller discussion, see chap. xviii below.

[114] J. Benda (*RP*, Aug. 20), using these words, condemned a television commentary attacking Švestka as an attempt to influence the CC elections. Cf. another criticism, *MF*, Aug. 10.

[115] *NYT*, Aug. 15, 18, 21; *RP*, Aug. 20. See also Rémi Gueyt, *La mutation tchécoslovaque* (Paris, 1969), p. 277.

communist journalists, but the purpose and the results of this meeting were not revealed. A brief report merely indicated that a consensus had been reached on the need for focusing attention on the preparations of the 14th congress. Whether, as reported by *The New York Times*, the journalists also consented to avoid anti-Soviet polemics cannot be verified.[116]

THE FINAL PRESIDIUM MEETING

These disputations were indices of the serious disunity within the party, the tension created by the impact of Čierna and Bratislava, and the nervous anticipation of the 14th congress. None of these events could objectively be interpreted as demonstrating that a counterrevolutionary situation existed or that the party had lost control, as was later argued in justification of the invasion. Far more serious was the growing split within the Presidium, although this was unknown to the general public or even to leading party strata. The controversy was touched off by an extensive report on the general political situation prepared by the information branch of the CC apparatus in connection with the forthcoming party congress.[117] Although its content and conclusions will be given detailed consideration later (chap. xvi), they must be briefly noted here as a crucial political factor on the eve of the invasion.

The report, based admittedly on incomplete information from party organizations, was tendentious and somewhat ambiguous, but in the main expressed conservative views on the uncertainty, and the dangers, of the future. It did note, however, the public confidence, representing

---

[116] *RP*, Aug. 18; *NYT*, Aug. 18. After the occupation, S. Budín reported on this meeting in *The New York Times* (Aug. 28, 1968) referring to appeals by Černík and others to the journalists that, in view of the gravity of the situation, they should avoid replies to Soviet attacks and any provocations that might be exploited by enemies of reform. Budín made no mention of any agreement on this point between government and journalists. The journalists, he wrote, expressed their support of the Presidium, or at least its liberal part, but accused them of being excessively pessimistic. All the leaders present (including Černík, Smrkovský, and Kriegel) said that military intervention was out of the question. Cf. J. Ruml's account of this meeting at which some Presidium members spoke of "a sword of Damocles" hanging over their heads but did not make the situation clear. He, too, did not refer to any agreement (*BBC*, ii, Aug. 28, 1968).

[117] Later published for inner party circulation under the title, *Zpráva o současné politické situaci Československé socialistické republiky a podmínkách činnosti Komunistické strany Československa (srpen 1968)* (Prague, Oct. 1968); henceforth cited as *Zpráva*. Dated July 23, this document, 116 pages long, with extensive appendices, was issued in printed form under the name of Dr. Jan Kašpar, head of the newly formed CC information branch, and was transmitted to the Presidium under the date Aug. 12. This report, without its appendices, was published in *Tribuna*, Feb. 5, July 2, 1969, and *Rudé právo*, July 2, 1969. According to Švestka, *Tribuna*, after publishing the first part in February, was forbidden by the party Presidium to publish the remainder at that time (*RP*, Aug. 21, 1969).

THE POLITICS OF CHANGE

almost 80 percent of the population, won by the party in preceding months and the national unity achieved at the time of Čierna. This unity, however, was associated with the questions of sovereignty and independence, and was therefore temporary and likely to disintegrate when faced with the grave problems to be dealt with before and after the congress. The divisions within the party reflected deep conflicts within society, and in particular the clash of "conservative" and "extremist" or "radical" views (pp. 31-34, 46-50). On the whole, the report believed, the conservatives who desired a return to pre-January conditions had been totally discredited and did not constitute a potential danger. There were others, employed mainly in the state and party apparatus who, although disapproving the pre-January system, were retarding the implementation of the Action Program. On the other hand, extremist elements, imbued with "romantic political opinions" and "certain political illusions," constituted a serious problem.

The divisions within the party would produce sharp conflicts at the forthcoming congress, at which an almost complete change of leadership cadres would also occur. In particular, the newly formed Czech party would be led by inexperienced functionaries who would face great difficulties in meeting the challenge of opposition forces, especially in Prague. If the party was not able to create a defense, for example by counterdemonstrations by workers, against such movements as the campaigns concerning the militia or the "ninety-nine," these could assume "the forms of dangerous conflicts" (p. 33). The party, however, lacked a clear and unified conception of its policy and concrete measures to implement it and was divided on basic problems.[118]

The domestic political situation was not consolidated, and could hardly be consolidated in a short time, the report concluded (p. 59). On the contrary repeated situations of conflicts and tensions were to be expected in the fall. Extremist forces would probably seek to achieve their aims of stirring up hostility toward the USSR; breaking up the People's Militia; weakening and splitting the party; dividing the unity of the working class by the creation of a social democratic party; organizing opposition forces; and discrediting those who were committed to counteractions (p. 44). Counterrevolutionary forces, which sought the return of capitalism, represented perhaps only 5 percent of the population, but might be

[118] Pages 47, 49, 52. The report perceived many other "disquieting" features in the situation, such as the divisions within the party (pp. 46-48); the disorientation of many of its functionaries (p. 44); a "crisis" in its aparát (p. 45); the unsatisfactory situation in the mass media (pp. 55-58); the growing activity of various non-communist political parties and organizations (p. 43); the lack of political consolidation in the security organs; partial consolidation but continuing questions in dispute within the army; continued attacks on the People's Militia and a certain "wavering" in its ranks (p. 59).

able to misuse "extreme situations and mass passions" to embark on political activity "through the medium of other forces and with apparently democratic demands and in an apparently democratic form" (p. 34).

On August 13, the Presidium had received, but not discussed, the Kašpar report and had requested Indra and Kolder to propose specific measures to be taken in the light of its information. When the Presidium met again on the 20th, this item was on the agenda, following the main business of the meeting—Dubček's draft report for the congress and the draft congress resolution.[119] Kolder unsuccessfully proposed that the Kašpar report be given priority inasmuch as the congress documents would be influenced by the Presidium's attitude to this report. The Presidium rejected this change in agenda and proceeded to discuss at length the congress documents, which were ultimately approved. Late in the evening, Indra and Kolder presented their prepared "standpoint" on the political situation, based on the conclusions of the Kašpar report and recommended a declaration by the Presidium, which would be published and used as the basis of a struggle against the extremist forces on the right prior to the congress.[120] Indra and Kolder had also prepared a list of definite measures to be taken to implement the proposed declaration, but for reasons that are obscure, did not present this to the Presidium.[121] These steps, nine in number, included a series of appearances by the top leaders in the various regions, and on radio and television, to defend the Presidium's evaluation of the situation. The major speeches of the CC delegates to the Slovak congress would be elaborated in the same spirit. A conference of seventy functionaries from the largest factories would be held to discuss the final phase of congress preparations. As a final point, the Indra-Kolder memorandum proposed "the consistent realiza-

[119] The following description of the Presidium session is based on an eyewitness report (by D. Havlíček) published in the illegal *Rudé právo*, Aug. 23, 1968 and reproduced in *Sedm pražských dnů, 21.-27. srpen 1968: Dokumentace* (Prague, Sept. 1968), pp. 8-13; in English, in Robert Littell, ed., *The Czech Black Book* (New York, 1969), pp. 12-18; and on a long interview by O. Švestka, *RP*, Aug. 21, 1969. See also Budín, *NYT*, Aug. 28. For Dubček's version, see his speech at the CC plenum in Sept. 1969 as reported in *Svědectví*, no. 38 (1970), pp. 277-78.

[120] Kolder, *RP*, Sept. 10, 1969. In this interview, Kolder quoted what presumably was a section of their standpoint, which embodied point by point the dangers listed in the Kašpar report (p. 44), but which added another referring to the "exalting" of certain individuals and the "branding" of others with the purpose of influencing 14th congress cadre preparations.

[121] What purports to be a text of these measures was made available by Kolder and published, *RP*, Aug. 13, 1969. These concrete measures, he reported, were to be introduced at a later stage of the Presidium discussions. In 1969 Dubček expressed surprise that these proposals, which Kolder and Indra had been specifically requested to prepare, had not been presented to the meeting on the 20th (*Svědectví*, no. 38, p. 277). He referred to them as measures for "carrying out and fulfilling the conclusions of Čierna and Bratislava."

tion of the conclusions and agreements of Čierna nad Tisou and Bratislava."

The discussion of the Indra-Kolder "standpoint" was bitter and excited and demonstrated the deep cleavage within the Presidium. Speaking in favor, according to Švestka, were Kolder, Bil'ak, Piller, and Kapek, and against, Kriegel and Smrkovský.[122] According to Švestka the discussion was not completed and no action was taken; the report was simply "taken under advisement."[123] A few moments later the news of the invasion of the country by Soviet and bloc forces was communicated by Černík to the meeting.

Whether the events described above were directly related to the invasion, as preliminary steps in preparing the political conditions for this action, is difficult to estimate. Indra and Kolder had presumably anticipated that the acceptance by the Presidium of their proposals would force the Dubček leadership to change its course and had perhaps hoped that it would eventually lead to Dubček's replacement by a more "realistic" colleague. Perhaps, too, the final decision on the report was regarded by Moscow as the ultimate test of Dubček's intentions and of his capacity to carry out the understandings of Čierna and Bratislava. At the very moment that the proposals were under consideration, however, the invading forces were already moving toward the frontier.[124]

[122] According to Havlíček, Rigo also supported the Kolder-Indra proposal and Černík opposed it. Piller spoke favorably of the Kašpar report but urged that nothing be published at that time.

[123] See also *Zpráva*, p. 60.

[124] See below, chap. XXII, for further discussion. According to Švestka (*RP*, Aug. 21, 1969) the archives revealed that some members of the Presidium knew, by 8:00 p.m., that Soviet troops were in motion. He also argued that "we all knew that there existed the possibility of an entry of troops . . . if the Čierna agreements were not fulfilled."

PART FOUR

THE NEW MODEL OF
SOCIALISM

CHAPTER XII

A New Political System

THE January overthrow, in part the product of deep dissatisfaction with the existing political system, opened the way for its reform but did not at once produce a blueprint for a new political model or even a set of specific reform proposals.[1] Prior to January, as noted in earlier chapters, the idea of "broadening" and "deepening" socialist democracy had been proclaimed officially at both the 12th and 13th congresses, but Novotný and his chief associates were reluctant to admit any changes that would seriously weaken the authority of the party or significantly alter its mode of operation. The January communiqué, and even the fuller unpublished resolution, gave only a few hints as to specific changes envisaged, and by citing the 13th congress and the October Theses and using well-worn and ambiguous terms such as collective leadership, democratic centralism, and inner-party democracy, cast doubt on the likelihood of genuine political reform.[2]

Until the publication of the Action Program in April, the shape of things to come in the political realm continued to be obscure. Dubček, in several major speeches, adumbrated, in fresh tones, a new conception of the party's leadership role within the context of a developing socialist democracy, but gave few precise details as to how these ideas would be implemented. The party's Institute of Political Science had not proceeded far enough with its studies to enable its chief, Václav Slavík, to offer anything more than general and familiar prescriptions for change.[3] The Mlynář team had also not gone far in its research on the optimum

[1] For general discussion, see A. H. Brown, "Political Change in Czechoslovakia," *Government and Opposition* 4 (Spring 1969), 169-94; Morton Schwartz, "Czechoslovakia's New Political Model: A Design for Renewal," *The Journal of Politics* 30 (1968), 966-84; H. G. Skilling, "Czechoslovakia's Interrupted Revolution," *Canadian Slavonic Papers* 10 (Winter 1968), 409-29; Boris Meissner, "Moskauer Orthodoxie und Reformkommunismus, Der politischer Aspekt," *Moderne Welt*, no. 2 (1970), pp. 133-56; Frederick M. Barnard, "Between Opposition and Political Opposition: The Search for Competitive Politics in Czechoslovakia," *Canadian Journal of Political Science* 5 (Dec. 1972), 533-52. See also Galia Golan, *The Czechoslovak Reform Movement* (Cambridge, 1971), pp. 299-308.

[2] See above, chapters v-vii. For a summary of pre-1968 discussions see the Presidium report issued on March 4, 1968, *Rok šedesátý osmý* (Prague, 1969), pp. 7-25. For the January resolution, see *Tribuna*, Oct. 15, 1969.

[3] Interview with Slavík, *Reportér*, Feb. 14-21, pp. 5-7; his articles in *Práce*, Feb. 7; *Rudé právo*, April 24; *Život strany*, no. 12 (1968), pp. 6-8; *Literární listy*, July 25. See also his speech at the Czechoslovak Political Science Association in which he referred to the contribution of "politology" to "the new political model" and urged its independence from "political power" (*RP*, June 25).

political model and, apart from the conflicting opinions expressed by Mlynář and other members, provided no firm guidelines for the future.[4] In the absence of direction from the leadership, party ideologists were at first relatively orthodox, citing both the October Theses and the January resolution, and not going much, if at all, beyond their pre-January obeisance to democratic procedures.[5] Little by little, however, a new note crept into these official expositions, as behind-the-scene preparations of the Action Program became known and gave significant clues as to the likely direction of reform.[6] Public panel discussions on radio and television, and in the weekly journals, provided more daring visions of the future but revealed substantial differences of viewpoint and considerable uncertainty.[7]

Prior to the Action Program the clearest statements on political reform appeared in a number of articles in the party daily by Zdeněk Mlynář who was deeply involved in preparing the program and was soon to be elevated to high party status. In the first of these, drawing on the experience of the economic reform, he warned of the danger of "half-heartedness and bad compromises" and spoke of "a qualitative reconstruction" of the political order.[8] Calling for a new and lucid policy, Mlynář indicated the need to revise or repeal certain earlier party decisions, referring explicitly to the October Theses.[9] Noting that the system had been severely criticized by Czech political theorists in the past four years, he described it as "a dictatorial system of centralistic directive decision-making," based on the monopoly of a single political subject, and designed to embody "one interest" and to "implement the directive of a single power center."[10] The logic of the new system would require the participation, "as independent political subjects," of various social groups and strata, interest groups and individuals, and also of the several institutional elements—state, party, and societal organizations. Within

[4] For Mlynář's articles, see below, n. 8. A symposium volume by members of the team was projected for publication in the fall of 1968 but was not completed owing to the summer crisis and Mlynář's involvement in high politics. See below for the views of other team members. For a memorandum prepared by Mlynář in 1975, see Appendix E.

[5] See especially various articles in *Nová mysl*, nos. 2-4 (1968); *ŽS*, nos. 2-4 (1968); J. Kučera, *RP*, Jan. 12; S. Provazník, ibid., Jan. 18.

[6] E.g. J. Fojtík referred to the improvement in practice after the 12th and 13th congresses and cited the October Theses, but expressed dissatisfaction with the "half-measures" taken before January. It was not enough, he said "to improve the system of direction and political leadership"; it was necessary to "rebuild" it (*NM*, no. 3, 1968, pp. 275-86).

[7] Cf., for instance, the panel discussions on Radio Prague, Feb. 20 and 28; on Czechoslovak television, Feb. 29; and in *Rep.*, March 6-13, 1968.

[8] *RP*, Feb. 13; in English, R. A. Remington, ed., *Winter in Prague* (Cambridge, Mass., 1969), pp. 43-47. See also his articles, *RP*, March 14, 26, 31, April 7; and his speech at the CC plenum, ibid., April 5.

[9] *RP*, March 31.   [10] Ibid., April 5.

each of the latter institutions there must be assured "mutual control and a certain equilibrium" of its various elements, and the possibility of expressing minority opinions.[11]

Mlynář rejected the idea of an "opposition party" and also of the monopolization of power by a single party. He advocated a National Front made up both of political parties and societal organizations, which would make possible "opposition" to various policy proposals, but would exclude a struggle for power. The Communist Party would have to win the support of the other parties and organizations; if it did not, it must modify or change its proposals. This would guarantee *"real politics,"* hitherto neglected in favor of "administration of society." Certainly "formal democracy," in the sense of legal guarantees and freedom for all citizens, would be required, but a socialist democracy would also have to guarantee the expression of opinion by the masses, e.g. by the working people at their place of work. "Mass participation" of the old style had led only to "crude bureaucracy" and the suppression of fundamental rights.[12] Mlynář praised the press and public opinion for raising the issue of political reform, and regretted the failure of the existing political institutions, including the party, to become active. If they did not show themselves capable of development, he warned, public opinion might turn against the existing system and favor its destruction or replacement, rather than its "rebuilding." It was necessary to publish the Action Program at once, for this would establish the conditions for the functioning of the political system in the new situation by giving a lead and coordinating the various institutions.[13] The goal should be a stabilization of development through the establishment of "definite democratic forms and necessary democratic rules," if spontaneity and pressures were to be counteracted.[14]

REFORM OF TOP PARTY ORGANS

The need for a substantial reform of the party was recognized as a corollary of the separation of the topmost party and state functions. There existed, said one communist scholar, "a permanent crisis in the work of the supreme party organs," with the apparatus supplanting the Central Committee, and even the Presidium.[15] The January resolution

[11] Ibid., Feb. 13. [12] Ibid., March 26.
[13] Ibid., March 14. [14] Ibid., April 5.

[15] V. Mencl, in an unpublished lecture to political workers in the army, on Feb. 22, 1968, in *50 let Československa 1918/1968* (Prague, Oct. 1968), p. 76. He spoke of the relatively insignificant role played by the CC plenum, which had ceased to be "a decision-making organ," and had become "a sort of broad plenum which applauded the speeches given and demonstratively approved proposals . . . already decided beforehand, either in the Presidium or in the secretariat of the First Sec-

had assigned to the Presidium and Secretariat the task of examining the work of these organs in the spirit of the October Theses and the CC plenum discussions, and had sketched out the general principles of reform. It had also assigned to the Presidium the task of submitting proposals on the relationship of the central organs of party, state, and societal organizations, and in particular had urged a division of labor between party and state organs. The fullest exposition of the goals contemplated was given in the March report of the Presidium which, although purporting to summarize the debates in the CC plena in October, December, and January, in fact outlined the general direction of intended reforms.[16] This document reflected the discontent with past operations of the party's top organs, the critical comments made during the plenum debates, and the de facto evolution of a new pattern of action.

In the past, it was said, the CPCz Presidium had become "the supreme decision-making organ, with an excessive concentration of power which was further aggravated by the cumulation of the two highest functions in the hands of one person." Yet, according to Šik, even the Presidium had not had the time or the expertise to handle its responsibilities adequately. The Presidium must now become, concluded the report, "the executive organ of the plenum," accounting to the latter for its activity and submitting its own plan of work for approval, on the principle that the plenum was responsible for "the solution of serious questions of principle." The January resolution described the Presidium's tasks as "to discuss the basic questions linked with the elaboration, realization, and preparation of decisions of the Central Committee" and "to solve strategic and programmatic questions of the party's policy." It should function "in a collective manner" and establish better relations with the regional committees.

The CC plenum in the past had been subordinated to the Presidium and had become "not an organ for deciding, but for approving," read the report. Its members had little participation in the implementation and supervision of decisions; were poorly informed about the activity of the Presidium and other top organs; and could not freely contribute to plenum discussions. As Šik later expressed it, it must be rehabilitated as

retary" (pp. 77-78). The Presidium itself, overwhelmed by an enormous agenda, including matters of detail, was also not able to fulfill its political function. "The actual direction of political work" fell to the *aparát*, through whose individual departments the ministries worked out their proposals for the Presidium or Secretariat (pp. 74-76). For a detailed critique of the past workings of the top party organs, see O. Šik, *Kulturní noviny*, March 29; also his December CC speech, chap. vi above.

[16] Quotations are from this document (*RŠO*, pp. 7-25). See also other Presidium statements, *RŠO*, pp. 26-34. Cf. a full criticism of the CC and proposals for reform, *ŽS*, no. 8-9 (April 1968), pp. 11-14.

the "party's parliament."[17] In accordance with the party statute, the report continued, the Central Committee must become "the supreme organ between congresses" and perform the function of "directing and supervising the other party organs, including the CC Presidium, CC Secretariat, the CC secretaries and departments, and the regions, so that it could assign them the basic tasks for elaboration and realization and check up on their activity. . . ." This would be accompanied by an improvement in the operations of the Central Committee, through guarantees to all members of full information and an opportunity freely to express their opinions. Along with this enhancement of the status of the Central Committee would go an improvement of its relationship with lower party organs, involving a widening of their leeway for action in their own affairs, and a greater use of the experience of the Slovak party organs.

These changes were to be coupled with reforms in the role of other central organs, such as the Central Commission of Supervision and Auditing and the CC *aparát*. The past activity of ÚKRK was sharply criticized, especially because it was subservient to the Presidium and Secretariat and was therefore unable to exert its function of "supervision (*kontrola*)" over these bodies. It should become "to a certain extent an independent supervisory organ," exercising a kind of "oppositional (*oponentský*)" function in relation to the Central Committee and its departments, watching over their adherence to Leninist norms.[18] A study of the work of the *aparát* was also under way. It was regarded as an indispensable but "auxiliary" agency which would be subordinated to the elected party organs and would no longer usurp the latter's authority.[19] This would require a reorganization of the entire information system of the party, so as to guarantee a two-way flow of information between the Central Committee and lower party organs.[20]

These reforms were regarded as but the first steps in the process of democratizing the party and were to serve as a model for the lower party organizations. The "cumulation of functions," for instance, was to be avoided at all levels of the party's structure.[21] The Action Program recognized that the party must itself be democratized if there were to be a development of democracy in society as a whole. The main responsibility

[17] *ŽS*, no. 17 (Aug. 1968), pp. 9-12.
[18] P. Hron, head of ÚKRK, *RP*, Feb. 8 and April 13; J. Frýbert, a member, ibid., March 21. Hron's severe self-criticism was followed by his replacement by M. Jakeš, whose attitude to ÚKRK's past and future role, however, was similar to Hron's. See *Pravda*, June 14.
[19] See Dubček's speeches on March 17, in Dubček, *K otázkam obrodzovacieho procesu v KSČ* (Bratislava, 1968), p. 77, and on April 1 (*RŠO*, pp. 75, 77-78).
[20] Presidium, March 4, *RŠO*, pp. 32-33. Cf. J. Kašpar's extensive discussion of the improvements needed in the party's information system, *RP*, Feb. 29.
[21] O. Podnecký and M. Hendl, *ŽS*, no. 5 (March 1968), pp. 35-38.

for drafting the final blueprint of a democratized party was later assigned to a committee whose proposals for the revision of the party statute will be discussed below.

The Presidium devoted attention also to the relationship of the party's leading organs with those of the state, economic institutions, and non-party associations.[22] The March report was highly critical of the party's administrative-directive and bureaucratic procedures and urged the need for "a basic turn in . . . the methods of exercising its leading role" and for a consistent "development of socialist democracy in the life of the whole society."[23] Party organs must put a stop to their tendency to usurp the functions of other organs, in particular to intervention in the activity of the government. The *aparát* and its departments had often taken over decision-making and had interfered in individual ministries. The independence of the government must be guaranteed, and its area of responsibility broadened, and it must be made responsible to the National Assembly in spheres previously controlled by the party.[24] The decumulation of functions at all levels, it was said, would bring about an improvement in the position of the government, the individual ministries, the presidency, the National Assembly, the National Front and its constituent organizations, and Slovak institutions.

THE ACTION PROGRAM

The Action Program represented the first attempt at a comprehensive statement of the changes necessary to constitute "a new political system, a new model of socialist democracy."[25] "The main thing was to transform the entire political system so as to make possible the dynamic development of socialist social relations, to combine broad democracy with scientific and professionally qualified management, to strengthen the social order, to stabilize socialist relations, and to foster . . . discipline." This new concept of the political system must be worked out preparatory to the 14th congress and ultimately embodied in a revised constitution. In the meantime, measures were necessary to open the door for "the creative activity of every individual, every collective, every element of management, lower, higher, and central."

The force of this proclamation was weakened by the fact that the changes were treated as a projection of earlier efforts to broaden socialist democracy, ever since 1956, and, in particular, after the 13th congress. It was admitted, however, that even during the sixties, the party had con-

---

[22] Presidium, *RŠO*, pp. 29-30, 38, 40, 45.
[23] *RŠO*, pp. 14-15, 18-20.   [24] J. Lenárt, *RP*, March 20.
[25] For text, see *RP*, April 10; in English, Remington, ed., *Winter in Prague*. For the quotations, see pp. 97, 102 (Eng.).

tinued to be characterized by "vestiges of, and reversions to, a bureaucratic and sectarian approach," and by "an inadequate development of socialist democracy." The main cause of this had been the "excessive concentration of decision-making within the party and the extraordinary position of individuals, first and foremost of comrade A. Novotný." This in turn had affected the leading role of the party and had led to "a weakening of the initiative and responsibility of state, economic, and societal institutions."

The reformation of the political system would not mean the abandonment by the party of its vanguard role but this role would be exercised in a new way, through winning popular support rather than imposing the party's will on the population. This would assure an opportunity for all group interests to express themselves and for all individuals to participate actively in political life. It would also assign an important position to science and expertise, and facilitate the presentation of alternative policy proposals, which would presume freedom of expression and of association. Nonetheless the party would exert its influence on society not merely through its ideas and its program, but also "through its political and organizational activity, would coordinate the practical efforts of people so as to ensure that the line and program of the party were implemented in all sectors . . . of society."[26]

This would not permit, as noted in an earlier chapter (VIII), the existence of opposition parties. The National Front, consisting of the political parties and societal organizations admitted to it, would share in the making of state policy, as "partners," having "a common political program." Its constituent elements would resolve controversies over policy through "political agreement," on the basis of "a common socialist concept of the National Front policy." This explicitly excluded opposition, either outside, or within the National Front, to its general policy. The CPCz would apply "the Marxist-Leninist concept as the guiding political concept in the National Front and throughout the political system" and would "assure its supremacy through democratic political means."

The Action Program was more precise in defining the future role of the state organs. All the elements of the political system, it was stated, must occupy "a position of independence," with "a division of competence and a system of mutual control" among them. This was tantamount to the acceptance of the hitherto heretical doctrine of the

---

[26] *RŠO*, p. 81. Cf. Dubček, *NM*, No. 5 (1968), p. 533, where he wrote of "a shift from direct party management to real party leadership." Stress would be laid on "a system of direction which is substantive, programmatic, and ideological and the corresponding functions which are organizational, supervisory and to a certain extent also operative." For post-occupation critiques of the Action Program's references to the leading role of the party, see A. Vanko, *RP*, Oct. 3, 1970; J. Pečen and K. Roubal, *ŽS*, no. 8 (1970), pp. 17-19.

separation of powers and would open the way for a more autonomous participation in politics by state institutions as well as by non-party associations. It was assumed that communists in the latter would vindicate party policy by persuasion rather than by coercion and domination, as in the past. Much would depend on the degree to which, although still under party discipline, they would be able to act independently and the degree to which officers would be freely elected and would include non-communists.

Dubček's plenum report indicated his desire to bring into being as soon as possible "a well-thought-out and well-functioning system of institutions, organs, and organizations."[27] In the words of the Action Program, the National Assembly, as "a socialist parliament," must "really make laws and decide important political questions and not just approve drafts submitted to it." It must also be strengthened as an agency of control of the whole of public life, in particular in relation to the government. The government had not sufficiently exploited "the scope for independent activity of the government and individual ministers" and had attempted "to shift responsibility to party organs and to avoid independent decision-making." As "the highest executive organ of state power," it must systematically deal with the entire range of political and administrative questions. In Dubček's terms, it must become "a collective organ which really governs the Republic and fulfills the needs of society, expressed in the policy of the Communist Party and the National Front."[28] The state apparatus as a whole must become "qualified, technically efficient, and rational" and "consistently supervised by democratic means." The national committees must become "the place where the line of state policy is democratically formulated in the localities, especially the districts and regions," and must act as organs of "local autonomy and popular administration," not as "local bureaucratic offices, managing communal enterprises."

The proposals of the Action Program, if implemented, would have produced a political system much more pluralistic and democratic than in the past. Yet, as Dubček admitted, the measures proposed were but "first steps," and the future model of a functioning socialist democracy could not yet be defined. Many crucial questions, in particular the relations of the party, the other elements of the National Front, and the National Assembly in the determination of policy, and the role of the

---

[27] *RŠO*, pp. 78, 81. Cf. the CC resolution on state organs (ibid., pp. 97-98).

[28] Ibid., p. 78. "In its activity," he went on, "it must respect fully the will of the supreme organ of state power—the National Assembly—actively cooperate with it, and systematically account to it for its activity. It must gradually free itself from the excessively and unsuitably directive form of operational management of the economy and culture and be primarily an organ of long-term strategic direction and effective state administration."

National Front in the future electoral system, were left unresolved, and would in some cases require legislation. In preparing for the 14th congress, said Dubček, they would have to think through proposals "how to develop the entire political system so that, using all branches of knowledge and international experience, it would represent a much fuller combination of democracy and socialism in specific Czechoslovak conditions."[29]

THE POLITICAL SYSTEM EVOLVES IN PRACTICE

During the period from January to August the key institutions of the political system went through an evolution which brought the principles of the Action Program into life to some degree. The time was short—essentially four months from April on—and did not permit the completion of this process or its full institutionalization. Nonetheless these de facto developments gave some indication as to how the system was likely to operate in the future.

The process of reducing the concentration of power had been initiated by the separation of the two highest party and state offices and by the election to the presidency of General Svoboda who, although a party member, held no high party post and was not even a member of the Central Committee. In the past, the fusion of the party first secretaryship and the presidency had meant the subordination of the latter, since the real source of power was in the party post. Separation of the two functions did not diminish the crucial importance of the secretaryship nor significantly alter the political status of the presidency. Under the constitution the President, however, possessed substantial powers, including the supreme command of the armed forces. Although nothing is known of the extent of General Svoboda's participation in key decisions—for instance, in military questions or in bloc relations—it seems doubtful that he played an important role in policy-making prior to August. His role was mainly a symbolic one, restoring to the office some of the prestige it had enjoyed under Masaryk and Beneš, and under Zápotocký and Gottwald, by virtue of their personal reputations and a popular appeal which differed in degree in each case. In a series of major addresses in various parts of the country Svoboda identified himself fully with the Action Program and the democratization process, in particular with federalism. Addressing himself to all sectors of the population and to all regions, he invoked the national tradition of both Czechs and Slovaks and emphasized the necessity of national unity. Frequently referring to his wartime experiences, the President declared that Czechoslovakia must remain closely allied with the Soviet Union and the socialist camp.

[29] Ibid., p. 82.

In July and August this was coupled with a firm defense of Prague's course and a strong espousal of the need for the socialist states to respect Czechoslovakia's "distinctive conditions."[30] As a person who enjoyed substantial popular support and presumably the respect of the Soviet leaders, he was included in the Czechoslovak delegation to the Čierna and Bratislava conferences, and although not a member of the Presidium, reportedly played an important part in these meetings. At the time of the invasion, in a manner not anticipated, nor fully justified by his office, Svoboda stepped into the forefront of political affairs and for a short time assumed a crucial role.

The elevation in status of both government and National Assembly, and a new definition of their mutual relationship, were other features of the process of change. In March, a joint meeting of the presidium of the assembly and the government criticized "past deformations" in this relationship and called on each to fulfill its constitutional rights and at the same time to cooperate with the other in elaborating a legislative program.[31] After the formation of the Černík government and the election of Smrkovský to the chairmanship of the assembly a new relationship began to take shape, embodying the complementary and somewhat contradictory principles of "the division of powers and the mutual control of state organs."[32] Smrkovský, in his initial address as chairman of the National Assembly, declared that the government, National Assembly, and the lower organs, should not be considered "mere instruments or transmission belts, but must develop a mutual relationship, defined by well-thought-out legal provisions, of reciprocal partnership, cooperation, and positive *oponentura*." This involved the separation of "the deciding and controlling authority (of the assembly), in the fundamental questions of state policy, from the executive activity of the government and its organs. The National Assembly must carry out its supervisory function over the whole executive apparatus, especially over the government and its individual members, uncompromisingly, but on the basis of objective analysis, and in no way by improvised interventions in the latter's executive and programmatic authority, which it is necessary to respect and defend."[33]

The new government started at once to assume an influential role in policy-formation. It was to be "the supreme organ of executive state power," said Černík, and was responsible for making decisions on "the

---

[30] See his addresses at Trenčín (*RP*, July 22) and Martin (ibid., Aug. 12). For other speeches, see ibid., April 19, 23, May 11, 22-24, 27, June 3, 11-13, 24-25, July 1, 4.

[31] Ibid., March 20.

[32] Government proclamation, April 25. See also Černík, *RP*, April 10, and Dubček, ibid., April 25.

[33] *RP*, April 19.

supreme and all-embracing questions of state administration." Both the government as a whole and each individual member would be accountable to the National Assembly and would facilitate supervision by the latter by more frequent policy statements and more abundant information. Each department, he promised, would have "full authority" in its own sector and at the same time would have "concrete controlled responsibility for each decision" so as to prevent "anonymity in decision-making." The government as a whole would coordinate the activity of the central organs, but would avoid decision-making in details or any usurpation of the authority of lower organs. In the work of the state organs, bureaucratization must be avoided, and democracy must be coupled with expertness and with respect for public opinion.[34]

The exercise of the government's authority was demonstrated in the manner in which it assumed the enormous burden of implementing the Action Program as set forth in its own policy declaration in April.[35] Regular meetings were held, usually once a week, and the subjects of discussion were fully reported in the press and in frequent press conferences. Responsibility for drafting the individual legislative statutes rested with the appropriate ministries, subject to the approval of the government as a whole.

Meanwhile the National Assembly was undergoing a similar metamorphosis and was beginning to resemble a genuine parliament. More life and independence had already been apparent in the plenary sessions of January and February and in the criticism of Novotný in parliamentary committees in March.[36] Although the part played by the assembly in the removal of Novotný and in the election of Svoboda (and later of Černík and Smrkovský) was a formal one, "secret voting" was introduced for the first time in these elections, and in the last case, negative votes were cast.[37] In mid-March a special commission was appointed to study the role of the National Assembly.[38] The inadequacy of the action taken by both the assembly presidium and the government to raise the assembly's authority was censured in committees and in the plenary session.[39] At the CC plenum in April, there were a number of speeches

[34] Černík, ibid., April 9. See also Černík's interview and the government proclamation, ibid., April 10, 25, resp. Cf. the views of the former Prime Minister, Lenárt, in a television broadcast in late March, in which he criticized at length the past usurpation by the party apparatus of the government's authority in certain fields such as foreign affairs, defense, and security, and its interference in the work of the government and individual ministries, and advocated changes similar to those proposed by his successor (*Mladá fronta*, March 19).

[35] See above, chapters IX, X.

[36] *RP*, Jan. 11-12; Feb. 28-29; March 21-23, 30, resp.

[37] For the removal of Novotný, *RP*, March 30; the election of Svoboda, ibid., March 31; the election of Smrkovský, ibid., April 19; vote of confidence in Černík's government, ibid., May 4.

[38] *RP*, March 15-16.   [39] Ibid., March 28, April 24-25.

highly critical of the past practices of the assembly as "a passive transformer of the party-political line"; extensive reforms were urged to make it "a dynamic political institution in creating and implementing the policy of party and state."[40]

Under the leadership of Smrkovský, however, the assembly entered, as *Rudé právo* put it, into a "new era" and became a democratic forum of discussion and debate.[41] The spirit of the assembly was evident both in its plenary sessions and in committee meetings. The plenary session devoted to the government proclamation was extended from two to four full days, filled with vigorous criticism of this document.[42] Although in the end it was approved unanimously, many suggestions and proposals were made and the majority of them, according to Černík, were incorporated in the government's policy.[43] Subsequently assembly committees, which were reported in some detail in the press, dealt in a lively way with government policies and measures, with frequent criticisms and occasional proposals for amendment. When measures on censorship and rehabilitation were submitted to the plenary session, the debate lasted for five days. Although the draft laws were ultimately adopted, there was vigorous argument, and in the former case, a substantial negative vote, and in the latter, the proposal of a significant amendment, which was defeated.[44]

In plenary sessions and in committees, individual departments were often censured and interpellations addressed to the responsible minister. One such interpellation, by General Kodaj, with reference to the Two Thousand Words, became a major political issue. The establishment of a military and security committee and reports to it by the Ministers of Defense and of the Interior, introduced parliamentary supervision of these sensitive areas for the first time in twenty years.[45]

By the late summer the responsibility of the government to the assembly had been well established. It was not surprising nor unusual that confidence in the government was expressed and that government policy was endorsed. What *was* remarkable, in a parliament whose members were mostly communists, was the keen criticism, amendments, interpellations, and negative votes—a confrontation unique in communist parliaments. The government was "responsible" to the assembly in the sense of having to defend its policy and its specific proposals before a critical legislature

---

[40] Š. Sádovský, *RP*, April 13. Cf. speeches by F. Tymeš and B. Laštovička, ibid., April 5, 21. Cf. the criticism of the National Assembly by V. Knapp, *Lidová demokracie*, March 18; a defense of the assembly by V. Škoda, and a reply to Škoda by M. Koutecký, *Literární noviny*, Jan. 13, Feb. 3.

[41] *RP*, April 20. [42] Ibid., April 25-26, May 3-4.

[43] Černík, ibid., May 4. [44] Ibid., June 25-29.

[45] Ibid., June 7.

and of having to take account of public opinion as reflected in the attitudes of the deputies.[46] These developments occurred without any change in the membership of the assembly, which had been elected on June 14, 1964. The date of new elections had not yet been fixed but were presumably to take place sometime after the national committee elections, scheduled for late May, and at the latest ninety days after the expiry of the electoral period in June. Preparations for the local elections had begun in January, but had been accompanied, it was said, by the persistence of old habits, for instance in selecting candidates.[47] There was criticism of the undemocratic character of the electoral law of November 1967, under which the elections were to be conducted.[48] Demands for the postponement of the elections were raised by party organizations, by parliamentary deputies, and by the press.[49] In April the Central Committee responded by proposing the deferral of the national committee elections to an unspecified date, at the latest in the fall.[50] There was a persistent anomaly in the continuance in office of those elected under pre-1967 procedures; yet it was equally inappropriate to hold the proposed elections under procedures which did not reflect the post-January democratization process. The need for a thorough revision of the electoral law; the as yet undefined role of the National Front; the impending federal reorganization of the state; the uncertain future of the regional committees; the possible establishment of a multicameral legislature—all these were additional factors suggesting the desirability of further postponement.[51] By late June it was decided to extend the period of tenure of the national committees, the assembly, and the Slovak National Council until elections were held, at the latest by the end of 1968.[52] In the meantime, the recall of individual deputies was theoretically possible, but only under a complicated procedure which in fact made this a remote possibility. Hence the National Assembly remained unchanged in its composition during the Prague spring, but nonetheless moved ahead with the program of reform.

[46] For comments on the successful exercise of the assembly's supervisory functions vis-à-vis the government, S. Vosecký, *Rep.*, July 10-17, pp. 8-9; also Smrkovský's interview, *Kulturní tvorba*, June 27. Cf. the bitter post-occupation attacks on the assembly in 1968 by V. Čermák, *Tribuna*, Sept. 17, 1969 and by B. Machačová-Dostálová, *ŽS*, no. 41 (1969), pp. 8-9. According to the latter, the assembly had pursued a policy independent of the party and had elevated itself above the party.

[47] V. Vedra, J. Meško, and the Central Electoral Commission report, *RP*, Feb. 20, 28, March 13, resp.

[48] Z. Kryštůfek, *Rep.*, April 17-24, pp. 6-8; M. Lakatoš, *KN*, March 15.

[49] Sádovský, *RP*, April 4. See also D. Plichta, *LL*, March 21.

[50] Sádovský, *RP*, April 4; CC decision, *RŠO*, pp. 94-95.

[51] Mlynář, *NM*, no. 5 (1968), pp. 626-27. He had initially opposed postponement, *RP*, March 26. Cf. his 1975 memorandum (Appendix E).

[52] Ibid., June 27; *Sbírka zákonů*, no. 83/1968.

THE NATIONAL FRONT

The performance of the National Front after 1948 was severely condemned, and the need for substantial reform was generally recognized.[53] To some extent there was a desire to revive the pattern characteristic of the years 1945 to 1948, although without the "struggle for power" which had culminated in February 1948. By the summer of 1968, however, the role of the National Front was still obscure and ambiguous. It was graphically described by a prominent Slovak writer as "a sleeping beauty."[54] Throughout the months from March on, its part had been largely nominal, limited to ratifying the Action Program and the government's program; confirming the party's nominations for the presidency, the government, the assembly's officers, and even of its own head, Kriegel; and later approving the composition of the Czech National Council. Its ceremonial meeting in June indicated that the front and its constituent organizations were ready to accept the leading role of the Communist Party and to endorse the concept of the front sketched out in the Action Program.[55] Thereafter work proceeded on the statute which was to define the front's position in political life and its relationship to the state, but was not completed until after the occupation, in late September.[56]

There was uncertainty as to the eventual composition of the National Front. Officially the desirability of the continued existence of the noncommunist parties was recognized and the National Front was regarded as a medium of cooperation of these parties and the mass associations with the ruling Communist Party. One thing had been made quite clear, namely, that political activity would be permissible only within the front and on the basis of its agreed program. On the part of some there was a strong feeling that the front should be "an open organization" in which other political forces should ultimately take part.[57] The official view was

[53] For instance B. Šimon spoke of the "stagnation, torpidity, and formality" of the National Front in the past and described its future role as "a partner-like rivalry of conceptions and qualified comradely *oponentura*" (*RP*, May 31). O. Klokoč said that the National Front had in fact "died" and had existed on paper only. It must now return to its original concept, with each element having its own life, and the CP being first among equals (*Pravda*, June 13). For other criticisms of the past and advocacy of reforms, see *RP*, April 6, and *Pravda*, April 7; Lakatoš, *KN*, April 5; Pithart, *LL*, April 18.

[54] J. Blažková, *Kultúrny život*, June 14.

[55] E.g. see the speeches by A. Pospíšil, *LD*, June 16, and B. Kučera, *Svobodné slovo*, June 16. See also above, chaps. IX, X.

[56] E. Erban, *RP*, June 27; S. Olšák, *SS*, July 26. The draft statute was ready in early August but was not made public (*RP*, Aug. 8, 15).

[57] Z. Pinc, *LL*, April 11; *KŽ*, June 28; J. Křen, *RP*, July 8. The idea of permitting political organizations outside the National Front, advanced by Křen, is said to have been approved by the Prague municipal party conference in July, but this was not reported in the *Rudé právo* account. See J. Pokštefl, in V. V. Kusin, ed., *The Czechoslovak Reform Movement 1968* (London, 1973), p. 170.

that new parties could come into existence only with the permission of the front, and on condition that their programs were consonant with that of the front. A reformed social democracy, as we have seen, was not to be permitted. Neither KAN nor K 231, both of which aspired to become members, although not to become political parties, had even been registered as legal organizations, let alone admitted to the front.[58] Their preparatory committees existed therefore in a kind of limbo of semi-legality, and were treated by some as illegal. In July several deputies, including Kriegel, Bil'ak, Kučera, and Pospíšil, proposed, as a matter of urgency, in view of the forthcoming federalization, the adoption of a constitutional law on the National Front which would regulate the formation and the activity of political parties on the basis of the front's statute, which in turn would set the conditions for membership. This proposal was adopted by the constitutional and legal committee of the assembly but had not been submitted to the plenary session by the time of the occupation.[59]

As for the interest organizations, a large number were already members of the front.[60] The original idea of differentiating the main mass associations from groups with a narrower range of interest was apparently dropped. It was probable, however, that only associations such as the

[58] According to A. I. Simon, in "Czechoslovakia's KAN: A Brief Venture in Democracy," *East Europe* 18 (June 1969), 20-22, KAN was orally promised admission to the front but on condition that the organization be "legalized." K 231, in direct negotiations with the government, had reached an agreement in mid-June that it would be recognized as legitimate but that it would wind up its activities after rehabilitation had been carried out. See Jaroslav Brodsky, "Czechoslovakia's 231 Club," ibid., pp. 23, 25.

[59] The proposal also provided for a decision by the Supreme Court, on the request of the National Front, as to "whether an organization which is not yet a NF member has or does not have the character of a political party." The text was not available except as reported in brief form in *RP*, July 10. A somewhat different version of this proposal, ascribed to Mlynář, is given in *Svědectví*, no. 38 (1970), p. 184, n. 15. See also P. Janyr, *LL*, July 25.

The statute ultimately adopted in September (*Sb. z.*, 128/1968) provided that "political parties and organizations fulfilling the same functions may act only as members of the National Front." If not approved by the front, such a party or organization would be banned by the Ministry of the Interior, subject to an appeal to a regional court within thirty days. This, it was explained, "closed" the "pluralistic system of the National Front," preventing activity outside it.

[60] In addition to the political parties, the National Front, as of mid-June, included the Central Council of Unions; the youth, women's, and cooperative peasants' unions; the Coordinating Committee of the Creative Unions; Magyar, Polish, and Ukrainian cultural associations; the Unions of Czechoslovak-Soviet Friendship, Anti-fascist Fighters, and Cooperation with the Army; the Central Council of Cooperatives; the Red Cross; the Scientific-Technical Society; the Unions of Physical Culture, Fire Fighting, and Invalids; the Committee of Defenders of the Peace; and the Socialist Academy. For this, and other documents, see *Informační zpravodaj Ústředního výboru Národní fronty* (Prague, Oct. 1968), published for internal use.

trade unions, the agricultural and youth organizations (eventually to be formed), and the creative unions would play a significant political role.

These uncertainties concerning the future composition of the front were compounded by lack of clarity as to its role in policy-making. Leading spokesmen had repeatedly stressed the significance of the front as a forum for the presentation of conflicting opinions, for the defense of the particular interests of its component organizations, and for ultimate agreement on the general line of policy to be followed.[61] Both the Socialist and the People's Parties anticipated a position of independent partnership in the front where they could express their distinctive viewpoints and hopefully influence policy. This assumed a willingness on the part of the Communist Party to modify its own proposals to meet the views of other parties and organizations and the capacity of the latter to influence, or even reject, communist proposals. It was unclear how the process of unification of views would be accomplished and what methods would be available for overcoming unresolved disagreements. It seemed likely that the party would usually be able to vindicate its own stand unless the other participating elements acquired greater power and independence than they had yet manifested.

Finally, the role of the National Front in elections had not been determined. The electoral law was not completed by August 21 and many questions remained open.[62] Since presumably the only participants in elections would be the approved components of the front and opposition parties would not be permitted, much would depend on whether any other parties and organizations were to be admitted to the National Front and how strong these would become. The front's part in confirming candidates and in determining the distribution of seats among the parties and organizations would also be defined in its statute, which, it may be assumed, would permit a certain degree of personal competition among candidates but would exclude unrestricted competition among rival parties and organizations.

THE PARTY: DE FACTO CHANGE

The commanding position of the party in political life was maintained intact from January to August, but its leadership was exercised in an unusual manner. As already noted, the government and assembly were able to act with a new independence and enjoyed an enhanced influence

[61] Kriegel, *RP*, April 7, 9, June 19; Dubček, and others, ibid,, June 16.

[62] Personal conversations with Slavík in May 1968 and with V. Šimek, official of the National Front, in October 1968, indicated that no decision had been reached as to whether there would be single or multi-member constituencies, whether there would be joint candidacies with a preferential vote, and whether there would be a kind of primary procedure in nominations.

in the detailed formulation and implementation of policy. Public opinion, and the views of the party rank and file, began to have some effect on the party's decisions, either directly, in the press and through public discussion, or indirectly, through the National Assembly, the Central Committee, and the lower organs of the party. The abolition of the traditional "*kádrový strop*" (cadre ceiling) which had prevented the holding of leading posts by non-communists, and of the "*nomenklatura*" system, which had given the party at various levels unfettered authority in all appointments,[63] made possible greater participation of non-communists in all spheres. The Communist Party, whose reputation had been seriously weakened by the revelation of its past crimes and mistakes, began gradually to recover its prestige, and as a result of its resistance to the pressures from Moscow, its authority became genuinely popular.

Nonetheless the party continued to hold a position of hegemony, without effective challenge from any other source. Although the personal fusion of the topmost posts had been terminated, party and state were still merged as a result of the domination of all state organs by high-ranking party persons. The supreme party organs, moreover, continued to be superior to governmental institutions in the governance of the country. The general line of policy, as adumbrated in the Action Program, and the crucial policy decisions all emanated from the topmost party organs and were not basically modified by state agencies. The selection of the key political leaders, such as the President and the Prime Minister, were made by the party's Presidium and then endorsed by assembly and government. Although much was said of the enhanced role of non-communists, their part was minimal, both in the government and the National Assembly, and in the National Front.[64]

Perhaps more significant were the changes within the party itself, in the functioning of its supreme organs, and in their relationship with lower organs and the members. This is not to imply that new methods of party work were accepted readily or were fully implemented. Functionaries and members, accustomed to the old ways, found it difficult to adjust and suffered uncertainty and fear, so that the process of change was slowed down. Yet progress was noticeable at all levels.

Dubček, as First Secretary, unquestionably remained the dominant figure, but was by no means as "all-powerful" as his predecessors. His was not a leadership based on "a firm hand"; indeed in some respects he was weak and indecisive. His lifelong experience as an *apparatchik*, ac-

[63] F. Zdobina, *RP*, July 23; M. Hysko, *Nové slovo*, July 25, 1968, resp. See the criticism of the *nomenklatura* system by Selucký, *Práce*, March 14.

[64] The formation of the Czech National Council was an interesting foretaste of change. The commission of the National Assembly, whose report was confirmed by the National Front, sought to select members in a representative manner and chose 85 CPCz members of the total of 150 (Kriegel, *RP*, July 11, 1968).

customed to wield power through the party and its organizational network, rather than through public opinion and non-party institutions, hampered his evolution as an authentic political leader. Nonetheless Dubček exhibited many democratic qualities, making himself accessible to the public, calling in many persons for consultation, and, on occasion, yielding to pressures of party opinion, for example, in respect of the calling of the 14th congress. His own decency and modesty, his articulation of deep national desires, and later his firmness toward Soviet demands, made him a popular national leader, even charismatic in his appeal. Although he lacked all the attributes of a demagogue or a dictator, he emerged as a real political personality, in a country, it was said, which for almost twenty years had known only the "cult of the personality."[65]

The Presidium continued to be the crucial wielder of power, both in the party and within the political system as a whole. Like executive bodies everywhere, it acted as an inner cabinet, meeting in secret, and determining the major lines of policy. Yet in contrast to its own tradition and the practice of other communist party presidia, it made a substantial effort to establish relations with the public, announcing regularly the agenda and the decisions of its weekly meetings. Its membership, although formally elected, was in reality co-opted and was not radically changed in successive reshuffles after January. Since it included persons of widely differing views, from conservative to progressive, the Presidium was weakened in its effort to exercise leadership and often took compromise decisions which papered over differences. Although sharp debates presumably occurred, divergencies were not revealed to the public. Even in the final months of crisis when the Presidium appeared to act in unity in opposition to Soviet pressure significant fissures in its ranks were forming behind the scenes.

The metamorphosis of the Central Committee was more pronounced. True, it did not meet at all until the end of March, and then only twice more prior to the invasion. Its composition remained almost entirely unchanged, apart from a few resignations and suspensions in April and May. Nor could it be said to have become a controlling, or even supervisory, body vis-à-vis the Presidium. In fact its decisions were almost all mere confirmations of those already taken by the Presidium or ÚKRK; its resolutions were adopted in their original version and reflected the contents of Dubček's opening reports. The Central Committee did approve the reform program but also adopted more conservative documents, such as the May plenum resolution. Yet later it endorsed firm resistance to Soviet pressure, and at its meeting in July after the Warsaw letter, gave unanimous acclamation of the policy presented by Dubček.

[65] *RP*, April 1.

What distinguished its other two sessions, in April and May, was the unusual, wide-ranging debate, reported in some detail in the press. Although these plenary sessions always culminated in unanimous approval of all policies, with no amendments submitted and no negative votes recorded, and did not lead to significant changes in leadership, they were valuable in transmitting to the latter the conflicting streams of party opinion and revealing to the public wide variations of viewpoints in its ranks. This transformation in the Central Committee, already initiated de facto in the turmoil of debate before January, was to be institutionalized in the form of "rules of procedures."[66]

The other high party organs experienced less noticeable but potentially important changes. ÚKRK, according to its new chief, Jakeš, ceased to be "a kind of gendarme," with the right to take disciplinary measures against members and concentrated on a study of its future role, the reexamination of earlier disciplinary measures, and the supervision of the observance of the party statute.[67] The Secretariat, whose membership was completely renovated, did not on the surface alter its pattern of activity. Its administrative arm, the CC central apparatus, drew some of the sharpest censure, particularly for its domination of the party and its elected organs in the past, and direct intervention in all spheres of public life.[68] Dubček and other leaders spoke of the indispensability of the apparatus, but also stressed the urgent need for its reform.[69] The demand most often raised was that the higher *apparatchiki* should become specialists, knowledgeable in management theory and other social sciences, and should serve, rather than run, the party.[70] The apparatus should no longer duplicate state agencies nor exercise a determining influence on all governmental affairs.

Apart from personnel shifts, the most important actual changes in the apparatus were the formation of a Department for Societal Organizations, and a Unit for Information Processing, Planning, and Management,[71] and the abolition of the Department for State Administration, which had previously supervised the military and security organs. Nonetheless the apparatus, and the Secretariat to which it was immediately responsible, remained influential in preparing the Action Program, the

[66] Proposed rules given by K. Mazač, *ŽS*, no. 11 (May 1968), pp. 48-51.

[67] ÚKRK meeting, *RŠO*, p. 224; M. Jakeš, *Pravda*, July 18, and *RP*, July 25.

[68] R. Selucký, *Práce*, March 14; E. Löbl, *KŽ*, May 24; M. Hysko, *NS*, July 25, and *Pravda*, June 1.

[69] Dubček (n. 19 above); Slavík, *RP*, April 24.

[70] J. Kučera, *RP*, March 1, 5.

[71] *RŠO*, p. 154. Jan Kašpar, its head, gave a long, sophisticated analysis of the functions of the information unit, which was to gather, process, and evaluate information, with the aid of computers, for the use of the party in its decision-making (*NM*, no. 8, 1968, pp. 1002-10).

party statutes, and the major documents of the CC plena and the forthcoming congress. There was, however, a greater share in this work by persons from outside the apparatus, especially by members of the scholarly teams and other intellectuals. The apparatus continued to be authoritative in cadre policy at the highest level, but lost control of many appointments and elections, for instance, of regional and district secretaries and congress delegates. It also lost some of its influence over the lower party organizations, the mass media, and non-party organizations, but still possessed a powerful weapon in its control of the distribution of information within the party.

Changes at the lower levels of the party organization, at the district and regional level, and in the membership meetings, were even more noteworthy. In January and February these had functioned in the old way, meeting only to endorse the January resolution. Two successive sets of district and regional conferences in March-April and June-July, however, were marked by unusual features—open expression of conflicting views, pungent criticism of local and even higher leaders, and democratic and secret elections. As a result local leaderships were often replaced. For instance, more than 71 percent of the members and candidates of regional committees were new. In the Prague municipal committee only seven of the previous seventy-six were reelected.[72] Of the leading district secretaries, thirteen resigned or were removed, and nine others were newly elected.[73] Rules of procedure, as well as reforms of the apparatus, were also introduced at the regional level.[74] Moreover, discussions in the local conferences and resolutions adopted sometimes had a noticeable effect on party policy, leading to a reversal of position, for instance, in regard to the date of the congress.

THE PARTY'S CONSTITUTION

The necessity of a fundamental reform in the party was recognized in the January resolution, and the need for appropriate changes in its statute was noted in the Action Program. The May plenum had devoted little attention to this theme but had appointed a working group to prepare a new statute for the consideration of the 14th congress. Šik, in his CC speech, had been one of the few to discuss the subject, noting the absence of "guarantees of democracy, built into the system, both within the party and outside."[75] In the discussion of the statute in the party press from mid-June on, rank-and-file members were alerted to what Martin Vaculík called the idea of "a radical reconstruction" of the party, in the

[72] *ŽS*, no. 12 (June 1968), p. 12.   [73] *RP*, Aug. 8.
[74] Ibid., June 22; *Průboj*, April 19.   [75] *RP*, June 5.

form of its democratization.[76] As one scholar put it, "the party had ceased to be a living democratic organism . . . and had become . . . a mechanism, a hierarchical structure of varied organs and *aparáts*, surrounded by a membership condemned to passivity." It must reform and regenerate itself and become "a modern political organization open to the society whose trust it seeks."[77]

The provisions of the draft statute reflected ideas raised in the discussion and the de facto changes which were occurring in the party's functioning, and as noted above, reflected the different perspectives of the working group and the Indra committee to which it was responsible.[78] It was the spirit, not the structure, of the party which was to be affected.

The definition of the responsibilities of the higher organs reflected in some degree the actual changes in their operation. The congress was defined as "the supreme organ," responsible for "setting the general line (*koncepce*) and tactics." The Central Committee was to be "the supreme organ" between congresses, responsible for "determining action for the solution of political, economic, ideological, cultural, and social problems." The Presidium in turn was described as the executive organ of the Central Committee which "elaborates questions of general strategy, ensures the fulfillment of the tasks flowing from the decisions of the congress and the Central Committee and carries on activity entrusted to it by the Central Committee." The responsibility of the Presidium to the Central Committee, and of the latter to the congress, was asserted. The Secretariat was assigned the task of "operative fulfillment" of tasks derived from decisions of the CC and the Presidium and of "organizing the current activity of the *aparát*," and was responsible to the Central Committee. The control commissions, including ÚKRK, were described as "impartial organs of supervision not dependent on the directing organs" and were designed to supervise the process of policy-making, protect the democratic principles of the party's activity and the observance of the statutes, and check on party finances.

Space prevents detailed examination of other features of the draft statute or extended comparison with the original version. In the preamble the party was defined in new terms as "a voluntary union of progressive, politically active members of all social strata (*vrstvy*) who have associated to implement in their country the programmatic aims of so-

---

[76] *Večerní Praha*, Aug. 1.

[77] J. Opat, in a lecture given in April 1968, in *50 let Československa*, pp. 15-17.

[78] See above, chaps. X, XI. For the text of the statute, and the original version, see J. Pelikán, ed., *Tanky proti sjezdu* (Vienna, 1970), pp. 137-82; in English, *The Secret Vysočany Congress* (London, 1971), pp. 128-87. Citations are translated from the Czech edition owing to faults in the English version. For the party statutes adopted in 1962 and 1966, see above, chap. V.

cialism and communism and thus to create the conditions for the full emancipation of man."[79] The fresh tone was perhaps most striking in the way in which democratic centralism was defined as embracing "the democratic formation of the party's program and political line . . . ; the confrontation of opinions and judgments on varied suggestions by communists and non-communists; participation of party members and the lower links of the organizational structure in the formation and implementation of party policy . . . ; an equal opportunity for all party members to express their standpoints toward the party's policy, to defend their views in party organizations, to make proposals and to criticize any members, organization or organ whatever" (para. 1).

Many other provisions of the statute—democratic election of officers (by secret ballot); the ban on the holding of several party, state, and other public posts; required rotation of officers; independence of lower party organs, etc.—provided evidence of its new content. The most notable break with the past, however, was effected by the measures to safeguard the rights of a minority viewpoint. "In the spirit of democratic centralism," read paragraph 3, "the minority is subordinate to the majority opinion and carries out decisions that are made." The minority, however, had "the right to formulate its own standpoints and to request that they be recorded in the minutes; to persist in their view and to request, on the basis of new information and the testing in practice of a decision taken, a fresh examination of their standpoints." "The organization of minority supporters, outside the framework of the statute, or the formation of groupings of party members with their own fractional discipline, is impermissible." Members and party organizations, however, may arrange, with the permission of higher party organs, "joint conferences to coordinate their activity or to elaborate standpoints or alternative proposals" (para. 6). Although these provisions were somewhat less innovative than those made by the working group, they constituted an unusual protection of those holding a minority viewpoint, who were expressly safeguarded against any but "ideological measures . . . as long as their opinions were not in fundamental conflict with the program and the statutes of the party" (para. 3).[80]

Party opinion was divided on this question. In a mid-July poll 49 percent favored provisions for protecting the right of the minority, 20 percent were against, and 30 percent were uncertain. However, 60 percent

---

[79] Cf. the 1962 statute, chap. V above.

[80] The original version also included the right of the minority to demand the publication of its opinions and allowed members to "group themselves temporarily," without the requirement of higher approval. Organizations were also permitted to "associate temporarily," after informing the competent higher organ of their intention (paras. 5, 21, 23). One discussant even suggested a suspensive veto for a minority (ŽS, no. 17, Aug. 1968, pp. 48-50).

believed that minority opinions should be published in the party press. Most party members (69 percent) believed that a minority was bound to fulfill party decisions, but a large majority (77 percent) agreed with the right of a minority to group together temporarily. There were slight differences between Slovak and Czech party opinion on these questions. A somewhat larger minority in Slovakia (28 percent as compared to 17 in the Czech lands) opposed provisions to protect a minority; a somewhat smaller majority (69 percent as compared to 81) favored the right to form groupings.[81]

Other clauses of the statute were reminiscent of former versions. For instance, the preamble of the final draft strongly emphasized the party's "leading political role" in the National Front, which "it constantly renews on the basis of unceasing initiative in the realm of ideas and politics and political organizational activity."[82] Other traditional features, such as the binding character of decisions and the necessity of discipline, were also contained in the original version. Certain provisions of the latter, however, were omitted, such as one that made meetings of the basic organizations generally open to the public, and another which gave a member the right to work in a party organization either at his place of work or at his place of residence.[83] The proposal to have "councils of elders" at the district and the all-national levels, as advisory bodies, was also dropped. In a somewhat ambiguous formulation which was broader than in the original version and in effect approximated previous statutes, the basic party organizations were "to direct communists" in public organs and societal organizations "toward an energetic activity in the fulfillment of tasks and of the special mission of these organizations and organs." At higher levels the party's right to direct elected deputies was even more explicit.[84] The original draft's provision for direct elections

[81] *RP*, Aug. 18. In August a poll of 1,905 CPCz members indicated an even more favorable attitude to minority rights. On the duty to fulfill decisions, 73 percent favored it; 36 percent did not. On the right to defend a minority position within the party and demand a new debate, 72 favored it; an additional 24 percent approved the right to defend this position outside the party also; only 4 percent "did not know." On the publication of minority opinion, 79 percent favored it; 18 percent did not. Very large majorities also favored various forms of greater independence for lower party organs. See Jaroslaw A. Piekalkiewicz, *Public Opinion Polling in Czechoslovakia, 1968-69* (New York, 1972), pp. 148-50.

[82] The preliminary draft had referred to the party "striving to gain" the leading role by "unceasing renewal of the confidence of the workers, by initiative in ideas and policy and by the creation of conditions for the fulfillment of the progressive interests of all classes and strata."

[83] The final draft provided that committees could call public meetings on important questions (para. 25). It stipulated that a communist should "in principle" be organized at his place of work, but permitted this at his place of residence with the approval of the basic organization (para. 17).

[84] Communist deputies were required to "work under the leadership" of the appropriate party committee and "in accord with its decisions." See paras. 28, 34, 44, 52.

of the highest party organs was replaced by election of congress delegates by the two national territorial organizations; of the CC by the congress; and of the Presidium and Secretariat by the CC. This flew in the face of the opinion of the overwhelming majority of party members (79 percent) who favored direct election of the highest organs.[85]

DEBATE OVER PLURALISM

Parallel with the day-to-day evolution of the political system and official planning of its reform, an intense debate went on in the press and on radio and television concerning the future political "model," in particular the "guarantees" of a socialist democracy. In the initial phase, until March, these discussions, conducted mainly by communist intellectuals, indicated a general consensus on the desirability of a form of limited "pluralism," confined within the framework of the party's leading position. This was regarded as a better way to achieve democracy than a multi-party system or an "opposition."[86] By mid-March, however, the latter ideas were being advanced, particularly by non-communist spokesmen, but also by prominent communist scholars, as the only guarantees of a real democracy and genuine pluralism and became the subject of heated discussion and of official condemnation.[87]

The first major statements in favor of a political opposition were made by two well-known non-communist writers, Alexander Kliment and Václav Havel, in *Literární listy*.[88] Kliment's essay was a plea to bring

[85] *RP*, Aug. 20. According to this poll, a majority of party members (57 percent) favored a secret ballot in all elections, including those of the highest organs, whereas 20 percent favored this for the highest offices only, but preferred to leave the matter open for the basic organizations. A large majority (77 percent) felt that there should be more candidates than vacancies in elections, and only 14 percent preferred the alternative of write-ins by the individual. For other polls of party opinion on the statute, see ibid., Aug. 15.

[86] Cf., for instance, the panel discussions on Prague radio, Feb. 28; Prague television, Feb. 29; and in *Rep.*, March 6-13, 1968, pp. i-viii. In all three cases, Mlynář cast doubt on the merits of a multi-party system and argued for the democratization of the party and democratic reconstruction of the political system along the lines indicated above. Other participants differed on the subject, but none strongly advocated a multi-party system.

[87] For this discussion, see Pavel Tigrid, *Le printemps de Prague* (Paris, 1968), chaps. 5 and 6; Leopold Grünwald, *ČSSR im Umbruch* (Vienna, 1968); Meissner, *Moderne Welt*, no. 2 (1970), pp. 141-43, 151-56. For translation of several important contributions, A. Oxley, A. Pravda and A. Ritchie, eds., *Czechoslovakia: The Party and the People* (London, 1973), part 4. For post-occupation critiques, see Jiří Hájek, *Mýtus a realita ledna 1968* (Prague, 1970), chap. 6; M. Formánek, "How Theory Contributed to the Destruction of the Political System of the ČSSR," *NM*, no. 8 (1970), pp. 1103-10, and L. Hrzal and M. Štěpanová, *ŽS*, no. 25 (1970), pp. 36-38.

[88] Kliment, "The Activity of the Unnamed," *LL*, March 14 and Havel, "On the Theme of Opposition," ibid., April 4 (in English, Remington, ed., *Winter in Prague*, pp. 64-71).

the non-communists (or non-party people) out of their "atomized isolation" and to facilitate their participation in politics. This would involve the growth of "an opposition of our own specific type," which would not be based on "class interests" nor seek to destroy the state or take over power, but would "cooperate in guaranteeing the state's democratic character." The opposition would have to establish itself by its own efforts and draft its own program.

Havel went even further, advocating a two-party model and calling for the formation of a "democratic party" based on "Czechoslovak democratic and humanist traditions." He did not consider the force of public opinion nor the democratization of the party to be adequate guarantees of democracy. Nor did he find sufficient safeguards in the participation of unorganized independent individuals, or societal organizations, in which non-communists exerted strong influence, nor in the revival of the seriously compromised non-communist parties. The only assurance was "a real choice . . . where the people have the possibility—from time to time—freely to select those who will govern them." This presumed the existence of at least "two independent, equal, and mutually independent political forces, each of which has the same chance of becoming the leading force in the state, if the people so decide."

A more radical stance was taken by Ivan Sviták, Marxist philosopher and ex-communist, who became a special target of attack by party spokesmen and later by Soviet propagandists.[89] He minced no words in stating that no essential structural changes had so far been made and that the Czechoslovak system remained a totalitarian dictatorship.[90] In a celebrated speech, "With Head Against the Wall," he set forth a detailed analysis of the nature of totalitarian dictatorship, which he termed "our enemy number 1," and appealed for a movement "from a totalitarian dictatorship to an open society." "We want democracy, not democratization. Democratization is a minimal program on the way to democracy." The aim must be to eliminate the monopoly of power by means of elections—free, secret, and democratic—"with a competition of alternative programs and personalities."[91]

In two major addresses to KAN groups, Sviták proposed the building of at least two new parties, on a Christian and socialist basis, which would provide "a healthy opposition to the communist program."[92] He severely criticized the existing non-communist "shadow parties" and

---

[89] See attacks by Z. Šulc and D. Kolder, *RP*, June 14, 21; the latter in English, in Remington, ed., *Winter in Prague*, pp. 80-86.

[90] *SS*, July 12.

[91] *Student*, April 10, 17 (partial text, Remington, pp. 73-80). For many of his articles and speeches in 1968, see Sviták, *The Czechoslovak Experiment, 1968-1969* (New York, 1971).

[92] *Student*, May 1, June 19.

condemned the banning of a Social Democratic Party. In his view, a new party would not be anti-communist but would form a partnership with the Communist Party. Free elections would involve separate lists and independent candidates and would be conducted according to rules defined in a new electoral law. Such procedures would in fact lead to the replacement of all existing deputies. Replying to the fear of opposition expressed in ruling circles, he said: "Without a political opposition there is no democracy. . . ." "A real opposition toward the past, which is not identical to an opposition to the Communist Party, nor with opposition to socialism, will penetrate both the center of power, the Communist Party, and the spontaneously emerging organizations and the National Front."

In a later article in *Literární listy*, Sviták expressed the opinion that the Communist Party could only win in free elections if it were able to change from "a military-bureaucratic organization into a civilian (*občanský*) party that respects fundamental human rights" and "the sovereignty of the people as the source of all power." The progressive communists, side by side with the non-communists, "could win an election on a program acceptable to the great majority of the nation" if its candidates were "people of a new type" for whom the non-communists could vote in good conscience.[93]

The Club of the Non-party Engagés had its own distinctive concept of a new political model that would replace the struggle for power by "constant confrontation of opinions, ideas and conceptions, an operative and free-flowing choice of the most suitable solutions of social, political, and economic problems, and . . . a natural selection of the morally and technically best qualified individuals as leading personalities." This would require an electoral system guaranteeing to all political parties and organizations the right to present candidates, and permitting also independent candidates, and would lead eventually, it was hoped, to a political model *without* political parties. The National Front was considered faulty in its very essence since it represented a system where decisions were made "behind the scenes (*kabinetní*)." It was in the parliament or government, however, that agreements should be reached. As for opposition, this was "a structural necessity" in almost all states, which could be eliminated or reduced if genuine possibilities of dialogue and participation in decision-making existed. The club itself did not seek to form either a parliamentary or extra-parliamentary opposition and hoped for "a state without opposition."[94]

Several legal scholars, notably Michal Lakatoš, Petr Pithart, and Ivan

[93] *LL*, July 18.
[94] An unpublished "Draft Perspective Program of the Club of the Non-party Engagés" (typescript).

Bystřina, put the case for a democratic system in somewhat different terms. Lakatoš contended that the guarantee of democratic government was to be found, not in a mere separation of functions or a change of personnel, but in what he called "civil (*občanský*) society."[95] This comprised, first, the societal organizations and parties in the National Front which ought to be autonomous genuine exponents of the varied interests they were supposed to represent and, second, the state representative bodies, which ought to be formed in elections based on "free choice." The National Front, although admittedly "dead," was a reality, and must be revived as "a real platform for the coordination and integration of a pluralist system." The representative bodies, as "the wheels of civil society," must cease to be mere transmission belts and "as autonomous organs of civil society," and responsible to it, should determine the line of state policy and supervise its execution.

Lakatoš rarely used the term "opposition" and when he did, usually referred to the "institutionalized opposition" within the National Front such as had existed from 1945 to 1948. Moreover, he accepted the necessity of the party as a vanguard whose authority would be based on its cognitive function of comprehending social and economic development and on its ability to coordinate and integrate the interests of civil society.[96] In a symposium in *Kulturní noviny*, however, he argued strongly for an opposition as a means of pressure on the making of policy and as a control over political direction. "Without an opposition political democracy simply cannot exist." Yet to be effective, the opposition must be "institutionalized" and must enjoy the elementary democratic conditions of freedom of speech and assembly.[97]

Petr Pithart, of the Faculty of Law of Charles University and a member of the Mlynář team, was a warm advocate of a multi-party system which, with freedom of speech, he regarded as the two conditions of Czechoslovak democracy. He was critical of the idea that the struggle for power was an evil that must be avoided. "The struggle of political parties for power is . . . the most reliable, although perhaps an imperfect, mechanism for the control of power that has yet been found." This argument presupposed more than one party, preferably more than two, since if there were only two parties, one would tend to become exclusively "oppositional." The formation of new parties should not, he thought, be in the hands of the National Front, whose members had a vested interest in discouraging competition, but should be defined in law by the National Assembly. Pithart was a sharp critic of the National Front for

[95] See especially his articles, *KN*, Feb. 24, April 5, 26. See also Lakatoš, *SS*, July 21.
[96] *KN*, Feb. 24.
[97] *KN*, April 19. Cf. Lakatoš's book, published after the occupation, *Úvahy o hodnotách demokracie* (Prague, 1968). See above, chap. v.

another reason, namely, that it would make parliament a mere "decoration," reduced to elaborating the legislative details of matters decided beforehand, in a secret manner, by the National Front. "A serious political line simply cannot be formed in two centers," he wrote; "either the National Front or parliament (and the government) will not function."[98]

Bystřina, who was also a member of the Mlynář team, in an unpublished contribution to the team's planned symposium, advocated a pluralist political system which would assure participation by several independent political parties, by interest organizations not subject to party control, and by economic enterprises and work collectives. He defended the right of "political opposition" and distinguished this from "a mere *oponentura* to the views of a governing majority," or "the defense of an alternative standpoint within the framework of the majority." Opposition he defined as the right to put forward programs for majority support and to seek to become "the leading force" in the state. Like Pithart, he opposed any limitations on the formation of political parties or organizations except in the form of law.[99]

The conception of political pluralism expounded by several other legal scholars, notably Zdeněk Mlynář and Vladimír Klokočka, was more moderate than those discussed above and closer to the spirit of the Action Program. Under the influence of the work of his team and some of its more radical members, Mlynář had apparently come to accept a model of pluralism that went beyond the official line, but continued to express more restrained views in public utterances. In May, in an important article in *Nová mysl*, although referring to a new system that would be the product of "radical reform," he still declined to identify political pluralism with a multi-party system and with opposition outside the National Front. He admitted that a two-party model was logically preferable and should certainly not be excluded, but felt that it was not suitable "in our situation" and that there was enough room "in principle" for opposition within the National Front.[100]

[98] See his articles in *LL*, May 1, June 20. In a personal interview in Prague in April 1969, Pithart expressed a preference for parties other than the existing ones. M. Kusý, on the other hand, considered the National Front an element of direct democracy which would serve as an *oponentura* to the representative bodies (*NS*, Aug. 1, 8).

[99] "K otázkám pluralitního politického systému socialismu" (typescript), 19 pp.

[100] See *NM*, no. 5 (1968), pp. 607-27. Cf. *RP*, June 6; *ŽS*, no. 13 (June 1968), pp. 1-4; and other articles cited above in this chapter. An unpublished draft article (typescript, 83 pp.), presumably intended as a chapter for the team's symposium, was submitted for publication to *Naše teme* (Zagreb) and was made available to the author. The two-party model was discussed still more positively there (p. 69, n. 13). This article (in French) was presumably the same as one in Czech prepared for publication in *Stát a právo*, cited by Mlynář in a 1975 memorandum (Appendix E).

The front would have to go through a substantial change, however. The development of political parties, either through reconstruction of the existing ones or the constitution of new ones, "on the basis of the National Front conception," was not excluded. Parties were, however, only one element of the political system and "a limited instrument" for guaranteeing the representation of the diverse interests of society. The problems that were associated with the crises of parliaments everywhere might be solved by the direct representation of interests and of economic entities in a multi-cameral representative institution. Such a legislature might include a political chamber, elected on a territorial basis by the National Front organzations, and four other chambers (industrial and commercial; agricultural; scientific and technological; and cultural) elected by the working collectives, probably indirectly.[101] The party would have to experience a rebirth (*obroda*) and only then, in his opinion, would be "fully capable of being the leading political force in a democratic pluralist socialist system."[102]

Another tempered version of pluralism was presented by Vladimír Klokočka, constitutional lawyer at Charles University, and head of the government's commission on the new political system. In a book on elections in pluralist democracies, published in 1968, he devoted a final chapter to a model of future elections in Czechoslovakia. This would be a pluralist system based on "a free play of political forces," but would exclude "an antagonistically conceived plurality of parties struggling for power." He opposed a monopoly of power in the hands of a single party, with "satellite pseudo-parties," and also a two-party system, and favored "a multi-party system of cohesive parties" grouped together in the National Front. Parties should be allowed to form freely, subject in the first stage to National Front approval, with an appeal possible to a constitutional court. Parties must accept the twin essentials, the socialist order and political democracy, both of which would be legally protected by law.[103] Although he would not permit an anti-socialist opposition,

[101] *NM*, no. 5, pp. 619-20. For further discussion of the idea of a multi-cameral parliament, see his unpublished article (pp. 72-74) and an interview with *Práca*, June 18. In the latter, Mlynář suggested three auxiliary chambers, industrial, agricultural, and social service (health, education, and culture), which would act in the manner of an "upper house," returning draft laws for reconsideration, supervising the government, making interpellations, etc. The materials prepared for the 14th congress also proposed a multichamber representative body, including industrial, agricultural, and social services chambers. Some members of the working body doubted the feasibility of introducing such a system at the same time as the federalization of the state and before self-management in the factories had begun to function (J. Pelikán, ed., *Vysočany Congress*, pp. 233-34).

[102] *NM*, no. 5, pp. 625-26.

[103] *Volby v pluralitních demokraciích* (Prague, 1968), chaps. 8-9; in German, *Demokratischer Sozialismus* (Hamburg, 1968). Quotations at pp. 263, 271; in

Klokočka regarded opposition as a necessary and a constructive (*státotvorný*) element in every state.[104] He even conceived of opposition parties within the National Front as well as independent deputies representing currents outside the National Front. He set forth a pluralist model of elections in some detail, stressing secrecy of voting and suggesting a candidate list system, with preferential voting. He favored a single chamber parliament, in which strengthened parliamentary committees would serve as the main arena for the confrontation of interests.

The debate over a multi-party system and the concept of opposition raged in the press and the mass media for several months, down to the crisis at the end of June,[105] and reflected a lack of consensus similar to that described above. Some reformers advocated a system of two or more parties,[106] and even recommended two separate communist parties.[107] Other persons, more official in spirit, denounced the idea of opposition parties and insisted on the leading role of the party and the preeminence of the National Front.[108] Even some reformers, however, spoke against a multi-party system, at least for the time being, and endorsed other forms of pluralism.[109] Those who supported a multi-party system sometimes rejected an opposition party and favored a partnership within the National Front.[110] Others strongly urged the necessity of "opposition," without specifying the form it would take.[111] According to another view, parliamentary democracy was not enough and must be supplemented by "direct democracy" in the form of free expression in the mass media, an

---

German, pp. 54, 65. See Barnard, "Between Opposition and Political Opposition," pp. 547 ff. See also Klokočka's discussion with Z. Jičínský, *RP*, May 30. The latter shared many of Klokočka's views, but advocated "a plurality of various political forces, elements, and organizations" and did not exclude "opposition within the framework of socialism." Like Mlynář, Klokočka considered a multi-party system, with opposition parties, as unrealistic at that time but acceptable if conditions became ripe (*LL*, March 21).

[104] Klokočka wrote elsewhere that free discussion presumed "opinion opposition" and spoke strongly in favor of "organized interest opposition" and opposition within the party (*LL*, March 21).

[105] In addition to sources cited in the following notes, see the panel discussions, *KN*, April 19 and *KT*, May 16, and the responses to questions on this theme in successive issues, *KŽ*, from June 14.

[106] M. Reiman, *RP*, May 4; P. Števček, *KŽ*, April 12.

[107] Ivan Klíma, *LL*, April 25; P. Kohout, ibid., May 16. See also Kohout, *KT*, June 6.

[108] K. Ondris and V. Karas, *ŽS*, no. 12 (June 1968), pp. 24-28; R. Rohan, ibid., no. 16 (Aug. 1968), pp. 10-11.

[109] See Z. Jesenská, *KŽ*, April 5; R. Kalivoda, *RP*, May 3, and *LL*, May 2 and 9; J. Fibich, *Rep.*, April 8-15. See also Šik, *NM*, nos. 9-10 (1968), pp. 1, 284-85.

[110] V. Chytil, *LL*, June 20; R. Kalivoda, ibid., May 9.

[111] J. Hanák, *Rep.*, April 17-24. Opposition of some kind was also endorsed by all participants in the symposium cited above (*KN*, May 16).

enhanced influence of the trade unions, and above all, workers' councils in the enterprises.[112]

PUBLIC OPINION ON THE POLITICAL SYSTEM

Meanwhile, the general public, which formed an attentive audience of this unusual debate, was also divided in its opinions. Even party members were not unanimous on the future of the party and on the idea of competing parties. When asked, in a poll in May, whether the exercise of the leading role by the party was a condition of socialist democracy, a majority of party members (61 percent) agreed it was; 25 percent did not agree; and 13 percent were uncertain. Conversely, 83 percent of non-members disagreed, only 11 agreed, and 6 were uncertain.

Two July polls on a similar theme in various parts of Bohemia and Moravia produced somewhat different results. When asked whether in politics there must be one political line valid for all, or whether many concepts and proposals of individual parties should exist side by side, 68 percent of the party members responding were for "many concepts," with 31 percent favoring one political line. Non-members were much more strongly in favor of many concepts—86 percent to 13 for one line. There was wide diversity as to who should determine the political line if there were "only one." Only 21 percent of party members, and 4 percent of non-members assigned this right to the CC of the Communist Party; 30 and 24 percent respectively, to the National Front; 19 and 18 percent, to the National Assembly; 13 and 24 percent, to public opinion through press, radio, and television; 6 and 10 percent, to other political parties; 3 and 7 percent respectively, to the government.

In August, however, a poll based on a larger sample in Bohemia, Moravia, and Prague, revealed more subtle variations, but suggested that the majority of the party members accepted "the present principle of the leading role of the party" (62 percent), as opposed to 38 who did not. In contrast, only 12 percent of non-members agreed with this principle, as compared with 88 percent who disagreed.[113]

---

[112] R. Kalivoda, *RP*, May 3; *LL*, May 9. On workers' councils, see below, chap. XIV. Petr Pithart warned that self-government (*samospráva*) in the factories could not replace democracy in the political sphere, especially in the crucial question of controlling power which could be accomplished only by political institutions proper (*LL*, Aug. 1).

[113] For the above, see Piekalkiewicz, *Polling*, pp. 135, 144; 81, 138; 136, resp. The May data were based on two polls in northern Bohemia: one a random mail sample of 524 party members; the other a newspaper poll of 636 non-party members. The July data represented a "combination" of two separate polls, one based on a "quota" sample of 269 persons in various parts of Bohemia and Moravia; the

Also in August, a random sample of 2,947 persons, in Bohemia, Moravia, and Prague, were asked to rank in order of importance the three "greatest guarantees of socialist democracy." The results are shown in Table XII.1.

TABLE XII.1
(in percentages)
GREATEST GUARANTEES OF SOCIALIST DEMOCRACY
(three choices in order of importance)

	Placement			Total in places 1, 2, or 3
	1	2	3	
Leading role of the party	43	10	8	61
National Front	21	36	16	73
Choice in elections among independent political parties	21	15	21	57
Public opinion in press, radio, and television	10	25	21	56
Non-communist parties	2	5	8	15
Large societal organizations	1	8	22	31

When party affiliation or non-affiliation was taken into consideration, the results were strikingly different. Party members placed the leading role of the CPCz in first place; National Front, second; public opinion, third; choice in elections, fourth; etc. Non-party members on the other hand ranked them in the following order: first, National Front; second and third (equally), CPCz leading role and choice in elections; fourth, public opinion. Both the People's Party members and the Socialists, however, ranked "choice in elections" in first place, followed by public opinion and the National Front (in that order by the Socialists, and in the opposite order by the People's Party), and placed the activity of the non-communist parties in fourth place.[114]

other, a random sample of 218 persons from Bohemia and Moravia as a whole. The August data were based on a mail poll of 1,905 party members and (presumably) on questionnaires returned by 2,966 persons of a quota sample of 3,600. Both polls were conducted in northern and eastern Bohemia, southern Moravia, and the city of Prague.

[114] *Polling*, pp. 101-6 (table from p. 102). The general poll was conducted, presumably by the National Front, between August 4 and 15, in northern and eastern Bohemia, southern Moravia, and Prague. It was supplemented by a poll of 1,008 Socialist Party (ČSS) members (Aug. 5-20) and 800 People's Party (ČSL) members (Aug. 5-Sept. 4), both based on a random sample from the total membership of each party. For a poll of *Rudé právo* readers, mainly party members, on this theme, see below, chap. XVI.

There were equally wide cleavages as to the role of the National Front. According to the July poll, a majority were ready to see it continue in its present form, but a substantial minority were not. Ideas also differed greatly as to the composition of the National Front, the degree of its "openness," and the extent of its authority over its members.[115]

There was a similar diversity as to electoral procedures. Although very few were satisfied with the previous system, there was no consensus as to what steps would contribute most to the democratization of elections, as Table XII.2 reveals.[116]

TABLE XII.2

(in percentages)

STEPS CONTRIBUTING TO DEMOCRATIZATION OF ELECTIONS

	All Respondents	CPCz members	Non-CPCz members
Free choice of candidates	29	40	26
Secrecy of elections	21	28	19
Real possibilities for the non-communist parties	22	12	25
Possibility of creating new parties	7	3	9
Participation of societal organizations such as ROH	6	4	6
Real possibility for use of mass media by all parties	7	4	8
No need to change	3	5	3
Don't know/no answer	4	3	3
Other conditions	1	1	1
	100	100	100

Opinion was divided on the mechanics of elections. In July, few respondents expressed support for the existing system of National Front candidacy (9 percent of all; 19 percent, CPCz; and 6 percent of non-CPCz). Most favored various forms of independent candidacy—either of "independents" (15, 15, 15 percent, respectively); independent candidates of political parties (26, 13, and 30 percent, respectively); independent candidates of parties and societal organizations (21, 22, 20 percent, respectively); or some combination of independent candidates of

---

[115] For full discussion of this and other polls, see below chap. XVII.
[116] July 8-16, *Polling*, p. 172 (Czech lands only).

political parties and societal organizations (19, 25, and 18 percent, respectively).[117]

HUMAN RIGHTS AND CONSTITUTIONAL REFORM

The discussion of a new political model naturally led to consideration of legal and constitutional guarantees of the fundamental rights and freedoms of citizens. This subject, which had not been mentioned in the January resolution or Dubček's early speeches, was treated in several paragraphs of the Action Program, which proclaimed "a broad democratic conception of the political and personal rights of citizens," extending beyond the limits of bourgeois democracy.[118] Černík, in his April declaration of government policy, made a comprehensive statement on "civil rights and freedoms" and "personal rights of man and citizen." Having referred to the rights of individual nationalities and freedom of religious faith, Černík enumerated the specific measures planned, including a law on assembly and association, a new press law, new regulations on travel, and reforms in criminal law procedures to guarantee "equality before the law."[119]

True, these rights, as leading spokesmen frequently emphasized, were not to be "misused" against socialism and the social order, but they represented a charter of freedoms which would have been unique in communist-ruled countries. Unofficial commentators were unconditional in their demands for legal guarantees of rights and freedoms, often citing the provisions of the United Nations Declaration of Human Rights and the two UN conventions in this sphere. Organizations for the defense of human rights were established, with the express purpose of securing their incorporation in Czechoslovak legislation. The government approved the signature and ratification of the UN pacts and recommended that individual ministries should take their principles into account in drafting new legislation.[120]

---

[117] July 8-16, *Polling*, p. 174. Polls in August revealed wide disparity of view on specific electoral procedures. See poll in Bohemia, Moravia, and Prague, August 4-15, and ČSS and ČSL polls, *Polling*, pp. 184-86, 182, 177, 181, resp. For other results, ibid., pp. 178, 187-88, 189-92. For a full analysis of these and other polls on elections (several of which were conducted under the auspices of the National Front), see D. Šmejc, *Rep.*, May 15, 1969, pp. v-viii.

[118] R. A. Remington, ed., *Winter in Prague*, p. 106. See above, chap. viii, p. 220. Cf. Dubček, *K otázkam*, p. 79.

[119] *RP*, April 25. See also Dubček, ibid., April 9; Černík, ibid., June 7.

[120] *RP*, July 19; also May 3, 17. See Z. Jesenská, *KŽ*, April 5 and E. Vidra, *KŽ*, April 12; E. Ludvík, *KN*, April 26; S. Luby, *Pravda*, May 2. J. Chaloupka (*RP*, April 16) advocated a constitutional court for human rights. See *Člověk a lidská práva* (Prague, 1969), containing the texts of the United Nations human rights documents and a commentary by Rudolf Bystrický. See also the special issue of the *Bulletin of Czechoslovak Law* 8, nos. 1-4 (Prague, 1967) which appeared in 1968

The central issue was freedom of expression, in particular freedom of the press. Throughout March there was a steady barrage of criticism of existing censorship practices and a growing stream of demands for the abrogation of preliminary censorship. This culminated in April and May in ever more insistent pressures for the complete abolition of censorship and for guarantees of freedom of expression in all spheres. Karl Marx was quoted as referring to the free press as "the ever-present open eye of the national spirit," "the spiritual mirror in which the nation sees itself."[121]

Dubček identified himself with this demand, although from time to time he spoke of the danger of the "abuse" of freedom of speech and urged the mass media to be "responsible."[122] Other political figures, in particular Bil'ak and Indra, spoke more critically of the proposal to end censorship and of the behavior of the mass media, and drew upon themselves sharp censure.[123] These latter statements were a stimulus for the formation, first in Ostrava and then elsewhere, of workers' committees for the defense of freedom of the press, which were designed, it was said, to take any constitutional steps, including strikes, to protect this freedom and to continue in existence at least until censorship was abolished and freedom of expression guaranteed by law.[124] At the May plenum Dubček again expressed his belief in freedom of expression, but was highly critical of the mass media, and deprecated the workers' committees as unnecessary.[125] The organization of journalists, however, welcomed this support from the working class and continued to press for the abolition of censorship and the passage of the press law amendment.[126] There were also complaints that censorship still existed in the form of concealment of important items of news, such as the steps to resurrect the Social Democratic Party, and that preliminary censorship could easily be re-

in honor of the 20th anniversary of the UN Declaration of Human Rights and contained a series of articles by Czech legal specialists on the implications of the declaration for Czechoslovak law. The essays were actually written in 1968. KAN also strongly advocated the guarantee of a wide array of civil rights, in accordance with the Declaration of Human Rights (*Svědectví* no. 45, 1973, pp. 154-56). See also M. Kalenská, *Socialistické soudnictví*, 1968, no. 4, pp. 9-20; no. 5, pp. 34-42; nos. 6-7, pp. 21-32.

[121] For articles defending the freedom of the press, see L. Šefčák, *KŽ*, March 29; Prague journalists' statement, *RP*, April 2; Union of Journalists, ibid., April 10, 18, 24; I. Klíma, *LL*, April 11; *Pravda*, April 13; K. Földvári, *KŽ*, April 19; J. Kapr, *Rep.*, May 1-7; S. Budín, ibid., May 8-15; L. Šefčák, *NS*, June 6; P. Pithart, *LL*, June 20; J. Wieser, *Pravda*, June 21.

[122] *RP*, April 21, but cf. ibid., April 9. See also Č. Císař, ibid., May 30.

[123] Bil'ak, *RP* and *Pravda*, April 11; Indra, Švestka, Bil'ak, and others at regional conferences, *RP*, April 21-30. See criticism by V. Maňák, *KŽ*, April 19; D. Hamšík, *LL*, June 13.

[124] *Rep.*, May 8-15; ibid., June 26-July 3; *LL*, May 23, 30, June 20, July 18.

[125] *RŠO*, pp. 197, 184, resp.

[126] *LD*, June 25; *RP*, May 25, June 28.

stored since the machinery for it had not been abolished. In fact the government abolished the Central Publication Administration responsible for censorship in mid-June.[127]

The adoption of the amendments to the press law in late June put an end to censorship by state organs, but did not fully satisfy those seeking guarantees of freedom of the press. The law was criticized for referring to intervention by state organs only, instead of excluding intervention by "any organ whatever," as proposed by the Union of Journalists.[128] There was considerable concern over the opposition in the assembly to the amendments and over the persisting criticism of the mass media by prominent figures. Unease was engendered by a list of secret items issued to the press by the Ministry of the Interior on July 30, consisting of thirty-five pages of "facts not to be published." It was feared that this might be abused to limit expression for reasons other than security.[129] There was some fear that the press law revision, which would contain provisions to protect the reputations of individuals and of state secrets, might in fact restrict the freedom of the press.[130] Radio and television, as state institutions, had a somewhat different status, but those holding positions of authority in them strongly asserted the necessity of assuring freedom of expression. Draft laws on radio and television, however, were envisaged as permitting some public influence through "advisory and initiating boards."[131] Neither these nor the press law were completed prior to the occupation.

The official reaction to the Two Thousand Words, on the heels of the passage of the press law amendment, confirmed fears that complete freedom of expression had by no means been fully accepted by the party leaders. They were, however, caught in a dilemma between the desire to satisfy the legitimate expectations of the people and of the journalists concerning freedom of expression and their wish not to give allies abroad any more reason for suspicion. The journalists faced a similar dilemma. They accepted the need to act responsibly in order not to complicate the position of the leaders.[132] Some even went so far as to accept the princi-

---

[127] *RP*, June 19. See P. Pithart and V. Škutina, *LL*, June 20; *Rep.*, June 26-July 3.

[128] Kryštůfek, *Rep.*, June 26-July 3; V. Vodička, *VP*, Aug. 8; R. Kaliský, *KŽ*, Aug. 9.

[129] *RP*, July 19, 30; *LD*, Aug. 6; A. J. Liehm, *MF*, June 25.

[130] On the new laws, see *RP*, May 23, July 26. Císař described the new press law as one which would guarantee the freedom of the press but would also require responsibility from journalists (*RP*, May 30). For criticism, see *Rep.*, June 19-26; *KŽ*, July 5; V. Kraus, *Práce*, Aug. 16; the Slovak journalists' organization, *RP*, May 15.

[131] D. Havlíček, *Rep.*, April 3-10; J. Pelikán, *RP*, June 6; Z. Hejzlar, *LD*, July 27.

[132] S. Budín, *Rep.*, May 8-15. For an advocacy of self-censorship, *Pravda*, June 22. Cf. the severe criticism of two series of articles on Radio Free Europe, based

ple of government regulation as essential in the interests of the whole society.[133] At the same time, they were determined to protect freedom of expression and reacted against indications of official limitations of information. The firm stand of the leadership in response to the Warsaw letter's criticism of the mass media was welcomed and warmly endorsed.[134] Later, however, after the Čierna and Bratislava conferences, there was widespread dissatisfaction with the lack of information given to the public and concern as to whether the party leaders had committed themselves to restrict the newly won press freedom. The struggle for freedom of expression, as Jiří Lederer put it, just prior to the occupation, was still continuing.[135]

The formulation of the law on assembly and association had not advanced as far. The establishment of new organizations and clubs was based legally on a 1951 law, which required approval in each case by the Ministry of the Interior or a regional national committee. Many associations were in fact coming into existence, often without the necessary approval. The desirability of a new law of association was generally recognized, but the final draft text was not expected to be completed until late August. The government intended to revise the 1951 law and had apparently reached agreement that it would apply to "voluntary associations" only, but not to political parties, trade unions, or cooperatives, or churches and religious associations. The alternatives included in the working draft differed in procedures and in the extent of the authority which state organs would have to grant approval to a proposed organization, but provided for limitations only in accordance with the law, subject to an appeal to a court. The law would also safeguard the right to hold public meetings or processions, subject to a ban by the national committee if the meeting was deemed to be in conflict with law or a threat to public order.[136]

---

on interviews at its headquarters in Munich, launched by *Obrana lidu* (July 20) and *Student* (July 24), both of which were voluntarily brought to an abrupt close. For the criticism, see *RP*, July 24; *VP*, July 24; *LL*, July 25. See a defense of *Student* for the series and censure of *LL* for its criticism by J. Müller (Aug. 1).

[133] See J. Brabec, *NS*, July 18; *Pravda*, Aug. 7. Some journalists were ready to accept "subsequent" censorship (symposium, *NS*, June 13). See a legal analysis suggesting "subsequent" censorship, subject to judicial review. Limitations on freedom of the press should be permitted only under "extraordinary circumstances" defined in law (M. Gašpar, *Právny obzor*, no. 7, 1968, pp. 590-96).

[134] For the official response, see *RŠO*, pp. 248, 254-55. See statements of support by Czech journalists, *RP*, July 13, 25, 27.

[135] *LL*, Aug. 15. See statements by the creative unions (*LL*, Aug. 8); by the scientific workers (ibid., Aug. 9); by the journalists, *MF*, Aug. 4. See above, chap. x.

[136] See statement by a deputy Minister of the Interior, Š. Demyan, *Pravda*, May 20; a critical analysis by F. Párek, *SS*, June 25; an anonymous summary, *Ľud*, Aug. 8; E. Palúch, *Hlas ľudu*, Aug. 14. See also Pavel, *RP*, June 19; government

Another human "right"—the freedom to travel—was to be assured by a new law on travel documents which was discussed in parliamentary committees in June and July and was expected to come into force in the fall. This would guarantee every citizen the right to have a permanent passport, valid for travel anywhere, without supplementary permits, and with the categories of any exceptions specified by law. Citizens would also have the right to emigrate and to return.[137]

The need for other "qualitative changes" in the legal order was officially recognized but it was stressed that in the meantime valid laws must be respected.[138] As the materials prepared for the 14th congress indicated, the first stage of future development would include specific and partial reforms in the legislative order, especially a new press law, a law on assembly and association, a system of guarantees of legality, including the independence of the courts, etc. The second stage, after the 14th congress, would involve the laws on federalization, the National Front and elections, and eventually, by the end of 1970 or early 1971, a new constitution.[139] A special committee, headed by Professor Viktor Knapp, was established to prepare the latter.[140] Legal experts discussed the main defects of the existing constitution and praised the earlier 1948 basic law and the traditions of the First Republic.[141] An entirely new constitution was needed, said one, not a mere amendment of the 1960 constitution, which was "an ideological document of low legal value."[142]

FOURTEENTH CONGRESS PERSPECTIVES

At the time of the invasion the Czechoslovak political model was still in flux. There was consensus on the need for "a qualitatively new politi-

---

report, ibid., July 6. For discussion, see P. Peška and R. Rychetský, *LL*, April 4; V. Pavlíček, ibid., Aug. 8. For a legal analysis advocating a law guaranteeing maximum rights of association, including the right to form trade unions, see M. Řehůřek, *PO*, no. 7 (1968), pp. 581-90; also Řehůřek, ibid., no. 3 (1968), pp. 216-28. Others, including Pavlíček, urged that the law also protect the right to form political parties, as well as trade unions. Cf. V. Pavlíček, *Bulletin of Czechoslovak Law* 8 (1967), pp. 90-95.

[137] For official statements, see *MF*, April 23; *RP*, June 13, July 10.

[138] CC resolution, *RŠO*, p. 210. Cf. a similar statement by the presidium of the National Assembly, *RP*, May 24.

[139] Pelikán, ed., *Vysočany Congress*, pp. 223-28, 239.

[140] Its first meeting was reported in *RP*, July 12. A committee was also established by the Academy of Sciences, headed by Prof. P. Peška (*Právník*, no. 6, 1968, pp. 547-50).

[141] See the positive evaluation of the 1948 constitution by J. Grospič and Z. Jičínský, *Právník*, no. 5 (1968), pp. 380-92; and the critical evaluation of the 1960 constitution by Peška, ibid., no. 6 (1968), pp. 551-57, and by B. Rattinger and Peška, *Rep.*, May 22-29. Cf. the round-table discussion by legal specialists in *Práce*, June 16, 1968.

[142] Peška, *RP*, July 12.

cal system," as the main draft report prepared for the 14th congress stated,[143] but no agreement on critical aspects of reform or on how the political system would in fact function in its more or less permanent form. Yet the report admitted that there were many obstacles to be overcome in the final elaboration of a new political system. The party was "linked to the organs of authoritarian administration, accustomed to the administrative 'handing down' of the party line . . ." and "had not yet learned to think in pluralistic terms, in terms of the equality and autonomy of the parties and organizations." If it were to become the "vanguard of a new life," it would have to change many of its methods and to carry through its own democratization. Thus, although "political pluralism" already existed, this was "in an embryonic form conditioned by the conception of the National Front as a common political platform which excludes a political struggle for the conquest of power." The National Front might attain a certain "internal pluralism" as "a forum for the elaboration of the political line"; it might even admit some other political organizations. But basically it would retain an "outwardly monopolistic" character, having the right to exclude certain political organizations from membership and therefore from political activity. Hence there would not really be an "open" political system, allowing a "free play" of political forces.[144]

Indeed, the authors of the draft report were themselves reluctant to see the National Front evolve in this direction and believed that this could not be permitted for at least the next five years. Without the front's monopoly it would be impossible "to rule out the danger of a conflict over political power aimed at the hegemony of the Communist Party" and such a struggle for power seemed highly probable. It was therefore necessary, concluded the report, to guarantee the hegemony of the CPCz and its majority position in the National Front, and in the federal and national parliaments (although not necessarily in the national committees), by "a set of well thought-out measures within the National Front and the electoral system." This would include a National Front statute that would forbid any party or political organization to function outside the front. As for elections, the report favored multi-member districts and a single National Front list of candidates, with the voters choosing certain candidates (say, 25 percent) as individuals and the rest as nominees, on the lists of the constituent National Front organizations, thus assuring the CPCz a likely majority from both processes of selection.[145]

Everything depended, it is clear, on the outcome of the 14th congress

---

[143] See Pelikán, ed., *Vysočany Congress*, pp. 195 ff.

[144] Ibid., pp. 196-228.

[145] Ibid., pp. 226-37. The report saw some advantage in the possibility of independent candidates since this would tend to divide anti-communist forces.

which would undoubtedly have witnessed a sharp clash of viewpoints, ranging from those who favored a completely open and competitive political system to those who sought to maintain the continued leadership of the Communist Party within a system of limited pluralism. The 14th congress material reflected this diversity, although it represented a compromise tending toward the latter view.[146] It was not at all certain, however, whether authoritative documents, such as the one discussed above, or the party statutes, would be accepted in their proposed form, or would be substantially amended. Moreover, much would depend on the nature of the leadership which resulted from the congress, and on the balance of political forces, within the party and both inside and outside the National Front. It was by no means assured, for instance, that the Communist Party, in spite of all precautions, would be able to achieve a substantial majority in the eventual elections. Whether the non-communist forces would be strong enough ever to influence seriously the party's policy, or to replace it in power, could not be foreseen. Nor could it be forecast how strong the progressive wing of the party would become nor how far it would go, in alliance with non-communist forces, toward permitting their own party's defeat in elections. The outlook therefore was for a much freer play of political forces, within a general atmosphere of free discussion, in a system more open and democratic than any other communist system in the world. In the long run this might have constituted a transition to an even more democratic system, going beyond mere "democratization" to a fully pluralist society. It might, however, also have represented an apex in the democratization process, to be followed by a gradual consolidation of communist power under firmer leadership and a restoration of some of the features of the older political system.

[146] An analysis of the Prague spring by Josef Pokštefl described the conflict over the issue of a "closed" or "open" political system, mirrored in the 14th congress documents, and concluded that the closed system was regarded as "transitional" and that the dominant current favoring an "open pluralistic system of democratic socialism" was likely to be endorsed at the congress. See *Svědectví* 11, no. 42 (1971), 231-38, and more briefly, in Kusin, ed., *Czechoslovak Reform Movement*, pp. 169-71.

CHAPTER XIII

Rehabilitation and Justice

ANGER over the illegalities of the fifties and resentment over the delays and inadequacies in the rehabilitation of the victims after 1956 was a major element in the developing political crisis of the sixties. After January the rectification of these injustices became a subject of fervent public discussion and by mid-March an essential component of the official program. The flood of revelations concerning the full dimensions of the evils of the fifties had a strong impact on public opinion, communist and non-communist, and intensified the determination to achieve a complete rehabilitation of those who had suffered persecution and to mete out appropriate punishment for those responsible. It led also to a probing inquiry into the basic causes of the liquidation of law and justice under Gottwald, the failure of Novotný to correct the situation, and the legal guarantees necessary to prevent a repetition of such events.[1]

REHABILITATION—INITIAL PHASE

Rehabilitation was not mentioned in the January resolution or in early statements by Dubček or the party Presidium. Smrkovský, however, in a major statement on reform in early February, included the need to rehabilitate all victims of injustice, communists and non-communists alike.[2] This theme was at once reiterated in a deluge of articles and speeches, including interviews with prominent communist victims of the fifties, such as Evžen Löbl and Marie Švermová, and with Josefa Slánská, wife of the executed party leader.[3] Common to most of these reports was severe criticism of the slowness and incompleteness of rehabilitation during the sixties. Even when justice had at last been done,

[1] The fullest analysis of the problems of rehabilitation and legal reform in English is given by Otto Ulč, "The Vagaries of Law," *Problems of Communism* 18, nos. 4-5 (July-Oct. 1969), 17-32. See also Harry Slapnicka, "Politische Verurteilungen und Rehabilitierungen in der Tschechoslowakei," *Osteuropa* 20 (June 1970), 410-18; Karel Kosik, "Reformtendenzen in der tschechoslowakischen Rechtslehre in den Jahren 1968-1969," *Jahrbuch für Ostrecht* 12 (Dec. 1971), 145-75. For a personal account of his experiences as a judge in Pilsen during the fifties, see Otto Ulč, *The Judge in a Communist State* (Columbus, Ohio, 1972).

[2] *Rudé právo*, Feb. 9. Cf. editorial, ibid., Feb. 8.

[3] *Lidová demokracie*, Feb. 15, March 16; Švermová, *Zemědělské noviny*, March 15; *Smena*, March 5-7; *RP*, March 14, 21; Löbl, *Kultúrny život*, March 15; Švermová, *ZN*, March 15; *Reportér*, March 20-27; *RP*, March 22; Slánská, *Rep.*, March 27-April 3.

this had occurred without publicity, and those legally exonerated remained under a shadow, usually receiving meager compensation and being debarred from public life or appropriate employment.[4] It was necessary, it was urged, fully to complete the process so as to include not only judicial, but also personal, social, and political rehabilitation, plus material indemnification, with as much publicity given to the exoneration as to the original condemnation. Normal procedures for the examination of past cases were inadequate, since they were not compulsory and were extremely time-consuming. What was required was a statute establishing special judicial procedures which would speedily guarantee justice and compensation to all who deserved it.

There was varying emphasis on the categories of victims who should be rehabilitated and differing estimates of their numbers. Most prominent were those unjustly sentenced by the State Court under the 1948 law for the defense of the Republic (Statute no. 231) whose cause was taken up by the newly formed club, K 231.[5] Of the total of 27,000 imprisoned under this law, only 2,000 had, it was said, been rehabilitated.[6] Particular stress was also laid on those who had participated in the various *odboj* (resistance) movements, including Spanish Civil War veterans, "Westerners," i.e. those who had fought with the RAF or other allied forces, and participants in the Slovak Uprising and the underground resistance. Their case was forcefully pressed by J. Hušek, head of the Union of Anti-Fascist Fighters (SPB), who estimated their number to be 30,000-40,000, of whom only 700 had been rehabilitated.[7] Others, including Bishop Tomášek, singled out the plight of Catholic priests, of whom the number of victims of injustice could only be guessed.[8] Peasants and small traders, who had been unjustly imprisoned or illegally deprived of their habitations and possessions, were also given special mention.[9] Although discussion centered initially on "political prisoners," it was urged that rehabilitation ought to extend to the hundreds of thousands who had suffered other forms of persecution, such as

[4] B. Fučík, *Literární listy*, April 4; O. Valeš, *Práce*, April 12.

[5] The club served as a center for collecting information on former prisoners and offered its services to the authorities. See the personal account by the club's general secretary, J. Brodský, *Řešení gama* (Toronto, 1970), in English, *Solution Gamma* (Toronto, 1971). Documents from K 231 archives on personal experiences of Czech victims of the fifties were later published abroad, O. Rambousek and L. Gruber, eds., *Zpráva dokumentační komise K 231* (Toronto, 1973). See also V. V. Kusin, *Political Grouping in the Czechoslovak Reform Movement* (London, 1972), pp. 173-83.

[6] J. Adamec, *ZN*, March 14.

[7] *ZN*, Feb. 29; *Roľnícke noviny*, March 13; *RP*, March 15.

[8] *LD*, March 13, 16, 21.

[9] *RN*, March 15; also M. Hric and T. Michal, *Pravda*, March 8.

dismissals from jobs, evictions from dwellings, confiscations of personal property, etc., usually without any form of judicial proceeding.

Intimately related to rehabilitation was the question of assessing the responsibility of those who had committed gross injustices in the fifties, as well as those who had later hindered rehabilitation of the victims, and the meting out of appropriate punishment. The press, radio, and television were filled with condemnations of the political leaders deemed to be ultimately responsible, including Gottwald, Bacílek, Čepička, and Novotný, but also of lesser figures—high officials, security investigators, judges, procurators, and lawyers—such as Josef Urválek, chief prosecutor in the Slánský trial or Miroslav Mamula, head of the party's 8th department.[10] Many, it was charged, still held public office and had blocked the implementation of rehabilitation. Certain incumbents, such as A. Neuman, the Minister of Justice, J. Kudrna, Minister of the Interior, J. Bartuška, Procurator General, J. Litera, Chairman of the Supreme Court, and others tried to defend themselves publicly, with varying degrees of admission of guilt and self-criticism, but were soon removed from office.[11] There were some references to a subject later to be discussed at length, namely, the role of the Soviet advisers, and of Stalin and Beria, in the conduct of the trials.[12] There was wide agreement that persons responsible for misdeeds should be removed from office and that none of them should be permitted to participate in the rehabilitation process. Some urged legal proceedings against those guilty of criminal actions, even though the statute of limitations excluded most crimes committed prior to 1958. In spite of the atmosphere generated by these charges and demands, and by the increasingly frank revelations of the horrors of the fifties, there were many, including well-known victims of that era, such as Löbl, Goldstücker, and Smrkovský, who warned against a policy of "revenge" and pleaded for "toleration."[13]

In the midst of this welter of discussion, the party Presidium referred to "the completion of rehabilitation" as "a moral and political obligation" and had under consideration measures for "giving moral, personal, and social satisfaction and material indemnification" to victims of illegality. Rehabilitation would be effected "on a legal basis which would fully guarantee the independence of the court and at the same time authorize

[10] For an early plea for punishing the guilty, see A. Tučková, Rep., Feb. 28-March 6, 1968. For a full discussion of past failures of rehabilitation, see M. Richter, Obrana lidu, March 23.

[11] For instance, Urválek, Rep., March 27-April 3; Neuman, RP, April 3; Litera, Student, April 3.

[12] E.g. Col. Z. Koudela, ZN, March 16; B. Rattinger, LD, March 22; Richter, OL, March 23; P. Hron, RP, April 13.

[13] Smena, March 5; Mladá fronta, April 2; RP, April 4, resp.

the government to take similar steps in the revision of demonstrably incorrect administrative measures." It was necessary, the statement emphasized, to distinguish "cases of fabricated accusations" from punishments that were "acts of legitimate revolutionary justice or that were justly pronounced on the basis of proven breaches of socialist legality." The Presidium recommended a commission to "complete" the rehabilitation of party members affected by the trials between 1952 and 1954.[14]

When the CC plenum met at the end of March, Smrkovský, by then a member of the Presidium, lamented the slowness of rehabilitation and emphasized the need for its speedy completion.[15] A number of other speakers, including even conservatives such as Auersperg, Chňoupek, and Novotný, endorsed the idea, although the latter criticized what he called the "campaign" on this theme and defended his own efforts to complete rehabilitation and to restore legality.[16] Kolder, reporting on the work of the rehabilitation commission which he had headed, vigorously defended its achievements, although admitting that it had been influenced by Novotný, especially in failing to rehabilitate Slánský and others politically as well as judicially. He exonerated Novotný from having played an "active role" in the trials, and reported that the archives had not revealed any evidence confirming Bacílek's assertions of Novotný's complicity. He criticized the commission headed by Barák, holding him responsible for its inadequacies, and accused him of responsibility for later trials.[17] There were similar disagreements about the work of the Barnabite commission and demands for the publication in full of its report. Its chairman, Koucký, sought to defend himself against charges concerning his leadership.[18]

The April plenum endorsed the Presidium's recommendations for a rehabilitation law, specifying, however, that it should relate only to the years from 1949 to 1954, and announced the formation of a special commission, headed by Jan Piller, to complete party rehabilitation for the same period.[19] The Action Program noted that rehabilitation of communists and non-communists had not been carried through "with all its po-

[14] March 14, 21, *Rok šedesátý osmý* (Prague, 1969), pp. 38, 40. Cf. other Presidium statements, March 25-26, ibid., pp. 45-46.
[15] *RP*, April 4.
[16] *RP*, April 5. He had acted on the principle, Novotný said, that rehabilitation must not revoke decisions reflecting "revolutionary power and legality against the class enemy" and must do the least harm to the party and to the reputations of Gottwald and Zápotocký.
[17] *RP*, April 6. The Kolder commission was censured by J. Frýbert, of ÚKRK (ibid., April 3) and praised by one of its members, P. Hron, who blamed Novotný for intervening in its work (ibid., April 13). K. Inneman, a member of both Barák commissions, sharply criticized Barák's role (ibid., April 12). See below for discussion of both commissions.
[18] Kladiva and Koucký, *RP*, April 3; V. Šalgovič, ibid., April 16.
[19] CC resolution, *RŠO*, p. 63.

litical and civil consequences" and reiterated the need to remove "any shadow of distrust and humiliation" from the victims and their families and to afford them the possibility of appropriate work and public activity. This must not "change the results of revolutionary measures" taken, "in the spirit of class legislation," against the bourgeoisie.

The formation of the Černík government at the end of April, pledged to the preparation of a law on rehabilitation, and certain personnel changes (although some were ambiguous) seemed to augur well for the completion of rehabilitation and for legal and security reforms. Leading progressives—Smrkovský, Husák, and Pavel—who had themselves suffered during the fifties and had early espoused the need for rehabilitation assumed key positions. Somewhat less encouraging was the replacement of Neuman, as Minister of Justice, by B. Kučera, a veteran Socialist Party leader, who soon proved, however, to be a strong proponent of rehabilitation, which fell under the jurisdiction of his department. The new Procurator General, M. Čeřovský, a former inmate of Nazi concentration camps, had been head of the Prague bar association from 1960. The new chairman of the Supreme Court, Otmar Boček, was an able lawyer, head of the Czechoslovak bar association for some years and then a Supreme Court justice. Černík, as Prime Minister, and Dubček were responsible for security questions in government and party respectively, with General Prchlík in charge of security affairs in the CC apparatus.

Initial speeches by Černík, Dubček, and Smrkovský left no doubt of their determination to carry through a thorough rehabilitation, including non-communists as well as communists, but made equally clear that they wished to avoid creating a general distrust of the party, or of the entire justice and security system, and did not intend to revise the post-1948 "revolutionary measures." Nor was it intended to rehabilitate genuine criminals or wartime collaborators.[20] It was clear, therefore, that opponents of the communist regime, who had broken existing laws, were not to be exonerated and those harmed by such measures as nationalization or collectivization were not to be compensated. Although the line between legal and illegal actions in the past was not easy to draw, subsequent actions by the courts in individual cases soon demonstrated that non-communists as well as communists were to be rehabilitated and compensated.

[20] Černík, RP, April 26, May 15, June 7; Smrkovský, Život strany, no. 10 (May 1968), pp. 16-19; Dubček, May plenum, RŠO, pp. 181, 188, 195; plenum resolution, ibid., pp. 210-11. See also warnings against rehabilitating large landowners or reversing collectivization (Piller, RP, May 24; Sádovský, ibid., May 25; Husák, Pravda, April 23). Husák described "the fine dividing-line between redressing wrongs and violating the principles of socialism"; it was necessary to "eliminate the wrongs . . . but keep the results," i.e. collectivization.

INDIVIDUAL CASES REEXAMINED

Encouraged, and indeed prodded, by the presidium of the National Assembly, the Supreme Court committed itself to accelerate the reconsideration of individual cases without waiting for the completion of legislative action.[21] Beginning in April a number of verdicts from the late forties or early fifties were canceled by the Supreme Court and certain regional courts. Notable were the cases of General H. Pika, head of the Czechoslovak military mission in Moscow during the war, and General K. Kutlvašr, military leader in the Prague uprising, who had been sentenced to death and life imprisonment respectively; Gen. K. Janoušek, commander of the Czechoslovak air force in Great Britain; Professor V. Kubeš, formerly of the Law Faculty, Brno University, and politically active as a National Socialist; V. Žingor, Slovak partisan leader; and Liberec and Ostrava social democrats. In some cases, although the original verdicts were quashed, new court proceedings were necessary before a final decision was taken. The death sentence imposed on Milada Horáková, prominent National Socialist deputy, and the verdicts in the case of those associated with her in the 1950 trial, were canceled by the Supreme Court in late July.[22] Much less serious but more recent cases from 1967 were also dealt with, leading to the release of Ivan Pfaff, author of the so-called writers' manifesto, and the pardoning of Jan Beneš. A presidential amnesty in early May had broader implications and was expected to lead to the release of some 500 political prisoners and to affect a total of 100,000 persons.[23]

Meanwhile many requests for reexamination of penalties meted out by the party were being handled by the Central Commission on Supervision and Auditing, and in lesser cases by regional and district control commissions and party committees. In late March ÚKRK recommended to the supreme party organs the annulment of the party penalties imposed on the dissident writers (Vaculík, etc.) in the fall of 1967, and the cancellation of the posthumous expulsion from the party of Slánský, Otto Šling, and other trial victims.[24] This was followed a month later by the macabre restoration of the high state orders conferred upon Slánský and Šling, and the award of new honors to other victims of the trials, such as the dead Clementis and Josef Frank, and the survivors, Husák, Pavel, Goldstücker, and Smrkovský.[25] Miloš Jakeš, the new head of ÚKRK (deputy Minister of the Interior since 1966), reported to the May plenum that the agency had dealt with 76 cases since January and had acted positively in 62 of them. There were several hundred more to

21 *RP*, March 10, 15, 22, 24.   22 Ibid., July 31.
23 Ibid., May 9.
24 ÚKRK, March 22-23; *RŠO*, pp. 42-43.
25 *RP*, April 30, May 1.

be handled, as well as several thousands of decisions relating to the work of the former Commission of Party Control (KSK).[26] Jakeš also reported on individual cases of rehabilitation, including Zdeněk Hejzlar, former head of the Union of Youth, expelled from the party in 1952 and later imprisoned; K. Lukeš and a group expelled in 1961 for alleged pro-Yugoslav views; and Charlotte Kreibichová, widow of Karl Kreibich, one of the party's founders, who had been expelled in 1957 for urging a reexamination of the trials and the rehabilitation of the condemned. Other rehabilitations occurred in subsequent months, including the lecturers dismissed from the Higher Party School in 1956 and 1964 and J. Grohman, removed in 1952 as chairman of the International Union of Students.[27]

The court hearings on the Barák case became a cause célèbre and brought out the political background of his arrest and trial in 1962 and his own role in the trials and rehabilitation. The original sentence, issued after a secret trial by military court, was appealed by the Procurator General on grounds of illegality, in particular that there was no basis for military proceedings and no evidence of economic espionage, and was quashed in its entirety by the Supreme Court in mid-July. The original charges concerning embezzlement were, however, to be investigated further.[28]

Barák and his defense lawyer used the occasion not only to deny all the original charges but to claim that the whole case had been a fabrication, prepared by Novotný for political reasons, and had involved various illegalities, including the use of confessions secured by psychological methods. Barák reported that he had been pressed to confess to his intention to seize power, but had refused, as had a codefendant, V. Jenyš. He cited other illegalities, including the cancellation of his parliamentary immunity and placed the blame on Fierlinger and Bartuška. He reported that he was arrested personally by Novotný, in the company of Široký, Štrougal, and Mamula.

Barák charged that Novotný, with whom he had a series of conflicts, had feared revelations of his involvement in the original political trials, and was worried about materials held by Barák concerning the wartime activities of high-placed personages. In fact, Barák said, by

[26] *RP*, June 6. Jakeš noted that between 1962 and 1966 some 1,500 cases had been dealt with, and in about 455 of them, wrongs were corrected. He stated that 29 former State Security officers had been given party penalties during that period. He later reported that a blanket abolition of all party penalties prior to the 13th congress would be recommended to the 14th congress (*RP*, June 20).

[27] *RŠO*, pp. 148-49, 155-59, 162, 172, 226, 232-33; *RP*, Aug. 2, 8, 21.

[28] For the procuracy's "complaint," see Richter, *RP*, April 24, 26, May 7, and Richter's statements during the trial. The trial was reported in some detail in *RP* and *Pravda*, July 17 and 18. See also the press conference of L. Schwarz, defense lawyer, *RP*, May 30, 31, July 12, and of Boček, ibid., July 26.

1962 he had come to the conclusion that Čepička and Novotný were the main instigators of the trials, especially that of Slánský, and just prior to his own arrest, had warned Novotný of his intention to bring this matter before a CC plenum in February 1962. Barák sought to depict his role as Minister of the Interior in positive terms, stating that he had at once forbidden the use of illegal interrogation methods and had unsuccessfully sought, with the support of his Soviet adviser, to drop the charges against Švermová and Husák in 1954, and in the same year, to secure the rehabilitation of Slánský.

The release of Barák in early May led to widespread press discussion of his past career, his conflicts with Novotný, his attitude to the trials, and the reasons for his arrest. A number of articles, including a series by his codefendant, J. Ondráček, discussed Barák's political career and his sudden fall in relatively favorable colors, depicting him as a man who had not only sought a revision of the trials but also basic reforms, including the decumulation of the highest party and state functions and a reduction in the power of the Ministry of the Interior, and who had been the victim of a political frameup by Novotný. Barák's popularity and the favor he enjoyed with Khrushchev were said to have made him a dangerous rival in the juggling for power among the top leadership.[29]

Other commentators were more critical, pointing to his responsibility for the trials of Švermová and Husák and his failure to carry through a serious rehabilitation.[30] In a statement to Rudé právo, Husák accused Barák of having staged his (Husák's) trial, with the use of brutal interrogation methods, and charged him with the failure to rehabilitate victims long after these methods were known. Švermová also blamed Barák for her original conviction and for his failure to fight for rehabilitation or even for an improvement of prison conditions.[31] A new issue was raised by a Slovak newspaper which charged Barák with responsibility for the kidnapping of Bohumil Laušman, the social democratic leader, in Aus-

[29] Kulturní noviny, March 22, 29, April 5. See also K. Hájek, Predvoj, May 2; Rep., June 5-12, pp. xiv-xvi. Alleged difference of view over policy toward the Chinese, and Khrushchev's admiration of Barák, were mentioned as sources of conflict with Novotný. A letter to Khrushchev from Barák just prior to his trial was referred to but almost nothing was revealed of its content. Boček referred to the letter in his post-trial press conference. He suggested that the main reason for Barák's removal might have been his special knowledge of the role of certain people during the Nazi occupation and of the extent of the economic crisis of the sixties.

[30] V. Kraus, Práce, July 18; Tučková, Rep., July 31-Aug. 7, p. 13.

[31] RP, July 21. A few days later the party daily published archival material from the Piller commission that indicated Barák's responsibility for the 1954 trial of Švermová, and somewhat ambiguously confirmed his efforts, in 1955 and 1956, to secure a reduction of her sentence and her release. Other archival material showed that Barák had shared the responsibility for Husák's original sentence and had opposed any change in the verdict in 1955 and 1957 (ibid., July 25, 28).

tria in 1953, the latter's fabricated press conference in 1954, his trial in 1957, and his death in 1963 in prison, after long years of solitary confinement.[32]

Another sensational event was the reopening of the question of Jan Masaryk's tragic death in March 1948, hitherto a mystery and a taboo subject. In an open letter dated March 10, addressed to the Procurator General, Ivan Sviták, referring to the promised rehabilitation of persons unjustly harmed by Stalinism, called for a thorough investigation of Masaryk's death to determine "whether he had been murdered as the first victim on the road to a totalitarian dictatorship." Citing extensively from an article in the West German magazine, *Der Spiegel* (April 7, 1965), Sviták expressed his own belief that Masaryk had been murdered, perhaps by Major Franz Schramm, prominent German-speaking member of the CPCz and former partisan leader, whom he described as a liaison officer between the State Security and the NKVD, and who was himself murdered later in 1948.[33] The twenty-year-old case was in fact taken up for examination by the procuracy, under the direction of J. Kotlář, head of the investigation department. It became the subject of widespread discussion and speculation in the press and on radio and television, which revealed sharply opposed differences of opinions and alternative theories of "murder" and "suicide" and touched occasionally on the possible involvement of Soviet security agents. Jiří Hochman, in a front-page article in *Rudé právo*, wrote that murder by "Beria gorillas," as he termed them, was sufficiently plausible to require a thorough examination but also cited views that favored suicide as an explanation.[34] The widow of Major Schramm, living in Hungary, denied the involvement of her former husband in Masaryk's death and criticized the press for their treatment of the whole affair, referring to forces wishing to evoke anti-Soviet feelings.[35] In this latter remark, she echoed the attitude of Tass, the Soviet press agency, which in a brief communiqué denounced "lies" and "provocation" in the Czechoslovak press and accused their authors of seeking to sow mistrust between the two countries.[36]

[32] *Smena*, July 25.
[33] Sviták's letter was published in *Student*, April 3, 1968. See also his interview, *Práce*, April 6.
[34] *RP*, April 16.
[35] A. Bebritsová, ibid., May 19. Her husband's name, she pointed out, was Gustav, not Franz, and he was employed, not in the security service, but in the CC *aparát* department concerned with partisans and liberation organizations. Cf. Rattinger's denial of Schramm's complicity, ibid., May 26. The press coverage of the Masaryk case was both subjected to severe criticism and defended as contributing to the ultimate establishment of the full truth. See E. Klinger, *Rep.*, May 8-15; *LD*, May 26.
[36] *RP*, May 8.

Meanwhile the official investigation proceeded, with a visit by Kotlář to England to interview the author of the *Spiegel* article and certain Czech exiles, including L. Soukup, Masaryk's former secretary, who publicly espoused the theory of suicide. In several interviews, Kotlář denied that there was any evidence of murder or of any connection of the death with Beria and leaned toward the suicide theory. It was not yet possible, he said, to reach a provisional conclusion between murder, suicide, or accident. The investigation would be completed by the end of the year, and the results, whatever they were, would be published.[37]

REVELATIONS AND ACCUSATIONS

In late March and April there was a veritable spate of revelations concerning the investigations and trials of the fifties, and the milder—in comparison—methods of interrogation and conditions of imprisonment in the sixties, throwing into sharp relief the horror of what had occurred during most of the party's twenty years of rule. There was much probing into the basic causes of the trials and of the delays in rehabilitation and a more explicit condemnation of those responsible. There were open references to the "forced confessions" of the past.[38]

The real break in the dam of public awareness came in late April when the book by Evžen Löbl, Testimony on the Trial, was published in Slovak, in an edition of 30,000 and several of its chapters were printed in Czech weeklies.[39] This book, by one of the three survivors of the

[37] For statements by Kotlář, see *RP*, April 6, 24, May 29, June 7; *LD*, April 10. There was occasional criticism of the investigation, in particular of Kotlář's decision not to exhume the body (e.g. *Večerní Praha*, May 18). See the full-length report of a private investigation conducted after the occupation by a Western journalist, Claire Sterling, *The Masaryk Case* (London, 1968, 1969). Her inquiry, based on many interviews in Prague and London, revealed the extraordinary cleavage of opinion among Czechs, some strongly convinced that Masaryk's death had been a suicide, and others equally persuaded that he was murdered. Sterling cast doubts on the official investigation and charged that Kotlář had deliberately misled her on many points. Her own conclusion—which, however, cannot be regarded as more than a hypothesis—was that Masaryk was murdered, probably by Czech communists, under NKVD direction.

[38] F. Janský, *LL*, March 28; J. Litera, *Student*, April 3; R. Slánský, *Smena*, April 6; K. Fukan, *KŽ*, April 12. On the sixties, *LL*, March 28; Jan Beneš, *LD*, March 31, April 26; *Student*, April 10, 17; V. Škutina, *Rep.*, April 17-24; V. Mandák, ibid., May 8-15.

[39] E. Löbl, *Svedectvo o procese s vedením protištátneho sprísahaneckého centra na čele s Rudolfom Slánskym*, with a foreword by Dušan Pokorný (Bratislava, 1968). This was later published in English as *Sentenced and Tried: The Stalinist Purges in Czechoslovakia* (London, 1969) and in an American edition, *Stalinism in Prague: The Löbl Story* (New York, 1969), the latter without the introduction by Pokorný. Both English editions included additional materials, especially excerpts from the original trial proceedings. For excerpts, see *LL*, April 25; *Rep.*, May 8-15; for reviews, see M. Hysko, *KŽ*, May 31; V. Vrabec, *RP*, July 5.

Another survivor of the Slánský trial, Artur London, published a revelatory book

Slánský trial, revealed some of the truth about the trial and sought to explain the causes of this ghastly episode in Czechoslovak history. Almost simultaneously there appeared a series of articles, "Report on My Husband," by Josefa Slánská, recounting in poignant detail her interrogation during her own detention without trial (from November 1951 to April 1953) and the discrimination against her and her son after their release.[40] This was followed by a series by Gustáv Husák in a Slovak weekly, describing the methods used during his interrogation and his ten-year imprisonment, the denial of full rehabilitation even after his release in 1960, and the historical background and political significance of the trials of the Slovak "bourgeois nationalists."[41] No less shocking were the reports of relatively minor figures, such as F. Přeučil, former National Socialist deputy, describing his fourteen years in prison; Nina Svobodová, former Catholic editor, condemned to prison in 1950, sentenced again in 1961, and released only in 1967, after a total of fifteen years' imprisonment; and M. Oren, Israeli socialist leader, who was forced to give evidence at the Slánský trial and was himself jailed from 1951 to 1956.[42] These explosive revelations were accentuated by the interviews given by two former Ministers of Public Security, Ladislav Kopřiva and Karol Bacílek.[43]

Löbl's book was outstanding for its appalling description of the manner in which the accused were forced to confess to crimes they had not committed and were thus rehearsed for their public "trial." The court scene was "stage managed" with the entire script and the parts of the various "actors" worked out by "the Teachers," as Löbl called the Soviet advisers.[44] The method was "simple," "a thing of genius." The interrogators used a combination of physical and psychological pressures, including interrogations for an average of sixteen hours at a time, deprival of sleep, hunger, drugs; appeals to party loyalty; threats to their own

---

on his arrest, interrogation, and trial, *L'aveu: Dans l'engrenage du procès de Prague* (Paris, 1968), later published, after the occupation, in Czech, *Doznání* (Prague, 1969); in English, *The Confession* (New York, 1970). See also the collection of moving letters exchanged from prison between Vladimír Clementis and his wife, Lída, *Listy z väzenia* (Bratislava, 1968), with an introduction by L. Novomeský.

[40] *LL*, April 26 to June 6, incl. These were chapters from a book later published in English, *Report on My Husband* (London, 1969). Cf. the account of the experiences of Šling's wife, in Marian Šlingová, *Truth Will Prevail* (London, 1968), and of the wife of the executed Rudolf Margolius, in H. Kovaly and E. Kohak, *The Victors and the Vanquished* (New York, 1973).

[41] Husák's seven articles were excerpts from two long letters addressed to the Central Committee in 1962 and 1963 and appeared weekly in *Nové slovo*, from June 13 to July 25.

[42] *Svobodné slovo*, July 17; *LD*, July 18; *Rep.*, July 17-24.

[43] Bacílek, *Smena*, April 28; *Pravda*, May 15; Kopřiva, *VP*, May 7; *Rep.*, June 12-19. See below for fuller discussion.

[44] Löbl, *Sentenced and Tried*, pp. 47-53.

lives and their families; and constant humiliation. "I was never once struck," he reported. "In the end I confessed to every conceivable crime." "I had lost all sense of human dignity." "I had ceased to be human." "I feel guilty," he admitted, "that I was not strong enough to stand up to the terror . . . ; to the end of my life I shall not be able to forgive myself that weakness."[45]

Husák confirmed that "their method was not physical violence but 'a psychological method.' . . . Every individual, every organism, every nervous system, has a certain limit to the enduring of a burden; when this is crossed, the nervous system gives way, breaks down, surrenders. . . . Thus were the 'confessions' achieved." "I signed what they wrote on paper. They wrote what they wished, not what I really said. He who signed was not a normal man, but one tormented, ill and in ruins, without the capacity to master his reason, his will, or his mind." Husák made three separate confessions, each followed by a retraction; his ultimate decision was "not to give way at any price, as a result of any violence, even at the price of life." As a result, his trial eventually had to be conducted in secret, with a faked record of the interrogation, including a falsified signature, and without any possibility of legal defense.[46] In other cases, the use of drugs, designed to achieve "a splitting of the personality," or outright physical torture, achieved the same goal, if the prisoner survived.[47] In the words of several commentators, the revelations confirmed the wildest fictional imaginings of Koestler's *Darkness at Noon*.[48]

A central issue of debate was the assessment of responsibility for the evils of the past. Some felt that the party as a whole could not escape ultimate responsibility for the system that produced the trials and carried out an incomplete revision.[49] Yet the notion that *all* were responsible, advanced by Novotný during his rule, was unacceptable to most. The

[45] *Sentenced and Tried*, pp. 9-20, esp. 17-19. Goldstücker confirmed the use by the security officers of "various levels of physical and psychical violence," which cannot be conceived even "in the fantasy of a decent person." As a result of the victim's faith in the party, confession was often achieved as a result of "an identification with the aggressor" (*LL*, May 30). London gave a similar description of the tortures used and concluded that, in view of the effectiveness of these measures, the use of drugs was not necessary (*L'aveu*, pp. 112, 369-70). Cf. the analysis of a clinical psychologist and former prisoner, I. Pondělíček, on the physical and psychical methods used to "destroy the human personality" (*LL*, July 11). See the essay on the same theme by a clinical psychologist, J. Čermerník, in the international edition of *Praxis* (Zagreb) 7, nos. 3-4 (1970), 434-40 (in French).

[46] Husák, *NS*, June 20, 27.

[47] On the use of drugs, see the interview with a doctor in the judicial service, *RP*, June 7; on torture, see Löbl, *Sentenced and Tried*, p. 18. Cf. the indictment of two state security investigators for the physical liquidation of two prisoners (*RP*, July 6).

[48] L. Sochor, *Rep.*, April 10-17; Pondělíček, *LL*, July 11.

[49] E.g. Vrabec, *Kulturní tvorba*, May 23. Others, for instance, Husák, rejected the notion of the guilt of the party as a whole (*Pravda*, April 23).

blame rested, it was argued, on individuals whose guilt varied according to their exact role in the hierarchy.[50] The chief responsibility rested with the topmost political leaders of the time, including Novotný.[51] A share had to be borne by all the lesser cogs in the machine of persecution, in the party organs and apparatus, the security service, and the judicial system. Individuals could not escape by invoking "orders from above," or "belief in the charges," or "ignorance of the methods used," or "faith in the party."[52] Nor could the onus be placed mainly on the "Beria agents," thus absolving Stalin and those Czechs, including Gottwald, who were also guilty.[53] Yet some thought that even the general public or ordinary citizen, who condoned, acquiesced in, or applauded the trials, bore a share of guilt. "We are all responsible for the political trials," wrote Dušan Hamšík—"the national *as a whole*, as a *continuum*." "It is a dark stain on our past, a burdening of our history, by which we are all determined for good or ill. . . ."[54]

The atmosphere of the time may be sensed from the charges and countercharges made in the public debate. Novotný, as already noted, disowned responsibility for the trials and the failure to rehabilitate, but was bitterly condemned by others, notably Husák, who pinned on him "the absolutely indubitable political responsibility" for "brutal reprisals, for imprisonment of innocent communists, for breach of the laws, and for fraudulent rehabilitation."[55] Alexej Čepička, who at first sought to avoid any public statement, asserted in early August, that, as a member of the Politburo, he had, like all other members, believed in the authenticity of the charges against Slánský, and that the later campaign against him, after 1946, had made him (Čepička) "a sacrificial lamb."[56] Viliam Široký, who shunned all publicity, was bitterly condemned by Husák as bearing the heaviest responsibility for the campaign against, and later the trials of, the so-called Slovak bourgeois nationalists.[57] Bacílek and Kopřiva, in their press interviews, claimed ignorance of the methods of investigation used by their own subordinate officials and placed much

[50] Mlynář, *RP*, April 17; Hysko, *KŽ*, May 31; Vrabec, *Rep.*, July 24-31; Pokorný, in Löbl, *Sentenced and Tried*, p. 263.
[51] Husák, *RP*, April 23; Mlynář, *LL*, May 16; Hysko, *KŽ*, May 31.
[52] Hric and Michal, *Pravda*, April 5; Mlynář, *RP*, April 17; Hysko, *KŽ*, May 31.
[53] B. Hájek, *Rep.*, Aug. 14-21, a reply to B. Maturová, ibid., July 17-24, pp. 11-12.
[54] Hamšík, *LL*, March 28.
[55] *RP*, June 15. See also his earlier article (*Pravda*, April 23) cited above, n. 20 (excerpts in R. A. Remington, ed., *Winter in Prague*, Cambridge, Mass., 1969, pp. 142-46), where he urged acceleration of the investigation of Novotný's past.
[56] *RP*, Aug. 5. Čepička noted that he had not been Minister of Justice during the Slánský trial and had never been Minister of Public Security. See criticisms of Čepička by *Hlas ľudu*, April 19; *VP*, May 22; *Práce*, July 23.
[57] *NS*, July 11, 18, 25. In these articles Husák criticized both Slánský and Kopecký, but was less harsh on Gottwald and Zápotocký.

blame on the Soviet advisers in the ministry. Both accused Stalin of direct responsibility in the arrest of Slánský, but they claimed to have been unaware of Mikoyan's visit to Prague in this connection.[58] Only after severe press criticism did Bacílek admit his errors as minister and his responsibility for collective decisions of the leadership.[59] Their successor, Barák, as we have seen, sought to evade responsibility for the 1954 trials and to justify his record but was challenged by Husák and Švermová.

At lower levels of the hierarchy, denials, or occasional admissions, of guilt, were usually coupled with attempts to shift the blame to higher levels. For instance, Josef Urválek, chief prosecutor in the Slánský trials, disclaimed any responsibility because he had known nothing of the interrogation methods and had believed in the guilt of the accused. He assigned the chief blame to State Security, the Soviet agents, and the Politburo members who had built up the entire machinery.[60] Mlynář and others ridiculed this plea of innocence and accused him of being "co-guilty" of "the crimes of justice behind closed doors."[61] Mamula, head of the CC's 8th department in the sixties, denied having had anything to do with the trials or with rehabilitation proceedings.[62] O. Valášek, former head of the Slovak CC's Security Department, threw the blame on the top Slovak leaders (Široký, Štefan Bašt'ovanský, and Bacílek), who had transformed the charge of bourgeois nationalism from an ideological fault to a criminal act, and on persons in central organs in Prague, particularly Kopřiva, Karel Šváb, and B. Doubek. Valášek denied that the Slovak security organs had any power after April 1950.[63] In contrast, B. Doubek, former head of the Investigation Department in the Ministry of the Interior (1951-1953), fully admitted his guilt, as he was, like others, such as Urválek, part of "the system"; although they had not created it, they did not *have* to remain in it. Both Novotný and Barák knew

[58] Interviews cited above, n. 43. Both former ministers noted that they had been charged with "softness" at the time. Kopřiva made much of the fact that he had been minister from May 1950 to January 1952 and hence *not* during the preparations of the Horáková trial or the conduct of the Slánský trial. See below for Mikoyan's visit.

[59] For criticisms of Bacílek, see in particular *Pravda*, May 15, 19, and for his admissions, ibid., May 19. B. Graca, in a retort to Bacílek's interview in *Smena*, blamed him both for the original condemnation of bourgeois nationalism and for his failure to rehabilitate the victims (*NS*, May 23).

[60] *RP*, April 14; *Rep.*, April 17-24.

[61] *RP*, April 17; *LL*, May 16. See the attack on Urválek for his part in the Horáková trial, and for his role in delaying rehabilitation as chairman of the Supreme Court, by R. Slánský, the son of the executed party leader, and K. Bartošek (*RP*, April 17). For other criticisms, see the statement by the Institute of State and Law, *RP*, April 21; I. Holý, ibid., April 26, May 21; letters, *Rep.*, April 17-24, April 24-May 1.

[62] *Rep.*, June 5-12.

[63] *Smena*, June 5-7. Husák, however, assigned heavy responsibility to Valášek, *NS*, July 25.

in 1955 of his confessions of illegal methods for which he was sentenced in 1957.[64] Another target of attack, Dr. Josef Sommer, chief physician at Ruzyně, who was charged by many with the drugging of prisoners and the neglect of the ill, denied any responsibility but committed suicide.[65]

Karel Kaplan, the historian, sought to assess the specific responsibility of individual persons in a systematic manner. Although the trials, he wrote, were the result of a complex of objective factors, "the bearers of deeds are people—concrete persons, individuals, organs, agencies or groups. Only their activity produced a whole series of illegalities culminating in the political trials, the result of which was scores of judicial and political murders." Although the Communist Party bore "the general or indirect responsibility" as "the main creator" of the trials, "the degree and quality of responsibility was, however, quite varied and corresponded to the significance of the various organs in the mechanism of power and decision-making." He then identified the party and state organs which bore "direct responsibility" in creating the trials: the security organs, including the Soviet advisers, which, together with the top political organs, had "the decisive voice," and the "implementers," namely, procurators, judges, and defense lawyers, and in the case of the political leaders, gave the names of the incumbents.[66]

"HOW WAS IT POSSIBLE?"

The Czechoslovak trials were, in Kaplan's words, "the greatest trials in post-war Europe," not only in extent but in the number of supreme penalties promulgated; they were also the last political trials to take place in Eastern Europe, the latter ones occurring at a time of transition from cold war to decreased tension.[67] How was it possible that such terrible events could occur in a country of humane tradition, and in the name of socialism? This worrying question gnawed at the minds and consciences of many Czechs and Slovaks, and the answer, or answers, to it, were closely related to the problem of how to avoid a repetition in the future.[68]

[64] *Smena*, June 19. A high-ranking security police official, under the pseudonym Marian Brázda, made a "confession" of how he came to accept and carry out the policies of the fifties and finally became unwilling to continue (*Pravda*, April 26).

[65] Sommer committed suicide on April 26 after he had been criticized by name in the Prague daily (*VP*, April 23) and interviewed by *Literární listy* (published posthumously, May 9). Löbl accused Sommer of brutality, but considered him also a victim of the system (*LL*, May 9).

[66] *Nová mysl*, no. 8 (1968), pp. 1057-60.

[67] *NM*, no. 8 (1968), p. 1054.

[68] See, for instance, Hamšík, "Trials that Made History," *LL*, March 28; Z. Jesenská, "The Roots of the Moral Crisis and the Trials," *KŽ*, March 29; panel discussion, "How Was It Possible?" *Rep.*, April 10-17, pp. I-VIII; Vrabec, "Mills and Millers," *Rep.*, July 24-31, pp. I-VI. For a translation of Hamšík's articles and other

387

It was recognized that the trials were not merely a matter of the responsibility of an individual, whether a Gottwald, a Bacílek, or a Doubek, but were the products of more profound forces and indeed of a general system in which even the guilty became victims.

Some commentators saw the trials not merely as a ghastly imitation of earlier trials in the USSR, but as an instrument to discredit the national path to socialism, and to justify and compel the adoption of Soviet patterns. What was on trial, stated Hamšík, was "the national path" and indeed its principal architect, Gottwald, although he himself had managed to shift the blame to Slánský, his chief lieutenant. Henceforth, said Löbl, Czechoslovakia was expected to subordinate its own interests unconditionally to those of the Soviet Union. Dušan Pokorný, in his introduction to Löbl's book, explained this as the result of a conscious decision by Stalin, who wished to eliminate plurality and diversity within his empire and to impose the Soviet model on the other communist-ruled states. Gottwald had to make a difficult choice—to accept or to refuse this edict. He accepted and thereby had "to condemn his own policy . . . to liquidate the Czechoslovak road to socialism and to condemn it, not just in words, abstractly, but also in the persons of those who had helped him prepare and implement it, and not just condemn them, but have them killed. . . . Nothing can relieve him of responsibility for the choice he made."[69]

Husák explained the trials of the Slovak leaders in similar terms. The Soviet leaders considered bourgeois nationalism ("Husákism") as the Slovak parallel of Titoism and other forms of the "nationalist danger." In order to reverse the policies advocated by those who had taken leading roles in the Uprising and had for a brief period occupied top positions in post-war Slovak politics, it was necessary to liquidate "the team of the Uprising" and to subordinate Slovakia to the centralized rule of Prague. This fitted well with the aims of Široký, who was not himself a participant in the Uprising and had already achieved a dominant position in Slovak affairs after 1945. The campaign against bourgeois nationalism from 1949 on permitted Široký to complete the elimination of his rivals (Clementis, Husák, etc.) and to make himself the absolute ruler of Slovakia, with a cult of his own personality. Široký, as the sole channel of contact between Slovakia and the Prague leadership, was able to exploit the Czech leaders' ignorance of Slovakia and to play on their fears of Slovak nationalism, and thus to implement a policy which neglected Slo-

---

commentaries on the trials, see A. Oxley, A. Pravda, and A. Ritchie, eds., *Czechoslovakia: The Party and the People* (London, 1973), part III.

[69] Hamšík, "Trials"; Löbl, *Sentenced and Tried*, pp. 20, 24, 40; Pokorný, ibid., pp. 259-63. Cf. J. Opat, symposium, *Rep.*, April 10-17.

vak national interests and to subordinate them to those of Prague and of Moscow.[70]

Karel Kaplan, who had been placed in charge of research for the Piller commission, in a series of articles published on the eve of the invasion, analyzed thoroughly the factors, international and domestic, that might offer an explanation of the gruesome events of the fifties.[71] The international context of the trials was produced by the "cold war," the division of the world into two camps, and the expulsion of Yugoslavia from the bloc. These conditions created an atmosphere of tension in the communist world and led to the appeal for "caution and vigilance," the demand for absolute unity, and the adoption of more militant policies. The CPCz, accepting the general argumentation of the Cominform resolutions, abandoned the "national path to socialism" in favor of the Soviet model; adopted harsher policies at home, including severe measures against farmers and tradesmen, the establishment of forced labor camps and trials of non-communists; and began the campaign against Slovak nationalism and the frenetic search for "enemies in the ranks." The trials in Hungary and other people's democracies served as a model and a warning, and in fact led to direct pressure from Rákosi for action against certain Czechs and Slovaks whose names had come up in the trial of László Rajk. This in turn led to the introduction of Soviet advisers in October 1949, and to the search for "a Czechoslovak Rajk," beginning with lesser functionaries, and moving up the hierarchy, ultimately, to Slánský. The broadening of the net, culminating in the selection of Slánský as the chief culprit, was the result of direct pressure from Stalin, who ordered first the removal of Slánský from the general secretaryship, and then his arrest and trial. It was also related in some degree to the rise of the campaign against Zionism by the world communist movement. In this process the Soviet advisers seemed to act sometimes as an independent force, persisting in their investigation of Slánský even without the knowledge, and against the will, of Gottwald and perhaps even of Stalin.[72]

The domestic causes of the trials, according to Kaplan, lay in the political system itself, which permitted supreme authority to reside in a small group at the party pinnacle, and thus rendered party and state organs impotent and eliminated any possibility of checking the abuse of power. This political order, contrary to Czechoslovak traditions, was a product of Bolshevik experience and was imported into Czechoslovakia

[70] This was Husák's 1962-1963 analysis given in his series in *Nové slovo*, cited in n. 41.
[71] *NM*, nos. 6-8 (1968). See also Kaplan, *RP*, Aug. 14; *ŽS*, no. 29, Nov. 27, 1968; Vrabec, *Rep.*, July 24-31.
[72] Kaplan, *NM*, no. 6 (1968), pp. 786-90; no. 7 (1968), pp. 925-33; no. 8 (1968), p. 1061.

as an essential feature of the policy of modeling all aspects of life on the Soviet pattern.[73]

A special feature of the system was the extraordinary power achieved by the security service which, after 1948, escaped from any control by the party, state, or judicial organs, and became so powerful that it not only determined security policy, but, through arrests, investigations, and trials was able to "decide a series of cadre questions concerning high party and state functionaries" and "indirectly influenced the political line of the state." Yet, in fact, political and security organs worked in close cooperation. "The leadership in such a political system needs the security to keep itself in power . . . at the same time the social and political tension, which is the source of the existence of the political system, is the source of the need for, and the power of, the security system."[74]

The power of the security forces was further enhanced, wrote Kaplan, with the arrival of the Soviet advisers who came to play a decisive role not only in security matters, but in the whole of political life. In Löbl's words, these agents were, "one might almost say, all-powerful," "the masters of our country."[75] According to Bacílek, there were advisers in all important ministries, twenty-six in the Ministry of Public Security alone, working in every department and exerting a great influence, in many cases "positive," he believed. They even made proposals for appointments and promotions.[76] Kopřiva confirmed the power of what the journal, *Reportér*, termed "czarist governors." "Their authority and influence was greater than that of the minister, not only on the officials of the ministry, but also on the party leadership," to both of whom they had direct access. "We all believed in them without reservations, informed them of everything, consulted with them."[77]

Another crucial feature of the political system was the discipline existing within the party itself, a discipline founded on total faith in the party and in its leadership. This belief in the party and in Stalin was cited by Bacílek and Kopřiva in explaining why they accepted all party decisions, and by some of the victims in explaining why they succumbed to their in-

[73] Kaplan, *RP*, Aug. 14. See also Kaplan, *NM*, no. 6 (1968), pp. 768-70, 790-92; M. Lakatoš, *SS*, June 30; Vrabec, *KT*, May 23; Vrabec, *Rep.*, July 24-31.

[74] Kaplan, *NM*, no. 6 (1968), p. 793; *RP*, Aug. 14. The security service was not itself immune from its own methods, as was shown by the almost complete purge of its ranks in January 1951 (Kaplan, *NM*, no. 7, 1968, p. 922) and the eventual arrest and trial of many of its leading figures.

[75] *NM*, no. 6 (1968), p. 793; Löbl, *Sentenced and Tried*, p. 32. Cf. his article in *Práca*, May 15, in which he spoke of the Republic turning over its sovereignty to the Beria agents. See also London, *Eaveu*, pp. 82-84, 377-78.

[76] *Smena*, April 28, May 13; *Pravda*, May 19.

[77] *Rep.*, June 12-19, 19-26; also VP, May 7. Bil'ak, at the May plenum, citing a letter from Stalin in 1951, argued that it was wrong to lay the blame for the presence of Soviet advisers on Stalin since the responsibility was the Czechoslovak party's (*RP*, June 5).

terrogators' pressures. Indeed, when their party loyalty was appealed to, the accused often indulged in acts of self-criticism at an early stage in their denunciation and later made humiliating and degrading confessions as a final service to the party.[78]

The whole of society was under the spell of the "evil atmosphere" fostered by massive propaganda concerning the trials, which led to mass appeals for death sentences or to general indifference to the fate of fellow citizens and intimate comrades.[79] Society, stated Kaplan, had suffered "a great moral shock," and "remained deaf to the fate of people. . . ." "Those who doubted were few, those who asked questions, still fewer, and those who protested and fought, fewest of all, perhaps only the closest relations."[80] It was difficult to explain this phenomenon. No doubt it was due in part to the distortion of information which deprived most people of a basis for rational judgment. Perhaps it was also due to the lowering of legal standards in the post-war trials of collaborators. Was it due to fears on the part of those not directly involved, and was that in turn due to the terrible system for "the mass manufacture of weak characters"?[81] Was it due to "a moral crisis" caused by the replacement of "conscience" by "discipline" as "the supreme principle"?[82] Was "the national character" at fault, perhaps affected by the German occupation?[83] Such questions were unanswerable but testified to the depth of the shock and to the serious self-examination occasioned by the revelations of past horrors.

The Law on Judicial Rehabilitation

Throughout April, May, and June, the rehabilitation law was being prepared under the direction of the Ministry of Justice, with widespread

[78] Kaplan, *RP*, Aug. 14; *NM*, no. 6 (1968), p. 791. See also Goldstücker, *LL*, May 30; London, *Ľaveu*, pp. 175, 273; Slánská, *Report on My Husband*, pp. 142-43, 166-67. See also Hamšík, "Trials," and B. Hájek, *Rep.*, Aug. 14-21, on party discipline and blind obedience. Bacílek is reported to have visited prisoners in jail and urged them to confess "in the interests of the party" (Kaplan, *NM*, no. 7, 1968, p. 936). Cf. London, *Ľaveu*, pp. 271-72.

[79] For a scholarly analysis of the mobilization of mass support for the trials, see Vrabec, "The Relationship of the CPCz and Public Opinion to the Political Trials at the Beginning of the Fifties," *Revue dějin socialismu*, no. 3 (1969), pp. 363-87.

[80] Kaplan, *NM*, no. 8 (1968), p. 1065. Cf. Pokorný, in Löbl, *Sentenced and Tried*, p. 264, "The silence of the great and of the small is the most dreadful testimony as to the state of the society in which all this had been enacted. It is a scream of impotence—coming also from those who perhaps originally were very powerful." An outstanding exception was Karl Kreibich, a founder of the CPCz, who protested the anti-Semitic character of the trials as early as 1952 (Vrabec, "CPCz and Public Opinion," p. 370), and in 1963, in an unpublished essay, characterized them as "judicial murders" (*Rep.*, July 3-10, 1968). See the description of the fate of persons who opposed the charges against Josef Frank (*RP*, June 16).

[81] Löbl, *Práca*, May 15.   [82] Jesenská, *KŽ*, March 29.

[83] Hamšík, *LL*, March 28. Cf. J. Ruml, *Rep.*, April 24-May 1, 1968.

391

consultation of legal experts and accompanied by vigorous discussion in parliamentary committees and in the press.[84] There was frequent criticism of the delay in the completion of this urgent task, and the government itself stressed the need for a speedy solution. It was, however, a difficult and complicated question, with differences of view in official quarters, and sharp public debate over crucial issues. The overwhelming majority (90 percent) of the public favored rehabilitation, but opinion was divided on the question of punishing the guilty, with a slight majority (58 percent) favoring judicial proceedings, and others (37 percent) their removal from all public posts.[85]

The dimensions of the task were enormous, potentially affecting many tens of thousand persons. The estimate of the exact number of victims depended on the choice of period to be covered, and on the categories of persons included. Although the period originally proposed was from October 24, 1948 to 1956, the government decided, under public pressure, to extend it to July 31, 1965.[86] A deputy, J. Šubrt, proposed that the initial date be shifted closer to February 1948, but this was generally rejected so as to make clear that "the socialist order" was not to be affected.[87] Originally the law was to embrace the major political cases of those illegally imprisoned by the State Court from 1948 to 1953 (some 27,000); by the regional courts from 1953 to 1956 (5,300); and by other courts from 1957 to 1967 (3,470), and to leave other so-called non-judicial cases to separate legislation. It was later decided to extend the law to include peasants and small tradesmen who had suffered from draconic administrative measures under certain laws of 1950 (some 25,000-30,000 and 16,000 persons respectively), as well as persons arbitrarily confined without trial in forced labor camps (22,000). In other words, some 100,000 individuals would be affected.[88]

Government spokesmen repeatedly specified that they would draw a line between citizens unjustly sentenced, although not guilty of criminal actions, and those who had engaged in criminal activity and were justly

---

[84] For government statements and discussions in parliamentary committee, see P. Colotka, *Pravda*, May 11; *RP*, May 24-25, June 7, 12-13, 15, 18, 26 (Kučera, fuller in *Pravda*, June 26). Among commentaries see in particular, J. Meško, *Pravda*, April 27; G. Přenosil, *RP*, April 30; J. Nezkusil, *LL*, May 23; L. Očenáš, *Práce*, May 24. See also Ulč, "Vagaries of Law," pp. 22-25.

[85] *RP*, May 5. A mimeographed report of the Institute for Public Opinion Research gave the first figure as 91 percent.

[86] *RP*, June 8. After 1965, it was argued, reforms in criminal law procedure had eliminated the dangers of illegality (Colotka, *NS*, July 18).

[87] *RP*, June 12.

[88] Meško, *Pravda*, April 27; Očenáš, *Práce*, May 24; J. Rychetský, *OL*, Aug. 4. Očenáš noted, in addition, lesser anti-state cases tried before district courts—35,000 from 1948 to 1956, and 27,000 from 1957 to 1967. Rychetský estimated these lesser cases at 50,000. Cf. various estimates given by Kusin, *Political Grouping*, pp. 173-75. Kusin's estimated total was approximately 80,000.

punished. Moreover, the familiar thesis was reiterated that the proposed statute would not cancel "acts which were the results of revolutionary changes and were derived from the historically justified class character of the legislation of the socialist revolution."[89]

There were those, in particular the organization K 231,[90] who pressed for a blanket cancellation of all sentences. The government, however, favored consideration of each individual case, contending that only this would distinguish between the guilty and the innocent; identify those responsible; and assist in defining the amount of compensation.[91] Another source of controversy was the question of punishment for those responsible for illegalities, with some calling for "tolerance" and "fair play," and others for "punishment" and "revenge." The opinion of the government, supported by the assembly's constitutional and legal committee, was that the "statute of limitations" (which varied from five to ten years in most cases, or twenty years in criminal actions involving the death penalty) must be observed and that retroactive legislation extending the period would be illegal.[92] Hence, no criminal prosecution could be launched against most of those responsible for crimes in the fifties. In any case, it was necessary to avoid a general condemnation of all judges or security officers, and the punishment of innocent persons. Those guilty of wrongdoing would be penalized mainly by removal from any positions held in the judicial or security services. The official viewpoint on "limitations" was shared by most legal specialists,[93] but some pressed for an extension of the period of limitation.[94] A deputy, G. Sekaninová, urged an extension to December 31, 1972, but did not receive the support of the constitutional and legal committee.[95] The government eventually agreed to extend the time limit for prosecution to 1972 only in those cases where the period of limitation had not yet expired.[96]

The statute on judicial rehabilitation was passed almost unanimously

[89] *RP*, June 7. Cf. government report, ibid., May 23; Kučera, ibid., June 26. V. Knapp, chairman of the constitutional and legal committee stated, "It is not a matter of revision of legislation, but of revision of incorrect verdicts" (ibid., May 25).

[90] V. Hejl, *LL*, June 27. See also interview with C. Nigrín, in M. Salomon, *Prague Notebook: The Strangled Revolution* (Boston, 1971), pp. 226-27, and Brodský, *Solution Gamma*, p. 215.

[91] Cf. Přenosil, Nezkusil, and Meško, cited above, n. 84.

[92] Colotka, *Pravda*, May 11; also *RP*, May 24, June 7. Kučera was quoted to the effect that only 100 of 1,400 judges had been involved in illegal judicial practices (*Práce*, May 14).

[93] Mlynář, *LL*, May 16; Solnář, *RP*, June 6.

[94] I. Bystřina, *LL*, May 30.

[95] *RP*, June 13. A private citizen, V. Mikeš, proposed Jan. 1, 1968 as the date from which the period of limitations should be calculated (*LD*, May 23). A similar proposal was made by the Society for Human Rights (*ZN*, June 11).

[96] *RP*, June 26.

on June 25, with one abstention, and was to come into effect on August 1.[97] As the preamble explained, its purpose was to facilitate and accelerate the rehabilitation of citizens wrongly punished as "offenders against socialism" and to restore "faith in socialist legality and justice." It was not, however, to "abolish acts of revolutionary legality, or weaken, still less, to negate, the socialist legal order." Rehabilitation would not encompass "enemies of socialist construction who, by their criminal acts against the republic or by other criminal activity, broke valid laws and were punished in accordance with them." It was to cover the period from October 1948 to July 31, 1965, leaving cases before or after these years of the worst repression to be dealt with by ordinary legal procedures.

The rehabilitation process was to be strictly legal in character, under the jurisdiction of special senates in the regional courts, with the right of appeal to a special senate of the Supreme Court. Although it was not specified in the law, the senate members were to be legally trained, usually judges by profession. Each case was to be examined separately, as a result of an initiative by the individual, his close relatives, or a procurator, within one year of the law. The decision would be made after a public hearing, and was to be published, and the right of defense was guaranteed. A special auxiliary role as societal defenders was granted to certain mass associations, including the Union of Anti-Fascist Fighters (but without mention of K 231).[98] The original sentences would be canceled or reduced if they were found to be "faulty" according to designated criteria. Several categories were to be rehabilitated by virtue of the law, without special proceedings, for instance, citizens sent to forced labor camp by administrative decisions, and peasants and tradesmen sentenced between 1950 and 1961 for the alleged hindering of the conduct of an enterprise, or for failure to carry out the obligations of the plan, such as compulsory deliveries. In the latter case, secondary sentences involving confiscation of personal property were declared null and void, although there was to be no restitution for the loss of land or means of production.

Compensation would be given to all whose prison sentences or deten-

[97] *Sbírka zákonů*, no. 82/1968. For text and official commentary, see *Zákon o súdnej rehabilitácii* (Bratislava, 1968). For fuller analysis, see Meško, *Pravda*, June 27; Colotka, *NS*, July 18; Rychetský, *OL*, Aug. 4; Boček, *Rep.*, Aug. 7-14; Kučera, *SS*, Aug. 20.

[98] After the occupation the National Front entrusted the union with advisory responsibilities, to be carried out through a network of consultation offices, and also defined its role as "societal defender" in rehabilitation proceedings. See *Informační zpravodaj Ústředního výboru Národní fronty* (Prague, Oct. 1968), pp. 28-31. According to Hejl, K 231 was to cooperate with national committees and ministries in rehabilitation (*SS*, Aug. 15, cited by R. Gueyt, *La mutation tchéco-slovaque*, Paris, 1969, p. 272). A statement to the same effect was reportedly made by Smrkovský (V. Čermák, *Tribuna*, Sept. 17, 1969). See also *Zpráva o současné politické situaci Československe socialistické republiky* . . . (pp. 25-26).

tion in camps was declared null and void. The maximum amount payable would be 20,000 Czechoslovak crowns (Kčs) per year; any payments above a grand total of 20,000 Kčs were to be paid in state bonds. This remuneration would cover not only loss of income during confinement, but also damage to health and the original trial costs, and was to be supplemented by the return of, or compensation for, personal property seized. Compensation would be paid to dependents in case of death of the breadwinner by execution or imprisonment.[99]

Finally, in regard to punishment of those guilty of illegal actions, criminal prosecution was permissible only if the period of limitation had not expired. This was extended until January 1973 if it had not already expired at the time of the enactment of the law. Those employed in the judicial and security services were to be dismissed if their responsibility for illegalities was established by special commissions to be set up in the Ministries of Justice and Interior, and in the Procuracy General, and in the case of judges, by disciplinary senates established by the National Assembly.

EXTRA-JUDICIAL REHABILITATION

Other serious injustices had resulted from administrative actions, either by national committees, ministries or other government agencies, or by institutions such as the universities or institutes. The reexamination of such cases raised distinctive problems which, it was finally decided, required special legislation, separate from the law on judicial rehabilitation. Throughout June and July work proceeded on such a statute, and in late July the general principles were approved by the government. The draft statute was not yet ready, but, it was expected, would be submitted to the National Assembly during August.[100]

The main purpose was not to give compensation (although this was provided in certain cases) but to afford moral satisfaction to the victims of injustice and to remove obstacles in the way of their employment and public activity. As in the case of judicial rehabilitation, it was not intended to question "revolutionary actions," such as collectivization or nationalization, or the activities of the action committees in 1948, but

[99] The probable amount of compensation was estimated as from 2½ to 3½ billion Kčs. The costs of the proceedings, which would involve the appointment of additional judges, administrative officers, and procuracy officials, would run to approximately 24,000,000 Kčs.

[100] For official summaries of the draft law, see L. Šmid, *RP*, June 13; Šmid, *Svět v obrázech*, Aug. 20; V. Lachout, *RP*, July 27; V. Adamus, *ZN*, July 27. See also for details, Meško, *Pravda*, May 25; M. Číž and J. Kabat, *NS*, Sept. 12; J. Inovecký, ibid., Nov. 28. Inovecký criticized the delay in the passage of legislation and the failure to handle some of these categories under the law on judicial rehabilitation.

395

rather to deal with a host of illegal and unjust measures taken by state authorities in implementing these basic post-1948 policies and with many other forms of persecution of citizens for ideological and political reasons. Included would be dismissals or transfers from jobs; evictions from living quarters, not only of peasants under 1950 laws, but also of city dwellers, in the so-called Action B between 1951 and 1953; confiscation of personal property; the arbitrary reduction or cessation of pension payments; expulsions from high schools or universities; illegal searches and detentions by the security police; and induction in the armed forces for compulsory labor in the so-called Auxiliary Technical Units. In some cases, the actions taken were declared null and void, or expunged from the record; in most cases, individual requests for reexamination, within one year after the law came into effect, could be made by the individual concerned. There were various channels for such appeals, usually through special rehabilitation commissions set up by the national committees, with a right of appeal to regional committees or regional courts. Compensation, up to a maximum of 20,000 Kčs, was provided in some cases. The individual was also entitled to the restoration of personal property or dwellings confiscated or to an assurance of alternative living space.

In the meantime, many government departments and other institutions began to carry out independent reexamination of injustices through their own commissions appointed for the purpose, thus assuming a responsibility which had been inadequately fulfilled during the sixties. For instance, the Ministry of Foreign Affairs considered some 350 requests for reconsideration of dismissals, and from time to time announced the rehabilitation of former diplomats.[101] The Ministry of National Defense had to deal with 1,500 requests from veterans of Western allied armies, of the Slovak Uprising, and of the resistance movement.[102] In the field of education, the Ministry of Education received over 1,500 requests; Czechoslovak higher schools, over 900; and regional committees, over 600. The Ministry restored 295 teachers to their jobs, and some eleven professors and eight docents.[103] At the Philosophical Faculty of Charles University, the faculty commission rehabilitated some 25 professors and 132 students.[104] Other organizations, such as the Writers' Union or the Revolutionary Trade Union Movement, also formed rehabilitation commissions. These procedures provided moral rehabilitation, and, in some cases, restoration of posts; complete rehabilitation, including compensation, had to await the enactment of the statute.[105]

[101] RP, June 8, 28. [102] Ibid., May 24.
[103] LL, Aug. 1. [104] RP, July 16.
[105] J. Seifert, ibid., June 2; V. Kadlec, LL, Aug. 1.

THE PILLER INVESTIGATION

The appointment of the Piller commission at the April plenum indicated that the party leadership intended to make a final study of the entire problem of the trials of leading communists and the delays in their subsequent rehabilitation. Its primary task was to reexamine the eight main political trials of the fifties, which had involved seventy-two persons, and to complete the rehabilitation of those not yet cleared. Its first report to the May plenum was not published, but its recommendations were adopted, namely, to remove Novotný from the Central Committee and to suspend the party membership of Novotný and other key figures. It was instructed to complete its work and present its final report by the end of the year. Meanwhile some sixty historians, lawyers, and economists continued the monumental task of going through some 50,000 pages of materials, drawn from party archives, and interviewed persons involved.[106]

The report was not ready at the time of the occupation and was published only abroad several years later.[107] Its potentially explosive character was revealed in the major articles by Karel Kaplan (referred to above) which were, in a sense, a preview of the report. The final report would have been even more comprehensive and would have contained recommendations for action by the Central Committee.

The report included a long historical analysis of the trials and of the international and domestic factors which influenced these events. The sword of persecution was turned first against non-communists in 1948, and then, in 1949, against communists—first, Šling and Švermová; then, Slánský and his topmost associates; later, certain groups in the economic sphere, security forces, the military, diplomatic service, etc.; and finally, Husák and the Slovak "bourgeois nationalists." Full data on all the arrests and trials in those fateful years were included; the number of death

[106] See CC communiqué, *RŠO*, p. 63; communiqué of the Piller commission, ibid., pp. 159-60; Piller's report to the May plenum, ibid., p. 164; Piller's interview, *RP*, June 19; K. Kaplan, *Práce*, July 23; M. Sedláková, *Pravda*, Aug. 12.

[107] Jiří Pelikán, ed., *Potlačená zpráva* (*Zpráva komise ÚV KSČ o politických procesech a rehabilitacích v Československu 1949-68*) (Vienna, 1970). The cover bears another title, *Zakázaný dokument*. It was published in several other languages, including English, *The Czechoslovak Political Trials, 1950-1954* (London, 1971). Henceforth cited as Piller report. All references are to the Czech edition. The report is well documented, footnotes citing CC and Ministry of Interior archives. The commission did not have full access to the Interior archives (p. 1), and as Pelikán notes in a long introduction, no access whatever to Soviet archives (p. xix). A book on this theme by Karel Kaplan was submitted to a Czech publisher in late 1968, but was not published. For a review, see V. V. Kusin, "The Trials: Czechoslovak Experience," *Soviet Studies* 22 (April 1971), 623-30. Cf. also Barbara Jancar, "The Great Purges and 'the Prague Spring,'" *Orbis* 15 (Summer 1971), 609-24.

sentences issued by the State Court from October 1948 to the end of 1952 was given as 233, of which 178 were carried out.[108] The analysis of international factors was similar to that in Kaplan's articles, and noted in particular the effect of the belief of some of its allies that Czechoslovakia was "the weakest link" in the communist camp and was lagging in its action against internal and external enemies.[109] The report documented Rákosi's letter of September 3, 1949, urging the arrest of certain persons (pp. 32-33); the Czechoslovak request for Soviet advisers (p. 33); and the personal intervention of Stalin in urging, on July 24, 1951, Slánský's removal from office and, on November 11, his arrest (pp. 55, 57). The latter message was apparently delivered personally by Anastas Mikoyan during a visit to Prague and was based on the alleged danger of Slánský's impending escape to the West.[110] His arrest was approved by the Political Secretariat, the Presidium, and the Central Committee on the basis of a single document, the notorious letter to "The Great Roadsweeper," allegedly from a Western intelligence agency, offering Slánský aid in escaping and asylum.[111] Three Soviet advisers (G. Gromov, G. Morozov, and J. Chernov) were sent for the express purpose of assisting Czechoslovak security officers in the preparation of the trial (p. 59).

In analyzing the domestic causes of the trials, the Piller report described the political evolution from 1948; growing opposition produced a serious crisis and led to the emergence of a political system characterized by "a hitherto unknown concentration of power." The "mechanism for the manufacture of the political trials," consisting of three main elements, was treated at some length. First, the "political organs," including the topmost party bodies and various other agencies and commissions, "gave the necessary directives . . . and ideological justification,"

[108] Piller report, pp. 17-18. An earlier action against a leading communist (in Sept. 1948) was the forced transfer to the Soviet Union of the academician, A. Kolman, ironically after his criticism of Gottwald's relatively "soft" policy (p. 25).

[109] Suspicion centered on the army and on General Svoboda personally. A message from the CPSU in April 1950 indicated that the Soviet military believed Svoboda was "not deserving of confidence" and could not be trusted with military secrets. In January 1951, Slánský admitted they had erred in leaving Svoboda too long in the Ministry of National Defense and in firing him only on Stalin's "urgent counsel" (Piller report, pp. 10-11). Svoboda was later arrested but shortly after, released, without trial. According to Svoboda, the original message from Moscow was false, and his release was due to a genuine telegram from Stalin (RN, March 26). The Barák commission had charged Svoboda and others with sabotage (Piller report, p. 114).

[110] Piller report, p. 57. Kaplan expressed uncertainty as to the purpose of Mikoyan's visit and suggested three alternative explanations (NM, no. 7, 1968, p. 932; no. 8, 1968, pp. 1061-62).

[111] The Piller commission was unable to ascertain the origin of the letter but believed that it was "a provocation" and that the arbitrary identification of Slánský as its addressee was the work of the security service and the Soviet advisers (p. 58).

decided on the arrests and participated directly in the preparation of the trials. Secondly, the security service was closely related to the party "in that party functionaries and members collaborated with the security organs and the party leadership either directly guided the security, or influenced it, or intervened in it." Thirdly, the courts, procurators, etc., were "the executors of decrees and decisions" made elsewhere, thus giving the proceedings "an appearance of legitimacy." This was a system of "justice behind closed doors" and involved "the complete liquidation of judicial independence" and "the degradation of law." "The court proceedings were changed into a great theatre, prepared by security workers. Everything was stage managed (*narežírováno*)."[112]

The role of the Soviet advisers was emphasized. "Their authority was great, their counsels, hints, and decisions had the force of command and the majority of members of the security system fulfilled them with a conviction of their correctness and advantage. . . . The minister also accepted the suggestions and recommendations of the advisers as correct and ordered their fulfillment" (p. 82). Their arrival in 1949 led to changes in the techniques of interrogation and the use of "inhuman methods, an elaborate system of physical and psychic violence" (pp. 36-37).[113]

The Piller report devoted much attention to past measures of rehabilitation and sought to fathom the reasons for their slowness and half-hearted character.[114] The death of Stalin, the execution of Beria, and the increasing evidence of illegal methods brought no immediate change in the attitude of the Czechoslovak regime to the trials. Indeed, *after* Stalin's death seven more major trials, including that of Husák and his fellow Slovaks, took place in Prague (pp. 70-75). The failure to carry through any serious revision of earlier trials was not due to lack of knowledge—the party leaders knew the main facts, including the methods used, by 1954.[115] The main reason for this failure was that the same mechanism "functioned without essential change": for ten years (from 1955 to 1966) there were almost no cadre changes in the security

[112] Piller report, pp. 19-22, 77-85. Cf. Kaplan's words (on the Slánský trial): ". . . a theatre piece . . . culminating in political and judicial murder" (*NM*, no. 7, 1968, pp. 938-39).

[113] These included long cross-examinations; beatings; torturing by hunger and thirst; confinement to dark cells; evoking fear for the fate of relatives; staged confrontations with others; planting of agents as fellow prisoners; bugging of cells, etc. (p. 37). A draft speech prepared for Piller noted that such methods had been used earlier, but developed to "unprecedented proportions" (pp. 208-9).

[114] Piller report, pp. 90-166. Cf. Kaplan, *NM*, no. 8 (1968), pp. 1065-74.

[115] The Piller report notes letters to the President and other government offices by J. Stavinoha, Husák, Smrkovský, Švermová, etc., in 1954, and the confessions of Doubek during his trial in 1955-1956, concerning the use of illegal methods (pp. 67-69, 116). Khrushchev, at the CPCz 10th Congress in June 1954, had also revealed some of the illegalities committed by Stalin (p. 66).

machine and "the same methods of work" were still used. The mechanism was thus a single "system for fabricating the political trials and for carrying through their revision."[116] This led the commission to seek to determine "the political responsibility for both the trials and their (sic) slow rehabilitation." This required an examination of the successive commissions appointed by the party to inquire into past trials and to effect rehabilitation.

The purpose of the successive Barák commissions, from 1955 to 1957, was described as not really "rehabilitation" at all, but merely a "revision" of the trials, mainly in respect to the length of the sentences.[117] The chairman, Barák, who was at the time Minister of the Interior, had been responsible for the trials of 1954. As he revealed in his final report, the commission had examined 300 cases and had recommended new proceedings in only 52 of them.[118] The revision proceedings were, according to the Piller report, highly illegal, since they were conducted in secret and their decisions were merely ratified by the courts, often in the form of new sentences. By the end of 1956 even this limited "revision" was brought to an end. The final report was not published for party consumption and was approved by the Central Committee in October 1957 without a dissenting voice.

The consequences of the Barák investigations were modest in the extreme. The main victim of the trials, Slánský, was not exonerated, but was indeed charged with being "a Czechoslovak Beria," responsible for setting the whole security machine in motion. A few persons were released, including London,[119] Pavel, Goldstücker, and Novomeský, but they did not receive political or even social rehabilitation. Some, such as Smrkovský, had their sentences reduced and were later released. The fate of others, for example, Husák and Löbl, remained unchanged. Still other cases were completely ignored. The commission did not seriously consider the question of responsibility and rarely recommended legal action against the guilty. B. Doubek and M. Kohoutek, who were detained in

[116] Ibid., pp. 219, 232-33. See also pp. 77, 106-7, 169-70.

[117] Ibid., pp. 90-134, 221-27. There were in fact two commissions, A and C, both headed by Barák. For their membership, see ibid., pp. 91, 109.

[118] Including the cases considered by the commission itself, the procurator and other bodies, there were 6,978 requests for reexamination, of which 263 were referred to new judicial proceedings. Only 50 verdicts were found to be completely unjustified; in 213 cases the original sentence was considered too high. In the remaining 6,715 cases (97.4 percent) the original sentence was deemed to be justified (p. 131).

[119] London described his long efforts to reveal the true nature of the trials and to secure his exoneration and release and reported on his interviews with members of the Barák commission (*L'aveu*, pp. 431 ff). His wife, Lise, who was French and the sister-in-law of Maurice Thorez, had at first been convinced of his guilt and had requested divorce; later persuaded of his innocence, she waged her own campaign, both in Prague and in Paris, for his release.

1955, confirmed, during their interrogation, the charges made by Husák and others concerning illegal methods, but were not tried until 1957 and were released a few months later, thus being freed before many of their victims. Sixty-four other security functionaries were removed from their positions or subjected to disciplinary measures, but were not tried. In the five years following the Barák commission's report, some other cases were reexamined and a few prisoners were released. General amnesties in 1957 and 1960 led to the release of thousands of political prisoners (without exoneration), including, in 1960, the last eleven of the seventy-two in the main trials.[120] Meanwhile critics of the trials and of the rehabilitation procedures, according to the Piller report, were often punished, even as late as 1961.[121]

The 22nd congress of the CPSU generated new demands for rehabilitation. After the trial and imprisonment of Barák in 1962,[122] Novotný laid the blame for previous errors in rehabilitation on him and proposed a new commission to investigate the trials between 1948 and 1954. This body, under the chairmanship of Kolder, which presented its report in April 1963, represented, in the judgment of the Piller commission, "the first extensive rehabilitation."[123] The Kolder report described the main trials as fabrications and completed the judicial rehabilitation of all the condemned. It made a partial attempt to explain the origins of the trials and to assign responsiblities for them. Yet the Kolder report suffered from serious inconsistencies, since it did not rehabilitate Slánský and certain others politically and did not retract the charge of bourgeois nationalism against Slovak communist leaders or restore them to public life. It also did not draw full conclusions concerning the question of responsibility, avoiding any mention of Novotný.[124] The result, therefore, the Piller report concluded, was a "compromise" and did not "settle ac-

---

[120] Piller report, pp. 133-46 for the events from 1957 to 1962. See also p. 137, n. 225, re Doubek and Kohoutek. In the 1957 amnesty, 4,811 were released, of a total of 26,412 in prison and 6,000 in detention (p. 136). In 1960, of some 31,000 still in prison, the "majority" were released (pp. 142-43).

[121] E.g. N. Kühnl and V. Kusín, C. Kreibichová, and O. Pavlík were expelled from the party in 1957, and some officers in the Military Political Academy were dismissed in 1958. K. Lukeš and others were expelled in 1961 (pp. 134-36, 145).

[122] The Piller report did not discuss the Barák case in any detail, referring only to its "political character," and noting that Barák had at his disposal a number of documents concerning the share of individual leaders in the trials (p. 146).

[123] For an examination of the Kolder commission's work see ibid., pp. 149-63, 228-31. The membership of the commission was at a higher level than the Barák commissions, including Dubček, Hron, Lenárt, P. Majling, Mamula, Prchlík, Štrougal, Laštovička, H. Leflerová, and Škoda. The Kolder report was not published in Prague during 1968. For Kolder's defense of his commission's work, see p. 376 in this chapter. See also chap. III above.

[124] The report of Politburo discussions in 1962 and 1963 revealed efforts by Novotný and others to shift the blame to Slánský, Čepička, Barák, etc. (Piller report, pp. 154-56, 158-59).

counts with the tragic legacy of the trials" (p. 162). Remaining cases of rehabilitation and punishment were assigned to party organs (ÚKRK) and to the Supreme Court, the Procuracy General, and the Ministries of the Interior and Justice. This led to the rehabilitation of 387 persons between 1963 and 1967 (with another 40 readmitted to party membership); the imposition of a few party penalties, in most cases relatively mild; and the dismissal of 58 security officers. Some organizational changes were made in the Ministry of Public Security but these left untouched "the mechanism for political trials in its most important link— interrogation," thus making a return to illegalities easily possible (p. 164).

Somewhat strangely, the Piller report devoted almost no attention to the Barnabite commission which had been set up in April 1963 to examine the political aspects of the Slovak trials in the wake of the juridical clearance of Husák and his associates by the Kolder commission. Headed at first by J. Lenárt, later by V. Koucký, it included a number of prominent Czech and Slovak politicians, and employed the services of some fifty scholars and experts, both Czech and Slovak.[125] The commission's work led to the removal of Široký from the prime ministership in September 1963; the complete repudiation of the original case against bourgeois nationalism; and the full party rehabilitation of Husák, Novomeský and Clementis in December 1963. During the spring of 1968 it was sharply criticized by former members and advisers. Although it had rehabilitated Husák and other Slovak leaders, it was censured for not restoring them to public life and for not proposing any solutions for Slovak economic, political, and constitutional problems. The blame was placed on Koucký and Novotný for this, and on Široký and Bacílek (before their removal) for trying to block a full reassessment of "bourgeois nationalism" and to maintain the status quo in Slovak politics.[126] According to some, the main purpose in creating the Barnabite commission, apart from meeting the pressure of Slovak demands for rehabilitation, was to prepare the ground for the removal of Široký from office but at the same time to prevent Husák's return to public life.[127]

The report of the Piller commission drew radical conclusions concerning the question of responsibility, linking together, as we have noted,

[125] For brief references, ibid., pp. 164-66, 231. The members of the commission included Biľak, R. Cvik, M. Lúčan, Valo, Šalgovič, Graca, Colotka, Macek, I. Skála, Kladiva, Sabolčík, and Laštovička.

[126] See above, p. 376, for plenum discussion. See also M. Hübl, RP, April 17; L. Kohout, KT, April 11 (reprinted in Pravda, April 14); F. Beer, A. Benčík, F. Janáček, and J. Křen, KT, May 2 (in Pravda, May 15); J. Kašpar, RP, May 16; Graca, NS, May 23, 30, 1968. There were apparently differences of opinion among the scholars and within the main commission, and the final report is said not to have embodied all the recommendations of the experts (Beer et al.; Graca).

[127] Kašpar, RP, May 16; Beer et al., KT, May 2.

both the trials and their revision.[128] It proclaimed the radical principle that "every political or public figure and worker in the organs and *aparáts* bears the responsibility for his own decisions, for the decisions of the organs of which he was a member, for the deeds which he performed in his posts, and for the tasks which belonged to him as a party or state functionary" (p. 232). There could be no excuse of any kind, whether external pressures, lack of knowledge, inability to do anything, belief in the correctness of the decisions, etc. (p. 239). The responsibility, however, must be differentiated, depending on the office held, and on the position of the particular agency in the system as a whole, as well as whether the person was responsible for the trials only, for their revision only, or for both (p. 240). Those in certain top positions bore the highest responsibility as "creators, initiators, and main ideologists of the entire mechanism"; next were those in the party and state apparatus who "actively elaborated the basic line and introduced it"; and finally, there were those who "carried out the instructions and decrees" (p. 179).

Applying these principles, the report indicated precisely the various party and state organs responsible for both the early and later trials or for successive revisions, and named the incumbents of the leading bodies. These included all members of the party's Political Secretariat or Presidium, and of other key bodies and commissions;[129] all members of the Central Committees elected at the 9th, 10th, 11th, and 12th congresses; all members of the Slovak Central Committee and its top organs from 1950 to 1954; all Ministers of National Security (V. Nosek, Kopřiva, Bacílek, and Barák); all Ministers of Justice (Čepička, Rais, and Škoda); the chairman of the Supreme Court, Urválek, and the Procurator General, Bartuška; and then, those officers (names were not given) in the judicial system and security service who had had a part in the trials and the revision process. There was special reference to the three Presidents since 1948: Gottwald, who was said to have yielded, after great inner struggle, to outside pressures, and to have borne the greatest responsibility; Zápotocký, concerning whom there was no evidence that he had differed from other leaders or made any effort at revision; and Novotný, who was not one of the main instigators of the Slánský trial, but shared in its execution, and was chiefly responsible for the later trials, for the failure to carry through rehabilitation after 1955, and for the limitations of the Kolder commission.

[128] Piller report, pp. 166-92, 232-40, 248-63 (draft CC decision).
[129] It listed the members of the Political Secretariat and all members of the Presidium (including Smrkovský to April 1951), the Secretariat, the Organizational Secretariat, the CC security commission of 1949-50 (including Pavel), other important commissions concerning the trials, as well as the Politburo from 1954 to 1958, the two Barák commissions, and the Kolder commission (ibid., pp. 170 ff., 235-38, 253-54).

The Piller report was clear and consistent in its specific recommendations (pp. 256-58). The 1963 decisions denying party rehabilitation to Slánský and others were revoked. The case of Novotný and others suspended from party membership in May was to be settled finally, within a month, by a special disciplinary committee. Although no recommendations were made for legal action against those responsible for the trials or their revision the political consequences were to be drastic. "Comrades who were members of organs and commissions actively participating in the construction of the political trials and their revision from 1955 to 1962" were to be withdrawn from any party and state offices still held. No one who was a member of the Central Committee (or KSK or ÚKRK) "uninterruptedly" since the 9th congress would be nominated as CC or ÚKRK members at the forthcoming CPCz or Czech party congresses. Finally, communists working in the judicial system, procuracy, or state security, who collaborated in the trials and revisions from 1955 to 1962, were never again to work in these areas, and those working in party and state organs were not to exercise important functions in these organs.[130]

GUARANTEES FOR THE FUTURE

The Piller report and the draft CC decision proposed a series of measures to guarantee against a repetition of the injustices and illegalities of the past. These recommendations were in the main similar to those which had been raised in the mass media, primarily by legal scholars and certain official personages.[131] Moreover, the party and government were

[130] There were certain differences in the formulations used by the report on these points, although none that was essential. For instance, the report declared that no one who was a member of the highest party organs between 1950 and 1954 and had continued as a member should hold high party office or be a member of the highest party organs (pp. 174-75). CC members elected by the 12th congress in 1962 were also included in this ban (p. 254). The report declared that those in the CC, elected at the 9th, 10th, and 11th congresses, or in leading party organs, should be removed if they were still members (p. 235).
One exception was to be allowed: those who had been expelled from their posts and tried between 1949 and 1953 (p. 257). This exception was presumably also covered by the use of the word "uninterruptedly" in the decision cited above and would have included a number of reformers such as Husák, Pavel, Smrkovský, and Švermová, who had been arrested, and perhaps others who were removed, or had resigned from the CC earlier, such as G. Bareš, Hejzlar, Svoboda, and Erban. The full list of those arrested or removed was given elsewhere in the report (p. 174).
[131] Piller report, pp. 192-99, 240-46, 258-63. See O. Ulč, "Vagaries of Law," pp. 25-27, for a summary of the discussion of legal reforms. Z. Mlynář, in an editorial comment in May, in the main legal journal, wrote that the lawyers were "sleeping," and that the discussions were conducted largely by publicists and political figures (Právník 107, no. 5, 377-79). Succeeding issues paid little direct attention to

firmly committed to specific reforms in this field, although apart from the judicial procedures established for rehabilitation, had not yet taken other concrete measures.

It was generally recognized that a primary prerequisite of avoiding repetition of past illegalities was what Karel Kaplan termed "a basic change," not a mere reform, of the political system as a whole, replacing the extreme concentration of power characteristic of the old system by a division of power and a plurality of forces, checking and balancing each other.[132] At the same time a democratic system required the rehabilitation of law and justice, a restoration of respect for law by the citizens and by those in authority.[133] In the words of the Piller report, the trials of the fifties created "a lawless state," "a state of complete and absolute legal uncertainty, even for those who stood at the apex of the ladder of power" (p. 83). What was required, wrote an eminent legal scholar, was the establishment of "a legal state," in which the state organs would be bound by legal norms and the citizens would be free to do everything *not* forbidden by law.[134] "Without law," said the Minister of Justice, Kučera, "there is no democracy." "For a democratic society socialist courts are just as necessary as parliament," just as "the judiciary could fully develop only within a democracy."[135]

There was a general consensus that a revision of the role of the party, in particular in its internal functioning, was central to political and legal reform. The Piller report endorsed the arguments advanced during the discussion of the party statute for a democratization of the party's inner life and an abandonment of the concept of unity based on "blind obedience." Most original was the suggestion of the report that the leading role of the party must not be effected "in conflict with the constitution and the valid laws." The party member therefore "has not only the right,

---

legal reform. The journal *Socialistická zákonnost*, published by the Ministry of Justice, devoted much space, from April on, to questions of legal reform and published the texts of resolutions by Communist Party organizations in the ministry, the Supreme Court, and the Faculty of Law of Charles University (no. 5, pp. 261-76; no. 6, pp. 330-41); the memorandum of the ministry's Research Institute of Criminology (no. 8, pp. 466-73); and the Action Program of the ministry (nos. 9-10, pp. 522-48). See also the statement, in early March, by legal scholars of the Slovak Institute of State and Law and the Faculty of Law at Komenský University, *Právny obzor*, no. 6 (1968), pp. 549-52.

[132] *RP*, Aug. 14; *NM*, no. 8, pp. 1075-78. Cf. symposium, *Rep.*, April 10-17; M. Lakatoš, *SS*, June 30. Lakatoš urged "a system legally guaranteeing political democracy and a legal state."

[133] J. Krupička, *LL*, June 20. The government, he wrote, had broken its own laws and hence encouraged others to break them, thus undermining "the basic pillars of the life of every human society—its legal order."

[134] Prof. J. Boguszak, *MF*, June 25, 27. This was best achieved by a division of powers, including the independence of the courts.

[135] *SS*, Aug. 11. See also *Socialistické soudnictví*, no. 4 (1968), pp. 5-8.

but also the duty not to fulfill those party decisions which are in conflict with the constitution and the valid laws.[136]

The general principles of legal reform were elaborated in more specific terms in many articles and documents.[137] The main prerequisite, enunciated in the Action Program in a brief reference to legal policy, was emphasized over and over again by commentators and reasserted in the Piller report—namely, the independence of the courts and of judges.[138] Past interference in judicial proceedings by party leaders, by the *aparát*, by the security service, by the Ministry of Justice and by public opinion, was roundly condemned. Boček, the chairman of the Supreme Court, and Kučera, the Minister of Justice, both favored the enactment of a special law that would guarantee the independence of the courts.[139] Some commentators advocated that any interference with the judicial process should be made a criminal act. Judges must be bound by law only, and protected in their independence by long-term, perhaps lifetime, tenure, and should be irremovable during their term of office. Some felt that judges should be appointed or chosen by the National Assembly, rather than elected by the people. There was also criticism of the practice of having lay judges. Judges should be required to have better legal training and more experience. They would have to overcome the "ethical crisis" through which they had passed and acquire "a moral profile."[140]

Other suggested legal reforms reflected the experiences of the fifties and the inadequacy of procedures in the sixties. The trial, it was contended, should be elevated to its rightful position as the crucial element in judicial proceedings. The procurator, who had acquired a dominating position and had in effect supplanted judge and lawyer, must serve only as prosecutor, in an adversary procedure in which the defense lawyer would be guaranteed an important role and the innocence of the accused would be presumed. The court should assume a greater responsibility in

---

[136] Piller report, pp. 194-95, 259-60.
[137] Among others, L. Richterová, *KT*, March 28; J. Koliášová, *ŽS*, no. 11 (May 1968), pp. 51-54; E. Husár, *NS*, July 11; J. Hrazdíra, *Rep.*, July 10-17; V. Mathern, *NS*, Aug. 1; J. Šustr, *Právník*, no. 10 (1968), pp. 848-56. See official statements by M. Čeřovský, *RP*, April 20, *Pravda*, April 24; Boček, *RP*, May 3, *Rep.*, Aug. 7-14; Kučera, *RP*, June 6; *Rep.*, June 19-26; *SS*, Aug. 11; *SZ*, no. 6 (1968), pp. 321-24. The Action Program of the Ministry of Justice, issued on June 3 (cited in n. 131) contained a full statement on legal reform, laying stress on guarantees of judicial independence, and proposing a reduction in the role of lay judges. The Slovak statement (cited in n. 131) urged the creation of special investigatory organs independent of the Ministry of the Interior or the procuracy, and special organs for supervising socialist legality in place of the procuracy. See also *Bulletin of Czechoslovak Law* 8, nos. 1-4 (1967), esp. J. Lukeš, on the work of the security apparatus, and A. Růžek, on penal procedures, pp. 108-19; pp. 247-57, resp.
[138] Piller report, p. 195.
[139] *RP*, May 3, 24; symposium, *Rep.*, June 19-26, pp. 15-16.
[140] Boček, *Rep.*, Aug. 7-14, pp. 8-9.

the pre-trial investigations, supervising their legality and perhaps even taking over the entire process.[141] The procurator should be free from control by the party, or the security police, and subordinated to effective parliamentary supervision.

Some felt that the procurator's rights to make complaints about breaches of law by the courts or to supervise the legality of actions by the state administration should be abolished; others that they should be reduced in extent. It was argued that the main responsibility in the latter sphere should rest with judicial organs and, in the opinion of some, be exercised by a system of administrative courts. In fact, a step in this direction was taken in August when a draft law was completed which made state organs responsible for damages done to citizens by illegal decisions and established procedures for determining whether such illegal actions had been taken and for awarding compensation.[142]

Drastic changes were also advocated in the sphere of security. The primary aim was to reduce the strength of the Ministry of the Interior which had become, in the words of its head, Pavel, "an enormous power apparatus which was to control everything and everyone."[143] It was crucially important to end the close association of the security service with, and its control by, the party apparatus, and to place it directly under the government as a whole and subject it to the general supervision of the newly established defense and security committee of the National Assembly.[144]

The Piller report did not deal with this problem in detail and recommended only a delimitation of the competence of the security system by law and, in particular, the restriction of the use of its materials against party functionaries or of its technical devices against citizens.[145] The Action Program had, however, been much more explicit in this area than in that of justice, and had already proposed measures which were often reiterated in other official statements and in public discussion.[146] The

[141] Šustr suggested a system of investigatory organs independent of any ministry, and subject to the National Assembly. Others proposed that investigations be handled by the procuracy, or by the courts or that the idea of "investigatory judges" be revived.

[142] *Pravda*, Aug. 13, for a summary. For analysis of the problem of judicial control of administration, see V. Mikule, *Právník*, no. 9 (1968), pp. 769-79; no. 10 (1968), pp. 857-73. See also Mikule, *Bulletin of Czechoslovak Law* (1967), pp. 258-65; J. Švestka and Z. Češka, ibid., pp. 266-73.

[143] *RP*, May 1. See his other statements, ibid., April 12, May 7. Pavel stated that both wiretapping and jamming had ceased, with some exceptions. His statement concerning wiretapping was criticized as insufficient by J. Štěpan, who described the practice as forbidden by law (*LL*, May 16).

[144] For the committee's first meetings, ibid., May 18, June 7 (Pavel). See also Prchlík, ibid., July 16.

[145] Piller report, pp. 195-96, 244, 262.

[146] For official statements, see Pavel, *RP*, May 1, 7; Prchlík, ibid., July 16.

power of the security network could be limited, according to the program, by removing certain departments from the Ministry of the Interior and by reorganizing what remained, especially by dividing the Corps of National Security (SNB) into two independent bodies, Public Security (VB) and State Security (STB).[147] Pre-trial investigation should be taken out of its hands altogether and assigned either to the procuracy or to the courts. The operation of the prison system, including places of pre-trial detention, and the so-called corrective educational institutions, should be transferred to the Ministry of Justice, and a general reform and modernization of the prison system effected. A draft amendment to the existing law to effect such a transfer was approved by parliamentary committees in June.[148]

The crucial reform of the security system—the need for a thorough purge of its personnel from top to bottom—was difficult to achieve. The official line, expounded by Dubček and others, was to assert the continuing need for the security service, to repudiate "wholesale (paušální)" attacks on it, and at the same time to argue for extensive cadre changes.[149] Pavel often stressed the need for such a purge but openly admitted that his efforts were hampered by resistance within his own department. He was able to replace his three deputy ministers only in late June, apparently after a bitter struggle.[150] He stated that many officers of the security organs were strongly opposed to his planned reforms, especially in State Security, and noted that they not only acted to preserve their own positions, but were exploiting "fears" for the fate of socialism as a screen for their opposition.[151] The continued presence of Soviet advisers in the ministry, which was publicly admitted on one occasion, no

---

[147] The program distinguished the two bodies as follows: the STB was for defense against hostile foreign centers, but was not to take action against citizens for their opinions, or to be used for settling domestic affairs; the VB was to fight against criminal activity and preserve public order.

[148] RP, June 11, 12, July 10. A revolt in the corrective educational institution at Minkovice on April 24 drew attention to the alarming conditions in such places (RP, April 24; cf. Rep., May 1-7, pp. 14-15). On these conditions see J. Zvár, RP, May 4; V. Mand'ák, Rep., May 8-15, pp. x-xi; LD, May 19.

[149] RŠO, pp. 78-79, 194-95. Cf. the CC resolution in May, ibid., pp. 210-11; the Slovak CC, RP, May 25, 31, and similar statements by Smrkovský (ŽS, May 1968, pp. 17-18) and by Mlynář, RP, June 6.

[150] RP, June 22. V. Šalgovič had already (in early June) been named deputy minister in charge of State Security. In a long interview in late 1969, Šalgovič bitterly criticized Pavel's performance as Minister of the Interior, especially his "sabotage" of a Presidium decision in May to separate intelligence and counter-intelligence from the ministry and to subordinate it to the government as a whole. He described another Presidium decision on August 20 on the reorganization of the ministry as a retreat from the May decision (Smena, Dec. 15, 1969). Šalgovič had submitted a plan for reorganizing the ministry but this had been rejected by Pavel, he complained (RP, Oct. 8, 1968).

[151] Pavel, RP, June 7; SS, July 2; Rep., July 17-24.

doubt strengthened this internal resistance.[152] The security service was defended publicly both by resolutions passed by security forces in certain regions and by articles praising the work of the State Security.[153] This led to an extraordinary situation in which the security and defense committee of the assembly had to defend publicly the position of Pavel, as Minister of the Interior, and to appeal to officials in his ministry to carry out their instructions.[154] It is not surprising that some were skeptical of the possibility of genuine reform in the security system, especially if the State Security were placed under another minister or transferred to the government as a whole.[155]

CONCLUSION

The passage of the law on rehabilitation was a humane step, rare in history, and unique in the communist world, to restore justice to the victims of illegalities of an entire historical period and to supplement the limited and inadequate measures of correction taken in the sixties. It was the first occasion in a communist country in which an action of such vast scope, embracing even discrimination and persecution by administrative agencies, was to be undertaken in accordance with strictly legal procedures. The entire process was expected to begin in early September, after the formation of senates during August, and to consume a two- to three-year period before its completion.[156] It was thus hoped, as the Czechoslovak reply to the Warsaw letter expressed it, that the problem of repression of innocent people would be solved, and public attention would no longer be concentrated on this painful matter.[157]

This reform sought to face a basically moral problem, created by the injustices of the past. As Lakatoš expressed it in a book published in late 1968, the crimes of the fifties had led to "a clash between law and justice," "a conflict between law and morality," in the minds of society.[158] Rehabilitation, quite apart from material compensation, offered moral

[152] J. Rypel, deputy Minister of Interior, *Práce*, June 28.
[153] For the former, *SS*, July 2; *OL*, July 13. For the latter, see the series of seven articles on the case of V. Veselý, sentenced in 1957 to 25 years for espionage and released in 1966. The author, Dr. M. Hladký, who had written a pamphlet concerning CIA espionage, sought to prove that Veselý was in fact a CIA agent and was therefore justly sentenced, and to refute charges made by Veselý in the press and on television that illegal methods were used during his investigation (*RP*, July 9 to July 17). Cf. *Rep.*, May 8-15, for Veselý's description of his interrogation in 1957. See letters by Veselý and Hladký (*RP*, Aug. 10).
[154] *RP*, July 11, 13. Cf. the defense of the work of security forces by deputy minister S. Padrůnek, ibid., July 26.
[155] *Rep.*, July 3-10. See reply by J. Aleš, ibid., Aug. 14-21.
[156] Kučera, *SS*, Aug. 20.   [157] *RŠO*, p. 247.
[158] *Úvahy o hodnotách demokracie* (Prague, 1968), pp. 149, 157.

vindication of the unjustly persecuted. At the same time the open discussion of these crimes and their rectification provided those less directly connected with a kind of moral purification, erasing to some degree their own feelings of guilt and revenge. A striking feature of the entire discussion was, however, the relative absence of a spirit of revenge or of demands for ruthless reprisals and the general insistence that justice be done, and by legal processes. As a result many who were guilty of criminal actions escaped their merited punishment.

More was necessary, however—namely, to erect safeguards against the repetition of such horrible events in the future. How could the link between justice and law be restored and respect for the law reestablished? In Lakatoš's view, only by guaranteeing "legal certainty" and this in turn by assuring "judicial independence." The latter, he wrote, "is anchored deeply in the recognition that the duty of the court is to concern itself first of all with 'justice', that is, to see to it that the law should be discovered in harmony with legal prescriptions. The court may not be an instrument of everyday political practice." This required the elimination of interference in the judicial process by the party. "If any political organ has the possibility of immediately influencing judicial decisions, or if judges are dependent on this political organ in the exercise of their function, it is hardly possible to speak of judicial independence."[159] The measures of legal reform discussed above, if implemented, would have gone far to reach that goal.

Political questions of vast magnitude were also involved. The report's ultimate publication would have revealed, in an official party-endorsed document, the full and horrifying truth of the trials, including the high degree of Soviet implication, and would have constituted a damning indictment of most of the party's past leaders and of much of its past record. Piller is said to have warned the leaders in the summer of 1968 that the report contained such "shocking facts" that its distribution could "seriously shake the authority of the CPCz and some of its chief representatives," and its publication was postponed for this reason.[160] Although the exact form and content of the final report would have been determined by the 14th congress and the highest party organs, there is

---

159 Ibid., pp. 179-81.
160 Pelikán, introduction, Piller report, p. xii. Actually, as internal evidence indicates, its final version was not yet ready; according to Sedláková (*Pravda*, Aug. 12), only a preliminary report was to be submitted to the 14th congress. The version published by Pelikán contains two appendices—a draft CC resolution and a draft speech by the commission's chairman. It is not known whether these materials were ready before August, nor is it possible to tell the form that the report itself would have taken in the final version. The CC decision drafted by the Piller commission requested the Presidium to elaborate a final report for the public and for the party (Piller report, p. 256).

little doubt that the sum and substance of the document and its recommendations were well known to Soviet authorities. To that degree the military occupation in August was no doubt motivated in part by the desire to prevent its publication and the legal and political consequences that would have followed.

CHAPTER XIV

Planned Market Socialism

THE INITIAL STAGE

January did not bring any immediate change in official policy with regard to persisting economic problems or the development of the system of economic management.[1] Neither the communiqué nor the resolution mentioned economic reform. Both asserted the need for concentrating attention on the economic tasks arising from the decisions of the December 1967 plenum and the plan for 1968. In the budget discussions in the National Assembly a few days after the plenum, Černík reviewed the economy in relatively positive terms, referring to the "correct" policy of the 13th congress and the growth in national income and in living standards in recent years. Admitting "structural imbalances" in the economy and inadequacies of housing, services, etc., Černík saw the key to their solution in the further development of economic reform, thereby intensifying market pressures and thus enhancing the effectiveness of production. Neither he, nor B. Sucharda, the Minister of Finance, went much beyond the degree of self-criticism and homage to economic reform that was customary before January.[2] Their colleague, M. Kohoutek, deputy chairman of the State Planning Commission, justified interventions by the "center" in order to establish the conditions for developing the new system of management and spoke of the latter as "a gradual process" requiring many specific government measures.[3]

Commentators in official publications wrote in similar terms, but with somewhat greater emphasis on the necessity of applying the principles of the economic reform. Early in January, Z. Šulc noted that only the "first steps" toward reform had been taken; observed tendencies of a return to the old directive system; and urged the need to go further, especially in establishing "economic" prices and creating "a functioning market."[4] J. Lipavský warned of the danger of administrative interferences in the economy and of the political obstacles to reform.[5] The organ for

---

[1] For analyses of economic reform written prior to 1968 and for major retrospective analyses, see above chap. III, n. 36. For post-occupation criticism, see Jan Stankovsky, *Osteuropa* 21 (Jan. 1971), 41-52.

[2] *Rudé právo*, Jan. 11, 1968. Cf. also Černík, "Restructuring the Czechoslovak Economy," *Hospodářské noviny*, Jan. 5, 1968.

[3] *HN*, Jan. 12. [4] *RP*, Jan. 12.

[5] *Literární noviny*, Jan. 6. See also Lipavský, *Reportér*, Jan. 10-17. Cf. J. Lúč, *Pravda*, Jan. 19. A Slovak economist, in a series of historical articles on the early Soviet economy, argued that the *NEP*, which involved "the combination of economic sectors through the market and through the state-regulated economy" was

party functionaries continued to deal with the role of the party in economic life in old-fashioned terms, expounding the hardly original ideas of distinguishing the role of party and state organs and of developing new methods of party work.[6] At the beginning of March a leading article in *Rudé právo*, commenting on the action program under preparation, wrote frankly of past errors and inadequacies in the economy and of the political barriers to improvement, and strongly advocated the broadening of enterprise authority.[7]

Dubček, in an early address, referred to the positive effects of the new economic system and the need to implement it in the whole economy, including agriculture, but spoke largely in terms of carrying out the decisions of the March 1967 plenum concerning agriculture.[8] Later in February the Presidium asserted the necessity of the "thorough implementation of the principles of the new economic system," a theme elaborated more fully by Dubček several days later in his first major discussion of economic policy.[9] He dealt critically with the inadequate use of economic scholarship and of progressive economic practice and of "the constant partial changes," dragged out over many years. Avowing the need to "systematically implement the new system of management in all its essentials," he described "democratization of the management of the economy" as "an integral part of the democratization of social life." This would not, Dubček admitted, be an easy or a short-term matter, and would require the efforts of the entire population. He warned against "illusions" that the "serious difficulties" in the economy could be overcome "tomorrow or the day after" and against "promises . . . which cannot be fulfilled."

In mid-March official circles began to speak more frankly of existing inadequacies and to urge the necessity of fundamental changes. Černík, who had long held responsible positions in the direction of the economy and was subjected to criticism for his past, took the first step in an article in the party daily. Acknowledging that the economic situation was not "rosy," and that many serious difficulties existed, he also warned against "illusions" or "irresponsible promises." He conceded that only the "first steps" toward the new system had been taken and that "no basic change" had been effected. The introduction of the new order could not be de-

---

"more suitable" for advanced socialist countries such as Czechoslovakia than later Stalinist theory (J. Ceconíc, *Pravda*, Jan. 19, 26, Feb. 2).

[6] *Život strany*, no. 3 (Feb. 1968), pp. 7-11; no. 5 (March 1968), pp. 22-27.

[7] *RP*, March 1.

[8] Feb. 1, in Dubček, *K otázkam obrodzovacieho procesu v KSČ* (Bratislava, 1968), pp. 19-25.

[9] *Rok šedesátý osmý* (Prague, 1969), p. 30; Dubček, *K otázkam*, pp. 44-46. See also Dubček's speeches in mid-March, ibid., pp. 79-80; and early April, *RP*, April 9.

layed, but it could not be accomplished in a few days. The eventual objective was a combination of plan and market, but this presumed the establishment of economic equilibrium, and this in turn required structural changes in the economy, a balancing of supply and demand, and institutional changes to guarantee democracy in decision-making. All these measures had to be carefully and thoroughly prepared. Černík dealt openly with concrete problems, such as pressures for improved living standards and the threat of unemployment under the new system, and saw a solution in more effective production, which would curb inflation and make possible wage increases, and in measures that would effect a transfer of employees from less to more effective places of employment.[10]

EXPERT OPINION ADVANCED

Meanwhile leading economists began to express more radical views. Otakar Turek characterized the main problem as the existence of monopoly in the economy, especially in the form of the general directorates, and various forms of state protectionism in the granting of subsidies and foreign trade supplements. The solution lay in liberating the enterprises from compulsory controls from above and subjecting them to the forces of competition, both domestic and international. He cautioned against too many compromises in the introduction of the new economic system and advocated a clear declaration that free trade and convertibility of the crown were the ultimate objectives.[11] Other economists expressed dissatisfaction with the slow and partial introduction of the new system of management and blamed this on the central organs, including the ministries, and the general directorates, which were fearful of their power position and their economic interests.[12] There were more and more frequent criticisms of the official failure to provide full information about the real state of the economy and the absence of a government program for correcting the many imbalances and for further implementing economic reform.[13] Economists echoed the warning of the political leaders that it was impossible to satisfy the mounting demands for increased wages and investments without the danger of inflation.[14]

[10] RP, March 15. See his defense of his past record, ibid., March 29, and his comments on economic policy, ibid., April 9. Cf. B. Sucharda, Rep., March 27-April 3.
[11] HN, Jan. 26. Cf. similar views by J. Řezníček, RP, Feb. 27; E. Löbl, Pravda, March 14.
[12] M. Sedlák, Pravda, March 28.
[13] Z. Vergner, director of the Research Institute of National Economic Planning, RP, March 28; V. Kadlec, L. Veltruský and other economists from the Higher School of Economics, ibid., April 1. Cf. similar criticism in the National Assembly committees (ibid., March 28).
[14] H. Kočtúch, Práca, April 5; economists from the Higher School of Politics, RP, April 7; R. Kostka, ibid., April 9.

Radoslav Selucký, who had visited most of the European communist countries (and Mongolia) in the fall of 1967, summed up his impressions in a series of articles in *Reportér* which had direct relevance for the Czechoslovak debate.[15] Frankly analyzing each country's economic inadequacies and difficulties (which were often similar to those of Czechoslovakia), Selucký described the different approaches to the "improvement" or "reform" of the economic system, with varying degrees of transition from "extensive" to "intensive" growth and with different combinations of plan and market. He did not hide his own reservations concerning the Soviet efforts to "improve" their economic system, comparing it to Czechoslovakia's 1958 reorganization. He revealed his sympathy with the Yugoslav model and with the Hungarian economic reform, which would go further, he thought, than the Czechoslovak. He was particularly critical of Poland's retreat since 1956 and warned that Czechoslovakia might also suffer a reversal of democratization unless economic reform was carried through without delay. On the other hand, he expressed doubt concerning the further development of the reforms in Bulgaria in the absence of a democratic system.

By the end of February, Ota Šik emerged as a sharp critic of the "halfway" and "inconsistent" implementation of economic reform and a persistent advocate of more decisive action. In many speeches, articles, and interviews, he waged a campaign against unnamed "demagogues" and "conservatives" who were throwing the blame for economic difficulties on the reform and were incorrectly predicting that its full introduction would have harmful effects on wages and employment. Prior to January, Šik argued, the political climate and the constellation of forces in the leading organs had blocked the application of the reform principles and had created an atmosphere of fear which discouraged frank discussion. Conservative forces were still seeking to hinder reform and to conserve old practices. He assigned the cause for economic difficulties and inadequacies to the administrative system of management and on the failure to replace it consistently and quickly with a new economic system.[16]

Concretely, Šik advocated the full implementation of economic reform, including those parts of the original proposals which had been excluded by the party authorities at the time as "a return to capitalism," in particular proposals for institutional and cadre changes. Plans had been drafted, he said, for changes both in the central organs and at the enterprise level, assuring the independence of the enterprise in relation to

[15] *Rep.*, nos. 6 to 14, and 16, from Feb. 7-14 on.
[16] For the fullest statement of his views, see his interview, *Práce*, March 5. See also Šik, *Mladá fronta*, Feb. 21; *Pravda*, Feb. 27; *Zemědělské noviny*, Feb. 27; *Rep.*, March 6-13; *RP*, March 15.

the general directorates.[17] According to these proposals the party should not duplicate nor interfere with economic and state organs but should concentrate on "supreme direction" of the economy and the settling of long-term aims. Cadre policy should be carried out by the responsible organs and should emphasize education and expertness as well as political maturity and organizational capacity. There should also be, Šik thought, a central organ (consisting of persons not directly responsible for a particular industrial sector), which would carry out "an anti-monopolistic policy" and which would exert an influence on the enterprises through economic and financial instruments and levers.

Šik acknowledged the need for a defined government policy of "consolidation" which would deal with certain burning questions and would seek to protect and improve living standards. The policy of wage controls must give way to a gradual rise in wages, say from 1.5 to 2 percent, with increasing differentiation of rewards according to the productivity of enterprises and of individual workers. He rejected "controlled inflation" as a threat to living standards and argued for increased production as the solution to inflationary pressures. In the meantime he recommended the inauguration of the second stage of price reform concerning retail and foreign trade prices. There should be an immediate shift of production toward a greater output of consumer goods, as well as an increase in the import of such goods; an expansion of the building industry; and encouragement of small and middle-sized private and cooperative production. These measures would help to raise the standard of living and would also help to counteract inflation.

Looking toward the future, Šik advocated the progressive elimination of the "protectionist" system which failed to discourage inefficient enterprises by giving them subsidies, surtaxes, and discounts, and by permitting general directorates to transfer profits from efficient enterprises to cover the losses of the inefficient. Similarly in foreign trade, "protectionist" and "monopolist" practices should be replaced so as to give the enterprises the opportunity to deal directly with foreign suppliers and buyers and require them to rely on their own competitive ability. Although these problems could not be solved quickly, their ultimate solution was a condition of the successful implementation of the economic reform, he said. In the meantime these measures should not be used as a pretext for delay in proceeding with the reform itself.

The most complete outline of the development of the economic system, prepared by four leading economists, was published in a special supplement of the party's economic journal, *Hospodářské noviny*, in

[17] *Práce*, March 5; *Rep.*, March 6-13. Two of the rejected documents were published by F. Vlasák, *RP*, March 29.

early April.[18] Although it was not an official document, this 77-point analysis, which went beyond the Action Program in its detailed analysis, offered an indication of likely future reforms. Reviewing the course of reform to date, the outline was severely critical of "half-successes" and "relapses" and placed much of the blame on the "forces affected" which continued to influence policy in their own interests. "Of the new system, we realized only that which caused no one any pain, and almost nothing that would have affected anyone." The old *aparáts* continued to "act in the old manner under the new conditions." The "obligatory indicators of the plan" were replaced by "manipulation from above," so that the enterprises had been disappointed or completely disillusioned and citizens had lost confidence in the new system. The latter could not be brought into being without "social and political conflicts," since the vital interests of a certain part of the state *aparát* would be affected and "social problems" (which were not explained) would be created. Success would depend on whether they could "sell" the idea of economic progress to the working people and "convince them that it would bring benefit to all in a short time" (no. 20).

The outline then set forth in some detail the major steps required to establish "a socialist market economy suitably combined with central planning." The key problem was to abolish the system of "protectionism" and to offer real freedom of decision-making to the enterprises. "The renaissance of the market, with its objective criteria," was the main objective (no. 2). This required several sets of measures. First and foremost was the debureaucratization of the central management system, replacing the old administrative system by democratic organs for decision-making at the center and creating conditions for the "priority of market criteria in enterprise decision-making." Next, the old forms of administrative monopoly must be replaced by economic monopolies where appropriate, or by free competition. Foreign trade would be released from state controls and monopolistic enterprises, and through a series of steps, ultimately made "free," with a convertible currency. Finally, an appropriate "income policy," including price, wage, finance, and credit policies, was expounded at considerable length, with market forces serving as the determining factor in all cases, and official organs creating a favorable context and, where necessary, exerting influence through indirect means.

---

[18] "Nástin koncepce dalšího rozvíjení ekonomické soustavy řízení," by M. Horálek, M. Sokol, Č. Kožušník and O. Turek, *HN*, April 5, 1968 (henceforth cited as *Nástin*). The complete text is available in German in K. P. Hensel, *Die sozialistische Marktwirtschaft in der Tschechoslowakei* (Stuttgart, 1968), pp. 337-79, summary at pp. 148-58.

THE APRIL PLENUM AND THE ACTION PROGRAM

At the CC plenum in early April, Dubček, in a review of economic questions, rejected the idea of a mere "improvement" of the system of management and committed himself to "a profound economic reform," based on "a synthesis of plan and market." He foretold a government program which would provide for measures to consolidate the economy and to meet the most urgent problems. He promised institutional reforms of enterprise management and referred to the need for "democratic managing organs" within the enterprises, thus raising an issue hitherto hardly mentioned. Subsequent plenum discussions, including statements by Sucharda, Šik, and F. Vlasák, introduced no novelties but indicated a general consensus on the necessity of an early promulgation of an official economic policy.[19]

The Action Program was not a radical economic document but represented an official endorsement of the main measures already under consideration.[20] There was an explicit commitment to "the idea of economic reform" which, it was said, had been approved by the 13th congress and had "triumphed." The aims were "a new economic system, a revival of the positive functions of the socialist market, unavoidable structural changes in the economy and a profound transformation of the function of the economic plan from an instrument which commands to an instrument by which society, in a scientific manner, discovers the most appropriate long-term direction of its development. . . ." It was essential, however, to remove the "inconsistencies and gaps" in the implementation of reform, and in particular "the vast network of protectionism" which encouraged "economic backwardness." Enterprises must be given freedom of decision-making and be obliged to react creatively to the requirements of a "demanding market" and to "economic competition." An enterprise would be free to withdraw from the association of enterprises of which it was a part, but only after the government had laid down rules for this procedure. The primary aim was the restoration of the market as "a necessary mechanism of the functioning of the socialist economy, . . . not a capitalist, but a socialist market, and its utilization not in a spontaneous, but in a regulated, manner."

Democratization of the economy would involve not only the freedom and independence of the enterprise, but also the right of the consumer to determine his own consumption needs and style of life, the right of

[19] Dubček, *RŠO*, pp. 83-84; Sucharda, *RP*, April 3; Šik, ibid., April 7; Vlasák, ibid., April 11. In Brno, Dubček had spoken of "collectives of workers" exerting a democratic influence in the factories (*RP*, March 17).

[20] Text in *RP*, April 10; in English, R. A. Remington, ed., *Winter in Prague* (Cambridge, Mass., 1969), pp. 88-137. References to international economic relations and to Slovakia will be discussed separately below.

"free choice of employment," and the right of social groups to express and defend their own economic interests. The program endorsed the creation of "democratic organs" of the work collectives in the enterprises, for which a statute was to be issued.

The program emphasized the desirability of the articulation of varied group interests in the process of formulating the general social interest. Decision-making must become "a process of mutual confrontation and harmonization of the various interests—entrepreneurial interests and the interests of consumers, employees, and various social groups of the population, the nations, etc." Accordingly, the mass societal organizations must no longer be mere transmission belts but must defend the interests of their members.

Responsibility for determining the state's economic policy, according to the Action Program, was to rest with the government, which would decide on appropriate organizational forms for performing this task. The central organs would be so formed as to make possible the expression of special interests and differing points of view and would be subject to democratic supervision by the National Assembly, as well as by scientific institutions.

CHANGES AT THE CENTER

The formation of the Černík government and attendant shifts in personnel in the central bodies were not entirely auspicious for the rapid reform of the economy or for decisive change in economic policy. Most of the persons assigned to responsible posts in the economic sphere had long been associated with the highest level of economic authority. This was true of the new Prime Minister, Černík, and several of his deputy prime ministers: Štrougal, who also became chief of the newly formed Economic Council, and F. Hamouz, who was placed in charge of Comecon relations; as well as F. Vlasák, chairman of the State Planning Commission; B. Sucharda, Minister of Finance; V. Valeš, Minister of Foreign Trade; and M. Hruškovič, chairman of the State Commission for Technology. It was also true of the key CC Presidium members, Kolder, responsible for the economy and heavy industry, and Sádovský, for agriculture and food, and light industry. Several of these veteran economic executives (for instance, Sucharda and Vlasák) were, however, experts and had long favored reform. The only new faces were J. Borůvka, Minister of Agriculture, and Šik, a deputy chairman in charge of economic reform and a member of the Economic Council. Šik, however, seemed likely to be in a position of relative weakness, since he dealt primarily with theoretical matters, as compared with Štrougal, who was in control of the operative aspects of economic policy.

419

Subsequent governmental and administrative reorganization did not suggest radical change. The most significant alteration was the transformation of the State Planning Commission into a ministry. Hitherto the supreme directing organ, superimposed above other departments, it was now to be responsible in the main for long-term theoretical work. Certain other departments were formed, including a Ministry of Labor and Social Affairs; a Ministry of Technology; and a State Price Office. The formation of an Economic Council (*Hospodářská rada*) seemed of greater significance even though its exact role was uncertain.[21] At first it was emphasized that this body, made up of ministers, was not to be another executive or bureaucratic agency but an instrument of coordination of current policy at the ministerial level, advisory and responsible to the government. Although it was officially denied that the council would constitute "a little economic government," and its strictly advisory position was stressed, its activities soon suggested that it was *in fact* a key agency for determining official economic policy, in particular for defining the fundamental strategy of such policy. In weekly meetings it discussed such vital matters as the economic directives for 1969 and concrete problems such as foreign loans, the five-day week, wage demands, and the improvement of housing and transport. It had its own staff, which was to number 100 to 120 specialists, and formed a series of commissions, which, it was said, would represent all important interest groups and make the council a "forum" for discussion of economic policy. But some felt that the division of labor between it and the government and other authoritative institutions, such as the Ministry of Planning, of Finance, and Šik's office, was unclear and that no effective economic center capable of adopting a strong program existed.[22]

In his first major policy statement to the National Assembly, Černík outlined the measures planned to consolidate the economy, amplifying the provisions of the Action Program.[23] Admitting the gross errors of earlier economic policies and the serious difficulties and disproportions that had resulted, Černík pressed strongly for structural changes in the economy and for a policy of intensive rather than extensive growth. This

[21] *Sbírka zákonů*, no. 53/1968. The members were Štrougal (chairman), Šik, Hruškovič, Vlasák, V. Valeš, Sucharda, M. Štancel (Minister of Labor and Social Affairs), V. Hůla (minister in charge of the State Price Office) and O. Pohl, Director of the State Bank, as well as the chairman of the Slovak Planning Commission.

For official explanation, see Vlasák, *RP*, April 13, 26. See also Indra, *RP*, March 30; Presidium, March 25, *RŠO*, p. 45; CC plenum, ibid., p. 64; *RP*, April 27, June 15, July 9; V. Komárek, *HN*, April 26; *RP*, June 12, July 3; *Rep.*, July 3-10.

[22] S. Vosecký, *HN*, April 26. Cf. Dalimil (pseud.), *Literární listy*, May 2 and 30.

[23] *RP*, April 25. See also his concluding remarks, ibid., May 4. Cf. detailed analyses by others, notably Sucharda, ibid., April 30, May 1, June 27, and *HN*, June 21, 28. Cf. B. Šimon and L. Říha, *ŽS*, no. 10-11 (May 1968), pp. 19-23, 44-48.

would place the main emphasis on the productive effectiveness of enterprises and would enhance competitive ability, at home and abroad, and make possible improved living standards. In particular he recommended the termination of protectionism for inefficient enterprises and foresaw a substantial reduction in subsidies within two years. He advocated a shift from heavy industry, mining, and power, toward the production of consumer goods, and larger investments in neglected sectors such as health, education, housing, and transportation. He rejected new demands for investment funds (amounting to 14 milliard crowns above what was planned) as certain to contribute to inflation and to detract from funds available for housing and other urgent needs.

Černík condemned the "directive system" of management, which he said "had permitted production for production's sake, isolated production from the market, worked with artificial prices and supported extensive development at the expense of quality, and did not make demands on expertness in work nor open the way to initiative." The introduction of the new economic system was of extraordinary importance, embracing appropriate changes in central organs and the branch directorates, and in the status of enterprises. He conceded that neither these institutional alterations nor the changes in the economy could be accomplished quickly, nor without serious conflicts. Measures must be taken to facilitate transfers to other employment for those displaced by shifts in production.

Černík devoted much attention to the problem of living standards, arguing that they were lower than they should be, and that whatever benefits the workers might have had under the old system, they had suffered, like all citizens, as consumers. He assured the assembly that the new economic policy would not cause a lowering of living standards but pointed out that an improvement would depend on higher productivity. A monetary reform was not intended, he said. There would be price changes but these would be kept under control by government action. A growth in real wages, estimated between 2.5 to 3 percent, would be possible, but negotiated wage increases would depend on increased productivity. Certain urgent measures to improve pensions, maternity and family allowances, would be proposed and steps would be taken to introduce the five-day week. Nonetheless, even though many of the wage demands which were being raised were legitimate, most of them could not be met for fear of inflation. Even the proposals of the Central Council of Trade Unions (ÚRO) concerning living standards could not be accepted in toto, but would have to be acted on according to their degree of urgency.

In ensuing weeks the government met a number of its specific commitments. In late April, the principles for the withdrawal of enterprises from general directorates were issued, subjecting this process to certain

421

rules and critieria.[24] In mid-May the government approved the guidelines for initiating the five-day week, which required inter alia that enterprises must fulfill the conditions of maintaining production and of not increasing wage payments.[25] In early June the government approved the principles for establishing enterprise councils.[26] In late June, the assembly adopted three laws which improved sickness insurance payments, maternity and children's allowances, and social insurance to cooperative farmers.[27] Černík announced also that a general increase of 8 percent in pension payments would be introduced as of January 1, 1969.[28] In early August, the draft economic directives for 1969 were approved.[29]

CONTINUING DISSATISFACTION AND DEMANDS

In spite of official proclamations and initial government measures, the experts remained dissatisfied and expressed their views openly, and with increasing sharpness, in ensuing months.[30] The chief complaint was that the new economic system had been introduced in a halfway manner and that the market system was not yet functioning. Kožušník, of the Institute of Economics, for instance, claimed that there had been few genuine changes in the system of management and that the old *aparáts* at the center were fighting a battle for "self-preservation." Karel Kouba, Šik's deputy at the institute, expressed the belief that the system was still basically centralist, with the ministries and the general directorates now using economic instruments, such as subsidies, surtaxes, etc., to control the economy. Others, such as the Slovak economist, J. Rosa, rector of the Higher School of Economics in Bratislava, also singled out the economic ministries and the directorates for blocking advance. Šik, although a member of the government, was still critical, lamenting that after a decade of struggle for economic reform, they were still at the very beginning of a transition to the new system. Like other experts, he placed the blame mainly on conservative forces defending their own "power" interests and their economic privileges. The immediate need was the consistent implementation of the principles of the new economic system—not a mere improvement of the old system, but its fundamental reform.[31]

---

[24] See below, in this chapter.
[25] *RP*, May 16. See *Sb. z.*, 63/1968 for the Ministry of Labor and Social Affairs' announcement.
[26] *RP*, June 7. See below in this chapter.
[27] *RP*, June 28; *Sb. z.*, 87, 88, 89/1968.
[28] Černík, *RP*, June 9.   [29] Ibid., Aug. 2.
[30] The fullest statement was that of Kožušník, *Nová mysl*, no. 5 (1968), pp. 589-95. Cf. his earlier article, *Rep.*, April 10-17. See also Dalimil, *LL*, May 2, July 11; K. Kouba, *RP*, May 21; J. Rosa, ibid., June 21; O. Čapo, *Nové slovo*, June 27; Turek, *RP*, July 2; Kadlec, *LL*, Aug. 1.
[31] Especially *MF*, June 26. See also Šik, *Kulturní tvorba*, May 2; *RP*, May 16,

Economic change, in the minds of the reformers, was closely intertwined with changes in the political system. Political obstacles had stood in the way of reform before January and still hampered its full implementation. Without complete democratization, it was argued, economic reform was not likely to be introduced systematically. Conversely, economic reform, in particular the introduction of the market system, would lay the foundations for a thorough reform of the political system. A system of pluralism in the economy, with independent and competing enterprises of differing kinds, the free play of interest groups, and democratic control within the enterprises, would represent economic democracy and would require a similar pluralism of autonomous "subjects," such as parties, pressure groups, etc., in political life.[32]

The implementation of economic reform could not take place without the adoption of appropriate economic policies by the central organs of government. As Šik stated, the effectiveness of economic reform would depend on the economic policy pursued.[33] Central organs would have to exert a strong influence if the economy were to break out of the "vicious circles" hampering progress and would have to establish "rules" and "principles" for the autonomous actions of economic entities.[34] Yet, in the opinion of most leading economists, the government had neglected to take the necessary steps to make reform feasible and effective. The authorities had not yet revealed the full truth concerning the economic situation nor offered the information needed for actions and decisions by others.[35] They had failed to develop a comprehensive program, either for correcting the imbalances or for introducing the new economic system.[36] They had failed also to make the necessary institutional changes, both at the center and at the lower levels, to democratize economic relations, as promised by the Action Program.[37]

22, June 18; *Práce*, July 7. Šik's address to the Czechoslovak Economic Association (*RP*, May 22) is given in English in *New Trends in Czechoslovak Economics*, no. 5 (1968), pp. 3-16.

[32] See especially J. Sláma, *RP*, March 21; Kožušník, *Rep.*, April 10-17; Sláma, ibid., May 15-21, *LL*, June 20. Similar views were expressed by V. Šilhán and others in a panel discussion of democracy in politics (*Rep.*, March 6-13). "The market is the basis of the functioning of democracy," said Šilhán. Šik later wrote that only one pillar of democracy had been achieved, namely, freedom of expression, and that two others, independent enterprises and enterprise councils, were necessary (*RP*, Aug. 2). Public opinion was divided on the question of the relative priority of economic and political change and did not remain constant. See below, chap. XVII.

[33] *KT*, May 2.

[34] Turek, *RP*, July 2; Kožušník, *NM*, no. 5 (1968).

[35] Selucký, *Práce*, April 23; Komárek, *RP*, July 3.

[36] Kouba, *RP*, May 21. See the resolution of the Czechoslovak Economic Association, of which Kouba was chairman (ibid.). Kočtúch also urged the drafting of a long-term program (*NS*, June 13).

[37] Kožušník, *NM*, no. 5 (1968).

The economists were more or less in agreement on the remedies for these ills. The crucial prerequisite was to assure genuine independence for the enterprises, freeing them from the hierarchical controls from above characteristic of the directive system.[38] Reform would also make necessary democratic organs in the enterprises and safeguards for the free and autonomous actions of interest groups, especially labor and agriculture. It would demand an end to the system of subsidies, which had involved substantial state expenditures for price control, foreign trade assistance, and support for unprofitable enterprises. It would necessitate drastic steps to control inflation, to limit investments, and to check the avalanche of wage demands set in motion by the January awakening.[39] The government would have to be prepared to deal with employment problems caused by the necessary structural shifts and by enterprise failures occasioned by the requirement of profitability.[40]

Šik, in a series of six television talks at the end of June and in early July, presented the case for reform in a style designed to have maximum impact on an audience unaccustomed to frank revelations of the truth by leading political figures.[41] Rejecting customary platitudes of growth and achievement, Šik painted, stroke by stroke, a devastating picture of Czechoslovakia's economic failures since the abandonment of her "own path to socialism" in 1948: the economy was using obsolete machinery; investing wastefully, primarily in heavy industry; producing goods in quantity but not of a quality sufficient to compete on world markets, and at extremely high cost; providing poor retail services; and offering inadequate housing and health facilities. Management was operating at a low level of competence, with few managers adequately trained. The impact of his assertions was heightened by the fact that they were based on official studies, many prepared before January, and that they were presented comparatively in relation to certain foreign countries. The standard of living was shown statistically to be very low in comparison with countries of comparable economic development, such as Austria or France.[42] The only way out, in Šik's view, was the change of the system of management, supplemented and buttressed by political reform. His purpose in these talks was not to adumbrate in detail the nature of the proposed changes, but rather, by revealing the black economic picture, past and

[38] Selucký, *Práce*, June 30; Turek, *RP*, July 2; J. Havelka, *Rep.*, April 24-May 1.
[39] Šik, *RP*, May 16; Selucký, *Práce*, April 23; Kadlec, *LL*, Aug. 1.
[40] Kouba, *RP*, May 21; Šik, ibid., May 22. See also K. Pinc, *Rep.*, July 24-31.
[41] These talks were reprinted in the daily newspapers and have been published abroad in many languages, including English, French, and German. See Ota Šik, *Czechoslovakia: The Bureaucratic Economy* (White Plains, N.Y., 1972).
[42] On the low level of Czechoslovak wages in relation to other European countries, see the articles by O. Schmidt, *LL*, May 23; I. Strup, *Rep.*, May 29-June 4, pp. VII-X; M. Hiršl, ibid., Aug. 7-14, pp. 21-22.

present, to persuade his listeners of their necessity. He depicted the future in sober but hopeful hues, based largely on the economic guidelines which had been prepared but not yet published.

REHABILITATION OF THE MARKET AND OF ENTERPRISE

The focal point of reform was to establish a market system in which the chief role would be taken by the enterprise.[43] Hence the key to success was a basic change in the position and the functioning of the individual enterprise (*podnik*) and a restoration of *podnikavost*—"entrepreneurship" or "the spirit of enterprise." In the past the state had in effect been the only "entrepreneur" (*podnikatel*), and the enterprise "had the position of a plant or shop within a 'large enterprise' represented and managed by the state and was an integrated component of a higher entity, from which was required, first of all, discipline in the fulfillment of the planned tasks." Under the new system "the enterprise must . . . become the real bearer of entrepreneurship." The enterprise would be "a relatively autonomous organism, separated from the state" and standing on its own feet, free from various state interventions, but also deprived of the possibility of relying on the state budget if its "own feet" were "unsteady." The central organs would merely define the boundaries and conditions of its entrepreneurship, so that "it was permitted to do all except that which was expressly forbidden." The motive force in the enterprise's actions would be its own "material interest" in the stability and growth of its income, which in turn would be based on its ability to satisfy the interests of other economic "subjects." The enterprise, consequently, must operate "economically" within a market, responsive to all the market's pressures in order to create a saleable product and to do so with due regard for costs so that the process would be profitable. As the 77-point outline put it, "it was necessary to throw the enterprises into the water so that they would learn to swim," but with the proviso that "their hands were unbound so that they could swim" and that they be freed of

---

[43] In addition to the 77-point outline (*Nástin*) referred to above, see articles by J. Toman, chairman of the State Commission for Management and Organization (SKŘO) and J. Řezníček, head of its working group on the status of the enterprise (*RP*, March 30 and April 17, resp.). These articles embodied the content of materials which were prepared by the working group and approved by the State Commission in 1967 but were not published at the time. These materials were discussed by the government and by party organs, including the Presidium (in August 1967). The final version was published by Řezníček and Toman under the title "Democratization of the Economy and the Position of the Enterprise" (*HN*, April 19 and 26, 1968, supplements). This detailed analysis of the position of the enterprise in the new system included the text of a draft law.

See also K. Suchan, *NM*, no. 6 (1968), pp. 712-21 and B. Šimon and L. Říha, *ŽS*, no. 14 (July 1968), pp. 34-37 (the latter based on the work of Řezníček).

"various stones which would pull them to the bottom." This could not be done all at once, however; some must be "loaned a life preserver for a certain time," but on the understanding that this was to be "only for a start" (*Nástin*, no. 14).

The market envisaged was to be a "variegated" one, with "a broad palette of organizational forms" (no. 33). Differing types of enterprise would exist. Some would be public or state enterprises, for instance, in undertakings such as railways or electric power. Others would be groupings of enterprises, under general directorates, either in the form of trusts, or of looser associations, in each case managed by collective organs representing the participating enterprises. Still others would be independent national enterprises, with or without associated smaller enterprises. Some would be cooperative enterprises, especially in small production, trade, and services. There would also be small-scale private enterprise. The almost total elimination of all private shops and stores in the fifties had admittedly lowered the standards of repairs and other services. The restoration of such small enterprises was frequently advocated and was officially endorsed by the Economic Council and the government as urgently necessary.[44]

A legal definition of the status and the rights of the enterprise was to be embodied in a statute, which was under active consideration by the government but had not yet been completed in August.[45] In the meantime, preliminary steps were required to permit an enterprise to withdraw, if it was felt necessary, from the association to which it belonged, and either to associate with other groupings of enterprises, or to act independently on its own. It was recognized that this freedom of the enterprise to decide voluntarily on its association was an essential feature of its new role, but would meet great resistance from the existing administrative monopolies.[46]

In order to regulate the process of disaggregation of existing enter-

[44] A draft law on small enterprises was in preparation (*RP*, July 17, *ZN*, July 31). See interview with the secretary of the Economic Council, *MF*, Aug. 2. For strong advocacy of the development of small and cooperative enterprise, see Löbl, *Pravda*, June 20 and *HN*, July 6; Selucký, *Svobodné slovo*, July 13.

[45] A first government draft was ready in July and discussed in scholarly and governmental institutions in early August but was not published. This draft was based on the Řezníček-Toman materials cited in n. 43. See M. Sedlák and M. Mejcher, *Pravda*, April 26, 1969. Another draft law on the enterprise was prepared by Bratislava lawyers and was available to the author in mimeographed form (henceforth cited as *Osnova, Zákon o podniku*).

[46] Löbl, *Pravda*, Aug. 14. As an example, J. Krejčí, Minister of Heavy Industry, although he endorsed the government principles, defended the many groupings within the jurisdiction of his ministry and argued that withdrawals must be fully justified on economic grounds (*RP*, June 13). See also the argument of his deputy minister, B. Belovský (*HN*, April 19, 1968).

prise groupings, which had already begun, the government, in late April, issued a set of fundamental principles concerning changes in organizational association.[47] Enterprise withdrawals were to take place according to specific economic criteria, and in agreement with all the organizations and enterprises under a general directorate and, if no agreement were reached, by a decision of the appropriate minister (in Slovakia, by the Slovak National Council). According to Šik, this would avert "spontaneity and subjectivism" and would assure careful analysis of proposed changes. This transitional measure, he noted, would prepare the ground for the future when the grouping of enterprises would mainly be decided by the enterprises according to "objective value criteria." The newly formed general directorates would no longer be superior administrative organs, as in the past, but would be the product of voluntary association and their policies would be determined by councils of enterprise directors.[48]

Just as important as the legal status of the enterprise would be its ability to act in an entrepreneurial manner, making its own major decisions concerning production, within the guidelines of government policy and the economic plan (*Nástin*, passim). Production would no longer be focused upon fulfilling the quantities specified by the plan, but would be guided by market criteria and would seek to meet the needs of the purchasers, both as to quality and assortment. Market criteria would eventually permeate all areas of enterprise behavior, including prices, wages, taxation, credits, and investments. Prices, which were still largely fixed by the state, would gradually be set freely according to supply and demand, both in retail and wholesale markets, subject only to certain state controls in the interest of avoiding inflation. Wages, hitherto largely frozen by state decree, would be determined by collective bargaining, within the framework of certain state restrictions. The enterprise would pay taxes according to fixed percentages, so as to encourage more effective procedures. Credit would be made available by banks operating on commercial principles, with defined interest rates and terms of repayment. Even investments would ultimately, subject to some restraints, be within the province of the enterprise, which would use its own resources or commercial credit.

The general principles of the new economic system were to apply equally to foreign economic relations.[49] The conduct of foreign trade had

---

[47] *RP*, April 27.

[48] Šik, *RP*, May 26. See also Šik, *RP*, April 7; *KT*, May 2; Suchan, *NM*, no. 6 (1968), pp. 717-18.

[49] On foreign economic policy, see *Nástin*, nos. 36-43; Valeš, *RP*, April 18; Šimon et al., *NM*, no. 4 (1968), pp. 428-39 (also in *NTCE*, no. 5, 1968, pp. 58-

been dominated for twenty years by practices similar to those in the domestic economy and had been strictly controlled by the Ministry of Foreign Trade and monopolistic foreign trade corporations. The state would in future lay down the general principles of foreign economic policy but would leave their implementation to the enterprises. The latter would operate primarily on the basis of economic criteria of effectiveness and profitability. The enterprises would themselves enter the foreign market, either directly through their own agencies, or indirectly through trading organizations of their own choice. Thus they would no longer be sheltered from the realities of the world market but would have to take them into consideration in making their decisions. They would also have the right to engage in new forms of international transaction, including direct cooperation with foreign enterprises.[50] These opportunities would be enjoyed equally by Slovak enterprises, with general supervision exercised by a special Slovak foreign trade agency in the Slovak National Council.[51]

No longer would enterprises engaged in foreign trade be able to depend on special aids and privileges which concealed their inefficiency and transferred their losses to the state budget. Although all surcharges and discounts could not be canceled at once, firm deadlines were to be established, five years at the maximum, for their abolition, so that enterprises would be forewarned that they would then have to compete on their own with foreign rivals, in both the domestic and the world market, in quality, prices, and other respects.[52] It was realized that this would require the gradual formation of "real" prices at home, reflecting supply and demand, and the establishment of a realistic exchange rate for the crown by devaluation, and, eventually, its convertibility. This could be achieved only in some five to seven years and would be conditioned by the "convertibility" of Czechoslovak goods, i.e. their saleability, on foreign markets.[53] Economic reform at home would contribute to the effectiveness of Czechoslovak production and thereby improve their competitive position on the world market. In turn, the pressures of foreign competition would be a spur and challenge to Czech and Slovak enterprises and thus fulfill a condition of the advance of economic reform.

---

77); Löbl, *HN*, April 19; M. Maruška and V. Nováček, ibid., July 6. See also chap. XIX below.

[50] F. Hamouz, *Práce*, June 26. According to an announcement of the Ministry of Foreign Trade (*Sb. z.*, 121/1968), foreign trade was no longer to be exclusively carried on by existing specialized organizations, but with the ministry's permission, by other organizations.

[51] Valeš, *Práca*, April 26; Ján Gregor, ibid., June 14.

[52] Černík, *RP*, April 25. Turek and others urged a declaration of intention to establish "free trade" and to abolish protective measures by a certain date (*HN*, Jan. 26; *Nástin*, no. 36).

[53] Černík, *RP*, April 25; Sucharda, ibid., April 30.

SLOVAKIA AND ECONOMIC REFORM

The application of economic reform in Slovakia was inseparably linked with the question of federalism, to be discussed in the following chapter. It was taken for granted that the principles of the new economic system would be applied to the entire economy. Slovak enterprises would operate independently; choose their affiliations with enterprise groupings; and compete on the all-state market on an equal basis. Most Slovak economists were as convinced of this as the Czechs, and assumed that there would be in principle a single unified market, with goods, labor, and capital moving freely between the two parts of the republic. There was general recognition that the Slovak economy would face certain distinctive problems and that special provisions would be required to prevent serious damage to Slovak enterprises facing Czech competition and to complete the economic equalization of the less developed region. Czechs regarded these as secondary matters and gave top priority to the rapid countrywide implementation of economic reform. Slovaks were more keenly aware that the market system would not be sufficient to deal with Slovakia's problems and in some respects would aggravate them. They urged that the region be given special consideration in the formulation of all-state economic policies and that special measures be taken to deal with them.[54]

When the debate on federation began, sharper differences began to emerge, not only between Czechs and Slovaks, but among Slovaks themselves. Czech economists, including Šik, recognized the desirability of federation from the beginning, but devoted little attention to this or to distinctive Slovak problems.[55] Their primary concern was to achieve the integration of the economy as a whole through the free play of economic forces and the independent action of enterprises. The idea of a separate or closed Slovak economy was condemned as a barrier to economic advance in both parts of the country and a danger to reform. When controversy began to develop over the authority of the federal and national organs, Czech economists emphasized stronger central powers in a unified market and opposed excessive national authority in the economic

[54] See articles by P. Turčan and A. Lantay, *Politická ekonomie*, no. 3 (1968), pp. 205-26, 227-38. Turčan advocated special policies by the center to promote the necessary restructuring of Slovak industry. Lantay suggested the creation of a special fund for Slovak development at the center, operating independently with resources from the federal budget. See also Lantay, *Ekonomický časopis* 16, no. 3 (1968), 225-41.
[55] Problems of Slovakia were hardly discussed in major works by Šik and Turek, or in other important declarations on economic reform (e.g. *Nástin*, no. 23). But see Šik's favorable reference to federation, CC plenum, *RP*, April 7. I. Rendek, a member of the Šik commission, reported that the commission, including Šik, had from 1963 accepted the need for the Slovak National Council to direct the Slovak economy (*Pravda*, March 16).

sphere. Šik, for example, contended that the central organs should be "real coordinators of two equal national organs and the articulators of their common interests."[56] Selucký accepted the desirability of federation but placed his main hope on the market system, identical in both parts of the federation. He foresaw the need for special measures to protect Slovak interests, suggesting certain privileges for entrepreneurs who desired to operate in Slovakia and an all-state fund to promote Slovak development.[57]

Slovak expert opinion underwent a substantial evolution after January and began to differentiate itself into several groups differing in subtle and not always easily distinguishable ways. No one was opposed in principle to economic reform.[58] Criticism had been voiced from the beginning, however, that the reform had been drafted from too general a standpoint, without taking into account its implications, possibly harmful, for Slovakia. By mid-March, the concept of federation had been generally accepted by all Slovak economists, although occasionally there was a warning that federation alone, without economic reform, was not enough.[59] Thereafter most Slovak economists emphasized the need for *both* economic reform and federalism and argued the compatibility between a national economy under Slovak controls and an integrated Czechoslovak economy.[60] The differences that gradually appeared concerned the relative priority of these two objectives and involved varying interpretation of the implications of economic reform for the Slovak economy and diverse views of the political and economic measures necessary to meet these problems. It also produced conflicting opinions (to be discussed in full in the following chapter) concerning the appropriate forms of the federal system.

Two major groups emerged. One, including Pavol Turčan, at the Institute of Economics, Ján Ferianc, of the Slovak Institute of Planning, and Evžen Löbl, of the State Bank, regarded economic reform as the most important objective.[61] This led them to place great emphasis on an in-

[56] Šik, *RP*, April 7.   [57] Selucký, *Rep.*, June 26-July 3.

[58] V. Pavlenda, in a series of articles in 1969 (*Pravda*, Nov. 14, 17-20, 1969), stated that the conception of a socialist market economy, in which the role of planning was not significant, had not found broad support in Slovakia, citing only Löbl as an advocate (Nov. 14). He contended that Slovaks had hardly participated in the formulation of the new economic system and that their observations had been ignored (Nov. 17). He distinguished, however, between the positive features of the original decisions concerning the new economic system and the later revision of these by the Šik group. But contrast his own defense of economic reform soon after the occupation (*RP*, Sept. 27, 1968).

[59] For example, Slovak Economic Association, *RP*, March 21; *Pravda*, April 1; Turčan, *Pravda*, April 6.

[60] Note especially Rendek, *Pravda*, March 16; Pavlenda, ibid., April 2.

[61] For instance, Löbl, *Ľud*, March 22; Turčan, *Pravda*, April 6, July 23-24; Ferianc, ibid., July 25, 30. Cf. the reports by J. Rosa and M. Sedlák at a confer-

tegrated economy and to reject any idea of "a closed (Slovak) economy." They accentuated the role of independent enterprises, freed from binding controls of the general directorates and from direct state interventions, and competing, both in foreign and domestic trade, on the basis of efficiency and quality. Slovak national organs should have the authority to guide and direct the development of the Slovak economy, but decisive authority must continue to rest with the organs at the center in Prague in setting the general principles of foreign trade, in drafting the general plan of development, and in regulating prices and wages on a uniform basis. There must be no separate price or wage levels, and no protectionist barriers to the movement of goods. Some special provisions would be essential, both in Prague and in the Slovak national center, to aid the weaker Slovak economy, but these must not be allowed to negate the general principles of economic reform. These economists, therefore, although fully aware of the peculiar exigencies of the Slovak economy and entirely in favor of federalism, were closer in their views to the Czech economists in their emphasis on the priority and urgency of reform.

The other school of thought, represented mainly by Viktor Pavlenda, a Slovak CC member, and Hvezdoň Kočtúch, both of the Higher School of Economics, argued that the economic reform must be fully adapted to special Slovak conditions and needs.[62] This would necessitate a Slovak strategic plan of development formulated by national organs exercising substantial authority. This would not take the form of a new Slovak bureaucracy, dictating to the enterprises, but of a regulated market economy, in which the national organs would have extensive powers, including their own budget and control of prices, wages, etc. The idea of a Slovak national economy was defended not as a "closed" economy, but as one in which national interests would be taken as a guiding consideration and harmonized with the needs of an integrated Czechoslovak economy. Federal authority would provide a coordinating mechanism to establish common principles and policies. Later, as the debate continued over the form of federation, Slovaks came to recognize that common policies in many fields were necessary and that Slovak interests must be protected at the center, too. The insistence on extensive national authority in the economic field was then supplemented by an equally

---

ence of Slovak economists in early May 1968. Both stressed the importance of the new economic system and enterprise independence and made little or no mention of the Slovak organs (*EC* 16, no. 6, 1968, pp. 557-71). See also Sedlák, *Pravda*, May 16, 21, 23; *NS*, July 4; *RP*, Aug. 16; Löbl, *Pravda*, Aug. 14.

[62] Pavlenda, *Pravda*, March 12; Kočtúch, *Kultúrny život*, March 15. See also J. Mališka and I. Zelinka, *KT*, Feb. 10; L. Kozar and F. Melísek (both of the Slovak Planning Commission), *HN*, May 31.

vocal insistence on measures assuring maximum Slovak influence in the formulation of central policies.

Space permits only brief mention of two crucial examples of these differences of viewpoint, one relating to the ability of Slovak enterprises to "hold their own" under the new economic system, and the other to the perennial problem of equalizing the level of Slovak and Czech development. These were in essence different sides of the same coin of the problem of developing and restructuring the Slovak economy, which involved the modernization of Slovak industry and the realization of an industrial complex competent to do the final processing of goods usually sent semifinished to the Czech lands for completion. Such a basic reorientation could hardly be achieved through the automatic working of a market economy but would have to be fostered by special measures taken by both federal and national organs. If accomplished, this would contribute both to the competitive ability of Slovak industry and to the more rapid attainment of equalization.

Slovak economists agreed on the main objectives, but differed on the methods to attain them. Although almost without exception they rejected the idea of a "closed" economy, or of protectionism, they varied in their degree of optimism as to whether Slovakia could solve these problems by her own efforts or would need aid from federal organs. Those who placed priority on economic reform believed strongly in the ability of Slovak firms to compete against Czech rivals and on the international market.[63] In any case, under the new economic system survival would depend on competitive ability and profitability, and inferior enterprises would have to be liquidated. Some special measures would be justified, in particular to encourage the "finalization" of production, but general protectionism must not be permitted. Moreover, Slovakia would not be able to develop her economy from her own resources and would have to depend for some time on the transfer of funds from the center. This required a strong federal budget, not dependent on the national organs for its sources. This would have the further advantage of avoiding bitter negotiations and misunderstandings between independent national organs over allocation of funds, and the risk of the stronger side vetoing unacceptable transfers.[64]

The position of the advocates of "national economies" was not always

[63] Löbl, Ľud, March 22; KŽ, April 26; Práce, May 24.
[64] Ferianc, Pravda, July 25, 30. Cf. the similar viewpoint of a Czech economist, L. Roubl (RP, Aug. 10). See statement by Czech economists, RP, June 21; Z. Jičínský and Č. Kožušník, Rep., Aug. 7-14. A Slovak, J. Petrenka, disapproved of making the federal organs dependent entirely on budgetary transfers from the national budgets and proposed subsidies to Slovakia for equalization and for large investments (Pravda, June 12). In addition to Lantay, Turčan also favored a special fund for promoting Slovak development (ibid., July 23, 24).

stated clearly and unambiguously.[65] They were confident that Slovakia could "go it alone," that is, had sufficient resources of its own, or could secure them, to carry out its development. This led them to insist on a strong "national" budget, controlling all sources of taxation, and transferring certain contributions to the federal budget, which would have no independent sources of its own. Sovereignty without money, they argued, was mere window-dressing (*atrapa*). If aid from the center were required, it could be secured by negotiation and should not depend on the decision of a federal organ. There were other possible sources of funds, namely foreign loans, interest-free loans from the central organs, or enterprises. On the other hand, these economists were less sanguine about the fate of Slovak firms in the freer economic system and argued for special measures to prevent wholesale liquidations and to promote the restructuring of the economy and its modernization. These would have to be implemented by the national organs. According to some, an independent Slovak price policy, with higher prices for some Slovak products, would help to assure the competitive ability of Slovak enterprises and would incidentally provide funds for investment and thus contribute to equalization.[66]

MANAGEMENT AND ENTERPRISE COUNCILS

The idea of introducing an element of workers' participation in factory management, which had been discussed in theoretical terms prior to January, was only occasionally raised in the first months of 1968, and then in vague and contradictory forms.[67] At the April CC plenum authoritative endorsement was given to "the democratic administration of enterprises" so as to afford the workers "the possibility of influencing the course of events" and to give them "the feeling that they were not mere employees but socialist owners."[68] The Action Program briefly developed this theme, calling for "democratic organs" which would appoint the

[65] Pavlenda was criticized for not discussing the effect of a "national economy" on the problem of equalization (Z. Hába, *Pravda*, July 12). For the following see Rendek, ibid., March 26; J. Horváth and J. Spišiak, *NS*, June 20; Spišiak, *Právny obzor*, no. 8 (1968), pp. 712-13; A. Nuoška, *Pravda*, Aug. 16.

[66] J. Lipták, *NS*, May 30; D. Plachtinský, *Práca*, July 2-3. Cf. a Czech criticism of such a price policy (*KT*, July 25).

[67] E.g. F. Velek expounded the pros and cons of workers' participation and proposed "consultative methods" (*ŽS*, no. 6, March 1968, pp. 40-43). Toman suggested that enterprise councils be given "real power" and not merely advisory influence, but should not replace the managing organs (*RP*, March 30). Kočtúch proposed organs that would be "supervisory," and not "co-deciding" (*Práca*, April 5). See also leading article, *RP*, March 1. For pre-1968 discussion, see above, chap. v, n. 42.

[68] *RŠO*, CC resolution, p. 98. See also above, n. 19.

enterprise director and to which he would be responsible. These organs would form "a direct component of the managing mechanism of the enterprise" and, unlike the trade unions, would not be societal organizations. On the other hand, the "indivisible authority and competence" of the leading officials would not be altered, it was said. The organs would include representatives elected by the "working collective," and also representatives from outside the enterprise, to assure the observance of all-societal interests and the technical level of decision-making. A statute, which would utilize the tradition of the factory councils of 1945-1948, was promised.

This pronouncement left the exact role and functions of the enterprise organs, and even their name, unclear. Authoritative articles by Mlynář and Šik offered further information, at least as to their own views.[69] Mlynář, who suggested alternative titles ("enterprise, administrative, or factory councils") stressed that they must have "a decisive voice" concerning the entire activity of the enterprise and should give to the "workers' collective" rights similar to stockholders in capitalist firms. According to Šik the "councils of the working people," as he called them, would have ten to thirty members, most of whom would be elected by the working people from their own ranks, supplemented in some cases by representatives of the state or banks, and outside experts. The director would be fully responsible for enterprise policy but would have to submit his basic conceptions to the councils. The latter would be free to express their views and even to exercise a veto in certain matters, or express lack of confidence in the management, but would not themselves assume responsibility for decisions. The directors would be approved and recalled by the councils. This would, in his view, effect a combination of "expertness" and "democracy" of leadership.

It was soon obvious that there was a wide variation of opinions as to the authority of the enterprise organs and as to their composition and the manner of their formation.[70] There were those, especially among the scholars (philosophers, sociologists, political scientists, and some economists), who adopted a "democratic" approach and saw in the councils of working people a form of self-management (*samospráva*) which would help to diminish the workers' sense of alienation and furnish a counterforce vis-à-vis the state bureaucracy and the managers. The councils would represent an important aspect of democratization in the eco-

[69] Mlynář, *RP*, April 20; Šik, ibid., May 22. Cf. Šik's earlier less definite views, ibid., April 7.

[70] Dalimil, *LL*, May 30; R. Budínová, *Rep.*, June 12-19; round-table discussion, *Rep.*, June 5-12. See also M. Tatu, *L'hérésie impossible* (Paris, 1968), pp. 125-31. The Řezníček-Toman materials on the enterprise (see n. 43 above) provided for enterprise organs and set forth various alternatives concerning their competence and composition (pp. VI-VII).

nomic sphere and would constitute a significant force in the political arena.[71] On the other hand, there were those, including some economists in the state organs and certain managers, who took a "managerial" or "technocratic" approach and tended to regard working people's councils as a threat to effective production, since they were likely to pursue their own short-run interest at the expense of the long-run interests of development. Some claimed that the working people were not able to contribute to the highly technical process of management, which should be left in the hands of experienced managers. "The worker," it was argued, "with exceptions, is not capable of deciding in a qualified manner how to develop the potential of the system of enterprise. This only an elite can do."[72]

There were also differing attitudes toward the authority and composition of enterprise organs. The "democratic" approach favored a council of working people with wide authority over enterprise policy and over the directors, and one composed mainly of representatives from the ranks of the enterprise employees. The "technocratic" approach opposed "a managing organ" of working people altogether, and supported either a body made up of representatives of managers, employees, state representatives, etc., or a managerial organ, consisting only of management experts, combined with some kind of "supervisory organ," elected from the ranks of workers but with strictly limited authority. There were others who advocated working people's councils as an element of "democratic supervision of expert leadership," with the composition varying according to the size of the enterprise and its position on the market.[73]

In spite of the lack of official guidelines, preparatory committees for the establishment of councils were formed in a number of enterprises during April and May.[74] For example, in the large ČKD Wm. Piece plant

[71] See esp. K. Bartošek, historian, and F. Šamalík, jurist, *Rep.*, June 5-12. Cf. R. Slánský, *RP*, June 8. Petr Pithart acknowledged that self-management could play a valuable political role in the enterprises but was concerned that its too rapid introduction, before independent enterprises and a market had been introduced and normal economic conditions established, would prevent it from performing its essential economic mission (*LL*, Aug. 1). There is no English equivalent to *samospráva* (*selbstvervaltung*, in German; *autogestion*, in French). It may be translated as self-rule, self-administration, or self-management.

[72] See esp. A. Mynář, of the Institute of Management, *Rep.*, June 5-12. Löbl opposed workers' participation in the "scientific" work of management (*Plánované hospodářství*, no. 6, 1968, pp. 67-72). See also articles in *RP*, April 23, p. 3; May 12, p. 3; May 14, p. 6.

[73] For example, *Nástin*, no. 26. See also Toman, *RP*, March 30; Budínová, *Rep.*, June 12-19. Belovský (cited above, n. 46) approved the idea of enterprise organs with a wide competence, and with two-thirds representation of the working people, but opposed the right of the council to appoint directors.

[74] See appeals to the workers to form such councils by Bartošek, *Rep.*, May 8-15; S. Budín, ibid., May 22-29. These appeals were sharply criticized by a conservative correspondent who called them appeals against the government and party (cited

in Prague, the draft principles of self-management left to the director full responsibility for "operative management" and for "organizing the work process," but assigned wide authority to the "self-administration of the working people." This would be exercised through a general "assembly of the working people"; a "council of self-administration" elected by the working people; and a smaller "administrative committee" of specialists and outside representatives, including the director. These several bodies would exercise the powers of self-administration, approving the plant's long-term plan of development, choosing and dismissing the director, and dividing the plant's income between personal income and the plant's funds.[75]

The May plenum announced that the formation of "democratic organs of management" was proceeding too slowly and appealed for greater discussion in the factories and among specialists, so that these organs, together with the enterprises under the new statute, could be functioning before the end of the year. Dubček in his report also urged speedier action in forming "collective organs of democratic administration of the enterprises," referring to them alternately as "enterprise councils" and "councils of the working people." Nonetheless, in a fuller discussion of the topic at a conference of union delegates, Dubček warned against hasty steps and urged that the councils should be set up only where their significance could be confirmed. He stressed the need for careful examination and experimentation before final legislation was adopted. In particular, the councils should be established simultaneously with the assurance of enterprise independence. They would be a constituent part of enterprise management but should not weaken the authority of the director and the enterprise leadership, nor must they be identified with the unions, whose task was primarily to defend the interests of the employees.[76]

COUNCILS OF THE WORKING PEOPLE

During June the government, after consultation with the ÚRO, decided to permit the formation of councils of the working people on a provisional basis prior to the adoption of the statute on enterprises and issued "a provisional framework of principles" as guidelines.[77] The coun-

---

by Budín, ibid., June 5-12) and by a progressive sociologist, M. Jodl (ibid., June 12-19) who advocated further study of the problem before a final decision.

[75] For text of principles and comment, Slánský, ibid., May 22-29.

[76] RŠO, pp. 206, 189; Dubček, RP, June 19. Smrkovský, Černík, and esp. Šik, advocated enterprise or working people's organs in their plenum speeches (RP, June 5-7).

[77] Text, RP, June 30; in English, NTCE, no. 6 (Sept. 1968), pp. 50-57. An excellent analysis is given by Robert Vitak, "Workers' Control: The Czechoslovak

cils were significantly not called "workers' councils" (*dělnické rady*),
but "councils of the working people" (*rady pracujících*), a broader term
including all employed persons, whether white- or blue-collar.[78] It was
hoped that the setting up of these bodies would proceed "in a deliberate
and organized" rather than a "spontaneous" fashion and that the whole
concept would thus be tested prior to legislation.

The government document described the director as "the executor of
the entrepreneurial function," "determining and implementing policy"
but responsible to the council in all his activity. The council, in turn, was
defined as "the representative of democratic enterprise administration,"
authorized to discuss fundamental questions of enterprise development,
especially the direction of investment policy, the division of gross income, and basic measures of management. In most cases, the director
could proceed with his proposed policy in the face of the council's disapproval, but the latter possessed a right of veto, subject to a two-thirds
vote, with regard to "large investment actions." The council of working
people was entitled, also by a two-thirds vote, to name and dismiss the
director and his deputies "after discussion with the superior organ," and
to approve their salary and bonuses. The director was to be appointed
on the basis of public competition and was to receive a six-year contract.
His dismissal could take place only after thorough analysis and for defined cause, such as a breach of legal provisions, or serious economic
failure, and not merely because of the council's disagreement with his
policy. The council of working people would consist of ten to thirty persons, depending on the size of the enterprise, and would be composed,
"in overwhelming proportion," of working people from the enterprise.
In large enterprises, or those dependent on complicated market conditions or technology, outside experts, numbering 10 to 30 percent of the
total, might be elected. In certain cases, nominated representatives of
state organs (not more than 20 percent), or of banks, might be included.

Experience," *Socialist Register*, 1971, pp. 245-64. See also J. Kosta, *Listy* (Feb.
1973), pp. 37-39.

[78] Cf. a similar distinction in German between "Arbeiter" and "Werktätige."
Although the name "workers' councils" is widely used in English in reference to
the Czechoslovak organs, the term used here, "working people's councils," is more
accurate and is indicative of their special character. There was isolated criticism
of the proposed councils by the extreme left which argued that a real socialist
democracy should be based on "workers' councils," or "workers' self-administration." There should also be an assembly of workers' councils delegates to supervise
the planning bureau and to enforce the general interests against individual enterprise decisions. See M. Borin and V. Plogen, *Management und Selbstverwaltung
in der ČSSR: Bürokratie und Widerstand* (Berlin, 1970), pp. 106-11.

From a conservative standpoint, Švestka emphasized that the councils were *not*
workers' councils in composition and were representative of the entire work collective, obliged to defend the interests not of one social group but of the enterprise
in general (*RP*, July 18).

These principles represented a kind of compromise between the democratic and technocratic conceptions, embodying much of the "self-rule" idea, both in the composition of the councils and their competence, but respecting the independent position of the director and the skilled character of his function. This official action did not by any means settle the future of the working people's councils or eliminate the clash of opposing viewpoints.[79] The sociologist, D. Slejška, strongly defended the concept of *samospráva* as the underlying principle of enterprise management and considered the councils of working people as only a partial expression of this principle.[80] He warned against the danger of managerial dominance and of a technocratic approach. Other exponents of this view recognized the dual role of the workers as both employees and sharers in the entrepreneurial function, but expressed the belief that the employees and the council would not interfere with the authority of the managers or hamper economic efficiency, and could be encouraged to develop a concern for the long-term interests of the enterprise. At the same time, proponents of *samospráva* recognized the crucial importance of expert management and the limitations of the management capacities of the working people.[81]

Others who endorsed the council idea criticized the abstractness of approach of some of its exponents and pointed out the practical problems to be overcome. The democratic procedure in the appointment of directors, for instance, would have to be combined with the use of expertise; this could be effected by advice tendered by an organization of managers, or by a state-appointed commission. The councils, it was thought, ought not have the final decision in formulating long-term enterprise policy or in dividing the gross income.[82]

In fact, although the sharp cleavage between the two extremes, *samospráva* and managerialism, was often referred to, most commentators

[79] See in particular the symposium at the end of June, *NM*, no. 8 (1968), pp. 947-62, and articles in the same issue by Löbl, pp. 963-69; D. Slejška, pp. 970-77; L. Tomášek, pp. 978-83. Other important articles were written by R. Kocanda, *RP*, July 23; P. Ernst, *RP*, July 23; Turek and M. Toms, *Rep.*, Aug. 7-14. See also round-table discussion (Bartošek, R. Kalivoda, Slejška, Šamalík, etc.) *Práce*, Aug. 8.

[80] Slejška, in *Nová mysl* symposium, and article cited. See also Slejška, "Le modèle d'autogestion et ses conditions en Tchécoslovaquie après janvier 1968," *L'homme et la société*, no. 14 (Oct.-Nov.-Dec. 1969), pp. 157-78.

[81] For instance, Slánský, *Rep.*, May 22-29; *RP*, June 8; Budínová, *Rep.*, June 12-19; Ján Zoubek, *Rep.*, July 24-31; Čapo, *NS*, June 27. In a television talk (*Czechoslovakia: The Bureaucratic Economy*, pp. 106-9), Šik admitted that councils might sometimes neglect long-term enterprise interests and select directors "responsive" to their own interests. He expressed confidence that the councils would learn by experience and would not produce worse results than previous methods of management.

[82] J. Mísař, *Rep.*, July 10-17; Turek and Toms, ibid., Aug. 7-14.

admitted advantages and weaknesses on both sides and saw the solution in a compromise. Some regarded the proposed councils of working people as an optimal solution which preserved the authority of the managers but subjected it to democratic control. What was needed, wrote Löbl, was a synthesis or symbiosis of "management" and *samospráva*, in which the director would neither be "absolutely independent of the council of working people," nor "completely dependent," with a Damocles sword hanging over him in the case of each unsuccessful action.[83] There was moreover a shift in attitude in favor of the working people's councils by some who had been concerned about their economic effect, particularly as to their willingess to make the difficult and unpopular decisions of the transitional period, but who now saw the economic and political value of the councils as a means of counteracting the power of the managers and ministries and of mobilizing the workers in support of the reform movement.

The complete rejection of the councils was rare. However, V. Šilhán, director of the Research Institute of the Economics of Industry and Construction, termed their formation a serious mistake, especially in the absence of full enterprise autonomy or of widespread popular demand or support. He strongly criticized the concept that the working people were co-owners of the enterprise property and argued that property assigned to the use of an enterprise could not properly be considered as under the ownership of the employees. He observed that the Yugoslav experience with workers' self-management had not been without negative features, especially in encouraging inflation.[84]

Others shared many of Šilhán's concerns, but few agreed with his conclusion that the councils were inappropriate.[85] Critical supporters contended that the councils were merely a first experimental step in the direction of *samospráva* and the final solution would be found in the light of their experience. Moreover, councils of the type authorized by the government constituted but one variant of the many possible combina-

[83] Löbl, *NM*, no. 8 (1968), pp. 968-69. Cf. Slejška on the "organic unity" of *samospráva* and expertness (ibid., p. 955).
[84] Šilhán, ibid., pp. 948-49, 956-58.
[85] F. Velek, ibid., pp. 958-59; Hrdinová, ibid., pp. 953-54; Ernst and Kocanda, *RP*, July 23. Cf. the Slovak lawyers' draft enterprise law, cited above, n. 45.
On ownership, see Löbl (*NM*, no. 8, 1968, p. 964), who took a view similar to Šilhán. Cf. Sedlák (ibid., pp. 954-55) and Slejška (ibid., pp. 971-72), who sought to respond to this criticism. The delicate theoretical question of the implications of the councils for social ownership was, however, not widely discussed, and "group" or "enterprise" ownership was not publicly advocated, in the sources cited in this section. Some commentators later argued that the councils would not infringe on the principle of social ownership, but would provide a means of participation by the working people in the management of the general social property of which they were co-owners. See for instance, Vitak, "Workers' Control," p. 255; R. Selucký, *Economic Reforms in Eastern Europe* (New York, 1972), pp. 95-99.

tions of management and self-rule. There should be a plurality of forms of enterprise councils corresponding to the plurality of types of enterprises, especially in this early period of experimentation. Self-rule would be fully applied in small and medium-sized private and cooperative enterprises, and in most national enterprises, but would be suitable only in limited degree in state enterprises. Other alternatives were suggested, including joint stock enterprises, in which representation in enterprise councils would be proportionate to stocks held by individual employees, the state, or other organs.[86]

The role of the party in the councils, although not so openly discussed, was another source of discord. Some party functionaries were rather noncommittal toward the councils of working people and emphasized the need to maintain the hegemony of the party in these bodies.[87] Exponents of the councils, on the other hand, believed that the councils and the directors should be free from party interference, especially from cadre controls.[88]

This spectrum of opinion among specialists was mirrored in varying interpretations of the councils of working people among the broader public. A poll conducted in four factories in Prague at the end of June 1968 revealed that 74 percent expected "an improvement" from the councils, 5 percent no change, and 3 percent a "worsening." As to the competence of the councils, 38 percent considered them as "organs of self-rule," and 24 percent as "managerial organs," neither term, however, being defined. The rest (37 percent) favored a neutral character. Although the responses concerning the role of the organs were not easily distinguished, the overwhelming majority supported an influential role, involving varying degrees of cooperation with the director. Ten percent favored "a decisive role" for the councils; 17 percent "a decisive role" for the director. Other responses endorsed a significant role in certain questions (15 percent) or a "deciding or co-deciding role" in strategic questions (16 percent); a supervisory role (14 percent); cooperation with the director (19 percent). As to the naming of the director, 52 percent thought the council should name the director; 26 percent that it should share in the naming of the director; and only 13 percent that it should not name the

---

[86] M. Čihák and Z. Kodet, *Rep.*, July 10-17; V. Chlumský, *LL*, Aug. 15. The latter presented a plan for representation on enterprise councils by only those employees who chose to become entrepreneurs by investing money in the enterprise.

[87] For example Šimon and Říha, *ŽS*, no. 14 (July 1968), pp. 34-37. Tomášek was even more restrained, arguing that the party should not declare itself for or against the councils and that "life" itself would verify their desirability and perhaps demonstrate their lack of suitability (*NM*, no. 8, 1968, p. 980). Some functionaries were strongly opposed to the councils, according to Slejška (*L'homme et la société*, p. 172).

[88] *Nástin*, no. 27; also Řezníček and Toman materials (n. 43 above), p. vi.

director. There was a substantial difference in the responses of workers, technical employees, and directing personnel.[89] In a poll conducted in July, lack of knowledge was admitted by 33 percent of those questioned. However, 53 percent expressed the view that the establishment of enterprise councils in all large enterprises would be advantageous; 10 percent thought they would not be beneficial. The proportion favorable to the councils was higher among skilled workers, university students, and party members.[90] The population at large then was not strongly opposed or attracted to the idea of works' councils prior to the occupation. In spite of this, and the somewhat tempered attitude both of the government and the unions to the formation of councils, preliminary steps were taken in a substantial number of enterprises. Few councils had actually come into existence by the time of the occupation.[91]

TRADE UNIONS AND THE COUNCILS

The proposal to form enterprise councils raised new problems for the trade unions. Were the councils necessary at all, if the unions resumed their proper role as defenders of the workers' interests? Would the councils become organizations which would compete with the unions or render the latter unnecessary? Should the unions themselves become the

[89] M. Bárta, Rep., Oct. 16-23, 1968; in English, NTCE, no. 8 (1968), pp. 57-66.

[90] RP, Aug. 20; Slejška, Rep., April 24, 1969. A general poll in March 1969 indicated a shift in favor of the councils: 59 percent for, 3 percent against (Slejška, Rep., April 24). In a poll in January 1969, based on responses of council chairmen, enterprise directors, and chairmen of party and union organizations, opinion was favorable to the councils, highly so among the council and union chairmen, somewhat less so among directors and party chairmen (M. Bárta, PE, no. 8, 1969, pp. 703-16).

See also Piekalkiewicz, Public Opinion Polling in Czechoslovakia 1968-69 (New York, 1972), pp. 280 ff.; Slejška, Politika, Sept. 19, 1968, pp. 14-15. For other 1968 and 1969 polls concerning works' councils see M. Bárta, Odbory a společnost, no. 4 (1969), pp. 54-69; O. Sedláček, ibid., pp. 79-88; F. Dvořák, ibid., pp. 88-92.

[91] Sources differ as to the number of preparatory committees or councils established. According to Bárta (Odbory a společnost), some 350 work collectives were planning, before August 21, to form enterprise councils. In a later article (PE, no. 8, 1969, pp. 703-16), he reported that 115 councils were formed by January 1969. Elsewhere Bárta referred to 120 councils in existence by that date, of which some 15 percent were formed by August. Only 4.2 percent of the total were formed in Slovakia (Odbory a společnost, no. 4, 1969, pp. 56, 61). According to Politika, Oct. 10, 1968, there were then 70 councils in existence and 267 preparatory committees. An editorial in Rudé právo (Nov. 27, 1968) referred to the formation of 140 preparatory committees and 46 councils, without, however, giving an exact date for these figures. By June 1969, 300 councils and 150 preparatory committees were said to be in existence (RP, July 22, 1970). A document approved by the ROH plenum in 1972 referred to 200 councils in the Czech lands and five in Slovakia (Práce, May 12, 1972, supp.). No date was given.

nucleus of the enterprise councils and merge with them? Or could they coexist, each fulfilling separate functions?

Party and union spokesmen responded by declaring that the unions should support the forming of the councils and take an active role in their work, especially by conducting the elections to these bodies, but should maintain their separateness and distinctiveness of purpose. The councils were a constituent part of enterprise management, sharing responsibility with the director and seeking to promote the general interest of the enterprise. In Mlynář's words, the council would be "an organ of the working people as co-owners" (and therefore as co-entrepreneurs). This involved a high degree of cooperation with the director in management, although frictions and conflicts were certainly not excluded. The councils would not by any means render the unions useless, however. The unions, representing the working people as "employees" and defending their interests, must provide a certain counterweight to management, exerting pressures in regard to wages and working conditions, thus spurring the management on to more efficient production. Although this would involve confrontation and conflict with management, and hence with the works' councils as part of management, it did not exclude cooperation between the two "sides" in the common interests of promoting production. However, if the unions were to give up their former role of mobilizing the workers for plan fulfillment, they should not weaken their new role by attempting to participate in the co-determination of the enterprise.[92]

In late June, the conference of the Revolutionary Trade Union Movement (ROH) delineated the relationship of the unions to the councils. ROH had already agreed with the government that an "experimental testing" of enterprise organs was desirable and set forth in considerable detail its proposals concerning these bodies and the unions.[93] The conference called on the unions to support the forming of councils; this was to be done, in the words of the main declaration, "in a deliberate and organized fashion." A positive attitude was indicated by the incorporation in the union statement of the government's principles in their entirety, almost without change. (The only addition was the stress on the provision that more than 50 percent of the councils' members would be working people from the enterprise.) The councils, it was declared, were

[92] Mlynář, *Práce*, June 18; K. Poláček, ibid., June 19, 21; Dubček, *RP*, June 19. Cf. also Slejška, *Práce*, June 14; J. Duži, *KT*, June 27; F. Lehr, *Rep.*, July 31-Aug. 7. On the importance of the unions under both the technocratic and "self-managing" models of management, see D. Slejška, *Odbory a společnost*, no. 4 (1968), pp. 1-16.

[93] *RP*, May 28. For text of draft statement, *Odbory a socialistický podnik* (Prague, July 1968); German version, Borin and Plogen, pp. 74-88. This draft was scheduled to be finally approved at the ROH congress in 1969.

the most suitable way of giving effect to the role of the producers as "co-owners and co-entrepreneurs," a role which could not be performed by the unions. At the same time, the unions had their own special functions to perform, namely the defense of the interests of the working people. Their relationship with the council would be close, involving cooperation and even participation in the council's deliberations. The unions would express their opinions on fundamental questions with "a right of suspension" of decisions on serious matters and would participate, in a way not specified, in the appointment of directors. They would, however, not be bound by the council's decisions, or responsible for its work, nor would the council or its members be responsible to the unions. The union would also cooperate with the director "in matters of an enterprise character" or those which "closely affect the interests of the working people" and would "co-decide" in such matters, which were specifically listed. Through the "collective agreement" in particular the unions and management would conclude a binding contract, especially on matters of social policy. At the same time the unions would check on the work of management, notably on its implementation of the "collective agreement" and of the principles governing the working people's councils. It was recognized that this did not exclude conflicts, and even strikes, if other measures failed, and special procedures for settling such disputes were set forth.

ECONOMIC REFORM IN TRANSITION

The January overthrow had been in large part a product of the economic crisis of the sixties and had been designed to remove the political obstacles previously blocking thoroughgoing economic reform. The change of leadership appeared to have opened the way for a more complete implementation of reform and for the correction of some of the chronic weaknesses of the national economy. The general concept of reform was accepted by the post-January leadership, by the academic experts, and by the public at large, and had, of course, already been introduced in partial form prior to January. Yet paradoxically the months from January to August did not witness dramatic or major steps forward in extending and implementing reform or in dealing with urgent and critical economic problems.

The slow progress provoked sharp criticism by some economists, a criticism perhaps exaggerated by their anxiety lest reform be neglected or inadequately pressed by the authorities. Šilhán, for instance, in an interview published on the eve of the invasion, expressed his concern that there had been insufficient progress in the theoretical elaboration of economic reform and that it had not advanced in practice as might have

443

been expected. "In essence," he said, "only little has changed in the centrally directive system of management of the national economy" and efforts had been characterized by "improvisation and lack of consistency." Neither the autonomy of the enterprise nor the reorganization of central administration had been achieved, nor had important elements of a market economy, such as markets for products, labor or capital, been introduced. It was urgently necessary, he said, to work out in detail a plan of economic reform.

Šilhán openly criticized the government's general economic policy, noting that there had been in effect "no qualitative change," but only "vacillation and compromises," and in some cases "politically oriented measures." There must be a profound and comprehensive analysis of the past and a program of "positive actions," which would have to try to "solve everything at once" and not ignore "a single essential relationship." While recognizing the close interrelationship of economic and political reform, he censured the lack of attention paid to economics and the high priority placed on politics, and warned that the fate of political democracy was linked with the positive development of the economy. Šilhán was particularly concerned by the failure to adopt the statute on enterprises and by the encouragement given to the formation of the enterprise councils prior to the assurance of enterprise autonomy.[94]

There was some evidence to confirm Šilhán's critique. In the eight months from January to August attention was concentrated overwhelmingly on the more exciting political aspects of change, such as rehabilitation, freedom of expression, reform of the political system, and changes in party leadership, and, in Slovakia, on federalization. Economic reform had not been ignored, especially by the academic experts, but had not assumed a central place in public attention. At the official level, meetings of the Presidium and Central Committee plena were devoted primarily to political questions and had offered almost no policy guidance on economic matters.[95] Dubček, in his major pronouncements, made only brief

---

[94] *RP*, Aug. 21. Cf. similar views expressed by Löbl, *Smena*, Aug. 15. From a more conservative standpoint, the political report prepared for the Presidium in August painted a black picture of the economic situation, referring to the disorganization of the system of management, inflationary pressures, and uncertainty of employment, and described agriculture as the only element of consolidation. Without a solution of these economic problems, there could be no solution of the basic political problems. The independence of enterprises and the establishment of enterprise organs would create serious problems and call forth political conflicts. "Although the economic situation of our country continues to move in a vicious circle, government leaders have not taken the necessary realistic measures in this connection and have not set forth a program which would make possible a solution at least within the foreseeable future" (*Zpráva o současné politické situaci Československé socialistické republiky* . . . , Prague, 1968, pp. 11-13).

[95] A Presidium statement on July 25 (*RŠO*, p. 260) stressed the need for fully introducing the new economic system of management throughout the economy.

references to this subject, couched in familiar terms. When the decision was made to advance the date of the party congress, it was decided not to discuss economic policy on that occasion.[96] The materials prepared for the congress did not include a detailed statement of reform or of economic policy and contained only general references to "a planned utilization of the market economy," freedom of enterprise action, working people's councils, and "indirect planned management" by "the economic center, the state." Although the congress, it was stated, would not formulate a long-term economic program, it would have to adopt an attitude to the serious economic difficulties and to major problems to be solved in connection with the transition to the new economic system. The materials included a general statement, along familiar lines, of desirable economic policy, but admitted that this would require elaboration and completion after the congress.[97]

Government circles were compelled by the situation to devote more attention to questions of economic policy but did not take any significant steps. The long-promised analysis of the state of the economy and of the mistakes of the past was not published before the invasion,[98] nor was the crucial law on enterprises yet ready for public discussion. The semi-annual report on the economy, published in July, conceded that economic reform had not been effectively carried out and that grave problems—for instance, "profound economic imbalances" and inflationary pressures—persisted.[99] In early August when the government issued its economic guidelines for 1969, Vlasák, Minister of National Economic Planning, warned that there could not be "any sort of leap as compared with previous development" and that the guidelines provided only for "a certain progress" in a situation that was "profoundly abnormal."

The guidelines, the only official document on the economy published prior to the invasion, did not go much beyond the government's April proclamation and provided further evidence that the authorities were

[96] Dubček, June plenum, ibid., p. 185; CC decision on congress preparations, ibid., pp. 218-19.

[97] J. Pelikán, ed., The Secret Vysočany Congress (London, 1969), pp. 112-15, 202-5, 217-19, 240-44.

[98] A report of this kind was discussed by the Economic Council in mid-July (RP, July 17). It was later said that a similar report had been prepared by the Institute of Economics before August but had not been published (A. Čechová, Rep., Dec. 18-25, 1969).

[99] RP, July 25. The rate of industrial growth slackened to 5.4 percent; in the second quarter to 4.6 percent. Real wages increased more quickly than in 1967, i.e. by 6.5 percent. Serious shortages continued; housing construction was less than in 1967. Cf. the retrospective evaluation of the whole year 1968 in relatively positive terms, with an 8.4 percent growth of national income, by J. Kosta and J. Sláma, "Die tschechoslowakische Wirtschaft in den sechziger Jahren, Das Schicksal einer Wirtschaftsreform," Jahrbücher für Nationalökonomie und Statistik 185 (July 1971), 489-97.

445

devoting their main attention to immediate practical problems. The guidelines did mention the necessity to "free the operation of the market," in particular to take further steps toward the freeing of prices, both retail and wholesale, and of foreign exchange purchases, and referred to the need for establishing an independent position for the enterprises. The bulk of the document, however, was devoted to a series of measures by which the government would seek to influence, directly or indirectly, the course of economic development.[100]

The guidelines did not constitute, it was stated, a binding plan or even a set of control figures determining enterprise planning, but were rather a statement of the government's general policy as a framework within which the enterprises would elaborate their own plans. The document projected a growth in national income of 7 percent; a growth in living standards, including a rise in real wages of 2 to 2.5 percent; and a rise in personal consumption of 9 percent. It declared, in terms similar to the April statement, the government's intention to direct investments so as to encourage the production of consumer goods and housing construction; to achieve a surplus budget, in spite of increased expenditures, by increased taxation of enterprises and wages; to limit investments and wage increases in order to avert inflation; to restrict the rise of retail prices to 2 to 2.5 percent while allowing prices to be more freely formed; to encourage efficient, and discourage inefficient, production through changes in taxes, levies, subsidies, and credits; and to direct foreign trade by detailed changes in previous regulations. It was clear that, in the immediate future, the economy would not be one in which market forces would predominate but one in which government regulations and stimuli would compel or encourage enterprises to move in the desired directions.

Yet any evaluation of the failure to move ahead in the economic field must acknowledge the obstacles that stood in the way. The time available was short in the extreme, and outside pressures distracted attention from urgent economic matters. The formulation of official attitudes was hindered by the absence of unified views at the administrative peak, produced in part by the division of jurisdiction between Štrougal and Šik. The relative lack of enthusiasm for radical economic change on the part of Štrougal, Indra, and perhaps Kolder, may also have blocked the efforts of Šik, Vlasák, and others to push ahead with more decisive measures. Šik, who had been effective in transmitting the conception of economic reform elaborated by the economic community to the political leadership before January, was less suited for the task of concretely implementing

<hr />

[100] Text, HN, Aug. 9. For exposition of the guidelines, see Štrougal, ibid., July 23, and Vlasák, ibid., Aug. 7. In approving the guidelines and a draft budget for 1969, the government spoke of further development of economic reform in 1969 (RP, Aug. 2).

the reforms and increasingly devoted his energies to the political aspects of reform and to influencing public opinion. At the same time, his direct involvement in the official hierarchy cut him off from his academic colleagues and subjected him to the administrative pressures of his day-to-day duties.[101]

In any case, the systematic reform of the economy was not something which could be accomplished quickly, or which, once initiated, would produce immediate improvements. This was understood by the specialists and was recognized also by the general public, which, in a poll in early July, showed itself both fully aware of the seriousness of the economic situation and realistic in assessing the time required for significant improvement. Seventy percent of the respondents regarded bad methods of management as the chief cause of economic difficulties. The overwhelming majority realized that reform could produce a change for the better only in two to three, five, or even more years.[102]

Moreover, the introduction of reform under extremely unfavorable objective economic conditions created a genuine dilemma for the advocates of radical change and posed many perplexities about the timing and sequence of measures to be adopted. Certain inherited features of the existing economy, such as obsolescence of equipment or the lack of qualified managers, could not be eliminated at once. Urgent, immediate problems demanded firm action by the government, often involving direct state intervention in economic matters, and requiring adjustments and compromises in the implementation of the new economic system. Inflationary pressures, always present in the economy, were stimulated by the freer atmosphere of the Prague spring and had to be checked, even at the cost of continuing price and wage controls. The reform would also require unpopular and tough measures, involving the changeover of unprofitable enterprises to other forms of production, or their liquidation altogether, and the transfer of displaced workers to other jobs. These considerations led the more cautious exponents of reform (as well as outright opponents) to argue that basic change could be attained only gradually, as and when concrete economic problems were solved. More radical reformers doubted the possibility of introducing reform piece-

[101] Šilhán (*RP*, Aug. 21) may have been implicitly criticizing Šik when he noted that theoretical economists were participating in the making of concrete economic policy and should rather concentrate on research and act as consultants and critics of official policy.

[102] *RP*, Aug. 20, 1968. The poll was based on a sample of 1,610 respondents from the entire Republic. The economic situation was evaluated as very critical, with improvement possible only after a long time, by 50 percent of those polled; as serious, with improvement possible in two to three years, by 30 percent; as good, with some deficiencies, by 6 percent; as hopeless, by 3 percent. A change for the better as a result of economic reform would take one year: 1 percent; two to three years: 19 percent; five years: 32 percent; longer than five years: 38 percent.

meal, within the existing system, and preferred rapid and drastic changes which would transcend the existing system. Furthermore, in spite of a high degree of consensus among the experts, there were still differences of opinion—for instance, on the enterprise statute, and on the role of the enterprise councils—which delayed final approval of the relevant measures.[103]

The January changeover had by no means fully eliminated political obstacles to reform, such as the veiled opposition, or lukewarm approval, by certain high-ranking leaders, as well as in some managerial and trade union circles and certain privileged sectors of the working class. Many reformers believed therefore that political and economic reform must go hand in hand, mutually supporting each other.[104] The establishment of democratic procedures in the central institutions, in the factories, farms, and in society as a whole, and particularly the elimination of direct party interference in economic administration, as projected by the Action Program, were regarded as a basic condition for attaining economic reform and hence an integral part of the struggle for the latter, thus justifying the high priority given to politics.

Notwithstanding what has been said above, the cause of economic reform, which had made a beginning prior to January, moved substantially forward in 1968. Although a market system had not been fully introduced, the old Soviet-type directive system had been dealt a serious, perhaps mortal, blow. The general principles of a planned market system had been accepted and fully endorsed by the political leadership and by the official planners. The government and its specific departments had made progress in planning the more detailed measures of change and would in due course have published the necessary basic materials on economic policy and reform.[105] Obligatory annual plans had, for the first time in 1968, been abandoned and replaced by economic guidelines that were indicative in character. Changes in price, wage, and tax policy, already initiated prior to 1968, were continued and extended. The general principles of enterprise independence and of the working peoples' coun-

---

[103] J. Kosta, at Reading conference, 1969, in V. V. Kusin, ed., *The Czechoslovak Reform Movement 1968* (London, 1973), pp. 192-94, 230, 235.

[104] Ibid., pp. 181-82, 190-92, 228-29.

[105] An official document, *Základní koncepce hospodářské politiky v nejbližších letech a vývoje soustavy řízení* (Aug. 1968), was available to the author in mimeographed form, but its source could not be determined. This outlined "a program of basic steps of economic policy," including a set of "liberalizing interventions at key (*uzlový*) points," "a new policy by the center aimed at creating a new climate of enterprise and developing the methods of planning in a market economy," and a set of measures for making the economy function more effectively. This memorandum outlined in great detail changes necessary in prices, wages, foreign trade, investments, subsidies, taxes, and cadre training, and dealt thoroughly and frankly with the problem of inflation and also the transfer of employees. It referred openly to the need for financially aiding and training displaced employees.

cils (as well as the federalization of the economy), had been officially approved. Preparatory steps were taken to establish enterprise councils, as well as new interest organizations of collective farmers and managers, and the trade unions were reviving as representatives of the interests of the workers.

A settlement of the international crisis occasioned by Soviet pressures would have opened the way for a more rapid advance toward economic reform. The 14th congress, and the changes in leadership it would have produced, would have eliminated the main political obstacles to the implementation of ideas of reform long advocated by economists and progressive political leaders and taken for granted in congress materials. This would not have guaranteed that the difficult problems of the Czechoslovak economy would have been easily or quickly resolved, but it would have created the possibility of a fundamentally different approach to their solution under a reformed economic system.

There was no evidence, in official planning or proclamations, or even in the more radical proposals by economists, of any intention to abandon socialism or to return to anything resembling capitalism.[106] Significantly, the Warsaw letter denied any desire to "interfere with the methods of planning" adopted by Czechoslovakia or with "actions to perfect the economic structure and develop socialist democracy."[107] Absent also was any criticism of economic reform or of Šik personally. Even the Soviet White Book, issued at the time of the invasion, devoted little attention to economic matters and only briefly condemned Šik and the idea of market socialism, but did claim that a planned socialist economy had been repudiated and criticized misrepresentations of Czechoslovak-Soviet trade relations.[108] After the occupation a comprehensive onslaught was made on the so-called revisionist theories of Šik and on his reform proposals, which were described as going beyond the legitimate reforms originally adopted in 1966 and as aiming at the conscious destruction of socialism and the planned economy.[109] Yet this was not the intention of

[106] See the critique of Czechoslovak reform by Benjamin Page, *Monthly Review* 21 (Oct. 1969), 36-47, and the response by O. Kyn and Howard Sherman, ibid. 22 (April 1971), 34-43. Page develops his ideas more fully in his book, *The Czechoslovak Reform Movement 1963-1968* (Amsterdam, 1973). See below, Conclusions, n. 34. For Marxist criticisms by Paul Sweezey and Charles Bettelheim, see *Monthly Review* 20 (Oct. 1968), 5-16, and 20 (March 1969), 1-19.

[107] Remington, ed., *Winter in Prague*, p. 226. The Czechoslovak reply did not mention economic reform at all (ibid., p. 241).

[108] *On Events in Czechoslovakia* (Moscow, 1968), pp. 42-44, 61-62.

[109] See in particular the article prepared by the CC's Economic Department, *NM*, no. 11 (1969), pp. 1363-76, published in part also in *Osteuropa*, no. 1 (1971), pp. A 5-10. Cf. series by R. Javořík, N. Zlocha, J. Musil, and J. Marek, *Tribuna*, nos. 39-42, Oct. 8, 15, 22, 31, 1969; series by V. Čermák and H. Kysilka, *RP*, Dec. 18, 19, 23, 1969; in fuller version, *HN*, nos. 46-52, Nov. 14-Dec. 19, 1969. This was later published in Slovak, V. Čermák and H. Kysilka, *Vývoj česko-*

the reformers, whether in the leadership, or among the experts. The overwhelming majority of economists remained convinced of the necessity of economic reform and rejected the idea that this represented a return to capitalism.[110] And the general public were overwhelmingly in favor of the continuation of socialist development and believed that the post-January revival process, including economic reform, would strengthen, rather than weaken, socialism.[111]

---

slovenskej ekonomickej reformy (Bratislava, 1971). See also an earlier series directed against Šik's economic views and political activity, by P. A. and K. R., *RP*, July 22, 24, 25, 1969. For exposition of these articles and commentary, *Osteuropa*, no. 1 (1971), pp. 42-47. Cf. Pavlenda's articles (*Pravda*, Nov. 14, 17-20, 1969) which condemned the new model of socialist democracy suggested by Šik as "right opportunist," involving the destruction of a unified direction of the economy and the planning system, their replacement by a market economy, the liquidation of socialist property, and the autonomy of producers.

[110] Declaration signed by leading Czech and Slovak economists, *RP*, Sept. 24, 1968.

[111] In late June and early July, 89 percent expressed their preference for the continuation of socialist development, and only 5 percent for a capitalist development (*RP*, July 13; Piekalkiewicz, *Polling*, p. 4). These results were based on 2,000 questionnaires (sent to a representative sample), from which a random sample of 297 was selected. For other polls, see below, chap. XVII.

CHAPTER XV

Federalism and the Slovak Problem

THE INITIAL January communiqué did not suggest, even by implication, that the unsatisfactory state of Czech-Slovak relations had been a significant causal factor in the shift of leadership or that any major changes. in these relations, other than an "improvement" in the activity of the Slovak National Council, was envisaged.[1] Even the choice of Dubček, as the first Slovak to be elected to the top post in the party's history, did not imply increased attention to the Slovak question, since he was not publicly known as a protagonist of reform in this respect. Moreover, in his early statements, while referring to the equality of Czechs and Slovaks, Dubček emphasized "Czechoslovak statehood" and the unity of the two nations.[2] Smrkovský, not then a Presidium member, was unique among leading party personalities when he described the Slovak question, in a speech in early February, as one of the main problems to be faced and advocated a solution on the basis of two equal national entities, the interests of each of which must be recognized.[3] But the unpublished January resolution, after repeating the usual clichés about "developing and bringing together (*sblížování*) the nations and nationalities" and strengthening "fraternal bonds" on the basis of proletarian internationalism, had referred to the need to elaborate a nationality policy in the new conditions and, on the basis of previous work done by the Presidium, to submit the results to the CC plenum.[4] Later in February, the Presidium revealed that the action program would include "a reform of nationality relations," resting on the equality of the two nations and the strengthening of "Czechoslovak statehood."[5]

At the end of February, the National Assembly, on the initiative of the Slovak National Council (SNR), took a significant step which suggested that some importance was being attached to the Slovak problem. This was the passage of several amendments to the constitution, and of certain related laws, which conferred on Bratislava the title of "the capital city of Slovakia" and gave its municipal national committee a status equivalent to that of a regional, rather than a district, committee as in the past.

---

[1] Cf. Presidium information, March 4, *Rok šedesátý osmý* (Prague, 1969), pp. 19-21 on the role of the Slovak question in the plenum meetings.

[2] February 1-3, Dubček, *K otázkam obrodzovacieho procesu v KSČ* (Bratislava, 1968), pp. 28-29. Cf. his unpublished speech at the Slovak Central Committee in late January, ibid., pp. 64-65.

[3] *Rudé právo*, Feb. 9.

[4] *Tribuna*, Oct. 15, 1969, p. 9.

[5] *RŠO*, p. 30.

Under the 1967 law on national committees, adopted only a few months earlier, Bratislava's national committee had been subordinated to the West Slovakia regional committee. It was now placed directly under the central government, and, where appropriate, under the SNR. Detailed provisions concerning its functioning were to be determined by the latter body.[6]

None of these early utterances or actions gave any hint that a solution of the Slovak question would become a principal objective of the reform movement, nor that a federalization of the Republic would become, in a short span of time, the primary aim of most Slovaks and would be generally accepted by Czechs.[7] No doubt, however, there was a widespread —although unexpressed—conviction among Slovaks that something must be done about the Slovak question and that federalism—an idea long discussed privately but, as we have noted earlier, taboo in public debate under Novotný—was the answer. Paradoxically, although most Czechs gave little attention to the matter, it was a Czech, Milan Hübl, long identified with Slovakia by virtue of earlier residence there and his scholarly study of Slovak history, who first openly broached the idea of federalism, both for state and party organizations, and pressed this solution in numerous articles.[8]

Beginning in early February, however, the Slovak question became

[6] *Sbírka zakonů*, no. 28, 29/1968. Cf. *Pravda*, Feb. 28. In 1967 the term "capital" was used in the original draft law but was deleted from the final text (*Sb. z.*, 69/1967). On March 14, 1968, the Slovak National Council unanimously adopted a law on the Bratislava national committee.

[7] Federation and the Slovak question are dealt with in two books which appeared in Czechoslovakia after the occupation, both by active participants in the official planning of federalism. One, by the Czech jurist, J. Grospič, ed., *Československá federace: Zákony o federalním uspořádání* (Prague, 1972), is a collection of documents, with a long formal introduction by the editor. The other, by the Slovak lawyer, V. Plevza, *Československá štátnost a slovenská otázka v politike KSČ* (Bratislava, 1971), is based on archival material and deals in detail with the federation discussions from the Slovak viewpoint (pp. 239-353). A Slovak jurist, Karol Rebro, gives a historical sketch of the problem, mainly prior to 1968, with documents, in *Cesta národa* (Bratislava, 1969); also in English, *The Road to Federation* (Bratislava, 1970). Western analysts of Czechoslovak reform have almost entirely neglected the Slovak problem and federation. An exception is Robert W. Dean, *Nationalism and Political Change in Eastern Europe* (Denver, 1973). For pre-1968 background, Stanislav J. Kirschbaum, "Le nationalisme minoritaire," *Canadian Journal of Political Science* 7 (June 1974), 248-67. Eugen Steiner, a Slovak journalist in exile, deals briefly and inadequately with these themes in *The Slovak Dilemma* (Cambridge, 1973), chaps. 17-20. Cf. two other articles of limited value: Peter A. Toma, "The Czechoslovak Question Under Communism," *East European Quarterly* 3 (March 1969), 15-30; M. George Zaninovich and Douglas A. Brown, "Political Integration in Czechoslovakia: The Implications of the Prague Spring and Soviet Intervention," *Journal of International Affairs* 27 (Spring 1973), 66-79.

[8] *Práce*, Feb. 21. Cf. *Literární listy*, March 14. In an earlier article Hübl had not mentioned federalism, but had invoked the Košice program (*Práce*, Jan. 28).

the subject of widespread public discussion, carried on mainly by Slovak political leaders and intellectuals. Not a single Slovak spokesman advocated a federal solution at this time, but some leaders struck a new note. M. Pecho, a high party functionary, and F. Hagara, a Slovak commissioner, criticized the lack of power of the Slovak national organs, especially under the 1960 constitution, and recommended a broadening of the authority of the Slovak National Council.[9] Another commissioner, A. Ťažký, responding to a question, had approved the idea of parallel Czech and Slovak national organs, as well as common organs to coordinate their relations, describing this as "the ideal of the Košice program."[10] The Slovak party leader, Bil'ak, also called for a return to the spirit of the Košice government program, terming it the Magna Carta of the Slovak nation and a good basis for reform.[11] Dubček, in a speech on February 22, stressed the urgency of establishing national equality as a guarantee of the stability of the common state and the necessity of repairing the damage done to Slovak national organs by the 1960 constitution.[12] Husák, who held no political post, had not even mentioned the Slovak question in his earliest post-January pronouncements and now spoke, in moderate terms, of establishing a new order in Czech-Slovak relations, based on equality, but did not offer specific proposals.[13] The prominent economist, Viktor Pavlenda, who was serving on an advisory group in the Slovak Central Committee and was later to become a leading advocate of federalism, expressed his preference for a genuinely symmetrical system, assigning extensive powers to the national organs, rather than a federation, which, he said, might well be "centralist" in character.[14]

[9] *Predvoj*, Feb. 22, 24, resp.

[10] *Predvoj* and *Kulturní tvorba*, Feb. 8. In fact, the Košice program (April 4, 1945) had proclaimed the equality of Czechs and Slovaks and proposed wide powers for the Slovak organs, but had not mentioned Czech organs or a federal system, nor had it defined a distribution of competence. An earlier proposal by the Slovak National Council (March 2, 1945) had also not mentioned Czech organs or used the term "federation" but had explicitly listed the proposed central powers, both exclusive and common, and exclusive national powers. For texts, see Rebro, *Road to Federation*, pp. 106-7, 101-5, resp.

[11] *Pravda*, Feb. 24. See his interview, *Květy*, March 9, pp. 22-25; also in V. Bil'ak, *Pravda zůstala pravdou* (Prague, 1971), pp. 51-69. The same collection of Bil'ak's speeches includes one made at the plenum of the Slovak CC in January, unpublished at the time, in which he described Czech-Slovak relations as unsatisfactory and called for a new nationality policy, to be worked out by all-state organs, with appropriate "initiative" by the Slovak organs. He cited the need for specific improvements in the SNR's position in regard to the budget, its relations with national committees and economic organizations, and Slovak economic and cultural development (ibid., pp. 36-50).

[12] *K otázkam*, pp. 47-48.

[13] *Kultúrny život*, Feb. 23, and *Pravda*, Feb. 25. See also his historical articles, *KŽ*, Feb. 9, 16. Cf. his earlier articles, *KŽ*, Jan. 12, Feb. 2.

[14] *Pravda*, March 12. Cf. Pavlenda, *Smena*, Feb. 11.

SLOVAK INITIATIVE

In mid-March, however, federation was openly proposed by legal scholars in the Communist Party organization at the Law Faculty of Komenský University in Bratislava as the only solution to Czech-Slovak relations.[15] Sharply criticizing the asymmetrical model which had developed after 1945 and the lack of authority of the Slovak National Council after 1960, their resolution urged a return not to the "compromise" of the Košice program, but rather to the federal proposals advanced by the Slovak National Council in early 1945. They submitted a plan for a symmetrical constitutional system embodying two parallel sets of government organs in the Czech lands and in Slovakia, together with common organs with equal representation of the two nations. Competence would be clearly divided between the common organs ("the most basic questions of all-state economic policy," national defense, and foreign policy) and the "national," i.e. Czech and Slovak, organs (the general direction of the national economy, including the economic plan and budget, within a framework set by the central government). Slovak interests could be safeguarded in all-state organs in various ways—either by a requirement that all-state legislation be approved by the national organs or by parity representation in a second federal chamber, or by the appointment of Slovak secretaries of state in common ministries headed by Czechs. The draft also proposed a constitutional law in the near future to define the authority of the Slovak National Council and to reestablish the Board of Commissioners; eventually, a new constitution incorporating the symmetrical system; and a corresponding reorganization of the Communist Party of Czechoslovakia. A few days after the publication of these recommendations, a symposium of legal experts, in the party weekly, *Predvoj*, pressed for a federal structure in both state and party, and in other organizations, as the only acceptable solution.[16]

The concept of a federal state was adopted officially by the Slovak National Council in a proclamation in mid-March, setting forth detailed proposals for immediate action (by mid-1968), which would assure the Slovak organs an enhanced position prior to the elections and to the preparation of the plan and budget for 1969.[17] The final establishment of federalism, it was recognized, could not be achieved in 1968 but

[15] *Pravda*, March 10. This resolution had been approved at a faculty party meeting on Feb. 29.

[16] *Predvoj*, March 14. The symposium included V. Hatala, K. Laco, L. Košťa, and others. On party reorganization, see also A. Kopčok (*Pravda*, March 6), who favored "autonomy and independence" for Slovak party organs.

[17] Text of declaration and of F. Barbírek's report to the SNR, *Pravda*, March 16. Only brief reports were given in *RP*, March 15-16. The text of the declaration, with favorable comment, was given in *Život strany*, no. 8-9 (April 1968), pp. 56-58.

would be contingent upon the adoption of a new constitution. In the meantime the immediate measures, which should be incorporated in the party's action program and then in a special constitutional law, would prepare the ground for the federal model, for which planning should begin at once and continue in the period up to the 14th Party Congress. These early steps would give the Slovak National Council legislative power, with a division of competence between it and the National Assembly "corresponding to the spirit of the Košice program." This would also establish a Council of Ministers as the organ of state power and administration in Slovakia and would permit the creation of appropriate ministries from the existing commissionerships, as well as new agencies in such spheres as industry, interior and security, labor and social affairs, and pricing, and an economic council.

The proposal, strangely enough, spoke only of Slovak organs, and not of parallel Czech and Slovak organs, and thus represented only an improved asymmetrical system, with expanded Slovak autonomy and enhanced Slovak influence in all-state affairs. The Slovak National Council would have full legislative authority in all areas except those enumerated as belonging exclusively to the National Assembly, namely, constitutional questions, foreign relations, national defense, and currency. Slovak executive power would extend to all except the three last-named spheres. The Slovak National Council would formulate a plan of development and its own budget, and would carry on foreign trade within general principles set by the central government. Its competence would specifically include education, culture, health, trade, construction, internal affairs, and the national committees. All-state bodies would be based on the principle of equality to avoid Slovak outvoting or *majorizácia*.[18] State secretaries of Slovak nationality would be appointed in the departments of foreign affairs and defense where the minister was Czech, and vice versa. There would be "equal" or "proportionate" representation in the state administration generally, including the foreign service, army, security, etc., and in societal and other organizations.

Once proclaimed, the concept of federalism was immediately adopted by the Slovak public and its leading spokesmen. A poll conducted in late March revealed that 94.3 percent of Slovaks recognized the necessity to settle anew the relationship of Czechs and Slovaks and of these, 73 percent favored a federal order, and 18 percent an improved asymmetrical system.[19] Bil'ak, not previously committed to federalism, identified himself fully with the proposal and with the general scheme of the SNR

---

[18] The term *majorizácia* (Czech, *majorizace*), equivalent to the German *Majorisierung*, cannot be exactly rendered in English. It will henceforth be used either in the original or translated as "majority-domination," in the sense of the outvoting of the Slovaks by the numerical Czech majority.

[19] *ŽS*, no. 19, May 7, 1969, p. 9.

declaration.[20] Husák, in several interviews in Czech newspapers, sought to reassure the Czechs that a federal solution would not threaten the unity of Czechoslovakia or a unified economy, and even argued that "common affairs" would predominate.[21] In historical discussions of Czech-Slovak relations there was an increasing emphasis on the need to base present solutions on the implicitly "federal" programs of the Slovak party and the SNR in early 1945, and sharp criticism of the "compromise" character of the Košice program and of the weakening of the position of Slovakia after 1948.[22] Several spokesmen stressed the interrelationship of democratization and federalization and contended that cadre changes and progressive policies were essential in Slovakia as a complement to widened autonomy.[23]

While Slovak opinion crystallized rapidly in favor of federalism, the Czech public evinced little or no interest in the matter. There was no outright opposition to federation, but there was also no sense of urgency, and suspicion of Slovak views was widespread. A number of commentators lamented this lack of concern and tried to dispel misunderstanding and prejudices concerning Slovakia.[24] The oft heard complaint that the Czechs were "paying" Slovakia in helping to raise the economic level of a backward region failed to take into account, it was said, the dire need for such equalization and the benefit to the economy as a whole. Slovak national feeling was a product of a deep sense of injustice and was in some measure justified. Moreover, the Czechs were also guilty of nationalism, as manifested in their attitude of condescension toward the "backward" Slovaks and their indifference to the Slovak question. The existence of Slovak organs, without parallel Czech organs, had not given a special advantage to Slovakia, since these organs had been more or less powerless since 1948 and Czechs controlled the all-state organs. The idea that Dubček's accession to power had placed the Slovaks in a ruling position ignored the fact that few Slovaks held leading positions in central party and state organs. The elimination of such misconceptions, and a greater Czech understanding of the Slovak position, were, it was contended, preconditions of a satisfactory settlement of the Czech-Slovak relationship.

Meanwhile, specific responses to the Slovak federalist proposals were

20 Bil'ak, *Pravda*, March 14, 16, April 4.
21 Husák, *RP*, March 21; *Práce* and *Zemědělské noviny*, March 22.
22 F. Hagara, *Pravda*, April 4; M. Dzvonik, ibid., April 5.
23 J. Strinka, *Pravda*, April 2; *KŽ*, April 5. Cf. Strinka's earlier article on federalism, *KŽ*, March 15. See also the Economic Institute's letter, *RP*, April 4, and the statement of the Slovak Economic Association, *Pravda*, April 1.
24 J. Šindelka, *RP*, March 16; J. Škaloud, *Pravda*, March 26; J. Putík, *LL*, April 4. In a symposium on democracy, no attention was given to Czech-Slovak relations (*Reportér*, March 6-13). In a symposium on this latter theme (*LL*, March 1), only one contributor, A. Kliment, proposed federalism.

few and far between. A meeting of the Mlynář team on the political system devoted to Czech-Slovak relations (to which little publicity was given) was held in Smolenice in Slovakia in early March and agreed that federalism was an integral part of an optimal political system.[25] A Czech legal specialist, Professor J. Grospič, endorsed the idea of federalism but accentuated the "common affairs" of the proposed central organs and estimated that it would take about two years to work out a federal system—views hardly likely to win Slovak approval.[26] Vilém Prečan, a Czech historian specializing in Slovak history, strongly supported federalism and urged that "something must be done now, at once," to remove Slovak doubts.[27] In two important articles, he analyzed the disadvantages of the asymmetrical system as it had evolved and condemned the "bureaucratic-centralist" system, which had liquidated not only the "phenomenon" of "Slovak politics," but also of "Czech politics," and had thus adversely affected Czechs as well as Slovaks. The Slovaks, Prečan argued, were *for* Czechoslovakia, which they regarded as "their own state," and were not seeking separation. It was the duty of the Czechs to dispel their prejudices and try to understand the Slovak problem.

THE OFFICIAL RESPONSE

Meanwhile the official leadership moved only slowly toward a recognition of the gravity of the Slovak problem and an acceptance of a federal solution. Party notables seldom included these matters in their discussion of reform, and not one advocated federalism.[28] Dubček, speaking a few days after the SNR declaration, urged that there be no delay in broadening the Slovak organs' authority "within the framework of the present situation." He stressed the need for "a certain time" to study "the forms of constitutional order" and did not use the term "federation."[29] The party Presidium, in a statement that aroused Slovak ire, spoke of "fulfilling, without residue, the possibilities of the asymmetrical model" and of initiating "intensive all-state preparations for the elaboration of a symmetrical system of legislative and executive power in the Czech

[25] Briefly reported in *Pravda*, March 19. See also *Právny obzor*, no. 6 (1968), pp. 552-53. Initial hesitations concerning federation were said to have been overcome. The meeting had been decided on in September 1967 when it was recognized that the solution of the national problem was a basic feature of a democratic political system.

[26] Grospič, *Lidová demokracie*, March 19; *Večerní Praha*, March 22.

[27] V. Prečan, *Rep.*, March 20-27, March 27-April 3.

[28] For instance, Černík, *RP*, March 14; Šik, ibid., March 15; J. Špaček, ibid., March 16; J. Lénart, ibid., March 20. V. Slavík, in a discussion of the Czech-Slovak question, made no reference to federalism, *Pravda*, March 13.

[29] *K otázkam*, p. 78.

lands and in Slovakia."[30] The plenum discussions at the end of March devoted little attention to the Czech-Slovak question, only a few speakers deeming it important and advocating a federal solution.[31] In the end, however, the Central Committee recommended that measures be taken at once to extend the authority of the Slovak organs and that there be an early "beginning of the elaboration of a symmetrical (federal) order."[32]

The adoption of the Action Program indicated that the party leadership, in spite of its delayed reaction to the initiative of the Slovaks, had come to accept, in somewhat more moderate form, their central demand.[33] A stamp of approval was given to a federal organization of the state, although ironically, reference was made only to Slovak, and *not* to Czech, organs. The program stated that the "unity" and the "strength" of the Republic depended on the recognition of national interests and the safeguarding of equality of rights of the nations. In a special section, the program severely criticized the asymmetrical system, under which the influence of the Slovak organs became "marginal," and recognized the need for a constitutional law which would remove at once the most glaring defects and prepare the ground for a symmetrical system in a new constitution.

Following in the main the SNR declaration of March 15, the Action Program proposed the establishment of the SNR as a legislative body and of a Council of Ministers as an executive agency, and an expansion of

[30] *RŠO*, p. 45. See critical comments by the Slovak Economic Association, *Pravda*, April 1; Pavlenda, ibid., April 2.

[31] For instance, Z. Fierlinger (*RP*, April 3), who favored a "powerful central government"; Smrkovský and J. Macek (ibid., April 4); Šik, who stressed "common economic interests" (ibid., April 7). Even Novotný declared: "If the Slovak working people today demand federation, then I am for it since it is up to them first of all how they wish to arrange their relations with the Czech nation and the Czechoslovak republic, and we Czechs must respect this without reservation. . . . If federation, then let it be done systematically." There should be a Czech National Council, he said, and a division of competence with all-state organs (ibid., April 6). The Slovak view was given in some detail by Barbírek (ibid., April 9) and supported by Lenárt (ibid., April 13). Both proposed wide economic competence for Slovak organs but emphasized the need for an integrated economy.

[32] *RŠO*, p. 64. The plenum recommended control of the national committees, and of the Slovak plan and budget, by the SNR, and the appointment of state secretaries in all-state ministries. See also Dubček's report, ibid., pp. 79-80.

[33] *RP*, April 10. According to Bil'ak, the Slovaks had to exert great pressure to get the idea of federation into the Action Program (*RP*, Aug. 17). F. Vašečka reported that in the preparation of the program there was a conflict of two views, one of which accepted "the advantages of federation," and the other which proposed that these advantages should be "considered" but in fact favored an improved application of the asymmetrical system (*Nové slovo*, July 18). According to Košťa, there was consensus on a federal solution in the Action Program's working groups, but a strong feeling that the general public in the Czech lands were not yet ready for it and should not be forced to set up Czech organs (*Predvoj*, March 14). See praise of the program by S. Falt'an, *RP*, April 8.

the competence of Slovak organs "according to the principles of the Košice program." Specifically, it recommended that the Slovak administration should include departments responsible for internal affairs and security, and should direct the Slovak national committees and determine the Slovak plan and budget. It suggested a return to the practice of having state secretaries in central departments, especially in foreign affairs, foreign trade, and national defense, as well as measures to exclude majority-domination in general constitutional questions and those affecting the constitutional position of Slovakia, and to guarantee equality of representation in the personnel of central organs. The party and societal organizations would also have to be organized "on the same principles."

Another section, dealing with the economy, placed emphasis on "the integration of two national economies," to be attained "through the rational use of sources and reserves of growth of both national-political regions." Criticizing the serious shortcomings in past policies in Slovakia, the program stressed that the Slovak economy must develop at a rate faster than that of the country as a whole so that the task of "economic equalization" would be accomplished by 1980. The need to define the competence of Slovak national organs was noted, as was the need to elaborate the new system of direction in such a way that "the territorial and national aspects of development would become equal and organic components of the system of direction of the entire national economy." It proposed that the competence of the Slovak national organs be extended to education and culture, including control of radio, television and films, scientific institutions and creative unions.

The Dubček regime was thus formally committed to the attainment of federalism and to early action to improve the position of Slovak organs, but seemed in no great hurry to achieve these two goals. The new government, under Černík, included, in its twenty-nine members, six Slovaks, of whom two, G. Husák, and P. Colotka were deputy chairmen, the former responsible for drafting the new constitutional ordering of Czech-Slovak relations. Smrkovský, in his inaugural speech as head of the National Assembly, acknowledged the urgency of federalism but warned against "improvisation" and for the first time officially raised the issue of creating Czech organs to parallel existing Slovak organs.[34] Dubček, also pressing for federation, continued to stress common Czechoslovak "statehood," the mutual interests of both nations, and the integration of the economy.[35] Husák's speeches were moderate and not very

[34] *Pravda*, April 19; see also his speech in Košice, ibid., April 28.
[35] In earlier speeches, he had made no mention of federation (*K otázkam*, pp. 123, 131-40). In Prague, early in April, he spoke somewhat defensively of the need for federation, almost as if it had not already been adopted as party policy (*RP*, April 9). In Bratislava, later in the month, however, he emphasized the urgency of federation (*K otázkam*, pp. 151-52).

specific concerning federation.[36] Černík, in the government declaration in late April, proclaimed the urgency of the constitutional reform of Czech-Slovak relations, but went no further than the Action Program in defining the form of federation.[37] In late May the appointment of a government commission, under Černík, and a commission of experts, under Husák, to formulate concrete proposals for the new federal system marked steps forward.[38]

Meanwhile the Slovak party, at its plenum in early April, had reasserted the necessity of elaborating a new constitutional order without delay, and assigned to the SNR the responsibility of working out a preliminary constitutional law and draft proposals on the economic aspects of federalism, and to a CC commission of experts the preparation of a project of federalism.[39] At this plenum Bil'ak forcefully advocated the cause of federalism and stated that this would require a corresponding reorganization of the party's structure.[40] In a later speech, Bil'ak put this latter point in even stronger terms, declaring that the Slovak CC's function could not be reduced "merely to the fulfillment of decisions of the CPCz Central Committee"; it must become "the creator and implementor of the conception of Slovak development and a co-creator, equal in rights, of all-state conceptions."[41]

At its plenum in early May, the Slovak CC raised for the first time the issue of deadlines, proposing June for the preparation of the initial constitutional law on federalism, and October 28, the anniversary of the founding of the Czechoslovak Republic, for its adoption. The plenum also urged that the appointment of the federalization commission be expedited and that a Czech committee be formed to share in the preparatory discussions. When the plenum met again at the end of the month, it restated the deadline of October 28 and issued the Slovak Action Program, which, however, offered no fresh concepts or details. Condemning the asymmetrical order as discredited, it reiterated the demand for a new constitution which would establish a symmetrical order and an immediate constitutional law to prepare the way for future federalism. Although not setting a deadline, the program urged that the forthcoming elections

[36] *Pravda*, April 23, May 9; *Nová mysl*, no. 6 (1968), pp. 659-60, 662.

[37] *RP*, April 25. Ján Marko, SNR deputy chairman, stated that no deadline could yet be set for federalization (ibid.).

[38] Ibid., May 18, 29, for the composition of both. The government commission had been instructed by the party Presidium to draft the general principles of the new system by June 1968 (*RŠO*, pp. 154-55). The expert commission was constructed on the principle of parity, with 15 Czechs and 15 Slovaks. Two more members, from North and South Moravia, were to be added. A separate commission, under Šik, was to deal with the economic aspects of federation (*RP*, June 2).

[39] *Pravda*, April 11. A few days later the SNR appointed a special commission to draw up a draft constitutional law.

[40] *Pravda*, April 10; *RP*, April 11.   [41] *Pravda*, April 27.

should bring into existence both Czech and Slovak national organs and a new common parliament. The state-right principle must also be applied to the party structure, and the out-of-date conception of the CPS as "a territorial organization of the CPCz" abandoned. All party organs (including presumably the Slovak) should be strengthened in their "independence," so that they would become not "mere mechanical implementors of the directives of central and higher organs, but institutions capable of working politically in an independent and creative fashion."[42]

CZECH AND SLOVAK OPINION DIVERGES

The provisions of the Action Program relating to Czech-Slovak relations were welcomed by both Czechs and Slovaks, although with greater enthusiasm by the latter. Of the entire sample in an April 20-21 opinion poll, 86 percent agreed fully or partially (60 and 20 percent, respectively); 7 percent disagreed. In the Czech lands, 83 percent (53 and 31 percent, respectively) agreed; 10 percent disagreed. In Slovakia, 94 percent (79 and 15 percent, respectively) agreed; none disagreed. Slovaks were also satisfied, although to a lesser degree, with the proposed solutions of the problem in the Slovak Action Program: 64.5 percent satisfied, and 23.8 percent, partially satisfied.[43]

In spite of official endorsement of federation, the Slovaks were impatient with what they considered the slow pace of advance. Their past experiences, under the First Republic, and again in 1945 and 1948, fostered doubts of Czech sincerity and fear of further disappointment. The memory of the hesitant efforts in 1956, and again in 1964, to expand the powers of the Slovak organs—followed in each case by renewed centralism—reinforced these uncertainties. The feeling was widespread that most Czechs were insensitive to the need for action and indeed indifferent to the problem. Criticisms were often aired concerning the prejudices against Slovakia held by the average Czech; the lack of serious discussion of the question by the Czech media; and the absence of any Czech representative organs which might prepare Czech opinion and draft proposals to match the Slovak initiative.[44] Only occasionally was there a positive statement on Czech attitudes and only rarely an admission that Slovaks shared the blame for past evils.[45]

---

[42] RP, May 7. For the Slovak Action Program, see Pravda, May 29. A summary for Czech readers was given in ŽS, no. 12 (June 1968), pp. 29-31.

[43] J. A. Piekalkiewicz, Public Opinion Polling in Czechoslovakia, 1968-69 (New York, 1972), p. 111; ŽS, May 7, 1969, p. 9.

[44] See the series of responses to questions, KŽ, April 12; R. Olšinský, ibid., April 5; M. Šimečka, ibid., May 17; Falt'an, NS, June 20.

[45] Husák, Rep., June 26-July 3; J. Kučerák and K. Pekník, NS, June 20. Cf. Karol Rosenbaum's analysis of Czech-Slovak relations which, although recognizing

Moreover, there was suspicion that the Prague leaders, in spite of their formal approval of federalism, were not really committed to a fully symmetrical order and that some still harbored notions of improving the asymmetrical system by merely broadening the scope of the Slovak organs.[46] These doubts were strengthened by reports that František Kriegel had expressed the opinion that the establishment of Czech national organs was contrary to Czech tradition.[47] This seemed to reflect a feeling common among Czechs, which had been expressed in its crudest form by Novotný at the April plenum, that federalization was a matter for the Slovaks and not, as the Slovaks claimed, for Czechs, too. It was not seen as a prerequisite of the stability and unity of Czechoslovakia as a whole. Some Slovaks even felt that, if such Czech attitudes persisted and federation were not fully and sincerely accepted, separation might become "the last resort."[48] Most spokesmen, however, including the poet and leading political figure, Ladislav Novomeský, although expressing their disgust with past Czech attitudes and disappointment with existing vestiges of these views, strongly supported the continuance of a common state, in a federal form, and rejected the idea of separation.[49] They usually contended, as Novomeský did, that there was no contradiction between federalization and democratization since these aims were closely interlocked and one without the other was impossible. A few Slovaks preferred confederation to a tighter federalist form of union.[50] Others, including two scholars, Hvezdoň Kočtúch and Karol Laco, although not rejecting confederation, expressed a preference for federation in some form.[51]

---

certain problems, was very positive in his emphasis on the common interests of the two nations (*RP*, March 10).

[46] Pavlenda, *Pravda*, April 2; J. Uher, *KŽ*, April 12; V. Mihálik and M. Holub, *Predvoj*, April 18.

[47] Kriegel's speech at the Bratislava party military conference (April 6) was not published, but in an interview granted during an intermission, he was reported as holding such views (Holub, *Predvoj*, April 18).

[48] M. Sklenka, *Roľnícke noviny*, April 20; F. Salaj, ibid., April 29. Expressing his conviction that Czechs would show understanding of Slovak demands, or would be pressed to accept them, Sklenka concluded: "If this should fail (which I cannot believe) there would remain for us only one last possibility—possibly as a last resort—to create an independent socialist state."

[49] Novomeský, *Pravda* and *RP*, April 19; M. Kusý, *NS*, June 20, 27. Novomeský defined the essential idea of federalization as follows: "Everyone to himself and in his own way, but not in an isolationist fashion, but in ceaseless mutual dialogue, in systematic reciprocal correspondence and in mutual control. Through mutual support and opposition toward a higher synthesis." In an interview with *Reportér* (June 19-26), Novomeský, referring to the Slovak Uprising in 1944, described it as the only case in history when a nation voluntarily relinquished its independence and actually carried through an armed uprising to attain its objective.

[50] M. Nadubinský, *Smena*, April 23.

[51] After an examination of several alternative solutions both rejected all forms other than a symmetrical one: either federation or confederation. Neither openly

Czech opinion, meanwhile, remained somewhat passive and disinterested, as many Czechs regretfully admitted, attributing this to such factors as traditional condescension, if not scorn, for Slovaks and the Slovak language; a lack of real knowledge of Slovakia and its disadvantageous position under the asymmetrical system; fears of Slovak nationalism, generated by the propaganda of the fifties, and of the danger of separatism, based on the experience of 1939; a failure to appreciate the full implications of a federal solution; and above all, the lack of serious study or discussion of the problem.[52] Even Czech intellectuals were, it was said, often ill-informed about Slovak problems and accepted federalism only because of Slovak insistence. Yet there was no overt opposition to federalism, and there were frequent efforts by more committed Czechs to explain the Slovak problem and to promote the idea of a federal solution.[53] Some contended that precious time was being lost and that the general principle of federalism ought to be given concrete form as soon as possible.[54]

The most serious effort to grapple with the problem was made by two constitutional specialists, Jiří Grospič and Zdeněk Jičínský, who gradually assumed the role of the main Czech advocates of federalism. In an article in Bratislava *Pravda*, they accepted the argument that the asymmetrical system was completely inadequate and that a return to the Košice agreement was impossible. Their conclusions in the main embodied the Slovak conception of a state based on two equal and sovereign nations, each having its own national organs, and conferring certain defined and enumerated powers on the common organs. Although they did not attempt at this stage to define the allocation of competence, the Czech jurists favored the assignment of legislative authority in most matters to all-state organs, and most of the executive authority to the national organs. They accepted the idea that Slovaks must be protected against majority-domination in all-state organs, suggesting that a qualified majority of Slovak deputies be required in decisions concerning the constitution or the position of Slovakia and Slovak organs. The two experts maintained that a federal solution could not be attained immediately, or even in a short time, since there were many difficult problems

---

advocated the latter; both implicitly argued for the former (Kočtúch, *KŽ*, March 22; Laco, *Pravda*, April 24-25).

[52] Symposium, "What Do Czechs Think of Slovaks?" *Rep.*, May 22-29. See K. Kosík, *LL*, May 2; Šimečka, *KŽ*, May 17; J. Patočka, *LL*, May 23; Z. Šisler, *RP*, May 23; *Filmové a televizné noviny*, May 29. See also Smrkovský, *My 1968*, no. 4 (1968).

[53] J. Bečvář, *RP*, April 17; M. Čermák, ibid., April 18; M. Hübl, ibid., April 17; *Smena*, May 3. Hübl emphasized the necessity of maintaining an integrated economy and of recognizing "a certain undeniable competence" of the central organs. See a sharp reaction to this by J. Rosa, *Pravda*, May 7.

[54] J. Kašpar, *ŽS*, no. 10 (May 1968), pp. 34-37.

to be solved, some of which should be left to the drafting of an eventual constitution.[55]

The gulf between Czech and Slovak opinion was a poor augury for the rapid implementation of federalism. By early May, the Czechs showed a greater understanding of the problem and of the imperative of a federal solution, but important differences of emphasis remained. For example, in major interviews in *Pravda*, Grospič and Jičínský pleaded for "full functions" for the federal organs so as to achieve "common solutions," whereas the Slovak jurists, Professors Laco and Vojtech Hatala, in the same paper, argued that "the center of gravity" should rest in the national organs and that federal powers should exist "only where unavoidable for the functioning of the whole federal organization."[56] There also began to emerge a serious divergence on the procedures to be followed and on the timing of federation measures.

In a report to the Academy of Sciences committee on constitutional reform in early May (ultimately adopted), Professor Grospič contended that, owing to the postponement of the elections, more time had become available for solving some of the critical problems connected with the new state-right order.[57] He envisaged that, by June, only a law to set up national organs would be drafted; the "theses" on the new federal order should be completed during the period prior to the 14th Party Congress. October 28 should be taken as a deadline, he suggested, *not* for a finished constitutional law on federalism, but rather for a political proclamation endorsing the principles of federation, followed by the elaboration of a law by the earliest realistic date—in the first quarter of 1969. Elections in the spring would make possible the immediate functioning of the new federal organs. Above all, this extension would permit the establishment of Czech national organs, in particular a Czech National Council (ČNR), which could arouse and inform Czech public opinion, prepare Czech proposals, and ultimately serve as co-sponsors, with the SNR, of the federal reform. It was important, Grospič stated, that the federal system be achieved, not "from above," by the central authorities, but "from

[55] *Pravda*, April 19. See also their joint article, *NM*, no. 5 (1968), pp. 596-616; and in *Právník* 107, no. 6 (1968), 481-96.

[56] *Pravda*, June 14, 21, resp. Husák, in an interview in early June, seemed to envisage all-state legislative unity, with executive power in the hands of the national organs. He spoke of the determination of economic policy by the federal organs, of legal unity in spheres such as economics, and even education and culture, and of reasonably strong central organs for the party (*Rep.*, June 26-July 3).

[57] J. Grospič, *Právník*, no. 9 (1968), pp. 798-805, and the Standpoint (*Stanovisko*) adopted by the commission, ibid., pp. 806-7 (also in *RP* and *Pravda*, May 21). The Standpoint still mentioned October 28 as a possible deadline. See also the joint articles by Grospič and Jičínský, *RP*, July 3, 4, and their joint interview, *Pravda*, June 14. Similar views were expressed by B. Rattinger, *Právník*, no. 8 (1968), pp. 732-33.

below," by agreement of both Czech and Slovak organs, and with the approval of the Czech and Slovak populations.

These concepts were in sharp contrast to those of the Slovaks who kept insisting that a proclamation of principle was not enough and that it *was* possible to prepare the draft law by June and to submit it for adoption by the assembly on October 28.[58] Moreover, the Slovaks wanted a detailed revision, not only of Chapter VI of the 1960 constitution, but of all other relevant parts, amounting to 40 or 50 percent of that document. This would represent what they called "a small constitution (*malá ústava*)" which would in turn become "an organic part" of the eventual new constitution. The Slovaks were also more concerned than the Czechs over the urgency of bringing Czech national organs into existence as soon as possible, so that the Czechs would become involved in preparing the federal order. This would, of course, create further complications, since the Czechs could not be expected to accept ready-made Slovak proposals and would have the right to advance their own concepts.[59] Since there were also serious differences on matters of substance, especially on the economic aspects of federation, it was clear that the task of reaching an agreement, through compromise, would not be easy.

Economic Aspects of Federalism

During the immediate post-January months discussion of Slovak economic problems concentrated on the traditional theme of the region's underdevelopment and the inadequacy of measures taken to "equalize" Czech and Slovak levels of development. Although much had been achieved, the Slovaks felt strongly that they had suffered from neglect and discrimination, even exploitation. There had been faulty methods and approaches and hence inadequate utilization of Slovak resources in serving not only Slovak interests, but also those of the economy as a whole.[60] Demands were made for greater economic powers for the Slovak national organs, especially in drafting their own plan and their own budget, but also in determining economic policies for the region and in directing the Slovak economy.[61]

At the same time Slovak economists emphatically denied that greater economic independence for Slovakia would in any way harm the continued existence of a unified Czechoslovak economy. Pavlenda and

[58] Pavlenda, *Pravda*, May 16; V. Plevza, *NS*, May 23, June 6; Laco and Hatala, *Pravda*, June 21; Husák, *RP*, June 21.

[59] Grospič, *Právník*, no. 9 (1968), p. 801.

[60] For instance, V. Komárek, *RP*, Feb. 6-8; J. Gráč and J. Lúč, *Pravda*, Feb. 9, 16; Pavlenda, *Smena*, Feb. 21; E. Pračko, *RP*, March 27-29.

[61] Gráč and Lúč, *Pravda*, Feb. 9, 16; J. Mal'iška and I. Zelinka, *KT*, Feb. 10; Pavlenda, ibid., March 12.

others rejected not only the previous economic centralism but also a closed or autarkic Slovak economy, and set forth the somewhat ambiguous goal of the integration of relatively independent "national economies" in a unified Czechoslovak economy.[62] Integration would be achieved, not by the previous administrative measures of central control, but by a freer play of economic forces, particularly through the relative freedom of action of individual enterprises under the new economic system of management.[63] Centralized bureaucratic management from Prague ministries would not be replaced, it was hoped, by a reincarnation of similar procedures in Bratislava. Relatively moderate controls by the Slovak regional authorities would leave the actual operation of industry to the enterprises.[64] Furthermore, the highly centralized "general directorates" in individual industrial sectors, with headquarters usually located in Prague, would be replaced by voluntary groupings of enterprises, located in either Slovak or Czech areas, or in both.[65]

Slovak organs would occupy a more important position in economic affairs, drafting their own plans and budgets, within the framework of the central plan and budget, and defining their own regional economic policies. They would be in a better position to influence all-state decisions in economic affairs. The exact sphere of competence of the national organs was not precisely defined but was intended to be very broad, with all-state powers limited in the main to the general plan, the federal budget, the general principles of foreign trade, etc. These procedures would ensure a fuller and more rational exploitation of Slovak resources, proper attention to specific Slovak interests, and an acceleration of the process of "equalization," and in that way would benefit the Czechoslovak economy as a whole, and hence serve the interests of Czechs, too.

In principle this approach did not collide with Czech interests and at first met with no serious objections from Czech economists. Radoslav Selucký, for example, proclaimed the need for federalization without delay but clearly indicated that his main concern was economic and political reform in the state as a whole. He was in favor of a single Czechoslovak economy, functioning without regard to the boundaries of the two national entities, according to the same rules and principles in the

---

[62] Pavlenda, in *ŽS*, no. 7 (March 1968), pp. 34-39; *Pravda*, March 12, 27; *NM*, no. 4 (1968), pp. 475-83; *LD*, May 31; and Kočtúch, *Práca*, April 20. The Slovaks used the term "national economy" (in Slovak *národna ekonomika*) to refer to the Slovak economy, as distinct from its customary usage in English to refer to the economy of the entire state (rendered in Slovak as *národne hospodárstvo* or *celoštátná* [or *Československá*] *ekonomika*).

[63] Löbl, *KŽ*, April 26; *Práce*, May 24; A. Nuoška, *Hospodářské noviny*, May 24.

[64] D. Hanes and M. Šimovič, *Pravda*, March 23; Pavlenda, ibid., April 2; letter of the Slovak Economic Institute, *RP*, April 4; Pavlenda and Kočtúch, *Pravda*, April 24.

[65] E. Löbl, *KŽ*, Feb. 9; *Ľud*, March 22.

whole Republic. Federalization, he concluded, should be primarily political and should preserve the integrated economy. "We are too small a state to permit two economic entities."[66]

A meeting of minds of Czech and Slovak economists was apparently reached at the end of April when, after discussions in Bratislava, a declaration of "The Principles of the Federalization of the Economy" was agreed upon and published.[67] This document accepted in general the conceptions propounded by Slovak economists, as set forth above, but made more precise the manner of their application. There must be "an economic and political federation," not "a great political" and "a small economic" federation. The declaration stated the familiar premise that the economy was "an integrated synthesis of two national economies" and contended that the sovereignty of the national states required "economic authority in the direction and utilization of the wealth created by them." An integrated economy required a unified market and "unified principles of management and economic policy." The national organs would be responsible for the development of their own economies, including long- and middle-range plans, the national budgets, instruments and rules of economic policies, etc., and would have "original" competence as to "policies regarding prices, wages, income, taxes, currency, et cetera." The national organs would apparently have been assigned the right to issue currency, to carry on foreign trade, and to collect taxes, making the federal budget dependent on contributions from the national budgets, these rights to be exercised, however, according to "unified principles, criteria, and methods" on the basis of agreement among the national organs. Certain powers would be delegated to the federal organs, including, apart from defense and foreign affairs, the shaping of the general principles of economic policy, especially in foreign trade, of currency policy, of the integration of the two economies, of the economic system of management, and of equalization of the national political regions.

It soon became evident that this declaration did not reflect a general consensus of Czechs and Slovaks on the economic aspects of federation. The legal experts, Grospič and Jičínský, expressed concern over the concept of "a political economic federation," as outlined in the declaration,

[66] *KŽ*, April 12. This article was sharply criticized by Kočtúch (*Pravda*, April 24) who stressed the need to break up the old institutional structure at the center through the new economic system and to carry through "a decentralization of economic power" as an integral part of democratization. This was hardly likely to be denied by Selucký.

[67] Reported in *RP* and *Pravda*, April 30, and given in full text, *Pravda*, May 18; English translation in R. A. Remington, ed., *Winter in Prague* (Cambridge, Mass., 1969), pp. 173-80. See commentary by I. Rendek, *Pravda*, May 22. Signatories included Hanes, Kočtúch, Löbl, Pavlenda, Turčan, and other Slovaks, and Č. Kožušník, L. Veltruský, and other Czechs. Šik was not present.

and criticized it as a project, not of federation, but of confederation.[68] A number of leading Czech economists (including L. Veltruský, who had been a signatory of "the principles"), issued a formal statement condemning this document and stressing the existence of a single all-state economy. Any step dividing the economy into two national economies was "a backward step," which would lead to the disintegration of many common activities and eventually to the danger of integration with other states. Repudiating the concept of the full sovereignty of the national states and the originality of their competence, Czech economists maintained that the federal organs should possess "certain original rights in the sphere of state sovereignty and economic policy," including the responsibility for the equalization of Slovakia. This would require a single bank of issue, a single currency, a unified balance of payments, and a federal budget greater in size than the expenditures on common activities. The federal organs must not be reduced to mere "coordinating" agencies, since this would stimulate conflicts between the two nations and might cripple the actions of the federal organs.[69]

Slovaks responded vigorously. Pavlenda defended himself against the charge of seeking an independent Slovak economy. Emphasizing the well-known theme of the integration of the entire economy and rejecting economic isolation, he declared his opposition to both a too powerful federal center and a too powerful national center, stating that both centers must be powerful "in their own way, in terms of the substantive competence logically belonging to them." He contended that he had always favored a full federation extending to the economic realm and had been opposed only to a narrowly political federation.[70] Several Slovak officials

[68] Grospič, Právník, no. 9 (1968), pp. 800-801; Grospič and Jičínský, Theses, ibid., pp. 815-16; B. Rattinger, ibid., no. 8 (1968), p. 733. Cf. also the appeals for strong central powers, Z. Valouch, RP, June 14; V. Vybral, LD, June 23.

[69] RP, June 21. A Czech, J. Sládek, waged a polemic against the principles and warned against limiting the powers of the federal organs in view of their responsibility for redistributing the national product in favor of less developed Slovakia. He urged that the conflict over federation should not be allowed to "drown out" the more important question of introducing the new economic system (RP, July 30). Another commentator (anonymous) sharply condemned the "economic dualism" of two separate national economies and proposed "unified management" through a powerful center (KT, July 25, pp. 1, 3). Another Czech, M. Tuček, speaking at a gathering of Slovak economists in May, wanted a unified economy and while favoring federalism politically, declared that "a systematic federal constitutional order without an economic system based on the market would lead to the dissolution of Czechoslovakia" (Ekonomický časopis 16, no. 6, 1968, pp. 562-66).

[70] Pravda, July 6, 13. Pavlenda had been personally attacked by another Slovak economist, Z. Hába, who claimed that he did not speak for all Slovak economists and was subordinating the economy to political considerations. Hába cited Pavlenda's writings from 1961 and 1966 to show his earlier opposition to federation (ibid., July 12). In his study, Ekonomické základy socialistického riešenia

468

of the Czechoslovak Bank in Bratislava sharply condemned the Czech economists' critique and claimed that it had distorted the original "principles" and represented "centralism under a new brand name."[71] Two other Slovaks expressed concern that the "common powers" proposed by the Czechs were so broad as to represent "a limitation of national sovereignty in important economic-financial relations"; they advocated "equality of competence" of Slovak and federal organs in all major economic matters.[72]

Delegates from Slovak enterprises demonstrated a strongly nationalist approach at a conference in mid-July.[73] The resolution adopted agreed to federal authority only in certain enumerated areas (such powers to be assigned by the national organs) and allocated to the national states all other powers, including planning, finance, labor and social affairs, industry, trade and agriculture, transportation and communications, education and culture, etc. The national organs would be invested with the primary power of taxation; would possess their own national banks of issue; would formulate their own scientific-technical policy; and within federal principles, would carry on foreign trade. Pricing policy would be settled in agreement with the national organs.

Certain leading Slovak economists expressed a less "nationalist" point of view which brought them closer to the Czech advocates of economic reform. Ján Ferianc, a Slovak member of the commission of experts, emphasized the need for "a regulated market socialist economy" without which the division of federal and national powers would be of little value.[74] Pavol Turčan, another commission member, wrote that economic integration should be accomplished by a genuinely functioning market, together with "common economic political organs" to promote the cohesion of the economy and to counteract the negative results of the market.[75] The economic development of Slovakia required "the coordinating function of federal organs" and funds provided from the federal budget. In the bodies which would elaborate common concepts and equalization measures, however, Turčan stressed the importance of a membership proportion corresponding to the two-nation composition of the country, thus indicating that his objective was not only to enhance

---

národnostnej otázky v Československu (Bratislava, 1968), completed in August 1966 but published only in June 1968, Pavlenda argued for greater power for the Slovak national organs and explicitly proposed federation as the best solution (pp. 253 ff, 264-65, 295-96). An earlier version, cited by Hába, was not available.

[71] *RP*, July 30. See a polemical response by D. Plachtinský who defended the concept of the "national economy" (*Práca*, July 2).

[72] J. Horváth and J. Spišiak, *NS*, June 20.

[73] *Pravda*, July 14.   [74] Ferianc, ibid., July 25, 30.

[75] Ibid., July 23-24. Both Turčan and Ferianc, as well as Löbl, had signed the May declaration in spite of its pronounced "nationalist" formulations.

the existing authority of the national organs but also to gain greater Slovak influence in all-state organs.

The Slovaks did not propound an official viewpoint on the economic aspects of federalization with any great speed. The original SNR declaration in mid-March had envisaged, in Barbírek's interpretation, an extremely limited federal authority and claimed wide powers for the Slovak organs. Barbírek, however, in his speech at the CPCz April plenum, referred to the direction of the national economy by the national organs, but within the framework of the Czechoslovak economy, and spoke also of the direction of the economy as a whole by all-state organs. "Isolated economies" would be against the interests of both nations.[76] The Slovak CC plenum revealed some uncertainty which reflected, according to Bil'ak, continuing differences among Slovak economists and indicated that further study was essential.[77] The Czechoslovak Action Program had accepted the federal idea, but had not been precise on the powers of the Slovak National Council. The Slovak Action Program, published two months later, was equally vague, saying nothing at all about the controversial question of competence. Playing on the two familiar themes of "an integrated synthesis of two national economies" and the Slovak organ's right to "direct its own economy," the program devoted much of its attention to the unfinished business of "equalization."[78] The Slovak National Council, meeting at the end of June, drew attention to "the two national economies," the sovereignty of the two "republics" and the original competence of their organs, but also spoke of economic integration, a united market, common currency, and the free movement of funds and labor force. Unlike the original March proclamation, however, the SNR spoke of "common," as well as exclusively federal, and national, affairs.[79] A statement by the Slovak CC's Economic Commission suggested that these critical issues were unresolved, since it spoke only in the vaguest terms of "an economically rational and nationally just federation" (neither "tight" nor "loose") and "an optimal joining of the activities of national and federal organs."[80]

TRIPARTITISM: A MORAVIAN ALTERNATIVE

The alternative idea of a tripartite (or "trialist") federation, including a Moravian-Silesian entity as an equal constituent partner with Bohemia and Slovakia, was first advanced in mid-April by the South Moravian regional national committee in Brno, and, after study by several working groups, was endorsed by an overwhelming majority of its

[76] Barbírek, ibid., March 16; *RP*, April 9.
[77] *Pravda*, April 11. [78] Ibid., May 29.
[79] Ibid., June 28. [80] Ibid., June 29.

plenum in early June.[81] The proposals were sent to the National Assembly and the government, and to Husák's committee on federation for their consideration. In late May a conference in Brno adopted a "Moravian declaration" which endorsed the principle of a tripartite federation and established the Society for Moravia and Silesia.[82] This society, which ultimately claimed a membership of 200,000, developed a campaign in favor of a tripartite system. Although the South Moravian party organization did not directly support the proposal, it did not condemn it and in fact urged that it be made the subject of nationwide discussion. Moreover, it agreed that the "community" of Moravia-Silesia constituted "a social, geographical, ethnic, historic, economic, and political fact," contended that "a specific status" for this entity, or a tripartite federation, was not contrary to Marxism, and demanded "a special solution for Moravia and Silesia in the constitutional law in preparation."[83]

The South Moravian proposal received support from certain local and national newspapers and from some national committees in Moravia, but was opposed in other areas and by the Brno cultural weekly, *Host do domu*. The North Moravian regional committee and individual cities in the Brno region, such as Olomouc, Gottwaldov, Jihlava, Vsetín, and Přerov, rejected the idea and favored the abolition of the regional link and a two-level system of more powerful district and local national committees. In Silesia there was a movement for a separate Silesian "land" (*země*) and even a demand for a quadripartite federation.[84]

The Moravian plan, in the detailed form published in August, envisaged a quite decentralized system, closer to Slovak than to Czech thinking. The federal organs would possess exclusive authority only in certain enumerated spheres (constitutional changes, state boundaries, international relations, defense and state security, Czechoslovak citizenship, common currency, etc.). In a wide array of "common affairs" (the greater part of economic activity, security, justice, transportation, and communications, etc.), the federal organs would determine "general principles" of policy, but would share authority with the three republics, which would possess executive competence in these spheres. In all other areas, the republic would have exclusive jurisdiction. Each republic would be

---

[81] *RP*, June 6; also V. Plevza, *NS*, June 6. Although three alternatives had been presented (including a restoration of the "land" [*země*] system and a bipartite structure) the majority for the tripartite order was overwhelming—114 for, 10 against, with one abstention.

[82] *RP*, May 21. The Moravian problem is fully discussed by Plevza, *Č. státnost*, pp. 275-96. He reported a flood of resolutions for a tripartite solution and ascribed the "artificial psychosis" on this question to the society's efforts.

[83] *RP*, June 21. See also ibid., July 27, Aug. 15 (Špaček). Šabata stated that Moravian interests should be defended "after careful consideration (*uvážlivě*) and in correct measure" (ibid., July 8).

[84] Ibid., May 31, June 6, Aug. 6; *LD*, May 4.

protected against being outvoted in a single-chamber parliament by the requirement that the deputies of each of the three republics must give approval, by a simple majority in each case, to laws relative to all exclusive federal and common affairs, and in a vote of confidence or non-confidence; and by a three-fifths majority in certain cases (declaration of war, conclusion of peace, changes in constitutional law, and state boundaries). The Moravian project embodied the principle of "autonomy" or "self-administration" (*samospráva*) which, it was argued, should also be extended to the local and district levels by enlarging the authority of the national committees (the regional committees would be abolished), thus reinforcing the safeguards against Prague centralism.[85]

The Moravian proposal became the subject of vigorous discussion, with both sides invoking Marxism and citing Lenin, and referring to the examples of Yugoslavia and other federal states. The advocates of tripartitism stressed the historical traditions of Moravia-Silesia in the pre-1914 period and the existence of an administrative territoriaι entity (*země*) under the First Republic and claimed that the Moravians, although members of the Czech nation, had their own cultural distinctiveness.[86] This area, including Brno, the second largest Czechoslovak city, had not, under the extreme centralism of communist rule, derived the economic benefits due to it as a highly developed industrial and cultural center. Neither the restoration of the Moravian-Silesian *země* nor a special status for the metropolitan city, Brno, was considered sufficient to protect the special interests of the region. Moravia-Silesia should be recognized as a constituent part of a tripartite federation, which would thus be based in part on the nationality principle, in the case of Slovakia, and in part on the territorial principle, in the case of Moravia-Silesia.

The case for a special status for Moravia met with considerable sympathy, but the idea of a federal system of three parts was strongly opposed.[87] The Moravians were, after all, Czechs. Moravian interests were not sharply separated from those of Bohemia, nor had they been more neglected than those of Bohemia, in particular of the capital city, Prague. The appeal to historical tradition was regarded as outdated and the ac-

---

[85] The detailed Moravian project was published in a special issue of *Index* (Brno), Aug. 1968, 31 pp.

[86] For instance, *RP*, May 31, July 5; round table, *LD*, June 23; B. Básta, ibid., June 7; V. Bánovský, *Rep.*, June 19-26; J. Solař, *RP*, July 26; V. Šaur, ibid., Aug. 14. See also *Index*, Aug. 1968, and a series of articles in *Moravskoslezský týden*, nos. 12-17 (n.d., presumably March and April 1969).

[87] For example, Z. Pátek, *RP*, May 18; K. Hártl and J. Slížka, ibid., June 11; Grospič and Jičínský, *Pravda*, June 14, *RP*, July 3; Hübl, *VP*, June 25; V. Vrabec, ibid., July 11; Holub, *NS*, July 11; J. Galendauer, *RP*, Aug. 3; O. Průša, ibid., Aug. 7; *NS*, Aug. 15; K. Ondris, *ŽS*, no. 15 (July 1968), pp. 6-9. An exception among Czechs was Martin Vaculík, former South Moravian party secretary, who gave his support to the Moravian demands (*MT*, no. 12, 1969, p. 4).

cent on local interests as threatening those of the economy as a whole. Certain Moravian complaints were legitimate enough, but could be met by establishing Brno as a city with a special statute, and perhaps making it the location of certain federal institutions such as the Supreme Court, and by placing branch offices of some federal ministries there. The restoration of the *země* as an intermediate administrative unit would create an additional level of government and was less satisfactory than a general administrative reorganization, involving the abolition of the regions, an increase in the powers of the districts, and perhaps the forming of "voluntary groupings of district committees" to articulate Moravian-Silesian interests. The federation itself, however, must be a dual system, based on the nationality principle, with two constituent parts, Slovakia and the Czech lands. Any other formula would not offer a solution to the urgent problem of Czech-Slovak relations and would be unconditionally rejected by the Slovaks. Indeed, Slovaks who spoke on this issue were almost unanimous in rejecting a tripartite system as one which would place them in a disadvantageous position vis-à-vis the two Czech "republics."[88]

From the beginning, the tripartite idea met with an almost completely negative reaction from leading Czech personalities and from the central party and state authorities. The federal committee of experts, under Husák, heard spokesmen for the South Moravian case, as well as Moravian opponents, on June 4, the so-called Moravian Day, but agreed overwhelmingly to proceed with federalism on a bipartite basis. This was endorsed by the government, as well as by the party.[89] Before the federalization law was passed in late June, alternative proposals were advanced by certain Moravian spokesmen but were not accepted; the only concession made was the recommendation that the Czech National Council study the Moravian comments.[90] South Moravia persisted in its efforts, however, elaborating its proposal in detail and submitting it to the assembly and government in July. Officially it was stated that legitimate Moravian complaints could be met within the framework of the new Czech national state.[91] The Society for Moravia and Silesia nonetheless continued its campaign and urged that a plebiscite be held on the issue. Complaints were made of inadequate attention in the mass media to the Moravian case, and of insufficient representation of Moravia in the

[88] Husák, *Práca*, May 25; Falt'an, *NS*, June 13; Laco, ibid., Aug. 1, 8. An exception was D. Rapant, who favored "trialism" (*KŽ*, Aug. 16).
[89] Husák, *RP*, June 21; *Rep.*, June 26-July 3; Černík, *RP*, June 8. In the government commission only K. Neubert, head of the South Moravian regional national committee, defended the tripartite system, but sought to dissociate himself from the Society for Moravia and Silesia (Plevza, *Č. štátnost*, pp. 292-93).
[90] *RP*, June 25.
[91] For instance, Husák, *KT*, July 18; Č. Císař, *Rep.*, Aug. 14-21, supplement. In his address to the Czech National Council on July 31, Císař did not mention the Moravian proposal.

federalization commissions and in the Czech National Council.[92] The approval of the principles of federation on a dual basis by the federal government and by the assembly presidium, as well as by the ČNR presidium, touched off a wave of protests and the beginning of a drive for signatures for a tripartite system. There was a renewed call for a popular referendum and demands for the resignation of Císař and Jičínský.[93]

The Moravian proposal raised the complex and difficult question of the future structure of local administration, especially in its plan for the abolition of the regional national committees and the expansion of the authority of the local and district committees. The Action Program and the April government proclamation had favored the strengthening of the role of the national committees and the democratization of their activity, but had made no other recommendation concerning the local organs.[94] The postponement of national committee elections had deferred this problem and encouraged passivity on the part of local organs uncertain of their future.[95] Meanwhile there was much public criticism of the committees, and many proposals for change, including demands for the creation of some new districts and the abolition of the regions. In Slovakia there was widespread support for the abolition of the three Slovak regional national committees, which were originally established to weaken the position of Slovak national organs and would hardly be required in the relatively small Slovak state.[96] On the official level there was a readiness to admit the weaknesses of the national committee system and the need to revise the 1967 law, but uncertainty as to the best solution. There was acknowledgment of the value of specific ideas in the Moravian draft, in particular the principle of "self-administration," but not of the restoration of the Moravian-Silesian "země," even within the Czech part of a bilateral federation. Official opinion tended to favor the abolition of the regional committees, a limited increase in the number of districts, and a new statute for Brno and other large cities. The entire question could best be considered, it was claimed, after the settlement of the federal problem, and within the framework of each republic.[97]

[92] RP, July 7, Aug. 18; Index, Aug. 1968, p. 30; MT (1969): no. 13, p. 6; no. 14, p. 4; no. 15, p. 4. The National Assembly presidium issued a statement appealing for patience and careful study of Moravian problems (RP, Aug. 9).

[93] RP, Aug. 21; MT, no. 16 (1969), p. 4.

[94] Černík, RP, April 25.

[95] Dubček, May plenum, RŠO, p. 194; J. Meško, Pravda, May 28.

[96] For instance, F. Červenka, RP, April 13; E. Litvajová, Pravda, May 14; M. Červený, RP, July 23. Löbl, however, urged the retention of the regional committees (Pravda, May 7).

[97] For this and the above, see Husák, RP, June 21; Rep., June 26-July 3; S. Švábenský, deputy chairman of the Brno municipal national committee, RP, June 28; V. Knapp, ibid., July 6; Husák and Černík, at a conference of national committee functionaries, ibid., July 12, 13; Císař, ibid., Aug. 1 and Rep., Aug. 24-31.

A subcommittee of the committee of experts on federalization, under the

OFFICIAL PLANNING: PROGRESS AND DEADLOCK

By the time of the CC plenum at the end of May the party had clarified its position on the procedures to be followed for the attainment of federation, and in particular had recognized the necessity of constituting Czech national organs. These would, it was said, articulate Czech interests and contribute to Czech understanding of the necessity and advantages of federation. The plenum recommended that the government and assembly establish a committee, under Špaček, the South Moravian leading secretary, to prepare the formation of Czech national organs, and that the Presidium establish a party committee, under Indra, consisting of regional organization representatives, to elaborate a party structure appropriate for a federal order. The plenum also commissioned Černík and Indra to report at the forthcoming congress on the federal order and the party structure respectively. It was not yet clear, however, what form party reorganization would take. Dubček referred only to "corresponding changes" in the party, which would, however, maintain its "international unity" and perform "an integrating role."[98] The Slovak party's committee on federalization endorsed these decisions, but reiterated the question of deadlines, not mentioned by the plenum resolution, urging the completion of a draft constitutional law by the time of the 14th congress, its enactment in October 1968, and the holding of elections in early 1969.[99]

Meanwhile the federal commissions had begun their work on the constitutional order.[100] The commission of experts, with various subcommittees, had been in session regularly from May 27 at the Zbraslav and later the Koloděj castles and had available for study not only a revised SNR draft, but other documents, such as the Principles of the Federalization of the Economy and studies by the government's presidium and by the Academy of Sciences. As Černík reported in June, at the governmental commission's first meeting, agreement had been reached on certain matters, with other contentious issues left for further discussion.[101] A general

---

chairmanship of Professor Průša, was studying the problem of local government and administration. A draft statute for Brno was under discussion in the National Assembly (*RP*, July 10). The idea of making Brno the capital city of the new Czech national state was not, however, officially favored.

[98] *RŠO*, pp. 208-9, 218-19, 223-24; Dubček, ibid., pp. 193-94. Smrkovský and Barbírek (*RP*, June 6-7) were the only persons to speak extensively on federation. Both rejected the tripartite approach.

[99] *Pravda*, June 4. Dubček had referred to the Oct. 28 deadline in his report to the plenum.

[100] For this, see the informative articles by V. Plevza, secretary of the government commission, *NS*, May 23, June 6; Plevza, *RP*, June 7; Husák and Knapp, ibid., June 21; Husák, *Rep.*, June 26-July 3.

[101] Černík, *RP*, June 8. According to him, federal competence in the economic

consensus had been reached on the idea of a bipartite federal system based on the nationality principle and on a division of competence between national and federal organs.

Most important, it had been recognized that Czech national organs must be formed at an early date. The first step in this direction was taken at the end of the month, when a draft constitutional law on the preparation of federation was passed, providing for the setting up of a Czech National Council; this body, together with the existing Slovak National Council, would prepare the federal system. It would serve, not as a legislative body, but as "a provisional organ of constitutional political representation of the Czech nation" until the elections, to express the Czech standpoint on the new Czech-Slovak order and to carry out the preparatory work of setting up permanent Czech state organs. Another provision of the law safeguarded Slovaks against being outvoted when the eventual constitutional law on federation was adopted, requiring that the law be approved by three-fifths of all deputies from the Czech regions and three-fifths of all from Slovakia, voting separately.[102]

At the beginning of July the Czech National Council was formed, consisting of all Czech National Assembly deputies, plus certain outstanding persons nominated by the National Front and elected by the assembly. Its first session, held in the building of the old Bohemian Diet in Prague at the end of July, in the midst of the Čierna crisis, was confined to appointing committees and hearing an address by its chairman, Čestmír Císař. The setting up of the council represented, he said, "a factual renewal of Czech statehood." The problem was to evoke "a Czech national consciousness," hitherto identified with "a Czechoslovak national consciousness." It was also necessary to work out "a policy for the Czech nation," for instance, in the economic and cultural fields, without, however, resorting to "national separation (*uzavřenost*)" in either field. Císař was ready to accept the concept of the sovereignty of the two nations and their states, and the derivative character of federal competence, but offered few details on the shape of such a federation. Each of the two republics would have its own national council and government. It would

---

sphere would include "the determination of the general directions of economic development and of the basic conditions of a unified market and a uniform currency, and the determination of the basic relations in the distribution of the social product and the national income," as well as of the conceptions and conditions of foreign economic relations and "the equalization of the level of the two national economies."

[102] *Sb. z.*, 77/1968; for Knapp and discussion, *RP*, June 25; for criticism of the procedures of selecting the additional deputies, *Práce*, July 5; *RP*, July 9. The law provided for the possible addition of others to the Slovak National Council. The SNR was later expanded by the addition of 47 persons (*Pravda*, Aug. 17).

also be necessary to develop a Czech party, a Czech National Front, and Czech mass associations and creative unions.[103] The ČNR was in a peculiar and difficult position, far behind the SNR and the federal commissions in the study of the problems of federation. Under these circumstances, the main arena of discussion continued to be the federal commission of experts, where, by early July, according to Husák, the conflict of views among the experts had reached such proportions as to constitute "a crisis situation." In an important speech to the Bratislava party conference, Husák made the public aware of this conflict, stating that the differences extended to "the whole complex of state-right and party questions" regarding federation. He charged the Czechs with rejecting the essential principles of parity and a ban on majority-domination in the federal organs, and with insisting on the principle of "majority rule" ("one citizen, one vote"). This he described as "a very dangerous tendency concealed by a democratic cloak," which would have led to Czech domination of the federal organs and hence a new form of asymmetry.[104]

Husák's political intervention, no doubt motivated in part by intra-Slovak political considerations, provoked heated charges and counter-charges, thus creating an atmosphere of crisis. Two Czech members of the commission, Grospič and Jičínský, denied the accusations made against the Czechs, stating that they recognized the need to protect Slovaks against "majority rule" in "basic matters of national political significance, especially constitutional," and in certain other matters directly "affecting national political interests," e.g. the budget and plan. Otherwise, they contended, there was no need for special guarantees against outvoting. Criticizing Husák's behavior as chairman, Grospič and Jičínský stated that the Slovak experts had "stressed the national principle one-sidedly and practically absolutized it" and had shown "no will to compromise on any basic question."[105] This produced a counterresponse by two Slovak commission members, Hatala and Rebro, who complained that the Czech defense of the principle of majority decision-making in many areas would create "a centralized and unitary federation" and re-asserted the principle of equality, particularly with regard to the division of competence and the application of parity.[106]

These divergencies among the experts, as Husák had said, reflected deeper "political trends and currents" on both sides and could only be

---

[103] Apart from his major address (RP, Aug. 1), see Cisář, ibid., July 14; his interview, Rep., Aug. 14-21 (supp.). Cf. the interview with Jičínský and Kožušník, Rep., Aug. 7-14.

[104] See above, chap. x, n. 73.   [105] RP, July 10.

[106] Pravda and RP, July 13. See also Vašečka, NS, July 18 and MF, Aug. 3.

resolved by higher authorities, either the government federalization commission or the topmost party organs. Some Slovaks, including Husák, were fearful that the CPCz Presidium would accept the Czech view and felt that the Slovaks must stake out their own position by holding their extraordinary congress prior to the CPCz congress. The alternative idea of a plebiscite was regarded as unacceptable inasmuch as Czech opinion was not really prepared to vote on this issue, and a different outcome in Czech and Slovak areas might contribute to a breakup of the state.[107] A common meeting of the two CC presidia, Slovak and Czechoslovak, was announced on July 9 by the CPCz Presidium whose report indicated the dilemma faced by this body and partially confirmed the doubts entertained by Husák. There must be no "majority rule" over Slovaks "in questions of their interests," said the Presidium, but "the federal organs must be capable of directing economic and other state policies from the standpoint of all-state interests and the needs of both our nations."[108]

This sober statement, which warned against "the abuse of national feeling" and "absurd argumentation" and called for a consideration of "objective and technically justified alternatives and material" contributed to cooler counsels. Husák, while openly admitting the continuance of differences among the experts on many questions, expressed his belief that a solution was possible within the commission by "dialogue" and "cold reason," excluding "national passions."[109] Even the question of the deadline did not appear to be a serious bone of contention. Some insisted on October 28; others, including Knapp and Laco, thought that this date was "possible."[110] Even Husák spoke of a decision by the fall or by the end of the year at the latest.[111] In the commission of experts attention therefore shifted to continued discussion of the points at issue, with the aim of composing a report embodying both items of agreement and disagreement. The ultimate reconciliation of differences would be left to the government commission.

SUBSTANTIVE QUESTIONS AT ISSUE

The work of the commission of experts had not been easy. At the outset it had no less than five major proposals to consider.[112] There was general agreement that two of these were not acceptable: the South Moravian tripartite draft, which was turned down after careful examination

[107] Rebro, *Ľud*, July 9. [108] *RŠO*, p. 234.

[109] Husák, *RP*, July 17. See also Laco, ibid., July 13 and *Pravda*, July 12.

[110] *RP*, July 13. See Laco, *Ľud*, July 21; *NS*, Aug. 1.

[111] *KT*, July 18. In an interview Husák had spoken of a rough draft by June and a completed law by Oct. 28, but admitted the possibility that this might not be accomplished until the end of the year (*Rep.*, June 26-July 3).

[112] *RP* and *Pravda*, July 5 (M. Hübl).

and the hearing of Moravian representatives; and the proposal for a quadripartite federation, submitted by the Opava district national committee, which was not formally discussed. This left the commission with three basically contradictory projects before it, and as Laco noted, two conflicting economic conceptions.[113]

The starting point of discussions in the commission was a Slovak proposal elaborated by the SNR's expert committee which placed the emphasis on the sovereignty of the two national states, the original competence of the national organs, and the derived and enumerated powers of the federal organs. Economic integration was endorsed, but in such a way as not to exclude the right of the national organs to direct their own "national economies." This conception was considered by Czechs to be a kind of "dualism," closer to confederation than to federation proper. The Slovaks denied this, terming their proposal a "compromise" which avoided either a purely "formal" federation or an excessive loosening of the federal link.[114]

Two draft proposals were presented by the Czechs. One, the work of Grospič and Jičínský, was referred to as a "tight" or "narrow," or alternatively, "rigid" or "closed" federation. Although recognizing the statehood and even the sovereignty of the national states, this approach also emphasized the sovereignty of the state as a whole and advocated strong federal powers. Condemning the idea of placing the center of gravity in the national states, this draft accented "unity" and "balance" in the division of jurisdiction, and sought means to coordinate the policies of the national states. Parity was accepted as a method of preventing majority-domination, but only in certain limited spheres and solely in legislative bodies, not in executive agencies. Otherwise, the federal organs would be unable to function effectively, and the very existence of the state would be threatened by constant crises. This plan, in the eyes of the Slovaks, represented, under the guise of federalism, a new kind of "unitary state."[115]

Another Czech proposal, known as an "open" or "loose" federation, was advanced by Prof. Jiří Boguszak as a response to the certainty of Slovak rejection of a "tight" or "closed" federation. Its author rejected the latter himself as likely to produce grave crises, but also disapproved

[113] *Pravda*, July 12.
[114] The Slovak draft was not published. For detailed references, see Rebro, *NS*, July 18 and K. Laco, ibid., Aug. 1, 15. Quotation from Rebro. See also Plevza, *Č. státnost*, pp. 303-6.
[115] "Theses on the ideological-political principles and the basic constitutional principles of Czechoslovak federation," *Právník* 107, no. 9 (1968), 808-23. This draft was discussed on June 10 by the Academy of Sciences federalization commission and evaluated positively by most participants (ibid., 798). O. Průša rejected the idea of a divided sovereignty altogether and argued that the sovereignty of the new federal state was "original" (*RP*, Aug. 6-8).

of the Slovak concept. He suggested a "loose dualism," which, he thought, would avoid the threat to the functioning of the federation which a parity system would pose and the threat to national equality which a system based on the majority principle involved. Exclusive federal powers should be "relatively limited," confined to foreign affairs, defense, and certain economic areas. The national states would possess all residual powers, but there would be a system of coordination, through a federal committee, headed by a minister, which would help to work out "federal agreements," subject to approval by the national organs. If agreement proved impossible, the national organs would be free to proceed on their own to formulate policy. "Integration" therefore would depend on "the sovereign will" of the two nation states, and "disintegration," if it occurred, would be peaceful, nonviolent, and would not lead to the breakup of the state.[116]

Faced with these sharply opposed viewpoints within its ranks, the federal commission had been able to reach a remarkable level of agreement considering the shortness of the time at its disposal. The idea of federation itself was not in dispute, but only its form and shape. There was consensus that the federation should be based on the national principle and consist of two, not three or more, constituent parts. There was general acceptance of the sovereignty and statehood of the two federating entities, and at the same time, of the sovereignty and statehood of Czechoslovakia as a whole, although some difference existed as to the relative emphasis to be placed on these twin concepts. Both sides concurred that federation should be based on the principle of "self-determination," manifested in a union for the sake of common interests, but that the right of "secession," in a state with only two parts, was not feasible. There was acceptance of the principle of certain exclusively federal, certain exclusively national, and certain common spheres of jurisdiction, and even some consensus on the actual division of competence. There was unanimity on the need for a corresponding reorganization of the

[116] *Právník*, no. 10 (1968), pp. 917-26. This alternative plan had been requested by the commission of the Academy of Sciences, which discussed it on July 1. Most participants favored the Grospič-Jičínský plan as the optimal solution but were willing to accept the Boguszak proposal, or even a looser confederal system, if the Slovaks were not willing to accede to the former (ibid., no. 10, 1968, p. 916). Prof. Pavel Peška opposed the dualist system and advocated a "closed" federation (ibid., no. 11, 1968, pp. 953-57).

Boguszak had advanced three alternatives, of which the one described was regarded as optimal and was embodied in a draft statute (*Právník*, no. 12, 1968, pp. 1039-49). A second alternative would have assigned residual powers to the federal organs, with a system of curial voting to prevent outvoting, and the transfer of any of these powers to national organs in the event of subsequent disagreement. A third alternative would have divided the residual powers between federal and national organs and provided for federal agreements in certain matters and the transfer of authority to the national organs in cases of disagreement.

party, the National Front, and other bodies, although no clear indication of what form this might take.

The areas of disagreement were, however, still substantial and related to two main topics, which require separate discussion: (1) the exact form and composition of the federal institutions, especially the National Assembly, and their procedures, in particular the question of parity and majority rule; (2) the division of competence between the federal and national organs in certain contentious areas.[117]

PARITY AND A BAN ON OUTVOTING

"Parity" and the prevention of *majorizácia* had become primary Slovak objectives, even though both these terms were ambiguous and could be, and were, interpreted in different ways. One without the other was considered insufficient to protect Slovak interests and to ensure Slovak influence on policy-making at the center. Some Slovaks stressed parity in the sense of equal Czech and Slovak representation in *all* significant federal or common organs, including the assembly, the government, federal committees, and the courts. This, it was admitted, would protect Slovaks fully against outvoting only if Slovak representatives were unanimous on a given issue and voted as a bloc. Hence it should be combined with special measures which would require more than a simple parliamentary majority for the adoption of laws and decisions. Simple majority rule on the principle of "one man, one vote" was, in Slovak eyes, a veiled form of Czech domination, reproducing asymmetrism in a new form. "Among nations," wrote J. Brabec, "only one arithmetic is valid: one nation, one vote."[118]

For the Czechs, the general application of parity and anti-majorization, as demanded by the Slovaks, was undemocratic, giving the minority an equal position in the state and enabling them to block all federal legislation or executive measures. The Slovak proposals would render the federal organs immobile and thus create serious crises and deadlocks, from which escape would be difficult. The federal powers should be firm and strong, so that the federal legislature and government could carry through a uniform policy in the major areas of political and economic life.

Slovaks differed, however, as to the best way to achieve their goal.

---

[117] For a summary of Czech and Slovak differences, see Rebro, *NS*, July 18; Laco, ibid., Aug. 1, 15. For Slovak and Czech views, in addition to those cited below, see D. Hanes, ibid., July 25; J. Průša, *RP*, Aug. 6-8; Císař, *Rep.*, Aug. 14-21 (supp.).

[118] *NS*, July 11. V. Hatala (*Pravda*, July 30) drew an analogy with international relations where the majority principle could not be applied against a sovereign national state.

Regarding the assembly, there were several alternative schemes, including, for instance, a single chamber, with equality of Czech and Slovak representation and separate voting by Czech and Slovak national *curiae*, or a two-chamber body, composed of a Chamber of the People, in which representation would be proportional to the population, and a Chamber of Nations, in which there would be equal representation of Czechs and Slovaks. This would be supplemented by measures to block majority-domination, including the stipulation that legislation must be approved by *both* Czech and Slovak representatives, perhaps in a two-thirds or three-fifths proportion. Some Slovaks were content to apply these provisions to certain defined spheres, such as constitutional relations, including a confidence vote in the government, and matters of basic economic significance.[119] Others seemed to favor anti-majorization measures in all, or almost all, decisions by the federal legislature.[120] They denied that this would create perpetual crises or lead to the immobility of the federal organs but recognized that provisions would be necessary to overcome deadlocks.

Some Slovaks demanded parity not only in the legislature but also in the executive, at a minimum in the form of state secretaries (of another nationality than the minister) in all central "exclusive affairs" ministries. Others wished to apply parity to the government as a whole, either through state secretaries, as members of the government, in all ministries, or through a simple equality of representation in the cabinet.[121] Another possibility, in the case of some or all "common affairs" ministries, and of all federal committees, would be to form collegial bodies, with equality of representation, in place of monocratic organs.

Another imperative was to improve the representation of Slovaks in the administrative service generally, especially in important departments such as foreign affairs, national defense, and foreign trade. As Professor Hájek, the Foreign Minister, admitted, only 14 percent of the members of the foreign service were Slovaks; there were ten Slovaks among fifty-five ambassadors abroad.[122] In National Defense, 20 percent of all mili-

---

[119] Rebro, *NS*, July 18. F. Vašečka (*MF*, Aug. 3) referred to "state-right questions" or "economic matters relating to livelihood." According to Laco (*NS*, Aug. 15), the commission reached agreement on constitutional affairs, and "social relations," including middle-range planning, budget, and taxes.

[120] Hatala (*NS*, July 11) contended that majority rule should be permitted "only in the degree necessary for the orderly functioning of the federal organs." The Slovak proclamation of August 1 insisted that Slovak agreement would be required not only in the enactment of constitutional laws, but also in the political and economic spheres, in legislative and governmental practice, and "in general wherever the interests of the whole state were involved, both in domestic and foreign policy" (ibid., Aug. 1).

[121] Respectively, D. Nikodým, *PO*, no. 8 (1968), p. 690; M. Gašpar, ibid., pp. 704, 707.

[122] *Pravda*, April 12.

tary officers were Slovaks, and in the leading posts in the ministry, there were even smaller percentages.[123] In foreign trade, Slovaks held only 5 percent of the posts abroad, and between 2 and 3 percent at home.[124] This gross underrepresentation of Slovaks and the slowness of action in correcting the situation was sharply criticized. Slovaks were not satisfied with Hájek's promise to appoint Slovaks gradually as places became available and contended that more Slovaks should be appointed at once to certain higher diplomatic posts.[125] The situation in other Prague ministries dealing with domestic affairs was no more favorable.[126] Yet the appointment of Slovaks was hindered by lack of housing in Prague: "without housing there is no federation," said one critic.[127]

The Czechs were not happy with the idea of parity in view of the numerical disparity in the population of the two nations. Some were willing to accept it in a second house of the legislature.[128] Others, such as Grospič and Jičínský, preferred a single chamber with separate voting in certain matters, but not in the form of national *curiae* or through numerically equal representation. They were willing to accept measures against majority-domination in carefully specified and limited spheres, notably constitutional relations, but not in economic matters.[129] The proponents of "open federation" proposed safeguards in the form of a three-fifths majority for the adoption of a constitutional law, together with subsequent approval by the national organs. In the event of a deadlock, the Czechs advocated the resignation of the government, or the dissolution of the assembly, or, in the case of the "open scheme," the actual transfer of authority to national organs.[130] Most Czechs were quite unwilling to accept parity of representation in the central government as a whole, and agreed only to state secretaries of another nationality for each "exclusive affairs" minister. In "common affairs" and coordinating committees, the Slovaks would have "appropriate proportionate

[123] M. Holub, *NS*, Aug. 8.
[124] Gašpar, *PO*, no. 8 (1968), p. 702; *Pravda*, April 26, p. 11. There were only three Slovaks among 127 heads or deputy heads of trade missions abroad.
[125] See P. Pollák, *Smena*, March 24; Ján Čierny, *Pravda*, May 12; Čierny, *NS*, July 11; D. Ruppeldt, ibid., Aug. 1; M. Andráš, ibid., Aug. 8; also a letter from former officers of the Ministry of Foreign Affairs to the minister, ibid., Aug. 8 (p. 6); Holub, ibid., Aug. 8. General Dzúr was criticized for not treating the national criterion as "decisive" or "primary" in cadre policy (Holub, *NS*, Aug. 8).
[126] Pavlenda (*Ekonomické základy*, p. 27, n. 15) gives the following figures for Slovak representation: State Planning Commission, 1.5 percent; Ministry of Finance, 3.4; Fuel, 1.3; Foundry Industry, 4.5; Transport, 5.1; Internal Trade, 5.0; Agriculture, 9.8; Construction, 6; Health, 4.3; Education, 1.2; Justice, 0.
[127] Čierny, *Pravda*, May 12.   [128] Průša, *RP*, Aug. 8.
[129] Grospič and Jičínský, *Právník*, no. 9 (1968), pp. 814, 815, 817.
[130] According to Rebro (*NS*, July 18), the "closed federation" advocates accepted a safeguard against outvoting in the case of a confidence vote, the plan, and the budget, but, in the latter two cases, only by a suspensive veto, with a subsequent three-fifths majority required.

representation."[131] The proponents of an open federation did accept parity in the government, in the form of state secretaries in all ministries, with the president casting a deciding vote in the case of a tie. The Czechs also recognized the need for "appropriate" representation of Slovaks in the personnel of the federal departments.[132]

No precise understanding had been reached concerning certain other federal institutions, notably the courts and general procuracy. Suggestions of rotating the office of presidency between Czechs and Slovaks, or of having a vice-president of a nationality other than that of the president, had been made, but not agreed upon.[133] It was assumed that the courts and the procuracy would be dealt with later in a special statute. There was no consensus as to whether there should be a federal court or federal procuracy, in addition to national organs of this kind.[134] There was, however, a consensus on the necessity of a constitutional court, with parity composition, to assess the constitutionality of federal and national laws.[135]

THE DIVISION OF JURISDICTION

The other main area of disagreement concerned the distribution of powers, particularly in the economic field.[136] The Slovaks continued to envisage "exclusive" federal powers in the realm of foreign affairs and national defense, and certain "exclusive" national powers, but had come to accept the notion of an intermediate group of "common affairs," where authority would be shared between federal and national organs. Nonetheless they considered the national state the center of gravity and sought to protect and enlarge the authority of the national organs. They also wished to have the latter share in, as well as to limit, the exercise of federal powers. They thus sought the best of both worlds—complete control of their own national affairs, and a decisive role in the forming of all-state policies.

Even in exclusively federal affairs, according to some suggestions, the national organs should play some part, for example, in the making of

[131] Grospič and Jičínský, *Právník*, no. 9 (1968), pp. 814, 820. Průša saw no need for parity in the government, since that body was responsible to the assembly, where Slovak interests were fully protected (*RP*, Aug. 8).

[132] Grospič and Jičínský, *Právník*, no. 9 (1968), p. 811.

[133] The former was suggested by Gašpar, *PO*, no. 5 (1968), p. 428, and conceded as a possibility by Grospič and Jičínský, *Právník*, no. 9 (1968), p. 821.

[134] This was accepted by Peška, *Právník*, no. 11 (1968), p. 955; doubted by Laco, *Ľud*, July 21; and opposed by Gašpar, *PO*, no. 5 (1968), pp. 428-29.

[135] Laco, *NS*, Aug. 15; Nikodým, *PO*, no. 8 (1968), p. 692; Peška, *Právník*, no. 11 (1968), pp. 955-57; V. Grál, *Pravda*, June 13.

[136] See sources cited in n. 117. On economic issues, see also J. Marko, *Práca*, July 13; J. Ferianc, *Pravda*, July 25, 30, Aug. 8; H. Kočtúch, *NS*, Aug. 15.

diplomatic appointments, or in the administration of "the foreign relations of the national states."[137] Some legal specialists, including a distinguished international lawyer and former Czech diplomat, saw no obstacle in international law to a certain international "capacity" for the nation states in certain spheres, including the right to negotiate and conclude treaties.[138]

The category of "common affairs" was to include not only "currency matters" (originally treated as exclusive) but also finance, planning, foreign trade, the price office, ,tatistical affairs, etc.[139] In these matters, authority would be shared, either through collegial bodies, with parity representation, or through various procedures or institutions for consultation between federal and national organs for the purpose of coordinating policies. For instance, parity committees to make decisions in fields such as currency issue and pricing were suggested, so that federal policy could not be formulated without Slovak approval. It was urged by some that budgetary power should be primarily national, with the federal state deriving its funds from the national states, or having powers of taxation only to meet needs in the areas of its exclusive competence.[140] Other Slovaks believed that a high proportion of administration, even in "common affairs," should be carried out by the national organs.[141] The national states would have exclusive competence in certain fields, especially in cultural and social affairs; general uniformity of action could be attained through coordinating committees, or through ad hoc consultation and agreement on common policies.[142]

The Czechs favored a federation with firm central powers, unhindered by parity provisions likely to produce deadlocks. Grospič and Jičínský in-

[137] Nikodým, PO, no. 8 (1968), p. 691; Gašpar, ibid., pp. 703, 706; Andráš, NS, Aug. 8. Andráš suggested a "state secretariat" for foreign relations in the Czech and Slovak governments and an international relations department in the CPS Secretariat.

[138] V. Outrata, Právník, no. 12 (1968), pp. 1019-26. Cf. a similar argument by the Slovak, G. Mencer, ibid., pp. 1027-30.

[139] Rebro, NS, July 18. See also Gašpar, PO, no. 8 (1968), pp. 706-7, for a full listing of federal (presumably common) competence, including currency, federal budget, federal taxation, the price system, water and air transport, and administration of federal enterprises.

[140] Nikodým, PO, no. 8 (1968), pp. 690-91; Spišiak, ibid., pp. 712-15; Spišiak and Chorváth, NS, Aug. 1.

[141] Gašpar, PO, no. 8 (1968), p. 704. Two-thirds of common affairs would be so administered, he said. In an earlier article (ibid., no. 5, 1968, pp. 434-35), Gašpar wrote that the national organs would administer everything except national defense and foreign affairs. The federal administrative organs would perform only the function of integrating the national economies and coordinating economic development.

[142] Gašpar, PO, no. 8 (1968), p. 707; Spišiak, ibid., p. 715. Laco, however, expressed doubts concerning such committees fearing they would acquire too much power (Ľud, July 21; NS, Aug. 15).

sisted on a precise delineation of common affairs to ensure that the federal organs had the capacity to maintain the unity of the political system, including the defense of state security, a single economic system, a unified currency and credit policy, and the uniform social and legal position of the citizen.[143] Others argued the need for substantial federal competence in the interests of the "equalization" of Slovakia and for "guarantees" in connection with the transfer of resources from the Czech lands.[144] Grospič and Jičínský also suggested that certain laws be adopted embodying "federal principles," thus establishing a unified legal order, even in such subjects as culture and economics. They proposed a wide area of direct federal executive power and mechanisms of coordination in regard to national policies.[145]

The "open federation" scheme also envisaged substantial "exclusively federal" affairs, including not only foreign affairs and national defense, but also financial affairs, currency, administration of federal enterprises and in part, the judicial sphere. Other competence would be treated either as common, or as exclusively national affairs, with the possibility of the transfer of the former to exclusive national jurisdiction in the event of insuperable conflict. In the field of administration the center of gravity would rest with the national organs, which would act as executive agencies in most areas of common competence.[146]

It is not entirely clear to what extent, by mid-August, a meeting of the minds had been achieved on the sensitive issues of the division of competence. According to Kočtúch, substantial agreement had been reached on all disputed questions, in particular on the number of federal ministries. In addition to the two exclusively federal departments (foreign affairs and national defense) there were to be six common ministries—finance, labor and social welfare, foreign trade, transportation, communications, and prices; and three economic councils, one federal and two national. Ján Ferianc reported accord on a sharing of powers between federal and national organs in planning and taxation, and on federal committees, based on parity, for pricing, and for currency, credit, and exchange policy. Other observers gave differing estimates of the areas of agreement and disagreement.[147] It was evident that much re-

---

[143] Grospič and Jičínský, *Právník*, no. 9 (1968), pp. 815-16. According to Rebro (*NS*, July 18), even stronger exclusive powers were claimed under this plan. Cf. the federal powers urged by Pruša, including "basic economic relations," currency, finance and income, foreign policy and trade, and "legal and economic unity" (*RP*, Aug. 6).

[144] Kožušník (a member of the commission of experts), *Rep.*, Aug. 7-14.

[145] Grospič and Jičínský, *Právník*, no. 9 (1968), pp. 818-20.

[146] Boguszak, *Právník*, no. 10 (1968), pp. 921-22; also Rebro, *NS*, July 18.

[147] Kočtúch, *NS*, Aug. 15; Ferianc, *Pravda*, July 30, Aug. 8. Cf. the analysis of agreements and disagreements by Ján Marko (*Práca*, July 25, 30, Aug. 8). See also Laco, *NS*, Aug. 15.

mained to be done before a full agreement was reached on all aspects of the division of powers.

By the time of the occupation Czechs and Slovaks stood on the threshold of federation but much remained to be done before the final step across could be taken. In mid-August the Presidium declared its intention to submit directives on the federalization of party and state to the 14th Party Congress.[148] The materials prepared for the congress anticipated that the constitutional law, or at least its principal clauses, would be completed by October 28, and that elections to the new federal representative organs would be held in the spring of 1969.[149] Meanwhile the government commission, and later the government, endorsed the report of the commission of experts—a statement of principles which included points of disagreement as well as agreed recommendations—and empowered the latter to prepare a draft law for submission to the National Assembly for action by October 28.[150] On the very eve of the invasion the expert commission had completed a revised version of a report on its standpoint on federalization, and turned it over to the Prime Minister, Černík, and the Slovak First Secretary, Bil'ak.[151] It was recognized that these materials would have to be submitted to the Czech and Slovak National Councils and that these two bodies would have to prepare a common proposal of their own as the basis of eventual action by the National Assembly. The Czech National Council had just begun to grapple with the economic and constitutional aspects of federalism and had taken a stand only with regard to the Moravian question.[152] The Slovak party Presidium had already examined the draft statement of principles and referred it to the SNR presidium.[153] The final outcome would undoubtedly be influenced by the party congresses—in the first place by the Slovak, scheduled to meet in late August, and then by the 14th CPCz Congress, at which the Slovaks might well demand safeguards to prevent their being outvoted at this crucial session.[154]

[148] RP, Aug. 14.
[149] J. Pelikan, ed., Tanky proti sjezdu (Vienna, 1970), p. 220.
[150] RP, Aug. 15-16. This statement of principles had been discussed and approved by the government presidium and by a CC Presidium commission on July 26 and submitted in final form, on Aug. 7, to the governmental commission and to other state and party bodies, including the ČNR and SNR (ibid., Sept. 26).
[151] Plevza, Č. štátnost, p. 331.
[152] ČNR presidium, RP, Aug. 2 and 20; economic commission, ibid., Aug. 10; constitutional commission, ibid., Aug. 15, and Pravda, Aug. 15.
Jičínský, head of the constitutional commission, in referring to the Oct. 28 deadline, spoke of the possibility of a declaration and a special law on that day as an alternative to a full constitutional law. Husák, however, was still insisting on Oct. 28 (above, chap. XI, p. 327). A full meeting of the ČNR was scheduled for Aug. 29.
[153] Pravda, Aug. 10.
[154] Bil'ak, in an impromptu interview with Literární listy (July 25, p. 4), re-

The situation was much less certain in regard to the reorganization of the party. The Slovaks had made clear their desire for a federalization of the party structure, and some CPS leaders, including Bil'ak, had spoken in favor of parity in the topmost party organs. Husák, however, had not committed himself on this point and indeed had mentioned the need for "strong central organs."[155] Czech spokesmen had come to accept the idea of a separate Czech party but had rejected parity in the top CPCz organs. Officially the party had been committed to some form of reorganization since the May plenum but Dubček often laid stress on the unity of the party and its integrative function. The draft statute had not applied the principle of federalism or of parity to the party and had been criticized for this by some Slovaks. It had, however, provided safeguards against the outvoting of the Slovaks. Opinion within the ranks was not yet known, although an official party questionnaire distributed in August had provided a wide array of alternatives, including two independent parties linked with a common Central Committee, and two national-territorial organizations as part of a unified CPCz (the option embodied in the statute), and had set forth various safeguards for "equality" in the central organs, including parity of representation, and separate voting by Czech and Slovak members, with a majority of both required for decisions.[156] Much would obviously depend on the attitude adopted by the Slovak party congress and by the founding congress of the Czech party, also likely to be held before the general congress. In the likely event of a confrontation of the viewpoints of the two parties, the final decision would have to be made by the joint meeting of the two presidia which was still planned, and by the 14th congress.

The situation was complicated by the continuing divergence of attitude among the Czech and Slovak publics. Individual Czechs, such as the historian, J. Opat, came out strongly for federation.[157] Opposition to federalism was rarely expressed, as in the case of an article by A. Pludek, in the radical paper, *Student*, which was sharply condemned in *Rudé*

---

ferred to the need for such safeguards in the congress voting, suggesting the requirement of a two-thirds majority of Czechs and Slovaks on certain questions. According to an unpublished speech by Pavlenda in mid-July (available in mimeographed form), the Slovak Central Committee had approved the principle that a congress decision, touching basic questions of the development of both nations, would require a one-half or two-thirds majority of both Czech and Slovak delegates.

[155] For this and the following, see above, chap. IX, p. 242; X, pp. 280-83; XI, pp. 319-22. Note also the argument for "a single all-state party with a firm and naturally authoritative center," and the rejection of parity in the Central Committee, by O. Jaroš (*NS*, Aug. 8).

[156] *ŽS*, no. 16 (Aug. 1968), insert at p. 28. The results of this poll are not known.

[157] *LL*, July 18, republished in *KŽ*, July 26.

právo.[158] More common was the censure of "loose" federation and of parity.[159] The ordinary Czech, however, as was often deplored, exhibited a general lack of interest in federalism and a lack of understanding of its importance.[160] The Slovaks, on the other hand, had a kind of obsession with the overriding importance of federalism, as the proclamation issued during the crisis of Čierna indicated.[161] Pludek's article was published in full in a Slovak paper and sharply condemned. Even Opat's plea for federation was censured for placing the blame for Slovak problems on the bureaucratic centralist system and neglecting "inner Czech pressures."[162] More moderate Slovaks, however, while supporting federalization, continued to assign even higher priority to democratization.[163] Such clashes of opinion indicated the hurdles to be overcome in formulating a final federal scheme. The chances, however, were favorable that, even without the invasion, a federal order would have been achieved by October 28.[164]

[158] *Student*, Aug. 7; J. Smíšek, *RP*, Aug. 13.

[159] The dangers of parity were demonstrated, it was said, by the split within the Czechoslovak football league (*RP*, July 1, p. 4; J. Gronský, *LL*, July 18; ibid., July 25, p. 7).

[160] J. Janů, *LL*, July 18; J. Škaloud, *MF*, July 23; interviews with Czech writers, *KŽ*, Aug. 16.

[161] See above, chap. XI, pp. 322-23.

[162] *NS*, Aug. 15, p. 12; M. Gašparík, ibid., Aug. 8.

[163] P. Števček, *LL*, July 25 and *KŽ*, Aug. 2; Löbl, *KŽ*, Aug. 16; D. Rapant, ibid., Aug. 16.

[164] For post-occupation developments and the enactment and inauguration of the federal system, see Appendix C.

PART FIVE

CONTENDING POLITICAL
AND SOCIAL FORCES

CHAPTER XVI

Conflicting Tendencies in the Party

THE REMOVAL of Novotný, the climax of a bitter clash of social and political forces, marked the opening of an intense conflict between rival tendencies, which crystallized into more and more distinct groups, divided in their attitudes toward the issues of reform. Old groupings realigned, and new ones emerged, each seeking to maintain, or to achieve, positions of power and thus to influence the future course of events. During the eight months from January to August the balance of forces was in constant flux and had not reached a stable equilibrium by the end of August. The two extraordinary party congresses (CPCz and CPS) would have produced a new, but by no means final, crystallization of relative strength.

A careful analysis of these contending forces and an estimate of their comparative power will provide a fuller understanding of the reform movement and its aftermath and may offer answers to certain key questions. To what extent was the Communist Party and its leading organs and personalities the directing factor in the reform movement? To what degree and in what way was the party divided on the issues of reform, both at the topmost level in the Politburo and the Central Committee, and at lower levels, among functionaries and the rank and file? What was the comparative strength of these trends in the party? How far were noncommunists involved in the struggle for reform? How strong were they as persons, parties, or organizations? How significant were divergencies between Czechs and Slovaks? What was the attitude of the general public to specific issues of reform, and to the party, its program, and its leaders?

The attempt to deal with these questions is beset with difficulties, and no claim to conclusive judgments can be made. General elections, which might have served as a barometer of the public mind, were not held prior to the invasion. Moreover, although "politics" came increasingly into the open after January, much remained hidden and obscure. Some persons spoke in veiled or Aesopian language and others resorted to anonymous letters or leaflets circulated privately. Shafts of light on strong anti-reform opinions were occasionally cast by documents such as the Praga letter, the message of the People's Militia, or the anonymous letter to Goldstücker. Important statements, such as that of the preliminary social democratic organization, or the letter of the Libeň "old communists," were not published. Nor were two of Novotný's speeches, one while he

493

was still President, in a Prague factory in February, and another, his address before the CC plenum in May. Other materials, prepared by the party, were circulated through intra-party channels but were unknown to the general public. Significant events within the party, for example, the resolutions of the Prague party conference in May and in July, were also not reported publicly.

On the other hand, the abolition of censorship and the emerging freedom of the press permitted individuals, groups, and organizations to express their views with greater freedom and for public opinion to become a political force. The attempt to measure opinion through systematic polling offered a rich mine of information on the distribution of views within the population as a whole, between party members and non-party, and between Czechs and Slovaks.[1] Studies of party opinion, although not published, provided some insight into the rival currents within the CPCz.[2] In this and the following chapter, these data, supplemented by other published materials on trends within the party and on non-communist political movements, will be used as a basis for tentative conclusions and rough estimates of the probable constellation of forces at the forthcoming party congresses and afterwards.[3]

"Conservatives," "Progressives," and "Anti-socialists"

The post-January period was often described at the time as involving a struggle between "the old and the new," or between "conservative and progressive tendencies."[4] Charges and countercharges against "conservative" or "anti-socialist" forces soon emerged. These designations were not well-defined scholarly concepts, but weapons of political combat, and were used in conflicting senses and in shifting connotations. For instance,

---

[1] For detailed analysis of public opinion polls, see below, chap. XVII. For poll results, see Jaroslaw Piekalkiewicz, *Public Opinion Polling in Czechoslovakia, 1968-69* (New York, 1972).

[2] The results of the principal polls of party opinion are contained in the appendices to the CC report, *Zpráva o současné politické situaci Československé socialistické republiky . . .* (Prague, Oct. 1968); henceforth cited as *Zpráva*. See also above, chap. XI, n. 117. The report was submitted to the Presidium and may have been circulated in the highest party circles. Although the report itself, with some deletions, was published after the occupation, the appendices were not, at that time or later. The full report, with appendices, was available to the author. The report bears the marks of hurried preparation and is characterized by a relatively conservative interpretation. Moreover, as its chief author, Jan Kašpar, admitted, the facilities for information gathering at the disposal of his office were less than satisfactory. For further discussion of the defects in the party's information system, see Jan Kašpar, *Nová mysl*, no. 8 (1968), pp. 1004, 1008-9.

[3] See the informative analysis of social groups and political organizations in V. V. Kusin, *Political Grouping in the Czechoslovak Reform Movement* (London, 1972). This study does not examine groupings within the Communist Party.

[4] E.g. editorial, *NM*, no. 4 (1968), pp. 403-14.

a prominent reformer, František Šamalík, admitted that the "structure of conservative or progressive thinking" had not been precisely analyzed and that these terms were mere short expressions for those supporting respectively the "pre-January bureaucratic model" and "the model of democratic and humanistic socialism." The Slovak scholar, Miroslav Kusý, in a rare attempt at systematic classification of the conflicting tendencies of post-January politics, admitted that the groupings which he identified were not "defined political groups unified on a definite, clearly formulated political platform" but were merely "orientations to which certain people within and outside the Communist Party incline," based on their differing evaluations of the process of reform.[5] Moreover, as another commentator observed, differentiation often varied with the specific issue. To a large extent, too, he argued, "the boundary line between progressive and conservative runs through each of us" (as individuals).[6] It is also clear that the informal group affiliations were not static, but altered with changes in the general political atmosphere and in the priority of successive issues of controversy.[7]

A factor complicating the definition of opposing forces was nationalism. Slovaks, for example, were more or less united in seeking to attain the common goals of national equality and federation, and thus formed in a sense a single national group. Among Slovaks, however, just as among Czechs, conservative and progressive trends could be distinguished, although the conservative element tended to be somewhat stronger and extremely radical views were largely absent. Nationalism affected the political alignments in another way. Soviet opposition to Czechoslovak reform kindled a general Czechoslovak nationalism, common to both Czechs and Slovaks, which created a high degree of national unity in resistance to outside interference. The issue of national independence and reform became intertwined, thus reducing the sharpness of differences of view concerning reform. Contradictorily, however, this outside interference also produced a polarization of forces, at least at the extremes of the political spectrum. The more conservative elements were alarmed by the increasing antagonism toward the Soviet Union and became more fearful of the program of change itself and more amenable to Soviet pressures. The reformers, on the other hand, hardened in their defiance of bloc pressures and in their insistence on swift and radical change.

According to Kusý's analysis, the original division marked off "a narrow defensive camp of conservatives and a broad mass camp of progres-

---

[5] Šamalík, *Politika*, Sept. 19, 1968, p. 12; Kusý, *Život strany*, no. 16 (Aug. 1968), pp. 25-28, 55-56. This was a shorter version of an article published in *Teoria in Praksa* (Ljubljana), nos. 5, 6, 7 (1968), not available.
[6] L. Papež, *ŽS*, no. 17 (Aug. 1968), pp. 24-25.
[7] K. Kaplan, *Rudé právo*, April 13, 1968.

sives." The lines of demarcation, however, soon shifted with a change in the orientation of the conservatives and an increasing differentiation among the progressives. In the new constellation he identified a "conservative wing," representing the old order, but recognizing the need for some changes; the supporters of a "palace revolution," who favored changes of persons and of practice, but not of the system as such; the Slovak national wing, which gave the highest priority to federation; and the progressive-democratic wing, whose opinions were first expressed in the Action Program but who were soon differentiated into several groups. Kusý's categories, however, are not clear-cut or exhaustive, and his analysis illustrates the difficulty of a precise classification of the contending forces.

Yet there can be no doubt that, on the issue of the reform of the socialist system, there was a wide gamut of opinion, ranging from reactionary or conservative to progressive or radical, with many nuances in between and with substantial overlapping. Although terms such as "progressive" and "conservative," and still more, "anti-socialist," lack exact meanings, they became the common currency of the political marketplace and did represent, however tenuously, significant political realities.[8] Some preliminary examination of these designations, and the groupings or tendencies which they sought to identify, is therefore desirable before proceeding to an examination of the available empirical data.

The "conservative forces," it may be assumed, included all those who, by reason of vested interests in positions held or as a result of the persistence of traditional ways of thinking and habits of action, were opposed to serious changes in the established system. Jiří Sláma, for instance, identified "a narrow elite which is conservative in consciousness and in program, both as a result of interests and of ideological stance."[9] This designation, however, did not distinguish between extreme conservatives or reactionaries, who were opposed to any change in the previous system, and more moderate conservatives who conceded the need for some reforms but wished to avoid basic alterations.[10] In Šamalík's

---

[8] See A. Ostrý, *Československý problém* (Cologne, 1972), pp. 91-95 for a discussion of the ambiguity of terms such as "conservative," "progressive," and "anti-socialist." In his own classification he uses the term "Marxist left" to refer to the "socialist and communist-oriented democrats" who were the dynamic force of reform. On the inexactitude of terms and the differences among "reform communists," see I. Bystřina, "Essays, Pamphlets, Concepts and Facts," *Svědectví* 12, no. 47 (1974), 451-53.

[9] *RP*, May 15. Cf. somewhat similar analyses by O. Šik, ibid., March 15; V. Gerloch and J. Kozel, ibid., July 6; Kaplan, *Reportér*, April 3-10, 1968, p. III; and by Papež, cited above.

[10] E. Löbl differentiated between conservatives and "outright" or "real reactionaries," but did not define or identify either group (*Kultúrny život*, July 26; *Práca*, July 28). Černík, on one occasion, strongly criticized conservatives who, he said,

view, this created an "optical illusion" that the only real conservatives were those, like the Jodas group, who expressed outright opposition to reform. Yet in fact there were also "conservatives" who, while ostensibly supporting the Dubček program, increasingly expressed fears and doubts as to a resulting threat to socialism. Such exponents of cautious reform or "conservative reformers," as they may perhaps be called, rejected the appellation of conservatives (and deplored "name-calling" in general) but employed the term themselves against undefined opponents of reform. After the occupation, official doctrine, while repudiating the pro-Novotný forces as dogmatist or sectarian defenders of the pre-January status quo, claimed that the term "conservative" had been wrongly used against the genuine Marxist-Leninist left.[11]

The term "progressive" was also somewhat ambiguous and was used with various connotations. Although it referred at first to all who supported the removal of Novotný, it became less precise as a differentiation took place between moderate reformers, who approved the Dubček program but urged relatively slow and deliberate advance, and more vigorous reformers who sought to accelerate the pace of change. There were others still more radical who pressed more impatiently for drastic change and sometimes charged that Dubček and other moderate reformers were not sufficiently progressive. The distinction between moderate, vigorous, and radical reformers is difficult to draw, but is useful in classifying "progressives" according to the intensity of their orientation toward change. Post-occupation analysis labeled all these so-called progressive elements "rightist opportunist" or "right revisionist," without distinction as to their precise attitude to reform, or even as to whether they were party members or not. Dubček and the moderate reformers were sometimes in retrospect called "centrists," as they occupied a position somewhere between the conservative "left" and the reform-oriented "right."[12] This was, however, an ambiguous term, freighted with unfavorable historical connotations, and was seldom used during 1968.

The term "anti-socialist" was even more imprecise and equivocal in its usage. Both conservatives and progressives were "socialist" in the

---

recognized the democratization process in words but in fact sought a return to the pre-January system (*RP*, June 7).

[11] For example, *Lessons Drawn From the Crisis Development in the Party and Society After the 13th Congress of the Communist Party of Czechoslovakia*, approved by the CC, Dec. 1970. Cf. O. Švestka, *RP*, May 16, June 23, 1968.

[12] For the term "centrists," see M. Kusý, *Politika*, March 27, 1969; I. Bystřina, in V. V. Kusin, ed., *The Czechoslovak Reform Movement 1968* (London, 1973), p. 156. See also Rémi Gueyt, *La mutation tchécoslovaque* (Paris, 1969), pp. 189-90. Cf. above, chap. IX, n. 102. Ostrý praises the role of the "centrists" in mediating between the extremes and thus making possible "progressive advance" but charges them with error when they tried to reconcile the irreconcilable, i.e. the conservatives and the "left" (*Československý problém*, p. 95).

sense of wishing to preserve the socialist system and not advocating a return to capitalism. Properly speaking, the term "anti-socialist" could be used to designate those who were opposed to the socialist system as established after 1948 and wished to restore the pre-February system, or even pre-war capitalist democracy. Thus the May 1968 plenum resolution expounded on the dangers threatening from "rightist anti-communist forces," referring to those whose property had been expropriated after 1948 and to their political exponents.[13] Such views were rarely expressed openly and were mainly contained in anonymous letters and pamphlets. There were others, however, who, while continuing their belief in socialism, were highly critical of the post-1948 system as not properly socialist and as not democratic. These, too, were condemned as "anti-socialist" by the conservatives, who singled out as targets of special attack individuals such as Ivan Sviták, groups such as KAN and K 231, and newspapers such as *Student*. Gradually, the term was used even more arbitrarily, not only by conservatives but by moderate reformers as well, as a blanket form of condemnation applied to more radical advocates of reform, whether communist or non-communist, and to the mass media as a whole. Even Dubček and vigorous reformers such as Šik and Smrkovský, sometimes warned, in a confusing manner, of "anti-socialist forces," thus drawing upon themselves disapprobation in the mass media.[14]

PARTY DIVISION: RANK AND FILE

Earlier chapters have shown that the CPCz was the main initiator of the reform movement and the channel through which it evolved during the subsequent eight months. Throughout this period the Communist Party remained the primary organized political force, exercising control over all the institutions of government and most of the mass associations. Its members, who constituted the majority of all elite groups, such as scholars and scientists, creative artists and journalists, manned the official agencies, the major organizations, and the mass media. The meetings of the Presidium and the Central Committee were the principal agencies by which the meaning of reform was officially elaborated. The extraordinary congress in September would have set the stage for further decisive developments.

Yet the word "party" was not precise in connotation, embracing as it did individuals and organs vastly different in function and in power, each playing a diverse part in the reform process. Moreover, the CPCz was

[13] *Rok šedesátý osmý* (Prague, 1969), p. 205.
[14] Smrkovský, Šik, and Dubček, *RP*, May 19, 22, June 4, resp. For criticism, V. Blažek and A. J. Liehm, *Literární listy*, May 23.

profoundly divided in every sphere and at every level—at the topmost pinnacle and among the middle and lower cadres, intellectual circles, and the rank and file. It was indeed experiencing "a profound crisis" and was, as some argued, "a party of two parties," which would either have to purify itself at the 14th congress, or divide into two or more separate movements.[15] Having lost many of its pre-January sources of strength, the party lacked widespread popular support after January, although it gradually gained an increasing measure of public confidence by its espousal of reform, and later by its resistance to outside pressure. The outcome of the congress was uncertain, but would undoubtedly affect profoundly the ability of the party to achieve a new legitimacy and thereby to maintain its leading position by other means than in the past.[16]

The party's membership was huge—1,698,002 in 1966—over 17 percent of the adult population 18 years of age and over.[17] Its size changed but little during the course of 1968. The entry of new members throughout the entire year was officially given as 38,369, an influx a little lower than in 1967, and almost the same as in 1966. Of these, over 18,000 joined the party between January 1 and July 1, averaging, that is, some 3,000 per month. Assuming a similar rate of growth during July and August, the total accretion may be estimated at approximately 24,000 prior to the invasion. New members were classified as follows: in the Czech lands, 58.3 percent; in Slovakia, 26 percent; and in the armed forces, 15.7 percent. These additions were more or less balanced by the customary attrition due to death (8,955 to July 1) and by cancellation of membership or expulsions (6,956 to July 1). During the second half of the year, there was a further loss of 19,340 persons for the same reasons. The total membership, therefore, showed a slight decline between 1966 and the end of 1968, as follows:[18]

TABLE XVI.1

CPCz MEMBERSHIP

Jan. 1, 1966	1,698,002
Jan. 1, 1968	1,670,977
July 1, 1968	1,687,565
Jan. 1, 1969	1,671,637

[15] Dalimil (pseud.), *LL*, May 9; P. Kohout, ibid., May 16. See also I. Klíma on differences within the party (ibid., July 4).

[16] Liehm, *LL*, June 13; M. Šimečka, *KŽ*, July 5; I. Sviták, *LL*, July 18.

[17] *XIII. sjezd Komunistické strany Československa* (Prague, 1967), p. 939.

[18] The figure of 18,282 new members to July was given in *RP*, Aug. 2; also *ŽS*, no. 27 (Aug. 1968), pp. 14-15. Cf. the later figure of 18,882 (*RP*, Oct. 4), and still later, of 20,694 (*ŽS*, no. 18, April 29, 1969, supp.). According to the latter source, over 17,000 new members joined in the second half of 1968. The number of recruits during the month of August was given as 5,178, occurring mostly, how-

Slovak party membership (included in the above figure) experienced a slight growth, rising from 305,221 in 1966, to 307,568 in 1968 and 311,656 on January 1, 1969. The number joining the Slovak party during the first half of 1968 was 4,679—a somewhat higher rate of entry than in the Czech lands. Only 86.9 percent of the Slovak party's total membership was, however, Slovak in nationality; it included 8.5 percent Magyar, 2.3 Ukrainian, and 2.1 Czech.[19]

Considering the relatively small number of new members, it may be assumed that the general composition of the party in terms of age, nationality, etc. did not seriously change during 1968. Data concerning the new entries revealed certain features, however, that might have been of some significance for the future.[20] Seventy percent of the new members (in the first six months) were 30 years or younger, and 20 percent below 40, suggesting a certain rejuvenation of the ranks of a party that had been experiencing a marked process of aging. Recruits in 1968 had a noticeably higher educational level—61 percent with a middle school or higher education. University students, very poorly represented in the past (0.4 percent in 1966) made up 9.8 percent of new members in 1968; teachers and professors (only 3.8 in 1966) constituted 6.8 percent of the entrants. Working class representation gained slightly, if at all, since 34.6 percent of new members were workers but 70 percent of those leaving the party belonged to this category. Finally, there was a trend toward more equitable nationality proportions in the party: 28.6 percent of the new members were Slovaks, 67 percent Czechs, as compared with ratios in 1966 of 18.1 and 79.2 percent respectively. Of some significance perhaps was the change in the organizational affiliation of members, represented by a decline in the number of members in factory and collective farm organizations (approximately 30,000 between January 1, 1968 and January 1, 1969) and an increase in the number in street and village organizations (10,000). This relatively slight increase in the latter category did not substantially alter the strong concentration of members in organizations in their place of work—67.5 percent in factories, 5 percent in collective farm organizations, at the end of 1968.[21]

The rank and file were profoundly affected by the events of January, in which they had played little part, and by the dramatic sequel in subsequent months when they began to exert a certain influence on the course of events. The report on the political situation, prepared by the

---

ever, after the invasion (*RP*, Oct. 4). For total membership figures, *RP*, Aug. 2; *ŽS*, no. 18, April 29, 1969, supp.

[19] *ŽS*, no. 17 (Aug. 1968), p. 15; no. 18 (1969), supp.

[20] For the analysis of new members, *ŽS*, no. 18 (1969), supp. For 1966 figures, see above, chap. v, p. 155, also *XIII. sjezd KSČ* (1967), pp. 909-13.

[21] *ŽS*, no. 18 (1969), supp.; *XIII. sjezd KSČ* (1967), p. 938.

CC secretariat in the summer of 1968, testified that "a characteristic feature of our Communist Party is the fact that in its mass base all the conflicts of our society are both hidden and most sharply expressed."[22] The party was divided on basic problems, such as the economic situation, political reform, and the role of the party; there was widespread distrust in the previous structure and methods, leaders, and tactics of the CPCz. The forces linked with pre-January conditions were "smashed and completely discredited in the public mind and had no mass basis whatever," the report proclaimed, but other conservative forces, who had repudiated pre-January policies, were "retarding elements in the realization of the Action Program." On the other hand, there were "very extreme" elements, especially in urban conglomerations such as Prague and to some extent Brno, who entertained "romantic political opinions" and "certain political illusions." They did not want "to recognize the existence of the hard reality of the world, our economic possibilities and the actual political struggle," and saw "no boundaries to democracy and freedom of expression." Both these extremes were said to be present particularly in organizations in places of residence where the party ranks were most divided and least consolidated, and where political activity during 1968 was greatest, but affected also what the report called "the stabilizing core"—communists of the "most productive age" and enjoying "a high level of qualification"—concentrated for the most part in the industrial factories where the party was most consolidated and compact.

This somewhat conservative appraisal was not based on any statistical data derived from systematic polling of the opinion of the rank and file membership. The closest approximation to such a poll was one conducted by the CC Institute of Political Science among Rudé právo readers in mid-May. It was based on the voluntary responses of some 38,000 readers, 62 percent of whom were CPCz members.[23] According to the

[22] Zpráva, pp. 46-48, 31-32.
[23] The questionnaire was published in RP, May 13; the results, ibid., June 26-27, July 28. The poll results were described as "a correct picture of the division of opinions in the politically most informed and committed part of our society." It was observed that the results showed that the party was not "an ideologically unified 'alliance of like-minded people'" (RP, June 27). For other results of this poll, see chap. IX, n. 58. Cf. somewhat different results in May and August polls, Piekalkiewicz, Polling, pp. 102 ff., 135-36, 144. In a poll of 1,118 party members and functionaries in the Czech lands and Slovakia in mid-July, 89 percent (93 percent Czech, 82, Slovak) favored the exercise of the leading role of the party by persuasion. Greater differences between Czechs and Slovaks were revealed in regard to the party's "leading position in the state," with 37 percent (39 percent Czech, 63 Slovak) believing that this meant that its decisions should be binding on state, economic, and societal organization. When asked as to whether they perceived a danger in having non-communists in responsible positions, 77 percent (82 percent Czech, 70 Slovak) replied "no" (RP, Aug. 13). For other polls on related questions, see chap. XII, pp. 363-67; XVII, n. 44 and passim.

501

poll, the majority of party members—73 percent with higher education and 66 with lower—were favorable to the April plenum and the Action Program, but a substantial minority—18 percent with higher education, 21 with lower—were uncertain; and 9 and 13 percent, respectively, were unfavorable. (Non-communist readers were favorable, 69 and 67 percent, respectively.) Confidence in the party had grown among its members—31 percent with higher education, 33 with lower education; had *not* grown, 43 and 47 percent, respectively (among non-communist readers, confidence had grown, 36 and 41 percent; had *not* grown, 44 and 43 percent, respectively).

When asked whether the leading role of the party was a necessary condition of socialist democracy, 52 percent with higher education (66 percent, with lower) replied in the affirmative; 38 and 27 percent, respectively, in the negative; and 10 and 7 percent, respectively, were uncertain (non-communists, with higher and lower education, 82 and 70 percent, respectively, negative). When asked whether the leading role of the party was in fact being exercised so as to serve rather than rule over society, communists were sharply divided, some agreeing (36 and 48 percent, respectively) and others disagreeing (49 and 34 percent, respectively). (Non-communists, negative, 71 and 55 percent, respectively.)

When asked to list, in order of importance, the three most important guarantees of democracy (from a list of five), the democratization of the party was put in the first place by 45 percent of party members with higher education, by 66 percent with lower education (16 and 28 percent, respectively, among non-communist readers). The possibility of choosing between several independent parties, on the other hand, was put in third place by those with higher education (57 percent) and in fourth place by those with lower education (54 percent; 89 and 91 percent, respectively, among non-communists).

Finally, when asked whether the Czechoslovak way of constructing socialism was "our domestic affair," to be decided by the sovereign will of the people, party members overwhelmingly favored this proposition (93 percent with higher, and 90 percent with lower education); most expected this to be so (74 and 77 percent, respectively); and 44 and 57 percent, respectively considered this in fact to be the case. (Non-communists, 97 and 94 percent, respectively, favored it; 72 and 80 percent, expected it; 36 and 48 percent believed it to be the case.)

The *Rudé právo* poll revealed that a majority of the party respondents held moderately progressive views, sometimes not sharply distinguished from those of non-communists. The poll also indicated the wide disparity of party opinions, which sometimes resembled and sometimes differed strikingly from non-communist opinions. The sample, however, could hardly be regarded as representative and the results therefore cannot be taken as reflecting accurately the thinking of the party membership as a whole. The more systematic polls conducted by the Institute for Public Opinion Research often distinguished the opinions of party members and non-party persons in their questionnaires and their published results. These will be examined below (chap. XVII) in connection with a discussion of general trends in public opinion, where the similarities and differences of party and non-party opinion can most conveniently be presented comparatively.

PARTY OFFICIALS AND FUNCTIONARIES

The regeneration process after January had produced, in the words of the CC report on the political situation, "a profound crisis within the (party's) *aparát*, which felt itself to be in a vacuum of its own dysfunctionality and uselessness." The more conservative elements in the CPCz were usually to be found within their ranks (or in the state apparatus). The unusual conditions both within the party and in relationship to the world communist movement, problems of the party's guilt for past crimes, and the "moral decline" of its leaders had resulted in "a collapse of internal party unity, a loss of confidence within the party *aktiv* . . . , generational distrust . . . , and distrust of lower levels of the party masses in the leading elements in the party." It had also caused substantial differences of opinion between the "professional functionaries" and the "ordinary members of the party" in the evaluation of party policy and the political system (even deeper, it was said, than the differences between party members and non-party).[24]

The *aparátníci* (from the Soviet *apparatchiki*), in the original meaning of the term, were the fulltime professional employees of the party's *aparát* or administrative offices and were distinguished from the "functionaries," the party's elected officers. Many of the latter were or had been *aparát* members and were appointed rather than elected, so that over the years the original distinction was smudged or erased. In popular parlance, at least, the terms *aparátníci* and functionaries became almost interchangeable and assumed a somewhat pejorative meaning.

The *aparát*, in the narrow and proper sense, included paid employees in the administrative offices at the center (in the Central Committee), in the regions and districts, and in certain functional committees (all-factory, university, and railway). As of September 1, 1968, there were 4,733 "political workers" in these offices, of whom 16 percent were said to be employed within the regional committees and 72.5 percent in district and factory committees. Assuming that those in the other categories were relatively few (or were included in these percentages), we may con-

[24] *Zpráva*, pp. 45, 31, 54.

clude that the balance (11.5 percent)—or somewhat over 500 persons —worked in the CC *aparát* in Prague. Of the grand total the majority were from 36 to 45 years old, but the *aparát* was said to be aging. Thirty-six percent had a university education; 27.3 percent, a high school education; the balance—36.7—had only elementary education. In the CC *aparát*, however, 69 percent had a higher education, but in view of frequent transfers from one position to another, they were presumably not treated as specialists.[25]

This body of bureaucrats, recruited and trained under Novotný, had become, in Kusý's words, "all-powerful and indispensable," "a power elite," duplicating and directing the state organs and providing a pool of cadres for elected party functions and state posts.[26] Their power was great, not only in the districts and regions, where they constituted a ruling local elite, but also in the Central Committee, where they represented a substantial bloc of more than half of the CC's total membership. The *aparát*, accustomed to solving problems by "power means," often mediocre in ability, and ambitious for power, feared that their position would be threatened by democratization.[27] They were used to obeying the central CPCz authorities and transmitting directives to others, and were totally unprepared to work in the atmosphere of controversy and discussion of the Prague spring. They had a strong vested interest in the status quo, to which they owed their power, prestige, and relative affluence, and feared meaningful changes, especially in the economic sphere, which might make their positions useless and unnecessary. Many, or perhaps most, were workers in origin, but, long removed from factory work, they possessed no industrial skills and, if dismissed, faced a difficult employment problem.

It was not surprising, therefore, that party officials were widely regarded as a strong conservative force, constituting the chief opposition to reform, and were subjected to frequent attack.[28] More conservative leaders, such as Bil'ak, but also Dubček, complained of "wholesale" assaults on these officials, defended the record of the overwhelming majority of them, and asserted the need for maintaining an administrative apparatus to serve the party.[29] The 14th congress materials reiterated this

[25] *RP*, Feb. 8, 1969: *ŽS*, Feb. 12, 1969, pp. 1-4.

[26] Kusý, *NM*, no. 11 (1968), p. 1320.

[27] M. Kubeš, ibid., no. 3 (1969), p. 335. For a discussion of the *aparátníci* and functionaries and their opposition to reform, see Ostrý, *Československý problém*, pp. 68-71, 79-80.

[28] The *aparát* was sharply criticized in the Two Thousand Words statement and was the chief target of many of Sviták's speeches and articles, e.g. *LL*, April 18, also *Práce*, May 19, and *Student*, May 22. A group of technical intelligentsia responded to Sviták by defending the *aparát*, although recognizing the need to reform it and subordinate it to the party's elected organs (*LL*, April 18).

[29] See above, chap. IX, p. 241; XII, p. 351.

need, and while admitting that there were deep cleavages among the functionaries, contended that the majority favored reform. The party should support "the qualified and honest administrative and economic officials of the party apparatus, the national committees and societal organizations, and employees in justice, security, and the army," while removing, by democratic and legal procedures, those guilty in the past, and others, in humane fashion, and with guarantees of their social security.[30]

The corps of party officials was by no means a homogeneous social group, either in function, age, or education; they also differed in their attitudes according to region and nationality. Those working in the repressive sections of the CC (police, army, etc.), and in the ideological and organizational departments, were, it may be assumed, more conservative; those in the economic sections, particularly if concerned with light industry, were more reform-oriented. The younger members (especially the generation in their forties who had joined the party during the war or post-war years up to 1948) were more likely to be progressive. This would presumably also be true of those who had received a higher education, especially those from the regional organizations and the CC apparatus who had studied at the Higher Party School under "liberal" instructors such as Hübl, Kouba, and Jičínský (all dismissed in 1964). Moreover, there was no watertight separation of intellectuals inside and outside the apparatus, as party officials were often in close contact with other intellectuals (a few of whom worked for short terms in the *aparát*) and were influenced by their books and articles, for instance, those by scholars of the Institute of Party History. Party committees in individual institutions of higher education (including the university committees), in party institutes, and in some Academy of Sciences institutes, were usually more reform-oriented.

There were also great contrasts between various regions of the country, with city committees, their *aparáts*, and their associated *aktivs*, in Prague, Brno, and Bratislava regarded as more markedly progressive, and the more rural and some industrial regions as more conservative. Ostrava, a center of heavy industry was, however, considered progressive. The Prague committee, initially a stronghold for Novotný, emerged in 1968, under the leadership of B. Šimon, as a focal point of reform and came under fire, after the occupation, as a "second center" which was seeking to rival the Central Committee. Certain borough committees, in particular Prague 1 (where many research institutes were located), but also industrial districts such as Prague 9, exerted a powerful influence for reform on the Prague party organization as a whole. In Brno, under the leadership of Josef Špaček and his successor, Josef Černý, the regional party organization was a proponent of change. Slovak organiza-

[30] Jiří Pelikán, ed., *Tanky proti sjezdu* (Vienna, 1970), pp. 195, 213.

tions tended to be more conservative but some, especially in Bratislava, were reform-oriented.[31]

Polls of *aparát* opinion were rare and partial in scope. For example, a poll of leading regional and district secretaries in northern Bohemia in May 1968 revealed moderately progressive views on issues of reform. They were almost unanimous in believing that the party's leading role was a necessary feature of socialist democracy (97 percent). They were overwhelmingly of the opinion that the party could fulfill its leading role, not by ruling, but by serving society (92 percent); a lesser proportion (73 percent) believed that this corresponded to existing reality. A large proportion (85 percent) agreed that the political system should make possible the free and democratic expression of the wants and desires of different groups, but fewer (71) thought that this was in fact the case. When asked whether the Czechoslovak way of constructing socialism was "our internal affair," 90 percent agreed that it should be so but only 78 percent thought that this corresponded to current reality. The same group, however, exhibited a conservative viewpoint with regard to the mass media: 82 percent agreeing with the criticism of them, and only 16 percent disagreeing.[32] In the absence of more comprehensive polling, however, estimates of the balance of conservative and progressive trends within the *aparát* can only be impressionistic, such as those given above, or those derived from somewhat arbitrary identifications based on votes and elections at district and regional conferences.[33]

[31] The above impressions are based on conversations in Prague in 1968 and 1969; papers and discussions at the Reading conference in 1971, especially those by Z. Hejzlar and A. H. Brown, in Kusin, ed., *Czechoslovak Reform*, pp. 109-47; comments by O. Šik at a conference in Windsor, England, in the summer of 1971; and evaluations in *Zpráva*, pp. 51, 84. Note Hübl's comment on the influence of the Higher Party School, *Mladá fronta*, Nov. 13, 1968. For attacks on the "second center," see A. Svárovská and J. Rous, *Tribuna*, Oct. 1, 8; J. Smrčina, *RP*, Sept. 16, 1969; K. Beránek, *Tvorba*, Dec. 3, 10, 17, 1969; for attacks on the "rightist" groups in Prague, Bratislava, Brno, etc., *RP*, Feb. 2, 1971.

[32] For the above, see Piekalkiewicz, *Polling*, pp. 135, 144; 79; 40, 85; 45; *Rep.*, April 10, 1969, p. xv, resp. The number of secretaries polled was 139. Piekalkiewicz in one place wrongly refers to this as a poll of leading secretaries in CC and district committees, instead of regional and district secretaries.

A poll of the highest functionaries (party and state, and directors of large enterprises), conducted in a single district in Bohemia in April 1968, revealed orthodox views that socialism was superior to capitalism (92 percent) and that socialist democracy as it existed in Czechoslovakia was democracy of the highest type (78.4 percent). Paradoxically, 42 percent considered that the leading role of the party had not been weakened after January, compared with 23 percent who thought that it had been. The rest believed that the leading role had been temporarily weakened but that the party was gaining authority once more (F. Zich, *Rep.*, Nov. 6-13, 1968, pp. 24-25).

[33] Barbara Jancar's attempt to classify regional functionaries illustrates the difficulties of this approach and can hardly be regarded as conclusive (*Czechoslovakia and the Absolute Monopoly of Power*, New York, 1971, pp. 119 ff.).

A broader segment of the party's officialdom included members who, while continuing in their own occupation, served the party, often for many years, in various capacities, including membership in district, regional, and municipal committees. No data were available as to the total number of these "functionaries," and no social and political profile can therefore be constructed. An excellent sample, however, of the entire corps of party officers was provided by the 57,000 delegates elected by their basic organizations to the extraordinary district conferences in late June; they represented 4 percent of the total party membership, and included, no doubt, most of the full-time officials and many of the part-time activists. A poll of these delegates was conducted by the CC apparatus on June 29-30, i.e. just after the Two Thousand Words statement and its official condemnation, and well after the May plenum. The responses of 40,000 (30,517 from Czech, and 9,423 from Slovak districts) which were received and accepted as valid, were tabulated and analyzed in the CC report on the political situation. The sample was said to correspond, in terms of social origin and length of membership, to the delegates as a whole and to the full party membership, although it was somewhat more representative of those of higher age and less education than these two latter groups. The questions and the results were unfortunately somewhat ambiguous, so that it is not easy to classify the delegates according to progressive or conservative criteria. The data did, however, reveal substantial differences of opinion, and on certain issues, a sharp polarization of viewpoint.[34]

The delegates greeted positively, by an overwhelming majority—88.8 percent (77.1 fully, 11.7 partially)—the plenum's decision to call the 14th congress. Only 1.6 percent disagreed, and 9.6 percent gave no answer. The delegates, however, showed dissatisfaction with other features of the May plenum. When asked to give their views of the plenum's evaluation of the political situation, and of the proclamation to the party and people, the responses could hardly offer clear-cut evidence of opinion, since these plenum documents, although tending in a somewhat conservative direction, were themselves ambiguous and contradictory. Disagreement, and substantial uncertainty, were, however, manifested in the fact that the two documents were fully approved by only 25.9 and 32.3 per-

[34] Some data were revealed by J. Kašpar at a press conference (*RP* and *Pravda*, Aug. 15), but in garbled form, with the results of the poll of 14th congress delegates sometimes mixed with those of the poll of district delegates. The full results, in tabulated form, were given in the appendices of the CC report, *Zpráva*, pp. 71-81, 95-98. Since this report is not available in the West, the full results are given below, Appendix B. The report's accompanying analysis was sketchy and incomplete, and contained inaccuracies and arbitrary interpretations. E.g. the delegates were asked, in a series of questions, whether the May plenum had "fulfilled their expectations," but the results were interpreted as indicating whether the delegates "agreed" or "were satisfied with" the plenum.

507

cent, respectively; and partially approved by 55.7 and 30.9 percent. Even wider differences and greater dissatisfaction were revealed in the responses concerning the solution of cadre problems at the plenum.

TABLE XVI.2

(in percentages)

	Fully	Partly	Did not Fulfill	No Reply
The cadre decision fulfilled your expectations	9.8	40.2	26.3	23.7

This was interpreted by the report, probably correctly, as indicating that the delegates were not fully satisfied with the current composition of the CC plenum, the Presidium, and the Secretariat, or with CC actions in this respect. Although the results seem in general to point to a somewhat progressive attitude among delegates, it is difficult to draw hard and fast conclusions, since the data provided no indication as to why the respondents found this and other plenum decisions satisfactory or unsatisfactory, or as to what distinguished full and partial satisfaction.

When the delegates were asked to evaluate the situation in the party, their reactions were on the whole more positive. A majority of delegates considered that the party's authority had been influenced positively by the plenum (62 percent, yes; 10.5 percent, no); that the party had sufficient resources to achieve the goals set (77 percent, yes; 2.4 percent, no); and that the functionary *aktiv* had reoriented itself to the new conditions of the party's leading role (60 percent, yes; 7.1 percent, no). On each question a substantial number of affirmative responses were qualified ("rather yes" as compared with "decidedly yes") and a number did not know, or did not care to reply at all. The replies were even more confusing as to the relative dangers of "forces hostile to the party and socialism" and of "conservative forces." Anti-socialist and anti-party forces were regarded as a danger by 56.3, and *not* as a danger by 22.9 percent; conservative forces were viewed as a danger by 57.9, and *not* as a danger by 21.1 percent. In other words, on these two important matters, the party was utterly divided; with more than half believing that either one or the other danger *did* exist, and one-fifth, in each case, believing that the danger did *not* exist. Since the aggregate of replies to all these questions varied from 78 to 88 percent of the total responses included in the analysis, a substantial proportion of delegates were evidently not ready to give an opinion on these crucial issues.

The delegates were also asked four questions on "methods of party work," which, although worded ambiguously, yielded somewhat interesting data on attitudes toward reform in these circles of the party. When asked to comment on whether it was "dangerous for the party to yield its position of power," 31.3 percent perceived a danger; 36.9 percent saw none. Asked to state whether the party was "evacuating its positions when it made it possible for other parties and organizations to share in decision-making," 59 percent responded in the negative (i.e. they viewed such action favorably), and 24 percent in the affirmative. When asked whether the party *should* give up direct management of state and economic organs, 61 percent answered affirmatively; 21.5 percent, negatively. When asked whether the party was doing enough in this direction, 43 percent said yes; 32 percent, no, suggesting a relative satisfaction with the moderate changes already accomplished. Once again, the responses to these questions were often qualified, and a substantial number of delegates did not reply at all. The results of the poll indicated that the party's lower functionaries were greatly divided on important issues, although their attitudes were not precisely revealed. A majority, relatively small, and manifesting considerable uncertainty, favored moderate political and econonic reforms, but a substantial minority was strongly opposed.

14TH CONGRESS DELEGATES

The delegates elected to the 14th congress were bound to have a profound impact on the outcome of that meeting and on the eventual composition of the party's leading organs. Proposed by the basic organizations and district conferences, and with some few changes, endorsed by the regional conferences, they had been selected with less interference by party secretaries than in the past and had already become an important political factor. The number of delegates was given officially as 1,543, of whom 1,251 (81 percent) were from the Czech lands, and 292 (18.9 percent) were from Slovakia. By nationality, they included 1,215 Czechs (78.6 percent); 300 Slovaks (19.4 percent); and 28 others (1.9 percent)—14 Magyars, 7 Ukrainians, and 7 Poles.[35]

Official data concerning the delegates yielded interesting results, especially in comparison with those attending the 13th congress in 1966. In nationality, the composition was somewhat more favorable to the Slovaks (265 Slovaks—17.1 percent; 1,192 Czechs—82.6 percent; and 33

---

[35] For the data, see *RP*, Aug. 14; *ŽS*, no. 17 (Aug. 1968), p. 13. These were final corrected figures, differing from those given earlier, *RP*, Aug. 3, and *ŽS*, no. 16 (Aug. 1968), p. 14. Cf. an initial figure of 1,539 in Presidium report of July 25 (*RŠO*, p. 260). The August 14 data were reproduced in *Zpráva* (pp. 92-94) and were used in calculating the proportions cited. *Zpráva* also gave slightly different figures of its own—1,585 delegates originally nominated, and 1,529 finally approved by the regional conferences (p. 82; also p. 50). For 1966, see *XIII. sjezd Komunistické strany Československa* (Prague, 1966), pp. 129-32.

others, in 1966). The delegates were relatively old, with not a single person 25 years of age or younger; only 2.3 percent up to 30, and with more than half (61 percent) over 40 years. On balance, however, they were somewhat younger than the 1966 delegates.

TABLE XVI.3

DELEGATES TO PARTY CONGRESS

Years of Age	Number 1968	Percentage 1968	Percentage 1966
18 to 25	—	0	
26 to 30	36	2.3	2.8 (18 to 30 years)
31 to 40	556	36.7	28.3
41 to 50	778	50.4	51.4
51 to 60	135	8.8	15.3
above 60	28	1.8	2.2
	1,533	100.0	100.0

As to length of membership in the CPCz, not many of the old guard, who had joined during the war or pre-war years, were included (pre-war: 4.4 percent in 1968; 6.9 percent in 1966). There was, however, a shift away from those who had become members in the early post-war democratic years (58 percent in 1968; 72.1 percent in 1966); and an increase in the post-1948 contingent (in 1968, 37.6 percent had joined between 1949 and 1966; in 1966, 21 percent between 1949 and 1965). Post-1958 members formed only 11.5 percent of the 1968 delegates. The congress was therefore to be a gathering of relatively seasoned party veterans, with few newcomers from the sixties. The educational level in 1968 was significantly higher than in 1966, with 45.2 percent having had university education (32.5 percent in 1966); 34 percent, a middle school education, complete or partial (31.4 percent in 1966); and 20.5 percent with only elementary education (26.3 percent in 1966). In terms of original employment, the 1968 congress delegates were somewhat less "proletarian" (60.3 percent, compared with 68.5 percent in 1966). But in terms of current employment, the 1968 delegates were drawn much less from the working class (17.4 percent, compared with 28.6 percent in 1966); less also from political workers, i.e. in party, state, and societal organizations (21.1 percent, compared with 31.2 percent in 1966); and with a substantial contingent from the engineering and technical intelligentsia (17.2 percent), from other intelligentsia (14.4 percent), and from administrative workers in the economy (11.9 percent).[36] It is of

[36] In addition to the 21.1 percent "political workers," data included 1.6 percent workers in central offices, and 4 percent, other officials. Comparison with 1966

interest that the representation of workers, according to the CC report, had been significantly higher (23.4 percent) prior to the final selection by the regional conferences; that of political workers had been much less (11.7 percent).

The CC report warned that the majority of the delegates were "new people" and that the composition of the congress would be so different from any preceding one that it was impossible to foresee what course it would take. The "polarity of opinions" between radicalism and conservatism assured, according to the report, that there would be "stormy discussion and conflict of views." The "very radical, frequently even extreme opinions" of some 10 percent of the delegates, who were likely to be "forceful (*průbojný*) and . . . erudite in pressing their opinions," and the "significantly reserved attitude toward the policy of the past half-year" on the part of another 10 percent, made it likely, the report concluded, that the "disputatiousness of these currents" would dominate the congress discussions and perhaps drown out the 80 percent of delegates with "matter-of-fact (*věcný*), progressive but at the same time realistic attitudes."[37]

The responses of the delegates, presumably during July, to the same questions posed to the district conference delegates, bore out the wide diversity of opinion, although not in the proportions referred to above in the report's analysis, and also revealed significant differences between delegates to the congress and to the district conferences.[38] Most congress delegates appeared to be more satisfied with the results of the May plenum: 87.3 percent endorsed the decision to call the congress; 92.1 percent, the plenum's evaluation of the political situation; and 87.5 percent, the CC's proclamation. The congress delegates evaluated the situation in the party more positively than the district conference delegates: 81 percent seeing the party's authority as strengthened; 87 percent judging favorably the party's capacity to fulfill its tasks; and 72 percent affirming the adaptability of the functionaries. One-third of the congress delegates were displeased with the May plenum's decisions on cadres, compared with one-quarter of the delegates to the district conferences. The dissatisfaction was more pronounced among Czechs (38.1 percent)

---

data is difficult since the 1966 figure of 31.2 percent referred to "party and public functionaries," and no data are given for technical intelligentsia. Other categories in 1968 were foremen (3.7 percent); tractor-drivers and machinists (0.5 percent); members of the armed forces (6.0 percent); pensioners (1.6 percent) and others (0.6 percent).

[37] *Zpráva*, pp. 50, 83-84.

[38] For the following, *Zpráva*, pp. 82-86 (analysis), 88-91 (tables), 97-101 (some correlations with the poll of district delegates). The report noted certain distinctions as between regions, but did not document these systematically. See below, Appendix B, for full results.

than Slovaks (23.3 percent); among the university-educated (40.2 percent); among those between 40 and 50 years of age (44.0 percent), and those below 40 (41.7 percent); and among the engineering and technical intelligentsia (37.4 percent). It was much less so among industrial workers (21.7 percent) and political workers (10.5 percent). The majority of delegates (61.7 percent) were fully or partly satisfied (14.2 and 47.5 percent, respectively) with the cadre decisions, however.

Perhaps the greatest diversity appeared in the evaluation of antisocialist and conservative forces, with a much higher proportion of congress delegates recognizing the existence of each of the two dangers: 63.8 percent regarded anti-socialist forces, and 65.8 percent regarded conservative forces, as a peril. Almost 28 percent of the congress delegates saw no anti-socialist danger; about 23 percent saw no conservative danger. More congress delegates (39.8 percent) than district conference delegates feared the results of the party "abandoning its position of power" as well as the sharing of decision-making with other parties (27 percent); but more took the opposite view, namely, that there was no threat from these developments: almost 50 and over 66 percent, respectively. The delegates exhibited a similar division of opinion and a more "progressive" attitude in regard to giving up direct party control of state and economic organs, with 74 percent favoring this withdrawal, and almost 20 percent opposing it. On the other hand, 53 percent expressed satisfaction, and 33 percent dissatisfaction, with the degree to which control had already been given up.

Pregnant with significance for the forthcoming congress was the priority given to its various tasks, although the ranking was not without ambiguity. The delegates placed CC cadre problems in first place and the economic situation in second, followed by constitutional arrangements (federalism), intra-party problems, and the political situation in the country and party tactics. (The district conference delegates had placed party tactics in second place ahead of the economic situation.) Of interest was the revelation that the delegates from both the Czech lands and Slovakia ranked federalization in third place (although Slovak district delegates had rated it third in priority, and the Czechs, fifth).

The results of the poll of congress delegates are not clear-cut and generalizations are difficult. On issues of reform, the delegates were strongly in favor of abandoning party control of state and economic organs, and also in favor, less strongly, of sharing power with other parties. This "progressive" attitude was coupled with an indication of its relative moderacy in the expression of a high degree of satisfaction with what had been accomplished, with the results of the May plenum, and with the rise in the party's authority and its capacity for leadership—a satisfaction which was somewhat more pronounced among congress delegates than

512

among district conference delegates. However, in all cases, there was a substantial minority holding different opinions: as many as 20 percent opposed to the abandonment of party control; as high as 27 to 40 percent opposed to sharing power with other parties. On the question of the dangers from the right or the left, confusion reigned, no less than among district conference delegates, but there were widespread fears of both "conservative" and "anti-socialist" dangers.

THE CENTRAL COMMITTEE

The composition of the Central Committee, essentially unchanged since Novotný's day, became a matter of acute controversy, not only within the party, but also among the general public. More than one-third of the total membership, it was asserted, no longer held the high offices which had justified their inclusion in the top party organ, and still others had forfeited public confidence by their past misdeeds or by their negative attitude to reform. The Slovak youth paper, *Smena*, listed by name thirty-eight members who had been removed or resigned from office and who should relinquish their CC membership.[39] The failure of more than a handful to resign voluntarily generated a rising tide of demands for their replacement and was a major cause for the decision to call a party congress—which alone could elect a new Central Committee—earlier than planned. Although discussion of this kind was officially condemned as a public branding of individuals, sometimes unjustly, and an interference in the internal affairs of the party, it continued, both inside and outside the party. The Prague municipal party conference, for instance, prepared what was called a "black list," giving the names of seventy CC members (full and alternates) and ÚKRK members who ought *not* to be nominated for CC membership.[40]

[39] *Smena*, May 22. The list included V. David, J. Dolanský, J. Hendrych, K. Hoffmann, L. Jankovcová, F. Krajčír, J. Kudrna, B. Laštovička, K. Mestek, A. Novotný, V. Nový, M. Pastyřík, O. Šimůnek, M. Vaculík, M. Zavadil, and from Slovakia, R. Cvik, F. Dvorský, and M. Chudík. The Czech youth weekly, *Mladý svět*, on May 11, published a list of all CC members, and without specifying names, argued that 35 of them no longer represented anyone and were discredited.

[40] A summary of the minutes of the conference, and the black list, were published in *Tribuna*, Oct. 8, 1969. The latter did not include some 14 persons on the *Smena* list (among them, for instance, Novotný) whose exclusion from the CC was presumably taken for granted, but named about 60 other full and alternate CC members and 9 ÚKRK members, thus rejecting well over half of the previous CC membership, and one-quarter of the ÚKRK membership. Included, in addition to many on the *Smena* list, were P. Auersperg, Z. Fierlinger, J. Fojtík, P. Hron, B. Chňoupek, A. Indra, J. Kladiva, D. Kolder, V. Koucký, A. Kapek, J. Lenárt, J. Macek, I. Skála, O. Rytíř, V. Ruml, F. Šorm, L. Štoll, L. Štrougal, O. Švestka, and O. Voleník. This list was not published at the time but was to be transmitted to the 14th congress and Central Committee.

The election of a new Central Committee was a high priority item on the agenda of the forthcoming 14th congress. In a manner unprecedented in communist party history, nominations for membership had been submitted by basic organizations and district conferences, and endorsed by the regional conferences. This provided a pool of 950 proposals, or after the elimination of duplications, 836 candidates, 719 for the CC, and 117 for ÚKRK.[41] The final selection was to be made by the congress according to procedures to be determined by it. An official candidates' list would be prepared by that assembly's electoral committee, with the number of names placed in nomination to exceed the 90 CC vacancies by 25 to 50 percent.[42] Additional candidates, it was indicated, could be submitted by delegates. The exact mode of voting was yet to be decided, but it would certainly have been by secret ballot. Although the party statute in its draft form made no reference to the process of CC elections or to any safeguards of adequate Slovak representation, equitable Slovak representation would have to be assured, either through prior agreement of the Czechoslovak and Slovak party presidia in their projected joint meeting, or by special arrangements approved by the electoral commission and the congress.

The general profile of the 719 candidates for the Central Committee from whom the delegates would make their choice was not unlike that of the actual CC selected in 1966 (indicated in parentheses) although there were some dissimilarities, especially in political outlook. According to nationality, Czechs constituted 79.6 percent (77.7 percent); Slovaks 18.7 (19.3 percent), of the total. Eighty percent of the candidates were between 35 and 50 years of age and, within this group, over 50 percent were between 40 and 50 (in 1966, 47 percent were up to 45; 53 percent, 46 and up). The candidates were somewhat better educated—53.7 percent with higher education (approximately 50) and 25.2 percent with middle school education (almost 16). In length of party membership, the candidates were drawn less from the pre-war and

---

[41] *Zpráva*, pp. 31, 102-5. Somewhat different figures were given in *RP*, Aug. 3: 735 for the CC, 99 for ÚKRK. The Presidium, in July, gave the number as 935 (*RŠO*, p. 260). All delegates nominated by district conferences (and even by individuals) were said to have been registered by the CC. However, some regional conferences selected a narrow list of preferred candidates from those nominated by the districts. Thus the Prague conference approved a short list of 70, drawn from the 120 nominated. These included, *inter alios*, M. Hübl, V. Šilhan, J. Hanzelka, S. Litera, S. Křen, O. Šik, and L. Sochor (*RP*, Sept. 16, 1969). The conference also added, over some opposition, seven former social democrats, including Prof. J. Hájek and E. Erban (*Tribuna*, Oct. 8).

[42] On procedures, see V. Pešička and E. Kučera, *RP*, July 30; *ŽS*, no. 17 (Aug. 1968), pp. 26-27; *RP*, Aug. 21, first part (second installment not published); CC decision, *RŠO*, pp. 219-20. Official statements mentioned various numbers of candidates on the final list, running from 25 percent more to as high as three times the places to be filled (*ŽS*, no. 14, July 1968, p. 3).

war years—8.5 percent (23.5); less, too, from the years 1945 to February 1948—47 percent (59.7); and much more from the post-1948 years (mainly from the 1949-1958 decade)—43 percent (16.8). Other striking features were the low representation of workers according to present occupation—only 12.2 percent; the relatively high representation of the scientific and technical intelligentsia—18.7 percent; and the very high representation of officials and administrators—63.8 percent (58.4).[43]

The future makeup of the Central Committee depended on a number of imponderables and as the CC report repeatedly stated, could not be predicted with any certainty.[44] It would, however, be overwhelmingly new. Only 25 percent of the former members and alternates had been nominated, stated the report's author, Jan Kašpar—"a unique phenomenon in the communist movement."[45] None of "the former conservative wing of the party leadership, or of those burdened by past errors," had been proposed. Unlike other communist parties, where changes were gradual and continuity was preserved, "practically the entire leading team (garnitura)" would be changed within less than a half year. Except for "a narrow part of the leading core of the party, practically the entire Central Committee would be replaced. Into the leadership would step people who were in the main politically unknown and who had become actively engaged in the political sphere for a short time only." As a result, warned the report, "the continuity of the previous party leadership would not be entirely certain and the future of the central organs and their cadre composition appeared very unclear . . ."—a fact which would have serious consequences for the party and for its policy in the post-congress period.[46]

Some possible clues as to the CC election may be derived from the results of a poll of congress delegates (as well as of the district congress delegates) concerning their preferences for CC membership among twenty-five top leaders, including all the full and alternate members of

[43] For the above, Zpráva, pp. 31, 102-3. Although exact figures for the other occupational categories in 1966 were not available, it is doubtful that the last Novotný CC had more than a handful of workers in its ranks. Incomplete information for the 1966 CC is given by Hendrych, XIII. sjezd KSČ (1967), pp. 560-62, and Jancar, Monopoly of Power, pp. 132-39.

The composition of the ÚKRK nominees (Zpráva, pp. 104-5) was similar in most respects to that of the CC, although the members were slightly older (88 percent from 31 to 50 years) and had longer membership in the party; and fewer were workers (6.0 percent).

[44] Zpráva, pp. 49, 52, 87.

[45] Kašpar, RP, Aug. 15. Zpráva (p. 31) gave an estimate of "not quite 30 percent" of former members nominated. In 1966, 56.7 percent of former full and alternate CC members were reelected; 43.3 percent were new (Hendrych, XIII. sjezd KSČ, 1967, p. 560).

[46] Zpráva, pp. 31, 48-49, 52.

the Presidium and Secretariat, supplemented by four deputy Prime Ministers (Šik, Husák, Štrougal, and Hamouz). This "popularity poll," included in the appendix of the Kašpar report, was an index of the relative appeal of the top leaders and indicated a substantial conformity between the various regions of the country, and also, with certain differences, between Slovakia and the Czech lands. The report was quick to point out that the popularity was based on "outward behavior" of the leaders, not on knowledge of their real activity; was in large part determined by the mass media; and was likely to be quite labile, shifting with changes in the political situation (p. 46), but offered no substantiation for these propositions. In any case the rating could only suggest which of these leaders were *more*, and which *less* likely to be supported, and offered no evidence as to how they would fare in competition with other candidates. The top thirteen in the accompanying table, who received more than 50 percent of the delegates' preferences (including conservatives such as Bil'ak, Piller, and Sádovský), were more likely to be elected; the bottom thirteen (including conservatives, such as Indra, Kolder, Štrougal, and Švestka, but also progressives, such as Kriegel, Slavík, and Šimon), with less than 50 percent support, were less likely to be elected.[47]

Much more uncertain—and more significant—was the outcome of what the Kašpar report foresaw as the main struggle at the congress, namely, the competition between the former leaders who were nominated and the newer candidates from the regions. It was not clear how far "local interests" would favor little-known regional candidates over well-known former leaders, many of whom might lose support owing to the very familiarity of the voters with their past. The report feared that the latter consideration would lead to as much as 5 percent negative voting against all the former leaders and that unknown candidates might get more votes than all the present Presidium and Secretariat members, including Dubček, so that only a third of the CC members nominated would come through the voting successfully.[48] However, although the individual local candidate (as indicated in the table) was ranked high on the delegates' preference list (always among the top eight), it seems more likely that such local support, divided among many regional candidates, would not be sufficient to guarantee their election. The strongest were likely to be nationally known nominees, from Prague, Brno, and Brati-

[47] *Zpráva*, pp. 76, 109 ff.; district delegates also at p. 81. Those receiving less than 40 percent of the votes included Kolder, Kapek, and E. Rigo, of the Presidium; and Voleník and Slavík, of the Secretariat. There were some variations in preferences among the regional delegations, but the same persons appeared, in varying order, among the top dozen. The most significant variation was the strong support given to Slovaks by the Slovak regions.

[48] *Zpráva*, pp. 51, 86-88. The report concluded that much would depend on the voting procedures, and in particular on the order of the listing of candidates.

516

TABLE XVI.4

PREFERENCES FOR CC MEMBERSHIP
(order and percentages)

	Delegates of district conferences	Delegates to 14th congress		
		Czechoslovakia as a whole	Czech regions	Slovak regions
Dubček	1 (85.4)	1 (88.6)	1 (87.4)	1 (92.0)
Šik	3 (73.9)	2 (74.5)	2 (76.7)	9 (68.5)
Císař	2 (75.9)	3 (72.4)	3 (74.7)	10 (65.9)
Černík	4 (70.6)	4 (72.1)	4 (69.9)	3 (77.9)
Husák	5 (65.4)	5 (67.2)	6 (63.8)	4 (76.5)
Lenárt	7 (61.4)	6 (66.4)	9 (60.6)	2 (82.0)
Špaček	6 (64.5)	7 (65.7)	5 (68.3)	12 (58.6)
(Candidate of region)	8 (60.4)	8 (63.6)	7 (61.7)	8 (68.7)
Bil'ak	10 (57.7)	9 (62.6)	11 (57.6)	5 (76.5)
Smrkovský	9 (59.5)	10 (61.5)	10 (59.8)	11 (65.9)
Mlynář	11 (52.0)	11 (58.5)	8 (61.0)	14 (51.5)
Piller	14 (44.1)	12 (53.4)	12 (52.0)	13 (57.4)
Sádovský	12 (44.4)	13 (50.4)	16 (43.0)	6 (70.6)
Šimon	16 (42.0)	14 (46.9)	13 (48.0)	22 (43.8)
Indra	17 (41.1)	15 (46.1)	15 (44.8)	15 (49.4)
Kriegel	15 (43.9)	16 (46.0)	14 (47.6)	23 (41.6)
Barbírek	13 (44.4)	17 (45.4)	20 (36.7)	7 (68.9)
Erban	19 (39.5)	18 (43.1)	17 (42.6)	20 (44.5)
Štrougal	18 (41.5)	19 (41.6)	18 (39.6)	17 (47.3)
Švestka	20 (39.5)	20 (40.8)	19 (39.1)	18 (45.4)
Hamouz	21 (39.3)	21 (38.4)	21 (35.9)	19 (44.9)
Rigo	24 (30.2)	22 (35.5)	22 (33.9)	24 (40.0)
Slavík	22 (33.0)	23 (34.5)	23 (31.1)	21 (43.8)
Kolder	23 (31.1)	24 (32.1)	25 (26.0)	16 (48.2)
Voleník	25 (29.2)	25 (31.2)	24 (28.7)	25 (37.9)
Kapek	26 (27.5)	26 (27.2)	26 (23.9)	26 (36.2)

slava, who would be supported not only by their own delegations, but also by others. At least a dozen or more of the former top leaders would probably have widespread backing by all regions. The distinct preference among Slovak delegates for Slovak candidates, especially Dubček, Lenárt, Husák, and Bil'ak, made their election almost certain. Other well-known figures, such as General Svoboda, Goldstücker, L. Novomeský, J. Pavel, General Dzúr, and perhaps even Jiří Hanzelka, Jiří Kantůrek, and Ludvík Vaculík, who were placed relatively high in general public opinion polls, might prove to be powerful candidates, if nominated.[49]

[49] See the following chapter; also Piekalkiewicz, *Polling*, pp. 253 ff. Communists at the Philosophical Faculty of Charles University proposed E. Goldstücker, J. Kopecký, and K. Kosík, and if these were nominated by other organizations, O. Starý and F. Šamalík (resolution, June 13, 1968, mimeo.).

The situation was indeed fluid. Šimon, the leading secretary in Prague, warned that democratic elections might lead to the choice of representatives of "partial interests," rather than "bearers and guarantors of all-society interests." Yet the highest party organs could perform their "integrating functions," he said, only if the CC included "spokesmen of autonomous organizations and representatives of concrete political viewpoints or variants."[50] There was no guarantee of the adequate representation of individual social groups which was mentioned as desirable by the CC decision of early June. In the final analysis, the selection would depend on the general atmosphere of the congress, including the degree of satisfaction with the official list of nominees and the actual course of the proceedings, including the role played by certain delegates. Although delegates were expected to vote for the preferred candidates of their regional organizations, they were not bound to do so, or to vote for those on the official list of nominees. Black lists and preferred listings would have an influence, as well as coalitions of certain groups, especially of the progressive and numerically strong delegations from Prague, Central Bohemia, South Moravia, and perhaps Bratislava and West Slovakia.[51]

PRESIDIUM AND SECRETARIAT

Prior to April, changes in the two top party organs were not great. There were fifteen holdovers from the Novotný period, and only five new

[50] *RP*, July 5.

[51] The size of the delegations was as follows:

Prague	158
Central Bohemia	179
South Bohemia	78
West Bohemia	94
North Bohemia	135
East Bohemia	151
South Moravia	190
North Moravia	175
West Slovakia	198
Central Slovakia	98
East Slovakia	129

The report omitted the Bratislava municipal organization, which was presumably included in the West Slovakia region (*Zpráva*, pp. 112-16). Interestingly, certain regions nominated a far larger proportion of the total CC candidates than others: for example, Prague, 23.1 percent, South Moravia, 13.8 percent, and North Moravia, 13.5 percent, as compared with 3 to 8 percent in all other cases. The four Slovak regions (including Bratislava) together nominated only 16.4 percent (*Zpráva*, p. 102). This was not based on membership strength (Prague, for instance, had 10 percent of the party's membership) but presumably resulted from the addition of candidates where there was dissatisfaction with the lists submitted. This disparity would not have affected the actual selection of the Central Committee, but would have provided the congress with a larger pool of candidates, presumably many of them progressives from the regions mentioned.

appointments in the Presidium; six holdovers, and only one new appointment, among the Secretaries; and three holdovers, and no new blood in the Secretariat. During the four months from April to August, greater shifts took place. Only five remained in the Presidium from the pre-January days; four of the five January additions continued; and five new persons were added. Only two pre-January Secretaries, and one post-January Secretary remained. In the Secretariat no one was left of the pre- or post-January incumbents, and four new persons were appointed.[52]

In other words, in the final phase of reform, the leadership was overwhelmingly of post-January vintage—fifteen of twenty-two. They were, however, not young nor were they new to party work. They were on the whole a middle-aged group, with eleven of the Presidium in their forties and three in their fifties; three of the Secretariat in their late thirties, three in their forties, and one in his fifties. Nearly all had been party members for at least twenty years; most had joined between 1945 and 1948, five before or during the war, and only one later, in 1950. Almost all had served extensively in the party apparatus, usually from the forties and fifties on, and had risen to high posts in Prague or Bratislava, and received membership in the Central Committee in the fifties and sixties. A number had held high ministerial or other state positions under Novotný. Almost all had had some form of higher education, most of them at party schools, either in Prague, or, in two cases, in Moscow. The majority were said to be workers in origin. The others had served in various occupations—as officials (five) or as doctor, lawyer, and journalist (one each).[53]

Employing the admittedly rather arbitrary terms discussed earlier, one may describe the political complexion of the top leadership from June as follows. In the Presidium there were three moderate reformers (Černík, Dubček, and Šimon); three more vigorous reformers (Špaček, Kriegel, and Smrkovský); the remaining eight (Lenárt, Kolder, Kapek, Bil'ak, Piller, Rigo, Barbírek, and Švestka) were conservative in varying degrees (five were 1968 newcomers). In the Secretariat, there were five moderate reformers (Dubček, Císař, Mlynář, Erban, and Slavík), and five conservatives (Kolder, Sádovský, Indra, Lenárt, and Voleník). Combining the two organs (and eliminating duplicates) we have then an uneasy balance of three vigorous reformers, seven moderate reformers or centrists, and eleven conservatives. There was no one who could be described as representative of the more radical reform currents.[54]

[52] See Appendix A below.
[53] The above was based on official biographies published in the press. See also Jancar, *Monopoly of Power*, pp. 148-49; 160-61. Jancar includes M. Vaculík but not B. Šimon who replaced the former in June, nor Erban and Mlynář, also appointed in June.
[54] See above, chap. VIII, pp. 215-16, IX, pp. 254-55.

How the leadership corps would be affected by the course of the 14th congress was difficult to predict. The party statutes had rejected the notion of the direct election of topmost party leaders favored by many, and had assigned to the Central Committee the responsibility of "electing" the Presidium, Secretariat, and the CC chairman and Secretaries. Neither the statutes nor the pre-congress discussions had given any hint as to the procedures by which the elections would be conducted. Presumably an official slate prepared by Dubček and his advisers would be submitted to the plenum. No doubt, in the freer post-congress atmosphere, the Central Committee would have been able to vote down some candidates and perhaps nominate alternatives, but it seems unlikely that there would have been an entirely free choice by direct nomination of the entire list.

If we take the delegates' list of preferences for CC membership, and assume that there was a relatively free choice among them, we may conclude that the first thirteen would be more likely than the others to be elected, so that the leading contenders would be those of the moderate center (Dubček, Černík, Husák, Císař, Mlynář); those of more vigorous progressive outlook (Šik, Špaček, Smrkovský); and several with a more conservative approach. (Lenárt, Bil'ak, Sádovský, Piller). However, a number of others were not far behind the first thirteen in percentage of vote (40 percent or more), so that the following would also have been likely competitors: Kriegel, a vigorous progressive; Šimon and Erban, of the center; and conservatives such as Indra, Barbírek, Štrougal, and Švestka. Others had less chance of election: Slavík, of the center; four conservatives, Rigo, Kolder, Voleník, and Kapek; and deputy premier Hamouz.

The preference polls would not, however, have been decisive. Some of the former leaders might not have been eligible by virtue of their defeat in the election of the Central Committee. A number of newcomers would probably have been placed on the official list of nominees, or might have been proposed from the floor. These would likely have included persons who would have augmented the ranks of the center (e.g. General Svoboda, Goldstücker, Pavel, and perhaps General Dzúr); the more conservative trade union chief (Poláček); and some well-known intellectuals (Kosík, Hanzelka, Hübl, V. Pavlenda, Novomeský, etc.). The final outcome would have depended on the composition of the new Central Committee and the members' degree of satisfaction with, and willingness to accept, the official slate. The balance would have shifted, perhaps decisively, in favor of reform as a result of an increase in moderate and vigorous reformers, and a decline in conservatives, but the chance of the inclusion of radical reformers was slim. The Kašpar report (p. 52) gloomily warned that a firm and stable leadership could not be expected, and that consolidation could not be anticipated until the end of 1968. Although this judgment seems too pessimistic, there was every reason to expect a leadership which, although more vigorously committed to reform, would be divided as to the pace and content of action to be taken.

THE SLOVAK PARTY

The Slovak wing of the party, under the leadership of Bil'ak, endorsed the reform program after January, but placed greater stress on federalization than on democratization and was accused by some of lagging behind the all-state party, particularly in making the necessary changes in leading cadres. Bil'ak had roundly denied these charges, but by early July, was challenged by Husák, who was pressing for an earlier scheduling of the extraordinary Slovak congress and for a new Slovak team. He was clearly engaged in a struggle with Bil'ak for the leading position in the Slovak party.[55]

Certainly the Slovak leadership underwent considerably less change after January than did the CPCz. In January M. Hruškovič was promoted to full membership in the Presidium, and M. Pecho and R. Harenčár were appointed candidates. In April four new members were added —O. Klokoč, V. Pavlenda, A. Ťažký, and J. Zrak. M. Chudík, F. Dvorský, and M. Sabolčík were removed from the Presidium in April and May. The Secretariat had been altered by the appointment of Bil'ak, as First Secretary, and of two new members, S. Falt'an and M. Sedláková, and by the removal of Sabolčík. Of the top group of sixteen, then, eight were carryovers from the pre-January period, and eight were post-January appointees. They were mainly post-war party members: two from the pre-war period; one from wartime; nine from 1945-1948; and only one from 1958. Seven had been in the Slovak Central Committee ever since the forties or fifties (two from 1945; five from the fifties); three from the early sixties; and three from 1966. As for membership in the Presidium and Secretariat, one had been an incumbent from the mid-fifties; one from the early sixties; seven from 1966; and seven from 1968. The Slovak leaders were therefore somewhat less seasoned veterans than those of the CPCz. Most of them were long-time members of the Central Committee, but had risen to the highest positions of authority only in 1966 or 1968.[56]

[55] See above, chap. IX, pp. 241-43; X, pp. 279-83; XI, pp. 320-22, M. Kusý, *Politika*, March 20, 1969. In an unpublished speech in mid-July (available in mimeographed form), Pavlenda, a member of the Presidium, expressed views somewhat similar to those of Husák, stating the need for a new team of leaders, including both those who had opposed Novotný and some fresh people.

[56] Based on official listings, in *Příspěvky k dějinám KSČ* 6 (Oct. 1966), 737-64, and in part on Jancar, *Monopoly of Power*, pp. 150-51, although the latter's data are frequently at variance with the official lists.

There is little doubt that the Slovak Presidium, under Bil'ak, adopted a more conservative attitude to reform than the Prague leadership, as was particularly evident at the CPS May plenum, in the Slovak Action Program, and in Bil'ak's speeches. As one of its more conservative members, Hruškovič, later admitted, the top Slovak organ, at the time of the May plenum, had a different conception of the situation than the CPCz. There were also differences with Dubček over the Warsaw conference. The Slovak party, however, according to him, was limited in its power even after January, and did not use the modest possibilities that it did have. Hruškovič lamented that, during July and August, divergencies began to appear within the Slovak Presidium, although what these were and who were the rival exponents was not revealed.[57] It would seem, however, that more important than such internal clashes was the open controversy between the Slovak leadership and prominent personalities outside, such as Husák.

There is little evidence on which to base an evaluation of the social and political profile of the Slovak party. It was, of course, a relatively small part of the whole CPCz, its membership of some 300,000 constituting less than 18 percent of the total. It represented an even smaller proportion of the population of Slovakia, 11.3 percent in 1968 (as compared with the party's 19.6 percent of the population in the Czech lands).[58] As mentioned earlier, the membership was not exclusively Slovak and included some 12-13 percent of Czechs and other nationalities. Little is known of the Slovak corps of functionaries. In 1966 the members and candidate members of the regional committees were somewhat less proletarian (15.6 percent, plus 2.8 percent on state farms) than in the Czech lands (20 percent, plus 0.8 percent); did not differ much in the number of political and administrative workers (40.1 percent, compared with 37.8 in the Czech lands); had somewhat more teachers and professors (9 percent, compared with 4.8), and fewer scholars and artists (0.5 percent, compared with 2.5).[59]

Post-occupation commentary sought to create the impression that the Slovak party was much less divided than were the Czech communists and that it was therefore "an element of consolidation" in the post-January period ("by which it earned the branding of conservative").[60] The determination of the political attitude of Slovak party members and functionaries, however, is hindered by lack of empirical data. Only one direct poll of Slovak party functionaries—members and candidates of district committees in the region of Central Slovakia, covering 465 persons—is available. It was conducted at the end of June, prior to the polls sum-

[57] Interview with Hruškovič, *Pravda*, Jan. 22, 1970.
[58] *XIII. sjezd KSČ* (1967), p. 939.   [59] Ibid., pp. 944 ff.
[60] *Pravda*, Sept. 15, 1969.

marized in the CC political report.[61] The results indicated a substantially progressive viewpoint, with a large majority favoring democratization: 409 judging that it would benefit the whole of society; 376 that it would improve the economic situation; and 240 that it would strengthen relations with the Soviet Union. Only 140 expressed satisfaction (212 partially so) with the extent of democratization in their district; 144 were satisfied with democratization in their place of work (188 partially so). Strong approval was voiced for the convocation of the 14th congress and for the Dubček leadership; somewhat less for the press, radio, and television. Indicative of a more conservative outlook was the fact that 192 feared a rightist danger; only 98 perceived a conservative danger; and 137 saw equal dangers on both sides. An overwhelming majority (418) favored federalization rather than an improvement of the asymmetrical system (54) or an independent state (21). As the authors of the report put it, the conservatives represented only 15 to 20 percent of the total, and even they backed Dubček and democratization.

Apart from this single poll, we are dependent on the CC Secretariat polls of district conference delegates, and of delegates elected to the 14th congress, which, it must be remembered, covered not Slovaks by nationality, but delegates from Slovak districts and regions. Unfortunately no comparable survey of the opinions of delegates elected to attend the Slovak party congress was made (or was available). The results, with all the shortcomings noted earlier, documented the relative similarity of Czech and Slovak functionaries in their attitude toward reform, but also revealed some differences between the two national groups, and wide divergences among Slovak functionaries, as well as between Slovak regions.[62]

Congress delegates from Slovak regions were on the whole satisfied with the May plenum's results, although they were, by a few percentage points, a little less satisfied than delegates from Czech regions. The widest difference related to the plenum's cadre decisions, with more Slovaks completely or partly satisfied (70.6 percent, as compared with 58.5 percent Czech), and fewer Slovaks dissatisfied (23.3 percent, as compared with 38.1 percent Czech). In the evaluation of the situation in the party, the differences between Czech and Slovak delegates were also

[61] The poll was prepared by workers of the Regional Political School, with the assistance of the regional party secretariat in Banská Bystrica, and was dated July 10. It was available to the author in mimeographed form. See also Slovak opinion on the party statute, above, chap. XII, pp. 354-55.

[62] *Zpráva*, pp. 78 ff., 88 ff. Space prevents a comparison of the opinions of delegates to the congress and the district conferences, although in the main the latter exhibited a somewhat less "progressive" view. It should be noted that Bratislava was not listed separately and was presumably included in the data for West Slovakia. See below, Appendix B, for full results.

minor. Slovaks were somewhat more satisfied with the party's gain in authority, and somewhat less satisfied with the party's capacity to fulfill its tasks and the ability of the functionaries to adapt to the new methods. Even on the key question of the relative danger of conservative and anti-socialist forces, Slovaks showed a little less fear of both, the discrepancy, however, not being substantial in either case. On the two questions concerning party control of the economy, the spread was also not great, although Slovaks were a little less positive regarding the giving up of such control, and a little more satisfied with the actual implementation of this policy. Somewhat greater divergence emerged in regard to the "dangers" of yielding the party's power and of sharing decision-making with other parties. For instance, Slovaks were more fearful on both points (38.8 and 54.3 percent, respectively, as compared with 23 and 52.7 percent for the Czechs). There was an even more striking difference in "the lack of fear" of such developments (40.2 and 28.2 percent among Slovaks, as compared with 53.4 and 73.3 percent among Czechs).

The comparison of the preferences of Czech and Slovak delegates concerning top party leaders yields interesting results, as can be seen from the table above. Certain Slovak leaders, notably Lenárt, Husák, Bil'ak, Sádovský, and Barbírek, were placed higher on Slovak preference lists—among the first seven of the twenty-five considered. Certain Czechs were, however, placed high on the list, e.g. Černík, in third place, after Dubček and Lenárt. Other Czechs, including Šik, Císař, Smrkovský, and Špaček, although placed below the favorite Slovak choices, were among the top twelve. Several Czech leaders, more progressive in outlook—Mlynář, Kriegel, Šimon, and Erban—who were ranked high by Czechs, were rated much lower by the Slovaks and dropped out of the top twelve. Several other Czechs, relatively conservative in outlook—Štrougal, Kolder, Švestka, and Piller, as well as the more progressive Slavík—were placed higher by Slovaks (although not among the top twelve) than by Czechs and were ranked higher than Kriegel, Šimon, and Erban.

These data suggest that nationality considerations affected Slovak preferences at least in the case of several of their topmost leaders, but were less decisive than ideological aspects in their choice of other leaders. Significant, too, were certain variations among Slovak regions. The West Slovak region showed top preference for certain Slovaks, as well as Černík, but ranked Czechs such as Šik, Smrkovský, Císař, and Špaček above other Slovaks, and much higher than more conservative Czechs. The East and Central Slovak regions placed greater accent on nationality, both placing seven Slovaks among the top eight, and ranking progressive Czechs—Císař, Šik, and Smrkovský—below them in all cases. Most interesting was the difference of attitude toward Husák, who was placed third on the lists of preference of delegates from West and Central Slovakia, but eighth on the East Slovak list.[63]

One can only speculate as to how these opinion trends might have affected the proceedings of the Slovak party congress and the subsequent 14th Party Congress, and the composition of the Slovak party's Central Committee and topmost organs. Hruškovič, in the interview cited, claimed that an effort was to be made, during the Slovak congress preparations, to elaborate a stand quite different from that of the CPCz, to confront Dubček with this position, and to present it to the Slovak congress. If this was indeed the intention of the more conservative leaders, it seems doubtful that the plan would have succeeded in the changed atmosphere of the congress. There was no systematic analysis of the social and political profile of the 630 delegates to the Slovak congress. Their opinions can be inferred only from the poll of 14th congress delegates from Slovakia. It seems probable that the congress of the CPS would have resulted in considerable changes in the composition of the Central Committee and a substantial shift in Slovak leadership, including the replacement of Biľak by Husák and the removal of other conservative leaders.[64] This in turn would no doubt have led to a more vigorous defense of the national interests of Slovakia in the discussion of federalization, but might well have also led to more energetic implementation of reform in Slovakia.

[63] Space again prevents a comparison with the preferences of district conference delegates. The general results were somewhat similar, thus tending to confirm the ratings of the leaders among congress delegates. Certain Slovak leaders (Lenárt, Husák, Biľak, Barbírek, and Sádovský) were placed higher on the Slovak list, although certain Czechs, notably Černik, Smrkovský, Šik, Špaček, and Císař, were ranked among the top twelve. There was a similar demotion of Kriegel, Šimon, and Erban (although not Mlynář) and a similar promotion of Štrougal, Kolder, and Slavík. Švestka, Indra, and Piller were rated about the same by Czech and Slovak delegates.

[64] No general data are available concerning the some 300 CC nominees selected by the regional conferences. For the number of delegates and some limited data, ŽS, no. 17 (Aug. 1968), p. 13. The Slovak Central Committee elected in 1966 consisted of 69 full members and 29 candidates. Cvik was removed in 1968. Perhaps indicative of the trend was the composition of the political commission for preparing the Slovak congress. Only 17 of the full CC members, and 6 of the candidates, were named to this key body of 34 persons (*Pravda*, June 21).

CHAPTER XVII

Non-Communists and Public Opinion

THE PRIVILEGED position of the Communist Party during the two decades after 1948 had as its obverse side the lack of privileges, or even of
ordinary rights, of non-communist citizens. These were "the nameless,"
as Alexander Kliment called them in an article in *Literární listy*, who
could be defined only in negative terms—"*non*-party, *non*-commu-
nist . . . , *bezpartijní*." Having no "public forum of their own" and holding usually "no significant position in society," they became "anonymous
and passive," "alienated." As a result of the party's monopolization, political life was "practically speaking annulled"; "society disintegrated into
powerless and resigned individuals. . . ."[1] Lip service had officially been
paid to the idea of the participation of the non-party masses in politics,
either through the several non-communist parties, or the mass associations, or as individuals, but this presupposed unconditional acceptance
of the party's line of policy and of its leadership, both in the political system and in the societal organizations, and the absence of any dissent or
opposition. The non-communist parties could function only within strict
confines: their membership was restricted; any activity in the factories
was prohibited; their participation in leadership was limited by the so-
called "cadre ceiling"; their electoral participation strictly circumscribed;
and their press subjected to the all-pervading censorship. As a result,
four-fifths of the population were relegated to the status of second-class
citizens, deprived even of the limited opportunities of expression available to party members.

The position of the non-communists did not immediately change after
January. They had played no direct part in the actual overthrow of
Novotný, except as an imponderable force of discontent, and their role
in the first three months of 1968 could only be minimal, as they had almost no representation in the government or in the leadership of mass
associations. The explosion of public discussion in March was largely the
work of communist editors and journalists; the population, non-communist and communist, served mainly as an audience. The mass media,
however, including the party organs, were articulating the discontents
and demands of the population, party and non-party alike, and provided
a forum for the airing of some non-communist opinions. The few non-
communist newspapers became bolder in their presentation of news and

---

[1] *Literární listy*, March 14.

views and exerted an influence on public opinion. As noted in previous chapters, there was a spirit of regeneration within the existing non-communist parties, and new organizations were formed and sought to play some part in politics. Certain individuals who were not communists, such as the writers, Alexander Kliment and Václav Havel, and the philosopher, Ivan Sviták, ventured to expound independent views.

The official attitude as expounded in the Action Program recognized the necessity of giving "the various strata and groups in society" a chance "to express their interests . . . and to bring to bear their opinions in public life," thus promoting the growth of "civic responsibility." Non-communist citizens must not "feel that their rights and freedoms are limited by the role of the party, but on the contrary must see in the party's activity a guarantee of their rights, freedoms, and interests." The party was to retain its leading role but to exercise it in such a way as to win the voluntary support of the majority of the people. Although "discrimination" and "the cadre ceiling" were to be abolished for "those not members of the party," the latter were clearly expected to perform a secondary and supporting role. Non-communist interests and opinions would be expressed through the medium of the National Front, but without the possibility of developing a real opposition to its common platform.

This was not regarded as satisfactory by some, including even certain party members. Karel Kaplan, the historian, commenting on the January plenum, shortly after the publication of the Action Program, expressed regret that the almost four-fifths of the population who were "without party (*bezpartijní*)" had "so far not joined in the democratization process with their full weight," and "practically speaking" still did not have the possibility of "political self-assertion" in the representative organs and the mass interest organizations. A primary task was "institutionally to guarantee, and de facto to create room for, the realization of the political activity of the non-party people." "One cannot talk of socialist democracy," Kaplan wrote, "if it does not offer full opportunity for realizing the political interests of this numerically dominant part of our society."[2] The sociologist, Rudolf Battek, advocated, "as part of the transition from totalitarianism to a democratic distribution of power," a "dialogue with our Christians, with our socialists, in other words, with our non-communists who form four-fifths of the nation," by which he meant not the National Front political parties but "those citizens who could not up to now express their views on matters political . . . or organize politically." "Without the *autonomous (svésprávný) political cooperation of non-communists* real democratization is unrealizable," he concluded.[3]

[2] *Rudé právo*, April 13.   [3] *LL*, March 21.

These and other critics contended that the non-communists had something to contribute to the process of change and were anxious to have the opportunity to do so. Kliment, in the article mentioned, urged that "political life must be renewed" and that the non-communists, while supporting the CPCz Action Program in everything with which they agreed, must take their own initiative. This required the "activization of opposition forces," even through old and discredited forms and methods, e.g. the non-communist political parties and societal organizations, but especially through the formulation of a new program. There must be an "open system, in which no one will be excluded from participation in common affairs, but all will be able, according to their conviction and their conscience, to commit themselves (*angažovat se*)." A leading role would go to the "more significant elements," but this would "rest on authority, and not on dictation." "The *neg*ativistic concept of *non*-party or *non*-communist will find an active expression, a positive name and a concrete program and will enter political life."[4]

Such motivations led Kliment to organize the Circle of Independent Writers. Although differing as to philosophical orientation, political thinking, and artistic opinions, they were united, said the initial declaration of the Circle, in believing that "all people were equal before the law and the executive power and had the same right freely to organize politically and to compete for participation in the administration of affairs, or freely to decide in free elections which of them was to guide the administration of these affairs." The non-communists were still in the stage of "programmatic and organizational crystallization, were starting so to speak from scratch . . . were beginning for the first time to express themselves politically in an independent fashion." They could, however, perform "a certain catalyzing role" and had "a duty to emerge from their role as outsiders and assume a commitment."[5]

That this declaration was not limited to cultural affairs and had broader political implications was evident from Kliment's article in the same issue of *Literární listy* in which he urged the National Front parties, the societal organizations, and newly forming independent groups to draft a document of their own which would be submitted publicly to the party congress and would offer "coalition collaboration and pragmatic *oponentura*." Thus the congress would be "truly confronted . . . with the public and not with a picture of the public created in a party fashion by a not yet thoroughly reformed *aparát*."[6] Professor V. Chytil, on the eve of the congress, expressed a similar view, describing as the crucial question "the relationship of the communist party to the other non-communist citizens of the nation, of which they were the majority." The party

---

[4] Ibid., March 14. See also Z. Pinc, ibid., April 11.
[5] Ibid., July 4. [6] Ibid., July 4.

would lose the confidence of the nation if its next Central Committee did not contain persons who were willing "to a certain extent to abandon their partisanry . . . and become politicians of the entire nation or nations . . . , willing with equal seriousness to listen to the voices and opinions of the non-communists as of the communists. . . ."[7]

It was clear to many, communists and non-communists, that a genuine role for non-communists in politics would require a thoroughly reformed political system. This point was often made by Ivan Sviták, for instance, in his arguments on behalf of the 6,000,000 *nestraníci*, who should have, he said, the right to form their own party or parties, and, prior to that, to express their views through the Club of the Non-party Engagés (KAN). He was not alone in advocating a political opposition, new parties, and free elections as the only firm guarantee of full participation by all, communist or not, party or non-party, in politics.[8] The exact form of the forthcoming political system and the nature of the electoral process were, however, not yet settled. In the meantime, the participation of the non-communists would necessarily remain limited and much less influential than anticipated in the demands cited above.

Nonetheless, their role was of some importance—in an organized form in the non-communist parties and the newly formed political clubs; in the creative unions, especially the Film Makers' Union; in the independent circles formed within the Writers' Union and other unions, and the Co-ordinating Committee of the Creative Unions; but also in a less organized manner among students, trade unionists, and the technical intelligentsia.[9] Still more significant was the inchoate force of public opinion, which, in the absence of elections and of a definitive crystallization of political movements, had a greater immediate impact on the course of politics.

PUBLIC OPINION AND POLITICS

From March on public opinion emerged as a serious factor which the leadership could not ignore. The awakening of public opinion was wel-

[7] *Práce*, Aug. 17.
[8] See in particular Sviták's speeches of April 18 and May 14, *Student*, May 1 and June 19. For similar views of others, see above, chap. xii.
[9] On the non-communist political organizations, see in particular V. V. Kusin, *Political Grouping in the Czechoslovak Reform Movement* (London, 1972), chap. 6. See also brief discussion in Kusin, ed., *The Czechoslovak Reform Movement 1968* (London, 1973), pp. 139-47, 157, 167-68. The materials prepared for the 14th congress contained no references to the non-communists and only brief analysis of the role of public opinion (J. Pelikán, ed., *The Secret Vysočany Congress* [London, 1971], pp. 237-39). The report of the CC secretariat of August 1968, *Zpráva o současné politické situaci Československé socialistické republiky* . . . (Prague, 1968) provided some information but admitted that its sources were not adequate (pp. 43-44). The sections dealing with the non-communist parties, public opinion, and the mass media were not included when the report was published after the occupation. See above, chap. xvi, n. 2.

comed by the reform leaders and endorsed in the Action Program which described freedom of expression as indispensable if the opinion of the working people was to have an effective influence on politics.[10] Prior to January, "public opinion," in party doctrine, was said to coincide with official policy, whereas in reality, in the opinion of a later commentator, there had been two separate "monologues"—the institutionalized "public opinion" of the controlled mass media, and the real, but unpublished, opinion of the public.[11] After January public opinion was often markedly different from official views, although the former steadily approximated the latter on many issues as the spring and summer proceeded. Yet public opinion was also "pluralistic," a mosaic of the opinions of many "publics," reflecting diverse interests and clashing beliefs.[12]

As the CC report on the political situation pointed out, public opinion was not only "a factor determining individual dynamic reversals of society" but also "a factor in the long-run forming of the movement of the masses." Although opinion was affected by "frequently accidental, quickly changing, and sensitively and powerfully operating factors, beneath this change of public opinion permanent factors of societal consciousness were operating in the social groups, forming a kind of underlay (*podloží*) for the effectiveness (*působnost*) of publicly expressed political opinions."[13] It was therefore a crucial element in affecting both the future constellation of forces and the direction of long-run policy.

Moreover, research on public opinion, which was conducted regularly throughout 1968, became a power in its own right, and as its practitioners argued, an integral part of the democratization process.[14] "Democratic socialism," said J. Zapletalová, head of the Institute for Public

10 R. A. Remington, ed., *Winter in Prague* (Cambridge, Mass., 1969), p. 104. See also Dubček, CC, April, *Rok šedesátý osmý* (Prague, 1969), p. 66.

11 H. Klímová, *Listy*, Feb. 13, 1969. In his book, *Úvahy o hodnotách demokracie* (Prague, 1968), Lakatoš devoted a chapter to public opinion, "the backbone of democratic governance" and concluded that "democracy cannot function without public opinion." Lakatoš distinguished "public" opinion "from above," expressed through press, radio, and television, coupled with censorship, and "public opinion" based on freedom of expression and association (pp. 92-104).

12 On the pluralism of public opinion see Z. Gitelman, "Public Opinion and the Political System in Eastern Europe," paper given at APSA conference, Sept. 1970, mimeo.

13 *Zpráva*, pp. 10, 53.

14 Polls were conducted throughout 1968 by the Institute for Public Opinion Research (ÚVVM) in the Academy of Sciences, by the Institute of Political Science in the Central Committee and by the CC of the National Front. The results were usually published in the press or were made available in mimeographed form. A useful compendium of the results of many polls, in table form, is given in Jaroslaw Piekalkiewicz, *Public Opinion Polling in Czechoslovakia, 1968-69* (New York, 1972). This collection omits some important published polls, and its value is reduced by a rather confusing organization and a number of factual errors and mistranslations. The commentary is hardly more than a summary of the tables, but sometimes draws strange and debatable conclusions.

Opinion Research (ÚVVM), "if understood as the genuine participation of citizens in society's decision-making, cannot be conceived without public opinion research . . . which can be an effective instrument of the democratization of public life."[15] The Action Program indeed urged that public opinion research be used systematically in the preparation of important decisions and that the results should be published.[16] In fact, the results of the public opinion polls became, in the judgment of a Western scholar, "a direct, powerful and effective input into the policy-making process."[17] They exerted an influence on the leaders, to whom the results were sent at once, and through their eventual publication, had an impact on the public, giving them a sense of participation in politics and a feeling of influence on the course of events. In Zapletalová's words, research on public opinion became "an important instrument of the self-consciousness of citizens. . . ."[18]

After the occupation the Soviet "White Book" censured the use by reactionary forces of "trumped up 'public opinion polls' . . . at a time when the population was misinformed and had lost the correct political orientation."[19] The CC report of August 12, somewhat more subtly, had expressed reservations on public opinion research and warned against the "uncritical use" of the results.[20] Admittedly, the concept of "public opinion" is not without certain weaknesses, and opinion polls, whether in Czechoslovakia or elsewhere, cannot be accepted without qualification. Scholarly investigators at the ÚVVM were ready to admit the difficulties and the problems involved in polling but defended their own methods as being as "scientific" as possible. In their view such research was a more effective means of estimating trends of opinion than other alternatives and was even superior in some respects to elections which occurred only at intervals and could not fully and accurately express all public attitudes.[21] The polls of party opinion contained in the August 12

---

[15] *Nová mysl*, no. 12 (1968), p. 1511.

[16] Remington, ed., *Winter in Prague*, p. 104.

[17] Gitelman, "Eastern Europe," pp. 6, 25; Gitelman, "Public Opinion and Politics in Czechoslovakia" (mimeo.) pp. 9-10, 12-14.

[18] J. Zapletalová, *Svět v obrazech*, April 30. Whereas before 1968 the institute's polls had required prior party approval (Č. Adamec, *Reportér*, April 3-10, 1968), they were now operating independently of party control, according to Zapletalová.

[19] *On Events in Czechoslovakia* (Moscow, 1968), p. 22.

[20] *Zpráva*, p. 53.

[21] For a discussion of problems and methods of public opinion research in Czechoslovakia, see Zapletalová, *Svět v obrazech*, April 30, and Zapletalová, with other colleagues, *NM*, no. 12 (1968), pp. 1510-24; Gitelman, "Eastern Europe," pp. 21-23. Between January and August 1968 the institute conducted nine major surveys of opinion on current political problems. The usual technique employed was that of the "representative" or "quota sample," numbering from 1,000 to 1,400 persons, with various social and age groups represented in the same proportions as in the total population.

report were conducted according to less strict standards and were less reliable than the ÚVVM polls.

In spite of the admitted weaknesses, the polls, in our opinion, provide an invaluable mass of data on public attitudes during the course of 1968 and offer important clues as to possible long-term trends of opinion on politics and the future constellation of forces after the 14th congress. The polls have merit in revealing likenesses and unlikenesses of Czech and Slovak opinion, although unfortunately many studies were confined to the Czech lands only. To a limited degree also they showed the particular views of members of certain social categories, distinguished according to sex, age, education, and occupation.[22]

Results of polls on major questions of reform, politics, and the future political system will be analyzed in some detail throughout the rest of this chapter. As an introduction, let us note certain attitudes to politics in general. Although interest in political affairs mounted after January and was substantial, attitudes were somewhat ambivalent. At the time of the April plenum, for instance, only 28 percent of those questioned in the Czech lands said they were very interested in politics; 40 percent were fairly interested; greater interest was evinced by party members (44 and 43 percent respectively) than by non-members (22 and 38 percent).[23] A few days later, however, in a poll covering the whole Republic, a much higher proportion of the sample said that they followed discussions of domestic politics—74 percent (CPCz, 87; non-party, 70); 23 percent followed such discussions partially; and 3 percent, not at all. Yet at the same time, only 16 percent had read the Action Program in its entirety; 25 percent had read some of it; 35 percent had learned its main ideas through the press, radio, and television; 18 percent knew about it only from hearsay; and 6 percent did not know it at all.[24] In Slovakia, a separate poll in mid-June which asked if the respondents knew of the Slovak Action Program elicited 32 percent, yes; 35.3 percent, partially; and 32.7 percent, no.[25]

In a poll in the Czech lands in April, participation in political life was favored by a very large proportion—81 percent (CPCz, 93; non-party,

[22] For brief summaries of the results, see Zapletalová, *NM*, no. 12 (1968), pp. 1520-22; Gitelman, "Eastern Europe," pp. 24-25; Gitelman, "Czechoslovakia," pp. 21-31; Klímová, *Listy*, Feb. 13, 1969; J. Hudeček, *Rep.*, April 10, 1969, pp. XIII-XVI; Ithiel de Sola Pool, "Public Opinion in Czechoslovakia," *Public Opinion Quarterly* 34 (Spring 1970), 10-25; J. Piekalkiewicz, "What the Czechoslovaks Want," *East Europe* 20 (May 1971), 2-8. See chap. XVIII below.

[23] April 8-16, representative sample of 2,183 persons, Piekalkiewicz, *Polling*, pp. 118-19.

[24] April 20-21, representative sample of 300, ibid., pp. 69-70.

[25] June 12-18, 1,160 questionnaires returned from a representative sample of 1,400 from the whole of Slovakia, ibid., p. 72.

77 percent).[26] This did not mean, however, that most people themselves wished to take an active part in an organized fashion. A month later, more than one-half of the respondents in the Republic as a whole either did not wish to be a member of any organization with a political program (49 percent) or were in an organization but preferred not to be (5 percent). Only 23 percent said they were already in such an organization; another 10, that they would like to be in one; 13 percent said that they did not think about this matter.[27] In Slovakia, the mid-June poll indicated a desire to contribute personally to the implementation of the Action Program by a large proportion (77.4 percent), including 18.4 percent who said they were already doing so, and 34.1 percent who said they did not know how to contribute. Only 5.1 percent did not wish to do so, usually because they had reservations about the program; 14.3 percent had not thought about it.[28]

Attitudes toward politics and politicians were not very positive. Politics was regarded as "dirty" by almost one-half of the respondents—49 percent, yes; 38 percent, no (CPCz members, 40 percent, yes, 52 percent, no; non-party, 51 percent, yes; 34 percent, no). Almost the same proportion—47 percent—thought politicians were seeking their own benefit (43 percent of CPCz members; 49 percent of non-members); only 19 percent thought politicians were trying to "carry out certain ideas." A clear majority—60 percent (67 percent, CPCz; 57 percent, non-members) felt that it was more important to have "good and honest politicians" than "a proper constitution and laws."[29]

The attitude of the public to the individual newspapers was also revealing. When asked in July (Czech lands only) to judge which newspaper was "most trustworthy" in its information, only 20 percent named *Rudé právo* (42 percent of CPCz members; 14 percent of non-party). An even smaller number—13 percent (5 percent of CPCz; 17 percent non-party) named the organs of the two non-communist parties, *Lidová demokracie* and *Svobodné slovo*. A larger proportion—39 percent (26 and 44 percent, respectively) named *Práce, Mladá fronta*, or *Zemědělské noviny*; 28 percent (27 and 25 percent, respectively) named other papers (including local) or did not answer.[30] A later poll produced rough-

[26] April 8-16, ibid., pp. 114-15.
[27] May 24-26, random sample of 317, *RP*, May 30; fuller account in *Polling*, p. 241.
[28] June 12-18, *Polling*, p. 24.
[29] April 8-16, ibid., pp. 126-27, 124, 128, resp.
[30] Ibid., p. 242. These results were based on two polls, both conducted July 8-16 in the Czech lands only, one using a representative sample of 269 persons drawn from various parts of Bohemia and Moravia, and the cities of Prague and Pilsen; the other, a random sample of 218 from the whole of Bohemia and Moravia (total 487).

ly similar results: 26 percent, *Rudé právo*; 15 percent, *Svobodné slovo* and *Lidová demokracie*; 38 percent, *Práce, Zemědělské noviny*, and *Mladá fronta*. However, unlike the earlier poll, 19 percent saw no difference between the newspapers or did not read them.[31] Members of the two non-socialist parties had greater confidence in their parties' own newspapers than in others, although the support was not overwhelming and many had other preferences.[32]

PUBLIC OPINION AND REFORM

The initial reaction to January was a mixed one, although on the whole favorable. In a mid-February poll less than 50 percent had read or heard of the plenum; 36 percent had heard or read "something"; and 14 percent, nothing. Less than 50 percent assigned "great significance"; 17.7 percent, "little," to this meeting. A substantial proportion expressed no opinion (31.7 percent). As Table XVII.1 indicates, a much higher proportion of party members were informed of the plenum and assigned significance to it. In Slovakia more respondents were informed about the plenum and more assigned great significance to it than in the Czech lands. There were somewhat similar reactions to a question as to whether the plenum conclusions would affect society favorably or unfavorably, or would produce no changes at all.[33]

The February poll, including an "open" and a "closed" question on "the most urgent problem" to be solved, revealed clearly that attention was focused on various kinds of economic questions. Ranked in the first place, in the open question, were the growth of the national economy—17.9 percent; housing—15.2 percent; and improvement of conditions in agriculture—9.1 percent, totaling 42.2 percent of the responses. When

[31] Aug. 4-15, 2,947 questionnaires returned from a representative sample of 4,310 persons, ibid., p. 94.

[32] Ibid., pp. 168-69. The ČSL poll (Aug. 5-Sept. 4) was based on 727 questionnaires returned from a random sample of 1,500 of the total ČSL membership; the ČSS poll (Aug. 5-20), on 1,008 questionnaires returned from 1,650 ČSS members. Thus among members of the People's Party (ČSL), *Lidová demokracie* was rated first by 55 percent, *Zemědělské noviny* by 14 percent, *Práce* by 8 percent, *Mladá fronta* by 5 percent, *Rudé právo* by 2 percent, and *Svobodné slovo*, by 1 percent; 13 percent saw no differences among the newspapers. Among Socialist Party (ČSS) members, their own paper, *Svobodné slovo* was rated first by 47 percent; *Práce*, by 17 percent; *Zemědělské noviny*, by 11 percent; *Lidová demokracie* and *Mladá fronta* by 7 percent each; *Rudé právo* by none; 11 percent saw no difference.

[33] Feb. 14-17, a representative sample of 1,444. For the above and the following paragraphs, see *ČSAV, výzkum*, Czechoslovak Academy of Sciences, Institute for Public Opinion Research, no. 68-2 (Feb. 1968), pp. 3-15, 16-40, resp. (tables at pp. 4, 7, 11). A useful table summarizing some of the results is given by Pool, "Public Opinion in Czechoslovakia," p. 22. Slightly different results were given in *Rep.*, April 3-10. These polls are not reported by Piekalkiewicz.

TABLE XVII.1

REACTIONS TO JANUARY PLENUM

(in percentages)

Respondents	All	CPCz members	Non-members	Czech lands	Slovakia
Had read or heard about plenum	49.9	74.8	40.9	48.5	53.6
Had read or heard something	36.1	21.0	41.5	37.5	32.5
Had read nothing	14.0	4.2	17.6	14.0	13.9
Assigned great significance to plenum	48.9	75.0	39.4	47.0	54.0
-little significance	17.7	12.1	19.8	18.7	15.1
-no opinion or no answer	31.7	11.1	39.7	32.8	30.2
Expected favorable results	55.3	75.4	48.0	51.7	64.3
-unfavorable results	1.2	1.6	1.1	1.3	1.0
-no changes	19.5	13.1	21.6	22.4	11.9
-no opinion or no answer	21.3	7.8	26.4	21.6	20.8

Source: See n. 33.

other economic questions, which were placed first by smaller proportions, are added, the total is raised to 72 percent. In contrast, the improvement of Czech-Slovak relations fell into fourth or fifth place and was ranked first by only 6.2 percent. The deepening of socialist democracy was also low on the list—seventh—and was named first by less than 5 percent. With a few exceptions, Czechs and Slovaks did not differ significantly in the priority which they assigned to various economic questions, but did diverge on the urgency of improving the Czech-Slovak relationship. Only 1 percent in the Czech lands placed this problem first; whereas 19.1 percent did so in Slovakia.

The responses to a "closed" list of eleven problems showed somewhat similar results. When asked to select and rank the three most urgent problems, economic questions were predominant, as follows: qualified cadres (50.8 percent of responses), housing (36.4 percent), higher wages for qualified work (34.7 percent), growth of national income (31 percent), raising of living standards of pensioners (26.8 percent) and of large families (26.4 percent). The deepening of socialist democracy was seventh on the list (21.2 percent); placed in first place by only 10.2

percent. Czech-Slovak relations was ranked eleventh, at the bottom of the list (16.8 percent); placed first by only 4 percent. Czechs and Slovaks sometimes differed in the relative priority assigned to various economic problems, but were alike in rating such questions high. "Deepening of democracy" was ranked seventh in the Czech lands (22 percent) and eleventh (last) in Slovakia (19.1 percent). The improvement of Czech-Slovak relations was rated eleventh in the Czech lands (11.9 percent); placed in the first place by only 1.6 percent; and third in Slovakia (29.1); in the first place by 10 percent. Functionaries generally placed greater stress on this problem (21.7 percent) than citizens (14.7) and did so also on "deepening democracy" (29.7 percent as compared with 18.3).[34]

A poll in March indicated a more positive attitude toward current developments, with 67 percent of the respondents expecting that changes would be "durable"; 14 percent, that everything would remain the same; and 19 percent, not knowing. An even higher proportion believed that the current development would strengthen socialism (76 percent); only 6 thought it would weaken it; and 18 percent, did not know. A still higher proportion expected that the development would strengthen democracy (88 percent); 1 percent, that it would weaken it; and 11 percent did not know. Most expected an improvement in the standard of living as a result of current development (68 percent); 7 percent, a lower standard; and 25 percent did not know. The differences between Czechs and Slovaks were slight, with the latter evincing a slightly more favorable attitude to current developments.[35]

Ten days after the publication of the Action Program, a telegraphic poll of 300 persons indicated a generally positive attitude toward the April plenum and the Action Program. The overwhelming majority (75 percent) believed it would have a positive effect; none thought its effect would be negative; a few (12 percent) thought it would change nothing, and some (13 percent) gave other answers or did not know. When asked to what degree the program would be fulfilled, 56 percent said partially;

[34] *ČSAV, výzkum*, pp. 17, 24, 34, 38.

[35] March 24-28, sample of 1,476, *RP*, May 4; fuller in ÚVVM mimeographed report, May 1968. Cf. the results of another poll in late March (268 citizens), three quarters of whom considered that the influence of the January plenum would be favorable; 12 percent expecting no change; 12 percent not knowing; and only 1 percent unfavorable (*RP*, March 27). Neither of these polls is reported by Piekalkiewicz. In a poll which was not fully reported, Czechs and Slovaks were said to differ on the importance of attaining national equality, with the latter ranking it first, and those in the Czech lands putting it in seventh place. The importance of "deepening of democracy," was put first by respondents in the Czech lands and second in Slovakia (*RP*, May 5). The date of the poll was not given, but was probably March 24-28. Nothing was given on this in ÚVVM reports or in Piekalkiewicz, *Polling*. This may have been one of the two poll results which were not published, according to Č. Adamec (*Pravda*, Oct. 21, 1968).

22 percent, fully; 1 percent thought it would not be implemented; and 21 percent did not know. Although the poll sample included people in the entire Republic, no data were published concerning differences between Czech and Slovak regions.[36] A separate poll in Slovakia, in mid-June, showed that 71.4 percent agreed that the Action Program would influence development positively; 21.5 percent that it would do so partially; 1 percent answered in the negative; and 6.1 percent had no opinion.[37]

A more comprehensive poll, conducted at the time of the April plenum, but limited to the Czech lands, indicated substantial approval of CPCz policy,[38] as shown in Table xvii.2.

TABLE XVII.2

ATTITUDES TO CPCz POLICY*

(in percentages)

Respondents	Approved CPCz Policy			Disapproved			No Answer
	Strongly	Rather	Total	Strongly	Rather	Total	
Total	37	39	76	3	9	12	13
CPCz members	56	32	90	1	6	7	4
Non-members	31	41	72	3	9	12	16

* Question: Do you approve or disapprove of contemporary CPCz policy?
Source: See n. 38.

Unfortunately no polls were conducted dealing explicitly with the June plenum and its results. Just prior to the meeting (May 24-26), a poll indicated mixed views as to who would benefit from democratization: 53 percent thought that it would benefit all; 21 percent, that it would benefit the intelligentsia and not the ordinary people; 3 percent, the reverse; 19 percent, that it would bring no change; and 4 percent, that it would bring little good but would rather harm all. When asked about the relative priority of economic or political questions, opinion was divided, with 46 percent giving preference to economic; 46 percent, to both in equal measure; and only 4 percent, to political questions.[39] In mid-July, two polls, in the Czech lands only, indicated a modest balance of favorable judgments of future development—very positive—17 per-

[36] RP, April 30; Polling, p. 15 (second poll not reported).
[37] Polling, p. 14. The Slovak poll was presumably that of June 12-18 (see n. 25 above), although elsewhere (ibid., p. 347) it was dated July 12-18.
[38] April 8-16, Polling, p. 21. Cf. the poll of Rudé právo readers in May, above, chap. xvi.
[39] May 24-26, RP, May 30; ÚVVM mimeographed report; Polling, p. 95 (first question only).

cent; positive—44 percent; some good, some bad—36 percent; bad and very bad—2 percent; no answer, 1 percent.[40]

Other polls in late June and early July demonstrated that public opinion, while strongly favorable to socialism, did not share the plenum's fears concerning anti-socialist forces. The majority had no fear that democratic development might stop and things return to pre-January conditions.[41]

In a poll in August in the Czech lands 84 percent expressed the belief that the many changes in political life since January were positive for the development of socialism. Another 11 percent answered "more yes than no," and only 5 percent, "no "[42] (see Table XVII.3).

Polls demonstrated a generally positive attitude to the leadership of the country, but a substantial minority felt partial trust or none at all. In April, for example, in the Republic as a whole, 51 percent of the respondents expressed satisfaction with the new Černík government; 39 percent, partial satisfaction; 3 percent were not satisfied; 7 percent gave no answer.[43] The following month, however, when asked whether confidence in the party had risen or not, 26 percent said that it had; 41 percent that it had remained the same; 20 percent, that it had fallen; 13 percent had no confidence in the party.[44] In late June and early July, a

[40] Polling, p. 19. Piekalkiewicz cites the Czech polls as having been conducted May 8-16. In fact they were the July 8-16 polls described in n. 30 above. The differences between party and non-party opinion were not great: very positive (14 and 17 percent, resp.); positive (49 and 42 percent, resp.); some good, some bad (31 and 39 percent, resp.); bad and very bad (5 and 1 percent, resp.); no opinion (1 percent in both cases).

[41] Czech lands, July 8-16, Polling, p. 7 (also pp. 8-11); p. 130. Cf. earlier poll, May 24-26, for Czechoslovakia as a whole indicating a similar denial of anti-socialist dangers (cited above, chap. IX, pp. 240-41, n. 60). In Slovakia (June 12-18), a rather ambiguous question was asked as to whether they supported the plenum's position rejecting anti-socialist views and tendencies—66.2 percent said yes; 4.4 percent, no; 26.4 percent either did not know or did not consider the matter (ibid., p. 23).

[42] Aug. 4-15, ibid., p. 13. Members of the non-communist parties in the Czech lands gave even stronger endorsement to the changes after January: 97 percent of the ČSL, and 100 percent of the ČSS, evaluating the changes as advantageous for socialism (ibid., pp. 17-18); 95 percent of each group expecting that the changes would have a positive influence on the economy (ibid., pp. 278-79). For poll descriptions, see above, n. 32. The response of the whole sample on the latter question was also affirmative: 65 percent, yes; 24 percent, more yes than no (total of 89 percent); 5 percent, no; don't know, 6 percent (p. 276).

[43] RP, April 30.

[44] May 24-26, RP, May 30; Polling, p. 141. Two other polls, in the Czech lands only, also indicated less than complete confidence in the party. When asked "whether there existed an organization defending the interests and opinions of people like you," only 29 percent said yes; 61 percent, no (April 8-16, Polling, p. 133). Even among party members the replies were 46 percent, yes, 49 no; among non-party, 22 percent, yes, and 65 no. When asked whether the party was in fact fulfilling its leading role, not by ruling society, but by serving its free advancement, only 49 percent of the CPCz members, and 15 percent of the non-

TABLE XVII.3

DANGER OF ANTI-SOCIALIST TENDENCIES
OR A RETURN TO CAPITALISM*
(in percentages)

Respondents	All	CPCz members	Non-members
Strongly do not subscribe	33 ⎤	27 ⎤	39 ⎤
	⎬82	⎬78	⎬87
Do not subscribe	49 ⎦	51 ⎦	48 ⎦
Sometimes yes, sometimes no	11	10	12
Subscribe or strongly subscribe	6	12	4
No answer	1	—	1
	100	100	104

* Question: Some people talk about the danger of anti-socialist tendencies and express fear of a return to capitalism. Do you subscribe to this fear?

FEAR DEMOCRATIC DEVELOPMENT WILL STOP AND WILL
BE A RETURN TO PRE-JANUARY CONDITIONS**

Share this fear	13	6	15
Sometimes yes, sometimes no	33	33	33
Do not share this fear	54	61	52
	100	100	100

** Question: Many fear that democratic developments will stop and that everything will return to pre-January conditions. Do you share this fear?

Source: See n. 41.

poll taken throughout the Republic produced somewhat ambiguous results. Of the respondents, 33 percent expressed satisfaction with the work of the leadership; 54 percent, partial satisfaction; 7 percent were not satisfied; 6 percent did not know. Yet, when asked what degree of trust they had in the CPCz, only 11 percent had "complete trust"; 40 percent, "trust" (a total of 51 percent with trust or complete trust); 33 percent, neither trust nor distrust; and 16 percent, distrust or complete

members, answered in the affirmative (May, 524 party members; 636 non-party, *Polling*, p. 144).

distrust. When asked whether the CPCz was capable of ensuring the development of socialism and democracy, 52 percent said yes; 21 percent, no; 27 percent did not know.[45]

A little later, in mid-July, trust in the new CPCz leadership, headed by Dubček, was expressed by large proportions of the population. Similarly, a large proportion (see Table XVII.4) responded affirmatively when

TABLE XVII.4

TRUST IN CPCz LEADERSHIP UNDER DUBČEK*
(in percentages)

	ČSSR	Czech lands	Slovakia
Trust	78	75	86
Distrust	7	9	2
No opinion or no answer	15	16	12
	100	100	100

* Question: Considering the political development in our Republic, do you have trust in the new leadership of the CPCz led by A. Dubček?

TRUST IN ČERNÍK GOVERNMENT IN EVENT OF ELECTIONS**

Yes	68	66	73
No	11	13	4
No opinion	21	21	23
	100	100	100

** Question: If your trust had to be declared during a general election, would you express trust in the existing government of the Republic led by Prime Minister Černík?

Source: See n. 46.

asked whether, in the event of an election, they would express trust in the Černík government.[46]

In Slovakia confidence in their own leadership was high, 81.2 percent agreeing that the Communist Party had the ability to formulate a pro-

[45] June 30-July 10, a random sample of 297 (397 also given, incorrectly) from 2,000 questionnaires sent to a representative sample of the population (*RP*, July 13; *Polling*, pp. 34, 143, 145). There was a substantial change in the direction of greater trust as compared with pre-January days. In retrospect, 23 percent of those polled said that they had had "complete trust" or trust before January; 48 percent professed distrust; and 29 percent were neutral.

[46] July 13-14; a representative sample of 1,772 (1,306 from the Czech lands, 466 from Slovakia), *RP*, July 18; *Polling*, pp. 29, 250.

gram for Slovak development, and only 3.1 percent disagreeing. Some 15 percent did not know or had not considered the matter.[47] Attitudes toward individual leaders were given in preference polls in April in which respondents were asked to identify the person or persons in whom they had the greatest confidence. The results were interesting but less than significant, since they presumably indicated merely a relative preference among certain leaders for the topmost place(s) and did not rank them in order of popularity.[48]

TABLE XVII.5

PUBLIC FIGURES IN WHOM YOU HAVE
THE GREATEST CONFIDENCE
(in percentages)

	Czecho-slovakia	Czech lands	Slovakia
1. Dubček	39.7	28.0	67.5
2. Smrkovský	17.1	23.1	2.7
3. Svoboda	12.5	14.9	6.8
4. Císař	11.5	15.9	1.6
5. Husák	6.7	1.7	18.8
6. Šik	5.1	6.9	.5
7. Goldstücker	4.8	6.8	–
8. Hanzelka	1.8	2.5	–
9. Novomeský	.8	.3	1.9
	100.0	100.1	99.8

Source: See n. 48.

A poll in late June and early July, when people were asked to name the three persons in whom they had the most confidence, produced somewhat similar results, with several significant differences. Dubček and Svoboda ranked high, each receiving 27 percent of the total votes (with 81 and 80 percent of the respondents voting for Dubček and Svoboda, respectively). Others followed with 11 to 1 percent of the total votes: Šik, Císař, Smrkovský, Černík, Goldstücker, Husák, Hanzelka, and Lenárt.[49] In mid-July respondents were asked to identify as many leaders in whom they had confidence as they wished: 100 percent named

[47] June 12-18, *Polling*, p. 146.
[48] April 20-21, *Polling*, p. 253. This was based on a telegraphic poll of 300 persons. Somewhat different results were given in two other separate polls in late March, with Císař and Šik ranking somewhat higher (*RP*, April 30). For a chart of the rise and fall of popularity in 1968, see Pool, "Public Opinion in Czechoslovakia," p. 15. Č. Adamec refers to a second case of concealing results (in an unspecified poll of trust in leading persons) for fear of incorrect interpretations (*Pravda*, Oct. 21).
[49] June 30-July 10, *RP*, July 13; *Polling*, p. 257.

541

Dubček; 25 percent, Císař and Šik; 21 percent, Svoboda; 17 percent, Smrkovský. Others listed were Husák, Černík, Hanzelka, Goldstücker, Bil'ak, Pavel, and Lenárt.[50]

Foreign policy was not made the subject of any public opinion polls in 1968. This topic evidently did not at first loom large in the minds of Czechs and Slovaks, since no one in the February polls was recorded as even mentioning it among the most urgent questions to be dealt with and only a small proportion referred to it in another poll, presumably in late March.[51] In May, in a poll in the Czech lands only, respondents were asked, on the basis of a quotation from the CC April resolution, whether they felt that the Czechoslovak way of constructing socialism was "our internal affair," based on the will of the people. An estimated 94 percent of the population agreed. Fewer, however, believed that this corresponded to current reality—an estimated 43 percent of the entire population.[52] Several months later, immediately after Čierna and Bratislava, a poll in northern Bohemia revealed that 100 percent (83 percent "decisively so") thought that "we should go by our own socialist path."[53]

Other polls demonstrated that the population was clearly alarmed by "foreign pressures" and "interference in internal affairs." In a poll in July in the Czech lands, in response to an open-ended question concerning the chief danger which might cause a return to pre-January conditions, the largest group (42 percent) saw this as "pressures from abroad," compared with 18 percent as the strength of conservatives, and 11 per-

[50] July 13-14, *RP*, July 18; *Polling*, p. 258. Separate figures for the Czech lands and Slovakia were not given. Another poll (July 8-16) in the Czech lands produced the following order: Dubček, Šik, Císař, Hanzelka, Černík, Smrkovský, Goldstücker, Husák, J. Kantůrek, Lenárt, and L. Vaculík, all with more than 30 percent of votes in a choice of 10 from a list of 30 (*Polling*, p. 259). A poll in Slovakia ("the five most trusted individuals") produced the following order: Dubček (90 percent), Svoboda (75 percent), Husák (64 percent), Smrkovský (42 percent), Černík (25 percent), followed by Bil'ak, Císař, Lenárt, Novomeský, and Dzúr (June 12-18, *Polling*, p. 256).

[51] *Rudé právo* (May 5) briefly reported that 1.5 percent had ranked "in the highest places" of matters to be improved a change in foreign policy or in foreign economic relations. The date of the poll was not given, nor were the results recorded elsewhere.

[52] May 1968, two polls, one based on a random mail sample of 524 party members, the other on a newspaper poll of 636 non-party members, *Polling*, p. 45. The difference between party members and non-party persons was slight on the first question (96 and 93 percent, resp.) but much greater on the second (61 and 38, resp.). Cf. similar results in a poll of *Rudé právo* readers, cited above, chap. XVI, p. 502. Several other polls (in North Bohemia, and among readers of the regional daily, *Průboj* and the Slovak edition of *Rudé právo*), confirmed these proportions, showing in each case 90 or more percent endorsing the first proposition (*RP*, July 28).

[53] *RP*, Aug. 7. This poll was conducted by the regional party committee in northern Bohemia. No information was given concerning the poll, other than that it had included "all strata of the population."

cent as political apathy. Other factors mentioned were the weaknesses and lack of skill of the progressive forces (9 percent); the indecisiveness of CPCz leadership (7 percent).[54] In August a closed question (Czech lands) produced similar results: interference from abroad was ranked as one of the three greatest dangers to "the positive development" of the country by 72 percent (49 percent put it in first place). Conservative opposition occupied second place, cited among the top three dangers by 48 percent (10 percent placed it first). The activity of anti-socialist forces was placed much lower, 29 percent placing it among the top three dangers (7 percent in first place). CPCz members and non-members were alike in placing foreign interference in the topmost category, and conservative opposition in second place, relegating anti-socialist forces to fourth and fifth places respectively.[55]

In early July, in a poll in the whole Republic, 84 percent of the respondents rejected the idea that the forces (*mocenské prostředky*) of another state should be used to crush "possible disorders." There were 16 percent of a different mind: 4 percent agreed with the idea; 6 percent accepted it as a possibility under certain conditions; and 6 percent expressed no opinion.[56] In mid-July, in answer to a question whether troops of allied armies should leave Czechoslovak territory immediately after the conclusion of the Warsaw pact exercises, there was an overwhelmingly affirmative response—91 percent (Czech, 93 percent; Slovak, 83 percent). Only 2 percent (2 and 3 percent, respectively) did not agree, and 7 percent (5 and 14 percent, respectively) did not know or gave no reply.[57]

THE NON-COMMUNIST PARTIES

The existing "satellite" parties were, at the beginning of the democratization process, weak in numbers and influence. The two Czechoslovak parties, which in spite of their name, were primarily Czech in scope, underwent a certain process of regeneration with some changes in leadership and some expansion of membership. The Czechoslovak People's Party (ČSL) rose from 20,642 members in 467 local organizations on January 1, to 46,028, in 859 organizations on July 1, 1968. The Czechoslovak Socialist Party (ČSS) increased from 10,715 members in 213 local organizations, to 17,323, in 334 organizations, between those two dates, and rose to 18,400 by August 1.[58] The two Slovak parties were so

---

[54] July 8-16, *Polling*, p. 44.   [55] Aug. 4-15, ibid., pp. 53-54.

[56] June 30-July 10, *RP*, July 13; *Polling*, p. 57 (the question was incorrectly translated). Pool, "Public Opinion in Czechoslovakia" (p. 18) gave slightly different results: 81, 5, 11, and 3 percent, resp.

[57] July 13-14, *RP*, July 18; *Polling*, p. 46.

[58] *Zpráva*, pp. 19, 22, 65-66. At the end of May, the Socialist Party claimed

minuscule as to warrant no further attention. Their membership was given, in the CC report, as follows: the Party of Freedom, 364, and the Party of Slovak Revival, 248.[59] These figures suggest that the non-communist parties, discredited by twenty years of unconditional support of the Communist Party, had not gained much ground by their modest efforts at reform after March.

That the People's Party and the Socialist Party would be able to become strong political forces capable of playing independent roles or of seriously challenging the massive Communist Party appeared doubtful. As already noted, both had adopted new programs but their objectives did not differ substantially from those set forth in the CPCz Action Program which both parties fully endorsed. Each party had expressed a desire for a more independent position within the National Front, but they accepted the front's concept of partnership and the leading role of the Communist Party.[60] Both parties were planning to hold congresses in the fall and to adopt more comprehensive new programs, and would no doubt, as the CC report warned, have increased their activities aimed at winning over public opinion and intensifying pressure on state and party organs, especially in connection with eventual elections.[61] The general public, however, as late as August, was not persuaded that they were "independent, autonomous parties conducting their own independent policies." Only 29 percent answered affirmatively to a question so

---

16,000 members (*Svobodné slovo*, June 8); in early July, the People's Party, 55,970 (*Lidová demokracie*, July 5); in August, 65,000 (ibid., Aug. 20). Cf. the figures given by Kusin, *Political Grouping*, p. 155, nn. 1, 2. Piekalkiewicz gives the figures of 57,231 and 18,144, for the People's and Socialist Parties resp., in early August (*Polling*, pp. 345-46).

Zpráva data on membership were based on information from the National Front. Estimates by CPCz district organizations, which were also given, were a little lower in each case. The data showed that the ČSL was stronger, and had experienced a greater increase, in South and North Moravia (12,000 and 10,000 members, resp.), and East Bohemia (6,500). Membership in Prague was given as 4,697. The ČSS membership was more evenly distributed but was strongest in South Moravia (3,321). Prague membership was 3,041.

[59] *Zpráva*, p. 24.

[60] See above, chap. IX, pp. 232-33; X, pp. 264-65; XII, p. 346.

[61] For scattered observations on these developments, see *Zpráva*, pp. 17-18, 19-23, 43-44. The CC report censured meetings of the ČSS for criticism of the CPCz and demands for the abolition of the People's Militia, and was particularly critical of the efforts of the Socialist Party, and of the National Front, to organize in the factories. The formation of NF organs in the factories would "open the door of the factories to the non-communist political parties and other organizations," thus introducing "a pluralist principle" inconsistent with the "monolithic principle" of unified expert leadership (p. 43). The report noted conflicting tendencies within the two parties and foresaw greater differentiation in the future. The inadequacy of the information sources used in the report was later sharply criticized by a Catholic newspaper, *Obroda*, Feb. 26, 1969.

worded, whereas 59 percent replied negatively (12 percent, "don't know," or no answer). Even their own members were skeptical of the parties' independence: ČSS members, 38 percent, yes, 59 percent, no; ČSL, 36 percent, yes, 63 percent, no.[62]

Nonetheless, the opinion was widely held that the non-communist parties should become more independent. In August strong majorities expressed the view that the two non-communist parties should be "really independent and autonomous, and equal partners of the Communists": 81 percent of the entire population; 71 percent of CPCz members; 85 percent of non-party; 100 percent of ČSL and ČSS members.[63]

The most telling evidence of the relative appeal of the existing parties was provided by two separate polls in July, in which respondents in certain parts of Bohemia and Moravia were asked to whom they would give their vote if there was an election that month, based on the independent candidacy of all political parties. The results were as shown in Table XVII.6.[64]

These polls clearly demonstrated the relatively weak support of the two non-communist parties among the population as a whole, and even among non-communists in general. The polls also showed that the Communist Party, although it would not have secured the support of a "majority" of the population as a whole, would have been supported overwhelmingly by its own members and would have been by far the strongest party. Significantly, a very high proportion of the respondents were undecided or did not respond—33 percent of the entire sample, and 41 percent of the non-communists. Because of this high degree of uncertainty, and the likelihood of serious changes of conditions by the time of elections, and in the absence of Slovak data, these preferences, even if they represent reliable data, could hardly offer an accurate prediction of the results of a future election.

[62] *Polling*, pp. 155-58, 160-61. The table at p. 155 is incorrectly titled, since it presumably refers to ČSL members (see pp. 345-46). The People's Party is wrongly referred to throughout as the Agrarian Party. These polls include those of Aug. 4-15, described in n. 31; those of the first half of August, 2,966 questionnaires returned from a representative sample of 3,600 persons; and the ČSS and ČSL polls described in n. 32.

[63] *Polling*, loc. cit. Cf. slightly different results in July, and for the ČSL in late August, ibid., pp. 163, 165. According to a July poll the necessary condition for achieving this desired state of affairs was believed by a substantial body of opinion to be free democratic elections (57 percent of all; 47 percent of CPCz members; and 60 percent of non-communists). A smaller group believed it to be equal access to the media (21, 22, and 21 percent, respectively). Source: July 8-16, ibid., p. 167.

[64] July 8-16 (n. 30 above), *Polling*, p. 247. Piekalkiewicz terms the results "a communist victory" and attributes this to the solid vote by CPCz members for their own party (p. 246). These numbered, however, only a million and a half as compared with some four and a half million non-party citizens.

TABLE XVII.6

VOTING IN ELECTIONS THIS MONTH

(in percentages)

Respondents would vote for:	All	Communists	Non-communists
Communist Party	43	90	28
Socialist Party	13	1	17
People's Party	9	2	12
Blank ballot, don't know, or no answer	33	7	41
	98	100	98

Source: See n. 64.

PROSPECTS FOR NEW PARTIES

The formation of other parties, including opposition parties, and free competition in elections among rival political groupings, was strongly pressed by advocates of a pluralist system as a sine qua non of a genuine democracy. Yet the prospect of the emergence of new parties as strong and effective forces capable of challenging the dominance of the Communist Party was uncertain, to say the least, and indeed unlikely as things stood prior to the 14th congress. The official view, repeatedly expressed by the leaders and in documents such as the Action Program and the June plenum resolution, was negative toward the idea of a political opposition and was not positive in general to the notion of forming additional parties. Nor was there great enthusiasm for the latter on the part of the existing non-communist parties.

Although the procedures for the forming of parties was not yet clearly established, the official viewpoint placed the decisive authority in the hands of the National Front and forbade the emergence of parties and organizations outside it. The NF was to include only the existing political parties, supplemented by the major societal organizations. In August other newly formed organizations were still in the stage of preparatory committees; few had been registered by the Ministry of the Interior, and none admitted to the front.

Only a few organizations could be regarded in any degree as political movements of potential importance—notably, the embryonic social democratic organization, and, less likely, the two political clubs, KAN and K 231. None of these, as far as can be estimated, had a really significant following. None had as yet been recognized as legitimate by either the

Ministry of the Interior or the National Front. All three had in fact been sharply condemned by party spokesmen, whose negative views reflected ingrained habits of thinking as well as fears of Soviet condemnation. Even more progressively oriented party members were inhibited from expressing favorable views by similar fears and by tactical caution.

The social democratic movement had been repudiated by the CPCz as a threat to the "unity" of the working class which had been attained by the fusion of the Social Democratic Party with the CPCz in 1948. The organizers of the movement themselves professed the desire not to oppose the latter but to cooperate with it in a political partnership. The exact size of the movement was unknown. According to the CC August report, 150 preparatory cells had been formed, including several in Prague, Brno, Pilsen, and Ostrava; only 1,700 membership applications had been received. The report, however, expected a renewal of social democratic activity after the 14th congress and feared the danger of its advance as a political party, thereby splitting the working class and creating "a real opposition force."[65] The movement's commitment to "socialism" might make it a force of some attractiveness since public opinion favored new parties with socialist programs and opposed any advocating a return to capitalism (see below). It was impossible to foresee, however, whether this movement would be able to vindicate its claims for political recognition and how far it would be able to attract popular support.

The future of KAN as a political force was even less bright. It claimed to be a spokesman for the non-communist majority of the nation and, although professing no desire to become a political party, or to oppose the Communist Party, it did seek to influence public opinion; it hoped to have representation in the National Front and in the elected representative bodies and to promote the election of other approved candidates. As of August 1968, however, its membership was small, restricted in the main to urban centers in the Czech lands, and there were few organizations in Slovakia. Its own leaders claimed 15,000 members.[66] The CC political report had information, as of June 30, of 55 KAN organizations, all in the Czechs lands, only five of them registered, with a total of 2,218 members. The report described it as an organization which was acting as a pressure group on the CPCz and which hoped to influence eventual elections, and was critical of the anti-communist views of some of its organizations, and of Sviták, one of its vocal supporters.[67] Al-

---

[65] Zpráva, pp. 25, 44.

[66] Rep., July 3-10. A. I. Simon gave an estimate of 4,000 in early May (EE 18, June 1969, 20-22); Tribuna gave the much larger figure of 40,000, without giving a date (March 19, 1969).

[67] Zpráva, pp. 67, 26-27. Both Sviták and former KAN leaders denied in private

though some of its members would have liked to see it become a political party, most were opposed to this, and some even rejected participation in the National Front. Although it had a defined goal—socialism of a democratic and humanist type—and had definite ideas concerning human rights and political reforms, it lacked the unified program necessary for effective action as a party.

The club of former political prisoners, K 231, had even less prospect of becoming a serious political force. Its leaders, like those of KAN, disavowed any intention of making it a party and, indeed, regarded its purpose as a limited and temporary one, which would end with the completion of rehabilitation. Officially it was regarded as having fulfilled its mission after the enactment of the rehabilitation law. Its potential membership was large, and its actual membership perhaps as high as 60,000 by August.[68] According to the CC report of August 12, K 231 had only 5,760 members in 74 organizations (30 registered), all but one in the Czech lands. The report claimed that there had been a decline in the influence of K 231 since May and a substantial differentiation within its ranks, but described it as "a potential political force" which was seeking to penetrate other parties, to influence elections, and to win places in public administration. Like KAN, claimed the CC statement, K 231 sought to act as "a pressure group" on public opinion, and was oriented toward "building a political opposition to the CPCz."[69] It seems doubtful, however, that this body, which consisted of older persons who had suffered greatly from many years in prison and which had no general political program, could have played any but a limited and transient role in political life. The Society for Human Rights, which was the one organization authorized by the Ministry of the Interior, had a more permanent task of acting as a watchdog for individual rights but seemed unlikely to seek a broader political role.[70]

Another embryonic movement, the "revolutionary left," should be mentioned for the sake of completeness, although its intrinsic importance appeared even less than those mentioned above. In May a declaration signed by Professor Zbyněk Fišer, former social democrat, and several others, in the name of "the revolutionary left," was published in *Rudé právo*, appealing to all those who wished "the continuation of the socialist revolution at home" and support of "really revolutionary forces"

conversations that he had been a founder or a leader of KAN. Although few clubs were formed in Slovakia, KAN planned to be an all-state organization, with a federal structure (*Svědectví* 12, no. 45, 1973, 156-57, 159).

[68] J. Brodský, *Řešení gama* (Toronto, 1970), pp. 163, 180. Also *LL*, July 4, p. 14.

[69] *Zpráva*, pp. 18-19, 25-26, 67. The report also alleged that K 231, KAN, and the social democratic organizations gave each other mutual support.

[70] Kusin, *Political Grouping*, pp. 193-95.

abroad. A month later at a meeting convoked by the Association of the Marxist and Non-Marxist Left spokesmen of the group urged "a deepening of socialism," an economic reform which would eliminate social inequality, and a broadening of the conception of "workers' councils." There was no desire "today or tomorrow to found a Maoist party," but "Maoism could not be rejected in advance" and the experiences of China, Cuba, and Albania, and the West European student radical movements, must be studied.[71]

Other proclamations of the movement were more radical in tone. A draft statement of April 18, for instance, condemned Šik's proposals of market socialism as "technocratic," urged a "Soviet (council) type" democracy, and suggested the study of works by Trotsky, Luxemburg, Zinoviev, Bukharin, Castro, and Che Guevara. The statement was also sharply critical of the proposed form of "workers' councils."[72] Other materials rejected self-management on the Yugoslav model as well as formal democracy of the bourgeois type, and declared that only power in the hands of "an authentic workers' revolutionary party," along with workers' self-management, would guarantee real socialist democracy.[73]

Somewhat later, a fuller statement of the objectives of what came to be called "The Prague Club" was drawn up by Professor Fišer for presentation to the 14th congress. This document, which was never published in Czechoslovakia, attacked the bureaucratic perversion of socialism that had occurred under Novotný and called for "a permanent revolution," implemented through the activization of the industrial workers and the democratization of the party. Emphasis was placed on a system of self-management of producers, not limited to factory management alone but including a central council of self-management, which would work in partnership with the government and other central institutions in all questions of importance. The right to strike must be guaranteed, as well as freedom of the press, opinion, and assembly for all socialist forces. The manifesto expressed support for January but warned of the danger of the establishment of rule by a new class of certain state and party bureaucrats—"either the so-called progressives or the conservatives"—together with some of the managers and intellectuals, which

---

[71] *RP*, May 11; *LL*, June 13, p. 12. See also P. Broué, *Le printemps des peuples commence à Prague* (Paris, n.d., pp. 85-86). Broué, a Trotskyist, admits that this, and other "leftist" phenomena, were "limited" in scope. See also Kusin, *Political Grouping*, pp. 183-85.

[72] See above, chap. xiv, n. 78. For a German version of the April statement see M. Borin and V. Plogen, *Management und Selbstverwaltung in der ČSSR: Bürokratie und Widerstand* (Berlin, 1970), pp. 106-11.

[73] These documents were published in two numbers of the movement's Information Material, available in French in *Le "complot trotskyste" en Tchécoslovaquie: Les textes de l'opposition révolutionnaire* (Paris, 1970), pp. 11-17.

would create, not a socialist democracy, but "a liberal pseudo-democracy."[74]

NEW PARTIES AND PUBLIC OPINION

There were widespread differences of view, as well as a certain ambiguity, as to whether the existing party system was satisfactory or whether new parties should be formed. The two July polls produced the results shown in Table XVII.7.[75]

TABLE XVII.7

SYSTEM OF POLITICAL PARTIES*
(in percentages)

Respondents	All	CPCz members	Non-members
The existing system is satisfactory	41	63	34
There should be only one party	7	10	5
There should be another political party	27⎫	16⎫	31⎫
There should be other political parties	23⎭ 50	9⎭ 25	27⎭ 58
Don't know	2	2	3
	100	100	100

* Question: Do you believe that the system of political parties that exists today in the Czech lands is satisfactory for the needs of socialist democracy?

Source: See n. 75.

The August poll (see Table XVII.8) revealed a similar diversity of opinion.[76]

One may conclude that most Communist Party members were satisfied with the existing party system, although a minority (25 percent) favored the addition of one or more parties. Non-communists were less satisfied, and a majority (58 percent) endorsed one or more additional parties. By August, however, the non-communists in general, and the members of the two non-communist parties, approved the existing sys-

[74] The program was published in English in *The Invasion of Czechoslovakia* (no author) (New York, 1969). Some forty of the fifty co-authors of the program were said to be party members.

[75] July 8-16, *Polling*, p. 230.

[76] Aug. 4-15, and ČSS and ČSL polls (n. 32), *Polling*, pp. 232-35.

TABLE XVII.8

SYSTEM OF POLITICAL PARTIES*

(in percentages)

Respondents	CPCz	Non-members	ČSS	ČSL
For retaining existing system	76	58	52	54
For one party only	7	4	–	–
For at least one additional party	13⎫	26⎫	38⎫	38⎫
For a few more parties	3⎭ 16	9⎭ 35	10⎭ 48	8⎭ 46
No answer	1	3	–	–
	100	100	100	100

* Question: Political parties are members of the National Front and in the Czech lands include the CPCz, ČSS, and ČSL. What do you think about this party combination?

Source: See n. 76.

tem by a majority in each case, but a good-sized minority of non-communists favored one or more other parties. A single-party system found favor with very few.[77]

When asked in the July polls what conditions should govern permission to form a new political party, the Czech respondents revealed substantial differences of view. Most favored the setting of some conditions, but they differed greatly as to what conditions should be required. When asked who should grant permission for the formation of a new political party, there was again great diversity of opinion (see Table XVII.9). A substantial minority thought that the members of the new party should simply "form themselves"—13 percent of the CPCz; 26 percent of the non-communists. A significant minority was opposed to the creation of a new party.[78]

Some further clues as to the trend of opinion concerning new parties were given by the results of a July poll concerning "the creation of an opposition party," in which the respondents were asked to express a preference among five alternatives (see Table XVII.10). A substantial minority were against any opposition party. Most, in all categories, were

[77] The support for forming other parties was later interpreted as reflecting a matter of principle, so as to assure that others would have the freedom to form a new party, and not as expressing the desire of the respondents to identify themselves with such a party (Klímová, Listy, Feb. 13, 1969).

[78] July 8-16, Polling, pp. 237-39.

TABLE XVII.9

CONDITIONS FOR PERMISSION TO FORM
A NEW POLITICAL PARTY
(in percentages)

Respondents	All	CPCz members	Non-party members
Against a new party	19	36	14
Recognition of CPCz leading role	6	10	5
Willingness to join the NF and respect its program	15	17	14
Program not contrary to law and constitution	18	11	20
Program not contrary to human rights or communism, or advocating war, racism or fascism	21	15	23
No restricting conditions	6	1	8
Socialist program	13	9	14
Don't know/no answer	2	1	2
	100	100	100

WHO SHOULD DECIDE ON THE CREATION
OF A NEW POLITICAL PARTY?

No new party should be created	19	33	14
The government	5	2	6
National Assembly	23	18	25
Constitutional Court	5	6	5
CC of the NF	21	22	20
Ministry of Interior	1	3	1
CPCz	2	3	1
Let new party form itself	23	13	26
No answer	1	–	2
	100	100	100

Source: See n. 78.

TABLE XVII.10

IDEA OF WHAT AN OPPOSITION PARTY SHOULD BE*
(in percentages)

Respondents	All	CPCz members	Non-members
Anti-socialist— a return to capitalism	–	–	–
A return to the 1945-47 system	7	4	7
A socialist program but differing from the communists in concept of socialism	22	9	27
A socialist program in agreement with the communists, but with a different concept for its realization	48	55	46
Against an opposition party	21	31	18
Don't know/no answer	2	1	2
	100	100	100

* Question: Often there is talk about the necessity of creating an opposition party as a basic foundation for the democratic control of power. However, people have greatly different ideas regarding the concept of an opposition party. We give you some possible characteristics of an opposition party. Mark the one that corresponds to your idea of what the opposition party should be.

Source: See n. 79.

ready to accept a party with some kind of socialist program. The largest number were ready to accept a party with a socialist program in agreement with the communists but with a different concept for its realization. None favored a party with an anti-socialist program, emphasizing a return to capitalism.[79]

When asked about the relationship of the new party to the CPCz, the largest group endorsed a party that "wished to share power with the communists and cooperate with them, but did not automatically recognize the party's leading role and sought to become the leading force of the coalition": 41 percent of the total; 32 percent of CPCz; 44 percent of non-party. Another substantial minority supported a party that "accepted the leading role of the CPCz, reserved the right to its own position,

[79] July 8-16, *Polling*, p. 227.

but did not attempt to broaden its power base": 33, 32, and 33 percent, respectively. Only a tiny fraction favored a party that "would refuse to share power and cooperate with the CPCz and wished to obtain power itself": 2, 0, and 3 percent respectively.[80]

These polls, in sum, revealed a somewhat ambiguous and variegated spectrum of opinion. The largest group—somewhat under 50 percent approximately—seemed to favor a party which had a concept of socialism similar to that of the communists and was willing to cooperate with the CPCz in a coalition, but one which would compete with it to become the leading force. There was no evidence of an overwhelming desire to see other parties established, even by non-communists. This was still less the case of members of the existing non-communist parties, who no doubt anticipated that new parties would be undesirable competitors. Other polls indicated that new parties were rated low as an assurance of democratic and free elections.[81]

The July polls tested voting preferences in the event of an election in which a "new political party" would take part.[82] The results are given in Table XVII.11.

TABLE XVII.11

VOTING IN ELECTIONS THIS MONTH*
(in percentages)

Respondents would vote for:	All	Communists	Non-communists
Communist Party	39	85	24
Socialist Party	9	1	11
People's Party	8	2	10
New political party	11	3	14
Don't know, no answer, or blank ballot	32	10	39
	99	101	98

* Question: To whom would you give your vote if there was an election this month, based on the independent candidacy of all political parties?

Source: See n. 82.

[80] Ibid., p. 229.　　　　　　　　　　　[81] See above, chap. XII, p. 365.

[82] July 8-16, Polling, p. 249. These polls indicated that CPCz strength was roughly comparable to its strength in a poll conducted in 1946 (35.8 percent) and in the actual elections of that year (40.2 percent). The 1968 polls showed that, since 1946, there had been a sharp drop (approximately 50 percent) in the support for the People's and Socialist Parties. In 1946, the other main party, the Social Democratic Party, had secured approximately one-fourth of the votes, both in the poll and in the actual elections (Č. Adamec, Sociologický časopis, no. 3, 1966, pp. 393-94).

When these data are compared with the voting preferences of the poll cited above (p. 546), it appears that the formation of a new party (even though its identity was not known), would have led to a decline in support for the Communist Party, even among party members. It would also have resulted in a decline in support for the existing non-communist parties, more serious for the Socialist than for the People's Party. The percentage who expressed no definite preference would have remained about the same—approximately one-third of the respondents. The unknown new party would have gained a modest degree of support —11 percent of all respondents (14 percent among non-communists, 3 percent among party members). These hypothetical results were hardly evidence of a strong showing by the Communist Party, or by the other parties, and demonstrated again the diversity of political preferences and the uncertainty of the outcome of a future election. Moreover, in the absence of any definition of the nature of a new party and of data for Slovakia, the polls provided no reliable forecast of eventual election results.

THE NATIONAL FRONT IN PUBLIC OPINION

A wide variation of opinion was also evident concerning the composition of the National Front and the role it should play. In the July polls there was more or less agreement among communists and non-communists that it should be an association of political parties and large societal organizations (42 and 36 percent, respectively), rather than a coalition of political parties alone (9 and 17 percent, respectively). There was a greater divergence as to whether a political party or societal organization should be permitted to exist outside the front: 39 percent of party members, 20 percent of non-communists, and 24 percent of the general public, favored such a restriction on political activity.

The functions of the National Front were described by both party members and non-communists in rather vague and general terms as being either to unify the working people of all classes and nationalities (45 percent in each case), or to serve as a base for political union of different orientations in a democratic association (34 and 33 percent, respectively). Significantly, however, few of either group (15 percent of CPCz members, and 5 percent of non-communists) believed it should direct, under CPCz leadership, other organizations and associations. Even fewer (3 percent of party members and 6 percent of non-members) believed that it should independently direct the work of free or voluntary organizations.[83]

[83] July 8-16, *Polling*, pp. 202, 204 (Czech lands only).

When asked about the mutual relations of NF members, most respondents advocated equal rights, with no party or organization playing a leading role. Even among party members only a little more than a third of the respondents assigned the leading role to the CPCz as shown in Table XVII.12.[84]

TABLE XVII.12

NATIONAL FRONT—MUTUAL TIES*
(in percentages)

Respondents	All	CPCz members	Non-members
The CPCz the leading force in NF	19	38	13
Another party may assume leading role in NF	16	8	19
All with equal rights; no one plays leading role in NF	64	53	67
Don't know	1	1	1
	100	100	100

* Question: Under the assumption that the National Front is formed by different voluntary organizations and political parties, what should be the principle of their mutual ties?

Source: See n. 84.

The polls revealed differences of opinion on whether National Front resolutions accepted by a majority vote should be binding on NF members or on other organizations. Thus 50 percent of the CPCz members and 39 percent of non-communists believed that resolutions should be binding on all NF members; 24 percent of CPCz members and 23 percent of non-communists thought that resolutions should also be binding on all organizations, even if not members of the NF. Others felt that no votes should be taken, and that resolutions should not be binding but should be accepted by organizations on their own volition (14 and 19 percent, respectively) or that resolutions should be binding only on those organizations whose representatives voted for them (11 and 17 percent, respectively).[85]

Polls in August gave evidence of the diverse opinion on the nature of the National Front and the degree of openness of the political system (see Table XVII.13). A majority of the public and of most specific cate-

[84] July 8-16, ibid., p. 214.　　　　　[85] Ibid., p. 206.

TABLE XVII.13

THE NATIONAL FRONT*
(in percentages)

Respondents	All	CPCz	Non-members	ČSS	ČSL
Yes	42 ⎫	49 ⎫	39 ⎫	40 ⎫	33 ⎫
	⎬ 62	⎬ 72	⎬ 58	⎬ 55	⎬ 48
More yes than no	20 ⎭	23 ⎭	19 ⎭	15 ⎭	15 ⎭
More no than yes	12 ⎫	10 ⎫	13 ⎫	14 ⎫	14 ⎫
	⎬ 26	⎬ 22	⎬ 28	⎬ 40	⎬ 46
No	14 ⎭	12 ⎭	15 ⎭	26 ⎭	32 ⎭
Don't know	12	6	14	5	6
	100	100	100	100	100

* Question: Do you think the National Front should continue in the same form as it is today?

Source: See n. 86.

gories expressed the view that the NF should continue in the same form, but there was a spread of opinion within each category, and greater doubt among the members of the two non-communist parties.[86]

Other polls in August probed into opinions concerning the specific composition of the National Front: whether it should be made up of political parties only, or of parties plus the most significant societal organizations, or of all parties, organizations, and movements. The results were diverse, somewhat ambiguous and difficult to interpret. It revealed a decided negative attitude to a NF made up of parties only, not only among party members but also among non-members (in each case reaching 75 percent). The opposition to this was less strong among members of the People's and Socialist Parties (33 and 41 percent, respectively). Apparently the latter parties perceived in such a front the advantage that they would confront the CPCz almost alone, without the danger of the communists receiving support from other organizations. There was considerable support for a National Front made up of parties and major organizations (a concept close to the standpoint of the CPCz), but this was not a majority among CPCz members (48 percent) and still less among non-members (34 percent); ČSS and ČSL, 40 and 39 percent, respectively. Much more enthusiasm was shown for a front including all political parties, organizations, and movements—a conception which might be interpreted as meaning a front open to all organizations desiring membership (57 percent CPCz members; 63 percent non-members). This was not, however, shared by the two non-communist parties who

[86] Aug. 4-15, ibid., p. 200 (Czech lands only).

perhaps feared competition to themselves from unknown parties or groups (69 and 74 percent, respectively, opposed). Significantly, no group of respondents (not even the non-communists) registered a strong majority supporting the idea that parties and organizations should be allowed to exist outside the NF, thus suggesting a common desire to restrict the political process and, in the case of the non-communist parties, to preserve their own privileged NF position (see Table XVII.14).[87]

TABLE XVII.14

COMPOSITION OF THE NATIONAL FRONT
(in percentages)

	All		CPCz		Non-communists		ČSS		ČSL	
Respondents	Yes	No	Yes	No	Yes	No	Yes	No	Yes	No
All political parties, voluntary organizations & movements	61	32	57	38	63	30	27	69	23	74
Political parties and only the most significant voluntary organizations	37	53	48	47	34	55	40	54	39	56
Political parties only	17	74	20	73	15	75	54	41	62	33
Should parties, organizations & movements exist outside the NF?	31	56	20	73	35	50	46	47	54	39

Source: See n. 87.

In the August poll a series of questions on admission to the National Front produced the usual checkered results but threw more light on the distribution of opinion concerning how "open" this gateway to political activity should be, as shown in Table XVII.15. The poll demonstrated that most categories overwhelmingly preferred that only organizations with socialist programs should become NF members. More controversial was the question of the recognition of the leading role of the Communist Party, on which a slight majority of CPCz members insisted but to which non-members, and the general public, were strongly opposed. The proposition that any organization could request membership in the front and that no conditions had to be fulfilled received little support. The ČSS and the ČSL members held distinctive views. Both groups decisively rejected the condition of the leading role of the Communist Party. Both were,

[87] Aug. 4-15, ibid., pp. 203, 209-11 (Czech lands only).

TABLE XVII.15

MEMBERSHIP IN THE NATIONAL FRONT
(in percentages)

Respondents	All		CPCz		Non-party		ČSS		ČSL	
	Yes	No	Yes	No	Yes	No	Yes	No	Yes	No
No limiting conditions	20	70	13	81	23	66	16	78	17	77
Only organizations with socialist program	74	19	84	13	71	21	63	33	47	48
Only organizations whose programs are not contrary to UN Declaration of Human Rights	76	11	75	14	77	10	90	6	90	5
Only organizations whose programs are in accord with the ČSSR constitution	81	12	84	11	80	12	81	14	80	14
Recognition of the leading role of the CPCz	32	59	52	44	26	64	7	90	10	86

Source: See n. 88.

however, opposed to membership in the NF without any limiting requirements. On the question of a socialist program, they were more divided, within and between themselves, with the ČSS members supporting this requirement and the ČSL evenly split.[88]

CONCLUSION

As of August 1968, the Communist Party still held the dominant place in the political system and exercised the leading role in the reform movement. No other organized political force confronted the CPCz as a serious rival. The National Front was a more or less closed organization, restricting political action to its members and guarding entry into its ranks with caution. The non-communist parties were weak in membership and in public support and had in fact lost ground since 1945-1948. New political organizations had so far attained no substantial strength and had not been permitted to assume leading roles on the political stage. Although the non-communist parties and organizations desired greater independence, they were willing to act as partners of the CPCz within the National Front and did not seek to form opposition movements. Their

[88] Aug. 4-15, ibid., pp. 219-24. Cf. other polls in July and August on the same subject, ibid., pp. 215, 217-18.

members, and public opinion in general, showed no strong desire for a completely open political system and seemed relatively satisfied with the present system of political parties and the National Front. In Slovakia the party's position was preeminent, the non-communist parties having no substance and the other embryonic organizations no branches. The Catholic Church was a factor of some magnitude, likely to affect the thinking of Slovaks, but it was not an organized political force and its political influence was difficult to measure.[89]

The party had the further advantage of strong public support in its pursuit of reform—a fact which strengthened the hands of the leadership but at the same time subjected it to the influence of public opinion and set certain ill-defined limits on its freedom of action. Although public opinion was sharply divided on most issues, and a significant minority was undecided and uncertain, a substantial majority supported the reforms and there was a high degree of consensus between progressive communists and non-communists. Opinion was almost unanimous throughout the Republic on the desirability of Czechoslovakia pursuing her own course without interference from outside. In spite of continuing distrust in politics and politicians, and substantial residues of doubts concerning the party and its leadership, there was widespread backing of the party and its leaders, increasing as time passed.

Slovak opinion, as mirrored in the polls, placed greater emphasis on the national question and the attainment of federation, but otherwise displayed no marked diversity as to the relative priority of desired changes and differed only in degree in support of reform. For instance in a poll in mid-July, concerning the law abolishing censorship, in Slovakia 74 percent of the respondents approved, 8 percent disapproved, and 18 percent had or gave no opinion, whereas in the Czech lands the proportions were 91, 3, and 6 percent, respectively.[90] When asked as to whether they desired to broaden individual freedom, 86.2 percent agreed; 8.6 percent agreed, but doubted it was possible; 1.5 percent had reservations; 3.7 percent did not respond; and 0.0 percent did not agree.[91] Slovaks showed confidence in the CPCz leadership, although tending to rank certain Slovaks, notably Lenárt, but also Husák and Bil'ak, higher than did the Czechs, and to prefer more conservative Czech leaders. As a relatively small minority of the total population and of the party membership, the Slovaks could not, of course, exercise a de-

[89] The CC report referred to the Church as representing in Slovakia "a potential political counterweight," taking the place of political parties (*Zpráva*, p. 24). An opinion poll in the fall of 1968 indicated that 70 percent of the Slovak population were believers, only 14 percent atheists, and 15 percent undetermined (*Sociologia*, no. 1, 1970).

[90] July 13-14 (n. 46 above), *Polling*, p. 84.

[91] July 12-18 (n. 37 above), ibid., p. 82.

cisive influence on the course of events. Their strongly nationalist and somewhat more conservative attitudes, however, constituted a problem with which the leadership, both in Prague and Bratislava, would have to reckon, but did not represent a fundamental cleavage threatening the cause of reform. There was uncertainty, however, as to how the balance would shift, within the party, and among Slovaks in general, between their wishes for federation and for democratization.

A crucial factor was the division within the party itself on the issues of reform, with some of the leaders, as well as substantial sections of the *aparát* and of the functionaries, lukewarm or opposed. A large majority of party members, and a substantial part of the functionaries, however, were favorable to significant change, at least in the form and degree espoused by the post-January leaders. The position of the conservatives was likely to be seriously weakened by the 14th congress, since the delegates, although sharply divided in their views, on the whole supported moderate reform and would have elected leaders likely to pursue that objective more vigorously.

The Slovak Communist Party was a distinctive element in the political scene, displaying strongly nationalist views and somewhat less progressive attitudes. Yet in general its leaders, functionaries, rank-and-file members, and congress delegates, according to polls, supported reform. Its own special congress in August was likely to bring about changes in leadership and to tip the balance both toward a greater accent on national demands and federation, and toward more vigorous measures of democratization. In what degree and in what proportion this would occur was uncertain because of the ambiguity of Husák's stance.

Yet the political situation contained many elements of uncertainty and was likely to be highly dynamic following the 14th congress, in the period leading up to the elections in the spring of 1969. The CC report of August, from a distinctly conservative point of view, described the situation as not "consolidated" and containing sources of conflict and tension.[92] The more progressive 14th congress materials referred to "disintegrating tendencies" on both right and left, and concluded that it was impossible to foresee which social groups would eventually emerge as "permanent [political] forces."[93] The elections would, needless to say, be decisive in establishing a new equilibrium, but as both the CC report and the 14th congress materials admitted, their outcome was fraught with uncertainty.[94] Polls of electoral preferences showed great indecision

---

[92] *Zpráva*, p. 59; see also chap. XI, pp. 327-29.
[93] Pelikán, ed., *Vysočany Congress*, p. 226.
[94] *Zpráva*, pp. 54-55; Pelikán, ed., *Vysočany Congress*, p. 231; also chap. XII, pp. 371 ff. A post-occupation analysis foresaw the victory of an "anti-communist coalition" including a CPCz under rightist leadership after the 14th congress, a Social Democratic Party, the Socialist and People's Parties, KAN, and some kind of Agrarian Party (Z. Dolejší, *ŽS*, no. 1, 1972, pp. 41-43).

on the part of at least one-third of the respondents, unaccustomed to making a free choice after twenty years of controlled elections. If these polls were in any way indicative of the actual results, however, the CPCz would emerge as the strongest party, but without a plurality, and would have to seek the support of other parties and organizations in a coalition government.

All organized political forces, without exception, professed a faith in socialism and a desire to retain this as the basic framework of life. Openly anti-socialist views were occasionally expressed, but organized forces espousing them could hardly be said to exist. Even the CC report concluded that those desiring a return to capitalism were minimal in number—some 400,000—no more than 5 percent of the voting population, and were not likely to engage in a struggle for this objective.[95] Active citizens, whether communist or non-communist, were, however, divided as to the optimal model of socialism. The conservative wing of the Communist Party adhered to an old-fashioned conception of the term, not basically different to the Novotný system, but were overwhelmingly outnumbered by advocates of change. The progressive majority of the party wanted to combine democracy with socialism and, with most non-communists, formed a kind of unofficial progressive bloc—an alliance of the committed—supporting a greatly reformed socialism.[96] Future controversy would center on the exact nature and extent of the reforms necessary, not on the existence of socialism as such.

[95] *Zpráva*, p. 34. The report expressed the belief that these individuals would provide support for an "eventual" group striving publicly for this objective. See above, chap. XI.

[96] J. Štern, *Práce*, Aug. 18.

CHAPTER XVIII

Social Groups and Organizations

CZECHOSLOVAK society, wrote the sociologist, Pavel Machonin, in 1969, had become a society "richly differentiated and clearly stratified and consequently differentiated also in interests and opinions." Before January, however, this "definite, objectively given interest orientation . . . could not be fully manifested in a clash of opinions or in political activity, thus creating a latent tension taking on the character of a crisis." This situation created "a powerful coalition of social forces" interested in the change of the existing "bureaucratic-egalitarian order" and produced, in January, "a radical political outburst of the social and cultural crisis." With the collapse of the old system, he wrote, the "real society" revealed itself. "The most varied macro-groupings of people, through meetings and through the medium of their organizations and spokesmen, strove to realize their interests and to achieve the correction of the wrongs (mostly real, although in some cases imaginary) committed by the pre-January regime against the Slovaks, and other national minorities, the youth, pensioners, women, workers, agriculturalists, the intelligentsia, employees of the health services, transportation, and consumer goods industry."[1]

This chapter will be devoted to a discussion of this explosion of group activity. We shall examine in turn certain social groupings distinguished by occupation—the intellectuals (writers, journalists, and scholars); the workers and the farmers; a number of other interest groups; and certain social categories based on age, religion, and nationality. These will not be analyzed as social groups in a system of social stratification, a task already accomplished by others.[2] Attention will be focused on the political actions taken by members of these groups and on the organizations created for the defense of their interests and the expression of their opinions. The analysis will attempt to identify the main groups involved in the struggle for reform, to estimate their relative weight and that of the diverse opinion groups within each, and to describe the process of institutionalization of group interests which occurred.[3]

---

[1] P. Machonin, *Politika*, March 13, 1969.

[2] Machonin, ed., *Československá společnost* (Bratislava, 1969); J. Krejčí, *Social Change and Stratification in Postwar Czechoslovakia* (London, 1972).

[3] For a more detailed study, V. V. Kusin, *Political Grouping in the Czechoslovak Reform Movement* (London, 1972). For a systematic analysis of the attitudes of social groups toward economic reform, see A. Korbonski, "Bureaucracy and Interest Groups in Communist Societies: The Case of Czechoslovakia," *Studies in Com-*

The Intellectuals

The intellectuals—in the sphere of creative culture as well as in science and scholarship—had played an important part in undermining the structure of Stalinism and preparing the ground for the overthrow of Novotný. After January articles at once began to appear in the press, condemning the previous hostility and suspicion toward the intelligentsia, deploring party interference in cultural and scientific work, and calling for cooperation between workers and intellectuals. It was contended that the general principles proclaimed by the 13th congress of the CPCz in 1966 with reference to culture and science had not been implemented. Intellectuals must be assured full freedom of creative and scientific work, self-administration of their own fields of activity, and participation in the formulation of public policy.[4] More orthodox spokesmen, seeking to maintain the doctrine of the leading role of the working class, described the intellectuals, especially scientific research workers and engineering-technical specialists, as the progressive core of the working class.[5] Others, more daringly, argued that the main criteria of social stratification were no longer class distinctions and concluded that certain social groups, consisting of those with education and technical competence, should be regarded as "a social avant-garde."[6]

Dubček, in late February, set the tone for a new attitude toward the intelligentsia when he deplored "the conflict situations which had characterized the relations between party organs and the creative artists and scientists" and declared that policy must be based on "confidence and fruitful comradely cooperation" vis-à-vis scientists, writers, film producers, artists, and other cultural and scientific workers.[7] The Action Program took a similar line, promising just remuneration for intellectual work and a proper recognition of education and ability in cadre policy. In sections devoted to culture and science the program rejected administrative methods of implementing cultural policy and declared that "artistic creation must not be subjected to censorship." Cultural workers must

---

parative Communism 4 (Jan. 1971), 57-79. For brief comments on conflicting group attitudes, see Z. Hejzlar and I. Bystrina, in V. V. Kusin, ed., *The Czechoslovak Reform Movement 1968* (London, 1973), pp. 124-26, 149-56; J. Pelikán, ed., *The Secret Vysočany Congress* (London, 1971), pp. 198-202. See also Šik's view cited below, n. 172.

4 For instance, M. Vacík, *Rudé právo*, Jan. 14; J. Klofáč, ibid., Jan. 17; M. Fiala, ibid., Feb. 4; editorial, ibid., March 2; J. Hermach, *Pravda*, Feb. 2; S. Falt'an, ibid., March 17; symposia, *RP*, March 17-18 and *Kultúrny život*, March 22; E. Goldstücker, *Nová mysl*, no. 4 (1968), pp. 461-65. Even J. Hendrych expressed himself in similar terms (*RP*, Feb. 17).

5 Z. Valenta, *NM*, no. 2 (1968), pp. 198-210.

6 Machonin, *RP*, March 7. Cf. his article in *NM*, no. 4 (1968), pp. 466-74.

7 Feb. 22, Dubček, *K otázkam obrodzovaciého procesu v KSČ* (Bratislava, 1968), pp. 49-50.

enjoy self-administration and become "indispensable partners" of the state organs. Intellectuals, communists and others, were capable of "responsibly and independently sharing in the creation of party policy and in implementing it in state, societal, cultural, and interest institutions. . . ." Similarly, science would be given an "autonomous position" and not be subordinated to outside interference or to any censorship. In particular the party must not intervene in the "creative scientific process" of the social sciences which must be assured "free development—similar to the natural sciences." Science as a whole must be guaranteed participation in the elaboration of political and economic decisions at all levels of society.[8]

How these principles would be implemented was not immediately clear. There were some, such as A. J. Liehm, who, at a conference of film and television artists in early April, raised the heretical idea that "no one should manage art and culture." This would assure "the human spirit" "a completely new, independent, and socially significant role" and presupposed "a constant struggle of culture and political power and technocracy."[9] The party made clear, however, that while it recognized freedom of artistic creation, it did not intend to abandon what it called its "inspiring role" and that party and state would continue to exercise some degree of direction in the cultural sphere.[10] The workers on the cultural front would be regarded as "partners," said the new Minister of Education, M. Galuška, who promised to replace the semiofficial commission for culture and information by regular contacts between the ministry and the creative unions.[11] The idea of a new cultural commission attached to the Central Committee was also broached.[12] These forms of participation at the center would be supplemented by what was called "self-adminis-

[8] For the corrected version of the section of the Action Program devoted to science, see *RP*, April 12 (*Pravda*, April 13). (See above, chap. IX, n. 67.) The Slovak Action Program (*Pravda*, May 29) spoke in somewhat similar terms of "incorporating" science and culture in the party's policy-making, and of increasing contact and consultation between the party organs and science. It also emphasized "freedom of artistic creation" and the task of communist artists within the creative unions in "formulating and assuring the policy of the party in a given artistic sphere."

The 14th congress materials endorsed the basic principles of "complete freedom of artistic creation" and "free and autonomous science and scholarly research." It described science as "an equal partner and . . . a significant co-creator of policy" and spoke of "cultural autonomy and self-administration, in the sense of a pluralism of ideas, nationalities and regions," with "specialists," who enjoyed public confidence, "administering and directing culture" (Pelikán, ed., *Vysočany Congress*, pp. 213-14, 244-47).

[9] *RP*, April 2.

[10] For instance, the Action Program. Cf. editorial, *RP*, March 2; Č. Císař, ibid., May 4; S. Vítek, ibid., May 26.

[11] *RP*, June 9. Cf. M. Brůžek, *Reportér*, Jan. 10-17, 1968.

[12] At a meeting of communist cultural and artistic workers and CC members of the creative unions (*RP*, June 7).

tration" in each cultural field, thus assuring, in Císař's words, a synthesis of "party aims and the needs of culture and art."[13]

Such official statements were pale reflections of the enhanced role that the intelligentsia, or at least a part of it, were already claiming. Direct political participation in the organs of policy-making was somewhat limited, although a number of outstanding intellectuals held high office, for instance, Šik, Colotka, and Kadlec in the government, and Mlynář, in the party Secretariat. Intellectuals were not numerous in the Central Committee and the National Assembly, but a few individuals such as Šik, Mlynář, Šorm, Starý, Macek, Kladiva, and O. Wichterle, raised their voices in these bodies in support of vigorous reform. Many other intellectuals exerted influence on policy-making as specialist advisers and consultants to party and government bodies or as molders of public opinion.

It would be untrue to say that all of the one million to one million and a half who might be considered intellectuals[14] took part actively in the reform movement or that they formed an organized cohesive force. Many thousands, were, however, involved, and these enjoyed widespread support in their individual fields and within the intellectual community as a whole. There was, to be sure, substantial difference in the degree of participation by the various sectors of the intelligentsia and in their social and political impact. As individuals they also varied in their opinions, with some holding radical, others moderate, and some conservative views. Nor did the intellectuals act through a single organization, although they gave each other mutual support and encouragement.

A special role was taken by the "creative unions" which grouped together, in separate organizations, the various sectors of the intelligentsia —architects, theatrical artists, film and television artists, journalists, composers, writers, and fine artists, and eventually also scholars and scientists, who formed an association of their own on the same model.[15] Most of the unions had originally been established as a means of controlling administratively all major fields of artistic endeavor and had functioned as transmission belts of the party. Some now suggested that the unions be abolished entirely, or at least divided, preserving in each case an organization for the defense of the economic and social needs of the members, but establishing less formal artistic associations for cultural

[13] Císař, *RP*, March 28; Vítek, ibid., April 23; Ministry of Culture and Information statement, ibid., July 14.
[14] Valenta, *NM*, no. 2 (1968), pp. 206-7; Kusin, *Political Grouping*, pp. 55-56; Krejčí, *Social Change*, p. 161.
[15] Kusin, *Political Grouping*, p. 75, where the membership of each union is given. Later a union of circus and stage performers was formed (*RP*, May 31). For the creative unions in general, see L. Pacovský, *Rep.*, Aug. 14-21.

purposes.[16] In any case, the unions must vindicate their independence vis-à-vis the party and state and carry through their own internal democratization so that they could function effectively as interest organizations, defending their members' economic, social, and cultural interests.[17]

The need for coordination of action was soon recognized, and led to the formation of the Coordinating Committee of the Creative Unions at the beginning of May. Although this was to be a loose association, exercising no authority over the member organizations, it provided a valuable framework for joint action, in particular through the issuance of declarations on such matters as the campaign against the mass media, the Two Thousand Words, the Warsaw letter, and the Čierna and Bratislava conferences. It was eventually agreed that each of the creative unions would have one representative in the central committee of the National Front and would have the right to nominate candidates for the National Assembly. The Coordinating Committee was granted a single representative in the NF presidium, Miroslav Holub, a non-communist who was a scholar in the field of medicine and a poet, and a member of both the Writers' Union and the preparatory committee of the Union of Scientific Workers. This representation was hardly more than symbolic since the National Front had little role in policy-making and the intellectuals could exert a far greater influence through direct impact on public opinion and pressures on the political leadership. Non-communist intellectuals sought to vindicate their claim to equal participation in the affairs of the unions and in public life by setting up "independent circles" within each union and by establishing a coordinating committee of their own.[18]

The creative unions soon indicated their desire to act as pressure groups on matters of special concern as well as those of broader political import. In a letter addressed to the CPCz Presidium in March, the Union of Writers and the Union of Film and Television Artists set forth their proposals for assuring "the free creative work of artists" and a cultural policy "free of all deformations" and gave their ideas concerning the party's policy in general. The Presidium expressed agreement with these proposals and promised further discussion in greater detail.[19] In meetings of their top organs, and at occasional conferences, the unions pressed for freedom of creative activity, including the abolition of cen-

[16] See *aktiv* of Prague artists (*RP*, April 2) and other comments regarding the Union of Fine Artists (ibid., March 8, April 7); L. Novák, *Vytvárná práce*, March 2.

[17] Joint declaration of the theatrical workers, architects, and fine artists (*RP*, March 13, 23).

[18] *RP*, June 8; *Literární listy*, June 13. It was suggested that "an association of independent culture," for politically non-organized artists and cultural workers, be formed.

[19] *Rok šedesátý osmý* (Prague, 1969), p. 46.

sorship and the relaxation of party and administrative controls; for the rehabilitation of former members unjustly persecuted in the past; and for the defense of human rights, including the right to travel; and also spoke out on more general political questions, such as the election of a successor to Novotný.[20] Their organs, especially those of the writers' union (*Literární listy*) and of the journalists' union (*Reportér*) became forums for intellectuals in all fields and helped to create a common intellectual front in favor of reform, and through their wide readership, to influence public opinion in this direction.

THE WRITERS

The Union of Writers, having served as a spearhead of opposition throughout the sixties, at once emerged as a focal point of reform strivings. In late January Professor Eduard Goldstücker, well known for his work in rehabilitating the works of Franz Kafka, was appointed to the post of chairman (vacant since 1967).[21] The union's immediate goal was described as the "normalization" of the relations between the writers and the party, through the correction of the "errors" of 1967 (the exclusion of Ludvík Vaculík and others from the party; the confiscation of the union's weekly; the cancellation of Mňačko's citizenship; and the jailing of Jan Beneš). The union recognized that one of its first tasks was to put its own affairs in order. Changes in the structure and purposes of the union would have to await its next congress in the autumn. In the meantime, the idea of federalization was accepted, and Czech and Slovak sections began to meet separately. The head of the union's publishing house, J. Pilař, was subjected to severe criticism and was superseded by his own predecessor, L. Fikar, who had been removed in 1959. Jiří Hájek, whose record during the sixties was sharply attacked, was replaced as editor-in-chief of the union's monthly, *Plamen*. Membership was restored to Professor Václav Černý, distinguished scholar in the field of Romance literature, who had been ousted from Charles University in 1948. The task of rehabilitating writers persecuted in the past was assigned to a commission headed by the distinguished poet, Jaroslav Seifert.[22]

A general report on Czech literature from 1948 to 1968, which would have fully revealed the effects of purges, censorship, and party controls,

[20] *RP*, April 2 (*aktiv* of Prague artists). See especially the conference of the film and television workers (*RP*, March 30-31; *Filmové a televizní noviny*, April 4).
[21] M. Válek and J. Procházka became vice-chairmen. The only change in the union's central committee was the resignation of J. Hanzlík, one of those elected in 1967 under pressure from the party (*LL*, June 6). See his letter, ibid., May 30.
[22] *RP*, May 29, 30; *LL*, June 6. Pilař's record as head of the union's publishing house was severely censured by the Circle of Independent Writers (*LL*, May 16). For Pilař's defense, see *LL*, May 23. Cf. M. Petříček, ibid., May 30.

568

was to be completed in time for the union's congress. Meanwhile there was sharp criticism of the organization and of individual writers, especially for their actions in the fifties, and demands for the rehabilitation of outstanding communist writers, such as Karel Teige, whose works had been banned, and Záviš Kalandra, who had been executed in 1950, as well as prominent non-communist writers. Feelings ran high on these matters and were countered by appeals for objectivity by Goldstücker and others.[23] One of the most powerful indictments of the political function of literature during the fifties, including support given the trials by individual writers, was penned by the esthetic theoretician, J. Chalupecký, who declared that post-1948 literature—an irrevocable part of Czech literary history—had resulted in "a sacrifice of moral, intellectual, and emotional integrity" and had produced "a political non-art and an anti-artistic policy."[24]

The writers claimed a broader political role. Art without politics, declared Goldstücker, quoting Berthold Brecht, was unthinkable. Literature, said the Slovak vice-chairman, M. Válek, must express its opinions on politics and become "a significant corrective of political thinking and action."[25] K. Chvatík, an esthetics scholar, in a cogent statement, called for a new meaning of the "political character" (*politićnost*) of art and literature as "the spokesman of the political opinions, needs, and yearnings of free citizens, endowed with full rights." Until political life was consolidated, he wrote, "the amateur and spontaneous activity of intellectuals in politics" was necessary. The writers must resume the active role played in the past, not only in 1967, or in 1956, but also in the prewar days. They must strive for "full freedom in thinking, work, and artistic and scientific expression" and in so doing, would become "a liberating force" for all citizens. Literature, as "the voice of the whole society," would remain "the conscience of the nation."[26] In pursuit of these wider objectives, the union established in late March a Club of Critical Thought, headed by M. Holub, K. Kosík, and M. Kundera, to facilitate the discussion of cultural and political affairs.[27]

It was in the columns of its weekly newspaper that the union had its greatest political impact. After some initial difficulties the union launched *Literární listy* with the issue of March 1. Since the title of the union's

[23] Union of Writers meetings, *LL*, April 4, 25, June 6; A. Kliment, ibid., April 11.
[24] "Literature and Freedom," *LL*, May 30, June 6.
[25] *RP*, Feb. 1, April 7, resp.
[26] "Literature and the Crisis of our Society," *LL*, May 16. Similarly, J. Chalupecký (*LL*, May 30, June 6), made a strong appeal for complete freedom for all artists and for society as a whole and defended literature and art as "a social and historic force." Cf. also articles by Ernst Fischer, describing literature as "the conscience of the nation" (*LL*, March 1) and by György Lukács, opposing party regulation of literature (*Kulturní noviny*, March 22).
[27] *LL*, March 21; *RP*, March 30.

569

original journal, *Literární noviny*, was still being used by its official "successor," a new name had perforce to be adopted, but its first issue indicated that it would continue the tradition of its predecessor. The editor-in-chief, Dušan Hamšík, described it as "a tribune for the entire writers' community" and declared that it would not confine itself to purely literary matters, since the freedom of writers was linked with the freedom of the whole society.[28] From the outset, its pages were filled with bold and critical comment on public affairs by scholars, writers, and persons from other walks of life. The size of its circulation, which reached 300,000, was evidence of its appeal to broad circles of the general public. The publication in its columns of declarations such as the Two Thousand Words, and the message to the central leadership before Čierna, were major political events which significantly affected public opinion and exerted substantial pressure on the leadership.

A special problem was that of the non-communist writers who had, as one of them said, not been able to publish at all in the fifties and even later were treated as " 'outsiders,' tolerated, suffered, allowed, lacking in full rights—potentially suspect and potentially unreliable. . . ." At the initiative of the playwright, Václav Havel, and the novelist, Alexander Kliment, a Circle of Independent Writers was established, with the support of some sixty non-communist writers and with Havel as chairman. This informal grouping was intended to assure non-communist writers equality of participation within the union and thus to counter the privileged position of the communists who had been able, in their prior party meetings, to prejudge the decisions of the union's general meetings. In their initial declaration the non-communists expressed the wish to make their own contribution, as equal partners, to the achievement of full democracy and to seek dialogue and cooperation with the communists. The statement contained a strong plea for the "independence of culture" from political controls of all kinds, and a demand for "equal opportunities for all opinions, philosophies and esthetic views," and equal participation by all, including non-communists, in the direction of cultural institutions. It urged the complete transformation of the Union of Writers to make it an "independent interest organization" and "a really democratic organization offering the same rights to all its members."[29]

[28] *LL*, March 1 (also in *KŽ*, Feb. 23). *Literární noviny* continued to appear, but changed its name to *Kulturní noviny*, and ceased publication in late April. Its editors defended their role both in 1967 and in 1968 (*Literární noviny*, Jan. 27; *KN*, April 26). It was decided to issue also a daily paper concentrating on news reporting, to be edited by A. J. Liehm and to appear under the name, *Lidové noviny*, the title of a well-known weekly during the First Republic and the early post-war years.

[29] *LL*, April 4, June 13; Kliment, *Lidová demokracie*, April 12; *LL*, July 4 for the full text of the declaration.

THE JOURNALISTS

Within weeks of the fall of Novotný the journalists emerged as active exponents of reform and as a powerful force without which the Prague spring can hardly be imagined. Almost all newspapers, both Czech and Slovak, experienced a "renaissance" and the press soon became, as a Slovak commentator described it, "a seventh great power." A Czech journalist termed the press "a standing parliament," offering the public a form of "direct democracy" and a means of influencing the course of events.[30] Enjoying an extraordinary degree of freedom from March on, the mass media provided a channel for the expression of public opinion as it gradually crystallized from day to day, and at the same time served as a catalyst and mobilizer of opinion, drawing the general public into the reform movement. Although the mass media were overwhelmingly on the side of reform, they offered a forum for a wide array of views, including the more conservative.[31]

The mass media served not only as the ally of the leadership but as its constant critic and opponent, thus creating a relationship of permanent tension. The revival of the media was welcomed by the party leaders as a source of public support for reform. Yet, faced with the problem of governing the country and placating their allies abroad, they often found the press a disturbing factor and called upon the journalists for self-control and responsibility. At the congress of journalists in late June Dubček praised the work of the press which had made possible "the participation of the public in political happenings" and thereby "the renaissance of political life," but spoke at some length about "one-sided tendencies," which negated the past and the party's achievements, and reminded the press that its function was not only to express, but also to influence, the opinion of citizens.[32] Later, in his reply to the Warsaw letter, Dubček evaluated the role of the media more positively and praised the responsibility shown by journalists. Admitting that certain articles had caused misunderstanding in allied countries, he rejected "intervention by force against freedom of the press and of expression" and referred to meetings held with journalists to seek a "common language."[33]

[30] Editorial, *Pravda*, June 25; J. Štern, *Práce*, Aug. 18.

[31] For discussion of the relationship of the mass media, public opinion and the leadership, see papers given at the Reading conference in 1969 by Dušan Havlíček and K. Jezdinský (Kusin, ed., *Czechoslovak Reform*, pp. 237-89). Havlíček's paper was published anonymously in *Svědectví* 11, no. 42 (1971), 193-211. Cf. William Shawcross' severe criticism of the journalists for their "uninhibited comment" on their own leaders and on the Soviet system as a factor contributing to the Soviet intervention (Kusin, pp. 280-89).

[32] *Novinář*, nos. 7-8 (1968), pp. 248-51. An interesting sidelight of Dubček's address was an extemporaneous defense of Švestka against charges concerning his actions in the sixties.

[33] *RŠO*, pp. 254-55.

The journalists defended the press against wholesale attacks, especially those by conservative critics, but conceded as necessary a certain degree of self-censorship. They were not willing to abandon what they regarded as the most precious achievement of January and the most effective guarantee of reform—freedom of expression. During and after the Čierna and Bratislava conferences, as we have noted, the mass media expressed their concern over lack of information and their fear of impending press controls and reiterated both the need for a guaranteed press freedom and their willingness to accept responsibility for its exercise. Public opinion polls indicated that the majority of the population had gained a new confidence in the media and were satisfied with the degree of freedom of expression achieved.[34]

The professional organization of journalists—the Union of Journalists—offered immediate support for the new regime, but was slow to condemn its own pre-January subservience to the Novotný regime. Criticism of this record and of the failure of the union's presidium to repudiate it was voiced, from early March, by various *aktivs* of journalists, by some of the union's commissions, by editors of *Rudé právo*, by regional journalist organizations, and by the Slovak CC of the organization. These commentaries usually urged the revocation of the decisions of the union's fifth congress, especially those relating to the writers' congress and *Literární noviny*, and changes in the union's leadership, and sometimes called for an extraordinary congress. These were coupled with demands for greater freedom of information and for changes in censorship practice.[35] Although the union's presidium indicated its willingness to engage in discussions with the writers and to revise the 1967 congress decisions, the Union of Writers was unwilling to meet until the Journalists' Union had changed its leadership and its attitude.[36]

Bowing to the pressure of its critics, the central committee of the Union of Journalists accepted the need to revise its 1967 attitude and removed A. Hradecký as general secretary, leaving the post vacant.[37] Soon afterwards a conference of Prague journalists formed an organization of their own, which called for a revocation of the fifth congress decisions and proposed an extraordinary congress of the union to elect a new central committee. They demanded that the union become an independent body designed to defend the professional and economic interests of its

[34] See above, chap. IX, p. 240 and nn. 58-59; also polls, *RP*, Aug. 7, 20.

[35] Statement of Jan. 16, *Novinář*, no. 2 (1968), p. 34; A. Hradecký, *Rep.*, Jan. 17-24; *RP*, Feb. 27, 29, March 1, 8, 15, 20; *Novinář*, no. 3 (1968) et seq.; *Pravda*, March 8, 9.

[36] *RP*, March 1; *Novinář*, no. 3 (1968), p. 72; *LL*, March 7; also D. Hamšík, ibid., March 1.

[37] *RP*, March 21, 22; *Novinář*, no. 4 (1968), pp. 111-12. This did not fully satisfy the critics who argued that Hradecký should not even remain in the union's presidium (*Rep.*, April 3-10).

members, and that a new statute be drafted. They advocated the abolition of any kind of preliminary censorship and the guarantee of full freedom of expression. The Prague group proposed that a committee on the mass media be set up within the National Assembly and that the union have the right to nominate several deputies. Offering to negotiate with the Union of Writers and with other creative unions, the Prague organization seemed to be presenting itself as a kind of alternative to the union of which it was a part.[38]

Faced with this challenge, the union made a complete retreat and at an extraordinary congress in late June, embarked on a new course.[39] The congress' political resolution called for "a rehabilitation of journalism"; an information system guaranteeing equal access to information for all journalists, without regard for political differentiation; and constitutional and legal guarantees of freedom of speech and the press. In a special resolution, the congress welcomed the proposed legal ban on censorship, but demanded that it be constitutionally prohibited and urged other laws which would define any specific limitations on freedom of expression, such as the nature of state secrets and the legal responsibility of journalists. Another resolution repudiated the action taken by the fifth congress relative to *Literární noviny* and the writers' congress. A new statute described the union as "a voluntary social creative organization of journalists defending professional, social, and other rights and guaranteeing freedom of journalistic work." The union was the first association to carry through its own federalization by forming two independent national organizations and a new all-state "center," headed by Vlado Kašpar.

Keynote addresses at the congress revealed differences of outlook. A. J. Liehm described the press as "the lungs through which society breathes," providing the full information needed by modern society and guaranteeing against the monopolization of power. The press would serve society by "striving that every one in this land should know everything" and would resist the natural efforts of the state to limit information. Goldstücker defended press freedom as a means of controlling power but called for self-discipline by journalists and "a gentleman's agreement" with the government in order not to hamper the latter and harm the interests of the Republic, especially in regard to foreign affairs. M. Hysko warmly praised the role of the press in expressing public opinion and thus making possible many of the achievements of the post-January period, at a time when the party's Central Committee, owing to its composition, could not take the lead. He went on, however, to deliver

---

[38] *RP*, April 2, 4; *LL*, April 18; *Novinář*, no. 4 (1968), pp. 112-14.

[39] *RP*, June 22-24; *Novinář*, nos. 7-8 (1968), pp. 229-70. For preceding CC meetings, see *Novinář*, no. 5 (1968), pp. 150-52; no. 6 (1968), pp. 199-200. For critical comment, see R. Olšinský, *KŽ*, June 28. For the Slovak Union of Writers, see *Nové slovo*, June 20.

a detailed critique of the weaknesses of journalism after January, including a certain sensationalism; insufficient concern over anti-socialist elements; unjust personal accusations; concentration on the negative aspects of the past; and idealization of the bourgeois Republic. Freedom of the press implied that there would be "no limitation on the discussion of any theme whatever," but journalists must defend the principles of socialism and avoid expressions of disrespect for the Communist Party or the Soviet Union.[40]

Much more conservative views persisted in certain circles, especially in the central apparatus, as was indicated in a special section on the means of communication in the August CC report on the political situation. This document criticized the one-sidedness of information and other features of the work of journalists, and lamented that the leadership had often yielded to their influence. The mass media, it was argued, were an "element of the operation of power" and should be used by party and government to mold public opinion.[41] Quite different was the spirit of the materials prepared for the 14th Party Congress which described the maximum availability of information and the open expression of opinions as guarantees of the free development of socialism and rejected "censorship, open or covert." The media would be limited, it was said, only by a sense of responsibility and by "impartial judicial guarantees, which, in accord with valid laws, protect the socialist and democratic basis of the state, its alliances and its most essential secrets, as well as the inviolability of the individual." Radio, television, and the Czechoslovak Press Agency, as all-national institutions, would be supervised by bodies representing the whole people.[42]

SCHOLARS AND SCIENTISTS

The January changeover awakened the hopes of scholars and scientists that the new conditions would facilitate the conduct of their research

[40] Liehm, *Mladá fronta*, June 25; Goldstücker, *Novinář*, nos. 7-8 (1968), p. 254. Hysko's reference to the CC was not included in the published version of the address (*Novinář*, nos. 7-8, 1968, pp. 241-48), but in a fuller version available to the author. Cf. Hysko's exposition of his conception of freedom of information, *NS*, Aug. 15.

[41] *Zpráva o současné politické situaci Československé socialistické republiky* . . . (Prague, 1968), pp. 55-58. Jiří Hájek, in *Mýtus a realita ledna 1968* (Prague, 1970) lamented the failure of the post-January leadership to set limits to freedom of expression (the necessity of such limits were recognized by the Action Program) and to maintain party influence over the mass media, which, as a result of the rightists' monopoly, became "an independent social force" (p. 182). For a fuller criticism, containing a potpourri of quotations, see Miloš Marko, *Čierne na bielom* (Bratislava, 1971). Cf. the Soviet "White Book," *On Events in Czechoslovakia* (Moscow, 1968), pp. 53-71.

[42] Pelikán, *Vysočany Congress*, pp. 237-39.

and enable them to contribute more effectively to the making of public policy. No distinction was drawn between scholarship and science, for which Czech (like other European languages) has only one word—*věda*—embracing all branches of scholarship, the humanities and social sciences as well as the natural sciences. Condemning past intervention by the party in this realm, various spokesmen lamented the failure of the authorities to base policy on the findings of science, in spite of frequent professions of this intent. There must be a basic change in the relations of science and political institutions, and institutional guarantees of the authority and equality of science so that it could be "a critical (*oponentský*) corrective" of policy. Science must cease to be an "apologist" or "propagandist" and become a source of "truth" and of criticism. What science needed, wrote O. Poupa, a corresponding member of the Academy of Sciences and prominent physiologist, was "absolute freedom." An enlightened state, which provided science with the necessary financial support and did not seek to subordinate science to ideology, as in the past, would find in science "a powerful, free, and wise partner."[43]

The Academy of Sciences, which, since its formation in 1952, had occupied a crucial position in the management and control of science and scholarship, bore the brunt of the criticism. Prominent scholars delivered slashing attacks on the role of the academy and on its highest organs for their policy during the fifties and also during the "improved" atmosphere of the sixties. Dr. J. Průšek, head of the Oriental Institute, condemned the academy's authoritative governance, its arbitrary interference, especially in the humanities and social sciences, and its failure to defend scholars against political persecution. He lamented the "absolute silence" of science compared with the outspokenness of writers and students.[44] Academician O. Wichterle, a leading chemist, was highly critical, although he tended to shift the main blame to the political authorities and also denied that there had been much political interference in the natural sciences. In the worst of times, in fact, he said, the academy had been an "oasis of quiet and relative justice."[45] A common target of attack was the academy's organs which were said to be unrepresentative, arbitrarily selected, and cut off from the rank and file of scientists in the institutes. The academy was described as "a bureaucratic office for the administration of science," or as "a medieval enclave" using "bureaucratic police

[43] Poupa, *Rep.*, May 15-21. See also B. Peleška, ibid., April 24-May 1; B. Valehrach, *KŽ*, April 26; Z. Servít, *LL*, May 9.

[44] *Práce*, March 27. M. Holub and O. Poupa also criticized the post-January "silence" of science, saying that it had stood aside from the democratization process (*LL*, April 11).

[45] *LL*, April 11.

methods."[46] Slovak scholars added a distinctive touch by criticizing the centralism of the control of science and the asymmetrical position of the Slovak Academy of Sciences as a mere branch of the Czechoslovak institution.[47]

The most caustic critique was embodied in the "protest" of a group of eleven scholars, former members of the Czechoslovak Academy of Sciences and Art, and of the Royal Scientific Society, both of which had been abolished in 1952. The signatories, mainly scholars from the humanities, included persons who had been denied membership in the Academy of Sciences or removed from scholarly posts, such as Professor Černý. Censuring the exclusion of qualified scholars and citing the poor quality of many of the academy's members or degree holders, the protest described the situation in science as "catastrophic" and spoke of the "decline of the academy's authority" and of the "level of its work." They urged its basic reform, the rehabilitation of persecuted scholars, and the restoration of the liquidated institutions.[48]

These criticisms touched directly on the past record of Dr. František Šorm, the academy's secretary from its formation, its president after 1962, and a member of the CPCz Central Committee from 1958, who had for years been the chief party spokesman on science.[49] In statements made soon after January he admitted past failures and advocated changes in the position of science. At the April CC plenum he went further, deploring the stagnation of the social sciences which had become instruments of politics and "transmitters of outdated principles" and expressed the academy's support for the process of democratization.[50] Šorm, however, rejected the indiscriminate attacks embodied in the pro-

[46] Statement by the state and law collegium of the Academy of Sciences, *RP*, April 5; M. Rektorisová, *LL*, April 11.

[47] Ján Uher, *Pravda*, March 26; E. Špaldoň, ibid., April 7; report on the 15th anniversary of the Slovak academy, ibid., June 21.

[48] *LL*, May 16. See also Černý's letter to Dubček, containing an appeal for permission to travel to a conference abroad, often denied to him previously. The Academy of Sciences, he said, had done nothing to defend the rights of scholars (*Host do domu*, no. 5, May 1968, pp. 53-56).

There were also demands for the restoration of the Czechoslovak Academy of Agricultural Science abolished in 1952 and absorbed in the Academy of Sciences and the Ministry of Agriculture (*RP*, July 16).

[49] See his book, *Věda v socialistické společnosti* (Prague, 1967), esp. pp. 19-25, 62. He admitted that there had been "serious errors" in the party's attitude toward science and regretted the insufficient use of "*oponentura*" in the elaboration of alternative economic and social policies, citing the Richta team as an example to be followed (pp. 25, 23).

[50] *RP*, April 3. His speech was sharply criticized by J. Bober, a Slovak scholar, who raised the question of the personal responsibility of Šorm (*Pravda*, April 4). During a meeting of communists from academy institutes, at which Šorm spoke, disapproval was expressed of the limited activity of the academy's leaders in the democratization process (*RP*, March 27, 28).

test of the eleven and defended the achievements of Czechoslovak science.[51] At a press conference in which he was joined by two other prominent scholars, Mlynář and Richta, Šorm admitted the responsibility of the academy's presidium for past policies, but sought to shift the main blame to the highest party organs. Mlynář denied that science had been "silent," in contrast to the cultural front, and praised the presidium for contributing to the renaissance of the social sciences in the sixties, making special reference to the work of the Institute of Economics and to the formation of the interdisciplinary teams.[52]

Meanwhile the academy began to take steps to reform itself and to improve the conditions of scientific work. The administration of science was to be democratized; science was to be assured autonomy and was to become an "equal partner" in decision-making. At the academy's assembly, in mid-April, committees were set up to prepare an action program, a new statute and a new draft law, and to conduct a rehabilitation study. It was not made clear whether the reorganization of the academy would include its federalization, but the relationship of the Slovak and the Czechoslovak academies was to be studied. The assembly accepted the resignation of two conservative scholars as directors, Ladislav Štoll, from the Institute of Czechoslovak Literature, and Václav Král, from the Institute for the History of the European Socialist Countries. Fifteen new members were accepted, including Šik (full member) and Richta (corresponding member).[53]

Dissatisfaction with the slow progress toward reform and the desire to participate more actively in public life led to attempts to form a special organization of scientists comparable to the creative unions of cultural workers. Curiously, steps were taken simultaneously by two separate groups to form what was called in each case an Association of Scientific Workers. The first initiative came from scholars at the Philosophical Faculty of Charles University who issued an appeal for such an associa-

[51] CC plenum, RP, June 5. See J. Průšek's criticism of this speech (LL, June 13) and Šorm's response (RP, July 2). Průšek found the "protest" by the eleven unacceptable, however, and defended the formation of the academy, and even the exclusion of certain scholars from its membership. Similar sentiments were expressed in a statement by the academy's presidium (RP, June 25). Černý responded with a bitter polemic against both Šorm and Průšek (LL, July 4).

Šorm became involved in another polemic, this time with the philosopher, A. Kolman, whom he criticized for his speech at the academy's assembly and for his past record under Novotný. Kolman in turn defended his record and blamed the academy for his enforced emigration to the Soviet Union in 1962, a charge which Šorm denied (RP, May 3, 15, 21).

[52] RP, April 12.

[53] RP, April 9, 18, 19; Šorm, ibid., April 10, May 3; presidium of the academy, ibid., June 29. The Slovak Action Program spoke of the need for "independent scientific work-places" in Slovakia but did not explicitly demand federalization of the academy (Pravda, May 29).

tion as a guarantee of the freedom of scientific work. This idea was endorsed by a meeting of communists from the academy's institutes and by the scientific council of the University. At a meeting on April 12 of over 400 scholars, mainly from Prague, a preparatory committee was formed, with J. Kejř, of the Institute of State and Law, as secretary. Other leading figures were Poupa, Holub, and J. Koryta, a polarographer. The purpose of the association was declared to be "political," to express the views of scientists on burning public issues, and representation in the National Front was demanded.[54]

The other committee, headed by a Slovak scientist, J. Čabelka (who had signed the original March appeal), emanated from the ROH Committee of Scientific Workers, which also envisaged a creative union comparable to those in the cultural fields. Characterizing its rival as representing only Prague scholars, it held a conference in Brno, where it formed a temporary committee on which places were reserved for representatives of the Prague committee.[55] In spite of differences of opinion and mutual criticism, unity was achieved and documented in a declaration issued in late June. The association was to group together scientists of all disciplines and to cooperate with other creative persons, especially in the arts, and was to defend truth and freedom of knowledge as well as the interests of its members. It would strive "to make the voice of scientists heard" and to achieve the "full use of scientific methods and knowledge in the direction of society."[56]

Two other sets of scholars were active. One was the Scientific and Technical Society, claiming 165,000 members, including scientific workers, engineers, technicians, etc. It held a meeting in Prague attended by some 2,000 persons in late May and sought to become an organization which would defend the interests of its members and would secure mem-

[54] RP, March 24, 28; April 13; May 4. See LL, April 11, for the text of the appeal. It was signed by J. Čabelka, M. Holub, L. Tondl, O. Poupa, and T. Syllaba, and by other distinguished scholars, such as Goldstücker, Kosík, Richta, Sviták, Starý, Šamalík, Šik, and Wichterle. As far as they can be identified, the signatories (thirty-five in number) included eleven natural scientists, seven social scientists, seven philosophers, and six others in the humanities (including history).
The distinguished philosopher, J. Patočka, delivered a very strong attack on the bureaucratization of science and defended the need for an association of scientists to protect the principle of "scientific conscience" (LL, June 27).
[55] RP, March 27, May 17, 24. Cf. a strong statement on April 5 in favor of freedom of science, and a share of science in the spiritual and moral leadership of society, by the All-Academic Committee of the ROH organizations in the Academy of Sciences (LL, April 18). For mutual criticism, see Čabelka, RP, April 13, May 17; Z. Fencl, ibid., May 22; Poupa, LD, May 20.
[56] Text, RP, June 23. This was signed by members of what was termed the preparatory committee of the Association of Scientific Workers—M. Jelínek, of the J. E. Purkyně University; Poupa; Tondl (a philosopher, from the academy); V. Vaněček, a legal scholar, corresponding member of the academy; and Wichterle.

578

bership in the National Front.[57] Another was the Socialist Academy, which was devoted to the popularization of science and claimed a membership of 34,000. Subjected to repression earlier in the sixties, it went through a process of revival, with Academician Ivan Málek, prominent biologist, elected as chairman, and R. Horák, purged in 1965, restored as general secretary. It also demanded National Front membership.[58]

Scholars and scientists found many other ways to make their views known on current issues of politics. In meetings of university and faculty councils, professional associations, party organizations in their institutions, or *aktivs* of communists in the academy or the universities, in the daily press and weekly journals, as well as in their scholarly periodicals, they contributed their knowledge and pressed their opinions on reform. Prominent scholars were members of the editorial boards or advisory councils of papers such as *Literární listy* and served as advisers or "ghost writers" for reform leaders. Many scholars "went to the people," delivering speeches in support of reform throughout the country. Although the scholarly teams fell into inactivity, their members played a prominent part in publicizing reforms and in consultative work, and the provisional results of the team studies had a marked impact on reform planning. Leading scholars participated in the drafting of the Action Program, in the work of official commissions for the study of federalization, party rehabilitation, and economic reform, and in the preparation of important documents for the 14th congress, such as the party statute and the draft program.

THE WORKING CLASS AND THE UNIONS

The attitude of the workers to reform was difficult to assess and became the subject of sharp dispute. It was at first characterized by considerable skepticism and passivity and in some degree by hostility.[59] Hav-

[57] Ibid., May 17, 24, June 28. Cf. statement by certain technical specialists supporting such an organization, ibid., May 13. A more conservative view was expressed by sixty-two members of the technical intelligentsia from the Doubrava mine in northern Moravia in a polemical reply to Ivan Sviták. For their letter and Sviták's reply, *LL*, April 18.

[58] *RP*, April 11, 18. Z. Šikl, also removed in 1965, was reappointed editor-in-chief of the academy's journal of popular history, *Dějiny a součásnost*.

[59] For this and the following, see L. Vaculík, "And What About the Workers?" *LL*, April 4, and subsequent articles in *LL* by Z. Fibich, April 18; J. Pokštefl, May 2; Z. Pochop, May 16; round table, May 30; M. Jodl, May 30; Šamalík, June 20. See also J. Kotrč, *Život strany*, no. 13 (June 1968), pp. 17-21; round table, *Pravda*, May 23; M. Hric and T. Michal, ibid., June 14; J. Sláma, *Rep.*, June 5-12.

For later analysis, see Alex Pravda, "Some Aspects of the Czechoslovak Economic Reform and the Working Class in 1968," *Soviet Studies* 25 (July 1973), 102-24; A. Oxley, A. Pravda, and A. Ritchie, eds. *Czechoslovakia: The Party and the People* (London, 1973), pp. 149-218; Jan Kavan, "Czechoslovakia 1968: Workers and Students," *Critique*, no. 2 (n.d.), pp. 61-69.

ing grown accustomed to the notion that they were "the ruling class" and having long been indoctrinated with suspicion of intellectuals, workers were often unhappy with the prominent part taken by journalists, scholars, and writers after January and feared a "hegemony" of the intellectuals. Many were disoriented by the free discussion in the mass media in which their own representatives had little part and which questioned old ideological maxims and long-established practices. Workers were naturally concerned primarily with economic problems, in particular with the maintenance or improvement of their standard of living, and were disturbed by the post-January concentration on political reforms. The economic reform itself was viewed with considerable reserve, and even opposition, raising as it did the specter of unemployment and by its emphasis on productivity and qualification, threatening the "equalization" of income under previous wage policy. The so-called workers' policy in the past had given them, they felt, "social security," assuring them both employment and a minimum and stable standard of living, and affording certain sectors of the working class a privileged position. Such attitudes were fostered by trade union and party functionaries, often of working-class origin, who saw their own positions endangered by reforms and speaking in the name of "their" class, inculcated the workers with their fears for the fate of socialism.

It was clear that the conservative elements in the leadership and in the *aparát* had broad social support for their resistance to reform and that the attitude of the working class would in the long run be decisive in determining the success or failure of democratization. Dubček, in a speech to factory workers in Kladno, tried to persuade them that the reform movement was not directed against the working class and indeed was in their general interests in the long run. Černík outlined the specific economic and social measures already planned and urged greater participation by the workers in the reform movement. Smrkovský proclaimed at the CC plenum that what had been called a "workers' policy" in the past had not in fact really benefited the workers, whereas the establishment of an effective economy was very much in their interests.[60] The Action Program reiterated the hackneyed dogma of the leading role of the working class, under the leadership of the party and in alliance with the cooperative farmers and the socialist intelligentsia, but struck a new note when it expressed the intention of the party to rely on the more qualified, efficient, and active workers and to give them scope to use their political and social rights and to influence management. The trade unions should be "independent democratic organizations and work out their own politi-

[60] For Dubček, see *RP*, March 3, 5. Cf. his CC speech, *RŠO*, pp. 68-73. For Černík, *MF*, March 13; *RP*, March 14, 15. Cf. Z. Šulc, *RP*, March 30. For Smrkovský, *RP*, April 4, also *Práce*, May 26.

cal line." Their primary function was to defend the interests of the working class and to act as a partner in economic management.[61]

The initial indifference and distrust of the workers began slowly to give way to a more active involvement in the post-January ferment. Workers became vocal in presenting demands for wage increases and for improvement of working conditions. There was a growing movement for the democratization and activization of the trade unions, leading to widespread replacement of union officials in elections. In some cases, although these were not many, the slogan of "unions without communists" was proclaimed and some newly elected union committees did not contain a single communist.[62] Workers were also becoming critical of management, even resorting to the occasional strike to secure the removal of a manager or greater independence for their enterprise or plant. The idea of works' councils in the enterprises began to catch on. Although polls indicated that the workers were not as yet well informed concerning the proposed councils and were not widely convinced of their value as organs of self-administration, preparatory committees were set up, from April on, in some factories, and by August, a goodly number of enterprises were planning to establish such councils.[63] Another indication of the changing mood of the workers was the formation of committees for the defense of a free press in Ostrava and other industrial centers. Although no precise evidence is available, it seems safe to conclude that the workers had begun to see the advantages of reform, but had not yet been won over on a large scale.

The most solid evidence of the increasing orientation of the workers to reform was the evolution of the Revolutionary Trade Union Movement (ROH).[64] Although long accustomed to supporting the party in every respect, the ROH was slow to react to the January changeover. By early March this passivity and the past course of the unions became the target of condemnation by union functionaries and rank-and-file members, and in the two chief dailies of the movement, the Czech *Práce* and the Slovak *Práca*. There were demands for the resignation of the ROH chairman, M. Pastyřík, and other officials; calls for a council meeting

[61] Remington, ed., *Winter in Prague*, pp. 94-95, 115.

[62] For instance, in the Mez enterprise in Vsetín (*RP*, June 21). *Rudé právo* reported that there had been sharp criticism of Stalinists and "despots" in the ROH committee and that not one communist was elected to the seventeen-member committee. In the fall of 1968, it was later reported, about 10 percent of ROH committees were without communist representation (ibid., Feb. 19, 1971).

[63] *RP*, June 30; *Práce*, Aug. 13. See also *Pravda*, "Reform and the Working Class," pp. 121-23. See above, chap. xiv, nn. 90, 91.

[64] In addition to Galia Golan, *The Czechoslovak Reform Movement* (Cambridge, 1971), pp. 283-87, see A. Rozehnal, "The Revival of the Czechoslovak Trade Unions," *East Europe* 18 (April 1969), 2-7; V. Holesovsky, *Planning and Market in the Czechoslovak Reform* (New Haven, September 1972).

and, in the near future, an extraordinary congress or a general conference. It was urged that the trade unions assume a fresh and independent role as organizations whose main purpose was the defense of the interests of the workers, instead of acting as the mere executor of party and government decisions.[65]

When the union council (ÚRO) gathered in plenary session on March 21-22, there was an explosion of criticism touching every aspect of work in the past—the subordination of the unions to party and government; the failure to adopt an independent policy in the interests of the members; the highly centralized control and subordination of the basic organizations and constituent unions to the center; the failure to give an autonomous position and appropriate representation at the center to the Slovak trade unions, etc. The council refused to accept Pastyřík's proffered resignation but instead removed him from office. He was replaced by Karel Poláček, head of the metallurgical union and a ÚRO vice-chairman, who had been for seven years Minister of Heavy Engineering under Novotný, a choice which at once aroused criticism. The final resolution endorsed the idea of the ROH as primarily an interest organization and recognized the necessity of reevaluating all aspects of its work and drafting a new program.[66]

At a meeting of the council in April, Poláček identified himself strongly with the new course and advocated a new role for the movement. While he recognized the leading role of the party and described the state as "our socialist state," he declared that the trade unions must be "neither an instrument nor an auxiliary of the state," and must be prepared for conflicts with the state and the economic organs.[67]

Having repudiated what one commentator termed its position as "a politically passive partner of the government and the ministries," the ÚRO opted to pursue its new policy by negotiating directly with the government, rather than by taking a more radical course, including the threat of strikes. In two meetings of the ÚRO presidium with the government, substantial agreement was reached on specific problems urgently requiring action: the raising of below-standard wages in certain industries (such as consumer goods production, agriculture, transportation, and education); a general rise in real wages by 3 percent in 1969; a reevaluation of the wage system, including a basic minimum, as well as of the taxes on wages; regulation of retail prices; introduction of the 40-hour week; improvement of sickness insurance payments; an early re-

[65] RP, March 9, 13, 15. See editorial article, Odbory a společnost, no. 3 (1968), pp. 1-13.

[66] RP, March 22-24. See also F. Röll and G. Rosenberger, ČSSR, 1962-1968: Dokumentation und Kritik (Munich, 1968), pp. 190-94. For criticism of K. Poláček, RP, March 23, April 3, 27; for his reply, ibid., March 27.

[67] RP, April 25, 26; ČSSR, Dokumentation, pp. 273-79.

appraisal of the entire social insurance system; measures to meet the desperate situation in housing and in facilities for travel to work; better health and safety regulations; improvement of working conditions for women. On certain matters the unions were not fully satisfied with the government's proposals, and amendments were proposed to the draft laws to be presented to the assembly. It was agreed that annual negotiations between ÚRO and the government were desirable and that the government should discuss with ÚRO all measures affecting the working people.[68]

Mounting demands for wage increases, sometimes backed by the threat of strikes, and even the occasional wildcat strike, created a dilemma for the trade union movement. Some commentators and union spokesmen contended that wage pressures on the enterprises were healthy phenomena, encouraging improvements in production to meet legitimate demands. The special need to increase the income of the groups lagging behind the more favored and to raise the wage level generally during the forthcoming year was emphasized. At the same time it was economically impossible to fulfill all demands at once and much would depend on increased productivity by the particular groups concerned. There was a similar dilemma about the use of the strike weapon. The trade union leaders insisted strongly on the right to strike, proposing that it be embodied in the state constitution and in the union statutes, but recognized that exercise of this right was a last resort to be used if the normal channels of negotiations had failed. They also publicly opposed wildcat strikes. The party Presidium expressed similar opinions and Dubček spoke out firmly on the dangers of employing this weapon of economic struggle and on the need sometimes to resist "popular demands."[69]

The trade union movement was also confronted with the problem of refashioning its own structure. There was general acceptance of federalization, in the form of separate and relatively autonomous Czech and Slovak councils within a single movement, but parity representation in ÚRO was not approved.[70] It was generally agreed that the individual associations (svazy) should be more independent than in the past and that the basic factory organizations should have greater freedom of action. A more difficult problem, however, was the tendency of many groups of workers to break away from existing svazy and to form their own organizations. The ÚRO showed a willingness to accept an increase, perhaps a doubling, in the number of svazy, so that there would be some

[68] J. Bartoš, RP, May 17; RP, May 28, June 4; Černík, ibid., June 9; Poláček, ibid., June 11; R. Frühauf, ibid., June 22.

[69] RŠO, p. 206; Dubček, RP, June 19. See also Bartoš, RP, May 17; Poláček, ibid., June 19; J. Duži, vice chairman, ÚRO, Kulturní tvorba, June 27; V. Daubner, ŽS, no. 14 (July 1968), pp. 9-13.

[70] Daubner, ŽS, no. 14 (July 1968), pp. 9-13; Poláček, Práce, Aug. 14.

twenty-five in each part of the Republic, and took the initiative in dividing one existing *svaz* into two, one for education and science, and another for art and culture. Three other *svazy* were later broken up to form nine independent associations.[71] The ROH leadership was, however, sharply opposed to other attempts to establish independent *svazy*, e.g. by the locomotive engineers. These, numbering 23,000, refused to remain within the railway workers' union and by brief passive resistance, secured de facto recognition by the Ministry of Transport. Such a splitting of the unions would, it was argued, weaken the union movement in carrying out its functions. On the other hand, there was recognition of the desirability of adapting the internal organization of each *svaz* so as to take account of the distinctive interest groups. In the individual enterprise the traditional policy of "one factory, one union" should be maintained so that the unions could confront the management as unified entities. These views received the strong endorsement of the party leadership which regarded efforts to divide the unions as a hindrance to their effectiveness.[72]

A special conference of delegates from basic union organizations in late June confirmed the trend toward a changing role for the unions. The two main documents adopted by the conference were a declaration concerning the new status of the enterprise and a draft program. The latter stated the essential purposes of the trade union movement as "an independent and democratic, unified interest organization of the employees" and reaffirmed the intention to carry out "an independent policy" vis-à-vis the state and political parties, and to seek to influence state and economic organs. It also demanded guarantees that the "existential security" of the working people not be threatened by the liquidation of ineffective production or other changes due to economic reform, and that there be "timely assurance of alternative opportunities of work." Dubček, in his address, paid tribute to the unions not only as an interest organization but also as a future political force within the National Front and within the enterprises, through the proposed councils.[73]

[71] *RP*, March 24, April 4, 25, June 6; Duži, *KT*, June 27. The union of transport and communications was divided into three unions (railway, highway transport, and communications); the union of employees of state organs and local economy, into four associations; the union of workers in mining and power, into two.

[72] For advocacy of the right of the locomotive crews to form their own union, see J. Lederer, *LL*, June 27 and *Rep.*, July 31-Aug. 7. On the need for unity, M. Kimlík, ÚRO secretary, *Práce*, June 4; ÚRO plenum decision, *RP*, June 5; Dubček, *RP*, June 19. See also CC Presidium, June 11, *RŠO*, p. 224.

[73] For the proceedings, *RP* and *Práce*, June 19-21. See also speeches by Poláček and Dubček at the preceding ÚRO plenum, *Práce*, June 5; *RŠO*, pp. 189-90. For the program, *Nástin programu revolučního odborového hnutí* (Prague, July 1968), German version, *ČSSR, Dokumentation*, pp. 314-24. For the declaration on the enterprise, see chap. XIV above.

Shortly thereafter the attitude of the workers became the subject of bitter dispute, provoked by controversial statements by Švestka on the subject of "social security" and "working class policy." In a major article in *Rudé právo* he described the "passivity" of the workers as a natural result of their fear of "social shocks," which would upset the social security hitherto enjoyed. The Action Program, he said, had offered "very little" to the workers, and they had been "excluded" from participation in the democratization process. He expressed the hope that the CPCz, true to its mission of defending the interests of the workers, would elaborate a new social policy which would allay their fears, meet their pressing demands, and assure their proper influence. These views were challenged by vigorous reformers (Machonin and others) who contended that the workers had not been excluded from political participation after January and that there had been at least a start in their activization, although this admittedly had not yet embraced a majority. It was contended that the workers had not really been the beneficiaries of past "working-class policy" and it was denied that there had been "an attack" on the working class or on socialism after January, as Švestka had claimed. The workers were right to demand a new social policy that would assure them "social security" and improved living standards, but should recognize that the economic reform would ultimately bring them real benefits. Other intellectuals, notably Kosík and Sviták, disputed the right of party functionaries to speak in the name of the workers and argued that the most reliable protection of the latter's interests were freedom of speech, democratic trade unions, and self-management through the working people's councils.[74]

FARMERS AND FARMERS' ORGANIZATIONS

The agricultural community, like the industrial class, did not take a leading part in the reform movement but were by no means as passive as was sometimes suggested.[75] No group had suffered more in the past, not only from the rapid and compulsory collectivization in the fifties, but from the ensuing neglect and ill-treatment of agriculture, both private and collective, in economic policy. On the other hand, the general living standard of the farming community had improved during the sixties and collective farming was a long-established reality, more or less accepted

[74] Švestka's articles, *RP*, July 14, 18, Aug. 13, 20; letters in support of his views, ibid., Aug. 21; replies by Machonin, *Večerní Praha*, July 15; K. Štregl and Sláma, *Práce*, July 18; K. Pinc, *Rep.*, July 24-31; I. Bystřina, *LL*, July 25; Machonin, *RP*, Aug. 13. For a series of articles criticizing pre-January social policy, see I. Tomeš, *LL*, June 20 and thereafter, esp. the issue of July 25. See also Sviták, *LL*, April 18, *Práce*, May 19; Kosík, *LL*, April 25.

[75] E.g. R. Selucký, *Economic Reforms in Eastern Europe* (New York, 1972), pp. 105-9.

by the farmers. If polls conducted in Slovakia in July were accurate, collective farming was regarded as more advantageous than individual farming, and was considered to have improved the cultural level and standard of the living of the countryside.[76] Certainly few sought to withdraw from the farms, as had occurred fifteen years earlier on a small scale during the New Course (or on a large scale in Hungary and Poland in 1956). The polls indicated, however, that there was substantial dissatisfaction with the living conditions of people in agriculture, especially in comparison with the city, and a widespread feeling that the countryside subsidized the cities.[77]

Not surprisingly, farmers and their spokesmen concentrated their attention on economic matters, seeking in particular a more equitable treatment of the agricultural sector and changes in the highly centralized and undemocratic organization in this sphere. There was sharp criticism of Karel Mestek, the Minister of Agriculture and Food, both in the agricultural committees of the National Assembly and by communists in the Ministry of Agriculture and Food. Moreover there was censure of the district agricultural organizations established in 1967 which had, it was thought, achieved some positive results but which were described as "arms of the ministry" rather than democratic organs. Discontent was expressed with the purchase and supply enterprises which had in the past controlled the market for agricultural produce and equipment. Above all, attention was focused on the desirability of establishing an organization or organizations to articulate the interests of the agricultural community in a democratic fashion, reversing the abolition of the union of farmers in 1948. Later, as the ferment in the countryside increased, there was discussion of the injustices done to many peasants during and after the period of collectivization, and although collectivization itself was not

[76] The poll, conducted July 18-24, 1968, was a random sample of 1,051 persons, of whom 165 were farmers. Of the farmers, 67.3 percent favored collective farming; 24.3 percent, individual farming. For all respondents the proportions were 61.5 and 19.5 percent, resp. Sixty-four percent of the farmers credited the improvement of the cultural level and the standard of living of rural areas to collectivization (42.4 percent, yes; 22.2 percent, partly so). Twenty-one percent of farmers (16.7 percent of all) thought this would have been achieved without collectivization. An even higher proportion thought that work was easier on collectives (74.6 percent of farmers; 76.3 percent of all). Source: J. Piekalkiewicz, *Public Opinion Polling in Czechoslovakia, 1968-69* (New York, 1972), pp. 310-12.

[77] Conditions were considered as good, or very good, by 37.6 percent of the farmers, and as poor, or not sufficient, by 60.6 percent (36.4 and 52.6 percent, respectively, of all respondents). According to 80 percent of the farmers, wages were lower as compared with industrial workers (67.8 percent of all shared this opinion). The countryside subsidized the cities in the opinion of 50.3 percent of the farmers; did not do so, according to 17.6 percent (33.0 and 26.7 percent, respectively, of all respondents). The present standard of living was better than in the city, thought 36.4 percent of the farmers (36.9 percent of all); was worse than in the city, thought 48.5 percent of farmers (48 percent of all). Ibid., pp. 313-19.

challenged, there were insistent demands that the victims be rehabilitated and compensated.[78]

As early as the beginning of February, the seventh congress of collective farm (JZD) representatives, already planned before 1968, aired the problems of the agricultural sector in what was described as an unusually democratic atmosphere. Dubček's address—his maiden public speech as First Secretary—was hailed as illustrating a fresh attitude toward the peasants and toward agriculture and won him substantial support among the farming community. True, his speech was couched largely in terms of implementing the March 1967 CC decision on agriculture and of introducing the new system of management in this area, and paid tribute to Gottwald for achieving collectivization, but it also spoke of deepening cooperative democracy and praised the work of small and middle-sized private farmers. Above all, in a reference which was widely interpreted as favoring the idea of an interest organization for agriculture, Dubček asserted the need to discuss "the completion of the structure of democratic organization in agriculture," both in the sphere of economic production and in the social field. The final resolution of the congress authorized the resolutions commission to elaborate "the best form of democratic organization of the management of agriculture," but made no specific mention of an interest organization, which had been raised by many speakers.[79]

The appointment of Josef Borůvka, a collective farm chairman with a progressive reputation, as Minister of Agriculture and Food, seemed to augur well for the "rehabilitation" of agriculture, although his simultaneous removal from the party Presidium aroused misgivings.[80] The Action Program, in brief references to agriculture, urged greater assistance to this neglected sector. Although it endorsed large-scale production in the form of cooperative and state farms, it also assured help to private farmers.[81] The government's program promised equal rights

---

[78] V. Vydra, *Hospodářské noviny*, Jan. 26; Z. Bendlová, *Rep.*, Feb. 14-21; J. Borůvka, *Zemědělské noviny*, March 6; J. Karlík, *Pravda*, March 11; *RP*, March 13, 20; E. Mand'ak, *RP*, April 13; B. Toman, *Rol'nické noviny*, April 27. See also the joint meeting of the resolutions committee with the National Assembly committee on agriculture, in which three alternatives were discussed (*RP*, March 28). For this and the following, see M. Klánský, *Rep.*, July 10-17; July 24-31. Cf. the post-occupation articles, by L. Klusáček and M. Pavlík, *RP*, Dec. 4, 16, 1969.

[79] *ZN*, Feb. 14; Dubček, *K otázkam*, pp. 17-25. Karel Mestek, the Minister of Agriculture and Food, was more positive in his evaluation of the progress in agriculture in recent years, commending in particular the formation of the district agricultural organizations and made no mention of the possibility of an association to defend the interests of agriculture (*ZN*, Feb. 2; also Feb. 4).

[80] Interview with Borůvka, *Pravda*, April 26. See also his unpublished article from 1963, *ZN*, April 13, 1968.

[81] Remington, ed., *Winter in Prague*, p. 116. See also Jan Havelka, former head of the CC agricultural department, on the department's favorable attitude to an independent cooperative organization in 1967 (*RP*, April 13).

for agriculture and an increase in investments in this sector.[82] Many official statements emphasized that there would be no retreat from collectivization and deplored the occasional demand for the abolition of the collectives and a return to small-scale farming. There were complaints that "kulaks" were becoming active and warnings that they would not be rehabilitated.[83] Special measures were, however, planned for rehabilitating some 30,000 small and middle peasants who had been incorrectly termed "kulaks" and had illegally been deprived of their property in the fifties.[84]

Official policy concerning a farmers' interest organization was slow in crystallizing. The Action Program approved what it called the JZD congress proposal for forming "an all-state organization of cooperative farmers" but did not give much guidance to those engaged in planning such an organization. In late May the CPCz Presidium endorsed the concept, said to be that of the Ministry of Agriculture and Food and the National Assembly's agricultural committee, of a Union of Cooperative Farmers which would be a component of the National Front and an exponent of the individual interests of this social group, but took no stand on the various suggestions for an economic interest organization.[85]

It was widely assumed that the congress had given the green light for the formation of a farmers' interest group, and the congress resolutions commission, headed by Jiří Karlík, deputy Minister of Agriculture and Food, was reproached for its slow progress. Although the members of this body were divided as to the most appropriate solution, the commission tended to focus at first on "an economic interest organization" which would group together some or all of the enterprises functioning in agriculture, for instance, collective farms, state farms, etc., and would concentrate on improving and democratizing the administration of agriculture. This presumably seemed most satisfactory to the leading functionaries of these enterprises who were fearful of the loss of their influence, and even of their posts, in a more radical reorganization.

Others, however, found this approach too conservative and production-oriented and proposed as an alternative a "social interest organization"

[82] RP, April 25.
[83] L. Hofman, for instance, proclaimed that there would be no rehabilitation of the "class enemy" who had opposed collectivization (RP, May 4). For the above, see also Borůvka, ibid., April 24, Pravda, April 26; RP, May 28, 29; Š. Sádovský, RP, June 5.
[84] On the regular rehabilitation laws, see chap. XIII above, and Borůvka, ZN, June 18, 21; on the special measures for agriculture, LD, June 18; P. Molnár, Pravda, June 20; J. Inovecký, KŽ, June 21. Consideration was also given to correcting the illegal transfer of collective farms to state farms. Borůvka spoke very cautiously on rehabilitation insisting that it should be undertaken only in consultation with the collective farmers and not at their expense (CC, RP, June 7).
[85] Remington, ed., Winter in Prague, pp. 95, 116; see also RŠO, p. 161.

which would embrace all farmers, and many others associated with agriculture, on an individual basis and would pursue broader social and political objectives. At the initiative of the Ministry of Agriculture and Food newspaper, *Zemědělské noviny*, and with the initial support of some agricultural deputies in the National Assembly, including V. Kučera, chairman of the agricultural committee, a movement was launched for the establishment of a Union of Farmers (*Svaz zemědělců*), including collective farmers, employees of state and training farms, machine-tractor stations, agricultural research institutes, and other agricultural enterprises and organizations, as well as private farmers and all inhabitants of villages and rural towns. Such an effort was initiated at a conference in Jičín in late March and was followed by the organization of preparatory committees throughout the Czech lands, and in early May by the formation of a general preparatory committee and the adoption of a program. In Slovakia a preparatory committee for a Club of Farmers was also established.[86]

It soon became obvious that the agricultural community was deeply divided by the conflicting interests of separate groups and by divergent opinions about the proper course to follow.[87] The proposed Union of Farmers was attractive to many working farmers, both collective and private, but was regarded with some fear by agricultural functionaries. Some criticized its ambitious political objectives of becoming a spokesman for agriculture through representation in the National Front and the organs of government and the assembly, and labeled it a reincarnation of the pre-war Agrarian Party.[88] A conference of district agricultural organization representatives, convoked by the Ministry of Agriculture and Food, proposed an alternative: a broad economic organization embracing the whole of agriculture and all enterprises within this field, a plan which would have preserved the district associations and made them the nucleus of the new organization.[89] The idea of a "social interest" organization, or even of an all-inclusive interest organization, caused apprehension in other quarters, for example, in the Union of Agricultural Employees (ROH), which regarded itself as the exponent of the social interests of the employees of state farms, tractor stations, and other agricultural enterprises. They suggested two separate associations, one for state farms and another for tractor stations, each grouping together these enterprises, without individual membership.[90] Another proposal was made by the workers (and later the functionaries) of the purchase and

---

[86] *RP*, March 26, 29; *ZN*, March 26, May 9, 20.
[87] For these differences, see V. Kučera, *RP*, May 3; J. Karlík, ibid., May 4; a round-table discussion including representatives of all tendencies (*RP*, May 24).
[88] These charges were denied by the *Svaz zemědělců*, *RP*, May 20.
[89] *RP*, April 11, 17; *ZN*, April 10-11.   [90] *RP*, May 8, 23; *ZN*, June 21.

supply organizations, who advocated replacing these state enterprises with economic cooperatives and forming an all-state association of cooperatives.[91]

Competing interest organizations began to come into existence, at least in the form of preparatory committees, for instance, an Economic Union of State Farms, a Union of Economic Cooperatives, a Union of Tractor Stations, etc. Jiří Karlík did not oppose these moves to set up economic organizations, but firmly rejected the idea of a Union of Farmers. He advocated a common federal organ to coordinate the many associations, as well as a social interest organization.[92] Meanwhile Slovak opinion was developing somewhat differently and favored a single economic and social interest organization.[93]

The final draft of the Karlík commission, published in full in early June,[94] represented a compromise but was designed to counteract the alternative idea of a Union of Farmers as proposed by the Jičín conference. It recommended the immediate formation of a Union of Cooperative Farmers as a "social interest" organization, to act as a spokesman for the cooperative farmers, to work with the organs of the state, and to participate in the National Front. Its local base would be the collective farms, as entities, but private farmers were to be permitted to join as individuals, and would have their own basic organizations and a special section of the union at the district and national levels. In addition there would be gradually developed an "economic interest" organization, based on the enterprises (collective farms, state farms, associations of enterprises, and food industry enterprises). At the district level, its units would be the district agricultural associations, which would form an "economic union of agricultural enterprises." If the state farms persisted in having a separate association, a new "economic union of agricultural cooperatives" would be formed. At the national level, there would be various national groupings (agricultural cooperatives, state farms, tractor stations, etc.) with a coordinating center. There would also be an organization of economic cooperatives in the fields of purchase and supply. Finally, there would be an all-state economic organization—a Central Union of Agriculture and Foodstuffs—representing the several associations and acting as a partner with government organs in the performance of regulatory functions in the market.

A conference was convened in early July in Nitra to consider these proposals and although it achieved some of its goals, it was something

[91] ZN, June 29.
[92] Karlík, RP, June 4 and NM, no. 7 (1968), pp. 826-34.
[93] Pravda, March 28 (declaration of Trusteeship of Agriculture and Food); J. Horváth, ibid., April 11; V. Mráz, ibid., May 28.
[94] Text, ZN, June 11. See also RP, May 24; also Karlík, ibid., June 4.

of an anticlimax. Since the participants were representatives chosen by the delegates to the 7th JZD congress (together with some representatives of the Union of Farmers), and since the Karlík draft was the main item on the agenda, there was little chance that the alternative of a broad Union of Farmers would be accepted. A major difference of opinion was manifested between Czechs and Slovaks who submitted two competing sets of draft statutes. The Czechs endorsed the Karlík proposals, whereas the Slovaks adhered to their plan of a single Union of Cooperative and Private Farmers which would serve both as an economic and social interest organization.[95] There was sharp disagreement at Nitra between the Czechs and Slovaks over the issue of parity in the central organs of the proposed associations, and this prevented the emergence of a single all-state organization. Hence the conference was able to approve only two organizations, with different names (the Czech Union of Cooperative Farmers and the Slovak Union of Cooperative and Private Farmers) and with different statutes, and had to postpone the formation of an all-state organization.[96]

The results of the Nitra conference were disappointing to both Czechs and Slovaks.[97] The failure to form an all-state organization was regretted, although it was assumed that it would be only a matter of time before such a body was created. Those Czechs who had endorsed the broader Union of Farmers felt that they had achieved a partial victory but expressed doubts as to whether an organization tied so closely to the collective farms as entities would satisfy the peasants. Some Slovaks voiced concern as to whether their single unified organization would be as politically effective as a distinctive social interest group representing a kind of "peasant socialist party." Nonetheless the conference had opened the way for creating not merely one but a series of interest organizations in agriculture. The preparatory committee of the Socialist Union of Farmers (the former Union of Farmers) disbanded and appealed to its members to join the Union of Cooperative Farmers. Separate meetings of organs of the Czech and Slovak unions were held from mid-July on;

[95] For the proceedings of the conference, see *RP, Pravda*, and *ZN*, July 10-12. Most of the delegates were collective farm chairmen with few "ordinary" farmers present (J. Bednařík, *RP*, July 3). See the pessimistic comment prior to the opening, Pavlík, *Rep.*, June 26-July 3. See also the conflicting views expressed in a symposium, *NS*, July 4. For the draft statutes, *ZN*, July 3 and *RN*, July 6, resp.

[96] Both organizations were to send representatives, in rotation, to meetings with the government (*RP*, July 18). In the meantime a provisional committee based on parity was formed to deal with common problems and to prepare for the formation of a unified organization (*Pravda*, July 11, 12).

[97] J. Lederer, before the conference, was critical of the Karlík proposals (*LL*, July 4). Klánský reconciled himself to the results but had reservations and noted continuing opposition to the proposed new organization (*Rep.*, July 24-31). See also J. Dunajovec, *NS*, July 18 and M. Pavlík, *RP*, July 30.

591

preparatory committees were set up in many places. Measures were soon taken to bring the new associations into existence and to assure their appropriate representation both in the National Front and in the elected representative bodies, but none of these goals had been fully reached at the time of the occupation.[98]

OTHER INTEREST GROUPS

After January the spontaneous outburst of activity by associations and organizations, new and old, expressing the interests and aims of a wide spectrum of social groups, was welcomed by the party Presidium which expressed the hope, however, that party members would spearhead this development. At the April plenum Dubček promised that there would be "a democratic right of way for the interests of all groups of society." The Action Program, as noted earlier, stressed the importance of recognizing the various interests of society and their articulation by societal organizations which would be voluntary in membership and would function democratically, and promised guarantees for this in a revised law on association.[99] The June plenum warned against mass organizations formed by each party and urged that the unity of existing associations be preserved through "umbrella" or federalized organizations embracing various sectors.[100]

The proliferation of interest groups in labor and agriculture has already been discussed. Many other organizations in the economic sphere, including one of managers, were also emerging.[101] The Union of Consumers' Cooperatives indicated its desire to become a "real organization" of consumers and to regain its former position of importance in the retail trade. A similar revival occurred within the Union of Producers' Cooperatives.[102] The prospect of a new statute for enterprises and the crea-

[98] ZN, July 24. Other steps were taken in the formation of the Economic Union of State Farms (RP, July 16, 18, 21), and of the Union of Economic Cooperatives (ZN, July 20). The Czech Union of Cooperative Farmers published its program (ZN, July 30). A meeting of the Czech union's central committee, and joint Czech and Slovak meetings, were scheduled for Aug. 22 and 23 but did not take place (ZN, Aug. 17).

[99] RŠO, pp. 30, 37, 69, 76-77, 81-82. See above, chap. XIV, p. 419; Remington, ed., Winter in Prague, pp. 103-4. Cf. S. Provazník, "The Action Program and Social Interests," NM, no. 5 (1968), pp. 561-68.

[100] RŠO, pp. 207-8. Cf. M. Řehůřek, "The New Concept of Societal Organizations," Pravda, June 28, where he discussed the role of the mass organizations as an "oponentura" in the political system.

[101] Vosecký, Rep., Aug. 7-14. See also reports on an association of engineer-economists (RP, April 11); of trade and catering services (RP, July 21); of small producers and services (ibid., July 12); and for scientific management (ibid., June 13). There were plans to form a Union of Towns and Municipalities (ZN, Oct. 8).

[102] RP, May 24, July 21, 31; March 19, 22, 27, May 1, July 17.

tion of enterprise councils provoked the idea of creating a Union of Industry to defend the interests of the industrial enterprises vis-à-vis the unions and the state organs and to become partners in negotiations with both.[103]

Other group interests based on generation, sex, profession, or the pursuit of common goals were articulated through the renaissance or reorganization of existing organizations, such as the youth movement or others to be described below; by breaking away from an established association; by the restoration of organizations liquidated in the fifties; or by the creation of new ones. The process of reviving long-dormant organizations and transforming them into genuine interest groups was remarkably similar in all cases, characterized by pungent criticism of their past record and their present leadership; demands for greater independence from party control and for the democratization of their structure; and the drafting of an action program stressing the defense of the interests of their members. In all cases there were plans for a federalization of their structure, usually with parity of Czech and Slovak representation in the all-state organs.[104]

Certain existing organizations had absorbed, in a monolithic structure, groups which had had distinctive traditions of their own and had once been independent entities, and these began to seek a more autonomous position or in some cases complete independence. For instance, the Union of Anti-Fascist Fighters was composed of former concentration camp prisoners, participants in the Prague and Slovak Uprisings, and veterans who had fought in the Spanish civil war, and on the eastern and western fronts in both world wars. Voices were raised exhorting the restoration of the tradition of the *odboj* or liberation movement, which had been downgraded or ignored, and for the rehabilitation of the individual participants, especially those who had fought on the western fronts or in the home partisan movement, who, during the fifties, had often been persecuted and ousted from public life.[105] Official spokesmen promised to rectify previous discrimination but urged the retention of a united organization. Nonetheless several separate organizations, such as the Union of Czechoslovak Officers and the Union of Airmen, were established. Overall unity was preserved, however, in a single organization under a new name, Union of Fighters for Freedom. Its structure was

---

[103] Ibid., July 13, 14, 31; S. Vosecký, *Rep.*, Aug. 7-14.

[104] *NS*, Aug. 8, 15. For a full list of the organizations admitted to the National Front by mid-June, see above, chap. XII, n. 60. For an excellent discussion, see Kusin, *Political Grouping*, pp. 186-97.

[105] F. Mišeje, *NS*, July 4. See esp. Smrkovský's call for a rehabilitation of the tradition of the liberation struggle, in particular that of the Prague Uprising (*RP*, June 19).

federal, with two national leagues, Czech and Slovak, and with autonomous associations for each of its several components.[106]

The Czechoslovak Union of Physical Training (ČSTV), which held a monopoly position in all sports, both competitive and recreational, was censured for its past activities and for its initial failure to recognize the need for reorganization. The ČSTV sections for individual sports began to express the wish to become distinctive bodies enjoying an autonomous position within a unified organization. By late March the ČSTV leadership was admitting past defects, conceding the idea of autonomy for its constituent elements, and contending for its own independence, free from outside interference. The process of transformation was complicated, however, by the demands put forward for a restoration of the Sokols. This famous organization, which had deep-rooted nationalist traditions dating from 19th century Bohemia, had been abolished after 1948, and its facilities expropriated, and many of its instructors absorbed, by the ČSTV. Some of its former functionaries strove to reestablish it as an independent organization, under the umbrella of a unified physical training movement. Sokol organizations were formed in various localities, sometimes withdrawing from the ČSTV and taking over its facilities.[107] A preparatory committee for the revival of Orel, the earlier Catholic physical training association, was formed, and a number of Orel units were established.[108]

The thorny question of the future of the Sokols continued to be the subject of vigorous discussion in the sports pages of *Rudé právo* and other newspapers. Although the ČSTV leaders were ready to recognize the Sokol tradition, they considered the restoration of this movement "a step backward," a position which was endorsed by the CPCz Presidium at the end of April. The ČSTV proposed the adoption of a federal structure, with separate Czech and Slovak leagues and autonomous sections for individual sports, including the so-called Basic Physical Training units. The latter had replaced the Sokols in recreational sport and in the intervening twenty years had developed into a vast network of 450,000 training places, with 35,000 instructors. In July these units announced that they would constitute a distinct entity, "Union of Physical Training —Sokol," which was, however, to remain a part of the unified ČSTV. Meanwhile official negotiations between the ČSTV and Sokol spokesmen had been broken off, to be resumed, it was said, only when the Sokols

---

[106] *RP*, April 18, 21, May 16, July 6, Aug. 6.

[107] Ibid., March 27-29, April 2, 4. According to *Zpráva*, p. 67, there were 70 registered, and 61 non-registered, Sokol organizations in the Czech lands, with a membership of 2,413.

[108] *RP*, April 23, May 6.

ceased their "splitting" activities and recognized the principle of unity. The stalemate had not been resolved prior to the invasion in August.[109]

Svazarm, a union for cooperation with the army, which supervised military and technical sports, was subjected to similar criticisms and was censured for its semimilitary character and the dominant role of high officers. Some groups within Svazarm, such as the air club and the clubs of motorists and radio amateurs, set up independent bodies. Other organizations, without breaking away from Svazarm, formed units of Junák, a scout organization which had been dissolved in the fifties. Svazarm, under changed leadership, sought to reform itelf as a federation of Czech and Slovak leagues composed of constituent associations such as motorists, divers, riflemen, and units of civilian defense and military preparedness. Negotiations with the groups which had already defected did not make rapid progress and were not completed by August.[110]

The Czechoslovak Union of Women, previously little more than a propaganda agency of the party, was galvanized into life. It severely condemned the neglect of women's interests by party and state and advanced plans to transform its own structure and activities. The new chairman, M. Fischerová, declared that the union wished to become, not a "charitable organization," like the Salvation Army, nor an organization of suffragettes, conducting "a holy crusade" against men, but a genuine societal and interest organization, defending the special interests of women, including equality of living and working conditions, and proper representation in political and state organizations.[111]

Even the Union of Czechoslovak-Soviet Friendship, which had claimed a huge membership on paper but had failed to attract genuine public support, was affected. In February it was still functioning in the old style, as indicated by a mass meeting in celebration of 1948, which was attended by the Soviet ambassador and held under the traditional slogan "With the Soviet Union for all time!" In April there were demands that the organization should become less ceremonial and formal in its activities and thus more appealing to young people. In July a change of spirit was reflected in a resolution pledging full support for the party's response to the Warsaw letter. The union proclaimed its desire for independence as a member of the National Front and announced measures to make its activities attractive and meaningful. A similar at-

---

[109] RP, April 18, 19, May 3, 4, June 20, 22, July 11, 19; RŠO, p. 153. The Sokol tradition was warmly defended (Svobodné slovo, July 11; ZN, April 6); its political role in the past was also attacked (J. Marek, RP, Aug. 17). Cf. a detailed proposal for a reorganization of the ČSTV which would give recognition to the Sokol tradition and include the name Sokol in its title (V. Fiala, RP, June 11).
[110] B. Toser and V. Doležal, Rep., April 10-17; J. Škubal, RP, Aug. 1.
[111] RP, April 12, 25, June 28, Aug. 6.

tempt at metamorphosis was made in another propaganda institution, the Committee of Defenders of the Peace, which, under the direction of Academician Josef Macek, sought to make itself a source of "genuine peace initiatives."[112]

YOUNG PEOPLE AND STUDENTS

For many years the youth had been driven into political passivity and alienated by a party that demonstrated little concern for their real interests and by a youth organization which had rejected their demands for distinctive treatment of their varied needs. Few young people were members of the party, and they formed a very small proportion of party committees.[113] The Strahov episode was still fresh in the minds of students and evoked anew critical discussion.[114] A report issued by the Ministry of the Interior in early March contained apologies to the injured students and promised compensation, but was criticized by the party university committee.[115]

Nonetheless, young people in general, especially the students, welcomed the reform course, although with some reservations reflecting their past experience. Mass rallies of youth in Prague, Bratislava, and elsewhere, including the huge meeting in the Congress Palace in March

[112] Ibid., Feb. 21, April 24 (E. Šíp), July 21, Aug. 8; April 3, 19.

[113] Cf. later remarks to this effect by Z. Vokrouhlický, acting ČSM head after March. As of Jan. 1, 1968, 6.4 percent of the total party membership were 25 years of age or younger, and 8.9 percent were between 26 and 30. Only one young person was a member of a regional committee (NM, nos. 9-10, 1968, pp. 1153-55). The Youth Union, Vokrouhlický admitted, had also little appeal. The situation was no better in Slovakia. Of 19,000 university students in Bratislava, only 410 were CPS members (Pravda, June 20). Cf. similar statements in materials prepared for the 14th Party Congress (Pelikán, Vysočany Congress, pp. 200-201). Cf. Kusin, Political Grouping, pp. 115 ff., 138-39, for this and the following. See also chap. III above. See also Galia Golan, "Youth and Politics in Czechoslovakia," Journal of Contemporary History 5, no. 1 (1970), 3-22; O. Ulč, "The Communist Party of Czechoslovakia and the Young Generation," East European Quarterly 6 (June 1972), 206-29.

[114] See above, chap. III, n. 121.

[115] The report (RP, March 12) described the Strahov conflict as "a most regrettable and unhappy event which arose by accident." It denied that the action taken by the police had been ordered by higher party or state functionaries and described the police intervention as "legal." The disproportionately harsh measures were, however, condemned; the students affected received apologies and compensation; and seven VB members were punished. The university committee contended that the events were "a logical result" of the line followed by the Ministry of the Interior and the Procuracy General, which had forbidden all demonstrations, without distinction, in conflict with the constitutionally guaranteed rights and freedoms of citizens. The ministry's statement had failed to recognize "the illegality of the entire action" and the responsibility of leading officials of the ministry (ibid., March 13).

(organized ironically by the Prague city ČSM), dissipated, as one observer noted, the myth of the apolitical character of youth and demonstrated their keen desire for reform, but also their skeptical attitude toward prominent reform leaders. One student spokesman, L. Holeček, at the Prague meeting, declared the readiness of youth to support Dubček for the present but observed that they might later advance a program of their own.[116]

The Czechoslovak Union of Youth (ČSM), thoroughly discredited in the eyes of the younger generation, particularly the students, showed signs of acute crisis. In January its leadership came under heavy attack by a Prague *aktiv* of ČSM student leaders. While admitting some weaknesses, the ČSM officials defended their behavior both in 1965 and in the Strahov case, but voiced their willingness to endorse the "political activity" of the students and their intention to articulate the interests of the students and other groups under their jurisdiction. This statement was rejected by the university party committee, and mounting criticism, especially by student members, caused the ČSM leadership to adopt a more reform-oriented stance and to recognize the need for democratic reorganization and greater independence from party control.[117] In late February the Prague municipal ČSM committee canceled the 1966 decision expelling Jiří Müller from membership in the union.[118] Such official actions and statements were regarded as "too little and too late" by many, including ČSM functionaries and organizations, and by the union's newspaper, *Mladá fronta*, and changes in the leadership and the convocation of an extraordinary congress were advocated. At its plenum in March the ČSM accepted the resignation of Zavadil as chairman and approved the idea of a federation of diverse youth organizations and of an extraordinary congress to delineate a new structure. The secretariat and presidium were abolished and a special committee, under Z. Vokrouhlický, was appointed to head the union in the interim and to prepare for the congress.[119]

[116] See *RP*, March 21, 22, for some of the speeches, including Holeček's. Note also comments by S. Budín, *Rep.*, April 3-10. See above, chap. VIII. For other meetings, *RP*, March 14, 15. A large demonstration was later held in the Old Town Square in support of freedom of expression, at which support was expressed for the Polish students (*RP*, May 4).
[117] *Student*, Jan. 31; Jelínek, *Rep.*, Feb. 21-28.
[118] *MF*, Feb. 23, 24. A month later Müller and Holeček were readmitted as students.
[119] *RP*, March 15, 20, 27, 28. At the CPCz Central Committee plenum, Zavadil admitted the faults of the ČSM and his own mistakes, but sought to deflect some of the responsibility onto higher party organs, which had allegedly not informed, or consulted, the ČSM leadership, and had instructed them as to the course to be followed (*RP*, April 11).

Meanwhile in the Action Program the party pledged itself to adopt a new approach which would treat the youth as allies and give them a voice in public matters, and to seek to improve their living and working conditions and recreational opportunities.[120] Vokrouhlický, in an open letter to Černík, described the most urgent problems requiring solution, such as housing, training for fifteen-year-olds, and payment according to merit, and suggested a special law on youth and a ministry for youth affairs. This resulted in a meeting with Černík and other ministers and an invitation to the ČSM to submit a draft "decision" regarding their main demands.[121] Although differences of opinion delayed official action, relations with the government were, in Vokrouhlický's opinion, good, but he was critical of the attitude of the National Assembly and the Czech National Council toward youth problems.[122] The various youth organizations were even more censorious of the National Front for the lack of youth representation in its topmost leadership.[123] Negotiations were conducted with Poláček, Goldstücker, and others, to discuss joint action with the trade unions, the writers' union, and other bodies.

The party leadership, in the Action Program and in a later Presidium report, accepted the idea of the independence of the Union of Youth from direct party control and the necessity for a differentiated approach to the various strata of youth, but still clung to the desire for a unified, perhaps federated, organization, to articulate the common interests of all young people and to exert an influence in the National Front and in the representative organs. Vokrouhlický, well aware of the serious crisis in the ČSM, was present at the Presidium meeting and endorsed the party's view. He warned that without a single organization the youth would not be a "powerful partner" or an influential "pressure group," and advocated some form of "integration," either through a coordinating committee or a federal structure. His Slovak colleague, R. Harenčár, proposed either a federation of independent organizations, or a unified organization with autonomy for each component, including Hungarian and Ukrainian organizations. Others spoke of a "confederation" of two federal organizations.[124]

The disintegration of the ČSM had proceeded so far that it was doubt-

---

[120] Remington, ed., *Winter in Prague*, pp. 96, 112-13.

[121] *RP*, April 10, May 28.

[122] *MF*, July 17. He had become doubtful of the value of a general law, but insisted on the creation of a ministry.

[123] Joint statement by all youth organizations (*RP*, June 20).

[124] Remington, ed., *Winter in Prague*, pp. 112-13. Cf. Dubček at April plenum, *RŠO*, pp. 75-76. For the May 21-22 Presidium, ibid., pp. 160-62. See also Vokrouhlický, *MF*, April 20 and *RP*, May 28; Harenčár, *Práca*, May 25, *Smena*, May 26, *Pravda*, June 27; V. Ryneš, *MF*, May 21.

ful whether a unified youth organization could be preserved at all.[125] It seemed more likely that it would be replaced by a federation of the separate youth organizations that were coming into existence, one after the other. The Pioneers, renamed "Czechoslovak Pioneers," proclaimed their independence but indicated willingness to cooperate with other youth organizations in a federation. *Junák* (Boy Scouts) was revived, and regarded federation as a possibility. Other emergent organizations (in addition to that of university students) included a union of campers (*Tábornická unie*); associations of middle school students and apprentices; village and agricultural youth; factory youth; military youth; and a Union of Youth Clubs. The chances of preserving a unified Slovak youth organization seemed greater than in the Czech lands, and it was envisaged as an equal partner with the Czech in a future all-state federal association.[126] Ukrainian and Hungarian youth also evinced a desire for autonomy or independence.

From the very beginning of 1968 most students looked upon the ČSM as moribund and mistrusted its leaders. Only some conservative student spokesmen, while voicing sharp criticism of the ČSM and urging the formation of separate youth groups, supported the party on the desirability of a single youth association to coordinate the individual groups and to defend their common interests.[127] For most, however, the idea of federalization, which had once been the major objective, was no longer regarded as a satisfactory solution except as the possible basis of an entirely reorganized movement. In the meantime students should form their own independent organization. Such opinions were expressed by more radical student spokesmen but also by many ČSM organizations and by the outspoken ČSM publication, *Student*. Meanwhile Academic Councils of Students (ARS), first formed in 1967 in the Philosophical Faculty at Charles University, were set up in other faculties in Prague and elsewhere to provide a foundation for regional and national student "parliaments." In March an all-state *aktiv* in Brno prepared the ground for a university students organization, and a similar development occurred in Slovakia. Finally, in late May, a congress in Olomouc brought into existence the Union of University Students as an independent organization. The union did not exclude association in a new federalized youth movement and revealed a readiness to cooperate with the National Front, although not as a constituent member.[128]

[125] K. Nývlt, *RP*, May 9.
[126] Ibid., April 8, May 27; V. Borodovčák, *MF*, May 11. The Pioneer organization opposed efforts to recreate *Junák*.
[127] J. Ondrouch, *RP*, March 6.
[128] D. Hanousek and J. Kavan, *Práce*, Feb. 29; *RP*, March 13, 24, April 18, May 27; *Student*, March 6; *Smena*, May 22; *NS*, June 6. See also P. Rybář, its chairman, *Rep.*, Oct. 2-9.

RELIGION AND THE CHURCH

The post-January climate encouraged churchmen and believers of all denominations to make known their demands.[129] The Roman Catholics, who formed the overwhelming majority of believers, expressed their support for democratization and for the Dubček regime, and a willingness to cooperate in reform. Condemning repressive actions against the church in the past and the suppression of freedom of religious profession, they called for a redress of injustices and a "normalization" of religious conditions. At the end of March a letter, signed by bishops, priests, monks and nuns, and laymen, setting forth their grievances, was presented to Dubček.[130] At the same time there was bitter criticism of those who had claimed to speak in the name of the Catholics, in particular the pro-regime Peace Movement of the Catholic Clergy, and its chairman, Father Plojhar, a cabinet minister after 1948. At a stormy meeting at the end of March, Plojhar was forced to resign his chairmanship, and Bishop Tomášek, apostolic administrator of Prague, was elected chairman of an action committee to prepare the way for a new organization.[131] It was hoped to carry through a "revival" of the church itself in line with the decisions of the Second Vatican Council. In mid-May, at a conference of churchmen and laymen at the Velehrad Basilica near Uherské Hradiště, a new association, the Cause of Conciliar Renewal (*Dílo koncilové obnovy*), headed by Bishop Tomášek, was formed to assist the hierarchy in fulfilling this goal.[132]

Letters and statements by Catholic spokesmen called for an open dialogue between church and state and listed the many grievances requiring correction. Bishop Tomášek defended religious freedom as an indispensable component of freedom in general and contended that believers should have equal rights with other citizens. "Today, when the word re-

---

[129] For general discussion of all religious groups see Kusin, *Political Groupings*, pp. 197-202; Jacques Marcelle, *Le deuxième coup de Prague* (Brussels, 1968), pp. 27-48, 89-92, 116-18. For the positive attitude of the Protestants toward the reform movement, see Jan Milic Lochman, *Church in a Marxist Society: A Czechoslovak View* (New York, 1970), pp. 106-10.

[130] This was one of many letters to Dubček from Catholics. Another was signed by 83 former prisoners whose sentences totaled 734 years (*LL*, March 21). For Bishop Tomášek's summary of the content of these missives and his pastoral letter read in all churches, see *LD*, March 22, 28. See also his article, "Religion and Socialism," *LL*, March 21; an interview with *L'Unità* (*RP*, May 21); *Rep.*, June 12-19; and an article by the Slovak bishop, E. Nécsey, *KŽ*, April 12. For a report of demands raised by various dioceses and institutions, see *Katolické noviny*, May 5.

[131] *LD*, March 22.

[132] *RP* and *LD*, May 15; also *Kat. nov.*, Aug. 4. The CC's report on the political situation (Aug. 12) stated that this organization, with almost one million members, could become "a very serious political force." It also spoke of tendencies toward "political clericalism," but offered no evidence (*Zpráva*, pp. 29-30).

habilitation is so frequently heard," said the bishop, "Christ, too, must be rehabilitated in our life."[133] More specifically, there were proposals for amendments of the existing laws concerning church and religion; the end of administrative interference in religious life; the abolition of the state hierarchy of church secretaries; the rehabilitation of bishops and priests unjustly confined or imprisoned, and the resumption of their religious functions; and the return of Cardinal Beran from his exile in the Vatican. Other goals were the abolition of censorship and other restrictions on the Catholic press, and of limitations on religious instruction in schools and on the training of priests; permission for religious broadcasts; the ending of discrimination against teachers and others who were believers; the establishment of a Slovak archbishopric and a Slovak theological academy. The restoration of the religious orders, liquidated in the fifties, and of the Greek Catholic Church, banned at that time, was also proposed. There was need for improved relations with the Vatican, including an official agreement which would make possible the appointment of bishops to vacant sees.

As the Action Program indicated in two brief references to religion, the party was ready to reckon with the participation in public life of all strata of the population, including believers, and to extend the projected law guaranteeing freedom of association and assembly to include "citizens of differing religious faith and confession." Černík, in his first declaration as head of the government, promised believers full rights as citizens and pledged "respect for freedom of religious profession and conviction." Gustáv Husák, who, as deputy Prime Minister, was responsible for relations with the church, spoke of a "reasonable" solution based on "respect for freedom of religious confession." An initial meeting of Husák and other government leaders with Bishop Tomášek and church spokesmen prepared the way for future state-church meetings.[134] Official talks with the Vatican were planned in the fall to deal with the problem of vacant bishoprics.

Another indication of the new attitude to religion was the appointment as head of the Secretariat for Religious Affairs in the Ministry of Culture and Information, of a sociologist, Erika Kadlecová, author of a study of religion in northern Moravia.[135] She recognized the need to modify the administrative directives which had deformed, she said, the principle of "freedom of confession" and to correct the injustices of past official policy toward religion and the churches. Kadlecová gave a fuller exposition of the government's intentions in an article published in *Rudé právo* in

[133] *LD*, July 27.
[134] Remington, ed., *Winter in Prague*, pp. 97, 104; *RP*, April 25; *NM*, no. 6 (1968), pp. 661-62; *Pravda*, May 1.
[135] E. Kadlecová, *Sociologický výzkum religiozity Severomoravského kraje* (Prague, 1967).

May in which she admitted the serious faults in the party's church policy and in the treatment of believers and conceded the legitimacy of many of the demands being raised.[136] It was difficult, she wrote, to incorporate into a democratic society an institution (the Roman Catholic Church) which was itself not democratic and to fit an international institution into the legal order without breach of sovereignty. Yet religious freedom was not a threat to society; since freedom was indivisible, its limitation threatened the freedom of all. In another statement, made privately to an *aktiv* of the CC Ideological Department, Kadlecová strongly defended the new policy toward the church and the believers as "a return to a Marxist starting-point" and rejected any reversion to terror and repression. On this occasion she categorically repudiated the idea of a return of property to the church—a declaration which she later repeated publicly. At the *aktiv* she also warned, more strongly than in public utterances, that cooperation with the church was based on certain conditions, the most notable of which was that the church must refrain from political activity and must not identify itself with any party (such as the People's Party), or seek to influence believers in a particular political direction.[137]

On July 14 the official Catholic newspaper, *Katolické noviny*, complained that almost nothing had been achieved, but state representatives claimed that many positive steps had been taken and that time was required to settle the host of outstanding problems. Certainly the Catholic press, like other newspapers, found itself free, from March on, openly to express Catholic views on matters religious and public. Dialogues between believers and Marxists, hitherto more or less confined to the international plane, occurred. Many priests and bishops were rehabilitated and permitted to take up their duties in parish or diocese. Religious instruction was to be in the hands of the churches and was to take place in church buildings, and in schools only if space in the former was not available. The Theological Faculty in Olomouc was reopened. Bishop Tomášek and others were able to visit the Vatican without hindrance.

The CPCz Presidium, in mid-July, reiterated its commitment to assure religious freedom and to encourage the cooperation of all citizens without regard to their beliefs, but voiced opposition to the use of religion for political purposes or the fomenting of religious dissensions. The church must respect socialism, be loyal to the state, and not seek to influence

---

136 *LD*, April 7; *RP*, May 18. See also V. Gardavský, *LL*, June 20.

137 *Naš vztah k věřícím; Některé současné církevně politické problémy* (Prague, June 19, 1968, for inner party circulation only). Cf. her more restrained public references, *LD*, April 7; *Kat. nov.*, Aug. 4. Catholic spokesmen, such as Bishop Tomášek, were highly critical of the People's Party for its earlier support of the regime and described it as a non-confessional party, including other than Catholics (*LD*, March 22).

citizens in civil matters. Similarly, no political party or organization could claim to be "the only or exclusive spokesman of believers."[138]

A most dramatic action was the restoration of the Greek Catholic Church. In 1950 some 300,000 Greek Catholics in eastern Slovakia, in and around Prešov, had been forced to "return" to Orthodoxy, and many of their priests had been arrested or had to seek other work. In April 1968 this was condemned as unjust by a gathering of Greek Catholic priests in Košice, and also by L. Holdoš, head of the Slovak Office of Church Affairs in 1950-1951.[139] A government decision on June 13 rescinded the 1950 ban and was accompanied by an ordinance providing for economic support of the newly forming Greek Catholic parishes. The believers themselves were to decide whether or not to leave the Orthodox churches and to reestablish Catholic churches. Where agreement had not been reached within six months through local commissions, the problem would be referred to the Slovak National Council or the Prague Ministry of Culture and Information.[140] After eighteen years of forced conversion and with few priests available, the changeover was not always easy, and sometimes led to sharp, and even violent, conflict over the control of churches between Orthodox and Greek Catholic rivals. A delegation of Orthodox priests went to Prague to present their complaints and demands to the government and to the President.[141]

THE NATIONALITIES

The January changeover awakened the hopes of the national minorities that their grievances would be dealt with and their national rights and interests better respected.[142] Their leaders, like those of the Slovaks, had been tarred with the brush of "bourgeois nationalism" in the past, and their cultural organizations had been either dissolved or severely restricted. There had been some improvement in their position after 1960, but there were no legal guarantees of their rights and no special institutions to protect their interests other than a department concerning

[138] July 16 (RŠO, p. 242).
[139] RP, April 12; Kat. nov., April 28, May 5; KŽ, May 17; O. R. Halaga, LL, June 20.
[140] Sbírka zákonů, no. 70/1968; RP, June 22, Východoslovenské noviny, June 23.
[141] RP, June 28. Incidents are mentioned in RP, June 22; Smena, July 21; Sľoboda, July 5; Z. Štastná, Rep., March 13, 1969.
[142] For this, and the following, see in particular the round-table discussion by members of the federal commission of experts, D. Okáli, L. Haraksim, and J. Fabian (Pravda, July 5); the excellent summary of minority demands by Okáli, NS, July 25; and the summary of the problem by J. Zvara and J. Šindelka, RP, Aug. 16. For population data, see Demografie, no. 2 (June 1968), pp. 179-80; also RP, Feb. 6. See also Kusin, Political Grouping, chap. 5; and a brief analysis in Zpráva pp. 38-41.

schools and culture in the central administration. The party had undertaken a study of the nationality problem prior to the 13th congress but the results had not been published or taken into account.[143]

The Action Program endorsed the right of each nation to live its own national life and enjoy all constitutional rights, and called for a special statute which would stipulate the rights of the nationalities and afford "constitutional and legal guarantees of complete and genuine political, economic and cultural equality." It proposed proportionate representation of the minorities in elected and executive bodies, and self-administration in matters of concern to them, and promised the promotion of the cultural individuality of each nationality through the establishment of its own institutions and through actions of the state organs and the national committees.[144] The Slovak Action Program also referred to constitutional guarantees of equality and contained several specific proposals—a nationalities secretariat in the Slovak Council of Ministers, a special committee in the Central Committee of the party, and nationality commissions in the lower party and state organs.[145] The preparation of more detailed plans, especially the proposed statute, rested with the governmental and expert commissions responsible for formulating the law on federalism.[146]

In the Czech lands the situation was less complicated than in Slovakia, since the nationalities were less vocal and their demands represented no threat to Czech national interests. The Germans, the vestige of the once large minority remaining after the expulsion in 1945, numbered some 124,000 at the end of 1966, living in scattered settlements in predominantly Czech areas, and were declining in numbers as a result of emigration and gradual assimilation. They had not been recognized as a nation-

[143] Zvara and Šindelka, *RP*, Aug. 16. See the vague general materials of the CC Presidium on the nationality question, *NM*, no. 12, June 13, 1967, pp. 7-8. See also Zvara, ibid., no. 2 (1969), pp. 194-202. According to Kusin, the study produced some constructive suggestions, including the idea of a nationality statute; the legal regulation of nationalities in mixed areas; a central body for minority problems; expansion of the rights of the cultural societies; and improvement in minority education (*Political Grouping*, p. 145).

[144] Remington, ed., *Winter in Prague*, pp. 96, 108-9, 132. The material prepared for the 14th congress did not mention the proposed statute and was confined to generalities and a few brief references (Pelikán, *Vysočany Congress*, pp. 110-11, 201 passim, 246-47). Curiously, the materials twice referred to secession as a possible form of national self-determination.

[145] *Pravda*, May 29. A meeting attended by M. Pecho, representatives of the Slovak National Council, other state and party officials, and communist functionaries of the Hungarian and Ukrainian cultural associations, at the end of April, stressed the need for economic development of the eastern and southern areas of Slovakia. The meeting expressed regret at the emotion and passion that had been aroused and called for concrete analysis and dialogue (ibid., May 1).

[146] See the noncommittal remarks on the nationality question by Husák, ibid., April 23, June 1; *Rep.*, June 26-July 3, pp. II-III.

al group in the 1960 constitution and were severely restricted in their cultural activities, having no association of their own and no schools using the German language. Their demands were modest in the extreme, concentrating on obligatory German instruction in schools and expanded cultural activities. They established a Kulturverband and planned to make their newspaper, *Volkszeitung*, a daily.[147]

The Polish minority was smaller, some 71,000 at the end of 1966, almost all domiciled in the Czech lands, in two districts in and near Těšín. Their Polish National Association numbered some 21,000 members, in 93 local branches. They proposed general nationality commissions in the National Assembly and the National Councils and state secretariats for nationality affairs in the two republic governments. They asked for official bilingualism in districts where the Polish population was substantial. Somewhat later, the idea of a Polish National Council was raised.[148]

A special case was the large Slovak population—at least 350,000—who had migrated to Ostrava and other industrial areas in northern Moravia to earn their livelihood and were subject to rapid assimilation. Although technically not a national minority, these Slovaks presented a serious national problem. They were concerned about the lack of Slovak schools (there were only two in Ostrava), insufficient representation in the national committees, and inadequacy of cultural facilities. It was hoped that the formation of local branches of the Matica Slovenská would help to correct some of these deficiencies and at least slow down the process of assimilation.[149]

In Slovakia there were two national minorities, the Ruthenians and Hungarians, and a third group, the gypsies, who wished to be treated as a distinct national entity. The Hungarians and Ruthenians were quite aggressive in their campaign for nationality rights and their demands produced a sharp counterresponse by the Slovaks. The gypsies, estimated at 165,000 at the end of 1968 (with an additional 61,000 in the Czech lands) were culturally backward and unorganized. Gypsy spokesmen, in Bratislava and Brno, separately put forward similar demands, requesting that the gypsies be recognized as a nationality and be given proportionate representation in elected bodies, and called for the formation of a Union of Gypsies.[150]

The Ruthenians (Ukrainians) were relatively few in number, some 36,000, living in fairly compact settlements in two districts, in and near Prešov (21,000 others were scattered in the Czech lands). This minority

147 P. Pokorný, *Rep.*, Oct. 23-30, 1968; I. Petřinová, ibid., April 17, 1969.
148 T. Siwek, ibid., April 10, 1969.
149 *Pravda*, July 31; J. Zíma, *Rep.*, March 6, 1969.
150 These demands were acceptable to the committee of experts (Okáli et al., *Pravda*, July 5). A preparatory committee for such a union was set up in 1968 (A. Tučková and V. Srb, *Rep.*, April 24, 1969).

605

had some difficulty in self-identification, some considering themselves Ukrainians, others Ruthenians (Rusyny). They had been subjected to official Ukrainianization after 1952 and many had preferred to call themselves Slovaks and send their children to Slovak schools. During the fifties they suffered other forms of repression in the liquidation of the Greek Catholic Church and the abolition of the Ukrainian National Council which had been established in 1945. The brief awakening of 1968 produced a swing toward Ruthenian self-identification which, however, collided with the Ukrainian orientation of the established intelligentsia in Prešov and produced friction with nationally minded Slovaks. The Cultural Union of the Ukrainian Working People (KSUT) advocated the restoration of the Ukrainian National Council, later renaming it the Council of Czechoslovak Ruthenians (Ukrainians), as "a political organ" with the right to propose legislation. Some favored a form of territorial autonomy, but others were content with the re-creation of the former predominantly Ruthenian districts. The KSUT was to continue as a cultural and scientific institution on the model of the Matica. A national congress, frequently postponed, was finally scheduled for August 23, but was never held owing to the occupation.[151]

Much more controversial were the demands raised by the Hungarians, who numbered 534,000 in the 1961 census and 559,000 at the end of 1966, and who lived mainly in southern and eastern Slovakia, often in compact settlements in certain cities and rural areas.[152] Taking advantage of the new freedom of expression, their organization, the Cultural Union of the Hungarian Working People (Csemadok) and the Hungarian party daily, Új Szó, aired pent-up grievances concerning the post-war exchange of population with Hungary; the forced transfer of many Hungarians from Slovakia to Bohemia; the campaign for "re-Slovakization" of those who had allegedly been compelled to Magyarize themselves; and the deprivation of cultural and educational rights.[153] Admittedly their lot had improved after 1948, and still more after 1956, but in their view the equality assured in the constitution of 1960 had remained largely on

---

[151] V. Kapišovský, Pravda, April 28, 1968; Z. Štastná, Rep., March 13, 1969. See also Paul Magoszi, "National Assimilation: The Case of the Rusyn-Ukrainians of Czechoslovakia" (mimeo.); and Grey Hodnett and Peter J. Potichnyj, The Ukraine and the Czechoslovak Crisis (Canberra, 1970), chap. 3.

[152] See the geographical analysis of nationality relations by E. Mazúr, NS, June 6, 13. Some stated that the Hungarian population was even higher, perhaps as many as 720,000-740,000. There was a Hungarian majority in 451 villages, constituting 13.5 percent of all Slovak villages (K. Douděra, RP, Oct. 18). For a valuable study of the Hungarian minority during 1968, see Robert R. King, Minorities under Communism: Nationalities as a Source of Tension among Balkan Communist States (Cambridge, Mass., 1973), chap. 6.

[153] J. Gyönyör, Új Szó, April 12. Cf. a historical analysis by M. Lavová (ibid., June 27).

paper. There were complaints of inadequate educational and cultural facilities, and the lack of an official agency where Hungarian interests could be presented.

In mid-March Csemadok issued a declaration which, although not published at the time in the Slovak press, became the target of bitter attack.[154] It stated that the nationalities should be regarded as "an inseparable organic part" of the Republic, which was formed, on an equal basis, of "nations and nationalities." This in effect placed the Hungarians and other minorities on the same constitutional basis as Czechs and Slovaks. The constitution should be revised in order to define the legal status of the nationalities and to guarantee them equality, not only as "individuals," but as "social groups." This would be assured by "nationality organs and institutions" which would share in the work of the all-state and republic-wide government agencies and would act as organs of national self-administration. These would include, within the Slovak National Council, a nationalities committee, and within the Board of Commissioners, a Commissionership of Nationality Affairs; within the National Assembly, a nationality committee; in the central government, a secretariat for nationality affairs, headed by a state secretary; and in the regional committees, nationality commissions and departments. Even more controversial was the proposal that nationally mixed districts should be reorganized to form districts as homogeneous as possible, with guarantees for minorities in those predominantly Hungarian or Slovak. The Hungarian school system should be greatly expanded and managed by Hungarian agencies. Cultural development required the establishment of appropriate scientific institutes and support from state institutions and national committees.

This charter of Hungarian rights was at once endorsed by other organizations, such as the Hungarian section of the Union of Slovak Writers, which added other far-reaching demands, for instance, that the Košice government program of 1945, the policy of re-Slovakization, and the post-war trials of Hungarians be repudiated, and that the victims of those years be rehabilitated and compensated. The writers also proposed the establishment of a Hungarian Scientific Institute, a national library, a theater in Pozsony (Bratislava), a publishing house, Hungarian television programs, an independent pioneer and youth association, and possibly autonomous unions of journalists and of writers. Others wanted a Hungarian theater in Košice and chairs of Hungarian studies at certain university faculties. Other suggestions were added later: a Hungarian National Council (or a Nationalities Council), a separate Slovak Minis-

154 *Új Szó*, March 15. Text in Slovak was published in *Pravda*, May 24, p. 6. Július Lörincz later revealed that the statement had been prepared at the request of the Slovak party (*Pravda*, May 24).

try for the Hungarian nationality, and the appointment of Hungarians to leading posts in other ministries, according to proportionate representation.[155]

Such demands evoked bitter reactions among Slovaks, who, while accepting the principle of national equality, criticized what they called "chauvinist" and "separatist" tendencies among the Hungarians and condemned Csemadok, Július Lőrincz, its chairman, and *Új Szó* for their attitude.[156] A reassessment of the Košice program was rejected, and the formation of a homogeneous Hungarian region was condemned as a threat to the Slovak minority in this area. With respect to the areas where the Hungarians were in the majority, the Slovaks complained about the failure of Hungarians to learn Slovak; the inadequacy of instruction in Slovak in schools; the lack of official use of Slovak in offices and at meetings; the use of Hungarian place-names (even Pozsony for Bratislava); inadequate representation of Slovaks in local party and government organs, etc. As a result, Slovaks were like "foreigners" in their own land and were often forced to give up their nationality or move to Slovak areas. Slovak repatriates from Hungary, it was said, found their situation worse in southern Slovakia than it had been in Hungary. It was asserted that the Slovaks in Hungary were treated much worse than the Hungarians in Slovakia. Hungarians were accused of disloyalty to Czechoslovakia and of making threats to appeal for aid to the Hungarian Communist Party. Slovak anger was also directed at Slovak leaders for their neglect of the fate of their kinsmen in southern Slovakia and for the "utter failure of Czechoslovakia's nationality policy."[157]

These Slovak utterances generated bitter counterresponses by the Hungarians who were particularly incensed by the comparison with the position of the Slovaks in Hungary, which they argued was completely different, and by the insinuation of interference from Hungary, which they denied. Passions increased in intensity on both sides. In southern Slovakia anti-Slovak and anti-Hungarian slogans appeared on walls; illegal leaflets were circulated; demonstrations led to minor violence, such as the breaking of windows. On both sides there were appeals for tolerance, for cooperation between Csemadok and the Matica, and for careful study of the nationality problem by the party's nationality commission and by the Slovak National Council.[158]

[155] *Új Szó*, March 24. See also *RP*, April 4, p. 6; Okáli, *NS*, July 25.
[156] For instance, Olšinský, "Hungarians against Slovaks?" *KŽ*, April 12; M. Gáfrík, ibid., April 19, May 31; Okáli, ibid., June 7. Contrast the defense of Hungarian rights by a Slovak, Z. Jesenská, *Új Szó*, April 12. See the impassioned letters from Hungarian and Slovak readers, *KŽ*, May 17, p. 7.
[157] Gáfrík, works cited above; also a statement by the party organization in the Institute of Slovak Literature, *Pravda*, June 12.
[158] M. Hric and T. Michal, ibid., May 17; V. Plevza, *NS*, May 23; Lőrincz,

Slovak fears of Hungarian nationalism led to two specific proposals. First, they asked for the constitutional endorsement of Czech and Slovak as state languages, as well as a special statute which would have proclaimed Slovak as the "national tongue of Slovaks," equal to Czech as a state language, and required its use as the official language in all spheres of public life in Slovakia.[159]

Secondly, there was a movement for the revival of Matica Slovenská, which had been founded in 1863 as an agency of cultural expression; had been banned by the Hungarian authorities in 1875; restored in 1919; liquidated again in 1953; and reestablished by law in 1954. During the First Republic, and in the early post-war years, it had been an important center of scholarship and cultural activity; had possessed a large library at its seat in Martin; and, between 1945 and 1948, had had 100,000 members, in a network of local branches. During the fifties it had lost its scientific institutes to the Academy of Sciences and had been greatly restricted in its other activities. When it was restored in 1954 it was not permitted to have local branches (or to concern itself with Slovaks abroad).

As a result, in 1968, Slovaks in southern and eastern Slovakia felt at a disadvantage in comparison with the Hungarians since they had no local organizations, comparable to those of Csemadok, to defend their interests.[160] Voices were soon heard calling for the revival of the Matica's cultural and popular functions, and "clubs of the friends of Matica" began to be formed, especially in southern Slovakia, in lieu of the former branches.[161] The Slovak Action Program paid tribute to the cultural mission of the Matica in the past and mentioned the desirability of transferring to it some of the competence of the Czechoslovak Foreign Institute, which had exclusive rights to deal with Slovaks abroad.[162]

In late June the Matica was formally established by statute as "an all-national institution," with a library, archive, and other institutes (includ-

---

Pravda, May 24, May 30, June 16; J. Bečvář, *RP*, June 8; P. Pokorný, *Rep.*, June 12-19. A seminar was held in Bratislava on May 21, with representatives of the minorities present, to discuss federalism and the nationality problem (*Pravda*, May 26, June 12). Its main recommendations were the formation of an interdisciplinary team in the Academy of Sciences for the study of the nationality problem and the establishment of an association and a periodical for nationality questions.

[159] This proposal was made by the Ľudovít Štúr Language Institute and was cited by J. Doruľa in an article in which he severely criticized the seminar for accepting the Csemadok demands (*NS*, June 20). See also J. Ružička's address to the Slovak Academy of Sciences, April 10, *Kultúra slova* (June 1968), pp. 193-97.

[160] Okáli, *KŽ*, June 7. For the history of the Matica, see J. Marták, *NS*, May 23; P. Vongrej, *Student*, May 29; Karol Rosenbaum, ibid., Aug. 8.

[161] *Pravda*, March 23; P. Vongrej, *RP*, April 14; ibid., April 21. See also D. Tatarka, *KŽ*, May 17; A. Hirner, *NS*, June 27.

[162] *Pravda*, May 29.

ing an institute for the study of Slovaks abroad), and with local branches coordinated by a center in Martin.[163] Some Slovaks were disappointed that it was to be a state organ, financed from the state budget, with its administrators appointed by the SNR presidium, and doubted that it would be able effectively to support the Slovaks in southern and eastern Slovakia.[164] Nonetheless, by the time of the Matica's first general assembly in early August, when President Svoboda paid tribute to its historical role, it had already begun to regain something of its old character and was composed of 300 clubs, with 100,000 members. The proclamation adopted by the assembly emphasized the Matica's function of protecting Slovaks in southern and eastern Slovakia and as "an active national political force" within the National Front.[165]

Meanwhile, the slowness of the government's commission of experts in reaching agreement on a plan of federation caused a delay in drafting a proposal of guarantees for the nationalities. The commission had decided to prepare a separate nationalities statute which would establish a "framework" of principles to be implemented by separate Czech and Slovak statutes. The opinions of the experts differed, however, from those of the nationalities' spokesmen. Among the latter there was a consensus that the nationalities should be regarded as fundamental components of Czechoslovakia, equal in status to the two principal nations, Czechs and Slovaks, and should possess their own institutions, especially national councils, as well as state organs for nationality affairs.[166] The experts, on the other hand, distinguished the nationalities from the "nations," who alone had a legitimate claim to "statehood." The interests of the nationalities should be safeguarded at the republican levels of the state structure, by means of nationality committees in elected bodies, organs to supervise the observance of the nationality statute in the Councils of Ministers, and departments in the Ministries of Education and Culture and Information. The experts rejected, however, the proposal of a federal secretariat or a national committee in the National Assembly, since nationality affairs did not, they argued, belong to the federal competence. They sought to protect bilingúalism in the mixed districts, to improve instruction in Slovak, and to establish Czech and Slovak as state languages. They also felt that the industrialization of southern Slovakia would be an effective contribution to the solution of national grievances.[167]

[163] *Sb. z.*, 97/1968.
[164] Editorial, *KŽ*, Aug. 16; D. Tatarka, ibid.
[165] *Pravda*, Aug. 10-12. See also I. Gegus, *NS*, July 11; Marták, *Život*, Aug. 7.
[166] Joint meeting of representatives of Hungarian, Ukrainian, and Polish organizations (*RP*, Aug. 15).
[167] Okáli et al., *Pravda*, July 5. See also editorial, ibid., June 30.

CONCLUSION

The foregoing analysis reveals the essential diversity of interests and opinions within Czechoslovak society, a diversity long concealed beneath a monolithic political system and behind an ideology which denied the existence of antagonistic conflict. In the absence of extensive quantitative data on group attitudes, the facts presented cannot claim to give an exact picture of the balance of forces within and among the various social groups. They show unmistakably, however, that there were substantial differences of attitude toward reform among the groups, reflecting their different roles in society and their specific grievances and demands. In each case, too, the identification with reform underwent a process of change between January and August. Moreover, no social group was homogeneous in its orientation. Within each of the categories there were significant divergences of interest and opinion, based on the economic and social diversity of each sector and reflecting a wide spectrum of varying attitudes among the individuals involved.

The spearhead of reform was the creative intelligentsia, especially the scholars and writers. In the forefront were the creative artists, some of whom had acquired a substantial income and prestige and enjoyed a unique position as self-employed persons. No less notable were the scholars in the humanities and social sciences, who, although usually public employees, utilized their professional knowledge and status in the interest of reform. Less active were the technical and scientific intelligentsia, although certain individuals played prominent roles. The journalists, who had for years served as mouthpieces of the regime, became vigorous advocates of reform. Students, less bound by the interests of professional position and inclined to be critical of the status quo, gave strong support to the reform cause. All of these groups, while pressing their own specific interests and ideas, also articulated the interests of broader sectors of society. Although most of the active intellectuals were communists, noncommunists played an important part, sometimes finding themselves in broad agreement with reform-oriented party members.

Leadership in the reform movement was thus assumed by certain elite groups and not by the "masses." The two largest occupational groups, the workers and farmers, at least initially, greeted the efforts of the intellectuals with indifference and sometimes with opposition. Moreover, the trade unions, thoroughly bureaucratized and party-controlled, were fearful of reform, as were officials in agricultural administration or in the collective farms. The rank-and-file workers and farmers were themselves divided, as a result of differing economic and social conditions. Some sectors defended vested interests threatened by reform; others pressed for the vindication of specific group interests. In the course of

611

time many workers and farmers became more and more active in pursuing their class or group interests and began gradually to endorse reform in general.

The reform movement was, however, not merely an exclusive affair of the elites but a matter of concern for the mass of the population, appealing to all who had grievances concerning past treatment and hopes for a new course. All economic and social groups took advantage of the post-January context to articulate their special interests. Reform was thus genuinely popular and all-national, winning support from almost all sectors of the population.

The public opinion polls revealed that reform was endorsed by the overwhelming majority of the population. Most of the published poll results—and especially those dealing with attitudes to reform or to the leadership—were unfortunately not broken down in terms of different social groups. Whenever differentiated data *were* given, there was some indication of a greater political interest and a more favorable attitude to reform among those under 40 years of age, and those with a higher level of education, and among men as compared with women. The differences were not, however, consistent, and were usually slight, and do not justify conclusions that opinion differed significantly according to age, education, or sex.[168] This was also true of the data on workers and collective farmers, both of whom showed themselves hardly less favorable to reform the national average. In some cases the farmers appeared to be somewhat less reform-minded, and certain other categories (such as "clerical staff and managers" and engineers, or in other polls, "other employees") more progressive, but the differences were in degree only and not significant enough to warrant serious attention.[169]

It is more difficult to analyze with any precision the social groups opposed to reform. Yet as the data set forth in this chapter clearly indicate, there were many who were lukewarm to change and sought to slow it down in their own particular sphere. The hard core of resistance, it is usually assumed, was to be found among the *aparátníci*—officials and functionaries of the party, the state, and the mass organizations.[170] More

<hr/>

[168] Piekalkiewicz, *Polling*, passim, especially polls cited at pp. 7 (anti-socialist danger), 17-19 (post-January changes), 21 (CPCz policy), 69 (interest in politics), 108 (guarantees of socialist democracy), 156-57 (non-communist parties), 230 ff. (existing party system), 270-71 (support for Dubček). Cf. Ithiel de Sola Pool, "Public Opinion in Czechoslovakia," *Public Opinion Quarterly* (Spring, 1970), p. 22.

[169] Piekalkiewicz, *Polling*, esp. pp. 104-5, 118-19, 133, 156-57, 184, 212, 221, 223, 269-73. For a subjective, impressionistic classification of attitudes of various social groups, based on demands and opinions expressed in certain newspapers, see *RP*, March 30.

[170] For instance, *Zpráva*, p. 31. On working-class origins of these officials, see Krejčí, *Social Change*, pp. 121-22.

specifically, the military and security police, legal and judicial personnel, and many managers—together with the relevant sectors of the party apparatus—were usually depicted as conservative defenders of the status quo. No doubt many, if not most, of these social categories had good reason to fear the reform movement, both because they were assigned the blame and guilt for past policies, and because their jobs, livelihood, and comforts were endangered. Yet it is also true that within these groups, there were differences of opinion and at least some, who, in varying degrees, endorsed reform. This was true of some party bureaucrats, as indicated above (chap. XVI). Managers, too, were divided on the issue of economic reform, some—the poorly educated—seeing it as a threat to their future, and others—the better educated—as an opportunity for the more efficient conduct of their enterprises.[171] Outright opposition was seldom expressed during 1968, however. Unfortunately, there are no empirical data based on polling of group attitudes which would permit any conclusions as to how many of these groups were opposed, and how many were in favor of reform, and in what degree.[172]

[171] Korbonski, "Bureaucracy and Interest Groups," pp. 76-77. On education of managers, Krejčí, Social Change, pp. 113-14.

[172] Ota Šik, at a conference in Windsor, England in 1971, offered a systematic but impressionistic classification of the attitude of various social groups toward reform as follows: (1) groups initiating the perception of the need for change—scientists, both natural and technical, some scholars in the humanities, writers and artists, students, journalists, etc.; (2) groups which had an interest in change but which had to be brought to this perception—workers in certain non-preferred branches of industry, and in transport and communications, farmers, women, and working youth; (3) groups which would join the reform movement under the pressure of public opinion—managers with education, the trade unions, a part of the party apparatus, and lower officers of the army; (4) groups who opposed reform for fear of losing their positions—the whole of the central economic bureaucracy, managers without education, workers in heavy industry, and certain parts of the party apparatus; (5) the "real enemies" of reform—the repressive and ideological sections of the party apparatus, security and judiciary officials, older communists, higher officers of the army, and the People's Militia (notes taken by author).

PART SIX

THE INTERNATIONAL CONTEXT

CHAPTER XIX

A Foreign Policy with "Its Own Face"

FOR SOME weeks after January it appeared that the changeover in leadership was not intended seriously to affect the sphere of external relations. The initial communiqué, as well as the unpublished resolution, emphasized unity with the Soviet Union and with the world socialist system and made no other references to foreign policy. The party daily refuted any speculations about changes, either in foreign policy proper, or in relations with the world communist movement.[1] Presidium statements did not touch on foreign affairs throughout the first three months.[2] Dubček's visit to Moscow on February 1 implied that there would be no break in the traditional intimacy with the Soviet Union, and his speeches during February and March repeatedly avowed loyalty to the alliance with the USSR and to the socialist bloc. There were references to "a more active policy" in Europe, greater "initiative" and "equality" in relations with socialist countries, and Czechoslovakia's national path, but nothing that would suggest that a major shift in international orientation was under consideration. In an article in *Pravda* (Moscow) on the anniversary of February 1948, Dubček reiterated the traditional slogan "With the Soviet Union for all time!" and described the essence of Czechoslovak policy as "proletarian internationalism" and its implementation in political, ideological, and economic relations with the Soviet Union and the socialist camp. He was convinced that "in spite of various difficulties and the complexity of problems which naturally and logically arise (but should not be exaggerated) cooperation . . . would continue along these lines."[3]

THE BUDAPEST CONFERENCE

It was in inter-party relations, at the Budapest conference held at the end of February to prepare a world communist assembly, that a new spirit in CPCz policy, in marked contrast to its traditional conformism, first became evident. As early as January 17, Karel Douděra, the foreign editor of *Rudé právo*, commenting on the forthcoming conference, referred to "the absolute sovereignty" of all communist parties and as-

---

[1] J. Hochman, *Rudé právo*, Jan. 10.
[2] A partial exception was that dated Feb. 19, which dealt with the forthcoming Budapest consultative conference of communist parties, *Rok šedesátý osmý* (Prague, 1969), p. 31.
[3] *Pravda* (Moscow), Feb. 21.

serted that unity in action could only be achieved if differences of opinion were taken into account and overcome in free discussion.[4] The Budapest meeting was marked by open debate, revealing substantial cleavages of opinion, and this unusual atmosphere was warmly welcomed in the Czechoslovak press. The final decision to hold a world communist conference in Moscow in November and to set up a preparatory commission in Budapest reflected the Soviet viewpoint and was supported by Czechoslovakia, but represented a compromise of conflicting views.[5]

Ironically, it fell to the old-time Novotný ideologist, Vladimír Koucký, to present the Czechoslovak view. He warmly espoused the need for unity in the struggle against imperialism and the necessity of a conference in November. "Real unity," he declared, "must respect the diversity and specificity of conditions and must assume . . . the possibility of differing opinions of fraternal parties on certain questions." He proclaimed his party's "full respect for the independence and equality of rights of all communist and workers' parties." Koucký advocated the widest possible participation in the preparation of the world conference, even by parties not present at Budapest, so that the preparatory commission would not represent a new "center."[6] He urged that all parties (including the Yugoslav and Chinese) be represented at the Moscow meeting and that a second conference, embracing all anti-imperialist forces, should be held soon afterwards.[7] Koucký did not exclude criticism of Chinese views at the eventual world gathering, but rejected any "condemnation" or "excommunication."

In the above matters Koucký's views were sometimes not far removed from those of Mikhail Suslov, the Soviet delegate. In other respects, however, the Czechoslovak position was more distinctive and closer to that of the Rumanians (who ultimately left the conference). Although Koucký expressly disapproved Rumania's withdrawal, he believed that this should not hinder her taking part in the preparatory work and in the eventual congress and would not affect the CPCz's relations with her.[8] As to the procedure of the later meeting, Koucký believed that it should

[4] *RP*, Jan. 17.

[5] The proceedings were fully reported in *Rudé právo* and *Pravda*, from March 1 to 8. See also K. Douděra, *RP*, March 8; Josef Šedivý, *Život strany*, no. 7 (March 1968), pp. 16-18; O. Kaderka, *Nová mysl*, no. 4 (1968), pp. 418-22. Cf. J. Dienstbier, *Reportér*, March 20-27, 1968. See also Roger Salloch, *Survey*, no. 68 (July 1968), pp. 44-55; L. U., *Yearbook of International Communist Affairs, 1969* (Stanford, 1970), pp. 997-1007.

[6] There was no place for a "center" or "several centers" in the communist movement, nor for a "binding general line," wrote O. Kaderka, head of the International Relations Department of the CPCz Central Committee (*NM*, no. 4, 1968, p. 419).

[7] At a press conference, Koucký specifically referred to China, although he had not done so in his address (*RP*, March 3).

[8] See also Josef Šedivý, *ŽS*, no. 7 (March 1968), p. 18.

involve more than a mere exchange of views, as some advocated, but that it ought not adopt "a single all-embracing document." Instead, the Czech delegate, like the Rumanian, favored a series of political resolutions on specific questions and concrete agreements for common political action. Moreover, unlike the Soviet Union, Czechoslovakia was openly critical of the declarations of previous Moscow conferences. These, observed Koucký, were still valid as a general line, but had become outdated, for instance, regarding Yugoslavia, "which we regard as an organic part of the international communist movement." The individual party could not claim as part of its sovereignty the right to lay down "the basic strategic directions" of the movement but should be given "enough room for creative implementation according to its specific conditions."

The Soviet position, from the outset, placed the main emphasis on "unity and again unity," in Suslov's words. Although he rejected the need for "any sort of leading international center of the communist movement," he urged the necessity for "unity and coordination of action" of the fraternal parties—a theme voiced repeatedly in Soviet commentary on the parley's purposes. Although conceding that not every letter of the 1957 and 1960 conference documents need be adhered to, Suslov avowed Soviet loyalty to "the general line" formulated in them and urged that the forthcoming conference adopt "a basic document." He accepted the idea that all communist parties would be welcomed to the conference and ruled out the condemning or "excommunicating" of any party. The final communiqué avoided contentious issues and included an appeal to all communist parties to attend the eventual congress.[9]

In the meeting of the preparatory commission in Budapest in April, Jozef Lenárt, who succeeded Koucký as party secretary responsible for international relations, spoke in the same vein as his predecessor, advocating wide participation and maximum publicity in the preparations and at the conference itself, and reiterating the CPCz's opposition to "a comprehensive document of a doctrinaire character."[10]

[9] For a very strong statement of the need for "concordance of policy," see *Pravda*, Feb. 22; also ibid., March 10. For texts of these, Suslov's speech, and the communiqué, see *The Current Digest of the Soviet Press* 20, nos. 8-9-10, pp. 8-11, 15-20, 3-5, resp. For CC statement of approval, see *Pravda*, March 12. The above documents are also given in *Reprints from the Soviet Press* (Compass Publications, N.Y., 1968) 6, no. 6 (March 22), 21-33; no. 7 (April 5), 3-9; no. 8 (April 19), 58-59. The idea of a "binding" general line was supported by E. Honecker, SED representative (British Broadcasting Corporation, Monitoring Service, *Summary of World Broadcasts*, Part II, Eastern Europe, March 1; henceforth cited as BBC.

[10] See his speech and interviews, *RP* April 26, 27, 30. The party daily opposed a "general theoretical code (*kodex*)" and preferred resolutions that would leave space for "independent activity" (ibid., April 24). See also Z. Klíma and I. Synek, ibid., April 21. In May the Presidium decided to "activize" the party's policy in the international communist movement, especially through bilateral contacts (*RŠO*, pp. 61-62). Cf. Dubček's article, *Problemy mira i sotsializma*, no. 6 (1968), p. 15.

Foreign Policy with "a New Face"

There were soon signs that a fresh approach was likely to characterize foreign policy proper as well as inter-party relations. An early sign was a resolution by the party group in the Ministry of Foreign Affairs (MFA), which was critical of past conduct of foreign policy, citing the failure of the Central Committee to deal systematically with this subject and of the MFA leadership to rectify the situation. Czechoslovak foreign policy, based on the alliance with the Soviet Union and the unity of the socialist community and the international communist movement, should acquire "its own defined face." The National Assembly and government, within the line set by the party's congress and Central Committee, should fully exercise their constitutional functions.[11] A week later, a commentary on the Action Program (as yet unpublished) after paying the usual tribute to the alliance with the Soviet Union, stated that Czechoslovakia could realize its own interests and make its own contribution without weakening the bases of its security and that there were unused opportunities for increasing "our active role in the formulation of a coordinated policy."[12] Two days later, J. Pudlák, first deputy foreign minister, asserted the need "to make our own analyses, to formulate our own views and to use our own arguments." The fundamental element of Czechoslovak foreign policy was, he declared, the alliance with the Soviet Union, and any idea of "noninvolvement" or "neutrality" was in conflict with the whole spirit of January. ". . . In the concert of the politics of the socialist states, it is a matter for us to have our own defined voice, our own defined face, so that it should be, not a monotone, but a real concert." The coincidence of Czechoslovak interests with the other socialist countries made possible "a common coordinated approach"; "specific conditions," however, required "a specific policy" for the individual parties, as recognized at Budapest.[13]

At the end of March, Václav Kotyk, of the Institute of International Politics and Economics (ÚMPE), contended that the democratization process should embrace foreign policy. The principle that every socialist country should have "the right to formulate its own domestic and foreign policy in harmony with the conditions and needs of the country" had been frequently proclaimed and should now be realized in practice. This did not involve changing "the orientation of foreign policy" but rather giving it a new "substantive content." "It was a question," he said, "of Czechoslovakia, within the framework of the basic orientation of foreign policy, utilizing to the maximum the conditions and possibilities of taking

---

[11] *RP*, March 14.
[12] A. Mikeštík, A. Müller, and I. Synek, ibid., March 22.
[13] *Pravda*, March 24. Pudlák announced that Clementis, the former foreign minister, executed in 1952, would be honored by a plaque in the Ministry.

its own foreign policy initiative, of having its own views on basic questions of international development and having its own foreign policy conceptions in relations to other countries, especially the socialist countries."[14]

Another commentator, J. Hanák, maintained that the basic concept "With the Soviet Union for all time!" required no change, but would become "more than a phrase" if Czechoslovakia became "an aide and a partner," rather than a child relying on a powerful brother. Specifically, he criticized Czechoslovakia's breach with Israel, called for an examination of aid to the developing countries in the light of "our real possibilities" and for "our own German policy."[15]

At the April plenum Dubček endorsed this general line of thought, without making any definite proposals. Describing the basic orientation of Czechoslovakia to the Soviet Union and the socialist countries as "untouchable" and defining proletarian internationalism as the keystone of its foreign policy, he expressed a determination to "activize the foreign policy activity of our state" and called for "an active contribution to the common scientifically based international political activity of the socialist countries," and in particular for "a more effective European, and especially Central European policy."[16] The plenum, in its main political resolution, did not touch on foreign policy, but by endorsing the Action Program, approved a similar approach.

In some respects, however, the program, in its brief reference to foreign policy, was anticlimactic in its vagueness and generality.[17] Restating the fundamental orientation based on alliance and cooperation with the Soviet Union and the other socialist states, it proclaimed the intention of seeking "a further deepening of the friendly relations with our allies . . . on the basis of mutual esteem, sovereignty, equality of rights, mutual respect, and international solidarity," and of "contributing more actively, and with a well-thought-out conception, to the joint activity of the Council of Mutual Economic Assistance (CMEA or Comecon) and the Warsaw pact." The program promised "a more active European policy aimed at developing mutually advantageous rela-

---

[14] RP, March 30. For an even stronger statement on these lines, see V. Kotyk, Mezinárodní vztahy, no. 2 (1968), pp. 3-11. See also Jaroslav Šedivý, NM, no. 4 (1968), pp. 496-503.

[15] Rep., March 27-April 3.

[16] RP, April 2 (RŠO, pp. 85-87). Cf. his speech to the Prague party aktiv when he spoke of measures to "deepen" the mechanism of the Warsaw treaty and the economic cooperation with the Soviet Union and other socialist countries (RP, April 9).

[17] RP, April 10 for the text. There had even been doubts about the desirability of including any reference to foreign affairs. The paragraphs on foreign policy were hastily written at the last minute by A. Šnejdárek, director of ÚMPE, and added to the "science and culture" section.

tions with all states and international organizations and safeguarding the collective security of the European continent." "Our foreign policy," the document continued, "has not taken advantage of all opportunities for conducting itself actively and has not taken the initiative in presenting its own views on a number of important international problems." The program also promised a more active role in the international communist and workers' movement, aimed at promoting the unity of world communism and cooperation of the communist parties with democratic forces. Finally, it endorsed the idea of the participation of citizens in the formulation of foreign policy.

FOREIGN POLICY DEFINED

The responsibility for the delineation of a more active foreign policy rested with persons newly appointed at almost every point of the official hierarchy dealing with external relations. The team included Černík, responsible as Prime Minister for defense and foreign policy; Professor J. Hájek, Minister of Foreign Affairs; V. Valeš, Minister of Foreign Trade; Gen. M. Dzúr, Minister of National Defense; F. Hamouz, as deputy Prime Minister for Comecon affairs; J. Lenárt, as Politburo member responsible for international relations; and J. Pelikán, as chairman of the assembly's foreign affairs committee. At lower levels, the appointment of Gen. V. Prchlík in place of M. Mamula, as head of the CC's 8th department; of Gen. E. Pepich, as head of the armed forces' Main Political Administration; and of Gen. K. Rusov as Chief of Staff, brought other new people into key posts. Old-timers, such as V. David, O. Šimůnek, Gen. B. Lomský, and others were removed from high office. Personnel replacements in the ministries of National Defense and Foreign Affairs were not made at once but were strongly pressed.[18]

Initial steps did not throw much light on the future direction of foreign policy. Dr. Hájek, in his earliest statements, stressed continuity but also indicated Czechoslovakia's desire to play its part in the "concert" of bloc relations, which he envisaged as "a polyphony as harmonious as possible." Smrkovský, in his inaugural address to the assembly, spoke of "a new spirit in our foreign policy," which "would more actively than hitherto use the possibilities of formulating our own standpoint on the basic

[18] The need for cadre changes, and in particular the reduction of security personnel in diplomatic representation, was propounded in *Mezinárodní politika*, no. 8 (1968), pp. 38-39. There was later censure of the practice of appointing discredited officials as ambassadors, e.g. David to Bulgaria and Koucký to the USSR (Hochman, *Rep.*, June 26-July 3). See also the criticism of Czechoslovak personnel at the United Nations, including those appointed to the secretariat, and the failure to make changes after January (X.Y., *Rep.*, July 17-24).

questions of world politics" and "would fully express both the international and national interests of Czechoslovakia."[19]

The government declaration in late April described the alliance with the Soviet Union and other socialist countries as one of "the firm permanent values," based on "the logic of historical development, the vital interests and needs of our country," and "the will, needs, and feelings of our people."[20] In the Warsaw alliance, Czechoslovakia would actively fulfill its tasks and support its defense power, and "at the same time, within the framework of the treaty, vindicate the democratic principles of collaboration and the interests of the Republic." Czechoslovakia would support the strengthening of the pact and "develop a greater initiative to deepen the work of the joint command." The needs of defense would be assured "in harmony with the possibilities of our state." Economic and scientific-technical cooperation with the socialist countries would be further developed, and proposals introduced in Comecon to "improve" the level of the division of labor, "which we regard as insufficient." On the question of peaceful coexistence with capitalist states and of European security, the responsibility for improvement of relations was placed on the other states. It was up to the United States, for instance, to take action to end discriminatory trade measures and to return Czechoslovak gold held since the war[21] and up to West Germany to recognize "existing realities." Pledging support for the Vietnamese, Czechoslovakia welcomed the efforts to find a peaceful settlement and suggested Prague as a meeting place for negotiations. A peaceful settlement in the Middle East must be based on the UN Security Council's 1967 resolution, including the withdrawal of Israeli troops from occupied territories.

The government proclaimed its intention to make foreign policy and defense "an affair of the whole people" through the activization of state organs and the elevation of their importance in relationship to party agencies. The main decisions would be made by the responsible ministers and the government as a whole, and by the proposed Council of Defense, and would be subject to the supervision and criticism of a vitalized National Assembly, of the parliamentary committee on foreign affairs, and of a new committee on defense and security.

Within the party itself, authority would no longer be concentrated in the Secretariat's 8th department but would be exercised by the Secretariat as a whole, the Main Political Administration in the Ministry of National Defense, and by party committees in the army which were to

[19] *RP*, April 12, 14, 19, resp.
[20] Ibid., April 25. David, former foreign minister, approved the government's foreign policy and the appointment of Professor Hájek (ibid., April 13).
[21] In a diplomatic note on May 2 Czechoslovakia reiterated its demand for the return of the gold and described the attitude of the USA as "unacceptable."

function in a more democratic fashion.[22] The Central Committee, and its defense and security committee, would also play a more active role. Other commentators endorsed the broadening of citizens' participation in diplomacy, including a greater contribution by scholars and experts, and an enhanced role for the mass media.[23]

A NATIONAL PATH TO SOCIALISM

On the anniversary of the February seizure of power in 1948, Dubček, in the presence of Brezhnev and other bloc leaders, proclaimed the party's intention, following the earlier example of Gottwald, to "realize the general principles of socialism by our distinctive (*svojrázný*) path, appropriate to Czechoslovak conditions."[24] The concept of a Czechoslovak model of socialism, corresponding to the special circumstances and the national traditions of the country, was restated in the Action Program, which referred pointedly to valuable elements in the policy of the Czechoslovak road to socialism pursued between 1945 and 1948. In the words of the political resolution of the April plenum, "we are seeking our Czechoslovak manner of constructing and developing socialism. This is our internal affair, to be decided by the sovereign will of our people and their honest labor."[25]

Almost at this very moment, V. Kozlov, a Soviet theoretician, was publicly condemning the ideas of "a specific path to socialism" and "a national form of Marxism" as un-Marxst, in their excessive emphasis on the national peculiarities of each state. Internationalism, he declared, was the main principle, and any weakening of it would harm not only the socialist community but also the country concerned.[26] Czechs and Slovaks were not slow in their response. Evžen Löbl directly refuted Kozlov's thesis, citing the Soviet declaration of October 1956 and arguing

[22] For discussion of the role of the party in military matters, see the articles by General Pepich, *Obrana lidu*, Feb. 24, March 30; *Pravda*, March 8; General Dzúr, *Práce*, April 11; *Pravda*, April 22; General Prchlík, *Práce*, April 21. Cf. a later article by V. Kovanda, *Rep.*, July 17-24.

[23] For instance, V. Janků, *NM*, no. 5 (1968), pp. 634-36; Josef Šedivý, *ŽS*, no. 11 (May 1968), pp. 58-59, 61; no. 12 (June 1968), p. 52. On the task of scholarly research in international relations see Šnejdárek's lecture, April 29, in A. Šnejdárek, *Výbor z přednášek a statí, 1968* (Prague, 1969), pp. 61-85. Hájek asserted the need for "maximum informedness," although recognizing that there had to be greater limitations in foreign, as compared to domestic, politics. He stressed the importance of scholars as "a critical opponent" in foreign policy, although the government and the minister bore the main responsibility (*NM*, no. 8, 1968, p. 990). See also Hájek, *RP*, April 12, May 17.

[24] Dubček, *K otázkam obrodzovacieho procesu v KSČ* (Bratislava, 1968), p. 33.

[25] *RŠO*, p. 102.

[26] *Sovetskaya Rossia*, April 4, cited in *RP*, April 5.

that Lenin and the Bolsheviks had themselves followed a specific path.[27] Having abandoned this idea in 1948, the Czechs and Slovaks must return to it. It was their international duty, he stated, to demonstrate whether a socialist system could be linked with the culture and tradition of its own nations, and with democratic and humanist traditions. Similarly, Ivan Synek denied that there was any universal model of socialism and, rejecting "mechanical copying" of one country's model by another, proclaimed "the inalienable right of every socialist country and every communist party to determine itself what forms of construction of socialism are chosen in its own country. . . . No one can dictate to any party or country what is and what is not its international duty."[28]

Čestmír Císař vigorously espoused a similar viewpoint in his address on the 150th birthday of Karl Marx, which was to earn him immediate condemnation in the Soviet press. He declared that "every Marxist-Leninist party must have its own policy, which takes into account national conditions and peculiarities and which naturally does not lose sight of the final revolutionary goal," and that this represented its contribution to the international communist movement and to the development of Marxist thought. This would not hinder fraternal cooperation, and "all our friends," he was convinced, "understood this." "In no case do we consider our approach as generally valid nor do we wish to force our policy on anyone. We reject intervention in our domestic affairs, but for this very reason, do not agree with efforts here to send advice to comrades over the borders. What we do not wish others to do to us, let us not do to them." Unity of the communist parties was urgently necessary, he stated, but, referring to the warning example of Maoism, it must be achieved, "not on the basis of any monopoly in the interpretation of Marxism in contemporary conditions, or on the basis of the subordination of a part of the movement to another part of the movement, but only on the basis of the recognition of the right of every party to an autonomous policy and on the basis of equality of rights and fraternal cooperation of all countries."[29]

The hostile reaction to Císař's speech, and the censure of Czechoslovak developments in the Soviet press from early May on, made it quite clear that the USSR and her closest supporters within the bloc were in fact challenging Czechoslovakia's right to follow its own course. Intensifying pressures, in the form of press polemics, military maneuvers, and

[27] Löbl, "The Right to a Specific Path," *Pravda*, April 12.
[28] Synek, "On the Specific Path to Socialism," *RP*, April 19.
[29] Ibid., May 7; also *ŽS*, no. 12 (June 1968), pp. 58-64. Cf. an article by V. Vrabec (*RP*, June 21) on the anniversary of the Cominform's expulsion of Yugoslavia in which he criticized this action and defended the value of "a wealth of forms of socialism."

exchanges of high-level visits, clashed with strong Czech and Slovak assertions of their right to formulate their own domestic policies and thus made what was, strictly speaking, an internal matter a major question of foreign relations.

Czechoslovak diplomacy was thus faced with a new and unusual problem. As Hájek put it in a major statement in the foreign affairs committee of the National Assembly in June, one of the principal purposes of Czechoslovak foreign policy was "to safeguard our process of revival against possible negative influences from outside pressures and at the same time to open up the possibility of exerting a positive influence abroad."[30] A major task, he said, was to explain the process of democratization to their allies and persuade them that it was not harmful to their mutual relations. Hájek's subsequent visits to Moscow and other bloc capitals, and the trip by Smrkovský at the head of a parliamentary delegation to the Soviet Union, were in large part devoted to this effort.[31]

BLOC AND FOREIGN RELATIONS

The bulk of Hájek's June statement was devoted to bloc relations. He described as a "constant" of their foreign policy the orientation toward the Soviet Union and toward the Warsaw Treaty Organization and Comecon, but he rejected "a static and stiff conception" of these commitments. Unity required respect for the sovereignty of the member countries and recognition of "the diversity of approaches to individual problems." They "would patiently and tirelessly work for an understanding and full vindication of this new element." Both sides should, in their statements, strive to recognize certain boundaries beyond which their comments would be regarded as "interference" and to avoid polemics that would negatively affect mutual relations and prevent "a coordinated approach" in the sphere of foreign policy. The process of democratization was not "aimed at weakening our bonds with the socialist countries in Europe, although it introduces new elements, new tasks and problems

[30] *RP*, June 12.
[31] Hájek, *RP*, May 17, June 20, 29; J. Pudlák, ibid., May 25; Smrkovský, ibid., June 20, 25. Hájek visited Moscow (May 6-8); Budapest (June 13-14); East Berlin (June 17-18); Sofia (July 8-10). After the occupation Hájek pointed out that no trips were made to non-socialist states (*Rep.*, Oct. 16-23). Pudlák denied any "cooling of relations" with their allies, but admitted "a certain differentiation in these relations—from the critical evaluation in the GDR to very positive and sympathetic expressions in Yugoslavia, and in part also in Hungary and Rumania." He reported "understanding" and "support" in official places in the USSR but some disquiet concerning the Czech press. "This leads them to the question whether this involves a threat to socialism, and thus a threat to the whole socialist camp. This is understandable—Czechoslovakia has one of the key positions in the Warsaw treaty, as, together with the GDR, the only country directly bordering on the GFR" (*RP*, May 25).

and leads to their more dynamic comprehension, and the consideration and vindication of new elements in their content." As for relations with non-communist states, Hájek's statement showed no signs of an impending shift.[32] Relations with the United States were admittedly "not normal," but improvement depended on actions by Washington. The relationship with Canada demonstrated the possibilities of improving relations with countries of a different social order. The renewal of diplomatic relations with Israel would not contribute to the solution of the problem of the Middle East unless Israel accepted the 1967 Security Council resolution. As for the developing countries, Czechoslovakia would continue to support progressive forces, but material aid was limited by her own economic difficulties and must take the form of scientific-technological and cultural assistance.[33]

In Europe there were good possibilities of developing relations with France, Italy, Great Britain, and especially with neighboring Austria[34] and within the Economic Commission for Europe. Although Czechoslovakia, as a country of medium size, could only make a contribution to European security based on the unity of the socialist countries, she would take "initiatives," which were, however, not specified. With regard to West Germany, Czechoslovakia would continue to act "in accord with the common interests of the socialist countries" but would seek actively to contribute to the defining of those interests. The dangerous growth of neo-Nazism must be noted, but "realistic tendencies," even in government circles, ought not to be ignored. The establishment of diplomatic relations, "an important step in the normalization of relations," was, however, "a long-term matter," and was linked with the creation of the conditions for European security by West Germany. This would include the recognition by Bonn of the invalidity of the Munich agreement *ab initio*, of the integrity of frontiers, and of the existence of two German states, one of which was "our close friend and ally."

In earnest of Czechoslovakia's continuing solidarity with her Warsaw

[32] In an interview with Zagreb *Vjesnik*, Hájek sharply rejected illusions or hopes in the West that Czechoslovakia might "go with you," and declared that NATO was the same coalition that had pressed them to the wall thirty years ago at Munich (*RP*, May 26). Describing the historical reasons and economic interests that made them wish to remain faithful to their "socialist friends" and to strengthen rather than weaken the alliance, Hájek declared: "We differ perhaps in practical implementation and method, but we are united in conception."

[33] In an article in *Nová mysl* (no. 8, 1968), Hájek urged coordination of the policies of the socialist states toward the developing countries, greater stress on the "human factor," i.e. the training of personnel, and the elaboration of "long-term conceptions" which would correspond both to developmental trends and to "our possibilities and interests" (p. 989).

[34] Conversations were held with the Austrian foreign minister in Bratislava in late June (Hájek, *RP*, June 29). See the strong advocacy of improved relations with Austria by Karel J. Matouš, *Rep.*, May 1-7.

627

pact comrades, the treaties of friendship, cooperation and mutual assistance were renewed with Bulgaria, in April, and with Hungary, in June.[35] As Hájek described them, these bilateral pacts, as well as the collective institutions of the Warsaw Treaty Organization and the Council of Mutual Economic Assistance, represented "the development of a type of international socialist unity and cooperation which would respect national and state independence and sovereignty."[36] The treaties were substantially the same in content, providing, "in case of an armed attack from any state or group of states" (without special reference to West Germany), for "immediate mutual assistance, including military, and support by all means available." Both treaties invoked the principles of "socialist internationalism" and also of "equality, mutual respect of state sovereignty and non-interference in the domestic affairs of the other party." Both proclaimed the invalidity of the Munich treaty *ab initio*.

Dubček availed himself of the opportunity provided by the high-level visits which accompanied the signature of the two pacts—Zhivkov's to Prague, and Dubček's to Budapest—to proclaim anew Czechoslovakia's solidarity with the socialist countries and the close friendship and cooperation of the countries concerned, with a reference, in the case of Hungary, to her understanding and support of the process of democratization. During Zhivkov's visit Dubček stated that they would "do everything possible and necessary so that the Warsaw treaty should be up to the level required by the time and the needs and should be firm and united." In Budapest, in Kádár's presence, Dubček declared that proletarian internationalism did not "exclude that each country should have its own domestic and foreign policy which would correspond to our common interests and its own historic development and specific conditions." Although admitting that anti-socialist tendencies existed, he firmly declared that they would not be given "a free field of activity." Accepting "the generally valid regularities of socialist development," Dubček also noted the need to take into account, and to respect and utilize, "the historical, political, and economic individualities" of each country.

On other occasions Dubček restated the fundamental orientation of Czechoslovakia to the Soviet Union and the socialist bloc and asserted that no change was intended in these relationships. He assured his listeners that "complete mutual confidence" existed between the Prague and

---

[35] For texts and speeches, see *RP*, April 24-28, June 14-16. The CPCz Presidium described an article praising Imre Nagy, published by *Literární listy* (June 13) on the eve of Dubček's visit to Budapest, as "inappropriate and untactful," and an action which could weaken "fraternal relations" (*RŠO*, p. 231). Šnejdárek wrote a personal letter to Kádár, stating that the article, which had been written by a member of ÚMPE, embodied the author's personal opinions and these were in conflict with the views of the institute (*RP*, July 30).

[36] *RP*, June 12.

Moscow leaders and that the principle of non-interference was accepted. This optimistic view was coupled, however, with vigorous assertions of the right to settle their own affairs and the rejection of any outside interference. At the same time he denied that Czechoslovakia was offering a model for other socialist states.[37] Occasionally Dubček made oblique references to the "realities" of the international situation and cautioned against "ill-considered" actions, such as the Two Thousand Words, which might lead to conflicts threatening the process of revival. He gave pointed reminders to the press of their responsibilities and made appeals to them to take foreign relations into account in their commentaries and reporting.[38] Smrkovský also referred to "the international situation" and urged "caution and responsibility." "Czechoslovakia does not live in a vacuum," he said. "She is a part of the socialist camp." Friendship with the Soviet Union was "untouchable," but these relations must be based on equality. He was ready to recognize the legitimacy of the concerns of their allies, and even to a certain degree the justice of some of their complaints, and to offer assurances that efforts were being made to remove the causes of their concern.[39]

PUBLIC OPINION EMERGES

Public opinion on matters of foreign policy could hardly be said to exist in the early post-January stage. In the upsurge of discussion from March on attention was focused on domestic aspects of reform and touched only tangentially on foreign affairs. Unfavorable Soviet press comments, coupled with other forms of pressure against Prague, awakened increasing resentment at what was regarded as outside interference in domestic affairs. This produced an increasingly critical mood concerning Soviet attitudes and policies and disparagement, open or implicit, of the Soviet political system as such—a development hardly conducive to the maintenance of good relations. As far as can be determined, public opinion continued to be convinced of the value of the alliance with the Soviet Union and with the other socialist countries, and rejected the alternative of neutrality.[40] There was, however, a growing realization that

[37] CC May plenum, *RŠO*, pp. 197-200; Dubček, *Problemy mira i sotsializma*, no. 6 (1968), p. 15; *RŠO*, p. 198. See also his speech in Brno, Dubček, *K otázkam*, pp. 191-92. Cf. his earlier comment on the Dresden conference, *RŠO*, p. 85. See also Smrkovský, *RP*, May 16, July 7; Černík, ibid., June 29. Cf. the plenum resolution cited above, chap. IX, pp. 256-57.

[38] Dubček, *K otázkam*, p. 206; CC plenum, *RŠO*, p. 197.

[39] *RP*, May 12, 20, June 20, 25, July 5.

[40] There were almost no opinion polls concerning foreign policy questions. See above, chap. XVII. The CC report in August cited an unidentified poll which indicated that the majority of the population considered the WTO and the alliance with

there were definite limitations on the possibilities of independent action by a small state and by a member of the socialist camp, and that there might be an inherent contradiction between the continuance of intimate relations with the Soviet Union and the desire to pursue Czechoslovakia's own course.

Commentators differed in their reaction to the dilemma of this clash of goals. In the more outspoken publications, such as *Literární listy* or *Reportér*, there was a certain willingness to recognize the necessity of adapting to the realities of the international situation, which, as a commentator, writing under the pseudonym Dalimil, expressed it, "strictly define the framework and the possibilities of the process" taking place in Czechoslovakia.[41] Jiří Hochman admitted that they would have to moderate their actions and agree to certain compromises, and should understand, and adjust to, the fact that the outlook for a full realization of Prague's Spring was not too promising. Some of our "hundred flowers," he wrote, "will be stunted; others will wither"; those that remain must be "carefully tended."[42] A major article in *Rudé právo* sought to clear up the "confusion," especially among the younger generation, concerning the alliance with the Soviet Union, describing it as a source of great benefit, far outweighing "negative deformations" of this relationship. Czechoslovakia was "one of the stones of the structure of world socialism" so that their friends had the right to express their doubts and fears concerning the fate of the whole structure. Asserting the desire to continue as a member of the Warsaw alliance, the commentator observed that this involved not only rights but also "certain obligations." It was "a voluntary agreement with a certain limitation of our sovereignty," but only in spheres affected by membership in WTO and Comecon.[43]

Specialists on foreign affairs also showed a difference of emphasis in resolving the dichotomy between the desire for a more independent course and the necessity of cooperation with fellow socialist states. Jaro-

---

the Soviet Union "a basic question of our security" and as "better than neutrality." The report also noted some reservations on economic and political relations with the USSR, "a lack of clarity and distorted views" on Czechoslovak-Soviet relations, and the presence of some anti-Soviet tendencies (*Zpráva o současné politické situaci Československé socialistické republiky*, . . . Prague, 1968, pp. 54, 17).

[41] *LL*, May 23. Among the realities mentioned were (1) that there could be no change in the general balance of power without a European or world conflict and (2) that any attempt to change the social order could lead only to a new Budapest. Cf. J. Procházka, who, in an interview with Agence Presse, said that Czechoslovakia had not had a diplomacy for twenty years and that the foreign ministry had been "a mere branch office." As a small country, he said, we should, however, have "a modest policy corresponding to our possibilities" and should not interfere in the affairs of Madagascar, Guatemala, or Nigeria (*LL*, May 16).

[42] *Rep.*, June 5-12.

[43] D. Spáčil, *RP*, May 19. Cf. J. Pal'o, *Pravda*, May 16.

slav Šedivý, for example, reiterated his earlier views concerning the errors of past Czechoslovak diplomacy, which, by always following Soviet policy, had in effect been conducting a "great power" policy, and he urged a more independent course and a long-term strategy based on the principle of peaceful coexistence, but with all states, not just with those having a different social system. In particular he advocated "a new conception of European policy based on the alliance with the USSR but bringing into proper harmony national and international aims." Like the GDR, Czechoslovakia should have a carefully thought out policy of defending its own national interests. This would include the diplomatic recognition of the German Federal Republic ("better sooner" than later); a renewal of diplomatic relations with Israel; improved relations with Austria; "real alliances" with Bulgaria, Rumania, and Hungary; the offer of a new treaty to Yugoslavia; and the ratification of the UN human rights pacts, already approved by the government. Šedivý suggested that Czechoslovakia make a concrete proposal for European security (without, however, specifying what form it might take). He proposed a reexamination of foreign economic policy, including dealings with the socialist countries, contacts with the Common Market and with international organizations such as the World Bank, and a thorough revision of relations with the developing countries.[44]

An interesting contrast of views was offered by Josef Šedivý, deputy head of the CC's International Relations Department, who endorsed the activization of foreign policy and the democratization of policy-making, but with greater recognition of common bloc interests. Agreeing with Jaroslav Šedivý that "new standpoints" were essential, he claimed that there was no need to "differentiate at any price, out of principle," "to break the chinaware," and that it was "not absolutely necessary to start anew," without regard for reasonable solutions already advanced, for instance, by the 13th congress. He rejected the idea that by supporting Soviet policy, Czechoslovakia had been pursuing a "great power policy" and contended that the Soviet Union was an ally and a great power with whom Czechoslovakia had many common interests and "an identity of many standpoints." As for bloc relations a more active policy required a concrete mechanism to facilitate the exchange of information, and bilateral and multilateral consultations so that, with due respect for differences, "a coordinated approach" could be achieved and "partial practical compromises" reached.[45]

Two other commentators, Lt. Col. B. Švarc, pro-rector of the Gottwald Military Political Academy, and his colleague M. Brož, advocated greater flexibility, activity, and independence in foreign policy, but rec-

[44] *LL*, April 18, pp. 10-11; *Rep.*, May 1-7.
[45] *ŽS*, no. 11 (May 1968), pp. 60-61; no. 12 (June 1968), p. 52.

ognized that the possibilities were restricted not only by Czechoslovakia's own strength and geopolitical position, but also by the limitations on freedom imposed by every alliance on its members. An alliance required loyalty, and mutual respect for the aims and interests of their partners, and excluded a purely "Czechoslovak" platform or "even a shadow of national narrow-mindedness."[46] "To carry out an active Czechoslovak policy," Švarc wrote elsewhere, "presupposed that we are loyal and active partners of our allies," although not necessarily "easy" partners. Moreover, the relations of the socialist community required "definite rules," excluding privileges and respecting differences. "If we are to be democrats at home, then we cannot be other than that in the socialist community."[47]

Václav Kotyk advanced a more uncompromising argument for basing the Czechoslovak party's policy on its own interests, just as, in his opinion, the Socialist Unity Party in East Germany had consistently done. Recognizing that national interests, when necessary, had to be subordinated to common interests, he flatly asserted "the right of individual parties to their own domestic and foreign policy." The case of Yugoslavia in 1948 had demonstrated, Kotyk said, the impossibility of forcing a communist party to abandon its own ideas and opinions. Within the bloc, there was "an objective process of mutual influencing" so that the Czechoslovak example might accelerate the process of change in other socialist countries. Czechoslovakia had the right to express its opinion on developments in the other countries. Noting the fears and doubts of other socialist countries concerning Czechoslovak development, he saw the solution in "open and public exchange of opinion."[48]

In another article published at about the same time, Kotyk went further, warning that any effort to exert pressure on the conduct of domestic affairs could threaten the country's basic orientation. Just as Czechoslovakia needed her alliance with the Soviet Union and the bloc, they also needed Czechoslovakia so that there were "certain limits" to attempts of this kind. Although he did not regard such an effort as realistic or likely, he warned that "only an evolution in this direction, which would give Czechoslovakia no other possible choice than subordination or isolation . . . would justify us in the consideration of neutrality for the ČSSR."[49]

[46] Report at a seminar, May 1968, *MV*, no. 3 (1968), p. 48. J. Bydžovský (*Pravda*, April 13) warned against basing foreign policy on myths and illusions and adopting "Messianic tones" by offering an example to Europe. As a small state, Czechoslovakia could not play a great power role, but could explore the unused potentialities of cooperation with other smaller European states.

[47] *Mezinárodní politika*, no. 5 (1968), pp. 29-30.

[48] *Rep.*, June 12-19.

[49] *MV*, no. 2 (1968), pp. 3-11. This was an expanded version of Kotyk's article

The idea of neutrality had already become matter of public discussion but was repudiated in official and semiofficial circles. Dubček, at the April plenum, said that neutrality was "excluded, from an ethical as well as a political standpoint, in the antagonistically divided world of today."[50] Alexander Ort, a specialist at ÚMPE, subjected to searching analysis the various forms of neutrality adopted by Sweden, Switzerland, Spain, Austria, and Yugoslavia, and drew the conclusion that none was suited to Czechoslovakia. Security—the search for which was one of the constants of Czechoslovak foreign policy—had been guaranteed by the alliance with the Soviet Union and through the Warsaw pact, and these guarantees would be lost by a policy of neutrality. Peace in Europe might eventually be assured by means other than the existing pacts, but only through an expanded European security system and not through neutrality. Moreover, Czechoslovakia could play a more significant international role as a member of the socialist community than as a neutral. Drawing attention to the way in which France, still a member of NATO, was able to develop French policy in a creative way, Ort concluded that others could do the same, even if little Czechoslovakia could not be mechanically compared with France.[51]

The strongest pressure by the public on a foreign policy issue was exercised, ironically, over Israel.[52] The breach of relations in 1967 had, as we have seen, aroused considerable dissatisfaction, and the reversal of this decision became the objective of students, certain scholars, such as Jaroslav Šedivý, and some writers. A meeting of young people in the Old Town Square on May 3 endorsed a call for the restoration of diplomatic relations with Israel. Shortly thereafter students at the Philosophical Faculty of Charles University circulated a petition proposing recognition and eventually presented it, with over 13,000 signatures, to the Ministry of Foreign Affairs.[53] The Slovak writer, L. Mňačko, who

---

in *RP*, March 30. This issue, although ready for the press in April, appeared only in June. The article was published in the Belgrade journal, *Medjunarodni problemi*, no. 2 (March-June 1968), pp. 17-27 (English translation, *U.S. Joint Publication Research Service, Eastern Europe*, 1967-1970, no. 46,771). This article may be part of the material on bloc relations elaborated in ÚMPE to which Šnejdárek referred in April (*Výbor*, pp. 76-77). See chap. III above for Kotyk's earlier writings on this theme.

[50] *RŠO*, p. 86. See also Pudlák (above), *RP*, March 24; J. Brabec, *Predvoj*, March 21; Mikeštík et al., *RP*, March 22.

[51] *Rep.*, April 10-17. For Ort's views in 1967, see above, chap. III. Jaroslav Šedivý also rejected neutrality for Czechoslovakia (*LL*, April 18). R. Břach, of the Gottwald Military Political Academy, in an analysis of pre-Munich Czechoslovak foreign policy, noted that neutrality had been unrealizable in that period (*MV*, no. 3, 1968, pp. 56-58). See also J. Brejchová, *Práce*, June 15.

[52] For the following, see also Paul Lendvai, *Anti-semitism without Jews* (Garden City, N.Y., 1971), pp. 267 ff. For 1967, see above, chap. III.

[53] Text in *Student*, May 29. A Society of Friends of Israel was later formed (ibid., June 26). See the interview with an Israeli diplomat, ibid., June 26.

had his citizenship restored in late April and returned to Czechoslovakia in mid-May, defended his action in leaving the country in 1967 and urged the resumption of relations with Israel.[54] Slovak writers, as already noted, were divided on the question of Israel, with some, such as Novomeský, criticizing what he termed the one-sided defense of Israel. His statement that the loss of 6,000,000 Jews in World War II did not justify Israeli atrocities against Arabs led to sharp condemnation by A. Lustig, a Czech writer, who castigated the regime for failing to recognize Israel and voiced suspicions that anti-Semitism existed in official circles.[55] In fact anti-Semitism and anti-Zionism in the form of anonymous letters and manifestos were reminiscent of the fifties when such arguments had been used to justify the trials. The issue of recognizing Israel thus became a "moral question" for many persons. The whole matter was complicated by events in Poland where a campaign against Zionism, with anti-Semitic overtones, was waged by the regime to justify actions against dissenters. This led to Czech protests against Warsaw's actions, both at the student rally on May 3 and in the form of an open letter to the Polish leaders by P. Kohout, J. Procházka, and Lustig; and to a Polish diplomatic protest to Prague.[56] Official policy remained unchanged, however. Although there was probably no great enthusiasm for the break of relations in 1967, the renewal of diplomatic relations was nonetheless rejected by the Ministry of Foreign Affairs.[57] Josef Šedivý, of the CC Secretariat, termed the breach a mistake but claimed that the basic issue was not that of restoring diplomatic relations, but of liquidating the conflict in the Middle East on the basis of the UN resolution.[58]

Strengthening the Warsaw Pact

The idea of strengthening the Warsaw pact, which had been urged by the Soviet Union for several years prior to 1968, was endorsed by Dubček in one of his earliest speeches after his accession to the leadership.[59] At the April plenum he suggested measures for "deepening the mechanism of the Warsaw treaty," in particular for "improving the activity of

[54] See Mňačko's interviews and articles, *Kultúrny život*, March 15, May 24, July 12; *Rep.*, March 20-27, pp. i-viii; *Svobodné slovo*, July 5; *Práca*, July 26. See above, chap. iii, n. 148.

[55] See his open letter to L. Novomeský, *LL*, May 23; Novomeský's letter (*RP*, May 12, also *Pravda*, May 7). Cf. an interview with an Arab editor employed by Radio Prague, who complained of the "pro-Israel dialogue" after January and opposed diplomatic relations (*Nové slovo*, July 18, 25).

[56] For the letter, *Práce*, May 4, as cited by Lendvai, *Anti-semitism*, pp. 269-70.

[57] On May 2 the ministry issued a denial of an early renewal of diplomatic relations with Israel and reiterated the necessity of the implementation of the Security Council resolution (*RP*, May 3). The MFA statement was sharply criticized in *Student*, June 26.

[58] *ŽS*, no. 12 (June 1968), pp. 54-55.   [59] Feb. 2, *K otázkam*, p. 27.

the joint command," and revealed that the latter had been the subject of discussion both at the Sofia meeting of the Warsaw pact powers in February and at the Dresden conference in March.[60] Both the Action Program and the government proclamation of late April referred to reforms of the Warsaw Treaty Organization without, however, giving any explanation of what might be involved.[61]

The exact nature of the Soviet Union's own ideas on this issue was also not revealed.[62] It was often rumored, but never conclusively proved, that the Soviet Union had requested the permanent location of Warsaw treaty forces on Czechoslovakia's western frontiers to strengthen the defensive capacity of the alliance at this critical point. Reports of a Soviet request for the stationing of troops, to the number of 10,000-12,000, emanated in late May from no less a source than the West German Chancellor, but were categorically and repeatedly denied by Czechoslovak military authorities.[63] These reports were no doubt associated with the discussions concerning Warsaw pact maneuvers on Czechoslovak soil during the visits of Marshal Yakubovsky and Grechko to Prague in early and late May, respectively. During Yakubovsky's visit, General Dzúr denied that

[60] *RSO*, pp. 86-87. The Dresden communiqué referred to concrete measures in this respect to be taken in the near future (ibid., p. 44). The Sofia communiqué did not mention this question, and referred only to other matters, including the nonproliferation treaty. Rumania expressed reservations about the latter and did not sign the joint statement. Czechoslovakia did so (*RP*, March 8). See Thomas W. Wolfe, *Soviet Power and Europe: 1945-70* (Baltimore, 1970), pp. 489, 491. General Dzúr, in a speech reported on Prague radio, Oct. 5, 1968, referred to the discussion of certain documents at Sofia which, he believed, would give "even greater responsibilities and independence to the defense ministers and general staffs." He spoke of Czech initiatives in certain respects and of Soviet support (BBC, II, Oct. 8, 1968).

[61] See also Hájek's references to this matter, *RP*, June 12, and *NM*, no. 8 (1968), p. 986.

[62] The content of Soviet proposals in 1968 may perhaps be deduced from the action taken at the Warsaw pact meeting in Budapest in March 1969 to establish a Council of Defense Ministers and a Military Council of the joint armed forces in order to "further perfect the structure and command bodies" of the Warsaw treaty (*RP*, March 18, 1969). Wolfe also reported a decision to remove each national defense minister from direct subordination to the Soviet commander-in-chief and to provide a senior national commander in charge of his country's pact forces who was to be accountable both to his own defense minister and to the Warsaw pact commander-in-chief (Wolfe, *Soviet Power*, pp. 496-97, n. 111).

[63] *RP*, May 23, June 1, 7. Bil'ak later reported that the Soviet Union had offered that troops be stationed on the western frontiers, thus making possible a reduction of Czechoslovak armed forces and hence a lowering of defense costs and the freeing of labor forces. This proposal, allegedly made during Dubček's visit to Moscow in early May, was rejected out of fears for "sovereignty." Bil'ak also stated that Dubček refused to go to the Warsaw meeting lest Brezhnev force them to permit the troops on maneuvers to remain in Czechoslovakia (CC plenum, September 1969, *Svědectví*, 10, no. 38, 1970, pp. 286).

See also L. W. Whetten, "Military Aspects of the Soviet Occupation of Czechoslovakia," *The World Today* 25 (Feb. 1969), 61-62; John Erickson, in V. V. Kusin, ed., *The Czechoslovak Reform Movement 1968* (London, 1973), p. 42.

a Soviet proposal for maneuvers in Czechoslovakia had been rejected and revealed that talks concerning staff exercises had in fact been held. During the Grechko visit, Dzúr contradicted reports concerning the permanent stationing of troops, but a Ministry of National Defense spokesman indicated that this did not mean that there would be no allied troops participating in the maneuvers, although the exact numbers would not be revealed.[64] It has been stated, but without substantiation, that Czechoslovakia sought the postponement of full-scale maneuvers on Czechoslovak soil during early 1968, and succeeded in having them replaced by limited staff exercises.[65] Such staff exercises with the participation of security (zabezpečovací), communications (spojovací), and transport (provozní) units, were in fact announced in early June and described as customary Warsaw pact operations.[66] The maneuvers, which began on June 20, were cited by Dubček as demonstrating Czechoslovak support for the Warsaw treaty and its defensive preparedness.[67] When, in late July, shortly after the Warsaw conference, rumors that requests had been made for troop stationing surfaced again, these reports were, perhaps significantly, not officially denied, but an extraordinary effort was made to publicize the ability of the Czechoslovak armed forces to defend the western frontier of the Soviet bloc.[68]

From time to time there were indications of Czechoslovak dissatisfaction with certain aspects of joint defense policy. Unofficial military commentaries contended that expenditures on conventional military forces imposed an excessive burden on the economy and prevented the modernization of the defense establishment.[69] The opinion was also expressed that advancing military techniques had negative economic effects and that defense policy should be brought into congruence with general economic policies.[70]

Other spokesmen wrote that a Czechoslovak "military doctrine" should be elaborated which, "within the framework of coalition defense," would take account of "the specificity of place and of responsibility."

[64] RP, May 4, 23, June 1. An announcement concerning Grechko's visit referred to "concrete measures agreed on for strengthening the friendship of the Soviet and Czechoslovak armies and their cooperation within the Warsaw Treaty Organization" (ibid., May 23).

[65] Whetten, "Soviet Occupation," p. 63.

[66] RP, June 7. General Čepický did deny that there was any question of the permanent stationing of Warsaw treaty troops.

[67] K otázkam, p. 192.

[68] RP, July 26. See above chap. XI, p. 298.

[69] See articles in the Czechoslovak military journal, A-revue, May 17, pp. 32-39, and July 12, pp. 28-30, cited by Roman Kolkowicz, ed., The Warsaw Pact (Institute for Defense Analyses, P-496, Arlington, Va., 1969), pp. 17-18. Cf. Whetten, "Soviet Occupation," pp. 63, 65; Erickson, in Kusin, ed., Czechoslovak Reform, p. 43.

[70] Lt. Col. J. Anger, letter, NM, no. 6 (1968), pp. 763-64.

Soviet military doctrine was not able to "solve on our behalf those tasks which stem from our own political, economic, geographical, technical and other conditions and possibilities." "We ourselves must decide how we want to fulfill our tasks within the framework of the coalition and how we want to defend our country."[71]

In mid-July the tendency of official Czechoslovak thinking was revealed in important pronouncements by Generals Dzúr and Prchlík. Dzúr, at an all-army conference of communists in Bratislava on July 10, was quoted as saying that Czechoslovakia, in the Warsaw Treaty Organization, intended to be "a more active factor than hitherto" and that "in spite of all particular (*dílčí*) problems, the Czechoslovak army was capable of fulfilling all the tasks which would be assigned to it."[72] Although his speech was not at first made public, some of his ideas were publicized a few days later in a major article in *Rudé právo* entitled "ČSSR—A Firm Link of the Warsaw Treaty."[73] Quoting the treaty's phrases concerning independence, sovereignty, and non-interference in domestic affairs, General Dzúr said that Czechoslovakia was "striving to increase its active share in the common defense" and that they did not want to be "mere passive members of the Warsaw treaty." Hence they supported proposals for "an international composition of the joint command" and the creation of "further organs which would create conditions for a more objective discussion of all serious questions of our common defense and the realization of more effective measures for safeguarding it." He urged the formulation of a Czechoslovak military doctrine as "our theoretical contribution to a coalition doctrine, optimally corresponding to the interests of the defense of the socialist community." This would serve as a basis for building the Czechoslovak armed forces in such a way that "with full respect for the demands of highest fighting

---

[71] Gen. E. Pepich, *Pravda*, March 8, and *OL*, March 30; General Knotek, *A-revue*, May 17, cited by Kolkowicz, ed., *The Warsaw Pact*, pp. 18-19. The right of Czechoslovakia to formulate its own military doctrine, which would reflect the specific conditions of the country, while not coming into conflict with the general interests and goals of the coalition, was developed at length in a post-occupation article by Gen. J. Čepický, *A-revue*, no. 20 (1968), pp. 18-22, available in English translation in *U.S., JPRS, East Europe*, 1967-1970, no. 47,010.

[72] *RP*, July 11. A fuller excerpt from this speech was published in *Práce*, Aug. 7 (cited from *OL*, no. 30, 1968, not available). Dzúr described Czechoslovakia as having been up to now "a disciplined and responsible implementer of the demands of the united command" and expressed their wish to "be an active participant in the coalition of armies." He recommended, in addition to a joint command of international composition, "the creation of a collective advisory organ for the commander-in-chief, a military council in which responsible members of all the armies would sit and which would discuss all serious questions, together with coalition military doctrine, which does not exist." He suggested the formation also of a technical committee representing all the armies to discuss "questions of technical perfection."

[73] *RP*, July 16.

capacity, we could use our resources with maximum effectiveness and without disproportions." He stated that the process of democratization did not conflict with the Warsaw treaty, but on the contrary, would make it possible for the Czechoslovak economy to keep pace with the rising demands of defense and "thus better defend the western frontier of the socialist community."

General Prchlík, in a press conference that became notorious and led to his dismissal, aired similar ideas.[74] He devoted a substantial part of his initial statement to recommended changes in the domestic making of defense policy, in particular the assurance of an "independent" role for the National Assembly (including its newly formed defense and security committee) and for the government in delineating, within the framework of the party's stand, the policy of the state. He stressed the responsibility of the party congress and the CC plenum in working out the basic concepts of military policy, suggesting that the forthcoming 14th congress, or an early CC plenum, should adopt a special resolution on these matters. The State Defense Council would have as its primary task the elaboration of a Czechoslovak military doctrine and a defense system which would avoid "an excessive emphasis on the military side of the matter."

General Prchlík's remarks on the Warsaw pact were even more explosive and revealing. There should be, he said, "qualitative changes" in the coalition, in particular a strengthening of the role of the political advisory committee, which should become "a regular, purposefully working organ," instead of functioning sporadically. This would assure that military matters should not take precedence over political matters and would guarantee "real equality of the individual members of the coalition . . . so that every member . . . could really achieve self-realization within it and actively share in its work." As for the joint command, it was criticized for being composed of Soviet officers only, apart from the representatives of the individual armies, who were actually "liaison officers" and took no part in decision-making. Referring to previous CPCz proposals concerning the joint command, Prchlík advocated that specialists be included from the individual armies who would be able to "co-create and participate . . . in the whole command system." The Ministers of

[74] Reports of his press conference varied considerably. This account is based on *RP*, July 16; a fuller report in *Pravda*, July 16; and a still fuller version from Radio Prague, given in translation in R. A. Remington, ed., *Winter in Prague* (Cambridge, Mass., 1969), pp. 214-17. Significantly, Prchlík's speech at the June CC plenum, which was said to have dealt with defense matters, was not published, even in abbreviated form. In a report on the CC proceedings, however, he was quoted as having proposed two CC commissions on security and defense to prepare materials for the 14th Party Congress (*RP*, June 2); also *RŠO*, p. 174). In 1971 Prchlík's statements at this press conference were taken as the basis of charges against him under the criminal code and he was sentenced to long-term imprisonment (*Listy*, no. 3, May 1971).

National Defense, who had been holding the posts of deputy commanders of the joint command, should have an improved position which would guarantee them "representation on the basis of equal rights." As for the stationing of troops on the territory of member states, he concluded, after careful study of the treaty and other documents, that this could occur only "according to the requirements of mutual defense against an external foe and after agreement among the participating states in this treaty."[75]

As noted in earlier chapters (x and xi), Prchlík's press conference took place at the time of the meeting in Warsaw of "the five" and of delays in the withdrawal of bloc forces, subjects to which he referred in the question and answer period following his principal statement. Official quarters in Prague, in commenting on Prchlík's remarks, accused him of distorting the facts and stressed that Czechoslovakia did have representation in the WTO Political Advisory Committee. In spite of denials that Prchlík spoke officially, it seems likely that the ideas expressed, which were not unlike those of General Dzúr, were being seriously considered in higher military circles in Prague.[76] These proposals, however, did not contemplate a breach with the Warsaw Treaty Organization, but rather were designed to improve and strengthen it as an agency of consultation and joint action.

A more radical critique of Czechoslovak defense policy was published in early July but did not receive public attention until after the occupation. This was embodied in a memorandum prepared by a group of staff members of the Gottwald Military Political Academy, including the rec-

---

[75] According to Prchlík, inquiries at the General Staff revealed no knowledge of any secret supplements to the official Warsaw pact documents. Cf. *The Christian Science Monitor*, July 31, 1968, where, it is reported, the existence of such secret clauses was implied by *Neues Deutschland* in June. In an earlier radio interview Prchlík was reported to have said that Warsaw pact military units might be stationed on the territory of member states in normal peacetime conditions but only by agreement, and in the interest of mutual defense (*Práce*, July 12).

[76] For discussion of the Prchlík episode, see above, chap. x, p. 287; chap. xi, pp. 298-300. See also Erickson in Kusin, ed., *Czechoslovak Reform*, pp. 44-46. Cf. a long interview given by Lt. Col. L. Kopecký to *Obrana lidu* (Aug. 17) in which he put the case, in guarded language, for changes within WTO, including "a modification of its statute," to take account of "the specific problems" of each country. He admitted that "conflicts" and "different opinions" existed and that cooperation could be threatened unless the problems were solved. The Czechoslovak political leadership had demonstrated by its acts its belief in the unity of the alliance, but took the view, he said, "that the international alliance and coalition system should be strengthened according to the principle of full state sovereignty." The military and security system required strengthening "in the sphere of interstate relations, strategic planning (*koncepčnost*), internal organizational structure, leadership, etc." The democratization process should extend to the sphere of military cooperation. While recognizing "the position of leadership of the Soviet military potential within the Warsaw alliance," the other partners should "increase their share in strengthening the bonds of military alliance."

tor, Col. V. Mencl and his associate, Lt. Col. B. Švarc. It was signed by thirty persons and was sent to twelve leading party and state officials.[77]

This brief document propounded the desirability of evolving "a state military doctrine" for Czechoslovakia which would be "a comprehensive formulation of the state's military interests and needs." Past military policy, elaborated in the fifties, was outdated, assuming an early military conflict in Europe and envisaging a transition from defense to a strategic attack to establish Soviet hegemony. The "threat" of a German attack had become mainly a lever for strengthening the unity of the socialist community in the absence of adequate economic and other forms of cooperation. In spite of the changed situation since 1956 Czechoslovakia had made no effort to devise her own military doctrine. That which existed had been based not on "an analysis of the real needs and interests of our national and state society" but on the "interests of the former sectarian leadership" and had simply taken over Soviet precepts as generally valid. The study of this problem, stated the memorandum, could not rely on traditional methods, but required "a systems approach, with the use of modern methods."

According to the memorandum, Czechoslovakia's military policy would take as its starting point "allied action with the other partners of the Warsaw treaty, and in particular the alliance with the USSR," but this would be "the policy of a sovereign state contributing its own standpoints to the formation of the common standpoints of the alliance." "The strengthening of the Warsaw alliance" would be designed to enhance the external security of the member states and thus "to open the way for the progressive development of the socialist countries and those of Western Europe." Czechoslovakia would not "abandon global risks" but would reckon with them only "as a partner, and not as a sacrifice to a development on which we have no influence." It was necessary to make "a scientific analysis of the whole scale of possible military situations in Europe" and, "with regard for our sovereign interests and needs" and "within the framework of the coalition, to determine our military possibilities in the individual situations."

[77] It was prepared in early May and published in Lidová armada, July 2, under the title, "On the Formulation and Constitution of Czechoslovak State Interests in the Military Sphere." This and other documents prepared by the academy were later described as the basis for a policy of neutrality and to have had the approval of the foreign minister, Professor Hájek, and of L. Hofman, chairman of the assembly's defense and security committee (RP, Sept. 6, 1969). Hájek denied this in a letter to the Minister of National Defense (RP, Sept. 20, 1969). Strong attacks on the academy's materials were made by M. Starosta, Tribuna, Aug. 20, 1969 (also given in East Europe 18, Oct. 1969, 20-22); ŽS, no. 42, Oct. 15, 1969, pp. 8-9, 11; J. Hečko, RP, Jan. 8, 1970 (also in Osteuropa 20, Dec. 1970, A 904-6). The memorandum was said to have been supported by some members of the Zápotocký Military Academy in Brno, but criticized by others.

The memorandum listed possible alternatives, ranging from absolute or limited wars, through various relationships of peace, to absolute peace based on general disarmament. Appropriate policies to meet each of these situations must be based not on "a stereotyped concept of class struggle dividing subjects into friend and foe" but on "a concrete analysis of a concrete situation, differentiating between foreign partners according to factual differences." For instance, Czechoslovakia must do everything possible to contribute to the elimination of the danger of "absolute war" which would mean the "national liquidation" of all the warring countries, including Czechoslovakia. For the contingency of "limited war," Czechoslovakia must prepare for defense within the framework of the Warsaw pact but should seek to exclude the use of violence in settling disputes. A "situation between war and peace," such as a serious crisis arising from the unsettled German question, particularly the Berlin problem, would have "catastrophic effects" on the Czechoslovak economy and must be averted by "an active foreign policy within the Warsaw alliance," including "a normalization of relations" with the German Federal Republic. The danger of "potential war" based on the mutual use of deterrents must be avoided by agreements with "potential enemies," including West Germany, for the non-use of the threat of violence. More than that, "peace between potential enemies" should be sought through non-aggression and arms limitation treaties.

In addition to the memorandum, the Gottwald Academy prepared a lengthy study relating to the army's action program, the content of which, however, was not published and can only be gleaned from post-occupation polemics.[78] This document was said to have accepted "the coalition principle, expressed in the Warsaw treaty and based on the nuclear potential of the USSR," as "the basis of the defensive systems of the individual socialist states of Europe" but advanced various alternative security systems for the ensuing ten to fifteen years. These included: (1) the Warsaw treaty framework, "but with the perspective of its bilateral or unilateral abolition in the near future"; (2) "security within the framework of the neutralization of territory or a neutral policy"; (3) disarmament measures (not specified); (4) a European regional collective security organization; and (5) "self-defense by one's own means." These alternatives were set forth for theoretical discussion only but suggested that military circles were, at least in theory, reassessing the assumption that the Warsaw Treaty Organization was the only source of security as long as a collective European system had not been brought into existence.

[78] The original document was not available. The following is based on Starosta, *Tribuna*, Aug. 20, 1969. See also Erickson in Kusin, ed., *Czechoslovak Reform*, pp. 43-44. Cf. Šnejdárek, ibid., p. 53.

Another associate of the academy, a scholar, Jozef Urban, in a detailed analysis of the rights and obligations of Warsaw pact members, emphasized, as Prchlík had done, that the temporary presence of Soviet troops, as in the case of East Germany, Poland, and Hungary, required the agreement of the states concerned, as did other measures such as joint exercises. Although each member was committed to collective self-defense, the extent of its military contribution would be based on the "possibilities" of each state and would be determined by "mutual agreement." Decisions of the political committee presupposed participation of representatives of all member states and would not be binding on non-participating states. Posing the question as to whether fears were justified as a result of recent events, Urban replied that the Warsaw treaty was directed against NATO aggressions and contained no provision justifying the use of armed forces "in event of a conflict between members of the coalition."[79]

In two other articles published on the eve of the invasion, under the title, "Our Approach to Neutrality," Urban dealt with the factors which had led certain states, such as Austria, Finland, Sweden, and Yugoslavia, to adopt neutrality, and commented favorably on such proposals as neutralized zones in Europe and neutralist tendencies in NATO. Yugoslavia's active neutrality was not, he said, derived from the socialist character of the state, but had been forced upon Yugoslavia by the action of other socialist states. "A socialist state can be compelled to adopt such a solution if serious disputes arise among the members of this system and if it wishes to maintain its original political program." Apart from this indirect warning, and a relatively objective discussion of the advantages of neutrality, Urban did *not* advocate this policy for Czechoslovakia and emphasized that the security of neutral states was assured by the existence of a unified socialist camp, or, in the future, could be assumed by a system of collective European security.[80]

Foreign Trade and Comecon

The Action Program severely criticized past foreign economic policy, in particular the "long isolation" from the world market, which had insulated Czechoslovak enterprises from the pressures of competition and had resulted in a serious lag in technical progress and in structural change in the economy. What was needed, it was said, was an end of the administrative monopoly of the conduct of foreign trade and of special protectionist measures which promoted inefficiency, and "an incorporation of our economy into the developing international division of

[79] *NS*, July 25.   [80] *Pravda*, Aug. 20-21.

labor."[81] This would require, declared Hamouz, an "active" foreign economic policy, in which exports would be regarded not as a "necessary evil" but as "a factor in economic growth."[82] The individual enterprises would assume a more significant and independent role, in direct contact with the foreign market.

This would not involve, it was argued, a fundamental shift in Czechoslovakia's foreign economic orientation which had, for two decades, been overwhelmingly directed toward the Soviet Union and the socialist bloc, the traditional links with the West having been abruptly cut off after 1948. The intimate economic association with the USSR was regarded not only as necessary politically, but also advantageous economically since it guaranteed a large and stable market and a source for needed raw materials.[83] Charges that this trade involved unfair prices and other disadvantages for Czechoslovakia were vehemently repudiated, although some difficulties and problems were admitted. Frequently quoted was a statement by Hamouz that the Soviet Union had indicated its willingness to accept the withdrawal of Czechoslovakia from any economic relationship that it regarded as disadvantageous. The party Presidium on April 16 approved a plan, which was not, however, published, for improving economic cooperation between the two countries.[84]

The Council of Mutual Economic Assistance was accepted as the basic framework of Czechoslovakia's relations with its fellow communist countries, but many aspects of its performance were regarded as unsatisfactory and official statements forecast concrete proposals for improvement. The Action Program referred to the need to base relations with Comecon countries more fully on "economic calculations and mutual advantage." Černík spoke of proposals for "higher forms of economic and scientific-technical cooperation" and "coordination of plans and financial cooperation in regard to foreign exchange," but did not otherwise indicate the nature of intended reforms.[85] Other official commentators pro-

[81] For the Action Program, see Remington, ed., *Winter in Prague*, pp. 120-21. See also Czechoslovak Economic Association, *RP*, April 9; B. Šimon et al., *NM*, no. 4 (1968), pp. 428-39; O. Šik, *Czechoslovakia: The Bureaucratic Economy* (White Plains, N.Y., 1972), pp. 71-80. See above, chap. xiv, pp. 427-28.

[82] *RP*, April 12.

[83] V. Valeš, *RP*, April 26, June 1; V. Vinklárek, *Hospodářské noviny*, June 21; J. Horský and R. Zukal, *RP*, Aug. 2; Zdeněk Šedivý, ibid., Aug. 16. For detailed analysis of Czechoslovakia's foreign trade, see Jan M. Michal, "Czechoslovakia's Foreign Trade," *Slavic Review* 27 (June 1968), 212-29; Z. M. Fallenbuchl, "The Role of International Trade in the Czechoslovak Economy," *Canadian Slavonic Papers* 10 (Winter 1968), 451-78.

[84] *RŠO*, p. 147.

[85] *RP*, April 25. See also O. Šimůnek, *RP*, Jan. 27; Šik, ibid., April 7; Hamouz, *Práce*, June 26. Valeš stated: "The previous work of CMEA is quite remote from our needs. In proclamations correct aims are emphasized, but meanwhile, in practical activity, almost nothing is realized. I do not dare to formulate a prescription as to how to achieve reforms quickly" (*RP*, April 18).

posed "the modernization of CMEA" and the stimulation of "intensive economic movement" among the members.[86] At the three meetings of the Executive Committee of Comecon during 1968, in February, May, and July, Czechoslovak representatives did not submit any suggestions for reform. In early August a draft proposal was approved by the government, but it was not published.[87]

The projected incorporation of the economy into the international division of labor presented distinctive difficulties in regard to both the socialist and capitalist countries. Within Comecon, trade was administratively controlled and had mainly taken the form of bilateral relations. In this situation no real integration of the economies had been achieved. The "openness of the economies of the individual socialist countries and the degree of their inclusion in the international division of labor" had not been adequate, wrote one official commentator. The "extent, level, and forms of economic cooperation" had not developed in accordance with the needs of the situation.[88] Although potentialities of development existed, these were hindered by the great differences in the level and the character of the national economies and the resulting differences in the interests of each country. Moreover, Comecon was not a supranational organization, so that cooperation depended on the voluntary agreement of the individual states.[89] Integration would have to take account of the "diversity of concrete national interests and the specific approaches of the individual countries to questions of economic integration" so that its achievement would be "a complicated and . . . a democratic process requiring respect for national specificity and the equal position of each country. . . ."[90]

A special problem had resulted from Czechoslovakia's decision to reform economic management. Šimon, in his report, noted that the opinion was growing in Comecon countries that there had been, in these countries, "insufficient utilization of market relations," "excessive centralization of decision-making," and lack of involvement of the "enterprise sphere."[91] Yet, it was argued, the only effective method of eco-

[86] E.g. B. Šimon et al., *NM*, no. 4 (1968), p. 432. See also Vinklárek, *Práce*, May 18; Jiří Hájek, *RP*, June 12; Josef Šedivý, *ŽS*, no. 12 (June 1968), p. 53; Hájek, *NM*, no. 8 (1968), p. 986.

[87] *RP*, Aug. 9.

[88] Šimon et al., *NM*, no. 4 (1968), pp. 430-31. K. Martinek, deputy secretary of CMEA, in a frank and critical interview on concrete problems facing CMEA, revealed that Czechoslovak officials in the organization had sent a resolution to the CPCz Central Committee urging greater inclusion of Czechoslovakia in the world economy and an improvement in cooperation within CMEA (*Pravda*, April 18, 19).

[89] Šimůnek, *RP*, April 13.

[90] Šimon et al., *NM*, no. 4 (1968), p. 432. Cf. Vinklárek, *Práce*, May 18; J. Štrba, *Pravda*, July 16.

[91] Šimon et al., *NM*, no. 4 (1968), p. 431.

nomic integration, whether at home or in international relationships, was a market system, with an increased role for the enterprise.[92] There were, however, different approaches to economic reform in the various member countries and the steps taken by individual countries were slow and uneven.[93] Much would therefore depend on the progress toward economic reform in the several countries of the bloc. Meanwhile, Czechoslovakia had no option but to develop closer relations with those countries resembling her in the extent of economic reform (e.g. Hungary) and to press for a greater role for the enterprises in her dealings with fellow bloc members.[94] Yet such an approach would probably conflict with Moscow's desire to integrate the bloc economies through more direct methods of control as in the past.

Most essential from the point of view of economic reform was the need to expand trade with non-socialist countries. In theory the Comecon association had not prohibited this, but in fact it had been hampered by the entrenched habit of dependence on trade with the USSR and with the other Comecon members and by the pressures of the political alliance with them, as well as by the lack of Western interest in trade with socialist countries and by the policy of boycott of such trade. Even more serious an obstacle was the relative inefficiency of Czechoslovak production. The transition to "a new institutional economic model incorporating our economy into the world division of labor" was, wrote Šimon, fraught with difficulties and could only be based on the method of "gradual approximation."[95]

Yet this goal must be achieved if the law of comparative advantage was to be applied and economic reform was to be promoted. The Action Program, while reaffirming economic cooperation with the Soviet Union and Comecon, called for expanded trade with non-socialist countries, on the basis of equality and mutual advantage, and without discrimination. This meant, as was often repeated, increased trade with the developed capitalist countries, especially the German Federal Republic, and the

[92] R. Selucký, *Rep.*, July 3-10. Selucký described Comecon as being in "deep crisis." For other articles on bloc integration, see K. Špaček and D. Libnar, *Rep.*, May 8-15; Štrba, *Pravda*, July 16.

[93] Valeš, *RP*, April 18. Šimůnek spoke of Czechoslovakia's decision to proceed with its own reform without waiting for agreement with other socialist states (ibid., April 13). Selucký distinguished two major groups, one, including Czechoslovakia and Hungary, which were making a transition to a market system, and the other, including the GDR, the USSR, Poland, and Bulgaria, which were merely improving the use of economic instruments while maintaining detailed planning (*MV*, no. 1, 1968, reprinted in English in *Soviet and East European Foreign Trade* 4, Fall 1968, pp. 72-86).

[94] Tomeš, *MV*, no. 4 (1968), pp. 14-15. See also Selucký, *MV*, no. 1 (1968); *RP*, April 13.

[95] Šimon et al., *NM*, no. 4 (1968), p. 437.

countries of the Common Market.[96] Although risks were involved, "a complete normalization of relations" with individual capitalist countries and with international economic organizations was imperative.[97]

The consideration of such problems led to the question of the desirability of a foreign loan, in hard currency, to speed up the restructuring and modernizing of Czechoslovak industry and to assist in the transition toward freer trade and currency convertibility. Official spokesmen stated that such a loan would be helpful, but was not absolutely necessary, and underlined the advisability of preparing a carefully worked out program for its utilization and for its eventual repayment.[98] The first approach, it was felt, must be made to the Soviet Union, but loans from capitalist sources were not excluded. In no case must any political conditions be attached. A request to the USSR for a loan, apparently in the amount of $300-500 million, was made in May, but no response was immediately forthcoming.[99] Zdeněk Šedivý, deputy Minister of National Economic Planning, in a rather cautious interview, described as "a most complicated question" the ascertainment of the most effective method of cooperation for modernizing Czechoslovak industry. He reported that, after the Moscow talks, experts had been assigned the task of studying "other ways" of meeting this problem, such as the import of Soviet installations manufactured at world standards.[100] Prague authorities apparently looked into other sources of funds, including the World Bank and private Western firms.[101] During Professor Hájek's press conference in

[96] V. Pleskot, RP, April 25; Tomeš, MV, no. 4 (1968), pp. 15-17; K. Špaček and Libnar, Rep., May 8-15; Černík, RP, May 15; Josef Šedivý, ŽS, no. 12 (June 1968), p. 53.

[97] Šimon et al., NM, no. 4 (1968), pp. 433-35. J. Vaněk advocated that Czechoslovakia rejoin the World Bank and Monetary Fund (Rep., July 17-24). An analysis of the future of Czechoslovak development and, with a plea for greater public discussion, was made by J. Texler, Rep., April 17-24.

[98] Hamouz, RP, April 12; Černík, ibid., April 25; Valeš, Pravda, April 26; Šik, RP, April 30; B. Sucharda, RP, April 30. The fullest explanation of the advantages of a loan was given by Šik in Pravda, May 21 (in response to a letter, ibid., May 8). He rejected the idea of a massive loan for restructuring Czechoslovak industry and favored a relatively small loan ($300 to $500 million) for meeting the problems of the transition to the new system. See also The Bureaucratic Economy, p. 125. Loans of various types were proposed by Vaněk (Rep., May 29-June 5) who argued that the "no conditions" principle should apply to all possible creditors. Cf. Č. Konečný's earlier article on long-term foreign credits (MV 2, no. 2, 1967, pp. 21-33).

[99] Z. Mlynář, The New York Times, May 1; Černík, RP and Pravda, May 15; Rol'nické noviny, June 22 (the figure of $260 million was mentioned). See chap. IX, above, and Appendix E.

[100] RP, Aug. 16.

[101] Černík, Mladá fronta, Aug. 19. He later disavowed an approach to the World Bank but expressed an interest in loans from enterprises in capitalist countries (RP, Aug. 20). Valeš denied official interest in a loan from West Germany (RP, May 7). Löbl openly proposed such a loan (KŽ, July 26).

August, Kohout, a deputy foreign minister, declared: "We will accept a loan from anyone, but naturally without political conditions."[102] Prior to the invasion little had in fact been accomplished in securing foreign credits or loans, owing in part to Prague's own caution, for political reasons, in approaching possible Western sources, and in part to the failure of Moscow to respond to Prague's request for such aid—in itself a subtle form of pressure.

THE GERMAN QUESTION AND EUROPEAN SECURITY

Prague's policy toward West Germany and European security remained almost completely static throughout the course of the reform period.[103] Dubček, in earlier speeches, spoke of the danger of "revanchist" forces in West Germany, and at Dresden had accepted the harsh comments of the communiqué on that subject. He seldom mentioned, however, the danger of imperialism and on one occasion declared that there was no threat from outside.[104] The Action Program and the government declaration said little on the subject of Germany, other than to stress the reality of the existence of two Germanies; Prague's solidarity with the GDR; and the dependence of "normalization of relations" on Bonn's "recognition of realities" and "the solution of certain questions." At the May plenum, Dubček advocated "good-neighborly and friendly relations" with the German Federal Republic but warned of neo-Nazi forces and the unwillingness of the Bonn regime to recognize the existing frontiers, the GDR, and the invalidity of the Munich treaty from the beginning.[105] During a visit to Budapest, Dubček again expressed an "interest in a real normalization of relations," but only on condition that Germany gave guarantees that it had broken with the heritage of Nazism.[106]

[102] *Pravda*, Aug. 18. Hájek was reported to have said that a loan would be helpful, that negotiations with the Soviet Union were not concluded, and that Western loans were not excluded. However, loans must be "without political or hard financial terms" (Tanjug, BBC, II, Aug. 20). A public opinion poll (*RP*, Aug. 20) revealed a wide spread of opinion as to whether a foreign loan should be accepted from the Soviet Union (15 percent); other socialist countries (5 percent); the USA (14 percent); other (or only) capitalist countries (23 percent); "from whomever was willing" (7 percent); neutral countries (5 percent); or the International Bank (4 percent). The responses of others questioned were not given.

[103] For a full review of this subject, see Adolf Müller, "Die Haltung der ČSSR gegenüber der Bundesrepublik Deutschland während des Prager Demokratisierungsprozesses," *Osteuropa* 19 (April 1969), 256-66; A. Müller and B. Utitz, *Deutschland und die Tschechoslowakei* (Freudenstadt, 1972), pp. 151-60.

[104] *RP*, Feb. 2, April 2; *RŠO*, p. 44.   [105] *RP*, June 4.

[106] Ibid., June 15. This statement was welcomed by Brandt, who reciprocated the wish for better relations and stated that Bonn was not pressing for diplomatic relations (ibid., June 19).

None of these statements suggested the likelihood of an early renewal of diplomatic relations. Those responsible for Czechoslovak diplomacy indeed made quite clear that recognition was a matter for the long run only and that in the meantime the newly established reciprocal trade representation should be utilized to the maximum to widen economic and cultural relations. Emphasis was laid, however, on the growing significance of "realist" forces in West Germany, even within the Bonn government, and on the need to give support to these tendencies.[107]

Public opinion was divided. Those who favored an initiative by Czechoslovakia complained that Prague had tended to accept the GDR's standpoint and had lacked a German policy of its own.[108] Others, without proposing diplomatic recognition, suggested that other kinds of relations be fully developed in order to influence opinion and support progressive forces in West Germany.[109] Some, such as Jaroslav Šedivý, openly advocated the resumption of diplomatic relations as soon as possible, believing that the remaining difficulties could be overcome.[110] Still others, such as Šnejdárek, warned against exaggerating the significance of diplomatic representation (although admitting that this must come eventually), for fear of complicating relations with the socialist countries, especially the GDR, and emphasized the greater immediate importance of developing economic and other ties.[111]

Right down to the occupation in August Prague persisted in its policy toward West Germany and sought to avoid even the appearance of an impending change. When the German leaders, Chancellor K. G. Kiesinger and H. Wehner, made statements concerning the invalidity of Munich, Prague diplomats pointed out their failure to recognize that this treaty was invalid *ab initio*.[112] Rumors of a forthcoming visit to Prague

[107] Hájek, *RP*, April 14, June 12; Černík, ibid., April 25; Pudlák, ibid., May 25. Cf. O. Václavík, ibid., March 16.

[108] A. Hradecký, *Rep.*, July 10-17. Cf. Václavík, *RP*, March 27. Following the example of the GDR, said Václavík, Czechoslovakia should take "its own initiative" on the German question.

[109] J. Hanák, *Rep.*, March 27-April 3; April 3-10; A. Polakovič, *Smena*, May 14.

[110] Jaroslav Šedivý, *LL*, April 18; *Rep.*, May 1-7. See also *Lidová demokracie*, April 24.

[111] Šnejdárek, *RP*, April 17. Cf. also Josef Šedivý, *ŽS*, no. 12 (June 1968), p. 54. At a seminar on European security in Moscow, Šnejdárek admitted that his own view that diplomatic relations were not necessary was not shared by all in Czechoslovakia and expressed the opinion that recognition would be possible if West Germany improved its relations with all socialist countries, especially Czechoslovakia, Poland, and the GDR. He urged contact with, and support for, the realist tendencies of German public opinion (*Výbor*, p. 57). On another occasion Šnejdárek recognized that there were "limits" to the possibilities of developing relations with West Germany, but argued that they should move up to those limits rather than do nothing until a right-wing government replaced the current Bonn regime (*Výbor*, pp. 82-83).

[112] Pudlák, *RP*, July 3; Hájek, *RP*, July 9, 11. When West Germany was re-

by Willy Brandt were disavowed, and a visit by Walter Scheel was described as purely private.[113] Denials were also made of reports that negotiations with Sudeten German leaders had taken place and that the return of some displaced Germans was being considered. The activity of Sudeten German organizations was cited as a major block to improved relations with the Federal Republic, and the Bonn government was called upon to repudiate them.[114] In mid-August Professor Hájek restated his belief that diplomatic relations, representing "complete normalization," were still remote and that the German question must be solved "in a broad common front with our allies and in the complex of European security." He reiterated the usual prerequisites for "normalizing relations" with West Germany and stated that economic relations should be further developed.[115]

Prague continued to proclaim as a basic aim of its diplomacy the attainment of a system of European security and to set forth familiar conditions—the recognition of the status quo, including the existence of the two German states; the convening of a European conference; and the preservation of Prague's close relationship with the GDR.[116] Although specific proposals were said to be under preparation, no concrete plan was advanced prior to August.

Specialists in international relations dealt with the problem in traditional terms, but offered some original recommendations. Šnejdárek, for instance, at a conference in Vienna in early March, expressed the belief that the existence of the two blocs (NATO and WTO) was not without danger (due to their military rivalry and West Germany's refusal to

---

portedly prepared to recognize Munich's invalidity *ab initio*, official quarters in Prague reiterated the other conditions of diplomatic relations (*NYT*, Aug. 17).

[113] *RP*, July 11, 23. After the occupation Hájek contradicted stories that he had met secretly with Brandt in Vienna on July 10 and claimed that he had been in Prague on that day (*Rep.*, Oct. 16-23). Apart from Scheel, of the Free Democratic Party, other visitors to Prague included H. Schmidt, of the Social Democratic Party; Karl Blessing, of the German Federal Bank; and Egon Bahr, special ambassador. Nothing is known of the content of Bahr's negotiations. See Müller and Utitz, *Deutschland u. die Tschechoslowakei*, pp. 158-59. No evidence has been found of secret negotiations with Bonn regarding financial credits referred to by R. V. Burks, in Morris Bornstein, ed., *Plan and Market, Economic Reform in Eastern Europe* (New Haven, 1973), pp. 385-86. Cf. similar charges of secret talks concerning diplomatic relations, economic credits, and a statement condemning the expulsion of the Germans in 1945, in V. Král, *Proč je Mníchov neplatný* (Prague, 1972), cited by J. W. Brügel, *Osteuropa* 24 (March 1974), 229.

[114] *RP*, July 14, Aug. 9, 12 (Černík).

[115] *Pravda*, Aug. 18; *NM*, no. 8 (1968), p. 988. See also the endorsement of these prerequisites in the communiqué issued after the visit by Ceauşescu (*RP*, Aug. 18). Hájek was quoted by the East German news agency as speaking in praise of the Karlovy Vary visit and as referring to "good relations" with the GDR and the latter's positive attitude to the ČSSR (BBC, II, Aug. 20).

[116] Hájek, *RP*, June 12; *Pravda*, Aug. 18; *NM*, no. 8 (1968), p. 987.

recognize the status quo) but observed that the blocs did provide a certain security and could not be immediately dissolved. A more likely solution could be found in the expansion of relations of all kinds between the members of both alliances, leading to "a gradual elimination of the blocs, based on cooperation among independent countries, irrespective of their social systems, and based on mutual respect." At a conference in Moscow on European security Šnejdárek stressed the need for unity of the socialist countries as a condition of European security, and the importance of working with non-communist forces in European countries, including those in West Germany. Declaring that security "without the Soviet Union" was impossible, he emphasized the value of cooperation among the smaller European states in elaborating a "democratic alternative for Europe."[117]

Some of his colleagues at ÚMPE offered alternative ideas. L. Líska saw the attainment of European security as a long-term process, with the liquidation of the blocs coming only at a later stage when an effective European system had been constructed.[118] Jaroslav Šedivý proposed that Czechoslovakia take the initiative to achieve a security system more reliable than dependence on the two blocs, and suggested as elements of such a move a European security conference; an expansion of trade with European countries, using the Economic Commission for Europe as a means of negotiation; and the codification of the principles of peaceful coexistence.[119] Alexander Ort thought that a solution might be found by expanding cooperation among the smaller states and suggested that Czechoslovakia convoke a conference of parliamentarians from the whole of Europe to discuss the eventual transformation of the Common Market into an "all-European" institution.[120]

FOREIGN POLICY IN CRISIS

The Warsaw conference opened a new phase in Czechoslovakia's foreign affairs, marked by open and grave crisis in her relations with the Soviet Union and her bloc allies. The Warsaw letter contained a sharp attack on Czechoslovak policies, domestic and foreign, as involving "the

[117] *Výbor*, pp. 9-21, 49-59. A European security system, he said, striking an unusual note, would prepare the way for "the final victory of socialism on the entire European continent" (p. 53).

[118] *RP*, May 14; *MV*, no. 3 (1968), p. 47.

[119] *Rep.*, May 1-7.

[120] Ibid., May 29-June 4. In other articles Ort noted the positive tradition of the Little Entente without, however, suggesting its restoration, and argued for the desirability of cooperation with Danubian states, including Hungary and Yugoslavia (*SS*, June 22). Cf. also Ort, *SS*, May 25. See an earlier article critical of the Little Entente by Robert Kvaček, *International Relations*, 1968-1969, pp. 58-72, originally published in *MV*, no. 1 (1968), pp. 26 ff.

danger of a break-away from the socialist camp" and described this as "the common affair" of the allied parties. It referred to voices in Czechoslovakia calling for a revision of "the common coordinated policy" toward West Germany, and the response in ruling circles to West Germany's "flirtation." This denunciation seemed to document the failure of Czechoslovakia's attempt to construct a foreign policy characterized both by continued loyal association with the Soviet Union and by some degree of autonomy and initiative, as well as of her effort to carry through a program of domestic reforms with the approval, or acquiescence, of her allies.

The Czechoslovak response was firm and decisive, rejecting the charges and proclaiming her continued solidarity with the USSR and the socialist camp.[121] "In the alliances and cooperation with the Soviet Union and with other socialist countries," read the CC statement of July 19, "the Central Committee of the CPCz sees the permanent international framework of socialist development in the ČSSR." Negotiations with their allies, preferably on a bilateral basis, would "overcome misunderstanding in the interests of comradely cooperation."[122] Theirs was "a thoroughly socialist foreign policy," based on the principles of socialist internationalism, declared the letter responding to the Warsaw condemnation. They would fulfill their commitments under the existing alliances and had concluded new treaties with Hungary and Bulgaria. As for West Germany, Czechoslovakia had been the last of the socialist countries partially to adjust its relations with its immediate neighbor and had consistently respected and defended the interests of the GDR. They would not, however, yield an inch in the course that had been adopted in January, declared Dubček in his television address on July 18. "We shall decide independently and according to our own considerations on the most suitable paths for the construction of socialism in our country, on the most acceptable model of our socialist life."[123]

Public opinion was more or less united in support of the party's stand, expressing no desire to break away from the socialist community or the alliance with the Soviet Union, but displaying an unyielding determination to defend the sovereignty of the country against outside pressure. No doubt some agreed with Dubček and his associates that the conflict resulted from a lack of information and misunderstandings on the part of their allies, and believed, or hoped, that it could be resolved by an exchange of views and by persistent explanation. Even in official party circles, however, there was recognition that the conflict resulted from

---

[121] See in particular the CPCz reply to the Warsaw letter (*RŠO*, pp. 243-50) and the resolution by a joint meeting of the National Assembly's foreign affairs and constitutional and legal committees, *RP*, July 16. See chap. x above, pp. 291-94.
[122] *RŠO*, p. 258.   [123] *K otázkam*, p. 223.

deeper causes. As Josef Šedivý put it, the allies held "an unfavorable view of our *entire* reality." The maintenance of such an attitude, he warned, "would only lead to an increased emphasis on the independence of the CPCz in the determination of its own policy and to the growth of the influence of negative forces."[124] Others were still less optimistic, expressing the belief that further talks could at the very best produce an agreement to disagree and a willingness to tolerate the Czechoslovak course. A complete solution would require a fundamental change of orientation within the communist movement as a whole, based on a new concept of unity in diversity.[125]

The most outspoken comment came from Václav Kotyk, who went so far as to admit the possibility of a break with the socialist bloc under certain conditions. In an article published in the widely read *Práce* immediately prior to the Warsaw meeting, he asserted the right of every socialist country to have its own domestic and foreign policy and demanded respect for the sovereignty and the specific conditions of each country. Explanation, he said, was not enough to win approval of the party's policy. It was necessary to make clear that "the CPCz leadership will not allow anyone, under any circumstances, to stop us in developing socialism according to our conditions." He restated his earlier warning that "only a policy which did not respect the right of the ČSSR to its own path and insisted on subordinating it to certain prevailing conceptions and practices" would lead Czechoslovakia to "reevaluate some of its basic standpoints on its relations with the socialist states." A few days after the Warsaw letter, in the same newspaper, Kotyk drew an analogy between the letter and the Cominform resolution of 1948, and lamented the fact that "concepts of monolithic unity" still governed the thinking and practice of certain communist parties. There were only two alternatives: "to capitulate to this pressure and restore . . . the pre-January administrative system, or to proceed consistently on our own path . . . even at the cost of serious complications in our relations with some socialist countries." It had been impossible twenty years ago to prevent a communist party from going its own way and it was all the more so today, "unless our party's leadership itself steps from this path."[126]

Kotyk elaborated his argument in even sharper terms in an article that appeared in *Nová mysl* in mid-July. Commenting on the trend toward a new formula of "unity in diversity" in the socialist camp, he regretted

---

[124] *ŽS*, no. 16 (Aug. 1968), pp. 1-3.
[125] For instance Synek, *RP*, July 13; I. Šetlík, ibid., July 26; Z. Bradáč, ibid., July 30. Synek wrote that relations among the socialist countries had not been "normal" for many years, and that the starting point for normalization was "the feeling of absolute equality and sovereignty." See also above, chap. XI, pp. 301-4. For Dubček, *RP*, July 28.
[126] *Práce*, July 11, 20, resp.

the countertrend toward outdated concepts, exemplified by the failure to invite Yugoslavia to Budapest, or Rumania to Dresden; the holding of the May conference in Moscow without Czechoslovak representation; as well as what he termed weaknesses both in the Moscow declaration of 1960 and in the Dresden communiqué. He censured the "subordination of one country to the prevailing opinions of a group of countries" or "the subordination of the majority of countries to the ideas of one country," citing the events of 1948, when the correct position had been taken by one country (Yugoslavia), not by the majority. The current goal should be not to subordinate national to international interests but to harmonize the two, accepting the inevitability of conflict among some parties, and cooperation among others. As far as Czechoslovak foreign policy was concerned, "task number one" was to develop "a stand that corresponds to these conditions as a whole and to our national needs, possibilities, and traditions," and "even in relations among socialist states to place the emphasis on the national interests and needs of Czechoslovakia." They must adopt "an unequivocal standpoint" toward the attitudes of the other socialist countries, seek to exert an influence on them and utilize the "new possibilities" offered by the support of countries such as Yugoslavia, as well as in relation with other countries of the world.[127]

BRATISLAVA AND AFTER

The outcome of the Čierna and Bratislava meetings seemed to have averted the crisis engendered by the Warsaw letter and to have warded off any danger of a Soviet resort to force against Czechoslovakia. From the reports given by Dubček and Černík it appeared as if Moscow had accepted the doctrine of "unity in diversity," dispelling fears concerning national sovereignty and interference in domestic affairs. It seemed to vindicate Czechoslovakia's idea that she could, in agreement with the Warsaw "five," continue on her reform course and at the same time maintain, and even deepen, her close relationship with them. Indeed, the two leaders laid great stress on the unity of the socialist camp and "the common interests" of its members and indicated Czechoslovakia's resolve to achieve an even more intimate cooperation with her allies, in particular by strengthening WTO and Comecon.[128]

Referring specifically to foreign policy, Černík, in his address of August 5, asserted that the Bratislava declaration did not oblige them "in a single respect, to amend our conceptions, as contained in the Action

[127] *NM*, no. 7 (1968), pp. 815-26.
[128] See above, chap. XI, p. 311, and the speeches by Dubček and Černík, *RP*, Aug. 3, 5, 6.

Program and the government declaration." Yet he went on to sound a new note. Czechoslovakia was not alone in Europe and had "an exceptional position," standing at the frontier of the two military blocs, as "the western promontory (*přiběžek*) of the socialist bloc." The leadership was convinced of the army's ability to perform the tasks assigned by the state and by membership in the Warsaw treaty and did not see any weakening in the external or domestic security of the country. "History has many times confirmed for us that we cannot be neutral," said Černík. "If we do not wish to be a plaything in the hands of the powers, then we must actively contribute to the strengthening of the defensive potential of the lands of the socialist camp."[129] Czechoslovakia, he said, could not be assured of raw materials and foodstuffs, or markets for its products, especially its machinery, without working with the members of Comecon. It was necessary, however, to improve the work of this organization, "to seek out new and more effective forms and to place cooperation on a new basis."[130]

The visits of Tito and Ceauşescu to Prague did not essentially change the situation. Like earlier statements of support from Yugoslav and Rumanian spokesmen, these visits raised the morale of the Czechoslovak public and strengthened their determination to resist pressure, but did not lead to the adoption of measures for political or military assistance.[131] The treaty of alliance signed with Rumania during Ceauşescu's visit did not differ significantly from the treaties concluded earlier with Bulgaria and Hungary. Like the others, it was in fact, if not in words, directed against the threat from West Germany and did not include possible action against a Soviet attack.[132] There were apparently no discussions

[129] *RP*, Aug. 6. During Ulbricht's later visit, Dubček, referring to the boundaries of the socialist camp with the Federal Republic, noted that the GDR was in one region, and the ČSSR in another. "The defense of the frontier of Czechoslovakia and West Germany is a matter for Czechoslovakia, which has assumed all the obligations flowing from its membership in the socialist community. It will carry out the defense of the frontiers as a sovereign socialist state. We have enough forces and means to assure the security of the frontier in a manner corresponding to our membership in the socialist community" (ibid., Aug. 14). Cf. Dubček's speech of Aug. 2 (*K otázkam*, p. 240). ". . . our army is not only a firm link in the defense of our socialist society but also a sufficient guarantee of the defense of our state boundaries and thus of the boundaries of socialism."

[130] During Ceauşescu's visit, Dubček expressed his strong dissatisfaction with the existing state of economic cooperation with the socialist countries and the need to augment the division of labor, both through Comecon and bilateral treaties (*RP*, Aug. 17).

[131] See above, chap. XI, pp. 313-17. There had been official visits by Yugoslav governmental or party delegations on May 13-14, June 3-6, July 14-24, and Aug. 1-2, and by Rumanian delegations on July 2-6 and Aug. 2-6; and firm statements of support on various occasions. See chap. XX below.

[132] The phrase "nonintervention in domestic affairs" was used twice, instead of once, as in the other treaties. Economic cooperation with "other socialist countries" as well as Comecon members, was mentioned. Professor Hájek defended the ref-

concerning the reform of the Warsaw Treaty Organization.[133] During Tito's visit no alliance was concluded, and according to him, it was not even discussed.[134] There was no attempt to organize any kind of trilateral alliance or communist Little Entente, directed against the Soviet Union —an alternative expressly rejected by Ceaușescu.[135] Nor presumably was any effort made, during either visit, to work out a strategy of political support for Czechoslovakia's resistance to outside pressures. The later visits of Kádár and Ulbricht afforded opportunities for Dubček once again to defend his course against criticism, but did not succeed in winning support for Czechoslovakia even from the Hungarian regime.

In the two weeks of uncertainty and renewed crisis after Bratislava, Czechoslovakia's strategy for dealing with the conflict with her bloc allies underwent therefore no reexamination or modification. Four days before the invasion, Professor Hájek, in an extended press conference, described Czechoslovak foreign policy as being conducted "in the spirit of Bratislava." His statements on this occasion and his article a week earlier in *Nová mysl* indicated that Czechoslovakia continued to regard the alliance with the Soviet Union and the socialist community as the "first constant" of her diplomacy. Hájek placed a new emphasis, however, on achieving a greater integration of action with the bloc as a whole, as exemplified by Bratislava. Declaring in familiar terms that unity should be based on the recognition of national diversity, the special responsibility of the USSR, and the interests of each state, Hájek observed that "the identity or at least parallelism (*souběžnost*) of the interests of the European socialist countries predominates over the diversity of national specifics." He revealed that Czechoslovakia was preparing a concrete proposal on European security and plans for strengthening Comecon, but did not divulge any details.[136]

Whether the 14th congress would have brought any change in Czechoslovakia's foreign policy or of her strategy in bloc relations is uncertain.

---

erences to the Warsaw treaty "during the period of its validity," explaining that this was in accord with the 1966 Bucharest declaration's reference to the dissolution of WTO if a collective security system came into existence (*RP*, July 16).
[133] Hájek, *Pravda*, Aug. 18.   [134] *RP*, Aug. 11.
[135] Ibid., Aug. 17.
[136] Ibid., Aug. 18, and more fully, *Pravda*, Aug. 18; *NM*, no. 8 (1968), pp. 984-90, quotation on p. 986. In his press conference Hájek was quoted by Tanjug as admitting that certain articles in the Czechoslovak press were not in keeping with the Bratislava spirit and as expressing the hope that Zhukov's article in Moscow *Pravda* did not represent a resumption of polemics (BBC, II, Aug. 20). See also Hájek's post-invasion interview, in which he reiterated the basic attitudes of Czechoslovakia on foreign relations and declared that he had no reason to withdraw anything from his article in *Nová mysl*. The Soviet ambassador, a few days before the invasion, had, he said, admitted that there was no reason to reproach the Czechoslovak Ministry of Foreign Affairs or the minister, or to criticize the foreign policy pursued (*Rep.*, Oct. 16-23).

The references to foreign policy in the congress materials reflected the familiar post-January ideas rather than the post-Bratislava "spirit." The usual emphasis on friendship and cooperation with the USSR was coupled with references to sovereignty and equality, and respect for the specific conditions of each country. It was "the exclusive right" of each party to determine "the optimal relation of national and international interests." "The active share of Czechoslovakia in forming and carrying out a joint strategy was regarded as a positive contribution to the formation of correct conclusions, and as the expression of reservations toward steps of whose correctness we are not convinced." Support for the GDR "did not exclude the formulation of our own standpoints on the German question." The draft concluded with "a resolute rejection of any denial of the right of each socialist country to go its own way, which would lead in practice to the break-up of the socialist system." Apart from this warning, the materials offered little that was new, and certainly not an outline of a radically different strategy.[137]

CONCLUSION

The basic assumption of Czechoslovak foreign policy after January had been that a certain degree of independence of action and the continued pursuit of reform was quite compatible with friendship and alliance with the USSR and the unity of the bloc. At no time was any fundamental change envisaged, such as withdrawal from the bloc, or a neutral course. Solidarity with the other members of the bloc was accepted as natural, and the tightening of this relationship by improvements in WTO and Comecon was endorsed. In the long run the trend toward a more active diplomacy and defense policy might have brought about substantial changes in Czechoslovakia's international orientation. In the meantime, however, her aim was to secure for Czechoslovakia greater influence in formulating the joint foreign policies of the alliance; any separate or more radical steps were deliberately avoided. After Bratislava, indeed, the concept of enhanced solidarity was given the highest priority, and a more active role was consigned to a secondary place. Yet even this modest version of independence collided with the overwhelming stress on unity and conformity which had of recent years become the hallmark of the Soviet attitude to the bloc.[138] The "double fidelity," as it has been called—a fidelity to the bloc and a fidelity to her own inde-

---

[137] Jiří Pelikán, *The Secret Vysočany Congress* (London, 1971), pp. 249-52. In the draft program a blank was left under the heading of international relations (ibid., p. 120).
[138] A "profound change in Soviet military concepts" was noted by Šnejdárek, in Kusin, ed., *Czechoslovak Reform*, pp. 51-52.

pendence of action—thus created a serious dilemma and produced constant oscillations between the two objectives.[139] In the end, at Bratislava, the pendulum swung decisively in the direction of unity and solidarity and away from independence and autonomy.

No serious thought was given to an alternative strategy of defying outside interference, as apparently proposed by some, by summoning at once the extraordinary party congress and by preparing for military defense against a Soviet attack. If the latter idea was broached, it was put aside as too provocative and as unnecessary by a leadership which considered military intervention highly improbable.[140] There were no discussions, during the visits by Tito and Ceauşescu, of joint measures for the contingency of a military attack. No diplomatic feelers were put out to the West in search of diplomatic or eventual military support, or even for substantial economic assistance. The idea of a conference of European communist parties, abandoned in favor of direct talks with Soviet representatives, was not revived after the apparent success of Bratislava. There was no thought of seeking support from China, in Albanian style, or even of attempting to balance between the Soviet and Chinese parties, following the Rumanian example. Finally, an appeal to the United Nations was not employed as a means of seeking a negotiated settlement of the conflict or as a possible buttress to diplomatic resistance.[141]

Many of these alternatives were no doubt unrealistic in view of Czechoslovakia's long-standing orientation to the USSR and her continuing faith in Soviet leadership. An appeal to China was ruled out by geography and by the general Czech and Slovak antipathy to the excesses of the Cultural Revolution. In any case, effective military help from China, or for that matter, from Yugoslavia or Rumania, or from Western countries, would not likely have been forthcoming.[142]

[139] Jacques Marcelle, *Le deuxième coup de Prague* (Brussels, 1968), pp. 236-39.

[140] In late July the Ministry of National Defense denied the report of a military plan for defense against the Soviet Union (*RP*, July 26). Presumably Czechoslovak military plans were predicated on a war against the Western states and did not include even contingency plans for defense against a Warsaw pact member. Warsaw pact strategy no doubt also excluded such a possibility. See Urban, above in this chapter. According to Pelikán, a contingency plan for the eventuality of a Soviet invasion had been drafted by General Prchlík but not discussed. It was passed on to the Soviet embassy, he reports, and constituted, in their eyes, Prchlík's "real guilt." See Pelikán in Kusin, ed., *Czechoslovak Reform*, p. 58; Erickson, ibid., p. 46; A. Ostrý, *Československý problém* (Cologne, 1972), pp. 155-56.

[141] When a Czechoslovak press agency representative at the United Nations publicly raised the issue of bloc pressure upon Czechoslovakia, this was repudiated by the Ministry of Foreign Affairs (*NYT*, July 20; *RP*, July 25).

[142] The CC report of August, in a few comments on the international situation, described the support of Rumania and Yugoslavia, and of certain Western European parties, as of "moral significance" only, and noted the West's lack of interest and the unlikelihood of anything but ideological and limited economic support. "For the capitalist world we remain an enemy, to whom support can be offered

Even with hindsight, it is impossible to speculate whether a more adroit and bold, and more realistic, diplomacy, coupled with measures to prepare the country for possible resistance, might have deterred the Soviet Union and its allies from invasion. A firm posture, consistently pursued on the Yugoslav pattern of 1948, would have strengthened the hand of Prague in dealing with Soviet pressures and might have increased the cost of invasion sufficiently to discourage the Soviet Union. The adoption of such a course, or even an attempt to introduce certain of these elements, especially preparations for defense, might simply have brought the invasion earlier. Such attempts, however, could hardly have been less effective in protecting Prague from outside intervention than the course actually pursued. Perhaps this objective was beyond the reach of any form of diplomacy and nothing except complete capitulation to Moscow's demands would have averted the final outcome.[143]

---

only within the framework of long-run conceptions of its own great power policy and of a possible economic penetration. Moreover, this aid must be offered as far as possible without public knowledge" (*Zpráva*, pp. 13-15).

[143] For analysis of Czechoslovak foreign policy, see André Gellert, "The Diplomacy of the Czechoslovak Crisis—Why They Failed?" *Studies for a New Central Europe* 2, nos. 3-4 (1968-1969), 43-53. For brief references to foreign policy, see also V. V. Kusin, *The Intellectual Origins of the Prague Spring* (Cambridge, 1971), pp. 124-30; Galia Golan, *The Czechoslovak Reform Movement* (Cambridge, 1971), pp. 312-15. For a post-occupation critique, see M. Šolc and V. Trvala, *Tribuna*, Aug. 20, 27, 1969. For criticism of the failure to formulate an alternative foreign policy strategy by pro-reform spokesmen, see A. Müller and J. Pelikán, in Kusin, ed., *Czechoslovak Reform*, pp. 63-66, 303-4; A. Müller, in C. Schmidt-Häuer and A. Müller, *Viva Dubček* (Cologne, 1968), pp. 184-85. Müller placed the blame on the conservatism and lack of experience of those in the Ministry of Foreign Affairs and the CC secretariat, and their failure to understand the significance of external factors in the conduct of domestic affairs in the modern world.

CHAPTER XX

The Reactions of the Ruling Communist Parties

THE HOSTILE response to Czechoslovak reform plans by the Soviet Union and the other members of the Warsaw "five" has already been discussed at many points in preceding chapters. The favorable reaction of Yugoslavia and Rumania, and some of the major non-ruling communist parties, has also been mentioned. In this chapter a more systematic analysis of the attitudes to Czechoslovakia of the other European communist regimes, including Albania, will be made on the basis of the statements of leading figures, press commentary, and radio broadcasts.[1] This will involve not a content analysis using quantitative measurements, but a qualitative assessment of the viewpoints, both positive and negative, of the ruling parties, comparing them as to relative emphasis on particular issues and as to variations at successive stages of the crisis. Needless to say, the avowed concerns about Czechoslovakia were not necessarily the real reasons for their actions, a matter which will be discussed in the subsequent chapter.

[1] The main sources were *Pravda* (Moscow); *Rudé právo*; the *U.S. Foreign Broadcast Information Service, Daily Report*, henceforth *FBIS* (all references to the USSR, unless otherwise specified, are to the USSR, International Affairs section); and the British Broadcasting Corporation, Monitoring Service, *Summary of World Broadcasts*, parts I (USSR) and II (Eastern Europe); henceforth BBC. To a limited extent, Soviet newspapers other than *Pravda* and the East European party organs were directly consulted. Radio Free Europe (RFE) publications were used for guidance but rarely as sources. Particularly useful was a series of RFE reports on East European reactions to Czechoslovakia, nos. I-XI, RFE, East Europe/5 to 17, from July 24 to Aug. 20; also RFE, East Europe, March 19, 1968. *The Current Digest of the Soviet Press* (*CDSP*), was used as a supplementary source, especially for Soviet papers other than *Pravda*. All translations are either my own, or those of *FBIS*, BBC, and *CDSP*, sometimes modified in the light of the original. Other Soviet documents are available in the biweekly *Reprints from the Soviet Press* (Compass Publications, N.Y.) based on translations from the Novosti Press Agency (Moscow). Not a single article on Czechoslovakia, however, was included in 1968 until the issues of Sept. 6 and 20 (vol. 7, nos. 5 and 6). There are two useful selective collections of important documents: R. A. Remington, ed., *Winter in Prague* (Cambridge, Mass., 1969) and Hanswilhelm Haefs, ed., *Die Ereignisse in der Tschechoslowakei* (Bonn, 1969). For analysis of Soviet and East European reactions, see William F. Robinson, "Czechoslovakia and Its Allies," *Studies in Comparative Communism* 1 (July-Oct. 1968), 141-70 (to the end of June only) and R. A. Remington, "Czechoslovakia and the Warsaw Pact," *East European Quarterly* 3 (Sept. 1969), 315-36 (also in R. A. Remington, *The Warsaw Pact*, Cambridge, Mass., 1971, chap. 5). See also the *Yearbook of International Communist Affairs, 1969* (Stanford, 1970), henceforth *YICA*.

INITIAL RESPONSE

There was at first no evidence that the changeover in Prague had awakened serious concern in Moscow or other bloc capitals. Dubček's visit to Moscow at the end of January was modestly reported in the Soviet press, in sharp contrast with the customary treatment accorded to visits by foreign leaders, but the communiqué announced "complete unity of views" on all questions.[2] Brezhnev, at the ceremonial meeting in Prague in commemoration of February 1948, was full of praise for the achievements of the CPCz and, in particular, singled out "its consistent internationalist position" within the Warsaw Treaty Organization and in its economic relations with the socialist countries.[3] The February anniversary was duly featured in the Soviet press, including an article by Dubček in *Pravda* (Feb. 21) and by Novotný in *Izvestia* (Feb. 22). Otherwise, until mid-March, no information was given about events in Czechoslovakia, and no criticism was voiced.

It was at the Dresden conference in late March that the first signs of friction appeared. The communiqué made no mention of Czechoslovakia but called for "vigilance against the aggressive and subversive tendencies of imperialist forces" and for "the further unification of the socialist countries on the basis of Marxism-Leninism and proletarian internationalism," referring specifically to concrete measures for strengthening the Warsaw treaty and the economic cooperation of the socialist countries. The document concluded by expressing confidence that "the working class, and all the working people of the ČSSR, under the leadership of the CPCz, would safeguard the further development of socialist construction in the country." Dubček's subsequent statement, however, that "a certain anxiety" about anti-socialist forces had been expressed was published in the Soviet and Czechoslovak press. *Rudé právo* also reported from Moscow that the Soviet Union, as "the economically and militarily strongest partner," was aware of the importance of its role and could not remain "indifferent" as to how socialist countries dealt with their problems. A Soviet commentator, writing under the pseudonym I. Aleksandrov, denied that Dresden represented in any way "interference" in Czechoslovakia's affairs, but described it as a rebuff to the designs of the imperialists.[4]

[2] *Pravda*, Jan. 30, 31. All references in this chapter are to *Pravda*, Moscow. Cf. Brezhnev's positive reference to Dubček's visit, cited from *Leningradská Pravda*, in *SCC* 1 (July-Oct. 1968), 171. On this occasion Brezhnev restated an oft-repeated theme that each communist party was autonomous and acted independently; that there could not be leadership of the world movement from any one center, but that there was need for "voluntary coordination of action in fighting the common enemy" (*FBIS*, USSR, Domestic Affairs, Feb. 19).

[3] *Pravda*, Feb. 23.

[4] For the communiqué and editorial, *Pravda*, March 25, 27. See also *Rudé právo*, March 27, 28; *Pravda*, March 28.

If later Soviet reports are to be believed, the Dresden conference was the occasion for open and frank censure of the Czechoslovak course and warnings that unless anti-socialist tendencies were rebuffed, it could lead to "a counterrevolutionary coup."[5] Otherwise information is lacking as to what occurred, except for a post-occupation interview given by Bil'ak, the reliability of which is highly uncertain. Bil'ak gave what purported to be a paraphrase of the statements of Brezhnev and others during the meeting. Brezhnev was said to have declared that they had had no objection to the change of leadership in the CPCz and in the state and that he had documented his full support of the new leaders at the February celebration. He and his associates had regarded certain anti-communist and anti-Soviet symptoms as "transitional phenomena" and had trusted in the promises of the Czechoslovak leaders to correct them. They found it difficult to understand, however, the "discrepancy between our (i.e. the Czechoslovak) words and deeds"—the tolerance of attacks on the party; the vilification of its history; the discrediting of the army, security, and the People's Militia, and of foreign policy and their closest allies; and the idealization of the bourgeois Republic and Masarykism. Reminding the Prague leaders of the course of counterrevolution in Hungary in 1956 and pointing to similar symptoms in Czechoslovakia, Brezhnev is said to have pleaded with them not to permit "chaos" and to "mobilize in time the party and the working class." Others were said to have spoken in similar terms. Gomułka referred to "Polish experiences" as well as those of the Hungarian counterrevolution. Kádár said: "Beware that a Czechoslovak Imre Nagy should not grow up!" Ulbricht warned that any weakening of the party or of socialism in Czechoslovakia meant "a weakening of the alliance with the socialist countries and of socialism in general."[6]

Throughout April the Soviet press relapsed into its previous reserve concerning Czechoslovak events, offering its readers a minimum of information, even, for instance, about the April plenum and the Action Program, and coupling official CPCz statements with Czech warnings of anti-socialist forces.[7] In sharp contrast with the CPCz's plenum, with its

---

[5] *Pravda*, Aug. 22.

[6] *RP*, Sept. 3, 1969; in English, *SCC* 3 (Jan. 1970), 120-24. Bil'ak cited an earlier version of the communiqué which was dropped, he said, at the request of the Czechoslovak delegation. It had referred to "the disquiet expressed over the activization of revisionist and anti-socialist elements . . . which sought . . . to undermine the political and economic bases of socialism in Czechoslovakia and the leading role of the CPCz and to weaken the relations of the ČSSR and the socialist countries." This could have "serious negative results" and required "decisive steps at once."

[7] See above, chap. VIII, p. 223. The brief reporting of Dubček's plenum speech contrasted with a two-page summary of Gomułka's address on the Polish situation on March 19 (*Pravda*, March 22). Rare were any objective comments on Czecho-

open discussion and plans for future change, was the CC plenum of the CPSU, held at the same time in almost complete secrecy and warning of the dangers of West German imperialism and of "anti-communist propaganda aimed at weakening the unity of the socialist countries and . . . attempting to undermine socialist society from within." The CC communiqué did not mention Czechoslovakia but emphasized the importance of the Dresden conference and reaffirmed Soviet "readiness to do everything necessary for the steady political, economic, and defensive consolidation of the socialist commonwealth." At home the plenum resolution called for an "implacable struggle against enemy ideology"—a goal that became the subject of many meetings and countless articles and speeches in ensuing weeks.[8]

Later in April, V. V. Grishin, Moscow city first secretary, in a major address on the anniversary of Lenin's birth, spoke even more strongly on the same themes, warning that imperialism was seeking " 'a weak point' in our ranks," and, relying on "revisionist, nationalist, and politically immature elements," was aiming at the "erosion of socialism" and the restoration of capitalism. Referring specifically to Dresden as demonstrating the will of the socialist countries to strengthen their commonwealth on the basis of Marxism-Leninism and proletarian internationalism, Grishin declared that the Soviet Union would provide "political, economic—and if necessary—military aid" to countries whose freedom and independence were threatened by imperialism. Grishin continued with a long exposition on the leading role of the party which, although referring to the Soviet Union, seemed more relevant to Czechoslovakia. Ascribing the party's strength to democratic centralism, he warned against "spontaneity, unlimited decentralization, and the reduction of the

---

slovakia such as those made in a Moscow radio symposium on April 21 by V. Nekrasov, deputy editor-in-chief of *Pravda* (*FBIS*, April 22).

[8] *Pravda*, April 11. Cf. editorials, ibid., April 9, 12. The latter reiterated the plenum's theme of the need for struggle against bourgeois ideology and for the unity of the socialist camp against imperialism, mentioning the Sofia and Dresden conferences (*Reprints* 6, May 3, pp. 33-40). It was at this plenum that General A. A. Yepishev was said to have announced that the Soviet army was "ready to do its duty" should "loyal communists" in Czechoslovakia request help in "safeguarding socialism." (Quoted from *Le Monde*, May 5, by ČTK, May 7 [BBC, II, May 8].)

Brezhnev's speech at the plenum was not published. In an address a few days earlier to the Moscow city party conference, he briefly referred to the use being made of nationalist and revisionist elements by imperialism to weaken the unity of the socialist countries and called for unity and discipline within the party. He alluded to the attempts of the enemy to make use of "the ideological immaturity and wavering" of individual members of the intelligentsia (*Pravda*, March 30; *Reprints* 6, April 19, pp. 19-20). Ten days later he was reported to have been very critical of Czechoslovakia and declared that socialism was endangered there and in other socialist states (M. Tatu, *Le Monde*, May 5-6, 1968, cited by Heinz Brahm, *Der Kreml und die ČSSR, 1968-1969*, Stuttgart, 1970, p. 24).

party to the level of a political-educational organization," as well as against "bureaucratic centralism," which signified the liquidation of intra-party democracy and collective party leadership.[9]

MOUNTING SOVIET CONCERN

The first ten days of May brought Czechoslovakia into the center of Soviet attention as a result of the one-day visit to Moscow by Dubček, followed a few days later by the Foreign Minister, Hájek, and the subsequent meeting in Moscow of the leaders of the CPSU and its four closest bloc associates. The Dubček visit, as officially admitted in Prague, was the occasion of renewed expression of Soviet concern over what was happening in Czechoslovakia, but little information is available on the course of the talks.[10] Again we have only a later report by Bil'ak (who was present with Černík and Smrkovský in the Czechoslovak delegation) according to which the Soviet spokesmen intimated that they saw no improvement in the situation since the Dresden conference and "literally implored us to realize the danger which threatened the CPCz and Czechoslovakia from the growth of counterrevolutionary forces." They warned that "rightist-opportunist and anti-socialist forces" were growing stronger and that "disorder and chaos were being organically transferred from the political sphere to the sphere of the national economy, which could have catastrophic consequences." "They begged us not to forget that the western frontiers of the ČSSR were also at the same time the western frontiers of the socialist world, and that on these frontiers things were now happening which were harmful for the security not only of the ČSSR, but also of the socialist camp in general." "The Soviet comrades," he said, "made no secret to us of the fact that under no circumstances was it possible to permit a development which sooner or later could lead to the liquidation of the achievements of socialism in the Czechoslovak Republic. This would be no longer only Czechoslovakia's 'internal' affair, but a matter of world socialism as a whole."[11]

In another retrospective version, the validity of which cannot be verified, Bil'ak reported that the Soviet leaders had told them "that Czechoslovakia is an important component of the socialist camp and that our

---

[9] *Pravda*, April 23. Full text in *Reprints* 6, May 17, pp. 3-27. Other authoritative commentaries in the Soviet press dealing with similar themes (vigilance against imperialist subversion and nationalist and revisionist elements, and the leading role of the party) could be interpreted as implicit criticisms of Czechoslovakia. Among the most important were V. Kozlov, *Sovetskaya Rossia*, April 4; editorial, ibid., April 13; T. Timofeyev, *Izvestia*, April 9; F. Petrenko, *Pravda*, April 17; P. Fedoseev, ibid., April 22; S. Kovalev, ibid., April 25; V. Zagladin, ibid., April 29.

[10] See above, chap. IX. The visits by Dubček and Hájek were briefly noted in *Pravda*, May 5, 7, 8, but without the fanfare customary on such occasions.

[11] *RP*, Sept. 3, 1969 (also *SCC* 3, Jan. 1970, pp. 124-25).

western frontier is at the same time also their western frontier. To permit Czechoslovakia to fall out of the socialist camp would mean the betrayal of socialism and the annulling of the results of the second world war in Europe . . . and this *they could not permit even at the cost of a third world war.*"[12]

The meeting of the "five" was still more ominous, coming as it did immediately after Dubček's visit and with no Czechoslovak representative present. Although the brief communiqué did not refer to Czechoslovakia, there can be little doubt that this was a major item on the agenda. *Rudé právo* noted that the communiqué had not included the customary phrase about unanimity of views, suggesting that there had been serious differences, and published Yugoslav reports that the Hungarian party had had reservations about the meeting and had opposed any efforts to influence the democratization process in Czechoslovakia by "intimidation."[13] A *Pravda* editorial, under the title, "In the Interests of Unity," discussed the Moscow gathering in the context of the previous ones in Budapest, Sofia, and Dresden, and of the April CC plenum, and concluded that the latest conference had been a rebuff to the efforts of imperialism to weaken the unity of the socialist countries and subvert socialist society from within.[14]

Meanwhile the Soviet press showed a somewhat ambivalent, but on the whole negative, attitude. The anniversary of Czechoslovakia's liberation in 1945 was marked by articles emphasizing the role of the Soviet army and extolling the accomplishments of subsequent decades. Among them were two by Czech leaders, General Svoboda, in *Pravda*, and Černík, in *Izvestia*, on May 9, the latter expounding in some detail on the

[12] Speech at the CC plenum, Sept. 1969, *Svědectví* 10, no. 38 (1970), 284-85. In his speech at the CC plenum in May 1968, as later reported, Bil'ak was said to have referred to the serious dissatisfaction voiced by the Soviet comrades during the Moscow visit. We stressed, he said, that "the seriousness of the situation demanded appropriate measures" with regard to the mass media, the army, security and the People's Militia, and "the adoption of clear positions" by the party. They warned of "an organized planned offensive against the party" and of "a struggle for power" that had already begun, but expressed confidence that the party would find "enough strength to deal with the situation" (Bil'ak, *Pravda zůstala pravdou*, Prague, 1971, pp. 108-10). According to this report the Soviet comrades revealed that the Czechoslovak situation had been discussed at the April plenum of the CPSU, but in "temperate terms."

[13] *Pravda*, May 9; *RP*, May 11, 12. See below in this chapter on Hungary's attitude.

[14] *Pravda*, May 10. Cf. similar comments by M. A. Suslov, in a major address on the 150th anniversary of Marx's birth, in which he attacked both "left" and "right" revisionism and called for unity of the international communist movement against the dangers of imperialism (*Pravda*, May 6; *CDSP* 20, no. 18, pp. 3-8). A major article in *Pravda* (May 12) by T. Kolesnichenko praised the May 8 meeting as a manifestation of proletarian internationalism and urged "a struggle against all deviations from Marxism-Leninism, and against nationalistic, dogmatist and revisionist distortions of its revolutionary principles."

new Czechoslovak course. This was, however, immediately preceded by a bitter Tass press release denying Soviet complicity in the death of Jan Masaryk.[15] Throughout the rest of May, major events in Czechoslovakia, such as addresses by Dubček and Svoboda, or the meeting of the Prague party *aktiv*, were reported, usually in such a way as to underline solidarity with the Soviet Union and the struggle against anti-socialist forces.[16]

Soviet concern was more sharply defined by a series of polemical articles attacking the authors of certain articles in the Czech press, charging them with misinterpreting Marxism, with proposing political changes that would undermine the leading role of the party, and with casting into doubt the foreign policy of Czechoslovakia and the alliance with the USSR.[17] Coupled with this was a series of major articles explaining in general terms the correct ideological understanding of the leading role of the party and of socialist democracy.[18] At the same time there were bitter attacks on imperialism, in particular the USA's policy of "building bridges," which was designed, it was said, to subvert the socialist countries from within and break up their unity with each other, and on West Germany's *Ostpolitik* and its aims in Czechoslovakia.[19] Marshal Yakubovsky, Warsaw pact commander-in-chief, in the pages of *Pravda* (May 14) spoke of the aggressiveness of imperialism and the increased danger of war and boasted of the unity and strength of the Warsaw alliance. He praised the coordination of policy through political and military conferences and joint military exercises.

The first half of June was characterized by the absence of polemics, no doubt owing to the CPCz plenum and the visit of the Smrkovský delegation to the USSR. Brief reports in the Soviet press informed readers of the plenum's decision to call the 14th congress on September 9 and

[15] *Pravda*, May 8. See also criticism by *Izvestia*, May 17.

[16] For the Prague *aktiv*, Pravda, May 15; for Dubček, ibid., May 29. See also D. Kolder's *Rudé právo* (May 29) article, in *Pravda* and *Izvestia*, May 30.

[17] For instance, censuring Jan Procházka for his anti-socialist views and his criticism of collectivized agriculture and of Czechoslovak foreign policy (*Literaturnaya gazeta*, May 8); *Student* for advocating a student organization independent of the party (*Komsomolskaya pravda*, May 11); L. Sochor for his interpretation of Marxism and defense of political pluralism (V. Gorin, *Trud*, May 15); V. Havel for his proposal of a multi-party system (N. Vladimirov, *LG*, May 15). See also the attack on T. G. Masaryk for his "anti-Soviet" role in 1918 (*SR*, May 14). For most of these articles, see *CDSP* 20, nos. 18-20, passim. The polemic with Procházka was resumed in *LG*, June 26.

[18] E.g. V. Stepanov, *Izvestia*, May 11; L. Onikov, *Pravda*, May 19; G. Kikalov, *Pravda Ukrainy*, May 24 (also *CDSP* 20, no. 20, passim). Cf. also editorial and articles, *Kommunist*, no. 8 (May 1968), pp. 3-12, 26-51.

[19] For example, A. Butenko, *Izvestia*, May 16; V. Kozyakov, *Krasnaya zvezda*, May 24; also *Izvestia*, May 15, 18, 27. Cf. V. Osipov, Moscow radio, May 16 (*FBIS*, May 17). Osipov assailed the efforts of West Germany to achieve a reorientation of Czechoslovakia's foreign and economic policy to the West.

of certain planned reforms, such as rehabilitation and federation, but gave no details. Lengthy accounts of Dubček's speech and the plenum resolution featured references to "anti-communist tendencies" and "anti-Sovietism," but also cited references to "sectarian" and "conservative" forces. It was stated that several plenum participants had mentioned anti-socialist forces and that some had underestimated this danger.[20] Smrkovský's tour was given front-page coverage in the Soviet press. He was quoted more than once on the unity of the two countries, and no Soviet criticism of Czechoslovak developments was reported.[21]

The relative calm was shattered in the midst of the tour, however, with the publication of a slashing attack on Císař by Academician F. Konstantinov in *Pravda* on June 14.[22] Shortly thereafter P. N. Demichev, candidate Politburo member and CC Secretary, delivered a major assault on revisionism, both left and right, especially in the field of the social sciences, which, although couched in general terms, seemed to point directly at Czechoslovakia's intellectual ferment.[23] The following day tension increased with the publication in *Pravda* of the letter from the conference of the People's Militia in Prague, succeeded, day after day, by resolutions adopted at factory meetings pledging support for their "class brethren" in Czechoslovakia in their struggle to defend socialism.[24] Parallel with this barrage was the publication of a series of polemical articles in selected Soviet newspapers, denouncing specific ideas published in certain Czech and Slovak papers and their authors.[25]

A foreign policy review by the Foreign Minister, Andrei Gromyko, at the Supreme Soviet session in late June included a severe condemnation of West Germany and its *Ostpolitik*, and although not mentioning Czechoslovakia, indirectly delivered a warning to that country in sharper terms than usual. Quoting the April plenum resolution on the subversive

---

[20] *Pravda*, May 31, June 1-4, 8. Cf. similar treatment of Dubček's speeches at a trade union conference and at the anniversary of the founding of the Social Democratic Party (*Pravda*, June 20, 29).

[21] *Pravda*, June 13-17.   [22] See above, chaps. x, xix.

[23] *Pravda* and *Izvestia*, June 20; fuller version, *Kommunist*, no. 10 (July 1968), pp. 14-35 (*FBIS*, Aug. 15). Among those criticized were economists who exaggerated the law of value and minimized the role of central planning. There was only one specific mention of Czechoslovakia—a reference to the technocratic idea of the management of the economy by the intelligentsia.

[24] See above, chap. x, p. 285.

[25] These included an attack on *Student* and I. Sviták for advocating a multi-party system, by G. Ognev, *KP*, June 21; on V. Havel for seeking to make the Union of Writers non-political, *Trud*, June 21; on *Literární listy* and J. Svoboda's idea of a multi-party system, by V. Platkovsky, *Izvestia*, June 25; on Jan Procházka, for belittling the role of the Soviet army in 1945, by Vladimirov, *LG*, June 26; and on M. Hübl and others for their comments on the Czechoslovak resistance movement, the role of the Soviet army in the liberation of Czechoslovakia, and the expulsion of the Sudeten Germans, by A. Nedorezov, *Izvestia*, June 29. For full or partial texts, *CDSP* 20, no. 26, pp. 7-12.

struggle of imperialism against the socialist community, Gromyko concluded: "But the calculations of those who want to break off even one single link from the socialist commonwealth are short-sighted and futile. The socialist commonwealth will not allow this to happen [Applause]. The commonwealth is an indissoluble entity." He cited more than once the efforts being made jointly with the other socialist countries to strengthen the commonwealth "in the political, economic, and defense spheres." Then, in a statement that went unreported in *Rudé právo*, but which clashed with Czechoslovak ideas of a more independent foreign policy, Gromyko spoke of various methods employed by the socialist countries to achieve "a coordination of efforts" and "a harmonizing of their actions in the international arena."[26]

CLIMAX AT WARSAW

During the first half of July, the stiffer attitude of the Soviet Union was displayed on several occasions in statements by leading Soviet personages. Brezhnev used the occasion of a visit of Kádár to Moscow to utter some thinly veiled warnings to the Prague leaders. At a ceremonial meeting in the Kremlin in honor of his guest, Brezhnev referred to "problems that do arise in relations among socialist countries" and declared that solutions are sought "on the basis of the principles of scientific socialism." He emphasized that "despite all the diversity of forms and all the specific national characteristics of each country," there were "common principles and a social-economic foundation common to all of them." As "internationalists," he continued, "we cannot and never will be indifferent to the fate of socialist construction in other countries and to the general cause of socialism and communism on earth," especially at a time when "apologists for bourgeois systems are prepared to dress up in any pseudo-socialist attire in attempting, behind the mask of 'national forms,' to shake and 'soften' socialism . . . and to weaken the fraternal ties among the socialist countries."[27]

His Politburo colleague, the Ukrainian party chief, P. Shelest, on the occasion of the 50th anniversary of the Communist Party of the Ukraine,

---

[26] *Pravda,* June 28 (*CDSP* 20, no. 28, pp. 11-16); also in *RP*, June 28. Cf. a strong statement (similar to his *Pravda* article in May) by Marshal Yakubovsky in *KZ*, June 22 or 23, BBC, I, June 25.

[27] Brezhnev, *Pravda*, July 4; *CDSP* 20, no. 27, pp. 5-8. *Rudé právo*, July 4, included the statements quoted. The communiqué on the visit stressed the need to strengthen the unity of the socialist commonwealth, including WTO and CMEA (*Pravda*, July 5). For Kádár's speech, see below in this chapter. Cf. Brezhnev's speech to a military graduation ceremony in which he referred to "ideological sabotage" against the armed forces of individual socialist countries and the need to "strengthen our collective defense" and to "perfect the mechanism of interaction" (*Pravda*, July 9; *CDSP* 20, no. 28, pp. 10-11).

was vitriolic in condemning "bourgeois nationalism" in the Ukraine and defending "proletarian internationalism," interpreting that to mean not just "the recognition of independence and equality of nations," but also "the necessity for the association, alliance, and mutual assistance of socialist nations." He scathingly condemned "theoreticians" who talked of " 'models of socialism,' abstract humanism, and abstract democracy" . . . and " 'national reforms,' " and lamented that "individual communists in some fraternal parties had swallowed the bait of bourgeois propaganda and its yes-men (*podpevala*), the opportunists of various stripes."[28]

At a press conference in Stockholm, the Soviet Prime Minister, Kosygin, expressed similar views and made specific mention of Czechoslovakia. Kosygin referred the press correspondents to an article published "the other day" in *Pravda* as representing "our appraisal" of Czechoslovak developments. He thus associated himself with the notorious statement by the pseudonymous Aleksandrov, in *Pravda*, July 11, condemning the Two Thousand Words as counterrevolutionary and comparing Czechoslovak developments with Hungarian events in 1956. This blast had concentrated its attack on the mass media, but also criticized certain leading party figures (unnamed) for their toleration of the manifesto.[29] Kosygin, it is true, went on to express confidence "that the Czechoslovak Communist Party will not yield its guiding role to anyone" and that "there are no forces that could break the friendship between the peoples of our two countries." But he also declared: "The Soviet Union and Czechoslovakia are Warsaw pact allies; we have mutual obligations under this pact; and we shall perform them unfailingly. . . ."[30]

Telling emphasis to Kosygin's warning was lent by subsequent articles in the government organ, *Izvestia*, one directed against the imperialist policy of "bridge-building," with specific reference to Czechoslovakia as the object of special attention, and another against the idea of "democratic socialism," polemicizing particularly with an article in the Czech newspaper, *Lidová demokracie*.[31] Even more vigorous endorsement was given by the organ of the armed forces, *Krasnaya zvezda* (July 12)

---

[28] Article, *Pravda*, July 5; speech, *Pravda* and *Izvestia*, July 6 (*CDSP* 20, no. 27, pp. 24-25).

[29] *CDSP* 20, no. 28, pp. 3-4. See also an attack on the Two Thousand Words, *LG*, July 10.

[30] *Pravda*, July 15 (*CDSP* 20, no. 28, p. 9); also *RP*, July 15. Cf. his speech in Stockholm, in which he predicted resistance to the efforts of imperialism to interfere in the internal affairs of countries and to change their system of government (*Pravda*, July 12).

[31] M. Volgin, *Izvestia*, July 11; V. Bakinsky, ibid., July 13 (both in *CDSP* 20, no. 28, pp. 4-8). See also *Izvestia* and *SR*, July 12. *Izvestia* (July 17) bitterly condemned NATO's psychological warfare which was seeking, in accordance with the concepts of Prof. Z. K. Brzezinski, to penetrate Eastern Europe and to isolate the GDR, and thus to export counterrevolution (Moscow, in Serbo-Croatian, July 17, BBC, I, July 19).

which declared that the socialist commonwealth was *"a unified entity . . .* which allows *none to sunder* our alliance or to break any of the ties that bind us." The Soviet Union was not forcing its strategic concepts on its allies. "The uniformity of opinion . . . on fundamental military questions" was "the result of free exchange of opinions and the joint efforts of the party, state and military leadership of the fraternal countries."[32]

The Warsaw conference in mid-July marked a climax in the controversy over Czechoslovakia and resulted in the first joint public statement on the reasons for Soviet and bloc concern. The meetings were veiled in secrecy, giving no reliable evidence of whether the delegates differed in interpretation or in recommendations. The brief communiqué was uninformative,[33] as was the report of the subsequent plenary session of the CPSU Central Committee which endorsed the actions taken at Warsaw.[34] Neither Brezhnev's address on the latter occasion, nor the speeches of the carefully selected participants, were published. The joint letter presented to the Czechoslovak party therefore constituted the only documentation of the viewpoints of the parties.

The Warsaw letter professed an "understanding" for the January decisions and disavowed any interference with plans for reform, specifically mentioning actions concerning socialist legality, planning and the economic system, socialist democracy, and the relations of Czechs and Slovaks. The object of their concern was the anti-socialist and revisionist

---

[32] BBC, I, July 15.

[33] Communiqué, *Pravda*, July 16; letter to CPCz, ibid., July 18. See also above chap. x. For a report on the proceedings by Gomułka's interpreter, see Erwin Weit, *At the Red Summit* (New York, 1973), originally published in *Der Spiegel*, Aug. 17, 24, 31, 1970. According to Weit, the most extreme positions were taken by Ulbricht and Zhivkov, and the least hostile by Kádár. Ulbricht was said to have been disappointed, and Kádár relieved, by the outcome of the conference. Ulbricht was supposed to have warned Kádár that Hungary was next in line and to have urged that action be taken before the CPCz 14th congress and the election of a new CC and Politburo.

[34] *Pravda*, July 18 (*CDSP* 20, no. 29, pp. 4-6). The speakers included P. Y. Shelest; V. V. Grishin, Moscow city party secretary; V. S. Tolstikov, Leningrad regional secretary; several other first secretaries (including the heads of the Kazakh and Latvian parties, and of the Moscow, Volgograd, Saratov, Donetsk, and the Transcarpathian regions); N. M. Gribachev, secretary of the Writers' Union; M. V. Keldysh, head of the Academy of Sciences; and S. G. Lapin, the general director of Tass. It has been pointed out that neither Suslov nor B. N. Ponomarev spoke, and that apart from Brezhnev, Shelest was the only member of the Warsaw delegation who made a speech (Richard Lowenthal, "The Sparrow in the Cage," *Problems of Communism* 17, Nov.-Dec. 1968, pp. 16-17). Kosygin and A. N. Shelepin were also silent.

Over half of the speakers represented non-Russian constituencies; three were Ukrainians, a fourth represented a Ukrainian region (Donetsk). Y. V. Il'nitsky, from the Transcarpathian region, was not a member of the CC and in other speeches had taken a hard line toward Czechoslovakia, to which his region had belonged prior to 1945 (Grey Hodnett and Peter J. Potichnyj, *The Ukraine and the Czechoslovak Crisis*, Canberra, 1970, pp. 86, 144, nn. 21-22).

forces (against which the May plenum of the CPCz Central Committee had warned) which threatened to liquidate the party's leading role and undermine the socialist system. In the face of this threat of counterrevolution, represented acutely by the Two Thousand Words, the CPCz had failed to act. The document had even found "outright champions" within the party's leadership; the flirtations of West Germany had also found "a response in ruling circles." Unlike the earlier press attacks and official statements, the letter thus trained its fire directly on the topmost leadership which was called upon to take certain specified measures and to rally "the healthy forces" in the party. Although focusing on domestic developments, the missive also criticized tendencies to change foreign policy. The domestic and external aspects were indeed inseparably intertwined, as the following quotation demonstrates. "The frontiers of the socialist world have shifted to the center of Europe, to the Elbe and the Bohemian Forest. And never will we consent to allow these historic gains of socialism and the independence and security of all our people to be jeopardized. Never will we consent to allow imperialism, by peaceful or non-peaceful means from within or without, to make a breach in the socialist system and change the balance of power in Europe in its favor."

Before the Czechoslovak response was received, a vitriolic campaign was launched in the Soviet media and continued with almost unrelieved intensity, after the reply, down to the final day of July and the opening of the Čierna conference. It was initiated in *Pravda* on July 19 with a scathing editorial declaring that the basic issue at stake was "socialist Czechoslovakia's to be or not to be." Warning that "indecisiveness, passivity, and slowness in mobilizing the party and nation" would mean "anarchy and political catastrophe," the editorial assured "the communists and the working people of Czechoslovakia" of "all necessary assistance in the defense of their socialist achievements."[35] *Izvestia* wrote that the situation in Czechoslovakia was "unacceptable" and required "concrete measures" by the CPCz, with "all necessary assistance" from the Soviet Union.[36]

N. V. Podgorny, Politburo member and chairman of the Supreme Soviet Presidium, in a speech before the RSFSR Supreme Soviet, declared that "hostile forces in and outside the country were clearly trying to push Czechoslovakia off the socialist road and to force it away from the socialist commonwealth." He expressed the belief that "the CPCz, the working class, and all the working people" would "bar the road to reaction" and

[35] On the same day, *Pravda* carried reports of caches of arms found in western Bohemia and of an alleged Pentagon secret plan for subversion and aggression against the socialist countries; on the next day, an article on West German machinations against Czechoslovakia.

[36] *Izvestia*, July 20, editorial (*FBIS*, July 22).

assured them, in the words of the Warsaw letter, that "fulfilling their internationalist duty, the communists and all Soviet people will give them every kind of assistance and support in this."[37] For the next ten days the campaign was fierce and unrelenting. In an editorial commenting on the Czechoslovak reply (which was not published), *Pravda* found it totally wanting, ignoring the Warsaw proposals, and failing to recognize the extent of the danger.[38] Other articles singled out specific Czech leaders for denunciation—General Prchlík for his "slander" of the WTO; Císař, for his distortion of Marxism-Leninism; and Josef Pavel, for his alleged role in the trials of the fifties.[39] There were personal attacks on individual Czech and Slovak intellectuals, both for their advocacy of political changes that would undermine the party's leading role and for their alleged sympathy for West German policies.[40] There were more general assaults on the plans of U.S. imperialism to interfere in Czechoslovakia and a constant stream of abuse concerning West Germany's *Ostpolitik* and its subversive measures, and on Sudeten German activities.[41] There was a concerted onslaught on the weakening of the party's democratic centralism, with specific mention of the proposed reform of the CPCz statute so as to guarantee the right of minorities or "fractions."[42] And on the very day when the opening of the Čierna conference was reported, *Pravda* carried a front-page editorial, entitled "Loyalty to Marxism-Leninism," which cited general support for the July CC plenum as an example of unity on the basis of Marxism-Leninism and denounced both left and right revisionists and nationalists, and "new variants" of Marxism.[43]

CALM BEFORE THE STORM

The Bratislava conference opened up a new phase during which, for almost ten days, criticism of Czechoslovakia was entirely suspended and

---

[37] *Pravda*, July 20 (radio version, *FBIS*, July 19). Cf. the speech on the same occasion by another Politburo member, G. I. Voronov, who made only passing reference to the Warsaw conference and concentrated on the achievements of the RSFSR, including the "triumph" of its nationality policy (*Pravda*, July 20).

[38] *Pravda*, July 22 (*CDSP* 20, no. 29, pp. 10-11). An article in *Práce*, July 20 (by V. Kotyk), concerning foreign policy was specifically condemned. For a more restrained but critical comment, *Izvestia*, July 22.

[39] *KZ*, July 23; F. Konstantinov, *Pravda*, July 24; and *Izvestia*, July 24, the last a reprint from the Bulgarian newspaper, *Otechestven front*, July 21 (*CDSP* 20, no. 30, pp. 3-5, and no. 31, pp. 7-8).

[40] Y. Zhukov, *Pravda*, July 26; "Journalist," *LG*, July 24, 31, resp. See also the Praga letter, *Pravda*, July 30 (*CDSP* 20, no. 31, pp. 9-10); above, chap. XI, pp. 302-3.

[41] In particular S. Vishnevsky, *Pravda*, July 26; B. Strelnikov, ibid., July 29; *Pravda*, July 22, 23, 27, 28; *Izvestia*, July 26, 27.

[42] S. Selyuk, *Pravda*, July 25.   [43] *Pravda*, July 30.

attention was centered on the theme of bloc solidarity. *Pravda*, in its editorial on August 5, under the heading "Strength in Unity," propounded the need of the socialist countries to "coordinate their action in the international arena" and described as the main task of all the parties "the fulfillment of all the provisions contained in the unanimously adopted document." On the following day *Pravda* reported at length Dubček's speech on Bratislava, giving the impression of full Czechoslovak support for the declaration, but carefully omitted most of his statements concerning post-January policies and the Action Program. His reference to the end of public polemics and his denial that any other agreements had been concluded were also deleted.[44] On the same day (Aug. 6), the CPSU Politburo endorsed the actions taken by its members at Bratislava and placed renewed stress on "putting into practice the theses of the declaration" as the paramount task of the fraternal parties.[45] In another editorial on August 8, entitled "Indestructible Solidarity," *Pravda* sounded the same note, again without mentioning an agreement to suspend polemics.[46] For the next six days, the Soviet press, with no noticeable difference in emphasis, continued to express similar sentiments of satisfaction with Bratislava and avoided any direct polemics with Czechoslovakia.[47]

A major change in Soviet attitude occurred on August 14, which, perhaps significantly, was the day following Ulbricht's short visit to Karlovy Vary. A carefully orchestrated barrage of attacks on Czechoslovakia began and continued without breakdown to the day of the invasion. Two of these, in *Literaturnaya gazeta* and *Pravda*, concentrated their fire on the Czech press and made the identical charge that commentaries had been "flagrantly contrary to the letter and spirit of Bratislava."[48] Even

[44] *Pravda*, Aug. 6. Cf. Dubček's speech, *Rok šedesátý osmý* (Prague, 1969), pp. 267-70. The sole reference to January included in *Pravda* was Dubček's statement that the new policy could be carried through to conclusion only in close solidarity with the socialist countries.

[45] *Pravda*, Aug. 7. This issue also contained the CPCz Presidium's statement concerning the preparations for the 14th congress, but omitted its references to the revised party statute or to the desirability of the press acting in the spirit of Bratislava.

[46] Commenting on this editorial, *Rudé právo* (Aug. 9) reported that the end of polemics was evident in the Soviet press and that foreign observers believed that its permanence would depend on the responsibility of the Czechoslovak media.

[47] For example, *SR*, Aug. 6; *KZ*, Aug. 6; *Pravda*, Aug. 11, 12; *Izvestia*, Aug. 6, 9, 13. Moscow radio (Aug. 8, 10, 11) spoke in the same vein, praising Bratislava for foiling the efforts of the imperialists, but lamenting the continuation of these efforts (BBC, I, Aug. 10, 12, 13). A distinctive note was struck by *Pravda Ukrainy* (Aug. 9) which repeatedly referred to the requirements of "proletarian internationalism," a term not used in the Bratislava communiqué. See also the invocation of this concept in an editorial in *Kommunist*, no. 12 (1968), pp. 24-31.

[48] "Journalist," *LG*, Aug. 14; Zhukov, *Pravda*, Aug. 16. The former attacked *Literární listy* and its editor, and criticized specifically J. Valka's commentary on

more unfavorable was the reportage by "Aleksandrov" on certain events in Prague, such as the activity of "hooligans" in downtown streets (including a demonstration at CC headquarters), the petition for the dissolution of the People's Militia, the campaign of persecution against the signatories of the Praga letter, and the press criticism of Bratislava. These were described as efforts by "right-wing reaction" to undermine the socialist order and to tear Czechoslovakia away from the socialist commonwealth, but were said to be doomed to failure in view of "the determination of the working people, relying on the solidarity and support of the fraternal parties, . . . to resist . . . the intrigues of domestic and external reaction." Ominous was the use of the term "working people" and the absence of any reference to the party.[49] In the same issue, a review of international events described the nefarious actions of West Germany and contained the menacing sentence that the fraternal parties "consider it necessary to assure the implementation of the decisions jointly taken at Bratislava."[50]

Interwoven with these direct attacks were more general commentaries with an indirect but clear bearing on the situation in Czechoslovakia. The most foreboding was a major article in the Soviet military newspaper on August 14 by the deputy head of the Polish general staff, Gen. W. Barański, who expatiated on the dangers of revisionism and imperialism and on the common responsibility to aid Czechoslovakia. "Even a partial weakening of one important link in the defense system weakens the whole system," he wrote.[51] On the same day, in *Pravda*, a Soviet theoretician, I. Pomelov, elaborated the common patterns of socialist development and the danger of exaggerating national peculiarities, thus in effect filling out in detail the obligations assumed by the Bratislava declaration.[52] On the following day (Aug. 15), in *Izvestia*, Ernst Henry wrote of an alleged West German plan for a military offensive against the GDR and Czechoslovakia.[53] Two days later, on the very day of Kádár's secret visit to Czechoslovakia, *Pravda* published a major article from

---

Bratislava. See also V. Matveyev, in *Izvestia* (Aug. 17) who, while primarily condemning Chinese and Albanian comments on Bratislava, also censured the Czech, L. Veselý. For all three, see *CDSP* 20, no. 33, pp. 7-10.

[49] *Pravda*, Aug. 18; fully reported *RP*, Aug. 19 (in English, Remington, ed., *Winter in Prague*, pp. 292-93).

[50] Kolesnichenko, *Pravda*, Aug. 18. The following day *Pravda* returned to the Praga letter, deploring the persecution of those who had spoken up for socialism and friendship with the Soviet Union. Although the letter had been condemned by the CPCz Presidium, attacks on socialist achievements by enemies of the working class continued, it was said (*Pravda*, Aug. 19).

[51] *KZ*, Aug. 14 (*CDSP* 20, no. 33, pp. 5-7). See also below in this chapter, in the section on Poland.

[52] *Pravda*, Aug. 14 (*CDSP* 20, no. 33, pp. 3-5).

[53] *Izvestia*, Aug. 15 (*Reprints* 7, Sept. 6, pp. 12-15).

Népszabadság on 1956 in Hungary, which termed the liquidation of the party's leading role the precondition for counterrevolution.[54] On the same day, *Krasnaya zvezda*, in a critique of American and West German policies, described Zionism as an imperialist tool and praised the rebuff given to it in Poland.[55] On August 20 *Izvestia*, concentrating its attack on West German revanchism, reiterated Henry's charge (after a West German denial); praised Bratislava as a barrier to subversion by imperialism and a step toward "a coordinated policy" of the socialist states; and endorsed the unity of the socialist camp as a guarantee against "a change in the correlation of forces" and of European security.[56] In a final blast, *Pravda*, in a front-page editorial on August 20, rejected peaceful co-existence in the sphere of ideology and endorsed the offensive against bourgeois ideology set forth at Bratislava.[57]

Thus, during the week prior to the invasion, Soviet commentary, while giving clear hints as to causes for concern, ironically gave no indications of worry on other crucial matters. The draft party statute, published in Prague on August 10, received no attention, although a major article on democratic centralism appeared in *Pravda* the day before. Without referring to the Czechoslovak statute, the author, P. Rodionov, elaborated the Leninist norms of party life and criticized revisionist ideas, such as "freedom of fractions."[58] The visits of Tito, Ulbricht, and Ceaușescu to Czechoslovakia were briefly reported in *Pravda*, but without comment.[59] There was only slight mention of the preparations for the forthcoming extraordinary party congress, and no serious comment on its likely character.[60]

The most telling evidence of the position of the Soviet leadership was the letter of August 17 sent from the Politburo to the CPCz Presidium, the text of which was revealed on the Czechoslovak radio one year after the occupation.[61] Referring to the fears of counterrevolution expressed

[54] I. Horváth, *Pravda*, Aug. 17. See below, in the section on Hungary.

[55] *KZ*, Aug. 17 (*CDSP* 20, no. 33, pp. 15-16). Cf. an earlier bitter attack on Zionism by K. Ivanov, who linked this with imperialism's effort at subversion in the socialist countries and made specific reference to events in Poland (although not to Czechoslovakia). See *International Affairs* (Moscow), no. 6 (June 1968).

[56] *Izvestia*, Aug. 20 (*Reprints* 7, Sept. 6, pp. 12-15).

[57] *Pravda*, Aug. 20 (*CDSP* 20, no. 33, p. 12). In the same issue reportage from West Bohemia cited the aims of Sudeten German revanchists to return to Czechoslovakia.

[58] P. Rodionov, *Pravda*, Aug. 9 (*CDSP* 20, no. 32, pp. 8-10).

[59] *Pravda*, Aug. 12, 14, 16-18.

[60] *Pravda*, Aug. 6, 7, 20. In the last issue, *Borba* was cited as having reported that there would be major changes in leadership at the congress and that at most 25 percent of the present CC would be reelected.

[61] English text, *SCC* 3 (Jan. 1970), 141-44; also BBC, II, Aug. 22, 1969. A Czech text was made available to the author by Radio Free Europe. There are minor inconsistencies and translation inaccuracies in the several texts. The BBC version seems to be more accurate than the one given in *SCC*.

at Čierna and the admission by the CPCz representatives that the situation required determined measures, the letter charged the CPCz with failure to implement their assurances that they would take specific actions, including control of the mass media, the banning of certain clubs and organizations, and steps to strengthen the leading role of the party. In other passages these assurances were referred to as "understandings" and "agreements." The missive buttressed Soviet complaints by pointing to the unsatisfactory development of events in Czechoslovakia (including the items listed in the Aleksandrov report in *Pravda*)—the hostile campaign of the mass media against the Soviet Union and the socialist countries, and in particular the "one-sided" and "nationalistic" interpretation of the Bratislava conference; the attacks against the Praga workers, the People's Militia, and the WTO; the actions of hooligans in downtown Prague; and the breach of Leninist principles and of the statutes of the party. The Prague municipal organization was censured for violating CPCz Presidium decisions, setting itself up as "a second CC," and seeking to influence the elections to the 14th congress. Although criticism was directed at the CPCz Presidium and the CC as a whole, there were references to certain unnamed authorities and "forces" in the Presidium, which suggested an effort to divide the leadership. Císař and Prchlík were explicitly condemned. The Politburo letter concluded by underlining "the immediate necessity of fulfilling the obligations which we jointly accepted at the meeting of brother parties. . . ."

EAST GERMAN HOSTILITY

For two months after the changeover in Prague, which had been reported only briefly, the mass media in the GDR avoided any direct comment on Czechoslovak events.[62] Indeed, Ulbricht, in his address at the 1948 celebrations in Prague, gave no evidence of concern or of hostility to the post-January course. On the contrary, he said that "the same fundamental problems" were being solved in the socialist countries "in accordance with the specific conditions of development in each country" and expressly approved Dubček's own speech on that occasion. "No force on earth can ever destroy the close fraternal relations between our two parties and peoples," he declared. He warned of the dangers of psychological warfare by imperialism in Eastern Europe and specifically of West German revanchism, but did not link these specifically with events in Czechoslovakia.[63]

[62] For this section see, apart from general sources (n. 1), A. Müller and B. Utitz, *Deutschland und die Tschechoslowakei* (Freudenstadt, 1972), pp. 100-13; also Haefs, ed., *Ereignisse.*
[63] *Neues Deutschland*, Feb. 23 (*FBIS*, East Germany, Feb. 27). All references to

From mid-March reports of the district conferences in Czechoslovakia, although brief, were tendentious, citing criticisms of the press by Kolder and others and charging that external forces were backing "liberalization" and hoping for a reorientation in foreign policy.[64] This kind of reporting continued, without commentary, during and after the Dresden conference. Such signs of uneasiness in the press were insignificant in comparison with the sudden and unexpected blast of censure by Kurt Hager, Politburo member of the Socialist Unity Party of Germany (SED), at a meeting in honor of the 150th anniversary of Marx's birth. Calling attention to the sympathy expressed in the West German press with the "transformation" in Czechoslovakia, Hager directly charged the Bonn government with having as its aim "to soften up the socialist countries from within, to separate them from each other and . . . to isolate the GDR." Singling out speeches by Smrkovský, Hager charged that the attitude of Smrkovský and others was imbuing the West Germans with hope that Czechoslovakia would be "drawn into the whirlpool of evolution."[65] This direct comment on Czechoslovakia's domestic affairs and unfavorable reference to a leader so closely identified with the new course stirred up resentment in Czechoslovakia and produced an official note of protest. Thereafter, throughout April, press coverage of Czechoslovak developments resumed its previously limited and selective character, without commentaries.

The scene shifted completely in early May, immediately following the Moscow meeting of the five parties. This, and the comprehensive onslaught on Czechoslovak reform ideas in *Literaturnaya gazeta*, reproduced in full in the German party daily, gave the green light for the opening of a wide-ranging polemic against Czechoslovakia.[66] Almost simultaneously, a diplomatic protest was presented to Prague by the GDR, complaining of an article in *Rudé právo* (May 3) which was critical of East German visa and passport measures for control of the passage of West Germans through East Berlin.[67] Also at this time a report in the GDR press of the presence of American tanks in Czechoslovakia (with-

---

FBIS in this part of the chapter are to the section on East Germany. Cf. the warning about the aggressive policies of West Germany in the resolution of the SED Central Committee (*Pravda*, Feb. 9).

[64] *ND*, March 12 and passim throughout the rest of March.

[65] *ND*, March 27; East Berlin domestic radio broadcast (*FBIS*, March 28). See above, chap. VIII, for Czechoslovak reactions. This was the second of two speeches given by Hager on this occasion. Cf. Haefs, *Ereignisse*, pp. 99-100.

[66] *ND*, May 9.

[67] Robinson, *SCC* 1 (July-Oct. 1968), 143, 169-70. The note was referred to only in *Berliner Zeitung*, May 11 and was not reported elsewhere. The original criticism appeared in *RP*, May 3 and was later retracted, ibid., May 29.

out mention of the fact that they were there for the shooting of a war film) contributed to Czechoslovak annoyance and to growing tension.[68] This was followed by a series of lengthy assaults on ideas raised by a number of Czech and Slovak reform spokesmen. Perhaps the most disturbing was the initial one, directed at two prominent Czech scholars, both party members, A. Šnejdárek and J. Filipec, who were castigated for appearing on a West German television program to advocate cooperation with West Germany, and even more seriously, for allegedly criticizing their country's foreign policy.[69] This was followed by a critique of ideas of neutrality, an opposition party, an independent foreign policy, and a Czechoslovak "model," which, according to the West German *Der Spiegel*, were being expounded in the Czech press.[70] Another lengthy onslaught was made by the deputy editor-in-chief of *Neues Deutschland*, H. Herbell, who expressed an understanding for the desire of the Czechoslovak party to "correct past mistakes," described this as "their own business," and voiced confidence that Czechoslovakia would solve these tasks successfully, but went on to warn of the efforts of imperialism to undermine the leading role of the working class and the party and to entice Czechoslovakia with the offer of economic aid.[71]

Although the censure in these articles was severe, there was no direct criticism of the party's leadership (other than the implicit one that they tolerated such things), and attacks on leading figures, such as that by Kurt Hager, were not resumed. A Czech newspaper reported that, according to a secret SED document, the German party had lost confidence in their Czechoslovak comrades and was beginning to think in terms of some kind of collective intervention, even in military form, to ward off the danger of counterrevolution.[72] There was no other evidence to confirm that things had yet reached this stage.

The visit of a high-level delegation to Moscow, headed by Ulbricht, produced a communiqué with sharp criticism of the USA's subversive

[68] *BZ*, May 9, also 15. For severe criticism, see *RP*, May 11, 19.

[69] *ND*, May 12 (*FBIS*, May 14). See a later attack on the same two by J. Rudolf, *BZ*, May 15 (*FBIS*, May 20). In their reply, the two Czech scholars referred to "falsifications, half-truths, and direct lies" and "interference in domestic affairs" (*RP*, June 14).

[70] H. Baierl, *ND*, May 12 (*FBIS*, May 14).

[71] *ND*, May 24 (*FBIS*, May 28; also Remington, ed., *Winter in Prague*, pp. 165-72).

[72] These instructional materials, circulated in the GDR for the use of party activists and editors, intimated that counterrevolution was already under way. The conclusion had been reached, according to this report, that the assurances given by Czechoslovak representatives were worthless and that collective measures of intervention, even military, were justified under the Warsaw treaty and might be necessary (*LL*, May 30). The document was not directly quoted but paraphrased. See the version given by F. Fejtö, "Moscow and Its Allies," *PC* 17 (Nov., Dec. 1968), 36.

activity against the socialist countries and bitter condemnation of the German Federal Republic (GFR) as on the road to a "military police dictatorship." Reiterating the usual conditions for European security, the document gave its approval to the visa measures proposed by the GDR.[73] A few days later, the SED Central Committee plenum heard hard-line speeches by Erik Honecker, who attacked ideas of "a new model of socialism" and defended the leading role of the party, and by Hermann Axen, who denounced the efforts of imperialism to break socialist unity and to undermine socialism and stressed the need to strengthen the bonds of unity. Neither made specific mention of Czechoslovakia.[74] A belated report on the CPCz Central Committee plenum, which played up Dubček's own criticism of excesses and his emphasis on bloc ties,[75] ushered in a period of relatively conciliatory treatment during the visit of the foreign minister, Dr. Hájek, to Berlin. Hájek reported that an end of polemics had been agreed upon and that there was understanding for Czechoslovak developments on the part of East Germany.[76] A few days later, *Pravda* (Moscow) published an article by Honecker, who, without naming Czechoslovakia, noted the "hysterical cries of some people concerning freedom of opinion and of the press" and declared that "only socialism signified genuine democracy, . . . real freedom, and humanity."[77]

Polemics were renewed in early July on the subject of the Two Thousand Words, which had originally been merely reported, then criticized, and finally two weeks later, subjected to a furious denunciation as a platform for counterrevolution. In a major article in *Neues Deutschland*, "The Strategy of Imperialism and the Czechoslovak Socialist Republic," published also in *Pravda*, the new methods of imperialism, in comparison with 1956, were described as "a refined effort to undermine and erode" socialism through "liberalization," or an inner transformation of the socialist countries. The article cited at length not only "imperialist" spokes-

---

[73] *Pravda*, June 1. The measures were adopted by the People's Chamber shortly thereafter and strongly defended by Ulbricht (BBC, II, June 13-14, 18).

[74] For brief reports of plenum speeches, *RP*, June 7, 9; also BBC, II, June 12. Ulbricht's own speech at the plenum was not published until June 21. Referring to the complete agreement of the leaders of the USSR and the GDR at their recent meeting and reiterating the customary conditions of "normalizing" relations between the two German states, Ulbricht termed the *Ostpolitik* "a variant of the cold war against the socialist countries" and attacked the freedom of press and radio in these countries as "an instrument for organizing reactionary counterrevolutionary forces." The *Ostpolitik*, he charged, sought to divide the socialist countries, to isolate the GDR, to abolish the socialist order in these countries, and, in particular, to dismember and to conquer Poland and Czechoslovakia" (*RP*, June 22).

[75] *ND*, June 15.

[76] On Hájek's visit, see *ND*, June 17, 19, 20. During his stay Hájek approved the GDR visa measures.

[77] *Pravda*, June 24.

men in the West, such as Professor Brzezinski, but also anti-socialist forces in Czechoslovakia (I. Sviták, V. Havel, Jan Procházka, and L. Vaculík were named), implying that both groups were working hand in hand. Summing up, the article declared: "The political offensive of imperialism is directed against the ČSSR, but thereby also against the vital interests of the socialist community."[78]

It was presumably about this time that the SED distributed an internal party document to regional party secretaries which indicated its hostility toward the Czechoslovak party. It contained a detailed censure of CPCz policy ever since 1948, charging a lack of knowledge of Marxism-Leninism on the part of Czech and Slovak communists; the influence of ideas derived from the struggle for national independence, including those of Masaryk and Beneš; and "a strong Western orientation" of the intellectuals. The document denounced the notion of "a specifically Czechoslovak way to socialism" and pointed to many distortions in the party's line, for instance, "leveling" of income; the use of administrative measures; the neglect of non-communist parties and other social groups; violations of party norms; and failure to solve the Slovak question. It condemned the Two Thousand Words and the subversive measures of West Germany, and expressed a readiness to take "all appropriate steps to strengthen . . . the positions of socialism in the ČSSR."[79]

By the time of the Warsaw conference East German hostility was clearly defined and was expressed during and after the meeting until the end of July. The twin dangers, inextricably interlocked in their exposition, were the imperialist strategy of subversion, and especially West Germany's part in this campaign, and the "creeping counterrevolution" in Czechoslovakia, which constituted a threat both to socialism in Czechoslovakia and to the entire socialist community. Authoritative articles gave detailed elaboration of both dangers, with frequent reference to Sudeten German revisionism. For instance, under the heading "Massive Intervention of Bonn in ČSSR's Internal Affairs," *Neues Deutschland* cited West German trade and credit offers and visits by Bonn leaders to Prague as aimed at a reorientation of Czechoslovak foreign policy away from the "jointly coordinated standpoint" of the socialist countries and toward the establishment of diplomatic relations.[80] Two days later the party organ described the GFR's "ideological interference" as the

[78] *ND*, July 13 (*Pravda*, July 15; *CDSP* 20, no. 28, pp. 9-10). See earlier articles, *ND*, June 29, July 6.

[79] This was published later in *Frankfurter Allgemeine Zeitung*, Aug. 27; also in Haefs, ed., *Ereignisse*, pp. 115-18; in English, *U.S., Joint Publications Research Service*, no. 46,667, pp. 46-56. No date was given. It was said to have been circulated in early summer and again at the World Youth Festival in Sofia at the end of July.

[80] *ND*, July 17 (*Pravda*, July 20; *CDSP* 20, no. 29, pp. 7-8).

main danger, condemning "bridge-building" and the *Ostpolitik* and lambasted "creeping counterrevolution."[81] Disturbing, too, were the reports of caches of arms discovered in Czechoslovak border regions, although these were described as false by Czechoslovak authorities.[82] This negative attitude received full endorsement by the SED Central Committee in a statement published on July 20, and by the Politburo, after the Czechoslovak reply to the Warsaw letter, on July 24. Although the CC, in the spirit of the Warsaw letter, expressed "the hope," and made an appeal, that the Czechoslovak leaders would take the firm measures which were recommended in this missive, the Politburo was openly critical of the Czechoslovak party for its failure to recognize the danger at home and for its underestimation of imperialist interference.[83] Hostile opinions continued to be expressed right to the opening of the Čierna conference and suggested that the GDR entertained no great hopes for its success and perhaps feared the possibility of a dangerous compromise.[84]

During the three weeks prior to the invasion there was a strange ebb and flow in East German comment. For a couple of days after the Čierna meeting convened the polemics against Czechoslovakia continued (unlike in other bloc countries), but from August 3 they ceased, although castigation of West Germany went on unabated. The Bratislava conference was warmly endorsed by the SED Central Committee on August 7,[85] and thereafter commentary was couched in terms of the declaration, with no criticism of Czechoslovakia. There were statements calling for an implementation of the Bratislava document by the parties which had signed it and assertions of readiness to provide the necessary assistance, but without mentioning Czechoslovakia.

There is no real evidence as to the purpose or result of Ulbricht's visit to Czechoslovakia on August 12. On the surface his evaluation of Czechoslovak policies at the Karlovy Vary press conference was relatively positive.[86] He referred more than once to differences in viewpoint and in practice but did not criticize specific Czechoslovak policies. Ulbricht, who claimed to have requested the meeting, described its purpose as twofold—first, to discuss the implementation of the Bratislava declaration, and second, to agree on concrete measures for cooperation of the two parties and states.

[81] *ND*, July 19 (*FBIS*, July 22).   [82] *ND*, July 31.

[83] *ND*, July 20, 24 (*FBIS*, July 22, 24). The Council of Ministers issued a statement along similar lines (*Pravda*, July 24).

[84] *ND*, July 27, 30-31, Aug. 1-2; *BZ*, July 21, 26, 28, Aug. 2.

[85] *FBIS*, Aug. 8; *Pravda*, Aug. 8.

[86] For the communiqué and press conference, see *RP*, Aug. 13, 14; for a slightly different version of the latter, Haefs, ed., *Ereignisse*, pp. 142-45; and for still another version as broadcast on the East German radio, BBC, II, Aug. 15. See also above, chap. XI.

The joint communiqué warned, as usual, of revanchism, militarism, and neo-Nazism in the GFR, but welcomed the recent East German initiative on European security and on the normalization of the two German states. This proposal, advanced in a speech by Ulbricht on August 9, had appeared to be more conciliatory, especially in dropping prior diplomatic recognition of the GDR as a condition for talks with the GFR.[87] Dubček, at the press conference, was reported, at least on the East German radio, to have given strong support to the East German proposition.

During the week that followed there was no overt sign of a decisive change in the East German attitude and certainly no buildup of propaganda to prepare the population for an invasion. There was the occasional article against West Germany and imperialist subversion, and even some criticism of the ČSSR, e.g. of Prchlík.[88] The big events of August in Czechoslovakia—such as the publication of the party statute, or the visits of Tito and Ceaușescu—were almost entirely ignored. Only on the eve of the invasion (Aug. 20) did *Neues Deutschland* publish a long essay on Bratislava, devoted to the twin themes of "socialist internationalism" and "imperialist interference." Socialist internationalism was said to include "the willingness and capability of a Marxist-Leninist party to demand assistance and support of the fraternal socialist countries." After citing the defeat of earlier frontal attacks of the imperialists by the solidarity of the socialist countries (such as the building of the Berlin wall in 1961), the article concluded: ". . . with the implementation of the Bratislava decisions, the socialist camp is preparing the same fate for new variants of the policy of interference."[89]

POLAND: MIXED REACTIONS

The initial Polish reaction to events in Prague was somewhat noncommittal and this continued, without significant change much longer

[87] For Ulbricht's speech in the People's Chamber on Aug. 9, BBC, II, Aug. 14. According to this version, as broadcast on the East German radio, Ulbricht referred to "diplomatic relations" between the GDR and the GFR as one of the measures for European security, to be "achieved step by step." At Karlovy Vary, in Haefs' version (*Ereignisse*, p. 142), Ulbricht denounced West Germany's *Ostpolitik* but spoke only of the need for diplomatic relations between all European states. The Karlovy Vary communiqué, however, reiterated the Bucharest and Karlovy Vary declarations of 1966 and 1967 as the bases of European security, thus endorsing the long-standing East German position. Hájek, in a press conference on Aug. 17, was reported by the East German radio to have referred to a decision by the Czechoslovak government to support the GDR's proposal (BBC, II, Aug. 20).

[88] *ND*, Aug. 15, 20; Aug. 17, resp.

[89] *ND*, Aug. 20 (*FBIS*, Aug. 21; BBC, II, Aug. 21).

than in the East German case.[90] Press coverage was scanty for several months, and direct evaluation was avoided, but some Czech liberal views, such as those of Smrkovský, were reported. General commentaries laid stress on the dangers of West Germay's *Ostpolitik* and on the need for communist camp unity. The meeting of Gomułka and Dubček in early February, according to the subsequent communiqué, revealed "full unanimity of views on all questions." No information was, however, given as to the substance of their discussions, nor of those held when the Polish foreign minister, Adam Rapacki, visited Prague at the end of the month. At the Prague celebrations of February 1948, Gomułka made no reference whatever to the January events or even to Dubček personally, and spoke of Polish-Czechoslovak collaboration mainly in historical terms, with specific mention of the renewal of their bilateral treaty in 1967.[91] Otherwise no comment was made by Polish leaders on Czechoslovakia, and nothing comparable to the Kurt Hager outburst occurred. As in the Soviet press, criticisms of the reform course were reported from the Czechoslovak party's district conferences in mid-March, but commentary was avoided, even during and after the Dresden conference.

Poland's domestic crisis in March, touched off by student demonstrations and creating a serious political situation, had no immediate effect on her publicly expressed attitude toward Czechoslovakia. Throughout March and April official statements concentrated on her own crisis, with repeated allusions to the role of Israel and the Zionists as causal factors; there were no direct references to Czechoslovakia.[92] Nonetheless, developments in the two countries were bound to have repercussions on each other and on their mutual relations. For one thing, widespread political sympathy for Czechoslovak reform was openly expressed by some of the students, and no doubt reflected views widely held among the population. Moreover, there was uninhibited criticism in the Czechoslovak press of Poland's handling of the crisis, including the stridently anti-Zionist overtones of official statements. Gomułka, in a major speech on March 19, blamed the Polish crisis on certain writers and students, and on a sector of the intelligentsia, an explanation highly relevant to Czechoslovakia.[93] Although he sought to downplay Zionism as a real danger to socialism, and denied that the fight against it had anything to do with anti-Semitism, he did speak of the problem of certain Jews

[90] Apart from general sources (n. 1), see Jan B. de Weydenthal, "Polish Politics and the Czechoslovak Crisis in 1968," *Canadian Slavonic Papers* 14 (Spring 1972), 31-56.
[91] *RP*, Feb. 23.
[92] For instance, see the strong statements in the Sejm by J. Cyrankiewicz, Z. Kliszko, and S. Kociołek (BBC, II, April 17). This was in response to the interpellation, strongly critical of official policy, made by the Znak group.
[93] BBC, II, March 21.

whose main loyalty was, he said, to Israel, not to Poland, an argument which encouraged some Poles to treat the Czechoslovak reform movement as also linked with Jews and Zionism.

In early May a sharp diplomatic note of protest to Prague expressed resentment at the Czechoslovak media's treatment of Polish events. Just prior to the deliverance of the note, an article by the Polish correspondent in Prague, W. Zralek, published in three newspapers, wrote of "disturbing" factors, including not only "tendentious" coverage of Polish events, but also advocacy of a multi-party system with an opposition party; of a dictatorship of the intelligentsia; of Slovak separatism; of neutralist and anti-Soviet tendencies; and of proposals of reconciliation with the GFR.[94] Even more serious was the editorial in *Trybuna Ludu* on May 9, on the occasion of Czechoslovakia's national holiday, castigating anti-socialist tendencies in Czechoslovakia which, with the support of imperialist subversion, were seeking to belittle the party's leading role, to liquidate the people's power, and to separate Czechoslovakia from the socialist camp. The Czechoslovak media were subjected to special censure for a campaign against Poland claimed to be similar to that of imperialist and Zionist centers. Confidence was expressed, however, that the communists and the working class would be able to paralyze the anti-socialist forces.[95]

Top Polish leaders were somewhat more restrained, at least in regard to Czechoslovakia. Gierek, for instance, speaking at a joint Czechoslovak-Polish celebration in Těšín, voiced his serious concern about the threat to both countries from West German imperialism, which was in alliance with anti-socialist forces, including Zionist elements, and warned that the response would be "never more!" to those "seeking to push us off the socialist road and to drive a wedge between our parties and nations."[96] A few days later, Premier Cyrankiewicz, in a long address on

[94] *Życie Warszawy, Sztandar Młodych*, and *Żolnierz Wolności*, May 4. A foretaste of this negative attitude was the publication of the *Pravda* (April 30) article on anti-socialist tendencies at the district conferences (*Trybuna Ludu*, April 30).

[95] *TL*, May 9. Cf. a broadcast along similar lines by a deputy editor-in-chief of the party daily, J. Barecki, two days later (RFE, Poland, May 22). Cf. C. Berenda (Radio Warsaw, May 18) who was critical of anti-socialist forces but expressed the belief that the Czechoslovak party would overcome them and described this as a "strictly internal affair." He commented positively on certain planned reforms, including rehabilitation, Czech-Slovak equality, and the revival of parliament (BBC, II, May 21). M. Moczar, on May 4, was particularly vitriolic in his condemnation of the GFR's revisionism and "the anti-Polish hue and cry by world Zionism," but made no reference to Czechoslovakia (BBC, II, May 7).

[96] *TL*, May 10, reprinted in *Pravda*, May 10 (*CDSP* 20, no. 19, p. 14; also BBC, II, May 11). See also statements by Cyrankiewicz and Kliszko (Weydenthal, "Polish Politics," pp. 38-39). According to Weydenthal, internal party instructions issued on May 7, after analyzing the differences among the Czechoslovak leaders between revisionists, centrists, and those following the "correct line,"

the anniversary of the defeat of Germany, made no reference to Czechoslovakia but referred to the danger from the GFR and proclaimed the need for unity of the socialist camp in order to "synchronize the national raison d'état of every socialist state with the raison d'état of the whole camp." Other leading figures, such as I. Loga-Sowiński and Z. Kliszko, also without referring to Czechoslovakia, were bitter in their condemnation of the campaign against Poland by international Zionist centers, allied with Bonn and Washington.[97]

Gomułka, whose position had been seriously shaken by the March events and by what appeared to be a sharp struggle for power, refrained from any direct comment on Czechoslovak affairs. However, during his visit to Budapest, to sign a renewed alliance with Hungary, he spoke in customary terms of the threats from imperialism and the need for unity. In remarks that no doubt related both to Poland and to Czechoslovakia, he condemned imperialism's subversive activity which was seeking to undermine socialism from within under the "mask of 'improving' socialism," and counterrevolution, which was advocating the "reshaping of socialist democracy on the pattern of bourgeois democracy." He was bitter in his censure of West Germany, which was "wooing us with the charms of the so-called new Eastern policy" and preparing a "new *Drang nach Osten.*" He rejected West Germany's proposals for normalization as "tactical moves" and reiterated the familiar conditions (recognition of frontiers, etc.) for normalization. He welcomed progressive forces in West Germany but lamented that they did not yet have any influence on Bonn's policy, which was increasingly affected by neo-Nazi and nationalist forces. This was not, he warned, merely an internal affair of the GFR.[98]

Polish press criticism, compared with that of the Soviet or East German, was more general in character, avoiding attacks on specific persons, and was usually coupled with expressions of "confidence" that the Czechoslovak party would take the necessary measures. Moreover, the polemics of early May did not develop into a sustained campaign, as in the Soviet Union, and subsided after May 10, particularly after the restrained Czechoslovak reply on May 24 to the Polish diplomatic protest. Isolated criticism continued, especially in the form of citations of Czech and Slovak warnings of dangers, but the coverage of events was more objective, not only during the rest of May but also throughout the whole

warned that this was "more than an internal affair" and that they could not allow counterrevolution to take over, but expressed conviction that the "healthy forces" in the CPCz would be able to prevent counterrevolution (pp. 35-37). See also *The New York Times*, May 12.

[97] BBC, II, May 14. Cf. an article on "the Tel Aviv-Bonn axis," condemning the alliance of Zionism and West German revisionism (*TL*, May 12; BBC, II, May 15).

[98] BBC, II, May 20; also *Pravda*, May 18.

of June (at a time of continuous Soviet polemics). Even the Two Thousand Words was at first merely reported and was not accompanied by condemnation. Notable, although not representative, was a lengthy account by a literary critic, W. Nawrocki, of his travels in Czechoslovakia, in the cultural political weekly, *Kultura* (June 23). He was objective and often quite positive in discussing the reforms under consideration, such as federation, and cited different Czech and Slovak views on this and other matters, such as the question of Zionism. He did not, however, neglect criticism of what he regarded as unfavorable features (including the "campaign" against Poland) which he supported by Czech and Slovak comments.[99]

In early July the Polish attitude veered sharply, well before the Warsaw meeting, and in accord with intensified Soviet polemics. The new line began with a denunciation of an article in the Czech paper, *Práce*, allegedly favoring the return of the Sudeten Germans to Czechoslovakia; the theme was continued a week later with a rejection of *Práce*'s denial. This was followed by the publication of the *Pravda* (July 7) article on the letter from the People's Militia and of the Aleksandrov attack on the Two Thousand Words.[100]

At this time (July 8-9) a CC plenum was held in an atmosphere of crisis reflecting the situation in Poland but having implications for Czechoslovak developments. Most speakers concerned themselves mainly with Polish problems, but several (Gierek and W. Kruczek, for instance) made brief but specific references to Czechoslovakia. Gomułka, in analyzing the March events, developed the theme of the failings of some students and intellectuals but admitted that the role of Zionism had not been properly understood. Although it was part of the anti-communist front, it was *not* the main danger. Kliszko delivered a long diatribe against revisionism which he identified as the main danger and argued that the struggle against it should take precedence over the struggle against Zionism. For the forthcoming party congress the plenum adopted theses which denounced West Germany's policies and condemned domestic revisionism as "the main ally of imperialism." In words that were applicable to Czechoslovakia, the theses, while admitting that there was no directing center in the world communist movement and that it was the sovereign right of every communist party and government to determine its policies, declared that this did not mean that "each party and each socialist country establishes its policy in international matters disregarding the voluntarily accepted alliance concepts as well as the opinions and policies of other parties and socialist states."[101]

[99] RFE, Poland, July 22.   [100] *TL*, July 7, 13; July 8, 12, resp.
[101] For plenum speeches, BBC, II, July 10-23 passim; for text of theses, *TL*, July 13.

In an important editorial in *Trybuna Ludu*, the Two Thousand Words was made the point of departure for a comprehensive assault on domestic and external developments in Czechoslovakia.[102] The main thrust of this article concerned foreign affairs and complained of voices in Czechoslovakia calling for the revision of Warsaw treaty policies to West Germany, and even for leaving WTO and for neutralization, of contacts with ruling circles in the GFR, and of plans for collaboration with the USA, the GFR, and Israel. Reaffirming the responsibilities of each party to international socialism and to the socialist countries, the editorial concluded: "If the forces of reaction threaten the bases of socialism in one of the socialist countries, this also threatens the interests of the remaining socialist countries. That is why we must be . . . united in the socialist camp in defense of socialist achievements and the international position of the entire socialist community of nations."[103]

These sentiments were, of course, those contained shortly thereafter in the Warsaw letter and continued to be articulated in Polish media in an ascending crescendo until the end of July. Two Politburo members, J. Cyrankiewicz and B. Jaszczuk, expressed themselves in similar terms,[104] but the main burden of denunciation of Czechoslovakia was carried by the press and by radio and television. Although the Czechoslovak reply to the Warsaw letter was not published in the main newspapers, it was made the target of particular attack, assigning to the Czechoslovak party leadership the main responsibility for this development and as in the Warsaw letter, appealing to them for action.[105]

The major offensive was conducted in editorials of *Trybuna Ludu* on July 19 and 25, both of which concentrated on two themes, impending foreign policy changes and domestic developments. These statements disavowed opposition to the Czechoslovak efforts to correct past mistakes,

[102] *TL*, July 14, also in *Pravda*, July 15 (*CDSP* 20, no. 28, p. 8). Contrast the treatment given by *Polityka* which gave a detailed summary of the Two Thousand Words, using many direct quotations, and of Czech and Slovak criticisms of it (July 13; *FBIS*, July 22). All *FBIS* references are to the section on Poland.

[103] Cited in *Pravda* and *RP*, July 15.

[104] *RP*, July 19; *TL*, July 20. Jaszczuk's references to Czechoslovakia were not quoted by the Polish radio. He is said to have reiterated the danger of anti-socialist forces in Czechoslovakia and of a rapprochement with West Germany and to have declared that the Poles would not "agree to having the security and independence of our nations infringed upon" and would not "allow imperialism to break through the socialist system and change the alignment of forces in Europe." Another Politburo member, R. Strzelecki, in a public speech, gave a negative evaluation of Czechoslovak events (also not cited on the radio). The newly appointed candidate member of the Politburo, Moczar, made no public statement at this time. For the above, see RFE, East Europe/5, July 24.

[105] The full text was published only in a newspaper with limited circulation, *Forum*. Otherwise the Polish press and radio did not cover events in Czechoslovakia except to cite the Soviet reports of alleged arms caches and to quote articles from *Pravda* and *Neues Deutschland* (RFE, Poland, July 24).

mentioning in particular economic reform and the Czech-Slovak relationship, and did not question the right of Czechoslovakia to decide these matters independently, but made clear that they were not satisfied with the actions taken in response to the Warsaw letter. Words were contradicted by facts, they charged. Developments on the domestic front were threatening the leading role of the party, but the leadership was passive to the danger. The editorials gave even more attention to the "trends toward revising the fundamental principles of Czechoslovakia's socialist foreign policy," in particular with regard to West Germany. Evidence of this was said to be the visits of West Germans, such as Walter Scheel and Karl Blessing, to Prague; the "open borders" between the two countries; the conduct of the West German media; offers of credits; and Czechoslovak promises to the Sudeten Germans. General Prchlík's comments on WTO, and the "anti-Soviet campaign" in connection with the maneuvers, were singled out as indications of hostility toward the socialist states and toward WTO.[106] These events, it was said, were more than "internal affairs" and threatened the very existence of socialism.[107]

The strongest assurances of "support" for Czechoslovakia, implying that it might take military form, came from the military journal, *Żolnierz Wolności*. Warning of the danger of "weakening the southern flank of WTO," where the German invasion had occurred in 1939, the newspaper declared that Poland, in unity with the Warsaw treaty powers, would give aid and support "by word and act." The following day it was proclaimed that, "faithful to their allied obligations resulting from Poland's membership in the Warsaw pact, they will do everything in their power to prevent the enemy from making a breach in the fraternal family of socialist countries."[108]

When the Bratislava conference was convened, Polish polemics against Czechoslovakia suddenly ceased, and a certain factual coverage of events was resumed. The Bratislava declaration was welcomed as "a program of action" whose "position and resolutions" were to be "carried out in practice by all the fraternal parties."[109] In the next two weeks events of importance in Prague, such as the visits of Tito and Ceauşescu, were ignored. Just before the latter visit, however, Rumania's foreign policy was severely criticized for weakening the unity of the socialist camp. In a response to a diplomatic protest by Rumania, an editorial in the Polish party daily recognized the right of each socialist country to

[106] This theme was emphasized in *TL*, July 25 (*FBIS*, July 30), also carried in *Pravda*, July 26. See the bitter attack on the Czech journalist, Hradecký, for his conciliatory attitude to West Germany (*Reportér*, July 10-17, in *TL*, July 24 and in *Dziennik Ludowy*, July 26; *FBIS*, July 29, Aug. 1).

[107] *TL*, July 19 (*FBIS*, July 25).

[108] July 29 (RFE, East Europe/12, Aug. 1); July 30 (*FBIS*, Aug. 6).

[109] *TL*, Aug. 5 (*FBIS*, Aug. 6).

establish its domestic and international policies independently but argued that it should take account of "the voluntarily undertaken alliance obligations and the opinions, policies, and interests of other parties." Criticism of a fraternal party was justified and did not amount to interference in internal affairs. Selected for censure were Rumania's recognition of West Germany; her withdrawal from the Budapest conference; and her opposition to the strengthening of Comecon. This statement was sharply condemned by the Rumanian party organ as "inadmissible meddling" in her internal affairs.[110]

A week later, Gen. W. Barański, writing in the Soviet military newspaper, expressed concern over dangerous tendencies in Czechoslovakia, especially revisionism and the undermining of defense principles, and expressed Poland's willingness to help.[111] Apart from this, no attempt was made to prepare the Polish people for the sudden announcement of invasion a week later, although, of course, the possibility of such a contingency had been widely sensed for some time, at least among party members.[112]

HUNGARY: SYMPATHETIC CONCERN

The Hungarian attitude to Czechoslovak reform was more positive from the beginning and persisted in this vein throughout the first six months of 1968.[113] In the early months after January, press coverage was, like that of other bloc members, selective, but provided Hungarian readers with much more information, and more positive interpretation, concerning the Action Program, economic reform, rehabilitation, freedom of speech, and not least, plans for improving the position of the nationalities, including the Hungarians. Direct commentary was, however, avoided, even during and after the Dresden conference.

Official reactions were not expressed openly at first. There is no information as to what transpired during the meeting of Kádár and Dubček at Komárno at the beginning of February, although "identity of views" on all questions discussed was reported. At the Prague celebrations Kádár referred only briefly to the January decision as "based on Marxist-Leninist principles and imbued with the idea of internationalism," and wished the Czechs and Slovaks well in implementing it as well as the

[110] *TL*, Aug. 7 (BBC, II, Aug. 8). See below on Rumania's position.
[111] *KZ*, Aug. 14. See above in this chapter.
[112] Almost the only reference to Czechoslovakia was by C. Berenda, on Warsaw radio (Aug. 19), who reported the "Hyde Parks" in Prague and the CPCz Presidium's condemnation of these events (BBC, II, Aug. 21).
[113] Apart from general sources (n. 1), see George Gomori, "Hungarian and Polish Attitudes on Czechoslovakia, 1968," in E. J. Czerwinski and J. Piekalkiewicz, eds., *The Soviet Invasion of Czechoslovakia* (New York, 1972), pp. 107-8.

directives of the 13th congress.[114] Just prior to Dresden, more positive comments were made. For instance, on March 21, J. Gosztonyi, editor-in-chief of *Népszabadság*, on the Hungarian radio, referred to "a renaissance full of political hopes" in Czechoslovakia and cited specific reforms, including rehabilitation. He noted, however, unfavorable developments reminiscent of the Hungarian counterrevolution in 1956.[115] On March 26, just after the Dresden conference, Z. Komócsin, Politburo member, also on the radio, gave a similar appraisal, commenting with approval on the plans for developing socialist democracy, economic reform, and changes in Czech-Slovak relations. He, too, noted the presence of anti-socialist forces, and bearing in mind the experience of 1956, counseled a battle on two fronts—against both conservative and rightist forces.[116]

During April there was full coverage of Czechoslovak developments, such as the April plenum and the Action Program, and relatively favorable official response. János Kádár, at a conference of the Hungarian People's Front, expressed his solidarity with both the Polish and Czechoslovak parties in their efforts at "strengthening socialism" and assured respect for the independence and sovereignty of each socialist country.[117] Jenö Fock, the Prime Minister, on the radio, made a strongly positive statement about Czechoslovak developments and although admitting that there might be "faults," did not expect them to be "serious" if the Czechs remained loyal to the Soviet Union and the other socialist countries.[118] István Szirmai, Politburo member, in an article in *Pravda* (April 20), without mentioning Czechoslovakia, insisted on the necessary combining of the universal laws of socialist revolution with the distinctive requirements of each country. Criticizing nationalism and "reliance on one's own forces," however, he advocated proletarian internationalism, which would not tolerate anti-Soviet attitudes or even a "neutral" stand on fundamental questions.[119]

Nothing is known with any certainty about the Hungarian role at the Moscow meeting of the "five" in early May. Yugoslav sources credited Kádár with having attended with some reluctance and having played a mediating role. He is said to have supported Czechoslovak democratization and opposed coercive measures against Prague, such as the stationing of troops on her territory.[120] Whatever the truth of these reports, the

---

[114] *RP*, Feb. 23. Politburo member Rezsö Nyers remained for a few days to discuss economic reform with the Czechoslovak leaders.

[115] *FBIS*, March 22. All *FBIS* references are to the section on Hungary.

[116] Ibid., March 27. Cf. the refutation of the parallel with Hungary by R. Hoffman, *Pravda* (Bratislava), April 6.

[117] *RP*, April 19.   [118] April 23 (*FBIS*, May 3).

[119] *FBIS*, April 29.

[120] This was proposed by Ulbricht and endorsed by Gomułka according to Tanjug

Hungarian press, at a time when other bloc countries were mounting offensives of varying intensity, avoided polemics and indeed was positive in its appraisal of Czechoslovak developments, for example, in *Népszabadság* on the occasion of the Czechoslovak national holiday in early May. This generally cordial tone was true of other papers and continued through May and June.[121] Although there were often references to anti-socialist forces, there was stress, too, on the need for a struggle on two fronts—against dogmatist as well as anti-socialist forces.

An extensive, favorable analysis was published in the organ of the People's Front, *Magyar Nemzet*, in a series of articles by Tamás Zala in late June.[122] The process of change in Czechoslovakia, he reported, was characterized by "cheerful optimism" and was thoroughly in accord with the national character. He paid special attention to economic reform, referring specifically to enterprise autonomy and factory councils, and quoted Ota Šik on political change as a necessary condition for economic change. He discussed the solution of the national question, mentioning a symmetrical federation and citing the need for improvement in the position of the Hungarians. He saw no reason for anxiety about this "renaissance of socialism," especially as Hungary had already completed similar reforms and could benefit from Czechoslovak experiences in making further improvements. "He had not come across anybody in Hungary," he said, "who has shown even the most minute bit of anxiety over the Prague events. I have not even seen any sign from which one could infer anxiety." There had been "friendly good advice and even warnings," but this did not constitute anxiety. Zala discussed at some length the danger of revisionism and the need for a struggle on two fronts, but held the opinion that the May plenum had pointed the correct way to a solution.

The appearance in *Literární listy* of an article favorable to Imre Nagy,

---

(Haefs, ed., *Ereignisse*, pp. 109-10). See also *Borba*, cited by T. Štepanková, Prague radio, May 12 (*FBIS*, May 13); Robinson, *SCC* 1 (July-Oct. 1968), 153; *NYT*, May 12. Kotyk also referred to Hungary's support at Moscow (*RP*, July 10). See Hájek's comments on Hungary's understanding and support during his visit to Budapest (*FBIS*, May 24).

[121] *Népszabadság*, May 9 (*FBIS*, May 16). Cf. *Népszabadság*, May 19, June 4 (*FBIS*, May 21, June 5). See also *Társadalmi Szemle*, May 1968 (Robinson, *SCC*, July-Oct. 1968, p. 153); K. Németh, May 8 (BBC, II, May 11). See also the reports from Prague, by Pál Fehér, literary historian and an editor of the literary weekly, *Élet és Irodalom*, which included interviews with Císař, Goldstücker, Galuška, and Novomeský. These dealt positively with projected reforms, including freedom of the press and of cultural activity, socialist democracy, federation, and the treatment of the Hungarians, and frankly discussed anti-socialist forces and Slovak nationalistic attitudes (*Élet és Irodalom*, May 4, 11, *Magyar Hirlap*, May 29, and *Népszabadság*, June 1).

[122] *Magyar Nemzet*, June 23, 25, 27, 30. For excerpts from the first article, Remington, ed., *Winter in Prague*, pp. 183-84; for the other three, *FBIS*, July 1, 9.

published at the very time of Dubček's visit to Budapest in mid-June for the signature of the new treaty between the two countries, was certainly not welcomed in official Hungarian circles but did not seem at first to affect their general attitude. In a belated reaction two weeks later, the Hungarian party daily lamented this event and expressed the opinion that whereas "wrong views" must be fought, not by force but by ideas, "it was necessary to fight against the class enemy with state power."[123] The postponement of comment suggested that the Hungarian regime did not wish to let this episode interfere with Dubček's visit. The good atmosphere fostered by this occasion reinforced the impression of a predominantly positive Hungarian attitude toward Dubček and Czechoslovak reform. However, Kádár, in his major address, chose to center his remarks not on the post-January struggle for reform, but rather on the offensive proclaimed by the May CPCz plenum against anti-socialist forces. Obviously the Czechoslovak party "knows the situation better than any one else," he said. Kádár declared Hungarian solidarity with the Czechoslovak party in its "struggle to overcome various obstacles hindering socialist development" and voiced the conviction that they would succeed in this effort. Although he did not discuss the planned reforms, he did speak of nationality relations, referring to the Slovaks in Hungary and the Hungarians in Czechoslovakia. He urged the necessity of dealing with these questions without "passion" and called on the Hungarians in Czechoslovakia to contribute to their solution.[124]

The position of the Hungarian party was put on record, albeit with some ambiguity, in a CC resolution a few days after Dubček's visit. It proclaimed full support for the CPCz in its "fight for the consolidation of the socialist order, for the defense of its achievements, and for its further development." It expressed the wish that "the endeavors of the party directed at the consistent correction of past mistakes, the development of socialist democracy and the overcoming of right-wing anti-communist tendencies will be successful."[125]

During a visit to Moscow in early July Kádár gave an important speech in the Kremlin, which, although not touching on Czechoslovakia, suggested a stiffening attitude.[126] Echoing Brezhnev's remarks concerning the unity of the socialist countries, Kádár stressed the need to strengthen all their common organizations, as well as bilateral and multi-

---

[123] *Népszabadság*, June 27; *RP*, June 28. See above, chap. xix, n. 35.

[124] *RP*, June 15. The Hungarian press and radio showed considerable interest in the demands of the Hungarian minority and the plans for nationality reform. See Robert R. King, *Minorities under Communism* (Cambridge, Mass., 1973), pp. 119-20.

[125] BBC, ii, June 25; also *RP*, June 22. None of this was included in *Pravda*, June 22.

[126] *Pravda*, July 4 (*CDSP* 20, no. 27, p. 8); *RP*, July 4.

lateral forms of cooperation. Opposing bourgeois ideas of constructing socialism "in isolation from the socialist countries," he declared that there was "no such thing as anti-Soviet communism" or "socialism without communism." Proclaiming the "duty" to defend the party's policy in each country against "all right and 'left' distortions" with the use of the weapon of Marxism-Leninism, he added that "as soon as our class enemies resort to organized and violent actions and attack the foundations of the socialist system, it is our right and duty also to use power to defend the cause of socialism, the cause of the working class." Rejecting the thesis that the class struggle automatically sharpened after the victory of socialism, he admitted that "in certain circumstances the struggle does become exacerbated." "And no matter in what country this struggle unfolds," the Hungarian party "expresses full solidarity . . . with those defending the rule of the working class and the cause of socialism against the encroachments of dogmatists, revisionists and the class enemy." He concluded with the statement (omitted by *Rudé právo*): "We understand the meaning of this struggle, and we are prepared to render every kind of international assistance."

That the Hungarian attitude to Czechoslovakia had not basically changed seemed evident from the treatment in the Hungarian press of the Two Thousand Words. Initial criticism (preceding that of other bloc countries) was accompanied by praise for the CPCz's attitude to the statement and for its policy in general.[127] Moreover, there was no wholesale condemnation in mid-July comparable to that in other bloc countries. At least one regional party organ, in Gyor, published lengthy extracts and gave a balanced and moderate evaluation of its content.[128] Václav Kotyk referred openly at that time to Hungarian support and sympathy for the Czechoslovak reform process. He praised Hungarian policy after 1956 which had carried through many reforms, both in the economy and in the political sphere, similar to those being sought by Czechoslovakia.[129]

There were several other illustrations of the fact that a distinctive Hungarian attitude persisted to the eve of the Warsaw conference. In the Hungarian parliament, János Péter, the Foreign Minister, in speaking of the treaty concluded with Czechoslovakia a month earlier, dealt favorably with Czechoslovak domestic developments. Another speaker, J. Gosztonyi, who had twice visited Czechoslovakia during 1968, explicitly denied that there was a counterrevolution in Czechoslovakia. Although admitting that a certain analogy existed between Hungary in 1956 and Czechoslovakia in 1968, he found this in the dogmatic and

---

[127] F. Varnai, *Népszabadság*, June 30.
[128] *Kisalföld*, July 7 (RFE, East Europe/6, July 25).
[129] *RP*, July 10.

sectarian leadership which had been a causal factor of crisis in both cases. He also described the danger of anti-socialist forces and referred to the article on Nagy as an example, but ended by quoting Kádár's conviction that the CPCz would be successful in its struggle against these forces.[130]

There is little or no reliable evidence as to the position taken by Hungary at the Warsaw conference. Kádár was reported to have met with Dubček and Černík a few days before and to have evinced a sympathetic attitude toward CPCz policy. According to Prchlík at his July press conference, the Hungarians had been worried by anti-socialist manifestations, such as the Nagy article, but were basically sympathetic to Prague's course and were resolved to act at Warsaw so as to avoid any action that would aggravate the dispute or violate Czechoslovak sovereignty.[131] The conference, however, produced a substantial shift in the Hungarian attitude, although press comment continued to be somewhat calmer and less abusive than the Soviet, Polish, and German media. The "sympathy" with the process of revival from January on had not changed, it was said, but the situation had changed, in particular by the failure of the CPCz to take a strong stand against the Two Thousand Words.[132] This theme was reiterated a week later, but with a more emphatic warning of the increased danger on the right and the need for action against it. The Nagy article and the Two Thousand Words were cited, and the unwillingness of the CPCz to use "administrative measures" against such "threats to power" was censured. A direct comparison was made between the Czechoslovak situation and the events leading

[130] For both speeches, given on July 13, see BBC, II, July 17; for Péter, also *RP*, July 14. Gosztonyi's speech was cited favorably by a Czech commentator, who himself deplored the Nagy article and praised the Hungarians, who, in spite of certain "fears," tried to understand and explain the Czechoslovak situation (O. Mohelský, *RP*, July 27).

[131] Remington, ed., *Winter in Prague*, p. 219. Erwin Weit reported a meeting of Kádár and Dubček just before Warsaw when Kádár received assurances that the party was in control (*At the Red Summit*, p. 247). Bil'ak also had a talk with Kádár a few days before Warsaw. In Bil'ak's version the latter expressed his concern over the Nagy article and over claims by the Czechs that their model of socialism was "better." Admitting that power had escaped from the Hungarian communists in 1956, Kádár is claimed to have said: "You have power in your hand —use it against . . . what harms socialism and your foreign policy" (Bil'ak, *Pravda zůstala pravdou*, p. 142).

[132] *Népszabadság*, July 17; also *Magyar Hirlap*, July 17 (*FBIS*, July 22). *Népszabadság* (July 19) urged a war on two fronts, against both revisionist and dogmatic forces. It criticized in particular the communications media and the efforts to restore the Social Democratic Party. *Magyar Nemzet* (July 19) called Czechoslovakia a pillar in the Warsaw pact defense system. "Even a microscopic crack in this pillar could have grave consequences not only for the European socialist countries but also in a larger sense for the balance of forces in the world" (for both, RFE, East Europe/5, July 24). According to this source the Czechoslovak reply to the Warsaw letter was broadcast after a delay of two days and summaries of it were given in the daily press.

up to the Hungarian "counterrevolution." The editorial concluded with an urgent appeal: "Comrades! Stop! Do not let the same things happen which led to open counterrevolution in Hungary!" This was no longer an "internal affair" of Czechoslovakia. "If the foundations of socialism in the ČSSR were shaken and its foreign policy orientation altered, we would be directly affected. In that case the common cause of socialism— and in the narrowest sense, the cause of Hungary, too—is at stake."[133]

Other papers, such as *Magyar Nemzet* and *Magyar Hirlap*, were even more emphatic in their expression of sympathy with the revival process and justified their warnings and advice by their desire for its success. There was constant reference to the Hungarian events of 1956 and a tone of regret that the Czechoslovak party was not taking this experience seriously enough. It was argued that the allies were not issuing orders against heretics (as in the case of Jan Hus), but had an obligation to tender their opinions. There was sharp criticism of the press in the ČSSR and the unwillingness of the authorities to use "power" against it. The *Literární listy* appeal for "sacred unity" of all Czechs and Slovaks on the eve of Čierna was particularly condemned as an example of "moral terror" exercised by the media. On the other hand, certain steps were praised, notably the removal of General Prchlík, the discontinuance of the press interviews at Radio Free Europe (RFE) in Munich, and a change in the direction of the media. This tone of regretful but sharp censure continued to the end of July and the opening of the Čierna talks.[134]

After Bratislava the Hungarian attitude was one of satisfaction. The declaration was hailed as an important document of unity showing that there was no question which could not be solved on the basis of "joint ideals—Marxism-Leninism—and joint interests." The Hungarian position, it was stressed in the party daily, was the same as that taken in previous negotiations and as expressed in the editorial of July 25.[135] Kádár, however, in remarks made at the Bratislava airport and repeated again on arrival in Budapest, admitted that some differences of opinion remained, but stated that the conferees had concentrated on what was "common." We will "oppose anybody who tries to act against it in one way or another," he said. The declaration was not "precisely understood by everybody" but "thinking, serious people understood, and all would

[133] *Népszabadság*, July 25 (*FBIS*, July 26). The appeal quoted above was given in *Pravda*, July 27, but not in *RP*, July 27.

[134] *Magyar Nemzet*, July 28 (*FBIS*, July 30); *Magyar Hirlap*, July 29 (*FBIS*, July 30). For other press comments, *FBIS*, Aug. 1, 2. Tanjug (July 16) claimed that Hungary's official attitude was still friendly but was changing as Kádár's confidence in the CPCz leadership declined (*FBIS*, Yugoslavia, July 18).

[135] *Népszabadság*, Aug. 6 (*FBIS*, Aug. 9). See also the CC statement of August 7, as broadcast (*FBIS*, Aug. 8).

in a week, a month, or later." He expressed the belief that the Hungarian standpoint would be supported by the party membership and the public, without the need for "special effort" or "against their convictions." These cryptic comments were presumably an appeal for understanding of the special attitude that Hungary had taken throughout the preceding months and not an indirect reference to the forthcoming invasion.[136]

His colleague, Z. Komócsin, in a television interview on August 9, expressed solidarity with Czechoslovak policy after January, although noting that they had stated "openly, and also not openly, at bilateral and multilateral meetings," the points on which they could not agree. He characterized Hungarian policy as being based on "collectivity" in the CC and the Politburo and as having a "popular foundation," suggesting a concern for popular acceptance of the Bratislava decisions. Unity had been restored after "a certain minor break"; the difficulties giving rise to serious anxiety had been eliminated so that they could again "cooperate in complete political unity."[137]

Until the invasion, therefore, Hungarian comment gave no evidence of increasing tension or an impending break. Iván Horváth, in a major article on August 16, in *Népszabadság*, reprinted in *Pravda*, termed the party's leading role "a question of the very existence of socialism" and described the effort in 1956 to liquidate this role as a precondition of counterrevolution, but made no direct reference to Czechoslovakia.[138] The party daily on August 18 referred to disquieting events, such as the attacks on the People's Militia and actions by certain newspapers "against the Bratislava spirit"; reported the visits of Tito and Ceaușescu; and cited the Ministry of Defense statement regarding General Prchlík.[139] On the same day the Hungarian President, Pál Losonczi, expressed satisfaction over Bratislava "which created favorable conditions for our Czechoslovak comrades to defend their socialist order against revisionist and anti-socialist attempts and to carry out the correct political aims set by the January plenum."[140]

Bulgaria: Belated Antagonism

The Bulgarian press and radio gave very brief attention to Czechoslovakia during January and February, and comment of any kind was absent. During his visit to the Prague celebration in late February, Todor

---

[136] *FBIS*, Aug. 6. These statements were repeated in *Népszabadság*, Aug. 6 (*FBIS*, Aug. 8). *Pravda* (Aug. 6) included the reference to "thinking serious people," but this was not given in *RP* (Aug. 5). *Pravda* omitted the references to "continuing differences," "special efforts" and "convictions."

[137] *FBIS*, Aug. 14.

[138] *Pravda*, Aug. 17 (*CDSP* 20, no. 33, pp. 17-18).

[139] *FBIS*, Aug. 19. [140] BBC, II, Aug. 21; *RP*, Aug. 20.

Zhivkov referred only in passing to the January resolution, as well as the 13th congress decision, but paid warm tribute to the Czechoslovak party and declared that there were "no disputed questions" between the two parties.[141] From mid-March to mid-April there was somewhat greater coverage of Czechoslovak events, usually factual and positive.[142] The Dresden conference, which Zhivkov was unable to attend owing to a visit to Turkey, passed without special Bulgarian comment.

Zhivkov's presence in Prague in April for the signing of a new bilateral treaty of mutual assistance produced several days of mutual compliments on radio and in the press. In his official addresses he avoided any direct mention of the post-January course and expressed himself in orthodox terms concerning the dangers of imperialism, the solidarity of the two countries and of the socialist camp, and the importance of the alliance with the Soviet Union. In radio interviews he emphasized that developments in Czechoslovakia were matters of internal affairs, and welcomed everything which contributed to the further development of socialism and to the leading role of the party. In response to a question from a Bratislava correspondent, Zhivkov claimed that the Bulgarian press had kept the people well informed but admitted that they had ignored articles that were "not written in the spirit of socialism and proletarian internationalism."[143]

The Moscow meeting in early May seemed to have no perceptible effect on Bulgarian attitudes. During May and June the Bulgarian media did not devote much attention to Czechoslovak developments. Zhivkov, on May 7, at the 150th anniversary of Karl Marx's birth, deplored the presence of right and left revisionism, and nationalism, in the socialist camp and the communist movement, but made no reference to Czechoslovakia. At the time of the Czechoslovak national holiday in early May there were articles featuring achievements in the ČSSR without reference to post-January developments. The only exception was the publication of several of the bitterest Soviet attacks, such as those in *Literaturnaya gazeta* on Jan Procházka and that of *Sovetskaya Rossia* on Masaryk.[144] Thereafter even this kind of treatment ceased. There were occasional theoretical articles, for example, one dealing with the leading role of the party, which indirectly referred to Czechoslovakia by making attacks on "rightist revisionism," expressed in trends toward "democratization," and on national isolation and chauvinism.[145] Not until July 1 was there

---

[141] *RP*, Feb. 23.

[142] *Pogled*, March 18, 25; *Otechestven front*, March 20.

[143] This statement was broadcast both by Bratislava and Sofia (*FBIS*, April 24, 29). All references are to the Bulgarian section of *FBIS*. For official statements see *FBIS*, April 22; *RP*, April 23-28.

[144] *Rabotnichesko delo*, May 9, 15.

[145] A. Kozharov, *RD*, June 7. Cf. P. Russev, *Trud*, June 15, on the same sub-

direct censure in an article which charged Czechoslovak theoreticians and journalists with minimizing the role of Leninism and its international significance.[146] This was followed a few days later with a slashing condemnation of the Two Thousand Words which was called "a camouflaged appeal for counterrevolution" to which Bulgaria could not remain indifferent.[147] Hájek, who visited Sofia on July 8, reported that both sides agreed that matters such as these were "the internal concern" of each country and that it would be improper to interfere. Yet the Bulgarian press persisted in its campaign, publishing Soviet and Polish attacks on the Two Thousand Words.[148]

The Warsaw conference marked a transition to a campaign even more intensive than in other bloc countries. The CC plenum on July 25, devoted mainly to the improvement of Bulgaria's system of management, condemned revisionist and counterrevolutionary elements in Czechoslovakia which were abusing the movement for reform in order to weaken socialism. The CPCz was censured for its disregard of the Warsaw proposals and for its underestimation of the danger.[149] Mass meetings of workers were held as in the Soviet Union. Beginning on July 18 the press had mounted a massive campaign, using dramatic headlines, against the threat of counterrevolution in Czechoslovakia.[150] The targets were the "ideological subversion" of American and West German imperialism and domestic anti-socialist forces serving as "a Trojan horse." Open distrust in the CPCz leadership was expressed and the "terror" exercised by the press was condemned. There were assertions that the leading role of the party was being undermined, and that its "ideological and organizational principles" were being attacked.[151] There were complaints that the defense system was being weakened, and assertions that "not even the smallest gap in the socialist alliance" could be permitted.[152] Kotyk was

---

ject; he accused certain leaders of entering an "open alliance with counterrevolution" (RFE, Bulgaria, June 19). See also B. Velchev (Politburo member), *Pravda*, May 11, on the relationship of party and masses, including criticism of right as well as left opportunist tendencies.

[146] *RD*, July 1 (RFE, Bulgaria, July 11).

[147] *RD*, July 4; *RP*, July 5. This article antedated Soviet condemnations of the Two Thousand Words and was cited by Aleksandrov in his own attack, *Pravda*, July 11.

[148] *RD*, July 12, printed the Aleksandrov article; *RD*, July 15, the *TL* editorial of July 14.

[149] Fully reported, *Pravda*, July 28; less fully *RP*, July 27 (also BBC, II, Aug. 1). Zhivkov and others were cited as specifically criticizing Czechoslovakia in their speeches.

[150] See in particular, *RD*, July 18, 21 (*FBIS*, July 22, 26). The newspapers did not publish the Czechoslovak reply to the Warsaw letter and gave almost no information concerning Czechoslovak events.

[151] P. Petrov, *RD*, July 20 (*JPRS*, no. 46,227, pp. 6-9).

[152] *RD*, July 19.

taken to task for his article in *Práce*. Much was made of the arms caches in western Bohemia. Although all newspapers were vehement in their denunciations, the organ of the army, *Narodna armiya*, was perhaps most vociferous, stressing the need for "collective measures to protect the common interests of the socialist community." It was "the duty of our armies to come to the aid of every fraternal country in which socialism is endangered."[153]

There was hardly any letup in polemics down to the end of July,[154] and even on August 1 the army newspaper was charging General Prchlík with treason to his fatherland.[155] The Bratislava conference produced the customary editorial glosses on the need for unity and solidarity and on the general laws for the construction of socialism.[156] *Pogled* commented that Bratislava offered a positive solution for the problems of constructing socialism and eliminating anti-socialist forces, but this would depend on "the energy and consistency with which each party acts . . . to apply the spirit and principles of the Bratislava declaration." This brought the accusation from Prague radio that *Pogled* was adding something to the Bratislava agreement.[157]

RUMANIA: OPEN SOLIDARITY

The three other ruling parties in Eastern Europe adopted from the outset a clear and unequivocal stance toward the Prague changes—in the case of Rumania and Yugoslavia, one of firm support, and in the case of Albania, unreserved hostility. The Rumanian position reflected her long-standing conflict with Soviet Russia and her own first tentative steps, at least in words, to move toward a somewhat freer and more liberal society.[158]

The Rumanian press and radio began to give extensive and positive

---

[153] *Nadodna armiya*, July 23 (*FBIS*, July 25); also *NA*, July 24, 26 (*FBIS*, July 30).

[154] Czech and Slovak media reported difficulties encountered by Czechoslovak delegates to the World Youth Festival in Sofia (July 28 to Aug. 6), and stated that a group of fifty were refused admission. Bulgaria denied "distorted" reports of this incident, but admitted that certain Czechs, "extremely improper in appearance," and without festival cards, had been denied entry at the border (BBC, II, July 31).

[155] *NA* (*FBIS*, Aug. 1).

[156] *RD*, Aug. 5. See an article in *Pravda* (Aug. 8) on these themes by B. Bulgaranov, Bulgarian Politburo member. He described as still valid Dimitrov's view that the touchstone of proletarian internationalism was the attitude to the CPSU.

[157] *Pogled*, Aug. 5 (*FBIS*, Aug. 8); Prague radio, Aug. 6.

[158] For brief treatment of Rumania, see E. Bennett Warnstrom, "Romania and the Invasion of Czechoslovakia," in Czerwinski and Piekalkiewicz, eds., *Soviet Invasion*, pp. 159-64. For a review of 1968 in Rumania, see *YICA*, 1969, pp. 714-27.

coverage of Czechoslovak events from the end of February, increasing in scope throughout March, April, and May. Since the mass media were tightly controlled, the treatment was selective, and did not give a full picture of the extraordinary outburst of democratic discussion, but left no doubt that Rumania's official attitude toward the major reforms was warmly sympathetic. There were occasional references to "non-socialist" as well as to "conservative tendencies," but these were coupled with assertions of the Czechoslovak party's readiness to combat both and of the broad popular support which the reform program enjoyed.[159] This harmonized well with Rumania's professed intentions to broaden her own system of "socialist democracy," including an expansion of the rights of the nationalities, although her efforts were very limited in substance compared to those of Prague.[160] The trend in this direction reached a peak at a CC plenum in late April, when Lucretiu Pătrăşçanu and others unjustly condemned in the fifties were fully rehabilitated and the blame placed squarely on the former Rumanian leaders.[161]

The central theme of Rumania's defense of Czechoslovakia's course, however, was one long popular in Rumanian pronouncements, namely, the independence of each communist party in determining its own domestic and foreign policies without interference from outside. In early March the Rumanian CC, in a communiqué justifying its withdrawal from the Budapest conference, charged that the meeting had failed to refrain (as previously agreed) from criticizing or judging the domestic or international position of any party, whether present or not, and asserted the right of each party to shape its internal and international policy line independently.[162]

The CC plenum in late April reaffirmed these principles in the strongest possible terms, again justifying its walkout from the Budapest gathering, and adding a new and somewhat belated criticism of the Dresden conference, to which Rumania had not been invited, for discussing matters relating to Comecon and the WTO.[163] In a major report on the plenum to a gathering of the party *aktiv* in Bucharest, Ceauşescu reiterated the censure of Dresden for discussing, in Rumania's absence, international bodies of which Rumania had been a founding member, and

---

[159] For example, E. Ionescu's report from Prague, *Scînteia*, May 29 (BBC, II, May 31).

[160] For example, *Scînteia*, March 14 (BBC, II, March 18); Ceauşescu, March 22 (BBC, II, March 26); D. Popescu (Secretariat member), *Scînteia*, April 2 (BBC, II, April 5). These steps awakened hopes, at least in Yugoslavia, that Rumania's domestic policy would thus be brought into accord with her traditional independence in foreign affairs (*Komunist* [Belgrade], May 9; *Vjesnik* [Zagreb], May 11).

[161] For the proceedings, BBC, II, April 27, 29.

[162] BBC, II, March 4; also *Scînteia*, March 3 (BBC, II, March 6).

[163] Resolution on international affairs, BBC, II, April 29.

in particular for the discussion of WTO only a few weeks after the Sofia conference of the Warsaw pact members.[164]

A month later, at the end of May, Ceauşescu paid a six-day official visit to Yugoslavia. The final communiqué contained no specific reference to Czechoslovakia, but proclaimed the support of the two leaders for the "democratic development of socialist society." It also endorsed the right of each party to "fashion independently its own policy" and underlined the desirability of nonintervention in the internal affairs of another country.[165]

As the crisis mounted during July, Rumanian support for Czechoslovakia's course became even more explicit and frequent. During and after his visit to Rumania in early July, foreign minister Jiří Hájek openly expressed his government's appreciation of Rumania's support.[166] When the leaders of the five parties gathered at Warsaw in mid-July (in the absence, of course, of Rumania as well as of Czechoslovakia), Rumania stood openly and strongly behind Czechoslovakia and opposed interference in her domestic affairs. An important article in Scînteia on July 15 by V. Iliescu declared that the individual national party "is the only one in a position to establish its strategy and tactics, its ways, forms, and methods of activity. This is its sovereign prerogative, its imprescriptible and inalienable obligation and right." Moreover, he went on, "the great diversity of conditions and national peculiarities excludes the use of single clichés, of universal recipes given once and for all."[167] On the same day Ceauşescu, in a major speech at Galaţi, was even more specific, declaring his full confidence in the CPCz and asserting that he did not share the views of those who were alarmed by Czechoslovak developments and who would like to interfere. No one could claim to have a "universal model"; it was the duty of each people and party to organize its internal life in compliance with its own conditions. Ceauşescu pointed out that the Warsaw pact was "organized for defense against an attack, against imperialist aggression from outside" and had never been thought of as "a pretext for justifying intervention in the internal affairs of other states."[168]

In the days immediately following the publication of the Warsaw letter

[164] Scînteia, April 28 (BBC, II, April 30). According to Ceauşescu it had been agreed at Sofia that proposals for WTO reform were to be submitted within a six-month period. He repeated Rumania's willingness to contribute to the strengthening of both WTO and Comecon.

[165] BBC, II, June 4.

[166] On July 12, Ceauşescu, in receiving Czechoslovakia's new ambassador, made a special point of speaking favorably of Czechoslovakia's efforts to develop democracy and to perfect her socialist system (BBC, II, July 15).

[167] FBIS, July 16; BBC, II, July 18. This article was featured by RP, July 16. All references to FBIS are to the section on Rumania.

[168] BBC, II, July 17; also RP, July 16.

and the CPCz reply (both of which were given equal prominence in the Rumanian press) the party organ, *Scînteia*, returned day after day to the same themes,[169] reasserting the right of each party to solve its own problems; declaring that outside interference was "harmful" and "alarming"; deploring the absence of correct information in the bloc press; professing its full confidence in the Czechoslovak party and proclaiming the "full solidarity and full active support" of the Rumanian Communist Party (RCP). Admittedly there were some anti-socialist forces, and also conservative forces, at work in Czechoslovakia, but there was "no reason for the present situation to be termed counterrevolutionary." There was public celebration (in both countries) of the 20th anniversary of the signing of the treaty between Czechoslovakia and Rumania, and the draft of its renewal was discussed in the Rumanian (as well as the Czechoslovak) parliament.[170]

In a closely related development, Rumania delivered a diplomatic note to Poland on July 31, at the very moment of the opening of the Čierna conference, which deplored the distortion of Rumania's foreign policy in the Polish media and reasserted the right of each state to shape its own domestic and foreign policies and the necessity of full and objective information on the part of other socialist countries. In response to the Polish reply, *Scînteia*, on August 9, reiterated the charges, complaining in particular of incorrect reporting of her policy toward West Germany and European security, to the CPCz, to the Budapest conference, and to Comecon. Linking this issue directly with Czechoslovakia, *Scînteia* described it as "part and parcel of a campaign of pressure and immixture in the internal affairs of other socialist states."[171]

The controversy with Poland coincided with the apparently successful conclusion of the Čierna and Bratislava conferences, which *Scînteia* at once welcomed for the "diminution of tension" and "the cessation of polemics" which these meetings had brought about. The party organ regretted, however, that important problems had been discussed at Bratislava that related to countries which had not been invited to attend. While recognizing the right of every party to meet within a bilateral or multilateral framework, binding decisions could only be taken, it was stated, "with the agreement and in the presence of the parties and the countries concerned."[172]

---

[169] For instance, *Scînteia*, July 19, 20, 24, 27, 31.

[170] Bucharest radio, July 18 (*FBIS*, July 19); also *Scînteia*, July 20, 21; RFE, Rumania, July 19. The twenty-year treaty with the Soviet Union, which had expired in February, had not yet been renewed.

[171] For the note, BBC, II, Aug. 1; for the reply, *Scînteia*, Aug. 9 (BBC, II, Aug. 12).

[172] *Scînteia*, Aug. 7 (BBC, II, Aug. 8); also *RP*, Aug. 8. This is given under the wrong date in Remington, ed., *Winter in Prague*, pp. 261-63.

Ceaușescu put the Rumanian position in even stronger terms in two speeches made prior to his departure for Prague. On August 11 he expressed satisfaction with the results of Čierna and Bratislava which indicated, he said, that if independence and the right of each party were recognized, nothing could prevent cooperation and unity. He openly endorsed the CPCz's policy of reform and condemned any interference in domestic affairs.[173] Three days later he announced Rumania's willingness to fight "shoulder to shoulder" with the Warsaw pact countries "in the case of imperialist aggression," but ruled out "the use of armed forces for intervention in the internal affairs of any of the Warsaw treaty member countries."[174]

Finally, during his triumphal journey to Czechoslovakia, Ceaușescu, on more than one occasion, articulated his confidence in the CPCz and reiterated his positive view of the results of Čierna and Bratislava. In his Prague press conference he observed that his visit had confirmed his belief in the support of the Dubček leadership by the entire people and he declared that any anti-socialist forces that existed were "isolated" and not harmful. Ceaușescu repeated his opinion that the WTO was created only for a possible attack by imperialist powers and not for interference in the domestic affairs of the member states.[175]

Yugoslavia: Firm Support

The January decisions in Prague were welcomed in official Yugoslav organs, such as *Komunist*, the party weekly, and *Borba*, the People's Front daily, and from the beginning events in Prague were given positive and objective coverage in newspapers and broadcasts, often based on reports from Yugoslav correspondents in Prague.[176] The analysis was fuller and more unrestrained than in the tightly controlled Rumanian press, and gave ample treatment to such matters as the Šejna case, abolition of censorship, rehabilitation, and the struggle of contending conservative and progressive forces. By mid-March the Prague correspondent of the official press agency, Tanjug, was terming the development "a peaceful revolution," no less significant than February 1948. In April the Action Program was warmly welcomed as offering a new model of social-

173 *FBIS*, Aug. 12. Ceaușescu again indicated Rumania's willingness to work for the "perfection" of Comecon and to cooperate, in unity with the other socialist countries, as well as the entire "anti-imperialist front," for the preservation of European security against imperialist aggression.
174 BBC, II, Aug. 16 (two separate versions of his speech are given).
175 For the press conference, BBC, II, Aug. 19; *RP*, Aug. 17; Haefs, ed., *Ereignisse*, p. 148.
176 There is a paucity of Western translations from the Yugoslav press and radio broadcasts as compared with the other communist countries. For a review of 1968 in Yugoslavia, see *YICA*, 1969, pp. 919-34.

ism, progressive and democratic in content.[177] During the Dresden conference the Yugoslav press and radio deplored the lack of information concerning Czechoslovakia in the communication media of the socialist countries (with the exception of Rumania) and condemned especially the attitude adopted by the GDR and Poland. At the same time, events in Poland, particularly the anti-Zionist campaign, were reported in critical fashion, and the more favorable attitude of Moscow toward Polish policy and Gomułka was noted.[178]

The official stance of the Yugoslav party and government was, however, more discreet than the Rumanian, with no strong statements of support at first from Tito or other top leaders. At the end of April, however, M. Ribičič, a member of the executive committee of the League of Communists of Yugoslavia (LCY), gave a long interview to the Belgrade newspaper, *Politika-Express*, in which he interpreted positively the democratization process in Czechoslovakia, which, he said, was in line with Czechoslovak democratic tradition and marked a break with the "grey socialism" which had hitherto prevailed. Although many difficulties would be encountered, he did not think that "conservative forces" would be able to prevent the progressive development. Stalinism was "no longer the dominant factor" that it used to be and was meeting with strong resistance both within the country and outside. He deplored the "complete misunderstanding" of the events in Czechoslovakia "in the East" and argued that the development of socialism was the affair of the individual socialist country.[179]

This coincided with a visit by Tito to Moscow (April 28-30) during which he had conversations with Brezhnev, the contents of which were not divulged at the time. It was later revealed, however, at the LCY Central Committee plenum in July, that Tito had expounded his views on Czechoslovakia, expressing confidence in the CPCz's efforts to develop socialism and his support for the party's struggle against "negative forces."[180] In late May, in an interview with C. L. Sulzberger of *The New York Times*, most of which was off the record, Tito permitted the publication of a brief reference to Czechoslovakia, in which he praised "democratization" but denied that it was "the same road" that the Yugoslavs had followed or that it should be called "Titoism."[181] In the mean-

---

[177] *RP*, Jan. 8, 19, March 15; *Komunist*, as reported by Tanjug, April 4 and Belgrade radio, April 13 (*FBIS*, April 4, 15, resp.) All *FBIS* references are to the section on Yugoslavia.

[178] RFE, East Europe, March 19, 26, 27; *YICA*, 1969, p. 930.

[179] *RP*, April 30. At the same time M. Sedmak, Moscow correspondent of *Vjesnik*, reported Soviet worries and an ideological campaign informing party members of an alliance of imperialism with nationalist and revisionist elements in Czechoslovakia (*Vjesnik*, April 30, May 1-3; RFE, Yugoslavia, May 7).

[180] See n. 194 below.   [181] *NYT*, May 22; *RP*, May 23.

time, M. Nikezić, State Secretary for Foreign Affairs, paid an official visit to Prague (May 13-15) during which he endorsed Czechoslovakia's "new road" and expressed his conviction that the party and government would be able to overcome their problems.[182] Ceaușescu, during his visit to Yugoslavia at the end of May, had ample opportunity to exchange opinions with Tito on Czechoslovakia, and the two leaders issued a joint communiqué giving indirect support.[183]

These relatively restrained professions of sympathy with Czechoslovakia were reenforced in a special statement on "changes in the world" issued by the LCY Presidium and Central Committee on May 23, which spoke of the transformation in Czechoslovakia opening up "new possibilities for socialism and socialist democracy." The socialist countries in general, it was said, were developing "fresh patterns" and eliminating contradictions "in a democratic spirit." This was the "sovereign right" of each party and country and should be respected, and relations among them should be based on "equality, mutual respect and trust."[184] Almost simultaneously, in the foreign affairs committee of the Federal Assembly, the chairman, V. Mićunović, evaluated positively the changes in Czechoslovakia as a contribution to the development of socialism in other European countries and in the world. It deserved the support of the socialist countries and of all progressive forces.[185]

Throughout the month of May the Yugoslav press and radio reiterated the sentiments already voiced. On May 14 Tanjug reported from Prague that as a result of the processes taking place, "socialism will emerge stronger in Czechoslovakia, with its prestige growing in the world. . . ."[186] Typical of press comment was the editorial of *Komunist* on May 16 which declared that the CPCz's program of radical change deserved the assistance of other socialist countries. The party organ criticized the attitude of the GDR, Poland, and the Soviet Union which evinced "an incomprehensible fear of the progress of socialist democracy." On May 20 *Borba* stated that the ruling parties should respect the principle of noninterference and lend support to the CPCz as evidence of their confidence. The Czechoslovak leaders recognized the existence of anti-socialist forces, it was said, and were in fact taking action against them.[187] There was complete coverage by the entire Yugoslav press of the CPCz

[182] BBC, II, May 17.   [183] See above, in this chapter.
[184] BBC, II, May 23.   [185] *RP*, May 23.
[186] *FBIS*, May 15. See also the praise for Czechoslovakia's "new road to socialism," especially the proposed economic reforms, in *Politika*, May 12 (RFE, Yugoslavia, May 14).
[187] *RP*, May 17, 21, resp. See also *Vjesnik*, May 18; *Borba*, May 18, as reported in RFE (Yugoslavia, May 20); Tanjug, May 14 (*FBIS*, May 15). According to RFE (Yugoslavia, May 10), there was a lull in Yugoslav press coverage between May 1 and 10, shortly after Tito's visit to Moscow, although the radio coverage continued to be favorable.

May plenum which was described as "a first victory over conservative currents." *Borba* noted particularly the decision to fight against both conservative forces and "anti-socialist demands."[188]

Throughout June, Yugoslavia was caught up in a serious domestic crisis of its own, generated by the stormy student protest movement, and attention was diverted from Czechoslovak events. At the close of the crisis, the guidelines adopted by the CC on June 9 emphasized the need for reforms, especially in the economic field; for special attention to the problems of young people; and for the further development of self-administration (*samospráva*) and of socialist democracy. There were sharp attacks on those who were seeking to block these reforms from "a bourgeois democratic or a bureaucratic étatist conservative position"; stern rejection of a return to a bureaucratic monopoly or a multi-party system; and a declaration of struggle against anti-socialist and oppositional forces.[189] In spite of what appeared to be a swing toward a somewhat more conservative course at home, Yugoslav sympathy with Czechoslovak democratization continued to be openly expressed.[190]

During the tense events of July, Yugoslav support of the ČSSR showed no signs of abating and indeed began to resemble the more defiant attitude taken by Rumania. The press was openly critical of outside pressures on Czechoslovakia which were often compared directly with the Cominform pressures of 1948 on Yugoslavia. *Borba* wrote of "Stalinists raising their heads"; of the danger of a frontal attack by "conservative forces with outside help"; and urged the need to stand behind the Czechoslovak leadership and to avoid outside interference.[191]

At the beginning of the Warsaw meeting, *Politika* was even firmer in backing Czechoslovakia against what it called the "groundless" censure contained in the letters addressed to Prague. "Certain extreme phenomena" did exist but were being dealt with by the Czechoslovak party. Czechoslovakia's "path of significant socialist changes was strengthening the socialist essence and position of this country in its internal and foreign policies." "The real cause of concern" of the five parties was "the fear of the influence of Czechoslovak changes in their own countries." The paper noted that the right of every party to make independent and

---

[188] *RP*, June 1.

[189] *RP*, June 16; full text, BBC, II, June 19.

[190] *Borba*, June 8; *Politika*, June 9 (RFE, Yugoslavia, June 11); *Borba*, June 18 (*RP*, June 19); statement by M. Nikezić on foreign affairs in the Yugoslav parliament, June 19 (*RP*, June 20).

[191] *Borba*, July 1 (*RP*, July 2). Cf. similar criticism of outside pressures by *Komunist*, July 11 and on the Belgrade radio (RFE, Yugoslavia, n.d.; BBC, II, July 16; *RP*, July 12). Although the Two Thousand Words declaration was criticized as containing certain "anarchistic elements," it was described by *Borba* as having the support of the majority of the people and as opening a new chapter in the struggle against the conservatives (RFE, Yugoslavia, July 3).

sovereign decisions was being tested for the first time in ten years and expressed fear of a return to the "old methods and forms of relations between parties and countries." Prague's defense of the principle of "equality and mutual respect" was not merely a matter of Czechoslovak national interest but was the concern of the entire communist and workers' movement.[192]

Official Yugoslav reaction was clearly articulated on two fronts. On July 15 the foreign affairs committee of the Federal Assembly, after hearing a report from Nikezić, approved the changes in Czechoslovakia as showing the "vitality of socialism." The resolution asserted the responsibility of each party for its own policy and unanimously condemned pressure and interference in domestic affairs as reminiscent of the old methods used against Yugoslavia. The committee stated that this matter had broader European implications since it was "a question of a sovereign and independent country and an active member of the European and world community of states."[193]

On July 16, at a meeting of the LCY Central Committee, M. Todorović praised the "democratic socialist transformation" in the socialist countries, including Czechoslovakia, and declared that the Czechoslovak party knew best their own conditions and had sufficient strength to overcome their difficulties. He openly proclaimed his support for the CPCz and its present leadership.[194] The CC plenum approved a statement giving its approval of the policy of the CPCz, including the Action Program, and urging other parties to support the CPCz's reform efforts, backed as it was by the enormous majority of the Czechoslovak working people.[195] At about the same time, Tito, in an interview with the Cairo newspaper, Al-Ahram, couched his views in moderate terms, saying that he saw no danger to socialism in Czechoslovkia and that interference would be a great mistake. He did not think that there were people in the Soviet Union so "shortsighted" as to resort to force.[196]

Following the publication of the Warsaw letter and the CPCz reply, the Yugoslav press continued its campaign for independence and non-

[192] V. D. Budimir, Politika, July 14 (FBIS, July 18). Cf. the strong defense of each party's right to follow its own independent course and rejection of outside interference by Borba, July 15, 17 (RFE, Yugoslavia, July 16, 18). See an even stronger statement by Z. Gluščević, in the Belgrade Književne novine (July 20) who argued that the Soviet attempt to subjugate other countries was based on "fear," especially of the "self-managing type of socialism" as a threat to their entire system (RFE, Yugoslavia, July 26).

[193] RP, July 16.

[194] BBC, II, July 18. Todorović revealed that the Yugoslav attitude had been set forth by Tito in his talks with Brezhnev in late April and had been conveyed to the CPCz and to all European and certain other communist parties. See also Tanjug, July 18 (FBIS, July 19), also reported in RP, July 19.

[195] BBC, II, July 20.   [196] Ibid., July 23.

interference. M. Ribičič, for instance, in *Komunist* (July 25) spoke of a new offensive of the "old Stalinism" and of dogmatic and conservative forces fighting against "new ideas" in all the socialist countries, including Yugoslavia, but predicted failure since Stalinism was no longer strong enough to prevent progress in socialist development. The Warsaw letter would be a "boomerang," as had been the case in Yugoslavia in 1948. In an editorial on the same day, *Komunist* asserted that the socialist countries were "sovereign members of the international community" and were not subordinated to "special rules" giving "a certain state or group of states" the right to act "in the name of higher common interests."[197] *Borba* condemned the thesis of the "right to intervene" as the revival of "the old bloc concept of the allegedly higher interest of the socialist community."[198] M. Sundić, in a commentary on Zagreb radio on July 26, saw a rebirth of Stalinism, according to which democratization and human rights were considered "a mortal danger to socialism." He warned of "the danger of open intervention" and doubted that the Čierna and Bratislava conferences were intended to do anything more than to legalize the use of force.[199]

No doubt with more hope than conviction, the Bratislava declaration was hailed by *Borba* as "a document of conciliation" since it contained not a word of the Warsaw letter; put an end to public polemics; and provided for the development of mutual cooperation. *Komunist*, however, recognized that the Bratislava declaration was a compromise and that its value would depend on whether "the conservatives would again try to undertake, through methods of pressure, to impose their will and put a stop to the development of socialism. . . ."[200] During his stay in Prague, Tito spoke positively of Bratislava as representing a solution through discussion and recognizing the right of each country to its own "specific road."[201] His visit, wrote *Borba*, documented "the unified support, without reservation, of the new trends."[202] The purpose of his visit, Tito said, was to "manifest friendly relations and support of Czechoslovakia's so-

---

[197] *Komunist*, July 25 (*RP*, July 26); Haefs, ed., *Ereignisse*, pp. 126-27, resp. Another article in *Komunist* on the same day was also quoted to the effect that Czechoslovakia was seeking "new forms of socialism" that would make socialism all the more attractive (*RP*, July 26).

[198] BBC, II, July 27. [199] Ibid., July 29.

[200] *Borba*, n.d. (*RP*, Aug. 8); *Komunist*, Aug. 7 (Haefs, ed., *Ereignisse*, pp. 138-39).

[201] Tito in his press conference stated that Rumania had a right to be dissatisfied at not being represented at Bratislava but Yugoslavia was not a member of WTO. The visit, originally scheduled for July, was postponed four times, according to *YICA*, 1969, p. 927, n. 2. J. Pelikán ascribed these delays to Soviet protests (V. V. Kusin, ed., *The Czechoslovak Reform Movement 1968*, London, 1973, pp. 300, 321).

[202] *Borba*, n.d. (*RP*, Aug. 10).

cialist development." He fully approved the Czechoslovak course and commented upon the deep confidence of the Czechoslovak people in the CPCz. Democratization not only met the needs of Czechoslovakia but was a contribution to the development of socialism in the world. He condemned as detrimental any criticism that represented interference in domestic affairs.[203]

ALBANIA: A PLAGUE ON BOTH HOUSES

Albania's attitude toward Czechoslovak reform reflected her indiscriminate hostility toward the communist countries of Eastern Europe, including the Soviet Union, all of which were regarded as revisionist states in which the dictatorship of the proletariat was being smashed and capitalism restored. Since 1966 the Hoxha regime had been waging an ideological campaign against bureaucratism, a more orderly and controlled version of the Chinese cultural revolution, designed to close the doors to the penetration of revisionist ideas. In a major analysis of the phenomenon of revisionism, *Zëri i Popullit* argued that the process of decline had begun with Krushchev's assault on Stalin and the subsequent betrayal of the essential principles of Marxism-Leninism in the Soviet Union and its subservient satellites. The main blame for the counterrevolutionary process was placed on the intelligentsia and the students, but even a section of the working class had been affected. As a result, power was held by "a new corrupted class of bureaucrats," characterized by "bureaucratism, intellectualism, and technocratism." The essential features of the revisionist states were the same; they differed only in tactics, and in some cases by resistance to the tutelage of the most powerful, namely, the Soviet Union. The ultimate result of these trends would be the breakup of the Warsaw Treaty Organization and Comecon and close cooperation with the West for the restoration of capitalism.[204]

At first Czechoslovakia was not singled out for distinctive treatment. In fact, for about two months after January, the Albanian press pre-

---

[203] *RP*, Aug. 11; BBC, II, Aug. 13. Other statements of support in the Yugoslav press (*Borba, Politika-Express, Vjesnik*, etc.) were cited in *RP*, Aug. 11.

[204] *Zëri i Popullit*, March 24. The Soviet Union, Hungary, Poland, and Czechoslovakia were singled out for special condemnation (BBC, II, April 2-3). There were, however, veiled references to certain countries that were "camouflaging" their revisionist line and also to "allegedly neutral countries or parties" which, in their revisionist course, were laying the main stress on foreign policy. Cf. the analysis of the Budapest conference, *ZIP*, March 15 (BBC, II, March 20); and other editorials, *ZIP*, April 3, May 5, 17 (BBC, II, April 6, May 9, 25, respectively).

Hoxha dealt with the subject in a speech on April 9 in a manner similar to the March 24 editorial, but warned that it should not be assumed that these revisionist trends contained no danger to Albania (*YICA*, 1969, pp. 3-4). For a review of 1968 in Albania, see *YICA*, 1969, pp. 3-12.

served complete silence concerning events in that country. In early April, however, Radio Tirana reported a fierce struggle between rival revisionist groups, headed by Novotný and Dubček.[205] The editorial of March 24 had referred to Czechoslovakia under Novotný as "the most powerful bastion and the most faithful country of the revisionists." Novotný had become "a dead horse" who had "sunk into the revisionist swamp which he created." "The other horse," Dubček, had "taken the bridle in his teeth" and was "running toward the Western fields" of the French and West German capitalists. Czechoslovakia was proceeding at a rapid tempo toward capitalism, and "the counterrevolution within the counterrevolution had fully triumphed."[206]

On April 21 *Zëri i Popullit* analyzed "the ultra-revisionist counter-revolution" in Czechoslovakia which was working more openly than under Novotný to restore capitalism and was intent on "changing all political, economic, state, organizational, and military structures." Czechoslovak revisionism was assuming distinctive forms of its own. Unlike Tito's Yugoslavia, with its so-called workers' self-management, Dubček's Czechoslovakia was openly returning to "the capitalist forms, methods and contents of the bourgeois capitalist Czechoslovakia of Masaryk and Beneš." Singled out for special condemnation was the creation of "a bureaucratic technocratic system of management"; a federal system which would promote Slovak chauvinism and produce conflicts of Czech and Slovak capitalists; the restoration of bourgeois political parties; the transformation of the CPCz into a party of "the social-democratic or Western socialist type"; the abolition of censorship, "even for the blackest reaction"; and radical changes in foreign policy, which would be oriented to the West and would involve diplomatic relations with Bonn. Whereas the Soviet leaders could accept the revisionism of Novotný as "a humble satellite," they could not tolerate this return to capitalism under Dubček, aided by West German and American imperialism for whom Czechoslovakia was "a pivot in Central and Southeastern Europe." What had occurred represented a serious defeat for the Soviet revisionists which would jeopardize Soviet control of Hungary and Poland and produce the collapse of WTO and Comecon.[207]

The mounting Soviet pressures on Czechoslovakia, in particular the Warsaw letter, produced even more vitriolic denunciation of what was termed the alliance of the Soviet Union and the USA. "The Czechoslovak crisis is neither a fortuitous and unexpected phenomenon, nor an isolated crisis. It is a part of the deep-going crisis of modern revisionism, the epicenter of which is in the Soviet Union. This crisis is felt also beyond

---

[205] April 4 (BBC, II, April 9).   [206] BBC, II, April 2.
[207] *ZIP*, April 21 (BBC, II, April 25). Published in pamphlet form, *Where is Czechoslovakia Heading For?* (Tirana, 1968).

the boundaries of the Soviet Union, in its satellites, which are seeking to free themselves from the yoke of Soviet revisionism."[208] Much stress was laid on the divisions within the Soviet leadership, one branch of which had been pro-Novotný, and another "more liberal," which had engineered his overthrow, contrary to the wishes of Gomułka and Ulbricht. Soviet pressures against Prague had failed, and in the process the support of Gomułka, Ulbricht, and even Kádár had been lost. Czechoslovakia had the solid backing of American and West German imperialism and the support of Tito and Ceauşescu.

The Warsaw powers, fearing a chain reaction, had delivered their letter, "a false sham document," "a piece of demagogy," quite in contrast to Stalin's letters to Tito in 1948—"immortal Marxist-Leninist documents." In reality the signatories agreed with the changes planned by Dubček, but wanted them achieved less openly and less quickly, "without making much noise, preserving the sham and demagogic forms." Faced with this new defeat, the Soviet Union would have to go to Canossa, agree to Dubček's conditions, and get him to accept at least the "appearance of friendship." "And they will do everything in their power, through all sorts of flatteries, maneuvers, and lies, in order to draw the Dubček clique nearer to them and normalize somewhat the situation, at least temporarily."

The Bratislava conference seemed to the Albanians to be a confirmation of their views, representing the kind of compromise predicted in the July 24 editorial. The meeting was considered a new defeat for the Soviet revisionists, who, for the sake of their alliance with the USA, had retreated before Czechoslovak demands. The Dubček revisionists had been victorious and had become a new center opposed to Moscow, an "attractive pole" for other revisionists. None of the contradictions among the revisionists had been resolved, however, and conflicts would continue.[209]

OTHER COMMUNIST PARTIES

The reactions of the Warsaw pact powers, and of Albania and Yugoslavia, have been depicted in all their variety, ranging from hostility to sympathy and support. Other ruling parties, such as the Chinese and other Asian parties, and the Cuban, publicly gave little or no attention to the events in faraway Prague before the invasion.[210] The Chinese, ab-

---

[208] ZIP, July 24 (BBC, II, Aug. 2, 5); in pamphlet form, The Soviet Revisionists and Czechoslovakia (Tirana, 1968).

[209] ZIP, Aug. 10 (BBC, II, Aug. 13).

[210] For an analysis of all communist parties, see YICA, 1969, passim; J. Pelikán, in Kusin, ed., Czechoslovak Reform, pp. 297-321. See also RFE, USSR and East Europe, March 27, 1968, and RFE, Non-Ruling CP's, May 10, 1968.

sorbed in the cultural revolution, did not adopt an official attitude but apparently shared the Albanian view that this was a quarrel among rival revisionist parties.[211] In Cuba the mass media did some reporting of events in Czechoslovakia from mid-July but the leadership took no position until after the occupation.[212]

The non-ruling communist parties also presented a mixed spectrum of response: enthusiastic support from the beginning given by the Italian party; a somewhat more restrained, but positive, reaction by the French; relatively strong support by the Austrian, British, Belgian, the exiled Spanish, and in Asia, the Indian, and the Japanese parties. Almost no European party, with the notable exception of the German Communist Party (in the GFR), supported the Soviet stance.

The positions of the powerful Italian and French parties were of most significance. The French communist press covered events in Czechoslovakia quite objectively and the party manifested a moderately positive attitude, for instance, in the speech of Waldeck Rochet at the CC meeting on April 18-19. In mid-July Rochet visited both Moscow and Prague and seemed to be serving in some degree as a "mediator." The party avoided taking a stand publicly, however, other than to propose a conference of European communist parties.[213]

The most positive response came from the Italian Communist Party, which was participating in an election in May and realized that the reform of Czechoslovak communism was likely to enhance the attractiveness of socialism and improve their own electoral chances. The party leader, Luigi Longo, expressed his approval of Czechoslovak policy at the CC plenum at the end of March, and, after a visit to Prague in early May, warmly praised the reform program as likely to "strengthen socialism." He recognized some dangers but counted on energetic action by the CPCz to counteract them.[214] The warm approval of the Italian Com-

[211] According to RFE, the only Chinese comment prior to the invasion was a long summary of the ZIP editorial of July 24 published by the media on Aug. 10 (RFE, China, Foreign Relations, Aug. 27, 1968). According to Pelikán, the other ruling Asian parties took a position closer to that of the Soviet Union (Kusin, ed., Czechoslovak Reform, p. 301).

[212] YICA, 1969, p. 208.

[213] On the French party, note in particular, YICA, 1969, pp. 328-29. On Rochet's mission, see above, chap. XI. Leo Figuères, in a post-occupation article, wrote that the French party had never believed that Czechoslovakia was on the verge of counterrevolution or that there was any need for preventive action from outside. There were no new developments between August 3 and August 21 that represented a threat to socialism. He wrote that the French party's position was made clear during the visits of July 16 and 18, and in a letter of July 23 to the CPSU (Politika, Prague, Oct. 24, 1968, pp. 42-43).

[214] RP, May 7, 8, 18. Longo, in an interview, stressed that the Italian communists did not regard the Czechoslovak "model" as one suitable for other countries. The Italian party was following their own "Italian path to socialism" in which socialism and democracy were closely linked.

munist Party continued after the elections. Two other leaders, G. Pajetta and C. Galluzzi, had talks with the CPSU in Moscow in July, and after their return, the party adopted a resolution supporting democratization and expressing solidarity with the CPCz.[215] On the eve of the invasion, the Prague correspondent of *L'Unità*, G. Boffa, who had given full and sympathetic coverage throughout, declared that there was no danger of counterrevolution and that the Czechoslovak party was in complete control.[216]

[215] *RP*, July 16, 18.
[216] *RP*, Aug. 21. Cf. his articles in *L'Unità*, July 3, 6, 8.

CHAPTER XXI

Military Intervention

THE INVASION

Without warning, just before midnight, during the night of August 20-21, the armed forces of the "five" entered Czechoslovakia, crossing four of its frontiers by road and by air, from the GDR, Hungary, Poland, and the USSR. This massive onslaught was followed, shortly after midnight, by a direct blow at the capital city, with the arrival at the Prague airport of several special planes, which then coordinated the landing in rapid succession of military planes bearing troops commissioned to seize the key points in the city and to arrest the leaders. Presumably, Bulgarian troops were either air-lifted or crossed Soviet territory to gain access to Czechoslovakia. The ground for this sudden action had been well prepared by the WTO Šumava maneuvers on Czechoslovak soil in June and July; by the subsequent Soviet "Nieman" logistic maneuvers on Soviet western territories from late July until August 11; and by joint maneuvers of the Soviet, German, and Polish forces on August 11, and of Soviet and Hungarian troops on August 15. Czechoslovak exercises, with the presence of allied representatives, were to take place in Central and West Bohemia on August 21-22 and presumably would have had the effect of distracting attention from the threatening invasion and of diverting Czechoslovak forces away from the endangered frontiers.[1]

The exact numbers of the invading troops are not known. Estimates have ranged from 250,000 to 500,000, and even as high as 650,000, perhaps as a result of a distinction between actual combat forces and supporting troops, some of which may have been outside Czechoslovakia proper or have entered later. The highest estimates are those of Czechoslovak authorities; the lower ones those of Western intelligence and military specialists. Table XXI.1 provides the estimates, presumably of front-line troops only, of two Western scholars. These were supplemented by airborne troops and by 400 to 700 combat aircraft.[2]

[1] H. Haefs, ed., *Die Ereignisse in der Tschechoslowakei* (Bonn, 1969), pp. 150-55. For the events at Ruzyně, see *Sedm pražských dnů, 21.-27. srpen 1968, Dokumentace* (Prague, 1968), pp. 1-4.

[2] Thomas W. Wolfe, *Soviet Power and Europe, 1945-70* (Baltimore, 1970), pp. 468-70; J. Erickson, in V. V. Kusin, ed., *The Czechoslovak Reform Movement 1968* (London, 1973), p. 31. The number of troops involved was estimated as 400,000 by Wolfe, and also by Philip Windsor and Adam Roberts, *Czechoslovakia, 1968* (London, 1969), p. 108. The high figure of 650,000 was that of General Dzúr (*The Times*, London, Aug. 28, 1968, cited by Windsor and Roberts, p. 107). Haefs' estimate was 250,000 (16 Soviet, 5 Polish, 2 Hungarian, and 2 East German

TABLE XXI.1

INVADING TROOPS

	Erickson No. of Troops	Wolfe No. of Divisions
Soviet	170,000 (from GDR, 70,000) (from USSR, 100,000)	22 (10-11 from the USSR; 10-11 from troops stationed in Eastern Europe)
Polish	40,000	2 to 4
East German	? (1 division)	2 to 3
Hungarian	10,000	less than 1
Bulgarian	5,000	less than 1
Total	225-230,000	28 to 31

The enormous size of the invasion forces was presumably designed to assure success even if there were resistance by the Czechoslovak armed forces, numbering some fourteen divisions or 175,000 troops, and to deter any Western intervention in support of Czechoslovakia, although neither was anticipated. The forces of the four smaller bloc countries were mere token contributions designed to give the appearance of collective action and to demonstrate the solidarity of these regimes with Moscow. In reality, the invasion was a predominantly Soviet operation. The Czechoslovak authorities were not officially forewarned of the invasion and had discounted the dangers implicit in the maneuvers on and around their territories, as well as the indirect warnings of Soviet statements and polemics. Nor did Czechoslovak intelligence apparently have any inkling of an impending invasion.[3] As noted above, no defense preparations had been made for such a contingency. In any case, General Svoboda, as commander-in-chief, on the decision of the Presidium, issued the command *not* to oppose the invading armies, and as far as is

divisions), later supplemented by another 250,000 (p. 158). Substantially lower estimates of 175,000 troops and 24 divisions were cited from British journalists' reports by S. W. Barton and Lawrence M. Martin, in G. Henderson, ed., *Public Diplomacy and Political Change* (New York, 1973), table 29, p. 280. According to U.S. Senator John Sherman Cooper, there were 22 Soviet divisions (8 from East Germany, 2 from Hungary), plus 1 airborne division, and 3 Warsaw treaty divisions (Wolfe, pp. 468-70).

[3] Czechoslovak intelligence, according to Barton and Martin, was largely controlled by the Soviet Union (Henderson, ed., *Public Diplomacy*, p. 281). Western intelligence services were better informed; some NATO officials expected an invasion on September 1 (ibid., p. 286). According to these authors a warning from an anonymous person was transmitted to Dubček by the Czechoslovak ambassador to Hungary about six hours before the invasion (ibid., n. 15, p. 289, cited from L. Bittman, *The Deception Game*, Syracuse, 1972, p. 198).

known, no efforts were made to resist by the armed forces either on the frontiers or later. Indeed, the soldiers were confined to barracks, so were effectively immobilized. Although this failure to fight was later condemned by some Czechs and Slovaks, others felt that opposition was not a feasible alternative in view of Czechoslovakia's geographical situation, the disparity of armed might, the lack of plans for defense against the Soviet Union, and the complete surprise effected. Resistance would have been hopeless, leading only to great loss of life and damage, without chance of success, and would have appeared to confirm the Soviet charges of Czechoslovak hostility.[4]

The conduct of the operations was regarded by some military specialists in the West as "impressive," carried out "almost with field-manual precision."[5] Yet the massive nature of the intervention, the lack of any direct warning, and the absence of forceful resistance, rendered an overwhelming triumph certain and reduced the significance of the "achievement." In view of these considerations, the operations were described by other Western commentators as "efficient," but not "brilliant."[6] Moreover, the occupying armies found themselves handicapped by a lack of food and water, sufficient supplies of which had not been brought with the troops. Nor did the invaders have the technical equipment for tracking down illegal radio stations. These defects in planning reflected the acute political failure of the operation—a result of the USSR's complete misjudgment of the political situation as shown by the lack of anticipated Czechoslovak support, and, most important, the absence of a new government willing to cooperate with the invaders. Those leaders anxious to collaborate were unable, because of the condemnation of the occupation and the passive resistance by the overwhelming majority of the population, to establish a new regime, even in the absence of Dubček and his closest colleagues (at first under arrest, and then in Moscow engaged in negotiations). Only a handful of lesser lights, who had been informed beforehand of the forthcoming occupation, gave some assistance in the early hours of the invasion.[7]

---

[4] General Dzúr later defended the decision not to fight as correct in view of the "great bloodshed" and the narrowed scope for continuing the post-January course that would have resulted (British Broadcasting Corporation, Monitoring Service, *Summary of World Broadcasts*, II, Oct. 8, 1968). The possibility of defense was also rejected by Windsor and Roberts, pp. 112-13; Erickson, in Kusin, ed., *Czechoslovak Reform*, pp. 47-48; J. Pelikán, ibid., pp. 307-8.

[5] Wolfe, *Soviet Power*, p. 473.

[6] Windsor and Roberts, *Czechoslovakia, 1968*, p. 111.

[7] See below, chap. XXII. These included Karel Hoffmann, former Minister of Information, who intervened at the radio to prevent the immediate broadcast of the Presidium declaration; M. Sulek, ČTK director (on leave) who returned and sought to prevent the issuance of reports without his permission; and Col. V. Šalgovič, chief of State Security in the Ministry of Interior, who coordinated the actions of pro-Soviet security officers and ousted or arrested those loyal to Dub-

WERE THE SOVIET TROOPS INVITED?

The final Presidium declaration during the night of August 20-21 proclaimed that the entry of Soviet and allied troops had occurred "without the knowledge of the President of the Republic, the chairman of the National Assembly, the chairman of the government, or the First Secretary of the CPCz Central Committee, and of these organs." Yet the Tass statement of August 21 on the invasion, and its communiqué on the following day, referred to "a request by party and state leaders" for "immediate assistance, including assistance with armed forces," a claim which was documented by the publication in *Pravda* (Aug. 22) of the text of an appeal by a group of members of the CC, the government, and National Assembly. This statement declared full support for the January plenum and for the Action Program and a desire to carry through the progressive ideas of January to conclusion. Attacking the "extremist right-wing forces," and especially their intensified efforts in late August (citing the events mentioned in the Aleksandrov article in *Pravda* on August 18), the document asserted that the "obligations of Bratislava" had been "violated" and that the "healthy progressive nucleus" of the party had decided to request the Soviet Union for "fraternal assistance." An appeal was made to citizens to "support the troops of our allies" and to rally around the "realistically minded nucleus of the party."[8]

The identity of the signatories, if there were any, was not given at the time and has never been revealed publicly since. The authenticity of the document was at once belied by the opposition to the invasion of the vast majority of the population and by public statements of condemnation by the party Presidium, the government, and the National Assembly. Moreover, the more conservative Czech and Slovak leaders, who were suspected of having desired Soviet intervention, made explicit denials that they had signed such an appeal. These included Bil'ak, Švestka, Piller,

---

ček (*Sedm dnů*, pp. 12, 67-72). For a description of the actions of pro-Soviet security officers and of newly arrived Soviet agents, see Bittman, *Deception Game*, pp. 196-204. According to Smrkovský, Švestka also sought to block publication of the Presidium declaration (Appendix D below).

[8] The appeal was also cited by the *Pravda* editorial of Aug. 22. For text in English, *The Current Digest of the Soviet Press* 20 (Sept. 11, 1968), 3-5; also R. A. Remington, ed., *Winter in Prague* (Cambridge, Mass., 1969), pp. 295-99. For the question of the "invitation," see *Listy* (Rome), no. 1 (Jan. 1971), pp. 10-12; no. 2 (March 1971), pp. 3-5; Wolfe, *Soviet Power*, p. 381, n. 158; *Der Spiegel*, Nov. 25, 1968, pp. 147-48; Feb. 10, 1969, p. 101. According to David Binder (*The New York Times*, Sept. 6, 1968), two appeals had been drawn up by M. Sulek and K. Hoffmann, in consultation with the Soviet ambassador, S. V. Chervonenko; one was an appeal to the "five" for aid, and the other a 1700-word address to the people. The former was sent by Chervonenko to Moscow, but the latter's transmission was blocked by officials at ČTK, so that it could not be used in the initial Tass statement. When it *was* published, no names were given as signatories.

Barbírek, Rigo, Kolder, and Indra.[9] At the CC plenum at the end of August, Bil'ak, Piller, Jakeš, Kolder, and "others" were reported to have declared "on their word of honor" that "never in the past ten days did they commit anything against our country or our party which was in conflict with the honor of a communist and a citizen of the Czechoslovak Socialist Republic."[10]

Although this protestation was ambiguous, other authoritative pronouncements seemed to indicate that no appeal for help had been made. Martin Vaculík, in his opening statement to the illegal 14th Party Congress on August 22, reported that at the meeting of the rump CC, the day before, at the Hotel Praha, which he had attended, "not even one member of the Presidium could confirm that any of our official representatives, whether leading officials of our party, the government, or the National Assembly, has asked for protection by allied forces."[11] Husák was even more emphatic, at the Slovak party's extraordinary congress a few days later, when he affirmed that in conversations in Bratislava, Prague, and Moscow, "each of the members of the CPCz and CPS leadership, without exception, gave their word of honor that he had not taken such a step and had not even known about it." He went on: "I know not a single leading personality of Czech or Slovak political life who could safely be said to have taken such a step."[12]

Faced with the failure to form a government of collaboration and with popular resistance to the occupation, the Soviet media, within a few days of the invasion, dropped all mention of the so-called invitation, although there were references to letters from individuals and groups of workers during the summer of 1968 expressing fear of counterrevolution and in some cases asking that the Soviet troops on maneuvers remain or that military aid be given.[13] When the Soviet authorities once again recog-

[9] Barbírek, *Mladá fronta*, Aug. 23; Bil'ak, *Pravda* (Bratislava), Aug. 23; Švestka, ibid., Sept. 5; Piller, *Svoboda*, Sept. 5; Bil'ak, *Smena*, Sept. 18. Bil'ak's statement in *Smena* was ambiguous in that he declared only that he did not know of the invasion beforehand. Concerning Kolder and Indra, see M. Tatu, *Le Monde*, Aug. 23, 1968 (Tatu, *L'hérésie impossible*, Paris, 1968, p. 19). See also Radio Free Europe, Czechoslovakia, Oct. 18, 1968, p. 3.

[10] *Rudé právo*, Sept. 3. The same text was given in the intra-party document, *o zasedání Ústředního Výboru KSČ dne 31. srpna 1968* (Prague, 1968), p. 4. According to *Listy*, no. 1 (1971), Piller and Indra made similar statements. It is not clear whether this was a joint statement or a series of individual statements. See, e.g. Bil'ak, Radio Prague, Aug. 31 (BBC, II, Sept. 4).

[11] J. Pelikán, ed., *The Secret Vysočany Congress* (London, 1971), pp. 19-20. *Rudé právo*, after having talked with Dubček and others at CC headquarters on the night of Aug. 20-21, also reported that none of the legal representatives had requested aid (*RP*, Aug. 21, 17.30 p.m. edition).

[12] *Pravda* (Bratislava), Aug. 28; also *Information Bulletin* (CPCz Central Committee, Prague, 1968), p. 53.

[13] Henry Kamm, *NYT*, Sept. 6, 1968. See also *Pravda* (Bratislava), Jan. 19, 1971, cited by M. Marko, *Čierne na bielom* (Bratislava, 1971), pp. 133-35.

nized Dubček and most of his colleagues as the legitimate authorities, the question of an "invitation" disappeared from public discussion.[14]

All the more surprising was its resurrection, over two years later, at the CC plenum of December 1970. In the document adopted, "Lesson Drawn from the Crisis Development in the Party and Society after the 13th Congress of the CPCz," it was stated that "thousands of communists, individual citizens and entire collectives of working people, representatives of all strata of the population and various organizations, including members of the Central Committee of the Communist Party of Czechoslovkia and the Central Committee of the Communist Party of Slovakia, as well as members of the government of the ČSSR and deputies of the National Assembly and of the Slovak National Council . . . began to turn to the leadership of the fraternal parties and to the governments of our allies with the request that . . . they should grant international assistance to the Czechoslovak people in the defense of socialism." Even this did not allege that a collective appeal had been signed by these leading figures, whose identity was not revealed then or later.[15] Bil'ak, in his address to the CC as published, merely cited the Lesson's reference to "thousands of communists and citizens," without mentioning "leading persons."[16] It cannot be confirmed whether, as has been claimed, he submitted to the CC a copy of the letter, with a list of signatories, forty in number.[17]

[14] In April 1969, just prior to Dubček's removal, the executive committee of the CPCz Presidium, without referring to the "invitation," exonerated certain leaders (Bil'ak, Barbírek, Kolder, Piller, Rigo, Švestka, Lenárt, Kapek, Indra, and Jakeš) of charges of "betrayal and collaboration" and denied that there was any evidence to support charges to this effect (*RP*, April 17, 1969). In September 1969, Bil'ak, at a CC plenum, in answering questions as to "who" had appealed for assistance, replied that the invasion was "evoked by disorder and disruption." "You all invited them, esteemed ones, who, by your irresponsible work and by your subversion of the party, helped in breaking up the party from within" (*Svědectví* 10, no. 38, 1968, pp. 289).

[15] English version (n.d.), p. 38; Czech version, *Poučení z krízového vývoje ve straně a společnosti po XIII. sjezdu KSČ* (*RP*, Jan. 14, 1971).

[16] *RP*, Dec. 21, 1970. Bil'ak was said to have stated: "We acted correctly when we invited the Soviet troops to help us" (Prague radio, Dec. 12, citing "Bulgarian papers," BBC, II, Dec. 16, 1968). Indra, in a speech in Most on December 14, prior to the CC session, was reported by Tanjug to have quoted the statement in full. This was not included in the ČTK report of his speech (BBC, II, Dec. 17, 1970). See M. Sundič's skeptical commentary on the alleged appeal (Radio Zagreb, Dec. 19, 1970 in BBC, II, Dec. 22, 1970). Several months later, at the 24th CPSU congress, Brezhnev referred to "the appeals of party and state leaders" (*Pravda*, March 31, 1971). Husák, on the same occasion, spoke of "their appeal for assistance" (ibid., April 2). Svoboda, in an interview in Moscow, spoke of the invasion as occurring "at the request of the Czechoslovak communists themselves" (*Pravda*, April 7, 1971).

[17] These were said to include Bil'ak, Indra, Kolder, Piller, Švestka, Barbírek, Rigo and Lenárt, as well as lesser figures such as V. David, J. Hendrych, K. Hoffmann, B. Chňoupek, A. Kapek, B. Laštovička, M. Mamula, K. Mestek, J. Němec,

THE DECISION TO INVADE—WHEN?

It is impossible to pinpoint the exact date of the decision to resort to military intervention. There can be little doubt that during the six or more months of search for a political settlement the ultimate use of force was regarded as an alternative if other measures failed. No doubt, too, preparations for such a contingency were made at an early date, perhaps as early as June.[18] Meanwhile, the military exercises, undertaken as a form of pressure on the Prague regime, were useful preparatory steps. The stationing of bloc troops in Czechoslovakia, frequently claimed (but without confirmation) to have been urged on the Czechoslovak leadership by the Soviet authorities, would not only have served as a means of exerting influence but would perhaps have obviated the need for an invasion.[19] Whether the use of force was seriously considered in the middle of July, as later reported by an East Berlin source, cannot be verified.[20]

In this context the apparent settlement of the crisis at Čierna and

---

V. Nový, J. Plojhar, J. Pecha, M. Sulek, V. Šalgovič, O. Rytíř, J. Kudrna, and others (Listy, nos. 1 and 2, 1971). According to Jiří Pelikán, editor of Listy, the "invitation" never really existed. Before the invasion the "signatories" had promised I. I. Udaltsov, of the Soviet embassy, to subscribe to such a statement in order to legalize an eventual invasion, but at the last minute did not do so, owing to fear of popular reaction and to the failure of a new government to be formed. The signatures were therefore added later (Kusin, ed., Czechoslovak Reform, pp. 304-5; Listy, no. 2, 1971, pp. 4-5).

[18] The best Western analysis of the motivation and the timing of the invasion continues to be that of Richard Lowenthal, "Sparrow in the Cage," Problems of Communism (Nov.-Dec. 1968), pp. 2-28. Reference at p. 14. Other useful commentaries are the following: Wolfe, Soviet Power; Windsor and Roberts, Czechoslovakia, 1968, esp. pp. 97-105; Kusin, ed., Czechoslovak Reform; Robert R. James, ed., The Czechoslovak Crisis 1968 (London, 1969); Fritz Ermarth, Internationalism, Security and Legitimacy: The Challenge to Soviet Interests in East Europe, 1964-1968 (Rand Corp., Santa Monica, Cal., March 1969); Wolfgang Klaiber, The Crisis in Czechoslovakia in 1968 (Institute for Defense Analyses, Arlington, Va., 1969); Pavel Tigrid, Why Dubček Fell (London, 1971), pp. 113-36; H. Brahm, Der Kreml und die ČSSR, 1968-1969 (Stuttgart, 1970), pp. 64-78; V. V. Aspaturian and others, in I. William Zartman, ed., Czechoslovakia: Intervention and Impact (New York, 1970), pp. 15-46; Sir William Hayter, Russia and the World (London, 1970), pp. 34-73; Isaac Don Levine, Intervention (New York, 1969); Anatol Shub, The New Russian Tragedy (New York, 1969); Herman Kahn, "How to Think About the Russians," Fortune (Nov. 1968), pp. 124 ff.; Shub, "Lessons of Czechoslovakia," Foreign Affairs 47 (Jan. 1969), 266-80; Adam Bromke, "Czechoslovakia and the World: 1968," Canadian Slavonic Papers 10 (Winter 1968), 581-91; Jacques Lévesque, "Problématique de l'intervention sovietique en Tchécoslovaquie," Socialisme 69 (Montreal), no. 16 (March 1969), pp. 27-46; Herbert Aptheker, Czechoslovakia and Counter-Revolution (New York, 1969).

[19] A diplomatic note to Prague containing this demand has been reported but not confirmed (Lowenthal, "Sparrow in the Cage," p. 18; NYT, July 23).

[20] NYT, Aug. 9. This was said to have been blocked by Soviet "moderates," in favor of the talks at Čierna, a compromise which, it was stated, satisfied Ulbricht at the time.

Bratislava, accompanied by the withdrawal of the remaining troops on maneuvers, has been differently interpreted. Some have concluded that the decision to invade had already been made and that the conferences may have been a mere deception.[21] Others, however, although also assuming a pre-Bratislava decision to invade, evaluated the meetings as a kind of "stay of execution," to use Lowenthal's term, providing a last test of Dubček's "sincerity" and leaving open the possibility of an invasion or the cancellation of such plans.[22] In other words, Čierna and Bratislava represented for the Soviet Union a provisional or conditional settlement, which did not exclude the option of intervention (in the event of Dubček's failure to act appropriately), but which, if implemented according to Soviet ideas, would have removed the necessity of forceful action. In the meantime it provided time to prepare public opinion in the Soviet Union and to complete the last-minute preparations for an eventual invasion should it prove necessary. The time available for a final judgment was short, however; at the most, three weeks to a month, inasmuch as the extraordinary party congresses were scheduled for August 26 and September 9, respectively. The legitimization of the reform movement and of a new leadership at the congresses would have made an invasion more than ever difficult, it has been argued.[23]

The appointment of General Sergei M. Shtemenko as chief of the general staff of the Warsaw treaty forces, announced in *Krasnaya zvezda* on August 6, the very day when the Bratislava conference ended, could be interpreted as signifying that the decision to invade had already been made and as confirming the deceptive character of Bratislava.[24] Shtemenko's Stalinist past and his continuing admiration of Stalin as re-

[21] Brahm, *Der Kreml*, pp. 64-65. This was doubted by Ermarth, *Internationalism*, pp. 98-99.

[22] Lowenthal, "Sparrow in the Cage," pp. 18-19; also L. Labedz and Erickson, in Kusin, ed., *Czechoslovak Reform*, p. 62; Ermarth, *Internationalism*, p. 107.

[23] James, ed., *Czechoslovak Crisis*, pp. 27, 110; Klaiber, *Crisis in Czechoslovakia*, p. 29. Klaiber cites a high-placed Czechoslovak informant as stating that, as late as August 20, the Soviet Union tried to get the CPCz to postpone the party congress (p. 20). Pelikán (*New Left Review*, Jan.-Feb. 1972, p. 25) also refers to Soviet efforts of this kind. According to A. Šnejdárek, the final Czech decision concerning the congress was made on August 20 (Kusin, ed., *Czechoslovak Reform*, p. 59).

[24] Actually the appointment was announced earlier by Tass in a Russian broadcast just before midnight on Aug. 4 (BBC, I, Aug. 6). It was also reported by the East German news agency in Berlin on Aug. 4 (*NYT*, Aug. 5) and by ČTK, in Prague, a day later (*RP*, Aug. 6). It was not mentioned at all in *Pravda*. The location of the announcement on the front page of *Krasnaya zvezda* was unusual, unlike similar cases in the past, for instance, the appointment of Shtemenko's predecessor, Gen. M. I. Kazakov in 1965, and might have been a form of subtle pressure by the Soviet military on Czechoslovakia. I am indebted to Prof. T. J. Colton for this and other information on Shtemenko's appointment.

vealed in his published memoirs[25] suggested a victory for the advocates of intervention and the preparation for it by the appointment of a younger and perhaps more enthusiastic commander.[26] On the other hand, if it was assumed that Bratislava represented a genuine conciliation, his appointment could also have been interpreted as a rebuff to the military's preference for armed intervention and possibly a personal demotion for its advocate, Gen. M. I. Kazakov, who had been in charge of bloc military exercises.[27] More simply, Shtemenko's appointment may have been merely a routine change, replacing an older by a younger man, and promoting an officer whose career had been advancing in recent years. Intervention, while still an option, may not yet have become a certainty. Moreover, although Kazakov's post was an important one, Marshal Yakubovsky was still the Warsaw treaty commander-in-chief, and actual military operations of the eventual invasion were placed in the hands of Gen. Ivan G. Pavlovsky, commander-in-chief of Soviet ground forces and a deputy Minister of Defense.

If it is presumed that Bratislava was not a subterfuge, the final decision to invade was made sometime between August 6 and 20, and more probably between August 14 and 18.[28] It is hard to identify the crucial events which precipitated the decision. Soviet propaganda after August 14 (in particular the Aleksandrov report of the 18th) and the final CPSU letter to the CPCz of the 17th, as well as post-occupation statements, placed heavy emphasis on the so-called failure of the CPCz to implement the Bratislava decisions, pointing in particular to the com-

---

[25] For biographical details concerning Shtemenko, see *KZ*, Aug. 6; *Prominent Personalities in the USSR* (New York, 1968), p. 570; *NYT*, Aug. 5, Sept. 4; *The Christian Science Monitor*, Aug. 22. At the time of his appointment Shtemenko was first deputy chief of the general staff in the USSR armed forces and he presumably retained this post. As operations chief on the general staff during World War II, with a distinguished record, he became deputy chief, and then chief, of the general staff, and later deputy Minister of Defense, with the rank of General of the Army. In 1952 he became a CC member. From 1952 to 1953 he served as chief of staff of Soviet occupation forces in Germany. After Stalin's death he was in eclipse, reappearing only in 1956 with a lower rank, but eventually becoming deputy chief of staff again, probably in 1965. In February 1968, he was known to be deputy chief of the general staff and regained his previous rank as General of the Army. According to *NYT* (Aug. 5) he had become chief of the general staff (James, ed., *Czechoslovak Crisis*, p. 53). In 1968 he published a history of staff work in World War II (*General'nyi shtab v gody voiny*, Moscow, 1968), which contained flattering accounts of Stalin's wartime activity. Ironically, in 1948, as chief of the general staff, he had been in charge of Soviet military movements before and during the February crisis in Czechoslovakia.
[26] Galia Golan, *The Czechoslovak Reform Movement* (Cambridge, 1971), p. 325.
[27] *CSM*, Aug. 22.
[28] According to Lowenthal, between Aug. 10 and 17 ("Sparrow in the Cage," p. 21); according to James, between Aug. 10 and 13 (*Czechoslovak Crisis*, p. 29). See also Ermarth, *Internationalism*, pp. 104-9 for the following.

mentaries in the Czech and Slovak press and to events in downtown Prague. Without discounting the significance of these factors, others, barely mentioned in Soviet statements, would seem to be more decisive, including the publication of the party statute, the ostentatious visits of Tito and Ceauşescu, and the failure of those of Ulbricht and Kádár.

The Soviet decision to invade may well have been made at a secret meeting of the Politburo said to have been held on August 16, when members were called back hurriedly from their vacations. Polemics had already resumed in the press, and Ulbricht's report on his Karlovy Vary conversations had been received. The decision may have been approved at a meeting of the "five," reportedly held on August 18, at which Kádár would have been able to report on his meeting with Dubček.[29] Meanwhile Marshal Grechko, accompanied by Yakubovsky and Generals Shtemenko and Yepishev, had held military conversations with top-ranking military leaders in East Germany and Poland.[30] By this time, too, the CPSU letter had been sent to Prague, and many of its crucial points had been published in the Aleksandrov article. The final step may have been the formal ratification of the invasion by the CPSU Central Committee at a meeting reportedly held on August 19 or 20.[31]

WERE COUNSELS DIVIDED?

Was there opposition within the Soviet leadership to the decision to invade? The answer to this question, as well as to the broader question—was there division of opinion at the top on the advisability and on the timing of this action—cannot be answered with any assurance. Some Western observers have emphasized the assumed disunity within Soviet decision-making circles and have even ascribed the delay in the decision to invade and the ultimate political failings of the operation to such divisions.[32] There has been speculation as to whether there were "hawks" and "doves" among the Soviet leaders, with persons such as Kosygin,

[29] Tigrid, *Why Dubček Fell*, pp. 95-96, for references to the two meetings. According to him, the Politburo was unanimous in its decision.

[30] *Pravda*, Aug. 17-18.

[31] Ermarth cites a report that a CC plenum on the 20th took the final decision, on recommendation of a Politburo majority, with Kosygin opposed (*Internationalism*, p. 116n.). Windsor and Roberts (*Czechoslovakia, 1968*, pp. 102-5), assume a hurried last-minute decision, on the 19th and 20th. Lowenthal ("Sparrow in the Cage," p. 3) casts doubts on this. According to Tigrid (*Why Dubček Fell*, p. 106n.) a CC plenum was held on Aug. 17 but did not take the final decision.

[32] This is particularly true of Windsor but the evidence offered and his speculations are dubious (Windsor and Roberts, *Czechoslovakia, 1968*, pp. 62-79). The journalist, Isaac Don Levine, in a book not remarkable for its accuracy, also stresses disunity and even assumes a possible putsch by the interventionists (*Intervention*, pp. 52 ff., 80-84). The latter idea is discounted by Ermarth (*Internationalism*, pp. 100-103) and by Lowenthal ("Sparrow in the Cage," p. 3).

Suslov, and perhaps Shelepin and Ponomarev identified as more conciliatory, others such as Shelest as more militant, and still others such as Brezhnev as occupying a middle position. These suppositions, however, remain highly speculative, based either on unconfirmed reports by journalists[33] or on Kremlinological or content analysis,[34] neither of which can be regarded as authoritative.

It is certainly probable that the question as to whether to invade or not, fraught with such serious consequences, generated differences of emphasis and perhaps basic clashes of opinion at various stages. It is possible that some favored early action against Czechoslovakia, perhaps at the time of the Warsaw conference, whereas others preferred renewed efforts at conciliation and perhaps had reservations or doubts about the ultimate decision to use force. Yet, without discounting these possibilities, it may equally well be assumed, on the basis of present evidence, that the Soviet leaders were in agreement at successive stages, including the final post-Bratislava period. Perhaps, as Ermarth has put it, "the collective leadership changed its collective mind" as a result of its perception of what transpired after Bratislava.[35] What is indisputable is that no Soviet leader openly opposed the invasion at the time or afterwards. Nor were there dismissals or resignations from high office. Indeed, no change in the Politburo occurred for some years after the invasion, which suggests a high degree of unity on the decision to invade.[36]

Only two serious scholarly efforts have so far been made to identify divisions within the Soviet leadership on attitudes toward Czechoslovakia and the ultimate decision to invade. Neither, in the opinion of this au-

[33] For example, a report in *NYT*, March 4, 1969, based on an East European source in East Berlin, quoting a Soviet secretariat official. According to this report, Kosygin, Shelepin, and Ponomarev were "doves," and Suslov actually abstained in the vote on the invasion. Ulbricht and Gomułka were said to have pleaded for an invasion and to have threatened to act on their own. Cf. H. Schwartz, *NYT*, Aug. 22; D. Binder, ibid., Aug. 25. See also Levine, *Intervention*; Shub, *Russian Tragedy*, pp. 101-2; Shub, *An Empire Loses Hope* (New York, 1970), p. 359n. Doubts on the validity of this type of evidence are expressed by Wolfe (*Soviet Power*, p. 413) and by Brahm (*Der Kreml*, pp. 74-77).

[34] See David Paul and Jiří Valenta below in this chapter.

[35] Ermarth, *Internationalism,* p. 104.

[36] When Shelest was removed from the Politburo in 1973, there were reports from Moscow that he was being blamed for the invasion, and charged with calling a meeting of the Politburo on Aug. 16 on the basis of faulty evidence provided by the Soviet ambassador in Prague, Chervonenko, and by Bil'ak. Tigrid did not exclude this possibility but admitted that there is no real evidence for it (*Le Monde*, May 17-18, 1973). According to M. Tatu (ibid., Sept. 23, 1968), Suslov blamed Chervonenko's reports for misleading the Politburo (cited by Lowenthal, "Sparrow in the Cage," p. 21). According to Tatu, Suslov and Shelepin had doubts about the final decision to invade (Tigrid, *Why Dubček Fell,* p. 96). Ponomarev and Katushev were said to have informed Lenárt in Budapest in September 1968 that they regretted the August events but had been in a minority against the dogmatists and the military (Tigrid, *Why Dubček Fell,* pp. 127-28; concerning Ponomarev, p. 128n.).

thor, can be regarded as providing conclusive, or even persuasive, evidence of actual divisions within the Politburo and among Soviet elites on these matters.

David W. Paul, in one such study, attempted "a data analysis of elite attitudes as reflected in their official newspapers," i.e. *Pravda, Izvestia, Krasnaya zvezda,* and *Trud,* which were taken to represent the government, the party, the military, and the trade union hierarchy.[37] It was assumed that differences in attitude in the newspapers reflected differences within the Politburo, especially with regard to the perception of "the threat to the alliance from within." Having uncovered certain differences in viewpoint expressed by individual papers at different periods, Paul drew the conclusion that there was no consensus within the Politburo, either in May or even after Čierna and Bratislava, when the decision to invade was made. According to him, the government elite, represented by Kosygin and perhaps Podgorny, did not share the panic of the party, the military, and the trade unions and indeed had "grave doubts" about the invasion. Two factions had emerged, one endorsing drastic action, and the other, a minority, led by Kosygin, tacitly and reluctantly supporting the decision "in a show of solidarity."[38]

Jiří Valenta, in the second study, using a bureaucratic model of politics, sought to identify conflicting "bureaucratic interests and pressures" affecting Soviet attitudes and decisions. He identified the divisions of the Politburo at the time of the Čierna conference as follows: the advocates of intervention, N. V. Podgorny, P. Y. Shelest, A. J. Pelshe; anti-interventionists, M. A. Suslov, N. A. Shelepin, A. N. Kosygin, B. N. Ponomarev; undecided, L. I. Brezhnev, P. N. Demichev, K. T. Mazurov, P. M. Masherov, K. F. Katushev, and G. I. Voronov. He regarded the Čierna agreement as a victory for Suslov and the moderates, and Bratislava as a compromise between the hard-liners and moderates. Brezhnev

[37] "Soviet Foreign Policy and the Invasion of Czechoslovakia, A Theory and a Case Study," *International Studies Quarterly* 15 (June 1971), 159-201. All articles relating to Czechoslovakia during three time periods were coded as favorable, neutral or ambiguous, or hostile. The time periods selected were each eleven days long, namely, Jan. 6-16, May 8-18, and Aug. 11-21, 1968. Paul's press coverage was highly selective for each period and omitted the important post-Warsaw conference period. For criticism of Paul's approach, see Arnold L. Horelick, A. Ross Johnson and John D. Steinbruner, *The Study of Soviet Foreign Policy, A Review of Decision-Theory-Related Approaches* (Rand Corp., Santa Monica, Cal., Dec. 1973), p. 47.

[38] Such conclusions can be justified only on the assumption that *Izvestia* in fact spoke for Kosygin and the government as a distinct faction. Moreover, a close reading of *Pravda* and *Izvestia* during the days following Bratislava does not provide conclusive evidence of a fundamental differentiation in attitude, but suggests a difference in tone and emphasis which may reflect a division of labor between the two papers. *Pravda* carried the main thrust of the polemics against Czechoslovakia, whereas *Izvestia* concentrated its attacks on West Germany, especially in the fiery article by Henry on August 15 and the editorial of August 20.

occupied a shifting position, vacillating between hard-line and moderate positions and hesitating before the final vote on invasion. The blame for the invasion is assigned to the Politburo hard-liners, supported by certain sections of the party apparatus, the military elite, and the secret service. Considerable responsibility for the decision to invade is assigned to Shelest who called a Politburo meeting on August 15-16 and pressed for intervention.[39]

There is wide difference of interpretation and no firm evidence as to the role of the armed forces. Some observers assumed that the military, aware of the threat to the Warsaw pact's defense position posed by Prague's increasingly independent course, were ardent exponents of a military solution. Others believed that the military, or some part of it, were opposed to the invasion.[40] Others placed heavy stress on the military factor, but did not claim that the military was primarily responsible.[41] Even if one assumed that military considerations tipped the scales, it does not follow that the military themselves played the decisive role. The invasion was presumably launched by the highest political authorities, and the military then carried out orders received from these authorities. There is no way to determine whether the military were from the start a strong pressure group pushing for action[42] or whether they

[39] J. Valenta, "Soviet Decisionmaking and the Czechoslovak Crisis of 1968," to be published, with a comment by Dimitri K. Simes, former staff member of the Institute of World Economics and World Politics in Moscow, in *Studies in Comparative Communism* 8 (Spring-Summer 1975). Valenta classified leading Soviet personalities as hard-liners and moderates according to the attitudes revealed in individual articles and speeches on major issues of Soviet domestic and foreign policy. In linking these attitudes with their assumed views on Czechoslovakia, Valenta gave substantial credence to reports by journalists and "witnesses" and sometimes offered only generalizations based on his own speculations. Shelest, for instance, is identified throughout as the leading interventionist, although no evidence is offered.

In his critique Simes argued that differences of opinion within the bureaucratic elite and the leadership normally reflected functional responsibilities rather than institutional affiliation and were based on conflicts among different Soviet foreign and domestic interests. He did, however, give a classification, presumably based on his own personal impressions, of the various party and government departments, according to their advocacy of, or opposition to, military intervention. There was, however, no hard evidence that there were outright opponents to intervention among the Soviet leaders, and voting on the final decision in the Central Committee was reportedly unanimous.

[40] Golan, *Czechoslovak Reform*, pp. 325, 327. John Thomas argued that some of the Soviet military (including General Kazakov) were opposed from a military point of view, but offered no evidence ("Soviet Foreign Policy and the Military," *Survey* 17, Summer 1971, 135-37).

[41] Erickson, in Kusin, ed., *Czechoslovak Reform*, p. 56. It has also been contended that the Politburo used the military argument to justify its own decision to invade (Kahn, "How to Think," p. 231).

[42] Mackintosh believed that the military favored the invasion but admitted there is no direct evidence of their views or of their influence on the final decision ("The Soviet Military: Influence on Foreign Policy," *PC* 22, Sept.-Oct. 1973, pp. 7-8).

were neutral, or perhaps even reluctant, executors of the party's decisions.

THE DECISION TO INVADE—WHY?

The fullest justification of the invasion was that set forth in a long editorial in *Pravda* (Aug. 22) which was widely distributed in pamphlet form by the invading troops. Its text is readily available and does not require detailed analysis.[43] This ex post facto rationale followed in the main the lines of pre-invasion propaganda given in detail in the preceding chapter. The attack on the Czechoslovak leadership as a whole was perhaps more unrestrained than in the Warsaw letter, but at one point there was an effort to distinguish between Dubček and a minority of the Presidium who had taken "right-wing opportunist stands" at Čierna, and the majority who had adopted "a principled line" against anti-socialist forces. Certain individuals—including Císař, Hájek, Špaček, Šik, and Prchlík—were singled out for special condemnation. There was a disavowal of hostility toward the reform objectives, although without the positive references to specific measures contained in the Warsaw letter, and with criticism of certain propositions of the Action Program. There was a more detailed critique of the proposed revision of the party statute, and more pointed censure of the preparations for the 14th congress and of the efforts of some delegates to exert pressure concerning the future CC.[44] There was explicit criticism of Hájek's alleged plan for revising foreign policy and of certain persons for seeking "independence" from the "unified policy" of the socialist commonwealth.[45]

These arguments and pretexts cannot, of course, be accepted as the genuine motives of the invasion. Yet in the subsequent years there have been no startling revelations accompanying leadership changes in the Soviet Union or Eastern Europe, and almost no other clues as to the real reasons for Soviet intervention. Consequently, our conclusions must remain speculative and tentative, subject to correction if and when more definitive evidence becomes available.

[43] Text in *CDSP* 20, Sept. 11, 1968, pp. 5-14; also *Reprints from the Soviet Press* (Compass Publications, N.Y., 1968), 7 (Sept. 5), 3-40; Remington, ed., *Winter in Prague*, pp. 299-323.

[44] Y. Zhukov, in a long article in *Pravda* (Aug. 21) described the plans for the overthrow of "people's power," mentioning specifically the election of a new leadership after the 14th congress and the drafting of a new party statute. He also referred to "the golden hook of promises of loans and credits" to isolate Czechoslovakia from CMEA (BBC, I, Aug. 22).

[45] V. Šilhan, at the secret 14th congress, was said to have urged "neutralization" and withdrawal from WTO. See V. Kudryavtsev, "Counterrevolution Disguised as 'Regeneration,'" *Izvestia*, Aug. 25 (*CDSP* 20, Sept. 18, 1968, pp. 7-8; also Remington, ed., *Winter in Prague*, pp. 365-71).

It may be assumed that the use of military force was not something inevitable, preordained from the beginning.[46] Certainly "intervention," without violence, began early in 1968, at least by March, and intensified steadily as the Soviet perception of the "danger" of Czechoslovakia's course became more acute. Although military action was no doubt contemplated as an ultimate possibility, probably from June on, it was evidently regarded as a last resort, to be used, with reluctance, only after all other means of influence—political and economic pressure, propaganda, and military maneuvers—had been tried and had clearly failed. The costs of military intervention were high, including the adverse effect that this would have on the projected world conference of communist parties, on the proposed European security conference, and on the progress of détente, including arms control and economic agreements with the USA. The costs of nonintervention were also deemed to be high, embodying all the major repercussions of Czechoslovakia's reform course, to be discussed in the following pages, as well as the blow to the prestige of the Soviet Union.[47] The ultimate decision to invade represented therefore a kind of conscious or unconscious calculation of benefits and costs, including among the latter the risks of various forms of American retaliation detrimental to Soviet interests.[48]

Three basic elements were presumably involved in the Soviet decision as to whether or not to resort to violence. One was primarily international, involving diplomatic and military-strategic considerations. The crucial factor here was that of "security," both of the USSR and of the East European bloc, which, it was perhaps thought, was threatened in the long run by American imperialism; by West German policies; by possible shifts in Czechoslovak defense and foreign policy; and by any weakening of the unity and defense capacity of the Warsaw pact. A second element was primarily domestic in character, namely, the fear of the effects of reforms on the stability of Czechoslovak socialism and on the dominant position of the Communist Party. This reflected ideological preconceptions concerning the superiority of the Soviet model of socialism over any

[46] Ermarth, *Internationalism*, pp. 112-14.

[47] Brezhnev is reported by Piller to have said to him in the autumn, "After the Hungarian experience the blood of a single Czechoslovak communist, of a single ordinary person, is dearer to us than a temporary loss of prestige in the world" (BBC, II, Aug. 22, 1969). Cf. the version given by Piller in *Rudé právo*, Sept. 17, 1969. Much later, B. Chňoupek, in a CC speech in Dec. 1970, spoke of the decision to invade as "a hard and unpopular alternative," "a tragic but unavoidable step." It was made, he said, only after all the disadvantages had been calculated: enormous international complications, complications in the communist movement, propagandistic and diplomatic exploitation of the action, etc. (*Tvorba*, Jan. 6, 1971, supp.).

[48] See Andrew M. Scott, "Military Intervention by the Great Powers, The Rules of the Game," in Zartman, ed., *Czechoslovakia*, pp. 85-104, for a cost-benefit analysis of the intervention. See also Klaiber, *Crisis in Czechoslovakia*, pp. 27-29.

form of "national model" differing in essentials from the Soviet. Finally, linking together both international and domestic considerations, there was the possible "spillover" effect of events in Czechoslovakia among its allies, either in the form of the contagion of reform ideas in other East European states, especially the GDR, Poland, and Hungary, perhaps in the Soviet Union itself, or in the form of a general loosening of bloc relations as a result of the example of Czechoslovakia's changing diplomatic and military orientation.[49]

Western commentators differ in their assessment of the relative significance of the several elements in the ultimate conclusions reached. Some stress the domestic danger, as perceived by the Soviet Union, and its spillover effect elsewhere, and argue that the international threat, in particular from West Germany, was secondary.[50] Others, especially military specialists, lay greater emphasis on the international aspects, in particular military-strategic considerations related to Czechoslovakia's position in the Warsaw pact defense system, although usually without claiming that this was the only, or even the decisive, factor.[51] The conclusion seems inescapable that many factors, domestic and international, were involved and that lack of evidence prevents any final judgment as to the relative weight of each. All elements were in any case so inextricably intertwined, both in Soviet and bloc propaganda, and in actual fact, that a separate weighting of each is impraticable and unrealistic.[52] Perhaps the final Soviet judgment, based on all the above factors, was that only

[49] There was also a fear that a group of several reform-minded countries might act with a certain independence (Kusin, in Kusin, ed., *Czechoslovak Reform*, p. 317).

[50] For instance Golan, *Czechoslovak Reform*, pp. 316, 327-28; Zartman, in Zartman, ed., *Czechoslovakia*, pp. 108-9; Roberts, in Windsor and Roberts, *Czechoslovakia, 1968*, pp. 100-101.

[51] For instance, Wolfe and Erickson (cited in n. 2) and Ermarth (cited in n. 18). M. K. Dziewanowski, in "The Aftermath of the Czechoslovak Crisis," *Studies for a New Central Europe*, ser. 2, no. 3 (1968-69), pp. 55, 57, believed that the threat from West Germany was the decisive factor.

[52] The American communist, Aptheker, believed that both domestic and external factors were interlocked and reinforced each other (*Czechoslovakia and Counter-Revolution*, p. 9). For other comments on the linking of many factors and the difficulty of separating them, see Ermarth, *Internationalism*, p. 110; Erickson, in Kusin, ed., *Czechoslovak Reform*, p. 46; James, ed., *Czechoslovak Crisis*, p. 111. On the multiple factors involved, see Lowenthal, "Sparrow in the Cage," p. 11; Wolfe, *Soviet Power*, pp. 386-92; Aspaturian in Zartman, ed., *Czechoslovakia*, pp. 31-42; Kahn, "How to Think," p. 127. Yuri Zhukov, in an article "Thank you for your Frankness, Mister Kahn!" (*Pravda*, Nov. 13, 1968) cited many of the "dangers" listed by Kahn (recognition of Bonn; political and economic changes in Czechoslovakia; the replacement of the Gomułka regime; attempts at the union of the GDR and the GFR; the weakening of WTO and a West German attack on the USSR), but omits others (denunciation of the Warsaw treaty by one or more members; Soviet loss of East Germany; Soviet retreat from East Europe; and liberalization in the USSR).

728

an invasion could consolidate Soviet hegemony and avert the danger of eventual loss of control of the Communist Party and of its policy in Czechoslovakia, and, ultimately, over the entire area of Eastern Europe still under its control or influence.[53]

This interweaving of domestic and international considerations and the concern for the control of Eastern Europe was clearly revealed in the justification advanced about a month after the event in the so-called Brezhnev doctrine. This was enunciated not by Brezhnev personally but by a scholar of the history of materialism, Professor S. Kovalev, in a major article in the pages of *Pravda*. Although he did not use the term "limited sovereignty" often ascribed to his theory in the West, Kovalev did advance a novel interpretation of sovereignty, denying that the invasion had "contradicted the principle of sovereignty and the right of nations to self-determination" and rejecting "the abstract and non-class approach" to these questions. Each socialist country and its party had the freedom to determine its own path of development, he wrote, but not in such a way as to "damage socialism in their own country, nor the fundamental interests of other socialist countries, nor the worldwide workers' movement." Self-determination in the form of "neutrality" would lead to the dismemberment of the socialist commonwealth and would infringe on the vital interests of the other member countries. The defense of the world socialist system was therefore "the common cause of all communists." The actions taken by the five were "aimed at defending the fundamental interests of the socialist commonwealth and primarily at defending Czechoslovakia's independence and sovereignty as a socialist state. . . ."[54]

Although couched in somewhat novel terms, this doctrine hardly broke new ground in asserting the right of the Soviet Union to intervene if events in a single socialist country threatened the common interests of the whole bloc. Indeed, a similar view had been enunciated in many polemical articles and statements during the summer of 1968, including the Warsaw letter, which had described the events in Czechoslovakia as "the common affair" of all and proclaimed the joint responsibility of all socialist countries to act in defense of "the common vital interests"

[53] Scott, "Military Intervention," p. 96; Hayter, *Russia and the World*, pp. 57-63. James, who concluded that the main motive was to preserve the status quo in Eastern Europe described the move as entirely defensive, without any aggressive or expansionist designs (*Czechoslovak Crisis*, pp. 55, 124).

[54] *Pravda*, Sept. 26 (*CDSP* 20, Oct. 16, 1968, pp. 10-12). V. Kudryavtsev advanced similar views immediately after the invasion. Expressing surprise at the use of the term "intervention" even by the Rumanian and Yugoslav leaders, he asked: "Don't they know that the Warsaw Pact was concluded not only to defend the signatory states' national borders and territories? It was concluded in order to defend socialism in response to the creation of the aggressive NATO military bloc . . ." (*Izvestia*, Aug. 25; *CDSP* 20, Sept. 18, 1968, pp. 7-8).

729

and to defend socialism and the unity of the commonwealth. In somewhat more subtle terms the Bratislava declaration had affirmed "the common international duty of all socialist countries to support, strengthen, and defend these (socialist) gains" and proclaimed their determination to act in solidarity against threats to socialism and the unity of the socialist states. The editorial of August 22 had used similar terms in jusifying the invasion, concluding with the statement: "The defense of socialism in Czechoslovakia is not only the internal affair of that country's people but also a problem of defending the positions of world socialism." The Kovalev doctrine simply put in formal legal terms a proposition frequently stated and reiterated anew the right of intervention so often asserted and implemented in earlier decades of Soviet rule.

Brezhnev himself, in an address to the Polish party congress in November 1968, while proclaiming "strict respect for the sovereignty of all countries," implicitly endorsed the doctrine by proclaiming the necessity of military action to protect the sovereignty of a socialist country if socialism were threatened by "external and internal forces hostile to socialism." Such military assistance, he declared, was "an extraordinary measure, dictated by necessity; it can be called forth only by the overt actions of enemies of socialism within the country and beyond its boundaries, actions that create a threat to the common interests of the socialist camp."[55]

THE INTERNATIONAL FACTOR

Soviet hostility and suspicion toward the United States were real and deep-rooted, based on ideological conceptions of "imperialism" and Soviet interpretations of American policies in Vietnam, the Middle East, and elsewhere. As far as Eastern Europe was concerned, the policies of "peaceful engagement" and "bridge-building," launched by President Lyndon B. Johnson in the fall of 1966, were regarded as a new form of intervention, replacing older, more militant doctrines of "containment" and "liberation" by subtle subversion through trade and cultural relations.

At the same time the Soviet Union considered it of vital interest to pursue a détente with the USA and to achieve its essential ingredients—the European security conference, arms limitations agreements, and a summit conference of the two super-powers. Military intervention in Czechoslovakia might have as its most serious debit the interruption of progress toward these goals. No doubt, however, the Soviet Union rated this cost

---

[55] *Pravda*, Nov. 13 (*CDSP* 20, Dec. 4, 1968, pp. 3-4). On the doctrine, see L. Labedz, "Czechoslovakia and After," *Survey*, no. 69 (Oct. 1968), pp. 10-13; Wolfe, *Soviet Power*, pp. 383-85.

as relatively low, consisting of delay rather than an irrevocable halting of this process. (In fact all three goals were eventually attained in spite of the invasion.) For her part the Soviet Union sought to reduce the risks of intervention by (a) holding out hopes for arms control agreements and a summit conference (the latter was actually to have been announced on August 21—the day after the invasion), and (b) by their massive deployment of troops prior to and during the invasion, thus accentuating the danger of war if the USA were to adopt a militant stance.[56] Although continuing to express hostility toward U.S. imperialism and to accuse the USA of intervention in Eastern Europe, the USSR was well aware that the USA was doing little or nothing to influence the course of events in Prague and could therefore reasonably hope that nothing serious would be done to combat Soviet military measures.

In fact the United States had deliberately decided to pursue a policy—often referred to as "silence" or "inactivity"—which offered neither positive nor negative inducements to the USSR to recede from her militant posture toward Czechoslovakia.[57] As one correspondent put it, Washington "loudly stood aside," giving every possible signal of her noninvolvement.[58] During the Prague Spring no decisive move was made to settle the question of Czechoslovak gold, held by the USA since the war, or to grant Czechoslovakia most-favored nation treatment in trade. No public statements were made that would have warned the Soviet Union of the harmful effects on her own interests of a resort to force. President Johnson, in several statements in June, indicated that the USA was giving highest priority to détente and made no references whatever to the gathering crisis. Dean Rusk, while denying charges of interference in Czechoslovakia, made clear that the U.S. did not regard itself as involved in the

---

[56] On the former point, Gromyko's foreign policy speech at the end of June, which showed a positive attitude toward arms control talks, may have been in part designed to encourage the non-engagement of the USA in Czechoslovakia (Ermarth, *Internationalism*, p. 116; Wolfe, *Soviet Power*, pp. 273-74). On the latter, see Henderson, ed., *Public Diplomacy*, pp. 254-55, 285.

[57] For a detailed exposition of the U.S. attitude, see S. W. Barton and L. M. Martin, "Public Diplomacy and the Soviet Invasion of Czechoslovakia in 1968," in Henderson, ed., *Public Diplomacy*, pp. 261-77. For severe criticism of American policy see ibid., pp. 265, 268, 292-94; William Griffith in Zartman, ed., *Czechoslovakia*, pp. 47-57; Ermarth, *Internationalism*, pp. 115-17; W. C. Clemens, Jr., *War/Peace Report*, Jan. 1970, pp. 14-19; George Liska, *Interplay* (Oct. 1968), pp. 21-24. The policy of inactivity pursued by the West, in particular by NATO, was praised by James, since warnings concerning Czechoslovakia would have been futile and détente was a major Western interest (*Czechoslovak Crisis*, pp. 78-80, 88-89). For a measured analysis of what the USA might have done, see John C. Campbell, "Czechoslovakia: American Choices, Past and Future," *CSP* 11 (Spring 1969), 10-22. He concluded that American actions would not have affected the Soviet decision but criticized the "silence" as seeming to confirm the existence of agreed spheres of influence (pp. 18-19).

[58] Joseph C. Harsch, *CSM*, July 29.

731

situation and had no intention of taking any action to support Czechoslovakia.[59] This policy may have been chosen as one which, by avoiding any appearance of interference, was likely to dissuade the Soviet Union from military action, but in fact it had the opposite effect of giving a "green light" to Moscow. It is, of course, dubious whether anything that the USA might have done would have deterred the Soviet Union from its military incursion. Serious American action might indeed have increased the risks of Soviet retaliation. Nonetheless the policy of studied indifference and unconcern reduced greatly the risks of invasion and no doubt was a factor encouraging the Soviet Union to intervene.[60]

The German Federal Republic represented, in Soviet eyes, an even more direct threat to the interests of the USSR, particularly in the light of the new *Ostpolitik* inaugurated by the Kiesinger-Brandt coalition government in late 1966 and its initial successes in regard to Rumania and Yugoslavia. Bonn's conciliatory policy was viewed by Moscow, and still more by East Berlin and Warsaw, as designed to achieve a peaceful penetration of Eastern Europe, thus threatening the post-war frontiers, especially those of Poland and Czechoslovakia; isolating the GDR; and in the long run undermining the socialist regimes themselves. Throughout 1968 Soviet, East German, and Polish propaganda laid heavy, indeed exaggerated, stress on this danger, citing as evidence Sudeten German agitation in the Federal Republic; visits by German politicians and by many tourists to Czechoslovakia; support of democratization by Western mass media; Western broadcasts to Czechoslovakia (including those of Radio Free Europe); offers of trade and credit; NATO maneuvers, etc. All this was linked with support from the USA, as demonstrated, it was charged, by the visit of Gerhard Schroeder, the West German Minister of Defense, to Washington in July. Worse still was the belief that Czechoslovakia, hitherto a staunch supporter of the bloc's hard-line policy toward the GFR, was showing signs of breaking with this "coordinated policy" and of preparing the way for ultimate diplomatic recognition on the Rumanian pattern. Czechoslovakia's denial of any such intention, and West Germany's sedulous efforts to disavow ulterior motives in its *Ostpolitik*, did not allay Soviet suspicions nor cause any diminution in the harsh anti-German line of Soviet propaganda throughout the crisis months.

Moscow's note of July 5 to Bonn on the proposed renunciation of

[59] It is not known whether Rusk, in his July 22 meeting with the Soviet ambassador, gave any private warnings (*NYT*, July 18, 20, 23). See also Barton and Martin (Henderson, ed., *Public Diplomacy*, pp. 262-68).

[60] There is no evidence that the USA gave prior consent or approval to the invasion. However, as one commentator put it, U.S. policy amounted to de facto collusion, recognizing a Soviet sphere of influence and treating Czechoslovakia as "an internal matter" (*CSM*, Sept. 16).

force agreement reiterated earlier Soviet statements claiming the right of equal participation by the GDR in such an agreement; denouncing the refusal of the GFR to recognize the post-war frontiers and the special position of West Berlin; and condemning the rise of neo-Nazism in West Germany. The July note also reasserted, somewhat ominously, the right, under the UN Charter, to employ sanctions in the case of "a restoration of aggressive policy" by the GFR.[61] In late July the West German decision to transfer NATO exercises away from the Czechoslovak frontier, and thus to avoid any provocative display of force, did not hinder Soviet condemnation of these exercises as a form of pressure on the bloc countries and continuing journalistic blasts at neo-Nazism and West German designs against Eastern Europe.[62] Indeed there were open charges that West Germany's "Eastern policy" was merely a new version of the pre-1914 Mitteleuropa plan for the domination of Eastern Europe and that there was already a military plan (Operation Deposit) providing for a "short 'limited war' " against the GDR and Czechoslovakia.[63] At the end of July the Soviet ambassador in Bonn refused to accept a West German note which protested against the wrong appraisal in the Soviet press of West German policy regarding Czechoslovakia.[64]

Czechoslovakia's aspirations for reform and greater independence coincided with a trend in Soviet policy toward intensified solidarity of the bloc, in particular toward enhanced military integration. The idea of a dissolution of both WTO and NATO receded into the background; the military and economic strengthening of the Soviet bloc, strongly stated by Brezhnev in his speech on July 8, moved into the foreground.[65] In this context Czechoslovak developments, presaging a more autonomous approach to defense strategy and foreign policy, seemed to constitute a dan-

[61] This and earlier notes were published in *Izvestia*, July 12-14 (*Reprints 7*, Oct. 4, 18, 1968, pp. 37-49, 14-30 resp.). Cf. the note along similar lines presented to Bonn on Dec. 8, 1967 (*Pravda*, Dec. 9, 1967; *Reprints 6*, Jan. 12, 1968, pp. 34-44). In each case there was reference to the rights of the great powers under the Potsdam conference to take action to curb Nazism and militarism, and mention of forces in West Germany which were opposed to these tendencies. See also the Soviet press conference on February 24 denouncing neo-Nazism and condemning West Germany's *Ostpolitik* (*Pravda*, Feb. 25; *Reprints 6*, March 22, 1968, pp. 50-55).

[62] For instance, E. Henry, *Pravda*, Aug. 1, 5, 10. Cf. Henry's earlier attack on what he termed the developing Bonn-Peking alliance (*Literaturnaya gazeta*, nos. 15-16; *Reprints 6*, June 14, pp. 3-17). See also *Pravda Ukrainy*, Aug. 1; *Krasnaya zvezda*, Aug. 8; *Sovetskaya Rossia*, Aug. 13. B. Orlov, in a short article in *Izvestia* (Aug. 16), attacked West Germany's negative attitude to the GDR's August proposals. See Orlov's condemnation of Bonn's "subtle subversion," and plans for possible military attack in an article which appeared on the day of the invasion (*Izvestia*, Aug. 21).

[63] Ernst Henry, *Izvestia*, Aug. 15. This was cited by Aptheker, *Czechoslovakia and Counter-Revolution*, pp. 13-14. A similar charge had been made earlier by V. Mayevsky, *Pravda*, April 2 (*Reprints 6*, May 3, pp. 41-45).

[64] *Neues Deutschland*, Aug. 3.   [65] *Pravda*, July 9.

ger signal, threatening to weaken the entire WTO security system, in particular the Northern Tier of East Germany, Poland, and Czechoslovakia.[66] Czechoslovakia's geographical location made her role in the WTO defense system crucial to its strength—more so, as has been pointed out, than that of Rumania.[67]

These fears were aggravated by what were thought to be dangerous trends in Czechoslovak foreign policy, including even the possibility of neutrality and withdrawal from the pact, or short of that, a more independent posture, comparable to that of Rumania, and compounding the latter in an even more sensitive area of Europe.[68] Even without such a drastic eventuality, any change in Czechoslovakia's attitude toward the WTO and West Germany might have caused a shift in the military and diplomatic balance of power in Europe and, if her example were followed by other East European countries, a gradual disintegration of the pact as a defensive entity.[69] Such dangers, of course, seem greatly overdrawn in the light of Czechoslovakia's constant professions of loyalty to the pact and her careful avoidance of any actions in foreign policy which were contrary to the bloc's interests. Equally overdrawn seem the professed Soviet fears concerning the German and American threats to Eastern Europe. These may have bulked large in the minds of the Soviet, and still more of East German and Polish leaders, and of their military au-

[66] Wolfe, *Soviet Power*, pp. 391, 493-94. Aptheker (*Czechoslovakia*, p. 23) cited an article in the *Bonner Rundschau* (July 26) concerning the danger to the "iron triangle" of the "removal of Prague." "The southern flank of Poland and the GDR would be exposed and a breakthrough to the Soviet frontier would become conceivable. The triangle would lose its value and the Warsaw pact its heart."

[67] V. V. Aspaturian, "The Aftermath of the Czech Invasion," *Current History*, no. 55 (Nov. 1968), pp. 306-8. Aspaturian called Czechoslovakia an "invasion funnel" (also Zartman, ed., *Czechoslovakia*, p. 36). The strategic importance of Czechoslovakia is discussed by Erickson, in Kusin, ed., *Czechoslovak Reform*, pp. 35 passim. See also L. W. Whetten, "Military Aspects of the Soviet Occupation of Czechoslovakia," *The World Today* 25 (Feb. 1969), 60-68; J. P. Fox, "Czechoslovakia 1968 and 1938," *Contemporary Review* 214 (March 1969), 122-27. Cf. Dubček's remark after the occupation that they had underestimated the Soviet "strategic interest" in Czechoslovakia (cited by Wolfe, *Soviet Power*, p. 390, n. 10). Černík, in his report of Aug. 26, referred to the Soviet view that the invasion was a strategic and military necessity (Tigrid, *Why Dubček Fell*, pp. 95-97).

[68] Neutrality was not mentioned in the Warsaw letter or in the Aug. 22 editorial, but was stressed in press polemics and was accented in post-occupation propaganda. The mention by Kotyk, in his *Práce* articles, of neutrality as an option that might be forced on Czechoslovakia as a result of Soviet pressures was cited. See also chap. XIX, n. 77, XXII, nn. 64, 70.

[69] Writing for foreign consumption, the Paris correspondent of *Novosti* described Czechoslovakia as "the main defense line of the socialist member states of the Warsaw treaty," a threat to which would have led to "a serious modification of power relations in Europe." The USSR had to consider what "the loss of Czechoslovakia or its transition to positions of nationalism and bourgeois revisionism would have meant" (*Le Monde*, Sept. 30, 1968, cited by Haefs, ed., *Ereignisse*, pp. 221-24).

thorities, but may also have been greatly exaggerated as an element of the propaganda barrage against Czechoslovakia and used as pretexts for an intervention motivated more by domestic developments.

DOMESTIC ISSUES

Soviet attitudes to Czechoslovakia's domestic reform were in large part concealed beneath the preoccupation of Soviet propaganda with what was called the deteriorating political situation. Major Soviet statements, as we have seen, disclaimed any opposition to the post-January reforms, and did not openly criticize the plans for federation or rehabilitation or even the projected economic and political reforms. What was condemned were the more radical unofficial plans for political change, especially ideas of pluralism and "democratic socialism," and the so-called anti-socialist forces, as represented by the political clubs and the non-communist parties, and especially by the mass media.

Yet there can be little doubt that the Soviet leadership was mortally afraid of the plan of reform in all its aspects. Their conception of the prerequisites of socialism, so often proclaimed in official documents, was fundamentally at odds with the new features of socialism envisaged by the Prague reformers. In particular, the Czechoslovak conception of the leading role of the party was in basic conflict with the traditional Soviet dogma concerning the party's dominant position and represented, in their eyes, a negation of the very essence of socialism.[70] Moreover, the proposed federal system, implicitly calling into question the authenticity of Soviet federalism, could scarcely be viewed with equanimity. Other major reforms were anathema to the Soviet leadership: a real democratization of the party, revising the dogma of democratic centralism; market socialism with enterprise autonomy and workers' participation; freedom of the press and of expression in general; full rehabilitation, condemnation of the guilty, and genuine legality; and autonomy of action in foreign relations. Finally, there was the dynamite of the Piller report, with its implication of the Soviet leaders in the terror of the fifties, its revelations of the preeminence of the security police, and its plans for legal reform and safeguards for human rights.[71]

---

[70] Z. Suda, *The Czechoslovak Socialist Republic* (Baltimore, 1969), pp. 137-38. Sviták, in an excellent analysis of the reasons for the invasion, written on Aug. 4, 1968, stressed the ideological aspects: the differing conceptions of the meaning of socialism and the danger of infection of other socialist countries with "socialist democracy" (*Student*, Aug. 29, 1968; Sviták, *The Czechoslovak Experiment, 1968-1969*, New York, 1971, pp. 131-34). For Smrkovský's views, see Appendix D.

[71] Great emphasis was laid on the development of human rights as a factor in the Soviet invasion by P. Bergmann, *Self-Determination: The case of Czechoslovakia, 1968-1969* (Lugano, 1972).

What was most feared was not the overthrow of the communist system in Czechoslovakia but its fundamental reform in such a way that a new model of socialism would exert a powerful attraction in other countries of Eastern Europe and perhaps in the Soviet Union itself.[72] This "spill-over" effect was never directly mentioned in Soviet propaganda, but the dangers to socialism and the party's leading role were constantly expounded in reference to all the socialist countries, including the Soviet Union. In several Eastern European countries the relevance of Prague's reform was more direct and frightening. Not only socialism, but the regimes themselves, including the personal interests of the leaders, were considered to be at stake.[73]

In the Soviet Union there was no actual political crisis (as contended by Windsor and Roberts), nor presumably any real threat to the system as such, except in the long run. Certainly there was no imminent danger from the projected Czech reforms which a reasonably conservative Soviet regime could not have tolerated. An all-pervasive "fear of change," as Lowenthal put it, on the part of a deeply conservative (perhaps, better, reactionary) leadership, however, made them fear even moderate reforms as a potential threat to their concept of socialism, and, therefore, ultimately, to their own vested interests in such a system.[74] Immediately disturbing was the attraction which some of the Prague reforms held for segments of the Soviet population, notably the nationalities and the intelligentsia, thus contributing to the conflict situations already existing between the regime and these groups.

THE UKRAINIAN FACTOR

The "Ukrainian factor" in the invasion has been subjected to probing and well-documented analysis by Grey Hodnett and Peter Potichnyj in their study, *The Ukraine and the Czechoslovak Crisis.* They do not argue

[72] This fear was mentioned by the Moscow correspondent, M. Syrůček, in *Mladá fronta,* April 25, 1968. See also J. Pelikán, ed., *Vysočany Congress,* p. 227.

[73] Philip Windsor, in discussing the relevance of Czechoslovak reform in the other socialist countries, uses the strange argument that its relevance in the GDR and Poland was largely "symbolic," and although not considered a real threat, was "used" by their leaders to deal with their own domestic problems (Windsor and Roberts, *Czechoslovakia, 1968,* pp. 29-32). Equally unconvincing is his argument that in the case of the Soviet Union the occupation was a result of a real political crisis, especially a split in the leadership over invasion (ibid., pp. 62-64, 66, 76).

[74] Lowenthal, "Sparrow in the Cage," p. 3. Tatu similarly argued that the Soviet Union after Khrushchev was "conservative" and "militant and aggressive" and that the leaders regarded Dubček's political reform as a matter of "life and death" for themselves (*Interplay,* Nov. 1968, pp. 4-5). Cf. Lévesque's analysis of the "fearful, conservative, and bureaucratic mentality" of the leadership which caused them to act on "risks and doubts" and not on "definitive or established facts" ("*Problématique,*" pp. 42-44).

that this was the single or even the most important factor in the decision to invade, nor do they try to estimate its weight. Their sober findings, however, suggest that there was an important "linkage" between the situation in the Ukraine and the developments in Czechoslovakia, especially in Slovakia, and particularly in the Prešov region with its Ukrainian (Ruthenian) population.[75]

The Soviet regime had been conducting a vigorous struggle against nationalism in the Ukraine, including "liberal national communist views" (p. 115) voiced most strongly by certain Ukrainian intellectuals, and also against the youth, including students, and the Ukrainian Catholics. As a result, the Ukrainian CC adopted in April 1968 a harder line against these groups, in full accord with the CPSU April plenum's position (pp. 24-25).[76] Secondly, Ukrainian intellectuals were made aware of events in Czechoslovakia by the Ukrainian broadcasts of the Prešov radio, which could be heard in the Ukraine, and by certain Prešov newspapers (notably *Nove Zhyttia* and *Duklia*), all of which carried favorable accounts of the democratization process and even occasional criticism of the situation in the Ukraine (pp. 54-75). There were frequent contacts between the Ukraine and Slovakia, often in the form of official Ukrainian delegations—a kind of "quasi-diplomacy" designed presumably to acquire information and to exert an influence in Czechoslovakia, but also more informally in the development of tourism, with visas not required. This was especially true of the border regions, including the Transcarpathian region, once, prior to 1945, a part of Czechoslovakia. Prešov thus offered "a window to the West" for the Ukraine (p. 74). Ukrainian intellectuals, sensing a certain common interest with Czechoslovak intellectuals, saw in the developments in the neighboring country an argument and support for their own strivings. On the other hand, certain Ukrainians played relatively prominent and "hawkish" roles in the crisis, notably Shelest and Podgorny in the Politburo, and others, such as Y. V. Il'nitsky, Transcarpathian secretary, Marshal Grechko, and the Soviet ambassador in Prague, S. V. Chervonenko (pp. 80-84, 96-97).

Finally, the more orthodox Soviet leaders, including those who were Ukrainian, shared a common attitude with Czechoslovak conservatives, viewing the developments in both the Ukraine and Czechoslovakia with

[75] Canberra, 1970, esp. pp. 77-91. See also above, chap. XVIII, concerning the Ruthenians.

[76] The situation was aggravated in 1968 by a visit from a delegation of the Canadian Communist Party, and by the publication abroad in 1968 of several books strongly critical of the situation in the Ukraine, one by the former Canadian communist, John Kolasky, *Education in Soviet Ukraine* (Toronto, 1968), another by the strongly nationalist Ukrainian Marxist dissenter, Ivan Dzuba, *Internationalism or Russification?* (London, 1968), and a third documenting the persecution of Ukrainian dissenters, *The Chornovil Papers* (New York, 1968).

anxiety, and having an "image" of the Czechoslovak problem which embraced both areas. The threat in the Ukraine affected their "image" of Czechoslovak developments and the latter were seen as dangerous to the Ukraine, each fear reinforcing the other (pp. 123-25). Perhaps the "threat" to the Ukraine was used as an argument by the hawks in favor of invasion, as suggested by the invitation to Il'nitsky to speak at the July plenum (pp. 86, 117, 121-23).[77]

Interpretation of the facts available is admittedly difficult and cannot yield hard and fast conclusions. The Ukrainian press and radio, although mounting a strong campaign against Czechoslovak developments in the spring and summer, did not differ in essentials from the general Soviet treatment (pp. 77-78). Even the emphasis on the danger of nationalism by Shelest and Podgorny was duplicated in statements by non-Ukrainian spokesmen. Plans for federation in the ČSSR were not referred to in Soviet polemics, even in the Ukraine, and were actually implemented, without Soviet opposition, after the occupation. Moreover, there was a certain moderacy in the stance taken by other Ukrainian leaders, including V. V. Shcherbitsky, a candidate member of the Soviet Politburo and chairman of the Ukrainian Council of Ministers, who perhaps represented a personal rival to Shelest (pp. 22-23, 84-85, 101-3).[78] Even Shelest, after his removal from office in 1973, was criticized as having been too tolerant of Ukrainian nationalism during his tenure of office.[79]

THE PROBLEM OF THE INTELLECTUALS

Throughout 1968 Soviet authorities continued to wrestle with the problem of ferment among the Soviet intelligentsia, in particular with the growing movement of dissent. *Samizdat* was becoming a familiar phenomenon, and the *Chronicle of Current Events* began to appear regularly in April of that year. Some intellectuals dared to criticize the continuance of censorship and efforts to rehabilitate Stalin. Such examples of dissent and nonconformity were in some cases met with repression, as, for example, in the trials of Y. Galanskov, A. Ginzburg, and others in January, resulting in heavy sentences for the accused and protests against the sentences by others. Some intellectuals became the target of attack in the mass media, especially Aleksandr Solzhenitsyn, whose books *The First Circle* and *Cancer Ward* were published abroad at this time. The April CC plenum set the tone for a sustained and vigorous drive

[77] See above, chap. xx, n. 34 re the CC plenum.

[78] Shcherbitsky did not take an active part in Soviet dealings with the Czechoslovak crisis, attending none of the key meetings at home or abroad.

[79] See an earlier criticism of Shelest for support of nationalists in the Writers' Union by A. D. Skaba, propaganda secretary in the Ukraine (Hodnett and Potichnyj, *The Ukraine and the Czechoslovak Crisis*, p. 23).

738

against the influence of bourgeois ideology in all fields, including literature and art.[80]

In May a major article in *Pravda* expressed concern about the intellectuals of some socialist countries who were advocating Western theories against socialism and Soviet intellectuals who were manifesting
"individualism and a-politicism" and succumbing to "foreign ideological
influence." Some, "under the guise of a struggle against administrative
methods (*administrirovaniya*), were trying to deny the significance of
the ideational influence of the party in the sphere of creative activity."
Individual "renegades" "questing in the direction of anti-communism"
would meet with "a stern rebuff."[81]

It is difficult to estimate the extent to which Czechoslovak events were
directly and/or indirectly involved in this toughening of the Soviet cultural line. The testimony of recent émigrés suggests widespread sympathy
among Soviet intellectuals with the reform measures in Czechoslovakia
and some hope that similar developments might occur in the Soviet
Union. Andrei Sakharov, in his unpublished memorandum, "Thoughts
on Progress, Peaceful Co-existence and Intellectual Freedom" (June
1968), urged support for the "bold initiative" of the Czechoslovaks,
which he called "valuable for the future of socialism and all mankind."[82]
In late July the dissident writer, A. Y. Kosterin, shortly before resigning
from the party, joined with four others in sending a letter to the Czechoslovak embassy praising Czechoslovakia and expressing fears of plans
for an invasion.[83] A. T. Marchenko, a worker and dissident writer, in an
open letter to *Rudé právo* and other Czech and foreign communist newspapers abroad, on July 22, expressed his support for Czechoslovak reform and condemned the Warsaw letter.[84] Even two establishment writers and journalists, B. Polevoi and K. Simonov, during a visit to Prague
in May, expressed sympathy for the Prague experiment, which would be,
said Simonov, "a great contribution for world socialism."[85] Other intellectuals were perturbed by Prague developments, or even hostile to them.
Although sharp discussions within the confines of institutes and offices

---

[80] *Yearbook of International Communist Affairs*, 1969 (Stanford, 1970), pp.
812-15; Wolfe, *Soviet Power*, pp. 250-56.

[81] R. Kosolapov and P. Simush, *Pravda*, May 25.

[82] H. E. Salisbury, ed., *Sakharov Speaks* (New York, 1974), p. 96. An article
by V. Cheprakov (*Izvestia*, Aug. 11) which sharply condemned capitalist ideology
and described capitalism and socialism as diametrically opposed systems, may
have been an indirect reply to Sakharov's theory of convergence. See also
G. Smirnov's article, "Socialism and Personality," contrasting the guarantees to
the individual offered by socialism in contrast to the denial of personal rights
under capitalism (*Izvestia*, Aug. 17).

[83] *PC* 17 (Sept.-Oct. 1968), 62-63.   [84] Ibid., pp. 59-61.

[85] *Reportér*, May 8-15. Cf. the strong statement advocating Soviet economic
reform by A. Birman, the Soviet economist, during a visit to Prague. He made no
reference, however, to Czechoslovakia's reform (ibid., May 22-29).

about Czechoslovak reform were reported, the pro-reform spokesmen were no doubt isolated and jeopardized their careers in expressing their opinions. Whether the majority of intellectuals favored Prague's course or condemned it cannot, in the absence of free expression or public opinion polling, be determined. Certainly the apprehensions of some, created in part by misinformation and in part by genuine ideological concern, provided implicit support to the regime in its treatment of the Prague challenge.[86] Nonetheless, the role of the intellectuals in Czechoslovakia, and the establishment of genuine intellectual freedom there, were matters of grave concern to the Soviet leadership and doubtless were factors in their decision to invade.

BLOC UNITY AND DIVERGENCY

The actual decision to invade seems to have been primarily a Soviet one, concurred in by the other associated Warsaw pact powers. The military operations were under Soviet command, and the participation of the allies more or less nominal in character. Nor was there an attempt, either in the Tass announcement or the *Pravda* August 22 editorial, to justify the invasion by reference to the obligations of the Warsaw treaty.[87] Certainly there were differences of attitude and particularly of emphasis between the USSR, GDR, Poland, Hungary, and Bulgaria, but these were overcome and the invasion approved by all its participants. It seems unlikely that there was outright opposition by any of the allies, and doubtful that if such opposition had been manifested, it would have deterred the Soviet Union from acting with force.

Apart from the Soviet Union, the GDR exhibited the most hostile attitude toward Czechoslovakia, rarely if ever striking a positive note, and

[86] M. Syrůček, Czech correspondent in Moscow, wrote of widespread fears, based on shortage of information and on the CPSU campaign against Czechoslovakia, as well as on "rigid habits of thinking" which had taken deep roots (*MF*, April 25). O. Marušiak, Slovak correspondent in Moscow, wrote of lack of information, especially in party and government circles, and also among the public, but of the sympathy of the artistic intelligentsia (*Pravda* [Bratislava], June 19). Cf. Peter H. Juviler, "Soviet Motivations for the Invasion, and Domestic Support," *Studies for a New Central Europe*, ser. 2, no. 3 (1968-69), pp. 97-100.

[87] The *Pravda* editorial did, however, make a number of references to the Warsaw treaty and its obligations, referring mainly to Czechoslovakia's commitments under the treaty and the determination of the other members not to tolerate a breach in the organization. It should be noted that the Warsaw machinery was not used in the earlier exercise of pressures (except for the military maneuvers). Only one full meeting of WTO was held, in Sofia; Dresden, Warsaw, Čierna, and even Bratislava, were not described as WTO meetings. On the above, see James, ed., *Czechoslovak Crisis*, pp. 51-54; also Klaiber, *Crisis in Czechoslovakia*, pp. 34-35. Malcolm Mackintosh writes of the transfer of responsibility from the Warsaw pact headquarters to the Soviet high command (under Generals Pavlovsky and Shtemenko) at the beginning of August ("The Soviet Military," p. 8).

expressing from the beginning the most vitriolic condemnation of the reform program.[88] This can hardly be explained in terms of any real threat to the regime, except in the long run, in view of the absolute control exercised by the SED and the continued presence in the GDR of twenty Soviet army divisions. This control was not in any way modified by the inauguration of a new constitution in April 1968 (as well as a new criminal code in July). Nor did the New Economic System adopted in 1963, and the measures adopted for its implementation in April 1968, seriously change the rigid system of centralized planning. The East German attitude reflected the strict system of socialism that prevailed in the GDR, the harsh neo-Stalinist ideological stance taken in all matters and their long-held conviction that their policy throughout the entire postwar period had been superior to that of the Czechoslovak party's. It also corresponded with their traditional solidarity with the USSR and their usual sedulous adherence to all major aspects of Soviet foreign policy.

Above all, East German hostility toward Czechoslovak reform was correlated with their hard-line policy toward the German Federal Republic, and the persistent conception of the GFR as a seat of militarism, imperialism, and neo-Nazism. This was evident in the reiteration of the terms required for normalization of relations with the GFR, and specifically in the harsher system of control over the passage of persons and goods from West Germany to East Berlin and East Germany. It is difficult to determine whether the apparently more conciliatory policy adopted in August represented a genuine change or merely a tactical shift.[89] No doubt there was a pronounced fear in the GDR that the new Czechoslovak regime would take a softer line toward the GFR and thus break from the united front of the bloc countries on the German question, perhaps precipitating similar actions by Poland and Hungary.[90] It may be assumed that the GDR pressed the Soviet Union to take drastic action against Czechoslovakia and no doubt favored, and perhaps advocated, the invasion. Although this may have exerted some influence on

[88] Indicative was the ban on the import of the Czechoslovak German language newspaper, *Volkszeitung*, and also the German version of the *Budapest Daily News*. For East Germany during 1968, *YICA*, 1969, pp. 336-48; Melvin Croan, "Czechoslovakia, Ulbricht, and the German Problem," *PC* 18 (Jan. Feb. 1969), 1-7.

[89] The GDR's conciliatory offer has been interpreted by Wolfe as designed to isolate Bonn from Prague and perhaps to lull West Germany in regard to the impending invasion (Wolfe, *Soviet Power*, p. 416, n. 84). V. V. Aspaturian interpreted it as raising the danger of an "autonomous" East Germany and as a reason for the Soviet decision to invade Czechoslovakia (Zartman, ed., *Czechoslovakia*, pp. 34-35). See above, chap. xx.

[90] This has been described as the fear of the "unfreezing" of the German question as a result of developments in Czechoslovakia (William E. Griffith, *Eastern Europe After the Soviet Invasion of Czechoslovakia*, Rand Corp., Santa Monica, Cal., Oct. 1968, pp. 22-24).

the leaders of the USSR, it is hard to believe that the ultimate decision was made elsewhere than in Moscow.

The Polish attitude differed markedly from that of the GDR and was affected greatly by official Soviet opinion as well as by Polish domestic affairs. There was considerable public support for the Dubček reforms, expressed openly by the Writers' Union in late February and by the students during the March days. Gomułka and some of his colleagues may conceivably have had some sympathy for Dubček's efforts, at least in their original moderate form.[91] The official stance changed after the March events, when student unrest, supported by many intellectuals, spread throughout the country, and when the Catholic Church and the Znak group publicly criticized the actions taken by the police against the students. The regime was preoccupied with the crisis at home and sensitive to the implications for Poland of Czechoslovak development, both in its domestic and external aspects. More realistic leaders perhaps perceived that there was no real threat from West Germany under Brandt's leadership or any danger of a NATO invasion, but were filled with panic at the thought of events in Czechoslovakia leading to similar changes throughout the whole bloc, and in Poland to the possibility of a new 1956. This negative position was consonant with the regime's generally hard-line policy during the sixties, including the failure to modify the strict system of central planning and stringent controls on intellectual life, with its continued harshness towards West Germany and with Gomułka's loyalty to the Soviet Union.

The March events undermined Gomułka's authority and offered an opportunity for rivals to challenge his leadership. His chief opponent was presumably Mieczysław Moczar, at that time not a member of the highest party bodies, but having strong bases of power as Minister of the Interior and as head of the influential veterans' organization. It is often assumed that, in the former capacity, he provoked the crisis in March by the use of force against the student demonstrations. When admitted to the Politburo as a candidate member and to the Secretariat in early July,

[91] According to a purported interview with Gomułka, published in a Polish newspaper in Israel, Dubček, at a meeting with Gomułka in early February, appealed for his support and assured him that Kádár would then join them. Gomułka is quoted as saying that he seriously considered accepting Dubček's proposal but in the end decided the risks were too great. Ten years earlier, if a Dubček had appeared, he would probably have supported him, said Gomułka. Referring to the student slogan of 1968, "We want a Polish Dubček," he is said to have stated: "In 1960 I was the 'Polish Dubček.' In 1968 I was no longer regarded as such and I simply could not risk any changes" (*Nowiny-Kurier*, Israel, June 1, 1973). Cf. a similar report in *CSM*, June 6, 1974 which referred to Gomułka's alleged memoirs smuggled out of Poland in typescript and published in Polish in Israel. The authenticity of these reports is doubtful and the attitude described seems hardly credible.

he became a powerful contender for the leadership. Although he did not publicly express pro-Czechoslovak views, he may have had some sympathy for Czechoslovakia's increasing resistance to Soviet pressures, but as a man reputed to be extremely conservative, was more likely to have been hostile to Prague's reforms. Another rival, Edward Gierek, also gave no signs of sympathy with Czechoslovakia, and like Moczar, laid heavy accent on Zionist involvement in both Polish and Czechoslovak developments.

Gomułka's settlement of the March crisis by repressive measures eliminated the danger of a mass movement in favor of Czechoslovkia, such as had developed in 1956 for Hungary, and consolidated his position. Gomułka also tended to deflate the anti-Zionist aspects of regime policies, at least in words, although the subsequent purges in the party, the universities, and government departments struck hard at Polish Jews as well as "revisionists." His increasingly hostile attitude toward Czechoslovakia, much more unwavering than Kádár's, endeared him to the Soviet Union, which, in any case, could ill afford a power struggle in Poland simultaneously with the Czechoslovak crisis. It is impossible to determine whether Gomułka was initially favorable or opposed to an invasion, or whether he pressed strongly for such action at the Warsaw conference and after.[92] Poland's eventual participation in the invasion won him the full support of the Soviet Union, undermined the position of his opponents, and saved him from a possible challenge. His policy was endorsed publicly by both Moczar and Gierek, and was approved at the 5th Party Congress in November.[93]

The more conciliatory attitude of Hungary reflected the fact that she was herself pursuing a reform-oriented course, similar in some respects to Czechoslovakia's.[94] The Hungarian economic reform, which came into force on January 1, 1968, was more far-reaching than the Czechoslovak 1967 reform, although not envisaging the more radical changes advo-

[92] Nothing is known with certainty of Gomułka's position at the Warsaw conference, although there is little question that he supported the "open letter." He is said to have criticized the "soft stand" of the Soviet Union at Čierna and to have been censured by Moczar and at least implicitly by Gierek. For this, see Jan B. de Weydenthal, "Polish Politics and the Czechoslovak Crisis in 1968," CSP 14 (Spring 1972), 46-47.

[93] Ibid., p. 48. Moczar's support was given in a speech on Sept. 15; Gierek's on Oct. 7 (ibid., p. 51). See also George Gomori, "Hungarian and Polish Attitudes on Czechoslovakia, 1968," in E. J. Czerwinski and J. Piekalkiewicz, eds., The Soviet Invasion of Czechoslovakia (New York, 1972), pp. 113-14. For a summary of events in Poland in 1968, see YICA, 1969, pp. 668-701.

[94] For the following, see the excellent analysis by Rudolf L. Tokes, "Hungarian Intellectuals' Reaction to the Invasion of Czechoslovakia," in Czerwinski and Piekalkiewicz, eds., Soviet Invasion, chap. 8; also YICA, 1969, pp. 414-28. For brief comment, see also G. Gomori, "Hungarian and Polish Attitudes on Czechoslovakia, 1968," pp. 107-9.

cated by Šik. Like the Czechoslovaks, the Hungarians hoped for reform in Comecon procedures, in line with the domestic economic reforms, and an expanded trade with Western countries. On January 1, 1968, a new labor code came into effect, substantially increasing the rights of the trade unions, even giving them the right to veto over certain actions of managements.

Some Hungarian leaders recognized that economic reform would require changes in the political superstructure.[95] Certain moderate steps, such as multiple candidacy in elections and an enhanced role for the parliament, had already been introduced. In line with the policy enunciated by Kádár in the early sixties, a greater role for non-communists as "partners" was also proclaimed. The leading role of the party was to be maintained, but was to be exercised in cooperation with the Patriotic People's Front. In the cultural field, too, a flexible and relatively tolerant policy was being pursued, and a certain modus vivendi between regime and intellectuals had been achieved. In the words of a competent observer, the Hungarians had already established a working "revisionist" socialist model which, although moderate in its approach, had given the regime a substantial degree of legitimacy and stability. Moreover, not without significance in affecting Hungary's attitude was the plan of the Czechoslovak reformers to improve the position of the 600,000 Hungarians in the Republic, although this was counterbalanced by the intense Slovak nationalism that developed and the resulting Slovak-Hungarian tension.[96]

Czechoslovakia, therefore, presented the Hungarian leadership with a genuine dilemma. They were sympathetic with the democratization process since its success would vindicate and support their own reforms. There was no threat to the existence of the Budapest regime, as in the case of Warsaw, and perhaps East Berlin, from the achievement of Czechoslovak reform, and as far as is known, no power conflict among Hungarian leaders. On the other hand, they were fearful, as time went on, that Prague would go too far and endanger socialism or require Soviet intervention, thus jeopardizing Hungary's own program and their relative independence from Soviet control. The memory of their experience in 1956 was ever present so that the threat of "counterrevolution" in the ČSSR awakened great concern.

Furthermore, a cardinal feature of Kádár's policy was solidarity with the Soviet Union and the other bloc members, demonstrated by his visit to Moscow in July, the renewal of the pact with Poland, and Hungary's leading part in planning the world communist conference. This solidarity was again revealed by their participation in the conferences in Dresden,

[95] Rezsö Nyers, *Társadalmi Szemle*, March 1968, cited in *YICA*, 1969, pp. 417-18.
[96] Tokes, "Hungarian Intellectuals' Reaction," pp. 146, 149, 151.

744

Moscow, Warsaw, and Bratislava, and their endorsement of the policies there adopted. Whether they sought to exert a "moderating influence" on those occasions, or to act as a "modest broker" or "go-between" between Prague and the more hostile bloc capitals cannot at present be documented.[97] When the decision to invade was taken, Hungary had literally no choice but to take part and termed it "unavoidable and necessary."[98]

Bulgaria's participation in the invasion was marginal in scope, but was to be expected owing to her customary complete identification with the USSR in foreign and bloc policy. The cordial relations with Czechoslovakia exemplified in the April visit to Prague by Zhivkov and the renewal of the alliance between the two countries, and the rather belated condemnation of the Prague course by Sofia, suggested that her part in the intervention was primarily a matter of "following the leader." Bulgaria had no immediate concern with developments in Czechoslovakia comparable to that of the GDR, Poland, and Hungary. The reforms represented a threat to Bulgaria only in the long run, if they contributed to the weakening of bloc solidarity and to the general spread of reformist ideas. Nor did the Bulgarians have any fear of West Germany comparable to that of the East Germans and Poles, and stood only to lose if the trend toward normalizing relations with the GFR, especially in the economic sphere, were interrupted. Prague's new course did, however, challenge the generally orthodox and conservative stance of Bulgaria on the nature of socialism and the leading role of the party. The July plenum of the Bulgarian CC proposed changes in almost every sphere of life, including measures to breathe life into the Fatherland Front, the National Assembly, and the trade unions; to further implement the new economic system; and to improve living standards. These were nonetheless modest reforms, still only on paper, and did not alter the essentially harsh nature of the political system, including the highly centralized control of the economy and the official domination of the arts in the spirit of socialist realism.[99]

Ex post facto justification of the intervention followed the familiar lines of pre-occupation polemics and exhibited no wavering on the part of Moscow's allies. The media of all four states explained the need to

[97] Such terms are used by *YICA*, 1969, p. 424; Tokes, "Hungarian Intellectuals' Reaction," p. 147; Gomori, "Hungarian and Polish Attitudes," p. 108, but no supporting evidence is given. See above, chap. xx.

[98] *MIT*, Aug. 21 (*FBIS*, Hungary, Aug. 22). The Politburo is also said to have stated that the decision to intervene had been difficult and had been much debated among party members (Gomori, "Hungarian and Polish Attitudes," p. 109). Tokes, also without giving any source, reports that pro-Dubček proposals by Kádár were turned down in the Politburo at least six times in the summer of 1968 (Tokes, "Hungarian Intellectuals' Reaction," p. 148).

[99] For a review of 1968 in Bulgaria, see *YICA*, 1969, pp. 71-84.

respond to the appeal for "assistance" in order to ward off the threats of counterrevolution at home and of West German imperialist subversion. East German and Polish spokesmen advanced the usual arguments that the WTO's southwestern flank would be exposed to West German and NATO offensive attacks, and thus imperil the defense of the alliance. The Polish army newspaper, quoting the famous phrase that "whoever holds Bohemia holds Europe," charged Bonn with aiming to establish "a military bridge-head" in Czechoslovakia. The decision to intervene was described in the same paper as "a step implementing the alliance obligations."[100] A commentator in the Polish party daily conducted a campaign against Bonn and insisted that Czechoslovakia was planning to adopt a position of neutralization.[101] Top leaders, such as Gomułka and Cyrankiewicz, also emphasized the German danger.[102] But the domestic dangers of counterrevolution were given equal play by all the participating states, which reiterated the familiar claims concerning the threat to the leading role of the party and the perils of "a free play of political forces."[103]

Some nuances of post-invasion polemics were, however, suggestive of certain differences of attitude and motivation. For the East Germans, whose line remained extremely harsh, the cardinal sin of the Czechoslovak party was its "betrayal of Bratislava," in particular the failure to implement the "agreements" reached at Čierna on the political management of the press, radio, and television, and the prohibition of anti-socialist parties and clubs.[104] The Poles also cited the broken promises of Čierna and Bratislava and described them as a maneuver designed to make possible the holding of the party congress and the transformation of the CPCz into a social democratic party. The Slovak congress was the first step in the direction of the elimination of reliable cadres.[105] The Poles added a special note in repeating the pre-invasion theme of the influence of Zionist forces in the Czechoslovak developments.[106]

[100] *Żolnierz Wolności*, Aug. 23 (*FBIS*, Poland, Aug. 30).

[101] T. M. Podkowinski, *Trybuna Ludu*, Aug. 24, 27, Sept. 25.

[102] Speeches of Sept. 1, 8, respectively (Haefs, ed., *Ereignisse*, pp. 217-20). See also Gomułka's speech of Nov. 11 (Remington, ed., *Winter in Prague*, pp. 426-30).

[103] *Polityka*, Aug. 31; *TL*, Sept. 13.

[104] See the joint statement of the SED Central Committee, Council of State, and Council of Ministers (*ND*, Aug. 21) and an editorial and long article, ibid., Aug. 25. Cf. Karl-Eduard von Schnitzler, on East Berlin television, Aug. 21 (Haefs, ed., *Ereignisse*, pp. 204-5). The charge was repeated by Ulbricht in his addresses in late October (*ND*, Oct. 18, 25).

[105] *TL*, Aug. 21, 22; also *Życie Warszawy*, Aug. 23. See also *TL*, Nov. 3 (*FBIS*, East Europe, Nov. 25) and A. Reisz, East Berlin radio, Aug. 21 (*FBIS*, East Germany, Aug. 22).

[106] Gen. Jan Czapla, *TL*, Aug. 25 (reprinted in *Żolnierz Wolności*, Aug. 26); C. Berenda, *TL*, Sept. 2; Moczar, Sept. 15, cited by Weydenthal, *Polish Politics and*

The Hungarian attitude was somewhat more defensive. L. Fehér, deputy Prime Minister and Politburo member, in an interview on radio and television on August 30, placed the usual stress on Hungary's sympathy with Prague's reforms and the "hopes" engendered by Bratislava, but defended the Hungarian participation in familiar terms, especially the danger of a repetition of 1956. Admitting that Hungarian information might be considered "one-sided," he argued that it had been "authentic" and that the Western radio, which had been widely listened to, had been "lying propaganda."[107] Official organs made serious efforts to assure the people that Hungary's own moderate course toward socialist democracy would not be affected by the August events.[108] Kádár addressed a joint meeting of the government and the party CC on August 23, but his speech was not reported, and he did not speak publicly for two months. Then on October 24, he justified the invasion with the customary phrases about the danger of counterrevolution and the threat to the security of the socialist countries.[109]

DIVERSITY OF COMMUNIST REACTIONS

Of the ruling communist parties in Europe (other than the CPCz and the "five") three—Rumania, Yugoslavia, and Albania—instantly condemned the invasion as unjustified aggression and did not change their viewpoint during ensuing weeks and months. Consistent with their earlier attitudes to Czechoslovak reform, both Ceauşescu and Tito proclaimed their solidarity with the Dubček regime. Albania was unique in repudiating both Prague and Moscow.

The Rumanian response was immediate and categorical. On August 21 a joint session of the party's CC, the State Council, and the government, attended by delegates from many organizations and the press, endorsed a declaration describing the invasion as "a flagrant violation of the national sovereignty of a fraternal, socialist, free and independent state, of the principles on which the relations of socialist countries are based and of the universally recognized norms of international law." Nothing could justify this interference in the internal affairs of Czechoslovakia; the only solution was the speedy withdrawal of troops. This declaration was read at a highly emotional mass rally in Bucharest, attended by thousands and addressed by Ceauşescu, who announced

---

the Czechoslovak Crisis in 1968, p. 53. Neues Deutschland was also reported to have alleged that Zionists had taken over the party (ND, Aug. 25; YICA, p. 345).
[107] FBIS, Hungary, Sept. 3. See also J. Fock, Sept. 25, 1968 (BBC, II, Sept. 27).
[108] Népszabadság, Sept. 1, 22.   [109] BBC, II, Oct. 26.

the formation of armed patriotic guards to defend Rumania's independence.[110]

On the next day at the Great National Assembly Ceaușescu reiterated his unambiguous position, rejecting the argument that the invasion could be called "international assistance." The assembly's proclamation, which was transmitted to all governments and to the United Nations, described the Warsaw treaty as "an instrument of defense . . . against external aggression, against imperialist attack," which could "in no case or in no form . . . be used for military action against a socialist country." A decision about the stationing of foreign troops was a matter within the jurisdiction of the parliament of each country, and any violation of this principle should be considered by the United Nations.[111]

On August 24 Ceaușescu met with Tito in Vrsac in Yugoslavia near the common frontier. In ensuing days, Ceaușescu bent every effort to mobilize the nation for a possible Soviet attack in speeches at various cities throughout the country and in Bucharest. Repeating his condemnation of the invasion, he also asserted his desire and his hope to maintain good relations and cooperation with the Soviet Union and all other socialist countries. After the conclusion of the Czechoslovak-Soviet negotiations in Moscow, the Rumanian party's executive committee again stated that the only solution lay in "the complete withdrawal of troops in the shortest possible time."

Yugoslav reaction was no less emphatic in its denunciation of the invasion. Although on August 21 Tito expressed only his concern, on the following day a government declaration portrayed the action of Moscow and its allies as "the grossest violation of the sovereignty and territorial integrity of an independent country and a direct disregard of generally recognized international law and the UN Charter." The declaration stated that there could be no justification for this military intervention and demanded "the withdrawal of the occupiers and respect for the independence and territorial integrity of Czechoslovakia." This document was transmitted to the United Nations with a request that it be circulated among the members. On the same day, a huge mass rally in Belgrade heard a sharp condemnation of the invasion by M. Todorović, who described it as an action that had "dishonored the proletarian red flag."[112]

110 *Scînteia*, Aug. 22 (Remington, ed., *Winter in Prague*, pp. 358-61). For an eyewitness report of the rally, see E. B. Warnstrom, in Czerwinski and Piekalkiewicz, eds., *Soviet Invasion*, pp. 164-66.

111 For the following, Haefs, ed., *Ereignisse*, pp. 230-32; RFE, East Europe, nos. 21-22, 26, 29 (Aug. 22, 23, 26, Sept. 1). On Aug. 23 Ceaușescu held talks with Ota Šik.

112 For this and the following, see W. Sichel, in Czerwinski and Piekalkiewicz, eds., *Soviet Invasion*, pp. 174-77; Haefs, ed., *Ereignisse*, pp. 234-45; Remington, ed., *Winter in Prague*, pp. 358 (n. 5), 361-67; RFE, Yugoslavia, Aug. 22, 23, 28,

At a meeting of the Central Committee of the LCY on August 23 Tito ridiculed the argument that there had been danger of an invasion of Czechoslovakia by West German and NATO forces and charged that the occupation had been designed to prevent developments in other socialist countries similar to those in Czechoslovakia. The resolution adopted included a strong protest against the exercise of "brute force . . . against the independence of a socialist country" and denied that it could be justi-fied either by "counterrevolution" or "any strategic interests," or by "ideological arguments" based on Marxism-Leninism. The resolution contended that the intervention was a manifestation of "bureaucratic statism" and "a big-power hegemonic policy of monopolism and national inequality"; and an illustration of the dangers of "the policy of blocs" and "spheres of interest." It demanded the immediate termination of the occupation and declared the resolve "to use all our forces and means to defend our independence, revolution, and our own way of socialist development."

In the days that followed, Yugoslavia took a number of measures to strengthen her own defenses, including the formation of civilian brigades and an increase in the defense budget. When the Yugoslav viewpoint was sharply criticized by the media of the Soviet Union and other bloc coun-tries, the Yugoslavs reiterated their condemnation of Soviet aggression. The Moscow agreement was criticized by *Borba* (Aug. 28) as a com-promise concluded under conditions of occupation and not likely to be lasting.

Albania's reaction was consistent with her earlier condemnation of both the Soviet and Czechoslovak parties. A joint declaration by the CC of the Albanian Party of Labor and the Council of Ministers on August 22 condemned the "fascist-type aggression . . . the most flagrant violation of the principle of the freedom and sovereignty of the peoples" which converted the Warsaw treaty from "a treaty of defense against imperial-ist aggression" into "an aggressive treaty against the socialist countries themselves." At the same time the statement denounced "the betrayal and capitulation by the Czechoslovak revisionist leadership" and pledged solidarity and support for the Czechoslovak people in their struggle against the invaders.[113]

The August events produced a number of shifts in Albania's diplo-matic and military policy. The most significant was the decision formally to withdraw from the Warsaw Treaty Organization from which she had been excluded de facto since 1961. Mehmet Shehu, chairman of the

30, Sept. 4. The CC resolution was broadcast on Aug. 25 and published in *Borba*, Aug. 26.

[113] Text in Remington, ed., *Winter in Prague*, pp. 329-31. For the following, see also Haefs, ed., *Ereignisse*, pp. 232-35.

Council of Ministers, in justifying this action before the Popular Assembly on September 12, complained that Albania had not been invited to WTO meetings since 1961 and that the organization's forces had been transformed into "component parts of the armed forces of the Soviet Union," dominated as it was by a Soviet commander and Soviet officers. Shehu denounced the "shameful capitulation of the Dubček revisionist clique" and their willingness to "perform the functions of a collaborationist and quisling government carrying out the orders dictated by the occupationist." The acquiescence of the USA in the invasion demonstrated anew the existence of "a U.S.-Soviet counterrevolutionary alliance for the domination of the world."[114] Meanwhile Albania began to strengthen its military defenses, including its military links with China, which had approved the withdrawal from WTO and had pledged support for Albania. Albania even relaxed its polemics against Yugoslavia.[115]

The governing communist parties in Asia had taken little interest in events in Czechoslovakia. Three of them (Mongolia, North Korea, and North Vietnam) added their voices to the chorus of approval of Soviet action. On the other hand, the Chinese position, set forth by the New China News Agency (Hsinhua) on August 22 and by a commentator in the party organ, Jen-min Jih-pao, on August 23 was identical with that of Albania, condemning Moscow and Prague as rival "revisionist renegade cliques." The invasion was carried through by the USSR in order to prevent the attempts of the Dubček clique to achieve independence and thus to ward off a "chain reaction" threatening the disintegration of the Soviet bloc in Eastern Europe. The invasion was carried out with the connivance of U.S. imperialism with which the Soviet Union was linked in an unholy alliance to divide the world. The invasion was "a crime against the Czechoslovak people." The "Dubček clique," however, received no sympathy from the Chinese, who criticized them for failing to adopt a policy of armed struggle against the invaders. The Moscow communiqué was "a dirty deal . . . made at the point of the bayonet."[116]

The Cuban position resembled the Chinese and Albanian in condemning Czechoslovak revisionism and similar tendencies in other so-

[114] Published in pamphlet form, On the Stand of the People's Republic of Albania Toward the Warsaw Treaty (Tirana, 1968), esp. pp. 13, 22, 27-29, 36.

[115] P. R. Prifti, Albanian Realignment?: A Potential By-Product of Soviet Invasion of Czechoslovakia (MIT, International Communism Project, Oct. 1968), pp. 7, 11; Prifti, "Albania and the Sino-Soviet Conflict," SCC 6 (Autumn 1973), 249-50.

[116] For the Hsinhua statement, see Haefs, ed., Ereignisse, pp. 245-46; for the commentary, Remington, ed., Winter in Prague, pp. 326-28; for an analysis of both and of other statements (esp. Jen-min Jih-pao, Aug. 30), see "Chinese Reactions to the Invasion of Czechoslovakia," SCC 2 (Jan. 1969), 115-24. See also YICA, 1969, pp. 162-63. For the other Asian parties, YICA, 1969, pp. 537-38, 603, 891.

cialist countries, but differed in endorsing the Soviet intervention, albeit with substantial reservations as to its legality. In a major address in Havana on August 23 Fidel Castro expressed the conviction that Czechoslovakia was "heading toward a counterrevolutionary situation, toward capitalism, and into the arms of imperialism."[117] The action taken by the five socialist countries was therefore "necessary to prevent this from happening at any cost, in one way or another." The socialist bloc, facing the danger of "the breakdown of a socialist country and its fall into the arms of imperialism . . . has the right to prevent it in one way or another." Nevertheless, this was a "flagrant" violation of Czechoslovak sovereignty which "cannot be justified from a legal standpoint," Castro admitted. Yet "the right of sovereignty . . . has to give way to the more important interest—the rights of the world revolutionary movement and of the people's struggle against imperialism."

Castro's view of the "inexorable necessity" of this "drastic and painful remedy" was based on his extremely negative attitude to Czechoslovakia's course, especially the "liberal" economic reform, the weakening of the leading role of the party, and the establishment of bourgeois "freedom" of the press. He criticized plans for credits from West Germany and the economic infiltration of Western imperialism. At the same time, Castro waxed indignant about developments in the other socialist countries, which, after twenty years of communism, had produced a "relaxation of the revolutionary spirit," bureaucratic methods of leadership, and neglect of communist ideals. "We acknowledge the bitter necessity that called for the sending of these forces into Czechoslovakia; we do not condemn the socialist countries that made that decision. But we, as revolutionaries, have the right to demand that they adopt a consistent position. . . ." Would Warsaw pact divisions be sent to Cuba if there were an attack by the Yankee imperialists?

The non-ruling communist parties throughout the world lined up on both sides of the issue, the majority supporting the action taken by Moscow and its allies, but a significant minority, including most of the European, opposing the invasion, although with varying degrees of intensity. One analysis identified thirty-five parties (including the Cuban, North Korean, Mongolian, and North Vietnamese) as being pro-invasion and eighteen (including Albania, Rumania, China, and Yugoslavia), as anti-invasion.[118] In North America, the United States party, after initial hesi-

---

[117] Full text, *Gramma* (Havana, in English), Aug. 25; partial text in Remington, ed., *Winter in Prague*, pp. 334-44.

[118] *Prag und die Linke* (Hamburg, 1968), pp. 137-38. For the standpoints of the parties, see, *inter alia, YICA*, 1969, passim; Haefs, ed., *Ereignisse*, p. 250; Pelikán, in Kusin, ed., *Czechoslovak Reform*, pp. 305-15; Kevin Devlin, "The New Crisis in European Communism," *PC* 17 (Nov.-Dec. 1968), 57-68; L. Labedz, "Czechoslovakia and After," *Survey*, no. 69 (Oct. 1968), pp. 13-21.

tation, approved the invasion, whereas the Canadian changed its original ambiguous position to one of support. Most of the Latin American parties approved Moscow's action, but Mexico dissented. In Asia, the strong Japanese party opposed the intervention; others (including Burma, Malaya, Indonesia, Thailand, and New Zealand) supported the Chinese position; one, the Australian, strongly opposed the invasion; another, the Indian, adopted a position of compromise. In the Middle East, the Arab parties and the pro-Soviet Israeli party (Rakach) approved Soviet action, whereas the other Israeli party (Maki) condemned it.

More significant than the approval of a Soviet action by a majority of the parties on a world scale was the fact that the majority of the European parties were opposed, especially the powerful Italian and French. Sanction was given only by communist parties in West Germany and West Berlin, the exiled Greek and Portuguese, and the tiny Luxemburg group. Certain European parties, notably the Italian, Austrian, and Swedish, revived the idea of a conference of West European parties as a means of supporting the Czechoslovak regime, and numerous interparty discussions took place on this issue. In the end, and especially after the French CP's negative statement on October 11, nothing came of this initiative.

The Italian party was more or less united in adopting one of the strongest statements in opposition to the Soviet action, describing it as "unjustified" and proclaiming full solidarity with the Czech policy of "renovation." Luigi Longo, who was in Moscow at the time of the Politburo meeting, elaborated his position in an interview in early September, in which he expressly repudiated the danger of counterrevolution and denied "the right of intervening militarily in the internal affairs of another communist party and another country."[119] He strongly defended the autonomy of each party and the independence of each country and the right of each party to follow its own path, in the Italian case, an "Italian path to socialism."

The French party, on the other hand, was less forthright. Initial declarations of the Politburo and the Central Committee disapproved of the intervention, but at the same time expressed concern over anti-socialist forces and proclaimed continuing solidarity with the CPSU. When the distinguished philosopher, Roger Garaudy, a Politburo member and a protagonist of the Czechoslovak course, expressed views critical of the revival of Stalinism in the Soviet party, he received a reprimand at the Central Committee in October, but this plenum reiterated the party's opposition to the intervention and censured Jeannette Vermeersch,

---

[119] Politburo statement, *L'Unità*, Aug. 22; Longo, at CC, ibid., Aug. 25; his interview with *L'Astrolabio*, in *L'Unità*, Sept. 8 (Remington, ed., *Winter in Prague*, pp. 331-32, 346-56, resp.).

widow of Thorez and a strong advocate of Moscow's action, who resigned from the Politburo.[120]

DISSIDENCE IN THE INVADING STATES

A number of courageous individuals in the countries participating in the occupation publicly expressed their opposition and were severely penalized for their actions. It is, of course, impossible to know whether these demonstrations or letters of protest were but isolated acts of defiance, or whether they represented the tip of an iceberg of widespread public disaffection, especially among the intellectuals. They deserve recording as illustrations of the refusal of at least some citizens to endorse the aggression committed by their governments.

The most notable was the demonstration in the Red Square in Moscow on August 25. Seven persons, bearing banners which expressed their solidarity with Czechoslovakia and protested Soviet intervention, quietly sat down in the midst of the square until they were carried off, within a matter of minutes, by the security police. Among them was Pavel Litvinov, grandson of the former Soviet foreign minister, a physicist and prominent dissenter, and Larisa Bogoraz-Daniel, wife of the dissenting writer, Yuli Daniel. The subsequent trial of five of them led to written protests by other individual citizens, including a joint letter to the Supreme Soviet by ninety-five persons, among them the well-known Soviet writer, Viktor Nekrasov.[121] Other letters expressing dissatisfaction with the invasion and solidarity with Czechoslovakia were also circulated in *samizdat* during the later months of 1968 and 1969.[122] There are reports of protests by the well-known dissenters, Ivan Yakhimovich and Gen. Pyotr Grigorenko, a letter from more than eighty Soviet writers to Prague, and an appeal to the UN Human Rights Commission by fifty-five persons, including Pyotr Yakir. The prominent Soviet poet, Yevgeny Yevtushenko, is reported to have written to Kosygin and Brezhnev deploring the Soviet action. Even more significant, if true, were letters of protest by some 800 party organizations and the refusal of many workers and intellectuals (including Aleksandr Tvardovsky, K. Simonov, and

[120] Haefs, ed., *Ereignisse*, pp. 247-48; Remington, ed., *Winter in Prague*, pp. 332-34. Cf. the strong pro-Czech stand by Leo Figuères, *Politika* (Prague), Oct. 24, pp. 42-43.

[121] For this event and the aftermath, see Natalia Gorbanevskaya, *Red Square at Noon* (New York, 1970); for a letter by her, and the final trial statements by Bogoraz-Daniel and Litvinov, *PC* 17 (Sept.-Oct. 1968), 63-65; for the letter of the ninety-five, *NYT*, Dec. 4, 1968.

[122] A. Boiter and P. Dornan, eds., *Register of Samizdat* (Munich[?], 1971), RO 93, RO 79, RO 69, RO 95, R 146, R 288, R 264, R 327. See also *Chronicle of Current Events*, no. 3 (Aug. 31, 1968); *NYT*, Oct. 20, Dec. 29, 1968; March 7, 27, April 13, June 4, 1969.

L. Leonov) to sign letters supporting the Soviet action.[123] In the Ukraine, it has been reported, many intellectuals and students did not accept the official explanation of the invasion and few prominent personalities were willing to endorse it publicly.[124]

Opposition has also been documented in the other invading countries, usually involving small groups of intellectuals or students, and in some cases workers. In Poland, for instance, the prominent writer, J. Andrzejewski, penned a letter of protest, published in Yugoslavia and France.[125] In the GDR, there were youth demonstrations, letters of protest, and visits of condolence to the Czechoslovak embassy in East Berlin. There were also reports of refusal by workers to sign letters approving the invasion. In trials in late October, seven young persons who had taken part in the demonstrations were charged with "anti-state incitement" and given heavy sentences. The Marxist philosopher, Ernst Bloch, published abroad a strong statement denouncing the action that turned Czechoslovakia into "a new Russian colony."[126] As for Hungary, five Hungarian participants in the annual *Praxis* conference in Korcula, Yugoslavia (three from the Philosophical Institute, and two from the Sociological Research group), signed a joint declaration condemning the invasion. In addition, Andreas Hegedüs, sociologist and former political leader, and György Lukács were reported to have protested the invasion.[127] Even in Bulgaria there was opposition by writers, a fact that was revealed only years later in a speech by Zhivkov.[128]

WESTERN RESPONSE: NATO AND THE UN

The reaction of Western governments consisted of sharp verbal condemnation of the invasion but did not include acts of retaliation or any serious change in the policy of détente with the Soviet Union.[129] In the

[123] Shub, *An Empire Loses Hope*, pp. 423-28; Tigrid, *Why Dubček Fell*, pp. 97-98; Levine, *Intervention*, pp. 123-28. For Yevtushenko's letter, see *PC* 17 (Sept.-Oct. 1968), p. 65.

[124] Hodnett and Potichnyj, *The Ukraine and the Czechoslovak Crisis*, pp. 104-5, 109-10.

[125] *Borba*, Sept. 26 (*YICA*, 1969, pp. 692-93); *Le Monde*, Sept. 27 (Weydenthal, "Polish Politics," p. 49).

[126] On the demonstrations and trials, *NYT*, Sept. 10, Oct. 24, 26, 30; *YICA*, 1969, pp. 345-46; on Bloch, Haefs, ed., *Ereignisse*, p. 250. One of the sentenced was the son of Prof. R. Havemann, scientist and dissident.

[127] Tokes, in Czerwinski and Piekalkiewicz, eds., *Soviet Invasion*, pp. 140-48; Gomori, ibid., pp. 110-13. Tokes reports a letter from Lukács, but Gomori casts doubt on this. Both Tokes and Gomori agree that there was no organized opposition by intellectuals or students.

[128] Zhivkov, April 1-2, 1974 (RFE, Bulgaria, April 26, 1974).

[129] For Western reactions, see Barton and Martin, in Henderson, ed., *Public Diplomacy*, pp. 265-68; Haefs, ed., *Ereignisse*, pp. 251-55, 267-76; Campbell, "Czechoslovakia," *CSP* 10 (Winter 1968), 19-20.

United States, President Johnson, on August 21, expressed his shock at the open breach of the UN Charter and called on the Soviet Union to withdraw its troops from Czechoslovakia. The State Department denied allegations that the United States had informed the Soviet Union beforehand that it was "indifferent" or that Washington's attitude reflected an acceptance of spheres of influence allegedly agreed upon at Yalta. Only later, on August 30, when the danger of an invasion of Rumania seemed acute, did Johnson react more strongly, expressing regret over the action in Czechoslovakia, which indicated, he said, that the Moscow leaders "felt that their interests were threatened by the emergence of even modest degrees of national independence and human liberty in Eastern Europe." Without specific mention of Rumania, he warned that "there would be no condoning of aggressors" and that "no one should unleash the dogs of war." On the same day Dean Rusk called in the Soviet ambassador, but the nature of the conversation remains unknown. It was later announced (Aug. 31) that the United States was reviewing with its allies the implications of Soviet action for their common security and, a week later (Sept. 6), that "some assurances" had been received. These statements were accompanied by decisions to put off the projected summit meeting between the Moscow and Washington leaders, to postpone also the strategic arms talks, and to delay the Senate's ratification of the nuclear test ban treaty. Certain other minor actions were taken, but nothing suggested that the desire to maintain good relations with the USSR and to continue the pursuit of détente had been in any way abandoned, or that the hope of eventual success had been seriously shaken.

Needless to say, among all the countries of NATO, the massive incursion of Soviet troops into Czechoslovakia created concern that the military balance had been significantly altered, severely strained confidence in the rationality and peacefulness of the Soviet leaders, and raised doubts concerning the possibility of détente. It also stirred up fears of the possibility of aggression against West Germany for which the invasion of Czechoslovakia was perhaps a preparatory step. The British, French, and West German official statements condemned the invasion as an intervention in the internal affairs of Czechoslovakia and as contrary to international law and the provisions of the Charter, and expressed concern as to its harmful effects on European security and détente, but also reasserted the desirability of a policy of conciliation aimed at attaining this goal. A West German proposal of an immediate NATO summit meeting was endorsed by some, including the British, but was not acted upon. West Germany was particularly concerned by the USSR's contention, expressed in its note of July 5, and reiterated in official radio and press statements in September, that it had the right, under the Potsdam treaty and the UN Charter, to intervene by force against the former

755

"enemy state" if its policy became aggressive. This claim was strongly denied by West Germany and by the United States and the other major European governments.[130] NATO presumably gave no consideration to the possibility of military intervention to counter the Soviet invasion, and did not even take any serious precautionary measures, such as an "alert" of its forces. Nonetheless, the intervention reinforced, in the minds of its members, the necessity of the organization's existence and impelled them to give serious thought as to how to maintain or increase its defensive strength. At a meeting of the Defense Planning Committee on September 4 it was agreed that no reduction or withdrawals of forces should take place. Two months later, at the Brussels meeting of the NATO council in November, the members agreed on the need to improve the state of their preparedness and each promised certain modest measures toward that end. Although the Czechoslovak events were admittedly a setback, it was stressed that European reconciliation was still the goal. Indirectly responding to the Brezhnev doctrine, the November communiqué urged the Soviet Union "to refrain from using force and interfering in the affairs of other states," and warned that "any Soviet intervention . . . in Europe or in the Mediterranean would create an international crisis with grave consequences."[131]

The role of the United Nations, in the immediate aftermath of the invasion, was not unlike that of the Western powers. It provided a forum for strong denunciation of the action taken by the "five" invading states but did not take, or even consider, any more effective or forceful measures.[132] The Secretary General, Kurt Waldheim, limited his participation to a statement deploring the use of force and the setback to détente and announcing the cancellation of a European trip, which had included a visit to Prague on the 22nd.[133]

A meeting of the Security Council was convened on August 21, not, however, at the request of Czechoslovakia but of a group of Western countries, including the USA, the United Kingdom, France, and Canada.

[130] Haefs, ed., *Ereignisse*, pp. 262-67; Wolfe, *Soviet Power*, pp. 414-18. In spite of rejections of the so-called right of intervention by all major Western governments, the Soviet press reiterated the claim (*Pravda*, Sept. 18, and *Izvestia*, Sept. 19, 20).

[131] On NATO reactions, see Wolfe, *Soviet Power*, pp. 407-14; James, ed., *Czechoslovak Crisis*, pp. 82-91; Andrew Pierre, in Zartman, ed., *Czechoslovakia*, pp. 59-83.

[132] A useful summary of UN discussions is given in A. G. Mezerik, *Invasion and Occupation of Czechoslovakia and the UN* (*International Review Service* 14, no. 100, New York, 1968). For verbatim report, see United Nations, Security Council, 1968, S/PV, 1441-45. See also James, ed., *Czechoslovak Crisis*, chap. 5; Haefs, ed., *Ereignisse*, pp. 255-61; *Sedm dnů*, pp. 481-94.

[133] See his regretful but not very forceful statements concerning Czechoslovakia in late September (Mezerik, pp. 64-66).

The Soviet effort to block discussion on the grounds that the "government" of that country had requested assistance was unsuccessful, with thirteen members voting to proceed, as against two (the USSR and Hungary) who opposed.

A long and highly polemical debate followed, lasting for four days, based on a resolution introduced by seven members (Brazil, Canada, Denmark, France, Paraguay, the UK, and the USA) condemning the "armed intervention in the internal affairs" of Czechoslovakia as a violation of the Charter and calling for withdrawal of the outside forces forthwith. The Soviet delegate, Mr. Yakov Malik, developed the theme of "imperialist machinations" against Czechoslovakia and cited in full the "appeal" for help published in the Soviet press. In his view the action had also been justified by the threat to the balance of forces in Europe and to the Western borders of the socialist community, as well as by the danger of counterrevolutionary forces. He made a point of expressing Soviet support for the January course and promised the withdrawal of forces as soon as the danger to socialism and to security had been dispelled. Malik described the matter as "an utterly internal affair of the Czechoslovak Socialist Republic and the common cause and affair of its partners in the socialist community under the Warsaw treaty" and denied the UN any right to discuss it. Similar views were expressed by the representative of Hungary, a member of the Council, and by those of Bulgaria and the German Democratic Republic, who, after long procedural discussions, were permitted to take part in the debate. Most of the other countries condemned the intervention and cast doubt on the authenticity of the so-called request. A representative of Czechoslovakia, Jan Mužík, a member of its UN mission in New York, described the situation in Czechoslovakia in the words of official statements by the government and National Assembly and denied that there had been a request for assistance. The outcome was an overwhelming vote in favor of the resolution, ten countries supporting it (Brazil, Canada, China, Denmark, Ethiopia, France, Paraguay, Senegal, the UK, and the USA), two opposing (USSR and Hungary), and three abstaining (Algeria, India, and Pakistan). The Soviet negative vote constituted a veto preventing adoption.

The debate continued on another resolution initiated by Canada requesting the Secretary General to send a Special Representative to Prague to seek the release and ensure the personal safety of the detained Czechoslovak leaders. This made it possible, late on Saturday, August 24, for Jiří Hájek, Czechoslovak foreign minister, who had just arrived in New York, to present a long statement as a member of the Czechoslovak government. "This act of use of force cannot be justified by anything," he declared, citing the declarations of party and government organs and expressing doubt that any demand for assistance was

757

ever made. In his exposition Hájek expressed himself positively both with regard to socialism and the alliance with the Soviet Union and denied the alleged danger of counterrevolution or any serious threat to socialism. He spoke, he said, "with sadness, but without hostility," in the belief that "this fateful act was done on the basis of incorrect consideration, incorrect information, incorrect analysis of the situation." Admitting that anti-socialist forces were present, he argued that Prague had not underestimated them and would have been able to resist them "through wide popular initiative," and where necessary, by "administrative steps." The occupation itself had contributed more than anything else to the growth of anti-socialist attitudes of a part of the population.

By this time the Moscow talks had already begun, resulting in a message from the Czechoslovak government stating that the Czechoslovak representative would no longer participate in the debate and that further discussion would not contribute to a solution of the problem. After the conclusion of the Moscow talks Czechoslovakia requested the withdrawal of the matter from the agenda, thus foreclosing further consideration or action. In the proceedings of the General Assembly which followed there was no specific discussion of Czechoslovakia, although the issue was raised in a number of speeches. Andrei Gromyko, in his address, implicitly evoked the Brezhnev doctrine by expressing the determination of the Soviet Union to preserve the socialist commonwealth at any cost. Both the American Secretary of State, Dean Rusk, and the British Foreign Secretary, Michael Stewart, declared that this attitude was in conflict with the basic principles of the Charter.

The United Nations, it has been said, acquitted itself reasonably effectively and offered at least a forum and a sounding board for the postoccupation discussion of the crisis.[134] Others have been more critical of the inaction of the UN, especially of the Secretary General.[135] By the nature of things, the UN was prevented by the Soviet veto power from taking any significant action and was hindered in prolonging discussion by the post-Moscow attitude of the Czechoslovak government. As a result, no effort was made to investigate the further development of the situation, so that even less was done than in the Hungarian crisis in 1956.

[134] Mezerik, p. 72; James, ed., *Czechoslovak Crisis*, p. 109.
[135] Barton and Martin, in Henderson, ed., *Public Diplomacy*, pp. 269-70.

CHAPTER XXII

Resistance and Capitulation

IN THE DAYS, weeks, and months following the invasion, there was a paradoxical medley of resistance and capitulation. The Presidium, in its fateful meeting during the night of August 20-21, did not even discuss the possibility of violent resistance. Its declaration, approved after midnight, noted that the army, security corps, and People's Militia had not been given the order to defend the country and called on the people not to oppose the invading troops "since the defense of our state frontiers is now impossible." The declaration, after condemning the invasion, called on all functionaries to remain at their posts and announced that meetings of the National Assembly, the government, and the Central Committee would be held.[1] This and the President's subsequent command to the armed forces not to resist the invading armies represented a capitulation in the sense of rejecting opposition by violent means. For the second time in a generation a well-trained Czechoslovak army surrendered to an outside force without firing a shot. Whether other forms of nonviolent resistance, political in character, would be attempted by the leaders remained to be seen. Simultaneously with this act of military surrender by the authorities there occurred a spontaneous outburst of nonviolent resistance by the population which clearly revealed the repudiation of the invasion by almost all Czechs and Slovaks. The holding of the 14th Party Congress, and meetings of the National Assembly and the government, demonstrated the unwillingness of the principal political institutions to reconcile themselves to the occupation and undermined efforts to form a government of collaboration. With these organs temporarily incapacitated by the arrest of their leading officers, the heavy burden of deciding what to do fell on the shoulders of the President, as he stated later in his address to the CC plenum on August 31. He faced a cruel dilemma—"whether to capitulate and accept any kind of solution that offered itself"—a course "ruled out by honor and conscience and my

---

[1] For English text, P. Windsor and A. Roberts, *Czechoslovakia, 1968* (London, 1969), pp. 174-75. According to them, the final phrase concerning the impossibility of defending the state frontiers was added only in later broadcasts. For the Czech text (including the phrase), *Sedm pražských dnů, 21.-27. srpen 1968* (Prague, Sept. 1968), p. 6. The phrase was omitted in later official published texts, e.g. *Rok šedesátý osmý* (Prague, 1968), p. 297.

For declarations of loyalty to Svoboda by General Dzúr and the Ministry of National Defense, BBC, II, Aug. 23. The People's Militia, in a letter of support for Dubček and Svoboda, declared that they would follow the instruction of the CC Presidium for the armed forces (*RP*, Aug. 25).

responsibility to the nation"—or "to resign"—"the simplest course but one which would have resulted in bloodshed and massacre." He chose a third course, which in fact embodied elements of resistance and capitulation. Refusing to endorse the formation of a government of collaboration, he decided to negotiate directly with the Soviet rulers in Moscow— a step which implied a willingness to reach some kind of settlement through compromise and in fact, as the Moscow talks soon revealed, opened the way to capitulation and collaboration in a different form.

THE FIASCO OF COLLABORATION ATTEMPTS

It has often been remarked that whereas the military side of the invasion was carefully prepared and eminently successful, the political side was unprepared and led to an initial debacle. There is little doubt that the Soviet authorities assumed that there would be widespread support among Czechs and Slovaks for their action and that a new government of collaboration would be formed at the time of the invasion.[2] This was suggested by the reference in the *Pravda* editorial of August 22 to the Dubček minority in the Presidium and the publication on the same day of the "appeal" for help. It was still more clearly implied by the immediate arrest of the Prime Minister, Černík, in his office; the arrest of Dubček, Smrkovský, Kriegel, and Špaček at CC headquarters; and the failure to apprehend other leading figures, such as Kolder, Bil'ak, and Indra.[3] It is not known with any certainty whether these three and other leading persons were informed beforehand of the invasion and were consulted as to the formation of an alternative government ready to welcome (or invite) the entry of troops.[4] It seems beyond doubt, however, that the

[2] On collaboration attempts, see, inter alia, *Sedm dnů*; M. Tatu, *L'hérésie impossible* (Paris, 1968), esp. pp. 250-56 (from *Le Monde*, Sept. 6); P. Tigrid, *Why Dubček Fell* (London, 1971), pp. 101 ff.; H. Brahm, *Der Kreml und die ČSSR, 1968-1969* (Stuttgart, 1970), pp. 81-84; M. Vaculík's report to the 14th congress in J. Pelikán, ed., *Tanky proti sjezdu* (Vienna, 1970), pp. 34-37; J. Piller, *Rudé právo*, Sept. 17, 1969; Tad Szulc, *Czechoslovakia Since World War II* (New York, 1971).

[3] Dubček, Smrkovský, and Kriegel were seized by a group of Soviet and Czechoslovak security officers who arrived at the CC headquarters sometime after 9 o'clock on August 21. A Czech officer was instructed to announce to Dubček: "You are taken under protection in the name of the revolutionary government headed by comrade Indra." The arrested were taken from the building sometime in the afternoon (*Sedm dnů*, pp. 51, 70). See also *Listy* (May 1971), pp. 32-34. According to an eyewitness, Kolder was allowed to move freely in the CC building (*Průboj*, Aug. 25, 1968). The arrest of Černík in his office was graphically described to the 14th congress by O. Boček, chairman of the Supreme Court, who had also been arrested and then released. For a full account of his detention and transport to the Soviet Union, see Smrkovský's testimony, *Listy*, March 1975, pp. 16-19 (Appendix D).

[4] Smrkovský claimed that Kolder, Indra, and Jakeš knew of the intervention

Soviet leaders expected collaboration and had identified those who were most likely to cooperate.

In this context the final meeting of the Presidium on the night of August 20 awakens strong suspicions of intended collaboration, and perhaps foreknowledge, by Kolder and Indra. Their efforts to have the Kašpar report on the political situation and their own proposals for action discussed *prior* to the report on the preparations for the 14th congress may well have been designed to place Dubček and his supporters in a minority and thus prepare the ground for his replacement as First Secretary, either at that meeting or subsequently.[5] If this had been accomplished during the afternoon or early evening, it would have made possible an open invitation to the Soviet authorities, whose troops were already moving toward the Czechoslovak frontiers. Whether Kolder and Indra were aware of the plan to invade and were preparing the ground for subsequent collaboration and whether the Soviet leaders were also aware of their intentions and counting on a favorable decision as a basis for a new regime, cannot at present be determined. The rejection of Kolder's proposal on the agenda, and the long discussion, first, of the 14th congress preparation and then of the Kolder-Indra proposals, prevented any action prior to the actual crossing of the frontiers. The ensuing debate on the proposed proclamation condemning the invasion was heated and angry but led to its adoption by a majority, with Kolder, Rigo, and Švestka, significantly, voting against.[6]

the day before and that Indra was to form "a revolutionary committee" (*Der Speigel*, Oct. 14, 1968, cited by H. Brahm, *Der Kreml und die ČSSR*, p. 136, n. 92). According to reports, based on information from the CC, given in a joint issue of the Ostrava newspapers on Aug. 29, 1968, Kolder, Indra, Bil'ak, Švestka, and Jakeš had counted on military intervention and a worker-peasant government. They had held a preparatory meeting in Orlík on August 18 and after the invasion participated in talks at the Soviet embassy concerning a new government. This source stated that those who knew of the occupation beforehand included Kolder, Indra, and Jakeš, and their subordinate helpers, M. Sulek, K. Hoffmann, M. Marko, M. Šalgovič, and Gen. O. Rytíř. For denials of collaboration, see above, chap. XXI.

[5] This is the contention of *Rudé právo*, Aug. 23 (*Sedm dnů*, pp. 12-13). According to Tad Szulc, Bil'ak, Kolder, Švestka, Indra, and Kapek all knew precisely when the invasion was to start, and assured the Kremlin that a resolution removing Dubček would be approved by the Presidium, that Indra would invite the Warsaw pact forces to save socialism, and that a pro-Soviet regime would be formed (*Czechoslovakia*, pp. 367-68, 372-73). According to J. Ruml's account Švestka, Kolder, and Indra, with Lenárt and Jakeš, had met earlier at Orlík to prepare the attack on Dubček. He also stated that General Dzúr knew of the impending invasion but was interned in his office. See British Broadcasting Corporation, Monitoring Service, *Summary of World Broadcasts*, II (Eastern Europe), Aug. 28; henceforth cited as BBC. For the entire episode see chap. XI above.

[6] According to Švestka their main objection was to the third paragraph describing the invasion as an "aggression" contrary to international law, which, he said, a year later, could have led to resistance and struggle, whereas it was "necessary to

The attempt to arrange some degree of collaboration with the occupying authorities, and to form a government in this spirit, was not abandoned during the twenty-four hours after the invasion. The events surrounding these efforts are, however, still clouded in uncertainty and can be documented only in part. What is known, with assurance, is that during the afternoon and evening of the first post-invasion day (Aug. 21) and extending into the night of August 21-22, a gathering of CC members took place in the Hotel Praha, the official party hotel for officials and foreign guests.[7] The exact number or the identity of the participants was not revealed, and little is known of the course of the discussions. Apparently an initial group of twenty-two persons grew to approximately fifty, or about one-third of the total CC membership, including candidates.

According to Martin Vaculík's speech to the 14th congress, as reported in the press, Bil'ak, Barbírek, Kolder, and Indra arrived at the Hotel Praha in the company of Soviet officers who were present throughout the balance of the proceedings. Also according to Vaculík, those who showed themselves most clearly as collaborators were Mestek, V. Nový, Jakeš, Indra, Kolder, and Piller. The latter three were said to have questioned the calling of the party congress and Piller the holding of a full CC meeting on that day.[8] Other delegates charged that Pastyřík, Pavlovský, and Mestek spoke in favor of the Soviet action, whereas others, including Academician Macek, Hrdinová, and Kabrna, urged that the meeting speak "in the language of the people" (i.e. to condemn it).

negotiate with the Soviet representatives." He implied that their negative vote was on this paragraph only (*RP*, Aug. 20, 1969). Indra, as a Secretary, had no vote but was also opposed, and was supported by Sádovský, also a Secretary (*Sedm dnů*, p. 13). According to Smrkovský, the vote was 7 to 4 in favor. Svoboda was present but did not express an opinion (Appendix D).

[7] The meeting was reported, on the basis of newspaper accounts, in *Sedm dnů*, pp. 64-65, 74-75; by M. Vaculík and others at the 14th congress, Pelikán, ed., *Tanky*, pp. 35-52; by J. Piller, in an interview with the regional party organ, *Svoboda*, cited by Tatu, *L'hérésie*, pp. 250-56, and in another interview a year later, *RP*, Sept. 17, 1969.

[8] Piller was said to have introduced a resolution expressing disapproval of the calling of the congress (*Sedm dnů*, p. 74). In his own account Piller reported the presence of three members of the Prague municipal party committee who urged approval of the holding of the congress, and admitted that he was opposed. According to him, a three-man delegation (Bil'ak, Barbírek, and A. Krček) was appointed to attend the congress, if it occurred.

Piller's role during these days remains ambiguous. In an interview with *Rudé právo* (Aug. 21, cyclostyled) he expressed support for Dubček and the legal organs and praised Svoboda with whom he had talked. He said that "negotiations" had already begun and praised talks by party and state organs in Central Bohemia (his own region) with the Soviet units to avoid conflicts and sacrifices. The regional committee later expressed its confidence in Piller (BBC, II, Aug. 29). See Smrkovský's favorable account of Piller's stand (*Listy*, March, 1975, p. 23).

Opinions apparently shifted during the course of the long meeting, perhaps as a result of the presence of Soviet officers. According to Vaculík the members present at an early stage adopted a resolution supporting the Presidium's stand on the invasion and demanding the release of the leaders. In the end a brief communiqué was adopted early in the morning of the 22nd, the content of which was somewhat less forthright and suggested a certain willingness to accept the reality of occupation.[9] Claiming that the Central Committee had met on the call of the Presidium, the communiqué endorsed that body's statement regarding the invasion and called upon all communists and citizens to "maintain unconditionally calm, balance, and responsibility" and thus "to respect the hard reality . . . which it is not possible to change at once." Appealing for "stabilization and normalization of conditions in working places and in localities," the communiqué declared that they would not permit a return to the pre-January conditions and that the Action Program would remain the basis of policy. It was resolved to remain in permanent session and to prepare a regular CC plenum as soon as possible. Then followed an ominous sentence: "Delegated members of the Presidium of the CPCz Central Committee are entering into contact with the commander of the troops of the five countries of the Warsaw treaty with the aim of assuring accelerated normalization." Although Vaculík apparently supported this resolution, he criticized it later (at the congress) for taking the occupation for granted and for ignoring the reality of public indignation and resistance. It was noted in the press that the communiqué made no reference to the release of the imprisoned leaders nor to the withdrawal of the occupying troops nor any mention of the 14th congress. According to the resolution the regional party committees were to follow only CC instructions and to act "in the spirit of these directives." According to the press, however, the committees received instructions to collaborate with the occupying forces.[10]

At some time, either before or after the passage of the resolution at the Hotel Praha, certain persons were apparently in direct contact with the Soviet authorities. Radio broadcasts, on August 22, reported that Indra, Bil'ak, Kolder, and Barbírek, were at the USSR's embassy discussing the formation of a new government. Another report said that Bil'ak, Lenárt, and Pavlovský had been authorized by the Hotel Praha meeting to do this and had reported back to the CC members after their visit. The majority of the Presidium and Secretariat members present were not satisfied and appointed Piller to continue the discussions, which were, according to him, designed to secure the release of the imprisoned

---

[9] The same text is given by Vaculík (Pelíkan, ed., *Tanky*, pp. 35-36) and by Piller (*RP*, Sept. 17, 1969). No names were given as signatories.

[10] Both M. Vaculík and Piller gave the former version of the appeal to the regional committees. For the alleged instructions, *Sedm dnů*, p. 75.

leaders.[11] Whether or not these meetings occurred, and what their purpose was, cannot be determined for want of evidence. If they did occur, they may have culminated in the often-reported visit to the Castle by several leaders, to request Svoboda's approval of the formation of "a government of workers and peasants" under Indra. It is not, however, clear whether this took place in the early morning hours after the Praha meeting, or as some reported, twenty-four hours earlier, on the very morning of the invasion. Accounts vary as to who were the participants and as to whether Svoboda refused to receive them, or summarily rebuffed their proposal.[12] Either before or after, the President had in any case decided to request conversations in Moscow before taking any further action. Although other efforts to form a government of collaboration were made, the meeting at the Castle marked in fact the end of the attempt to find a Czechoslovak leader willing and capable of assuming the responsibility of leadership under Soviet sponsorship, as Kádár had done in Hungary in 1956.

AN EXTRAORDINARY PARTY CONGRESS

The 14th Party Congress, originally scheduled to meet on September 9, in fact met, under truly extraordinary circumstances, on the sec-

[11] Rémi Gueyt, *La mutation tchécoslovaque* (Paris, 1969), pp. 308-9. In his *Svoboda* interview, Piller admitted visiting the embassy and also President Svoboda, but denied that there were any discussions about a new government (Tatu, *L'hérésie*, pp. 253, 255). According to Piller a meeting of the Presidium and Secretariat was held in the morning of the 22nd at which he was entrusted with the direction of the two top organs during Dubček's absence. All members were to associate themselves with discussions for the release of Dubček and to participate in the congress when these efforts had succeeded. Vaculík confirmed that talks were held concerning the release of the imprisoned leaders, but said that these were with the military authorities. Tad Szulc, on the other hand, reported a meeting of a dozen Czechs and Slovaks at the Soviet embassy during the night of Aug. 21-22, which led to the appointment of a troika (Bil'ak, Indra, and Kolder) to run the party and which drew up a list of members of a new government headed by Indra (*Czechoslovakia*, pp. 404-5).

[12] Indra was said to have later (Feb. 17, 1969) confirmed the attempt to constitute a workers' and peasants' government while denying that it was his idea or that he was to head it (Gueyt, *Mutation*, p. 309). Complete confusion reigns as to who visited Svoboda. They were variously reported as Piller and Ambassador Chervonenko, and later in the day, Bil'ak, Kolder, and others (Szulc, *Czechoslovakia*, pp. 405, 412); Indra and O. Pavlovský (Journalist M, *A Year Is Eight Months: Czechoslovakia, 1968*, New York, 1970, p. 170); Indra and Pavlovský, with Chervonenko (Tigrid, *Why Dubček Fell*, pp. 109-10); Indra and Lenárt, with the Soviet General Pavlovsky (Brahm, *Kreml*, p. 81); General Pavlovsky and Ambassador Chervonenko, and later Kolder, Bil'ak, and others (*Sedm dnů*, p. 313). Members of the Indra government, according to various reports, were to include O. Pavlovský, K. Hoffmann, Sulek, General Rytíř, Šalgovič, Chňoupek, Voleník, Švestka, Barbírek, Kolder, and Bil'ak (H. Haefs, ed., *Ereignisse in der Tschechoslowakei*, Bonn, 1969, p. 48; Christian Schmidt-Häuer and Adolf Müller, *Viva Dubček*, Cologne, 1968, p. 113.

ond day of occupation, on Thursday, August 22, at 10:00 a.m. Although it had been publicly announced by press and radio, the assembly took place secretly, in a location successfully hidden from the occupying authorities, in one of the buildings of a very large enterprise in the industrial district of Vysočany. Over 1,000 delegates assembled from all over the Czech part of the Republic, and some from Slovakia, traveling by car and train and by other means of conveyance through the occupied country, and were directed to the hastily improvised meeting place by local and factory party organizations in Prague. Dressed in working-class garb, they entered the factory individually and in the evening, after some eleven hours of hectic proceedings, departed in buses, just prior to the 10:00 p.m. curfew imposed by the occupation authorities.[13]

With the party Presidium partly under arrest, and partly engaged in collaborationist attempts, and with the Central Committee unwilling or unable to gather in full force, the initiative for convoking the congress was taken by the Prague municipal party committee which had been in session from the early morning hours of Wednesday the 21st. As early as 2:00 a.m., barely two to three hours after the first troops had crossed the frontiers, Bohumil Šimon, Prague leading secretary, is reported to have proposed to Dubček (not yet in captivity) the calling of "a conference of delegates to the 14th extraordinary congress." An hour later Šimon was called back to CC headquarters, this time without being able to establish contact with the party leader.[14] Meanwhile, during the early morning hours, appeals were made by congress delegates in Prague and

---

[13] The proceedings of the congress, based on tape-recordings, and its major documents, were published abroad, under the editorship of Jiří Pelikán, at first in German, then in Czech and other languages. See J. Pelikán, ed., *Panzer überrollen den Parteitag* (Vienna, 1969); *Tanky proti sjezdu* (Vienna, 1970); *Le congrès clandestin* (Paris, 1970); *The Secret Vysočany Congress* (London, 1971). Page references refer to the Czech edition (with pages in the English edition sometimes given in brackets). The main documents were published in the press at the time, in particular the special congress issue of *Rudé právo* (n.d.) and are given in *Tanky*, pp. 99-109; *Sedm dnů*, pp. 93-108. A briefer "protocol" was published by A. Zvarovská in *Tribuna*, Oct. 22, 31, Nov. 5, 1969. Although this version is distorted and much is deleted, it included some credible information missing in the Pelikán version. For highly biased anti-congress analysis, see V. Král, *Život strany*, Oct. 15, 22, 29, 1969; M. Jakeš, ibid., Oct. 1, 1969; for critical reports by participants, *RP*, Sept. 25, Nov. 6, 19, Dec. 2, 1969. For defense of the congress, see L. Pacovský, *Reportér*, (n.d., Aug. 26?); Z. Hejzlar, *Listy* (May 1971), pp. 14-17. Cf. also brief accounts, from a hostile standpoint, in M. Marko, *Čierne na bielom* (Bratislava, 1971), pp. 202-8; and from a Trotskyite viewpoint in P. Broué, *Le printemps des peuples commence à Prague* (Paris, n.d.), pp. 114-19.

[14] *Sedm dnů*, pp. 7-8. It is not known whether Šimon actually spoke to Dubček nor whether the latter approved the convening of the congress. Messages from Dubček were read over the radio about 7:00 a.m. appealing to workers to proceed to their places of work and to the population to act calmly and with dignity (*Sedm dnů*, pp. 24, 30). These messages were said to have been smuggled out prior to his arrest (BBC, II, Aug. 26).

significantly, Bratislava, and by individual organizations, that the 14th congress be convened.[15] After the arrest of Šimon, J. Litera, a secretary of the Prague municipal committee, consulted regional and borough committees and assumed the task of organizing the meeting. In an appeal broadcast repeatedly during the day and published in the cyclostyled version of *Rudé právo* of August 21, the Prague municipal committee called on all elected delegates to proceed to Prague at once by all available means for the "immediate opening of the 14th Party Congress."

Once the delegates had assembled in large numbers—at the outset 935 of the 1,500 delegates previously elected—the question was immediately posed by Litera as to whether the gathering should be changed from "a conference of delegates" to a meeting of the 14th congress, or alternatively, in the absence of most Slovak delegates (only five were present), to a constituent congress or conference of Czech communists. The urgency of speedy action to form a new party leadership, including a new Central Committee, was apparent when the delegates heard from Martin Vaculík and others of the rump meeting of the CC the day before (including Indra's opposition to the convening of the congress) and from Litera of continuing efforts by Indra to prevent the holding of the congress. A race was clearly in progress between those in the CC who were seeking to form a new leadership and a government of collaboration, and those at the congress who were seeking to bring into existence a progressive Central Committee and Presidium, including Dubček and the other imprisoned leaders, and excluding those suspected of collaboration.

The absence of most Slovak delegates was the greatest single obstacle to considering the meeting an actual party congress. A Slovak delegate, however, noted that other Slovak delegates, reportedly held up at Břeclav en route to Prague, evidently considered this a meeting of the party congress, and speaking on behalf of four of those present, expressed approval of the constitution of the meeting as such. The chairman made a special point that, in the interests of guaranteeing Slovak delegates complete equality and safeguarding them against "outvoting," a majority of them would eventually have to agree to all questions discussed, including this one. Without further debate, the delegates, by an overwhelming majority, approved the inauguration of the extraordinary congress.[16]

The proceedings that followed were characterized by a serious effort to proceed in an orderly and democratic fashion, observing the formalities of past party congresses, and, at the same time, by confusion and disorder occasioned by inadequate facilities, the atmosphere of tense excite-

[15] *RP*, Aug. 21 (cyclostyled); *Pravda*, Aug. 22. The editorial board of the latter paper also asked that the congress be held.

[16] Pelikán, ed., *Tanky*, pp. 45-46.

ment, and the pressure of time. The sense of the urgency to proclaim to the public their attitude toward the situation and to bring into being a new leadership was compounded by the knowledge that at any time the congress might be closed down by the occupation forces. More than once there were warnings of the nearby presence of Soviet military forces and the necessity for dispatch in transacting business. Many of the delegates were without credentials and had to be certified by their regional or district delegations. There had been no time to prepare documentation, so that all business had to be conducted orally. Microphones were not available on the floor and speakers, in the noise and commotion, could not be clearly heard, and their statements were not recorded. Secret balloting had to be abandoned, and voting was by voice or the raising of hands. The chairmen (the chair was occupied by different persons) ruled on votes according to their own perception, and in their haste often neglected to announce the results. Substantial time was devoted to organizing the session for business, with the election of a "working presidium" to determine program and procedures, a credentials commission (the Slovaks agreed not to be included in it until a larger number arrived), and the important electoral committee for nominating members for the CC.

As the meeting progressed, the delegates seemed to gain greater confidence in the legitimacy of the proceedings. Much time was consumed in debate, sometimes on secondary questions. Leading roles were assumed by Prague personalities such as Litera, Pelikán, Šilhán, and Hejzlar, and by Šabata, from Brno. The report of the credentials commission revealed that a total of 1,112 delegates were present, that is, 72.6 percent of the more than 1,500 regularly elected delegates and more than the two-thirds majority required for decisions. The number later rose to 1,182, and by the end of the meeting, to 1,219.[17] More Slovaks arrived, numbering, it was officially reported, some fifty in all.[18] Significant was the relatively poor attendance of CC members, even though several direct appeals were made to them to attend. According to a supplementary report of the credentials committee, only twenty-nine CC members, and nine members of ÚKRK, were present.[19] The ranks of the delegates were strengthened by the arrival of some fifteen members of the government,

---

[17] Ibid., pp. 66-67, 95, 105. The chairman, perhaps inadvertently, at the close of the session, referred to 1,290 delegates present (p. 97).

[18] Ibid., p. 105.

[19] Ibid., p. 77. A letter to the CC members urging them to participate was approved by the congress. Vaculík and Litera were also reported to have called on them to attend (Tribuna, Oct. 22). It was reported that the CC and ÚKRK had appealed to all members to go to the congress (Tanky, p. 61). Of the three persons appointed by the Hotel Praha meeting only one apparently appeared, Křcek, who was elected to the working presidium (Tanky, p. 32).

including a deputy Prime Minister, Božena Machačová, who read the text of the government's declaration and reported on a meeting with President Svoboda and of his support for the government.[20] Later, the leader of a delegation from the National Assembly, which was then in session, declared its support for the congress.

Considerable obscurity surrounds the adoption of two major documents which were approved during the early part of the proceedings and (apparently) subsequently revised—these were a proclamation on the situation and an appeal to the communist parties of the world. Although the protocol published abroad contained the final text of both documents, it includes nothing of the apparently contentious discussion which preceded their adoption and led to their revision in a more moderate direction by two commissions headed by the original sponsors, Hejzlar and Šabata. The proclamation in its final form asserted that Czechoslovakia's "sovereignty" had been breached by "the occupation" and that "no competent party or constitutional organ had requested such an intervention." Denying that there was any counterrevolution or any threat to socialism, the statement declared that Czechoslovakia had not "broken its alliance obligations and duties." It was the invading forces that had "broken these obligations" and "trampled on Czechoslovakia's sovereignty." The declaration demanded that the imprisoned leaders be released and that "normal conditions be created for the functioning of all constitutional and political organs." Czechoslovakia would never accept "either a military occupation administration or a domestic collaborationist power. . . ." The congress recognized only Svoboda, Smrkovský, Černík, and Dubček as legitimate leaders. The fundamental demand was the withdrawal of troops. If this was not met, or if negotiations for withdrawal, "with our free constitutional and party authorities," did not begin within twenty-four hours, the congress called on the workers to begin a "one-hour protest strike" at 12:00 noon on Friday, August 23. If this had no result, the congress or the newly elected Central Committee would decide on "other necessary measures."[21]

[20] Valeš gave a full list of those ministers present at the congress (including Pavel and Kadlec) and explained the absence of others, such as Šik and Hájek, etc., who were abroad, and Hamouz and Štrougal who were in hiding, but who were reported to have approved the government's actions. General Dzúr was said not to have freedom of movement. The Slovaks, Husák, Colotka, and Hruškovič, who were in Bratislava, had not attended the government's first meeting. There was no contact with Pavlovský and Hoffmann (*Tanky*, pp. 63-65, 79).

[21] According to a post-occupation version the original declaration had called for "a general strike" to begin at 6:00 a.m. on Aug. 23 and had appealed to the armed forces to be in a state of readiness and to "fulfill their oath" if the situation demanded it. Discussion apparently revealed substantial opposition to the original proposal and caused Hejzlar himself to reconsider his position (Král, *ŽS*, Oct. 22, 29; Svarovská, *Tribuna*, Oct. 22). In Pelikán's version Hejzlar is quoted only as making a later correction for the press, changing the wording from a general, to

The original appeal to the communist parties, introduced by Šabata, was also apparently modified after reconsideration by a commission. Reiterating its condemnation of the occupation, the appeal in its final form called for the release of all interned leaders, restoration of civil freedoms and rights, and the "immediate beginning of the speedy withdrawal of the occupation armies," and called upon the other parties to support "our just cause" and consider the possibility of a conference of communist and workers' parties, in which Czechoslovakia would participate, represented by persons elected at the congress.[22]

During the course of the day, the congress, alarmed by reports of incidents in Prague, issued a brief appeal to all citizens, and especially to youth, urging them to avoid "ill-considered meetings or manifestations" or any actions that would lead to "useless clashes and conflicts, and irreplaceable losses of life, health, and national property." "Do not aid the foreign troops, pay no attention to them, ignore them!" Near the end of the congress, a letter to Dubček was adopted, telling him that "thy name has become a symbol of our sovereignty" and that "we still see in thee our chief representative."[23]

The election of a new Central Committee was accomplished only in the closing hours of the meeting. During the preliminary discussion some voices were raised warning against haste in carrying through the election. Others, including the representative of the working presidium, described the election as a "provisional" action, which could be changed at a later session. Pelikán, however, warned of the claims made by a part of the former CC and Presidium, a minority, to be the party's "leading representatives" and expressed doubts that the congress would be able to meet again. The main purpose of the invasion, he said, had been to prevent the congress, which he described as "the only—the most representative —embodiment of the party." The most urgent task was to elect a Central Committee "so composed as to correspond in a maximum degree to today's thinking of the majority of party members or delegates." This body

---

a one-hour, strike (*Tanky*, p. 66). In a later article Hejzlar referred to more radical demands such as immediate withdrawal of forces as a condition of negotiations, preparation of armed resistance, a permanent general strike, and a breach of relations with the CPSU, which were, he said, not accepted by the congress (*Listy*, May 1971, p. 16).

[22] Originally the draft had apparently included proposals to boycott the Moscow communist conference and to consider whether the CPSU and its allied parties could any longer be considered "revolutionary Marxist parties." Also dropped from the final version was harsher wording which condemned "the blind deeds of a group of bureaucratized leaders" who were using "brute force" in place of "material arguments" (Svarovská, *Tribuna*, Oct. 22, 29, 1969).

[23] For the appeal, *Tanky*, pp. 104-5, also 77-78; for the letter, pp. 93-94. A Slovak delegate brought greetings from Dubček's mother whom he had seen in Trenčin, "tearful and worn." She had called on all delegates to be "courageous" as in the past.

would then be able to negotiate with the representatives of the five parties and with other communist parties for a solution of the situation "on the basis of respect for our sovereignty and for the common interests of the international workers' movement." The discussion that followed (much of which was not recorded) was evidently heated and prolonged.[24] The chairman reported that the military command had issued an ultimatum to the rump CC Presidium to form a new Presidium including Bil'ak, Barbírek, Indra, and others, who were to set up a new government by evening. He also informed the delegates that a group of CC Secretaries (Lenárt, Kolder, Indra, and others) had called a CC plenum in the Hotel Praha for 4 o'clock that afternoon. He declared that the congress, during its sittings, was the supreme organ of the party and that all former CC members were subordinate to it, and indeed had relinquished their mandates from the moment of the beginning of the congress. They must be "compelled to observe party discipline," he said.[25]

An electoral committee was eventually constituted, consisting of representatives of the regions, together with representatives of the army and the security forces, and two spokesmen of the working presidium (Litera and V. Šimeček). It was agreed that all Slovak delegates present should sit on the committee and that eventually the entire Slovak delegation would determine its own CC members. The committee's recommendation that the rules of election procedures be changed to meet the extraordinary conditions (the secret ballot, for instance, would be replaced by "acclamation") was approved. Its proposal of a change in the party statute so as to reduce the rule of eligibility to five years' party membership gave rise to long discussion before it was finally agreed that there be no membership condition for nomination.

Still more time-consuming was the actual selection of nominees for the CC. In view of the delay in submitting its list of candidates, the committee proposed, as an interim measure, the immediate election of the eight interned CC members, each of whom was voted upon separately: Svoboda, Dubček, and Černík, unanimously, Smrkovský, Kriegel, Špaček, Císař, and Šimon, with a handful of negative votes or abstentions in each case. The eventual full list of approximately 150 was based primarily on the nominations and short-listings of the regional conferences and could not be adjusted to reflect the size of the regions or to include

[24] *Tanky*, pp. 48-51.
[25] Ibid., p. 58. It was later reported that Kolder, Indra, Bil'ak, Pavlovský, and Rytíř were willing to join a new Presidium being formed under instructions of the Soviet army but that Šimon, Sádovský, and Mlynář had refused (ibid., p. 89). L. Pacovský, chairman of the electoral committee, was said to have raised the question as to whether the congress should declare the existing CC and its Presidium invalid and even expel or suspend some of its members from the party. Šilhán's view that this should be left to the new CC was approved (*Tribuna*, Nov. 5).

appropriate social strata. Slovak representatives were included, but with the proviso that the vote would be valid only when the entire Slovak delegation approved the list by a two-thirds vote or made the necessary changes.[26] A number of additional names were proposed from the floor, including Vodsloň, Vaculík, Mlynář, and Borůvka, all of whom were eventually accepted.[27] In the final vote the full list of nominees—144— including Slovaks, was presented, with each person voted upon individually. The ÚKRK slate of 37 was read and voted upon en bloc. The election of candidate members was postponed. Of former CC members, only 25 were included in the new supreme organ, 65 having been dropped. The 119 new members included all leading officeholders and well known progressive spokesmen, including sixteen outstanding intellectuals.[28]

The relationship of the Slovak delegates to the congress and its decisions was a delicate question and later became the subject of great controversy. As we have noted, the organizers of the congress, including the chairmen and the committee spokesmen, were most sensitive to the need to assure the Slovak delegates their proper place on the Central Committee and to reserve for them the right to question decisions taken or persons selected. The congress itself, in a special message to Slovak communists and the Slovak people, declared that the Action Program and the guarantee of equality in the form of federation would be implemented. The message called upon the Slovaks to support the congress decisions which would all be "discussed" with the absent Slovak delegates. Those Slovaks present, it was said, considered the acceptance of these decisions a fundamental condition of united action by the party as a whole. All Slovak communists were asked to follow the instructions of the newly elected CC and to carry out the tasks adopted by the congress. A part of the old CC, they were warned, still remained in session in Prague and were disorienting the work of the party, and especially of communists in Slovakia.[29]

Apart from the attitude expressed by Slovak delegates in Prague, there were several indications that Slovak communists would respond favorably to the congress's appeal. It was reported to the congress, for in-

[26] This was to apply to all CC members, not only to Slovaks (*Tanky*, pp. 82-83).

[27] According to *Tribuna* (Nov. 5) Machačová was also added. Piller's name was put forward but withdrawn because of reports of his collaborationist activity.

[28] Full list is given in *Tanky*, pp. 107-9 (96-97). The actual votes for each candidate were not recorded. General Prchlík was proposed from the floor but was not approved. There were strong objections to a certain candidate from North Bohemia (A. Kábele) but in the end he was elected. Among the more conservative *not* included were Kolder, Indra, Bil'ak, Lenárt, Barbírek, Piller, Rigo, Švestka, Kapek, and Voleník. Among those elected were the prominent intellectuals, Šabata, Goldstücker, Hanzelka, Hübl, Kosík, Mlynář, Colotka and others; the well-known reform politicians, Galuška, Pavel, and Hejzlar; and General Dzúr and Erban.

[29] Ibid., pp. 103-5 (92-94), for text. This statement was not mentioned in post-occupation party reports of the congress.

771

stance, that at a meeting in Košice, forty-seven delegates and the East Slovak regional committee demanded the return to political life of the imprisoned leaders and repudiated "any group in the CC or any other group" seeking to elevate itself to the leadership of the party. They requested that their statement be considered "a valid contribution to the deliberations" and endorsed the idea of declaring the congress as "permanent."[30] In another message, from Bratislava, Slovak delegates, who were planning to go to Prague, were said to have expressed their support for Dubček and "the legal government" and condemned the traitors who were aiding the occupiers.[31] Eleven Slovak delegates who reached Prague too late to attend the congress met with the newly elected CC and asked to be considered as "regularly present" delegates.[32]

In its concluding resolution the congress restated its loyalty to the Action Program and its will to develop "democratic and humanist socialism" and reiterated its demand for the immediate withdrawal of the occupation troops and the "restoration of the activity of the legal state and political organs" headed by the imprisoned leaders. It declared itself to be in "permanent session," ready to discuss the party statutes, the constitutional reordering of the Republic, and other matters at a further sitting. As Vodsloň expressed it, in his closing remarks, "the impossible had become possible." The congress, the convocation of which had been considered unrealistic by many, had been successful and would, he said, have extraordinary significance for the party, the country, and internationally.

The congress was immediately denounced by the Soviet Union as an "illegal" effort by the rightists to seize control of the party.[33] In fact, under the difficult conditions of military occupation, it constituted the most representative and legitimate embodiment of the party and played a decisive role in preventing the formation of a collaborationist regime and in effecting the release of Dubček and his associates for participation in the Moscow talks. It became a symbol and a stimulus to the popular resistance which had already begun and which contributed, in the ensuing week, to the same results.

National Defiance

The Czech and Slovak people reacted to the invasion in virtual unanimity, condemning it unconditionally and expressing their feelings

---

[30] Ibid., p. 93 (81-82). [31] *Tribuna*, Oct. 31.

[32] *RP*, Aug. 24; *Sedm dnů*, pp. 173-74. See also below, p. 789.

[33] *Pravda* (Moscow), Aug. 24; *Sedm dnů*, pp. 216-21. A special pro-Soviet edition of *Rudé právo* also repudiated the 14th congress and the CC elected by it and called itself "the organ of the officially elected CC" headed by Dubček (*RP*, Aug. 26; *Sedm dnů*, pp. 353-56).

in a spontaneous and widespread resistance without parallel in Czech or Slovak history and rare in human experience.[34] This extraordinary display of defiance embraced those in authority and the ordinary man in the street and assumed almost identical content in all parts of the country, among both Czechs and Slovaks, and even among the national minorities, in town and country, in official institutions of both party and state, in social organizations of all kinds, and among individual citizens of whatever occupation or standing. This was an outgrowth and a dramatic intensification of what had gradually developed during the summer—the remarkable national unity and solidarity of leadership and people, the increasing participation of citizens in public affairs, and the determination to continue the movement for reform in spite of outside pressures. It reflected the sense of outrage at the flagrant invasion and imprisonment of the leaders, a desire to support and protect those leaders, and a resolution to defend the cause of reform and national independence.

This explosion of popular defiance, so contrary to the usual concept of the Czechs as a nation of Švejks, came as a surprise, not least to the Czechs and Slovaks themselves. For many Czechs it restored faith in their nation, a faith that had been badly shaken by their failure to act at critical turning points in their history. Although nonviolent, the resistance was not in any sense passive as it involved intense activity on the part of tens of thousands of persons. The variety of ingenious and original forms of defiance that were devised is richly documented in the contents of the radio and television broadcasts, and of the clandestine newspapers, and in the official statements by party and state organs. Much of this material was collated in the so-called Black Book produced by a group of historians, a unique attempt at the instant documentation of history and itself a daring act of resistance.[35] The events of that rare and remarkable week have often been described, especially by eyewitnesses, whose attention was focused, perhaps naturally, on the dramatic events that occurred in the streets of Prague and on the extraordinary role played by the radio and television and by the clandestine press, to be

[34] For studies of other cases of political resistance, see Adam Roberts, ed., *The Strategy of Civilian Defence* (London, 1967), and V. V. Sveics, *Small Nation Survival: Political Defense in Unequal Conflicts* (Jericho, N.Y., 1970). Roberts included as case studies the *Ruhrkampf* of 1923, the Norwegian and Danish resistance to German occupation, and the East German revolt in 1953.

[35] The Black Book (*Sedm pražských dnů*) was published in Sept. 1968 as "study material—for inner use only." Although openly sponsored by the Historical Institute of the Academy of Sciences, the names of its editors were not given. For a description of the preparation of the Black Book, see interview with two historians who had taken part, V. Prečan and M. Otáhal (*Rep.*, Jan. 23, 1969). It has appeared in several foreign languages including English—Robert Littell, ed., *The Czech Black Book* (New York, 1969). Citations are to the Czech edition. The English version omits a number of documents, without indicating it in the text, and also all the appendices.

773

summarized briefly in the following section. Equally significant, and requiring more analytical treatment, was the resistance of the official organs, to be examined thereafter.[36]

Although the resistance was spontaneous and unplanned, and occurred largely without prior organization or centralized guidance, there was an amazing identity in the spirit and in the dominant goals of the individual acts of resistance. These were: an unconditional condemnation of the occupation as unjustified politically, illegal under international law, and contrary to the basic principles of communist solidarity; continued loyalty to the established leaders, Svoboda, Dubček, Černík, Smrkovský, and Kriegel, and demands for the release of those under arrest; a refusal to cooperate with the invaders and repudiation of all efforts to form a collaborationist regime, coupled with personal denunciation of the individuals suspected of such action; a reassertion of faith in the program of reform and the right of Czechoslovakia to proceed on this course in spite of armed intervention; and repeated demands for the withdrawal of the invading forces as the only basis for negotiations. The decision by Svoboda to go to Moscow and to negotiate with the Soviet leaders did not affect these crucial demands or dampen the initial wave of emotional and intellectual resistance. Rare, almost nonexistent, were demands for violent resistance, or any actions of that kind. Although the idea of a declaration of "neutrality" was often raised, it was officially

[36] Brief analyses of the resistance are given by Adam Roberts in his contribution to P. Windsor and A. Roberts, eds., *Czechoslovakia, 1968*, esp. pp. 111-31, and by Theodore Ebert, "Civilian Resistance in Czechoslovakia," *The World Today* 21 (Feb. 1969), 52-59. See also Constantin C. Menges, "Resistance in Czechoslovakia —An Underground in the Open," *Trans-action* 6 (Dec. 1968), 36-41 (originally published as a Rand Corporation memorandum, *Prague Resistance, 1968: The Ingenuity of Conviction* [Santa Monica, Cal., 1968]); Milton Mayer, *The Art of the Impossible: A Study of the Czech Resistance* (Center for the Study of Democratic Institutions, Santa Barbara, Cal., 1969). Among many books of journalistic reportage, the following may be mentioned: Tad Szulc, *Czechoslovakia Since World War II*, pp. 405 ff.; Michel Tatu, *L'hérésie impossible*, pp. 174-221; Gerard de Sède et al., *Pourquoi Prague?* (Paris, 1968), pp. 462-83; C. Schmidt-Häuer and A. Müller, *Viva Dubček*, pp. 130-49; J. Wechsberg, *The Voices* (New York, 1969); Ladislav Mňačko, *The Seventh Night* (New York, 1969); Jaroslav Kučera, *Pražský srpen* (Munich, 1971).

For graphic day-by-day documentation, cf., in addition to *Sedm dnů*, the radio broadcasts, BBC, II, Aug. 22 on, and the clandestine press (see below, n. 46). The Soviet press, although very biased, provided the Russian reader with detailed coverage of the activities of the "counterrevolution," including references to the 14th congress, the illegal radio and press, and the widespread opposition of the population to the invading forces (e.g. *Pravda* and *Izvestia*, Aug. 22 on).

Major official documents of the resistance are given in Slovak, in *Dokumenty o okupácii ČSSR* (Bratislava, 1968). For National Assembly documents, see *Dokumenty o Národní shromáždění ve dnech 21.-28. srpna 1968* (n.d.). Some documents are given also in *Tanky*, pp. 245-63. Party documents, including those of the 14th congress, with a single exception, are omitted from the official party collection, *RŠO*.

rejected as a harmful and futile strategy and an ineffective means of attaining the main goals.[37]

Most striking, considering the spontaneity of the resistance, was its disciplined and nonviolent character. Soviet propaganda talked of "white terror," of 40,000 armed counterrevolutionaries, of arms caches, and of armed actions against the invading forces.[38] In fact, losses of life were few (perhaps fifty in all) and there were some hundreds of wounded, in both cases mainly Czechs and Slovaks. These casualties resulted from occasional incidents when the invading troops fired on unarmed civilians.[39] The Czechoslovak armed forces, although not disarmed, remained in their barracks and offered no armed resistance at any time. The civilian population, with extraordinary self-control, obeyed the original order of the President and commander-in-chief, and of the highest party authority not to resist the invaders and responded to the repeated appeals of the mass media and leading spokesmen to preserve "calm and composure (*klid a rozvaha*)" and to avoid incidents that might lead to violence. Even mass demonstrations, such as the one announced for the morning of August 22 on *Václávské náměstí* (Wencelas Square) in downtown Prague, was abandoned as a result of radio warnings. Strikes, too, were for the most part avoided, again in response to repeated appeals. The single exception was the one-hour protest strike at 12:00 noon on August 23, called by the 14th congress and endorsed by the trade unions, which produced an almost complete stoppage of work in factories and work-places throughout the Republic.[40]

This civil resistance proved in many ways to be a remarkably effective substitute for military resistance and scored some important results, even though these were limited and short-lived. For a brief period, at least, it produced an extraordinary popular unity and created a solidarity of people and leaders which had a significant effect on the course of events. In all probability it strengthened the hand of Svoboda in his effort to secure the release of Dubček and the other interned leaders, and their participation in the Moscow talks. There is little doubt that it blocked the forma-

[37] See below, pp. 785, 787, 794. The idea of neutrality appeared in posters and the press and on the radio, and a campaign for signatures developed on this issue. It was "the dominant word" in the capital on Friday, the 23rd, according to *Rudé právo* (Aug. 24). For favorable comment, see *LL*, Aug. 23; *Mladá fronta*, Aug. 23; *Svobodné slovo*, Aug. 24; *Student* (n.d.), and *My 1968*, Aug. 24.

[38] *On Events in Czechoslovakia* (Moscow, 1968), pp. 129-57.

[39] Haefs, ed., *Ereignisse*, p. 164. According to the letter from the National Assembly to President Svoboda in Moscow, there were 30 dead and 300 wounded in Prague alone (*Sedm dnů*, p. 284). Mlynář, in September, spoke of 70 dead in the whole Republic (BBC, II, Sept. 17).

[40] On the demonstration, *Sedm dnů*, pp. 122-25; on the strike, ibid., pp. 185-89. Another protest against the occupation took the form of the blowing of sirens and automobile horns, and the ringing of bells, from 9:00 to 9:15 a.m. on Aug. 26 (ibid., pp. 322, 325).

tion of a collaboration government. Another important effect was to discredit the Soviet Union and its allies in the eyes of the world, and to win worldwide sympathy for the Czechoslovak cause, including that of many communist parties and rank-and-file party members. It has been termed a "political victory" in that it successfully denied to the invaders "the political control" that was their main objective in intervention.[41] In this respect it may have been more effective than military resistance, since the latter would have been brief and easily countered by overwhelming force. The nonviolent, but active resistance, for which the Soviet Union was ill-prepared, was difficult to counter by political means. Yet in the last analysis the resistance was a Pyrrhic victory, brought to a close by the conclusion of the Moscow agreement which was eventually to lead to the legitimizing of the occupation and in the end to the extinction of the reform movement. Hence, after the initial political fiasco, the Kremlin actually attained its major political ends, and the resistance failed.

CIVILIAN RESISTANCE

Opposition in the streets of Prague and other cities began during the first day of occupation and continued unbroken for more than a week until after the return of the delegation from Moscow. As the radio expressed it (Aug. 24), this was a strange occupation, "the strangest occupation which history has ever recorded—a situation when someone is attacked and wishes to defend himself, and must defend himself mainly by not firing a single shot, when he must defend himself against the most terrible weapons only by his calm and composure and by a joke." As *Rudé právo* (Aug. 24) put it, "They have guns and rockets. Our weapons are chalk, pen, word, and the consistent ignoring of them!" The first reaction had been to talk to the invading troops, asking them why they had come and trying to convince them that there was no reason or justification for their intervention. When this had utterly no effect, except perhaps to shake the morale of some individuals, the citizens turned almost at once (after the first day) to a new tactic—evincing their hostility by "ignoring" the invading forces. This included not only refraining from conversations but also refusing to provide them with water or food or any assistance whatever. This was accompanied by a conscious effort to hinder the work of the occupation forces by removing all highway and street signs, house numbers, and plaques identifying institutions. Broadcasts and posters even gave the license numbers of automobiles believed

[41] Sveics, *Small Nation Survival*, pp. 97, 264. Both Sveics and Roberts (*Civilian Defence*) drew similar conclusions concerning the effectiveness of nonviolent civilian resistance to aggression. See also Eberts, "Resistance in Czechoslovakia," pp. 58-59; Windsor and Roberts, *Czechoslovakia, 1968*, pp. 124-31.

to be proceeding to make arrests so that citizens could try to block their passage.

Most effective of all was the posting of signs and placards, and the drawing of graffiti on walls and pavements, often in Russian, denouncing the invaders and the Soviet leaders, as well as suspected collaborators, and expressing loyalty to Dubček and the other leaders. Pictures of Dubček and Svoboda were everywhere. Prague, wrote the regional party paper, *Svoboda* (Aug. 25), became "one great poster." Even when it was announced that anyone writing slogans and putting up posters would be shot, the campaign continued. When the walls were cleaned during the night, the posters and inscriptions went up again the next day. Small demonstrations occurred frequently, particularly at the famous statue of St. Wenceslas at the head of *Václavské náměstí*, which was covered with pictures and posters and became a rostrum for youthful speakers.

Soviet tanks were everywhere and occupied or blockaded, one after the other, buildings regarded as dangerous, including the Union of Writers, the Academy of Sciences and Charles University, the editorial and publishing houses of most of the newspapers, including *Rudé právo*, the railway stations, telephone and telegraph centrals, government ministries, the government presidium, radio and television studios, bridges and communication points, the CC building, and local party headquarters. Production and transportation ground to a halt, and supplies of provisions became scarce. The people, however, remained unconquered, and their institutions and associations continued to function.[42]

Of crucial importance was the continued functioning of the radio, and even television, and the appearance of clandestine newspapers.[43] Although radio and broadcasting stations were soon occupied by Soviet troops (sometimes after a violent struggle) broadcasting was at once resumed in improvised stations which frequently changed their location and wavelength. According to those who were associated with this unique undertaking, the broadcasting system was not planned beforehand, but improvised under occupation conditions in a kind of "partisan" manner under rules of strict conspiracy. Full advantage was taken of existing facilities designed for use against a Western invasion and of the assistance offered by the Ministry of the Interior, the Ministry of National

---

[42] For the above, *Sedm dnů*, pp. 226-27, 237, 256, 262. The scene in the streets of Prague is best portrayed pictorially in Vaclav Svoboda, *Genosse Aggressor: Prag im August 1968* (Vienna, 1968). Examples of street signs and posters are given in *Sedm dnů*, appendix, pp. 471-80.

[43] For the role of the mass media see D. Havlicek and K. Jezdinsky, in V. V. Kusin, ed., *The Czechoslovak Reform Movement 1968* (London, 1973), pp. 253-58, 271-75, resp. For broadcasting, see Slava Volny, "The Saga of Czechoslovak Broadcasting," *East Europe* 17 (Dec. 1968), 10-15. Even the Soviet White Book dealt with the "counterrevolution on the air" and admitted the existence of nineteen stations which "coordinated the counterrevolutionary underground" (p. 132).

Defense, and the party. There gradually evolved a network of stations throughout Bohemia, Moravia, and Slovakia, sometimes in factories or barracks, or wherever transmitters could be found or installed. Even television was eventually organized on a limited and irregular basis. The Soviet forces found themselves unable to locate the frequently moving transmitters. The arrival of locating and jamming equipment from the USSR was delayed by railwaymen who blocked the passage of the train carrying it. The broadcasting station of the occupation forces, named Radio Vltava, which began operating early in the morning of August 21, could not compete with the "free and legal" Czechoslovak radio, in which the listeners placed complete confidence.

The continuance of broadcasting (and of the press) performed a vital function in both the civilian and the official resistance. Above all, it served as a link between the various party and state institutions and between these and the people, so that all knew what was happening in the otherwise chaotic conditions of military occupation. The radio has sometimes been evaluated, in view of its important role and the often spontaneous and uninstructed content of its broadcasting, as a kind of de facto government, operating in what was otherwise a partial vacuum of power.[44] In fact, although much of its action was carried on independently, it was in regular contact with the organs of state and party, which continued to function and gave general guidance to the media by their decisions and declarations. They, in turn, found the media an indispensable means of communicating with the population. The radio served as a kind of command-point for the popular resistance, issuing instructions, appealing for calm, maintaining morale and unity, and transmitting information from abroad and from within the country. There was also an attempt to shake the morale of the troops through broadcasts in their own languages.

Hardly less important was the clandestine press. With their offices and presses occupied by Soviet troops, editors and their staffs took emergency measures to issue their newspapers, sometimes in the form of handbills and leaflets, but soon in their regular formats. *Rudé právo* and *Pravda* appeared regularly from August 21 on,[45] as did all the major daily newspapers, often in more than one edition to keep up with the rapidly changing course of events, and were distributed free of charge to the population. In Brno and Ostrava, joint editions of several local newspapers were published. Even illustrated, humorous, and cultural weeklies put out special editions from time to time. The regional party organs,

---

[44] Wechsberg, *Voices*, p. 30; Tigrid, *Why Dubček Fell*, p. 101. Cf. the analysis of Havlicek and Jezdinsky above.

[45] *Rudé právo* appeared in a special Brno edition as well as in Prague. The Slovak *Rudé právo* did not appear, but its staff assisted in the production of *Pravda*.

including the two main city papers, *Večerník* and *Večerní Praha*, appeared without exception, as did the organs of the non-communist parties. In addition to the prominent dailies and weeklies, many lesser known papers were published. Two new Central Committee weeklies— *Politika* and *Tribuna*—appeared for the first time, in clandestine form. Important factories such as ČKD and Škoda published issues of their factory newspapers, *Kovák* and *Škodovák*.[46] There was also a vast outpouring of leaflets of all kinds, some anonymous, others issued by organizations and associations. In this flood of anti-invasion material the Czech-language newspaper, *Zprávy*, published by unnamed persons on behalf of the occupation forces and dumped in bundles on streets and at Soviet military command posts, awakened little interest and was in fact scorned by most of the population. All papers carried the texts of the important decisions of the 14th congress and of party and state organs, as well as news from abroad and at home, thus providing a written record for the public and supplementing the radio as a link between the official organs and the people at large.

It is impossible to give more than a brief summary of the unanimous reaction of the mass associations, specialized organizations, semiofficial agencies, and lesser governmental organs and their employees, all of which reacted, as though by one accord, to condemn the invasion, to pledge loyalty to Svoboda and Dubček, and to repudiate the collaborators. The stand of the trade union movement, for instance, was unequivocal from the very first day. The secretariat and the chairmen of the individual unions issued an appeal for support to the trade unions of the world, and urged the formation of strike committees and preparations for a general strike should it be necessary. The union leadership endorsed the protest strike called by the party congress and although thereafter they emphasized the necessity of maintaining normal economic life, they did not exclude a long-term general strike if the situation demanded it.[47]

Declarations in similar vein were issued by each of the creative unions, who also made a joint appeal to the intellectuals of the world. The

---

[46] A rich collection of these newspapers and leaflets is in the possession of the writer and in 1968 a special collection on Czechoslovakia will be deposited in the University of Toronto Thomas Fisher Rare Book Library. Apart from those mentioned above, the collection includes issues of *Nové slovo, Literární noviny, Kultúrny život, Reportér, Mladá fronta, Mladý svět, Smena, Obrana lidu, Práce, Práca, Zemědělské noviny, Rol'nické noviny, Svobodné slovo, Lidová demokracie, Ľud, Sloboda, Občanské noviny, Signál, Vlasta, Květy, Svět v obrazech, Roháč, Československý rozhlas, Československý voják, Československý šport* (Bratislava), *Stadion, Svět motorů, Letectví a kosmonautika,* etc. The regional party organs include *Jihočeska pravda, Pochodeň, Pravda* (West Bohemia), *Svoboda, Průboj, Nová svoboda, Rovnost, Hlas ľudu, Smer,* and *Východoslovenské noviny.*

[47] For the above, *RP,* Aug. 25; *Sedm dnů,* pp. 44-45, 120-21, 174-75, 247-50.

Czechoslovak Olympic Committee delivered a protest to the Olympic Committees of the five countries, and later called for the exclusion of the Soviet Union from the Olympic games. Even the Union of Czechoslovak-Soviet Friendship, through the person of Zdeněk Fierlinger, associated itself with the wave of public opinion. The National Front and the two major non-communist parties issued similar statements, as did the two Slovak parties. The Czechoslovak Academy of Sciences condemned the invasion in the early morning hours of the first day and sent appeals to their fellow scholars in the Soviet Academy. The Military Historical Institute in Prague and the Zápotocký Military Academy in Brno made strong protests. The Roman Catholic bishops, in a joint statement, pledged support for the government and defended religious freedom. Statements of loyalty were made by various branches of the People's Militia, public and state security, officers of the armed forces, the Ministry of the Interior, and the press agency (ČTK). Even signatories of the notorious July letter from Praga employees condemned the action of the Soviet Union and pledged support for Dubček.[48]

OFFICIAL RESISTANCE

During the six days following the invasion supreme government and party institutions operated under difficult conditions. The CC headquarters, the government presidium and many government ministries were occupied, and other buildings, such as the Castle and the National Assembly, were blockaded by Soviet forces. In the case of the assembly, government, party Presidium and National Front, their topmost leaders had been interned. Nonetheless all agencies of party and state continued to function, usually meeting in semi-legal conditions, and were able to keep in touch with each other by exchange of visits, by telephone, and by radio reports.

President Svoboda was in a somewhat unique position, since he had not been arrested and had freedom of movement within the Castle.[49] He originally planned to drive through the city but gave up the idea. He was able to communicate, through personal meetings, with spokesmen of the government and the assembly, and by radio and television with the population. In a brief radio address in the early morning of August 21, the President called on the people to maintain "absolute calm" and to await further steps by the constitutional organs. In the evening, at 10:30, he spoke in less noncommittal terms. Although not explicitly condemning the invasion, he observed that the entry of troops had been "without the

---

[48] For the above, see *Sedm dnů*, passim; *Večerní Praha*, Aug. 25; *SS*, Aug. 22, 25; *Lidová demokracie*, Aug. 21, 22.

[49] For the following, see *Sedm dnů*, pp. 32-33, 63-64, 129, 172, 176-77, 191, 201, 313.

agreement of the constitutional authorities" and they (the latter) must seek their "early withdrawal." There was no way back from the course outlined in the Action Program and the government declaration of policy, he declared. He had called a plenary session of the National Assembly and had held talks that evening with the government which would be continued on the following day, he hoped with the presence of Černík. He made no reference to any discussions with Soviet representatives or party leaders concerning the formation of a new government.

By Friday the 23rd, in spite of the urging of the National Assembly presidium that he should under no circumstances leave the country, President Svoboda had made up his mind, with the approval of the government, to proceed to Moscow for talks. In his address to the nation at 8:45 a.m., on that day, he explained that negotiations in Prague with Soviet representatives had not produced satisfactory results and that he had requested, and received approval of, negotiations with the supreme leaders in Moscow. He would be accompanied, he said, by two members of the government, Husák and General Dzúr (who had been selected by the government), by Dr. Kučera of the Socialist Party (delegated by the National Front), and by Piller, Bil'ak, and Indra.[50] Once more he appealed for calm and expressed his intention to continue on the January course. The National Assembly, in a special resolution, expressed their confidence in the President, and in Husák and Dzúr, both of whom had been elected to the party Presidium at the 14th congress, and expressed the belief that they would negotiate in accordance with the congress's principles, that this would lead to the restoration of Dubček and the others to their posts, and that there would be "no capitulation." The assembly endorsed Svoboda's appeal for the avoidance of any actions that would render the negotiations difficult and agreed to refrain from any measures until his return. Šilhán, acting party Secretary, in a radio speech, also pledged support for the President and for Husák and Dzúr, and indicated that the others would be judged in the light of their behavior in the negotiations and their attitude to the 14th congress decisions. At a stopover at the Bratislava airport en route to Moscow, the presidential party was joined by Husák and greeted by members of the Slovak party Presidium, which expressly confirmed Husák's mandate to act in the name of Slovak communists.[51]

[50] The radio and press reported later that the President had himself requested the visit and had not agreed to the establishment of a collaborationist government (ibid., p. 178). The government had received assurances that he would not negotiate any changes in the leadership of the top state and political organs (p. 201). There was criticism of the inclusion of Piller, Bil'ak, and Indra in the delegation and no information as to how they had been selected (p. 236). All three had been repudiated by the 14th congress.

[51] *Pravda* (Bratislava), Aug. 23. See also below in this chapter. P. Colotka reported from Bratislava that the President had assured them that they intended to

The government, its chairman under arrest and many of its ministries under occupation or guard, was severely handicapped in the performance of its activities, but met at least once every day in improvised quarters, at first under the chairmanship of Božena Machačová, the Minister of the Consumer Goods Industry, and later under one of its deputy chairmen, Štrougal.[52] During the afternoon of the first day of invasion the government endorsed a statement made earlier in the day by a group of government members who had denounced the occupation as an illegal act, and confirmed a note of the Ministry of Foreign Affairs, to be delivered to the governments of the five states, demanding the withdrawal of troops. It also called on these governments to issue orders for the release of the interned government members and for the creation of conditions permitting the orderly operations of the constitutional and political organs. In the evening, the government issued a declaration to the people along similar lines and urged them not to permit the installation of any other government.

On Thursday, the 22nd, in the morning, the government reiterated its demands and stressed the need to assure the functioning of the economy and the provisioning of the population, expressly declaring that the use of such supplies by the invading armies was "an act of violence." During the evening, with twenty-two members present and Štrougal in the chair, the government declared itself bound by the Action Program and its own April declaration of policy and assumed the duties of the presidency during Svoboda's absence.

During Saturday, the 24th, two press conferences were held to inform the public of the government's activities and to air grievances concerning Soviet behavior in Prague.[53] It was declared that Černík continued to be the head of the government and that none of the ministers would enter a collaborationist government. Complete support was expressed for the 14th congress and for the newly elected CC. It was announced, however, that the Minister of Domestic Trade, Pavlovský, had attended only one meeting and that his ministry had been placed under the direction of the first deputy minister.[54] General Šalgovič was suspended from his duties as deputy minister in charge of State Security, and the Minister of the Interior, Josef Pavel, who remained free, took over direct supervision

---

negotiate as representatives of a sovereign state and could be "trusted to defend our interests" (BBC, II, Aug. 27).

[52] For the following, *Sedm dnů*, pp. 55-56, 60-61, 119-20, 129-30.

[53] Ibid., pp. 235-36, 277-78. The first was conducted by V. Valeš and S. Rázl; the second by M. Galuška and V. Kadlec.

[54] Ibid., pp. 235-36. Yet on Aug. 23 the radio reported that Pavlovský had attended the government meeting that day and approved its work, including the decision concerning the occupation (BBC, II, Aug. 26).

of this department.[55] P. Colotka, deputy Prime Minister, who was in Bratislava, was reported to have expressed the full solidarity of the Slovak party and state organs and was, with the government's consent, remaining in Bratislava.[56] Certain government members who were abroad, notably Šik, Hájek, and others, issued strong statements condemning the invasion and collaboration efforts and appealed to the communist parties and the governments of the world.[57]

Over the weekend the government devoted its attention to the failure of the commander-in-chief of the invading forces, General Pavlovsky, to fulfill promises made to President Svoboda that steps would be taken to facilitate the functioning of the government, particularly by removing troops from the occupied or blockaded ministries.[58] Moreover, it was said, the military authorities had failed to honor their commitment not to disarm Czechoslovak forces or to use force against the civilian population, or even to withdraw their troops from small towns and villages and from areas of dense traffic in the cities. These complaints were expressed in a diplomatic note from the Ministry of Foreign Affairs on Sunday and by a government protest on Monday which bitterly condemned "the incomprehensible improprieties" committed by the invading troops. The Ministry of Foreign Trade issued a note protesting the suspension of the fulfillment of agreements for the exchange of goods.[59]

In the afternoon of the first day of the occupation, on the call of the President, the National Assembly held a plenary session in its regular meeting place.[60] Since the building was surrounded by military units and access to it was uncertain, most of the deputies took up residence inside, sleeping on the floor and leaving only for special reasons. In spite of the

[55] *Sedm dnů*, pp. 223-25, 235-36. The situation in the security service was confused, with many rumors rife concerning collaboration and arrests of Czechoslovak citizens by the State Security. The CPCz's main organizations in the Ministry of the Interior and in the State Security department both issued declarations of loyalty to Dubček and opposition to the occupation. The reports of arrests by the State Security were officially denied. Pavel, in a statement on August 25, described the situation in the Public Security (VB) as good but admitted that there were cases of illegalities committed by some State Security (STB) officers. He dismissed certain officials but warned against indiscriminate charges and promised careful future study of all cases (ibid., pp. 196, 198-99, 228, 296-97, 321). For Pavel's statement concerning the dismissal of Šalgovič and others, BBC, II, Aug. 27. See also statement of the assembly's defense and security committee praising the overwhelming majority of Ministry of Interior employees, including part of the State Security (*VP*, Aug. 26). For a report on the situation in State Security, *Práce*, Aug. 24.
[56] *Sedm dnů*, p. 235; BBC, II, Aug. 27.
[57] *RP*, Aug. 27; BBC, II, Aug. 26, 27.
[58] *Sedm dnů*, pp. 278-80, 324-25. See the order on these matters issued by the occupation command on Aug. 22, ibid., p. 123.
[59] BBC, II, Aug. 28.
[60] For the following, *Sedm dnů*, pp. 40-41, 51-52, 81-84, 117-18, 126, 182-84, 200-201, 222-23.

difficulties of travel through the occupied country, a majority of deputies (eventually numbering approximately 200) were present. In the absence of Smrkovský, the Slovak, Jozef Valo, first deputy chairman, acted in his place. Thus began what was in effect a permanent session for the next six days. The assembly established direct contact through specially appointed delegations not only with the President (before his departure) and the party congress, but also with the government and the new party Presidium, and with the Soviet embassy.

In its first session the assembly, endorsing a declaration already issued by its presidium in the morning, condemned the occupation and the arrests of the leaders, and demanded the release of the latter and the withdrawal of troops. On the following morning, a declaration of protest to the governments and parliaments of the five invading countries was adopted, and delivered to the Soviet embassy by a special delegation. Only one deputy, Karel Mestek, abstained from what was otherwise a unanimous decision of the 162 deputies then present.[61] The assembly adopted an address to the people, appealing for support and calm and warning against strikes. It endorsed a letter of warm support for the President.

On Friday morning the assembly approved a letter to the newly elected party CC, acknowledging it as the party's "highest organ" and approving the actions taken by the 14th congress. It addressed to the mass media a message of gratitude for the role they were playing and the support thus given to the assembly and other legal organs. During a meeting with representatives of the government (S. Rázl, B. Sucharda, and V. Valeš), the assembly declared its full confidence in the Černík government and both bodies agreed on the need for coordinating their actions.

By Saturday morning the number of deputies present had risen to 196, including 47 Slovaks. Plans for coordinating the assembly's work with the government and with the Slovak National Council were discussed, and a joint meeting was held with some members of the party's Presidium, including Šilhan. A session with representatives of the Prague national committee was devoted mainly to the consideration of measures relating to the maintenance of supplies, transportation, and health, and the opening of the school year. The work of the national

[61] Mestek was later reported to have written to the National Assembly, saying that he repudiated the occupation, even though he had disagreed with the assembly's first declaration (ibid., p. 239). In Gottwaldov, 50,000 voters signed a petition that Indra be deprived of his parliamentary seat (*RP* [Brno], Aug. 23). A similar petition was launched against Kolder (Ostrava joint newspaper, Aug. 23). The Ostrava regional committee of the National Front backed this petition (signed by 34,000 persons) as did the presidium of the National Assembly (BBC, II, Sept. 3).

committees in general was also discussed. Once again an appeal was made to the workers not to engage in strikes in the interest of avoiding losses of production. The committees of the assembly were at work, including the foreign affairs committee, under J. Pelikán, which adopted a letter of protest to the invading powers demanding the withdrawal of troops.[62]

Sunday was not a day of rest for the assembly and witnessed two important actions. Concerned by the duration of the talks in Moscow, the assembly (jointly with the government and the party Presidium) adopted a long letter to President Svoboda which gave a full description of the situation in the Republic (including news of arrests and deaths, and of economic disruption) and of the overwhelming rejection of the occupation by the people and the legal organs. Although the letter referred to the "relative calm" of the population, it warned of "dangerous tension." In the light of these facts the letter advocated one of two courses: either a group representing the assembly, the government, and the party CC should be permitted to go to Moscow to describe the atmosphere of the country and the spirit of the people, or Svoboda should break off negotiations for a short time and return to Prague, with Dubček and others, for consultations.[63]

No less important was a declaration on neutrality, a subject widely discussed in the mass media and strongly pressed by some individuals. A unilateral declaration of neutrality would, in the assembly's opinion, be useless and indeed harmful. Czechoslovakia considered itself still bound by the Warsaw treaty, which was, however, also binding on its other members. The basic needs of the moment were, however, the withdrawal of the occupation armies, the restoration of Dubček and the other leaders to their posts, and the assurance of normal conditions for the functioning of government and party organs.[64]

On Monday the assembly, with some 200 deputies present (excluding those Slovaks who had left for the Slovak party congress) took two other important steps. One was the approval of a letter to the Slovak nation, celebrating the anniversary of the Slovak National Uprising, and proclaiming the need for a common state of Czechs and Slovaks and for

[62] BBC, II, Aug. 27. For a meeting of the Prague national committee, ibid., Aug. 28.

[63] *Sedm dnů*, pp. 282-85. This letter bore the signatures of J. Valo, L. Štrougal, and V. Šilhan.

[64] Ibid., pp. 291-93. See below for Šilhan's rejection of neutrality. Other negative views were expressed in *Pravda*, Aug. 23 (S. Breier); *Politika*, Aug. 26; *Student*, n.d.; *VP*, Aug. 26. On Sept. 13 Smrkovský announced in the assembly that a diplomatic note had been sent to Warsaw denying as untrue a report in *Trybuna Ludu* (Aug. 27) that the assembly's foreign affairs committee had, on Aug. 23, identified itself with the demand for neutrality. In fact it had condemned and rejected it (*RP*, Sept. 14).

achieving federation by October 28. The second was a proclamation to the working people, issued jointly with the government and the Central Council of Trade Unions (ÚRO), declaring that long-term strikes (as distinct from a symbolic protest strike of a few minutes) would be harmful to the economy and helpful to the occupation.[65]

The two national councils were less active than the National Assembly and differed somewhat in their initial reaction to the occupation. In a meeting on August 21, the Czech National Council protested the arrest of its chairman, Císař, and issued a brief message to the Slovaks assuring them of the Czech desire to achieve federation by October 28 and appealing for solidarity of the two nations. On the 24th the ČNR reiterated this message, expressed its strong support for the legal organs of the Republic and for the 14th congress, and called for the withdrawal of foreign troops.[66] The Slovak National Council, meeting on the 21st under its chairman, O. Klokoč (who had not been arrested), gave support to the legitimate representatives of the Republic and to the declarations of the presidia of both parties, but expressed only "dissatisfaction with the presence of allied troops" and voiced the hope of a solution by peaceful negotiations. The SNR presidium on August 23 gave its backing to the legally established organs and their leaders, and to Dubček's policy and the Action Program, but did not respond to the Czech appeal for solidarity. However, a meeting on August 25 of the SNR presidium with representatives of the ČNR brought the two councils together in a strong common statement favoring the unity of the state, the release of Dubček and the withdrawal of troops, and supporting the post-January course and the passage of a federation law on October 28.[67]

The party's new Central Committee met during the night immediately following the congress to elect a new Presidium, to confirm Dubček unanimously as First Secretary, and to entrust to V. Šilhan, elected as Secretary, the direction of the Presidium during Dubček's absence. Šilhan, a worker by origin, had studied at the Higher Party School and in Leningrad. He was a prominent economist, the director of the Research Institute of the Economics of Industry and Construction, a university professor, and a member of the Prague party municipal committee.[68] The membership of the Presidium included the following: Dubček, Smrkovský, Černík, Špaček, Kriegel, Šimon, Císař, Šik, Šilhan, Slavík, L. Hrdinová, V. Matějíček, B. Kabrna, Hejzlar, Litera, Goldstücker, B. Vojáček,

[65] *Sedm dnů*, pp. 336-39.

[66] Ibid., pp. 55, 245-47. Císař soon escaped from arrest and may have presided at the second meeting. See his statement, ibid., pp. 193-94.

[67] *Pravda*, Aug. 22, 23, 26. O. Klokoč, in his initial statement, had been rather reserved, speaking of the "hard reality" of the occupation, calling for calm, and expressing the hope that the occupation would not last long.

[68] Biography given in *RP* (Brno), Aug. 25.

Hübl, Z. Moc, Šimeček, Husák, J. Zrak, Ťažký, Sádovský, Colotka, J. Turček, Pavlenda, and A. Zamek.[69] On Friday at 12:30 a.m., on the radio, Šilhan read the standpoint of the new Presidium on the Moscow negotiations. Pledging support for Svoboda, he declared that there could be no compromise on the question of withdrawal of troops or the restoration of sovereignty, but that this did not exclude "a reasonable agreement." As for the idea of neutrality, this offered no safeguard of a country's sovereignty. Czechoslovakia still regarded the Warsaw alliance and its obligations as the basis of its foreign policy but desired a profound renaissance of relations among socialist countries based on "real internationalism."[70]

The Presidium at once set to work under the difficult conditions of the time to direct party activities and to coordinate these with the government and the assembly. Deprived of its headquarters in the CC building, it established temporary quarters elsewhere and placed its apparatus under the direction of Martin Vaculík. Almost all former party officials were ready to continue under the new leadership, it was said, only one department head, Jan Kolář, having refused to do so. Švestka, however, was replaced as general editor of *Rudé právo*. It was assumed that a plenary CC session would soon be held and that the 14th congress would resume its deliberations, especially to deal with the question of federalism and to add others, such as Prchlík, to the Central Committee. The Presidium also strongly favored the holding of the Slovak congress without delay, warning against efforts to postpone it, and appointed a delegation to attend.

The Presidium sought to keep the public informed through a number of radio statements and press conferences by Šilhan, Hejzlar, and Slavík. In particular, these spokesmen warned against mass demonstrations and "certain slogans," and against strikes which would harm the economy. On Sunday the 25th, the Presidium issued an important proclamation, "What communists must do today," summing up the familiar demands for the withdrawal of troops and the restoration of the leaders to their

[69] *RP*, Aug. 24 (*Sedm dnů*, p. 173). The Presidium was large, consisting of 28 members, of whom only 6 were pre-August members (Černík, Dubček, Šimon, Špaček, Kriegel, and Smrkovský plus Císař, Mlynář, and Sádovský (pre-August Secretariat members). The Secretariat showed more continuity, except for the dropping of Indra, Lenárt, and Voleník. Excluded from both bodies were almost all the more conservative former leaders.

[70] *RP* (Brno), Aug. 25 (also *Sedm dnů*, pp. 190-93; *Tanky*, pp. 248-51). Moscow *Pravda* (Aug. 24, 27) falsely reported that Šilhan, on the radio, had initially demanded neutrality and then retracted the demand. Haefs, ed. *Ereignisse*, incorrectly stated that Šilhan transmitted a proposal of neutralization made by the CPCz Central Committee (p. 168). The Czechoslovak Information Service officially informed Svoboda that a spontaneous call for neutrality was going through the country, but neither the government nor the assembly nor the new CC had identified themselves with this demand (BBC, II, Aug. 27).

posts, and calling on communists "never to leave the ranks of the CPCz" and to fight for the vital interests of the entire population. The declaration called on every party organization to decide whether it recognized the CC elected at the congress as the supreme party organ and appealed to the People's Militia, the security service and army, the trade unions and all party functionaries to accept the authority of the newly elected party leadership.[71]

Party organizations, at the regional and district level, and in institutions and enterprises throughout the country, reacted independently to the invasion with a surprising degree of unanimity, lacking as they did any central guidance other than what they heard on the radio about the actions of central party and state organs. The common themes were repeated in resolution after resolution, from the party organizations in the ministries, universities, factories, institutes, etc. Without exception, the regional party organizations and their newspapers condemned the occupation and pledged loyalty to Dubček and his colleagues. There were, of course, some differences in tone and emphasis, especially on the first day or two, but in general there was an identity of outlook in all parts of the country.[72] No voice was raised publicly by any party organization approving the occupation or advocating collaboration. Most of the regional party committees entered into negotiations with the local military commanders of the invading armies, but they used these meetings to express their hostility to the occupation, to complain about the behavior of the occupying troops, and to demand that the forces be withdrawn from the cities and not interfere with the restoration of normal economic and social life. Soviet complaints concerning the actions of the population and the mass media were rejected.[73]

[71] Text, *RP*, Aug. 25; *Sedm dnů*, pp. 271-77. For the above, see *Sedm dnů*, pp. 192, 203, 227-28, 230-34, 238-39. For the press conferences, ibid., pp. 294-96; *RP*, Aug. 25, 26. Note the editorial (*RP*, Aug. 27) which warned of the continuing danger of a harsh occupation regime such as the protectorate in World War II and a collaborationist government under domestic quislings.

[72] This is based on a comparative analysis of regional committee statements published in the regional newspapers listed above, n. 46. For Slovak statements, see *Pravda* and *Smena*, Aug. 21. The regional party organ, *Svoboda* (Aug. 24) complained that the initial statement of the Central Bohemia regional committee, of which Piller was the leading secretary, had been weak in comparison with all others. Its later statements, however, were no less strong than that of other regional committees and even suggested the desirability of neutrality (*Svoboda*, Aug. 25).

[73] See the descriptions of such negotiations in East Bohemia, *Pochodeň*, Aug. 23; North Bohemia, *Průboj*, Aug. 22, 23; West Bohemia, *Pravda*, Aug. 25; Brno, *Rovnost*, Aug. 24 and *SS*, Aug. 24; in North Moravia, Ostrava joint newspaper, Aug. 23; Central Slovakia (BBC, II, Aug. 27). Cf. the letter of the Prague municipal committee to the military command protesting the occupation and demanding the release of Šimon (*VP*, Aug. 26).

788

SLOVAK REACTIONS

The response of Slovak public opinion was hardly different from that
of the Czechs. The same spontaneous demonstration of hostility to the
invaders was evident in the streets of Bratislava and other centers, and
the same attitudes were manifested by the clandestine press and radio.[74]
The unanimity of opinion in condemning the occupation and any attempts at collaboration was clearly demonstrated in strongly worded
common statements signed by spokesmen of the more nationally oriented
and liberally oriented wings of the intelligentsia and published in the
rival journals, *Kultúrny život* and *Nové slovo*.[75] The Slovak National
Front issued a firm statement, as did the Slovak writers, composers, and
artists, the Union of Journalists, the Bratislava university party committee, and the workers of two large enterprises, Slovnaft and the Dimitrov
Chemical Plant.[76]

Public opinion was not, however, fully mirrored in the initial statements of party and state organs, e.g. those of the Slovak National Council (see above) and the Slovak party Presidium. The latter announced
support for Dubček and for the reform movement, but did not expressly
condemn the occupation and appealed for discipline and order on the
part of the population. The early pronouncements of the three regional
party organizations, in East, West, and Central Slovakia, especially the
last, were relatively mild in content, usually stressing the need for calm
and order and in only one case referring to the illegality of the occupation.[77] The Bratislava municipal committee, meeting with delegates to
the two congresses on August 22, was much more vigorous in denouncing the illegality of the occupation and asserting the legal status of
the constituted state and party organs. It justified the Action Programs
of the two parties and empowered the delegates to express these views
at the 14th congress.[78] A joint statement of the party Presidium and Secretariat on August 22 was more forceful, criticizing the entry of troops
and opposing any actions taken "outside the legal, democratically elected

---

[74] The following is based mainly on the radio and the Slovak press, since the
Black Book gives inadequate coverage of events in Slovakia.

[75] One statement (*Kultúrny život*, Aug. 21) was signed by M. Válek, R. Kaliský,
L. Mňačko, V. Mihálik, L. Novomeský, P. Števček, L. Holdoš, R. Olšinský, L.
Ťažký, D. Tatarka, and many others from both wings. The other (*Nové slovo*,
Aug. 23) was signed by a smaller group, including Holdoš, Olšinský, Tatarka,
Mihálik, Mňačko, Števček, and Válek. The editorial boards of both newspapers
also published declarations condemning the occupation.

[76] *Pravda*, Aug. 21; *KŽ*, Aug. 21; *Hlas l'udu*, Aug. 22; *Pravda*, Aug. 25.

[77] *Pravda*, Aug. 21, 22; *Smena*, Aug. 21.

[78] *Pravda*, Aug. 23. The municipal committee also took a certain initiative concerning the Slovak party congress, calling on delegates to come to Bratislava and
report to the large factories (BBC, II, Aug. 24).

party and state leadership." They expressed the hope of "an honorable political solution" which would be in the interests of the two nations and in accordance with the post-January course. Accepting the reality that "the troops are here," the statement warned against provocations that would cause bloodshed. On the 23rd, the Presidium conferred on Husák the mandate to speak in Moscow "within the intentions" of its August 22nd statement and called on him to demand the release of the interned comrades, the normalization of the legal organs of party and state, and the withdrawal of troops.[79]

The utterances of the top party organs aroused considerable misgivings and doubts, especially as they made no references to either the 14th Party Congress or to the Slovak extraordinary party congress, scheduled to take place on August 26. Yet the proceedings of the Vysočany congress were widely publicized in the press and on the radio, and were, without exception, greeted positively and held up as an example for the Slovaks.[80] The desirability of convening the Slovak congress immediately, at the latest on the scheduled date, was advocated by many. It was argued that the congress was all the more important because of the divisions within the Slovak party Presidium which included, it was claimed, some who approved the occupation and favored collaboration.[81] Lurking in the background, too, was the unspoken concern to document without equivocation the unity of Czechs and Slovaks and to demonstrate the lack of support for any idea of separation of Slovakia and its incorporation in the Soviet Union.[82]

[79] *Pravda*, Aug. 23. The Žilina district party committee criticized the joint statement for not stressing the illegality of the occupation and called for an immediate convocation of the Slovak congress (ibid). In a strange episode, O. Klokoč, SNR chairman, expressed the wish to go to Moscow and was given a mandate to represent the SNR by its presidium. He apparently tried to board the plane carrying the President's party but was barred by troops (BBC, II, Sept. 3).

[80] For positive appraisals of the 14th congress, see, e.g. *Roľnícke noviny*, Aug. 24; Š. Hanakovič and B. Graca, *Pravda*, Aug. 25; other delegates, ibid., Aug. 26; for a full report of the 14th congress, *Pravda*, Aug. 27. See also the positive statement by Saml, a Slovak who had attended the Prague congress, who believed that the whole CPS would support the congress. He called for a CPS congress at once (BBC, II, Aug. 27). Saml was identified on the radio as a CPCz Central Committee member, but such a name does not appear in the list of CC members, or among Slovak leaders. The reference may be to A. Zamek, a Slovak, who, although not listed as a CC member, was elected to the new CPCz Presidium (see above, p. 787).

[81] Radio reports, Aug. 24 (BBC, II, Aug. 27). Among those favoring the immediate convocation of the congress were Hanakovič, Graca, H. Kočtúch, Saml (above), and the Central Slovak Regional Committee.

[82] Several radio reports of such proposals were broadcast (BBC, II, Aug. 27, 28, Sept. 3). *Roľnícke noviny* (Aug. 26) reported that leaflets proposing Slovak incorporation in the USSR were dropped by helicopter. The presidium of the East Slovak CPCz regional committee denied such reports as absurd and called for unity of the Republic (*Východoslovenské noviny*, Aug. 28). A similar viewpoint

Meanwhile delegates were already preparing to go to Bratislava for the congress and some had already arrived on the assumption that it would be held at once. They were met with official reports that Dubček, Husák, and others, by telephone from Moscow, were pressing for a delay, at least until their return from Moscow, so that they could participate.[83] The mood of some delegates was so suspicious, however, that they were unwilling to believe such reports without verification but reluctantly agreed to accept a postponement if this was really Dubček's wish. The Bratislava municipal committee believed that the congress should be held on the scheduled date and urged contact with Dubček and Husák to verify their attitude.[84] Telephonic connection was in fact established on August 24th, at 6:00 in the evening, between four CC members (J. Janík, Klokoč, Pavlenda, and Zrak) and Dubček and others in Moscow. Dubček strongly urged the postponement of the congress for a short time, saying that he spoke in the name of Husák and his other partners in the Moscow talks. The Presidium decided to accede to Dubček's wish and to so inform the Central Committee, to be convened on August 25, at 10:00 a.m., and appealed to the delegates to accept this delay.[85]

The CC plenum adopted a resolute and unambiguous stand that was almost identical to that taken by the CPCz and the state organs. In its final decision the plenum disapproved the occupation and demanded the withdrawal of troops, asserted its full recognition of the legal organs of party and state, and demanded the release of the interned leaders. Most significantly, the CC decision associated itself (*hlasiti se*) with the results of the 14th congress and approved the results of its first session. Although, it was said, the situation demanded that the Slovak congress be held at once, it was postponed at the personal request of Dubček and would meet at a date to be set in agreement with him after his return. The decision declared the firm unity of Slovaks with the Czech communists and with the Czech nation, and their desire for a unified federal Republic. The CC plenum made certain important changes in leadership, expelling M. Chudík from the CC, adding to the Presidium J. Kosce-

---

was expressed by Husák at the Slovak CC plenum in early September where he ridiculed the idea of Slovak separation or incorporation in the Soviet Union (*Pravda*, Sept. 6).

[83] V. Pavlenda, for instance, reported a call from Husák to this effect (*RP* [Brno] Aug. 25). There is some mystery surrounding this call. It was variously reported to have taken place in the evening of the 23rd or early in the morning of the 24th and to have involved Husák *and* Bil'ak (BBC, II, Aug. 26). See also *Svědectví*, nos. 34-36 (1969), p. 225. On the views of Slovak delegates, see *Pochodeň*, Aug. 25; *Pravda*, Aug. 26; *RP* (Bratislava), Aug. 26; BBC, II, Aug. 27.

[84] *Pravda*, Aug. 26.

[85] This report was broadcast on the evening of the 24th (BBC, II, Aug. 27); also given in *Dokumenty o okupácii ČSSR*, p. 20.

lanský, Š. Sádovský, P. Colotka, V. Mihálik, and the former candidates, R. Harenčár and K. Boďa, and appointing to the Secretariat L. Novomeský and L. Abrahám. It also adopted a message to the parties of the five invading states condemning the occupation and urging withdrawal.[86]

The decisive position adopted at the plenum was warmly welcomed by Bratislava *Pravda* (Aug. 26) which admitted that it had entertained serious doubts as to the stand taken by the party leadership and fears as to the position the CC would adopt. The congress delegates present were assigned the main credit for the outcome of the plenum, and certain leading secretaries showed, by their attitudes, that they no longer belonged in the ranks of the CC. The overwhelming majority had wanted an immediate convening of the Slovak congress and had been willing to wait only as a result of the personal request of Dubček and Husák. As for the 14th congress, Milan Lajčiak had argued that no stand be taken on this question, but all subsequent speakers favored support of the congress "as a matter of principle." In the words of the *Pravda* editorial, "firm unity and solidarity with the Czech communists and with the Czech nation is for us at the time a sacred matter, for on this depends our common fate." By its decision the CC had "preserved the honor of the party and the nation," and by its approval of the 14th congress, had "expressed its firm will to preserve the unity of the party and the unity of the Republic."

THE SLOVAK CONGRESS

In fact, the extraordinary Slovak congress convened prior to the return of the leaders from Moscow but in the knowledge that this was imminent. Its first meeting was held late at night on the date originally scheduled—August 26—under semilegal conditions in a large factory in Bratislava.[87] In attendance were Slovak delegates to the 14th congress and the official CPCz delegation, F. Vodsloň, L. Hrdinová, Š. Sádovský, and J. Zuda. According to an unofficial report, the proceedings began as

[86] For the proceedings, see *Pravda*, Aug. 25-27. According to *RN* (n.d., Aug. 26?), there was sharp criticism of the Presidium's earlier indecisiveness with regard to the two congresses, e.g. by L. Holdoš.

[87] The proceedings were officially reported in *Pravda*, Aug. 27 (in three editions), Aug. 28-29, and in a booklet, *Mimoriadny zjazd Komunistickej strany Slovenska* (Bratislava, 1968). Only Husák's speech was given; those of 41 others went unrecorded. For an English text of Husák's speech, see the CPCz Central Committee's *Information Bulletin*, no. 4 (Prague, 1968), pp. 49-66. His closing remarks were not published. For other reports, see BBC, II, Aug. 28-30. For an account by a delegate, see M. Dvulitová, *VN*, Sept. 1. See the report of the congress by B. Chudý who criticized the early calling of the night session in spite of Dubček's appeal and in the absence of the First Secretary, Biľak. He claimed that this was done by certain members of the Presidium, with the assistance of the Bratislava municipal party committee, and that the CC apparatus, which had already completed the congress preparations, was bypassed (*Pravda*, Jan. 8, 1971).

soon as a quorum was present with an address by A. Ťažký who strongly urged the replacement of compromised functionaries in the election of the new leading organs.[88] The congress decided at once to declare itself in "permanent" session since it would be unable to deal with all the items on the original agenda. It proceeded to take the significant step of endorsing the conclusions and the results of the 14th congress in Prague. It also confirmed the Slovak CC's appeal to the parties of the five invading countries. By the time of the second sitting at 10:00 the following morning the leaders had already returned to Prague (in the early morning hours). Husák requested, however, that discussion of substantive questions be postponed until he or Dubček could participate. Meanwhile the congress approved a letter of welcome to Dubček and his colleagues and to the CPCz CC (which was to meet that day), and prepared itself for action by selecting a working presidium and other committees.[89]

In any event, Dubček did not attend the congress, excusing himself in a letter which authorized Husák to speak in his name. On Husák's arrival, he met at some length with the working presidium, thus delaying the sitting of the congress until late in the afternoon. Paradoxically, and to the concern of many delegates, two of the CPCz delegates were excluded from the presidium meeting.[90] When the plenary session finally came to order at 17:40, it did so under more legal circumstances, in the originally planned location, the Park of Culture and Recreation. Its business was confined, however, to the reading of letters from Dubček and the other leaders and a relatively brief report from Husák, who postponed his main address to the following day.[91]

The main work of the congress was done on the third and final day. In his full report on the Moscow talks Husák justified the "political solution" that had been found at these meetings, rejected the alternative of "resistance," and declared that there was "no third way." They had been able to attain their main aims—the return of the leaders, the restoration

---

[88] *Smena*, Aug. 27. Initially, of the 638 delegates, only 358 were present (BBC, II, Aug. 28), but the number rose to 536 the following morning and 604 by the end of the congress (*Pravda*, Aug. 27 [III] and Aug. 29).

[89] The congress presidium was said to have assumed the right of party leadership from the old CC plenum. Two former CPS Presidium members, M. Hruškovič and H. Ďurkovič, were not included. For full list of names, see BBC, II, Aug. 28. There was some opposition to the election of Klokoč because of his "indecisiveness" in regard to the occupation, but he was defended by Zrak and elected (ibid., Aug. 29). One person was rejected as a member of the resolutions committee due to his actions in preceding days (*Pravda*, Aug. 27).

[90] These were Vodsloň and Hrdinová. All four delegates had originally been welcomed to the congress. In the final communiqué, the CPCz delegation was, however, listed entirely differently—G. Husák, F. Barbírek, and Š. Sádovský. Vodsloň and Hodinová were listed as guests. Of the three, Husák had been elected to the CPCz Central Committee for the first time at the 14th congress; Sádovský was reelected; and Barbírek had not been reelected.

[91] BBC, II, Aug. 28.

of the legal organs, and the gradual withdrawal of troops "within a relatively short period," when normalization had been achieved. At the same time Husák pledged himself to continue the post-January course, describing the eight months as "a great and bright period," but admitted the defects in that course and the need to correct them. He warned of the danger of a split in the party (especially among the Czechs) but expressed confidence that the Slovak party would be united and that there would be no "great oppositional current" to what he called the "Dubček concept" of policy.[92]

It is not known to what extent his arguments were countered by other speakers. The final communiqué reported that the congress had given its full support to the Moscow negotiators and had seen no other possibility than to endorse the implementation of the results of the negotiations. In the main resolution the congress announced determination to continue on the January path and to fulfill the Action Program, and called for unity around Dubček. Neutrality was rejected as contrary to the interests of the two nations. The principle of federation would be embodied in legislation, they were convinced, by October 28, as the Czech National Council had proclaimed.

A source of potential conflict was the issue of the 14th congress and the attitude adopted by Husák toward it. Although professing not to wish to judge or to criticize the congress, Husák contended that it had been called without consultation with the Slovak CC or Presidium, or with any Slovak politician, whether in Bratislava or Prague. In the absence of most of the Slovak delegates (only 10 percent were present) the Central Committee had not been democratically elected. Moreover, he noted, the communist parties of the five invading countries did not recognize the new CC. Although he was in Prague the day before, he said, he had not been consulted or invited to the meeting of that body. He was therefore not willing to accept a position in the new CPCz Central Committee or its Presidium and urged other Slovaks to give up their posts in these bodies. There were, he said, two Central Committees in Prague but he was confident that Dubček would find a solution that would assure the unity necessary to avoid another crisis.

The acceptance of Husák's position would represent a complete volte-face on the part of most Slovaks on the question of the 14th congress. According to an eyewitness there was substantial opposition on this issue, but this was not revealed in official reports. Just prior to the opening of the Slovak congress, however, according to *Pravda* (Aug. 29), the delegates had given their approval to the 14th congress in their meetings, and during the proceedings in Bratislava, a number of delegates endorsed

[92] For the congress documents, including Husák's speech, *Pravda*, Aug. 27-29.

its legality in interviews with the press.[93] Husák, however, won substantial support, especially in a declaration signed by 30 CC members. This stated that, although they had originally approved the 14th congress, they currently felt, in light of the Moscow talks, that they could not be members of an organ "at the head of which the Dubček leadership does not stand." (In fact, of course, Dubček had been elected First Secretary!) They expressed the hope that "the 14th congress" would be called in the shortest possible time so as to avoid a split in the party. This declaration bore the signatures of progressive leaders such as Zrak, Ťažký, Pavlenda, Števček, Kočtúch, and Graca, as well as Husák and Novomeský. In the end the Bratislava congress, noting that 247 Slovak delegates to the 14th congress had agreed, formally adopted a stand that the CC created at that congress "cannot be considered as an all-state leading organ of the party" and called for unity of Czech and Slovak communists under Dubček. Finally, in its letter to Dubček, the congress stressed the need to create a CPCz Central Committee "which would have authority in the whole party, in Bohemia and in Slovakia, and which would . . . assure the continuance on the path embarked upon by the January and May plenums. . . ." It also urged that the 14th congress should meet quickly to elect such a committee.[94]

The decision to deny the legality of the Vysočany congress (presumably taken under the influence of Husák's arguments) undercut the legitimacy of the progressive post-congress leadership of the CPCz as a whole and raised the danger of a split between Czechs and Slovaks. On the other hand, the Slovak congress had a positive result in electing a predominantly new Central Committee of 107 members, of whom only sixteen were carryovers, and a Supervision and Auditing Commission (KRK) with only four previous high officeholders.[95] This in turn led to

[93] E.g. L. Holdoš, D. Okáli, Š. Hanakovič, I. Hutíra, I. Laluha and S. Fal'tan. Two others favored resignation from the CPCz Central Committee (*Pravda*, Aug. 28, 29). In radio commentaries, Husák's position was both justified and criticized. The critics spoke of the general support of the 14th congress by regional and district committees and by thousands of letters, resolutions, and telegrams, and implied that Husák's tactic was aimed at Dubček's leadership—a charge denied by the more positive commentary (BBC, II, Aug. 30).

[94] For the above, *Pravda*, Aug. 29.

[95] Of the 107 full CC members, only 12 had belonged to the 1966 CC: Barbírek, Bod'a, Colotka, V. Daubner, Dubček, J. Janík, Klokoč, S. Lupták, Š. Sádovský, Ťažký, J. Valo, and J. Zrak. Five others had been candidates: R. Harenčár, S. Kodaj, L. Kompiš, S. Martinka, and V. Pavlenda. Ninety were new members. Of the 24 candidates, all were new except two former full members, V. Mihálik and J. Vrabec. Of the 28 KRK members, four were carry-overs from 1966 (two from KRK, and two from the CC). Of the 1966 CC, only 15 of the 69 full members were given positions in the new bodies. Of the 29 CC candidates in 1966, only two became full members; the rest were dropped. Of KRK, only two were carried over. According to Chudý (*Pravda*, Jan. 8, 1971) the selection of CC members from the

the formation, at the first CC plenum, of a Presidium and Secretariat that were also new and relatively progressive in membership.[96] The Presidium was almost entirely of 1968 vintage—Klokoč, Pavlenda, Ťažký, Zrak, Harenčár (hitherto a candidate), Falt'an, and Sedláková (appointed to the Secretariat in 1968), and included several new members—Husák, Novomeský, Sádovský, and S. Lupták. Only Bod'a (then a candidate) remained from the 1966 Presidium. In the Secretariat only Zrak was retained from 1966 and six others who had not been members previously were added—Husák, Pavlenda, Graca, Sádovský, L. Abrahám, and J. Turček. The head of the KRK was Ján Koscelanský, a 1966 CC member. Of greatest significance was the omission from the two top bodies of Bil'ak and Barbírek, and the absence of Bil'ak even from the CC.

THE MOSCOW TALKS

President Svoboda and his party, having left Prague at approximately 9:30 a.m. on Friday, the 23rd, received an ostentatious reception, with full military honors, at the Vnukovo airport, with most of the top-ranking Soviet leaders present. Most of the first day seems to have been consumed with discussion of Brezhnev's renewed appeal for the formation of a new government (which Svoboda rejected), and Svoboda's insistence on the participation of the interned leaders in the talks.[97] Brezhnev ultimately gave in and at some point, perhaps during that evening or night, Dubček, Smrkovský, and Černík were brought to the Kremlin. Early Saturday morning broadcasts in Czechoslovakia brought the news that Dubček and others were taking part in the parleys but this was not officially confirmed until 10:45 that evening when a message from Svoboda was carried by the Czechoslovak radio. Other Czech and Slovak leaders arrived in Moscow a day or two later, probably on Saturday or Sunday, including notably Mlynař and Šimon, but also Barbírek, Rigo, Švestka, and Jakeš. This constituted the entire pre-congress Presidium, with the exception of Kolder (who was in Prague) and Kriegel, still imprisoned. By the end of the talks, according to the final communiqué, there were nineteen present on the Czechoslovak side, including also Špaček, Lenárt, and the Czechoslovak ambassador in Moscow, Koucký. On the Soviet side almost the entire Politburo took part, along with two CC Secretaries (K. F. Katushev and B. N. Ponomarev), Marshal Grechko, and A. A. Gromyko, the foreign minister.[98]

---

324 nominees was based mainly on the criterion of the individual's attitude toward the occupation.

[96] Names were given in *Pravda*, Aug. 29, biographies, ibid., Aug. 31.

[97] Reports of a threat of suicide by Svoboda, if his demands were not met, cannot be confirmed.

[98] The communiqué described the Czechoslovak participants by their pre-14th

Throughout the talks the Czech and Slovak negotiators had few and limited communications with Prague. As Smrkovský later said, "We had at first little or no information" about the situation at home. Yet they must have had some knowledge of the dramatic resistance to the occupation since it had commenced (and the 14th congress had ended) prior to Svoboda's departure and it was no doubt described by later arrivals and in the occasional telephone conversations with Prague and Bratislava.[99] Prague was even less informed about the progress of the talks. Svoboda, who had expected to return on the very day of his arrival, sent back occasional terse messages, including the one which was broadcast on Saturday evening, but these were confined mainly to appeals for calm and support. Dubček was in touch with the Slovaks on the 24th, as has been mentioned, in connection with the postponement of the Slovak congress. The lack of information about the talks and the length of the negotiations had led to the August 25th appeal from Prague to President Svoboda to return but it is not known whether it was ever received. The discussions were in any case nearing conclusion by that time. The communiqué was finally signed on the 26th and the delegation departed at dawn for home, arriving in the early morning hours of Tuesday the 27th, after four days of exhausting negotiations.[100]

Little or nothing is known with any assurance concerning the content of the negotiations or the attitudes taken by the two sides, or by individual members of the two delegations. In a laconic announcement each day

---

congress designation, thus ignoring the changes made at the 14th congress. Husák was at first wrongly identified as a CC member, but this was corrected. For the communiqué, *Pravda* (Moscow), Aug. 28; for the protocol, see below.

For the Moscow talks and the immediate aftermath, see in particular P. Tigrid, *Why Dubček Fell*, pp. 112-23; also *Sedm dnů*, pp. 380 ff.; *The Current Digest of the Soviet Press* 20, Sept. 18-25. Other accounts are given in Windsor and Roberts, *Czechoslovakia, 1968*, pp. 131-36; Gueyt, *Mutation*, pp. 311 ff.; Szulc, *Czechoslovakia*, pp. 412-44; Brahm, *Der Kreml*, pp. 84-88. Documents are given in R. A. Remington, ed., *Winter in Prague* (Cambridge, Mass., 1969), part v; Haefs, ed., *Ereignisse*, pp. 17-91. For Smrkovský's account, *Listy*, March, 1975, pp. 19-22 (also Appendix D).

[99] Štrougal (Aug. 26) reported several phone conversations with Svoboda, and also some with Dubček; they were, he said, informed of the situation in Czechoslovakia (BBC, II, Aug. 26). Svoboda was reported to have spoken with his wife on the evening of his arrival and to have received from her a description of the situation at home (Tigrid, *Why Dubček Fell*, pp. 113-14). According to a typescript report which circulated in Prague, by a participant in the talks, the discussions were influenced, and the position of the delegation strengthened, by the election of the interned leaders at the 14th congress and by Mlynář's detailed description of the situation at home. This was confirmed by Smrkovský (Appendix D).

[100] For the altercation between the Czechoslovak and Soviet leaders over permission to Kriegel to return home with the others, see Smrkovský's testimony, *Listy*, March 1975, p. 22. Kriegel was not a participant in the talks and refused to sign the protocol (p. 21). See also Appendix D below. Indra remained in Moscow for reasons of health.

Pravda reported that the talks were proceeding "in a frank and comradely manner." The final communiqué was vague and ambiguous. The 14th point of the secret protocol provided that the talks, as well as all other contacts between the two parties after August 20, should remain "strictly confidential."

The situation on the Czechoslovak side is obscure and can be gleaned only from later reports from some of the participants. According to Husák's initial statement on his return, the original purpose of Svoboda's trip had been twofold and had related to the internment of the leaders and the prevention of the functioning of the legal organs of party and state. Apart from that, the main objective was to search for "a political way out of the situation in which we had landed ourselves" and in particular to effect the departure of the invading armies. Although the Czechoslovak delegates adopted "the same attitude" on these matters and ultimately agreed unanimously with the solution adopted, there were, Husák admitted, "heated discussions" within the ranks of their own delegation and he hinted that one or other had threatened to refuse to continue. Husák reported that "we insisted that we should continue with the development which began . . . with the January plenum . . ." and were met with Soviet professions that they did not seek to pressure the Czechoslovaks to revert to the pre-January situation or to interfere in their internal affairs.[101]

Smrkovský, in his later radio address, also reported that they had "clashed sharply—with our partners, and among ourselves." Admittedly "they might have rejected any type of compromise" and "they had borne in mind that at a certain point there is nothing left but to reject any kind of accommodating solution . . . and to expose one's breast to the bayonets in the interests of the honor and the character of the nation." In the end, however, they had agreed on another possibility—"a way out based on an acceptable compromise"—a possibility which emerged, he said, as a result of the clearly demonstrated attitude of the Czech and Slovak people to the occupation and its influence on their own situation and the stance of their partners.[102]

The Soviet views as presented at the outset are not known and can be deduced only from the communiqué and the secret protocol. When it became clear, both from Svoboda's adamant stance and from the continuing loyalty of the Czech and Slovak people to their leaders, that no

---

[101] *RP*, Aug. 29; also Czechoslovak radio Aug. 28 (BBC, II, Aug. 29); for another version, *CDSP* 20, Sept. 18, p. 6. Svoboda, in his address to the CC plenum on Aug. 31, described his objectives in somewhat broader terms; the restoration of the country's sovereignty through "a political solution," the renewal of the functions of the principal organs and their representatives, and the continuation on the January path.

[102] *Sedm dnů*, pp. 402-3.

alternative regime could be formed, Brezhnev and his colleagues reluctantly accepted Dubček and the other interned leaders as participants in the talks and sought to secure the delegation's consent to their principal demands. There have been unconfirmed reports of Soviet threats to bombard Prague into submission, to form a military government, and even to separate Slovakia from the Republic. The danger of the latter, although seldom mentioned publicly, was often indirectly implied and was no doubt an ominous contingency ever present in the minds of the Czechoslovak negotiators.[103] In any case, the enormous psychological pressure exerted on the participants, backed by the total occupation of their homeland by half a million troops, which was only partially counteracted by the massive popular and official resistance at home, allowed little leeway for effective counterargument and forced the Czechoslovak side to yield to the main Soviet demands. The Soviet delegates, on their side, were willing to agree to an ambiguous and hypocritical communiqué, coupled with the secret protocol which incorporated their main demands.[104] It then remained only for the other invading partners to

[103] Grey Hodnett and Peter J. Potichnyj found no convincing evidence that the Soviet Union was seriously considering the annexation of Slovakia (*The Ukraine and the Czechoslovak Crisis*, Canberra, 1970, pp. 87-89).

[104] The most authentic version of the protocol is given by Tigrid, in Czech, in *Svědectví*, nos. 34-36 (1969), pp. 228-31; in English, in *Why Dubček Fell*, pp. 210-14 (also in Remington, ed., *Winter in Prague*, pp. 379-82). For French and German versions, Tigrid, *La chute irrésistible d'Alexander Dubček* (Paris, 1969), pp. 293-99 and E. Löbl and L. Grünwald, *Die intellectuelle Revolution* (Düsseldorf, 1969), pp. 302-8. A mimeographed typewritten version (identical to that of Tigrid's), which circulated in Prague, is in the author's possession. An official party document for intra-party circulation on the CC plenum of Aug. 31 referred explicitly to the protocol and summarized some of its major provisions (*O zasedání Ústředního Výboru KSČ dne 31. srpna 1968*, Prague, 1968, pp. 34-37). Smrkovský, in a speech on Sept. 9, expressly referred to the 15-point document without revealing its content (BBC, II, Sept. 10). Mlynář also referred to the protocol in a television address (*RP*, Sept. 15) but mentioned only several of its commitments. Another version of the protocol was published by Tad Szulc in *The New York Times*, Sept. 8. In his book *Czechoslovakia* (pp. 422-23) Szulc described this as the list of Soviet demands presented to the Czechoslovak delegates. It differs somewhat from the Tigrid version, mainly in demanding (by name) the dismissal of Pavel, Šik, and Hájek, and in requiring recognition by the Czechoslovak side that there was a counterrevolutionary situation and that the Czechoslovak border was not prepared for defense. The Szulc account provided for a commission on possible reparations for damages caused by the invasion and stipulated that the invalidation of the 14th congress would occur only when the occupation troops left. It also provided for the withdrawal of Soviet security agents from Czechoslovakia. The Western press published a number of different versions of the protocol and of Soviet demands. *Der Spiegel* (Sept. 30), for instance, printed a 17-point document which differs substantially from the Tigrid document, including a number of quite different demands: the expulsion of certain foreign correspondents; censorship of letters and telephone conversations; replacement of the chairmen of the Writers' and Journalists' Unions; punishment of persons guilty of anti-Soviet actions; a ban on the formation of a Czech Communist Party; requirement of exit permits for Czechoslovak citizens and limits on visits from the West; abolition of

accept the outcome in a brief communiqué which announced merely that the representatives had discussed the Czechoslovak situation and had "unanimously adopted an appropriate decision."[105]

The final communiqué, at least by implication, in listing the participants with their pre-invasion positions, indicated that the Soviet Union had reconciled itself to the continuance in office of the pre-invasion party and state leadership. The Soviet representatives expressed a desire for friendship and cooperation with Czechoslovakia on the basis of "equality" and "independence" and endorsed the CPCz's intention to proceed on the basis of the January and May CC plenums (the April plenum was omitted). At the same time the statement referred to the necessity of implementing the joint decisions made at Čierna and the principles proclaimed at Bratislava, as well as "the practical steps" stemming from the understanding reached at the two meetings. There was no reference to a counterrevolutionary situation in Czechoslovakia or to an official appeal for help, nor even an explicit endorsement of the occupation, or, as it was called, "the entry of troops." The latter would not, it was said, interfere in the internal affairs of the country and would be withdrawn "as the situation normalized." The "swiftest possible normalization of the situation" in Czechoslovakia was said to be the goal and undefined "measures" to achieve this goal were agreed upon. Czechoslovak delegates indicated their intention to demand the removal of the Czechoslovak question from the agenda of the United Nations Security Council. Both sides avowed their intention to rebuff revanchist and neo-Nazi forces seeking to "breach the inviolability of the frontiers," and to strengthen the defense might of the socialist commonwealth and enhance the effectiveness of the Warsaw pact.

The protocol, which, it should be remembered, was never revealed to the public, gave a much clearer picture of the real meaning of the Moscow talks. The document restated the need to put into practice the "principles and obligations" of Bratislava and the "agreements" made at Čierna nad Tisou and to apply the resolutions of the January and May plena. The fifteen points included several that were statements of intention by the CPCz Presidium and others that represented agreements of the two parties. The measures of normalization were specified as follows: the invalidation of the 14th Party Congress; the convocation of a

---

the West German trade mission; a ban on negotiations with Yugoslavia and Rumania and on agreements with the West; a Czechoslovak share in provisioning of allied troops (Haefs, ed., *Ereignisse*, p. 75).

[105] *Pravda*, Aug. 28. According to Smrkovský's testimony, Ulbricht, Gomułka, Kádár, and Zhivkov were present in Moscow and, unknown to the Czechoslovak delegates, were consulted and gave their approval to the final protocol. See Appendix D.

CC plenum within six to ten days to discuss "questions of normalization"; and other measures, including the dismissal of certain persons; the rapid imposition of control over the mass media, including personnel changes; the banning of the activity of certain anti-socialist organizations, including the Social Democratic Party; measures against government members outside the country; measures to strengthen the leadership of the Ministry of the Interior; no reprisals against those who had struggled against anti-socialist forces. On the important question of troops, point 5 provided for the conclusion of a treaty for the complete withdrawal of troops in stages "as soon as the threat to socialism in Czechoslovakia and to the security of the countries of the socialist community had passed," and in the meantime for their restationing in barracks and military places away from cities and villages wherever the local authorities could maintain order. The question of the security of Czechoslovakia's border with the GFR was to be studied. In the sphere of foreign affairs the protocol provided for early economic negotiations between the two countries; strengthening the defense system of the Warsaw treaty and other organizations; "coordinated action in international relations," including opposition to revisionist and imperialist forces; the withdrawal of the Czechoslovak question from the UN; and further negotiations between the two regimes in the near future.

REPORT TO THE PEOPLE

Within a few hours after their return the top party and government leaders delivered reports on the Moscow negotiations to the principal governing organs—Černík to the government (with Svoboda present at a later stage); Smrkovský to the National Assembly; and Dubček to the Central Committee. The National Assembly, in a strong statement, reiterated its positions on the occupation, on the earliest withdrawal of troops, and on the reform program, and announced its intention of discussing the government's report on the Moscow talks. It issued an appeal to the population which followed similar lines and also proclaimed its support for the party organs legally elected by the 14th congress. The government did not make any public announcement, but began to prepare measures to control the media. The party CC, in an initial statement published in leaflet form, expressed its agreement with the public's "bitterness and . . . disillusionment" with the Moscow talks. "We yield to superior odds, but we shall never give up the demand for sovereignty and freedom. . . . Socialism with a human face still remains the mission of our nations." In a later communiqué, however, it was reported that the CC elected by the 14th congress "had decided in a disciplined manner to

801

support the party leadership headed by A. Dubček . . . and to implement the political procedures unanimously agreed upon. . . ."[106]

The population at large received the bitter news in the form of the communiqué, read over the radio at 14:40 in the afternoon, followed at once by a brief speech by Svoboda, and at 17:30 by a longer address by Dubček, delivered under great stress and broken by long pauses. Meanwhile the four leaders issued a joint statement, begging citizens "not to allow their emotions to carry them into actions that would result in a national catastrophe" and pleading for support for "consolidation so that the troops could begin gradually to withdraw from our land and finally leave entirely."[107] On the two following days, Černík and Smrkovský also reported to the nation, the latter in a frank and moving manner which provoked the ire of Moscow.[108] The secret protocol, with the grim reality of its fifteen points, was not, however, revealed or even mentioned.

All four leaders referred to the difficulties of the talks, Smrkovský calling it "the most difficult experience" of his entire life, and spoke warmly of the strength which they had derived from the confidence expressed by the people and their disciplined behavior. Great emphasis was laid on what had been achieved in Moscow, especially the safe return of all the leaders and their restoration to their rightful positions, and the possibility of resuming the post-January course. All four declared their intention to proceed with the program of reform as outlined in the Action Program and at the January, April, and May plenums (not omitting, as the communiqué had done, the April session). Černík and Smrkovský paid special tribute to the Slovak respect for the unity of the Republic and the latter restated that October 28th was the target date for federation. All the leaders spoke of the paramount task of achieving "normalization," without, however, giving much concrete meaning to this ambiguous term.

The requirements of order, discipline, and circumspection were stressed, and as Černík put it, the need to avoid "ill-considered radicalism," or in Dubček's words, "passions and psychoses." Svoboda and Dubček warned particularly of the danger of "bloodshed" if the Moscow agreements were not carried out. It was admitted that certain "extraordinary" and "temporary" measures would be necessary, which would, as Dubček put it, "restrain, in some degree, democracy and freedom of ex-

[106] For the leaflet (n.d.), *Práce*, Aug. 29; also Pelikán, ed., *Tanky*, p. 263; for the other statements, *Sedm dnů*, pp. 393-94, 384-85, 391-92, resp. For Smrkovský's account of the post-Moscow events, see his testimony, *Listy*, March, 1975, pp. 22-25 (also Appendix D).

[107] *RP*, Aug. 28; *Sedm dnů*, pp. 392-93.

[108] Texts of all four speeches are given in *Sedm dnů*, passim. Dubček's and Svoboda's speeches (but not Smrkovský's), and Husák's initial report to the Slovak congress were briefly reported in *Pravda* (Moscow), Aug. 28, 31 (*CDSP*, Sept. 18).

pression." These measures, said Smrkovský, would slow down and make more difficult the building of democratic socialism.

All emphasized the Soviet commitment to withdraw their troops gradually, "in stages," although only Smrkovský frankly admitted that the troops would remain for some time and would leave only "after normalization of the situation." Dubček, on the other hand, was so bold as to declare that the main aim was "to effect the withdrawal of troops as soon as possible" and termed groundless and harmful any doubts about withdrawal.

Smrkovský described most poignantly the dilemma facing the negotiators in Moscow—whether to reject any compromise, with the result of a permanent military occupation of the country, or to seek "an acceptable compromise," which he felt they had found. Only history, and the people, however, would judge whether in fact it *was* acceptable or "a betrayal." Only Smrkovský, too, referred to the fact that the National Assembly would debate the government statement on the negotiations and would have to approve any agreement.

The reaction of the population to these grim reports (with the protocol still unknown to all but a few) was uniform in its bitter disillusionment with the outcome of the talks. This was demonstrated in hundreds of resolutions and dozens of broadcasts and newspaper comments.[109] To some it seemed "the only way out" as their leaders had argued. For most the agreement at Moscow, concluded under duress, was "unacceptable" —"a Diktat by force," bearing all too close a resemblance to Munich in 1938. It was generally conceded, however, that the Czechoslovak representatives had achieved the maximum possible under difficult circumstances and deserved praise for their efforts. The presence of "collaborators," who no longer had any right to speak for the nation, was bitterly condemned. Resolution after resolution reasserted full trust and confidence in Dubček, Svoboda, and their colleagues, and demanded that they retain their posts. Without exception the resolutions expressed belief in the legality of the 14th congress, and recognized the new Presidium and

109 For representative samples of resolutions see *Sedm dnů*, pp. 408-69, in particular the resolution of the ÚRO presidium, the National Front central committee, the youth organization representatives, the party's university committee, the Academy of Sciences presidium, and many factory groups. The English version, *The Czech Black Book*, inexcusably omits, without acknowledging the fact, a number of these documents. For other reports, see BBC, II, Aug. 29, 30, Sept. 3. The resolutions adopted by the regional party committees and the national committees followed the same uniform pattern. See, for instance, those adopted in Košice and East Slovakia (*VN*, Aug. 29, 30); in Brno (*Lidová demokracie* [Brno], Aug. 28; *SS*, Aug. 28); South Moravia (*Rovnost*, Aug. 28); East Bohemia (*Pochodeň*, Aug. 29); South Bohemia (*Jihočeská pravda*, Aug. 30); West Bohemia (*Pravda*, Aug. 28, 29); Central Bohemia (*Svoboda*, Aug. 29); North Moravia (Haefs, ed., *Ereignisse*, p. 179).

CC as the only legitimate leading party organs. Devotion to the democratization process and to the Action Program, to democratic rights and socialist legality, and to the sovereignty and freedom of the Republic was constantly reiterated. Demands were made for immediate withdrawal of troops and compensation for material damages done. Some called for final action by the National Assembly; a few for a popular referendum or discussion by the United Nations or a world communist conference; others, but rarely, for a general strike. Almost no one advocated armed resistance, and only occasionally did someone urge the continuance of the passive resistance of the preceding week.[110] Most statements urged calm and order, and the avoidance of actions likely to lead to bloodshed.

CC APPROVAL OF MOSCOW AGREEMENTS

At its meeting on August 31, the CC plenum put the seal of approval on the outcome of the talks and the policy of implementing the obligations accepted at Moscow. It did so, however, in "a specifically Czech way," wrote Michel Tatu—"neither submission nor rebellion."[111] President Svoboda admitted that the results were neither "some kind of triumphal victory" nor were they "capitulation," but they did offer a way out of the situation. The other main speakers whose speeches are available—Dubček, Husák, and Černík—argued that accepting the Moscow terms was the only solution possible under the circumstances and that the alternative of rejecting them was not realistic and would have brought even worse consequences. All agreed with Dubček that the fulfillment of these commitments was imperative as a means of restoring the USSR's shattered confidence in the Czechoslovak leadership and that there must not even be a suspicion that they were trying to avoid this obligation.

The major decision of the plenum gave explicit approval to the actions of the Presidium in Moscow and called on the party to "fulfill the conclusions of these negotiations . . . as a condition of normalization of relations in Czechoslovakia and of relations with the five socialist states of the Warsaw treaty." In a phrase not reported in Moscow *Pravda*, the CC empowered the Presidium to do everything possible for the quickest withdrawal of foreign troops and for creating the conditions for the implementation of the January policy.[112] The plenum did not specifically

---

[110] For the latter, *Literární listy*, Aug. 28 (*Sedm dnů*, pp. 426-27). *Student*, in an initial reaction, called the acceptance of the Moscow terms "treason" and demanded that the National Assembly not ratify the agreement. In a later statement, the editors, however, retracted these comments (*Student*, Aug. 27; *MF*, Aug. 31; *Sedm dnů*, pp. 419-20).

[111] Tatu, *L'hérésie*, p. 233.

[112] Official report of the CC plenum, *RP*, Sept. 3; *RŠO*, pp. 299-309. This in-

invalidate the Vysočany congress, but did so implicitly by "postponing" the scheduled convocation of the 14th congress on September 9 and assigning to the Presidium the decision on an alternative date. It also established a commission, headed by Špaček, to prepare a constituent congress of the Czech party.

It was apparently left to Smrkovský to perform the grim task of giving the terms of the secret protocol, but neither his speech nor the protocol were published. Dubček himself noted some of the necessary steps: strengthening the army and the security organs; reorganization of the Ministry of the Interior; "extraordinary and temporary measures" for the "control" of the information media (the term "censorship" was used in the published version of his address); prevention of the organization of social democracy, or the political activity of KAN and K 231; cadre changes (without persecution of those who had defended the alliance with the Soviet Union); the withdrawal of the Czechoslovak question from the Security Council's agenda; the "evaluation of the Vysočany meeting of congress delegates." On this crucial point Dubček was much more reticent than Husák had been in Bratislava, or than Černík, who endorsed Husák's views; he made no statement concerning the invalidity of the Vysočany meeting. He even praised it for contributing to the authority of the party and suggested that the "14th congress" should not meet too soon, and only after party statutes and federalization theses had been completed.

In his long speech justifying the Moscow decisions Dubček put the best face on it by arguing strongly that meeting these obligations was the only way to avoid "another catastrophic . . . solution" ("another intervention of Warsaw treaty troops," he said later), but also the only way to secure the fulfillment of Soviet obligations, namely, the withdrawal of troops, non-interference by the occupying army in Czechoslovakia's internal affairs, and compensation for damages. Above all it was a condition of implementing the post-January policy, which, he admitted, would be "slower and more complicated" under the new conditions. He expressed belief in Moscow's assurance that this policy had not been the cause of the intervention. The mistakes of the past—both "extreme liberalistic" and "conservative, dogmatic" tendencies—must be avoided, but there could be no return to the pre-January policies. On the with-

---

cluded short summaries of the addresses by Dubček and Svoboda, the major decisions, and the cadre changes. The speeches of Dubček, Svoboda, Husák, and Černík were given more fully for inner party information in *O zasedání*. Most of these were given in English in the CPCz Central Committee's *Information Bulletin*, no. 4 (1968). For brief versions see also *Pravda* (Moscow), Sept. 3 (*CDSP* 20, Sept. 25, pp. 3-4). Smrkovský's speech was omitted from all accounts, as were the other 29 speeches recorded as having been given.

drawal of troops, Dubček was more than optimistic, at least in words, speaking of three stages: (1) removal of the troops from cities and villages to special military areas; (2) the retention of troops on the borders with the German Federal Republic and in places where consolidation had not been achieved; and (3) complete withdrawal on the basis of negotiations with Moscow. He made clear that this depended on the "consolidation" of the situation and set no date or time limit on the succession of stages.

In his analysis of the past, especially of the military intervention, Dubček was adamant in defending the Czechoslovak interpretation of events as correct. He even gave a positive evaluation of Čierna and Bratislava, and described the measures that they had intended to take (concerning the media and other parties and organizations) to correct the situation. He was contradictory, however, in his explanation of the real Soviet motive for the intervention, at one point defining it as their "declining confidence" in "the capacity of the party's leadership to solve its problems," and at another point, as the Soviet "evaluation of the domestic situation" in Czechoslovakia and/or international factors (including strategic) which they had not taken sufficiently into account. Dubček firmly declared that no social group accepted the justification of the intervention. All were agreed that it was not "aid, but an unjustified measure contrary to socialist relations." Still more strongly, he declared that the people did not consider this intervention as "defense against counter-revolution but as an intervention against their civil rights, freedoms, and state and national sovereignty."[113]

Almost nothing is known of the course of the plenum's debate. According to the official summary the majority rejected "isolated views" which cast doubt on the post-January policy, as well as those which "ignored the reality of today's situation from extreme positions" and advocated "the breach of the conclusions of the Moscow talks" and "an adventurous, irresponsible policy." One of those latter voices was no doubt that of Jaroslav Šabata of Brno, who argued that "normalization was conditioned by the withdrawal of troops, and not at all the reverse," and that the *Diktat* of the document read by Smrkovský was not realistic and could not be carried out.[114]

Some degree of continuing resistance to Moscow was displayed in the personnel changes made by the plenum. The session itself had been an

[113] The published version of Dubček's remarks was a pale reflection of his real statements and did not include any of the latter comments.

[114] Part of his speech was given in *Listy*, July 1971, p. 23, also in J. Pelikán, ed., *Ici Prague* (Paris, 1973), pp. 87-89. He sharply attacked General Rytíř, who identified himself with the position of the Warsaw letter and the *Pravda* editorial of Aug. 22, Šabata charged.

enlarged one, supplementing the old Central Committee with many of the delegates to the 14th congress. The new CC was similarly increased by the addition of some eighty new members, of whom seven were previously candidates, and approximately fifty were persons who had been elected to the 14th congress CC, together with the new regional secretaries.[115] The newly formed Presidium and Secretariat were also of mixed character, after the removal from the former of a number of hard-liners (Rigo, Švestka, Kolder, and Kapek), as well as the outstanding reformer, Dr. Kriegel, and from the latter of Císař, Voleník, Sádovský, and Erban. The much larger Presidium created was a compromise, retaining Dubček, Bil'ak, Černík, Piller, Smrkovský, and Špaček; adding Svoboda, as an honorary member, but with full rights; and including Husák and many others who had been elected to the 14th congress Presidium.[116] Candidates were Barbírek, Lenárt, and Poláček. Added to the Secretariat were Špaček, L. Kovalčík, and J. Sekera, newly appointed chief editor of *Rudé právo*. Similarly in the case of ÚKRK, a number of delegates to the 14th congress who had been nominated for this body were included, and a collective leadership of fourteen persons was formed. Erban was appointed chairman of the National Front CC in place of Kriegel.

THE DILEMMA AFTER MOSCOW

The Moscow negotiations presented both leaders and the people at home with a dilemma similar to that of August 20-21—to accept the terms or refuse them, in other words, to give in or to resist. The reaction depended on the meaning given to Moscow—was it a compromise, based on reciprocal concessions?[117] Or was it a *Diktat*, accepted under duress? The leaders, or some of them, had considered the alternative of breaking off the talks and rejecting the cruel terms imposed, which would have

[115] Gueyt, *Mutation*, p. 332. The names of the new CC members were not published. Chudík was formally removed from the CC. Ironically Husák justified the coopting of new members on the ground of loss of confidence in so many CC members. The formal provisions of the party statute should not stand in the way of such an urgent political question, he said. The changes in leadership came as a surprise to Moscow which felt it should have been consulted (V. V. Kuznetsov, Soviet First Deputy Foreign Minister, in an interview with Smrkovský, *Der Spiegel*, Oct. 14, 1968, p. 162).

[116] The newcomers were Šimon (formerly candidate), Erban, and Mlynář (formerly on the Secretariat), eight others who had been elected to the 14th congress Presidium (Hrdinová, Husák, Kabrna, Sádovský, Slavík, V. Šimeček, A. Ťažký, and J. Zrak); and three new members (J. Hetteš, K. Neubert, and J. Pinkas). Members of the 14th congress Presidium who were dropped were Císař, Šik, Litera, Colotka, Šilhan, Hejzlar, Goldstücker, Hübl, Pavlenda, and others. See below, Appendix A.

[117] Windsor and Roberts described the agreement as a compromise with concessions made on both sides (*Czechoslovakia, 1968*, pp. 133-36).

involved serious risks—violent resistance, with destruction and bloodshed; a permanent military occupation, or a government of collaboration; continued detention of the arrested leaders; and perhaps even the partition of the country. Faced with such possibilities, the Czechoslovak leaders sought a way out through "a political solution" and believed that they had found one in an "agreement" embodying certain gains as well as the inevitable losses. They had not had to admit the existence of counterrevolution or to recognize the intervention as justified. The unity of the Czechoslovak state and its formal sovereignty and independence had been maintained. The leaders could return home as free men and even resume their pre-occupation posts. The post-January course could be continued, subject to certain limitations. Even the military occupation would be temporary and the evacuation of Soviet troops was assured, once normalization was achieved.

The people at home faced the same dilemma, accentuated by the fact that their leaders had signed the agreements in Moscow without even requiring subsequent approval by the legitimate party and state organs. The joy occasioned by the safe return of Dubček and his colleagues was counterbalanced by the shock of the Moscow agreement as revealed in the radio and television reports given by the negotiators. For many people the agreement represented surrender rather than a compromise. Even some of the delegates believed that, in view of the weakness of Moscow's political situation resulting from the absence of collaborators and the almost universal denunciation of the intervention, more might have been attained in the negotiations.[118] Others believed that the protocol should not have been signed, but at the very least, should have been taken back to Prague for consideration by the government and the National Assembly.[119] A few persons, but only a few, insisted that the only honorable course was to reject the Moscow accord and to resist, if necessary, by violence.[120]

[118] Tigrid, *Why Dubček Fell*, pp. 116-17.

[119] A radio commentary (n.d.) insisted on the need for approval of the agreement by the National Assembly and the Central Committee (*Svědectví*, nos. 34-36 [1969], p. 227). Jiří Pelikán later expressed the opinion that it would have been better not to sign the agreement, considering Moscow's difficult situation (*New Left Review*, Jan.-Feb. 1972, pp. 30-31).

[120] Ivan Sviták argued that the *Diktat* should not have been accepted and that the leaders, by doing so, were performing a service for Moscow, executing Soviet policies under the slogan of "normalization." The path taken would only lead to "camouflaged collaboration" and hence "the betrayal of the nation," he predicted (*Die Presse*, Oct. 12, 1968, available in English in mimeographed form, pp. 38-40, and substantially the same in *Studies in Comparative Communism* 2, April 1969, 74-76). See also Sviták, *The Czechoslovak Experiment, 1968-69*, pp. 161-63, 174-75.

For statements which were tantamount to advocating rejection and resistance, see Karel Sidon, *LL*, Aug. 28; *Reportér*, Aug. 26; R. Olšinský, *KŽ*, Aug. 30; radio commentary, Aug. 30 (BBC, II, Sept. 3).

Yet most Czechs and Slovaks were soon convinced that there was no real alternative to a reluctant acquiescence in the conditions imposed in Moscow.[121] The terms of the so-called agreement were onerous, it was realized, but were probably the best that could have been secured under the circumstances. Their leaders deserved praise for what they had accomplished and merited continued trust and support. Public opinion polls revealed overwhelming confidence in Svoboda, Dubček, and their closest associates.[122] The population shared their fears of the dangers of resistance and their hopes for the outcome of the policy adopted. In particular, it was expected that acceptance of the terms would lead to the gradual and complete withdrawal of troops and the resumption of the post-January course.[123] Doubts and skepticism were sublimated in the

[121] For arguments favoring acceptance, see the radio commentaries of Z. Jezdinský and J. Dienstbier, on Aug. 27 (*Smena*, Aug. 28; BBC, II, Aug. 31, resp.); Jonaš, *KŽ*, Aug. 30. On the fear of an uprising, see L. Veselý, *Die Zeit*, Sept. 6.

[122] All-Republic polls in mid-September (Sept. 14-16; 1,882 respondents, a quota sample) revealed that 97.8 percent had complete confidence in Svoboda; 97.2 percent, in Dubček; 90.4 percent, in Černík; and 90.1 percent, in Smrkovský. For this and the following, see Jaroslaw A. Piekalkiewicz, *Public Opinion Polling in Czechoslovakia, 1968-69* (New York, 1972), p. 264; also pp. 31, 33. When the respondents were asked to name those in whom they had most trust and confidence, the results were as follows:

	percent
Dubček	96.1
Svoboda	95.6
Smrkovský	73.3
Černík	72.6
Císař	37.6
Husák	23.6
Šik	15.7

The same poll revealed a positive response (85.2 percent) to Svoboda after the Moscow agreement, and a negative response of 9.4 percent (ibid., p. 260). Similar results were produced by a Prague poll (a quota sample of 208 persons was used) (*Rep.*, Sept. 18-25, 1968, p. 8). For Slovakia, this poll and a separate one in Slovakia (Sept. 16-22; 1,182 responses from a random sample) produced similar percentages for Dubček, Svoboda, Černík, and Smrkovský, with Husák ranking either immediately behind the top four, or in fourth place, above Černík (Piekalkiewicz, *Polling*, pp. 262-63). Trust in CPS leaders in the latter poll was greater than before the Slovak party congress (59.7 percent); the same (17.1 percent); trust, but with reservations about some members (12.4 percent) (ibid., p. 30).

[123] The all-Republic poll of Sept. 14-16 showed that 27 percent thought that the Warsaw troops would leave; 45.5 percent that they would leave partially; 14.4 percent that they would stay forever; 13.2 percent gave "other" or no answers. The attitude in the Czech parts of the Republic was slightly more optimistic than in Slovakia (Piekalkiewicz, *Polling*, p. 58). There was overwhelming support for CPCz efforts to implement the Action Program—94.6 percent, with no appreciable difference shown between the Czech and Slovak areas (ibid., p. 27). For positive attitudes in Slovakia toward the press, radio, and television during the Moscow talks, and toward the CPCz and its policies, see ibid., pp. 41-42, 64-65. The Prague poll cited in the preceding footnote produced similar results concerning the Action Program and the activity of the journalists, and indicated that

belief or hope that ultimately the policy recommended by Svoboda and Dubček would prove successful. Thus the brave and spectacular seven days' nonviolent resistance was brought to an end, even to the point of the replacement of street signs, the removal of posters and the wiping of slogans from the walls by the youth.

Unfortunately, the true meaning of Moscow was not known, concealed as it was in the secret protocol (which the leaders did not reveal to the people) and distorted by the wishful thinking and self-deception of the leaders and of the population. As events unfolded in subsequent months and years, the grim reality of Moscow was revealed—it was not a genuine compromise, but an arbitrary and harsh edict imposed on a weak and helpless delegation. The major hopes entertained by both leaders and people were to be gradually dissipated and ultimately destroyed. "Normalization"—upon which all else depended—was ambiguous and ill-defined and its meaning was to be determined by Moscow. The withdrawal of troops was to be indefinitely postponed, and the so-called temporary stationing of troops was to become a permanent occupation. The January course was to be curbed in its very essentials and eventually terminated, with the single and partial exception of federalization of the state. The top leaders, although restored to their positions, were to become in effect conditional "collaborators" and ultimately ousted by wholehearted collaborators of the ocupying powers.

---

93 percent of those polled believed that there was no danger of counterrevolution prior to the invasion.

DUBČEK'S DECLINE AND FALL / REFORM REVOLUTION
OR COUNTERREVOLUTION

Dubček's Decline and Fall

WITH THE return of Dubček and the others from Moscow life began slowly to return to normal in occupied Czechoslovakia. During the first week of September work in the factories and on the farms resumed; the provisioning of the population was assured; transportation was restored. Gradually the occupying troops were withdrawn from the printing presses and broadcasting stations, and radio, television, and the press began to function normally. The troops evacuated other public buildings and were withdrawn from urban centers to less noticeable bases in the countryside. Much more difficult, however, was the "normalization" of political conditions, and still more, of the thinking of the population after the shock of the invasion and occupation.[1]

Indeed, for eight months after the occupation a paradoxical situation, full of strange contradictions, prevailed.[2] Although the context of politics had been fundamentally changed by the occupation, the two sets of opposing forces which had been present from January to August continued to operate—the persisting counterpoise of Moscow and Prague, and the action and interaction of the Prague regime and domestic forces. The Dubček leadership again found itself between two mutually opposed pressures, internal and external.[3] On the one hand, Moscow, in spite of the enormous shift of the balance of power in its favor, was unable to impose its will fully on occupied Prague. On the other hand, the Prague regime was unable to win complete support for its policy of compromise from the Czech and Slovak people. Progressive forces were still active, both outside and within the regime, seeking to defend something of the post-January line and urging greater resistance to outside pressures. Con-

---

[1] A. Ostrý, *Československý problém* (Cologne, 1972), p. 178.
[2] On the post-August period, see Jan Provaznik, "The Politics of Retrenchment," *Problems of Communism* 18 (July-Oct. 1969), 2-16; J. Ruml, *Reportér*, Jan. 8, 1969, pp. I-VIII; A. Müller, "Zur Lage in der Tschechoslowakei," *Osteuropa* 23 (Aug. 1973), 599-617; E. Taborsky, "Czechoslovakia: The Return to 'Normalcy,'" *PC*, 19 (Nov.-Dec. 1970), 31-41. See also the following books: Rémi Gueyt, *La mutation tchécoslovaque* (Paris, 1969), part IV; P. Broué, *Le printemps des peuples commence à Prague* (Paris, n.d.) pp. 337-420; P. Tigrid, *Why Dubček Fell* (London, 1969), pp. 124-67 (longer version in *Svědectví*, nos. 34-36, 1969, pp. 239-52); M. Tatu, *L'hérésie impossible* (Paris, 1968); H. Brahm, *Der Kreml und die ČSSR, 1968-1969* (Stuttgart, 1970), pp. 89-126. For documents, see H. Haefs, ed., *Die Ereignisse in der Tschechoslowakei* (Bonn, 1969), pp. 277-93; R. A. Remington, ed., *Winter in Prague* (Cambridge, Mass., 1969), part V.
[3] M. Lakatoš, *Zítřek*, Jan. 8, 1969.

servative forces were equally active urging speedier adaptation to the "reality" of the occupation and a more decisive correction of the "negative aspects" of the post-January policy.

The domestic balance of forces had not shifted as much as might have been expected. The Big Four remained in their key positions, and the leading party organs were in fact more progressive in composition than before the invasion. The removal from their posts of key reform spokesmen, such as Šik, Hájek, and Pavel, however, marked a shift away from reform. Hejzlar and Pelikán, who had been active at the 14th congress, were ousted from their positions in radio and television; on the other hand, Sulek, a collaborator, was replaced as head of ČTK.

Initial retreats on fundamental aspects of the post-January program were indicated in the decision of the Ministry of the Interior not to register K 231 or KAN, thus in effect banning these organizations, and the passage of legislation restricting the press and political activity. A law on press control established an Office of Press and Information to exercise supervision of the means of communication and placed the responsibility for actual censorship on the editors themselves. The statute on the National Front restricted political activity to members of the front, thus in effect "closing" the system of political parties, and barring the formation of new parties such as a Social Democratic Party. A third law authorized restrictive measures on assembly and association to "guarantee public order."[4] It soon became clear (and this was formally announced at the November plenum) that the regular 14th Party Congress, and the Czech party congress, which had been designed to bring into existence a Czech party, were to be postponed indefinitely, and in the latter case, as events turned out, permanently. In place of a separate Czech party, a CC bureau for the Czech lands was established, following the Soviet pattern for the Russian branch of the CPSU. The postponement of the 14th congress indicated that the proposed revision of the party statute was to be abandoned. Elections to the representative bodies were also deferred.

At first these measures were justified as elements of a "realist" policy necessary to create the conditions for the eventual withdrawal of Soviet troops. It was soon evident, however, that total withdrawal would depend on the achievement of "normalization" to the satisfaction of the Soviet Union and would in fact be indefinitely delayed. The leaders themselves became aware of this hard reality at a top-level meeting in Moscow at the beginning of October, at which the Soviet leaders made clear their dissatisfaction with the measures taken to achieve normalization and proposed a special treaty on the presence of military forces in Czechoslovakia. Another meeting in Moscow in mid-October led to an

---

[4] *Sbírka zákonů*, 126-7-8/1968.

agreement which legitimized the "temporary" presence of occupation forces, without, however, indicating the number of forces to remain, or giving any date of withdrawal. This treaty, concluded in secret, was revealed to the public only just prior to its ratification by the National Assembly, and represented a major step backward from the original hopes entertained by leaders and people alike. Only four deputies had the courage to vote against the treaty—Vodsloň, G. Sekaninová-Čakrtová, Prchlík, and Kriegel. Ten others abstained; some sixty deputies were absent.[5]

Yet the retreat was not complete. In his report to the November plenum Dubček defended the necessity of "normalization" and criticized the "negative features" of the post-January policy and the "anti-socialist forces" currently active. Nonetheless he made a spirited defense of the main tendencies of the pre-invasion course and did not accept the thesis of "counterrevolution" or the legitimacy of the occupation. He emphatically declared his determination to continue to implement the positive features of the post-January program.[6] In other respects, however, the November plenum was less encouraging as there was a strong offensive by the conservatives against the post-January course and a more muted response by the progressives. Following Dubček's lead, the resolution directed its main criticism against anti-socialist forces and emphasized the need to fulfill the Bratislava agreement and the Moscow protocol. There were no fundamental changes in leadership, however, apart from the inclusion of Bil'ak in the Secretariat and the resignation of Mlynář. Both the enlarged Presidium and the new eight-man Executive Committee maintained a relatively centrist character. Two men emerged into positions of prominence. Štrougal, a minister under Novotný (including five years as Minister of the Interior) and deputy Prime Minister under Dubček, became a key figure, as a member of both the Presidium and the Executive Committee and as the head of the newly created bureau for the Czech party. Husák, with a firm base in Slovakia as First Secretary, also won membership in the two top organs of the party.

In some respects Dubček's hopes of salvaging some elements of re-

---

[5] For the Moscow communiqué and the treaty on stationing of troops, see *Rudé právo* and *Pravda* (Moscow), Oct. 19 (Remington, ed., *Winter in Prague*, pp. 417-24). For Sekaninová's critical speech against the treaty, V. David's defense of it, and sharp critique by J. Hochman, see *Rep.*, Oct. 30-Nov. 6, 1968. Part of the occupying forces (at first those of Moscow's allies and then Soviet troops) were withdrawn, beginning in late October. The number of troops remaining was estimated to be approximately 60,000 to 100,000 (Thomas Wolfe, *Soviet Power and Europe, 1945-1970*, Baltimore, 1970, p. 470).

[6] For the November plenum, *RP*, Nov. 15-19; for the CC resolution, Remington, ed., *Winter in Prague*, pp. 430-41. For Dubček's report, *RP*, Nov. 15; a fuller version is given in *Zasedání Ústředního Výboru KSČ ve dnech 14.-17. listopadu 1968* (Prague, 1968), pp. 3-34.

form were justified. The establishment of a federal system was achieved, as planned, on October 28, the fiftieth anniversary of the Republic. On January 1, 1969 the federal state of two equal republics, Czech and Slovak, came into existence. At the same time a statute on nationality rights was adopted.[7] Rehabilitation continued, although at a slow pace, and individual cases were reviewed before the special tribunals and in various organizations and state institutions. Work proceeded on the drafting of the statute on extra-judicial rehabilitation. Legal reform moved forward in discussion of draft laws to reorganize the procuracy, to safeguard the independence of the judiciary, to regulate investigation procedures, and to establish a constitutional court. Individual cases of party rehabilitation proceeded, but the Piller report, although completed, had not yet been submitted to the CC. The formation of interest groups, such as a new youth association, continued apace, usually as federal organizations, including separate Czech and Slovak organizations and constituent specialized associations. Economic reform was strongly advocated, and the draft law on the status of enterprises aroused considerable controversy. Working peoples' councils were set up in many enterprises, and their formation as bodies of self-administration was warmly advocated, even after a government announcement (October 24) forbidding any new councils.

There were strong pressures from below by reform elements, seeking to discourage Dubček from excessive retreats and urging him to preserve as much of the Action Program as possible. Letters, resolutions, and articles expressed confidence in the leadership, while warning of the danger of concessions to Moscow's pressure and condemning the continuous criticism in the Soviet press. In spite of censorship, the press was remarkably open in its discussion of issues, and public opinion continued to be a powerful force. A wide range of critical views on public policy were published in the press, especially in the newspaper of the Writers' Union, reborn under the name *Listy*, in the Union of Journalists' magazine, *Reportér*, and in two new weeklies, *Zítřek*, associated with the Socialist Party, and *Politika*, organ of the party's Central Committee. There was also lively activity by the mass organizations, including the reinvigorated trade unions, the creative unions, the Academy of Sciences (especially its institutes in the social sciences), and party organizations and institutions.

Students at the universities took a leading role, with a successful three-day general strike in late November in support of the post-January program. The Ten Points advanced by the student strikers included statements in favor of the Action Program, the temporary nature of censor-

_____
[7] See below, Appendix C.

ship, freedom of assembly and association, freedom of research and of literary and cultural expression, and personal and legal security of the citizen. The trade unions also became a powerful force for reform, especially the metal workers, 900,000 strong, who threw their weight behind the student strike and later concluded a formal alliance with the Union of Students. This provided for cooperation in opposing "the policy of continual concessions to external pressure" and in pressing for freedom of expression, workers' councils, elections, and other progressive demands.[8] Mass demonstrations in the streets on the anniversaries of October 28 and November 7 contributed to the spirit of resistance.

Dubček's conditional retreat and his permissive attitude toward oppositional forces could only awaken profound dissatisfaction among conservative forces at home and in the invading countries. The Moscow protocol and the troop treaty had promised that the occupation forces would not interfere in internal affairs. Nonetheless the Prague leaders were under direct and constant pressure from the Soviet Union, through high-level talks during visits to Moscow in October, Warsaw in November, and Kiev in December; through frequent exchanges of visits by other party and government leaders; and through the influence of First Deputy Foreign Minister Kuznetsov during a stay in Prague in September, and party Secretary K. F. Katushev during a two-week visit at the end of the year, and through the daily influence of the Soviet ambassador. Kuznetsov, in his conversations with Smrkovský and other leaders, made clear that Moscow was profoundly dissatisfied with the "failure" of Prague to implement fully the Moscow protocol and with the manner in which persons such as Bil'ak, Kolder, and Indra were treated.[9] The Czechoslovak situation was sharply criticized in the Soviet and bloc mass media, as well as by the Czech-language newspaper Zprávy, distributed by the occupation forces,[10] and by the Czech-language radio station Vltava, operating until February from East German soil.

This unrelieved outside intervention was intertwined with internal pressures from conservative Czechs and Slovaks. The most extreme "leftist" critics voiced their discontent with Dubček and his policy in closed

[8] For the student strike, the Ten Points, and the text of the student-union agreement, see Pavel Tomalek, Czechoslovakia 1968-1969: The Worker-Student Alliance (Center for International Studies, M.I.T., Cambridge, Mass., 1971). The Ten Points are also given in J. Pelikán, ed., Ici Prague (Paris, 1973), pp. 98-99.

[9] For the minutes of the talks between Kuznetsov and Smrkovský on September 11, 1968 (originally published in Der Spiegel, Oct. 14, 1968), see Tigrid, Why Dubček Fell, pp. 215-29.

[10] In late November the National Assembly presidium protested the continuance of Zprávy, and a month later a diplomatic note was transmitted to Moscow requesting its cessation, but in each case to no avail. The first issue was that of Aug. 30; the final one, May 10, 1969. Selected articles were published in Zprávy v boji proti kontrarevoluci, Výbor članků z časopisu Zprávy (Prague, 1971).

meetings[11] and in the organ of the Czech party bureau, *Tribuna*, edited by Švestka. Similar, although less extreme, views were expressed in the Central Committee and in the press by conservative leaders, such as Štrougal, Bil'ak, and Husák. Indeed the latter adopted an increasingly conservative position, emphasizing the need for normalization of relations with the Soviet Union and its allies, and criticizing ever more sharply the negative features of the reform period. He went so far as to speak of two stages of "deformation" of Marxism-Leninism, the first under Novotný, and the second after January 1968, thus condemning equally the Novotný and the Dubček courses.[12]

The period from September 1968 to April 1969 was therefore one of intense political conflict, characterized by a succession of serious crises. The student strike in November was followed by efforts of reform-oriented groups in December 1968 and January 1969 to prevent the barring of Smrkovský from the chairmanship of the new Federal Assembly created in the federal reorganization. Husák articulated the Slovak insistence that this post be occupied by a Slovak (the President and the Prime Minister being Czechs).[13] Smrkovský had already been pushed aside by exclusion from participation in the high-level talks in Moscow and Kiev, and was viewed with suspicion and hostility by the Moscow leaders. The trade unions, the students, the creative unions and the press rallied to his defense, regarding these as moves to oust from high office a person still regarded as one of the strongest defenders of reform. The metal workers, then in congress in Prague, threatened a general strike if he were removed. The crisis was settled by a compromise, when Professor Colotka, a progressive Slovak, was appointed to the position in question, and Smrkovský, retaining his top party posts, became deputy chairman of the assembly and chairman of one of its two houses, the People's Chamber. This episode brought into relief the instability of the political balance.

Almost immediately thereafter the self-immolation by fire of the student Jan Palach re-created for a few days the atmosphere of August and intensified political tension. His two simple demands for the abolition of censorship and the banning of the distribution of *Zprávy* not only crystallized the popular desire for freedom of expression and the ending of outside intervention but stimulated anew a spirit of national unity against the occupation. From January on the struggle of conflicting

[11] For instance, the meeting on October 9 in the Libeň district of Prague, addressed by A. Kapek and J. Jodas, and the meeting in the Lucerna hall in Prague in November, addressed by Václav David, foreign minister under Novotný. For the text of the Libeň resolution, see *Dějiny a současnost*, no. 11 (1968), pp. 44-47; also *Život strany*, Oct. 8, 1969.

[12] *RP*, Nov. 14, 1968.

[13] Ibid., Dec. 23, 1968. For Smrkovský's account, see *Listy*, March 1975, pp. 24-25.

forces continued, as was evident at the CC plenum in January; at another gathering of conservatives in Libeň; at an anti-reform conference of the People's Militia; and in reform-oriented conferences of the Czech trade unions, of representatives of working people's councils, and of the all-union ROH. The latter meeting, in March, represented a high point in the activity of the progressive forces and in the democratization of the trade unions when a democratic charter was adopted for the movement. Moreover, the discussion of concrete reforms, including those in the economic and legal spheres, continued in the press and in public bodies.

In retrospect the months after the invasion were a transition period which was bound sooner or later to come to an end because of its inherent contradictions. Dubček tried to steer a middle course between total surrender and outright resistance to Soviet demands, but his popular support declined and his reputation was increasingly tarnished by his concessions to Moscow and his retreats from the January program. Among his critics there were some who bitterly condemned the entire policy of "surrender"; there were others who had serious reservations about the official "realist" policy, but who sought to strengthen Dubček's hand in withstanding pressures from Moscow. On the other side were those who advocated a policy of even closer collaboration and a harder line against opponents at home.

In fact Dubček was attempting the impossible—to satisfy both the people and the Russians. It was an effort to square the circle: to follow a reform course condemned by the Russians and to maintain the independence of an occupied country. The population was caught up in a dilemma of its own—between their desire, on the one hand, to trust Dubček and to believe in his assurances of the continuance of reform, and on the other hand, an increasing disappointment at his failure to resist Moscow and a gradual decline in their confidence in his leadership. Indeed, in sharply condemning his progressive critics, Dubček contributed to this crisis of confidence and undermined the very forces on which he must depend to stay in office and to maintain his policy of moderate reform.[14]

The Soviet Union no doubt estimated Dubček as a person who could be cajoled and coerced into carrying out the measures of normalization, but who could eventually be dropped in favor of a more subservient successor. Their opportunity came with a new political crisis at the end of March when Czechoslovak ice hockey victories over the Russians in Stockholm led to massive popular demonstrations in many cities and to violent actions, in several places, against Soviet installations, including the Aeroflot offices in the center of Prague. The Soviet deputy foreign minister Vladimir Semyenov and Marshal Grechko suddenly arrived

---

[14] Cf. the comments by Provaznik, "Retrenchment," p. 10; Broué, *Le printemps*, p. 131; Ostrý, *Československý problém*, pp. 187, 201.

in Prague, reportedly to present a Soviet ultimatum demanding drastic political changes and threatening the renewal of military intervention. There were rumors of an effort at a take-over by high-ranking Czechoslovak army officers. The party Presidium, describing the situation as being "on the edge of catastrophe," immediately took special measures, particularly against certain newspapers.[15] Under heavy pressures at home and from abroad Dubček yielded. At a Central Committee plenum in mid-April, he resigned as First Secretary, proposing Husák as his successor. This appointment was approved and a smaller Presidium, including Dubček, but excluding Smrkovský, was formed. Within the Central Committee opposition to the change was minimal (twenty-two negative votes, and four abstentions). Popular resistance did not materialize since the opposition forces were tired and dispirited and Dubček himself had proposed the changeover. The press was already muzzled. A student strike fizzled out. Anticipated action by the trade unions did not take place.

Husák had already emerged as a possible alternative leader in the preceding months. Increasingly vigorous in his criticism of so-called pressure groups which were creating constant tension, he had offered, as a model for the entire country, the "middle-of-the-road current" in Slovakia, where the relative weakness of extreme conservative or progressive tendencies and his own strict control had in fact produced a quieter political scene than in the Czech lands.[16] As Husák had become deputy Prime Minister only in April 1968 and had held no high party position until after the invasion, his responsibility for post-January "excesses" could be minimized.

In April 1969 Husák assumed the full burden of finding "a way out of the difficult crisis situation." There was to be no change in the political line, he declared, but a change in the attitude toward its implementation. Once the situation had been consolidated, all problems with the Soviet Union—"without exception"—could be solved.[17] There were some hopes that Husák, a victim of persecution under Novotný and a supporter of the January reform movement, would avert a return to the "fifties" and total subjugation to Soviet demands, and by "normalizing the situation," through draconic measures, might even create the conditions for the withdrawal of Soviet troops and for a resumption of at least part of the reform movement. At the same time, many feared that his past record of ruthless and autocratic leadership and his current hard line, coupled with continuing Soviet pressures and the influence of extremists

[15] Presidium statement, *RP*, April 3, 1969. For the Soviet ultimatum, see Tigrid, *Svědectví*, no. 37 (1969), p. 94.

[16] *RP*, Nov. 20, 1968. See his speech on "pressure groups," ibid., Jan. 11, 1969.

[17] See Husák's speech at the close of the CC plenum, ibid., April 18, 1969.

at home, would lead to a complete reversal of the post-January gains and pave the way for a return to the "fifties," either under his aegis or under even tougher successors. In the words of a slogan used by students during the November strike which played on the meaning of the name Husák (a male goose), "socialism with a human face" seemed to have been replaced by "socialism with goose-flesh."

The ensuing months witnessed the gradual unfolding of Husák's neo-conservative policy of "consolidation."[18] Attention was first given to the systematic replacement of party functionaries, especially at the regional and district levels, and of leading figures in the mass associations, radio and television, party and government institutions, and newspapers and journals. At the May plenum Šik, Kriegel, and Vodsloň were removed from the CC and Kriegel was expelled from the party. The appointments of Miloslav Brůžek as Minister of Culture and of Jaromír Hrbek as Minister of Education initiated a policy of drastic repression of so-called revisionist ideas and persons. Freedom of expression was limited by the banning of reformist journals, such as *Politika, Listy*, and *Reportér*, the removal of editors from other key newspapers, and tighter control and censorship of the mass media in general. This was accompanied by a mounting campaign against "rightists" and a reevaluation of the post-January period, replete with sharp criticism of leading persons, including Dubček himself. Significantly, the Soviet paper *Zprávy* ceased publication, since its purposes were being fulfilled by other means.

There was continued moral and intellectual resistance to the new course, especially by the creative unions, by the rank and file of the party and the trade unions, and by intellectuals in research and educational institutions, but the tightening repression made overt opposition increasingly difficult. Nonetheless a Ten Points Manifesto, signed by a dozen leading intellectuals, was circulated illegally in Czechoslovakia and published abroad. The manifesto, addressed to the governmental organs and the Central Committee, condemned the Moscow protocol and described the presence of Soviet troops as the "cause of unrest." The document expressed disagreement with "the policy of constant concessions" and with the abolition, "point by point," of the Action Program, and criticized the introduction of censorship, the abandonment of economic reform, the postponement of elections, and other actions of the regime.[19]

Street demonstrations during the week of the anniversary of the invasion were crushed by strict police action and served as the grounds for

---

[18] See Husák's speech at the May plenum, ibid., June 2, 1969. For a review of events, see Wolf Oschliess, "Die Tschechoslowakei nach Dubček," *Osteuropa* 19, no. 8 (Aug. 1969), 575-88, and Oschliess, "Prags schwarzes Jubiläum: Nach dem 21. August 1969," ibid. 20, no. 1 (January 1970), 1-25.

[19] Reprinted in Pelikán, ed., *Ici Prague*, pp. 124-30.

issuing emergency measures for preserving public order. The campaign against Dubček intensified.[20] At the September 1969 plenum he continued to defend himself against attacks but was removed from the Presidium; at the same time seven persons, including Smrkovský, were expelled from the Central Committee, and nineteen others resigned; conservative veterans such as Švestka, Kolder, and Kapek were given responsible posts. Major Central Committee resolutions from July and August 1968, including those condemning the invasion, were rescinded. This was followed in October by the removal of Smrkovský, Dubček, and others from their posts in the National Assembly presidium, the resignation or removal of a number of deputies, and the annulment of many 1968 assembly resolutions. Several months later Smrkovský and others were forced to resign their parliamentary seats. A new stage in the drive against the "guilty" rightists came in January 1970 when Dubček resigned from the Central Committee (following his appointment as ambassador to Turkey) and Černík was removed as Prime Minister and from the Presidium. The January plenum initiated a mass screening of party members which was intended to reduce the membership substantially and to eliminate those regarded as "rightists."[21] In May 1970 Dubček was recalled from Ankara and a month later, after he had made a vigorous defense of his record, he was expelled from the party.

This unrelenting purge of public life was accompanied by an ever closer rapprochement with the Soviet Union and the other bloc members. From May 1969 on, Husák paid formal visits to each of the invading states, including four trips to the Soviet Union. At a meeting in Moscow in late October an economic agreement was reached placing Czechoslovakia in even greater dependence on the USSR. Husák used the occasion to go far beyond his previous statements on the invasion, terming it an "act of international assistance."[22] A new treaty between Prague and Moscow, in the spirit of the Brezhnev doctrine, placed the emphasis on solidarity and integration of the bloc as a whole and put the final seal on Czechoslovakia's subordination to Moscow.

By the spring of 1970 almost nothing was left of the democratization program, although Husák continued to pay lip service to the post-January policy. Freedom of expression had been completely curbed, and no independent organs of opinion were left. Discipline was being restored in the party, with mass expulsions used to deal with dissent. The intellec-

[20] This was initiated by Husák's speech, *RP*, Aug. 20, 1969.

[21] Kriegel was the first post-January leader expelled from the party, in May. Three others were ousted at the Central Committee plenum in September. Šik was expelled in October 1969, and Smrkovský in March 1970.

[22] *RP*, Oct. 29, 1969. In his speech at the September plenum he had spoken of the presence of "counterrevolutionary forces," without, however, actually accepting the Soviet view that there was in fact a counterrevolution, ibid., Sept. 29, 1969.

tual world, especially the Academy of Sciences, the universities, and cultural institutions, were subjected to ever closer party and state control. The idea of economic reform was almost dead, as indicated by the reassertion of the necessity of centralized planning and state control and the dissolution of the enterprise councils. The press, radio, and television spouted only ideological propaganda and conducted vicious polemics against heretical ideas and individual persons. Rehabilitation was slowed down, modified, and ultimately abandoned. The National Front and its constituent elements became nothing but mouthpieces of the Communist Party and lacked even the potentiality for independence. The federal structure remained formally intact, but was steadily weakened by an emphasis on the need for integration, by various centralizing measures, and above all, by the abandonment of the idea of federalizing the party.

By mid-1970 Husák had thus achieved a kind of domestic stabilization by coercive measures. Overt opposition had ceased and political crises no longer occurred. After his accession to power Husák had tried to create an image of himself as a centrist. There would be no return, he said in Pilsen in October, either to "Novotný bureaucracy" or to "Dubček anarchy."[23] In many statements, however, he still upheld the January change as inevitable and abjured any return to the pre-January system.[24] In particular he ridiculed the notion that there would be a resumption of the terror of the early fifties. Arrests were relatively few and no political trials of the topmost leaders took place.

In fact, however, Husák's regime was an extreme, conservative one, which had abandoned or reversed most of the post-January reforms and was committed to intimate collaboration with the Soviet Union. The situation could best be described as analogous to those of the late fifties, prior to the relaxation and ferment of the sixties. In other words, the Novotný system had been restored, not in its earlier and worst form, but with the traits of its middle phase; its final stage, in the sixties, appeared favorable in comparison to Husák's rule. An element reminiscent of the Stalinist years, however, was the resumption of direct Soviet interference and control, this time by means of military occupation. As long as Soviet troops remained and Soviet pressure continued, Husák had little room to maneuver in his relationship with the USSR and could entertain no hope of a more independent course. He had adopted a role resembling Gomułka's after 1956 and showed no signs of following the moderate pattern of Kádár, or still less, the independent course of Tito or Ceaușescu. In Czechoslovak terms Husák had come to resemble not so much President Hacha, a conservative but reluctant collaborator of Hitler, but rather of Father Tiso, who ruled Slovakia, under Hitler's auspices, with a strong commitment to Nazi policy.

[23] Ibid., Oct. 15, 1969.   [24] For instance, ibid., Jan. 20, 1970.

Reform, Revolution, or Counterrevolution?

DURING the first eight months of 1968 communism in Czechoslovakia underwent a process of radical change which, although only in its initial stage, was unequaled in the history of communist reform. In the eight months following the invasion, this process was interrupted, at least partially, and then, after the fall of Dubček in April 1969, reversed in all its major aspects. The traditional dualism of Czechoslovak communism, discussed at the outset of this book, was thus once again illustrated in the persons of Dubček, the reform leader, and his successor, Husák. Although by no means free of pro-Soviet and authoritarian attitudes, Dubček represented the more nationalist and democratic characteristics of the movement. Husák, on the other hand, although he had associated himself with the post-January democratization and was strongly nationalist vis-à-vis the Czechs, personified the more authoritarian and subservient face of Czechoslovak communism, especially after August. Even during the period of reform there were other evidences of the duplexity characteristic of the CPCz in the reluctant acceptance of reform and the strongly pro-Soviet attitudes of persons such as Bil'ak and Kolder; in the more democratic and independent tendencies of men such as Smrkovský and Špaček; and in the contradictory and ambivalent attitudes of most of the leaders, including Dubček.

THE CRISIS OF STALINISM

The post-January process of change was deeply rooted in the profound crisis of the whole society under Novotný and the gradual ripening of the forces of opposition during the sixties. The crisis was in large part the product of the imposition of an alien system, Stalinism, on a country with vastly different circumstances and traditions, and of the impulse for substantial changes in that system given by Khrushchev's denunciation of Stalinism and his call for the elimination of its worst evils. In this sense it was but part of a general crisis of communism in most of Eastern Europe where both the initial Sovietization and the subsequent steps toward de-Stalinization were, so to speak, "time-bombs," whose explosive effects were manifested at different times and in different ways in each country. In Czechoslovakia the special intensity of Stalinism and the slowness of

824

de-Stalinization made the outburst of demands for change all the more unrestrained when the dam finally broke in 1968.[1]

It is difficult to explain why Stalinism took such extreme forms in a country whose strong democratic traditions made this Soviet system particularly inappropriate. Moreover, in the years from 1945 to 1948, Czechs and Slovaks had experienced a relatively democratic phase of development during which the "national path to socialism" had a more authentic character than in most "people's democracies." Stalinism during the fifties represented therefore an even more abrupt and sharp break with the past than in other countries, and assumed a special ruthlessness which was in a sense proportionate to the democratic traditions which had to be destroyed. Likewise the tardiness of the official reaction to Soviet signals for de-Stalinization left Czechoslovakia far behind its neighbors, Poland and Hungary, and was no doubt linked with official realization of the strength of the oppositional forces that might be unloosed. There was a peculiar poignancy, too, in the fact that the Stalinist system, although external in origin, had been in some measure self-imposed by leaders who chose slavishly to establish the Soviet model of socialism in their country and by many rank-and-file communists who endorsed this course with enthusiasm, at least initially.

The crisis of Czechoslovak communism affected every facet of life and evoked discontent among all social groups, especially the youth, the nationalities, and the intellectuals, but also the workers and peasants, and, in increasing degree, the rank and file and the functionaries of the party. The terror of the fifties, continuing in less draconic form in the sixties, created not only widespread political anomie, reflecting a general feeling of impotence, but also a mounting tide of criticism, particularly among the intellectuals, who became the chief articulators of the need for social change. The crisis had a special moral aspect arising out of a sense of guilt which many felt for having contributed, by deed or by acquiescence, to past evils, and for having failed to resist after Stalin's death. Although oppositional tendencies had been curbed by repression for almost a decade after his demise, they gathered momentum during the sixties and brought about a gradual erosion of the Stalinist system. Novotný bent every effort to avoid fundamental reform but his intermittent concessions, his inability to resort to extreme forms of coercion, and his own political ineptitude resulted, paradoxically, in Czechoslovakia ceasing

[1] For a good analysis of Stalinism, its effect in Czechoslovakia, and its gradual disintegration, see K. Bartošek, "Revolution against bureaucratism?" *Rudé právo*, July 18, 24, 26, 30, 31, 1968. See also Radoslav Selucký, *Czechoslovakia: The Plan that failed* (London, 1970); Barbara Jancar, *Czechoslovakia: The Absolute Monopoly of Power* (New York, 1971).

to be genuinely Stalinist and becoming, in a sense, "the most liberal country" in the socialist camp.[2]

THE MEANING OF JANUARY

The January overthrow was a climax in this slow process of decline when the crisis permeated the topmost reaches of the party command. The outcome came as a surprise even to the advocates of reform. This "palace coup," as it has been termed,[3] was to become the starting point of a momentous course of events, the true significance of which was not at first evident. It was in fact "a revolt without theory," as Černík is reported to have called it (after the occupation), in the sense that the new leadership did not really know what they wanted.[4] The potential meaning of "January" began only slowly to appear, from March and April on, with the emergence of "the civic public (*občanská veřejnost*)," but then in the form of a clash of rival interpretations.[5] The official Action Program was based on theoretical studies made in the years before January, but was outdated by the time of its publication. The reform program took definite shape only gradually in subsequent months as more detailed plans were elaborated and forces capable of implementing them crystallized. Nonetheless the direction of change remained unclear since conflicting tendencies were present, differing proposals were advanced, and distinctive stages followed each other in a highly dynamic process of development.[6] Furthermore, what happened in Prague varied in some degree from what happened in Bratislava, where national demands were in the forefront and democratic aims, although similar in substance, were less strongly and widely voiced. The ferment of discussion and activity was weaker, too, in smaller towns and in the countryside than in the larger cities.[7] In any case, as events transpired, the time was to be too short for the further elaboration and for achievement of the reform goals. "Democratic socialism," at the time of the occupation, still remained ahead, "a new and unknown field."[8]

[2] E.g. Bartošek, *RP*, July 26.   [3] Ibid., July 24.
[4] J. Šabata, "Revolta bez teorie?" *Index* (Brno), April 1969.
[5] P. Pithart, *Listy*, Jan. 9, 1969.
[6] For an analysis of these complex elements, see Ivan Sviták, *The Czechoslovak Experiment, 1968-1969* (New York, 1971), Introduction, pp. 5-6. The differences among the "reform communists" as well as among the "reform non-communists" were well analyzed by I. Byštřina, *Svědectví* 12, no. 47 (1974), 453.
[7] Sviták, *Czechoslovak Experiment*, p. 78. Cf. Ludvík Vaculík's articles on the lagging of the democratization process in the town of Semily, *Literární listy*, June 27, 1968; *Listy*, March 19, 1969; given in translation in A. Oxley, A. Pravda and A. Ritchie, eds., *Czechoslovakia: The Party and the People* (London, 1973), pp. 6-17, 285-303. Cf. similar comments in Vaculík's Two Thousand Words (*LL*, June 27, 1968; in translation, Oxley et al., pp. 261-68).
[8] F. Šamalík, *Politika*, Sept. 19, 1968.

REFORM OR REVOLUTION?

Did the "post-January development," as the 1968 events were often called, constitute a reform or a revolution? The designation chosen is a matter of definition and depends also on one's assessment of those events and of their future potentialities. The choice of terms may obscure, distort, or clarify the course of events often known as the "Prague Spring." The latter widely used term was, of course, a metaphor without precise meaning, although it implied a phenomenon of short duration, to be followed inexorably by summer, fall, and winter, a seasonal sequence which in fact acquired an unexpected validity. Officially "January" (in Czech *Leden*, derived ironically from the word for "ice") was usually described as initiating a process of "democratization" or of "regeneration" (*obrodný proces*), the latter term harking back to the national renascence (*obrození*) of the early nineteenth century. The Action Program referred to "a new model of socialist democracy" and to "fundamental reforms . . . of the socialist economy," without defining the general process of change as either a reform or a revolution. Dubček usually employed relatively moderate terms, implying that reform, not revolution, was involved. At the April plenum he spoke of eliminating everything that was "out-of-date and incorrect" and developing everything "positive," and discouraged the condemnation of the entire past. At the May plenum he described the aim as "not the destruction, but the qualitative transformation and development of the socialist system." Only in late July did he use the famous phrase—"socialism with a human face,"[9] another metaphor lacking precision, but implying a humanist type of socialism, and, for many of his listeners, reflecting Dubček's own personal qualities.

Some Western commentators, mainly journalists, loosely used the word "revolution" to describe the Prague Spring.[10] Scholars, however, preferred more moderate concepts, such as "political change" (A. H. Brown) or "the reform movement" (Galia Golan and V. V. Kusin).[11]

[9] July 27, in Dubček, *K otázkam obrodzovacieho procesu v KSČ* (Bratislava, 1968), p. 237.

[10] E.g. M. Salomon, in *La révolution étranglée* (Paris, 1968), referred to "la révolution tranquille" (pp. 10, 15); L. Grünwald, in *ČSSR im Umbruch* (Vienna, 1969), to "die stille Revolution" (p. 73). Cf. the curious and unexplained term "controlled revolution," used by the Czech journalist, Josef Maxa (pseudo.), *Die kontrollierte Revolution* (Vienna, 1969).

[11] E.g. A. H. Brown, "Political Change in Czechoslovakia," *Government and Opposition* 4 (Spring 1969), 969-90 (reprinted in Leonard Schapiro, ed., *Political Opposition in One-Party States* [London, 1972]); Galia Golan, *The Czechoslovak Reform Movement* (Cambridge, 1971); V. V. Kusin, *Political Grouping in the Czechoslovak Reform Movement* (London, 1972). Golan did not define "reform" but wrote of "a process of fundamental change." Cf. her second book, *Reform Rule in Czechoslovakia* (Cambridge, 1973), p. 19.

Kusin, in *The Intellectual Origins of the Prague Spring*, persuasively defended the view that what transpired in 1968 was a "reform" and not "a revolution." The aim was not "the destruction of socialism" but "a reformed socialism, non-Stalinist, democratic." It would lack the essential elements of a revolution since it was to be gradual and not accompanied by violence, and would not involve non-constitutional forms of struggle, or the overthrow of government and the seizure of political power. Kusin distinguished the "profound change" sought by the intellectual reformers and the more restricted aims of those inside the power apparatus, but did not treat even the former as revolutionary in character and described Dubček as "the point of contact between the two reformatory concepts."[12]

There is much to be said in favor of Kusin's position. In addition to the absence of violence and other points made by Kusin, an outstanding feature of the Prague Spring was that the main changes were to be effected by legal procedures, through existing institutions, without even an immediate change in the composition of the National Assembly through general elections. Moreover, the pace of legislative change was relatively slow. Only two major laws were adopted prior to the August invasion. One, abolishing censorship, was an amendment of the existing press law, which was to be followed in due course by a new statute. The other, providing for rehabilitation, was enacted but had not been implemented. The prospects for the future were a series of similar specific changes in many other spheres, to be introduced one by one by statute, and elections in early 1969, to be conducted according to more democratic procedures than in the past. This was reminiscent, as one Czech cynically remarked, of the party jokingly founded by Jaroslav Hašek, the author of *The Good Soldier Švejk*, which he, with conscious irony, entitled "The Party of Moderate and Peaceful Progress Within the Limits of the Law."[13]

Whether 1968 was a reform or a revolution depends, of course, on the definition of the two terms and the essential differences drawn between them. Among Western scholars there is no generally accepted theory of revolution, and the meanings of the term are as numerous and varied as the authors who have attempted to define it.[14] Crane Brinton, in his clas-

---

[12] *The Intellectual Origins of the Prague Spring* (Cambridge, 1971), esp. pp. 140-42. Bystřina distinguished "reforms of the system," to be carried through within the framework of the party, and the more radical aims of the intellectuals as the "catalyzers of revolution," seeking "a real change of the system" (*Svědectví* 12, no. 47 [1974], 451-60).

[13] Bartošek, *RP*, July 31. See also Jaroslav Hašek, *The Good Soldier Švejk* (London, 1973), tr. by Cecil Parrott, p. x.

[14] For a critical analysis of recent works on revolution, see Lawrence Stone, "Theories of Revolution," *World Politics* 18 (Jan. 1966), 159-66. See also Perez Zagorin, "Theories of Revolution in Contemporary Historiography," *Political Science Quarterly* 88 (March 1973), 23-52. For varied definitions, see J. H. Meisel, *Counter-Revolution: How Revolutions Die* (New York, 1966), pp. 210-11.

sic study *The Anatomy of Revolution*, deliberately refrained from offering an exact definition of "revolution," or even from drawing a border line between it and other changes, suggesting that the difference was comparable to that between a mountain and a hill.[15] Others have been more precise and have regarded violence as an integral component of revolution. Cyril Black, for instance, defined revolution as the employment of "illegitimate violence . . . within a country to effect political change." Carl Friedrich termed it "a sudden and violent overthrow of an established political order." Chalmers Johnson expressed similar views and regarded "a non-violent revolution" as a contradiction in terms. Samuel Huntington conceived of revolution as "a rapid, fundamental, and violent domestic change in the dominant values and myths of society, in its political institutions, social structure, leadership, government activity and policies."[16] If, as suggested by these authors, violence is indeed the touchstone of a revolution, the Prague reforms of 1968, although otherwise largely conforming to Huntington's analysis, clearly do not fall within the category of revolution.

Some scholars, however, such as Alfred Meusel, regarded "social change," *not* the use of violence, as more characteristic of revolution and defined it as "a sudden and far-reaching change, a major break in the continuity of development." Others, although admitting that violence often accompanied a revolution, have written in similar terms. Walter Laqueur, for instance, described a revolution as "an attempt to make a radical change in the system of government," or "any fundamentally new development in the economy, culture or social fabric." Sigmund Neuman referred to it as "a sweeping fundamental change in political organization, social structure, economic property control and the predominant myth of a social order, thus indicating a major break in the continuity of development."[17] If such analyses are correct, the description of the Czechoslovak process of change as a revolution becomes more tenable.

[15] *The Anatomy of Revolution* (New York, rev. 1965), pp. 24-25. Elsewhere Brinton implied a difference between revolution and "orderly, peaceable gradual change" (p. 5) and stated his intention to focus on "drastic, sudden substitution of one group in charge of the running of a territorial and political entity by another group not hitherto running that government" (p. 4). He implied that it was usually, if not always, associated with violence.

[16] Cyril E. Black, in Black and T. P. Thornton, eds., *Communism and Revolution* (Princeton, 1964), p. 4; Friedrich, in Carl J. Friedrich, ed., *Revolution* (Nomos VIII, New York, 1966), p. 5; Chalmers Johnson, *Revolutionary Change* (Boston, 1966), p. 7; Samuel P. Huntington, *Political Order in Changing Societies* (New Haven, 1968), p. 264.

[17] Alfred Meusel, "Revolution and Counter-revolution," *Encyclopaedia of the Social Sciences* 13 (1934), 367-76; Walter Laqueur, *International Encyclopaedia of the Social Sciences* 13 (1968), 501-7; Sigmund Neuman, "The International Civil War," *WP* 1 (April 1949), 333-34, n. 1. Neuman, however, considered it an error to identify revolution with "significant change" or "persistent transformations that were accomplished within the framework of existing institutions," and insisted on the presence of a radical break in continuity of development.

Some Marxist Views

From a Marxist standpoint the 1968 events, on first thought, do not seem to exhibit the features customarily regarded as characteristic of revolution. This was certainly not a revolutionary transition from one historical form of society to another in accordance with the stages envisaged by historical materialism. It involved a transformation of socialism itself, but not in the direction of a higher stage of communism, as conceived by Marx. Nor was it the product of stern class struggle, with one social class succeeding another in power. Moreover, force or violence, normally regarded by Marx as a hallmark of revolution, and elevated by Lenin as a *sine qua non* of the transition from capitalism to socialism, was not present.[18] Marxists, however, have varied significantly on the latter issue. A peaceful transition to socialism was considered as a possibility in more democratic countries by Marx himself, and was expounded as official dogma by Nikita Khrushchev. The Western specialist on Marx, Professor Robert Tucker, disregarded the element of violence in Marx's analysis and identified the core of the revolutionary process as a social revolution—"a change in the mode of production with consequent change of all subordinate elements of the social complex."[19] Although Tucker's approach eliminated the thorny issue of violence, it raised the question as to whether the changes in Czechoslovakia constituted a social revolution in terms of an essential change in the mode of production.

Several prominent Czech and Slovak Marxists described the development in 1968 as "revolutionary" and advanced interesting arguments in support of their interpretations. The views of four—two Czech and two Slovak—deserve attention.

In January 1968, the Czech historian, Karel Bartošek, made a distinction between reform and revolution, one seeking to improve the existing system, and the other "to change the system from its foundation." "Structural reforms" could be "gradual in a time sense, but in their en-

[18] Michael Waller, *The Language of Communism: A Commentary* (London, 1972), pp. 72-74, 93-98. A. C. Janos, in an essay on the communist theory of revolution, stressed the element of "force" (Black and Thornton, eds., *Communism and Revolution*, pp. 36-39).

[19] Robert C. Tucker, "The Marxist Revolutionary Idea," in Friedrich, ed., *Revolution*, chap. 10, quotation at p. 226. This approach was endorsed by another contributor to that volume, David Braybrook, on p. 241. For a similar view, see Waller, *The Language of Communism*, p. 93. The Polish Marxist, Marek Waldenberg, in *Rewolucja* (Warsaw, 1964), claimed that a revolution need not be violent but could be "a peaceful, legal, transformation of power." The Czech sociologist, Jaroslav Krejčí, rejected this view because it erased the difference between revolution and evolution, and defined a revolution proper as "an overwhelmingly violent change of power relations within one and the same state." For this, see J. Krejčí, "Sociologický model revolučního procesu," *Sociologický časopis* 4 (1968), no. 2, 159-63, and no. 6, 635-49, citation at p. 161 and n. 16.

tirety will mean a qualitative, i.e. revolutionary, change." Under socialism, he wrote, the reformists regarded "revolution as forever finished";
the revolutionaries consideerd it as "continuing, if you wish, permanent,
as a condition of unceasing dynamics. . . ." The situation required not
mere "reforms putting the situation right," but "structural reforms"
which would lead to "the destruction of the system (bureaucratic-etatist
socialism)" and would perhaps offer "a new model of civilization and
human life." He warned, however, of "the developed sense of compromisingness" in Czech politics in the past, even under socialism, and concluded: "Perhaps everything would depend on whether they would find
the path from reforms to revolution."[20]

In his historical series on "the revolution against bureaucratism," published in the late summer of 1968, Bartošek spoke of the "explosion of
freedom" in March as "the initial act of the 'anti-bureaucratic revolution,' " and referred to a possible "new stage" in the future which would
involve "not just partial reform of the old system but a reconstruction of
the whole political structure." Again he warned of "historical complexes
and illnesses" and the possibility of a mere revolt leading to a consumer
society. He clearly regarded revolution only as a future possibility, part
of a revolution against bureaucratism in the whole of Europe.[21]

The Czech philosopher, Ivan Sviták, who viewed events during 1968
with a skeptical eye, distinguished sharply between "democratization"
and democracy, and doubted the possibility of the success of the former.
Democratization of a totalitarian dictatorship, he said, in his lecture
"Heads against the Wall," was like squaring the circle. "Round squares
do not exist."[22] But in July 1969, in an address in Vienna, Sviták spoke
of a unique historical event in 1968: "a Czechoslovak Democratic Revolution based on a socialist society," which had grown, just before the
occupation, into "a revolutionary movement calling for a radical structural change in Stalinist institutions." Generalizing from this experience,
Sviták concluded that, unlike previous revolutions, the modern democratic revolution "was not just a political change, but a radical structural

---

[20] *Plamen* 10 (Feb. 1968), 63-65.

[21] *RP*, July 31. In a lecture in June 1969, Bartošek developed the theme of an
"anti-bureaucratic revolution" as "a continuation (a component part) of the anti-
capitalist revolution." It would be based on "a strategy of revolution in developed
societies, on a Gramsci-Šmeral strategy of trench warfare, seeking to win spiritual
hegemony, to gain one enemy trench after another, to understand the real relation
between reforms and revolution." The revolution could not be "a single act but
a series of structural reforms" and would require violence. It would have to take
place on an international scale as "a *common* struggle of the smaller nations of
central, eastern and southeastern Europe for equality of rights," aimed at abolishing the relationship of subordination to the USSR. "Our Present Crisis and Revolution," *Svědectví* 10, no. 38 (1970), 231-40; quotations at pp. 237-38.

[22] March 20, 1968 (*Student*, April 10), in Sviták, *Czechoslovak Experiment*,
pp. 25-26, 36, 44.

change of the system, a transformation of the social order, combining revolution and reform, its course being a sequence of revolutionary reforms, not merely a change of persons or of parties in power." It was "a permanent revolution, a sequence of changes requiring a long period of time and a long, or possibly permanent, effort by a democratic, revolutionary movement which is not an opposition within the system, but an opposition against the system." This revolution was the product of "a sudden crisis" which had resulted from "the latent contradiction between the explosively growing productive forces and the archaic productive relations" and generated "an avalanche-like sequence of spontaneous movements in the direction of radical reforms. . . ." In this analysis Sviták was referring not to the actions of the leaders, but to the more radical performance of "spontaneous groups . . ." which created "a unified front against the elite." Although communists might take part in such "a pluralistic movement," the party itself, as a bureaucratic-elitist organization, was incompatible with the democratization movement and could not provide the leadership for it.[23]

Miroslav Kusý, prominent Slovak philosopher (who for a time after the occupation was a CPS Secretary until dismissed by Husák), considered the post-January developments as involving "a qualitative leap in the development of our model of socialist democracy" which could best be described as "an institutional revolution." The socialist revolution in 1948 established rule by the working class, abolished private property, and socialized the means of production. The present need was "a revolution whose aim was to change qualitatively our whole system of rule, the entire institutional structure of our society so that this system and this structure would reflect in an optimal manner the new changed social structure of our society." This would be "an institutional revolution, a revolution in the sphere of the institutional superstructure of our social base." The superstructure did not automatically change with the change in the economic base, and might lag behind, and become, as it did in the form of the centralized system of power and the dominance of an all-powerful and irresponsible *aparát*, "a conservative and regressive factor." This had given rise to a long-term process of opposition, involving many social forces, under party leadership, and culminating in 1968 in "a profound and all-embracing institutional revolution." This must be carried through to the end by "rebuilding the old institutional structure from its foundations" and by creating "a new Czechoslovak model of socialist democracy. . . ."[24]

The Slovak economist, Evžen Löbl, advanced the view that the revolu-

---

[23] Ibid., pp. 221-23. In later essays, Sviták adopted a very different stance, highly critical of the reform efforts of 1968. See below.

[24] Kusý, *Nová mysl*, no. 11, 1968, pp. 1315-28; also *Nové slovo*, Oct. 24, 1968.

tion in Czechoslovakia had been "an intellectual revolution," the first of its kind in history, synthesizing the scientific-technological revolution with a socialist revolution.[25] As a result of the former revolution and the crucial importance of science in modern production, the intellectuals, as the bearers of knowledge, had become the main source and creator of national wealth and had replaced the proletariat as the only stratum (*Schicht*) capable of leading society. Only in Czechoslovakia, as a result of a deep crisis, had the intelligentsia actually assumed this leading role and become "a tremendous political power." Contrary to the belief of Marx, the mere nationalization of the means of production had not established socialism. State ownership, on the Soviet model, had simply made the party Presidium the "owners" of nationalized property. A new "socialist revolution" would expropriate the Presidium and place property under the control of the organs of the working class in the enterprises. Such co-determination would establish for the first time a genuine form of socialized ownership.[26] This would have to be combined with political democracy, attained, not through the classic form of a multi-party system, but through the democratization of the Communist Party and the political participation of social organizations.[27] Economic democracy would be achieved through an extended role for the market, coupled with enterprise independence, vigorous trade unionsim, and state intervention to protect the consumers. Such an "intellectual revolution" in Czechoslovakia would bring into being an authentic and humanist form of socialism, "socialism with a human face."

REVOLUTIONARY ASPECTS OF 1968

The Marxist interpretations cited above, in most cases retrospective and not entirely consistent with each other, are individual appraisals which cannot be taken as representative of general opinion in Czechoslovakia or as decisive in determining the nature and meaning of 1968.[28]

[25] E. Löbl, in Löbl and L. Grünwald, *Die intellektuelle Revolution* (Düsseldorf, 1969), pp. 7-104. See also Löbl, in V. V. Kusin, ed., *The Czechoslovak Reform Movement 1968* (London, 1973), pp. 329-40. See Löbl's earlier study identifying "mental work" as the source of "the wealth of nations," *Úvahy o duševnej práci a bohatstve národa* (Bratislava, 1967); also in German, cited above chap. IV, n. 125.

[26] Löbl explicitly rejected, however, a comprehensive form of co-determination which would have placed the manager in a subordinate position, and opted for a more limited form of participation including the election of managers and consultation (*Intellektuelle Revolution*, pp. 55-56). See also his article, *NM*, no. 8 (1968), pp. 963-69, and above, chap. XIV, p. 439, nn. 72, 83, 85.

[27] For a severe criticism of the multi-party system, see *Intellektuelle Revolution*, pp. 60-66.

[28] Others, including non-communists, have taken similar views that 1968 was not a reform but a revolution. E.g. Josef Škvorecký, in a lecture at Yale University on March 13, 1974, "1968: Reform, Revolution or Counter-Revolution" (available

Moreover the four theorists, in varying degrees, regarded the "revolution" as unfinished, or as a future perspective, not as a completed action. The differences between them demonstrate anew the difficulty of developing a theory of revolution and the absence of one that will fit all cases.[29] The Czechoslovak "revolution," if one calls it that, was unique in character, differing in essential features from other revolutions and not easily subsumed in the categories set forth by Marx or by modern scholars, Marxist and non-Marxist.

In my own opinion reform is too mild a term to describe accurately what was happening in 1968 and what was likely to happen thereafter. Many features of the post-January development were revolutionary in character, and might well have culminated, if not interrupted from the outside, in a revolution of profound dimensions. January was the product of a breakdown of the old order conforming to Lenin's classic recipe for a revolutionary situation: the rulers were unable to continue to rule in the old way, and the ruled were unwilling to be so ruled. It involved the gradual loss of power by a strong ruling group—the bureaucratic or *apparatchik* class, some 100,000 in number—and a portentous shift in the balance of forces within the party and in society as a whole. Although the impetus for reform was initially given by party leaders (who were certainly not revolutionaries) and by certain intellectual elites, all social groups were eventually drawn into the quickening currents of political action, so that by August that which had started as an affair of elites and leaders had become a mass movement for substantial change, differing only in degree, but not in essentials, among Slovaks and Czechs.

Moreover, the changes envisaged were many and substantial, and affected all aspects of life without exception. At least three major reforms were extremely radical in the context of the Soviet model. The extent of freedom of expression was a complete break with the Soviet pattern of censorship and indoctrination. The rehabilitation process was intended to correct gross injustices in a thorough and systematic manner unequaled in other communist countries, and was to be accompanied by radical changes in legal procedures. Federalization, designed to reorder Czech-Slovak relations on a federal basis, was without parallel in Czechoslovakia either before or under communist rule, and was the antithesis of the pretenses of Soviet federalism.

Other matters on the agenda, such as economic and political reform, and foreign policy, were dealt with in a relatively moderate fashion prior to August, but were likely to assume more drastic form in due course.

---

in typescript), described it as "a democratic revolution which was purely socialist in character." Radical changes in the political superstructure were to be made, but without changing the socialist character of the economy.

[29] Zagorin, "Theories of Revolution," *PSQ*, p. 52.

Economic reform did not advance much beyond its original pre-January stage. However, planned changes (the statute on the enterprise and the working people's councils) would have constituted basic transformations in the economic system in the direction of market socialism and workers' participation, breaking completely with the previous system of central-ized administrative management. From a Marxist viewpoint, this could well be regarded as a fundamental change in the productive relations of society. In the political realm the leading role of the party was to be retained, and the National Front was to remain a barrier to an open political system. Nonetheless, significant changes had already occurred, or were definitely planned, in the process of government, including the revival of the assembly, the democratic reform of the party, the proliferation of interest groups and the democratization of their organizations, and guarantees of human rights. Proposals for greater initiative in foreign and defense policy and in bloc relations were at first modest, but clear hints of a desire for much greater independence in these spheres were given. Whether these and other changes would assume a more drastic character depended indeed on the fate of the leading role of the party. Would the claim to communist hegemony be vindicated in fact, or would it be replaced by a genuine political pluralism as demanded by many in the free and wide-ranging discussion of the political model?

The scope and nature of the reform program would therefore have been determined not merely by the pre-August actualities of 1968 (significant as they were) but also by the potentialities unleashed by the on-rush of events. The process of democratization was in its initial stage only and represented a combination of reformist and revolutionary elements. Much had been accomplished in the eight months (only 227 days!) before the invasion, especially when one takes into account the unexpectedness of the January overthrow, the absence of detailed plans, the bitter struggle of contending forces, and the intense pressures against reform from outside. Although the future was in some degree open, what seemed most likely was a continuing sequence of individual reforms, each drastic in its own sphere and reinforcing one another, the cumulative effect of which would have been a metamorphosis of the entire system.[30] This would have been a kind of "uninterrupted" or "permanent" revolution, not in the Leninist or Trotskyist sense of telescoping the historical changes anticipated by Marxism (in the case of Russia, the bourgeois-democratic and proletarian revolutions) but in the sense of successive stages of radical change, each one leading on to the next, over a

---

[30] Waller noted that earlier Marxists were preoccupied with the "cataclysmic" French revolution and neglected the English revolution which might have led to "a more cumulative, epochal model (of revolution), with more than one critical transition" (*Language of Communism*, p. 73, n. 1).

period of years, or even decades. The ultimate result would probably have been a transformation, in Marxist terms, of both base and super-structure for which Bartošek's concept of "structural" change would have been more appropriate than Kusý's weaker term "institutional."

From this standpoint the intervention of the Warsaw "five" did in fact, "interrupt" a process of revolutionary transformation, the depth and breadth of which was demonstrated by the time required to bring it to a complete halt. Indeed the nonviolent resistance to the invasion during the first week, and the continuing opposition manifested in the students' strike, public demonstrations, the suicides of Palach and others, and radi-cal oppositional declarations by various social groups, demonstrated that attitudes, especially among workers, students, and intellectuals, were rad-icalized by the invasion. The revolutionary process was paradoxically accelerated and deepened as a result of the military intervention, and assumed also a nationalist character in the effort to defend the continu-ance of reforms against outside interference. In spite of the unfavorable conditions, certain basic reforms were consummated, notably federation, although this was greatly marred by the absence of democracy. Despite censorship, freedom of expression was substantial and radical views were voiced on all issues. Preparatory work for implementing drastic reforms of the economy and of the judicial system proceeded apace. It took an-other eight months for the Soviet Union to apply sufficient pressure and to mobilize the domestic forces needed to throttle the process of radical change initiated in January.

COUNTERREVOLUTION?

Were the changes under way in Czechoslovakia of such a character as to constitute a counterrevolution? Did 1968 represent a reversal of 1948 and the "socialist revolution" of that year? Did it involve a return to capitalism and bourgeois democracy? Such were the claims made by the Soviet Union and expounded by Czech and Slovak apologists of the intervention.[31] Official Albanian and Chinese commentaries took a simi-lar line, although they made no distinction between what was happening in Prague and what they considered the general advance of counterrevo-lutionary revisionism in the other states of Eastern Europe and in the USSR. Castro also condemned counterrevolutionary tendencies in Czechoslovakia.

[31] For a full post-occupation analysis, see the report adopted by the CC, Dec. 1970, *Poučení z krízového vývoje strany a společnosti po XIII. sjezdu KSČ* (Prague, 1971); in English, *Lesson Drawn from the Crisis Development in the Party and Society after the 13th Congress of the Communist Party of Czechoslo-vakia* (no place, n.d.).

Yet, prior to the occupation, Soviet statements, at least in public, did not condemn the reforms as such, or even the Dubček regime, as counterrevolutionary, but limited their criticism to the anti-socialist forces which, they argued, constituted an acute danger of counterrevolution of which the Prague leadership seemed to be unaware. The central theme of Soviet propaganda and the main pretext for intervention was the potential danger of counterrevolution rather than its actual existence. The leadership was censured for permitting the activities of these forces and whatever its intentions might be, for in effect losing control of the situation, thus running the risk of having power wrested from it by anti-socialist elements. After the occupation, however, Soviet propaganda openly indicted the reform program itself as likely to move, through economic reform, toward the restoration of capitalism, and through political reform, toward bourgeois democracy and the end of communist rule. This was coupled with the charge that Czechoslovakia was planning to leave the Warsaw Treaty Organization and would thus weaken the defense capacity of the bloc and endanger socialism in Eastern Europe as a whole.

In the long run the dynamics of the revolutionary process in Prague *might* have led to the gradual erosion of socialism and the loss of communist power. This was not, however, the purpose of the reform leaders, nor was it the most likely immediate perspective, nor an inevitable result even in the more distant future. In actuality the Communist Party and its leadership were still in relatively firm command of the situation, although, in the more democratic environment of 1968, this control was not total nor was it effected by coercive means. The party leaders themselves admitted the existence of anti-socialist, and even counterrevolutionary tendencies (as expressed, for instance, in the Two Thousand Words), but denied that these were a predominant feature of the situation and insisted that they could be controlled and ultimately eliminated by political, rather than violent measures.[32] The leadership was subject to the pressure of public opinion and organized reform groups, but was confident that it could maintain its primary position and guide and direct, and if necessary, limit, the pace and direction of change. It had no intention of abolishing socialism and returning to capitalism, but sought a fusion or synthesis of planning and the market. Public ownership would be retained, but would be combined with entrepreneurial independence and workers' participation. Cooperative agriculture would also be re-

[32] See Dubček's defense of his policy at the CC, Sept. 1969, *Svědectví* 10, no. 38 (1970), 267-80. See also his letter to Smrkovský's widow, *Listy*, no. 2 (May 1974), pp. 4-6. For Dubček's 1969 CC speech and that of Smrkovský on the same occasion, see J. Pelikán, ed., *Ici Prague* (Paris, 1973), pp. 153-76. See also Smrkovský's oral memoir published (after his death) in *Listy*, no. 2 (March 1975), pp. 3-25 (Appendix D) and Mlynář's memorandum, Appendix E.

tained, but would be democratized through organized representation of agricultural interests. There was no intention of abandoning the alliance with the Soviet Union, or leaving WTO or Comecon, but a belief that greater independence of action would transform the alliance into a genuine partnership based on equality and common interest.

Admittedly socialism, as a Czech commentator later said, was a "hazy" term and was conceived in many different ways by different persons.[33] This is abundantly clear from the diversity of views, even among Western Marxists, in their analysis of the Czechoslovak movement for reform. For instance, an American economist, Benjamin Page, although not without sympathy for the Czechoslovak experiment, did not acknowledge the Prague reform model as "socialist," but considered it as a new class society in which the dominant position would be held by the managerial and technical experts, not by the workers. This represented, however, not a return to capitalism, nor was it a managerial revolution, but the eventual result would have been a consumer-oriented, elite-dominated society resembling capitalism in many ways.[34] Another American economist, George Wheeler, whose faith in socialism had led him to live in Czechoslovakia from 1947 on, and who had become a member of the Institute of Economics in 1954, believed that 1948 had been a socialist revolution and that the subsequent highly centralized system of planning had many achievements to its credit. The breakdown of the system in the sixties and its many failures, however, demonstrated in his view the need for a profound economic reform, combining planning and elements of the market, as a means of achieving a higher stage of socialism.[35] Western Trotskyist analysis, although ambiguous, may also be cited as evidence of the variety of Marxist interpretations. According to this view the Czechoslovak crisis was part of the general crisis of bureaucratic socialism, and the events of 1968 constituted an "anti-bureaucratic revolution," at least in embryo. Šik's economic reform, although it was an attempt by one wing of the bureaucracy to maintain the system and could not solve the crisis, was not described as a return to capitalism, nor was the situation deemed to be counterrevolutionary. The weakness of Dubček's movement for reform lay in his failure to enlist the working class and the masses, and his willingness to compromise both with the bureaucratic system and with the Soviet Union.[36]

[33] V. Stupka, *Politika*, Oct. 31, 1968, p. 13.

[34] Benjamin B. Page, *The Czechoslovak Reform Movement, 1963-1968* (Amsterdam, 1973). Page described the Action Program as "a managerial and technocratic manifesto," based on the writings of Šik, Richta, and Mlynář.

[35] George S. Wheeler, *The Human Face of Socialism* (New York, 1973).

[36] The most informed Trotskyist study, and the most positive, was that of Pierre Broué, *Le printemps des peuples commence à Prague* (Paris, n.d.). More critical but less well documented was Chris Harman, *Bureaucracy and Revolution*

Czech and Slovak Marxists, as we have seen, did not share these views, nor were they willing to acknowledge that the Soviet Union had a monopoly over the definition of socialism. They insisted on their right to interpret socialism in their own way and to create their own version, independently fashioned according to their requirements. In the words of Šamalík, the goal was "a Czechoslovak model of socialism," formed "on the basis of a more authentic conception of the ideas of Marx and Engels, Lenin and Plekhanov, Luxemburg, Gramsci and other Marxists and on the basis of the thought and practice of progressive socialist movements of all countries." "We wished," he said, "more firmly and organically to incorporate Marxism into the culture and tradition of our nations. . . ."[37] The new system, as another commentator wrote after the occupation, would be "a humanist socialism" in the spirit of the earlier Marx, ending alienation and liberating man.[38]

It was this very objective of a thoroughly reformed communist system, a democratic model of socialism, which awakened most alarm in Moscow.[39] They feared *not* a return to capitalism, or the end of socialism, but a return to democracy—indeed an advance toward a system of popular participation which might have gone beyond the traditional forms of parliamentary democracy. Freedom, not private enterprise and the market, was the real danger. What the Czechs and Slovaks sought to do was to reverse the worst consequences of the assumption of power in 1948, but not to restore the status quo ante. This was indeed a counterrevolution, not in the sense of a negation of socialism as such, but of the replacement of an obsolete and unsuited Soviet model of socialism with a new one. As the Italians and other European communists perceived, this would have made socialism in Czechoslovakia more viable and would have enhanced its appeal to the people of Western Europe. In Eastern Europe, however, apart from Hungary, such a radically reformed socialism, although still under communist leadership, would have endangered the system of Soviet-style socialism, the very existence of the regimes, and hence the personal positions of those in power.

If considered from this standpoint, the Soviet intervention was itself counterrevolutionary, designed to ward off these dangers, to defend the political and social status quo, and to crush by force a revolutionary transformation under way.[40] By the summer of 1969, with the coopera-

---

in Eastern Europe (London, 1974), chap. 8 and the conclusion. See also the booklet, *L'intervention en Tchécoslovaquie, Pourquoi?* (Paris, 1969).

[37] *Politika*, Sept. 19, 1968.   [38] Stupka, ibid., Oct. 31, pp. 14, 16.

[39] Bystřina, *Svědectví*, 12, no. 47 (1974), 454.

[40] The role of the Soviet intervention, ironically, resembled "counterrevolutionary interventions" by imperialist countries analyzed by the Soviet author, E. B. Chernyak, *Zhandarmy istorii (Kontrrevolyutionnye interventsii i zagovory)* (Moscow, 1969). D. Aleksandrov, in a review of this historical study, described

tion of Husák and his colleagues, the USSR had succeeded in attaining this goal. Unlike some counterrevolutions,[41] no attempt was made to retain some of the elements of the antecedent reform, and all the major reforms planned or introduced were reversed and the status quo ante restored in full.

COULD THE EXPERIMENT SUCCEED?

The history of past revolutions warns against the assumption that the Prague Spring, even in the absence of intervention, would have proceeded directly, without zigzags and setbacks, to a preordained victory for fundamental reform. Crane Brinton in his study of four great revolutions sought to generalize about their common features and to discern a uniform sequence of stages of development. His conclusions, however, do not satisfactorily cover the extraordinary variety of types and phases of revolution and seem particularly inapplicable to Czechoslovakia.[42] The Czech sociologist, Jaroslav Krejčí, in a comparative analysis of selected revolutions, revealed the diversity of the successive stages and the conflicting forces involved at each stage, and demonstrated the length and complexity of the course of a revolution and the unpredictability of its ultimate outcome.[43] One must assume, therefore, that the process of

---

it as having great "actuality." The purpose of such "outside counterrevolution," he wrote, was to restore power to a defeated class or to preserve the power of a ruling class threatened by revolution. An important aspect of intervention was to slow down the tempo of social progress and to restore an obsolete political and social order, making possible the victory of more conservative variants of social development. It was most likely to succeed if the intervening power had military superiority and the help of domestic counterrevolution (*Novy mir*, no. 5, 1970, pp. 274-77).

[41] Meisel, *Counter-Revolution*, pp. 20, 32; Meusel, "Revolution and Counter-revolution," pp. 371-74.

[42] Brinton, *The Anatomy of Revolution*, passim, pp. 249-50; 267-69. According to Brinton, an initial stage of "rule of the moderates" led to "accession of the extremists," which was followed by a reign of terror and, eventually, a Thermidorean reaction. For critical comment on Brinton's stages, see Zagorin, "Theories of Revolution," *PSQ*, pp. 30-31. Cf. another sequence suggested by Rex D. Hopper, cited by Stone, "Theories of Revolution," *WP*, p. 175.

[43] Krejčí, "Sociologický model revolučního procesu," cited in n. 19 above. Generalizing from three "vertical" revolutions (the Hussite, English, and French), Krejčí distinguished the following phases: the start of the revolutionary process, repression, revolutionary eruption, revolutionary oscillation, seizure of power, deformation, expansion, reversal, and consolidation. The forces involved were labeled counterrevolutionaries, revolutionary right, revolutionary center, revolutionary left, and extreme left. A revolution, he wrote, was "usually a long-term process during the course of which the social organism experienced many changes, some transitional (short-term) and some permanent (long-term)." In the three cases studied the period lasted from 35 to 60 years. In his second article Krejčí studied three examples of "horizontal" revolution, the Dutch, British American, and Spanish American revolutions.

radical change in Czechoslovakia was likely to take strange turns, and that its future course and final result could not be forecast with certainty.

Some analysts have expressed strong doubts as to whether the process of change in Czechoslovakia would have ever been completed. Could Czechoslovak communism be reformed by its own efforts? Even if it were conceded that this might have been possible in an international vacuum, could it have been achieved within the limits set by the power of the Soviet Union?

For instance, Pavel Tigrid, in his study *Why Dubček Fell*, concluded that the Dubček experiment was not possible. The Czech and Slovak party leaders would not have gone beyond a certain point (in reform) at which the loss of their own power was threatened. "A communist dictatorship is by its very nature permanent, able to change its costume but never its skin."[44] Ivan Sviták, in one of his more pessimistic essays, presented a strong case that the movement for democratization was doomed to failure. The reformers were filled with illusions as to the possibilities of market socialism, an "open Marxism," and the reform of a totalitarian dictatorship. As long as the party retained its monopoly of power, he believed, the radical reforms envisaged by some intellectuals were unrealizable.[45]

Undoubtedly there were elements of uncertainty on the eve of the August invasion, and there were some factors which might have impeded the ultimate success of the reform movement. The very structure of the system of power and the existence of strong vested interests in the status quo made the achievement of radical change difficult. Within the leadership, among the party rank and file, and within the body of *apparatchiki* and functionaries, there were substantial numbers who were afraid of serious reform and susceptible to Soviet persuasion and enticement. Even more progressive reform leaders were fearful of radical change. Within the party the balance of forces would have almost certainly shifted in favor of more drastic reform at the 14th Party Congress, but the new leaders would have been divided on the pace and direction of reform. A polarization of views would have presented Dubček with the dilemma of whether to identify himself with the more moderate or the more radical tendencies. It is not excluded that he might have sought to moderate the course of change in the style of Kádár, or even to reverse it, in the manner of Gomułka. Nor can one even exclude the possibility that the ousted conservatives, using the armed forces or security police, might have tried to overthrow him and to restore the old order.

To predict the certainty of the ultimate failure of the Czechoslovak

[44] *Why Dubček Fell* (London, 1971), pp. 194-209; quotations at pp. 198, 204.
[45] "The Errors of the Prague Spring," Sviták, *Dialektika moci* (Cologne, 1973), pp. 69-83.

experiment, is, however, risky, and indeed perhaps more so than to forecast its likely success. The contingencies mentioned above were possibilities, and not the most probable ones. Other factors in the situation suggested a greater likelihood of the victory of the cause of fundamental change, but with the Communist Party retaining its commanding position. For the immediate future the party had no serious challengers, and enjoyed a great increase in popularity as the inspirer of the movement for reform and as the defender of national independence. Its victory in relatively free elections was probable (and a fully democratic electoral system would not likely be introduced, at least for the polls in early 1969). In the new constellation of forces within the CPCz after the 14th congress, Dubček, surrounded by firm believers in reform and under the strong pressure of public opinion and progressive party opinion, might well have identified himself with the more radical tendencies and forged ahead with drastic reforms. If he had refused, he might have been pushed aside as too cautious and too willing to compromise and replaced by more radical leaders. In general, prior to August, there was a powerful dynamic at work, within the party and in society at large, which suggested that, barring outside intervention, the process of change would have been accelerated rather than slowed down or blocked, and would eventually have produced a thoroughly revised socialism, democratic in form, and national in content.

Much less favorable were the external conditions for success. Was Soviet intervention not inevitable under almost any foreseeable conditions except a complete retreat by the reform leaders? As we have argued in an earlier chapter, the motivations for the decision to invade were many and related both to the domestic course followed by Prague and to its international implications. The Czechoslovak program struck at the heart of the Soviet conception of socialism and offered an alternative model not only distasteful in itself but likely to infect other communist states and parties with heretical ideas, thus threatening the Soviet position in Eastern Europe and in the world communist movement, and in the long run, raising the specter of a challenge to the Soviet system at home. These fears were compounded by the assumption that such developments in Prague and other communist capitals, coupled with their aspirations for greater independence of action in the international field, would weaken the defenses of the bloc against the assumed menace of American and German imperialism. Herman Kahn, in a persuasive but somewhat exaggerated argument, concluded that "from the Soviet leaders' point of view the case for intervention was on balance an overwhelming one."[46]

[46] *Fortune*, Nov. 1968, p. 125.

Although Soviet leaders were no doubt united in their antipathy to the Czechoslovak course, all, or most of them, were reluctant to resort to military force. In fact the decision to invade came only after long and persistent efforts to persuade and pressure the Prague regime into changing or moderating its plans. In the end, when these political measures failed, military intervention seemed to have been accepted as unavoidable by the entire leadership. There was a certain logic to this conclusion, but it was a reactionary logic, rooted in a rigid conception of socialism and the fear that any serious changes in that model would lead to even greater and more fundamental changes in the future. This "logic" was not inherent in the communist outlook itself, as indicated by the pro-reform attitudes of the Italian, Yugoslav, and even the Rumanian parties, but was convincing to Moscow's East German, Polish, and Bulgarian comrades, and to the more conservative and pro-Soviet parties elsewhere in the world. The Hungarian communists, who had initially had some sympathy for the Czechoslovak reform, accepted, perhaps reluctantly, the "necessity" of intervention, fearing that Prague's program, and Soviet hostility to it, endangered their own more moderate reforms. Given the extremely conservative character of the Soviet regime, the incompatibility of their concepts of socialism and those of the Czechoslovak regime, and the unwillingness of the latter to yield in essentials, the intervention, in retrospect, appears to have been more or less unavoidable. Barring perhaps a different strategy and tactics by Dubček, the Prague experiment seemed doomed to failure for external reasons rather than inherent domestic ones.

Was Dubček's Strategy at Fault?

Could the Czechs and Slovaks have averted military intervention by following a different strategy? It has sometimes beem contended that a more restrained and moderate course, especially one limiting the freedom of expression so characteristic of the Prague Spring, might have lessened Soviet fears and made possible a stable compromise under which much of the reform program might have been achieved.[47] More often, however, Dubček has been censured by Czechs and Slovaks for the opposite reasons—for his excessive caution and moderacy, and his failure to resist outside interference more firmly.[48]

[47] This has been put most strongly by the British journalist, W. Shawcross, in Kusin, ed., *Czechoslovak Reform*, pp. 280-89. See above, chap. XVIII, n. 31. For a fuller critique along this line, embracing also the reform leaders' errors, see the 1975 memorandum by Z. Mlynář, given in Appendix E.

[48] For criticism along these lines, see Šabata, "Revolta bez teoria?" pp. 18-21; J. Pelikán, "Socialist Opposition in East Europe and the International Left," *New*

In fact, of course, Dubček did seek to moderate the reform course and to conciliate the Russians, especially at the June plenum and at the Čierna and Bratislava conferences. His insistence on the leading role of the party; his condemnation of anti-socialist forces; and his constant asseveration of his loyalty to the Soviet bloc, were examples of his efforts in this direction. To have exercised still greater circumspection was well-nigh impossible in the face of an aroused public opinion and might have cost him his popular support. In any case, once a spontaneous movement for radical reform, or revolutionary change, has been launched, it is difficult, if not impossible, to set limits to it without depriving it of its essence and preparing the ground for its reversal. Such a retreat might have won Soviet approval, or tolerance, but only at the cost of the basic goals themselves.

Dubček was more open to criticism for his failure to comprehend that his reform program could not be reconciled with friendship and alliance with the USSR and the bloc, and that military action by his so-called allies was a real possibility. He has been blamed for treating Soviet concern with Czechoslovak domestic affairs as legitimate and, by engaging in joint deliberations with his bloc partners, acquiescing in their interference. Unlike Yugoslavia, Albania, and Rumania, in somewhat analogous circumstances, he thus accepted the Soviet "rules of the game."[49] Even the brief interlude of "defiance" during and after the Warsaw conference did not mean that Czech hopes of reconciling the irreconcilable were relinquished, as Čierna and Bratislava demonstrated. Above all, Dubček underestimated or ignored the possibility of military intervention and failed to make clear that Czechoslovakia would resist such action by force.[50]

Politics 11, no. 1 (1974), 76-77; A. Černý, *Stanovisko k XIV. sjezdu*, mimeo. (in French, J. Pelikán, ed., *Ici Prague*, pp. 287-308; in English [under Šabata's name], *Critique* 1, Spring 1973, pp. 64-75; A. Ostrý, *Československý problém* (Cologne, 1972), pp. 41-45, 155-56; J. Pokštefl, in Kusin, ed., *Czechoslovak Reform*, pp. 351-52; A. Müller, in C. Schmidt-Häuer and A. Müller, *Viva Dubček* (Cologne, 1968), pp. 184-86. See also Selucky's evaluation of Dubček's strategy, "The Dubček Era Revisited," *Problems of Communism* 24 (Jan.-Feb. 1975), 38-43.

[49] Moravus (pseud.), *Listy*, no. 6 (1971), pp. 28-29; in English in *Survey* (Autumn 1971), pp. 203-15; in French, in Pelikán, ed., *Ici Prague*, pp. 364-66. For a contrasting view, see Mlynář's memorandum, below, Appendix E.

[50] Smrkovský, in his testimony published in 1975, denied that they had received any warning of intervention from the Soviet Union. "I can say that until half an hour before midnight on the night of August 20 I never heard either directly from anyone on the Soviet side or from other socialist countries, or through another person, that they were determined to enter our country and occupy it with their army. If I had heard anything of this kind, even at second hand, I would certainly have had to deal with it concretely; it would have had to be discussed at the party Presidium; I simply could not pass over it. I never

His critics have argued that a more decisive stance would have required the convocation of the 14th Party congress at the time of the Warsaw conference, thereby removing the lukewarm and conservative members from the leading party organs, and making possible a united front against outside interference. At the same time support should have been sought abroad, from the non-governing European communist parties, from Yugoslavia and Rumania, from Western countries and the United Nations, perhaps even from China. It is hardly likely that this would have elicited military aid from any quarter, but it would have produced an acute international crisis and forced all governments and communist parties to seek a solution by diplomatic and political means. Whether the threat to resist would have deterred the Soviet Union from invading, as in the case of Yugoslavia in 1948, cannot be determined. The Soviet leaders would have been confronted by a united and newly legitimated Czechoslovak leadership, backed by overwhelming popular support, and would have faced the certainty of violent resistance by Czechoslovakia, and the strong disapproval of many communist parties, including perhaps even the Hungarian. This would have raised the costs of invasion; would perhaps have aroused doubts among some Soviet leaders; and certainly would have made the decision to invade more difficult.

Many factors militated against such a firm stand. A threat of resistance was rendered difficult by the presence of Soviet troops in Czechoslovakia during the critical period of mid-summer, and by the absence of any military plans for such a contingency. The presence of pro-Soviet conservatives in the Presidium and the Central Committee hampered the adoption of such a strategy. Preparations for resistance would have become known at once to the Soviet Union through its agents in the armed forces and police, and might have triggered the invasion at an earlier date. Prague's attitude was undoubtedly influenced by the country's geographical situation, which made military resistance a hopeless affair, likely to be crushed in a few days. History, too, was against it, having woven for Czechoslovakia a tradition of seeking conciliation or accepting capitulation, rather than using the threat of violence or resorting to force. Most important of all, the personality of Dubček and his intimate association with the Soviet Union in the past led him to exclude the very idea of a Soviet invasion—and this in spite of many hints and warnings, direct and indirect, that it was a real possibility—and therefore to neglect any plans for resistance by force.

heard anything of this kind and as far as I was a participant in several conversations with the Soviet leaders, such words were never uttered" (*Listy*, March 1975, p. 9). See also below, Appendix D.

CONCLUSION

There were some who felt that the failure to resist in August, even against hopeless odds, was a fatal error. As Sviták expressed it after the event, resistance was required by the very "essence of sovereignty" and was morally imperative, too. "No nation can expect to thrive if its backbone is broken every twenty years." The course taken in August would only lead, he said, to "camouflaged collaboration" and hence "the betrayal of the nation."[51] Others, more realistically, disputed the feasibility or wisdom of resistance in August, but contended, as did Jiří Pelikán, that there should have been a "firm stand" against Soviet pressures earlier and a warning of resistance. Even in August other forms of resistance, such as a general strike, might have been taken by the leaders to mobilize the population against the occupation.[52] The more radically minded also condemned the participation of Dubček and others in the Moscow discussions, the acceptance of the Moscow protocol, and the subsequent collaboration with the occupying powers.[53] These steps were regarded as natural outcomes of the original decision not to resist and prepared the way for complete capitulation later on. The final outcome was not the preservation of the balance of the reform program, but its ultimate liquidation and Dubček's removal from office, his reputation tarnished.

THE "CZECH QUESTION" IN NEW FORM

The fate of the Czechoslovak experiment in 1968 illustrated once again—and in highly dramatic form—the perennial problem of this small state in the heart of Europe and its two nations, who have sought, usually in vain, to elaborate a democratic way of life in an unfavorable environment and to protect these aspirations against the pressures of that environment. "The Czech question," once posed by Masaryk in a celebrated essay of the 1890s (*Česká otázka*), presented itself anew, this time as

[51] *Die Presse*, Oct. 12, 1968 (available in English in mimeo). The substance of this statement is given in *Studies in Comparative Communism* 2 (April 1969), 74-76. See also Sviták, *Czechoslovak Experiment*, pp. 159, 181. Similar views were expressed by Pokštefl, in Kusin, ed., *Czechoslovak Reform*, pp. 351-52, and opposed by A. Šnejdárek, ibid., p. 356. For a symposium of conflicting views on the question of resistance by a number of anonymous intellectuals, see *SCC* 2 (April 1969), 74-89. In an interview just prior to his death, Smrkovský implied regret that they did not resist in 1968 (*Svědectví* 12, no. 47, 1974, pp. 426, 432; also in Pelikán, ed., *Ici Prague*, pp. 334-43). Contrast Mlynář's view, Appendix E.

[52] J. Pelikán, *New Left Review* (Jan.-Feb. 1972), pp. 27-29. After Prchlík's dismissal the Kremlin could be sure that there would be no hostilities. Pelikán criticized Dubček for not having taken the opportunity to escape arrest by leaving the CC building and organizing an underground resistance "in a revolutionary spirit."

[53] Ostrý, *Československý problém*, pp. 197-203; Šabata, "Revolta bez teoria?" p. 20.

a Czech and Slovak question, different in form than in the past, but essentially similar in substance.

After the occupation, in a symposium on "The Czech Question,"[54] one of the participants, Brabec, observed: "The August events confirmed once again the actuality and the permanent validity of the question—how can a small nation maintain and develop itself in the modern world?" The central problem, said Blažek, was the Czech society's "permanent state of being threatened," and "the insufficiency of certainty and of guarantees that we shall be able to carry through to the end any activity begun. . . ." He found the source of this uncertainty in "powerful external forces" always threatening Czech society. Vodička used similar terms: ". . . the Czech national community often finds itself in situations which make it impossible for it to develop its activity in the totality of all its needs, both existential and conceptual." He also saw the chief obstacle as "the resistance of those forces around us which jointly decide, by means of power, as to the maintenance of the existence of the Czech community."

The symposium touched on the varied forms that the Czech question had assumed in history, and the responses which had been given to a problem which, at one point, was characterized as one "permanently incapable of complete resolution." Vodička expressed what seemed, in spite of difference of emphasis, to be a consensus among the discussants, namely, that there were two sides to the Czech question, one concerning "questions of existential preservation," and the other, "questions which express the content and meaning of the existence of the given national community." These were closely connected. "Preserving, confirming, and assuring the existence of national life is the precondition for the acceptance of a definite historical task which gives meaning to this existence and in its significance goes beyond the sphere of national reality." Kosík, however, perceived a conflict between what he termed two responses given in the past. One, derived merely from "the smallness of the nation and its threatenedness," led to the "predominance of tactics over principles," to the popular "philosophy: bow down and survive; be reasonable." The other, derived from a search for the "meaning of existence," led to the conclusion that "the political nation" was "capable, of itself and from itself, of creating the bases of its existence and while reckoning with influences, pressures, threats and compulsions, is not their plaything . . . and can therefore develop its culture, statehood, public life and morality as its own . . . non-derivative and non-changeable forms of life."[55]

[54] *Listy*, March 27, 1969. The participants were Karel Bartošek, Vladimír Blažek, Jiří Brabec, Karel Kosík, and Felix Vodička.
[55] Kosík put it in somewhat similar terms in another post-occupation essay,

Prior to the invasion, Kosík had attempted a serious and sustained examination of the "Czech question" in its contemporary form in a series of penetrating articles on "Our Current Crisis"[56] (a title borrowed from another of Masaryk's essays of the nineties). He described the crisis as not just a struggle for "bare existence," but, in the spirit of Masaryk, "a discussion over the meaning (*smysl*) of national and human existence." "Have we fallen to the level of an anonymous mass for whom conscience, human dignity, the sense of truth and justice, honor, decency, and courage are unnecessary ballast . . . or are we capable of remembering and solving all our economic, political and other questions in harmony with the claims of human being and national existence?" (April 18). In spite of the doubts implied in his question, Kosík saw the solution clearly—in socialism and democracy. The goals were "political equality of rights and fullness of rights derived from the principles of socialism and humanism. Socialist democracy is *integral* democracy, or it is not democracy at all" (April 25). Posing the question as to what in fact socialism was, Kosík denied that it was merely "a *scientifically managed* society" and asserted, "Its historical meaning is *the liberation of man* . . . a revolutionary and liberating alternative to poverty, exploitation, oppression, and injustice, to lying and mystification, to lack of freedom, indignity and humiliation" (May 16). He believed, too, that the Czech question, often considered primarily "a question of *national* independence," was also a matter of *state* independence," and hence was closely linked with the solution of the Slovak question. "The relationship to the Slovak problem is . . . a test of the *statesmanship* of Czech policy" (May 2).

His hope for a new and more satisfactory solution of the Czechoslovak question reflected the mood of greater optimism prior to the invasion and the renaissance of respect for the Czech and Slovak past, especially of its more positive accomplishments. Democratic and national traditions, submerged under Nazism and Stalinism, somewhat miraculously came to the surface again. Scholars, journalists, and leaders reconsidered significant episodes of modern history and, freeing them from earlier dogmatic misinterpretation, evaluated them as progressive events having a certain continuity with the developments of 1968. Among Czechs there was a revival of interest in the First Republic and the restoration of democracy between 1945 and 1948, and a new appreciation of the

---

"Illusion and Reality," in which he defined the Czech question as "the problem of a political nation in Central Europe," and whether it can exist as "a progressive and sovereign nation." "We are a political nation only to the degree that the nation . . . is not only able to endure the tension of currents and influences, but shows itself able to transform this into an independent political, cultural, and spiritual synthesis" (*Listy*, Nov. 7, 1968).

[56] *LL*, April 11 to May 16, 1968.

achievement of independence in 1918, the struggle for liberation during both world wars, and the Prague revolt in 1945. Among Slovaks there was a reawakening of interest in the achievements *and* the failures of the First Republic, and in the idea of Slovak independence, expressed paradoxically both in the wartime Slovak state and in the National Uprising against that state. The sense of mutual solidarity of Czechs and Slovaks, often marred by friction or even hostility, was also revived, reaching a high point in the consensus on the desirability of a federal system and later in the common opposition to Soviet intervention.

Another feature of the revived respect for the past was the rehabilitation of persons from the pre-communist period whose role had been hidden or distorted for more than a decade. The ideas and deeds of Tomaš Masaryk, the central figure of modern Czechoslovak history, which had been distorted by falsification for more than a decade, were reassessed, critically but objectively, and were linked with the current trend toward democratization.[57] Masaryk's Slovak associate during World War I, Milan Štefánik (whose career was cut short by death in 1919), was reappraised as a symbol of the struggle for liberation and of Czechoslovak unity, and was given a positive contemporary significance.[58] The ordinary people demonstrated their affirmative attitude by massive pilgrimages to Lány and Brádlo, the burial places of these two outstanding historical figures who personified the positive features of the First Republic and the solidarity of the two nations.

This revival of past traditions lends support to the view that the movement for reform in 1968 was a product of certain crucial elements in the traditional political culture, such as the humanist values of Masaryk, democracy, freedom of expression, Slovak independence, and Czech-Slovak solidarity, and as a rebirth of these traditions.[59] Yet 1968 was more than a renaissance of the past. It represented an advance toward

[57] See, for example, J. L. Fischer, *LL*, March 7; J. B. Čapek, ibid., June 20; J. Karola, *Kulturní tvorba*, May 9; O. Janeček, *NM*, no. 6 (1968), pp. 680-89; V. Olivová, *RP*, Aug. 21; J. Galandauer, *Život strany*, no. 17 (Aug. 1968) pp. 29-31. For replies to the attack on Masaryk in *Sovetskaya Rossia* (May 14) see Z. Sládek, *RP*, May 16. A book by Milan Machovec, *Tomaš G. Masaryk* (Prague, 1968), appeared and was favorably reviewed (V. Vrabec, *RP*, May 3). Statues of Masaryk were erected; pictures and postcards of him appeared on sale.

[58] See, for example, the polemical articles condemning a book on Štefánik by Prof. L. Holotík and calling on him to revise his hostile interpretation (*Roľnické noviny*, March 14, 19, 20, April 3; M. Dzvoník, *Pravda*, May 4). See also J. Mésáros, *NS*, April 17, 1969; Dzvoník, ibid., April 24, 1969. On the pilgrimage to Brádlo, *Pravda*, May 6.

[59] E.g. A. H. Brown, "Political Change," pp. 189-93; Kusin, *Intellectual Origins*, pp. 15-17, 70-75, 144-45. For a fuller argument, see David Paul, "The Repluralization of Czechoslovak Politics in the 1960s," *Slavic Review* 33 (Dec. 1974), 721-40. Doubt is cast on the role of traditional culture in the Prague Spring by F. A. Barnard, *Socialism with a Human Face: Slogan and Substance* (Saskatoon, 1973), pp. 4, 15.

a more humane social order embodying in some degree the traditions of Masaryk *and* Marx, both critically reinterpreted, and synthesizing the basic ideas of democracy and socialism in a manner not only new to Czechoslovak history but unduplicated elsewhere in the world. Yet there were negative aspects of the Czech and Slovak past which could not be ignored even in the heady atmosphere of the Prague Spring and which were bound to loom larger in the depressing post-occupation times. It was recognizied, in a characteristic spirit of self-criticism, that Czechs and Slovaks had often failed to find a satisfactory answer to their problems and that this was sometimes due, not only to external factors, but to the lack of will and the failings of the Czech and Slovak people and their leaders.

Karel Bartošek expressed these feelings in the most radical terms. In an article in May 1968 in praise of the revolt in Prague in 1945, he lamented the fact that acts of "self-criticism by deed," such as the revolt, were rare in Czech history and were usually hampered at the time by doubt and hesitation and often forgotten or ignored after the event. He reminded his readers of "the massive character of past opportunism," "the poison of mediocrity," "the distaste of revolt," and the widely held feelings of "the 'reasonableness' of surviving."[60] After August 21, negative attitudes toward the past were naturally expressed more frequently and strongly, no doubt reflecting dissatisfaction with the tactics pursued before, during, and after the invasion. In the symposium cited above, Bartošek, as usual more critical than others, discerned in the nation's history two "historical constants"—one, "the objective smallness of the national society, demographic and geographic smallness," but also "political smallness," "the mediocrity and smallness of conceptions and actions." Blažek spoke of "the multitude of illusions which accompany attempts to solve the Czech problem . . . illusions of enlightenment, of liberalism, of democracy, of the possibilities of nationalism, of socialism and communism, illusions of our place in the world, of our allies, of the example which we will evoke by our deeds." "Yes, to abolish the Czech question means to abolish the endangerment of this society," said Blažek, "but no one has so far succeeded in achieving this."[61]

The views expressed in this symposium, abstract and radical as they were, and confined to the Czech side of the problem, have been quoted at length since they present so well the inescapable and apparently insoluble character of the Czech and Slovak question in modern times. The "dialectic of Czechoslovak history," as I have termed it elsewhere, has been a succession of triumphs and disasters, each triumph seeming to offer a solution to the problem, but each one followed, at ever shorter

---

[60] *Reportér*, May 8-15, 1968. [61] *Listy*, March 29, 1969.

intervals, by disaster.[62] Discontinuity, rather than continuity, has been the central feature of that history. Liberation in 1918 was followed by partition and German occupation twenty years later. Independence, restored in 1945, lasted only three years until the communist takeover in 1948. The democratization efforts of 1968 ended abruptly, after eight months, with a Soviet occupation. As on earlier occasions, the Czechs and Slovaks were again blocked in their attempt to proceed with a program of democratic and independent action.

The historical record thus offers little comfort or encouragment for the future, either in the behavior of the great powers to the West or East, or of Czechoslovakia's smaller neighbors in Central Europe, or in the efficacy of the many alternatives tried and found wanting. As a state Czechoslovakia has sought in turn to rely on alliance with the West and alliance with the East and has had twice to endure occupation, by Germany and by Soviet Russia. The two nations have known a bewildering sequence of political forms of government—the absolutism of the Habsburg monarchy, democracy and independence, fascism and occupation, Stalinism and terror, and reformed communism. The Slovaks, in their relations with the Czechs, have had the diverse associations of union and subordination under democracy, independence under fascism, and subjugation, and federalization, under communism. Yet in none of these contradictory political experiences has this country and its two nations found a lasting and satisfactory recipe for solving the question of national existence and progress.

A MODEL FOR THE FUTURE?

Will this exciting and innovative period of Czechoslovak life, cut short by intervention, be repeated at some time in the future? Will the "interrupted" revolution be resumed under similar circumstances and with similar goals? Will the short-lived experiment, like the even briefer Paris Commune of 1870, remain an inspiration for future reform in Eastern Europe, a model of orderly but radical social change in communist countries, including even the USSR? Or will the experience, with its abrupt conclusion in August, remain a warning against an attempt at repetition either in Czechoslovakia or elsewhere?

These are questions that defy an answer. The Prague Spring represented a program of fundamental change more comprehensive and radical than anything previously attempted in Eastern Europe. It undoubtedly struck a responsive chord in other countries where similar objectives have been sought in the past, even if in less ambitious form,

[62] Skilling, "The dialectic of Czechoslovak history," *The Canadian Forum* 49, no. 585 (Oct. 1969), 155-57.

and where forces resembling those that produced the Prague Spring continue to exist. Yet the experience of 1968 demonstrated all too clearly the narrow limits to reform and independence set by Moscow and counseled future caution. All are conscious of the Damocles sword of Soviet intervention hanging over any future effort at radical reform along Czechoslovak lines. In any case historical experiences and national circumstances are so diverse that the pattern of change will no doubt exhibit the same variety in the future as in the past and will not likely follow the model of 1968.

As for Czechoslovakia the likelihood of a repetition of the experiment in the foreseeable future seems most unlikely. The experience of 1968, still relatively fresh in every one's mind, would seem to discourage the hope of gradual and peaceful change under the auspices of the Communist Party. A renewed effort toward radical change might possibly repudiate communist rule and even socialism itself. At present political apathy and stagnation prevail, in a disillusioned country, relieved only by a certain economic recovery, and the occasional spark of opposition by brave individuals. Yet the present dispensation of neo-Stalinism and Soviet occupation certainly offer no enduring solution for the Czech and Slovak questions, which remain unsolved. In due course Czechs and Slovaks will again, as in the past, seek a new solution for the ever present problem of survival and progress. The year 1968, like other periods of Czech and Slovak triumph, was a time of greatness, both in aims and accomplishments, and undoubtedly will remain embedded in the historical consciousness of the two nations. So, too, will the memory of the electrifying week of nonviolent resistance after August 21, and the months of opposition until Dubček's fall. In that sense 1968 will remain an inspiration and in some degree a guide for the future, and the revolution will perhaps be resumed, but under changed conditions and in new forms that cannot now be known.

MEMBERS OF CPCz PRESIDIUM AND SECRETARIAT, 1968

PRESIDIUM OF CPCz IN 1968

Before Jan. 5	Jan. 5 to April 5	April 5 to Aug. 31	14th Congress	Aug. 31 to Nov. 17	After Nov. 17
Černík	Černík	Černík	Černík	Černík	Černík
Dolanský	Dolanský				
Dubček	Dubček	Dubček	Dubček	Dubček	Dubček
Hendrych	Hendrych				
Chudík	Chudík				
Kolder	Kolder	Kolder			
Laštovička	Laštovička				
Lenárt	Lenárt	Lenárt (cand.)		Lenárt (cand.)	Lenárt (cand.)
Novotný	Novotný				
Šimůnek	Šimůnek				
Kapek (cand.)	Kapek (cand.)	Kapek (cand.)			
Pastyřík (cand.)	Pastyřík (cand.)				
Sabolčík (cand.)	Sabolčík (cand.)				
Sádovský (cand.)	Sádovský (cand.)		Sádovský	Sádovský	Sádovský
M. Vaculík (cand.)	M. Vaculík (cand.)				
	Biľak	Biľak		Biľak	Biľak
	Borůvka				
	Piller	Piller		Piller	Piller
	Rigo	Rigo			
	Špaček	Špaček	Špaček	Špaček	Špaček
		Barbírek		Barbírek (cand.)	Barbírek (cand.)
		Kriegel	Kriegel		
		Smrkovský	Smrkovský	Smrkovský	Smrkovský
		Švestka			
		Šimon (cand.)	Šimon	Šimon	Šimon
			Císař		
			Šik		
			Slavík	Slavík	Slavík
			Hrdinová	Hrdinová	Hrdinová
			Litera		
			Colotka		
			Šilhán		
			Matějíček		
			Kabrna	Kabrna	Kabrna
			Hejzlar		
			Goldstücker		
			Hübl		
			Moc		
			Šimeček	Šimeček	Šimeček
			Husák	Husák	Husák
			Zrak	Zrak	Zrak
			Ťažký	Ťažký	Ťažký
			Pavlenda		
			Turček		
			Zamek		
			Vojáček		
				Mlynář	
				Erban	Erban
				Hetteš	Hetteš
				Neubert	Neubert
				Pinkava	Pinkava
				Svoboda	Svoboda
					Štrougal
				Poláček (cand.)	Poláček (cand.)

SECRETARIAT OF CPCz IN 1968

Before Jan. 5	Jan. 5 to April 5	April 5 to Aug. 31	14th Congress	Aug. 31 to Nov. 17	After Nov. 17
		Secretaries			
Novotný	Novotný				
Hendrych	Hendrych				
Kolder	Kolder	Kolder			
Koucký	Koucký				
Štrougal	Štrougal				Štrougal
Sádovský	Sádovský	Sádovský	Sádovský		
	Dubček	Dubček	Dubček	Dubček	Dubček
		Císař	Císař		
		Indra		Indra	Indra
		Lenárt		Lenárt	Lenárt
		Mlynář (June)	Mlynář	Mlynář	
			Slavík		
				Špaček	Špaček
				Biľak	Biľak
				Hetteš	Hetteš
				Kempný	Kempný
				Penc	Penc
		Members of Secretariat			
Pastyřík	Pastyřík				
Pecha	Pecha				
M. Vaculík	M. Vaculík				
		Mlynář			
		Slavík		Slavík	Slavík
		Voleník		Kovalčík	
		Erban (June)		Sekera	Sekera

POLL OF PARTY DELEGATES (1968)
(in percentages)

Question	District Conference Delegates				14th Congress Delegates			
	Completely	Partially	Did not	No reply	Completely	Partially	Did not	No reply
I. Evaluation of the May CC plenum. Your expectation was fulfilled by:								
(a) decision on calling the congress								
ČSSR	77.1	11.7	1.6	9.6	82.9	4.4	1.6	11.1
Czech lands					84.5	13.5	1.3	0.8
Slovakia					78.6	16.7	2.4	2.3
(b) evaluation of the contemporary political situation								
ČSSR	25.9	55.7	4.0	14.4	30.7	61.4	3.7	4.2
Czech lands					27.3	65.0	4.4	3.3
Slovakia					39.0	51.5	1.9	6.8
(c) solution of cadre problems at Central Committee								
ČSSR	9.8	40.2	26.3	23.7	14.2	47.5	34.1	4.2
Czech lands					10.8	47.7	38.1	3.4
Slovakia					23.5	47.1	23.3	6.1
(d) CC proclamation to party members and the whole population								
ČSSR	32.3	30.9	3.8	33.0	45.9	41.6	5.2	7.3
Czech lands					42.0	46.0	5.7	6.3
Slovakia					56.7	29.4	4.0	9.9

POLL OF PARTY DELEGATES (cont'd.)

(in percentages)

Question	District Conference Delegates					14th Congress Delegates				
	Decidedly Yes	Rather Yes	Don't Know	Rather No	Decidedly No	Decidedly Yes	Rather Yes	Don't Know	Rather No	Decidedly No
II. Evaluation of the situation in party:										
(1) Do you believe that the results of the May plenum positively influenced the party's authority										
ČSSR	23.7	38.2	5.7	8.6	1.9	30.2	51.4	6.8	7.3	2.5
Czech lands	20.8	41.4	6.1	10.2	2.1	24.4	55.9	6.8	8.8	2.2
Slovakia	33.0	27.8	4.5	3.4	1.4	46.1	39.1	6.6	3.3	3.3
(2) Does the party in your opinion have sufficient resources (a) to realize and implement tasks set forth										
ČSSR	52.0	25.4	5.4	4.7	0.8	57.5	29.7	4.4	5.2	1.2
Czech lands	51.1	27.5	5.6	5.2	0.8	55.5	31.9	4.5	5.5	1.2
Slovakia	54.9	18.9	4.7	3.1	0.8	63.1	23.8	4.0	4.2	1.2
(b) to reorient the aktiv of functionaries for the new conditions of implementing the leading role of the party										
ČSSR	30.9	29.5	9.7	10.5	2.4	35.2	36.0	8.5	13.2	2.5
Czech lands	30.7	30.7	10.1	11.3	2.6	33.5	38.4	8.9	13.4	2.6
Slovakia	31.3	25.7	8.3	8.2	2.1	39.8	29.2	7.3	12.7	2.4
(3) Do you believe there is danger for the party (a) that forces hostile to the party and socialism will become active										
ČSSR	29.8	26.5	4.5	15.7	8.3	33.8	30.0	4.3	18.4	9.5
Czech lands	30.3	27.6	4.3	16.5	8.5	33.4	30.7	4.1	19.2	9.5
Slovakia	28.3	22.9	5.2	13.3	7.8	34.6	28.0	4.9	16.2	9.4
(b) that progress will be hampered by conservative forces in the party										
ČSSR	30.1	27.8	4.6	13.8	7.3	33.6	32.2	4.8	15.1	8.2
Czech lands	30.2	29.2	4.8	14.6	7.3	34.5	33.6	4.5	15.5	7.2
									13.0	10.8

POLL OF PARTY DELEGATES (cont'd.)

Question	District Conference Delegates					14th Congress Delegates				
	Yes Decidedly	Yes Rather	Don't Know	No Rather	No Decidedly	Yes Decidedly	Yes Rather	Don't Know	No Rather	No Decidedly
III. Opinions on methods of party work:										
(1) Do you believe that it is quite dangerous for the party to give up its power position										
ČSSR	18.1	13.2	3.1	15.1	21.8	22.8	17.0	4.4	19.2	30.7
Czech lands	8.9	13.3	3.6	20.7	43.2	20.5	17.8	3.9	20.6	32.8
Slovakia	18.6	11.0	3.6	13.0	17.0	29.2	14.6	5.6	15.5	24.7
(2) Do you believe that the party is relinquishing its positions if it makes it possible for other parties and organizations to share in decision-making										
ČSSR	10.2	13.6	4.5	20.3	39.0	13.1	14.1	4.9	21.4	45.2
Czech lands	8.9	13.3	3.6	20.7	43.2	10.1	12.9	2.7	22.6	50.7
Slovakia	14.3	14.7	7.3	18.9	23.5	21.4	17.4	10.8	18.1	10.1
(3) Do you think that the party is giving up to a sufficient degree direct management of state and economic organs										
ČSSR	16.8	26.5	11.9	22.0	9.9	20.8	32.4	11.8	23.7	9.5
Czech lands	16.6	27.1	12.2	23.3	10.0	19.1	33.6	11.8	24.9	8.8
Slovakia	17.4	24.5	10.6	17.9	9.6	25.4	28.9	11.8	20.2	11.3
(4) Are you of the opinion that it is in the party's interest to give up direct management of state and economic organs										
ČSSR	42.0	19.2	4.6	11.2	10.3	53.8	20.9	4.2	10.0	9.8
Czech lands	44.4	19.5	4.3	11.4	9.9	55.4	20.7	3.2	10.6	9.0
Slovakia	34.5	18.1	5.5	10.6	11.5	49.2	21.4	6.8	8.2	12.2

Source: Zpráva o současné politické situaci Československé socialistické republiky a podmínkách činnosti Komunistické strany Československa (srpen 1968) (Prague, Oct. 1968), pp. 78-80, 88-91.

Federation and the Nationalities Law

THE FEDERALIZATION of the Republic was accomplished as planned on October 28, with the adoption of the constitutional law on federation by the National Assembly.[1] Many Czechs, and even some Slovaks, had some doubts as to whether it was worthwhile proceeding with federalization in the vastly changed circumstances produced by the occupation on August 21. On the other hand, the August events had demonstrated the unity of Czechs and Slovaks in their rejection of Soviet intervention and their insistence on the integrity of the Republic, thus dissipating suspicions that may have lingered in Czech minds of Slovak separatist tendencies. The Slovak reaction to the invasion was partly due to a greater feeling of confidence in the future of their association with the Czechs, based on the acceptance by the latter of their demand for federalization. Yet the immediate aftermath of the intervention revealed continuing political differences between Czechs and Slovaks, particularly regarding the relative priority of democratization and federalization. There were fears on both sides that the Soviet Union would seek to exploit any disunity in its own interests and this strengthened their belief in the urgency of completing federalization to ward off this threat.[2]

During the days of crisis, official declarations made it clear that both nations were still committed to the goal of achieving federation by October 28.[3] Yet time had been lost as a result of the invasion and the schedule for preparing the federation had been seriously interrupted. The position of the Czechs was particularly difficult since they had not had time to draft a proposal of their own and had perforce to take a position on

[1] See above, chap. xv, n. 7, for sources on federation, most of which deal briefly with post-occupation developments and with federation as finally established. For a full analysis of the latter, see Lothar Schultz, "Die tschechoslowakische Föderation," *Osteuropa-Recht* 15 (1969), 318-32.

[2] For some Slovak views, see Novomeský (on Sept. 5), *Politika*, Oct. 3, pp. 34-35; M. Hysko, *Nové slovo*, Sept. 26; for Czech views, Císař (at the SNR session), *Pravda*, Sept. 7; editorial, ibid., Oct. 3. See the joint interview, V. Hatala and Z. Jičínský, ibid., Sept. 24. There were references to foreign "speculation" on disunity by Hatala and Jičínský, ibid.; Klokoč, *Pravda*, Oct. 8; *Smena*, Oct. 8. On the unity of the Republic, Z. Eis and K. Jech, *Reportér*, Sept. 18-25.

[3] See declarations of the 14th congress, National Assembly, ČNR and SNR, CPS Central Committee, and CPS congress, chap. XXII above, passim (pp. 771, 786, 791, 794). A poll conducted in Slovakia in Sept. 1968 indicated that 88.1 percent approved decisions concerning Czech-Slovak equality and the national minorities; 6.3 percent approved but doubted their fulfillment; 2.1 percent had reservations (*Život strany*, no. 19, May 7, 1969, p. 9).

explicit Slovak demands and the fully elaborated plan of the federal commission of experts.[4] Moreover, in the absence of a Czech party congress, it was left to the Czech legal experts on the federal commission and in the Czech National Council to formulate a "Czech" standpoint, without the benefit of widespread public discussion or of any authoritative Czech statement of policy. A lesser problem, but one that could not be ignored, was the continued pressure from some Moravians, either for a tripartite federation, or since this had been rejected in official Czech and Czechoslovak quarters, for some recognition of a special Moravian position within the future Czech republic.[5]

At the time of the occupation the federal commission of experts had completed a draft statement of principles.[6] Discussions in both the Czech and Slovak National Councils in early September indicated a willingness to accept this draft as a general basis for discussion but also revealed certain crucial differences of opinion which were again manifested in Czech and Slovak statements in mid-September.[7] The ČNR Standpoint (Stanovisko), for instance, which summed up the Czech position, warned the Slovaks that in view of the changes in the political system brought about by external influences, "it was not necessary to double or triple the constitutional legal guarantees of equality of the Slovak national-territorial whole." The Standpoint was praised by Slovaks for its exposition of general principles, but sharply criticized for some of its specific proposals, which would have produced, it was argued, "a symmetrical system of powerless national states in a powerful centralized federation once again dominated in the federal sphere by the most numerous of the two partners."[8]

Moreover, although the Czechs were ready to accept October 28 as the deadline for federation, there was a feeling that on many crucial issues only general principles could be endorsed by that date and that detailed decisions would need more time. It was also observed that the actual implementation of federalism would require many additional steps, including the holding of elections to the assembly and the two

[4] Císař, *Rudé právo*, Oct. 3, 10.

[5] On Sept. 6, the Society for Moravia and Silesia issued a proclamation favoring the tripartite system (*Moravskoslezský týden*, no. 17, p. 4). For later statements indicating that the Moravians were reconciled to something short of trialism, such as the recognition of the Moravian land (*země*), see C. Procházka, *RP*, Sept. 19; conference in Brno, ibid., Oct. 14; A. Rusek, ibid., Oct. 17; Jičínský, ibid., Oct. 24.

[6] See above, chap. xv.

[7] For the Slovak viewpoint see CPS Central Committee (*Pravda*, Sept. 6); SNR, ibid., Sept. 7; F. Barbírek, ibid., Sept. 10. The Slovak draft proposal of Sept. 15 was not published. For the Czech position, see Císař at the SNR (*Pravda*, Sept. 7) and in the ČNR (*RP*, Sept. 19); "Stanovisko České národní rady k federativnímu uspořádání ČSSR" (*RP* and *Pravda*, Sept. 20), henceforth ČNR Stanovisko.

[8] Hatala and H. Kočtúch, *Pravda*, Sept. 27. Cf. Kočtúch, ibid., Sept. 25; K. Rebro, *NS*, Sept. 26.

councils, which could hardly be completed by January 1st.[9] These reservations on timing, as well as opposition on matters of substance, awakened disquiet and suspicion on the Slovak side and a stiffer insistence on the acceptance of their viewpoint and their own conception of timing.[10]

The CPCz Presidium, however, on September 17, reiterated the goal of achieving a constitutional law by October 28, and stressed the need quickly to publish an agreed document in the name of the organs of the National Assembly, the ČNR and SNR, and the government.[11] By the end of the month the penultimate stage of deliberations began with the completion of a detailed draft law on federation by the commission of experts, its adoption by the government commission and by the government, and its transmission to the two councils for their consideration.[12] A joint meeting in Brno of the presidia of the two councils, and the simultaneous plenary meetings which followed immediately in Bratislava and Prague, indicated that although there was wide agreement on general principles, there were significant gaps on specific issues. The Brno meeting, the first direct Czech-Slovak confrontation, achieved a compromise on some matters, especially in the economic field, but left a number of questions open. Similarly, at the plenary sessions of the two councils, the draft constitutional law was endorsed but significant reservations were expressed by both sides.[13] When a common draft was submitted by the two councils to the National Assembly, on October 7, points of differences were not concealed but were in fact included in the document as alternatives. The party's Presidium, however, still described the original deadline of October 28 as the target.[14]

[9] For instance, L. Veltruský, *RP*, Sept. 10; A. Pokorná, *RP* and *Pravda*, Sept. 19; Z. Jičínský, speech in ČNR, *RP*, Sept. 19, and fuller, *Právník* 107, no. 12 (1968), 1050-57.

[10] SNR presidium, *Pravda*, Sept. 24; Pavlenda, ibid., Sept. 25.

[11] *Rok šedesátý osmý* (Prague, 1969), p. 323.

[12] The draft constitutional law was formally approved by the government commission on Oct. 1 (*RP* and *Pravda*, Oct. 2). Its text was published later in *NS*, Oct. 10, as a supplement, but not elsewhere. The draft principles were also published in final form over the signatures of Černík, Husák, Císař, and Klokoč, "Stanovisko k federalizaci ČSSR" (*RP*, Sept. 26 and elsewhere), henceforth joint Stanovisko. Comments and amendments were requested, to be submitted by Oct. 15. Císař later explained that he was able to sign only because it was noted that the views of the ČNR could not be fully taken into consideration due to the shortness of time (*NS*, Oct. 24).

[13] For the Brno meeting, especially the speeches by Císař and Klokoč, *RP*, Oct. 3. For a full analysis of the conference, see Kočtúch, and Hatala and K. Laco, *NS*, Oct. 10. For ČNR session, *RP* and *Pravda*, Oct. 5; for SNR session, *Pravda*, Oct. 5. At the ČNR meeting there was some opposition to a vote at that time and to the January 1st deadline for the coming into force of the law on federation, but the draft law was ultimately approved overwhelmingly. Similarly, although a number of suggestions and criticisms were offered, the SNR also approved the draft law.

[14] *RŠO*, pp. 326-27.

Although the Moravian demand for tripartitism was once again formally rejected by official Czech spokesmen, the problem of local government or *samospráva* raised by the Moravians was left unsettled as a task to be dealt with by the future Czech republic. There was no indication of any willingness to accept the idea of Moravia as a "land" (*země*) or province, nor any clarification of the future of the national committee system.[15]

Major Points at Issue

The main controversies after the Brno meeting related to the same questions as prior to the occupation, namely, parity and majority-domination in the federal organs, and the distribution of competence between federal and national organs.[16] Subsequent discussions had resolved some differences, but also pinpointed persistent conflicts. Even the title of the new federal state, for instance, became a bone of contention, with Czechs favoring the retention of the previous title and Slovaks proposing a new one, the Federative Czechoslovak Socialist Republic.[17] The timing of the establishment of federation was still a source of controversy, with Slovaks opposing any postponement beyond January 1st of the federation's coming into existence and arguing for provisional arrangements thereafter until elections could be held. The Czechs, convinced that without elections federation could not be effectively implemented, wanted a more flexible deadline, linked with elections, and a gradual establishment of the new federal and national organs.[18] As to substantive matters, there were not only differences *among* Czechs, and to a lesser extent among Slovaks, but also a clash between the government's viewpoint, as expressed in the draft constitutional law, which approached in many re-

[15] ČNR Stanovisko, *RP*, Sept. 20; Císař, ibid., Oct. 3; Jičínský, *Mladá fronta*, Oct. 4. The ČNR Stanovisko described the position of Moravia and Silesia and of the regions as a domestic matter for the Czech republic and promised to consider Moravian ideas of *samospráva* in preparing the future administrative organization of the republic. Jičínský flatly stated that no change in the regional system was possible under existing conditions (*Právník*, no. 12, 1968, p. 1054). The government's draft constitutional law did not refer to Moravia or the national committees. The joint Stanovisko referred to a new law on national committees in two or three years, and certain specific changes to be introduced, on the suggestion of the two national councils, by Oct. 28.

[16] The differences were set forth by Rebro, *NS*, Sept. 26; Grospič and Hatala, *Rep.*, Oct. 9-16; A. Pšenička, *Politika*, Oct. 17; Laco, *Pravda*, Oct. 18. For expositions of Czech views, see the ČNR Stanovisko; Jičínský, ČNR speech, *Právník*, no. 12 (1968), pp. 1050-57; Císař, *RP*, Oct. 3, 9; Grospič, *Nová mysl*, nos. 9-10 (1968), pp. 1103-6. For Slovak views, see Rebro, *NS*, Sept. 26; Hatala and Kočtúch, *Pravda*, Sept. 27; Kočtúch, *NS*, Oct. 10; Law Faculty, Komenský University, *Pravda*, Oct. 10; M. Gašpar, *NS*, Oct. 17; J. Ferianc, *NS*, Oct. 24.

[17] SNR, *Pravda*, Oct. 24.

[18] Jičínský, *Právník*, no. 12 (1968), p. 1056.

spects the Slovak standpoint, and the attitude of other Czech official spokesmen. There were also divergent opinions within the various assembly committees, and perhaps within the government, and differences among these official organs. Ultimate agreement, it was clear, would require, within a very short space of time, complicated and difficult negotiations and a willingness to compromise on both sides.

The differences, to be discussed in greater detail in the following pages, reflected persisting diversity concerning the underlying principles of the federal system. Slovaks continued to emphasize the principles of "national equality," expressed in parity and a ban on majority-domination in federal organs, and of self-determination, expressed in wide authority for the Slovak organs, thus seeking to achieve maximum influence in decision-making in the center, and maximum control of their own affairs in Slovakia. The Czechs, on the other hand, stressed the principle of democracy, or rule by the majority, and firm central powers, thus seeking to achieve a maximum of unity and uniformity in all spheres of political action and to assure the efficient functioning of the federal organs. Both sides professed a willingness to accept a compromise between these opposed principles and objectives but found it difficult in fact to reconcile conflicting views.

This was most clearly exemplified in the economic sphere in the difficult problem of striking a balance between all-state integration and national economic independence. The Czech Stanovisko, for instance, devoted much attention to the desirability of attaining economic integration, economic equalization, a unified market, uniform currency and tax policies, and a common approach to economic reform. Although recognizing that all tasks of economic policy not assigned to the federal organs would be within the province of the national organs, the Standpoint urged that federal institutions should have the necessary competence to fulfill their tasks, and warned against "absolutizing" the ban on majority-domination, especially in economic politics, "so as not to affect the efficiency of direction and the flexibility of the economy." Slovak experts, however, while stressing the desirability of "a higher synthesis of the two national economies," warned against measures that would take key branches out of the Slovak national economy and thus deprive self-determination of "its basic economic dimension."[19] The government draft sought to bridge the gap between these concepts, at least in words, by warning that "the unified market, advantageous for both partners, objectively required that the independence of the economic policy of the national organs should not be absolutized, that economic integration should not be weakened and that the mobility of the federal organs be assured.

[19] Hatala and Kočtúch, *Pravda*, Sept. 27; Kočtúch, *NS*, Oct. 10.

On the other hand, it did not require an excessive centralization of competence in the federal organs. This economic system will create the conditions for a flexible economic policy, respecting the diversity of conditions (level of development, structure, etc.) and variegated forms of integration."[20]

These divergent points of departure expressed themselves more concretely in clashes of opinion concerning the role and the procedures of the federal organs. With regard to the National Assembly, Czechs and Slovaks had reached agreement on the desirability of a two-chamber body, which would reconcile the principles of democratic rule and national equality. Although some Czechs continued to advocate a single-chamber parliament,[21] most had accepted the bicameral system, on condition, however, that the two chambers would be clearly distinguished, both as to their competence and the manner of their formation. It was proposed that the Chamber of the People should be directly elected by popular vote and should have authority in all spheres of federal jurisdiction. The Chamber of Nations, on the other hand, should be composed of delegations from the two national councils, and should deal only with questions relating to national interests, including constitutional matters. The need for a qualified majority in certain cases affecting national interests was recognized.

This scheme, in the Slovak view, would reduce the Chamber of Nations to hardly more than a "formality" and assign the main authority to the Chamber of the People, with its Czech majority. Their preference was for two houses of equal status, both directly elected, and taking an equal part in legislation in all spheres of activity. This would assure that Slovak interests and opinions could be clearly articulated, and would in effect give Slovak representatives a veto power in all questions. In Czech eyes this would make the Chamber of the People, representing the population as a whole, a "useless" body since the real power would lie with the national delegations.[22] This suggested to some the desirability of reverting to the idea of a one-chamber legislature. Slovaks were just as convinced that theirs was the "only solution" that would guarantee equality in the federal parliament. If it were not accepted, the whole question of the division of jurisdiction and the composition of the federal government would have to be reexamined.[23]

[20] NS, Oct. 10. See the detailed formulation of the economic aspects of federation in the joint Stanovisko.

[21] Pšenička (*Politika*, Oct. 17) referred to a minority report, supported by 31 members of the ČNR, favoring this.

[22] Císař, RP, Oct. 3.

[23] Hatala and Laco, NS, Oct. 10; Laco, *Pravda*, Oct. 18. The government draft law provided for equality of competence of the two chambers, as the Slovaks wished, but required the indirect election of the Chamber of Nations and a

This controversy raised other problems concerning the assembly, notably the procedures for a vote of confidence or non-confidence, and for settling deadlocks. The Czechs proposed, and Slovaks opposed, a provision that a qualified majority of the Chamber of the People would have the right to adopt a vote of non-confidence; the Slovaks proposed, and the Czechs rejected, a provision which permitted either house alone to do so. In cases of dispute, where no solution had been reached in "agreement procedures," the Czechs favored the application of the rule of a simple, or perhaps a qualified, majority. The Slovaks suggested other measures, including in the last resort a vote of non-confidence in the government or the dissolution of the assembly.

Differences also persisted concerning the structure and operation of the government. Although the Slovaks preferred full parity, they were willing to accede to something less, namely, that state secretaries be appointed, as full members of the government, in all departments, and that parity be required in all federal committees.[24] They apparently were ready to accept the principle of decisions by majority vote in the executive organ.[25] They advocated a constitutional endorsement of the principle of the "balanced" appointment of Czechs and Slovaks to head up mutually related departments, so as to assure Slovaks key posts in important spheres of activity.[26]

The Czechs were unconditionally opposed to full parity in the government, arguing that this would make federal administration "clumsy" and "complex" and create the danger of immobility.[27] Although originally they had been willing to accept state secretaries only in the two departments dealing with exclusive affairs (foreign affairs and defense) they had by this time agreed to such posts in all federal ministries (although not in federal committees), and to parity representation in some federal

---

3/5 majority vote in both houses in constitutional questions. A simple majority in both parts of the Chamber of Nations was required in a long series of cases where "majority-domination" was forbidden, including laws concerning plans, budgets, currency questions, taxation, etc. A vote of non-confidence could be adopted by a majority in either house. There was also a provision for parity within the National Assembly presidium.

[24] See Gašpar, NS, Oct. 17, for full treatment of this question.

[25] Cf., however, G. Oláh (Pravda, Oct. 5) who proposed the requirement of a 2/3 vote if there were opposition on national grounds.

[26] Kočtúch, NS, Oct. 10. Thus if a Slovak were Minister of Foreign Affairs, a Czech would be Minister of National Defense; if a Czech headed the bank of issue, a Slovak would be Minister of Finance, etc. According to Kočtúch, the Brno conference had demonstrated the need for a government of no more than eighteen members, including a chairman, two deputy chairmen, ten ministers, and five state secretaries. A Czech proposal, he reported, envisaged a government including thirteen to fourteen Czechs, and six to seven Slovaks.

[27] Jičínský, Právník, no. 12 (1968), pp. 1053-54.

committees.[28] They accepted the need, as did the Slovaks, for proportionate representation of Slovaks in the federal administrative service. The actual composition of the federal government, and the manner of determining and creating the individual ministries and other organs, were also sources of dispute, relating, however, more to the thorny problem of federal competence.

On the division of competence, there was consensus on the three types of jurisdiction (exclusively federal, common, and exclusively national), and on the assignment of certain spheres to these categories, but there was not yet agreement on some matters of general principle or on the locus of authority in certain fields. The Czechs contended that the constitutional law should settle the division of competence only in terms of general principle, leaving it to later laws to delimit the exact spheres. Similarly the constitutional law on federation should establish only the "types and character" of federal organs, especially ministries and committees, and future statutes would establish the individual ministries. In areas where national authority would be exclusive, the Czechs insisted on the maintenance of a unified legal order, to be assured through federal committees, a supreme federal court as the highest judicial instance, and a federal general procuracy. The Slovak position was diametrically opposed on all these issues. The exact distribution of competence and the formation of individual ministries should be included in the draft constitutional law, and should not be left to later ordinary laws. The distribution of authority would thus be firmly established from the beginning, avoiding future conflicts and preventing easy later changes. Legal unity could be safeguarded through consultation or coordinating committees and did not require a federal judicial system, apart from a constitutional court.[29]

It was still more difficult to settle opposing views concerning certain specific spheres of government action and the appropriate federal ministries and committees. Pressures from existing ministries and Czech de-

[28] The government's draft law provided for state secretaries in all departments, parity in all federal committees, but a simple majority vote in the government.

[29] The government draft law left open the question as to whether federal ministries would be created by laws requiring a majority in both parts of the Chamber of Nations or by ordinary laws. It set forth detailed provisions for a constitutional court, but left the judicial structure to be defined later by separate constitutional laws. Although accepting the three main categories of competence, the draft also provided for different kinds of legislative competence for the National Assembly. This included not only competence in areas of exclusive and common federal jurisdiction, but also in certain matters where administration was in exclusive national hands. Although the draft law purported to set forth only "basic criteria" for the division of competence, in fact it prescribed extensive federal authority in all common affairs (arts. 10 to 24), and gave a long listing of federal ministries (4) and federal committees (6, of which 2 were not settled) (art. 77).

mands for strong federal authority often clashed with Slovak desires for unfettered national control. According to Kočtúch agreement had been reached at Brno in early October on five federal ministries: defense and foreign affairs (exclusive); planning, finance, and foreign trade (common); and on five federal committees: labor and social affairs, prices, transport, post and telecommunications, and internal affairs. He also reported that no federal committees would be established in technology, internal trade, and agriculture and food, assigning these to exclusive national organs.[30] The government draft law envisaged a somewhat different structure, adding a Ministry of Labor and Social Affairs, and listing as possibilities federal committees for industry and domestic trade, and science and technology. It also provided for a parity-based organ in the Federal Bank.[31] It had been agreed that there would be no Ministry of Culture, and that there would be both federal and national Commissions of People's Control.[32] In other areas, such as health, industry, domestic trade, technology, construction, agriculture, and even security, continuing discussion had led to no consensus as to whether federal committees would be established or not.[33] Some Slovaks pressed hard for purely national organs in such fields, as well as in justice and transport.[34] They also proposed that international relations should be a "common," rather than exclusively federal, responsibility, and that appropriate national organs be set up.[35]

FEDERATION ENACTED

The final stage of deliberations began in mid-October when the debate was transferred to the National Assembly, particularly to its committees, which met jointly and separately, with spokesmen of the two councils present and taking an active part, and then to the committees and plenary sessions of the ČNR and SNR.[36] These discussions revealed cleavages on important issues and persistent doubts as to whether the full federation law could be completed by the deadline of October 28 or

[30] NS, Oct. 10. Kočtúch complained that these questions were later reopened by the Czechs and by the government (ibid., Nov. 28).

[31] NS, Oct. 10.

[32] RP, Sept. 19; Pravda, Oct. 16; Š. Gašparík, RP, Sept. 25, Oct. 17.

[33] For instance, RP, Oct. 5, 9, 16, 17, 22, 24, 27; Pravda, Oct. 16.

[34] Pravda, Oct. 2; Sept. 23, 25, Oct. 2, 11. The Minister of Transport was criticized for his resistance to the proposal of Slovak control of their own railway system, which they strongly urged.

[35] Ibid., Oct. 14. A secretariat for international relations was established in the SNR presidium (ibid., Oct. 1).

[36] For assembly committees, RP, Oct. 5, 9, 12, 15-17, 22-23; for the ČNR's organizational committee, ibid., Oct. 12, 17; for its plenary session, ibid., Oct. 24, 25; for the SNR, Pravda, Oct. 22, 24. Jičínský reported that some 300 suggestions had come in from the public. The SNR received some 1,000 proposals for change.

whether a "framework" law should be approved on that date, leaving detailed settlement until later. There were also doubts as to whether the federal system could be inaugurated by January 1st in the absence of elections to the new representative bodies. The government offered a mediating proposal which apparently came closer to the Slovak viewpoint than to the Czech.[37] The Slovak National Council in its meeting of October 23 reiterated its familiar views and appointed a delegation, under Klokoč, to defend these in Prague. A stormy debate in the Czech National Council on the morning of October 24 was followed by negotiations with the government in the afternoon, and this in turn led to an acceptance of the government's mediation proposal and of the January 1st deadline. It was resolved, however, that the Czech delegation to the final sessions of the assembly's constitutional and legal committee should continue to defend the Czech position and if no agreement ensued, should propose the postponement of a decision.

The climax was reached at a meeting of the government on October 24, when, with delegations of the two councils present, a compromise proposal was adopted, endorsing the establishment of federal committees for industry, and for agriculture and food, and the indirect elections of the Chamber of Nations.[38] Even then the assembly's committees still had a part to play. On October 25 the constitutional and legal committee accepted the two additional federal committees, but postponed its decision on the other recommendation.[39] Finally, in a concluding joint meeting of the parliamentary committees on October 26 (unreported), the direct system of electing the Chamber of Nations was reintroduced and the agreed draft approved. The constitutional law was then adopted without serious debate, and by unanimous vote in the plenary session of the National Assembly on Sunday, October 27.[40] The ceremonial signing of the law on federalization followed on October 30 in the Bratislava Castle, the restoration of which was completed just in time for the occasion.

The constitutional law was achieved, as Professor Viktor Knapp admitted, in spite of "the pressure of time," a "disturbing stubbornness" on both sides, and "the inadequacies of preparations."[41] Moreover, it was

[37] Laco, *Pravda*, Oct. 24. According to Laco, the government proposal accepted the indirect election of the Chamber of Nations, the establishment of federal organs by constitutional law, the retention of the present title of the country, and a constitutional provisorium until elections were held, and added industry, and agriculture and food, to the category of common affairs.
[38] *RP*, Oct. 25.　　　　　　　　　　[39] Ibid., Oct. 26.
[40] For speeches on this occasion, see *RP* and *Pravda*, Oct. 28. The author was privileged to attend this historic session held in the Spanish Hall of the Prague Castle.
[41] *RP*, Oct. 28. For text of law, *Sbírka zákonů*, no. 143/1968. For a summary, see *Pravda*, Nov. 1, and for a detailed analysis in a series of nine articles, *RP*, Nov. 5-19, passim. See also the booklet, with text and commentary, by J. Chova-

negotiated in the difficult environment produced by the Soviet occupation. It is not known whether there was direct Soviet intervention in the last weeks of debate, and hence impossible to judge whether any such interference may have affected the ultimate form of federation. The document was certainly the product of intense controversy in the three months after the occupation and represented a genuine compromise between Czech and Slovak views. In the following brief analysis of the text, indication is given of those elements in the law enacted which represented a primarily Czech (C) or Slovak (S) point of view.[42]

The new state, its title unchanged (C), was described as "a voluntary union of equal national states," based on "the right of self-determination" of each nation and on "their will . . . to live in a common federative state" (S). Sovereignty would rest with each republic, as well as with the federal republic as a whole. Although the 1960 constitution remained valid, large sections, including the whole of chapters 3, 4, 5 and 6, and many other individual articles, were replaced by the constitutional law (S). A new constitution was to be introduced later, as well as constitutions for each of the republics (S).

The individual republics, through their own independent organs of government, were to exercise a broad range of exclusive powers including education, culture, justice, health, trade, construction, forest and water resources, and the supervision of the national committees (S). The federal organs, on the other hand, were to possess a limited number of exclusive powers, encompassing, in addition to foreign affairs and defense, federal state material reserves, federal legislation and administration, and the protection of constitutionality. But there was to be a wide array of "common affairs," not initially envisaged by the Slovaks, including certain areas, such as agriculture and food, and industry, which were to the last minute regarded by them as exclusively national (C).[43] Moreover, the federal organs were assigned substantial authority in the common economic spheres through articles 10 to 26, empowering them to establish "general principles" and to encourage "coordination" of action (C).[44] Federal power was further enhanced by the definition of the com-

---

nec, L. Káčer, S. Matoušek, and R. Trella, *ČSSR: Federatívny socialistický štát* (Bratislava, 1969).

[42] These designations are approximate only. Some original Slovak views had come to be accepted by Czechs, and vice versa.

[43] The common affairs listed in art. 8 were: planning, finance, currency issue, price questions, foreign economic relations, industry,* agriculture and food,* transport, post and telecommunications, science and technology, labor, wages and social policy, social and economic information, legal settlement of the socialist enterprise,* normalization, weights and measures and patent rights, internal order and state security, press and other information media.* The ones starred* were added to the government's original draft law.

[44] Černík laid great stress on the factors making for unity in his address (*RP*,

petence of the National Assembly (arts. 36-39) which was given the right to legislate, not only in regard to exclusive and common affairs, but also in spheres where the executive power rested solely with the republics (e.g. family law, civil and criminal law, higher education laws, etc.) or where "the unity of the legal order" required it (e.g. health, education, association and assembly, nationality and religion, etc.) (C).[45] In addition, the powers allocated to the President were substantial, thus giving him "a quite powerful position" (C).[46]

Although the Slovaks had yielded substantial power to the federal organs, they had attained many, although not all, of their demands concerning their status at the center. The National Assembly was to consist of two chambers, equal in status and competence (S), and both directly elected (S). Each house would have to pass a proposed law by a simple majority, or in certain defined spheres, mainly constitutional, by a three-fifths majority (S). In other areas, embracing most federal economic activities, laws had to be approved in the Chamber of Nations by a majority of deputies elected in each of the two republics, voting separately (art. 42)(S). This was also true of the ratification of the government's program and of a vote of confidence in the government (S). A vote of non-confidence, on the other hand, could be adopted by a simple majority in the Chamber of the People or in either section of the Chamber of Nations.[47] In the event of different decisions by the two chambers, agreement proceedings were to be conducted by a parity committee, and if this failed, the dissolution of the assembly might follow, at the discretion of the President (S). Finally, the presidium of the National Assembly was to be formed on the basis of parity, and with the same safeguards against majority-domination as applied to the assembly as a whole (S). These provisions, taken together, did not grant full parity nor the complete ban on majorization demanded by the Slovaks, but afforded them substantial safeguards against outvoting and assured them a powerful position in the enactment of all-state legislation.

In the government parity was not established (C), and a simple majority vote was sufficient for a decision (C). State secretaries were, however, to be appointed in all ministries (art. 67)(S).[48] Federal organs

Oct. 28). In this "sensitive sphere," wrote certain commentators, there would be need for "intimate cooperation" of the federal and republican governments so as to "avoid possible conflict situations by preventive political measures" (Chovanec et al., p. 66).

[45] Chovanec et al., pp. 47-48.   [46] *RP*, Nov. 8.

[47] This could mean, in the Chamber of Nations, a vote of only 38 Czech or Slovak deputies (ibid., Nov. 7).

[48] The state secretaries were described not as persons of Czech or Slovak nationality but as "citizens" of the Czech or Slovak Republic. It was not excluded, therefore, although unlikely, that a state secretary might *not* be of the opposite nationality.

were not listed in the constitutional law (C), as had been proposed in the draft, but were to be formed by separate constitutional laws, requiring a three-fifths majority (S). Other federal organs, such as the bank of issue, were to be established by an ordinary law, subject to the ban on majorization. Federal committees were to be based on parity (S), with the possibility of an appeal by the minister, or by "one of its national parts," to the government as a whole (art. 82).

A constitutional court was to be established, as the Slovaks had urged, in the constitutional law itself and was to be composed on a parity basis (S). Its purpose was primarily to watch over the constitutionality of actions taken by both federal and republican organs and to settle disputes over jurisdiction, but it was also to protect the rights of citizens against decisions of the federal organs. It was empowered to make suggestions for the improvement of federal or republican legislation, thus giving it a significant influence in the promotion of uniformity of the legal order.[49] Republican constitutional courts were to be established later (S), and other courts and the procuracy were to be settled by a special constitutional law (C).

Implementing Federation

The constitutional law on federation was welcomed by both Czechs and Slovaks. The Slovaks saw it as the culmination of their long struggle for national equality and as a repudiation of any thought of separation.[50] Husák, in a speech at the ceremonial signing, declared that the "idea of a common Czechoslovak state" was deeply rooted in Slovak consciousness and that there should "never be any doubt, today or in future, either at home or in the world," of Slovak intentions.[51] Czech commentators characterized the law as strengthening the stability of the common state, but noted persisting Czech doubts, aggravated by the absence of adequate time for the crystallization of Czech opinion.[52] It was generally recognized, however, that the adoption of the statute was only the first stage in introducing the federal system and that its consummation on January 1 would require many complex organizational steps. This second stage, just like the first, had to be accomplished in a relatively short time and under the unfavorable conditions of the occupation. The impossibility of holding elections in these circumstances meant that certain transitional measures would have to be taken. These were set forth in the

[49] RP, Nov. 13.
[50] For instance, articles by F. Vašečka, M. Kusý, J. Spišiak, and D. M. Krno, NS, Oct. 31; Husák, ibid., Nov. 7; R. Olšinský, Politika, Nov. 7.
[51] RP, Oct. 31.
[52] Z. Eis, Rep., Oct. 23-30; Jičínský, Politika, Oct. 24; Císař, RP, Oct. 28; M. Filip, ibid., Oct. 31; J. Lipavský, ibid., Nov. 1.

law itself and provided for the National Assembly to continue in existence as the new Chamber of the People, for the Chamber of Nations to be formed by indirect delegation from the two national councils, and for the two councils to expand their own membership by cooptation.

The preparatory work for the inauguration of federation on January 1 involved the adoption of a whole series of laws, including the crucial constitutional law concerning the formation of federal ministries and committees. From late November the preparation of these measures proceeded in the government, the assembly committees, and finally in plenary sessions of the assembly in late December.[53] Although press reports were terse and uninformative, they revealed continuing differences, in particular as to whether federal organs should be established in certain spheres or not. For instance, five of the assembly committees, and most of the ČNR committees, urged a federal committee for health, but this was opposed by the government and the decision was postponed for later legislation. There were disputes over whether there should be a federal committee for press and information, as proposed by the government, or merely an office, as suggested by the ČNR.[54] The Slovaks voiced complaints concerning what they deemed to be an expansion of federal competence contrary to the federation law.[55] They demanded increased Slovak representation in the federal administrative organs, where they were grossly underrepresented.[56] There were also those who advocated that Slovak influence should be assured in treaty-making and that national organs in the sphere of international relations be established.[57]

The outcome was a batch of federal laws passed in late December 1968 just in time to make possible the inauguration of federation in January. The important constitutional law on federal ministries and committees (Sb. z., no. 171) established seven ministries, each with a state secretary, and seven federal committees. Two were exclusively federal: foreign affairs and national defense. Five were common: interior, planning, finance, foreign trade, and labor and social affairs. The federal committees were as follows: prices, technical and investment development, industry, agriculture and food, transport, posts and telecommunications, and press and information. A separate law on federal committees provided that these would be organized on the basis of parity and headed by a minister-chairman, with a deputy chairman of another na-

---

[53] RP, Nov. 26-28; Dec. 4 on; Dec. 19-22.

[54] Ibid., Dec. 5, 10, resp.

[55] Klokoč, ibid., Nov. 15; M. Mitošinka, NS, Dec. 12.

[56] J. Meško, Pravda, Nov. 15. There were only 521 Slovaks of 14,000 employees (i.e. 3.7 percent) in the federal organs, he reported. Slovaks numbered only 15 of 109 deputy ministers; 53 of 605 directors and division heads; and 39 of 1,144 department heads.

[57] J. Tomko and J. Azud, NS, Dec. 12. Cf. J. Čierný, Pravda, Nov. 28.

tionality (*Sb. z.*, no. 172).[58] Another law stipulated that Czechoslovak citizenship was derived from citizenship in either of the two republics, to be determined normally by the place of birth (*Sb. z.*, no. 165). A federal statute defined the city of Brno as "an independent territorial-administrative entity," with its own national committee directly under the government of the Czech republic, and described in detail the assistance to be offered by the Czech government and its organs in assuring the development of the city and of its neighboring territory (*Sb. z.*, no. 175).

The two national councils were confronted with a huge agenda to be completed in the short interim before January 1.[59] Both had to expand their membership by cooptation and to elect delegates to the Chamber of Nations. Both had to consider and approve the draft federal laws and elaborate their own legislative measures, for example, concerning rules of procedure, citizenship, etc.[60] Most important of all, the councils had to determine the number of national ministries and their spheres of activity. The ČNR finally decided to establish seventeen ministries, plus a Price Office.[61] The Slovaks at first had contemplated the same number of ministries, but as a result of public criticism of excessive bureaucracy, reduced the number to fifteen.[62]

[58] Another law established a Federal Statistical Office, with a chairman and deputy chairman of the two nationalities, and with a parity council, and an Administration of Federal Material Reserves, and prolonged the existence of certain agencies, including the State Bank, until later legislative settlement (*Sb. z.*, no. 170). The Czech and Slovak Insurance and State Savings institutions were divided into two Czech and Slovak agencies (*Sb. z.*, nos. 162-63). The state budget for 1969 was also adopted, with provision for its reworking into three separate budgets, in agreement with the Czech and Slovak governments, by May 31 (*Sb. z.*, no. 158). Federal competence was established in specified areas of internal affairs and security (*Sb. z.*, no. 166) and in the formulation of the general principles for, and the legislative regulation of, press and other information media, including publishing enterprises (*Sb. z.*, no. 167). All references to *Sb. z.* in text and notes are to 1968, unless otherwise noted.

[59] See interviews with Císař, *RP*, Nov. 14; Klokoč, ibid., Nov. 15 and *Pravda*, Nov. 13.

[60] For rules of procedure, *Sb. z.*, ČNR, no. 1; SNR, no. 204. For citizenship laws, *Sb. z.*, SNR, no. 206; ČNR, no. 39/1969.

[61] *Sb. z.*, ČNR, no. 2. The law listed the ministries and defined the primary function of each. The ministries were: planning, finance, labor and social affairs, construction and technology (originally construction and building), education, culture, youth and physical training, health, justice, interior, industry, building, agriculture and food, forest and water resources, transport, posts and telecommunication, and commerce. In addition there was to be a Czech Statistical Office, a Price Office, etc.

[62] *Sb. z.*, SNR, no. 207. See also Husák, *Pravda*, Dec. 23. The ministries were the same as those listed in the Czech law, without, however, the ministry for youth and physical training, and with transport, post and telecommunications combined. In addition the Slovak law established a Slovak Statistical Office, a Price Office, and an Office for Press and Information.

Certain questions, such as the structure of the courts and new electoral laws, were left to future legislation. The decision on the territorial-administrative structure, in particular the fate of the regional committees, was also deferred. Differences of opinion on the latter questions were already evident. The Czechs were still uncertain about the future shape of the administrative system, including the place of Moravia.[63] The Slovaks had already decided that a two-tier system of national committees was adequate and that the regional committees in Slovakia should be abolished as soon as possible.[64]

The shape of federation as embodied in these implementing laws was somewhat more centralist than had been originally expected and aroused some Slovak criticism.[65] The leadership had evidently concluded that although the forms, and much of the reality, of the federal system were to be respected, special efforts must be made to strengthen the central powers and safeguard the unity of the legal and political order. Černík, in a major speech at the CC plenum in mid-December, stressed "common interests," "integration," and "unified economic policy" and warned against "unhealthy disintegrating and centrifugal tendencies." Černík also emphasized the responsibility of the federal organs for setting the basic policy through legislation and referred to the need for "advisory and coordinating organs" to assure the necessary unity in fields which were under national competence, such as education, health, etc.[66] Ten days later, Husák expressed the opinion that the federation would "not weaken the firmness and unity of our common Czechoslovak state" and declared that the CPS "will strive for this all-state unity with all its means."[67]

A factor pointing in this same direction was the failure to carry through the original idea of federalizing the Communist Party. It is reported, without confirmation, that the Soviet authorities, although not opposing the establishment of the federal system, had forbidden the application of the same principle to the party. Certainly the congress of the Czech party was *not* held, even though delegates had been selected and

[63] Císař (*RP*, Nov. 15) mentioned as possibilities the establishment of regional administrations for certain spheres such as planning, education and health, and a special Ministry of Moravia and Silesia, with its seat in Brno.

[64] CPS Central Committee decision, *Pravda*, Dec. 23; Husák, ibid. The regional committees were in fact abolished in July 1969 but restored again in Dec. 1970. See Robert W. Dean, *Nationalism and Political Change in Eastern Europe* (Denver, 1973), pp. 44-45.

[65] Hatala, *NS*, Christmas, 1968; M. Lakatoš, *Ži:ťek*, Dec. 18.

[66] *RP*, Dec. 13. Cf. the CC decision which also underlined the need for the closest cooperation of the two republics (ibid., Dec. 16).

[67] CPS Central Committee, *Pravda*, Dec. 23. A strong trend toward recentralization began in Sept. 1969 and reached a high point in Dec. 1970 and Jan. 1971 (Dean, *Nationalism*, pp. 38-47).

preparations made. The joint Stanovisko of September 26 had referred openly to the need to establish federal forms in the National Front and the Communist Party. Other commentators, before and after the ratification of the constitutional law, regretted that there had been no opportunity for the Czech party, or for that matter, the Czechoslovak party as a whole, to discuss the project.[68] The concept of federalizing the party was, however, replaced by an alternative: the forming of a bureau for the Czech lands in the CPCz Central Committee. This was announced on October 22 and created in November.[69] The CPCz Central Committee, through the bureau and the Slovak CC, would perform, it was said, "an integrating function by linking together the national and international elements in the structure and life of the party."[70] Dubček dispelled any doubt that might remain. "Any breach of the unity of the party," he warned, "or of its all-state character, would be a serious error." The party can "best express and best co-create the integrated unity of Czechs and Slovaks, represent its international content, unify the national and all-society interests of the people, and represent the idea of Czechoslovak unity (*československskost*) in the best sense of the word."[71] Clearly such a conception of the role of the party would deprive the federal state structure of much of its significance.

There was, however, a much more serious drawback, namely, that the new federation was to be initiated not as a component of democratization, as originally anticipated, but within a political system in which the basic elements of democracy were lacking. For Czechs and for those Slovaks who had regarded democratization as the primary goal, and had considered federalization without this almost meaningless, this was a confirmation of their worst fears.[72] Even for those Slovaks who had con-

[68] Eis, Jičínský, and others, cited above, n. 52.

[69] Presidium, Oct. 22, *RŠO*, p. 328; CC decision, *RP*, Nov. 18 (also *RŠO*, pp. 368-69, 371). This arrangement was described as "transitional" until the 14th congress. The bureau, headed by Štrougal, was to prepare the eventual Czech founding party congress—a congress which was in fact never held. The position of the bureau was weakened somewhat in Dec. 1968, and it was ultimately abolished in May 1971. The unitary character of the party was stressed increasingly from June 1969 on (Dean, *Nationalism*, pp. 39-43).

[70] Cf. Husák, *RP*, Oct. 31, on the party as "a politically integrating force." According to the CC decision, the CPCz's unity would be expressed in the common program, common membership and common statute, and in the binding character of CC decisions.

[71] *RP*, Oct. 31. Cf. Dubček at CPS Central Committee, *Pravda*, Dec. 22.

[72] Nevertheless, a poll of Slovak opinion in Feb. 1969 revealed that 61.4 percent believed that the creation of the Slovak republic would deepen the democratization process; only 14.5 percent did not agree. In response to a question as to whether the development of Slovakia would be quicker and better as a result, 57.3 percent replied affirmatively; 15.4 percent replied "neither better nor worse"; and 15.3 percent, "worse" (*ŽS*, no. 19, May 7, 1969). The February poll also yielded the interesting result that 70 percent of those polled believed that the most positive

sidered federalization as the primary goal, and democratization as secondary, the outcome was a severe disappointment. Could the theoretical sovereignty of the two republics, or of Czechoslovakia as a whole, have any substance in view of the limits on sovereignty imposed by the Soviet invasion? Moreover, if federation were to weaken the bonds between the two nations, some elements, within or outside the state, might be able to manipulate this disunity for their own purposes. If, on the other hand, federalization contributed to a strengthening of Czech-Slovak bonds, as many believed, the two nations could ward off this "mortal danger" by presenting a united front to "any efforts to divide us, from within or from outside."[73]

THE NATIONALITIES LAW

The idea of legal guarantees for the rights of the nationalities was not abandoned in the wake of the occupation but was embodied in a constitutional law adopted by the assembly at the same session at which the law on federation was enacted. The "loyal" attitude of the nationalities had been frequently noted and had provided a basis for improved relations, especially between Slovaks and Hungarians. Husák, in a major address to the Hungarian association, Csemadok, less than a month after the occupation, praised their reaction to the invasion and assured them of the passage of a federal law, as well as separate Czech and Slovak nationality laws, which would take cognizance of the different nationality problems of the two republics.[74]

In early October, a draft law elaborated by government experts and approved by the Slovak party Presidium, became, however, the subject of sharp controversy before its ultimate adoption, with some significant changes, on October 27.[75] Its proposals were regarded as relatively satisfactory by the Hungarians but were censured by many sectors of the Slovak public as ignoring their demands and threatening national interests.

---

element after January was the deepening of democratization (*RP*, March 20, 1969)—a result in sharp contrast to the usual assumption of the greater interest of Slovaks in federalization.

[73] Jičínský, *Rep.*, Nov. 26-Dec. 3; Eis, ibid., Dec. 25. The quotation is from Eis. On this last point, see also Olšinský, *Politika*, Nov. 7; M. Gosiorovský, *RP*, Oct. 30.

[74] *Pravda*, Sept. 12; *NS*, Sept. 12. For praise of the behavior of local Hungarians and Ukrainians during the invasion, see *Pravda*, Sept. 6; L. Šulc, *RP*, Sept. 23, Oct. 18.

[75] Text of draft law, *Pravda* and *RP*, Oct. 4. For exposition and defense, V. Plevza, *NS*, Oct. 10. The Slovak National Council established a Commission for Nationalities, made up of deputies of Slovak, Hungarian, and Ukrainian nationality living in mixed areas. Its first task was to prepare a Slovak nationality law (*Pravda*, Oct. 5).

In particular, the guarantee of the right of citizens of the nationalities to receive instruction in their own language and to use their language in relations with offices and other state organs (art. 3) was said to endanger the position of Slovaks in the mixed regions of southern Slovakia. Since the draft law did not establish Slovak as the state language or require the Hungarians to learn Slovak in school, Slovaks would be forced to become bilingual or to leave these districts of their own homeland. This led to the reiteration of the demand for legislation establishing Slovak as the state language and to suggestions that the passage of the law be deferred to allow time for further discussion.[76]

The law finally adopted recognized four nationalities—Hungarian, German, Polish, and Ukrainian (Ruthenian)—as constituting, with the Czech and Slovak nations, "in an inseparable community," the working people as the source of state power, and assured them "participation in state power" and "effective guarantees of their further development."[77] The nationalities were to be represented in proportion to their numbers in the representative bodies and other elected organs. The citizens of the four nationalities would be guaranteed the right to instruction in their own language; the right to full cultural development; the right to use their languages in official relations in regions inhabited by the relevant nationality; the right to associate in cultural organizations; and the right to a press and media of information in their languages. The extent and conditions of these rights would be defined by law. Each citizen would freely decide his nationality "according to his own conviction." All forms of pressure tending toward denationalization were forbidden. The constitutional law would be implemented by federal and national laws. The latter would designate the representative and executive bodies in which organs to guarantee the realization of nationality rights would be established.[78]

[76] For Hungarian approval, *RP* (Slovak ed.), Oct. 15. Ukrainians were less pleased, ibid., Oct. 12. For criticism by the Matica Slovenská, the Slovak Writer's Union, members of the Law Faculty of Komenský University, and in letters to the press, see *RP* (Slovak ed.), Oct. 9, 12; *RP*, Oct. 18 (K. Douděra); *Pravda*, Oct. 14, 22, 23. For a detailed critique, see J. Dorul'a, *NS*, Oct. 10.

[77] *Sb. z.*, 144/1968. The designation Ruthenian was not included in the original draft law. The Germans had not been mentioned in the 1960 constitution. The gypsies were not included in the nationality law, but in the meantime formed a Union of Gypsies (*RP*, Oct. 22, Nov. 1, Dec. 18).

[78] The draft law had been stronger and more specific than the final text, assuring the nationalities "equal position and participation in the formation of the state will and in the performance of state power" and "legal guarantees of further development." Proportional representation in "political organs, representative bodies, and other state organs" and "an equal position in economic and cultural life" had been guaranteed. Moreover, the right to use their own languages in official relations had been expressed more generally, without reference to areas inhabited by the nationality. The "special organs" in the representative bodies and executive organs were also to "decide independently concerning their specific interests."

The nationalities law was greeted with relative satisfaction by Hungarian spokesmen and with considerable discontent by Slovaks. Csemadok, for instance, welcomed it as defining the nationalities, for the first time in a constitutional law, as "constitutional factors (*státotvorní činitelé*)" but regretted that it did not proclaim their political, economic, and cultural equality and did not guarantee their right to their own nationality organs or the right to proportional representation in executive as well as representative organs.[79] Slovaks claimed that the law took no account of their earlier criticisms and hoped that the detailed provisions of the republican law would give protection to their interests.[80]

[79] *RP*, Dec. 18.
[80] Doruľa, *Pravda na weekend*, Nov. 1. See also J. Meško, *Pravda*, Oct. 30, Nov. 14.

Smrkovský's Testimony

THE FIRST personal account of 1968 by a major participant was given by Josef Smrkovský some six years later, not long before his death in January 1974, in the form of a taped interview given from his hospital bed. It was published abroad in a weekly close to the Communist Party of Italy, *Giorni: Vie nuove* (Feb. 20 and after, 1975) and in its original Czech form in a special issue of *Listy* (March 1975, pp. 4-25). Extemporaneous in character, this memoir makes no startling revelations, but provides new information and personal judgments of considerable interest. This brief summary (to which reference has been added in a number of footnotes above) gives only important highlights of the document.

OCTOBER 1967-JANUARY 1968

Smrkovský said little concerning the CC meetings or other events during this period, but described two conversations with Novotný just prior to the December plenum. In the first, Novotný informed him of changes he planned to make in the Presidium, including Smrkovský's own appointment. Smrkovský urged the need for more extensive changes, including the separation of the functions of the President and First Secretary, and suggested Lenárt as the most suitable candidate for the latter post. A few days later Novotný told Smrkovský that, on the advice of "old comrades," he had decided not to resign. Following the plenum, Smrkovský learned indirectly of a conversation which three persons had with Mestek who reported that Novotný was determined to resist, using the army and the militia, and that warrants had been prepared for the arrest of certain persons, including Smrkovský. The latter thereupon redrafted his plenum speech (prepared originally for the December sitting) in "more militant" terms and delivered it in January, referring in it to his conversations with Novotný.

Concerning Brezhnev's visit, Smrkovský sought in vain to learn the content of his talks with Novotný and was told that "Brezhnev listened ... but refused to interfere in the matter—this was the well-known statement—*'eto vashe dyelo.'* "

THE JANUARY DECISION AND AFTER

Concerning Dubček's appointment, Smrkovský heard that he was selected as the only person who would be acceptable to all and took the post unwillingly. Smrkovský and others were dissatisfied with the CC's original intention not to give a report to the public and urged the issuance of a decision giving the main principles of future party policy. Thereafter they pressed for the speedy elaboration of a relatively simple provisional document on post-January policy and were disappointed that the Action Program was so lengthy and so much delayed. He, and others, were embarrassed when reporting to party organizations, not knowing "what to say, and what not to say." Hendrych finally informed them that they could speak of "all matters dealt with by the Central Committee" but without indicating the standpoint of individual members.

Smrkovský related his own efforts to secure the political rehabilitation of Husák in 1964 or 1965, when Novotný had agreed to appoint Husák as deputy Minister of Justice but had rejected certain conditions set by Husák. In mid-January 1968, Smrkovský secured Dubček's immediate approval of the idea of activizing Husák "on the state level" and prepared the way for his appointment to the government by conversations with Bil'ak and Husák in Bratislava.

Smrkovský stated that between January and March Svoboda visited him almost daily to inform himself concerning the political situation (of which he knew little, said Smrkovský) and later traveled widely throughout the country. When he learned of the likelihood of Svoboda's becoming President in the event of Novotný's fall, Smrkovský viewed it "on the whole positively," and later supported it.

MOSCOW TALKS IN MAY

The Czechoslovak delegates had to listen, he said, to an enumeration of Soviet complaints about events in Czechoslovakia (which he likened to the White Book) and sought to "deny or explain" these matters and to provide more substantial information. The Soviet delegates were not interested in "the imposing and spontaneous participation of the people" on May 1st, involving millions, but only in meetings of KAN and K 231 attended by 50 to 100 people. They spoke only marginally of the April plenum and expressed reservations concerning the Action Program. "We saw they were not interested in facts or in our situation in its entirety but were seeking pretexts for a stand against us." Bil'ak argued for their position so that "we were three against five, not four against four." They demanded "strict administrative—I should say police—action against any one who . . . was not fully in agreement . . . with party policy." We stressed that "we would gain control of the outburst of political activity by democratic discussion and negotiation but . . . would use administrative measures against extremes if things went beyond the bounds of law and discussion did not meet with success."

Smrkovský referred to their request for a Soviet loan of 400 to 500 million rubles, and if this were impossible, "a loan from the international bank or somewhere else" but "without political conditions." Kosygin promised to examine their request but expressed himself negatively as to the prospect of Czechoslovakia's exporting consumer goods either to the West or to the Soviet Union. The purpose of Soviet trade policy was, said Smrkovský, "calculatedly political," designed to make "our economy . . . completely dependent" and to "subordinate us firmly to their policy."

Smrkovský denied that any warning of the possibility of military intervention was given either then or at any other meeting prior to August 20. "[There was] nothing from which one could logically deduce that their words could lead to military intervention. There were only criticisms and charges, everything possible, but a threat of such a kind—even indirect or veiled—I did not hear."

THE MAY PLENUM

The Dubček report and the plenum resolution were affected by "the spirit with which we came away from Moscow." Smrkovský himself recognized the existence of "extremes and extremists" and published a sharp article against them (*Rudé právo*, May 19). He took the view that "if the radical extremists wanted to push things still further, toward some kind of conflict, . . . I would not have hesitated to use tough measures against all who threatened the very existence of the Republic." Although he recognized extremes on the right, Smrkovský also stressed the extremes on the left, the conservatives or dogmatists, and regretted that the May resolution was predominantly directed against the right. This was due to "pressure from outside, from the Soviet Union." After the plenum, however, things quieted down, and "the prospect of a power clash practically disappeared from the horizon."

THE TWO THOUSAND WORDS

Smrkovský strongly opposed the conclusions drawn by this document and when Černík informed him that he had been unable to convince the government to oppose it, he requested permission to attend a night session of this body. He warned that if the government did not take a firm stand, "a different government" would do so a week later. He approved Černík's eventual statement and issued one of his own. He recognized that the authors intended no harm, certainly not a counterrevolution, and that the declaration reflected "fears of the people that the old times could return"—fears, he said, which were shown to be justified by later events —and the inadequacy of the party's actions against the dogmatists.

Smrkovský told of a planned student demonstration against the Warsaw pact and of his own role in the preparation of measures by the Prague city committee to ward off this danger by persuasion, or by action by the militia if necessary. As a result, there was no meeting and no demonstration.

PARLIAMENTARY DELEGATION TO MOSCOW

During this visit Smrkovský spoke so openly of the problems at home that he was asked not to do so, since the Soviet people were "not enough informed" and "their heads would be confused." At his Moscow press conference, he spoke out clearly, for instance, on foreign loans, but almost nothing appeared in the Soviet press. He reported a private meeting with Brezhnev in which the latter expressed his dissatisfaction with Dubček and implied that Smrkovský had the responsibility for effecting a change. Smrkovský defended Dubček and "rejected the offer which was in fact made to me."

THE WARSAW CONFERENCE

The meeting was "not a conference at all, but a summons to an accounting." Dubček's description of the course of events before Warsaw at the CC in September 1969 was correct, he said. He reported a decision by the Presidium, he thought at Černík's suggestion, that "our party Presidium should not leave the territory of our Republic." It was the Slovak Presidium which first proposed that they not go to Warsaw, a decision which was published in *Rudé právo* and *Pravda* on July 16 or 17 and brought to Prague by Bil'ak. (This did not in fact appear in either newspaper and seems most improbable.)

CONFERENCE AT ČIERNA

Their task, he said, was to defend the post-January program and to prevent a split with the Soviet Union. Brezhnev had "assistants on our Czechoslovak side"—Bil'ak, Kolder, Švestka, and others, who "spoke from the position of the Soviet arguments." The Soviet delegates were united. The talks were broken off at one point when Dubček and others left the meeting because of charges by Shelest that they were responsible for leaflets distributed in Subcarpathian Russia demanding its separation from the Soviet Union. Negotiations were resumed after the Soviet delegates apologized.

The Soviet side raised six concrete demands: the removal of Kriegel from the National Front chairmanship, and of Císař from his post as Secretary; a ban on the Social Democratic Party, and on KAN and K 231; and "the communications media." "We said . . . we did not wish to introduce censorship anew . . . but wished to do it democratically, to reach agreement—by the discipline of the journalists; we shall undertake the necessary steps in this direction. After our return from Čierna we talked much with them (the journalists) . . . and finally took various governmental measures to prevent various excesses in the communications media." Almost at once the Soviet side complained that the Czechs were not fulfilling the agreement. "There were no agreements; we said either that this was decided or that this will be decided and how it will be decided."

Smrkovský admitted that he did not know whether the Soviet leaders had "a completely clear idea of what would come next and how." He was not convinced that they had already decided upon military intervention. He realized that "it was not a matter of concrete particulars, but rather of the entire concept of our policy. That was the cause of everything that was done. But it was difficult to step forward and say: we are against democratization of the party; we are against democratization of the social order; we are against humanism; we are against modernization of the management of the socialist state. They could not take up such a stand. But this was in fact the issue. Everything they said there were pretexts; hence the difficulty in coming to an agreement. These were details which could not give reasons for a conflict of any kind, because we were solving or had resolved them."

The Czechs urged Brezhnev to come to Czechoslovakia and see for himself. In Moscow Smrkovský had complained that Chervonenko (the Soviet ambassador) was not informing Moscow correctly and urged his removal.

Dubček and Brezhnev had agreed to a meeting in Bratislava in a private talk at Čierna. At Bratislava there was no negotiation, but merely an editorial council which elaborated the declaration.

PRESIDIUM—AUGUST 20-21

Smrkovský's report on the final Presidium meeting is confined to the proceedings after the invasion. Both Dubček and Černík had "broken down" and "were not capable of acting." When discussions concerning a standpoint to be made public reached no conclusion, Smrkovský demanded an end to further debate and called upon each member to vote for or against a communiqué drafted by Mlynář. The result was seven to four, Bil'ak and others opposing that part relating to the breach of the Warsaw pact and international law. Sádovský and Piller, who as Secretaries, did not have a vote, expressed themselves in favor. Svoboda was present but without a vote, and did not express an opinion. The broadcast of the resolution was interrupted by Karel Hoffmann, and its publication in *Rudé právo* prevented by Švestka, but in each case, after receiving assurances from Smrkovský, radio and newspaper employees took steps to assure that the Presidium's decision was made public. In spite of urgings, Smrkovský and Dubček refused to leave the CC building, and when the tanks arrived at 5:00 a.m., were confined, along with Špaček, Kriegel, and perhaps Šimon, and later taken to Ruzyně airport. Smrkovský, Špaček, and Kriegel were transported by plane to Legnica in Poland, and then to Subcarpathian Russia, where they were joined by Černík, who had been flown from Prague with Dubček. They were later called to Moscow to join Dubček—first Černík alone, and then Smrkovský, Špaček, and Kriegel.

THE MOSCOW TALKS

In Moscow Smrkovský and Špaček met with Brezhnev, Kosygin, and Podgorny in the CC headquarters where they learned for the first time of the 14th Party Congress, of the general strike, and of the popular resistance from Brezhnev, who told them they must return and "liquidate" the congress. They were then taken to the Kremlin to join Dubček and some twenty to thirty others. Mlynář informed them of the events in Czechoslovakia, including the congress. The negotiations were "chaotic," with Dubček lying down most of the time in an adjacent room, suffering from heart trouble (as was Indra); the others in the "Dubček camp" conducted the negotiations, constantly consulting Dubček; others who had come to Moscow with Svoboda "wandered around and were always off somewhere." All, he admitted, had suffered a "nervous shock" and "wept," either in Prague, or in Moscow when they read in Russian the original Soviet draft: "one after the other they broke down." They found the Soviet draft protocol "absolutely unacceptable" and submitted their own. "Officially, so to speak formally, in all discussions no one in our delegation supported the original Soviet proposal. I do not know anyone who agreed with it, so that our rejection was unanimous." Smrkovský, as head of a delegation, which included Lenárt and Švestka, informed Ponomarev that they could not sign it, and were told that their draft was unacceptable to the Soviet Union. They managed to have some changes made in the original draft, such as the omission of references to counter-revolution and "international aid," the addition of the word "temporarily" to the mention of troops "remaining," and the inclusion of a reference to the continuance of the post-January policy. When the Czechoslovaks informed Ponomarev that the protocol was still unacceptable and that they would not sign it, he replied that they would sign it in a week, or two weeks, or a month. No alternative was left but to take the Soviet draft as the basis of negotiations and to seek "tiny corrections." Only Kriegel refused to sign the document when it was taken to him in another building, and again when he was brought to the Kremlin.

At the final session the talks were close to breakdown when Dubček sought to reply to Brezhnev's renewed charges and were saved only by the intervention of Svoboda who urged that "they take the protocol and begin to discuss it point by point, word by word. He said that all will be well and that when the Soviet troops . . . leave our land, they will be inundated with flowers." "So in the end we signed it. . . . We all hesitated. I hesitated long—should I? should I not? . . . Today it would be difficult to say who resisted more or who was more willing to sign, because we all more or less resisted. No one wanted to. . . . In my address (after returning home) I said that history will sometime judge whether we did well or whether we committed treason. I do not know. But under the circumstances in which we were, I acted on my own decision. But I long, long hesitated."

Only later, after the signing, did they learn that Ulbricht, Gomułka, Kádár, and Zhivkov were there and that "everything had been agreed" with them. When told that the others wished to drink a glass of cognac with them, the Czechoslovak delegates firmly refused, saying that they did not want even to see them, let alone drink together. Even at this point the entire agreement was threatened again when they learned that the Soviet leaders did not want to permit Kriegel to return to Prague, as originally promised. In a new conversation between Dubček, Svoboda, Černík, and Smrkovský, and Brezhnev, Kosygin, Podgorny, and Suslov, Dubček declared that they would not return home without Kriegel. The Soviet representatives eventually yielded, and Kriegel was waiting in the plane at the airport.

The Return Home

For ten days the delegates lived in the Castle. Meetings were held with the government, with the assembly, and with the party officials elected at the 14th congress. Dubček had to inform the latter of the provision of the Moscow protocol that the congress should not be recognized. "The negotiation was very complex, complicated, and emotional—in effect it was designed to overturn the result of the congress." In the end Dubček's conclusions were accepted. Smrkovský had to report to parliament and to negotiate with General Pavlovsky concerning the removal of wall inscriptions all over Prague. Major addresses to the nation were given. Smrkovský's speech awakened dissatisfaction in Moscow. He was convinced that everything depended on maintaining unity between the leadership and the people. Unity within the leadership began to crumble in September and culminated in the crisis surrounding his exclusion from the chairmanship of the assembly.

The Mlynář Memorandum

Zdeněk Mlynář, in early 1975, prepared a memorandum on the theory and practice of reform in 1968 which included a critique of the reform leadership. Dated January-February 1975, signed by the author, and entitled "*Teorie a praxe pokusu o reformu politického systému socialismu v Československu roku 1968*," it circulated in typescript (249 pp.) in Czechoslovakia and was sent abroad for publication in Czech and other languages. It was intended to provide a basis for discussion of the Czechoslovak question among the Communist Parties of Europe at a forthcoming conference. The document is significant as the first critical analysis by a leading scholar who was also in the ranks of the top leadership. His comments are relevant to many of the issues discussed in the conclusion of this book (which was completed before the memorandum became available). No page references are given owing to its typewritten form.

The first part, entitled "The Theoretical Conception of the Optimal Development of the Political System of Socialism," was devoted to a defense of the work of the Mlynář team on political reform and of his own views in this respect (see chap. IV, n. 97, and chap. XII, n. 100). Highly polemical in tone, it was directed against Jaroslav Matějíček, and his article "Criticism of the right-wing revisionist construction of a 'new model' of the political system in the ČSSR," *Právník*, no. 9 (1974). Mlynář, citing his own writings of 1967 and 1968, reasserted his conception of pluralism under the leadership of the party. Although admitting that a two-party system was an optimal solution, he repeated his earlier denial of the feasibility or the desirability of such a system in Czechoslovak circumstances. Mlynář stressed the fact that the team's work was in its initial phase only. Its tentative conceptions were embodied, in most positive form, in the Action Program.

The second, longer, part of the memorandum, entitled "Political Practice and the Actual Development of the Political System in Czechoslovakia in the Year 1968," was a systematic analysis of certain crucial aspects of the movement for reform and of the strategy and tactics of the CPCz leadership. Apart from the issues discussed below, the memorandum also contained a discussion of the social forces involved (in particular the working class and the intelligentsia) and the situation within the party, relevant to chapters XVI and XVII of this book.

Mlynář contended that what was involved in 1968 was a reform, not a revolution, and strongly denied that there was any tendency toward a restoration of capitalism or any threat of counterrevolution. He rejected charges that the CPCz leadership had lost control of the situation and emphasized the overwhelming support of reform by the population and the widespread public participation. He admitted that there were serious differences of opinion within the party, and some opposition to the reform, but was convinced that these problems would have been solved at the 14th Party Congress. He considered the Action Program a realistic solution of the most pressing problems and condemned "radical" elements who sought to go beyond it. Because of the distortion of socialism after 1948, pre-revolutionary ideas of bourgeois democracy had come to the fore, and a certain "idealization of the First Republic" had taken place. This tendency was, in Mlynář's view, a positive support for the policy of democratizing socialism, and removed the danger of violence which might have occurred had such traditions been absent. Although recognizing faults on the part of the leaders, Mlynář left no doubt that the responsibility for the military intervention rested, not with them, but with the Soviet leaders.

Mlynář was sharply critical of the "radical" wing of the intelligentsia, expressing itself principally in the mass media. The radicals did not recognize that politics was "the art of the possible" and created difficulties for the leadership, especially in the international context. He was particularly severe in his censure of the Two Thousand Words. Nonetheless Mlynář recognized the positive aspects of the mass media in mobilizing the population for reform.

Mlynář charged the leadership with the following errors of tactics, stating that he had warned against most of them at the time: 1) the failure of the party to retain the initiative for reform after January by offering a fully elaborated political program. The Action Program was ready in late February and should have been published earlier.

2) the abolition of censorship before the publication of the program, thus allowing the mass media to become the main vehicle of reform ideas, and the failure to set certain limits on the media during subsequent months. Mlynář criticized the press law amendment for abolishing all limits on freedom of expression, contrary to the June 14 proposals of the Legal Commission, of which he was the chairman.

3) the failure to call the 14th congress earlier and to hold elections to the National Assembly, thus leaving the leading personnel largely unchanged.

4) the failure to take certain measures in July, such as the adoption of the draft statute on the National Front, which would have set limits to

887

the activity of certain new political organizations; also, there should have been restrictions on the mass media, including the banning of *Student*.

5) the failure to devote sufficient attention to the economic aspects of reform and thus to satisfy the main concern of the workers.

6) delay in carrying through the democratization of the CPCz itself.

These errors in leadership, and the activity of the radicals, led to the continuance of the "eruptive" character of the post-January development and delayed political stabilization. This strengthened the hands of those against reform; gave some of the reform-minded the impression that the leadership had lost control; and pushed some leaders (such as Kolder and Švestka) into opposition to the reform. Nonetheless, in Mlynář's view, the leading role of the party was maintained, and no counterrevolutionary situation developed. The Communist Party was united in favor of the Action Program, enjoyed great authority, and faced no serious competing force. It was able to operate as "a decisively regulating force." The armed forces, including the People's Militia, were strong and united, and could have been used in case of need. Negotiations had been successful in dealing with the problem of KAN and K 231, so as to prevent the development of an "opposition," and like measures would have solved the problem of the proposed Social Democratic Party. The formation of this party would have brought about a competition for power, having grave international repercussions and involving the "destruction," not the reform, of the political system. Although he approved the avoidance of the use of force against certain tendencies, Mlynář was not averse to the employment of "measures of power," even against party members who sought radical steps.

In a final section dealing with the "international context," Mlynář presented views which he described as retrospective, not held at the time. He rejected the charge that the reform policy desired changes in foreign policy. The objective was to express specific Czechoslovak interests within the "common foreign policy" of the socialist countries. Owing to their lack of experience in international affairs, the Prague leaders, however, gave insufficient attention to the international implications of the reform. They failed to recognize that it was bound to have grave repercussions in the entire socialist system, and particularly to create problems for the leaders of the GDR and Poland (although not, in his view, for those of the USSR). Instead of insisting that their reform was a purely domestic affair, the Prague leaders should have recognized that it was a problem of the entire communist movement and seized the initiative in seeking a solution jointly with the other socialist countries and with the European Communist Parties. This would have required setting certain limits to the reform and effecting them so as to avoid causing complications among their allies. Although some of the radicals were ready to contemplate a rupture with the Soviet Union, in the style of Yugoslavia in 1948, the reform leaders rejected any thought of such a break, and, quite rightly, accepted the necessity of the "integration" of the socialist bloc. Mlynář categorically condemned any resort to armed force by Czechoslovakia, arguing that this would have offered evidence of counterrevolution and produced another Hungary.

In Mlynář's opinion the cause of the invasion was not the Action Program or general ideological differences, but the misunderstanding by the Soviet Union and its allies of the actual situation in Czechoslovakia, and their fear of its ultimate outcome and its implications in other bloc countries. The developments in Czechoslovakia were also seen as complicating the Soviet strategy of relaxing tensions—especially, he thought, in matters such as the size and disposition of the Soviet armed forces and relations with the world communist movement—thus giving the Western countries opportunities to take advantage of these problems. Mlynář expressed doubts that the reform movement could have succeeded, even if the Prague leaders had avoided the errors mentioned above, because certain responses would also have been required by the other side. The USSR would have had to change its attitude, especially in respect of the relationship of the "common" and the "specific" features of socialism. This would have involved the abandonment of the concept that the features of socialism adopted in the Soviet Union were obligatory for all, and the recognition that variant forms, such as those of Yugoslavia or Czechoslovakia, were legitimate "embodiments of the general in the specific."

HUNDREDS of books and thousands of articles have been published in connection with the events of 1968 in Czechoslovakia. A comprehensive bibliography, edited by V. V. Kusin and Z. Hejzlar, *Czechoslovakia 1968-1969: Annotation, Bibliography, Chronology* (Garland Publishing Inc., New York, 1974) (which appeared after the completion of this book) lists more than 600 books published in the West and over 1,000 Czech and Slovak articles which relate to the Prague Spring and its aftermath. An earlier brief bibliography was compiled by Michael Parrish, *The 1968 Czechoslovak Crisis: A Bibliography, 1968-1970* (Clio Press, Santa Barbara, Cal., 1971). See also my review articles, "Thaw and Freeze-up: Prague 1968," *International Journal* 25 (Winter 1969-70), 192-201; "Reform aborted: Czechoslovakia in retrospect," ibid. 28 (Summer 1973), 431-445; correction, ibid. (Autumn 1973), p. 800.

In writing my own book, I consulted all available books that have appeared in English, French, German, and Czech, including the four outstanding works by Vladimir V. Kusin and Galia Golan listed below. With one exception, all these works were utilized and where appropriate, cited. The exception was Galia Golan's study, *Reform Rule in Czechoslovakia: The Dubček Era 1968-1969* (Cambridge, 1973), which covered approximately the same ground as mine and which I read only after the completion of my own work.

Research for this book started from a detailed chronology, based on a specially constructed index of the events of 1968 as reported in *The New York Times* and *The Christian Science Monitor*, Moscow *Pravda*, *Rudé právo*, and *Pravda* (Bratislava), *East Europe*, and the *Situation Reports* of Radio Free Europe. The most useful chronologies were: B. Kříženecká and Z. Šel, eds., *Československo 1968: Přehled událostí* (Prague, 1969), and J. Hronek, ed., *ČSSR: The Road to Democratic Socialism: Facts on Events from January to May 1968* (Prague, 1968).

The main sources were the newspapers, journals, and books which appeared in 1968 and 1969. Research was based on specially prepared indexes of *Rudé právo*, Bratislava *Pravda*, *Literární listy*, *Kultúrny život*, *Nové slovo*, *Reportér*, *Nová mysl*, and *Život strany*.

These sources were supplemented by the use of Czech and Slovak articles selected by Radio Free Europe for publication in its *Přehled tisku (Prehľad tlače)* and by clippings from the Prague press prepared by myself and by a research assistant in Prague. Radio broadcasts, which sometimes suffered from poor reception and hurried translation, were used sparingly, with the exception of certain chapters where other sources were not available. The Soviet press, apart from *Pravda*, was covered in *The Current Digest of the Soviet Press*.

Party documents and speeches by Dubček and others were taken from the press and from the useful collections of party decisions and documents, *Rok šedesátý osmý* (Prague, 1969) and of Dubček's speeches, *K otázkam obrodzovacieho procesu v KSČ* (Bratislava, 1968). A number of party documents published for intra-party use were also available to the author.

Only books used extensively are listed in the bibliography that follows. Similarly, only newspapers and periodicals examined systematically are listed. For fuller lists of sources, see footnotes in each chapter.

Books, newspapers, and other materials used in preparing this volume will be deposited in a special collection on Czechoslovakia in 1968 in the University of Toronto Thomas Fisher Rare Book Library.

SELECTIVE BIBLIOGRAPHY

A. Scholarly and Interpretative Studies

Aptheker, Herbert. *Czechoslovakia and Counter-Revolution* (New York, 1969).

Barton, S. W. and Martin, L. M. "Prague," in Gregory Henderson, ed. *Public Diplomacy and Political Change: Four Case Studies: Okinawa, Peru, Czechoslovakia, Guinea* (New York, 1973).

Borin, M. and Plogen, V. *Management und Selbstverwaltung in der ČSSR: Bürokratie und Widerstand* (Berlin, 1970).

Brahm, Heinz. *Der Kreml und die ČSSR, 1968-1969* (Stuttgart, 1970).

Broué, Pierre. *Le printemps des peuples commence à Prague* (Paris, n.d.).

Czerwinski, E. J. and Piekalkiewicz, Jaroslaw A., eds. *The Soviet Invasion of Czechoslovakia: Its Effects on Eastern Europe* (New York, 1972).

Dean, Robert W. *Nationalism and Political Change in Eastern Europe: The Slovak Question and the Czechoslovak Reform Movement* (Denver, 1973).

Ermarth, Fritz. *Internationalism, Security, and Legitimacy: The Challenge to Soviet Interests in East Europe, 1964-1968* (Santa Monica, Cal., 1969).

Feiwel, George R. *New Economic Patterns in Czechoslovakia* (New York, 1968).

Golan, Galia. *Reform Rule in Czechoslovakia: The Dubček Era 1968-1969* (Cambridge, 1973).

————. *The Czechoslovak Reform Movement: Communism in Crisis, 1962-1968* (Cambridge, 1971).

Gueyt, Rémi. *La mutation tchécoslovaque* (Paris, 1969).

Hájek, Jiří. *Mýtus a realita ledna 1968* (Prague, 1970).

————, trans. *Demokratiserung oder Demontage? Ein Prager Handbuch.* Translated by Peter Lux (Munich, 1969).

Hensel, K. Paul, et al. *Die sozialistische Marktwirtschaft in der Tschechoslowakei* (Stuttgart, 1968).

Hodnett, Grey and Potichnyj, P. J. *The Ukraine and the Czechoslovak Crisis* (Camberra, 1970).

James, Robert R., ed. *The Czechoslovak Crisis 1968* (London, 1969).

Jancar, Barbara. *Czechoslovakia and the Absolute Monopoly of Power* (New York, 1971).

King, Robert R. *Minorities under Communism: Nationalities as a Source of Tension among Balkan Communist States* (Cambridge, Mass., 1973).

Klaiber, Wolfgang. *The Crisis in Czechoslovakia in 1968* (Institute for Defense Analyses, Arlington, Va., 1969).

Krejčí, Jaroslav. *Social Change and Stratification in Postwar Czechoslovakia* (London, 1972).

Kusin, Vladimir V. *Political Grouping in the Czechoslovak Reform Movement* (London, 1972).

————, ed. *The Czechoslovak Reform Movement 1968* (London, 1973).

————. *The Intellectual Origins of the Prague Spring* (Cambridge, 1971).

Löbl, E. and Grünwald, L. *Die intellektuelle Revolution* (Düsseldorf, 1969).

Müller, A. and Utitz, B. *Deutschland und die Tschechoslowakei: Zwei Nachbarvölker auf dem Weg zur Verständigung* (Freudenstadt, 1972).

Ostrý, Antonín. *Československý problém* (Cologne, 1972).

Page, Benjamin B. *The Czechoslovak Reform Movement 1963-1968: A Study in the Theory of Socialism* (Amsterdam, 1973).

Piekalkiewicz, Jaroslaw A. *Public Opinion Polling in Czechoslovakia, 1968-69: Results and Analysis of Surveys Conducted During the Dubcek Era* (New York, 1972).

BIBLIOGRAPHY

Plevza, V. *Československá štátnost a slovenská otázka v politike KSČ* (Bratislava, 1971).
Prag und die Linke (Hamburg, 1968).
Remington, Robin A. *The Warsaw Pact* (Cambridge, Mass., 1971).
Sborník, Systemové změny (Cologne, 1972).
Selucký, Radoslav. *Czechoslovakia: The Plan that failed* (London, 1970).
Shawcross, William. *Dubček* (London, 1970).
Steiner, Eugen. *The Slovak Dilemma* (Cambridge, 1973).
Sterling, Claire. *The Masaryk Case* (London, 1968, 1969).
Suda, Zdeněk. *The Czechoslovak Socialist Republic* (Baltimore, 1969).
Tigrid, Pavel. *Le printemps de Prague* (Paris, 1968).
———. *La chute irrésistible d'Alexander Dubcek* (Paris, 1969).
———, trans. *Why Dubcek Fell* (London, 1971). Although an accent on Dubček is not given in the title of Tigrid's books as published, it has been included in all citations given.
Ulč, Otto. *Politics in Czechoslovakia* (San Francisco, 1974).
Veselý, Ludvík. *Dubček* (Munich, 1970).
Wheeler, George W. *The Human Face of Socialism: The Political Economy of Change in Czechoslovakia* (New York, 1973).
Windsor, Philip and Roberts, Adam. *Czechoslovakia, 1968* (London, 1969).
Wolfe, Thomas W. *Soviet Power and Europe: 1945-1970* (Baltimore, 1970).
Zartman, I. William, ed. *Czechoslovakia: Intervention and Impact* (New York, 1970).
Zeman, Z.A.B. *Prague Spring: A Report on Czechoslovakia, 1968* (Harmondsworth, 1968).

B. SCHOLARLY AND LITERARY WORKS BY CZECHS AND SLOVAKS

Dziedzinská, Libuše. *Inteligence a dnešek* (Prague, 1968).
Faľtan, Samo. *K problémom národnej a demokratickej revolucie na Slovensku* (Bratislava, 1965).
Goldmann, J. and Kouba, K. *Hospodářský růst v ČSSR* (Prague, 1967, 2nd ed., 1969).
———, trans. *Economic Growth in Czechoslovakia* (New York, 1969).
Hamšík, Dušan. *Spisovatelé a moc* (Prague, 1969).
———, trans. *Writers Against Rulers* (London, 1971).
Kalivoda, Robert. *Moderní duchovní skutečnost a marxismus* (Prague, 1968).
Klokočka, Vladimír. *Volby v pluralitních demokraciích* (Prague, 1968).
———, trans. *Demokratischer Sozialismus* (Hamburg, 1968).
Kosík, Karel. *Dialektika konkretního* (Prague, 1963).
———, trans. *Die Dialektik des Konkreten* (Frankfurt, 1967).
Kotyk, Václav. *Světová socialistická soustava* (Prague, 1967).
Kouba, Karel et al. *Úvahy o socialistické ekonomice* (Prague, 1968).
Král, Miroslav, ed. *Věda a řízení společnosti* (Prague, 1967).
Lakatoš, Michal. *Občan, právo a demokracie* (Prague, 1966).
———. *Úvahy o hodnotách demokracie* (Prague, 1968).
Liehm, Antonín J. *Generace* (Vienna, 1968).
———, trans. *The Politics of Culture* (New York, 1967, 1968).
———, trans. *Trois Générations* (Paris, 1970).
Löbl, Evžen. *Úvahy o duševnej práci a bohatstve národa* (Bratislava, 1967).
———, trans. *Geistige Arbeit: Die Wahre Quelle des Reichtums* (Vienna, 1967).
Machonin, Pavel, ed. *Československá společnost* (Bratislava, 1969).
———, ed. *Sociální struktura socialistické společnosti* (Prague, 1967).
Mlynář, Zdeněk. *Stát a člověk* (Prague, 1964).
50 let Československa 1918/1968: K některým politickým a ekonomickým problémům let 1948-1968 (Prague, 1968).

Pavlenda, V. *Ekonomické základy socialistického riesenia národnostnej otázky v Československu* (Bratislava, 1968).

Rebro, Karol. *Cesta národa* (Bratislava, 1969).

———, trans. *The Road to Federation* (Bratislava, 1970).

Richta, Radovan, et al. *Civilizace na rozcestí: Společenské a lidské souvislosti vědeckotechnické revoluce* (Prague, 1966; 3rd ed., Prague, 1969).

———, trans. *Civilization at the Crossroads: Social and Human Implications of the Scientific and Technological Revolution* (Prague and New York, 1969).

Rohan, René. *Politické strany* (Prague, 1968).

Šamalík, František. *Člověk a instituce* (Prague, 1968).

———. *Právo a společnost* (Prague, 1965).

Selucký, Radoslav and Milada. *Člověk a hospodářství* (Prague, 1967).

Šik, Ota. *Czechoslovakia, The Bureaucratic Economy* (White Plains, N.Y., 1972) radio speeches given in 1968.

———. *Ekonomika, zájmy, politika* (Prague, 1962; revised ed. *Ekonomika a zájmy*, Prague, 1968).

———, trans. *Ekonomika, interesy, politika* (Moscow, 1964).

———. *Plán a trh za socialismu* (Prague, 1968).

———, trans. *Plan und Markt im Sozialismus* (Vienna, 1967).

———, trans. *Plan and Market Under Socialism* (White Plains, N.Y., and Prague, 1967).

Škvorecký, Josef. *All the Bright Young Men and Women: A Personal History of the Czech Cinema* (Toronto, 1971).

Slováci a ich národný vývin (Bratislava, 1969).

Šnejdárek, Antonín. *Výbor z přednášek a statí, 1968* (Prague, 1968).

Šorm, František. *Věda v socialistické společnosti* (Prague, 1967).

Sviták, Ivan. *Man and His World: A Marxian View* (New York, 1970).

———. *The Czechoslovak Experiment, 1968-1969* (New York, 1971).

———. *Verbotene Horizonte* (Freiburg im Breisgau, 1969).

Tomášek, L., Litera, J., and Večeřa, J. *Strana a dnešek* (Prague, 1967).

Tomášek, Ladislav. *Vedúca úloha strany a politický systém* (Bratislava, 1968).

Turek, Otakar. *O plánu, trhu a hospodářské politice* (Prague, 1967).

C. NEWSPAPERS AND PERIODICALS

A-revue
Dějiny a současnost
Ekonomický časopis
Hospodářské noviny
International Relations
Kulturní noviny
Kulturní tvorba
Kultúrny život
Lidová democracie
Listy (Rome)
Literární noviny
Literární listy
Mezinárodní vztahy
Mladá fronta
Nová mysl
Nové slovo
Novinář
Obrana lidu
Plánované hospodářství
Práca

Práce
Právník
Příspěvky k dějinám KSČ
† *Pravda* (Bratislava)
‡ *Pravda* (Moscow)
Právny obzor
Reportér
Roľnické noviny
Rudé právo
Socialistická zákonnost
Sociologický časopis
Student
Svědectví (Paris)
Svobodné slovo
The Christian Science Monitor
The New York Times
Tribuna
Večerní Praha
Zemědělské noviny
Život strany

† Cited as *Pravda* throughout except in chap. xx and xxi.
‡ Cited as *Pravda* throughout chap. xx, xxi.

BIBLIOGRAPHY

D. Party Documents

(i) Congresses (in chronological order; date in parentheses is that of publication)
XII. sjezd Komunistické strany Československa (Prague, 1963).
XIII. sjezd Komunistické strany Československa (Prague, 1966).
XIII. sjezd Komunistické strany Československa (Prague, 1967). A fuller version
of preceding.
Sjazd Komunistickej strany Slovenska (Bratislava, 1966).
Pelikán, Jiří, ed. Tanky proti sjezdu: Protokol a dokumenty XIV. sjezdu KSČ
(Vienna, 1970). Title as given on cover of book. Alternative title also given:
XIV. mimořádný sjezd KSČ (Protokol a dokumenty).
———, trans. The Secret Vysočany Congress: Proceedings and Documents of the
Communist Party of Czechoslovakia, 22 August 1968 (London, 1971).
———, trans. Le congrès clandestin, protocole secret et documents du xiv⁰ congrès
extraordinaire du p. c. tchécoslovaque (Paris, 1970).
———, trans. Panzer überrollen den Parteitag, Protokoll und Dokumente des 14.
Parteitags der KPTsch am 22. August 1968 (Vienna, 1969).
Mimoriadny zjazd Komunistickej strany Slovenska (Vybrané dokumenty) (Bratislava, 1968).

(ii) CC Plena
Plenární zasedání ÚV KSČ 29. května - 1. června 1968 (Prague, 1968).
O zasedání Ústředního Výboru KSČ dne 31. srpna 1968 (Prague, 1968).
Zasedání Ústředního Výboru KSČ ve dnech 14.-17. listopadu 1968 (Prague, 1968).

(iii) Decisions and Documents
Akční program komunistické strany Československa přijatý na plenárním zasedání
ÚV KSČ dne 5. dubna 1968 (Prague, 1968).
———, trans. The Action Programme of the Communist Party of Czechoslovakia
(Prague, April 1968).
Rok šedesátý osmý v usneseních a dokumentech ÚV KSČ (Prague, 1969).
Usnesení a dokumenty ÚV KSČ, Od xi. sjezdu do celostátní konference, 1960
(Prague, 1960).
Usnesení a dokumenty ÚV KSČ, Od celostátní konference KSČ 1960 do xii. sjezdu
KSČ, 2 vols. (Prague, 1962).
Usnesení a dokumenty ÚV KSČ, 1962-63 (Prague, 1964).
Usnesení a dokumenty ÚV KSČ, 1964 (Prague, 1965).

(iv) Speeches and Articles
Bil'ak Vasil. Pravdá zůstala pravdou: Projevy a články, říjen 1967-prosinec 1970
(Prague, 1971).
Dubček, Alexander. Komunisti a národné dedičtvo (Bratislava, Nov. 1968).
———. K otázkam obrodzovacieho procesu v KSČ, Vybrané prejavy prvého
tajomníka ÚV KSČ súdruha Alexandra Dubčeka (Bratislava, 1968).

(v) Reports
Pelikán, Jiří, ed. Pervertierte Justiz (Vienna, 1972).
———, ed. Potlačená zpráva (Zpráva Komise ÚV KSČ o politických procesech a
rehabilitacích v Československu 1949-68) (Vienna, 1970). Title on cover:
Zakázaný Dokument.
———, ed. trans. Das unterdrückte Dossier, Bericht der Kommission des ZK der
KPTsch über politische Prozesse und "Rehabilitierungen" in der Tschechoslowakei 1949-1968 (Vienna, 1970).
———, ed. trans. The Czechoslovak Political Trials, 1950-1954 (London, 1971).
Poučení z krízového vývoje ve straně a společnosti po XIII. sjezdu KSČ (Prague,
1971).

Trans. *Lesson Drawn from the Crisis Development in the Party and Society after the 13th Congress of the Communist Party of Czechoslovakia* (approved by the plenary session of the CC CPCz in December 1970; n.p., n.d.).
Zpráva o současné politické situaci Československé socialistické republiky a podmínkách činnosti Komunistické strany Československa (*srpen 1968*) (Prague, Oct. 1968).

E. OTHER DOCUMENTS

IV. sjezd Svazu československých spisovatelů (Protokol), Praha, 27.-29. června 1967 (Prague, 1968).
Dokumenty o Národním shromáždění ve dnech 21.-28. srpna 1968 (Prague, n.d.).
Dokumenty o okupácii ČSSR (Bratislava, 1968).
Grospič, J., ed. *Československá federace, Zákony o federativním uspořádání* (Prague, 1972).
Informační zpravodaj Ústředního výboru Narodní fronty (Prague, Oct. 1968).
Littell, Robert, ed. *The Czech Black Book* (New York, 1969). Translation of *Sedm pražských dnů*, below.
Rambousek, O. and Gruber, L., eds. *Zpráva dokumentační komise K231* (Toronto, 1973).
Sbírka zákonů Československé socialistické republiky.
Sedm pražských dnů, 21.-27. srpen 1968, Dokumentace (Prague, Sept. 1968). (The so-called Black Book)
Zákon o súdnej rehabilitácii (Bratislava, 1968).

F. PRESS AND RADIO BROADCASTS (IN TRANSLATION)

British Broadcasting Corp., Monitoring Service, *Summary of World Broadcasts*, I (USSR), II (Eastern Europe).
The Current Digest of the Soviet Press (New York).
Reprints from the Soviet Press (Compass Publications, N.Y.).
U.S. Foreign Broadcast Information Service, Daily Report.
U.S. Joint Publication Research Service, Eastern Europe.

G. DOCUMENTS AND MATERIALS (IN TRANSLATION)

de Sède, Gérard, ed. *Pourquoi Prague?* (Paris, 1968).
Ello, Paul, ed. *Czechoslovakia's Blueprint for "Freedom"* (Washington, D.C., 1968).
Grünwald, Leopold. *ČSSR im Umbruch* (Vienna, 1968).
Haefs, Hanswilhelm, ed. *Die Ereignisse in der Tschechoslowakei vom 27. 6. 1967 bis 18. 10. 1968, Ein dokumentarischer Bericht* (Bonn, 1969).
Information Bulletin (Central Committee, CPCz, Prague, 1968).
K sobytiyam v Chekhoslovakii, Fakty, dokumenty, svidetelstva pressy i ochevidtsev (Moscow, 1968). (The so-called White Book)
———, trans. *K událostem v Československu, Fakta, dokumenty, svědectví tisku a očitých svědků* (Moscow, 1968).
———, trans. *On Events in Czechoslovakia, Facts, documents, press reports and eye-witness accounts* (Moscow, 1968).
Oxley, Andrew, Pravda, Alex, and Ritchie, Andrew, eds. *Czechoslovakia: The Party and the People* (London, 1973).
Pelikán, Jiří, ed. *Ici Prague: L'Opposition intérieure parle* (Paris, 1973).
Remington, Robin A., ed. *Winter in Prague: Documents on Czechoslovak Communism in Crisis* (Cambridge, Mass., 1969).
Röll, F. and Rosenberger, G., eds. *ČSSR, 1962-1968: Dokumentation und Kritik* (Munich, 1968).
Škvorecký, Josef, ed. *Nachrichten aus der ČSSR* (Frankfurt, 1968).

BIBLIOGRAPHY

H. Personal Memoirs and Commentaries

Brodský, Jaroslav. *Řešení gama* (Toronto, 1970).
——, trans. *Solution Gamma* (Toronto, 1971).
Clementis, Vladimír and Clementisová, Lída. *Listy z väzenia* (Bratislava, 1968).
Kohout, Pavel. *From the Diary of a Counter-revolutionary* (New York, 1972).
——. *Journal d'un contre-révolutionnaire* (n.p., 1971).
Kovaly, H. and Kohak, E. *The Victors and the Vanquished* (New York, 1973).
Löbl, Evžen. *Svedectvo o procese s vedením protištátného sprísahaneckého centra na čele s Rudolfom Slánským* (Bratislava, 1968).
——, trans. *Sentenced and Tried: The Stalinist Purges in Czechoslovakia* (London, 1969).
——, trans. *Stalinism in Prague: The Löbl Story* (New York, 1969).
London, Artur. *Doznání* (Prague, 1969).
——, trans. *L'aveu, Dans l'engrenage du procès de Prague* (Paris, 1968).
——, trans. *The Confession* (New York, 1970).
Mňačko, Ladislav. *The Seventh Night* (New York, 1969).
Slánská, Josefa. *Report on my Husband* (London, 1969).
Slingová, Marian. *Truth Will Prevail* (London, 1968).

I. Reportage

Daix, Pierre. *Journal de Prague* (Paris, 1968).
Journalist M. *A Year Is Eight Months: Czechoslovakia, 1968* (New York, 1970). Translation of Maxa below.
Kučera, Jaroslav. *Pražský srpen* (Munich, 1971).
Marcelle, Jacques. *Le deuxième coup de Prague* (Brussels, 1968).
Marko, Miloš. *Čierne na bielom* (Bratislava, 1971).
Maxa, Josef. *Die kontrollierte Revolution, Anatomie des Prager Frühlings* (Vienna, 1969).
Salomon, Michel. *Prague, La révolution étranglée, Janvier-Août 1968* (Paris, 1968).
——, trans. *Prague Notebook: The Strangled Revolution* (Boston, 1971).
Schmidt-Häuer, Christian and Müller, Adolf. *Viva Dubček* (Cologne, 1968).
Schwartz, Harry. *Prague's 200 Days: The Struggle for Democracy in Czechoslovakia* (New York, 1969).
Szulc, Tad. *Czechoslovakia Since World War II* (New York, 1971).
Tatu, Michel. *L'hérésie impossible* (Paris, 1968).
Wechsberg, Joseph. *The Voices* (New York, 1969).

J. Addenda

Alex Pravda. *Reform and Change in the Czechoslovak System: January-August 1968* (Sage Publications, Beverley Hills and London, 1975).
Pravda pobezhdaet (Moscow, 1971), transl. of *Poučení* . . . , cited above under D (v), and other Czechoslovak post-occupation materials.

Index

Abrahám, L., 792, 796
Academic Council of Students (ARS),
202, 599
Academy of Agricultural Science, 576n
Academy of Sciences, 90, 93, 145, 232,
575-77; federalization of, 53. *See also*
individual institutes (by name)
Academy of Sciences (Slovak), 53, 576
Academy of Sciences and Art, 576
Action Program, 191, 207, 211, 214,
215, 217-21, 222, 564-65, 580-81,
587-88, 592, 597, 598, 601, 604, 726,
786, 802, 804, 810n, 827, 879, 887,
888; CPS extraordinary congress on,
794; and economic reform, 221, 418-
19; on federation, 458-59; 14th
extraordinary congress and, 771, 772;
implementation of, 255, 258, 343; on
party's role, 339; and political reform, 218-19, 221, 337-41; public
opinion on, 502, 530, 531, 536-37;
on rehabilitation, 376-77; Soviet
Union on, 250, 879. *See also* individual subjects (by topic)
administrative measures, 37, 56, 63, 94,
105, 147, 158, 879-80, 888
administrative procedure, law on,
110-11
Agricultural Cooperatives, Congress of,
186, 188
agriculture, 413, 587-88; Slovak public
opinion on, 586. *See also* farmers
Albania, 38, 39; attitude to ČSSR,
708-10, 749-50; on Warsaw letter,
710
Aleksandrov, I. (pseud.), 285, 326,
660, 668, 685; article in Moscow
Pravda (August 18), 673, 675, 716,
721, 722
all people's state: and ČSSR, 136, 137,
138-39, 141, 142, 145, 151-52, 153;
and Soviet Union, 135, 141
amnesties, general, 378, 401
Andrzejewski, J., 754
anti-Semitism, 200, 273, 634, 682
anti-socialist forces, 209, 223, 236-41
passim, 249, 254, 259, 272, 273, 292,
295, 296, 303, 326, 494, 628, 661,
679, 683, 697, 699-705 *passim*, 815,
857; analysis of, 497-98; Dresden conference on, 660, 661; Hájek on, at
UN, 758; Hungary on, 689, 690, 693,
695; party polls on, 508, 512, 523,

524; and political leaders (ČSSR),
238-40; public opinion polls on, 538,
543; Soviet Union on, 663, 837;
Warsaw letter on, 669-70
aparát, 134, 150, 335, 337, 338, 503-9;
attitudes to reform, 506-9, 612; defined, 503; opinion polls of, 506-9.
See also party functionaries
apparatchiki, 61, 834, 841
apparatus (party), 343n, 351-52. *See
also aparát*
armed forces, and the invasion, 714-15,
759, 768n, 775. *See also* invasion
and armed resistance
arms caches, reports of, 297, 670n,
680, 698
army: action program for, 641; role of,
in Novotný's removal, 172-74, 197
assembly and association, law on, 369
assembly, right of (post-August), 814
Association of the Marxist and Non-
Marxist Left, 549
asymmetrical system, 51, 454-58
passim, 462, 463, 477, 481
Auersperg, Pavel, 151-52, 212, 376
Austria, Czechoslovak relations with,
87, 627, 631
Austria-Hungary, 4, 17, 18
Axen, Hermann, 678

Bacílek, Karol, 29, 35, 46-47, 48, 49,
54, 185, 223, 254, 375, 376, 383,
385-86, 390, 403
Barák, Rudolf, 31, 48, 376, 386, 400,
401, 403; trial of, 40-41, 379-81
Barák commission, 32, 35, 376, 400-
401
Barański, W., 673, 688
Barbírek, František, 216, 470, 519, 520,
524, 717, 762, 763, 770, 796, 807
Barnabite commission report, 50, 376,
402
Bartošek, Karel, 830-31, 850
Bartuška, Jan, 204, 375, 379, 403
Bašťovanský, Štefan, 386
Battek, Rudolf, 527
Benada, Ľudovít, 54
Beneš, Edvard, 4-8 *passim*, 13-17
passim, 21-26 *passim*, 102, 236, 341,
679
Beneš, Jan, 71, 205, 378, 568
Beran, Cardinal Josef, 203, 601
Beria, L. P., 375, 381, 382, 385

828; abolition of, 198, 262-63, 368, 887; public opinion on, 560. *See also* press law

Central Commission of Supervision and Auditing (CPCz), *see* ÚKRK

Centràl Committee (CPCz), 138, 143, 231, 350-51, 513; bureau for Czech lands, 814, 874; commissions of, 139-40; Department for Societal Organizations, 351; Department for State Administration (8th), 172, 193, 299, 351; division of opinion in, 166-67, 168, 171-72, 183; Ideological Commission, 93, 99, 100, 125, 193, 215; Ideological Department, 63, 66, 67; Legal Commission, 109, 113, 887; members of, meeting at Hotel Praha, 762-63, 766, 767n; and Moscow talks, 801-2; opposition in, 164; in party statute, 319-20; report on political situation (*Zpráva*), 444n, 494n, 500-501, 507-9, 511, 516-17, 520-21, 523, 530, 531-32, 544, 547, 548, 561, 562, 574, 600n, 629n, 657n; role of, 140, 335, 336-37, 350-51, 353; Unit for Information, 351

elections: candidates for, 514-15; candidates for, blacklisted, 513, 518; nominations to, 269, 317; preferences for, in party polls, 515-17, 524-25; preferences of Slovak delegates for Slovaks in, 524; probable choices in, 515-16, 518; procedures of, 514; Slovak candidates for, 514; Slovaks and extraordinary congress, 771

plena, pre-1968: November 1961, 39-40; December 1963, 66, 92; November 1964, 142; January and August 1965, 142-45, 152; February and March 1967, 163, 587; September 1967, 71, 157, 163-64; October 1967, 165-68; December 1967, 169-72; October-December 1967 plena, Biľak on, 184-85, and fall of Novotný, 162-77

January 1968 plenum, 174-77, 451, 879; communiqué of, 183-84; lack of information on, 210; public opinion on, 534-35, 536n; resolution of, 183n; significance of, 186-87

April 1968 plenum, 211-15; Action Program approved, 217-21; Dubček's report to, 210-11, 214; on federation, 458; and leadership changes, 215-16; on rehabilitation, 376; on political situation, 214;

public opinion on, 502; significance of, 222; Soviet reaction to, 223

May 1968 plenum, 251-57, 258-59, 880; party poll on, 507-8, 511; as political offensive, 252, 253, 258; poll of Slovak congress delegates on, 523; resolution of, 255-57; Soviet press on, 665-66; Yugoslav press on, 704-5

July 1968 plenum, 292-93

August 31, 1968 plenum, 759, 806-7; approval of Moscow negotiations, 804-7; and 14th extraordinary congress, 805

November 1968 plenum, 815

plena, January and May 1969, 819, 821; December 1970, "Lesson," 718

Central Publication Administration (ÚPS), 68, 368

Central Union of Agriculture and Foodstuffs, 590

centrists, 216, 222, 497

Čepička, Alexej, 33, 48, 375, 380, 385, 403

Čepický, Josef, 177

Černík, Oldřich, 61, 163, 168, 176, 196, 208, 212, 216, 254, 274, 277, 287, 307, 309, 311, 326, 342-43, 344, 366, 377, 519, 520, 524, 541, 542, 580, 598, 601, 622, 663, 664, 768, 770, 774, 782, 786, 796, 807, 822, 873, 880, 882; arrest of, 760, 883; cabinet under, 225-26; on economic reform, 412, 413-14, 419, 420-21, 422; report after Bratislava, 653-54; speech at May plenum, 253; speech to National Assembly (April), 225-27, 228; on Moscow talks, 801, 802

Černý, Josef, 505

Černý, Václav, 568, 576

Čeřovský, M., 377

Chalupecký, J., 569

Chamber of Nations, 482, 863, 865n, 867, 869, 871, 872

Chamber of the People, 482, 863, 864, 869, 871

Charles University, Philosophical Faculty of, 235, 396, 577-78

Chervonenko, S. V., 723n, 737, 882

China, 38-39, 41, 657; attitude to ČSSR, 710-11; on the invasion, 750

Chňoupek, B., 212-13, 242n, 376

Chudík, Michal, 47, 54, 55, 170, 172, 175, 203, 204, 212, 215, 227, 241, 521, 791

Chvatík, K., 569

Chytil, V., 528-29

INDEX

Jenyš, V., 379
Jesenská, Zora, 245, 246, 247
Jews: Poland and, 682, 683; in political
  trials, 26
Jičínský, Zdeněk, 111, 463-64, 467-68,
  474, 477, 479, 485-86, 505
Jirásek, Alois, 14
Jodas, Josef, 193, 204, 238, 272, 497
Jodl, Miroslav, 72-73, 100, 237, 324,
  325
Johnson, Chalmers, 829
Johnson, Lyndon B., 730, 731, 755
journalists, 571-74; and Bratislava con-
  ference, 312; and freedom of expres-
  sion, 367-68, 368-69, 572, 573; as
  interest group, 573; meeting of, with
  Presidium, 326-27; organization of, in
  Prague, 572-73; party attitude to,
  571, 574; and self-censorship, 572.
  See also Union of Journalists
judicial independence, 109, 110, 406,
  410
Junák, 595, 599

Kabrna, B., 762, 786
Kádár, János, 288, 628, 661, 691, 743,
  744, 884; on Bratislava declaration,
  694-95; meetings with Dubček, 186,
  289n, 313, 316-17, 655, 688, 722;
  role at Moscow meeting (May), 689;
  visit to Moscow (July), 667, 691-92;
  visit to Prague, 688-89
Kadlec, Prof. V., 226, 254, 566
Kadlecová, Erika, 601-2
Kafka, Franz, 14, 97, 568
Kahn, Herman, 842
Kaláb, Miloš, 99, 101
Kalandra, Záviš, 569
Kalecki, M., 123
Kaliský, Roman, 50
KAN, 202, 233, 307, 347, 498, 529,
  546, 547-48, 879, 882, 888; banned
  (post-August), 814; on civil rights,
  367n; Moscow protocol on, 805; as
  political party, 265-66; and political
  reform, 358; in Slovakia, 547; Sviták
  and, 547
Kantůrek, Jirí, 517
Kapek, Antonín, 41, 216, 254, 330, 519,
  520, 807, 822
Kaplan, Karel, 387, 389-91, 397, 405,
  527
Karlík, Jiří, 588, 590
Karlík commission, 588, 590, 591
Karvaš, Peter, 245
Kašpar, Jan, 515
Kašpar, Vlado, 573

Kašpar report, see CC report on politi-
  cal situation (Zpráva)
Katolické noviny, 602
Katushev, K. F., 723n, 724, 796, 817
Kazakov, M. I., 721
Kejř, J., 578
Khrushchev, Nikita, 35-39 passim, 51,
  135, 380, 830
Kiesinger, Kurt G., 87, 648
Kirilenko, A. P., 304
Kladiva, Jaroslav, 81, 164, 254, 566
Klíma, Ivan, 69, 71
Kliment, Alexander, 69, 356-57, 527,
  528, 570
Kliszko, Z., 684, 685
Klofáč, Jaroslav, 99, 100
Klokoč, O., 241, 521, 786, 790n, 791,
  793n, 796, 867
Klokočka, Vladimír, 361-62
Knapp, Viktor, 108, 263, 370, 478, 867
Kočtúch, Hvezdoň, 431, 462, 486, 795
Kodaj, Samuel, 276, 278
Köhler, Bruno, 46-47, 48, 49, 254
Kohout, J., 647
Kohout, Pavel, 69, 200, 201, 274, 301,
  634
Kohoutek, Miloslav, 125, 400-401, 412
Kolár, F. J., 104
Kolář, Jan, 787
Kolder, Drahomír, 41, 47, 61, 168, 189,
  197, 212, 215, 216, 217, 223, 229,
  239, 268, 269, 329, 330, 419, 446, 516,
  519, 520, 524, 717, 761, 784n, 796,
  807, 817, 822, 824, 881; and col-
  laboration, 760-63 passim, 770;
  memorandum of, on Warsaw
  meeting, 288-89; on rehabilitation,
  376
Kolder commission, 41, 376; Piller
  report on, 401-2; report of, 47-49,
  107
Kolder-Indra memorandum, 329-30,
  761
Kolman, A., 577n
Komenda, B., 119
Komenský, Jan Amos, 18
Komócsin, Z., 689, 695
Komunist, 702, 704, 707
Konev, I. S., 248
Konstantinov, F., 666
Kopecký, Václav, 65
Kopřiva, Ladislav, 48, 383, 385-86, 390,
  403
Koryta, J., 578
Koscelanský, Ján, 791-92, 796
Košice program, 9, 175, 453, 459, 607,
  608

910

911

Feeding the Russian Fur Trade. By James R. Gibson. (University of Wisconsin Press, Madison, Wisconsin, 1969)

The Czech Renascence of the Nineteenth Century. Edited by Peter Brock and H. Gordon Skilling. (University of Toronto Press, Toronto, 1970)

The Soviet Wood-Processing Industry: A Linear Programming Analysis of the Role of Transportation Costs in Location and Flow Patterns. By Brenton M. Barr. (University of Toronto Press, Toronto, 1970)

Interest Groups in Soviet Politics. Edited by H. Gordon Skilling and Franklyn Griffiths. (Princeton University Press, Princeton, New Jersey, 1971)

Between Gogol' and Ševčenko. By George S. N. Luckyj. (Harvard Series in Ukrainian Studies. Wilhelm Fink Verlag, Munich, Germany, 1971)

Narrative Modes in Czech Literature. By Lubomir Dolezel. (University of Toronto Press, Toronto, 1973)

The Collective Farm in Soviet Agriculture. By Robert C. Stuart. (D. C. Heath and Company, Lexington, Mass., 1972)

Leon Trotsky and the Politics of Economic Isolation. By Richard B. Day. (Cambridge University Press, Cambridge, England, 1973)

Literature and Ideology in Soviet Education. By Norman Shneidman. (D. C. Heath and Company, Lexington, Mass., 1973)

Guide to the Decisions of the Communist Party of the Soviet Union, 1917-1967. By Robert H. McNeal. (University of Toronto Press, Toronto, 1974)

Resolutions and Decisions of the Communist Party of the Soviet Union 1898-1964. General Editor, Robert H. McNeal. Four Volumes. (University of Toronto Press, Toronto, 1974).

Dated: June 13, 1975

Library of Congress Cataloging in Publication Data

Skilling, Harold Gordon.
  Czechoslovakia's interrupted revolution.

  Bibliography: p.
  Includes index.
  1. Czechoslovak Republic—History—Intervention,
1968-   2. Czechoslovak Republic—Politics and
government—1968-   I. Title.
DB215.6.S58   943.7′04   75-30209
ISBN 0-691-05234-4
ISBN 0-691-10040-3 pbk.